Social Perspectives

on Behavior

Social Perspectives on Behavior

A READER IN SOCIAL SCIENCE FOR SOCIAL WORK
AND RELATED PROFESSIONS

EDITED BY

Herman D. Stein AND Richard A. Cloward

With a Foreword by GORDON HAMILTON

THE FREE PRESS, NEW YORK
COLLIER-MACMILLAN LIMITED, LONDON

Library of Congress Catalog Card Number: 57–12960

Seventh Printing March 1966

Contents

Section I
FAMILY STRUCTURE
AND ETHNIC PATTERNS

(v)

Section II

SOCIAL ROLES

The Social Location of Selected Attitudes and Behavior

Section V

DEVIANT BEHAVIOR
AS A PROPERTY OF GROUPS

Section VI
BUREAUCRATIC STRUCTURE

Foreword

by Gordon Hamilton

Social Perspectives on Behavior, edited by Professors Herman D. Stein and Richard A. Cloward, of the New York School of Social Work, Columbia University, is designed for the practitioner by practitioners. Why is this volume so timely—so much needed today?

The preoccupation of social work was first with economic phenomena—relief of poverty, then, gradually, income maintenance and standard of living. The next swing was to an understanding of personality and the development of a psychosocial approach to all problems. For over a quarter century social workers have been familiar with a theory of personality which enabled them, as never before, to understand the individual and his behavior in certain important respects. The advent of dynamic psychology, chiefly due to the creative genius of Freud, changed the whole approach of the profession toward relationships, especially those of the family, children, and worker-client. It was not as possible, however, to derive comparable insights from the social sciences whose concepts, problems, and even terminology remained obscure to social work. The current revolution of which we are slowly becoming aware lies in this very area of social and cultural insights for which social workers require a new sophistication in social science.

This *Reader in Social Science for Social Work and Related Professions* contributes vitally to a new dimension, therefore, one that is indispensable for the practitioner in the complex world within which he moves and works. It will stimulate him to think about society in a new way, just as in the twenties and thirties he had to think about people in a new way. The readings are grouped into several key areas, all of which hold meaning for those interested in individual and group treatment, as well as in administration, community planning, and social action. The social worker of tomorrow can no longer restrict himself to consideration of how the client feels about his situation—he must be equally attuned to the effects on the client of ethnic, class, and other significant group determinants of behavior.

Social work, like any of the humanistic professions, is culturally molded in goal and in method. Each client selectively incorporates and exemplifies the cultural environment. Every treatment objective is a value judgment, culturally shaped. Cultural patterns influence the kind and amount of self-expression and life satisfactions. It is too easy to forget that every treatment goal, just as every bit of community planning, is influenced by our value system. But except for a few axiomatic postulates of democracy which are regarded as the very basis of social work's characteristic method—the right to participate in one's own destiny, acceptance of differences (cultural pluralism), the worth of the individual, the duty and responsibility of society for human betterment—there has been little systematic study of the very value system which underlies practice. Contrary to popular misconception, social workers cannot be "non-judgmental"; "acceptance" never means indifference to the act, the mores. Even so common a notion as that of "adjustment" can have no usefulness unless viewed from the perspective of some explicit value system. Norms must be examined, criticized, reacted to, as well as imparted.

What practical use will practitioners make of theories and insights deriving from such topics as Value Systems, Family Structure and Ethnic Patterns, Social Roles, Social Stratification, Bureaucratic Structure, and Deviant Behavior? It is not too much to say that the characteristic process of study, diagnosis, and treatment in social work becomes deeper and more effective as attention is given to different family structures and various ways of life, to occupational, ethnic, and class variations. Light is thrown on many of the major problems of our times, such as parent-youth conflict and family instability. We have long been taught to try to discover the client's self-image which, in part, conditions his strivings and group identification, his probable degree of self-involvement in treatment. We have not been quite as sensitive to ethnic and class factors which enter as well into the client's view of the agency, a strategic variable in treatment. What class and cultural framework distinguishes a particular client's approach to a child guidance clinic, to adoption, to institutional or foster home placement for the child? If the only concept of significant relationship is, as is likely for the Mexican, a purely informal and "personal" one, what happens when such a client is exposed to the zealously guarded psychotherapeutically conditioned worker-client relationship of our professional sub-culture?

One defense against either over-use or under-use of social science material is assimilation of its best concepts into an invigorated art of professional helping. It is possibly not so important that one knows all the details of ethnic and class differences but that every worker start with the recognition that *there will be* patterned differences among clients which should affect both diagnosis and treatment. It is no longer admissible to overlook the differential effects of the matriarchal and patriarchal family on the personalities of family members, or to fail to observe what happens when traditional family roles are threatened or disturbed in a new environment. The impact of immigration and urbanization cannot be intuitively handled or naively avoided. The "hard core" family cannot be fully explained as one merely showing character disorders. Resistance is a many-faceted expression of the total personality with cultural as well as unconscious roots. The stronger personality will mobilize normal defenses against outer stresses—the threats and hazards of existence, discrimination, unemployment, restriction of rights, inferior status; the weaker personality will erect defenses against inner stresses. Practitioners attuned to the importance of the social environment as well as to psychodynamics, will find in this volume significant keys to environmental stresses against which the client's reactions may be evaluated, and appropriate treatment approaches thereby clarified. The social worker can no longer regard himself as competent in psychosocial diagnosis, able to distinguish between neurotic and normal defenses, unless he is well equipped to weigh the balance between inner and outer stresses.

Social workers, in particular those chiefly engaged in casework, are familiar with the mechanism of identification in the learning experience and the treatment situation, but few have given attention to group identifications deriving from social institutions beyond the family circle. Social reality, including group customs and behavior, ultimately affects the total functioning of the personality. If we are to develop, now and in the future, our characteristic method in psychosocial study, diagnosis, and treatment, knowledge of group and cultural patterns must match our not inconsiderable knowledge of internal personality organization.

The section of the *Readings* on deviant behavior as a property of groups throws a light particularly on the *sources* of deviance. Intrapsychic pressures, such as those stemming from the oedipal situation, are usually accepted as essential for diagnosis by the practitioner. We have not been equally aware of the ways in which the social environment conditions the individual's behavior towards deviance. Who should know better than the social worker how culturally patterned limitations operate; how especially tragic is the situation when the individual seeks goals which the social structure does not permit him to attain?

The concept of social role has, perhaps, been better assimilated in the practice of group work than of casework, but as individual and group "specialists" become qualified as *social workers,* knowledge about status and role press for wider attention and use in treatment. An understanding of role conflict, in the client, in the worker-client relationship, often in the practitioner's own roles, is especially important because of the strains such conflicts can create. The concept of role in terms of age, sex, occupation, and other factors takes on flesh and blood meaning as one sees with fresh insight how culturally induced role perceptions assist or play havoc with the successful functioning of the personality.

Along with role, theories of social stratification come alive and challenge new thinking and treatment direction in case after case of mental discord, vocational guidance, housing, and standards of living. Already familiar with the psychodynamic theory of frustration-aggression, how much more clearly the social worker can see individual, group, and even mass reactions when the dispossessed minorities and stigmatized groups do not have ready access to socially valued goals. One recognizes again, in stronger color, problems of relationship, the effects on families and neighborhoods of competing or conflicting value systems; the effect of stress on men and women through prolonged unemployment, illness, or other hazards, and the degree to which such stresses disrupt already tenuous family and group relations.

Social workers have often been criticized for not moving more strongly into social action. As we better understand the nature of social stratification, the effects of value systems, the importance of community power structure as it affects established practice, we will certainly be more effective both in the formulation of social policy and the methods of social action.

To one who has spent most of her professional career at the New York School of Social Work, it is gratifying to note the extent to which the climate and development of the School are reflected in the publication of this volume. This climate has been strongly affected by the educational leadership of the School, and by the influence of teachers like the late Eduard C. Lindeman, who inspired generations of students to become aware of how their values enter into every level of practice and sometimes come into conflict with the value systems of client groups, agency boards, and the surrounding community. The creative re-development of course material on the relationship of social science to social work practice by Professor Stein, together with Professor Cloward who later joined him in this work, after the pioneering efforts in introducing cultural subject matter by Professor Emeritus Mary Hurlbutt, was made possible by the receptive atmosphere generated in the School. This course material in turn, under the outstanding leadership of the two editors of this volume, has had an electric effect on the entire curriculum. It was their work in this field of teaching that provided the impetus for *Social Perspectives on Behavior,* a reader for practitioners that signalizes the advent of a fresh new influence on practice and theory.

Social work is indebted to these two scholars who, themselves qualified practitioners, have brought so much that is important within reach of us all. This volume will also stimulate many social workers to go further and deeper as students and so make an informed contribution to their own and related professions.

New York School of Social Work
Columbia University

July, 1957

Preface

This book of readings is intended to enable both the student and the experienced social worker—as well as the teacher, psychologist, and psychiatrist—to familiarize himself with concepts and findings in the social sciences which are relevant to professional practice. Although each section of the volume contains at least one theoretical contribution, most of the selections are factual and empirical, describing and analyzing variations in the behavior of individuals from different segments of the American social structure. This book is not, in other words, designed as a text in social science; no attempt has been made to cover all interpretations of the social order or to give a rounded view of the social sciences. The themes have been chosen for their applicability to practice, the selections within the themes for their scope and clarity. No integrated theory is presented throughout the volume; moreover, inconsistencies and even contradictions appear, as these too are part of development in the social sciences. It is our hope, however, that the total comprises organized, illuminating, and provocative ideas that can be incorporated into the thinking and practice of the social worker and other professionals.

The field of social work is, for the most part, only beginning to evolve a sophisticated set of operational assumptions regarding the influence of the social environment upon behavior. We have often viewed the social environment, if only implicitly, as either a repressive barrier against which the individual struggles for self-expression and to whose pressures he must accede, or as oppressive and depriving. However, the social environment is more than a source of restraint or deprivation. It is a dynamic complex of forces which participate in the shaping of personality and the determination of behavior. If we view the individual as being independent of his environment, or being set against it, or being what he is despite his environment, we will not be likely to search out and to identify the linkages, the bonds between the individual and the social structure. The social environment is not self-evident and unproblematical; in fact, it is extraordinarily complex and subtle. To the extent that we have not recognized this, we have neglected to give it the detailed attention and analysis that we have given to the biological and psychological components of behavior.

There is little doubt that in recent years social workers have recognized the need for an increasing investment in the social sciences. While social work and social science were intimately related in the early years of the development of professional social work, their contact was relatively meager from the 1920's to the 1940's. During this period social work was primarily concerned with incorporating the insights of dynamic psychology into its theory and practice. While continued interest in the social sciences was not entirely absent, we did not keep abreast of the marked technical and theoretical advances of sociology, cultural anthropology, and social psychology.

More recently, particularly since World War II, there has been an intellectual ferment in social work which has led inevitably to renewed concern with the social sciences. This ferment has been fed by many sources, including the interest of social scientists in working with social agencies and social work data; the enlivened curiosity of social work students whose undergraduate preparation in the social sciences had substantially improved; the growth of interdisciplinary research, with greater availability of funds as the result of the increased interest of large foundations; the search for answers to new questions of social work theory and practice, a search which often borrowed both research method and theory from social science. As a consequence, there has been a potently revived interest in the nature of society in terms that do not neglect social work's continuing concern with housing, unemployment, and minorities, but include as well a deeper and more sophisticated perspective on the social environment.* This book is both an outgrowth and reflection of this renewed interest in the social environment.

Practitioners who seek to become better acquainted with the literature of social science should bear in mind two points regarding socio-cultural perspectives which distinguish it from other perspectives on behavior. *First, the social scientist is not so much concerned with the incidence of a particular aspect of behavior as he is with the rate of its occurrence.* The fact that criminals may be found in all walks of life is of less interest to the social scientist than the fact that proportionately they are found more frequently in some walks of life than in others (e.g., proportionately more frequently in some occupational spheres, or social classes, or ethnic groups). He is concerned with the fact that *various forms of behavior—including deviant behavior—are not randomly distributed throughout the social structure, but vary in a predictable way from one social position to another.* Thus, Durkheim, in his famous study of suicide, did not ask why a particular individual committed suicide, but rather why Protestants were more likely than Catholics or Jews to take their own lives. In a similar way, one may inquire about patterned variations in the rates of mental illness, divorce, delinquency, and a whole host of behavioral phenomena.

The second point to be made about the sociocultural approach is that

---

*See especially, Herman D. Stein, "Social Science in Social Work Practice and Education," *Social Casework*, April 1955, pp. 147-155; see also Ernest Greenwood, "Social Science and Socal Work: A Theory of Their Relationship," *Social Service Review*, March 1955, pp. 20-33; Roger Little, "The Social Side of Casework," *Socal Casework*, April 1950, pp. 162-164; Otto Pollak, *et al.*, *Social Science and Psychotherapy for Children* (New York, Russell Sage Foundation, 1952); Kimball Young, "Social Psychology and Social Casework," *American Sociological Review*, February 1951, pp. 54-61; Peter L. Sandi, "A Cultural Approach to Social Work," *Human Organization*, Vol. 8, No. 2, 1949, pp. 15-19; Sol Ginsburg, "The Impact of the Social Worker's Cultural Structure on Social Therapy," *Social Casework*, October 1951, pp. 319-25; Herman D. Stein, "Sociocultural Factors in Psychiatric Clinics for Children," *Social Service Review*, March 1956, pp. 9-19.

explanations of differing rates of behavior are sought in the nature of the social environment itself. The sociocultural perspective contributes to our understanding of human behavior because it provides a basis for assessing *the consequences of patterned exposure to different locations in the social structure.* To find out why middle-class individuals are more likely to exhibit neurotic behavior than lower-class individuals, one might, for example, look at typical differences in social classes with regard to child-rearing mores, or family structures, or occupational roles. For just as no two individuals experience the social environment in quite the same way, neither are any two positions in the social structure quite the same. Each location has its own unique features. It is of precisely this variability in the social environment that we have not been altogether mindful. Although we readily acknowledge the hazards to health which typify various occupational pursuits, the way in which different occupational roles affect the individual's values, family relationships, or psychological well-being are not equally apparent to us. One frequently encounters case histories of marital conflict or parent-child difficulty which fail even to note the occupation of the father, much less the meaning of this occupational role for diagnosis and treatment. This should not be construed to mean that pressures arising from occupational pursuits (or socioeconomic position, or ethnicity, or any other specific sociocultural factor) are immediately relevant to the case in hand; nonetheless, *some* sociocultural factors are relevant in *every* case. To omit consideration of them defeats the purpose of diagnostic procedures and can deflect treatment processes from the most appropriate and beneficial goals, for it presumes that the individual has an existence and can be understood apart from the particular social milieu in which he is enmeshed.

The sociocultural perspective, accordingly, directs attention to the relationship between social position and human behavior. Knowledge of the social environment alerts and sensitizes us to the pressures which predispose the individual, depending on his location in the social structure, to engage in one rather than another form of behavior. And once we have defined the salient environment of a given individual, our diagnostic framework may be elaborated and refined by weaving in knowledge of intrapsychic, organic, and other relevant factors.

As in the case of any generalizations based on group data, the reader should be cautioned against applying sociocultural generalizations to any individual without very careful study of the individual to determine whether the generalization really holds in his case. The distinction between rates of behavior and the behavior of a single individual is obviously fundamental. For those who deal with individual behavior as such, any attempt to adapt a theory which explains general rates of behavior to a single instance is perilous and should be approached with the greatest caution. However, generalizations (e.g., regarding child-rearing, etc.) may still be useful even when they do not apply to a particular individual or family. When the generalization fits the individual, it can be the source of clues for the practitioner as to life goals, attitudes, and actual or potential strains. When the individual does not conform to generalizations that apply to his group, however, the absence of such conformity may be just as significant clinically as its presence. The sources of non-conformity are often illuminating and thus diagnostically vital; the consequences of non-conformity—in terms of satis-factions and of problems—may often become the focus of treatment.

In viewing social science material—whether in this book or elsewhere—the practitioner should be careful to retain his perspective as a practitioner, rather than to regard himself as a social scientist. He does not have to be a social scientist in order to be a good practitioner, and his ultimate function as a practitioner is quite distinct from that of the social scientist. The heart of the distinction lies in the difference between the function of an academic discipline and the function of a professional discipline. The underlying func-tion of the academic discipline, as of all science, is to acquire and disseminate knowledge, even if it is knowledge for its own sake. The task of developing means for applying the knowledge in practice belongs to the professional discipline. The objective of the professions is to help people—through social planning and through preventive and direct services, with the acquisition of knowledge being subordinated to this end.

This volume presents an array of salient materials on the social environ-ment which provide a deeper understanding of human behavior. Many of the implications of this material for diagnostic processes will no doubt be evident to the experienced practitioner. Since there is continuity between diagnostic appraisals and treatment plans, the fuller utilization of social science knowledge in the former must inevitably affect the latter. This continuity requires that those responsible for practice do not stop with the understand-ing of such material, but pursue its implications for a revised professional methodology. What the academic discipline provides by way of understanding, the professional discipline transforms into prescriptions for action. This is the essential and the ultimate task—a task which has not been attempted in this book. It is our conviction that the social work profession of the future will be characterized by a vigorous emphasis on the development of new techniques of change—applicable to individuals, groups, and communities—based on a more sophisticated understanding of the social environment and its relationship to psychodynamics.

If we look at any one social determinant of behavior, such as socio-economic position, some of the possible implications for professional method-ology become evident. On the basis of existing data, for example, there appear to be different types of delinquency which vary by class position, because of different pressures and different alternatives available at different social levels. Treatment, therefore, could be more specifically shaped to these distinct pressures and alternatives, as well as to characteristic modes of behavior. Techniques suitable for the middle-class child may be relatively ineffective for the lower-class child. Thus, the emphasis on treatment of the delinquent through verbalizing both by the therapist and child, the very use of one-to-one clinical relationships, the objective of stimulating emotional growth through self-awareness, the utilization of formal structure in treatment, may all be more related to the responses of the middle-class than the lower-class youth. For the latter, non-verbal techniques, a minimum of intellectualization, the utilization of peer groups (as in the case of workers attached to "street gangs") may be far more effective in stimulating change than the characteristic battery of devices accenting "rational" types of communication and control. In the case of group work services, similarly, there should be sharper inquiry into whether techniques that may be relevant to middle-class youth, such as those of adult group leadership, of requirements for group organization, of methods of resolving disputes, or of defining standards of acceptable behavior, do not require substantial modification when directed to lower-class youth.

When we consider that class position is only one social variable that may affect treatment, the importance of a comprehensive view of the social environment for the practitioner becomes more sharply evident. Whether it is the treatment of delinquency, programing of leisure-time activities for youth, or the provision of casework services, greater concentration on the social determinants of behavior, together with psychological or biological factors, will lead to development of more effective techniques and clearer treatment objectives. This is not, of course, to say that no such developments have been taking place; there have been many innovations in which use was made of social perspectives. It is a question, rather, of emphasis; we are convinced that the present needs of the profession require a much stronger emphasis on knowledge of the social environment both for the construction of a more potent arsenal of techniques and methods, and for the more incisive definition of the practitioner's role.

By blending the psychological and the social, as our knowledge in both areas increases, the uniqueness of our professional discipline will be increasingly clarified. The growing body of social science knowledge will permit us to fulfill, more effectively than in the past, that definition of our function that has always been central: namely, that we help people by affecting the relationship between them and their social environment.

We wish to express our gratitude first to the New York School of Social Work, Columbia University. The educational leadership and the intellectual climate of the New York School of Social Work, Columbia University, made it possible for us to experiment with course material, and provided stimulus and encouragement in the production of this volume. Furthermore, the School's liberal policy in providing clerical assistance was of great help and is much appreciated.

The cooperation and interest of The Free Press, and particularly of Jeremiah Kaplan, has been sustaining and encouraging. It should be noted that this is the first venture of The Free Press in publishing a volume directed primarily towards a social work audience. We wish to acknowledge as well the valuable technical assistance of Sidney Solomon and Elaine Cohen.

To Alice Horowitz, our secretary, we express our thanks for an arduous task excellently performed.

Our deep appreciation is extended to the publishers and authors of the selections included in this volume for their kind permission to reprint material.

HERMAN D. STEIN
RICHARD A. CLOWARD

August 1957
New York School of Social Work
Columbia University

SECTION I
Family Structure and Ethnic Patterns

Social workers have always regarded the family as being of primary importance in the development of individuals, and have treated the well-being of family life as a major objective of professional service. Our attention has been invested principally in the psychological relationships between husbands and wives and between parents and children, the latter relationship, in particular, having life-long consequences for the personality development of the child.

The relationship of the family to society, the influence of the social environment on family structure and values, have had much less recognition in our theoretical understanding and therefore less impact on practice. As the content in the following section will demonstrate, it is through the family that the social system most effectively molds the individual. It is the family that most decisively prepares the individual to assume his appropriate roles in society, imparts its norms and values, and imbues him with patterns of behavior.

The family, as the mediating agent between the larger social environment and the individual, is itself shaped by social determinants. Families in different societies, and often in different segments of the same society, vary in structure, by which we mean that such factors as the particular individuals comprising a family, the basis of marriage, and the relationship of spouses to their own parents, may differ considerably. In most extended kinship families in many parts of the world the household would normally consist of three or more generations, the choice of marital partner would be by parental decision, and the bride would (in the typical patriarchal type of extended kinship family) take up residence with her husband in the home of his father. In many such family structures, the primary obligation of the husband is to his parents rather than to his wife, and the underlying objective of the family is the continuation of the family line, rather than the immediate welfare of parents and children.

(1)

By contrast, the American nuclear family, the prototype of the American middle-class family, characteristically begins with marital partners who choose one another on the basis of a romantic attachment, set up a household separated from either set of their own parents, and raise children who eventually marry and similarly leave the parental household. This family is therefore described as an isolated, conjugal, open choice type of family. Whereas the extended kinship family is typically found in agrarian societies, the nuclear family arises in highly industrialized societies, although there are occasional variations in both kinds of societies.

While there has been considerable comparative social anthropological study of family structures, little is known of the differential effect of a particular family structure on personality development. However, being raised in an extended kinship family (where there would characteristically be several significant adults in the household other than parents) as against growing up in an isolated nuclear family, undoubtedly has differential consequences for personality formation.

The American nuclear family has been subject to intensive study in the past decades. While there are variations by class and ethnic group, the middle-class nuclear family is the modal type, and in that sense the most significant for study. Many authorities, such as Kingsley Davis and Talcott Parsons, point out the "intensity" of emotional relationships in this family as a source of strain between parents and children. In the smaller American family, the absence of strong kinship ties (other than between parents and children), in contrast to those existing in most European societies, compel a virtually exclusive dependence of children on their parents, and particularly of the child on his mother. Where the mother has emotional problems, the intensity of the relationship between mother and offspring, undiluted by interaction with other significant adults in the household, can easily lead to emotional problems in the child.

Arnold Green analyzes the nuclear family in terms of the neurotic conflict often generated in the middle-class child, who is engaged in a frustrating attempt both to submit to parental dominance and to achieve in order to fulfill parental demands. In many middle-class families, he suggests, "love" becomes a currency to be given or withheld depending on the extent of the child's conformity to parental expectation, with consequences of permanent underlying insecurity.

There are strengths in middle-class family structure. It is highly adaptable to an industrialized society which calls for ease and frequency of geographical mobility. It presupposes free choice in marriage between spouses based on mutual love and respect with an accent on individual rights and independence, values highly regarded in our society. There are also characteristic strains. Status, depending mainly on the occupation of the father, is achieved rather than ascribed. The pressure on the father to be upwardly mobile in order to achieve higher status may be great and induce family tension, and for the child the pressure to achieve may be beyond his capacity. When the romantic basis for marriage is not sustained, the marriage itself is subject to severe pressure. Unlike the extended kinship family, where marriage is often more a union of two families than two individuals, and the major objective is continuity rather than marital happiness, the nuclear family rests on the frail fulcrum of mutual consent between two individuals.

It is apparent that social work requires a deep understanding of this kind of family, in order to maximize the family's strengths and minimize its strains. At the same time, we need to know the variations in family structure in our society as influenced particularly by social class and ethnic factors. We will reserve consideration of class influences to a later section and concentrate here on the ethnic component, which is particularly potent in determining family structure and roles.

The concept and term "ethnic" encompasses, and has gradually come to replace, such unsatisfactory expressions as race and nationality, when reference is intended to groups which are each identifiable by a core of cultural homogeneity. Thus, Negroes, Jews, Italians, and Puerto Ricans are all ethnic groups. The influence of ethnic background ranks with that of social class position as among the key societal determinants of individual and family behavior.

Ethnic determinants of behavior are deep and ramified, stemming as they do from cultural patterns which penetrate the individual's values, and his roles in life, and define the norms which provide him with a sense of location, identity, and continuity with his cultural group. When ethnic patterns are challenged by conflicting norms, as in the case of the new immigrant, conflict and strain are bound to develop. In the Italian group, we see the breakdown of ethnic solidarity in Ware's description of the Italian immigrant in New York City's Greenwich Village; in Campisi's analysis of the Italian family in the United States, we see the ways in which family structure and roles have been affected by the new environment.

The Southern Italian family, characteristic of the bulk of Italian immigration to the United States, was of a modified extended kinship type, strongly patriarchal, with arranged marriages and a deep feeling of family solidarity. While a husband was not expected to take his bride to the home of his father, obligations to his family and particularly to his father continued throughout life. Family roles were highly differentiated, the obligations and rights of each member of the family clearly defined. Girls and boys were separated, and virginity among girls rigidly guarded, the boys responsible with their father for the protection of their sisters' virtue in particular, and the family honor in all respects.

The virtually total control exercised by the father in the Italian village was gradually undermined in the family's interaction with a metropolitan community in New York City. Schools, social agencies, police and courts, the sons' employers whom the father did not know, all impinged on the paternal authority. Total protection of girls became an impossibility. The intense filial loyalty of sons could easily become deflected by the influence of new norms transmitted by children encountered in street and school and by conflicting values communicated by movies, press, and official agencies. With the second and third generations, the accent on large families as the fulfillment of the mother's role waned drastically, arranged marriages were no longer the rule, boys and girls tended to strike out for an independence which to the immigrant father could seem no less than rank rebellion. The conflict between first and second generations, in the Italian as well as in other groups where ethnic patterns collided with contrasting values of the dominant society, sometimes led to delinquency among youth, as pointed out in the Introduction to the section on Deviance.

Similar conflicts were experienced by the East European Orthodox Jewish family, where patriarchal authority also tended to break down and tension was created by the resistance of second generation children to the religious tenets of their parents. As mentioned in connection with Deviant Behavior, such conflict is now being experienced by the Puerto Rican immigrant, where the father's role as breadwinner is threatened by the greater availability of jobs for Puerto Rican women. Children of such families are often confused as to parental roles, caught between ethnic values transmitted by parents, the inability of their parents to live up to these values in the new environment, and the pressure of the surrounding society toward other norms of behavior.

While in the United States immigrant groups have tended, with acculturation through the generations, to lose their old world ethnic patterns, some traces of varying intensity remain An interesting hypothesis, developed by the historian Marcus Hansen, is that the third generation—who have no problem about being "American"—manifest an inevitable tendency to identify once again with the cultural tradition, if not the specific ethnic pattern, of their immigrant forbears. While there is evidence that traces of ethnicity tend to persist through generations, we know relatively little about the forms such persistence takes in the various ethnic groups. We have, however, become sensitized to the almost inevitable problems of the first and second generations. The moving account by Oscar Handlin of the experience of the peasant immigrant in his transition to the New World graphically brings some of these problems to our attention.

Social workers have, by inclination and by training, relatively little difficulty in accepting cultural differences, for the acceptance of difference is a cardinal tenet in the social worker's professional ideology. The general lack, however, of a systematic appraisal of ethnic factors in their more subtle forms, impairs the fullest use of the social worker's psychological understanding and philosophic orientations. Where the caseworker, in particular, is dealing with a client from an ethnic group not completely familiar to him, certain key questions should inevitably occur to him. What, for example, is the client's image of the agency, in view of his ethnic background? He may be culturally oriented to see the agency as distant and authoritative, as in the case of the Spanish-American, or as an opponent he must pressure, cajole, and match wits with. What may seem like a manipulative quality in a client may turn out to be simply a natural tendency carried over from previous experience and having little bearing on his basic personality. The image of the worker to which the client is ethnically conditioned should also be systematically viewed. The client may have a clear idea of the worker's role, and of his own role as client; his perception of both, however, may be clearly at variance with the worker's. He may view the worker as a powerful representative of authority, a person who can use pressure, a threatening and potentially hostile figure, or a friendly, informal person in whom to confide. His own role may be seen as appropriately passive and helpless, as demanding, informal and egalitarian, or respectful and distant. The tendency of many Puerto Rican clients to refer only to material needs and to refrain from discussion of personal feelings bespeaks a culturally conditioned perception of the social worker as an external, influential agent to whom one may turn only in the event of material necessity. To many a European client, the intimate discussion of feelings may fix the worker's role as personal, not professional. The Southern lower-class Negro may view the white worker as essentially hostile, or unduly powerful, bringing to the fore culturally shaped attitudes of resistance or subservience. The Eastern European Jewish client may tend to view the Jewish agency's service as his right, anticipating that pressure and demands would be quite expected behavior on his part, but may be intimidated by the public agency or the non-sectarian agency. What, furthermore, is the client's image of his problem as culturally determined? To the "old-American" middle-class woman a child born out of wedlock may represent a calamity deeply fraught with complex emotions, to the rural Southern lower-class Negro girl it may be a natural event, relatively uncomplicated by feelings of self-censure.

Such considerations of the ethnic component should be a consistent part of the social worker's approach. In agencies dealing with substantial numbers of a particular ethnic group, it would seem logical for the agency to have a thorough knowledge of the particular group. Generally, it would be unreasonable to expect expert knowledge by the social worker of every ethnic group that could possibly be represented by clients in casework or group work agencies; we should, however, know as much as we can about relevant ethnic backgrounds. Having the appropriate questions in mind as to the possible ethnic influences operating would go a long way, moreover, to minimize distorted perceptions on the part of the worker.

As with any other group determinant of personality and behavior, one cannot know beforehand that any given individual shares the patterns characteristic of his group. But the modal tendencies in these cultural patterns suggest where to look for possible or probable influences. The Spanish-American's different values concerning time, or the East European Jew's reaction to pain and medical treatment, are both in contrast to those of the "old American" and failure to view such behavior in ethnic terms risks distortion in diagnostic appraisal. At the same time, the very absence in a client of characteristics dominant in the group (a condition which need not at all connote pathology) provides cues for diagnostic exploration.

The fact, on the other hand, that a given aspect of behavior may be ethnic in character, or "cultural" does not make it automatically "normal," for ethnic patterns may be used neurotically. The father in a patriarchal family may exploit his role to express a neurotic need to control and punish, but the worker would have to be sensitive to the ethnically defined role in order to deal with its pathologic manifestations in any given case. An awareness of the ethnic component and its ramifications thus becomes essential to the social worker's professional equipment.

THE KINSHIP SYSTEM OF THE
CONTEMPORARY UNITED STATES

Talcott Parsons

IT IS A REMARKABLE fact that, in spite of the important interrelations between sociology and social anthropology, no attempt to describe and analyze the kinship system of the United States in the structural terms current in the literature of anthropological field studies exists. This is probably mainly accounted for by two facts; on the sociological side, family studies have overwhelmingly been oriented to problems of individual adjustment rather than comparative structural perspective; while from the anthropological side, a barrier has grown out of the fact that a major structural aspect of a large-scale society cannot be observed in a single program of field research. To a considerable extent the material must come from the kind of common sense and general experience which have been widely held to be of dubious scientific standing.

There are two particularly cogent reasons why an attempt to fill this gap is highly desirable. In the first place, an understanding of the kinship system on precisely this structural level is of the greatest importance to the understanding of the American family, its place in the more general social structure, and the strains and psychological patterning to which it is subject.[1] Secondly, our kinship system is of a structural type which is of extraordinary interest in relation to the broader problems of typology and systematic functional dynamics of kinship generally. As a type which, to the writer's knowledge, is not closely approached in any known non-literate society, its incorporation in the range dealt with by students of kinship should significantly enrich their comparative perspective.[2]

It can perhaps be regarded as established that, with proper precautions, analysis of kinship terminology can serve as a highly useful approach to the study of the functioning social structure. In the case of the English language two precautions in particular, over and above those commonly observed, need to be explicitly mentioned. Such analysis alone cannot serve to bring out what is distinctively American because the terminology has been essentially stable since before the settlement of America, and today there is no significant terminological difference between England and the United States. Moreover, the differences in this respect between English and the other modern European languages are minor. Hence all analysis of terminology can do is indicate a very broad type within which the more distinctively American system falls.

Reprinted from *The American Anthropologist* (January 1943), pp. 22-38, by permission of the author and the publisher. (Copyright, 1943, by the American Anthropological Society.)

As shown in the accompanying diagram[3] the American family is perhaps best characterized as an "open, multilineal, conjugal system."

The American Kinship System

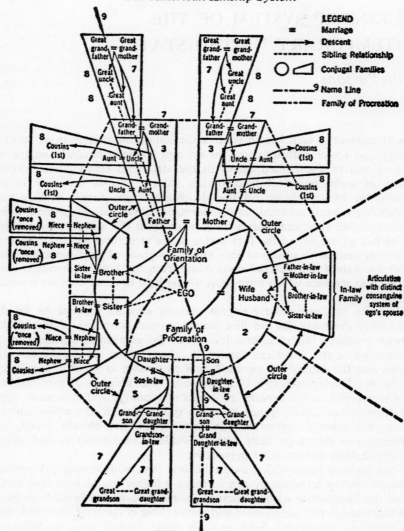

Types of Families:

1. Ego's family of orientation (1 only)
2. Ego's family of procreation (1 only)
3. First-degree ascendant families (2)
4. First-degree collateral families (number indefinite, 2 types)
5. First-degree descendant families (number indefinite, 2 types)
6. In-law family (1 only)
7. Second-degree ascendant and descendant families (4 ascendant, descendant indefinite, 4 types)
8. Second-degree collateral families (all children ego's cousins)

Structural Groupings of Families:

I. 1 + 2 — Inner circle
II. 3, 4, 5 + 6 — Outer circle
III. 1, 2, 3, 5, 7 — Families in line of descent
IV. 4, 8 — Collateral families
V. 2, 6 — Articulation of consanguine systems
   No difference according to sex of ego, except in the term for spouse and the fact that, if ego is female, name line does not extend below ego in line of descent.

The conjugal family unit of parents and children is one of basic signifi-cance in any kinship system. What is distinctive about our system is the absence of any important terminologically recognized units which cut across conjugal families, including some members and excluding others. The only instances of such units are *pairs* of conjugal families each with *one* common number. Terminologically, in common speech, it is significant that we have only the words "family," which generally[4] refers to the conjugal unit, and "relatives," which does not refer to *any* solidarity unit at all, but only to anyone who is a kinsman.

Ours then is a "conjugal"[5] system in that it is made up *exclusively* of interlocking conjugal families. The principle of structural relation of these families is founded on the fact that, as a consequence of the incest tabu, *ego* is always in the structurally normal[6] case a member not of one but of two conjugal families, those which Warner usefully distinguishes as the "family of orientation," into which he is born as a child, and the "family of procreation," which is founded by his marriage. Moreover, he is the *only*[7] common member of the two families.

From *ego's* point of view, then, the core, of the kinship system is consti-tuted by families 1 and 2 in the diagram, in the one case his father, mother, brothers and sisters, in the other his spouse (wife or husband according to *ego's* sex), sons and daughters. Monogamy is reflected in the fact that *parent* and *other parent's spouse* are terminologically identical, modified only by the prefix "step" to take account of second or later marriages, and in the fact that the terms "father" and "mother," "husband" and "wife" can each apply to only *one* person at a time. It is also notable that no distinction on the basis of birth order is made—all brothers are terminologically alike. But most notable of all is the fact that *none* of these seven kinship personalities is terminologically identified with *any* relative outside the particular conjugal family in which he is placed. A brother is specifically distinguished from any male cousin, the father from any uncle, the mother from any aunt, etc. These two conjugal families may conveniently be treated as constituting the "inner circle" of kinship structure. Relative priorities within them will be discussed below.

Now *each* member of *ego's* inner kinship circle is the connecting link with one other terminologically recognized conjugal family. Moreover he links the family of orientation or procreation, as the case may be, with *only* one farther conjugal family, and each individual with a separate one. The kinship personalities of this "outer circle" are not, however, always terminologically separate, a fact which will be shown to be of paramount importance.

The first pair of outer circle families, which may be called the "first ascendant," are the families of orientation of *ego's* parents. Besides the articulating personality, each consists of the four kinship personalities of grandfather, grandmother, uncle, and aunt. The most significant fact is the lack of terminological distinction between the paternal and the maternal families of orientation—grandparents, uncles, and aunts are alike regardless of which "side" they are on. The only important exception to this lies, not in kinship terminology as such but in the patrilineal inheritance of the family name, giving rise to a unilateral "name line" (9). Since the same principle of lack of distinction by sex of intervening relative applies to still higher ascendant generations—the four great- and eight great-great-grandfathers—it is perhaps more accurate to speak of a "multilineal" than a "bilateral" system. Anyone of an indefinite number of lines of descent *may* be treated as significant. Above all, the extension from the principle of *bi*laterality, as applied to the first ascendant (and descendant) families, to that of *multi*lineality in succeeding generations is completely incompatible with any tendency to bifurcate the kin group on the basis of lines of descent.

The same fundamental principles govern the terminology of the first collateral families (4), the families of procreation of *ego's* siblings; and the first descendant families (5), the families of procreation of his children. It is noteworthy that siblings' spouses are terminologically assimilated to sibling status with the suffix "in-law"—generally not used in address or the more intimate occasions of reference—and that nephews and nieces are the same whether they are brothers' or sisters' children and regardless of the sex of *ego*. Similarly, spouses of children are assimilated to the status of children by the same terminological device and sons' and daughters' children are all indiscriminately grandchildren. Finally, both siblings-in-law and children-in-law are terminologically segregated from *any* kinship status relative to *ego* except that in the particular conjugal family which is under consideration.

The last outer circle family, the "in-law" family (6), has a very particular significance. It is the only one of those to which *ego's* inner circle is linked to which he is not bound by descent and consanguinity but only by affinity, and this fact is of paramount importance, signalizing as it does the openness of our system. Preferential mating on a kinship basis, that is, is completely without structural significance, and every marriage in founding a new conjugal family brings together (in the type case) two completely unrelated kinship groups which are articulated on a kinship basis *only* in this one particular marriage. Seen from a somewhat more generalized point of view, if we take the total inner and outer circle group of *ego's* kin as a "system," it is articulated to another entirely distinct system of the same structure by *every* peripheral relative (i.e., who is not a connecting link between the inner and outer circles), except in the direct lines of descent. The consequence is a maximum of dispersion of the lines of descent and the prevention of the structuring of kinship groups on any other principle than the "onion" principle, which implies proportionately increasing "distantness" with each "circle" of linked conjugal families.[8]

Another way of throwing the significance of this basic open-multilineal structure into relief is to recall the fact that *ego's* family of orientation and his in-law family are, from the point of view of his children, both first ascendant families whose members are equally grandparents, aunts, and uncles.

In principle it is possible to distinguish, beyond the outer circle, further layers of the "onion" indefinitely. It is, however, significant that our kinship terminology ceases at this point to apply at all specific terms, fundamentally recognizing only two elements. First is the line of descent (8) designated by the ascendant and descendant family terms with the addition of the reduplicating prefix "great"—e.g., great-grandfather and great-grandson. Second is the indiscriminate category "cousins" into which all "collaterals" are thrown, with only the descriptive[9] devices of "first," "third," "once removed," etc., to distinguish them by.

How far can this distinctive terminology be said to "reflect" the actual institutional structure of kinship? In a broad way it certainly does. We clearly have none of the "extended" kin groupings so prevalent among non-literate peoples, such as patrilineal or matrilineal clans. We have no exogamy except that based on "degree" of relationship. We have no preferential mating—all these are a matter of the simplest common knowledge. But to get a clearer conception of the more specific structure it is essential to turn to a different order of evidence.

In the first place, the importance of the isolated conjugal family is brought out by the fact that it is the normal "household" unit. This means it is the unit of residence and the unit whose members, as a matter of course, pool a common basis of economic support, money income, especially in our society. Moreover, in the typical case neither the household arrangements nor the source of income bear any specific relation to the family of orientation of either spouse, or, if there is any, it is about as likely to be to the one as to the other. But the typical conjugal family lives in a home segregated from those of both pairs of parents (if living) and is economically independent of both. In a very large proportion of cases the geographical separation is considerable. Furthermore, the primary basis of economic support and of many other elements of social status lies typically in the husband's occupational status, his "job," which he typically holds independently of any particularistic relation to kinsmen.

The isolation of the conjugal unit in this country is in strong contrast to much of the historic structure of European society where a much larger and more important element have inherited home, source of economic support, and specific occupational status (especially a farm or family enterprise) from their fathers. This of course has had to involve discrimination between siblings since the whole complex of property and status had to be inherited intact.[10]

Hence considerable significance attaches to our patterns of inheritance of property. Here the important thing is the absence of any specific favoring of any particular line of descent. Formally, subject to protection of the interests of widows, complete testamentary freedom exists. The American law of intestacy, however, in specific contrast to the older English Common Law tradition, gives all children, regardless of birth order or sex, equal shares. But even more important, the actual practice of wills overwhelmingly conforms to this pattern. Where deviations exist they are not bound up with the kinship structure as such but are determined by particular relationships or situations of need. There is also noticeable in our society a relative weakness of pressure to leave all or even most property to kin.[11]

It is probably safe to assume that an essentially open system, with a primary stress on the conjugal family and corresponding absence of groupings of collaterals cutting across conjugal families, has existed in Western society since the period when the kinship terminology of the European languages took shape. The above evidence, however, is sufficient to show that within this broad type the American system has, by contrast with its European forbears, developed far in the direction of a *symmetrically multilineal type.* This relative absence of any structural bias in favor of solidarity with the ascendant and descendant families in any one line of descent has enormously increased the structural isolation of the individual conjugal family. This isolation, the almost symmetrical "onion" structure, is the most distinctive feature of the American kinship system and underlies most of its peculiar functional and dynamic problems.

Before entering into a few of these, it should be made clear that the incidence of the fully developed type in the American social structure is uneven and important tendencies to deviation from it are found in certain structural areas. In the first place, in spite of the extent to which American agriculture has become "commercialized," the economic and social conditions of rural life place more of a premium on continuity of occupation and status from generation to generation than do urban conditions, and hence, especially perhaps among the more solidly established rural population, something approaching Le Play's *famille souche* is not unusual.

Secondly, there are important upper class elements in this country for which elite status is closely bound up with the status of ancestry, hence the continuity of kinship solidarity in a—mainly patrilineal—line of descent, in "lineages."[12] Therefore, in these "family élite" elements the symmetry of the multilineal kinship structure is sharply skewed in the direction of a patrilineal system with a tendency to primogeniture—one in many respects resembling that historically prevalent among European aristocracies, though considerably looser. There is a tendency for this in turn to be bound up with family property, especially an ancestral home, and continuity of status in a particular local community.

Finally, thirdly, there is evidence that in lower class situations, in different ways both rural and urban, there is another type of deviance from this main kinship pattern. This type is connected with a strong tendency to instability of marriage and a " mother-centered" type of family structure—found both in Negro and white population elements.[13] It would not disturb the multilineal symmetry of the system but would favor a very different type of conjugal family, even if it tended to be as nearly isolated as the main type from other kinship groups. This situation has not, however, been at all adequately studied from a functional point of view.

Thus what is here treated as the focal American type of kinship structure is most conspicuously developed in the urban middle class areas of the society. This fact is strong evidence of the interdependence of kinship structure with other structural aspects of the same society, some of which will be briefly discussed below.

In approaching the functional analysis of the central American kinship type, the focal point of departure must lie in the crucial fact that *ego* is a member not of one but of two conjugal families. This fact is of course of central significance in all kinship systems, but in our own it acquires a special importance because of the structural prominence of the conjugal family and its peculiar isolation. In most kinship systems many persons retain throughout the life cycle a fundamentally stable—though changing—status in one or more extended kinship units.[14] In our system this is not the case for anyone.

The most immediate consequences lie in the structural significance of the marriage relationship, especially in relation to the lines of descent and to the sibling tie. *Ego,* by marriage, that is, is by comparison with other kinship systems drastically segregated from his family of orientation, both from his parents—and their forbears—and from his siblings. His first kinship loyalty is unequivocally to his spouse and then to their children if and when any are born. Moreover, his family of procreation, by virtue of a common household, income, and community status, becomes a solidarity unit in the sense in which the segregation of the interests of individuals is relatively meaningless, whereas the segregation of these interests of *ego* from those of the family of orientation tends relatively to minimize solidarity with the latter.

The strong emphasis for *ego* as an adult on the marriage relationship at the expense of relationships to parents and siblings is directly correlative with the symmetrical multilineality of the system. From the point of view of the marriage pair, that is, neither family of orientation, particularly neither parental couple, has structurally sanctioned priority of status. It is thus in a sense a balance of power situation in which independence of the family of procreation is favored by the necessity of maintaining impartiality as between the two families of orientation.[15]

From this it seems legitimate to conclude that in a peculiar sense which is not equally applicable to other systems the marriage bond is, in our society, the main structural keystone of the kinship system. This results from the structural isolation of the conjugal family and the fact that the married couple are not supported by comparably strong kinship ties to other adults. Closely related to this situation is that of choice of marriage partner. It is not only an open system in that there is no preferential mating on a kinship basis, but since the new marriage is not typically "incorporated" into an already existing kinship unit, the primary structural reasons for an important influence on marriage choice being exerted by the kin of the prospective partners are missing or at least minimized.

It is true that something approaching a system of "arranged" marriages does persist in some situations, especially where couples brought up in the same local community marry and expect to settle down there—or where there are other particularistic elements present, as in cases of "marrying the boss's daughter." Our open system, however, tends very strongly to a pattern of purely personal choice of marriage partner without important parental influence. With increasing social mobility, residential, occupational, and other, it has clearly become the dominant pattern. Though not positively required by the kinship structure, freedom of choice is not impeded by it, and the structure is probably, in various ways, connected with the motivation of this freedom, an important aspect of the "romantic love" complex.

A closely related functional problem touches the character of the marriage relationship itself. Social systems in which a considerable number of individuals are in a complex and delicate state of mutual interdependence tend greatly to limit the scope of "personal" emotional feeling or, at least, its direct expression in action. Any considerable range of affective spontaneity would tend to impinge on the statuses and interests of too many others, with disequilibrating consequences for the system as a whole. This need to limit affective spontaneity is fundamentally why arranged marriages tend to be found in kinship systems where the newly married couple is incorporated into a larger kin group, but it also strongly colors the character of the marriage relationship itself, tending to place the primary institutional sanctions upon matters of objective status and obligations to other kin, not on subjective sentiment.[16] Thus the structural isolation of the conjugal family tends to free the affective inclinations of the couple from a whole series of hampering restrictions.

These restrictive forces, which in other kinship systems inhibit affective expression, have, however, positive functional significance in maintaining the solidarity of the effective kinship unit. Very definite expectations in the definition of role, combined with a complex system of interrelated sanctions, both positive and negative, go far to guarantee stability and the maintenance of standards of performance. In the American kinship system this kind of institutionalized support of the role of marriage partner through its inter- locking with other kinship roles is, if not entirely lacking, at least very much weaker. A functionally equivalent substitute in motivation to conformity with the expectations of the role is clearly needed. It may hence be suggested that the *institutional* sanction placed on the proper subjective sentiments of spouses, in short the expectation that they have an obligation to be "in love" has this significance. This in turn is related to personal choice of marriage partner, since affective devotion is, particularly in our culture, linked to a presumption of the absence of any element of coercion. This would seem to be a second important basis of the prominence of the "romantic complex."

Much evidence has accumulated to show that conformity with the expectations of socially structured roles is not to be taken as a matter of course, but that often there are typically structured sources of psychological strain which underlie socially structured manifestations of the kind which Kardiner has called "secondary institutions."[17]

Much psychological research has suggested the very great importance to the individual of his affective ties, established in early childhood, to other members of his family of orientation. When strong affective ties have been formed, it seems reasonable to believe that situational pressures which force their drastic modification will impose important strains upon the individual.

Since all known kinship systems impose an incest tabu, the transition from asexual intrafamilial relationships to the sexual relation of marriage—generally to a previously relatively unknown person—is general. But with us this transition is accompanied by a process of "emancipation" from the ties both to parents and to siblings, which is considerably more drastic than in most kinship systems, especially in that it applies to both sexes about equally, and includes emancipation from solidarity with *all* members of the family of orientation about equally, so that there is relatively little continuity with *any* kinship ties established by birth for anyone.

The effect of these factors is reinforced by two others. Since the effective kinship unit is normally the small conjugal family, the child's emotional attachments to kin are confined to relatively few persons instead of being distributed more widely. Especially important, perhaps, is the fact that no other adult woman has a role remotely similar to that of the mother. Hence the average intensity of affective involvement in family relations is likely to be high. Secondly, the child's relations outside the family are only to a small extent ascribed. Both in the play group and in the school he must to a large extent "find his own level" in competition with others. Hence the psychological significance of his security within the family is heightened.

We have then a situation where at the same time the inevitable importance of family ties is intensified and a necessity to become emancipated from them is imposed. This situation would seem to have a good deal to do with the fact that with us adolescence—and beyond—is, as has been frequently noted, a "difficult" period in the life cycle.[18] In particular, associated with this situation is the prominence in our society of what has been called a "youth culture," a distinctive pattern of values and attitudes of the age groups between childhood and the assumption of full adult responsibilities. This youth culture, with its irresponsibility, its pleasure-seeking, its "rating and dating," and its intensification of the romantic love pattern, is not a simple matter of "apprenticeship" in adult values and responsibilities. It bears many of the marks of reaction to emotional tension and insecurity, and in all probability has among its functions that of easing the difficult process of adjustment from childhood emotional dependency to full "maturity."[19] In it we find still a third element underlying the prominence of the romantic love complex in American society.

The emphasis which has here been placed on the multilineal symmetry of our kinship structure might be taken to imply that our society was characterized by a correspondingly striking assimilation of the roles of the sexes to each other. It is true that American society manifests a high level of the "emancipation" of women, which in important respects involves relative assimilation to masculine roles, in accessibility to occupational opportunity, in legal rights relative to property holding, and in various other respects. Undoubtedly the kinship system constitutes one of the important sets of factors underlying this emancipation since it does not, as do so many kinship systems, place a structural premium on the role of either sex in the maintenance of the continuity of kinship relations.

But the elements of sex-role assimilation in our society are conspicuously combined with elements of segregation which in many respects are even more striking than in other societies, as for instance in the matter of the much greater attention given by women to style and refinement of taste in dress and personal appearance. This and other aspects of segregation are connected with the structure of kinship, but not so much by itself as in its interrelations with the occupational system.

The members of the conjugal family in our urban society normally share a common basis of economic support in the form of money income, but this income is not derived from the co-operative efforts of the family as a unit— its principal source lies in the remuneration of occupational roles performed by individual members of the family. Status in an occupational role is generally, however, specifically segregated from kinship status—a person holds a "job" as an individual, not by virtue of his status in a family.

Among the occupational statuses of members of a family, if there is more than one, much the most important is that of the husband and father, not only because it is usually the primary source of family income, but also because it is the most important single basis of the status of the family in the community at large. To be the main "breadwinner" of his family is a primary role of the normal adult man in our society. The corollary of this role is his far smaller participation than that of his wife in the internal affairs of the household. Consequently, "housekeeping" and the care of children is still the primary functional content of the adult feminine role in the "utilitarian" division of labor. Even if the married woman has a job, it is, at least in the middle classes, in the great majority of cases not one which in status or remuneration competes closely with those held by men of her own class. Hence there is a typically asymmetrical relation of the marriage pair to the occupational structure.

This asymmetrical relation apparently has both exceedingly important positive functional significance, and is at the same time an important source of strain in relation to the patterning of sex roles.[20]

On the positive functional side, a high incidence of certain types of patterns is essential to our occupational system and to the institutional complex in such fields as property and exchange which more immediately surround this system. In relatively common-sense terms it requires scope for the valuation of personal achievement, for equality of opportunity, for mobility in response to technical requirements, for devotion to occupational goals and interests relatively unhampered by "personal" considerations. In more technical terms it requires a high incidence of technical competence, of rationality, of universalistic norms, and of functional specificity.[21] All these are drastically different from the patterns which are dominant in the area of kinship relations, where ascription of status by birth plays a prominent part, and where roles are defined primarily in particularistic and functionally diffuse terms.

It is quite clear that the type of occupational structure which is so essential to our society requires a far-reaching structural segregation of occupational roles from the kinship roles of the *same* individuals. They must, in the occupational system, be treated primarily as individuals. This is a situation drastically different from that found in practically all non-literate societies and in many that are literate.

At the same time, it cannot be doubted that a solidary kinship unit has functional significance of the highest order, especially in relation to the socialization of individuals and to the deeper aspects of their psychological security. What would appear to have happened is a process of mutual accommodation between these two fundamental aspects of our social structure. On the one hand our kinship system is of a structural type which, broadly speaking, interferes least with the functional needs of the occupational system, above all in that it exerts *relatively* little pressure for the ascription of an individual's social status—through class affiliation, property, and of course particular "jobs"—by virtue of his kinship status. The conjugal unit can be mobile in status independently of the other kinship ties of its members, that is, those of the spouses to the members of their families of orientation.

But at the same time this small conjugal unit can be a strongly solidary unit. This is facilitated by the prevalence of the pattern that normally only *one* of its members has an occupational role which is of determinate significance for the status of the family as a whole. Minor children, that is, as a rule do not "work," and when they do, it is already a major step in the process of emancipation from the family of orientation. The wife and mother is either exclusively a "housewife" or at most has a "job" rather than a "career."

There are perhaps two primary functional aspects of this situation. In the first place, by confining the number of status-giving occupational roles of the members of the effective conjugal unit to one, it eliminates any competition for status, especially as between husband and wife, which might be disruptive of the solidarity of marriage. So long as lines of achievement are segregated and not directly comparable, there is less opportunity for jealousy, a sense of inferiority, etc., to develop. Secondly, it aids in clarity of definition of the situation by making the status of the family in the community relatively definite and unequivocal. There is much evidence that this relative definiteness of status is an important factor in psychological security.[22]

The same structural arrangements which have this positive functional significance also give rise to important strains. What has been said above about the pressure for thoroughgoing emancipation from the family of orientation is a case in point. But in connection with the sex-role problem there is another important source of strain.

Historically, in Western culture, it may perhaps be fairly said that there has been a strong tendency to define the feminine role psychologically as one strongly marked by elements of dependency. One of the best symbols perhaps was the fact that until rather recently the married woman was not *sui juris,* could not hold property, make contracts, or sue in her own right. But in the modern American kinship system, to say nothing of other aspects of the culture and social structure, there are at least two pressures which tend to counteract this dependency and have undoubtedly played a part in the movement for feminine emancipation.

The first, already much discussed, is the multilineal symmetry of the kinship system which gives no basis of sex discrimination, and which in kinship terms favors equal rights and responsibilities for both parties to a marriage. The second is the character of the marriage relationship. Resting as it does primarily on affective attachment for the other person as a concrete human individual, a "personality," rather than on more objective considerations of status, it puts a premium on a certain kind of mutuality and equality. There is no clearly structural superordination-subordination pattern. Each is a fully responsible "partner" with a claim to a voice in decisions, to a certain human dignity, to be "taken seriously." Surely the pattern of romantic love which makes his relation to the "woman he loves" the most important single thing in a man's life, is incompatible with the view that she is an inferior creature, fit only for dependency on him.

In our society, however, occupational status has tremendous weight in the scale of prestige values. The fact that the normal married woman is debarred from testing or demonstrating her fundamental equality with her husband in competitive occupational achievement, creates a demand for a functional equivalent. At least in the middle classes, however, this cannot be found in the utilitarian functions of the role of housewife since these are treated as relatively menial functions. To be, for instance, an excellent cook, does not give a hired maid a moral claim to a higher status than that of a domestic servant.

This situation helps perhaps to account for a conspicuous tendency for the feminine role to emphasize broadly humanstic rather than technically specialized achievement values. One of the key patterns is that of "good taste," in personal appearance, house furnishings, cultural things like literature and music. To a large and perhaps increasing extent the more humanistic cultural traditions and amenities of life are carried on by women. Since these things are of high intrinsic importance in the scale of values of our culture, and since by virtue of the system of occupational specialization even many highly superior men are greatly handicapped in respect to them, there is some genuine redressing of the balance between the sexes.

There is also, however, a good deal of direct evidence of tension in the feminine role. In the "glamor girl" pattern, use of specifically feminine devices as an instrument of compulsive search for power and exclusive attention are conspicuous. Many women succumb to their dependency cravings through such channels as neurotic illness or compulsive domesticity and thereby abdicate both their responsibilities and the opportunities for genuine independence. Many of the attempts to excel in approved channels of achievement are marred by garishness of taste, by instability in response to fad and fashion, by a seriousness in community or club activities which is out of proportion to the intrinsic importance of the task. In all these and other fields there are conspicuous signs of insecurity and ambivalence. Hence it may be concluded that the feminine role is a conspicuous focus of the strains inherent in our social structure, and not the least of the sources of these strains is to be found in the functional difficulties in the integration of our kinship system with the rest of the social structure.[23]

Finally, a word may be said about one further problem of American society in which kinship plays a prominent part, the situation of the aged. In various ways our society is oriented to values particularly appropriate to the younger age groups so that there is a tendency for older people to be "left out of it." The abruptness of "retirement" from occupational roles also contributes. But a primary present concern is one implication of the structural isolation of the conjugal family. The obverse of the emancipation, upon marriage and occupational independence, of children from their families of orientation is the depletion of that family until the older couple is finally left alone. This situation is in strong contrast to kinship systems in which membership in a kinship unit is continuous throughout the life cycle. There, very frequently, it is the oldest members who are treated with the most respect and have the greatest responsibility and authority. But with us there is no one left to respect them, for them to take responsibility for or have authority over.

For young people not to break away from their parental families at the proper time is a failure to live up to expectations, an unwarranted expression of dependency. But just as they have a duty to break away, they also have a right to independence. Hence for an older couple—or a widow or widower—to join the household of a married child is not, in the terms of the kinship structure, a "natural" arrangement. This is proved by the fact that it is seldom done at all except under pressure, either for economic support or to mitigate extreme loneliness and social isolation.[24] Even though in such situations it may be the best solution of a difficult problem it very frequently involves considerable strain, which is by no means confined to one side. The whole situation would be radically different in a different kind of kinship structure. It may be surmised that this situation, as well as "purely economic" questions, underlies much of the current agitation for old age pensions and the appeal of such apparently fantastic schemes as the Townsend Plan.

In this brief paper there can be no pretense of anything approaching an exhaustive functional analysis of the American kinship system or of its structural interdependence with other aspects of our social structure. A few problems of this order have been presented, beyond a direct descriptive analysis of the kinship structure as such, to illustrate the importance of a clear and thorough grasp of this structure in the understanding of many problems of the functioning of American society, including its specific pathology. This, by and large, sociological students of the American family have failed to provide or use systematically. It is as a contribution toward filling the gap in our working analytical equipment that the present paper has been conceived.

THE CONTEMPORARY AMERICAN FAMILY AS AN ANTHROPOLOGIST SEES IT

Margaret Mead

AN ANTHROPOLOGIST looks at the American family as one of the many forms which the family has taken throughout human history since human beings first invented ways in which adult males could become more or less permanently responsible for the care of females and their children.[1] With a few exceptions which are so curious and contrived that they only emphasize the ubiquitousness of the institution of the family, all human societies have patterned the relationship between sexually paired adults and dependent young. The tie between the father and adult child may not be recognized as biological. It may be conceived as fostering only or as a spiritual contribution only in which the father gives spirit, the mother body. The children of other men may be accepted readily; children of several brothers may be regarded as having equivalent claims on the care of one of the brothers; brothers may be treated interchangeably in their access to each other's wives; or sisters may be regarded as potential wives of the same man. The primary fostering tie between parent and child may be extended to include a three-generation family with many collateral lines or shrunk to the tiny biological family of the modern three-room apartment dwellers who have no kin within a thousand miles. The authority of the father may last until death, or all social relations between father and son, even speech, may end at puberty. Women may become completely absorbed into the kin group of their husbands, taking their names and their burial places, or they may even retain control over their own dowries. The life of the next generation may be minutely described in terms of family relationships or family choices made by the parents, or each generation may construct its family life for itself. Marriages may be for life between one man and one woman, or serially monogamous, or between one man and several women, or, less usually, between one woman and two or more men.

But nowhere are these crucial relationships, within which women are protected and cared for during childbearing and little children nurtured and reared, left unpatterned and unregulated. During periods of very rapid social change, of migration, of war and epidemic, the carefully devised and delicate patterns, which rely far more for their preservation on the habituated bodies and vivid expectations of those who were reared within them than upon any external sanctions, may break down. Then, for a period, the primary unit tends to become what it is among the primates, females and young, with the males exercising a nonspecific dominative and protective function in regard to the whole group. During such periods or in certain sections of a population almost the whole support of the children may fall on the mother, as in certain lower economic groups in large cities, or among ethnic groups at the moment of cultural breakdown. Old forms of legal marriage may become so expensive and cumbersome that a large part of a population may

Reprinted from *The American Journal of Sociology* (May 1948), pp. 453-59, by permission of the author and publisher. (Copyright, 1948, by the University of Chicago Press.)

be said, at some period, to be living out of wedlock, but the new, altered, or simplified form will in time again become the recognized form of the family for that group.

Traditionally, societies have depended upon reproducing their orderly forms of family life by rearing children within families, who will regard that form of family life within which they were reared as normal, natural, and desirable. Children absorb during infancy and early childhood the whole pattern of family interrelationships which they then will be able to repeat, subject to the distortions introduced by hiatuses in their own experience, or idiosyncracies of their own constitution and personality. Even in a society which changes as rapidly as our own, a large proportion of our patterns of family life are attempts—often faulty attempts because circumstances are so changed or the other partner has learned such different patterns—to reproduce the family behavior learned in childhood. A large part of the disorganization of family life today, the frequency of divorce, the incidence of neurosis and disease, may be laid to the discrepancies and contradictions between the expectations learned in childhood and the actualities of the present time.

The American family pattern is an urban middle-class pattern, although upper-class patterns occur, and lower-class practice deviates sharply from middle-class standards, and rural family life still retains the stamp of an earlier historical period. Films, comic strips, radio, and magazines presuppose a middle-class family. This family is typically formed at marriage, when young people finally cease to speak of "my family" as referring to the parental family and begin to look toward a family of their own. It is expected to consist exclusively of husband, wife, and minor children, with the presence of in-laws to be prevented if possible and almost universally to be deplored, particularly by the unrelated spouse. Support from parents to married children is not expected, and, where married children have to give support to their parents, this is regarded as a handicap, a burden on the young marriage. Nor are married children expected to plan their lives on the expectations of ultimately inheriting from either set of parents-in-law; such inheritances when they come along are windfalls, good luck rather than something which may be properly looked forward to. While married children will acknowledge some responsibility for the support of aging parents, especially when widowed, almost no responsibility is taken for brothers and sisters and their children, except in cases of extreme emergency or disaster. Unmarried adult women are expected to support themselves and are often also expected to assume a larger share of the support of a parent than that which is shouldered by married sons and daughters.

The orientation of the new family is forward, and the young couple are normally expected to provide their own establishment. The parents may provide for a wedding or give them a house or a car, but these are works of supererogation, not expected parental behavior, such as is expected in countries in which the parents have to set the young couple up with full household equipment. The assumption is that the parents have given their children of both sexes a "good education" which equips them to choose a mate, earn a living, and manage their lives for themselves with a minimum of help, advice, or interference.

The new family is expected to be formed entirely on the choice of the young people, with the young man taking the formal initiative in making the actual proposal. In selecting a mate, the primary considerations are personal attractiveness in the girl and attractiveness and ability as a breadwinner in the boy; all other considerations, even health, are regarded as subsidiary to them. Common background is very often subsumed under personal attractiveness and congeniality, and the skills which may be necessary to homemaking and mating are regarded as appropriately learned after marriage by practicing them on and with the chosen partner. Here a convention of premarital chastity for the girl and a preference for minimal premarital experience for the boy combine with an equal expectation that the girl will know nothing about running a house or a man about budgeting his income and that during the early years of marriage romantic ardor must balance ignorance and lack of skill. Young people may, without criticism, marry without any accumulation of property of any sort, without any certainty of where they are going to live, and, provided they have a little cash in hand and the man has proved earning power, without his having a job at the moment. Very few human societies have encouraged young people to start a new family with such very small backing from parents and the wider kin group. Actually a great deal of help, both formal and informal, is given to new marriages, but it is not only not something which may be legitimately expected, but is actually something about which young people may feel considerable hesitation if not a real sense of inadequacy in accepting.

The American wife is expected to be educated, as well educated although not as highly trained as the husband, for there is more expectation that he will have a special money-bringing skill than that she will. Differences in education between men and women vary from couple to couple, and the only consistencies are a generally accepted delegation of earning to the husband and management of consumption to the wife. Which spouse prefers driving the car, listening to the radio, keeping up with the news, or participating in the community is a matter of individual adjustment subject to the rules of local groups or cliques but not a matter which is patterned by role for husband and wife. Until marriage the girl has been almost as free as her brother; if she has had a job, she has spent her money as she wished, giving her family something for her board where circumstances dictate such a course, and in recent years often leaving home to work and live in another city, with steadily decreasing protests from parents. For an unmarried son to leave home is still regarded as more usual than for an unmarried daughter. Until her decision to marry she is expected to be guided by the same considerations in the choice of a job which influence her brother—chance for advancement or security, interest, or money, or any combination of these. Once engaged, however, her life-orientation is expected to undergo a sharp change—ambition to shift from job to home.

The new home, so unsupported by parents or kin, is designed and planned by the young couple, very often an ill-assorted compromise between home memories and the new standards of contemporaries, of the department stores, and of women's magazines. Even the simplest middle-class home in the United States is a sort of stage set, constructed with thought, on which the family are going to enact their parts, against which the wife sees herself and the rest of the family. If the furniture is not new, it is at least newly bought second hand, and refurnished and rearranged with care. Within this home, the wife is expected to occupy herself, using it also as a platform from which she goes out into community life, of which, however, she has very little during the early years of her marriage. Where marriages have not taken place inside an existing youthful clique, it is expected that former friends of either spouse will prove trying and uncongenial and that new social groups will be formed based on neighborhood and community ties cultivated by the wife and on business ties cultivated by the husband. The claims of the wife for the local ties grow stronger when there are children and when their neighborhood companionships have to be considered. Husband and wife are expected to rely exclusively on each other as far as cross sex relationships are concerned and never to go out in mixed company without the other partner. On the whole, where men continue social relations with men after marriage, they are either labeled rather dubiously as "business" or frankly regarded as periods of relaxation—fishing, card-playing, yarning—antithetical to the more regulated home life. Women's relations with women outside the home are patterned either as parts of a local prestige game or as earnest endeavors to "do something worth while," and the grounds upon which men and women resent their spouses' outside interests tend to be very different.

A small family, with at least one child of each sex, for whom the parents can make adequate educational allowance, is regarded as more commendable than a larger family of children in which the children have to forego an education. A large family, however, all of whom receive good educations through a combination of parental help and their own energies is a great credit to everyone. It is regarded as unfortunate when children are born within the first two years after marriage, as this ties the young couple down too soon. Parenthood is a responsible anxious matter, in which the mother must keep herself continually up to date with changing standards of child care. Having children, for a woman, is pretty close in feeling to having a job, for a man—a necessary proof of adequacy and wholeness as a human being, something which one does not so much enjoy but something which one would be unwilling not to have done. Unemployed married women without children are under some compulsion to explain their lack of occupation to themselves or to their neighbors; until recently women who had successfully reared even one child felt that they had made an appropriate and dignified social contribution for which they deserved recognition and support for the rest of their lives. When the children marry and leave the home, the American woman is faced with the same type of readjustment as that facing her husband perhaps two decades later when he retires. The discrepancy in the timing of the husband and wife's retirement periods presents one of the problems of American marriage, as it is motherhood rather than housewifeliness which is the source of pride and self-sacrifice in the urban married woman. The period between the children's leaving home and old age is the main source of voluntary civic and social activity in the United States, as the married woman, trained to years of responsible social behavior in the care of family, finds her task cut in half while her strength is still unimpaired.

Marriage is for life, and all breaks in marriage are treated as failures, and failures which involve some degree of moral turpitude—either sexual or economic irresponsibility. At the same time, the extremely wide prevalence of divorce means that the possibility of divorce, defined as failure and as a disaster, is included in the picture of marriage. Women learn that they must keep their husbands, not merely from casual adventures or time spent wastefully elsewhere, but as husbands; and men learn that it is their wives' duty to keep them and that the world is filled with other women, married or unmarried, who, having failed or decided not to keep their own husbands, will try to attract them away from their present wives. This question of a wife's maintaining her attractiveness, in the face of the domestic routines, the sick bay, the broken drain, the unwashed coffee cups after last night's party, is felt to be a test of her adequacy and her sense of responsibility. A wife is not expected to try to keep her husband's love simply because love is a warm and pleasant thing or simply because she loves him and wants him to love her. Rather she must be continually on the alert to be a successful wife who is making a good job of her marriage. The moral alternatives are whether a woman is regarded as selfish because she "is just interested in keeping her husband" or is "unselfishly working to make a success of her marriage," which includes a sense of responsibility to her husband and children. With this burden of making the marriage relationship a continuous articulately happy experience in which each partner would choose the other over again each day—which puts a premium on never being unshaven or in curlers—there goes an explicit recognition that it is wrong to insist on the trappings of success where one has failed. The husband or wife who holds an unwilling partner—whatever the reason for the unwillingness—to a marriage from which he or she is trying to escape is regarded as behaving in an unsportsman-like manner. It is the wife's duty to make her husband want to stay and to shy away from taking too great risks with other women's efforts to impress him with their superior attractiveness. Similarly it is the husband's duty to provide for his wife and children so that she will want to stay with him. But, except within orthodox religious groups who still regard marriage as a sacrament, it is neither husband nor wife's duty to stay, once they are sure they want to leave, and, indeed, they may be regarded as doing harm to the other spouse and the children by bringing them up in a "home without love." The average American male's job insecurity, the fear that his maturity, which is based on his ability to earn his own living and provide completely for his family, may be taken from him by personal failure or by a depression, is matched by the average American wife's fear that she may fail at her job of homemaking and end up without a husband and perhaps with children to support.

Within this family, children are given an extraordinary amount of attention when judged by the standards of most other societies. Their needs, their wishes, and their performances are regarded as central and worthy of adult attention. The mother is the principal disciplining and character-molding parent and must both give love, comfort, and care, and stimulate and goad the child to achievement and outside contacts. Her inevitable oscillation between demanding achievement as a proof of the child's love and threatening to withhold her love if the child does not achieve produces some of the typical conflicts in American character which were especially apparent in young draftees in World War II. The mother also has to train the male child in assertiveness, bidding him at the same time to be peaceful and co-operative and to stand up for himself, which training is responsible for some of the characteristic American uncertainties about their own strength. The father's role is to provide at one time a more horizontal fraternal relationship, supporting the growing child, especially the son, in conflicts with his mother when her demands are excessive or she is too unwilling to let the child grow up, and occasionally introducing a sharp unpredictable bit of violent disapproval in reinforcement of the mother's discipline. While the relationship to the mother introduces into the American child's character the principal strains and conflicts in regard to ethical behavior and giving and receiving of love, the relationship to the father provides a fairly steady, although not very aggressive, support of the child's individuality and pressure toward maturity. Both parents offer the child an appreciative audience for his growing independence, achievement, and autonomy and thus establish firmly his habit of acting, while young, weak, and inexperienced, with the overemphasis which is not regarded as inappropriate because the child is so small that it is all right to show off.

In the training of the young child there is a strong emphasis upon habit training, his learning to eat and eliminate and to sleep at the right times, and an enormous interweaving of beliefs about health and hygiene with morality. Next in importance is the attainment of some degree of motor autonomy. Training of the emotions is a matter more of teaching a child that it should not feel disapproved emotions, like jealousy, hate, or envy, than of any great attending to manners or minutiae of interpersonal relationships, and an ethical insisting that the other person's feelings, rights, etc., must be taken into account. Children are expected to develop consciences modeled upon the admonitions and supported by the rewards and punishments administered by parents. Each child is given its own property; a room to itself is the ideal, and toys and books and tools are personal possessions, respect for which is enforced among brothers and sisters. The custom of paying children for small jobs in the home, and encouraging them to undertake small money-earning jobs outside the home as good for their characters, is widespread. Children are permitted to exert considerable pressure upon the family's choice of food, magazines, and radio programs, and the American advertisers regularly exploit this willingness to take consumption cues from children. Weaning is a gradual matter, punctuated by new privileges granted on birthdays and culminating in the period when either son or daughter becomes self-supporting. Self-support is defined not as actual ability to support one's self outside the home but as having a full-time paid job, all of which may actually go into clothes and pleasure, while the parents continue to provide most or all of the board. The tendency to overestimate and overstate an earning child's own money—so sharply contrasted with urban working-class practice in many European countries—has a later reflection in the tendency to treat a married woman's earnings as in some peculiar sense her own and not simply the resource of the whole family—which is the view held of the husband's earnings. The expectation is that children will press toward maturity and that parents will provide an admiring audience, practical help, and a certain check on their impetuosity, which, however, should actually serve as a further stimulus to make them take on more responsibilities.

The relationship between the character formation of the child and the life-history of its own immediate family, its financial ups and downs, accidents, illnesses, etc., is extraordinarily close, because of the isolation of each small family. Events which would be blurred or reinterpreted by the behavior of neighbors and relatives here become crucial in forming the personalities of the children. This extreme importance of the small, intimate family is to some degree compensated for by the great importance of the age group and by the extent to which group standards supersede family standards at adolescence.

The theme of American parenthood was well summarized by the head of a great high school, who turned to the group of assembled parents, many of them foreign born, many of them showing the marks of sacrifice which had made it possible for their children to attend high school, and said: "Let us rise to greet the children," and then added: "They offer you, their parents, the only thing they have to offer you—their success."

Two major readjustments are taking place in the American family pattern today. The first is the new ways of life which are becoming necessary as the isolated biological family becomes more and more usual, at a period when the demands made on the housewife as a result of new knowledge of nutrition, pediatrics, psychology, and home management in general have also greatly increased. Society is expecting more of the wife and mother at the very period when she, through isolation and lack of help and resources, is less able to meet these demands. Community services of all sorts—all-year-round school facilities, housekeeping services, twenty-four-hour boarding for children during illness in the home, prepared foods, expert advisory services to supplement the homemaker's traditional behavior, which is no longer adequate—are the results.

These innovations find cultural support in our American focus on the welfare of children and in the major contribution to future success which is given by careful education in childhood. Resistance to these changes and a continued insistence that, because families managed in the past to meet every emergency of illness, unemployment, insanity, accident, death, without formalized outside help, they should continue to do so now are rooted in the American cultural belief in the importance of autonomy, independence, and responsibility. Only by a widespread recognition that the family of today is being asked to do a much more difficult task of child-rearing, with much fewer resources than were available to the farm and small-town family, nested among relatives and neighbors and informed by a trusted tradition, can this resistance be shifted.

The second great readjustment which is occurring in the family pattern is the terminability of American marriage. As the old religious sanctions which enjoined fidelity until death, regardless of such ephemeral considerations as congeniality or "happiness," have faded for large sections of the population and have been powerless to save many more marriages from dissolution, new ways of holding marriages together are developing. The life of a family is coming to be seen as a ship which may be wrecked by any turn of the tide unless every member of the family, but especially the two parents, are actively and co-operatively engaged in sailing the boat, vigilantly tacking, trimming their sails, resetting their course, bailing in storms —all to save something which is worth their continuous care. This new ideal, in which all the members of a family work together to keep alive an ever changing relationship, may in time provide us with the necessary new ethical sanction within which to give our changing family dignity and safety.

THE MIDDLE-CLASS MALE CHILD
AND NEUROSIS

Arnold W. Green

IN ANOTHER PUBLICATION,[1] Erich Fromm's and Karen Horney's use of general cultural data to explain neurosis was criticized. It was pointed out that while these two analysts have a concept of cultural neurosis (Horney) and pathological normalcy (Fromm), from which "the culture" is suffering, at the same time a clinical picture of neurosis is presented without reference to culture—the going awry of personal relationships, particularly of the child-in-family. While in her earlier work in this country Dr. Horney found love-frustration the key to the individual etiology of neurosis,[2] later, and indicating Dr. Fromm's influence, the key became the arbitrary imposition of authority within the family of orientation.[3]

Two things are being attempted in this paper: first, by a brief discussion of the socialization process taking place in a specific Polish industrial community to demonstrate the inadequacy of a clinical etiology of neurosis in terms of either love-thwarting or the arbitrary exercise of authority; second, to explain in sociological terms the context in which "lack of genuine love" and "authority" operate to produce neurotic symptoms.

1. Sinclair Lewis failed to "see" Sauk Center until he had spent some time at Yale and in New York. Similarly, to evaluate what parts the "lack of genuine love" and "arbitrary authority" in themselves play in the etiology of neurosis a comparison should be made of their effects in different contexts.[4]

The author spent his childhood and young adulthood in a Massachusetts industrial village of some three thousand population, most of which is made up of immigrant Poles and their native-born children. It was previously pointed out how the middle-class norms governing courtship and marriage do not apply within this local Polish colony.[5] This is also true of parent-child relationships.

The local Polish parents emigrated before marriage from farm villages and small towns in Poland. While the old familistic tradition has been slowly deteriorating in rural Poland for several decades, enough of that tradition was brought with them so that their expectations of their American-born children's conduct reflected an alien peasant system of values.

Reprinted from *The American Sociological Review*, (February 1946) pp. 31-41, by permission of the author and the publisher. (Copyright, 1946, by the American Sociological Society.)

An outstanding feature of peasant family life, in contradistinction to that of modern middle-class family organization, is the stress placed upon rules and work-functions rather than personal sentiment; and parental authority is excessive by the standards of any comparative segment of the American population.[6] These rules of conduct and this parental authority are out of place in the American industrial slum. Second-generation Poles participate in a social world outside the home which their parents, because of language difficulties and previous conditioning, are incapable of sharing or even of understanding. As bewildered parents attempt to enforce old-world standards, they are met with the anger and ridicule of their children. In answer to this, the parents have final recourse to a kind of authority which was unsanctioned in Poland: a vengeful, personal, irrational authority, which no longer finds support in the future hopes and ambitions of the children; and this new authority is no longer controlled by both parents' families and a cohesive community. But this personal authority will not suffice to curb their wayward progeny, who have little respect for their parents as persons, and who soon come to learn that their "American" playmates are not subjected to anything like it in their homes.

It is through this tragically antagonistic, mutually distrustful clash of wills that the relations of parents and children tend to be lacking in "love" (which is alien to the peasant *mores* anyway). At the same time, there is plenty of "irrational authority." In exasperation and fear of losing all control over their Americanized youngsters, parents apply the fist and whip rather indiscriminately. The sounds of blows, screams, howls, vexatious wails of torment and hatred are so commonplace along the rows of dilapidated millhouses that the passer-by pays them scant attention. *But those children do not become neurotic.*[7] Why? Because parental authority, however harsh and brutal, is, in a sense, casual and external to the "core of the self." The Polish parents do not have the techniques and opportunity to *absorb the personality* of the child. In the first place, the child has many models of behavior to adopt both within the family (five to eight children are, in estimate, modal in the Polish section of the village) and outside. Siblings present a more or less united front in their rebellion against their parents. Parent-avoidance techniques are easily acquired because of the parents' halting use of English and the fact that both parents, typically, work in the local factory, leaving the younger children to the daytime supervision of older children, which frequently results in no supervision at all. The open woods and fields are close at hand and the children roam far. The homes are not particularly clean, nor do they contain bric-a-brac or furniture of any value, so that the local Polish child is spared the endless admonitions which bedevil the middle-class child not to touch this or that.

The children also develop a tolerant or openly malicious contempt for their parents as stupid, unknowing of American ways, concerning which the children regard themselves authorities. By and large, the parents are obstacles to be avoided, or circumvented wherever possible. And while the resulting lack of identification with the parents virtually obviates demonstrations of affection, it also saves the children from feelings of guilt and repressed hostility.[8] The training of the child becomes, then, casual, haphazard, "free" in a sense, very similar to the training received in many primitive tribes, except for the negative other-regarding attitude of parent and child so typical in the village.

2. The claim has been made that "lack of love" and "irrational authority" do not, in and of themselves, cause the development of neurotic symptoms. These phenomena do operate, however, in individual etiologies of neurosis, but only within a certain context. The term "personality absorption" has already been used. Personality absorption is the physical and emotional blanketing of the child, bringing about a slavish dependence upon the parents. It is personality absorption, in conjunction with factors other than lack of love or irrational authority, that produces a certain type of neurosis.

To delineate the kind of socialization which maximizes personality absorption, it will be necessary to conceive of a parental type which simultaneously occupies several population segments: native-white, Protestant urban, college-educated, middle-class.[9] The training of children born to parents who can thus be characterized, is so experientially consistent it has a certain range of predictive value.

Now, how can we define the middle-class child's situation?[10] It has already been said that his personality is "absorbed,"[11] and to the extent that it has been absorbed, he is in danger of developing neurotic symptoms. But why is it absorbed?

Perhaps the best way to view his social conditioning is to consider his parents, and their position in relation to him.[12] The father's work takes him far from the place of residence, where most of his associates are only slightly less strangers to him than they are to his family. He is a white-collar worker. As a salesman, office worker, minor bureaucrat, or professional man, his job-techniques revolve around manipulating the personalties of others, instead of tools. Since he has internalized the supreme middle-class value, individual success, he tries to use his associates as means to further his career; in fact, he has himself been conditioned to view his associates, education, hobbies, intellectual interests, in terms of their possible value to his career.[13] On the job he views himself not so much as functionally associated with others in a common purpose, as a self-contained unit establishing "contacts" with others. His work relations are not defined in fixed terms of status and role to the extent that they were in the past for he is on the move, or views himself in that way. He has, then, a well-developed tendency to view his relations with others *in terms of what he, as a mobile, displaced person, can get out of them.*

Yet the modern middle-class father cannot use his *child* in the new sense of manipulating others to his own advantage, nor, be it noted, in the ways available in the past. In the old rural-familistic system, the child served well three predominant interests of the father: he would soon work on the farm, or during the earlier days of the industrial revolution, in the factory, become an economic asset to the father; in other words, he would provide economic security in the father's old age,[14] and finally, he would provide psychological security by preserving the family name, a form of this-worldly immortality in a society which made the family the primary repository of most social values.

In terms of dollars alone, the cost of raising a modern middle-class child represents a serious threat to the personal ambition of the father.[15] At the very time when, in terms of his primary success-goal, he should have time and money available for further study if a professional man, money for clothes, entertaining, household furniture and an automobile for purposes of presenting a "front" in any event; at this time when his career is in its initial and hence its crucial stage, the presence of the child represents a diversion of energy and funds, so long, of course, as the career remains his primary goal. A certain degree of ambivalence directed toward the child is inevitable. Not the depth, but the present height of the middle-class birth-rate is the noteworthy phenomenon, indicating an amazing vitality of the old rural-familistic values which find little support in modern social structure.

With the advancing individuation of modern society, not only has individual success become a supreme value, but also individual, hedonistic enjoyment. The child again presents an interference with most of the recreation available to the middle-class father, for whether commercialized (movies, sports events, plays) or social (golf, bridge, tennis, dinner parties), these are designed not for family-wide participation, but individual- or couple-participation.

In conjunction with the above factors, the growing middle-class emphasis upon "scientific child care"[16] and the child's higher education further increase the father's duties and obligations, while his rights steadily diminish. What emerges from his total situation is an ambivalence toward his child which is more or less widespread, though very rarely admitted, even with confidantes.[17] Finally, children interfere with the companion and partner roles of husband and wife, which are more and more displacing the traditional patriarchal and housewife-and-mother roles.[18]

And how about the mother? She enters marriage and perhaps bears a child with no definite role and series of functions, as formerly. Her old role within the patriarchal family, with its many functions, its economic and emotional security, its round of community participations, is lost, but no well-defined role has taken its place. She feels inferior to men because comparatively she has been and is more restricted.[19] If she works after marriage she faces sex discrimination on the job and perhaps her husband's criticism if his traditional role of bread-winner is important to him.

Half-seriously she prepared for a career prior to marriage, half-seriously because a career is regarded by most middle-class girls as insurance against the grim possibility they will not be married; through a "good" marriage (the folk phrase "she married well" refers not to personality adjustment but to the bank balance and career prospects of the husband) the middle-class girl attains far more status than is possible through a career of her own. But the period of phantasy dalliance with a career, or an embarkation upon one, leave her ill-fitted for the drudgery of housecleaning, diapers, and the preparation of meals. The freedom which the urban apartment and modern household devices have brought the middle-class housewife has been commonly misinterpreted as well as exaggerated. While the Victorian housewife had more work to do, that work was part of a well-integrated system of household and community activities. While the modern middle-class housewife has more leisure-time than either her mother or grandmother, she must still work at a number of household jobs for which she has not been trained, which are usually not an essential part of her value-system, and which are isolated from her social activities. One sociologist has expressed this dilemma facetiously:

half her working day is spent doing something she does not like, the rest is spent thinking up ways of getting even with her husband. The resulting boredom frequently leads to a period of indecision early in the marriage over whether to have children or resume the career. This internal conflict has been well-expressed by Thompson:

> In the present economic situation in the United States increase of population is not desired. The fact that small families are the rule is one of the factors driving women out of the home. Now that they are not in the home a kind of vicious circle is formed, for it is no longer convenient to be occupied in the home by one or two children. Much conflict centers here, for it is one of the problems of the culture which as yet has no generally satisfactory solution. Individual women have worked out ways of having both children and a career, but most women still do one or the other; and in either case there are regrets and often neurotic discontent ... the problem is not solved by going to the other extreme and trying to prove one's adequacy by having a child or two. The women of past generations had no choice but to bear children. Since their lives were organized around this concept of duty, they seldom became aware of dislike of the situation. .... Nowadays, when women have a choice, the illusion is to the effect that unwanted children are less common, but women still from neurotic compulsion bear children they cannot love.[20]

And so it is inevitable that the child shall be viewed with some degree of ambivalence by both father and mother, for he represents a direct interference with most of the dominant values and compulsions of the modern middle class: career, social and economic success, hedonistic enjoyment. There is some doubt that *under modern middle-class conditions,* children automatically bring husband and wife closer together.[21]

To return to the consideration of the middle-class child. Personality absorption takes place against a background of parental ambivalence. The mother has little to do, in or out of the home; she is her single child's sole companion.[22] Modern "scientific child care" enforces a constant supervision and diffused worrying over the child's health, eating spinach, and ego-development; this is complicated by the fact that much energy is spent forcing early walking, toilet-training, talking, because in an intensively competitive milieu middle-class parents from the day of birth on are constantly comparing their own child's development with that of the neighbors' children. The child must also be constantly guarded from the danger of contacting various electrical gadgets and from kicking valuable furniture. The middle-class child's discovery that the living-room furniture is more important to his mother than his impulse to crawl over it unquestionably finds a place in the background of the etiology of a certain type of neurosis, however absurd it may appear.

Under constant supervision, with limited play-area in a house touching other homes on all sides, or in an apartment, and lacking companions, the child's physiological expansiveness, fed by his boredom, persists in getting him into trouble: screaming, running around the apartment, upsetting daddy's shaving mug, rending teddy-bear in two, emptying his milk on the rug to observe what pattern will be formed. This "trouble" is all a matter of definition. Similar behavior, in modified form, would not be interpreted in primitive society as "trouble," and neither would it be by Polish parents in the community above described.

Already the parents have made "love" of supreme importance in their relation to the child, theirs for him and his for them, partly because of the love-complex of our time, which is particularly ramified within the middle class,[23] and partly as a compensation for the many sacrifices they have made for the child, long debated before and after its arrival. *The child's need for love is experienced precisely because he has been conditioned to need it.* That the need is biological seems unlikely.[24] Now, the more ambivalent the parents are toward the child, the more seriously is the "trouble" he causes them interpreted. He should not act in such a way because of the sacrifices they have made in his behalf, and the least he can do is show his gratitude by "loving" them in turn, *i.e.,* keeping out of "trouble." When the trouble inevitably occurs, *the most effective punishment imaginable is the threat to withdraw their love from him.* He "needs" that love because his personality has been absorbed by these two persons, because he has been conditioned to have a slavish-emotional dependence upon them. *Not the need for parental love, but the constant threat of its withdrawal after the child has been conditioned to the need, lies at the root of the most characteristic modern neurosis.* Mamma won't like you if you don't eat your spinach, or stop dribbling your milk, or get down from that davenport. To the extent that a child's personality has been absorbed, he will be thrown into a panic by this sort of treatment, and develop guilt feelings to help prevent himself from getting into further trouble. In such a child a disapproving glance may produce more terror than a twenty-minute lashing in little Stanislaus Wojcik.

The threat of love-withdrawal is usually the mother's technique for controlling the child. At first the father may threaten to withdraw love, but as the child grows older the father finds a more subtle control—the expression of disapproval. The child is limited to his parents for modelling his behavior. While very young, he wants to set the table and sweep the floor "like mummy." In a few years standards of manly conduct are imposed and he wants to do things "like daddy." The father now controls him through the child's new self-conception, and it is not so much the use of "authority" as threatening the child's self-respect.[25] The child is not a person who amounts to very much, how does he ever expect to get along when he gets old enough to go to school, or join the Boy Scouts, or go to college, or get a job? Again, to the extent that the child's personality has been absorbed, he will be made to feel small, insignificant, unworthy. And, feeling absorbed, caught and helpless, must propitiate these combined god-monsters that he needs so desperately. Hence anxiety, guilt feelings, the sense of inferiority; seek security at all costs for he is living alone and afraid, in a world he never made.[26]

As for authority, its exercise generates neurotic symptoms only under two conditions, both of which must be present; close identification of the child with at least one parent; the effective blocking-off of all avenues of authority-avoidance for twenty-four hours of the day. Neither of these conditions is met in the Polish homes described, and thus while the authority wielded by Polish parents is far more "irrational" (as defined by Fromm) than that likely to be encountered in many middle-class homes, neuroses are not developed. Indeed, it seems unlikely that Fromm's differentiation between rational and irrational authority has much psychological relevance. The *child* is hardly in a position to understand when authority is ". . . based on the competency of the person in authority to function properly with respect to the task of guidance he has to perform . . ."[27] and when it is ". . . based on the power which the authority has over those subjected to it and on the fear and awe with which the latter reciprocate."[28] Perhaps the Polish children do not experience irrational authority exactly as defined by Fromm, for while they fear parental authority they also are hostile toward and contemptuous of their parents, and thus are not in awe of them. Nevertheless, the important differentiation is not between rational and irrational authority but the extent to which any parental authority succeeds in absorbing the child's personality, *which is itself dependent upon factors other than the imposition of arbitrary authority.*

Yet when we have used the term "personality absorption" we have not by any means explained a neurosis etiology. The personality of the middle-class girl of the late nineteenth century was "absorbed" by her parents, she was subjected to the demands of "love" and unquestioning obedience, at least ideally; nevertheless, the rate of neurosis under those conditions was probably not too high, as nearly as can be judged at this later date. Why? Because she was not faced with inconsistent expectations of conduct on the part of others and herself. Because love and obedience were integrated within a role which changed relatively slightly from childhood into adolescence, courtship, and finally into marriage. In other words, her initial goals and self-conceptions were constantly re-enforced with each new life experience.

The modern middle-class child on the other hand, particularly the boy, who has found surcease from anxiety and guilt by blind obedience and "love" for his parents, is not allowed to stabilize his relationships with others on that basis. His play-group, which may be denied him until he has reached school age, makes him feel a certain shame and inadequacy in attempting to approach its members with familiar techniques.[29] He also early discovers that he is involved in competition with others, as an individual with his contemporaries, and as a representative of his family unit with other families.

If the abstraction "ours is a competitive society" is translated into terms of what happens to the child born to modern middle-class parents, it becomes quite relevant to the present discussion. Before the child has developed a real self-awareness he becomes part of a process of invidious comparison with other families: he uttered his first word two months earlier than the Jones' boy; he weighed so many pounds at the end of his first year. At Sunday School he received the Bible for perfect attendance; at public school his grades in arithmetic were higher than two-thirds of the other members of the class. He may take piano lessons in view of the day when Mrs. Smythe's pupils will be on public exhibition before the parents of the neighborhood. Everything he accomplishes or fails to accomplish becomes an inevitable part of the family's attempt to maintain or improve its standing in the community.

But effective competition demands a certain degree of independence, firmness of purpose, perhaps aggressiveness. Even for the "normal" middle-class child the transition from submission to some degree of independent behavior is made difficult.[30] And for the child whose personality has been absorbed, an especially exacerbated conflict arises. He is expected to "do things," to accomplish, perhaps to lead in some endeavor, like other children, but his earliest social conditioning was dependence, submission, inferiority; his accomplishments, if any, are on a god-scale—in phantasy. He is desperately attempting to stabilize all later relationships on the basis of his earliest conditioning. Any pressure to compete only exaggerates his anxiety, guilt, and feelings of inadequacy. Life in the modern middle-class home insures that he shall feel that pressure.

There are, then, three elements in the etiology of what has been called the most characteristic neurosis of modern society—personality absorption; the reiterated threat to withdraw a love which has been made of paramount importance; a conflict between the resulting initial adjustment of submissive propitiation and the later assumption of goals of achievement and roles of independent action.

The child is not able to establish an integrated self-conception. Propitiation has meant obedience and "love" for the parents, leading to a compulsive repression of self-will. But he soon discovers that propitiation, in the sense of meeting new parental expectancies, means exhibiting independence, self-assertiveness, aggressiveness, *outside* the home. The father, as the child's mediator of the outside male world, rather than the mother, makes this demand uncompromisingly which may, incidentally, be one of the unsuspected sources of the so-called oedipus complex. This seems more than likely since male neurotics often recall facing the father's ridicule of their first fumbling efforts to meet the father's expectations of "manly" conduct.

With the new conflicting expectations on the part of parents and contemporaries, the child's anxiety reaches new heights, a *double set of guilt-feelings appears where previously there was only one:* at first he felt guilty only if he failed to love and obey, and his guilt could be assuaged by the propitiation of submission; now, however, the god-monsters will be appeased only by a combination of submission in his role of child-in-family, and assertiveness in his play-group, school-pupil, and other roles enacted outside of home. An integration of these conflicting roles is impossible. His conception of himself becomes one of abject failure. Any striving is painful for it violates the initial submissive adjustment. But he feels equally guilty for not making the effort to achieve. This is a key to much of his contradictory and self-blocking behavior: his desire to be the last man in the last regiment and his desire to conquer the world; his demand that everyone shall love him, and his settled conviction that no one could love a person as base as he; his inability to erect a hierarchy of values; his endless debate over the value of his own goals. He is damned if he does and damned if he doesn't. He is embraced by a psychological Iron Maiden; any lunge forward or backward only impales him more securely on the spikes.

THE SOCIOLOGY OF
PARENT-YOUTH CONFLICT

Kingsley Davis

IT IS IN SOCIOLOGICAL TERMS that this paper attempts to frame and solve the sole question with which it deals, namely: Why does contemporary western civilization manifest an extraodinary amount of parent-adolescent conflict?[1] In other cultures, the outstanding fact is generally not the rebelliousness of youth, but its docility. There is practically no custom, no matter how tedious or painful, to which youth in primitive tribes or archaic civilizations will not willingly submit.[2] What, then, are the peculiar features of our society which give us one of the extremest examples of endemic filial friction in human history?

Our answer to this question makes use of constants and variables, the constants being the universal factors in the parent-youth relation, the variables being the factors which differ from one society to another. Though one's attention, in explaining the parent-youth relations of a given milieu, is focused on the variables, one cannot comprehend the action of the variables without also understanding the constants, for the latter constitute the structural and functional basis of the family as a part of society.

The Rate of Social Change. The first important variable is the rate of social change. Extremely rapid change in modern civilization, in contrast to most societies, tends to increase parent-youth conflict, for within a fast-changing social order the time-interval between generations, ordinarily but a mere moment in the life of a social system, become historically significant, thereby creating a hiatus between one generation and the next. Inevitably, under such a condition, youth is reared in a milieu different from that of the parents; hence the parents become old-fashioned, youth rebellious, and clashes occur which, in the closely confined circle of the immediate family, generate sharp emotion.

That rapidity of change is a significant variable can be demonstrated by three lines of evidence: a comparison of stable and nonstable societies;[3] a consideration of immigrant families; and an analysis of revolutionary epochs. If, for example, the conflict is sharper in the immigrant household, this can be due to one thing only, that the immigrant family generally undergoes the most rapid social change of any type of family in a given society. Similarly, a revolution (an abrupt form of societal alteration), by concentrating great change in a short span, catapults the younger generation into power—a generation which has absorbed and pushed the new ideas, acquired the habit of force, and which, accordingly, dominates those hangovers from the old regime, its parents.[4]

The Birth-Cycle, Decelerating Socialization, and Parent-Child Differences. Note, however, that rapid social change would have no power to produce conflict were it not for two universal factors: first, the family's duration; and

Reprinted from *The American Sociological Review* (August 1940), pp. 523-35, by permission of the author and the publisher. (Copyright, 1940, by the American Sociological Society.)

second, the decelerating rate of socialization in the development of personality. "A family" is not a static entity but a process in time, a process ordinarily so brief compared with historical time that it is unimportant, but which, when history is "full" (i.e., marked by rapid social change), strongly influences the mutual adjustment of the generations. This "span" is basically the birth-cycle—the length of time between the birth of one person and his procreation of another. It is biological and inescapable. It would, however, have no effect in producing parent-youth conflicts, even with social change, if it were not for the additional fact, intimately related and equally universal, that the sequential development of personality involves a constantly decelerating rate of socialization. This deceleration is due both to organic factors (age—which ties it to the birth-cycle) and to social factors (the cumulative character of social experience). Its effect is to make the birth-cycle interval, which is the period of youth, the time of major socialization, subsequent periods of socialization being subsidiary.

Given these constant features, rapid social change creates conflict because *to* the intrinsic (universal, inescapable) differences between parents and children it adds an extrinsic (variable) difference derived from the acquisition, at the same stage of life, of differential cultural content by each successive generation. Not only are parent and child, at any given moment, in different stages of development, but the content which the parent acquired at the stage where the child now is, was a different content from that which the child is now acquiring. Since the parent is supposed to socialize the child, he tends to apply the erstwhile but now inappropriate content (see Diagram). He makes this mistake, and cannot remedy it, because, due to the logic of personality growth, his basic orientation was formed by the experiences of his

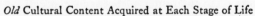

Old Cultural Content Acquired at Each Stage of Life

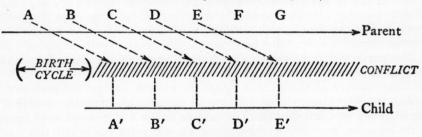

New Cultural Content at Each Stage

The Birth-Cycle, Social Change, and Parent-Child Relations at Different Stages of Life*

*Because the birth-cycle interval persists throughout their conjoint life, parent and child are always at a different stage of development and their relations are always therefore potentially subject to conflict. E.g., when the parent is at stage D, the child is at stage B. But social change adds another source of conflict, for it means that the parent, when at the stage where the child now is, acquired a different cultural content from that which the child must now acquire at that stage. This places the parent in the predicament of trying to transmit old content no longer suited to the offspring's needs in a changed world. In a stable society, B and B' would have the same cultural content. In a changing society, they do not, yet the parent tries to apply the content of A, B, C, etc., to the corresponding stages in the child's development, A', B', C', etc., which supposedly and actually have a different content. Thus, a constant (the birth-cycle) and a variable (social change) combine to produce parent-youth conflict.

Though the birth-cycle remains absolutely the same, it does not remain relatively the same, because it occupies, as time goes on, a successively smaller percentage of the total time lived. Furthermore, because of the decelerating rate of socialization, the difference in the total amount of cultural content as between parent and child becomes less pronounced. After the period of adolescence, for example, the margin is reduced to a minimum, which explains why a minimum of conflict is achieved after that stage.

own childhood. He cannot "modernize" his point of view, because *he* is the product of those experiences. He can change in superficial ways, such as learning a new tune, but he cannot change (or *want* to change) the initial modes of thinking upon which his subsequent social experience has been built. To change the basic conceptions by which he has learned to judge the rightness and reality of all specific situations would be to render subsequent experience meaningless, to make an empty caricature of what had been his life.

Although, in the birth-cycle gap between parent and offspring, astronomical time constitutes the basic point of disparity, the actual sequences, and hence the actual differences significant for us, are physiological, psychosocial, and sociological—each with an acceleration of its own within, but to some degree independent of, sidereal time, and each containing a divergence between parent and child which must be taken into account in explaining parent-youth conflict.

Physiological Differences. Though the disparity in chronological age remains constant through life, the precise physiological differences between parent and offspring vary radically from one period to another. The organic contrasts between parent and *infant,* for example, are far different from those between parent and adolescent. Yet whatever the period, the organic differences produce contrasts (as between young and old) in those desires which, at least in part, are organically determined. Thus, at the time of adolescence the contrast is between an organism which is just reaching its full powers and one which is just losing them. The physiological need of the latter is for security and conservation, because as the superabundance of energy diminishes, the organism seems to hoard what remains.

Such differences, often alleged (under the heading of "disturbing physiological changes accompanying adolescence") as the primary cause of parent-adolescent strife, are undoubtedly a factor in such conflict, but, like other universal differences to be discussed, they form a constant factor present in every community, and therefore cannot in themselves explain the peculiar heightening of parent-youth conflict in our culture.

The fact is that most societies avoid the potential clash of old and young by using sociological position as a neutralizing agent. They assign definite and separate positions to persons of different ages, thereby eliminating competition between them for the same position and avoiding the competitive emotions of jealousy and envy. Also, since the expected behavior of old and young is thus made complementary rather than identical, the performance of cooperative functions is accomplished by different but mutually related activities suited to the disparate organic needs of each, with no coercion to behave in a manner unsuited to one's organic age. In our culture, where most positions are *theoretically* based on accomplishment rather than age, interage competition arises, superior organic propensities lead to a high evaluation of youth (the so-called "accent on youth"), a disproportionate lack of opportunity for youth manifests itself, and consequently, arrogance and frustration appear in the young, fear and envy, in the old.

Psychosocial Differences: Adult Realism versus Youthful Idealism. The decelerating rate of socialization (an outgrowth both of the human being's organic development, from infant plasticity to senile rigidity, and of his cumulative cultural and social development), when taken with rapid social change and other conditions of our society, tends to produce certain differences of orientation between parent and youth. Though lack of space makes it impossible to discuss all of these ramifications, we shall attempt to delineate at least one sector of difference in terms of the conflict between adult realism (or pragmatism) and youthful idealism.

Though both youth and age claim to see the truth, the old are more conservatively realistic than the young, because on the one hand they take Utopian ideals less seriously and on the other hand they take what may be called operating ideals, if not more seriously, at least more for granted. Thus, middle-aged people notoriously forget the poetic ideals of a new social order which they cherished when young. In their place, they put simply the working ideals current in the society. There is, in short, a persistent tendency for the ideology of a person as he grows older to gravitate more and more toward the status quo ideology, unless other facts (such as a social crisis or hypnotic suggestion) intervene.[5] With advancing age, he becomes less and less bothered by inconsistencies in ideals. He tends to judge ideals according to whether they are widespread and hence effective in thinking about practical life, not according to whether they are logically consistent. Furthermore, he gradually ceases to bother about the *untruth* of his ideals, in the sense of their failure to correspond to reality. He assumes through long habit that, though they do not correspond perfectly, the discrepancy is not significant. The reality of an ideal is defined for him in terms of how many people accept it rather than how completely it is mirrored in actual behavior.[6] Thus, we call him, as he approaches middle age, a realist.

The young, however, are idealists, partly because they take working ideals literally and partly because they acquire ideals not fully operative in the social organization. Those in authority over children are obligated as a requirement of their status to inculcate ideals as a part of the official culture given the new generation.[7] The children are receptive because they have little social experience—experience being systematically kept from them (by such means as censorship, for example, a large part of which is to "protect" children). Consequently, young people possess little ballast for their acquired ideals, which therefore soar to the sky, whereas the middle-aged, by contrast, have plenty of ballast.

This relatively unchecked idealism in youth is eventually complicated by the fact that young people possess keen reasoning ability. The mind, simply as a logical machine, works as well at sixteen as at thirty-six.[8] Such logical capacity, combined with high ideals and an initial lack of experience, means that youth soon discovers with increasing age that the ideals it has been taught are true and consistent are not so in fact. Mental conflict thereupon ensues, for the young person has not learned that ideals may be useful without being true and consistent. As a solution, youth is likely to take action designed to remove inconsistencies or force actual conduct into line with ideals, such action assuming one of several typical adolescent forms—from religious withdrawal to the militant support of some Utopian scheme—but in any case consisting essentially in serious allegiance to one or more of the ideal moral systems present in the culture.[9]

A different, usually later reaction to disillusionment is the cynical or sophomoric attitude; for, if the ideals one has imbibed cannot be reconciled and do not fit reality, then why not dismiss them as worthless? Cynicism has the advantage of giving justification for behavior that young organisms crave anyway. It might be mistaken for genuine realism if it were not for two things. The first is the emotional strain behind the "don't care" attitude. The cynic, in his judgment that the world is bad because of inconsistency and untruth of ideals, clearly implies that he still values the ideals. The true realist sees the inconsistency and untruth, but without emotion; he uses either ideals or reality whenever it suits his purpose. The second is the early disappearance of the cynical attitude. Increased experience usually teaches the adolescent that overt cynicism is unpopular and unworkable, that to deny and deride all beliefs which fail to cohere or to correspond to facts, and to act in opposition to them, is to alienate oneself from any group,[10] because these beliefs, however unreal, are precisely what makes group unity possible. Soon, therefore, the youthful cynic finds himself bound up with some group having a system of working ideals, and becomes merely another conformist, cynical only about the beliefs of other groups.[11]

. While the germ of this contrast between youthful idealism and adult realism may spring from the universal logic of personality development, it receives in our culture a peculiar exaggeration. Social change, complexity, and specialization (by compartmentalizing different aspects of life) segregate ideals from fact and throw together incompatible ideologies, while at the same time providing the intellectual tools for discerning logical inconsistencies and empirical errors. Our highly elaborated burden of culture, correlated with a variegated system of achieved vertical mobility, necessitates long years of formal education which separate youth from adulthood, theory from practice, school from life. Insofar, then, as youth's reformist zeal or cynical negativism produces conflict with parents, the peculiar conditions of our culture are responsible.

Sociological Differences: Parental Authority. Since social status and office are everywhere partly distributed on the basis of age, personality development is intimately linked with the network of social positions successively occupied during life. Western society, in spite of an unusual amount of interage competition, maintains differences of social position between parent and child, the developmental gap between them being too clearcut, the symbiotic needs too fundamental, to escape being made a basis of social organization. Hence, parent and child, in a variety of ways, find themselves enmeshed in different social contexts and possessed of different outlooks. The much publicized critical attitude of youth toward established ways, for example, is partly a matter of being on the outside looking in. The "established ways" under criticism are usually institutions (such as property, marriage, profession) which the adolescent has not yet entered. He looks at them from the point of view of the outsider (especially since they affect him in a restrictive manner), either failing to imagine himself finding satisfaction in such patterns or else feeling resentful that the old have in them a vested interest from which he is excluded.

Not only is there differential position, but also *mutually* differential position, status being in many ways specific for and reciprocal between parent and child. Some of these differences, relating to the birth-cycle and constituting part of the family structure, are universal. This is particularly true of the super- and subordination summed up in the term *parental authority*.

Since sociological differences between parent and child are inherent in family organization, they constitute a universal factor potentially capable of producing conflict. Like the biological differences, however, they do not in themselves produce such conflict. In fact, they may help to avoid it. To understand how our society brings to expression the potentiality for conflict, indeed to deal realistically with the relation between the generations, we must do so not in generalized terms but in terms of the specific "power situation." Therefore, the remainder of our discussion will center upon the nature of parental authority and its vicissitudes in our society.

Because of his strategic position with reference to the new-born child (at least in the familial type of reproductive institution), the parent is given considerable authority. Charged by his social group with the responsibility of controlling and training the child in conformity with the mores and thereby insuring the maintenance of the cultural structure, the parent, to fulfill his duties, must have the privileges as well as the obligations of authority, and the surrounding community ordinarily guarantees both.

The first thing to note about parental authority, in addition to its function in socialization, is that it is a case of authority within a primary group. Simmel has pointed out that authority is bearable for the subordinate because it touches only one aspect of life. Impersonal and objective, it permits all other aspects to be free from its particularistic dominance. This escape, however, is lacking in parental authority, for since the family includes most aspects of life, its authority is not limited, specific, or impersonal. What, then, can make this authority bearable? Three factors associated with the familial primary group help to give the answer: (1) the child is socialized within the family, and therefore knowing nothing else and being utterly dependent, the authority of the parent is internalized, accepted; (2) the family, like other primary groups, implies identification, in such sense that one person understands and responds emphatically to the sentiments of the other, so that the harshness of authority is ameliorated;[12] (3) in the intimate interaction of the primary group control can never be purely one-sided; there are too many ways in which the subordinated can exert the pressure of his will. When, therefore, the family system is a going concern, parental authority, however inclusive, is not felt as despotic.

A second thing to note about parental authority is that while its duration is variable (lasting in some societies a few years and in others a lifetime), it inevitably involves a change, a progressive readjustment, in the respective positions of parent and child—in some cases an almost complete reversal of roles, in others at least a cumulative allowance for the fact of maturity in the subordinated offspring. Age is a unique basis for social stratification. Unlike birth, sex, wealth, or occupation, it implies that the stratification is temporary, that the person, if he lives a full life, will eventually traverse all of the strata having it as a basis. Therefore, there is a peculiar ambivalence attached to this kind of differentiation, as well as a constant directional movement. On the one hand, the young person, in the stage of maximum socialization, is, so to speak, *moving into* the social organization. His social personality is expanding, i.e., acquiring an increased amount of the cultural heritage, filling more powerful and numerous positions. His future is before him, in what the older person is leaving behind. The latter, on the other hand, has a future before him only in the sense that the offspring represents it. Therefore, there is a disparity of interest, the young person placing his thoughts upon a future which, once the first stages of dependence are passed, does not include the parent, the old person placing his hopes vicariously upon the young. This situation, representing a *tendency* in every society, is avoided in many places by a system of respect for the aged and an imaginary projection of life beyond the grave. In the absence of such a religio-ancestral system, the role of the aged is a tragic one.[13]

Let us now take up, point by point, the manner in which western civilization has affected this *gemeinschaftliche* and processual form of authority.

1. Conflicting Norms. To begin with, rapid change has, as we saw, given old and young a different social content, so that they possess conflicting norms. There is a loss of mutual identification, and the parent will not "catch up" with the child's point of view, because he is supposed to dominate rather than follow. More than this, social complexity has confused the standards *within* the generation. Faced with conflicting goals, parents become inconsistent and confused in their own minds in rearing their children. The children, for example, acquire an argument against discipline by being able to point to some family wherein discipline is less severe, while the parent can retaliate by pointing to still other families wherein it is firmer. The acceptance of parental attitudes is less complete than formerly.

2. Competing Authorities. We took it for granted, when discussing rapid social change, that youth acquires new ideas, but we did not ask how. The truth is that, in a specialized and complex culture, they learn from competing authorities. Today, for example, education is largely in the hands of professional specialists, some of whom, as college professors, resemble the sophists of ancient Athens by virtue of their work of accumulating and purveying knowledge, and who consequently have ideas in advance of the populace at large (i.e., the parents). By giving the younger generation these advanced ideas, they (and many other extrafamilial agencies, including youth's contemporaries) widen the intellectual gap between parent and child.[14]

3. Little Explicit Institutionalization of Steps in Parental Authority. Our society provides little explicit institutionalization of the progressive readjustments of authority as between parent and child. We are intermediate between the extreme of virtually permanent parental authority and the extreme of very early emancipation, because we encourage release in late adolescence. Unfortunately, this is a time of enhanced sexual desire, so that the problem of sex and the problem of emancipation occur simultaneously and complicate each other. Yet even this would doubtless be satisfactory if it were not for the fact that among us the exact time when authority is relinquished, the exact amount, and the proper ceremonial behavior are not clearly defined. Not only do different groups and families have conflicting patterns, and new situations arise to which old definitions will not apply, but the different spheres of life (legal, economic, religious, intellectual) do not synchronize, maturity in one sphere and immaturity in another often coexisting. The readjustment of authority between individuals is always a ticklish process, and when it is a matter of such close authority as that between parent and child it is apt to be still more ticklish. The failure of our culture to institutionalize this readjustment by a series of well-defined, well-publicized steps is undoubtedly a cause of much parent-youth dissension. The adolescent's sociological exit from his family, via education, work, marriage, and change of residence, is fraught with potential conflicts of interest which only a definite system of institutional controls can neutralize. The parents have a vital stake in what the offspring will do. Because his acquisition of independence will free the parents of many obligations, they are willing to relinquish their authority; yet, precisely because their own status is socially identified with that of their offspring, they wish to insure satisfactory conduct on the latter's part and are tempted to prolong their authority by making the decisions themselves. In the absence of institutional prescriptions, the conflict of interest may lead to a struggle for power, the parents fighting to keep control in matters of importance to themselves, the son or daughter clinging to personally indispensable family services while seeking to evade the concomitant control.

4. *Concentration within the Small Family.* Our family system is peculiar in that it manifests a paradoxical combination of concentration and dispersion. On the one hand, the unusual smallness of the family unit makes for a strange intensity of family feeling, while on the other, the fact that most pursuits take place outside the home makes for a dispersion of activities. Though apparently contradictory, the two phenomena are really interrelated and traceable ultimately to the same factors in our social structure. Since the first refers to that type of affection and antagonism found between relatives, and the second to activities, it can be seen that the second (dispersion) isolates and increases the intensity of the affectional element by sheering away common activities and the extended kin. Whereas ordinarily the sentiments of kinship are organically related to a number of common activities and spread over a wide circle of relatives, in our mobile society they are associated with only a few common activities and concentrated within only the immediate family. This makes them at once more instable (because ungrounded) and more intense. With the diminishing birth rate, our family is the world's smallest kinship unit, a tiny closed circle. Consequently, a great deal of family sentiment is directed toward a few individuals, who are so important to the emotional life that complexes easily develop. This emotional intensity and situational instability increase both the probability and severity of conflict.

In a familistic society, where there are several adult male and female relatives within the effective kinship group to whom the child turns for affection and aid, and many members of the younger generation in whom the parents have a paternal interest, there appears to be less intensity of emotion for any particular kinsman and consequently less chance for severe conflict.[15] Also, if conflict between any two relatives does arise, it may be handled by shifting mutual rights and obligations to another relative.[16]

5. *Open Competition for Socioeconomic Position.* Our emphasis upon individual initiative and vertical mobility, in contrast to rural-stable regimes, means that one's future occupation and destiny are determined more at adolescence than at birth, the adolescent himself (as well as the parents) having some part in the decision. Before him spread a panorama of possible occupations and avenues of advancement, all of them fraught with the uncertainties of competitive vicissitude. The youth is ignorant of most of the

facts. So is the parent, but less so. Both attempt to collaborate on the future, but because of previously mentioned sources of friction, the collaboration is frequently stormy. They evaluate future possibilities differently, and since the decision is uncertain yet important, a clash of wills results. The necessity of choice at adolescence extends beyond the occupational field to practically every phase of life, the parents having an interest in each decision. A culture in which more of the choices of life were settled beforehand by ascription, where the possibilities were fewer and the responsibilities of choice less urgent, would have much less parent-youth conflict.[17]

6. *Sex Tension.* If until now we have ignored sex taboos, the omission has represented a deliberate attempt to place them in their proper context with other factors, rather than in the unduly prominent place usually given them.[18] Undoubtedly, because of a constellation of cultural conditions, sex looms as an important bone of parent-youth contention. Our morality, for instance, demands both premarital chastity and postponement of marriage, thus creating a long period of desperate eagerness when young persons practically at the peak of their sexual capacity are forbidden to enjoy it. Naturally, tensions arise—tensions which adolescents try to relieve, and adults hope they will relieve, in some socially acceptable form. Such tensions not only make the adolescent intractable and capricious, but create a genuine conflict of interest between the two generations. The parent, with respect to the child's behavior, represents morality, while the offspring reflects morality *plus* his organic cravings. The stage is thereby set for conflict, evasion, and deceit. For the mass of parents, toleration is never possible. For the mass of adolescents, sublimation is never sufficient. Given our system of morality, conflict seems well nigh inevitable.

Yet it is not sex itself but the way it is handled that causes conflict. If sex patterns were carefully, definitely, and uniformly geared with nonsexual patterns in the social structure, there would be no parent-youth conflict over sex. As it is, rapid change has opposed the sex standards of different groups and generations, leaving impulse only chaotically controlled.

The extraordinary preoccupation of modern parents with the sex life of their adolescent offspring is easily understandable. First, our morality is sex-centered. The strength of the impulse which it seeks to control, the consequent stringency of its rules, and the importance of reproductive institutions for society, make sex so morally important that being moral and being sexually discreet are synonymous. Small wonder, then, that parents, charged with responsibility for their children and fearful of their own status in the eyes of the moral community, are preoccupied with what their offspring will do in this matter. Moreover, sex is intrinsically involved in the family structure and is therefore of unusual significance to family members *qua* family members. Offspring and parent are not simply two persons who happen to live together; they are two persons who happen to live together because of past sex relations between the parents. Also, between parent and child there stand strong incest taboos, and doubtless the unvoiced possibility of violating these unconsciously intensifies the interest of each in the other's sexual conduct. In addition, since sexual behavior is connected with the offspring's formation of a new family of his own, it is naturally of concern to the parent. Finally, these factors taken in combination with the delicacy of the authoritarian relation, the emotional intensity within the small family, and the confusion of sex standards, make it easy to explain the parental interest in adolescent sexuality. Yet because sex is a tabooed topic between parent and child,[19] parental control must be indirect and devious, which creates additional possibilities of conflict.

Summary and Conclusion. Our parent-youth conflict thus results from the interaction of certain universals of the parent-child relation and certain variables the values of which are peculiar to modern culture. The universals are (1) the basic age or birth-cycle differential between parent and child, (2) the decelerating rate of socialization with advancing age, and (3) the resulting intrinsic differences between old and young on the physiological, psychosocial, and sociological planes.

Though these universal factors *tend* to produce conflict between parent and child, whether or not they do so depends upon the variables. We have seen that the distinctive general features of our society are responsible for our excessive parent-adolescent friction. Indeed, they are the same features which are affecting *all* family relations. The delineation of these variables has not been systematic, because the scientific classification of whole societies has not yet been accomplished; and it has been difficult, in view of the interrelated character of societal traits, to seize upon certain features and ignore others. Yet certainly the following four complex variables are important: (1) the rate of social change; (2) the extent of complexity in the social structure; (3) the degree of integration in the culture; and (4) the velocity of movement (e.g., vertical mobility) within the structure and its relation to the cultural values.

Our rapid social change, for example, has crowded historical meaning into the family time-span, has thereby given the offspring a different social content from that which the parent acquired, and consequently has added to the already existent intrinsic differences between parent and youth, a set of extrinsic ones which double the chance of alienation. Moreover, our great societal complexity, our evident cultural conflict, and our emphasis upon open competition for socioeconomic status have all added to this initial effect. We have seen, for instance, that they have disorganized the important relation of parental authority by confusing the goals of child control, setting up competing authorities, creating a small family system, making necessary certain significant choices at the time of adolescence, and leading to an absence of definite institutional mechanisms to symbolize and enforce the progressively changing stages of parental power.

If ours were a simple rural-stable society, mainly familistic, the emancipation from parental authority being gradual and marked by definite institutionalized steps, with no great postponement of marriage, sex taboo, or open competition for status, parents and youth would not be in conflict. Hence, the presence of parent-youth conflict in our civilization is one more specific manifestation of the incompatibility between an urban-industrial-mobile social system and the familial type of reproductive institutions.[20]

CLASS DIFFERENCES IN
FAMILY STABILITY

August B. Hollingshead

SOCIOLOGISTS IN RECENT YEARS have become aware of the interdependence that exists between the family and status systems in American society, but no studies have been focused on the analysis of the problem of class differences in family stability. Consequently there is no comprehensive body of either quantitative or qualitative data that we may draw upon for a statement of similarities and differences in family stability and instability in the several classes found in our society. Official city, county, state, and national statistics on marriage and divorce do not recognize the existence of social classes, so these data are not appropriate for our purposes. In view of these limitations, this paper will merely outline some of the major differences in family stability revealed by studies of social stratification at the community level.[1] However, before we turn to a discussion of the problem of family stability and the status structure, a few paragraphs of theoretical orientation are in order.

RELATION OF FAMILY AND CLASS SYSTEMS

The nexus between the family and class systems arises from the fact that every individual is simultaneously a member of both systems. He is created in the family and placed in the class system whether he wills it or not. However, the functions of the two systems are essentially different; the family is the procreative and primary training institution, whereas the class system functions as a ranking device. The two systems are interwoven at many points in ways that are too intricate for us to unravel here. It is sufficient for present purposes to point out that each individual's original position in the class system is ascribed to him on the basis of a combination of social and biological characteristics inherited from his family through genetic and social processes. This position may be modified, and in some cases changed sharply, during the course of the individual's life; but the point of origin in the status system for every individual is the family into which he is born.

The nuclear group of husband, wife, and dependent children constitutes the primary family and common household unit throughout our society. This group normally passes through a family cycle[2] which begins with marriage and extends through the childbearing and child-rearing years and on into the old age of the parental pair. It is the maintenance of the family cycle from marriage to old age that we will take as our criterion of a stable family. Each marriage of a man and a woman brings into being a new family cycle. Upon the birth of their first child the nuclear pair becomes a family of procreation, but for the child this family of origin is his family of orientation. Thus, each individual who marries and rears children has a family of orientation and a family of procreation. He also has an ascribed status which

Reprinted from *The Annals of the American Academy of Political and Social Science*, (November 1950), pp. 39-46, by permission of the author and the publisher. (Copyright, 1950, by The American Academy of Political and Social Science.)

he inherits from his family of orientation, and an achieved status which he acquires in the course of his life. His achieved status may be different from his ascribed status, but not necessarily, particularly from the viewpoint of class position; but his family of procreation, of necessity, is different from his family of orientation. In the case of a man, his achieved status normally becomes the status of his wife and of his children during their early years.

Each nuclear family is related to a number of other nuclear families by consanguineal and affinal ties. Also, each family in the kin group occupies a position in the status system. All nuclear families in a kin group may be in the same class or may be in different class positions from others. The latter situation is produced by mobility on the part of some individual families, while other families remain in the approximate status position ascribed to them by their family of orientation. This movement of the individual nuclear family in the status system, while it is approved, and often lauded as "the American way," has important effects on kin group relations.[3]

With these considerations in mind, we turn to the discussion of class and family stability. We wish to warn the reader, however, that the statements presented in the following analysis are based on a few community studies in different parts of the Nation, and therefore the bases of the generalizations are fragmentary; heuristic observations are made in the hope that they will draw attention to this area of the social structure, and that they will give readers new insight into these facets of our society.

THE UPPER CLASS

Families in the upper class may be divided into two categories on the basis of the length of time they have occupied upper-class position: (1) *established* families, which have been in the upper class for two or more generations; and (2) *new* families, which have achieved their position through the success of the present adult generation.

Who one's ancestors were, and who one's relatives are, count for more in the established family group than what one has achieved in one's own lifetime. "Background" is stressed most heavily when it comes to the crucial question of whom a member may or may not marry, for marriage is the institution that determines membership in the family group. Indeed, one of the perennial problems of the established family is the control of the marriage choices of its young men. Young women can be controlled more easily than young men, because of the sheltered life they lead and their passive role in courtship. The passivity of the upper-class female, coupled with sex exploitation of females from lower social positions by upper-class males that sometimes leads to marriage, results in a considerable number of old maids in established upper-class families. Strong emphasis on family background is accompanied by the selection of marriage mates from within the old-family group in an exceptionally high percentage of cases, and if not from the old-family group, then from the new-family segment of the upper class. The degree of kinship solidarity, combined with intraclass marriages, found in this level results in a high order of stability in the upper class, in the extended kin group, and in the nuclear family within it.

The established upper-class family is basically an extended kin group, solidified by lineage and a heritage of common experience in a communal setting. A complicated network of consanguineal and affinal ties unites nuclear families of orientation and procreation into an in-group that rallies when its position is threatened by the behavior of one of its members, particularly where out-marriage is involved; this principle will be illustrated below. Each nuclear family usually maintains a separate household, but it does not conceive of itself as a unit apart from the larger kin group. The nuclear family is viewed as only a part of a broader kin group that includes the consanguineal descendants of a known ancestral pair, plus kin that have been brought into the group by marriage.

An important factor in the extended established family's ability to maintain its position through several generations is its economic security. Usually a number of different nuclear families within a kin group are supported, in part at least, by income from a family estate held in trust. Also, because of the practice of intramarriage it is not unusual for a family to be the beneficiary of two or more estates held in trust. For example, in an eastern community of some 80,000 population, one of these extended family groups is the beneficiary of a trust established a century ago that yields something over $300,000 annually, after taxes. This income is divided among 37 different nuclear families descended from the founder, 28 of whom live in the community; 23 of these families are beneficiaries of one other trust fund, and 14 receive income from two or more other trust funds. These different nuclear families regard themselves as parts of the Scott[4] family; moreover, they are so regarded by other upper-class families, as well as by persons lower in the status system who know something of the details of the family history.

The Scott family has maintained its upper-class position locally for more than two centuries by a combination of property ownership, educational, legal, and political leadership, and control of marriages generation after generation. Its members are proud that it has never had a non-Protestant marriage in seven generations; only five divorces have been traced, but these are not mentioned; one desertion has been hinted, but not confirmed.

The In-Group Marriage Test. The tradition relative to Protestant intra-upper-class marriages had a severe test in recent years. A son in one family, who had spent four years in the armed services in the late war, asked a middle-class Catholic girl to marry him. The engagement was announced by the girl's family, to the consternation of the Scotts. The Scotts immediately brought pressure on the boy to "break off the affair." His mother "bristled" at the very idea of her son's marriage; his father "had a talk with him"; his 84-year-old paternal grandmother snorted, "A Scott marry a Flaherty, never!" A great-aunt remarked icily, "No Scott is dissolute enough to *have* to marry a Flaherty." After the first shock of indignation had passed, the young man was told he was welcome in "any Scott home" without that "Flaherty flip." A few weeks later his maternal grandfather told him he would be disinherited if he "demeaned" himself by marrying "that girl."

After several months of family and class pressure against the marriage, the young man "saw his error" and broke the engagement. A year later he married a family-approved "nice" girl from one of the other "old" families in the city. Today he is assistant cashier in his wife's family's bank, and his father is building him a fine suburban home.

Nancy Flaherty, when the storm broke over her engagement, quit her job as a secretary in an insurance office. A few weeks later she left home to seek a job in another city. After the engagement was broken she quit this job and went to New York City. Today she is unmarried, living alone, and working in New York.

This case illustrates a number of characteristics typical of the established upper-class family. It is stable, extended, tends to pull together when its position is threatened—in this instance by an out-marriage—exerts powerful controls on its members to ensure that their behavior conforms to family and class codes, and provides for its members economically by trust funds and appropriate positions.

The New Family. The new upper-class family is characterized most decisively by phenomenal economic success during a short interval of time. Its meteoric rise in the economic system is normally the personal triumph of the money-maker. While its head is busy making a "million bucks," the family acquires the purchasable symbols associated with the wealthy American family: a large house, fine furniture, big automobiles, and expensive clothes. The new tycoon knows the power of money in the market place, and he often attempts to buy a high position in the status system. The new family is able to meet *the means test,* but not *the lineage test* of the established families. Consequently, it is generally systematically excluded from membership in the most prestigeful cliques and associations in the community. This is resented, especially by the wife and children; less often by the tycoon.

The new family is very unstable in comparison with the established family. It lacks the security of accepted position at the top of the local status system—a position that will come only through time; it cannot be purchased. The stabilizing influence exerted on the deviant individual by an extended family group, as well as friends, is absent. (Many upwardly mobile families break with their kin group as part of the price they pay for their mobility.) Then, too, the new family is composed of adults who are self-directing, full of initiative, believe in the freedom of the individual, and rely upon themselves rather than upon a kin group. The result is, speaking broadly, conspicuous expenditure, fast living, insecurity, and family instability. Thus, we find divorces, broken homes, alcoholism, and other symptoms of disorganization in a large number of new families. Because new families are so conspicuous in their consumption and behavior they become, in the judgment of the general population, symbolic of upper-class actions and values, much to the detriment, and resentment, of established families.

THE MIDDLE CLASSES

The nuclear upper-middle-class family, composed of husband, wife, and two or three dependent children during the major years of the family cycle, is a very stable unit in comparison with the new upper-class family and the working-class family. Divorce is rare, desertion by the husband or wife is most infrequent, and premature death rates are low.

During the past half-century, changes that have taken place in American society have created a demand for technically trained personnel in such large numbers that the old middle class could not provide enough recruits to fill the new positions. Concomitantly, our educational institutions expanded enormously to meet the need for professionally, scientifically, and administratively trained personnel. A vast area of opportunity opened for boys and girls in the lower-middle and working classes to move upward in the economic and status structures. Thus, the majority of upper-middle-class persons now above 35 years of age are upward mobile. Their mobility has been made possible by education, self-discipline, and opportunity in the professional and administrative channels of our economic system.

Geographic mobility has been a second concomitant in this process. The man—or woman—who is now in the upper-middle class more often than not left his home community as a young adult to attend college. After his formal schooling was completed he generally took a job in a different community from the one where he was trained, and often-times it was in a different one from his home town. If he began his adult work career with a national business firm, the chances are high that he was transferred from one city to another as he moved up the job ladder.

Geographic movement is typical of an upward mobile family, even when it lives out the family cycle in its home community. In a large number of cases, when a mobile couple is newly married, both partners work. The couple often lives in an apartment or flat in a residential area that is not desirable as a permanent residence. As the husband achieves a higher economic status, the new family generally moves to a small single-family house, or a two-family one, farther from the center of the city, where there are yards and trees. Often about this time the wife quits work and the first of two or three children is born. A third or fourth move, some years later, into a six- to eight-room single-family house on a well landscaped lot in the better residential areas of the city or the suburbs normally completes the family's odyssey. While it is moving from house to house, many of its social contacts change as the husband passes through the successive stages of his business or professional career.

Even though there is a high prevalence of social and geographic mobility, and no extended kin group to bring pressure on the family, there is a negligible amount of instability. Self-discipline, the demands of the job, and the moral pressures exerted by friends and associates keep the nuclear family together. The principal family goals are success in business or a profession, a good college or university education for the children, and economic security for the parents in their old age. These goals are realized in the vast majority of cases, and the family is generally a happy, well-knit group.

The Lower-Middle Class. The lower-middle-class family, like the upper middle, is a stable unit for the most part. In fact, there is no essential difference between these two levels of the status system in so far as family stability is concerned. In Elmtown 85 per cent of the upper-middle (class II) and 82 per cent of the lower-middle families (class III) were intact after fifteen and more years of marriage.[5] Oren found in an industrial city in Connecticut that 93 per cent of the lower-middle families with adolescent children were unbroken after eighteen and more years of marriage.[6]

Probably a higher proportion of lower-middle-class individuals have achieved their positions through their own efforts than is true of any other status level except the new family group in the upper class. The majority of lower-middle-class adults have come from a working-class background; many have an ethnic background of recent immigrant origin. Through ability, hard work, and an element of luck they have founded small businesses, operated by the family members, and a few employees, or acquired some technical training which has enabled them to obtain clerical, sales, and minor administrative posts in industry and government.

The major problems of the lower-middle-class family are connected with the security of its economic position and the education of its children. Parents generally have high educational aspirations for their children, but income limitations often compel them to compromise with less education than they desire, and possibly a different kind from what they would choose. Parents acutely see the need for a good formal education, and they make heavy sacrifices to give their children the educational training that will enable them to take over positions held by persons in the upper-middle class. By stressing education for the child, parents many times unwittingly create conflicts for themselves and their children, because the educational goals they set for the child train him in values that lead him away from his family. This process, while it does not have a direct bearing on the stability of the nuclear family, acts as a divisive factor that splits parents and children apart, as well as brothers and sisters who have received different amounts of education and follow different job channels.

THE WORKING CLASS

The family cycle is broken prematurely in the working class about twice as frequently as it is in the middle classes. Community studies indicate that from one-fourth to one-third of working-class families are broken by divorce, desertion, and death of a marital partner, after a family of procreation has been started but before it is reared. This generalization does not include families broken before the birth of children or after they leave the parental home. In Elmtown I found that 33 per cent of the working-class families (class IV) had been broken after 15 and more years of marriage;[7] Oren[8] reported that 29 per cent of his working-class families with adolescent children were broken ones. The norm and the ideal in the working class are a stable family, but broken homes occur with such frequency that most parents realize that they are, along with unemployment, a constant hazard.

Family instability is a product of the conditions under which most working-class families live. In the first place, they are completely dependent on the swings of the business cycle in our wage-price-profits system, for the working-class family is almost invariably supported by wages earned by the hour, the piece, the day, or the week. Ideally, its wages are earned by the male head, but in a considerable proportion of families the wife too is employed as a wage earner outside the home. When a working-class wife takes a job it is for a substantial reason, usually necessity, rather than the desire for "a career."[9]

Factors of Stress. The home is the center of family life, and the hope of most working-class families is a single-family dwelling with a yard; but from a fifth to one-half are forced to live in multiple dwelling units with inadequate space for family living. Added to this is the working-class *mos* that one is obligated to give shelter and care in a crisis to a husband's or wife's relatives or to a married child. Thus, in a considerable percentage of these families the home is shared with some relative. Then, too, resources are stringently limited, so when a family is faced with unemployment, illness, and death it must turn to someone for help. In such crises, a relative is called upon in most instances before some public agency. The relative normally has little to offer, but in most cases that little is shared with the family in need, even though grudgingly.

While crises draw family members together, they also act as divisive agents; for when a family has to share its limited living space and meager income with relatives, kin ties are soon strained, often to the breaking point. One family is not able to give aid to another on an extensive scale without impairing its own standard of living; possibly its own security may be jeopardized. In view of this risk, some persons do everything short of absolute refusal to aid a relative in distress; some even violate the "blood is thicker than water" *mos* and refuse to give help when it is requested. This ordinarily results in the permanent destruction of kin ties, but it is justified by the belief that one's own family's needs come first.

Although the principle is stressed here that the working-class family lives very close to the limits of its economic resources at all times, and when a crisis comes its effects upon family stability are profound, we should not overlook the fact that moral, personal, and emotional factors contribute to family instability. It is possible that these factors are as important as the economic ones, but this and other observations made here need to be verified by field studies. Actually, while we know that the family at this level of the status structure is susceptible to instability, we have little knowledge derived from systematic research to tell us what cultural conditions are associated with unstable, in contrast to stable, families. A carefully planned series of studies of stable and unstable families with class level held constant is needed. Until this is done, we can only guess about the factors which condition stability and instability in family life.

THE LOWER CLASS

Lower-class families exhibit the highest prevalence of instability of any class in the status structure. If we view the lower-class family in terms of a continuum, we find at one end stable families throughout the family cycle; at the other end, the nuclear family of a legally wedded husband and wife and dependent children has given way to a reciprocal companionate relationship between a man and a woman. This latter relationship, in most cases, is the result of their personal desire to live together; it is not legally sanctioned. A companionate family is often a complicated one. It may include the natural children of the couple, plus the woman's children from a previous legal or companionate relationship; also there may be dependent children of the man living with the woman. Normally, when the lower-class family is broken, as in the higher classes, the mother keeps the children. However, the mother may desert her "man" for another man, and leave her children with him, her mother or sister, or a social agency. In the Deep South and Elmtown, from 50 to 60 per cent of lower-class family groups are broken once, and often more, by desertion, divorce, death, or separation, often due to imprisonment of the man, between marriage, legal or companionate, and its normal dissolution through the marriage of adult children and the death of aged parents.[10]

Economic insecurity is but one of a number of factors that give rise to this amount of instability. Lower-class people are employed in the most menial, the poorest-paid, and the dirtiest jobs; these jobs also tend to be seasonal and cyclical, and of short duration. Moreover, from one-half to two-thirds of the wives are gainfully employed outside the home; in many cases they are the sole support of the family. However, the problem of economic insecurity does not account for amoral behavior that ranges from the flagrant violation of conventional sex mores to open rebellion against formal agencies of social control.

The very nature of our society may be responsible, in large part, for the number, the intensity, and the variety of social problems associated with the lower class. Such cultural values as individualism, wealth, position, and power must be considered in an analysis of social problems from the viewpoint of the class system. Ours is a competitive, acquisitive society where individuals successful in the competitive arena are admired by most other Americans; they achieve positions of prestige and of power desired by many and attained by few. Less successful individuals may struggle as hard but not be able to do more than hold the status in which they were born; their goal may be to avoid the sorry drift toward lower-class existence. Other individuals may fail in the struggle and sink to the bottom. To be sure, some were born there and failed to rise from the unenviable position they inherited at birth.

RESEARCH NEEDED

The interdependence between the family and status systems sketched here needs to be studied systematically before we can draw definitive generalizations that may be used as the basis for an action program to increase family stability. Isolated community studies indicate that there are functional linkages between the types as well as the amounts of family instability at different levels of the status structure. These indications ought to be analyzed by carefully designed research. If and when this is done, I believe we shall gain some valuable new insights into family and individual stability and instability.

THE NEGRO FAMILY IN
THE UNITED STATES

E. Franklin Frazier

AS THE RESULT OF THE MANNER in which the Negro was enslaved, the African cultural heritage has had practically no effect upon the evolution of Negro family life in the United States. The destruction of the African family system began in Africa, where the slave-traders gathered their human cargo, consisting largely of young males. The process of "breaking" the Negroes into the slave system and the scattering of them on numerous and relatively small plantations and farms left little opportunity for the slaves to reknit the threads of their ancestral culture. Memories of the homeland were effaced, and what they retained of African ways and conceptions of life ceased to have meaning in the new environment. There were no longer marriages according to African customs; hence mating became subject to individual impulses and wishes and to the control of the white masters. The type of family system which developed was determined by the requirements of the slave system. Likewise, in later stages of its development, the character of the Negro family was shaped by social and economic forces in American life.

Under the system of slavery the Negro family emerged first as a natural organization based upon the physical and emotional ties between the mother and her offspring. The father and husband played a less important role in family relations because his interest in the family was less fundamental and his relations with his wife and children were influenced to a larger extent by the fortunes of the slave regime. The attitudes of both "husband" and "wife" toward "marriage," which had no legal basis, were influenced by the degree to which they had assimilated the sex and family mores of the whites. The process of assimilation proceeded most rapidly with the house servants who lived in close association with the whites and shared in the lives of the latter. Where slavery became a settled way of life, and the plantation became a social as well as an industrial institution, the slave family was likely to acquire considerable stability. Moreover, in the organization of the plantation there was a division of labor and social distinctions among the slaves which tended to reinforce the family mores of the whites.

The process of assimilating the family mores of the whites was facilitated and accelerated by racial amalgamation under the slave system. The very fact of white ancestry tended to make the mixed-blood identify himself with the whites. Largely as the result of race mixture, a class of free Negroes came into existence, especially in those areas of the South where the economic basis

Reprinted from *The American Journal of Sociology* (May 1948), pp. 435-38, by permission of the author and the publisher. (Copyright, 1948, by the University of Chicago Press.)

of slavery was being undermined. Among the half-million free Negroes, nearly 40 per cent of whom were of mixed blood, there was a substantial element with a secure economic position, especially in the South. It was among this element that the Negro family acquired an institutional character with traditions of conventional sex and family mores.

The social upheaval occasioned by the Civil War, emancipation, and reconstruction tended to destroy the customary forms of family relations that had taken root during slavery. Moreover, the stability and privileged position of the mixed-blood families were affected by the emergence of Negro communities composed largely of Negroes with a background of slavery. From emancipation to the first decade of the present century, two general tendencies are apparent in the development of the Negro family. In the families which had acquired considerable stability during slavery, the father's position was more firmly established, especially if he became a landowner or a home-owner. This class grew in importance during the first fifty years of freedom, and, together with the descendants of the free Negro with whom they intermarried, formed what represented the conventional and stable elements in the family life of the Negro. On the other hand, among the great mass of rural Negroes, who became accommodated to a modified form of life on southern plantations, there developed a form of family life based largely upon mutual interests and mutual sympathies. It lacked an institutional basis, since both legal marriage and divorce were not generally observed. The family often grew out of unmarried motherhood and the common interests which developed from the association of men and women in the struggle for existence.

Around the opening of the century public attention was focused upon the widespread family disorganization among Negroes in the cities of the country. Hundreds of thousands of Negroes had gradually drifted into the seven hundred or more cities of the South. Then came the First World War, which carried nearly a million Negro migrants, with their simple family folkways, to the metropolitan regions of the North. The small Negro communities in the North were overwhelmed, and race riots often ensued as the Negro communities spilled over into the adjacent white areas. Following the First World War, the northward migrations continued, along with the cityward movements of Negroes in the South. By the outbreak of World War II nearly half of the Negroes were in cities. As the result of urbanization and widening contacts, Negro family life had to adjust to a new social and economic environment. The type of family life which took shape among the rural folk in the South could no longer function in the urban environment. There has been much disorganization, but at the same time the family has adjusted itself increasingly to the demands of city living.

In order to secure a true picture of familial relations among Negroes, it would be necessary to study groups of families in the cultural and economic life of the various communities of the country. Statistics on family relations for the general population obscure the important differences among Negroes. Nevertheless, when one studies the distribution of whites and Negroes in households for 1940, certain differences, significant in view of the social history of the Negro family, appear (see Table). It should be noted, first, that about 5 per cent more white males than Negro males are heads of households. This is in accord with the fact that 28 per cent of white males as compared with 32 per cent of Negro males fourteen years old and over were single in 1947.[1] A more important difference between the races is indicated by the fact that 10.3 per cent of the Negro females, in comparison with 6.5 per cent of the white females, were heads of households and 9 per cent fewer Negro females were wives in households. The fewer Negroes than whites who are children of the head of the household is not so significant as the larger proportion of Negroes than whites who are grandchildren to the head of the household. This is undoubtedly related to the fact that Negro families, especially in rural areas, include several generations. Moreover, very often in the Negro maternal households the grandmother becomes the head of the family. Probably this also accounts for the larger proportion of male parents of heads of white households than males who stand in the same relation in Negro households.

The larger proportion of the Negro population than the white population classified as "other relatives" is indicative of what has been called the "amorphous" character of the Negro family. The amorphous character of the Negro family is owing to the fact that it has retained many of the characteristics of a purely primary group. It is likely that the term "other relatives" includes not only uncles, cousins, and other persons related by "blood," such as illegitimate children, but even adopted children. The larger proportion of servants and hired hands in Negro households than in white households would be misleading if one took these terms literally. Among the rural Negroes, servants and hired hands are more likely to represent those who are taken into the household because of human sympathy, and who share the responsibilities of the household. The larger proportion of lodgers in Negro households than in white households confirms what all statistics show concerning the housing of Negroes in cities.

Although these figures provide a rough index to the general characteristics of Negro families, they do not show some of the important differences between rural and urban families. There is no indication of the large number of childless couples among urban Negroes and the smaller number of children in urban families. Then, in regard to female heads of families it is found that in the rural South between a ninth and an eighth of the Negro families have a female head, while in the rural nonfarm areas between a fifth and a fourth have a woman as head.[2] On the other hand, nearly a third of the Negro families in the cities of the South have a woman as head of the family. In the rural areas the landlords want families with an adult male; thus Negro men and women gain mutual advantages in marriage and family relations. In the rural nonfarm areas Negro women are able to earn a living for themselves and their children without a husband or father. In the urban areas, family desertion on the part of the men and the opportunity for employment for women, especially in domestic service, swell the number of families with female heads.

Nor do the figures on the distribution of Negroes in households reveal the important differences in the character of the Negro family which are related to the class structure of the Negro community. As the result of urbanization the class structure of the Negro community has become more complex, and there are three fairly well-defined socioeconomic classes. Among the lower class, which comprises between 60 and 70 per cent of the Negro population, family relations still reflect the influence of rural folk traditions. It is among these that one finds the majority of families with female heads.

Percentage Distribution of Population in Private Households by Relation to Head and by Color and Sex for the South, 1940*

Relationship to Head	Nonwhite		White	
	Male	Female	Male	Female
Head	39.5	10.3	44.4	6.5
Wife		31.9		40.9
Child	41.5	38.2	45.2	40.8
Grandchild	5.4	4.8	2.1	1.9
Parent	0.6	2.4	0.9	2.5
Other relative	6.3	6.7	4.1	4.3
Lodger	6.2	4.8	3.1	2.3
Servant or hired hand	0.5	0.9	0.2	0.5

*Sixteenth Census of the United States: 1940, Vol. IV: Population, Part 1: "Characteristics by Age," p. 114.

The statistics on the marital status of the female heads of Negro families indicate the loose family ties among this class. Although a larger proportion of owner families—24.5 per cent as compared with 20.9 per cent—have female heads, the marital status of the owners as given in the statistics indicates that there is greater conformity to legal and conventional relations.[3] Among the female heads who are tenants, 25.4 per cent of the husbands are absent, 12.7 per cent of the women are single, and only 56.5 per cent are widowed. On the other hand, 77.4 per cent of the female heads who are owners are widowed, 11.5 per cent have husbands absent, and only 7.7 per cent are single. These figures provide only a rough index of the absence of stable and conventional family relations in the lower class.

It is in the middle class, which is assuming greater importance in the Negro community, that one can note the increasing stabilization of Negro family life under the new conditions of city life. The increase in the size and importance of the middle class is the result of the increasing opportunities for employment and education in the city and the integration of the Negro into institutional and associational life of the city such as churches, lodges, and labor unions. The stability and conventionality of family relations among this class rest partly upon the desire to achieve and maintain respectability. It is among this class that family traditions are built up and merged with the traditions of stable family life already established among the descendants of Negroes free before the Civil War and the more steady elements that emerged from slavery. The middle class constitutes from 25 to 30 per cent of the Negro population. Because of the social mobility in the Negro community, this group merges with the upper class, which is becoming more sharply differentiated from the middle class on the basis of money and style of life. The upper class is relatively small in the Negro group, but it has a style of life and values similar to those among the white upper class. There are relatively few children, and there is considerable emphasis upon conspicuous consumption and leisure. There is intermarriage among prominent families, whose aim is to conserve their wealth and maintain their status and family name. Such families are circumscribed both by the limitations placed upon the earning capacity of Negroes and by the fact that the upper class represents an artificial growth behind the walls of segregation.

The deviations in the character of the Negro family from the dominant American patterns have been owing chiefly to the social isolation and economic position of the Negro. As the Negro acquires education and enjoys greater economic opportunities and participates in all phases of American life, he is taking over the American patterns of behavior characteristic of different classes and regions. His family life increasingly conforms to the American pattern, which is becoming a part of his cultural heritage.

HYPOTHESES CONCERNING THE EASTERN EUROPEAN JEWISH FAMILY

Ruth Landes and Mark Zborowski

THE PRESENT DISCUSSION is directed towards phrasing hypotheses about the form and functioning of the Jewish family in the now destroyed Eastern European[1] small town known in Yiddish as the *shtetl.* The shtetl life, organized into characteristic, richly detailed patterns of behavior, was destroyed under the German occupation of World War II. Persons reared in shtetl culture, however, constituted the bulk of the East European Jewish migration to the United States; in the absence of exact figures, there is a belief among authorities that it constituted 90 per cent or even more of the total, in the aggregate.

Our hypotheses are drawn from a mass of data collected by the Columbia University Project, Research in Contemporary Cultures, inaugurated by the late Dr. Ruth Benedict. The data were assembled during two years of work in New York City which included intensive interviewing of 128 informants who had migrated to New York from the shtetl, and of 10 more born here of shtetl parentage,[2] besides the combing of a variety of literature relevant to shtetl culture. Research in Contemporary Cultures based its general picture on conditions in Ukrainian Jewish communities before the Russian Revolution of 1917 and in the Polish, Hungarian, and Romanian villages or small towns before their destruction in the years 1939-1945. The data were not collected for the purposes of this paper, however, but in order to yield a rounded picture of the total life.[3]

Our purpose, reported in this paper, is to develop enough understanding of Eastern European Jewish family life to provide us with a theoretical base line from which to start field inquiries among American Jewish families descended from this tradition. The Research in Contemporary Cultures data, for our particular purpose, left lacunae that we have tried to span with our hypotheses, testing them against facts in the literature,[4] against our own scattered interviews, and against Eastern European Jewish films which we have analyzed. Having blocked out these hypotheses rather completely, we offer them now with two objectives: for the insights they may provide the sociocultural, psychological, and psychiatric specialists; and for critical appraisal as tools for our own proposed field research into American Jewish family life. It came as a surprise to all of the researchers to realize the seemingly considerable perseverance of traditional European modes in American surroundings, even in the third generation, despite some evidence of important changes or, at least, of shifts of emphasis. Shtetl Jews themselves expect perseverance, and in orthodox religious circles decry any of the changes in family life.

Family Relationships. Though there were two major ranked groups of high social mobility in the shtetl,[5] called *sheyne* (Yiddish, beautiful, fine) and

Reprinted, by special permission of the William Alanson White Institute, from *Psychiatry* (November 1950), pp. 447-64, vol. 13.

proste (Yiddish, common), our hypotheses of family life appear to apply to both, except for situational details. This is because the family behavior of traditional Jews everywhere has been painstakingly guided for centuries by written codes that standardized conduct. The ideals of the codes held for all, though they were often ignored in practice.

This family of our hypotheses obviously belongs to Western civilization. In its general outlines, it is patrilineal, even patriarchal, fostering obligations among members of the biological family, weakening them with more distant kin. Within these outlines, however, there are developments which we may call institutional, and behavioristic emphases and nuances which vary markedly and consistently enough to make this family distinct among the others in the European tradition, including Jewish families of central and western Europe.[6]

There are three dynamic relationships within the shtetl family that constitute an institutional universe and a field of tensions. These are: the bonds between man and wife, between mother and son, and between father and daughter. Other blood and kin ties flow from, support, and otherwise are consequences of these three.

A man and woman marry primarily to have offspring, and their duties and roles are carefully detailed by tradition. The *Schulchan Aruch,* or Jewish Code of Law,[7] covers the subject precisely, as do many portions of the Talmud and many folk sayings. Our informants carried these injunctions clearly in their minds, both the regular ones and those covering special individual cases like sterility and quarrelsomeness, and special social cases like defined *mésalliances.*[8]

We differentiated three aspects of behavior: prescribed conduct as formulated in the Jewish Code of Law; customary behavior which varies with social position and geographical area, and which is manifest in folklore, folk sayings, proverbs, institutions; and behavior not verbalized by the inhabitants of the shtetl, but manifest to the scientific observer. Thus, we distinguished between "formalized" and "unformalized" family behavior to facilitate our understanding of the dynamics of both equilibrium and change within the family. By formalized, we mean the codified and customary conduct of relatives. By unformalized, we mean the motivations and emotions of persons occupying the different roles, which are often unconscious or unverbalized, and often not evident in behavior; these are deeply intertwined with the formal structures, giving them fresh connotations, producing tensions and resolving them, but all contained within the confines of an equilibrium-directed logic termed *Sholem Bayis* (Hebrew, domestic peace).

The formal structuring of the husband's role places upon the man the responsibility for propagating the family, which carries his name, but attributes the failure to the wife; so that after ten years of barren marriage, the man is enjoined by Jewish law to request a divorce that will enable him to remarry fruitfully, though he and his wife may care deeply for each other.[9] The husband should study sacred literature and promote the book learning tradition of Israel, and this is so heavily stressed that devotion to study is the one condition allowed by the Schulchan Aruch for delaying marriage.[10] A scholar is expected to delegate the family's economic responsibilities to his wife; she is secondary to him in the spiritual or intellectual sphere, but is expected to be fully responsible in mundane affairs. However, the ideal, sometimes realized, is for a man to be both learned and successful in business. The husband is responsible for certain important domestic ritual, such as the *Kiddush* prayers said over wine on the Sabbath and holidays, the feast of the Passover, the pinning of the mezuzah on the house door-jamb.[11] And always he is responsible for his wife's general well-being, an injunction which was often so interpreted as to allow the Eastern European Jewish woman latitude and opportunities for movement, to conduct business, seek employment, and visit relatives in other parts.

The wife's role, from a legalistic point of view, is regarded as complementary to her husband's. From a functional point of view, it is subordinated to and dependent upon her husband's. This is perhaps symbolized by the belief that a woman enters heaven at her husband's footstool regardless of her possibly superior virtue and despite the fact that theoretically she enters heaven just as her husband does because "every Jew has his share in the world to come."[12] The fear of infertility threatens a Jewish woman with a heavy penalty of shame, producing anxieties, and may lead to social subterfuges like the adoption of children. A wife serves her husband and children in prescribed ways, and she is trained to be ready to assume the economic burdens of the family. In emergencies, like illness, her husband will carry out her duties, and one informant even told of a Jewish father giving the breast to his motherless infant to stop his crying. The wife shares responsibility for the Kashruth [Kosher diet] ritual[13] with her husband, but bears the burden of its correct functioning within the home; and she is responsible for fulfilling her own female ritual bearing on the family's well-being, such as observing the Mikvah[14] [ritual bath for women], lighting and blessing the Sabbath candles, offering God a portion of the dough from the Sabbath loaf.

This clear-cut understanding of the specialized functions of a husband and a wife, with its emphatic suggestion of male and female worlds of acts and values does not preclude overlapping and interchange in specific situations of need. In time of need, women may carry out a large part of the sacred activity normally assigned to men, and this is permissible because they are far less completely covered by regulations than are men; that is, when necessary, women may do anything unforbidden to them, even if normally it is bidden only to men. It is the universal obligation of all Jews to fulfill the obligations of the Jewish way of living, and in emergencies formal specializations of sex-typed roles are largely ignored.

A couple fulfills its Jewish mission by raising its offspring, hopefully numerous and favored with sons, in traditional detailed ways. Both parents support the children, educate them, and provide for the "crisis rites" of circumcision, confirmation, marriage, even death and apostasy. The male child is officially preferred by both parents, and the eldest boy (Hebrew, *B'chor*) is singled out as his father's legal heir, to receive respect from the youngest siblings all of his life.[15] Birth of a son is announced joyously by the father in the synagogue, in contrast with the flat announcement of a daughter's birth; the son carries the responsibility of the mourning prayers for the parents, called *Kaddish*. However a boy, like his sister, develops relationships with each parent that are culturally characteristic, and qualitatively different, partly in consequence of the different roles of the sexes in the community and of the differently structured ties with the parent of either sex, partly in consequence of the unformalized developments around the structuring. The father supervises the son's education. A daughter is not encouraged in advanced study but may teach herself from any available source.[16] The mother is the representative and administrator of the father's wishes, as she is the effective disciplinarian; her daughters however are her own full responsibility. She is always in or near the home with her sons and daughters, tending their physical needs, while the father is usually out of the home, studying in the synagogue or occupied with business. The father's presence and interests are remote from domestic concerns. But the mother prepares the food and serves it; she is always associated with the tangibles of existence. The father has the further obligation of supporting his married daughter and her husband in his home during the first few years of marriage, if his son-in-law is a promising scholar; this is known as supporting the young couple in *kest,* and is regarded by the bride's parents as an ideal arrangement. A divorcee or widow may return to her parents, but this is not expected of a son.

The reciprocally correct conduct of children is to respect and obey the parents unconditionally. This has many manifestations, prescribed in the Schulchan Aruch; symbolically, the son is obliged to rise whenever his father enters the room. The daughter serves her father, and helps and serves her mother, and the daughter is expected to influence her husband to support her parents when necessary. When mature, that is, married, all children are officially expected to support parents, though proverbs indicate how distasteful this can be to both parties since it connotes frailty or deficiency of the parents.

Relationships among siblings are guided by the parents, systematized along the lines of sex difference or identity, and of relative age. It appears that children introject parental standards successfully, and much of their behavior can be understood as modeled after that of the parent of the same sex. This does not of course preclude rebellion, or introjection of other ideals or adult models such as the teacher; priority of the teacher is even enjoined by law.[17]

Parents discourage opposite-sex siblings from playing together by reminding them of their sex differences, and attaching to these implications of prestige. Thus, a boy attending *cheder,* Hebrew school, is told it is beneath him to play girls' games, if he is found playing with his sister.[18]

Siblings are prohibited as sex partners by the Levitical code. In the shtetl, the prohibition is realized by avoidance[19] devices which include full body covering and segregated seating of the sexes except on rare formal occasions. Avoidance seems to increase with the maturity of brother and sister, as does the tension between them. Communication between them is fostered by the mother, when she initiates matters of interest to them but insists on functioning as their intermediary in such a way as to maintain their avoidance.

Parents are frequent intermediaries in the cross-sex sibling relationship, either on their own initiative or at the call of the children. Consistent with the indoctrinated habits of avoidance, mutual aid among these siblings is expected, and is often initiated by the parents. A practice of third-party mediation is in fact a feature of other aspects of the culture, notably in marriage and business arrangements.

Any sibling can develop into a parent-substitute as need arises. This adds to the strains in all sibling relationships, for authority, avoidances, and intimacies are differently organized between the parents and children. Siblings do not participate in each other's private lives until one assumes the role of substitute parent. Males and females are equally responsible for maintaining a traditionally prescribed standard of respectability and integrity that is contained in the word *yiddishkeit* (literally "Jewishness," roughly analogous to the United States' "our own way of life").

Brothers do not maintain avoidance in the sense cultivated by opposite-sex siblings, but it seems to us they manifest only a slight amount of interest in each other except when forcibly called upon in a family crisis. Then, after having raised requested funds, or provided for needy youngsters, they are likely to relapse into their distant ways. Even quarrels do not bring them together, as they do sisters, for angry men characteristically withdraw into sulky silences.

All women are presumed to quarrel more violently than men, in speech and act. This release of expression actually serves to bring sisters close together, at least socially, into a community little known to brothers.

A convention stresses marriage for siblings in their age sequence; this is emphasized for sisters, because, as rationalized by informants, it serves to minimize envy and quarrels, and to stress the authority of age.

The structuring of roles within this small biological family, the traditional allowances accorded each—either explicitly or by oversight—and the interrelationships among them result in role functions peculiar to this Eastern European Jewish culture. The functions or uses of the roles appear to be affected less by necessities of the family structure itself than by the ethos of the people,[20] by their "prevalent tone of sentiment"[21] or collective "emotional emphases."[22]

The most striking instance of ethological variation is the behavior of the woman as mother, particularly in relations with her son; she behaves similarly however as wife, and as sister in relationships with her brother. In other words, it is in association with these three relatives of the opposite sex that she most fully evolves her emotional or sentimental potentialities. Our data suggest that it is the women who initiates these opposite-sex interactions, who arouses them and conditions them. It was a practice, in the time of arranged marriages, for a mother to select a wife for her son; in memoirs written by Jewish men recording marriages, it was often the woman who instigated the negotiations and "had her way";[23] in folk and published stories, and in films, a sister assumes the role of mother when necessary. There is a saying that domestic harmony rests with the wife, and another that "a wife sets you on your feet, or knocks you off them."[24] It often happens that the mother's relatives are the ones best known to her children, even, in cases, to the entire ignorance of the father's kin. Informants born and reared in the shtetl area have told us of never having met paternal grandparents, especially the paternal grandfather, until the age of thirteen or fourteen. One male informant explained that the "mother's side was closer [because] first of all the very word *mameh* [Yiddish, mother] is closer to you than the word *tateh* [Yiddish, father]."[25] And a proverb declares, "A son always takes after his mother's brother."[26] Indeed, the wife is the actual head of the household, and responsible for its "Jewish way of life."

The house is the place for rearing the children. "She kills herself," people say of a good mother, in order to bring up her children. The father too becomes like a child to her in the home, except when he is studying or performing ritual acts; only outside of the home, in the synagogue or in business, does he enter upon a fully adult role. Mother is frequently described as "a loving despot,"[27] always busy, always nagging, "the last and highest court of appeal."[28] Generally her conduct is understood, tolerated, loved. In retrospect it is idealized, as shown in the published memoirs of Jewish men. Levin says, recalling his childhood, ". . . One figure emerges . . . my mother. In that image I recognize the beginning of my life and feel the first pulse beat of my being. . . . My mother was in my eyes the personification of all that is loveliest and most lovable. . . . In my eyes she was a saint. . . . Though my head was drawn toward [my] father, [my] heart [was drawn] toward [my] mother, and I was forever swinging like a pendulum between these two forces."[29] A folk tale that has even crept into American lore tells of a mother's devotion: A young man begs his mother for her heart, which his betrothed has demanded as a gift; having torn it out of his mother's proffered breast, he races away with it; and as he stumbles, the heart falls to the ground, and he hears it question protectively, "Did you hurt yourself, my son?"

The woman in the home personifies emotionality—the mother most of all. A young son often sleeps with her, unlike her husband who is prohibited by sacred law from remaining in her bed. In one memoir a boy slept with his mother until he was thirteen, that is, ritually a man. Although displays of endearment between husband and wife are frowned upon, regarded as vulgar whether in speech or gesture, a great deal of demonstrativeness is allowed between mother and son, which mothers encourage. The father is also unwontedly demonstrative to his daughter, but less so than the mother to her son.

It seems to us that though the marital obligations are fulfilled with the husband, the romance exists with the son. In the *New York Times* of October 29, 1949, an Associated Press story from Capetown, South Africa, reports, "A mother who had traced her missing sailor son around the globe fell dead of shock here when she faced him. The story was related today by the woman's husband as last rites were said at her grave. . . . Mrs. R. Levi of Aden saw her 19-year-old son early in World War II when he kissed her good-bye and left to join the Royal Navy. After several months she was advised that his ship had been torpedoed and all hands lost. . . . She refused to believe her son dead and wandered through Mediterranean ports seeking him. Mrs. Levi visited Britain, the United States and Australia in her weary search. . . . Then, in an asylum at Observatory, near Capetown, she found her son. He was a human wreck who could only mutter 'shalom, shalom,'—the Hebrew word for 'peace.' She looked at him, fell to the floor, and died." The same theme appeared in a Polish Jewish film, "Long Is the Road," where mother and son, separated by the Nazi occupation of Warsaw, sought each other after the Nazi defeat, searching devastated cities and concentration camps of Central Europe, until eventually the son located his mother in a hospital to which she had been taken in a state of breakdown. In the film, the woman's acceptance of her husband's murder by the Nazis contrasts with her agonized search for her son. Again, in the film "The Eternal Song" is depicted a

Polish woman's tragic love and desperate search for her son, ending in her own death. Another Polish Jewish film, "Bar Mitsvah," dramatically depicts the attachment between mother and son in another setting, and here too it causes all other relationships to pale.[30]

In actuality, a boy avoids[31] his sister, especially if she is a coeval, the avoidance increasing as they age; among most orthodox Jews, especially the very numerous Chassidic sect, a man avoids all women except his wife, mother, and daughter.[32] The interest in the sister however is powerful, revealed in indirect ways: in the Talmud[33] where dreams of incest with mother and sister are described coolly as "opening the way to wisdom," and where another dream symbol of incest with sister is to see one eye kiss another; in European Jewish films—"I Want To Be a Mother," "Bar Mitsvah," "Mamele"—brother-sister interest ranged from violent horseplay to one suggestion of romance and another of marriage, where however the siblings were unaware of their biological kinship.

There is no avoidance between mother and son, except that intercourse is forbidden. Mother is the embodiment of warmth, intimacy, food, unconditional love, security, practical reality. This inclusive libidinal character, of which the sisters partake to a lesser extent—the coeval sister partaking the least so that she is as much a stranger as a relative—is in complete contrast with the spiritualized, remote character of the father. Father's life is as dedicated to the study of the Law as mother's is to material comforts for the family; he is remote from his son physically and emotionally, being mentor and guide rather than comforter and nurse, and occupied outside of the home. Insofar as is possible to a living creature, a father's personality is delibidinized. Levin observes, "Toward my father my attitude was one of the deepest respect, but in that respect there was not lacking an element of fear. . . . I would say that my father's influence was to intellectualize me, my mother's to inspire me: From my father streamed a cool, clear light: from my mother, warmth and emotion. . . ."[34] Yet the father and son bear a similar relationship to the wife and mother, except that the woman owes respect to the husband because such is her defined obligation, and the son owes respect to the mother because that is his obligation. Indeed, rivalry between father and son is a familiar theme, expressed in large and small ways, privately and publicly. It is a commonplace that a man prefers his son-in-law to his son, and a proverb says, "Every son-in-law has in him something of his father-in-law."[35] Partly for this reason, it is proverbial that a man, though legally his father's heir, feuds with his sister's husband who stands to inherit his father-in-law's goodwill and perhaps his property; this is particularly striking in the history of some noted Chassidic "courts" or "dynasties."[36]

The mother-son relationship does not run smoothly, with all of the woman's high feeling. The Jewish mother of our informants is known for nagging, quarreling, worrying, and hypochondria. She overstresses her concern and her criticism, and offers or so manipulates the serving of the food as to indicate which.[37] Her husband and son are used to this. When she becomes too difficult, the man withdraws psychologically, silently picking up a book, or bodily, silently leaving for the synagogue; sometimes he deserts the family. By her conduct the woman manipulates her traditionally subordinate status to win some advantages: in many directions, she thus persuades her husband and her son to do her will.[38]

We have found the involvements between mother and son to be so far-reaching and intense as to approximate a kind of adoration. The mother is extremely jealous or resentful of her son's interest in another woman, even though she wants him to marry, for that is a Jew's obligation, and to have children, for that is also his duty and will besides bring her the joy, the *nakhes,* of grandmotherhood. Even though she may choose his wife, the feeling of treason is such that there is a folk saying, "When the son marries, he gives the wife a contract and the mother a divorce."[39] The bitterest mother-in-law stories are told by Jewish women, and here we see one element determining the greater closeness with the mother's kin.

What enters into the son's adoration of his mother? It appears to us that fundamentally there is her great concentration of loving, admiring attention on him, creating an interacting libidinal universe of two. To no one else will he ever be so desirable and important, nowhere else will he receive the indulgences shown a helpless child. If the son does not know this, the mother and the whole tradition so inform him. Besides, we think, the son early experiences the threat of being deprived of her. This happens when his parents start training him for adulthood. At three or four years of age, a "man" ready for study, he is carried in his father's arms away from the all-permissive home to the Hebrew school, or cheder, where he meets a harsh, indifferent teacher. He is sent away from home to the accompaniment of his mother's heartbroken sobs, to spend ten hours daily in the cold company of books and scholars, eating scantily whereas before he had overeaten, obliged in these surroundings to be "a man." If at home he now complains to mother about his teacher's whippings, she does not sympathize, but supports the brutal teacher. She steadily reminds him that in the area of Jewish studies he stands on his own as a man. Levin recalls, ". . . at the age of four I was treated like a big boy. Whenever I forgot to put on my *Arba Kanfoth* [ritual male body-garment], my mother would speak to me seriously, as to a grownup, and tell me how shameful it was for an adult Jew to be running about like a heathen without the reminder of his Jewishness hung about his body."[40] Such recollections are repeated in the memoirs of Eastern European Jewish men.

From this time on, the son is subject to continuing uncertainties of the same sort. We hear of boys of nine and ten being sent off to other cities to study with famous teachers, living with relatives or friends and dreaming of the indulgent mother far away. One informant, now a rabbi, said he actually dreaded returning home for the holidays, knowing how he would suffer when it came time to leave his mother's endless love and attentions and return to school. Sometimes one parent would die, necessitating distributing the children among relatives. Here enters the miserable state of orphanhood. Charney describes the tragic parting from his widowed mother at the age of thirteen, when she left for another city to marry.[41] She had been even more thoughtful than other mothers in waiting until he reached legal manhood before leaving. They both wept over the separation, and the boy said courageously, "If it will be good for you—it will be good for me. You will see." His feeling of loss and of personal helplessness come clearly to the reader. And it appears characteristic of Jewish males to regard the mother as a retreating figure of shelter, a most desirable warm figure always just out of reach, a poignant symbol of tenderness. Morris Raphael Cohen writes thus of his mother and his wife.[42] Indeed we believe that the Jewish man hopes to find a mother again in his wife, and is happiest in his marriage when this search is fulfilled.[43] Besides, the culture aids him, for in the time of arranged marriages his mother selected his wife, and a proverb states, "Every daughter-in-law has something of her mother-in-law."[44]

A girl's place in the family is a reflection of her mother's, but her truly affectionate tie is with her father. She is peculiarly his; when she is little, her father calls her his "queen" and "princess." At all ages she is the one family member in whose company he can relax; and when she marries, he finds joy in her husband[45] that he cannot find in his own son. If, as the people say, "a man sees himself in his son-in-law," they understand why he takes particular pleasure in his daughter's children. The mother observes all this and complains that the father spoils his daughter, though he may be severe to his son; she herself nags her daughter, especially before marriage, but conveys none of the overtones of affection and play that temper her nagging of husband and son.

The daughter responds readily to these highly specialized interpersonal situations. In all respects she follows her mother's example. In case of need, she takes over her mother's duties.[46] In *proste*, or "common" families, that do not maintain the highest Jewish standards, the father may be harsher and ruder with his family, including his daughter.

This easy relationship between father and daughter is comparable to the mother-son bond only in its selective coupling. Just as the mother imbues her activities with powerful emotion, the father gives his the culturally standardized spiritual and intellectual leanings demanded of a male. With his daughter, the father is indulgent and undemanding; his daughter is the only female other than his wife and mother with whom he may remain alone,[47] for to him she is not sexual. Real intimacy is not expected of a Jewish father, especially of *sheyne* class or aspirations, but he shows his daughter a unique affection and comradeship.[48]

Actually, short of incest, there are no norms prescribed in the Codes or elsewhere in tradition to guide a father in relations with his daughter; and he appears to follow a need to cultivate in this rather overlooked relationship a haven fairly free of tension.[49] This is in contrast with his prescribed relationships with his son, which are authoritarian and didactic, for a father represents all of traditional Law and is the personal model for his son to emulate. Comfortable as the father-daughter bond is, it lacks the obvious drama belonging to the mother-son and the muted tension—often expressed in rivalry and rebellion in adulthood—inherent in the father-son.[50] However, the content of a film, based on a classic Yiddish play,[51] indicates the powerful emotional current that possibly underlies relations of father and daughter, threatening to draw them together and to displace the mother from her wifely status. It was reported to us that occasional instances of this sort actually occurred among Eastern European Jewish immigrants. Perhaps in daily life, the mother, unaware, anticipates this eventuality when she repeatedly attacks her unmarried daughter; indeed a monotonous theme in her nagging is her articulated anticipatory refusal to be supplanted in any capacity by her daughter. We suggest that the interchangeability of any individual's role in shtetl society functions in a woman's life as a threat of replaceability that may color her total personality with anxiety and tension. Since her status is defined in terms of her domestic roles, she expresses her anxieties in this area.

The mother-daughter relationship contains more rivalry and even hostility than do the other family couplings. The mother cues this development as clearly as she does her different relationship with her son. Though she nags at all members of the family, in her special woman's idiom of communication, she nags at her daughter in a consistently hostile manner, while her husband and her son can be nagged at with affectionate purposes apparent to everyone. The mother knows she must rear her daughter to be like herself, but she is determined to keep the daughter in her place as a junior female as long as the latter lives in the parental home. Informants indicate that the mother does not really wish to teach the daughter cooking or any other skill that might replace her own services, and so she rails, for example, "Keep out of my kitchen! This is *my* kitchen! You don't know how to cook! You just waste time and food."[52] Her negativism is a striking contrast to the emphasis of many other cultures, where girlhood also is the mandatory period of training for housewifely responsibilities. And in fact the Jewish girl's goals in life are precisely to function as wife and mother.[53] However, the Jewish mother confines her daughter to the role of unskilled assistant. When the daughter makes a household suggestion or any other suggestion touching upon the mother's sphere of influence, the mother may react as to a challenge and strive to confine her. This can be interpreted as the mother's jealous protection of the adult status she acquired by marriage; it is consistent with a probable predisposition of the women to react defensively or hostilely. Upon the daughter's marriage there is an important shift in the interaction, from authoritarion to egalitarian, since the daughter's new status approaches that of her mother, and since she may for the first time leave the home if she does not remain on kest.

The relations between siblings of opposite sex are polarized about regulations of avoidance and incest, and, depending upon the relative age of the two siblings, are characterized by avoidance-quarrelsomeness or by permissiveness. Actually there appears to be a gradient of these attitudes. Much tension is frequently found between opposite-sex siblings of about the same age, expressed in quarrelsome or silent hostility; our film analyses suggest that we regard this conduct as possibly a barrier to incest. As age differences between such siblings increase, permissiveness is allowed increasingly by the elder along the lines of permissiveness between mother-son, father-daughter; as age differences between the siblings decrease, avoidance increases. The role of mother-substitute need not be adopted by the chronologically senior sister, though that is the expectation; as is commonly known, and is illustrated in the film "Mamele," a less senior sister whose personality is more congenial to the role can actually function as mother-substitute. (The adaptability of personality to the traditionally sex-typed roles appears in all aspects of Eastern European Jewish culture.) Considering males of the family from the viewpoint of a girl: one might say that there is a maximum permissiveness with the father, although the incest taboo is always observed; with the elder brother there is considerable permissiveness, and some degree of avoidance; with the coeval brother there is more avoidance than permissiveness; the relationship with the younger brother is a mirror-image of the father-daughter relationship, since here is displayed a maximum permissiveness following the mother-son pattern, and a minimum of avoidance barring incest. The same gradient behavior patterns a boy's relationship with his mother and sisters within the poles of parental permissiveness and sibling avoidance.

Behavior among siblings of the same sex follows a gradient that is comparable in extent but different in qualities. Thus among brothers, the father represents ritual and statutory authority, in which the older brother shares; between coevals there is a mutual ignoring of this authority, but in the relationship with the younger brother, authority must reappear. Among sisters, the mother enforces her authority over her daughters largely through generation-linked attributes; the elder sister partakes of this authority, but coeval sisters quarrel over any manifestations of privilege or even of equality; the generation-bred authority reappears in the relationship with the younger sister. All of these relationships become more equalized after marriage, since the status of the women is then referred not to the parental authority but to the conjugal role.

Parents distinguish between the eldest child who, if male, is the heir, and the youngest, who is the beloved baby. Beyond these two, singled out by traditional appellations, the various children are often indicated by affectionate, somewhat ironical appelations descriptive of personal qualities like beauty, brains, skills, idiosyncracies. Daughters employ these identifications in the rivalrous quarrels, especially when the identifications derive from the father. Sons however tend to substitute sulky silences and ignoring for quarrels and thus drive themselves further apart.

Affinal Behavior. Affinal behavior is intelligible as a function of the behavior of the blood kin, especially as functions of the mother-son, father-daughter, and brother-sister relationships. In the period of arranged marriages,[54] a woman chose her prospective daughter-in-law carefully, appraising the social and financial standing of her parents, demanding dowry and kest to correspond to her son's intellectual talents, examining the future bride's housewifely abilities, and generally measuring her by severe personal and role specifications. As informants said half-humorously, a prospective mother-in-law "knows" no girl is good enough for her boy, yet Jewish law obliges each man to marry. Even after marriages by personal choice were accepted—and today in this country—a woman impresses her son with her caustic opinions, and in informal ways subjects his prospective mate to examination. One woman raised in the shtetl but now living in New York told us with real chagrin, "I can't find anything wrong with my son's girl! But I've got to criticize her! All her buttons are sewed on right, the seams of her stockings are straight, there are no tears or holes in her clothing even when she doesn't expect to see me!"

The relationship between a woman and her daughter-in-law is expected to be one of tension despite the hopeful proverb that "a woman sees herself mirrored in her daughter-in-law," for in effect she has chosen her. At the wedding ceremony itself the two dance the *broiges tants,* or "angry dance." Tradition has stressed the son's marriage as the mother's divorce.[55] And the people love to tell a comical story, in many variations, having the point that whatever the daughter-in-law has, does, or enjoys is an exploitation of the son in the eyes of the doting mother; whereas the same circumstances in the life of the daughter are testimony to the virtues of the son-in-law.

Not until a young matron gives birth to a child can she face her mother-in-law with something like equality, when the older woman must admit that the marriage has been justified and that she has been blessed with grand-motherhood. Nevertheless she is ever alert to comment that her daughter-in-law does not cook or indulge or otherwise take care of the son as adequately as she did;[56] and an angry husband will rebuke his wife as though in his mother's behalf saying, "You can't cook as well as she did!"[57] Soon, too, a woman becomes highly critical of her daughter-in-law's methods of rearing the grandchild, her son's child, the more so as the harassed daughter-in-law turns to her own mother for help, and avoids or excludes her possessive mother-in-law. This may be one reason why the maternal kin are closer than the paternal. The son is caught between the complaints of mother and wife. The father-in-law has a fairly conventional, formal relationship with his daughter-in-law, growing out of sex avoidance and tension with the son.

It is some relief to the strain between a woman and her mother-in-law if the former begins her married life at a distance, if possible taking her husband to live in kest with her own parents. The typical mother-daughter rivalry in the wife's family is now moderated by the accomplishment of marriage, which elevates the status of all parties, and which introduces a new and much desired member into the family circle. Father and mother both welcome the son-in-law with open arms. We suggest that this welcome contains nuances that differ with the mother and with the father, growing out of their differing relationships to their daughter. It appears to us as a possibility that the mother's characteristically rivalrous relationship with her daughter employs the entrance of the son-in-law into the family as a situation offering additional potentialities for expressing or cultivating her well-established feeling of rivalry. For example, a woman will belittle her daughter in conversation with her son-in-law, even at the risk of arousing his antagonism. The son-in-law comes to resent his mother-in-law because she disparages and nags his wife, for his wife is *his,* and she is not his mother-in-law's property any longer. A man may scold his wife, saying for example, that she doesn't run the house as well as his own mother, but he will quarrel with his mother-in-law when she scolds his wife. Thus, a woman's relationship with her son-in-law contains elements that derive in part from her characteristic relationship with her daughter, since her rivalrous relationship with her daughter-in-law derives in part from her special relationship with her son. On the other hand, the father employs the entrance of his son-in-law into the family as an additional opportunity for expressing his habitual affection for his daughter. We have no unequivocal documentary evidence for this interpretation, but we offer it because it seems to us consistent with the other family relationships and suggests those roots in the filial bonds out of which are elaborated details in affinal behavior.

The father, in the days of arranged marriages, chose the son-in-law after testing him for family and personal qualities, stressing scholarly accomplishments over physical and economic qualifications. The mother welcomed the son-in-law as a kind of son, with a warmth that the young man often found objectionable and in conflict with his mother-son bond. He often rejected her as a "witch" (Yiddish, *machasheifeh*) telling her so and quarrelling with her, unlike her silent, often resigned husband and son. The special, poorly reciprocated fondness of a woman for her son-in-law is a familiar matter among the people. It is equally understood that real affection and camaraderie exist between a man and his son-in-law—if the son-in-law fulfills expectations —when the relationship assumes an ease and warmth foreign to the relationship of father and son.[58]

However, this unusually amiable tie, prettily consistent with the amiable father-daughter relationship, is sensed with hostility by the unmarried brothers-in-law who see in the newcomer a competitor for everybody's affections[59] and an unjustified beneficiary of the family's goods, since the son-in-law receives a dowry and kest support. Ordinarily the brothers-in-law operate with the distance characteristic of males, but after the father's death they are likely to quarrel over his estate, such as his seat in the synagogue, or the loyalty of his followers, should he be a Chassidic leader. The unmarried sisters-in-law behave differently however, prevented by inter-sex avoidance from manifesting fully the parental attitude of welcome. Siblings-in-law come into their true importance as aunt and uncle, potential guardians of the children.

However, an unmarried girl is predisposed to dislike strongly her coeval brother's wife, considering her inferior, unattractive, stupid, thus supporting her mother's feelings about her daughter-in-law. When sisters-in-law first meet however, before or after the marriage, they greet each other with a show of kindness that may conceal hostile anticipations, even from their own conscious thoughts. The formal kindness is related to the recurring admonition in the Schulchan Aruch, "You must receive [everybody] with a friendly countenance and joyful feeling."[60] The mother-in-law and daughter-in-law also meet thus, the former being very "kind" to her son's wife, cooking special dishes, serving elaborately, keeping the young woman from domestic chores. However, friction soon develops, which the mother-in-law initiates with ironical remarks that grow more stinging, alternating with prolonged silences (*broiges,* Yiddish, angry), continuing in noisy quarrels and arguments about any detail of everyday life but especially over the inadequate care that the daughter-in-law gives her husband. It is probably the "kind" period that produces behavior reflected in the folk saying (woman speaking), "Scold your daughter, but mean your daughter-in-law." The saying also reveals some of the pressure that is placed on the unmarried daughter at this time.

It appears to us that in the relations between the sisters-in-law, it is the unmarried girl who originates the hostilities. She complains in idioms taken from her mother that her sister-in-law does not feed her brother properly, and that she acts as though she were more important than the sister. Thus family ranking is introduced between the sisters-in-law to establish their interacting roles. The sister feels sincerely that her brother's wife's family is not as good as her own, and that her brother's intellectual and other attainments are superior to his wife's.

We infer that where avoidance characterizes the relationship between sister and brother, the marriage of the brother may prod the sister to displace her concealed feelings about him onto his wife in the form of resentment.

Thus from one point of view, affinal behavior is determined by sibling avoidance: the sister is driven by unconscious jealousy of the advantages which the wife possesses in her relationship with her husband. The wife responds by stressing her enviable married status. These interactions produce a mounting tension, eventually relieved for the sister through the channel of affection for her brother's children. Nonetheless this sister in one way or another puts the scornful question, "Why should anyone want to marry my brother?" This seems to reflect the Jewish family's habit of belittling the son in comparison with his father, and to be also an expression of sibling avoidance.

Our data suggest that the marriage of the sister leads to a lessening of her resentment against the sister-in-law. This is attributable not to any change in the relationship with the brother but to the equalization of the statuses of the two young matrons. Rivalry continues however on the new level of common married interests. It is voiced through quarrels and nagging, which are a recognized style of communication by women—although men should quarrel only about important matters, such as business, or points of learning. With time, the sisters-in-law drift apart, as each family tends to cultivate its own flesh-and-blood maternal kin and to overlook its more indifferent paternal kin.[61]

The Character of Marriages. It seems to us that the distinct kinship roles cultivated by members of the small two-generation family guide and even determine the character of the marriages into which the children enter. Traditional law contains few indicators for the choice of partner; mainly the chief restriction is that from among his kin a man may marry only in collateral lines of descent, that is, nieces, and that an unmarried man must honor the obligation of the levirate[62] within specified limits. Actually when marriage was by parental arrangement, the preference of the opposite-sexed parent allowed little or no choice.

We think that this preference in fact matched, and still matches, needs in the child of opposite sex. If one examines the nature of marriages taking place through free personal choice, it seems that a young woman is guided in these private relations with men by two male models from within her own family universe: her father and her brother.[63] As already shown, she behaves quite differently with each. Roughly, one is a permissive, secure situation, the other is tense and uncertain. We suggest that father is the model for the "husband," in which relationship the woman ideally expects security, status, unconditional affection, spiritual and intellectual qualities, a minimizing of youthful traits however these are defined locally, and a certain kinship feeling of "belonging." We suggest that brother is the model for "lover" in extramarital experience, a relationship which holds for the woman libidinal attractions, nonintellectual interests (in keeping with the father's lower valuation of his son), physical appeals of youthfulness and play, and the quality of being a "stranger" (which probably roots in coeval avoidance) instead of kin.

Similarly, a young man is guided in his private relations with women by two female models from within his family universe: his mother and his sister. With the first there is great permissiveness, with the second there is avoidance. We suggest that mother is the model for "wife," with whom the man ideally expects security, protection, warmth, unconditional affection, practical support, and the kinship quality of "belonging." We suggest that sister is the model for "lover," containing expectations of libidinal appeals, physical characteristics of youth, independence and an aspect of "strangeness" instead of kinship; it is in this context that we understand the affair with the gentile girl.

Under the system of arranged marriage, the father selected his son-in-law, the mother chose her daughter-in-law. As the proverbs quoted earlier indicate,[64] the bride is married to someone expected to be like her father, the groom is married to someone expected to be like his mother. Hence, the bride responds to the groom somewhat as to her father; the groom responds to the bride somewhat as to his mother. One of our scholarly informants was of the opinion that those marriages succeeded where the husband really did find mother-qualities in his wife: he thought that the frequent desertions by men[65] could be related to the inability of the wife to function in the mother-role; for instance an extramarital affair usually would not of itself lead to desertion or divorce. Thus, it seems to us that the arranged marriage, in its selection of the young couple, corresponds to the sucessful marriage by free choice. Shtetl marriages were usually regarded as successful, despite the ease of divorce. Also, couples often considered themselves happy. This shtetl saying offered pertinent advice: "First marry, then love."

Family Obligations. When the Jew speaks of his family, he means the biological family of parents, children, and siblings. Ancient codes prescribe specifically the reciprocal obligations within it and override completely personal preferences. The informal, ethologically influenced aspects still function within the codified framework. The only codified behavior outside of the biological family is the incest taboo extended to grandparents and grandchildren. As relationships move out from the biological family, personal preferences operate with increased freedom and variety, filling a vacuum otherwise occupied by institutional prescriptions. In this area the only codifications are those covering the behavior of the total society, such as deference and respect toward older people and scholars, as well as general avoidance of women.

The shtetl Jews consider all members of the Jewish community to be related to each other through kinship ties, a belief expressed formally in the collective term *B'nai Israel,* Children of Israel, and in the acceptance of the three Biblical patriarchs as the ancestors of all Jews. In actual practice, two Jews who meet try to identify themselves in the expectation of establishing some kin connection, no matter how remote or indirect. This is regarded as a pleasurable circumstance and holds the assurance of mutual aid. It is considered good Jewish behavior to refer social interests to the framework of family thinking.

The interaction of family roles produces a field of tensions whose balance is a goal periodically striven for, but regularly disturbed by the complications of the mother-son, father-daughter, and opposite-sex sibling relationships. This goal of balanced tensions, domestic harmony, is termed *Sholem Bayis.* Within its dynamics, of striving and of briefly-held fulfillment, are patterned the differentiated effects of being cared for reliably and intensively by mother, and of being disciplined or loved irregularly and distantly by father. It is a pattern offering all participants comfort, excitement, and security; but it is also tyrannical and in its strong demands promotes much individual strain and often revolt. For the boy, the filial role provides the prototypes of adult relationships, since he will act with his wife much as he acts with his mother, and with older men much as he acts with his father. The filial role is somewhat different for the girl, since she must early learn to accept her obligation to be a mother, and will discover her widest opportunities in this sex-typed function only after her marriage. Modifications of these relationships are practiced and fixed in the sibling interrelationships, and from here carried out in the contacts outside the home.

Traditional family rearing lays great emphasis on sex differences, defining social functions in terms of sex. Tradition views the differentiation as complementary, but in actuality there are frequent implications of male status-superiority and of female status-inferiority. Ritual and learning are honorific male occupations; and homely family duties including economic responsibility and childbearing and physical child-care are less exalted female pursuits. There is thus a complete dichotomy between the intellectual burdens and opportunities charged to men, and the earthy ones charged to women. This is true under the ordinary circumstances of living, but under stress, practically without restriction, a person can carry out needed functions of the other sex;[66] this adaptive elasticity obtains also in other aspects of the culture, enjoined by traditional law. Our data suggest that women, being less honorifically placed and as such neglected by the codified prescriptions, found widening opportunities exactly under conditions of stress. They took on the responsibilities brought to them, and we have no record of large-scale female rebellion in the traditional communities.[67] But history is replete with rebellions led by men and composed of men. These range from simple open rivalry between father and son, noted even in folk sayings, to great social movements.[68]

Within the traditional community, where almost all values and ideals and honorific activities are cast in male terms and references, and are understood to be such when not explicit, the private life of the family emerges as the responsibility of women and is largely dominated by them. A man, busy outside the home with holy study or his livelihood, often appears as a guest[69] on the domestic scene, as his wife orders space and quiet for his rest and study. This is the complement to the place of the woman in the synagogue which, as a community house for studious men, reserves a place for her in a separated section. However, there is considerable understanding and cooperation between the sex-separated functions of shtetl society, both in the family and outside in the general community; no secrets exist between them; the two spheres of male and female activities are welded into interdependent wholes by severe bonds of ritual and of specialized responsibility.

Summary. Our hypotheses concern the form and functioning of the Jewish family in the recently destroyed Eastern European small town containing the indigenous Jewish culture. We emphasize that these are not definite findings, nor can these hypotheses ever be tested in the field, since the Jewish communities no longer exist. We risk the additional conjecture that this was a distinct culture, and therefore a distinct set of family phenomena, since it employed its own common language, Yiddish, and its own sacred language, Hebrew; it boasted of its ancient and special history and its religious and scholarly traditions, known to all the Western world; and it always functioned under highly precarious conditions among hostile peoples.

Within the space and objectives of this article, we cannot attempt systematically to compare Jewish and other European and American cultures. We can illustrate important differences however by pointing out that whereas among Eastern European Jews no man hopes to be outstripped by his son, the opposite is often described as true in middle-class urban American life. This may be a value adopted by Jewish immigrants. Again, Eastern European Jewry stresses the superiority of the arranged durable marriage, and the attendant responsibilities of the elder generations; the opposite is known to obtain widely in the United States where romantic and rather impermanent unions are standard. And again, the authority of the Eastern European Jewish father rests ideally and primarily upon his status as an exponent of the religious and scholarly tradition, and only secondarily upon his reliability as an earner; but in the United States no man escapes the primary pressure to provide economically for his family, and failure can be punished by state law.

In the recently flourishing Eastern European Jewish family, the traditionally codified standards underwent local and temporal modifications, and among certain kin were often interpreted or acted out unexpectedly under the pressures of living. Its most dynamic relationships were those between husband-wife, mother-son, and father-daughter; other blood and kin ties flowed from, supported, and otherwise were consequences of these three. All the relationships were keyed to operate under conditions of high psychological tension that often threatened to break down, but peace-making machinery was set in motion at the point of rupture; thus family harmony or balance, Sholem Bayis, was restored. In the overcrowded shtetl where there could be no privacy within the home, or among the homes, where all men attended synagogue daily, all boys attended chedar daily, and the women met at their work, the community was always reckoned with in connection with Sholem Bayis: each family felt it important to maintain a respectable front in the face of public opinion.

In the family, as throughout the culture, there are provisions for male and female worlds of acts and values. But this does not preclude overlapping and interchange in specific situations of need. Women may sense this interchangeability as a threat of replacement in spouse relations, against which they see a principal safeguard in fecundity.

Relationships among siblings are patterned after those between parents and children especially where age differences exist, but a stressed avoidance separates opposite-sexed coeval siblings. Patterned avoidance appears with variations among all family kin of opposite sex, and also among men and women in the general community. After the spouses, the least avoidance obtains between mother and son, and then between father and daughter. Considerable tension exists between parents and children of the same sex. Important aspects of relationships among affinal kin appear as functions of the behavior of the blood kin. Consistent with the avoidance practices, parents are frequent intermediaries in the cross-sibling relationships; besides, third-party mediation is a feature of other aspects of the culture, notably in marriage and business arrangements.

The functions or uses of the family roles appear to be strongly influenced by ethological emphases of the people. This is strikingly so in the behavior of women within the family; the home is traditionally specified as the only area where they possess status. Legalistically, men have higher status everywhere; actually, as scholars, their preferred sphere lies outisde the home in the synagogue. Women are often the effective breadwinners and adapt better to necessity than their husbands, but this does not confer status on them. Women symbolize emotionality, men symbolize spirituality.

Marriage marks the complete adulthood of men and women, and leads to changed relationships with the families of origin. Marriage should be arranged by the parents, who keep in mind traditional criteria as well as personal preferences. The institution of kest roots here, where a young scholar is supported by his father-in-law during the first years of marriage. Generally, families try to live separately. Modern marriages by free choice may actually correspond in values to the arranged marriage.

THE ITALIAN FAMILY IN
THE UNITED STATES

Paul J. Campisi

THE CHANGES IN THE ITALIAN FAMILY in America can be visualized in terms of a continuum which ranges from an unacculturated Old World type to a highly acculturated and urbanized American type of family. This transformation can be understood by an analysis of three types of families which have characterized Italian family living in America: the Old World peasant Italian family which existed at the time of the mass migration from Italy (1890-1910) and which can be placed at the unacculturated end of the continuum; the first-generation Italian family in America, which at the beginning of contact with American culture was much like the first but which changed and continues to change increasingly so that it occupies a position somewhere between the two extremes; and, finally, the second-generation Italian family which represents a cross-fertilization of the first-generation Italian family and the American contemporary urban family, with the trend being in the direction of the American type. Consequently, the position this family assumes is near the American-urban end of the continuum.

Since there are significant differences between the northern Italian and southern Italian families and since there are even greater differences between peasant, middle-class, and upper-class families, it seems expedient to single out one type of family for discussion and analysis, namely, the southern Italian peasant family. During the period of mass migration from Italy the bulk of the immigrants were from southern Italy (including Sicily).[1] These immigrants came mostly from small-village backgrounds as peasant farmers, peasant workers, or simple artisans, and as such they brought with them a southern Italian folk-peasant culture. It is this type of background which the majority of Italian families in America have today.[2]

This paper cannot possibly present an adequate analysis of all the important changes observed in the Italian family. Therefore, a simple tabular form (see Table) is used to display the most important details.

The Southern Italian Peasant Family in America. At the time of the great population movement from Italy to America, beginning at the end of the nineteenth century, the southern Italian peasant family was a folk societal family. One of the chief characteristics of the folk society is that its culture is highly integrated, the separate parts forming a strongly geared and functionally meaningful whole.[3] This intimate interconnection between the various parts of a folk culture indicates that it would be artificial and fruitless to attempt to isolate, even for the sake of study and analysis, any one part, such as the family, and to proceed to discuss that as a discrete and distinct entity. All the characteristics of the Old World Italian peasant family are intimately tied in with such institutions and practices as religion, the planting and gathering of food, the celebrations of feasts and holidays, the education

Reprinted from *The American Journal of Sociology* (May 1948), pp. 443-49, by permission of the author and the publisher. (Copyright, 1948, by the University of Chicago Press.)

of the children, the treatment of the sick, the protection of the person, and with all other aspects of small-village folk culture. In the final analysis Old World peasant-family life meant small-village life, and the two were inseparable aspects of a coercive folk-peasant culture. This fact sharply distinguishes the Old World peasant family from the first- and second-generation families in America.

The First-Generation Southern Italian Peasant Family in America. By the first-generation Italian family is simply meant that organization of parents and offspring wherein both parents are of foreign birth and wherein an attempt is made to perpetuate an Italian way of life in the transplanted household. This is a family in transition, still struggling against great odds to keep alive those customs and traditions which were sacred in the Old World culture. As a result of many internal and external pressures which have cut it off from its Old World foundations, the first-generation family is marked by considerable confusion, conflict, and disorganization. The uncertain and precarious position of the first-generation Italian family today is further aggravated by the loss of that strong family and community culture which had been such an indispensable part of the Old World peasant family. It is this loss in the first-generation family which pushes it away from the unacculturated end of the continuum to a position somewhere in the middle.[4]

The Second-Generation Southern Italian Family in America. This refers to that organization of parents and offspring wherein both the parents are native American born but have foreign-born parents who attempted to

Differences between the Southern Italian Peasant Family in Italy and the First- and Second-Generation Italian Family in America

Southern Italian Peasant Family in Italy	First-Generation Southern Italian Family in America	Second-Generation Southern Italian Family in America
A. General characteristics:		
1. Patriarchal	Fictitiously patriarchal	Tends to be democratic
2. Folk-peasant	Quasi-urban	Urban and modern
3. Well integrated	Disorganized and in conflict	Variable, depending on the particular family situation
4. Stationary	Mobile	High degree of mobility
5. Active community life	Inactive in the American community but somewhat active in the Italian neighborhood	Inactive in the Italian neighborhood, but increasingly active in American community
6. Emphasis on the sacred	Emphasis on the sacred is weakened	Emphasis on the secular
7. Home and land owned by family	In the small city the home may be owned, but in a large city the home is usually a flat or an apartment	Ownership of home is an ideal, but many are satisfied with flat
8. Strong family and community culture	Family culture in conflict	Weakened family culture reflecting vague American situation
9. Sharing of common goals	No sharing of common goals	No sharing of common goals
10. Children live for the parents	Children live for themselves	Parents live for the children
11. Children are an economic asset	Children are an economic asset for few working years only and may be an economic liability	Children are an economic liability
12. Many family celebrations of special feasts, holidays, etc.	Few family celebrations of feasts and holidays	Christmas only family affair, with Thanksgiving being variable
13. Culture is transmitted only by the family	Italian culture is transmitted only by family, but American culture is transmitted by American institutions other than the family	American culture is transmitted by the family and by other American institutions
14. Strong in-group solidarity	Weakened in-group solidarity	Little in-group solidarity
15. Many functions: economic, recreational, religious, social, affectional, and protective	Functions include semirecreational, social, and affectional	Functions reduced to affectional, in the main

Southern Italian Peasant Family in Italy	First-Generation Southern Italian Family in America	Second-Generation Southern Italian Family in America
B. Size:		
1. Large-family system	Believe in a large-family system but cannot achieve it because of migration	Small-family system
2. Many children (10 is not unusual)	Fair number of children (10 is unusual)	Few children (10 is rare)
3. Extended kinship to godparents	Extended kinship, but godparent relationship is weakened	No extended kinship to godparents
C. Roles and statuses:		
1. Father has highest status	Father loses high status, or it is fictitiously maintained	Father shares high status with mother and children; slight patriarchal survival
2. Primogeniture: eldest son has high status	Rule of primogeniture is variable; success more important than position	No primogeniture; all children tend to have equal status
3. Mother center of domestic life only and must not work for wages	Mother center of domestic life but may work for wages and belong to some clubs	Mother acknowledges domestic duties but reserves time for much social life and may work for wages
4. Father can punish children severely	Father has learned that American law forbids this	Father has learned it is poor psychology to do so
5. Family regards itself as having high status and role in the community	Family does not have high status and role in the American community but may have it in the Italian colony	Family struggles for high status and role in the American community and tends to reject high status and role in the Italian community
6. Women are educated for marriage only	Women receive some formal education as well as family education for marriage	Emphasis is on general education with reference to personality development rather than to future marriage
7. The individual is subordinate to the family	Rights of the individual increasingly recognized	The family is subordinate to the individual
8. Daughter-in-law is subservient to the husband's family	Daughter-in-law is in conflict with husband's family	Daughter-in-law is more or less independent of husband's family
9. Son is expected to work hard and contribute to family income	Son is expected to work hard and contribute to family income, but this is a seldom-realized goal	Son expected to do well in school and need not contribute to family income
D. Interpersonal relations:		
1. Husband and wife must not show affection in the family or in public	Husband and wife are not demonstrative in public or in the family but tolerate it in their married children	Husband and wife may be demonstrative in the family and in public
2. Boys are superior to girls	Boys are regarded as superior to girls	Boys tend to be regarded as superior to girls, but girls have high status also
3. Father is consciously feared, respected, and imitated	Father is not consciously feared or imitated but is respected	Father is not consciously feared. He may be imitated and may be admired
4. Great love for mother	Great love for mother but much ambivalence from cultural tensions	Love for mother is shared with father
5. Baby indulgently treated by all	Baby indulgently treated by all	Baby indulgently treated by all with increasing concern regarding sanitation, discipline, and sibling rivalry
E. Marriage:		
1. Marriage in early teens	Marriage in late teens or early twenties	Marriage in early or middle twenties
2. Selection of mate by parents	Selection of mate by individual with parental consent	Selection of mate by individual regardless of parental consent
3. Must marry someone from the same village	This is an ideal, but marriage with someone from same region (i.e., province) is tolerated; very reluctant permission granted to marry outside nationality; no permission for marriage outside religion	Increasing number of marriages outside nationality and outside religion
4. Dowry rights	No dowry	No dowry
5. Marriage always involves a religious ceremony	Marriage almost always involves both a religious and a secular ceremony	Marriage usually involves both, but there is an increasing number of marriages without benefit of religious ceremony
F. Birth and child care:		
1. Many magical and superstitious beliefs in connection with pregnancy	Many survivals of old beliefs and superstitions	Few magical and superstitious notions in connection with pregnancy
2. Delivery takes place in a special confinement room in the home; midwife assists	Delivery takes place generally in a hospital; may take place in home; family doctor displaces midwife	Delivery takes place almost always in a hospital; specialist, obstetrician, or general practitioner assists
3. Child illnesses are treated by folk remedies; local physician only in emergencies or crises	Child illnesses are treated partially by folk remedies but mostly by the family doctor	Child illnesses are treated by a pediatrician; much use of latest developments in medicine (vaccines, etc.)

Southern Italian Peasant Family in Italy	First-Generation Southern Italian Family in America	Second-Generation Southern Italian Family in America
4. Child is breast-fed either by the mother or by a wet nurse; weaning takes place at about end of 2d or 3d year by camouflaging the breasts	Child is breast-fed if possible; if not, it is bottle-fed; same practice with variations regarding weaning	Child is bottle-fed as soon as possible; breast-feeding is rare; no weaning problems
5. No birth control	Some birth control	Birth control is the rule
G. Sex attitudes:		
1. Child is allowed to go naked about the house up to the age of 5 or 6; after this there is rigid enforcement of the rule of modesty	Variable, depending on the individual family's situation	This is variable, depending on the individual family; development of modesty is much earlier than in Old World peasant family
2. Sex matters are not discussed in family	Sex matters are not discussed in family	Sex matters increasingly discussed in family but not as freely as in "old" American family
3. Adultery is severely punished by the man's taking matters into his own hands	Adultery results in divorce or separation	Adultery may result in divorce or separation
4. Chastity rule rigidly enforced by chaperonage; lack of it grounds for immediate separation at wedding night	Attempts to chaperon fail, but chastity is an expectation; lack of it is grounds for separation, but there are few cases of this kind in America	No chaperonage; chastity is expected, but lack of it may be reluctantly tolerated
5. No premarital kissing and petting are allowed	No premarital kissing and petting are allowed openly	Premarital kissing and petting are allowed openly
6. Boys and girls attend separate schools	Schools are coeducational	Schools are coeducational
H. Divorce and separation:		
1. No divorce allowed	No divorce allowed, but some do divorce	Religion forbids it, but it is practiced
2. Desertion is rare	Desertion is rare	Desertion is rare
I. Psychological aspects:		
1. Fosters security in the individual	Fostered conflict in the individual	Fosters security with some conflict lags
2. The family provides a specific way of life; hence, there is little personal disorganization	Family is in conflict, hence cannot provide a specific way of life; yields marginal American-Italian way of life	Family reflects confused American situation, does not give individual a specific way of life, but marginality is weakened
3. Recreation is within family	Recreation is both within and outside the family	Recreation is in the main outside the family; this is variable, depending on individual family situation

transmit to them an Italian way of life in the original first-generation family in America.

Among the significant characteristics of this type of family is the orientation which the American-born parents make to the American culture. This adjustment tends to take three forms. One is that of complete abandonment of the Old World way of life. The individual changes his Italian name, moves away from the Italian neighborhood and in some cases from the community, and has little to do with his foreign-born parents and relatives.[5] The ideal is to become acculturated in as short a time as possible. This type of second-generation Italian generally passes for an American family and is rare. A second form of second-generation Italian family is a marginal one. In this type there is a seriously felt need to become Americanized and hence to shape the structure and functions of the family in accordance with the contemporary urban American type of family. The parental way of life is not wholly repudiated, although there is some degree of rejection. This family is likely to move out of the Italian neighborhood and to communicate less and less with first-generation Italians, but the bond with the first-generation family is not broken completely. Intimate communication is maintained with the parental household, and the relationships with the parents as well as with immigrant relatives are affectionate and understanding. A third form which the second-generation family takes is of orientation inward toward an Italian way of life. This type of family generally prefers to remain in the Italian neighborhood, close to the parental home. Its interaction with the non-Italian world is at a minimum, and its interests are tied up with those of the Italian community. Of the three, the second type is the most representative second-generation Italian family in America. This is the family depicted in the table.

The table reveals the movement of the first- and second-generation Italian families away from the Old World peasant pattern and toward the contemporary American family type. In this persistent and continuous process of acculturation there are three stages: (1) the initial-contact stage, (2) the conflict stage, and (3) the accommodation stage.

The Initial-Contact Stage. In the first decade of Italian living in America the structure of the Old World family is still fairly well intact, but pressures from within and outside the family are beginning to crack, albeit imperceptibly, the Old World peasant pattern. Producing this incipient distortion are the following: the very act of physical separation from the parental family and village culture; the necessity to work and operate with a somewhat strange and foreign body of household tools, equipment, gadgets, furniture, cooking utensils, and other physical objects, in addition to making an adjustment to a different physical environment, including climate, urban ecological conditions, and tenement living arrangements; the birth of children and the increasing contact with American medical practices regarding child care; the necessity to work for wages at unfamiliar tasks, a new experience for the peasant farmer; the attendance of Italian children in American parochial and public schools; the informal interaction of the children with the settlement house, the church associations, the neighborhood clubs, the neighborhood gang, and other organizations; the continuing residence in America and increasing period of isolation from the Old World; the acceptance of work by the housewife outside the home for wages; the increasing recognition by both parents and children that the Italian way of life in the American community means low status, social and economic discrimination, and prejudice; and the increasing pressure by American legal, educational, political, and economic institutions for the Americanization of the foreigner.

Nonetheless, the first-generation Italian family in this phase is a highly integrated one, as in the Old World. The demands of the American community are not seriously felt in the insulated Italian colony, and the children are too young to articulate seriously their newly acquired needs and wishes. The Italian family is stabilized by the strong drive to return to Italy.

The Conflict Stage. In this period the first-generation family experiences its most profound changes and is finally wrenched from its Old World foundation. It is now chiefly characterized by the conflict between two ways of life, the one American and the other Italian, and by the incompatibility of parents and children. This phase begins roughly during the second decade of living in America—specifically, when the children unhesitatingly express their acquired American expectations and attempt to transmit them in the family situation, and when the parents in turn attempt to reinforce the pattern of the Old World peasant family. Conflicting definitions of various family situations threaten to destroy whatever stability the family had maintained through the first period. This is the period of great frustration and of misunderstanding between parents and children. In this undeclared state of war between two ways of life it is the parents who have the most to lose, for their complete acceptance of the American way of living means the destruction of the Old World ideal.

The first-generation Italian family is also constantly made to feel the force of external pressures coming from outside the Italian colony. It is inevitable that the family structure should crumble under the incessant hammering. Not able to draw upon a complete culture and social system to support its position, the family pattern, already weakened, now begins to change radically: the father loses his importance, the daughters acquire unheard-of independence; in short, the children press down upon the first-generation family an American way of life.

Accommodation Stage. This period begins with the realization by parents and children that the continuation of hostility, misunderstanding, and contraventive behavior can result only in complete deterioration of the family. The ambivalent attitude of the children toward the parents, of great affection, on the one hand, and hostility, on the other, now tends to be replaced by a more tolerant disposition. This stage begins when the offspring reach adulthood and marry and establish households of their own, for by this time the control by the parents is greatly lessened.

Among the many factors which operate to bring about a new stability in the family are the realization on the part of the parents that life in America is to be permanent; the adult age of the offspring; the almost complete dependence of the parents on the offspring, including use of the children as informants, interpreters, guides, and translators of the American world; recognition on the part of the parents that social and economic success can come to the offspring only as they become more and more like "old Americans"; the conscious and unconscious acculturation of the parents themselves with a consequent minimizing of many potential conflicts; the long period of isolation from the Old World which makes the small-village culture and peasant family seem less real; the decisions by the parents to sacrifice certain aspects of the Old World family for the sake of retaining the affection of the children; the acknowledgment by the children that the first-generation family is a truncated one and that complete repudiation of the parents would leave them completely isolated; the success of the first-generation family in instilling in the offspring respect and affection for the parents; and the gradual understanding by the children that successful interaction with the American world is possible by accepting marginal roles and that complete denial of the Old World family is unnecessary.

The accommodation between parents and offspring permits the second-generation Italians to orientate themselves increasingly toward an American way of life. The second-generation household, therefore, tends to pattern itself after the contemporary urban American family. Considerable intermarriage, the advanced age of the parents, the loosening of ties with the Italian neighborhood, and the development of intimate relationships with non-Italians make the transition of the second-generation family comparatively easy.

CULTURE PATTERNS OF PUERTO RICO

Julian H. Steward

THIS ESSAY WILL DEAL PRIMARILY with the culture patterns or life-ways of certain classes or segments of the Puerto Rican people, with special attention to how the processes of industrialization have modified a predominantly agrarian population.[1] The term "industrialization" used in connection with rural people refers rather broadly not only to their involvement in a system of cash crop production and of consumption of mass manufactured commodities, but also, at least in the Western world, to the development of political democracy, an augmented role of the state in controlling and directing change and in providing services to its people, religious freedom, and other patterns which have accompanied technological progress and the growth of economic free enterprise.

In Puerto Rico, industrialization has produced certain general trends which provide a kind of common denominator to all classes of people. These trends began during the nineteenth century, but they were greatly accelerated during the twentieth century after the island came under United States sovereignty. Industrialization in Puerto Rico today is developing rapidly, and it involves not only general tendencies but certain economic patterns, a political ideology, a legal and governmental system, and other features specific to the United States.

URBAN CHANGES

All segments of the Puerto Rican population have been influenced by industrialization, but the town and urban centers have responded most uniformly. Urbanization, itself a major trend, has entailed a number of characteristic changes. Not only do towns become much larger and comprise an ever greater percentage of the total population, but their functions and internal composition are being altered. The local communities mediate the national institutions to the countryside by serving as centers for marketing, wholesaling, retail trade, and credit; for governmental administration and for education, farm extension, health, and other public services; for the servicing and building trades and the transportational workers; for local political parties and labor unions; for religious and recreational functions; and for the distribution of certain mass media of communication.

While these new urban functions tend to create greater similarity between towns, they also differentiate the population within each town into special segments, classes, or sociocultural groups: wealthy commercial and professional personnel; civil servants, transportational workers, and servicing and building trades groups; and skilled and unskilled laborers. Most characteristic of these are the new middle classes of varied occupation and income. They represent a new trend, a new set of values which ascribes major importance to the symbols of personal achievement and wealth. Upward mobility in the

Reprinted from *The Annals of the American Academy of Political and Social Science* (January 1953), pp. 95-103, by permission of the author and the publisher. (Copyright, 1953, by The American Academy of Political and Social Science.)

socio-economic hierarchy becomes a crucial goal; and individual effort, thrift, education, and utilization of governmental services and opportunities become means to the goal.

RURAL CHANGES

The rural population also is affected by these industrial trends. Cash crops or wage labor provides money with which to purchase desired items in the rising tide of manufactured goods offered by the town merchants, and to maintain a standard of living that carries prestige. The farm population is acquiring a cash-oriented value system, which is supplanting the older rationale of personal relations and services. The traditional patterns of labor exchange between small farmers, of personal favors and perquisites between landowners and laborers, and of kinship and ritual kinship duties and obligations are disappearing or being seriously modified.

However, the sociocultural groups created in the rural areas by industrialization are less uniform than those in the urban centers. Each rural region has a distinctive environment, and therefore particular crop potentials. In each region the productive arrangement—the kind of crop, mechanization in field production or in processing, land tenure, capitalization and credit, and the nature of labor and of owner-worker relations—has created distinctive subcultures among the people involved. The present article is primarily concerned with the subcultures of the rural workers.

PUERTO RICAN CULTURE AND SUBCULTURES

In order to understand the cultural patterns of contemporary Puerto Rico, it is necessary to view the processes of industrialization against the background of the cultural tradition of the island. For four centuries the culture was essentially Hispanic, both in its national institutions and in its folk aspects. Early in the island's history there were probably important subcultural differences between landowners, ecclesiastical and lay officials, craftsmen, merchants, subsistence farmers, and other groups. For an undetermined period there were probably also differences between ethnic groups—Indians native to Puerto Rico and from the continent, Africans, and Europeans of various origins and classes. But true ethnic minorities are not now important. The Hispanic heritage, however, was the basis of Puerto Rican culture and subcultures, and, despite the effects of industrial trends, many features of the tradition survive today: the Spanish language, certain familial patterns, religious practices, forms of recreation, food habits, and others.

Today, the Puerto Rican subcultures, or special regional and class groups, represent distinctive interactions between the Hispanic patterns, the local productive arrangements, the effects of industrialization, and the specific influence of Americanization. The subcultures are many and varied. Only certain of the more important types were selected for analysis: a representative *municipio* of the small farmers of subsistence crops and tobacco in the mountains, the so-called *jíbaro,* who are in the tradition of the isolated and independent farmers of the island; the growers of coffee, both landlords and workers, who are of interest because they exemplify the traditional Hispanic paternalistic pattern of two closely interrelated classes; the sugar-cane workers on a corporate plantation and on a government-owned, profit-sharing plantation, both groups of whom comprise a rural proletariat; and the insular upper class, which consists of a few hundred families who live in San Juan, the capital, who represent United States commercial enterprises, and who are by far the most Americanized of any segment of the population.

In spite of these subcultural differences there is an over-all Puerto Rican culture, in that the Hispanic heritage provides a common background, the processes of industrialization are creating insular-wide trends, and most of the Puerto Rican people feel a sense of common origin and destiny. But the cultural common denominator can be overemphasized. The following pages will be concerned with the more important subcultures which have emerged from Puerto Rico's complex historical background.

THE SMALL FARMERS

The mountain farmers who grow their own foods as well as a cash crop of tobacco are of interest not only because they are numerically important but because they exemplify the adaptation of a formerly self-sufficient, isolated, and independent folk society to the demands of modern industrialization. During much of its history, Puerto Rico was somewhat distinctive among Spanish possessions in lacking important mineral wealth and in having little access to markets for such crops as it could grow. Until the nineteenth century the country was underpopulated, and there was ample opportunity for squatter farmers of Indian, Negro, and white ancestry to clear lands in the interior where they lived in comparative self-sufficiency and isolation from the state, the church, and the currents of world economy.

During the last century, however, world trends began to reach these farmers. Improved communications drew them more into the orbit of national affairs. The lure of manufactured goods stimulated their desire for cash, which they obtained primarily through growing tobacco. Tobacco can be grown at little risk, it can be rotated with other crops on small plots, and it requires no expensive field or processing machinery. Moderate credit facilities will carry the producer over a year. Neither losses nor profits can be great. Owing to market restrictions, Puerto Rican tobacco production has not run to large plantations. It is the small farmer's source of cash income, whether he be landowner or share cropper.

Our study of a tobacco *municipio* shows that certain changes have accompanied the introduction of the cash crop. As the people still grow their own food, subsistence is not so vital a problem as it is in the monocrop sugar area, where all food must be purchased from wages. But cash goals have led to individualization of landownership, and, since population has increased beyond the agricultural resources, farms tend to be divided among heirs to the extent that individual holdings are often insufficient to support the family. This individualization of landownership has been a major factor in disrupting the extended family. Duties and obligations to the extended kin group have become secondary to responsibility for the immediate family.

The trends in land use and landownership have reduced the functional household and familial unit to the nuclear family. The somewhat patrilineal and patrilocal traditional Hispanic family has been modified in that residence and affiliation tend to follow lines of property, which may be inherited on either side of the family. The nature of the marital union, moreover, is affected by economic and social considerations. Where property or social status is involved, marriage is usually religious or civil; where neither counts, it tends to be consensual.

These tobacco farmers have a new value orientation based on monetary standards and the importance of individual effort. It is known that upward mobility in the socio-economic scheme can be achieved, and the people are eager to take advantage of all aids: education, farm extension services, health facilities, and the like. Simultaneously, interfamily relations based on labor exchange and other services lacking a monetary standard have declined. The goal of upward mobility has been facilitated by the constant fragmentation of landholdings, for it is possible for a thirfty and successful small farmer or sharecropper to purchase small parcels of land. Although few persons can acquire great wealth, there is considerable opportunity for upward as well as downward mobility in the socio-economic hierarchy.

Social, Political, Religious Features. The socio-economic mobility in the tobacco region has influenced social relations. Class lines cannot be sharp, even though there are differences in wealth and corresponding differences in social participation, recreation, standard of living, and other features. Comparative equality is manifest in various ways, including the nature of the *compadrazgo. Compardres* (coparents, that is, godparents of one's children) are selected from among one's economic superiors and inferiors as well as among one's equals.

Political ideology of the tobacco farmers is consistent with other aspects of their culture. They are independent in their political as well as economic and social attitudes. Since they are actual or potential landowners, they stand less to gain than the proletariat of the sugar areas from a political program designed to benefit landless workers. The greatly expanded governmental services have been to their advantage, and they have utilized them perhaps more than any other rural group. But in the 1948 election, a much larger portion of the tobacco farmers than of any other rural group voted for the rather militant *Independentistas* rather than for the dominant Popular Democratic party which has stood for rural and social reform.

The small mountain farmers are traditionally and nominally Catholic, but Protestant sects have begun to penetrate the area. It is perhaps too early to appraise this trend, but a factor which appears to favor the new faiths is the ideal of individual initiative and the concept of individual responsibility—the "Protestant ethic," which is part and parcel of the new socio-economic trends. Another aspect of religious change is that the Catholic festivals, although still observed, have assumed a recreational rather than religious character.

THE COFFEE HACIENDA CULTURE

The coffee haciendas are of interest less because they involve large numbers of persons today than because they still exemplify in many ways a typically Hispanic pattern which once characterized much of the sugar area as well as the coffee area. The earlier pattern has been perpetuated through several factors.

First, coffee cannot be the poor man's cash crop, for it requires a fairly large capital outlay. Unlike tobacco, which can be grown on plots of any size and during brief periods, coffee requires a fairly large acreage in order to justify the processing equipment; and, since it does not bear for several years after planting, the owner must have resources to carry him over. There are a few small and medium coffee farms, but the tendency is toward large holdings which are worked by peasants or landless laborers. Because needed capitalization for coffee production has increased, coffee haciendas tend to become fewer and larger.

Second, since coffee production can be carried on profitably in isolated areas which lack improved roads and communications, the farm population tends to remain socially and culturally isolated from the urban centers. Public services, political ideologies, and the effects of mass media of communication have been slow to reach the coffee workers.

Owner-Worker Relations. The productive arrangements of the large haciendas set the framework for the survival of the traditional culture. The owners are largely Spaniards, often third or fourth generation, and they constitute a well-defined upper class of highly educated and sophisticated persons who maintain close ties with the town. The laborers, both peasants and landless workers, are mostly native Puerto Ricans. The relationship between owner and worker is typically paternalistic, personal, face to face, and variable, as compared with the impersonal wage-based and legalized relationship in sugar production. Between owner and laborer there is a mutual dependency, a system of personal understandings and perquisites. The laborer is paid in wages, but since work is seasonal he is also granted favors in lieu of wages, such as a subsistence plot on which to grow foods, or the chance to burn charcoal on shares. The owner takes a personal interest in him, advising him in his affairs and looking to his welfare. In return, the worker renders unpaid services to his landlord and may even supply daughters as servants in the landlord's household.

The culture of the workers and peasants reflects the isolation and traditionalism perpetuated by the productive arrangement. The family is strongly paternalistic. The father manages its property and income, directs the labor of all its members, including the children, who usually perform useful tasks, and dictates the social behavior and marriages of his offspring.

Solidarity and reciprocity within the working class are manifest in many traditional ways. There is labor exchange based on reciprocity rather than on monetary standards; there is visiting and participation in socioreligious events; there is choice of *compadres;* and there is intermarriage.

Between owners and workers, relations are reciprocal but unequal. They include the system of favors and services already mentioned. The workers seek *compadres* among the owners in order to strengthen their position, but the reverse is not true. They look to the owners for leadership in political as well as economic and social affairs. They are not yet sufficiently sophisticated to recognize the program of the Popular Democratic party as their own. They have too little economic opportunity to place value on individual effort, too little access to and use for education to recognize it as a means of upward mobility, and too little chance to utilize governmental services to feel that these are vital to them. They depend upon their landlord rather than upon unions, political parties, or the government.

Religion. The coffee workers are perhaps the most thoroughly Catholic of all farm people, but their Catholicism is not wholly orthodox. Partly because of limited contact with the church and the priests, the religion tends to center in a cult of saints. Formal church rites and priestly administrations are secondary to a system of household and village saints which constitute the principal supernatural functionaries. These saints receive prayers and supplications, and if they fail to respond they may be punished. At the same time, certain church rites such as baptism sanction *compadre* relationships and hence have great sociological importance. Moreover, the many religious festivals provide a traditional form of recreation, in contrast to other regions, where social dancing and sports have become popular.

THE SUGAR PLANTATION CULTURES

The sugar regions of Puerto Rico exhibit the most pronounced effects of industrialization upon the rural cultures. Since sugar is produced competitively for an outside market, it is necessary that the most modernized methods be used in field production and processing. The mills cost a half-million dollars or more, and in order for them to operate at maximum efficiency, cane from a vast acreage must be fed into them. Sugar, therefore, tends to be monocrop, and subsistence farming, which is so vital to the rural people of other areas, is virtually eliminated.

Earlier in Puerto Rican history, when sugar plantations had ox-driven mills and simple steam boilers, they were family owned. At one time they depended partly upon slave labor; later upon free labor. The productive and social arrangement was the family hacienda type. As technology advanced and the necessary capital outlay increased, there became fewer and larger mills and plantations. Less opulent families, which could not afford mills, contracted to have their cane ground at the large plants. On the arid south coast, however, where cattle ranching had prevailed and where irrigation projects were essential to sugar expansion, the costs were best met by corporate credit. Meanwhile, through its program of land reform, the government finally bought up many production units and made them into profit-sharing mills and plantations.

The Corporate Sugar Plantation. The corporate community on the south coast consists almost entirely of a very homogeneous group of workers who have a considerable Negro admixture, having descended in part from slaves. There is no upper class today, for the private owners have sold out and moved away. Their economic functions have been taken over by a handful of managers representing the American corporation. The middle classes of the community are small, for many of the services they would normally perform are carried out by the corporation.

The working class differs profoundly from that of the tobacco and coffee regions. It consists entirely of wage earners, whose employment is seasonal and whose income is barely adequate for survival. There are no subsistence plots, and there is no system of personal favors between owner and worker, as on the family hacienda. The workers even have difficulty in finding dwellings. They live in clusters of houses on small plots on some of the older hacienda centers, along public highways, and on the beach.

There is remarkable similarity among all members of this class, since opportunities for advancement are absent, and the position of everyone is fixed by a uniform system of wages and agreements. The ideal of self-improvement which characterizes the tobacco farmers is absent. Escape from the fixed socioeconomic status can be achieved only through out-migration or through winning a stake in illegal gambling or bootlegging, both of which would be regarded by the highland people as unwarranted risks rather than as opportunities.

The sugar workers place little value on individual initiative. Their hope is not to achieve upward mobility through education, thrift, or effort, for the job hierarchy holds no place for them. Instead, they seek common goals through the collective means of the labor union, which is used not only to bargain with management but which is a political instrument that lends mass support to the Popular Democratic party in its legislative struggle for improvement of wages, hours, and working conditions.

In the typical labor-class family, all members who are old enough work for wages, which give a measure of independence to each individual. Since neither property nor considerations of religious orthodoxy are important, marriage unions are largely consensual. Because divorce is frequent and children generally remain with the mother, the family has a matrilineal and matriarchal character. The *compadrazgo* has proliferated among the sugar workers, and a person may have thirty to forty *compadres*. *Compadres* are always chosen within the working class, however, for the American managerial staff will have no part in such arrangements. Ritual kinship, therefore, instead of binding together members of different socioeconomic classes as in the tobacco and coffee areas, serves as a surrogate for extended kin ties and as a means of furthering the security of the individual within his class.

The homogeneity and solidarity of the working group is also expressed to some extent in religion. Here more than anywhere else on the island, evangelical sects of Protestantism have made considerable progress. This seemingly reflects in part the traditional association of orthodox Catholicism with the ruling upper-class whites, and in part the need for a common emotional outlet which such religions frequently provide insecure groups. Despite the large Negro element in this community, no religious beliefs or practices of unquestioned African provenience were found.

The Profit-Sharing Sugar Plantation. The culture patterns and the attitudes of the workers on the government-owned, profit-sharing sugar plantations are very similar to those of the corporation employees. The workers do not have a sense of proprietorship and participation in plant affairs, because they do not manage the plant. In fact, they speak of it as "the corporation." The line of authority from worker to mill runs a devious course. The worker belongs to a union and supports the Popular Democratic party through the local organization. The party controls the government, which in turn appoints the plantation managers. The workers bargain directly with the managers through their union.

Two features distinguish the profit-sharing plantations from the corporate ones, but these have made little difference in the lives of the workers. First, the workers receive proportional benefits, but this provision has been counterbalanced by the need to spread work as widely as possible, so the labor force is several times as large as it need be, and individual income is very low. Second, subsistence plots have been provided the workers, but since little value is attached to owning land and growing one's own food, the people turn during the "dead" season to activities which yield cash, and make slight use of their plots.

Fixed essentially in a proletariat class, the workers constitute a fairly homogeneous sociocultural group. The processes of industrialization have not affected them as deeply as on the corporate plantation, for they were fairly recently on family haciendas, and the older patterns survive in slight degree. But the nature of the family, life goals, economic activity and union organization, and political attitudes are substantially the same as under the corporation.

The greatest differerence between government and corporation workers is in religion. The saint cult survives in some strength among the former, and there is considerable fear of witchcraft. A plausible explanation of witchcraft is that the general insecurity of the people has led them to channel hostility toward competitors—in this case especially migrants from the highlands seeking jobs—into a fear of supernatural measures rather than to express it overtly.

THE UPPER CLASS

The Puerto Rican upper class is limited to a few hundred families which are distinguished by their wealth, their social prominence, and their extreme Americanization. Their income is usually over $10,000 a year. Most of them are engaged in commerce, especially as representatives of United States business firms, although some also derive income from the land. Unlike the wealthy agrarian families, such as the coffee growers, the primary economic allegiance of these families to the United States has been a major factor in their Americanization.

The necessity of carrying out business activities on American terms has profoundly affected the lives of the upper-class people. Children are indoctrinated at an early age in the status and role they will assume. They become accustomed to luxurious housing, automobiles, servants, and other evidences of a very high standard of living. They are educated in American social customs and business practices. Many of them are sent to the United States for their high school education and most of them for college education, which is taken in the business and professional fields. As adults, they are largely business executives.

Cultural characteristics of the Hispanic heritage are rapidly disappearing among upper-class families. They are bilingual, but it can hardly be said that they are bicultural. The nuclear family of man, wife, and children is acquiring independence of the extended kin ties, just as it is in the United States. There is a great love of children, but the number of children has decreased despite prevalent Catholicism which disapproves of birth control.

These families must deal with Puerto Ricans in their business activities, and consequently they understand Puerto Rican behavior. But to a large extent they force their own terms upon business associates and thus become an acculturating influence.

In their relationship to one another, the upper-class families constitute a strong in-group which moves in restricted circles. They belong to highly exclusive social clubs, and their patterns of visiting and entertainment involve only their equals. Social and recreational activities have assumed a predominantly American character. Political attitudes are conservative. The upper class has been opposed to the program of the Popular Democratic party, but since the latter seems to have moderated its social reform program, most of the class has supported it. These classes may also be described as conservative in religion, in that Catholic orthodoxy continues to characterize them.

SOME CONCLUSIONS

The acculturation of the upper-class families has resulted not only from the general processes of industrialization but also from conscious borrowing of the patterns of upper-class business families of the United States. These Puerto Rican families, however, have played only a minor role in acculturating other local groups. They have, do doubt, strongly influenced the lower echelons of the business classes with whom they have direct contact, but their subculture presupposes an economic basis and opportunities which are absent among the workers, the peasants, and the small farmers.

The tobacco farmers and the sugar workers are similar in many respects to their counterparts in the United States, but similarities are less the result of borrowing (these groups have had little contact with one another) than of the industrial trends which have introduced national institutions of a North American type into Puerto Rico. Many North American culture elements, such as manufactured goods, clothes, sports, and motion pictures, have also spread very widely in Puerto Rico, but they have been incorporated in local subcultures which are patterned quite differently.

This article has emphasized the subcultural differences, the distinctive lifeways, found among certain segments of the rural population, rather than the common denominator of Puerto Rican culture. There is, of course, much that all Puerto Ricans share. All groups speak Spanish, and they have in common something of the Hispanic tradition of familial patterns, the Catholic religion, the *compadrazgo,* music, dancing, and recreation. They were all once under Spanish political, economic, and religious domination, and they have been under United States sovereignty for a half-century.

The new goals, values, and patterns created by industrialization have been mediated specifically by the United States, but they would undoubtedly have been much the same under any other sovereignty. They have set up new currents of political, social, economic, and religious activity. Fundamental and rapid change is always disturbing. Most Puerto Ricans quite understandably react to some degree against these trends; that is, they exhibit evidences of insecurity. Some are openly antagonistic to the United States, which they hold responsible for what is happening to them. If Puerto Rico can be said to manifest nationalism, however, it is a form of cultural rather than overtly political nationalism. It is the spontaneous and inevitable reaction of all segments of the population to profound changes brought about by a set of institutions which has been imposed upon them from the outside.

THE FAMILY IN OLD WORLD AND NEW

Oscar Handlin

SOMETIMES AT NIGHT she'd wake and turn to feel if he were there. She'd reach the space across to where he lay, sense the reassuring bulk of him. She'd hug the thought. *All else has passed away with our passing from that place. But this will never change. By holy matrimony he has made me wife and mother to his family. That* (fiercely) *we can hold intact.*

In the morning's light the certainty was gone. Through the day the fear came that this most intimate part of life would not remain the same. At the stove later she paused while the long spoon in her hand continued its mechanical stirring; she looked in bewilderment at the gathering table. Would the strangeness of the setting make strangers also of these her dear ones? Resolve came back, but confidence not altogether. It would be a desperate battle to hold firm in these relationships, outside the context that had nurtured them.

The difficulty was that formerly the family had not been a thing in itself, but an integral element of the village community. It had been fixed in a framework of numerous links and knots that held each individual within it in his place. As the functioning unit within the economy, it was the means through which bread was produced and consumed. No one could live except as the member of a family.

As the medium for holding and transmitting land, its stability had been vital to social order. Every change in its structure affected the whole community. On the quality of a single marriage depended the welfare of all the brothers and sisters and less directly a widening circle of other persons. The connection with the soil had also been an element in extending these affiliations beyond the single household to a broad range of other kin tied together by inheritance, of blood and of possible claims to a common patrimony.

The family had therefore never been isolated. Its concerns were those of the entire village. While each home was expected to be the source of its own discipline, the community stood ready with sanctions of its own to make sure that the children were obedient, that parents were good, and that relatives were helpful to each other. The network of mutual rights and obligations had thus the support of both an inner and outer control.

Emigration took the family out of the village. The mere going was disruptive. The struggles of departure and resettlement subjected the household to a severe strain under most trying and most unusual conditions, and at the same time deprived it of the counsel and assistance upon which it had traditionally depended. When so many new decisions were to be made, they had to be made alone. That alone distinguished the new family from the old.

Reprinted from *The Uprooted* (1951), pp. 227-58, by permission of the author and the publisher. (Copyright, 1951, by Little, Brown and Co.) The chapter appears in that volume under the title "Generations" (Chapter IX).

In America also the economic unity of the common household enterprise disappeared. The minority who found their way to the farms or who, by their labors, maintained little businesses where wife and children could work along with the father, held on to the former ways. Vestiges of the old order also remained in the sweating homework system; as the father brought back the bundles that would be sewn into shirts or twisted into artificial flowers, the gathered group in the tenement room recaptured the sense of common effort familiar in recollection from the Other Side.

These were, however, but byways in the economy. In the characteristic immigrant employment, the individual was hired as an integer. He was one line in the ledger, one pair of hands on the floor, one pay envelope at the window, with no reference to who was there at home. Ultimately this pattern supplanted all others. Would they continue to take his bidding, to toil in the dim room with him, the one to pocket all, when they could go out to be their own wage earners? There was no point to it. Of what inheritance could he deprive them?

Properly speaking, the family no longer had an income; there were only the combined incomes of its members. The larger unit was now a source of weakness rather than of strength. Those who could, broke away; it was madness for a man who was capable of supporting himself to maintain the ties of uncle or cousin when those ties would only draw off a share of his earnings. Those who remembered the old obligations, alas, were generally those more likely to consume than to produce—the aged, the weak, the ill. With these the circumstances, and with no outside force to assign the blame, the extensive family of the Old World disintegrated. *So it is now, a brother stabs his brother, a sister drowns her sister, for profit's sake.*

Steadily the relatives dropped away; the husband, wife, and children were left alone. Where need compelled additions to the income of this narrower household, it was better to take in boarders, tenants, on an impersonal, cash-down basis. The more compelling duties of the old extended family were treacherous here; it was safer by avoiding them to transform the relationship into one of mere occasional sociability.

The bonds to those left at home also disintegrated. There was a piece of land, and if he had not gone away it would have been his; but having gone away he ought not ask that it be sold and money sent to him in America. Endless quarreling followed. Or the old folks, staying, bitterly resented the departed son who should have been the staff on which they might lean in age. *You went to make money and you forgot that you left parents; may God and your own children care for you as you for us.*

Is it the loss of income they minded, or the sadness of being abandoned? *We cannot know whether we shall yet speak with you, embrace you, at least once before our death.* It does not matter. The demands are too heavy on both emotions and purse. The old ties gradually are loosened. The family steadily tapers down to the conjugal unit, a father, a mother, and their immediate offspring. The New World has separated them from all the others who would have been one with them in the Old.

Perhaps for that reason she wished so intensely to hold together what was left. From mistress in an extensive household she had become mother of a more intimate group; that hard core she would labor to keep intact.

The early experiences of the new family entity fed her hopes. That they were cut off from all else that was familiar led the members to value each other the more. With whom else could they discuss the memories of the past and the problems of the present? Depending upon each other because there was no one else upon whom they could depend, they drew steadily together.

The very process of migration had been shared. Mostly they had come together, together faced the open road and the close quarters of the steerage. In the long lapse of time between departure and arrival, they were deprived of the busying occupations of the farm, of the comradeship of neighbors, and had for company only one another. The occasion was one for deeper understanding; and long after the final settlement, recollections would come back of the joys and tribulations of the way, come back to unite those who had made the journey together.

The warmth of participation in the enterprise of crossing cheered even those later immigrants who divided for the critical steps, husband first to make a start, wife and children after. Such a separation created problems of its own, but it did not of itself lessen the attachment of the partners to it. Though the ocean lay between, they were joined by the gravity of the common effort.

That is why, as the years passed and they thought back to the first exploratory days in America, it seemed to them that the family had been strongest and purest before its exposure to the new life. As strangers they had known no one. Evening brought them always back together. Excited with discoveries or downcast with disappointments, they communicated to one another the freshness of each occurrence. They knew then they were one like the meager loaf from which they would begin each to slice the sustenance of all. It was a tenement room or a sod hut. But it was home; and those who came to it worn out with wandering acquired for home an enduring devotion.

Only soon, the conditions of their being in the United States would break in upon them. The narrow family would not remain alone together. Individually, its members in going out would make each their own adjustments to the society about them, and coming back would be less alike. Man and woman, boy and girl, they would find for themselves new roles and establish for themselves new relationships. It would happen more quickly in the cities than on the farms where a rural environment extended the family's isolation. But ultimately it would happen everywhere. The woman meditating by the stove would resist it. But already as they took their places her heart chilled to the fear of failure.

Across the long table they confronted each other, the two who were now central to all. It was as if daily they felt the need of a fresh view of the familiar features in the light of the new experiences. In the anxious regards were mingled two questions. Is this the same being united to me those many years ago and now still unchanged? How adequate will this union be to the present demands upon it?

Indeed these were no longer the man and woman joined in wedlock at at that distant date; they had never then imagined that such questions might ever arise. Then marriage had not been the product of an individual passion, but a social arrangement under the oversight of the community. She had accepted the obligations of her situation, to be obedient and faithful, to further his health and comfort, to be a good and kindly wife, the crown of her husband's life. He had taken on the responsibilities of the efficient provider who would safeguard her from degrading work, keep want away, and mildly satisfy her will. The union upon which fortune smiled was one blessed with the dignified respect of the partners for their rights and duties.

The day they turned their backs upon the old home, the relationship began to change. At the very outset, the course of the crossing led to troubles. In the long suspended period between departure and arrival, neither he nor she had duties or could expect fixed dues. They were then thrown more together than ever before, but as never before found it difficult to judge one another. The intimacy of shared miseries brought them together, but, as it were, only to be the more conscious of each other's deficiencies. A sorry figure he made, lounging about from day to day with nothing to do; while her derelictions of housewifely obligations were served up in the stale biscuits of every meal.

If migration involved a temporary separation as, after 1880, it often did, the results were more disruptive still. He went away to the sound of the children's crying; and heard it echo through the months apart. In his unaccustomed singleness, he came to miss what before he had taken for granted, the warmth of the woman's presence. *As the fish thirst for water, so I long for you.*

It is hard to know what may happen across that far dividing distance. *Only I beg you write more often.* As the letters fail to appear, for she is not familiar to the pen, worries take their place, and suspicions. Resentful, he asks a friend in the village to inform him of her doings. Does she hold to the home? At the same time the fear will rise lest she be unable to manage. The stock of grain may be too small, the labor in the field too hard. Cautionary advice covers the pages he sends home.

She has the advantage of waiting in a known place in the company of the children. But her double role is burdensome; she cannot be as he was, head of the household. The boys are unruly and, though she gives them some of the broomstick, they are slow to obey. She hires a hand to help in the field, but he is negligent; he has not for her the fear as for a master. Often she thinks of her husband and what a life he must lead there among strangers, his work heavier than a stone, his strength being drained away into a foreign soil. *The day passes in labor but in the evening I long very much and at night I cannot sleep. We can be united in heart and thought but that satisfies me not. Take us or come back; let it be so or so; as it is I exist neither upon ice nor upon water.*

Sometimes the months stretch out and the separateness widens. He sets himself a goal: I will have a thousand rubles and then send for them. But the goal is never attained. Meanwhile he is hardened in his bachelor life and puts off indefinitely the day of reunion. Or she at home grows reluctant. The dread of the new place mounts up in her and feeds off the complaints in his letters. She wishes him back—enough of this America—and when the call comes, procrastinates.

Whatever division, long or short, appeared in the transplantation was not mended in the resettlement. On the farms, the man could resume his place as head of the household enterprise; but the millions who stayed in the cities found their positions drastically altered. She could not think that he was here satisfying his obligations toward the family. No longer the sole or even the main provider, he seemed to her wanting in the most critical duty of all. Why, there were times when she herself or the children earned more than he, times when he sat home idle while they went out to bring home his bread. When he was taken on, it was not at work she understood or could respect. Away at some menial task, she could not regard him as she had that husbandman who had once managed their tiny plot and had brought up her sons to follow in his steps.

Nor could he be satisfied as to her adequacy for the life of the New World. Deprived of the usual household chores of the garden, the needle, and the loom, she appeared often lethargic; the blood hardly ran in her veins. On the other hand management of the domestic economy under American conditions was frequently beyond her comprehension. When the results were unhappy—disorderly quarters, poor food—it was hard to draw the line between the effects of negligence and the effects of poverty and ignorance. The necessity that drove her to labor for others was the source of resentment, both because it reflected upon his own abilities and because it took her away from her proper job in the home.

Roles once thoroughly defined were now altogether confounded. The two got on under the continual strain of uncertainty as to their place in the family, as to their relationships to each other. And their experience, no longer one for the two, added constantly to that underlying uncertainty. Sometimes it was he went out to the wide world, learned the language of the country, and grew sophisticated in the ways of the place, while she was confined to the flat and remained ignorant of the rudiments of English. *I at least know where there's an Eighth Street, and a One Hundred and Thirtieth Street with tin works, and an Eighty-fourth Street with a match factory. I know every block around the World Building and the place where the car line stops. But you know no more than if you had just landed.* Sometimes it was she, in service in some other's home, who earlier learned the ways—what food they ate and clothes they wore and how they sat of an evening in the polished sitting room. It was bitter hard to be the satisfying helpmate when one could hardly guess what wants the other had.

As the situation clarified, aspects at first hidden emerged with oppressive distinctness. In the Old World her status had been fixed by a variety of elements—whose daughter she was, what dowry she brought, into what family she married. Let her husband be unfortunate or unskillful or unthrifty, she had still a set place in the village. Here her fate was completely tied up in his success. What she was or had been mattered nothing, only what he could do. Well, it was galling to see what other, lesser women had, to watch their men push their way ahead. The utter dependence on his efforts put an acrimonious tone in her greetings as he came nightly home no better than before.

Nagging demands he could not meet confirmed his own inner doubts about himself. Was not the whole migration the story of his succession of failures? He had been unable to hold on to the land, to direct the family comfortably across the ocean or to establish it securely on this side. He felt respect ebb away and carried about a gnawing shame at his own lack of capacity. Most of all, he resented his loss of authority. Indeed he became accustomed to request, not to order, but knew it was not right it should be so; and he resented his wife's growing dominance over the household. It was a poor state of affairs when the cow showed the way to the ox.

In the secret night when her stirring waked him he did not move. Fatigue pinned him down. Yet sleep would not return. Instead an angry tension crept into his heart. Her body's presence intruded on his consciousness. Limbs rigid, he pushed the thought away; to this demand too he would not respond, by so much had he now lost his manhood.

Clenched eyelids would not keep the moonlight out. Not a beam came down the narrow airshaft; still his sight tingled to the streaks reflected from a distant meadow where they had walked amidst the long grasses, and had been young, eager for the enjoyment of each other to which marriage had opened the way. There had been no strain then; what the community had to that day forbidden, it now welcomed; and these two had been carried along by confidence in the rightness of their acts, by certainty they would each be gratified.

It was coming away that had first added wormwood to the taste. They had lost the benevolent oversight of the village which by its insistence on traditional propriety had answered every how and when. Now the deed required ever a decision; it raised ever some question; and it involved ever some clash of wills, his or hers. By leaving they had created doubts they knew not how to resolve.

He remembered the darkness of successive borrowed beds. In the enforced closeness of boardinghouses and shipboard he had stifled the groping desires. Years later, the confined warmth of many bodies would come back to assault his senses, would bring the painful recollection of urges never satisfied. And in this place that was their own it was rare that wish and opportunity coincided. In the cramped quarters they had been never alone and therefore never really together. Often there was the startling chill of interruption—the uneasy stirring of a child, the banging progress of a neighbor through the ill-lit hall. Always there was the uncertainty of when and how. Even the times when, flushed with the cheap certitude of liquor or with the passing exuberance of some new job, he had asserted his passion, there had followed inevitably an aftermath of regret and doubt. What had really been given and what received in these exchanges?

Perhaps he should not have expected more. He himself knew the dull indifference that came with being often tired. He knew too her deep fear of recurrent childbirth. Not that this was a subject of conversation between them; but it took no words to convey her dismay at each discovery of her condition. But the terms must be accepted, the price paid. Worse would follow the attempt to avoid it; often enough she had heard the stories of such a one, desperate at the approach of an eighth or ninth, who had sought the relief of self-abortion and had found only the painful death of blood poisoning.

Vaguely also they suspected that there were ways of forestalling pregnancy. But the old wives' knowledge did not extend that far; in this matter the midwife was not helpful; and, as for doctors—why, if a woman had thought of them, she would have found it difficult even to frame the terms of her inquiry. The husband had once cautiously sounded out an apothecary, but got only a jocular response: *Better sleep out on the fire escape, Joe.* Besides it all smacked of the illicit and the shameful. The law frowned on it; the priest cautioned against it; and deep inner forebodings conjured up the visions of nature's reprisals for interference with her processes.

There was, therefore, not much joy to their desiring; the shadow of the reckoning was too close. There was no blame. Only, sometimes, as she nursed her discontent, the thought came to her that, if only he had managed better, all would be otherwise. And he, reading the accusations in her eyes, felt the pangs of a sudden guilt, the acknowledgment of his own inadequacies. At such times, a sullen anger entered the household, lingered unexpressed for days. The mornings when he went to work, he carried off a pained exasperation. Suspicions might come; the scandal of that other's wife, who with the boarder shamed her home, might cross his mind. The memory galled his wounds and, returned that night, edged his answers with acerbity. Peace then departed in an exchange of taunting words, then blows, and sad conciliation.

Some men surrendered. Confronted by intolerable burdens they deserted their families, lost themselves alone somewhere and put thus an end to this striving. Then the fatherless home, adrift, was not long from its foundering.

Mostly however they held together, the man and woman. Yes, partly it was the thought of the children that kept the family whole and partly it was the consciousness that in abandoning each other they would sever every last tie with their own past, diminish thereby their own human identity. Yes, often as they lay there, longing for escape to an undefined freedom, there was no move simply because the effort seemed too great, the means far out of reach.

But it was more than that that curbed the passing wish to flee. But it was more than that that drew them at last to each other. The old fixed order of respect between husband and wife had disappeared as the obligations on which it rested became irrelevant in the New World. Without the protective cover of well-defined roles they faced each other as individuals under the most trying conditions. That was difficult. But then as he looked upon this person who shared his bed and recalled the long way she had come, the sufferings she had borne, his heart went out to her. And then as she sensed the turning of his eyes upon her and thought of the little pleasure all his efforts brought, her heart went out to him.

It was not pity that sealed them in this attachment, but the brief glimmers of comprehension that they shared a life as they shared a bed. They were individuals, separate, two, and had been so since they left the village. But they had been two together. In those moments of recognition they knew they had been partners in a common experience and were now involved in a common situation. Only in each other could these beings find the complete understanding that would alone bring what they so desperately wanted, some reaffirmation of their own human dignity. For warmth they moved toward each other, for the warmth that came from the knowledge that here was consolation. Another knew and understood. That was a precious certainty, where all else was insecure.

About the children they can feel no certainty whatever.

This country is full of children. In the morning their clatter down the staircase fills the house. In the afternoon they occupy the streets. In the evening they pour back into the waiting flat which they quickly distend with the clamor of their ceaseless activity.

The immigrants were by no means strange to the idea of full families. The little ones had always made up a sizable part of the village population. But the spot had not been so taken up with their presence. They had had each their places, where they ought to be and where they ought not to be. They had had each their functions, what they ought to do and what they ought not to do. They had not been, therefore, so prominent in the sight of their elders.

Perhaps it was because, in these matters as in so much else, the Old World community had been very specific in its definitions of proper behavior. What a parent owed his offspring was clear. The child was to be fed, clothed, and housed decently as befitted the status and the resources of his father. The boys and girls were to be properly brought up, taught the skills necessary for their own adulthood and imbued with the beliefs necessary for continued memberhip in the community. It was their due at maturity to receive the land or dowry that would permit them to take the rank their ancestors had held; and one was not unduly to be favored at the expense of his brothers and sisters.

The obligations of the young were equally plain. They were to obey their elders and particularly him who stood at the head of the family, him whom they were to approach always in fear and with respect as the source of all authority. They were to assist, to the extent they were able, in the labors of the common enterprise; every age had its appropriate tasks. Even those fully grown but without households of their own were still to work for their parents. The unmarried had strictly speaking no property, no possessions of their own; if they went out to toil for strangers they were expected still to hand over their earnings to the father.

The neat balance of rights and duties was enforced by the village as a whole. Parents delinquent in the support or the discipline of their progeny, children remiss in compliance, could expect the swift censure of the organized opinion of their neighbors. There was no breaking the pattern of these relationships without a complete break with the community. But conversely, separation from the community by emigration would altogether disrupt the relationships of parents and children.

They might suppose it was the same as they strolled to worship on a holiday, Papa, Mama, and the boys and girls, covering the paved walk in a pair of uneven rows. They were wrong. Even then they knew the momentary solidarity would disintegrate before the day was over. They no longer cohered as a family and, as individuals, could scarcely say how they stood to one another.

The divisions created by differences of experience were too great. The older ones, sedately in the rear, had been eight or nine or in their teens in the year of the crossing. They had vivid memories of the Old Country, of the troubles that drove them off, and of the hardships of the journey. They spoke their mother's language and their unaccustomed English bore a heavy accent that united them with their past. Trained under the discipline of the household that had been, they were still ready to accept obligations. Necessity had long since heaped responsibilities upon them: no doubt they had been wage earners since soon after their arrival.

There was impatience in their scrutiny of the younger ones. Before them were two to be watched, scrabbling along without regard for appearances. These had been infants or little more when the migration came; their early childhood had passed under the unsettled conditions of the transition. They had never learned the proper ways at home, and a brief attendance at the public school had confused them so they knew not where they stood. They were clumsy in the speech of both the old land and the new; their names came from abroad but had already been corrupted into nicknames here. They were neither one thing nor the other.

At the head of the procession toddled the citizens. These more fortunate ones had been born into their environment. They had never known the Old World; they had not shared the experience of coming. They were Americans from the start, had lisped the words in English, and often received names appropriated from the older inhabitants.

It was at such times the parents were fullest of their responsibilities. As they led the way on these occasions they became gravely conscious of a disturbing uncertainty. What if the children should cease to follow, should take it into their heads to march off in some altogether strange direction! It was difficult enough to show them the right ways around the corners of the city blocks; it was infinitely more difficult to show them the right ways around the twisting curves of the new way of life.

As they consider the heaviness of their tasks, the mother and father grow somber. They remember the failures. Their minds go to that one who came to them as if on a visit, then sickened and went away. It occurs to them that they cannot possibly meet their obligations to the children. Not only that the food will hardly go around to nurture all, not only that the mended garments pass from one to another, but that by the act of migration, they, the parents, have destroyed the birthright of their sons and daughters. These boys who should be picking berries or hunting nuts, these girls who should be approaching mastery of the stove, have all been robbed and must endure the present, enter the future without their proper due. To each other, the parents acknowledge the guilt: *Yes, dear, and therefore let us sacrifice ourselves and live only for them. If there is any hope in this world, it is not for us but for them.*

It was easier to bend the neck in readiness than to be certain that the yoke would fit. With bewilderment the immigrants learned that to be willing to sacrifice was not enough, that their children must be also willing to accept the sacrifice; and of that there could be no confidence. The initial dissimilarities of experience widened with time as youngsters ventured out from the home and subjected themselves to influences foreign to their elders. The life of school and the life of street completed the separation between the generations.

If it did nothing else to the child, the school introduced into his life a rival source of authority. The day the little boy hesitantly made his way into the classroom, the image of the teacher began to compete with that of the father. The one like the other laid down a rigid code of behavior, demanded absolute obedience, and stood ready to punish infractions with swift severity. The day the youngster came back to criticize his home (*They say in school that . . .*) his parents knew they would have to struggle for his loyalty.

That was an additional reason why the immigrants labored to create educational institutions of their own; they hoped thereby to minimize the contest. But the parochial schools were expensive and spread very slowly; they accommodated at best only a small fraction of the children. The strong-minded and well-to-do could hold out against the pleas of their offspring who wished to go where everyone else went; mostly the newcomers were compelled by circumstances and by the law to depend on public instruction.

The building itself was familiar enough; this was one of the known landmarks of the neighborhood. The idea of attendance was also familiar; this had happened already to older brothers and friends. And as the lad entered the yard, even sight of the fellows playing or waiting in line had the appearance of familiarity; he recognized some from around his own block, the others were much like himself. The public school was universal, but each nevertheless reflected the quality of the homogeneous residential district within which it was situated. In effect is was Irish or Jewish or German or Polish; the first impression it made on the new scholar was that of the altogether familiar and the altogether expected.

The ringing bell broke the continuity of his life; as he walked up the cast-iron staircase he left the narrow orbit of his home and moved into the limitless world. He stood in the stiff lines and sat motionless in the formal rows of seats. He learned silence and passivity who had never before felt restraints on his actions. He came to conform to rules: there were ways of rising and of sitting, ways to come dressed, ways to leave the room on certain occasions, and ways without words to signal the need. This order would now be his life.

Mostly the boys accede, and the girls too. At least the youngest do. There are truancies, some from their stubborn will, some from their shame at the poverty of clothing, some from necessity that keeps them home or sends them out to work. But mostly they give in and come. There is vaguely an understanding that the school will help them get on; and everyone else goes, so they go along. Besides they fear the law, want no trouble.

Only often, as they sat in the torpid classrooms, their attention wandered from the drone of recitations. Through the windows, gray filmed-over, they could see the bustle of purposeful men. By contrast, the school seemed empty of achievements, empty of the possibility of achievement. For what reason were they thus confined? What could they hope to gain from all this?

They did not ask those questions. They had long ago heard the trite answers. They came in order to grow up good and useful citizens. How would the school help them? By teaching them what was in these books.

Idly the boys fingered the battered volumes from which wisdom was to flow. There was no need to open them; the bold type of their pages was familiar enough from constant drilling.

THIS IS JACK. THIS IS JACK'S HOUSE. THIS IS JACK'S DADDY. JACK GOES SHOPPING. JACK GOES TO SCHOOL. ON THE WAY HE MEETS A COW. ON THE WAY HE MEETS A SHEEP. JACK COMES HOME. JACK FALLS ASLEEP.

And surely enough, across the top from page to page the brightly colored pictures show it all. Blue-eyed and blond, Jack himself stares out over the nice white collar and the neatly buttoned jacket. Across the green lawn, from the porch of the pretty yellow house, a miraculously slim mother waves.

By the side of a road that dips through the fields of corn, the animals wait, each in turn to extend its greeting. There it all is, real as life.

Except that it is all a lie. There is no Jack, no house, no brightly smiling "Mummy." In the whole room there is not a boy with such a name, with such an appearance. One can walk streets without end and there will be never a glimpse of the yellow clapboards, of the close-cropped grass. Who sleeps like Jack alone in the prim room by the window to be wakened by singing birds? *Good morning, Mr. Robin.* The whole book is false because nothing in it touches on the experience of its readers and no element in their experience creeps into its pages.

Falsity runs through all their books, which all were written to be used by other pupils in other schools; even the arithmetic sets its problems in terms of the rural countryside. Falsity runs through all their education. They learn the songs their mothers never sang. They mouth the words of precepts with no meaning: *A rolling stone gathers no moss. Make hay while the sun shines.* But what stone, what moss, what hay? The time that man appeared to speak from the platform and roused them, he shook them with his talk until they cheered the thin line at Bunker Hill, at Plymouth through the snow. *Our fathers' God, to Thee. . . .* Then later they thought, *Whose fathers?* Again a deception!

They themselves compounded the enormity of the untruth by the inability to give it the lie. From the desk the teacher looked down, a challenge they dared not meet. It was foolhardy of course to question her rightness. What an arsenal was at her command to destroy them! The steel-edged ruler across the knuckles was the least of her weapons. Casually she could twist the knife of ridicule in the soreness of their sensibilities; there was so much in their accent, appearance, and manners that was open to mockery. Without effort she could make them doubt themselves; the contrast of positions was too great. As she snapped shut the closet upon the symbols of her ladyhood within—the white gloves, the rolled-up umbrella, and the sedate hat—she indicated at once the superiority of her own status. There was visible evidence of her correctness in her speech and in her bearing, in her dress, and in the frequent intimations of the quality of her upbringing.

Perhaps a few were touched with sympathy at the condition of their charges. But what these offered was pity, nobler than contempt, but to the children no more acceptable. It was rare indeed to find the dedicated woman whose understanding of her students brought a touch of love into her work. After all, it was not of this they had dreamed in normal school when they had surrendered a part of their girlhood to acquire a profession, that they would devote the rest of their lives to the surveillance of a pack of unwashed ruffians. Mostly the teachers kept their distance, kept flickering the hope that a transfer might take them to a nicer district with nicer pupils from nicer homes. When that hope died, bitterness was born; and there was thereafter more savagery than love in their instruction. To admit the least question of the rightness of what they taught would undermine the whole structure of their self-esteem. So a boy should look and be, so a home, and so a parent. Many a woman, tired with all the years of it, looked out at her "scholars" tumbling into the street, and discovered a hidden crumb of satisfaction in the thought they were not so, nor the homes to which they'd go, nor the parents who'd greet them.

It took no uncommon sagacity to learn it was better not to question the teacher's world. The wise fellow kept his mouth shut and accepted it; he came to believe in a universe, divided as it were into two realms, one for school and one for home, and each with rules and modes of behavior of its own.

Acquiescence was no solution, however. Their lives could not be so divided. As the children of the immigrants grew up, they felt increasingly the compulsion to choose between the one way and the other. For some, the vision of the yellow house was peremptory. The kindness of a teacher, taken with the earnestness of the exceptional good student, may have opened the prospect of attaining it. Or the intense will of the ambitious youngster may have done so. Or the desperate dislike of a repressive home may have made this the only tolerable alternative. In any case, this way involved the complete identification with Jack, and that meant the total rejection of the origins and the background Jack could not have had.

Only a few, however, had the ability or the desire to make the radical break. The much greater number recognized the existence of the world they saw through school, were even willing to acknowledge its superiority, but they were not willing or, perhaps, not able to enter it themselves; their ties with their families were still binding. They developed perforce a kind of life of their own, an intermediary ground from which they could enter when necessary both the life of the school and the life of the home.

The setting generally was the street, where the young were free of oversight and masters of themselves. The boys and girls of an age who played together fell spontaneously into little coteries, for the very acts of play depended upon a sense of community and upon some degree of organization. There could be no games without rules and without subjection to the sanctions that enforced them. The interests of these groups changed as their members matured, from childhood to youth to adolescence to adulthood. But with notable persistence the members held together at least until marriage made them heads of families in their own rights or until they moved out of the neighborhood.

The structure of these organizations was simple, although they were endowed with a certain formality that mirrored the associational forms of the immigrant parents. There was a consciousness of belonging; you were in the gang and that set you off from outsiders. The sense of participation was tied to a specific place, a street or a district that was their own. Within the group each individual had a role which reflected his own capacities and qualities— the leader, the fighter, the buffoon, the clever one. And the whole was held together by a code of loyalty; they were in a common situation, understood one another and felt understood, and found strength in being together. In these matters the young folk followed the behavior and adopted the standards of their elders.

But the boys in the gang had also learned something from the school and from the world it represented. The teacher had told them, and the books, that the end was to get ahead, to make good, to strive so that success might come. They must not repeat the errors of their fathers who had not made good, had not gotten ahead. The consequences of failure were everywhere apparent about them.

They could see the point of such injunctions. Only the hoary aphorisms did not ring true. A penny saved was not in their lives a penny earned; or the best policy. They were not much in demand to fill posts as office boys, so that road to a vice presidency was closed to them; and the runaway carriage of the banker's daughter came rarely into their neighborhood. The atmosphere of the street, where so much of reality was in open view, was not congenial to the ideal of the self-made businessman.

The impulse toward success found expression in terms dictated by the nature of their own group life. In childhood they strove in the competitive play of the alley, games of pursuit and capture, of sides that struggled against each other for a goal. As the boys grew older and their gangs took form, there were fighting forays in the rivalry of block against block; or (and it was not much different), where space permitted, there were savage athletic contests for the winning's sake.

The growth of professionalism gave an enormous impetus to this interest in sports which, after 1880, persisted on through adolescence to adulthood. On the baseball diamond, in the boxing ring, a lad could win fame and fortune. In these arenas, opportunity was free and only ability counted. The tone of one's name, the manners of speech and behavior, antecedents and affiliation were matters of no consequence. The pure capacity to succeed, with no other advantages, would bring the acclaim of the newspapers and wealth beyond the reach of these boys in any other way. The outstanding athletes who actually won such prizes were, of course, few in number. But each had his tremendous following of boys and young men who gained a kind of derivative satisfaction from his achievements and who sought within their own gangs to emulate his exploits. Increasingly the thoughts of the children were preoccupied with the events of the world of sport within which were played out the vivid dramas of American success and failure.

Down by the corner where the older fellows congregated another kind of game held out the excitement of winning and losing. Watching the parades at campaign time, the youngsters looked forward with anticipation to the age when they too might be old enough to carry a banner. Meanwhile on the outskirts of the crowd around the ladder, they heard the orators' stirring periods and yelled the slogans of their partisanship. Its members were not yet voters when the gang was pressed into service, performing the menial jobs that might nevertheless win it the boss's notice. Here too was the possibility of rewards and of public esteem; and here too they need not labor against the liability of their own background.

The pursuit of success might take still another form. On the same corner, or on another much like it, the same boys or others much like them waited to turn the fight within them to riches. The violence of their childish play would grow up into racketeering; there were opportunities in plenty for such efforts.

For some the chance came through politics itself; perhaps they gained a proper "in" through roughing-up intransigent voters near the polls. For others the knock came in connection with gambling, or boxing, or labor organization, or in illicit liquor dealing. In whatever form, the ability to amass force in the gang, the willingness to defy rules the binding quality of which they did not recognize, and the burning desire by whatever means to elevate themselves above their origins, led such young men into organized criminality.

There were still other ways of rising, of course—the church, the stage, and the professions, for instance. But sports, politics, and the rackets had a larger importance even for the passive mass of the young who never ventured to be more than followers, who married and reconciled themselves to a stolid family life without the hope for success. For in these three endeavors were the closest approximations to the American standards of achievement open to persons like themselves. In no other way could the children of newcomers readily earn the appreciation of the whole society.

In the face of this whole development the immigrants were helpless. They had neither the will nor the ability to turn their offspring into other directions. The nominal authority of the fathers was only halfheartedly used; they were cruelly torn by the conflicting wishes that their sons be like themselves and yet lead better lives than they. Sensing that the school and street would tear the next generation away, the parents knew not how to counteract those forces without injuring their own flesh and blood.

If there was a serious one favored by the teachers who came home to sneer at the family ways, it was clear enough that when he could he would break away, change names, and drop all old connections. Could or should the father therefore stand in the way of his becoming a doctor?

That the brothers ran about all day with a crowd of wild ones was also disquieting. The worried parents could see no sense in the athletics, the infantile antics of grown men playing at ball. The immigrants had a deep fear of the consequences of the use of force in the rackets and an uneasy distrust of politics. But they could not deny that these were the ways to success, that these were the means of gaining the approval of the American onlookers. Even the older folk indeed derived a kind of satisfaction from the fame of men who bore names like their own, as if John L. Sullivan or Honus Wagner or Benny Leonard, somehow, testified to their own acceptance by American society. How could they then hold the youngsters to the traditional ideals of status and propriety?

In truth, the children were more in this world than they the parents. Often it was necessary for the fathers to turn for enlightenment to their sons. *We also keep a paper, but you have read more and studied in school.* The young wore their nativity like a badge that marked their superiority over their immigrant elders. It was this superiority that gave the second generation its role as mediator between the culture of the home and the culture of the wider society in the United States.

Accepting that role, the immigrants nevertheless resented it. It reversed the proper order of things. They could remember how they themselves had feared and respected the father; and they were embittered by their own failure to evoke the same fear and respect from their children. Beyond the loose behavior at the table and in the streets, these parents sensed the tones of ridicule. In their eyes the young Americans were undisciplined and ungrateful, good only at throwing stones and snow at strangers. When the boys and girls were small, it was still possible to curb their rebelliousness; the swift punishment of the strap held them temporarily in line. But as age increased their power, they were not so amenable to authority. As they grew in knowledge and in craftiness, as their earnings rose above those of the head of the family, they ceased to bow to restraints and would no longer be ordered about.

Adolescence was therefore a time of acute crisis, and particularly for the girls. As infants they had played with their brothers, but already at seven or eight they were excluded from the society of the gang and thereafter had little to do with boys. In girlhood they stayed close to their mothers since the home was to be their place. But even they could not be shut off from the world outside. They went to school or to work, observed the American familiarity of association between men and women, and soon enough revolted against the old restrictions. They learned to dress like others, with petticoats dragging behind to shut out the air and with their waists laced up in corsets so tightly the blood could not flow; and they lost their health—or so it seemed to their elders.

The worry was that they could not be guided by the safe rules of the Old World. They knew too much, boys as well as girls. Coming down Ann Street, they could not help but notice the "jilt shops" open for the dubious satisfaction of the sailors. Sometimes they could earn pennies distributing the cards of the brothels that flourished in their neighborhoods; and it was often years before they got to understand that a hotel could be other than a house of assignation. Why, even at home, through the thin walls, through the open windows, across the narrow courts, came the revealing sights and sounds. It was all familiar enough by the time they were of an age to conduct their own exploratory operations.

Well, such a girl or boy was open to error, by betrayal or by the longing for a withheld joy. Having spent the day in the closeness of the factory, having come back to the dank room where there was no room, it was release they sought and the assertion of themselves as individuals. Everywhere crowds hemmed them in so they had never the feeling of being one, uniquely one and not one of many. And so it might happen once when the sense of inner powers would no longer tolerate constriction, and the still night offered unaccustomed privacy, and there was a yearning for identity—to be a being, to desire and be desired.

Or, it might not happen; and then only the empty wish remained, returning evening after empty evening as the moody hours went by before sleep came.

Here was the ultimate barrier between the generations: they would never understand each other's conception of marriage. Sure, the parents tried to explain the nature of this most crucial step, that this was a means of extending on in time the continuity of the family, that it involved the sacrifice of personality toward some larger end: *From a maiden you will become a married woman, from a free being a slave of your husband and fortune.* The children would not listen. For them, marriage was an act of liberation by which they cast off the family ties and expressed themselves as persons through the power to love.

Nor could the children make their parents understand the longing for individuality. To enter upon such a relationship without consultation with one's elders, to make such decisions on the basis of chance impressions, to undertake this partnership with a stranger of unknown antecedents, was a madness of the reason. To many a saddened father and mother it seemed that their sons and daughters had moved gross passion to the center of marriage and had thereby obscured the true end of the family, perpetuation of the succession of generations.

Often enough, then, the old couple were left alone. Looking back across the years, they realized they had been incapable of controlling the course of events. Out of the village context and without the support of the community, the family as they had known it had been doomed. Though they clung to the vestige of home and urged their children to hold together, they would never recapture the essential solidarity.

Perhaps sometimes it occurred to them how much of these tribulations they would have avoided if only they had been able to find that farm and there to work united together. They need not have grieved over it. Certainly the immigrants in agriculture did not need to guard their boys and girls against the influences of the street; and there, where the father was still effective head of the household, his authority was not readily questioned. But the parents could no more keep America away in the country than in the city. As the young matured and discovered wills of their own in school and in more frequent worldly contacts, they too were rebellious and refused to be bound.

Indeed, the impact of separation, when it came, was more decisive on the farm. Lacking as rich an associational life as was possible in the urban places, the second generation had not so full a function as mediators between the cultures. The sparseness of settlement, moreover, was more likely to encourage marriage with strangers that cut the children completely off from their parents. Only here and there was an occasional township, closely knit, homogeneous, stubbornly resisting all changes in a declared antagonism to America. There the family might survive a generation in its traditional form because there the family could call on the support of communal sanctions analogous to those of the Old World. Nowhere else could it survive with its roots pulled out of the village soil.

Perhaps they never took the time to make a balance sheet of their lives, those two old ones left alone, never stopped to reckon up how much they had gained and how much lost by coming. But certainly they must occasionally have faced the wry irony of their relationships with their offspring. What hope the early seasons of their years had held was hope of efforts for their children's sake. What dreams they had had were dreams of the family transplanted, that generation after generation would bear witness to the achievement of migration.

In the end, all was tinged with vanity, with success as cruel as failure. Whatever lot their sons had drawn in this new contentious world, the family's oneness would not survive it. It was a sad satisfaction to watch the young advance, knowing that every step forward was a step away from home.

RELIGION IN OLD WORLD AND NEW

Oscar Handlin

A MAN HOLDS DEAR what little is left. When much is lost, there is no risking the remainder.

As his stable place in a whole universe slipped away from under him, the peasant come to America grasped convulsively at the familiar supports, pulled along with him the traditional bulwarks of his security. He did not learn until later that, wrenched out of context, these would no longer bear the weight of his needs.

Even in the Old World, these men's thoughts had led ineluctably to God. In the New, they were as certain to do so. The very process of adjusting immigrant ideas to the conditions of the United States made religion paramount as a way of life. When the natural world, the former context of the peasant ideas, faded behind the transatlantic horizon, the newcomers found themselves stripped to those religious institutions they could bring along with them. Well, the trolls and fairies will stay behind, but church and priest at very least will come.

The more thorough the separation from the other aspects of the old life, the greater was the hold of the religion that alone survived the transfer. Struggling against heavy odds to save something of the old ways, the immigrants directed into their faith the whole weight of their longing to be connected with the past.

As peasants at home, awed by the hazardous nature of the universe and by their own helplessness, these people had fled to religion as a refuge from the anguish of the world. Their view of their own lives had generated a body of conceptions and of practices that intimately expressed their inmost emotions. It was not only that they held certain theological doctrines; but their beliefs were most closely enwrapped in the day-to-day events of their existence. The specific acts of being religious were the regular incidents of the village year. Their coming needed no forethought, indeed no consciousness. Their regularity was an aspect of the total order of the village. That was a feature of their attractiveness.

The peasants found also attractive the outward aspects of their religious institutions. The very formality of structure and organization had a meaning of consequence to them. They were all communicants of established churches, whether Roman Catholic, Lutheran, Anglican, or Orthodox In some lands, where the monarch professed the same faith, to be "established" meant that the Church and State were closely united. That was true in Italy, Germany, Scandinavia, England, and Russia. But that link was not the essential element in establishment which also existed in countries such as Poland and Ireland, where Catholic peasants lived under non-Catholic rulers.

Recognition by the government and special treatment in law were only the surface indications of a deeper signficance. To the peasants, establish-

Reprinted from *The Uprooted* (1951), pp. 117-31, by permission of the author and the publisher. (Copyright, 1951, by Little, Brown and Co.) The chapter, which appears in that volume under the title "Religion as a Way of Life," has been abridged.

ment meant that their religion held a fixed, well-defined place in their society, that it was identified with the village, that it took in all those who belonged, all those who were not outcasts. Establishments in that sense gave these people a reassuring conviction that they belonged, were parts of a whole, insiders not outsiders.

The other attributes of establishment were appropriate also. About these churches was no confusing cloud of uncertainty. Their claim to men's allegiance rested on a solid basis of authority. It was not an individual choice that was involved in the process of belonging, but conformity. So, everyone else did. So it had been done year before year, generation before generation, as far back as the peasant could reckon . . . ever. The very rights and privileges of the Church, its lands and possessions, were evidence of its legitimacy and longevity. It was unthinkable not to be a member; it demanded a considerable feat of the imagination to conceive of what it would mean to be excluded, to draw down the censure of the entire community, to be barred from every social occasion.

There was no need to argue about these matters, to weigh alternatives, to consider. The Church gave no reasons for being; it was. Its communicants were within if not because they had rationally accepted its doctrines; they had faith because they were in it. Explanation in terms of reasonable propositions was superfluous; the Church was accepted as a mystery, which called for no explanation. These peasants felt the attractiveness of the demand on their faith as of the demand on their odebience to authority. Such, their own ideas had led them to believe, were the sources of certainty.

Village religion was, as a matter of course, conservative. Peasants and priests alike resisted change. They valued in the Church its placed conviction of eternal and universal sameness, of continuity through the ages, of catholicity through Christendom. The very practices that stirred them now reached back to the earliest times. Here and in precisely this manner, generations of untold ancestors had worshiped. Dimly over the gap of years, fathers and sons engaged in a common communion, assured by the permanence of forms.

The peasants were certain of the fixity of their church in space as well as in time. This priest who ministered to them in this parish was not an isolated individual but one who had an established place in a great hierarchical structure that extended through society. Above the priest was a sequence of other dignitaries rising to loftier and loftier eminence to the one supereminent above all, pope or patriarch, king or emperor. When the retinue of the bishop pranced through the village, when that personage himself appeared attired in all the magnificence of his vestiture, when his distant countenance framed in the miter of his majesty looked down on the assembled community, then the people, humble in his presence, were elevated through the dignity of his own imposing power. He had ordained the priest, stood guarantor of the efficacy of the parish rites, brought the village into communion with the whole world of true believers, made the peasant certain there was order in the Church and security of place for each soul within it.

Yet the grandeur of religion did not leave it aloof from its communicants. Splendid though it was in appearance, extensive and powerful in its compass, it was still close to the life of each man. The hierarchy that reached up to the most exalted also reached down to the most humble.

The Church was familiar to the peasants' day-to-day existence. Its outward forms and ceremonies were established in the round of the year. By long usage, each festival had a seasonal connotation through which, in the same celebration, were commingled the meanings of the distant Christian event and of the proximate changes in the immediate world of nature. All the acts of worship were embedded in a setting of which the landscape, the weather, and the sight of the heavens all were aspects. Each holiday thus had substance and individuality, a whole and entire character of its own. Its coming filled the whole place and the whole day, spread out from the church through the road where the procession passed to the blessed field around, extended on from the early service at the altar to the feast and the accompanying jubilation. Each occasion was thus local to the particular village, the possession of each participant, a part of his way of life. This the peasants had in mind when they hoped, most eagerly, to re-establish their religion in the New World.

It was not only the attractiveness of such elements of form that moved the immigrants to reconstruct their churches in America; it was also the substance embraced in those forms. These people were anxious that religion do and mean in the United States all that it had back there before the Atlantic crossing.

At home, worship had brought to the worshiper a pleasure that was aesthetic in nature. If in the new land he had the occasion, which he had rarely had in the old, to talk about the quality of that satisfaction, the peasant put the words of his description around specific impressions of the service— the stately manners, the inspiring liturgy, the magnificent furnishing. But such descriptions he knew were inadequate; for beyond the beauty that adhered to these things in their own right was a beauty of essence that grew out of their relationship to his own experience as a human being. Lacking the habit of introspection, the peasant could not set words to that satisfaction. He could only feel the lack of it.

How comforting were the ceremonial movements of the priest and how stirring his sermon—not at all a bickering argument but a be-gestured incantation! Here was not so much an effort to persuade man to be good as a reminder that he was bad, in effect magically to cleanse him. Indeed, magical qualities inhered in all the acts of worship. Touching on sin and the remission of sin, on evil and the warding-off of evil, these practices made sense in terms of peasant ideas.

In the rite before his eyes, the man could see that the world in which he lived was not whole, did not of itself justify itself. No. This was merely a dreary vestibule through which the Christian entered the life eternal that lay beyond the door of death. Long and narrow was the passage and bitter dark. With utmost striving was the crossing made, and little joy was in it. But there was a goal, and there would be an arrival. The bells that tolled at the culmination of each service would toll also at each soul's release, when the hard journey, over, would lead to its own compensation for the troubles of the way.

The promise of life to come, and the meaning of the life of the present, was consolation. At that expected future, retribution, rewarded good and punished evil, would make whole the order of mundane things, explain the lapses of justice, the incongruity of achievements, the neglect of merit in the existence of the peasant. To the congregation, devoutly silent under the plaster images, the monotonous chant affirmed over and over that the perspective of eternity would correct all the disturbing distortion in the perspective of today.

Faith brought the affirmation that man, though the creature of chance that appearances made him to be, was also an actor in the great drama that had begun with the miracle of creation and would end in the miracle of redemption. For him, God had come to earth, had suffered, and had sacrificed Himself to save all humanity. That sacrifice, repeated at every mass, was the visible assurance of meaning in the universe.

The same sacrifice transfigured the communicants who shared the mystery. Wafers and wine, blood and flesh, united them in the togetherness of their common experience. Not only they within the village, but through the village to the uncounted numbers elsewhere, to their own ancestors in the churchyard who had also once shared, still shared. In the salving rite of Communion, there mingled with the satisfaction of the act itself the sentiments of village loyalty, the emotions of family love, and the awareness of fullment of the ideal of solidarity.

If the peasants made a way of life of the establishment of their religion, so those who were not peasants made a way of life of their dissent.

The dissenting churches made no claims to universality, could imbue their members with no general sense of belonging, indeed left them with the consciousness of being outsiders. But, as outsiders, the Jews or Quakers or Baptists had to cherish the differences which were the marks of their election. Such sects could not take their membership for granted; they had to stress a continuing process of conversion and dedication, whether that be intellectually or emotionally arrived at. Out of the desire to protect their distinctive differences from obliteration in societies so much oriented around the peasant and out of the need to lend dignity to the process of conversion, these groups had also achieved an order of holidays, a formality of services, and a rigid mode of observances that, together, constituted a way of life.

Religion for these people was not as much tied to a locality as for the peasants. The appearance of things played not so prominent a role in the dissenting as in the established churches. Chapel and synagogue by their nature were not so likely to make a visual appeal, and rite was not so conspicuous in their practices. The congregations were more likely to be attached to the evidences of their own participation in worship as individuals—how they sang this psalm or offered up this prayer. For these evidences reminded them of their own consciousness of community as a group; and though they were a community of noncommunicant outsiders, still that consciousness was precious to them, worthy of preservation wherever they were.

Become immigrants and arrived in America, peasants and dissenters alike therefore struggled to reconstruct their churches. In the manner of doing, there were differences among the various groups. But the problem of all was the same: how to transplant a way of religious life to a new environment.

The immigrants began with the determination that their emigration would not destroy the ties that bound them to the church. For years they kept alive a connection with the Old Country parish. Letters from the other side brought news of the place and the people; letters from this side brought gifts to embellish the building, and, sometimes, requests for counsel from the priest.

But the immigrants thought it more important still to bring their churches to the United States, to reconstitute in their new homes the old forms of worship. At heavy cost and despite imposing obstacles, they endeavored to do so. Often when a phase of the struggle was over—say, a new edifice dedicated—they would look back with relief and surprise at the height of the difficulties surmounted.

The conditions of emigration and the hardships of the crossing were immediate sources of confusion. On the way, in the ships, the terrible disorder made troublesome any ritual observance. The prolonged lapse of unsettled time obscured the calendar; on the move, no day was individual from any other. Without the ministrations of a priest, without the sustenance of a whole community, the worshiper was limited to his own humble resources of prayer. It would take an effort to regain the richness of experience he had once enjoyed.

The end of the journey was the start of new tribulations. In the United States the immigrants encountered a most discouraging situation. All the conditions of religious life in America were different from those in the Old World. As the newcomers struggled to adjust themselves, they discovered a maze of barriers that separated them from the desired objective, transplantation of the old churches.

It was difficult, for instance, to understand the diversity of religious affiliations. In Europe the established church was universal; only a few outsiders dissented. Here a vast variety of sects divided the population, and did so according to no meaningful pattern of social, economic, or sectional status. In outward aspect, in occupations, in respectability, one could not distinguish the members of one denomination from another. All these people furthermore associated with each other on terms of complete equality. There seemed no reason therefore why a man should not change his church as freely as his hat. Indeed, to the immigrants it seemed the Americans were perilously near to doing so all the time.

Every religion therefore was in open competition for adherents with every other. There was no establishment in the United States; no church was connected with the State or favored by the laws. What was more, no sect had so secure or commanding a position in any other way that it could compel members to come to it or penalize those who did not. In all the great cities, throughout the West, and in many parts of the South, the churches were almost all equally new and stood on approximately the same footing. Even rural New England, where the Congregationalists had at first held an exceptional position, after 1850 approached the general condition.

The absence of an authoritative national, or even a regional or local, church was unfamiliar and disturbing. The privacy of beliefs, the freedom to enter what denomination he wished—or none at all—placed before the immigrant the necessity of giving answers to questions that had never been asked of him before. Without the aid of priests, for it was in the nature of the movement that laymen came in advance of the clergy, these humble people had to make the most difficult of decisions. That they insisted on re-creating the old churches testifies to the strength of the old ties.

Such decisions involved not principles alone, but all sorts of concrete, practical considerations. With the most devout will in the world, a church would not appear unless there were funds for an edifice and a staff for its service.

The problem of finances was sufficiently oppressive. At home the peasants had never to consider the means of paying the expenses. The Church supported itself by grants either from the State or from the income of its own lands; the communicants contributed only the fees for particular services and these were fixed by the force of age-old custom. All such revenues disappeared with immigration. New ones to replace them were the minimal cost of reconstituting the churches in America.

Then the immigrants discovered that costs could not be minimal in the New World which compelled them to take on many additional charges not known in the Old. Here the pious had to create afresh, and at once, what in Europe had always been at hand, the product of centuries of growth. Everywhere the newcomers went they purchased buildings or, where they were able, erected new ones. They accumulated all the furnishings and the appurtenances necessary for the service and for all that raised what funds their own efforts brought them.

They could count on little help. The Roman Catholics occasionally benefited from the assistance of philanthropic monarchs like King Ludwig of Bavaria, or from the donations of missionary organizations, the Austrian Leopoldine Verein and the French Society for the Propagation of the Faith, or most of all, from the services of the international orders. But such aid, valuable as it was, was trifling against the enormity of the need. By and large, the money that built the churches and other religious institutions was assembled from the earnings of human laborers who painfully accumulated what they scarcely could spare and devotedly gave what they could.

The magnitude of the task was multiplied by the circumstance that it was executed without the support of the kind of authority that had familiarly operated on the peasants at home. There was, to begin with at least, only a skeletal hierarchy and no corps of clerics to supply leadership. Under the American voluntary system, the churches had no sanctions. They counted for support on the good will and loyalty of their communicants. A bishop could not simply command and expect to be obeyed; his orders evoked a response only to the degree that he catered to the wishes of his flock. Law in the United States increased the uncertainty by defining the congregation as the church incorporate, and naming the laymen rather than the priest as owners of its property. Yet there were limits to the powers of a majority of the membership, for a minority was always free to secede and drift off in its own direction. If the immigrants held together and achieved as much as they did, it was because the longing that moved them sprang from a common stem in their life before emigration.

The transition from establishment to voluntarism was more difficult for peasants than for dissenters. The latter had known, at home, how it was to support a church through their own efforts. In America indeed their situation improved, for the neutrality of the state was better than its hostility. Here all sects were in the same position.

Paradoxically that very equality of situation threatened the survival of the dissenting groups. The sense of election grew weaker in the absence of persecution by a dominating church. Unless constantly reminded of the particularity and uniqueness of their own form of dissent, individuals might be tempted to drift off into other analogous denominations.

Dissenters and peasants both, therefore, saw a danger in the pervasive latitudinarianism of religion in the United States. Too many Americans were ready to believe that salvation could come through any faith or none, that ethical behavior and a good life rather than adherence to a specific creed would earn a share in the heavenly kingdom.

There was a double menace to this delusion. To begin with, it put to nought the sacrifices of establishing the immigrant religions. If all roads led to salvation, why trouble with great difficulty and enormous expense to hack out one's own? Why not follow the well-established easy paths others had already marked? Experience shouted the denial. In the missions, in the chapels, where the strangers came to pray, there the voices were of aliens and the ways were not the same. There were not the satisfactions that a full religion brought. No salvation could be there.

There was also a more subtle threat in latitudinarianism. The American ideas might penetrate the immigrant churches themselves, undermine the old ideas. That would deprive the newcomers, in particular the peasants, of their promised reward. For these people salvation was the compensation for faith and suffering, not for good behavior. They would not have the shift in emphasis.

The problem was, the whole effort, no matter how earnest, was out of context. You can build a church, but you cannot re-create the site, wipe out the surrounding city, restore the village background. You can reassemble the communicants; but can you re-create the communion, wipe out the effects of the crossing, and restore the old piety? A new environment has disorganized the old order. Determined men long for reorganization, struggle to effect it.

Invariably the way seemed to be the complete transfer of the old religious system to the New World. It was not simply the Gospel and priest the immigrants would bring with them, but holidays and processions, ancient costumes and traditional rites, the whole life of religion at home. All these they wished to replant in the unreceptive soil of America. The only way to be sure of survival was to insist on the rigid preservation of the whole.

THE BREAKDOWN OF ETHNIC SOLIDARITY: THE CASE OF THE ITALIAN IN GREENWICH VILLAGE

Caroline F. Ware

Social Organization. The Italians of Greenwich Village, largest of local ethnic groups, experienced in the post-War [World War I] years a fundamental shift in the social organization of their community and a rapid disruption and dislocation of their social standards under the impact of the American environment. Virtually no part of American culture except the acquisitive drive was incorporated into their social code, and the only major institution which became an integral part of their life—namely, the Tammany brand of politics as developed by the Irish—was less the product of American tradition than the creation of an earlier immigrant group. The social history of this Italian group is not only the story of half of the people of this locality, but a fairly representative sample of the process through which the mass of city-dwelling "new" immigrants were passing during the years when their children were growing to maturity.

The beginnings of the Italian community of Greenwich Village dated back into the 1880's, though the rapid development of the area into an Italian district was a matter of the twentieth century. Before 1900, when the South Italians began to come in, it was made up chiefly of North Italians who came both as an overflow from the East Side and directly from the ship to the immigrant hotels which were opened in the West Side district.

As the number of Italians multiplied, the community took shape. To the Italian mission church which had been located in the area since 1859, a special Italian-language parish was added in 1892. In the manner common to the ghettos of every nationality whose distinctive habits constitute distinctive needs, Italian stores were set up to sell products appropriate to the Italian taste. Macaroni, olive oil and cheese, fish, pork, and live poultry—these, along with such distinctive vegetables as red peppers, broccoli, and squash blossoms, all began to appear on sidewalk stalls, in stores, and on the inevitable pushcarts.

Social organizations were formed on the basis of the part of Italy from which people had come. Village and provincial groups from both North and South Italy organized mutual benefit societies for mutual aid in case of sickness and death and for carrying on their social life. The number of these societies was legion, and even their names were often not known outside of their own membership. In 1930, nobody could be found who knew the names of all the societies which had survived, and a newspaper editor who was attempting to compile a city-wide list reported that when his list was completed, it would be unique. Upwards of seventy-five were said to have drawn their membership from the local district. One doctor, who in 1930

Reprinted from *Greenwich Village, 1920-1930* (1935), pp. 152-202, by permission of the author and the publisher. (Copyright, 1935, by Houghton Mifflin Co.) The chapter has been abridged.

was "lodge doctor" for twenty-five different societies, had "had" as many as fifty societies at one time or another, all from South Italy, as the North Italians never would use him because he was a southerner. Fifty per cent of the local Italian men in 1910 were estimated to have held membership in town or provincial societies. A few of the more prosperous of these societies had had their own clubrooms, but most had held their meetings in the various public halls.

Informal social relations, as well as formal organization, were almost wholly restricted to people from the same town or province. Difference in dialect made it easier to communicate with *paesani* than with other Italians. Although this community differed from other Italian areas of first settlement in the city in that it contained a large number of provincial groups within a smaller radius—the local schools had children from nearly every province in contrast to the East Side where solidly Neapolitan and solidly Sicilian schools served adjacent territories—houses and, usually, blocks were homogenous. In fact, it was only the experience of being in a foreign land which made many of the immigrants feel themselves to be Italians at all rather than citizens of the particular town or province.

In the years that followed, this Italian community disintegrated rapidly. Its social structure was broken, partly through the loss of members in the migration to outlying boroughs, partly through the impact of American institutions, and partly because the old provincial alignment ceased to be relevant and newly developed interests cut across old lines. Organization on the basis of Old World backgrounds gave way either to disorganization or to the reorientation of local Italian life in terms of American interests and especially, American politics.

Many of the institutions which served the Italian community lost their vitality. Most of the stores which supplied the Italian population in 1930 were relics of the period of community building, many having served the area for upwards of twenty years. Though stores had gone out, new ones had not come in. A few had shifted their locations slightly, usually moving a block or two farther to the west in the direction of the population drift. Street and subway construction had forced pushcarts to move. But, on the whole, the same storekeepers as before the War, located at the same places, continued to offer the same favorite Italian wares.

As the provincial ties became weaker, the provincial mutual benefit societies dwindled and many died. When the stream of immigration stopped, both the constant supply of new members and the close connection with home villages were cut off. By 1930, all informants agreed that these societies had almost ceased to constitute an important element in the social organization of the community. . . .

The provincial societies made no appeal to the younger generation raised in the community, or to those foreign-born who had transferred their center of interest to America. In contrast to the ethnic organizations of some other groups in America whose educational and cultural programs have attracted and held at least part of the younger generation within the bonds of ethnic consciousness, the provincial emphasis of these organizations tended to represent to the young Italo-American the worst aspect of his heritage and to be associated with the "backwardness" of his parents. Some few young people retained membership in their fathers' lodges because they hoped to gain either political backing or if they were professional men, clients, but they complained that they had never been able to count on either the professional or political support of fellow members.

Yet, though time destroyed provincial cohesion and subordinated provincial difference, it did not eliminate provincial jealousies altogether. These lines remained to divide the Italian community when they had ceased to give it a basis for social organization. As people moved in and out, blocks no longer were so solidly of one or another province, but not all lost their provincial identity. . . .

The younger generation, too, moved largely, though less exclusively, in provincial groups. When several second generation young men were being selected to interview a body of Italians in the community, the boy who was choosing the group made his selection on the basis of the part of the country from which each boy's people came, saying that this would be the way to get a representative body of interviews, since each one would be sure to know the people from the same part of the country as his parents. Out of 144 persons of both generations who were directly questioned, 10 expressed an unwillingness to marry, or have a member of his or her family marry, someone from a different province. At a local mental hygiene clinic, the psychiatrist reported having to deal with cases where even American-born girls objected to marriage with men from another province. A stranger from the same province was regarded with much less suspicion than one from another province. . . .

Certain elements in the American situation helped to keep provincial differences alive, in spite of time, distance, and the irrelevance of these differences to American affairs. The North Italians were at pains to maintain the distinction between themselves and the southerners, not alone on traditional grounds, but because they felt more Americanized and therefore superior. They had found adaptation to American customs somewhat easier, both because of longer residence, and because, on the points at which the clash between the Italian and American cultures were most acute, they had traditionally been less insistent than the southerners. They could meet the problem of freedom of girls in America, since they had not been so strict at home as had the South Italians and the Sicilians. A larger proportion came from cities and were literate and thus had an advantage in making the transition into an American urban situation.

Whenever a North Italian thought that a question implied criticism of something which was not American, he took pains, often gratuitously, to insist that the particular thing was done by the South Italians and to turn the question into a criticism of the latter. . . .

Where home attitudes had been thus reinforced by American circumstances, it was not surprising to find the expression "low" and "high" Italian, which in Italian merely referred to geographical areas used to denote differences in quality and social status. While provincial consciousness remained strongest at the two extremes—Piedmontese and Sicilian—even violent insistence on differences was not limited to them. . . .

To the younger generation, provincial differences had ceased to be of major importance in determining their associates—except through accident of residence or family friends—or their points of view, but they still produced a strong automatic reaction—a readiness to hurl the stock phrase about the person from the other part of Italy if a quarrel should arise.

As essentially Italian organizations dwindled, local politics, or, to a slight extent, local social agencies, furnished the basis for new groupings. Those who left their Italian lodges and joined political clubs looked upon the benefit society leaders as "those little people." Political aims had so largely superseded fraternal interests by 1930 that people frequently insisted, "there are no such things as non-political Italian clubs or societies." One social club felt obliged to protest its non-political character by stating on its entertainment program, "This club has no other purpose than to provide pleasant hours for its members."

A few attempts to salvage what remained of the mutual benefit societies by uniting the small-town groups into provincial and regional units showed some signs of achieving success by virtue of their political purpose. As the president of one of the united groups put it, "We are not satisfied with what we have been getting from Tammany. We want not only jobs but patronage. We want a number of commissioners and judges *and what goes with them. . . ."*

The single flourishing organization within the local Italian community in 1930 was an Italian business and professional men's society which was exclusively Italian—it was rumored that a prominent Jewish clothing merchant had not been admitted even though he sent the club five hundred coat hangers—and which was known both in the locality and by Italian organizations outside the locality as an essentially political club, though it insisted that it was purely social. Its officer acknowledged, however, that it would be its policy to support an Italian political candidate. Most of the political organizations in which the Italians took part were not the outgrowth of provincial or other Italian societies, but were newly formed under individual political leaders.

Where affiliation with one or another of the social agencies became a basis for association, the social realignment which was involved was more extreme. In this situation, not only did the New World interests supplant those of the Old, but they centered around the associations and interests of women and children—members of the community who had no place in the old structure which involved only men. Such new groupings had not become numerically very important by 1930, for the membership of Italian lodges was probably still greater than that of the mothers' clubs at the centers which their children attended. A large part of the community, moreover, belonged to no formal organization whatever, and informal associations were most likely to involve the men and to follow traditional rather than newly developed lines. Even a slight trend toward making women's groups important, however, was significant because it fundamentally altered the structure of the Italian community and reversed the roles of its members.

The effect of time and of the American environment did more to disrupt the Italian community than to reorganize it. By 1930 the community had ceased to acknowledge any leadership. To all questions about local leaders, those consulted replied with a negative answer. When pressed with individual names there was always some good reason for not regarding the individual mentioned as a leader—"He would have nothing to do with people of the locality," "We know too much about him to respect him," "He takes no interest and will not contribute anything to the neighborhood." The only person for whom everyone was ready to say a good word was one of the old Genoese leaders who had died. With his passing the community felt that it had no one to look to.

Those who had risen in the community during its 30 or more years of development had gone their several ways. The various positions in relation to the community which they occupied in 1930 revealed much about the social forces which had been at work. Most of the old Genoese families had moved away, and among those who remained the sons were very much less highly regarded than the parents had been. A few of the earliest South Italians and their sons had been distinctly "neighborhood" leaders in the period of community building—active in organizing lodges of such American fraternal orders as the Moose as well as in the Italian societies, "hail-fellow-well-met" with everybody, whether Italian or non-Italian, and ready to support all types of community ventures.

With the disappearance of the social neighborhood, their position had gone. The one who remained most prominent in 1930 had made his way into politics and had become one of the outstanding Italian politicians to whom people came from all over the city for help in getting jobs. A second, who had held the presidency of several lodges, had moved out of the locality and had concentrated his interest on American fraternal societies and politics; another continued as lodge doctor for a number of societies whose membership was widely scattered, but the lodges now furnished only his income and not the basis for his social life. . . .

The professional people, both those who had come into the community already trained and those who grew up in it, differed in their adjustment to changing conditions, but agreed in having little to do with the neighborhood.

There were the aggressively American young doctors with conspicuously up-to-date offices who wanted an American practice and only remained to serve their compatriots until they could get firmly enough established to leave them behind.

There were well-known and prosperous doctors who at one time had served the locality, but who, in 1930, were specialists with offices on lower Fifth Avenue and a city-wide American clientele. One of these was an ardent supporter of all efforts to promote Italian culture and an active member of the Italian Historical Society and the exclusive Italy-America Society. His interest, however, was in the culture of Italy, not its people; his associations were with cultivated people, both Italians and Americans, all over the city and he had nothing to do with the local community.

Some of the successful, whose business relations were entirely with Americans, belonged to the upper "four hundred" of the Italian metropolitan community, and though their social life was led completely within an Italian circle they had no contacts with the local community, even with its professional members. Others, who were not numbered among the city-wide Italian upper crust, moved within a small circle of well-to-do Italian friends, largely but not exclusively drawn from the professional and business people of the locality. Some of these who had made a lot of money were generous in their donations to local institutions such as the Italian church and even to non-Italian agencies working with Italians, but they had no social dealings with the community beyond their own group and were constantly on the defensive for fear of being approached for money. A third type of the prosperous and successful Italian was represented by the business men who had moved out into a definitely American neighborhood, would have no social relations with Italians except with those few whose prestige in the American community was high, would contribute nothing to the support of local activities—"they are always trying to get us to contribute to the Church or a society because we are Italians"—and were emphatic in their opposition to all forms of Italian-American solidarity.

At the opposite extreme were those who remained completely immersed in their Italian point of view, doctors who withdrew from the Association of Italian Physicians because it used the English language—"They call themselves 'Italian Physicians' but it seemed as if they wanted to forget everything Italian when they gave up the language"—and who were determined to shield themselves and their families from the contamination of the American scene. These had little to do with the local Italian community, partly because it was low-class and partly because they feared that if they let their children play in the neighborhood, even with Italian children, they would pick up "those foreign ways." They sent them to private church schools, confined their own associations to other like-minded Italian professionals, and undertook to maintain a solidly Italian culture spot in spite of the rest of the community.

Among the younger generation which was beginning a professional or business career in 1930, only those few who had political ambitions showed any interest in the local community, any desire to occupy a position of local leadership, or any feeling of responsibility toward the group among whom they had been brought up. "We educated Italians are too few in all the city to get anywhere through leadership of our people. We have no choice but to fight our way up individually." The hard-working wife of a struggling attorney insisted that it was all right for people who had made money to lead and help the Italians, but a person who was poor and had to make his own way could not afford to jeopardize his position and his earning power by identifying himself with the Italian group.

The failure of the local Italian community to develop local leadership reflected a combination of factors—class distinction in Italy which produced a wide gap between the cultivated Italians with background and money and the immigrant mass; the fact that those who achieved business or professional success looked rather toward the avenues into American life which money opened to them than to prestige among their own people; and the fact that their success came in terms of money rather than of fame, and hence did not attract a following.

Most of the conscious pressures to which the Italian community was subjected had sought to break up its solidarity and transform its members as individuals from Italians into Americans. It has never been part of the American code to treat its ethnic minorities, in any official or positive way, as groups rather than as individuals. The assumption that all persons may become "Americans" simply by setting foot on American soil and going through the legal form of naturalization has had its counterpart in the policy of the public school to treat all children as nearly alike as possible without regard to the ethnic background from which they have come. Only when the War revealed the fact that hyphenism had survived this process of laissez-faire individualism, and that the country was made up, not of a mass of "Americans," but of a number of undigested lumps of different nationalities, was official cognizance taken of ethnic differences. The Immigration Act of 1921 gave legal status to this consciousness of difference as far as the exclusion of future immigrants was concerned, and the publicity for Nordic superiority which accompanied the passage of this act greatly increased public awareness of nationality differences. But the awakened consciousness extended only to external, not to internal, policy; while immigrants at Ellis Island were rigidly scrutinized for their national origin, public schools and other agencies continued to ignore ethnic differences and to make individual "Americans" out of the children of foreign origin who came under their sway.

In this respect, most of the schools and agencies of this district, as well, of course, as the indirect influences of movies, radio, and press, worked in the same direction. One of the local agencies gave instruction in the Italian language and put on Italian plays. In another, the director treated the patrons as part of the Italian community of the city by securing publicity in the Italian press for affairs at the center. The local branch of the public library kept a large collection of Italian books. But the local schools were indifferent to the loyalties and customs of the Italian group and did not consider it necessary to be familiar with the ethnic background of the children in order to prepare them for their role in American life. Health agencies accused patients of "trusting only their own" in following their own doctors in preference to those of the outside agencies. The few constructive local efforts to deal with the Italians as a group were made in the face of American public opinion and the pressure of those supplying the funds. When an Italian woman—selected for her administrative skill rather than because she was Italian—was put in charge of one of the local agencies, a principal sponsor of the agency threatened to withdraw her support. A health center which used a corps of Italian girls as assistants and interpreters in its work of health education had to justify itself to its patrons for spending money in this way.

Unconsciously many agencies bewildered the Italians with whom they came in contact. "My people understand two things, kindness and force," explained an observant Italian woman. "The rational, temperate attitude of the Americans does not move them." "You must reckon with the intense loyalty of the Italian," a prominent Italian advised a group of local social workers, "and remember that he expects loyalty, not reason or justice, in return, and is very quick to suspect that by the latter treatment you are letting him down."

To a considerable extent, the conscious and unconscious efforts to make individuals lose their identity with their own group has been successful and the solidarity of the Italian group had been undermined. Those who had gone to college had little good to say of the neighborhood and its association, and of Italians and their ways; they repudiated the suggestion that they were potential leaders of their own people. Only occasionally did they show any other attitude. . . .

But the sense of being Italian was very far from having been destroyed. The second generation as well as the first had retained a sufficiently strong "consciousness of kind" to make Italian boys bet on an Italian prize-fighter even when their best judgment told them that he was the weaker combatant; to make Italians overcome their age-long prejudice against investment in stocks when an Italian enterprise was involved; to make an appreciable change in the balance of votes when an Italian candidate appeared on the ballot; to make an Italian college student remark that he always felt un-comfortable when an Italian recited badly in class; to make an Italian girl whose associates had been largely non-Italian wonder why it was that she felt more at home and got on better with Italian people; or to make 10 per cent of the persons directly questioned state that they would object to mar-riage on the part of a member of their family with anyone who was not an Italian.

In a large measure, consciousness of being Italian was a defense reaction against the attitude of others—against being treated as a "Wop"—rather than a positive manifestation of group solidarity. There were plenty of situations which brought to the Italian a consciousness of his nationality. So long as his life was led strictly within his own community, he might escape such con-sciousness. The women who lived out their lives between their tenement kitchen, their church, and the market were aware of their nationality only indirectly, through the experiences of the children or the men. But those men and young people who went out of the neighborhood to work were not allowed to forget.

The post-War [World War I] drive for "Americanization" took the con-crete form of bringing every possible pressure to bear upon aliens to become American citizens, often to the point of excluding aliens from jobs or at least giving preference to citizens. Among the industries of the locality, many of the managers or owners interviewed asserted, quite gratuitously, that their employees were all citizens. In a number of cases there was good reason to doubt the truth of this assertion, a fact which only emphasized more strongly the presumption in favor of citizens as against alien workers. The three building-trade unions which local Italians were most likely to want to join—tile-setters, masons and bricklayers, and carpenters—all required at least first citizenship papers for membership. The fear of deportation which was awakened during and after the War persisted through the following years and increased with the depression when the drive to rid the country of "reds" and alien criminals was supplemented by the expulsion of unemployed as "public charges." In view of their treatment under the quota immigration law and the tendency to assume them to be gangsters, the Italians were left in no doubt of the fact that they had been classed among the "undesirables" and were in the country on sufferance. . . . Those who had not become citizens by 1930 had apparently largely abandoned the effort, for little de-mand for citizenship classes was reported, though English classes continued.

The younger generation had not the opportunity to forget its ethnic origin if it would. The alien tongue spoken in their homes remained as a constant reminder. Though as children they might, perhaps, have played

with children of other nationalities with only slight consciousness of difference, as they reached maturity they became aware of parental pressure to
marry within the group. They stood a good chance of being rejected by
employment agencies—and if they had not had such an experience personally,
their friends probably had. Practically all of the young people interviewed
could volunteer stories of discrimination which they or friends or relatives
had experienced. Ten per cent of the younger people questioned admitted
that they would hide their Italian nationality if it turned out to be a handicap
to them in getting ahead. In contrast to the intense nationalism which immigrant groups of other nationalities brought with them, especially those with
experience of oppression such as Irish, Polish, or Slovak, the Italians had
their Italian consciousness thrust upon them by the conditions of their
American life.

   The Distortion of its Culture. When the Italians arrived in the community, they brought with them not only their Old World associations but their
inherited culture. Like that of the many other immigrants who have made
America their home, this Old World culture was severely modified by New
World experience. At the same time, it modified the life of the community
into which it came.

   The fate which the culture of each immigrant group has met in its new
home has depended partly upon the extent to which the central features of
its life could survive transplanting and partly upon the social situation into
which it was transferred. For the Italian group of this community, conditions were almost equally unfavorable to the maintenance of much in Italian
culture, and to the adoption by the Italian immigrants of the traditional pattern of the American community. The result was that during these years
the disintegration of the old pattern was rapid and violent, while the confusion
in the American situation gave little opportunity for the successful acquisition of new standards. The Italian community in 1930 was almost wholly
lacking in cultural coherence.

   A culture is in a position to be transplanted and to survive in a different
environment if it is self-conscious and articulate and if it has organized
institutions integral with it. Especially is it able to survive when severed from
its roots if it has been strengthened by persecution—a fact amply attested
by the experience of the Jews, Armenians, or Poles. It is weak if its distinctive features rest in any important measure upon relation to any particular
place, if its organized institutions are not fundamental to it and if it has not
been on the defensive.

   Of the cultures brought into America by various immigrant groups, none
has been in a weaker position for survival than that of the Italians. Never
the object of persecution, it has not had the fortifying experience of fighting
for survival. Its articulate expression has been confined to the cultivated
minority, which has been almost entirely unrepresented among the body of
immigrants and which, when present, has been separated by a wide social
gulf from the illiterate peasantry. Its folk culture has been poor in articulate
content—in the folktales, dances, and the wealth of strong group customs
characteristic of the Slavic peasantries. It has lacked even a common language for the many who have known only a local dialect. No important
institutions have been integral with it, for the Church has never played the

central role among Italians that it has among such others as Irish or Poles, and nothing comparable to the Slavish *Sokol* or the German *Turnverein* has furnished a center for cultural and political activity. Place associations, which cannot be transported, have been important to it.

The family has always been the central institution of Italian culture. This has, in one way, made their culture easier to transplant than those which depend upon more complex institutions. Embedded in the intimacy of family relations, the most fundamental Italian attitudes have been beyond the reach of many influences that have affected external relations and practices.

At the same time, their culture pattern has been peculiarly vulnerable, for any weakening of its foundations has undermined the fundamental basis of social organization. Were the family less central, it could continue to function socially, though the culture pattern were disrupted. Were the culture less tied up with the institution of the family, its destruction or modification would be less socially disorganizing in its effect. But whatever tended to place the Italian tradition in disrepute or to draw the members of the group, either first or second generation, away from it, struck directly at the institution of the Italian family, while the American influences which loosened the bonds of that family produced a collapse of the whole inherited code of behavior. In contrast to the American who could retain many of his institutions—the community, for instance, or certain codes of honesty, fair play, and decency—though his family might be destroyed, or could lose many of his traditional values and still retain his family, the tradition of the Italian made his family and his culture inseparable. Any agencies which sought to amalgamate this group with the American community thus had the choice of accepting its Italianness and dealing with it in family groups or of attempting to deal with a group of individuals who were not only traditionless but socially disorganized as well. In this community, the line of development has followed the latter course.

The culture which the Italian peasant brought with him to America was closely rooted in the soil, and centered in the family which was patriarchal in form and integral with the land. It rested on oral tradition rather than literacy. It accorded a place of dignity to manual skill and fine craftsmanship. It took for granted the Catholic faith, but accepted religious indifference as well as piety. It contained a body of superstitions revolving about the "evil eye" and the use of occult powers. It contained no element of community participation or social organization beyond the family group. Although this pattern had been substantially modified before emigration among some emigrants, especially those who had lived in cities in Italy and some of those from the north who were more literate, most of those who came to America brought with them this pattern intact.

In 1930, it could still be found in Greenwich Village. A middle-aged woman from the South who was described by the young local Italian man who interviewed her as "a type prevalent in the neighborhood among the older Italians" and "the stubborn kind whose opinions you cannot budge," gave her views in no uncertain terms. According to this woman, every girl should marry, the man to be determined by the parents' choice with particular reference to the reputation of his family, his health, and his having steady work. A girl's qualifications as a wife consisted in her ability to bear many children. Prior to her marriage she should not be permitted to go out unchaperoned even with other girls or to entertain a man at her house. The husband should have complete authority in the home, and on no account should there be divorce or even separation. Parental authority must be complete. Children must obey their parents absolutely all their lives, be guided by them even after marriage, bring home to their parents all their pay if they were at work, and always be prepared to sacrifice their own interests or ambition in order to promote the welfare of the family group. A boy should be allowed a little spending money, while a girl should have none at all.

She desired no education for her children, except that they should learn a trade; a son should follow the trade of his father. It was preferable for a girl to work in a factory rather than in an office, presumably because of the necessary association with men in an office and the fact that a dress factory would call for a suitable type of manual skill. She was a devout Catholic, celebrating all Holy Days and appropriate saints' days, attending confession regularly, and sending her children to parochial school. She had retained such superstitious practices as protecting a baby with charms against the evil eye because "it is always best to be sure of everything," and insisting that a pregnant woman eat whatever her fancy dictated lest failure to do so should disfigure the child. She thought that America was not a good place to live or to raise children because there was "no respect for family or parents" and the atmosphere was "too free and instructive." Her ambitions for her children were that the boys should be good workers and respect their parents, and the girls good housewives. The outstanding change in the life of the local Italian community which she had observed was the loss of respect on the part of children. She deplored this as "un-Italian," and hoped for a return of filial love and respect. Children and a comfortable home she considered more essential to a good life than money, friends, prestige, leisure, education, or congenial work. She retained her provincial prejudices as well as her Italianness unshaken. She was opposed to intermarriage by Italians, not only with non-Italians, but also with someone from a different province. She herself did not associate with people from other parts of Italy because she "did not like them," and she not only did not think that the people of different provinces had become more friendly, but doubted that they ever would. She hoped to return to Italy to live.

Of all the elements in this traditional pattern, none has been in more fundamental conflict with the new environment than the patriarchal family. It has been under fire from practically every American institution with which it has come in contact, for, with the exception of the family welfare agencies, American institutions have normally been designed to deal with people as individuals rather than in family or other groups. Democracy, community participation, public school education, have all rested on individualistic assumptions. Recreational agencies such as settlement houses dealt with their members in individual terms, and Protestant churches have still further stressed the ultimate separateness of the individual. Activities of all types have been characteristically planned for and carried on by the several age groups rather than by young and old acting together. In the community in which this Italian population thus found itself, there was little or nothing to reinforce and everything to undermine the unity of the family group.

American pressures penetrated below its external unity and gave its internal structure a severe wrench. Whatever operated to individualize the women and the children upset their subordination to the group as a whole, and to the man who was its dominant head. As this occurred, the most fundamental of all traditional Italian relationships was destroyed. The breakdown of Italian culture can, thus, be traced in the changing position of Italian women and girls.

In many communities, immigrant women have hardly felt the direct impact of American institutions, since they have largely led their lives within the confines of their own homes. In this community, however, social agencies, and especially health agencies, undertook to reach these women in their homes and to modify their lives. Where such modifications involved only minor matters of housekeeping technique, they did not necessarily influence the family structure. But where they gave to the women independence and a sense of importance, especially where they took them out of the home, organized them into classes or clubs, and offered them recreation, or where they forced the mothers to take responsibility for decisions about the children without deferring to the head of the house, they pried these women loose from their positions within their family units.

Health agencies and recreation and church groups, during the years under review, all joined in taking the married women out of the home and building up a taste for club activities. The principal health center, starting first with baby, prenatal, and children's clinics, added classes for mothers which began to take on the aspect of clubs so completely that a group of younger women, ignoring the fact that they were dealing with a health agency, asked to have a club which could simply run dances. In connection with the kindergartens at several centers, mothers' groups all developed into social clubs which shifted their interests from the problems of their children that had first brought them together to affairs of their own. Children, in fact, were brought along and set to play in the corner or allowed to sleep in their mothers' laps while the club meeting was going on. When in 1930 one center organized a new women's club—which, significantly enough, called itself a "women's club" and not a "mothers' club" as the others had—the membership mounted rapidly. Inside of a few months it numbered 200 and at the end of six months it claimed 400 members. There was pressure during these years to turn Italian wives and mothers into American clubwomen.

The proportion of women who had joined clubs by 1930 was somewhat difficult to estimate, as membership was not drawn from a limited area and there was considerable duplication. Certainly, the great mass of Italian women, especially the older ones, belonged to no organizations. Nevertheless, several hundred women were enrolled and the men were beginning to mutter, "Oh, Italian women will join anything. . . ."

In their organizations, the women quickly developed all the attitudes and sense of importance of clubwomen. They spent a great deal of time over problems of organization, appointing committees, and planning activities. They had the requisite number of quarrels among people who were trying to run things. On one occasion an effort to hold a joint meeting of several clubs was very nearly broken up over the question of whether a woman who was a member of two clubs should walk to the meeting with one club member or the other.

The development of these clubs was opposed in the home by the more conservative men. As one husband expressed it, when a worker from the center at which the club met called to find out why his wife had not been attending, "I won't have her go because they learn her things there." This attitude, however, was absent in a sufficient number of cases to permit the enrollment of the clubs to rise rapidly. One center, in fact, reported that some husbands were actually cooperating with their wives by taking care of the children in order to enable them to attend club meetings.

Though it was not possible to make a scientific appraisal of the effect of such activity upon the women, there was no doubt that it had very importantly altered the relation of the women to their families and their homes, primarily by giving them the idea of living for themselves rather than exclusively for the family group of which they were a part. In fact, the organizer of one club whose purpose had been to give them this sense feared that the change in point of view might carry them too far. She acknowledged that she was shocked to see how selfish her group of women had become and commented, "If I really thought that this was the result of my work I should feel very much distressed."

At the same time that the American environment gave Italian women a life outside of their families, it removed the traditional basis for their prestige. In a patriarchal family, child-bearing was a woman's principal source of distinction, for the economic usefulness of children in an agricultural society, reinforced by the teaching of the Church, made a large family proverbially a blessing—"It is better to be rich in flesh than rich in goods." In the local community, pressure toward family limitation was very strong. Virtually every agency dealing with this group tacitly assumed, if it did not directly express, the position that large families were evidences of irresponsibility and foreignness and that the basis for the size of a family should be the economic capacity of the parents to support their children. When a questionnaire including a question as to how many children they wanted was submitted to a girls' club at a settlement, the girls' worker reported that she found the girls not taking the questions seriously, but putting down that they wanted six children. She upbraided them for their levity, and the questionnaires as finally filled out all gave the desired number as two. . . .

The school added its pressure by its stress on standard of living. In the words of one local young man, "They made us feel at school as if we were being actually unpatriotic—almost traitors—if we did not achieve a high standard of living." In these families, whose earnings were low, a high standard of living was incompatible with a large family, and it became almost heresy among the younger people to maintain the traditional "rich in flesh" attitude.

The burden of carrying out a changed attitude toward family limitation fell, in the older generation, entirely upon the women. The evidence from doctors and individuals consistently agreed that the older men would take no precautions. The women, moreover, were under pressure from their husbands, their tradition, and their Church not to practice birth control. The clinics, in spite of the fact that their health education pointed directly toward infrequent pregnancies, had nevertheless been scrupulous in withholding the necessary information out of regard for the fact that the community was Catholic and they were unwilling to jeopardize their position by antagonizing the Church. . . .

Among the younger generation, the traditional idea that the more children a family had the better had been very generally abandoned. Three quarters of the younger people directly questioned gave a negative answer to the question, "Do you favor large families?" That they disagreed over what constituted a "small" or a "large" family was immaterial for the purpose under discussion. Among the boys interviewed, the use of contraceptives was known and taken for granted; among the girls, somewhat less so. The attitude of the Church on the subject was not found to be of great importance to the younger Italians interviewed. There were, of course, some young people in the community, chiefly girls, who took their attitude from the instruction of the Church, but, at least among the boys, disregard of the Church on this point was widespread.

By setting up the small family as the standard, and at the same time placing legal and social obstacles in the way of securing birth-control information, the American situation was doubly destructive of the integrity of the Italian women, first by undermining their status in the family group and attacking the tenets of their Church, and second, by forcing them to resort to subterfuge and to be exposed to physical danger and exploitation in the process. The result was a state of conflict in the older generation and, among the younger generation, very frequent abandonment of the traditional attitude, and with it much that was essential to the structure of the family. Though the loss of personal integrity which this situation produced was very far from universal and did not involve the many women who were scarcely touched by these pressures it made the conflict and breakdown at this point peculiarly disorganizing—more especially as the woman had always been the stabilizing element in Italian life and as the influences of the American community were certainly not likely to give any added stability to the men. An Italian social worker who knew her people well realized the serious implications of this development. "It is important to talk about the boy as the future citizen and to develop a program of 'boys' work' and to help him," she agreed, "but what about his companion and the mother of his children who has been overlooked? We cannot afford to let these girls grow up without any focus to their lives."

It was around the position and activity of the girls who were growing up that the clash between the tradition of rural Italy and the dynamics of modern America really centered. Traditionally, a girl's marriage ability depended upon her chastity, and fear that she might lose her virginity before marriage led parents to establish the strictest sort of surveillance from the time of adolescence. Supervision, in fact, was increased at adolescence beyond that accorded to young children. When a group of seventh- and eighth-grade girls was required to go to a more distant school by the closing of upper grades in a smaller building, the mothers objected that the girls were too old to be walking such a distance, and they sent their girls to the near-by parochial school instead. Traditionally, contact between the sexes from adolescence to marriage was assumed to be solely with a view to marriage. No outside play contacts were favored and work contacts were restricted to the necessary minimum. All contacts must theoretically be made under the supervision of parents or relatives, and no man might enter the girl's home unless serious in his intention to seek her hand. All intimate acquaintance began with marriage, or, among the more lenient, with betrothal. All physical contact was regarded as defiling and was completely taboo.

There were still some girls in 1930 who actually never left the house unaccompanied by a member of the family from adolescence until marriage and who accepted the candidate of their parents' choice as husband. But every American institution and every influence with which she came into contact tended to dislodge the girl from this position and to transfer responsibility from parents to the girl herself. The school, the neighborhood, the example of everything which she read and saw, and the opportunities resulting from the necessity of going out to work all combined to make her seek the "freedom" which American girls enjoyed in place of the restrictions which were normal in her parents' eyes.

Her traditional position fitted a rural and small-town situation where marriage was a matter of families rather than of individuals, where the houses containing marriageable men were all known and the problem of each family was simple to choose among them in an effort to better their social position and landed holdings. In a strange land among strange people, the parents could not know those who were eligible for their daughter's hand. In an industrial civilization, where each marriage meant a new household rather than the carrying on of an inherited farm, marriage tended to be more an individual and less a family matter. Under these circumstances, it became extremely difficult for the parents to find suitable husbands for their daughters and for the daughters to accept as a matter of course the husbands provided for them.

This situation inevitably bred conflict and strain. The negative parts were held on to when the positive could no longer be supplied. The prohibitions on girls' going out, and particularly on their associating with men, lasted when the parents no longer had the power to find a husband which had made it unnecessary for a girl to do her own hunting. "Our parents think you can just sit home and wait for a man to come asking for your hand—like a small town in Italy. They don't realize that here a girl has got to get out and do something about it."

The situation which resulted was curious and anomalous. In the stricter families, and even in those families which had departed appreciably from the pattern and had acquired some understanding of and tolerance for American ways, it remained the rule that a girl could bring no man to the house unless he was to marry her. Even in the families where this rule had been set aside, girls still complained, "Whenever I bring a boy to the house, my father starts propositioning him." Prohibitions against going out with men alone, and, usually, even in groups, were equally rigorous. In fact, every effort was made to prevent contacts between men and girls, thereby making it most difficult for a girl to find herself a man. At the same time, she was expected to find such a man, since her parents were not in a position to do the hunting, and it was taken for granted that she would walk in some day with a man whom she never was supposed to have had the opportunity to meet and to announce, "This is the man I am going to marry." Such a method of finding a mate placed great reliance indeed upon the traditional matchmaker—Fate.

By 1930, the local community contained Italian families ranging all the way from those where the girl continued to occupy her traditional position to those where none of the traditional controls had been retained. All evidence agreed that girls were on the whole less strictly supervised and accorded more liberty than they had been in the past. Efforts to discover how far a change in this respect had permeated the community and what factors in the family situation went along with the modification of the traditional attitudes, brought out conflicting and inconclusive evidence. The one point upon which testimony was united, however, was that the relations between girls and their parents were very frequently characterized by subterfuge, defiance, or resentment—precarious foundations for the maintenance of stable family relations.

The evidence of those who had come in contact with Italian girls in the neighborhood varied according to the group with which they had been dealing. At one center, the girls' worker declared that so far as her experience was concerned, the idea that Italian girls were strictly kept was a myth. She had never had any difficulty in getting them to come to athletic clubs and there had always been enough to make her teams. On the other hand, one of the Italian priests found it difficult to fill his girls' clubs because either the parents would not let the girls out even to the church or else the girls were engaged to be married. Another worker was engaged in a special effort to overcome parental objections, running her girls' clubs as nearly in accordance with the attitudes of the mothers as was possible.

The socially élite of the metropolitan Italian community included people as eager to bring their daughters up in the old ways as the poor and "backward" laborer. The daughter of a prosperous and cultivated business man had been sent back to Italy for part of her schooling and was attending a Catholic college in the suburbs. She had made few contacts through college, however, for her friends were carefully selected by her parents from among the children of their friends. She belonged to a select Italian cultural society and her mother took immense pride in the fact that her daughter spoke Italian beautifully.

Many of the girls interviewed expressed interest in attending dances at the local settlement house, but reported that they could not do so because they were not allowed to go out to dance. Some had never danced, others only at dances given by their fathers' benefit societies.

At the opposite extreme were those who were entirely unrestricted because their parents did not pay any attention to them at all. . . .

Much more general, however, than complete parental indifference were situations in which efforts at varying degrees of supervision and restriction were met by subterfuge on the part of the girls. In probably a majority of the families, though it was not possible to establish the proportion with any certainty, the old controls were first eluded and then worn away by evasion and deception. "What mother doesn't know won't hurt her," was the standard comment of the girl who would tell her parents that she was earning less than she was and pocket the difference; who met boys around the corner if she was allowed out for a walk; who sneaked out to a dance and got home without being caught; or who went to a movie outside of the neighborhood and "happened" to find a boy friend sitting in the next seat.

Once the rigidity of restriction had been relaxed, the way was open for activities not at all within the family's code. The first step—being allowed to go down and sit on the stoop in front of the house—did not offer much opening, but to be allowed to go out for an evening stroll with another girl gave an enormous loophole. Groups of girls started out in one direction and then worked around the block so that they would meet their boy friends in a place where they would not be likely to be found. Neighborhood boys took it for granted that if they met a girl and walked with her, they would have to leave her a couple of blocks away from her door. One group of girls went night after night to a clubroom maintained by a group of boys to listen to a detective story over the radio—all as part of their "walk." A number of girls said they could slip away to a dance and get home without being caught, as they had done so before. Nearly everybody had a ready fund of stories of things that they had done in defiance of parental prescript, and the tales of how their older sisters got their men were well stocked with episodes involving deception.

Even those who were allowed to go out were required to be in at an early hour. This put them at a certain disadvantage in competition with the girls who were under fewer restrictions. Boys complained at having to deliver their companions home when the evening was still young. The girls complained that to be kept under these restrictions made it very difficult for them to find a man because boys went with girls of other nationalities, or Italian girls from other communities who were less strictly kept, while they had no chance even to go with the neighborhood boys let alone to forage outside. Boys confirmed the grounds for these complaints with accounts of their discomfort when irate parents scolded them about the hour at which they brought girls home. Among girls who were subject to the fewest restrictions, the hour of home-coming was quite universally the sorest point, probably because it was the one on which evasion was most difficult. Girls who wanted to move to another neighborhood gave as their reason the desire to escape from the lash of local gossip, for even if their own parents were lenient, the tongues of the neighbors on the solidly Italian blocks certainly were not.

Not all, however, who did not submit to the old controls and yet were not ignored completely by their parents took to deception as the normal course. Some were allowed to go out if the parents knew exactly where they were. Others were allowed to go freely to the settlement house or the dances, but they still could not go out alone with a man. Still others could go with men specifically approved by their parents. A very occasional parent was actively sympathetic with the interests of her children, like the mother of a girl interested in athletics who never missed a match game if she could help it and, when questioned about her attitude, saw nothing out of the way in it.

What girls of nearly all types were struggling for, whether successfully or unsuccessfully, was the negative advantage of freedom from restraint rather than any of the positive opportunities or responsibilities which went with a different sort of position on the part of women. Where they had acquired any positive aim, it was the bourgeois-romantic ideal—*True Story Magazine's* version of "love" and the *Ladies' Home Journal* style of a "lovely home."

Other aspects of the traditional Italian family—masculine dominance, filial obedience, and the subordination of the interests of children to the welfare of the family group—were subject to modification, while those features such as the dowry which went with the more strictly agricultural society of which it was a part were dropped. The vital point, however, was the place of women.

At other points, less essential to Italian culture but nevertheless a part of it, American influences broke down inherited attitudes and institutions. Economic pressures swiftly and completely routed the work habits which had been brought in. Neither the spirit and working conditions of American factories nor the drive of American business methods permitted the survival of the sense of craftsmanship and the high regard for manual skill which distinguished many Italian groups. Except in a few determined families which made arrangements to apprentice their children—like one man who opened a barber shop of his own in order to keep his boys off the street by apprenticing them in his shop—the second generation grew up almost entirely free from the craftsman's point of view. In the effort to make use of the traditional skills or to sharpen them, one of the local settlement houses opened a workshop in charge of an Italian master who undertook to train boys in woodcarving and stonecutting by the apprentice method. But even this organized attempt to preserve crafts and skills was faced with an economic set-up which had little place for such types of work. It was disheartening to those in charge of the shop to find scarcely any of their graduates who had been out any length of time still employed in the crafts to which they had been trained.

The Church, never so prominently a part of Italian as of other Catholic cultures, was nevertheless the one formal institution which the Italians brought with them. It had to struggle in this community against the tendency of the American-born to link it with the old culture from which they were breaking away. Its effort to maintain itself by out-Americanizing the Americans is a story in itself.

A very few families were drawn away from their Church completely and brought within the Protestant fold by the work of Protestant missions. These were introduced to the traditional American pattern in a somewhat more coherent form, but a form which took little or no account of the newer influences which were modifying the attitudes of the American community. For most who attended the Protestant missions without, however, turning Protestant, the influence of these centers did not go beyond that exerted by schools and non-sectarian agencies to disrupt the old attitudes without introducing a body of new ones.

One of the adjectives which the young "Americanized" element was most ready to apply to the older generation was "superstitious." The type of superstition most at variance with the institutions of the American community was that which substituted the practice of magic for scientific medicine. In view of the statement from all sides that these superstitions had been dropped by an increasing proportion of people in the neighborhood, efforts were made to discover how far witchcraft had survived and charms were still used. It was very difficult to get people to talk about witches and fortune-tellers, and their very hesitancy revealed the fear which they felt for the power of the witch or *strega*. One woman acknowledged that her daughter had gone to a *strega* to secure a powder to put on her pay envelope so that her pay would not be cut, while others had sought love potions. Doctors and health centers still complained of the patronage of witches, although one doctor reported that for some time he had not seen a case of mumps with the black marks which the witch made behind the ears.

Some who ceased to use horns, fishes, or red string as charms against the evil eye substituted religious medals to secure the protection of God and the aid of the Saints. The most general form of this was the habitual carrying of the picture of Saint Christopher by all who had cars or were in the habit of driving. In some cases there seemed to be an important distinction between the use of charms and religious medals, but in others they were regarded as essentially the same—either potent or evidence of superstition. Some of the younger generation who dropped away from the Church altogether classed all religious observances with the rest of their parents' traditional beliefs as "superstitions."

Certain practices which were considered superstitious or which were part of an older medical tradition came into conflict with the health practices prescribed by the agencies in the locality. . . . Since health standards were among the American attitudes most vigorously forced to the attention of the immigrants and were among the things most easily recognized by them as "American," the pressure to disregard superstitious beliefs and practices was strong. Their interrelation with religion and the basic insecurity of the immigrant group which made every possible aid seem important, however, tended to permit the survival of these beliefs.

Customs which were not in conflict with local conditions survived, while the more basic social attitudes did not. Spaghetti remained the staple in the diet, and the social worker who valued her relation with her client was well advised not to try to stop her from "wasting" money on good olive oil. Weddings continued to be celebrated in the customary manner, with the guests giving presents in money which were counted on to more than defray the expense of the affair. Customs which were attached to the land and those, such as swaddling, which were directly attacked by local agencies, did not survive.

Neither the absolute extent to which the Italian culture pattern was modified, nor the rate of change could be determined, for there was no adequate measuring stick by which to test the degree of modification. It was possible, however, to get some indication of the kinds of distortion resulting from the fact that traditional attitudes had broken down much more thoroughly and more generally at certain points than at others. The process of distortion was not confined to the post-War years, but had been going on ever since the group arrived in America. In these years, however, influences combined to hasten the shift, and other influences which had retarded it disappeared. It was only after the War that large numbers of children reached maturity; that the community shifted its orientation from Europe to America with the cessation of immigration and the decision of many to make their American residence permanent; that their lives were invaded by radio crooners and Villagers.

In an effort to determine where the pattern was crumbling fastest and where it was holding most firm, an interview schedule was drawn up and used by local Italians with 144 local residents. Younger residents were especially sought, since they were most involved in the shift. Ninety-three of the 144 cases were between 18 and 35 years of age and 51 were over 35. The sample was biased partly by accident and partly by design, in the direction of those who were more self-conscious and articulate, better educated and more Americanized than the mass of the community. For a study of the cultural disequilibrium which has been produced in the Italian community by contact with the American influences, these interviews reached the appropriate element, for unless future developments should thrust the immigrant group farther back into its ghetto, American influences can be expected to spread through those who have made the first contacts and adjustments.

The results of these interviews were in no sense a measure of the absolute extent of disintegration. Because 60 per cent of those interviewed maintained a certain attitude, there was no reason to assume that 60 per cent of the community shared that attitude. But by comparing the questions with each other, it was possible to see where the process of modification was proceeding fastest and where more slowly. If 90 per cent of the answers repudiated one attitude and only 40 per cent another, there was at least *prima-facie* evidence that the first was breaking down more rapidly than the second.

Direction of the Distortion of the Italian Culture Pattern
PROPORTION WHOSE ANSWERS DEPARTED FROM THE TRADITIONAL PATTERN[a]

	Over[b] 35 years	Under[c] 35 years
Family		
Does *not* believe that:		
Marriages should be arranged by parents	70%	99%
Large families are a blessing	48%	86%
Girls should not associate with men unless engaged	45%	83%
Husband's authority should be supreme	34%	64%
A child should sacrifice his personal ambition to welfare of family group	31%	54%
Divorce is never permissible	12%	61%
Children owe absolute obedience to parents	2%	15%
Church		
Person does not attend church	4%	16%
Person does not observe Holy Days of Obligation	33%	70%
Superstitions		
Does not believe in either "evil eye" or superstition about pregnancy	40%	61%
Does not believe in "evil eye" (though may about pregnancy)	70%	81%
Does not believe in pregnancy superstition (though may believe in "evil eye")	46%	69%
Italian Civilization		
Cannot dance Italian dances	58%	93%
Cannot name familiar Italian operas	15%	9%
Cannot name familiar Italian songs	8%	15%
Unable to speak Italian language[d]	57%	50%
Cannot name great Italian artist, scientist	3%	2%
Italian Neighborhood		
Italian neighborhood not preferred	49%	72%
American neighborhood	9%	28%

[a]144 questionnaires. Where question is not answered, the percent of those answering has been taken.
[b]51 cases.
[c]93 cases.
[d]Knowledge of Italian vernacular, not dialect.

This inquiry showed that different aspects of the patriarchal family institution were breaking down at different rates, those which had been bound up with land and family estate—i.e., the arrangement of marriage by parents and the giving of dowries—going the fastest. The younger people were nearly unanimous, and over two-thirds of the older agreed, that the choice of a husband should fall to the girl rather than to her parents. The younger people had clearly dropped the idea that marriage involved a union of families and had adopted the bourgeois-romantic assumption that it united individuals, for they included only personal attributes among the qualifications of a good husband or wife, while a majority of the older group regarded the reputation of the girl or man's family as an important consideration. There was some slight indication that the man had become more completely individualized and distinguished from the family group than the girl in the fact that a few among the younger element included family reputation as a consideration in viewing a girl's qualifications, but none regarded it as relevant in the case of the man.

The central patriarchal assumption that large families are a blessing had broken down only less completely than the idea that marriage unites families rather than individuals. Again it was the younger group that had repudiated the assumption, but half of the older group joined in this view. The difference between the older men and women hinted that social influences weighed in this shift rather than the economic consideration that children were less likely to be economic assets under city conditions. Although the younger people, and many of the older, had ceased to regard children as an economic asset, many still, in 1930, did not look upon them as heavy economic burdens. . . .

The positive drive toward a higher standard of living was a more potent influence in making a small family the ideal than the fear of being unable to support children. The girls, especially, longed for a nice home and escape from the "dumps" in which they had been brought up. All evidence agreed in indicating that a home was the central interest in marriage for local girls of all types, and Italian girls were no exception. The homes of girls who had married and left the locality reflected care, effort, expenditure, and the influence of advertisements. . . .

Personal appearance was also part of the higher standard of living. "I wouldn't think of letting my appearance go after I married," declared a carefully dressed young girl. She and her friends intended to continue to spend money on themselves after marriage. Nor did they expect to sacrifice their own pleasures in order to be like their mothers who didn't have a chance even to go to a show.

There were no indications that any idea of a "career" attracted Italian girls as an alternative to complete absorption with childrearing. One Italian woman lawyer was found who resented having to give the necessary time and attention to her child because of her professional interest, but the case appeared to be virtually unique.

All agreed that the only reason why a girl might work after marriage would be economic, in order to provide a better home. The alternative value which the young Italian had substituted for the traditional pride in many children was a high standard of material culture.

There were even some—more than a third of the younger group and a tenth of the older—who were ready to apply the term "successful" to a marriage where there were no children at all. Here was a striking confirmation of the extent to which the patriarchal ideal had broken down with respect to its chief purpose—the raising of children.

The younger group had discarded the principle that there should be no free association between boys and girls before marriage nearly as generally as they had the larger family ideal. Among the older group, too, this part of the traditional code was next in the frequency with which it had been dropped.

Masculine authority continued to be accepted by a larger proportion than held to the ideal of a large family, but it was challenged by two-thirds of the younger and a third of the older groups. Again the women in both age groups were, quite naturally this time, more opposed to the traditional attitude than the men. Though professed views on this score may frequently not have accorded with practice—women refusing to acknowledge an authority which in practice they accepted, and men asserting a position which factually they could not maintain—there was little doubt that the head of the household would have to be alert in order to maintain his traditional position and exact unquestioning obedience from his wife.

Masculine authority was still strongly enough entrenched for social agencies to find it impracticable to go against it in working out their program for a family. One of the health centers introduced night visiting because it felt that its educational work with the mother was ineffective unless the husband's support was gained. Another agency reported cases of refusing to act at the request of the wife, even though its judgment concurred with hers, unless the husband were agreed. But the traditional authority had begun to be referred to as "tyranny" by some of the younger members of the Italian community. . . .

But though the individual rather than the family group had become the center as far as marriage itself was concerned, and slightly less so in the drift away from the large family principle and in the challenge to masculine domination, over two-thirds of the older, and nearly half of the younger group, maintained that a child would be expected to sacrifice his own ambition and advancement to the interests of the family group—interrupting his educational or his professional career to aid the family, for instance. For many of the families of the locality, the question was a purely academic one because family need was so great that the child could not choose but aid if called on to do so. . . .

Parental authority was not called into question with anything like the frequency of other relationships. The older group was practically unanimous in expecting absolute obedience from children, at least to the age of about eighteen, and all except a seventh of the younger group agreed, frequently admitting that it was due up to marriage and even beyond. Among all the young Italians encountered in the course of the study, respect and obedience were taken for granted in principle, however little they might be observed in fact.

Though children were ashamed of their parents and though those parents failed in their responsibility to their children, the filial relation remained, and parental authority was entitled to recognition. The father who came home drunk, beat up the mother, was mean to the children, and was entitled to little or no respect as a human being, was still to be looked at by his children as a father and honored accordingly.

The two aspects of the traditional family least subject to question in the older group were its absolute permanency and its economic solidarity. The younger element agreed in placing the economic unity of the family group among the features unanimously retained, but it was far more ready to admit the dissolution of the family bonds. Only 12 per cent of the elders admitted divorce on any count, though some were willing to accept a separation. Sixty-one per cent of the younger element, on the other hand, expressed themselves as not wholly opposed to divorce. The difference between younger and older was greater on this score than on any other. This difference was doubly significant in that tolerance of divorce by the younger people reflected the weakening of the hold of the Catholic Church on the group questioned as well as the loosening of the family ties. The attitude on the question of divorce was closely correlated with the attitude of the individual toward the Church, but it did not follow the latter exactly. Where the permanence of the marriage bond was firmly maintained, the motive was not always religious scruples, but frequently a conviction, independent of the Church's teaching, that the family was too valuable an institution to break on any account. The women, as might be expected, were less willing to admit of divorce than the men, both because their lot was more closely tied up with the family and because of their greater adherence to the Church.

In the matter of the economic solidarity of the group, the low income level of the families in the locality readily accounted for the unanimity of the entire 144 in agreeing that the earnings of a working child should go toward the family's support, but contributing these earnings had a social as well as an economic sanction. The only question was whether all the earnings should be so devoted or only a part turned in and the rest retained. The latter arrangement was favored by half of the younger persons, but admitted by few of the older ones. Cases of family friction over the disposition of the children's earnings were found, but on the whole the principle of economic solidarity seemed to have been so firmly grounded that money disagreements did not constitute a major source of friction in the Italian home. . . .

Distortion of the central Italian cultural institution, the patriarchal family, thus involved the loss of its central drive—many children—and the partial individualization of its members, especially in the courtship and marriage relationship. Subordination, obedience, and responsibility of children to the group and, especially, their parents, continued, and was reinforced by economic necessity which remained the strongest binding force. The elements which tended to survive were those common to the patriarchal and the bourgeois-romantic family forms—male superiority, permanence, filial respect. Those who had departed from the traditional attitudes on the points most frequently discarded had almost as little in common with the Villagers who held by the independence of women and a highly individualized, experimental family form as had their more patriarchal elders.

Though the group as a whole had abandoned Italian social attitudes on many points, it had retained a sense, at least, of Italian culture. Few, either old or young, were unable to name promptly Italian songs which they knew,

Italian operas with which they were familiar, and great Italian artists or scientists who had made their mark on the world. The circulation of Italian books at the local public library branch, after falling off by 57 per cent from 1920 to 1926, increased again by almost 50 per cent of the 1926 low figure between that year and 1930.

Only half of the younger, however, and an even smaller proportion of the older, could speak the Italian language, other than a local dialect. Folk culture, moreover, had not been imported. Scarcely any of the younger, and less than half of the older, knew how to dance such traditional Italian dances as the tarantella or the quadrille.

The group questioned was not interested in maintaining solidarity with its Italian compatriots, at least as far as living among them was concerned. Half of the older, and nearly three-quarters of the younger, had no preference for an Italian neighborhood as a place to live. In fact, 9 per cent of the older, and 28 per cent of the younger, specified to the contrary—that they definitely preferred the American to an Italian locality.

When the various aspects of the pattern are put together and compared for their differential rates of change, distortion of the whole becomes apparent. Institutions difficult to maintain and at most direct variance with the environment, such as arranged marriages, were going fastest. Distinctive forms of amusement, as represented by Italian dances, were disappearing as far as the younger group was concerned. The husband's authority was being undermined while parental authority was maintained. The assumption that many children are a blessing was being dropped more generally than the attitude that the interests of the family group are paramount over the interests of the child. The lapse in church observance was not keeping pace with the spread of the idea of family limitation, but it was going farther than the acceptance of divorce. Indifference to living in an Italian neighborhood was slightly greater than the average of the divergences on specific points—perhaps a reflection of the corresponding desire to be free from community pressure to Italian conformity. Although some superstitions were being widely abandoned, others were persisting, and less difference appeared between young and old on this than on important points of conduct. The evil eye was surviving American pressures slightly more successfully than was the large family or the supervision of girls, as far as the younger element was concerned.

As between younger and older groups important differences in rates of change appeared. Whereas the younger group quite naturally departed more generally from the tradition than did the older, it was moving relatively faster on some points than on others. This was especially true in respect to divorce, where the difference between the per cent of younger and of older approving of divorce was 49 per cent as against an average of 25 per cent by which the younger exceeded the older group in its divergence on the items listed under family, church, and superstitions. Large families too, were disproportionately opposed by the younger group, as were restrictions on girls. The younger were also relatively more negligent in church attendance, though not in complete disregard of church observances. In respect to superstitions and to the obedience and submission of children, they were relatively closer to the older group than on the other points.

Among the older group, the men were stronger in their support of virtually everything relating to the traditional patriarchal family than the women. The latter remained relatively more religious than their husbands, doubtless because they started so in Italy. Among the younger ones, there was little difference between the sexes on any point except, quite naturally, the husband's authority, approval of divorce, and loyalty to the Church. While the younger men showed greater sympathy with masculine dominance than the young women, they were more ready to approve of divorce and to neglect their religious duties.

There was some noticeable difference between North and South Italians, but less than the familiar generalizations about them would lead one to expect. The southerners were more favorably disposed toward large families, were more ready to maintain the husband's authority, and took more account of family reputation in considering the qualifications of a husband or wife. On parental authority, divorce, and the supervision of girls, however, this sample showed no important difference between southerners and northerners. The former were slightly more faithful in matters of religion and more tenacious of superstitions about pregnancy, but no more in awe of the evil eye. . . . But this material indicated that those differences tended to be unimportant in the adaptation of the younger group which had been subjected to Americanizing influences.

THE THIRD GENERATION:
SEARCH FOR CONTINUITY

Marcus L. Hansen

BY LONG ESTABLISHED CUSTOM whoever speaks of immigration must refer to it as a "problem." It was a problem to the first English pioneers in the New World scattered up and down the Atlantic coast. Whenever a vessel anchored in the James River and a few score weary and emaciated gentlemen, worn out by three months upon the Atlantic, stumbled up the bank, the veterans who had survived Nature's rigorous "seasoning" looked at one another in despair and asked: "Who is to feed them? Who is to teach them to fight the Indians, or grow tobacco, or clear the marshy lands and build a home in the malaria-infested swamps? These immigrants certainly are a problem." And three hundred years later when in the course of a summer more than a million Europeans walked down the gangplanks of the ocean greyhounds into the large reception halls built to receive them, government officials, social workers, journalists said: "How are these people from the peasant farms of the Mediterranean going to adjust themselves to the routine of mines and industries, and how are they going to live in a country where the language is strange, and how are they, former subjects of monarchs and lords, going to partake in the business of governing themselves? These immigrants certainly are a problem."

They certainly were. The adventurers (call them colonists or immigrants) who transferred civilization across the Atlantic numbered more than forty million souls. Every one of them was a problem to his family and himself, to the officials and landlords from whom he parted, to the officials and land-lords whom he joined. On every mile of the journey, on land and on sea, they caused concern to someone. The public authorities at the ports of embarkation sighed the traditional sigh of relief when the emigrant vessel was warped away from the dock and stood out to the open sea carrying the bewildered persons who for a week or more had wandered about the streets; the captain of that vessel was happy when the last of his passengers who had complained of everything from food to weather said good-bye—often with a clenched fist; and the officers of New York and Baltimore were no less happy when the newly-arrived American set out for the West. How much of a problem the forty million actually were will not be known until their history is written with realism as well as sympathy.

The problem of the immigrant was not solved; it disappeared. Foreign-born to the number of almost fifteen million are still part of the American population, but they are no longer immigrants. By one adjustment after the other they have accommodated themselves and reconciled themselves to the surrounding world of society, and when they became what the natives called "Americanized" (which was often nothing but a treaty of peace with society) they ceased to be a problem. This was the normal evolution of an individual, but as long as the group classified as immigrants was being constantly recruited by the continual influx of Europeans the problem remained. The quota law of 1924 erected the first dam against the current, and the depression of 1929 cut off the stream entirely. Statistics reveal what has happened. During the year ended June 30, 1936, there were admitted as immigrants only 36,329 aliens. During the same period 35,817 aliens left the United States for permanent residence abroad—a net gain of only 512. But this was the first year since 1931 that there had been any gain at all. The great historic westward tide of Europeans has come to an end and there is no indication in American conditions or sentiment that it will ever be revived.

Thus there has been removed from the pages of magazines, from the debates in Congress, and from the thoughts of social workers the well-known expression: the problem of the immigrant. Its going has foreshadowed the disappearance of a related matter of concern which was almost as troublesome as the first, a rather uncertain worry which was called "the problem of the second generation."

The sons and the daughters of the immigrants were really in a most uncomfortable position. They were subjected to the criticism and taunts of the native Americans and to the criticism and taunts of their elders as well. All who exercised any authority over them found fault with the response. Too often in the schoolroom the Yankee schoolmistress regarded them as mere dullards hardly worthy of her valuable attention. Thus neglected they strayed about the streets where the truant officer picked them up and reported them as incorrigible. The delinquency of the second generation was talked about so incessantly that finally little Fritz and little Hans became convinced that they were not like the children from the other side of the tracks. They were not slow in comprehending the source of all their woes; it lay in the strange dualism into which they had been born.

Life at home was hardly more pleasant. Whereas in the schoolroom they were too foreign, at home they were too American. Even the immigrant father who compromised most willingly in adjusting his outside affairs to the realities that surrounded him insisted that family life, at least, should retain the pattern that he had known as a boy. Language, religion, customs, and parental authority were not to be modified simply because the home had been moved four or five thousand miles to the westward. When the son and the daughter refused to conform, their action was considered a rebellion of ungrateful children for whom so many advantages had been provided. The gap between the two generations was widened and the family spirit was embittered by repeated misunderstanding. How to inhabit two worlds at the same time was the problem of the second generation.

That problem was solved by escape. As soon as he was free economically, an independence that usually came several years before he was free legally, the son struck out for himself. He wanted to forget everything: the foreign language that left an unmistakable trace in his English speech, the religion that continually recalled childhood struggles, the family customs that should have been the happiest of all memories. He wanted to be away from all physical reminders of early days, in an environment so different, so American, that all associates naturally assumed that he was an American as they. This picture has been deliberately overdrawn, but who will deny that the second generation wanted to forget, and even when the ties of family affection were strong, wanted to lose as many of the evidences of foreign origin as they could shuffle off?

Most easy to lose was that which, if retained, might have meant the most to the civilization of the American republic. The immigrant brought with him European culture. This does not mean that the man who wielded the pickaxe was really a Michael Angelo or that the one who took to house painting was in fact an unrecognized Rembrandt. They brought a popular though uncritical appreciation of art and music; they felt at home in an environment where such aspects of culture were taken for granted and (what is not to be overlooked in any consideration of the development of American life) they did not subscribe to the prevailing American sentiment that it was not quite moral for a strong, able-bodied man to earn his living by playing a fiddle. If they did not come in loaded down with culture, at least they were plentifully supplied with the seeds of culture that, scattered in a fertile soil, could flourish mightily.

The soil was not fertile. Americans of the nineteenth century were not entirely unfriendly to a little art now and then if it were limited to the front parlor and restricted to the women. Even a man might play a little, sing a little, and paint a little if he did it in a straightforward, wholesome way and for relaxation only. But these foreigners, most of whom had been in Paris and set up what they called a studio where they dawdled away the hours, day and night, were not to be trusted. Let them earn their living by doing a man's work instead of singing arias at the meetings of the woman's club in the middle of the afternoon or giving piano lessons to the young girls, thereby taking away the source of livelihood from the village spinster who also gave lessons and willingly sang for nothing. The second generation was entirely aware of the contempt in which such activities were held and they hastened to prove that they knew nothing about casts, symphonies, or canvas. Nothing was more Yankee than a Yankeeized person of foreign descent.

The leaders among the natives proclaimed loudly: It is wonderful how these young people catch the spirit of American institutions. The leaders among the foreign-born sighed and said to themselves: This apostasy means nothing good. It is not good for the sons and daughters who give up a heritage richer than farm acres and city lots; it is not good for this uncouth pioneer nation which has spent its time chopping down trees and rolling stones and has never learned how the genius of one might brighten the life of many and satisfy some human longings that corn bread and apple pie can never appease. Blind, stupid America, they said, the one nation of the globe which has had offered to it the rich gifts that every people of Europe brought and laid at its feet and it spurned them all. The immigrants, perhaps, may be excused. Their thoughts and efforts were taken up with material cares and they were naturally under some suspicion. But nothing can absolve the traitors of the second generation who deliberately threw away what had been preserved in the home. When they are gone all the hope will be lost and the immigration of the nineteenth century will have contributed nothing to the development of America but what came out of the strong muscles of a few million patient plodders.

These pessimists were wrong. All has not been lost. After the second generation comes the third and with the third appears a new force and a new opportunity which, if recognized in time, can not only do a good job of salvaging but probably can accomplish more than either the first or the second could ever have achieved.

Anyone who has the courage to codify the laws of history must include what can be designated "the principle of third generation interest." The principle is applicable in all fields of historical study. It explains the recurrence of movements that seemingly are dead; it is a factor that should be kept in mind particularly in literary or cultural history; it makes it possible for the present to know something about the future.

The theory is derived from the almost universal phenomenon that what the son wishes to forget the grandson wishes to remember. The tendency might be illustrated by a hundred examples. The case of the Civil War may be cited. The Southerners who survived the four years of that struggle never forgot. In politics and in conversation the "lost cause" was an endless theme. Those who listened became weary and the sons of the Confederate veterans were among them. *That* second generation made little effort to justify the action of their fathers. Their expressed opinion was that, after all, the result was inevitable and undoubtedly for the best. These sons went North and won success in every field of business and in every branch of learning. But now the grandsons of the Confederates rule in the place of the sons and there is no apologizing for the events of 1861; instead there is a belligerency that asserts the moral and constitutional justice of their grandfathers' policy. The South has been revived. Its history is taught with a fervid patriotism in the universities and schools. Recently there has been formed the Southern Historical Association as an evidence of the growing interest. The great novel of the Civil War and Reconstruction era was not written by one who had participated in the events or witnessed the scenes. It did not come from the pen of one who had listened to a father's reminiscences. *Gone with the Wind* was written by a granddaughter of the Confederacy, in the year 1936, approximately sixty years after the period with which it dealt had come to an end.

Immigration not only has its history, it has its historiography. The writing of descriptions of that great epic movement began almost as early as the movement itself. Every immigrant letter written from new shores was history, very personal and very uncritical. Every sheaf of reminiscences written by one of the participants in his later years was also history, a little more uncritical. There was much to be recounted and since sons would not listen the grayheaded participants got together and, organized as pioneer societies, they told one another of the glorious deeds that they had seen and sometimes performed and listened to the reading of the obituaries of the giants that had fallen. When the last of them had joined his ancestors the pioneer society automatically disbanded, leaving behind as the first chapter of immigrant historiography a conglomerate mass of literature, much and often most of it useless. All of it seemed useless to the son who cleared out his father's desk, and he resolved not to waste any of his time on such pointless pursuits.

As a broad generalization it may be said that the second generation is not interested in and does not write any history. That is just another aspect of their policy of forgetting. Then, however, appears the "third generation." They have no reason to feel any inferiority when they look about them. They are American born. Their speech is the same as that of those with whom they associate. Their material wealth is the average possession of the typical citizen. When anyone speaks to them about immigrants he always makes it clear that he has in mind the more recent hordes that have been pouring through the gates and any suggestion that the onrush should be stemmed is usually prefaced with the remark that recent immigrants are not so desirable as the pioneers that arrived in earlier times. It is in an attitude of pride that the substantial landowner or merchant looks about him and says: "This prosperity is our achievement, that of myself and of my fathers; it is a sign of the hardy stock from which we have sprung; who were they and why did they come?" And so their curiosity is projected back into the family beginnings. Those who are acquainted with the universities of the Middle West, where a large proportion of the students are grandchildren and great-grandchildren of the nineteenth century immigrants can sense this attitude of inquiry and can not escape the feeling of pride in which they study the history and culture of the nations from which their ancestors came.

To show how universal this spirit has been we can retrace some periodic resurgences of national spirit and relate them to the time of immigration. There were Irishmen in America before the Revolution, but there is no reason to question the generalization that until 1840 two-thirds of the emigrants from Ireland were the so-called Scotch-Irish. In the 1830's their influx was particularly large; in fact, the great proportion of Ulstermen who came to America arrived in the course of that decade. Sixty years later (at the time of the third generation) a renaissance of Scotch-Irish sentiment in the United States was strikingly apparent. Local societies were formed that met in monthly or quarterly conclave to sing the praises of their forbears and to glory in the achievements of the Presbyterian Church. Beginning in 1889, and continuing for more than a decade, representatives of these societies met in an annual national meeting called a "Scotch-Irish Congress." Then the movement lost its impetus. Leaders died or took up other activities; members refrained from paying dues; attendance at sessions dwindled. After 1903 no more Scotch-Irish congresses were held.

We can pass to another example. The large German immigration reached its crest in the late 1840's and early 1850's. A little over half a century later, in the first decade of the twentieth century, a breeze of historical interest stirred the German-American community. One of the number was moved to offer a prize for the best historical discussion of the contribution of the German element to American life. Not only the prize-winning work (the well-known volume by A. B. Faust) but many of the manuscripts that had been submitted in the competition were published, forming a library of German-American activity in many fields. Several local and state historical societies were formed, and the study of German literature in universities and schools enjoyed an amazing popularity that later observers could ascribe only to the propaganda of an intriguing nation. The Theodore Roosevelt Professorship established at the University of Berlin in 1907 was an expression of the same revival. The war naturally put an end to this activity and obscured much of the valuable work that the investigators had performed.

. . . The large Scandinavian immigration began in the 1850's, and after the interruption of the Civil War reached its culmination in the 1880's. True to expectations we find that at present the most lively interest in history of this nature is exhibited in Scandinavian circles in America. Among Scandinavians, Norwegians were pioneers and in historical research they are also a step in advance. The Swedes came a little later and an intelligent prophet of that period, looking forward to the cultural development of the nationality in their new home, would have said: "About 1930 a historical society will be formed." It was. In June, 1930, the Augustana Historical Society was organized among the members of the Augustana Synod which so faithfully represents the more than a million people of Swedish descent who are citizens of the American republic. . . .

As problems go, the problem of the third generation immigrant is not one to cause worry or to be shunned. It has none of the bitterness or heart-breaking features of its predecessors. It is welcome. In summary form it may be stated as follows: Whenever any immigrant group reaches the third genera-tion stage in its development a spontaneous and almost irresistible impulse arises which forces the thoughts of many people of different professions, different positions in life, and different points of view to interest themselves in that one factor which they have in common: heritage—the heritage of blood. The problem is: how can this impulse be organized and directed so that the results growing therefrom will be worthy of the high instincts from which it has sprung and a dignified tribute to the pioneers, and at the same time be a contribution to the history of the United States which has received all Europeans on a basis of equality and which should record their achieve-ments in the same spirit of impartiality.

CULTURAL COMPONENTS IN RESPONSES TO PAIN

Mark Zborowski

THIS PAPER REPORTS on one aspect of a larger study: that concerned with discovering the role of cultural patterns in attitudes towards and reactions to pain which is caused by disease and injury—in other words, responses to spontaneous pain.

Some Basic Distinctions. In human societies biological processes vital for man's survival acquire social and cultural significance. Intake of food, sexual intercourse or elimination—physiological phenomena which are universal for the entire living world—become institutions regulated by cultural and social norms, thus fulfilling not only biological functions but social and cultural ones as well. Metabolic and endocrinal changes in the human organism may provoke hunger and sexual desire, but culture and society dictate to man the kind of food he may eat, the social setting for eating or the adequate partner for mating.

Moreover, the role of cultural and social patterns in human physiological activities is so great that they may in specific situations act against the direct biological needs of the individual, even to the point of endangering his survival. Only a human being may prefer starvation to the breaking of a religious dietary law or may abstain from sexual intercourse because of specific incest regulations. Voluntary fasting and celibacy exist only where food and sex fulfill more than strictly physiological functions.

Thus, the understanding of the significance and role of social and cultural patterns in human physiology is necessary to clarify those aspects of human experience which remain puzzling if studied only within the physiological frame of reference.

Pain is basically a physiological phenomenon and as such has been studied by physiologists and neurologists such as Harold Wolff, James Hardy, Helen Goodell, C. S. Lewis, W. K. Livingston and others. By using the most ingenious methods of investigation they have succeeded in clarifying complex problems of the physiology of pain. Many aspects of perception and reaction to pain were studied in experimental situations involving most careful preparation and complicated equipment. These investigators have come to the conclusion that "from the physiological point of view pain qualifies as a sensation of importance to the self-preservation of the individual."[1] The biological function of pain is to provoke special reactive patterns directed toward avoidance of the noxious stimulus which presents a threat to the individual. In this respect the function of pain is basically the same for man as for the rest of the animal world.

However, the physiology of pain and the understanding of the biological function of pain do not explain other aspects of what Wolff, Hardy and

Reprinted from the *Journal of Social Issues* (No. 4, 1952), pp. 16-30, by permission of the author and the publisher. (Copyright, 1952, by the Society for the Psychological Study of Social Issues.)

Goodell call the *pain experience,* which includes not only the pain sensation and certain automatic reactive responses but also certain "associated feeling states."[2] It would not explain, for example, the acceptance of intense pain in torture, which is part of the initiation rites of many primitive societies, nor will it explain the strong emotional reactions of certain individuals to the slight sting of the hypodermic needle.

In human society, pain, like so many other physiological phenomena, acquires specific social and cultural significance, and, accordingly, certain reactions to pain can be understood in the light of this significance. As Drs. Hardy, Wolff and Goodell state in their recent book, ". . . the culture in which a man finds himself becomes the conditioning influence in the formation of the individual reaction patterns to pain. . . . A knowledge of group attitudes toward pain is extremely important to an understanding of the individual reaction."[3]

In analyzing pain it is useful to distinguish between self-inflicted, other-inflicted and spontaneous pain. Self-inflicted pain is defined as deliberately self-inflicted. It is experienced as a result of injuries performed voluntarily upon oneself, e.g., self-mutilation. Usually these injuries have a culturally defined purpose, such as achieving a special status in the society. It can be observed not only in primitive cultures but also in contemporary societies on a higher level of civilization. In Germany, for instance, members of certain student or military organizations would cut their faces with a razor in order to acquire scars which would identify them as members of a distinctive social group. By other-inflicted pain is meant pain inflicted upon the individual in the process of culturally accepted and expected activities (regardless of whether approved or disapproved), such as sports, fights, war, etc. To this category belongs also pain inflicted by the physician in the process of medical treatment. Spontaneous pain usually denotes the pain sensation which results from disease or injury. This term also covers pains of psychogenic nature.

Members of different cultures may assume differing attitudes towards these various types of pain. Two of these attitudes may be described as pain expectancy and pain acceptance. Pain expectancy is anticipation of pain as being unavoidable in a given situation, for instance, in childbirth, in sports activities or in battle. Pain acceptance is characterized by a willingness to experience pain. This attitude is manifested mostly as an inevitable component of culturally accepted experiences, for instance, as part of initiation rites or part of medical treatment. The following example will help to clarify the differences between pain expectancy and pain acceptance: Labor pain is expected as part of childbirth, but while in one culture, such as in the United States, it is not accepted and therefore various means are used to alleviate it, in some other cultures, for instance in Poland, it is not only expected but also accepted, and consequently nothing or little is done to relieve it. Similarly, cultures which emphasize military achievements expect and accept battle wounds, while cultures which emphasize pacifistic values may expect them but will not accept them.

In the process of investigating cultural attitudes toward pain it is also important to distinguish between pain apprehension and pain anxiety. Pain apprehension reflects the tendency to avoid the pain sensation as such, regardless of whether the pain is spontaneous or inflicted, whether it is accepted or not. Pain anxiety, on the other hand, is a state of anxiety provoked by the pain experience, focused upon various aspects of the causes of pain, the meaning of pain or its significance for the welfare of the individual.

Moreover, members of various cultures may react differently in terms of their manifest behavior toward various pain experiences, and this behavior is often dictated by the culture which provides specific norms according to the age, sex and social position of the individual.

The fact that other elements as well as cultural factors are involved in the response to a spontaneous pain should be taken into consideration. These other factors are the pathological aspect of pain, the specific physiological characteristics of the pain experience, such as the intensity, the duration and the quality of the pain sensation, and, finally, the personality of the individual. Nevertheless, it was felt that in the process of a careful investigation it would be possible to detect the role of the cultural components in the pain experience.

The Research Setting. In setting up the research we were interested not only in the purely theoretical aspects of the findings in terms of possible contribution to the understanding of the pain experience in general; we also had in mind the practical goal of a contribution to the field of medicine. In the relationship between a doctor and his patient the respective attitudes toward pain may play a crucial role, especially when the doctor feels that the patient exaggerates his pain while the patient feels that the doctor minimizes his suffering. The same may be true, for instance, in a hospital where the members of the medical and nursing staff may have attitudes toward pain different from those held by the patient, or when they expect a certain pattern of behavior according to their cultural background while the patient may manifest a behavior pattern which is acceptable in his culture. These differences may play an important part in the evaluation of the individual pain experience, in dealing with pain at home and in the hospital, in administration of analgesics, etc. Moreover, we expected that this study of pain would offer opportunities to gain insight into related attitudes toward health, disease, medication, hospitalization, medicine in general, etc.

With these aims in mind the project was set up at the Kingsbridge Veterans Hospital, Bronx, New York, where four ethno-cultural groups were selected for an intensive study. These groups included patients of Jewish, Italian, Irish and "Old American" stock. Three groups—Jews, Italians and Irish—were selected because they were described by medical people as manifesting striking differences in their reaction to pain. Italians and Jews were described as tending to "exaggerate" their pain, while the Irish were often depicted as stoical individuals who are able to take a great deal of pain. The fourth group, the "Old Americans," were chosen because the values and attitudes of this group dominate in the country and are held by many members of the medical profession and by many descendants of the immigrants who, in the process of Americanization, tend to adopt American patterns of behavior. The members of this group can be defined as white, native-born individuals, usually Protestant, whose grandparents, at least, were born in the United States and who do not identify themselves with any foreign group, either nationally, socially or culturally.

The Kingsbridge Veterans Hospital was chosen because its population represents roughly the ethnic composition of New York City, thus offering access to a fair sample of the four selected groups, and also because various age groups were represented among the hospitalized veterans of World War I, World War II and the Korean War. In one major respect this hospital was not adequate, namely, in not offering the opportunity to investigate sex differences in attitude toward pain. This aspect of research will be carried out in a hospital with a large female population.

In setting up this project we were mainly interested in discovering certain regularities in reactions and attitudes toward pain characteristic of the four groups. Therefore, the study has a qualitative character, and the efforts of the researchers were not directed toward a collection of material suitable for quantitative analysis. The main techniques used in the collection of the material were interviews with patients of the selected groups, observation of their behavior when in pain and discussion of the individual cases with doctors, nurses and other people directly or indirectly involved in the pain experience of the individual. In addition to the interviews with patients, "healthy" members of the respective groups were interviewed on their attitudes toward pain, because in terms of the original hypothesis those attitudes and reactions which are displayed by the patients of the given cultural groups are held by all members of the group regardless of whether or not they are in pain although in pain these attitudes may come more sharply into focus. In certain cases the researchers have interviewed a member of the patient's immediate family in order to check the report of the patient on his pain experience and in order to find out what are the attitudes and reactions of the family toward the patient's experience.

These interviews, based on a series of open-ended questions, were focused upon the past and present pain experiences of the interviewee. However, many other areas were considered important for the understanding of this experience. For instance, it was felt that complaints of pain may play an important role in manipulating relationships in the family and the larger social environment. It was also felt that in order to understand the specific reactive patterns in controlling pain it is important to know certain aspects of child-rearing in the culture, relationships between parents and children, the role of infliction of pain in punishment, the attitudes of various members of the family toward specific expected, accepted pain experiences, and so on. The interviews were recorded on wire and transcribed verbatim for an ultimate detailed analysis. The interviews usually lasted for approximately two hours, the time being limited by the condition of the interviewee and by the amount and quality of his answers. When it was considered necessary an interview was repeated. In most of the cases the study of the interviewee was followed by informal conversations and by observation of his behavior in the hospital.

The information gathered from the interviews was discussed with members of the medical staff, especially in the areas related to the medical aspects of the problem, in order to get their evaluation of the pain experience of the patient. Information as to the personality of the patient was checked against results of psychological testing by members of the psychological staff of the hospital when these were available.

The discussion of the material presented in this paper is based on interviews with 103 respondents, including 87 hospital patients in pain and 16 healthy subjects. According to their ethno-cultural background the respondents are distributed as follows: "Old Americans," 26; Italians, 24; Jews, 31; Irish, 11; and others, 11.[4] In addition, there were the collateral interviews and conversations noted above with family members, doctors, nurses and other members of the hospital staff.

With regard to the pathological causes of pain the majority of the interviewees fall into the group of patients suffering from neurological diseases, mainly herniated discs and spinal lesions. The focusing upon a group of patients suffering from a similar pathology offered the opportunity to investigate reactions and attitudes toward spontaneous pain which is symptomatic of one group of diseases. Nevertheless, a number of patients suffering from other diseases were also interviewed.

This paper is based upon the material collected during the first stage of study. The generalizations are to a great extent tentative formulations on a descriptive level. There has been no attempt as yet to integrate the results with the value system and the cultural pattern of the group, though here and there there will be indications to the effect that they are part of the culture pattern. The discussions will be limited to main regularities within three groups, namely, the Italians, the Jews and the "Old Americans." Factors related to variations within each group will be discussed after the main prevailing patterns have been presented.

Pain Among Patients of Jewish and Italian Origin. As already mentioned, the Jews and Italians were selected mainly because interviews with medical experts suggested that they display similar reactions to pain. The investigation of this similarity provided the opportunity to check a rather popular assumption that similar reactions reflect similar attitudes. The differences between the Italian and Jewish culture are great enough to suggest that if the attitudes are related to cultural pattern they will also be different despite the apparent similarity in manifest behavior.

Members of both groups were described as being very emotional in their responses to pain. They were described as tending to exaggerate their pain experience and being very sensitive to pain. Some of the doctors stated that in their opinion Jews and Italians have a lower threshold of pain than members of other ethnic groups, especially members of the so-called Nordic group. This statement seems to indicate a certain confusion as to the concept of the threshold of pain. According to people who have studied the problem of the threshold of pain, for instance Harold Wolff and his associates, the threshold of pain is more or less the same for all human beings regardless of nationality, sex or age.

In the course of the investigation the general impressions of doctors were confirmed to a great extent by the interview material and by the observation of the patients' behavior. However, even a superficial study of the interviews has revealed that though reactions to pain appear to be similar the underlying attitudes toward pain are different in the two groups. While the Italian patients seemed to be mainly concerned with the immediacy of the pain experience and were disturbed by the actual pain sensation which they experienced in a given situation, the concern of patients of Jewish origin was focused mainly upon the symptomatic meaning of pain and upon the significance of pain in relation to their health, welfare and, eventually, for the welfare of the families. The Italian patient expressed in his behavior and in his complaints the discomfort caused by pain as such, and he manifested his emotions with regard to the effects of this pain experience upon his immediate situation in terms of occupation, economic situation and so on; the Jewish patient expressed primarily his worries and anxieties as to the extent to which the pain indicated a threat to his health. In this connection it is worth mentioning that one of the Jewish words to describe strong pain is *yessurim*, a word which is also used to describe worries and anxieties.

Attitudes of Italian and Jewish patients toward pain-relieving drugs can serve as an indication of their attitude toward pain. When in pain the Italian calls for pain relief and is mainly concerned with the analgesic effects of the drugs which are administered to him. Once the pain is relieved the Italian patient easily forgets his sufferings and manifests a happy and joyful disposition. The Jewish patient, however, often is reluctant to accept the drug, and he explains this reluctance in terms of concern about the effects of the drug upon his health in general. He is apprehensive about the habit-forming aspects of the analgesic. Moreover, he feels that the drug relieves his pain only temporarily and does not cure him of the disease which may cause the pain. Nurses and doctors have reported cases in which patients would hide the pill which was given to them to relieve their pain and would prefer to suffer. These reports were confirmed in the interviews with the patients. It was also observed that many Jewish patients after being relieved from pain often continued to display the same depressed and worried behavior because they felt that though the pain was currently absent it may recur as long as the disease was not cured completely. From these observations it appears that when one deals with a Jewish and an Italian patient in pain, in the first case it is more important to relieve the anxieties with regard to the sources of pain, while in the second it is more important to relieve the actual pain.

Another indication as to the significance of pain for Jewish and Italian patients is their respective attitudes toward the doctor. The Italian patient seems to display a most confident attitude toward the doctor which is usually reinforced after the doctor has succeeded in relieving pain, whereas the Jewish patient manifests a skeptical attitude, feeling that the fact that the doctor has relieved his pain by some drug does not mean at all that he is skillful enough to take care of the basic illness. Consequently, even when the pain is relieved, he tends to check the diagnosis and the treatment of one doctor against the opinions of other specialists in the field. Summarizing the difference between the Italian and Jewish attitudes, one can say that the Italian attitude is characterized by a present-oriented apprehension with regard to the actual sensation of pain, and the Jew tends to manifest a future-oriented anxiety as to the symptomatic and general meaning of the pain experience.

It has been stated that the Italians and Jews tend to manifest similar behavior in terms of their reactions to pain. As both cultures allow for free expression of feelings and emotions by words, sounds and gestures, both the Italians and Jews feel free to talk about their pain, complain about it and manifest their sufferings by groaning, moaning, crying, etc. They are not ashamed of this expression. They admit willingly that when they are in pain they do complain a great deal, call for help and expect sympathy and assistance from other members of their immediate social environment, especially from members of their family. When in pain they are reluctant to be alone and prefer the presence and attention of other people. This behavior, which is expected, accepted and approved by the Italian and Jewish cultures often conflicts with the patterns of behavior expected from a patient by American or Americanized medical people. Thus they tend to describe the behavior of the Italian and Jewish patient as exaggerated and over-emotional. The material suggests that they do tend to minimize the actual pain experiences of the Italian and Jewish patient, regardless of whether they have the objective criteria for evaluating the actual amount of pain which the patient experiences. It seems that the uninhibited display of reaction to pain as manifested by the Jewish and Italian patient provokes distrust in American culture instead of provoking sympathy.

Despite the close similarity between the manifest reactions among Jews and Italians, there seem to be differences in emphasis especially with regard to what the patient achieves by these reactions and as to the specific manifestations of these reactions in the various social settings. For instance, they differ in their behavior at home and in the hospital. The Italian husband, who is aware of his role as an adult male, tends to avoid verbal complaining at home, leaving this type of behavior to the women. In the hospital, where he is less concerned with his role as a male, he tends to be more verbal and more emotional. The Jewish patient, on the contrary, seems to be more calm in the hospital than at home. Traditionally the Jewish male does not emphasize his masculinity through such traits as stoicism, and he does not equate verbal complaints with weakness. Moreover, the Jewish culture allows the patient to be demanding and complaining. Therefore, he tends more to use his pain in order to control interpersonal relationships within the family. Though similar use of pain to manipulate the relationships between members of the family may be present also in some other cultures it seems that in the Jewish culture this is not disapproved, while in others it is. In the hospital one can also distinguish variations in the reactive patterns among Jews and Italians. Upon his admission to the hospital and in the presence of the doctor the Jewish patient tends to complain, ask for help, be emotional even to the point of crying. However, as soon as he feels that adequate care is given to him he becomes more restrained. This suggests that the display of pain reaction serves less as an indication of the amount of pain experienced than as a means to create an atmosphere and setting in which the pathological causes of pain will be best taken care of. The Italian patient, on the other hand, seems to be less concerned with setting up a favorable situation for treatment. He takes for granted that adequate care will be given to him, and in the presence of the doctor he seems to be somewhat calmer than the Jewish patient. The mere presence of the doctor reassures the Italian patient, while the skepticism of the Jewish patient limits the reassuring role of the physician.

To summarize the description of the reactive patterns of the Jewish and Italian patients, the material suggests that on a semi-conscious level the Jewish patient tends to provoke worry and concern in his social environment as to the state of his health and the symptomatic character of his pain, while the Italian tends to provoke sympathy toward his suffering. In one case the function of the pain reaction will be the mobilization of the efforts of the family and the doctors toward a complete cure, while in the second case the function of the reaction will be focused upon the mobilization of effort toward relieving the pain sensation.

On the basis of the discussion of the Jewish and Italian material two generalizations can be made: 1) Similar reactions to pain manifested by members of different ethno-cultural groups do not necessarily reflect similar attitudes to pain. 2) Reactive patterns similar in terms of their manifestations may have different functions and serve different purposes in various cultures.

Pain Among Patients of "Old American" Origin. There is little emphasis on emotional complaining about pain among "Old American" patients. Their complaints about pain can best be described as reporting on pain. In describing his pain, the "Old American" patient tries to find the most appropriate ways of defining the quality of pain, its localization, duration, etc. When examined by the doctor he gives the impression of trying to assume the detached role of an unemotional observer who gives the most efficient description of his state for a correct diagnosis and treatment. The interviewees repeatedly state that there is no point in complaining and groaning and moaning, etc., because "it won't help anybody." However, they readily admit that when pain is unbearable they may react strongly, even to the point of crying, but they tend to do it when they are alone. Withdrawal from society seems to be a frequent reaction to strong pain.

There seem to be different patterns in reacting to pain depending on the situation. One pattern, manifested in the presence of members of the family, friends, etc., consists of attempts to minimize pain, to avoid complaining and provoking pity; when pain becomes too strong there is a tendency to withdraw and express freely such reactions as groaning, moaning, etc. A different pattern is manifested in the presence of people who, on account of their profession, should know the character of the pain experience because they are expected to make the appropriate diagnosis, advise the proper cure and give the adequate help. The tendency to avoid deviation from certain expected patterns of behavior plays an important role in the reaction to pain. This is also controlled by the desire to seek approval on the part of the social environment, especially in the hospital, where the "Old American" patient tries to avoid being a "nuisance" on the ward. He seems to be, more than any other patient, aware of an ideal pattern of behavior which is identified as "American," and he tends to conform to it. This was characteristically expressed by a patient who answered the question how he reacts to pain by saying, "I react like a good American."

An important element in controlling the pain reaction is the wish of the patient to cooperate with those who are expected to take care of him. The situation is often viewed as a team composed of the patient, the doctor, the nurse, the attendant, etc., and in this team everybody has a function and is supposed to do his share in order to achieve the most successful result. Emotionality is seen as a purposeless and hindering factor in a situation which calls for knowledge, skill, training and efficiency. It is important to note that this behavior is also expected by American or Americanized members of the medical or nursing staff, and the patients who do not fall into this pattern are viewed as deviants, hypochondriacs and neurotics.

As in the case of the Jewish patients, the American attitude toward pain can be best defined as a future-oriented anxiety. The "Old American" patient is also concerned with the symptomatic significance of pain which is correlated with a pronounced health-consciousness. It seems that the "Old American" is conscious of various threats to his health which are present in his environment and therefore feels vulnerable and is prone to interpret his pain sensation as a warning signal indicating that something is wrong with his health and therefore must be reported to the physician. With some exceptions, pain is considered bad and unnecessary and therefore must be immediately taken care of. In those situations where pain is expected and accepted, such as in the process of medical treatment or as a result of sports activities, there is less concern with the pain sensation. In general, however, there is a feeling that suffering pain is unnecessary when there are means of relieving it.

Though the attitudes of the Jewish and "Old American" patients can be defined as pain anxiety they differ greatly. The future-oriented anxiety of the Jewish interviewee is characterized by pessimism or, at best, by skepticism, while the "Old American" patient is rather optimistic in his future-orientation. This attitude is fostered by the mechanistic approach to the body and its functions and by the confidence in the skill of the expert which are so frequent in the American culture. The body is often viewed as a machine which has to be well taken care of, be periodically checked for disfunctioning and eventually, when out of order, be taken to an expert who will "fix" the defect. In the case of pain the expert is the medical man who has the "know-how" because of his training and experience and therefore is entitled to full confidence. An important element in the optimistic outlook is faith in the progress of science. Patients with intractable pain often stated that though at the present moment the doctors do not have the "drug" they will eventually discover it, and they will give the examples of sulpha, penicillin, etc.

The anxieties of a pain-experiencing "Old American" patient are greatly relieved when he feels that something is being done about it in terms of specific activities involved in the treatment. It seems that his security and confidence increases in direct proportion to the number of tests, X-rays, examinations, injections, etc. that are given to him. Accordingly, "Old American" patients seem to have a positive attitude toward hospitalization, because the hospital is the adequate institution which is equipped for the necessary treatment. While a Jewish and an Italian patient seem to be disturbed by the impersonal character of the hospital and by the necessity of being treated there instead of at home, the "Old American" patient, on the contrary, prefers the hospital treatment to the home treatment, and neither he nor his family seems to be disturbed by hospitalization.

To summarize the attitude of the "Old American" toward pain, he is disturbed by the symptomatic aspect of pain and is concerned with its incapacitating aspects, but he tends to view the future in rather optimistic colors, having confidence in the science and skill of the professional people who treat his condition.

Some Sources of Intra-Group Variation. In the description of the reactive patterns and attitudes toward pain among patients of Jewish and "Old American" origin certain regularities have been observed for each particular group regardless of individual differences and variations. This does not mean that each individual in each group manifests the same reactions and attitudes. Individual variations are often due to specific aspects of pain experience, to the character of the disease which causes the pain or to elements in the personality of the patient. However, there are also other factors that are instrumental in provoking these differences and which can still be traced back to the cultural backgrounds of the individual patients. Such variables as the degree of Americanization of the patient, his socio-economic background, education and religiosity may play an important role in shaping individual variations in the reactive patterns. For instance, it was found that the patterns described are manifested most consistently among immigrants, while their descendants tend to differ in terms of adopting American forms of behavior and American attitudes toward the role of the medical expert, medical institutions and equipment in controlling pain. It is safe to say that the further the individual is from the immigrant generation the more American is his behavior. This is less true for the attitudes toward pain, which seem to persist to a great extent even among members of the third generation and even though the reactive patterns are radically changed. A Jewish or Italian patient born in this country of American-born parents tends to *behave* like an "Old American" but often expresses *attitudes* similar to those which are expressed by the Jewish or Italian people. They try to appear unemotional and efficient in situations where the immigrant would be excited and disturbed. However, in the process of the interview, if a patient is of Jewish origin he is likely to express attitudes of anxiety as to the meaning of his pain, and if he is an Italian he is likely to be rather unconcerned about the significance of his pain for his future.

The occupational factor plays an important role when pain affects a specific area of the body. For instance, manual workers with herniated discs are more disturbed by their pain than are professional or business people with a similar disease because of the immediate significance of this particular pain for their respective abilities to earn a living. It was also observed that headaches cause more concern among intellectuals than among manual workers.

The educational background of the patient also plays an important role in his attitude with regard to the symptomatic meaning of a pain sensation. The more educated patients are more health-conscious and more aware of pain as a possible symptom of a dangerous disease. However, this factor plays a less important role than might be expected. The less educated "Old American" or Jewish patient is still more health-conscious than the more educated Italian. On the other hand, the less educated Jew is as much worried about the significance of pain as the more educated one. The education of the patient seems to be an important factor in fostering specific reactive patterns. The more educated patient, who may have more anxiety with regard to illness, may be more reserved in specific reactions to pain than an unsophisticated individual, who feels free to express his feelings and emotions.

The Transmission of Cultural Attitudes Toward Pain. In interpreting the differences which may be attributed to different socio-economic and education backgrounds there is enough evidence to conclude that these differences appear mainly on the manifest and behavioral level, whereas attitudinal patterns toward pain tend to be more uniform and to be common to most of the members of the group regardless of their specific backgrounds.

These attitudes toward pain and the expected reactive patterns are acquired by the individual members of the society from the earliest childhood along with other cultural attitudes and values which are learned from the parents, parent-substitutes, siblings, peer groups, etc. Each culture offers to its members an ideal pattern of attitudes and reactions, which may differ for various subcultures in a given society, and each individual is expected to conform to this ideal pattern. Here, the role of the family seems to be of primary importance. Directly and indirectly the family environment effects the individual's ultimate response to pain. In each culture the parents teach the child how to react to pain, and by approval or disapproval they promote specific forms of behavior. This conclusion is amply supported by the interviews. Thus, the Jewish and Italian respondents are unanimous in relating how their parents, especially mothers, manifested over-protective and over-concerned attitudes toward the child's health, participation in sports, games, fights, etc. In these families the child is constantly reminded of the advisability of avoiding colds, injuries, fights and other threatening situations. Crying in complaint is responded to by the parents with sympathy, concern and help. By their over-protective and worried attitude they foster complaining and tears. The child learns to pay attention to each painful experience and to look for help and sympathy which are readily given to him. In Jewish families, where not only a slight sensation of pain but also each deviation from the child's normal behavior is looked upon as a sign of illness, the child is prone to acquire anxieties with regard to the meaning and significance of these manifestations. The Italian parents do not seem to be concerned with the symptomatic meaning of the child's pains and aches, but instead there is a great deal of verbal expression of emotions and feelings of sympathy toward the "poor child" who happens to be in discomfort because of illness or because of an injury in play. In these families a child is praised when he avoids physical injuries and is scolded when he does not pay enough attention to bad weather, to drafts or when he takes part in rough games and fights. The injury and pain are often interpreted to the child as punishment for the wrong behavior, and physical punishment is the usual consequence of misbehavior.

In the "Old American" family the parental attitude is quite different. The child is told not to "run to mother with every little thing." He is told to take pain "like a man," not to be a "sissy," not to cry. The child's participation in physical sports and games is not only approved but is also strongly stimulated. Moreover, the child is taught to expect to be hurt in sports and games and is taught to fight back if he happens to be attacked by other boys. However, it seems that the American parents are conscious of the threats to the child's health, and they teach the child to take immediate care of any injury. When hurt, the right thing to do is not to cry and get emotional but to avoid unnecessary pain and prevent unpleasant consequences by applying the proper first aid medicine and by calling a doctor.

Often attitudes and behavior fostered in a family conflict with those patterns which are accepted by the larger social environment. This is especially true in the case of children of immigrants. The Italian or Jewish immigrant parents promote patterns which they consider correct, while the peer groups in the streets and in the school criticize this behavior and foster a different one. In consequence, the child may acquire the attitudes which are part of his home-life but may also adopt behavior patterns which conform to those of his friends.

The direct promotion of certain behavior described as part of the child-rearing explains only in part the influence of the general family environment and the specific role of the parents in shaping responses to pain. They are also formed indirectly by observing the behavior of other members of the family and by imitating their responses to pain. Moreover, attitudes toward pain are also influenced by various aspects of parent-child relationship in a culture. The material suggests that differences in attitudes toward pain in Jewish, Italian and "Old American" families are closely related to the role and image of the father in the respective cultures in terms of his authority and masculinity. Often the father and mother assume different roles in promoting specific patterns of behavior and specific attitudes. For example, it seems that in the "Old American" family it is chiefly the mother who stimulates the child's ability to resist pain, thus emphasizing his masculinity. In the Italian family it seems that the mother is the one who inspires the child's emotionality, while in the Jewish family both parents express attitudes of worry and concern which are transmitted to the children.

Specific deviations from expected reactive and attitudinal patterns can often be understood in terms of a particular structure of the family. This became especially clear from the interviews of two Italian patients and one Jewish patient. All three subjects revealed reactions and attitudes diametrically opposite to those which the investigator would expect on the basis of his experience. In the process of the interview, however, it appeared that one of the Italian patients was adopted into an Italian family, found out about his adoption at the age of fourteen, created a phantasy of being of Anglo-Saxon origin because of his physical appearance and accordingly began to eradicate everything "Italian" in his personality and behavior. For instance, he denied knowledge of the Italian language despite that fact that he always spoke Italian in the family and even learned to abstain from smiling, because he felt that being happy and joyful is an indication of Italian origin. The other Italian patient lost his family at a very early age because of family disorganization and was brought up in an Irish foster home. The Jewish patient consciously adopted a "non-Jewish" pattern of behavior and attitude because of strong sibling rivalry. According to the respondent, his brother, a favored son in the immigrant Jewish family, always manifested "typical" Jewish reactions toward disease, and the patient, who strongly disliked the brother and was jealous of him, decided to be "completely different."

This analysis of cultural factors in responses to pain is tentative and incomplete. It is based upon only one year of research which has been devoted exclusively to collection of raw material and formulation of working hypotheses. A detailed analysis of the interviews may call for revisions and reformulations of certain observations described in this paper. Nevertheless, the first objectives of our research have been attained in establishing the importance of the role of cultural factors in an area relatively little explored by the social sciences. We hope that in the course of further research we shall be able to expand our investigation into other areas of the pain problem, such as sex differences in attitudes toward pain, the role of age differences and the role of religious beliefs in the pain experience. We hope also that the final findings of the study will contribute to the growing field of collaboration between the social sciences and medicine for the better understanding of human problems.

ENGLISH-SPEAKING AND SPANISH-SPEAKING PEOPLE OF THE SOUTHWEST

Lyle Saunders

Differences in Orientation to Time. The cultural characteristics of any people are not a haphazard, random collection of elements unrelated to each other or to the environmental situation in which that people finds itself. They are rather a closely knit, interrelated, and interdependent set of traits that have been developed, not by the application of any predetermined logical scheme, but through the slow, unplanned series of accretions resulting from trial-and-error attempts of the group to find ways of adjusting to its environment.[1] The principal function of culture is a purely utilitarian one, to enable the group to survive. Each trait has—or once had, since some traits tend to persist long after changing circumstances have made them unnecessary—some relationship to other traits and some relevance for the environment in which the particular group happens to live. Culture has its locus in the personalities of people, and personality is built up by successive layers of experience. New layers may be added; old ones cannot be taken away, although they may be greatly compressed. When people move, their culture goes with them. And, if one wishes to know the "why" of their behavior, he must look to the old environment as well as to the new.

Many of the traits that distinguish the Spanish-speaking and Anglos in the Southwest can be seen as related to the particular historical and environmental circumstances the two groups have experienced. An example is the well-known and frequently mentioned difference in their orientation to time.[2] Stated in somewhat extreme form the difference is this: The Anglo is primarily oriented toward the future; the Spanish-speaking person is oriented toward the present and, to a lesser extent, the immediate past. Anglos tend to be much preoccupied with time. They carry watches and make a point of referring to them frequently. Huge clocks are a prominent part of many public buildings. Clocks are also displayed in windows of stores and offices. Radio and television programs frequently remind their audiences of the correct time. Appointments are made for a specific hour and minute, and a high value is placed on being "on time." Days are broken up into small segments of time and certain amounts of the precious stuff are allotted to each activity. The rhythm of living is primarily a daily one, and a person tends to do the same thing at the same hour each day. "Time is money" the Anglos tell each other, and to "waste" time—that is, to fail to do something designed to influence the future in some way—while not exactly sinful is subject to disapproval.

Not only clocks but also calendars are important elements in the time orientation of Anglos. Nearly every home has at least one and most offices have several. They are consulted frequently, and most Anglos would feel a little apologetic if they were unable to give on request the date, month, and year. In fact, one test of sanity in the Anglo culture consists in asking what day and year it is. Many Anglos have their time scheduled or at least tentatively planned far in advance; they know what they are likely to be doing at a given time weeks, months, and in some cases, even years in the future, health and other factors permitting. Relatively few of the activities Anglos engage in have much significance for the moment. Many are oriented toward the future and are essentially attempts to control the future. Thus, the present is important not for itself, but because it offers an opportunity to engage in activities that can affect the future. In other words, for Anglos most activities are not ends in themselves but are rather means to ends, the attainment of which lies somewhere in the future.

Unlike the Anglo, the Spanish-American or Mexican-American is likely to be strongly oriented toward the present or the immediate past. He is not a visionary, with his eyes on the golden promise of the future. Nor is he a dreamer brooding over the glories of the past. Rather he is a realist who is concerned with the problems and rewards of the immediate present. The past, since he comes from a folk culture with no tradition of writing, was not carefully recorded, contained little that was sufficiently out of the ordinary to justify recording, and has been almost forgotten. The future, since for hundreds of years it brought almost nothing different from what he already had, offers no particular promise and is neither to be anticipated with joy nor feared. But the present cannot be ignored. Its demands must be coped with, its rewards must be enjoyed—now.

The Spanish-speaking person, whether Spanish-American, Mexican-American, or Mexican, has had in his immediate past some contact, direct or through his parents, with a village, agricultural society. In the village the rhythms of life were seasonal rather than diurnal. What one did on a particular day did not matter; what one did during the year mattered a great deal. The community was small and the division of labor not very complex, and most people did what others of their age and sex were doing and at approximately the same time. There was no need for the intricate interrelating of activities that is so necessary in an urban-industrial society. A man awoke in the morning knowing from the season what tasks he might engage in that day. But the tasks were seldom urgent, and if he chose to do them in one order or another or put them off until another day, neither he nor anyone else was inconvenienced. There being no "jobs," no first-of-the-month bills, no pressure toward competition, nor formal organizations, no particular value placed on preciseness of any kind, few clocks, and no resources or skills with which more could readily be constructed, there was no pressure to develop any particular concern with time. And so the villagers, both in Mexico and along the Rio Grande, developed through many generations of almost imperceptible change cultures in which time was a matter of no particular consequence.

As Arthur Campa pointed out fifteen years ago, Anglos have developed some peculiar and erroneous notions about Spanish-speaking people's conceptions of time.[3] We have already mentioned that there is a widespread misconception among Anglos in the Southwest which holds that the "Mexican" is lazy and that he will not work unless coerced. "Mexicans" are believed to have a *mañana* attitude which leads them to put off until tomorrow many things that they should do today, and as a result little ever gets done.

Actually this generalization is based on accurate, although incomplete, observations. What throws it off is the failure of the Anglos who make or accept the generalization to take into account the "Mexican" attitude toward time. The Anglo works now in order to be rewarded in the future. The Spanish-speaking person, having no very definite concept of the future, prefers immediate rewards. What the *mañana* attitude actually involves is that the Spanish-speaking person puts off for an indefinite *mañana* those things that can be put off and does today those that can be done only today. If what must be done today is work—as in the case of a harvest or the need to earn money—the work is done, not gladly perhaps or with any sense of dedication, but with an uncomplaining acceptance of the responsibility of the moment. When what must be done today is something else—participation in a fiesta, say, or in the celebration of the birthday of a patron saint, or embracing an opportunity to visit distant relatives—then what must be done now or never is done and what can be postponed until another time—work perhaps—is postponed. In a very real sense the Spanish-speaking person lives in and for the present, a fact that frequently bothers and confuses Anglos who live in today but for tomorrow.

There are many illustrations of difficulties caused by the different time orientations of Spanish-speaking and Anglos. Some are trivial, as for example the bewilderment of some Spanish-speaking people when asked by a physician, "What day would you like to come to clinic next week?" How are they to reply to this strange question? How can they know how they may feel next week or what they will be doing? What is there to make one day preferable to another? And why come next week, anyway, when they are at the clinic now? Some are more serious, as for example the irritation of employers at employees who fail to appear for work or who habitually arrive late, and the resulting closing down of employment opportunities to Spanish-speaking workers. Some have extremely serious consequences. Consider, for example, the case of the Spanish-speaking woman who is known to have tuberculosis in an early stage, but refuses treatment because she feels well at the moment and sees no point in inconveniencing herself now in order to avoid a possible consequence in the nebulous future.

Like other aspects of culture our attitudes toward time are so much a part of us and seem so right and natural that it is difficult to understand how anyone could have a different point of view. That a person could have no particular concern for the future is almost inconceivable to an Anglo. That an Anglo will sacrifice the present for some possible gain in the dubious future is likely to be equally inconceivable to anyone reared in a Spanish-American or Mexican village. The difference in point of view could be well illustrated by the old story of the grasshopper and the ant were it not for the fact that the story, as told by Anglos, is already interpreted from the Anglo point of view, in that the attention throughout is focused on the ultimate fate of the improvident grasshopper and the certain—although also temporary—survival of the industrious ant. By passing lightly over the values deriving to the grasshopper during his long summer and emphasizing the tragedy that befalls him as a result of his unconcern for the future, the story seems to demonstrate beyond doubt the wisdom and rightness of the Anglo attitude toward time. (It also illustrates the value the Anglo places on the accumulation of material possessions!) But with only a slight change of emphasis it could be made to illustrate the orientation of the Spanish-speaking people. The eminently sensible grasshopper lives each day according to the imperatives of the day, enjoying what may be enjoyed, enduring what must be endured. The coming of winter brings more than he can endure, and he perishes, having lived fully and well, albeit briefly. The foolish ant, with an eye to the future, toils throughout the summer, storing up food against the coming cold. He survives the winter and is rewarded with another summer's toil. The version one prefers depends on his values. There is no way of proving that one story is better than the other, or that one point of view about the relative importance of present and future is better than the other. The most that can be expected is that one be aware of the possibility that there can be a point of view other than his own and that persons having different attitudes toward time may be expected to behave somewhat differently in given situations, at least some of the time.

Differences in Attitudes Toward Change. Closely related to a group's attitudes toward time are the views of its members about change and progress. Anglos, of course, are highly oriented toward change. For nearly three hundred years they have been living in a period of accelerating change. Hardly a day passes that does not bring its quota of new things—new discoveries, new inventions, new products, new relationships, new perspectives, new ideologies, new problems. New automobiles are introduced with the announcement of 85 "important new improvements" over the models of only a year ago. A soap that just weeks ago was only slightly less than miraculous in its cleansing power is replaced by an "entirely new and greatly improved" formula. A new source of power—atomic energy—is bringing new promises, new worries, and new fears. Newness among the Anglos has come to be valued for its own sake, and oldness alone, quite apart from any other characteristic a person or object or event may have, is enough to make it or him somewhat undesirable.

Much of the attractiveness of new things derives from their being thought to be somehow better than the old, and thus the notion of progress becomes associated with the fact of change. To the Anglo progress is a self-evident fact. How can he doubt it when the evidence is all about him? Not only is he the recipient of a multitude of new things—but each is bigger, better, more efficient, more durable, brighter, more powerful, more convenient, more mechanized, more accurate, more comfortable, than its predecessors. Not only is this the best of all possible worlds, but by the minute it is getting better. There are problems, of course, and many imperfections, but progress is being made toward their solution and they will not exist, or will be greatly diminished, in the future. There is probably nothing the Anglo more completely accepts than the notion that change is good and progress inevitable.[4]

The Spanish-speaking person, coming from another background, has a somewhat different orientation toward change and progress. He and his ancestors have lived for many generations in an environment in which there was almost no change and in which efforts toward innovation, had they occurred, might have been seen as dangerous. Isolated from the main stream of western civilization, cut off from all but the most meager of contacts with urban centers, and living, for the most part, in a somewhat precarious equilibrium with their environment, the Spanish-speaking people had but little opportunity either to experience or initiate change. Until very recently the change that occurred within the lifetime of a man was almost unnoticeable. The village of an old man was essentially the village into which he had been born. Neither people, nor objects, nor events changed very much or very rapidly. The future, if envisioned at all, was seen as an extension of the present. There being little or no change, there could be no notion of progress. There being no conception of progress, there could be no desire for change. Security and stability lay in the old, the familiar, and the well-tested ways and techniques. Uncertainty, and possibly danger, came with the new, the unfamiliar, the untried.

The present-day Spanish-speaking person, living in an Anglo world, may be handicapped in his efforts to understand and be understood by the persistence of attitudes toward progress and change which he inherited from the village. He may mistrust and fear the changing future into which the Anglo so buoyantly rushes. He may want to hold onto whatever he can of the old and familiar rather than pursue the new. He may be confused by the effort to adjust to a constant succession of new elements and fail to grasp the principle that it is the succession, the flow, that one must adjust to and not the elements that make up the stream. His attitudes and his behavior may be such as to make Anglos impatient or exasperated at what they interpret as being lack of initiative, backwardness, unprogressiveness, or satisfaction with things as they are. Some Spanish-speaking persons, of course, have caught the Anglo point of view and, like recent converts to a religion who are more zealous in their observance than older members of the faith, have become enthusiastic devotees of change and progress. But these are likely to be the more acculturated members of the Spanish-speaking group who are rapidly becoming culturally indistinguishable from the Anglos. For the less acculturated members—older persons or those who have had relatively little contact with Anglo ways—the old attitudes persist to some degree and operate to interpose barriers to good understanding and effective interaction between them and Anglo professional people.

Differences in Attitudes Toward Work and Efficiency. Closely related to a group's orientation to time and its attitudes toward change and progress are the values its members place on work, achievement and success, and on efficiency. Here again one can note wide differences between the Anglo and Spanish-speaking ideals.

Anglos are doers. They like to be busy. As a group they value activity above contemplation. As a group, too, they see industriousness as a virtue. Work for them is a value in itself, regardless of the return it may bring. It is simply better to work than not to work, and one of the worst things that can be said of an individual is that he is lazy—that is, that he does not like to work. Idleness is thought to be very close to sinfulness and those who do not work or work only with reluctance are regarded as being deficient in character. Anglos identify themselves with and are identified by their work. One of the best ways for an Anglo to answer the question "Who is he?" is to say what he does. If one Anglo asks another, "Who is that man?" and receives the reply that "he is a banker" or "he is a plumber" the question is considered adequately answered. The extent to which Anglos identify themselves with their work can be seen in the reluctance of many of them to retire, even when they could well afford to do so, and in the tremendous sense of loss of identity and purpose that came to many people in the 1930's when, as a result of the depression, they lost their jobs. Reduction of income and of the security that in our culture derives from income was psychologically traumatic, but almost equally so was the lack of "something to do."

Associated with the emphasis on work is the Anglo's preoccupation with success. Indeed, if work has any meaning beyond itself, it is that it is a road to success—which may be defined as anything from a greatly increased income to achieving notoriety or attaining an upward social and occupational mobility. Success, as the term is commonly used, refers less to a subjective satisfaction with one's performance than to an objective recognition by others that one has attained commonly esteemed goals. Success is such a valued goal that the means by which one reaches it are not always critically judged. The ideal of success extends even across generations, and parents are eager to give their children "the right kind of start" so that they will have successful careers and an easier life than their parents. The notion that they somehow ought to be a success acts as a constant incentive to Anglos to "keep their noses to the grindstone" and work for a successful—although seldom accurately envisioned—future.[5]

Minor, but nonetheless important, values of working Anglos are efficiency and practicality. As a group they pride themselves on their practicality and on the "know-how" that makes them and their products efficient. They are inclined to be a bit impatient with theoretical considerations or with the philosophical implications of their activities and want to get on with the "practical" business of "getting the job done." The statement frequently heard in discussions among Anglos, "I agree with you in theory, but it just isn't practical," illustrates their concern with practicality, which usually takes the form of action directed toward the attainment of short-run, isolated goals. It is thought "practical," for example, to pass and enforce laws providing for the capture and incarceration of tuberculous persons who refuse to go to sanitariums for treatment, since this provides an "efficient" way of removing possible sources of infection from the community. Practicality and efficiency are both high values and no "right-minded" Anglo would think of questioning the validity of such a statement as "it is better to be practical than impractical," or "it is better to be efficient than inefficient."

In attitudes toward work, success, efficiency, and practicality the ideal viewpoint of the Spanish-speaking person is far from that of the Anglo. The Spanish-speaking ideal is *to be* rather than *to do*. This may be related to the fact that in the villages it would have been almost impossible to identify a given individual by telling what he did, since there were few, if any, specialized occupations and no one did anything very different from anyone else. To place a villager one needed to know his age and sex, what family he belonged to, and what was his position in the family. Further identification was in terms of his personal characteristics. Or the emphasis on being may be related to the fact that in the villages opportunities for "doing" were quite limited, so that the only way a person could have a differentiated status was in terms of what he was. At any rate, there never developed among the Spanish-speaking any great concern for doing. Activity was not highly valued and work was looked upon as something necessary but of no particular importance in itself. Work was the lot of man, and one did what he needed to and no more. And, indeed, why do more, when it would only result in more food than one could eat or more clothes than one could wear or more houses than one could live in? When the results of one's work are products that must be immediately consumed or utilized, work beyond the ability to consume or use is meaningless. And so the Spanish-American and Mexican villagers, having few storage facilities and little opportunity for trade, developed no tradition of work either as an end in itself or as a means to a possibly more abundant life.

Circumstances that might have led to the development of a drive toward success were also absent in the villages. A person was esteemed on the basis of his possession of qualities that for the most part were the qualities of others of his sex and age and that were definitely self-limiting. Where everyone has the same characteristics and skills, it is almost impossible for anyone to be outstanding; and where esteem is based on such uncontrollable factors as sex, age, family membership and centers in such limited areas as being a good son, a just father, a good provider, a faithful wife, the ability of an individual to command very much of it through his own efforts is definitely restricted. There were simply no avenues in the village through which "success" as the Anglo knows it could be achieved, and so no cult of success and no particular awareness that one must be either a "success" or "failure" developed.

Nor was there much concern for practicality or efficiency. The one was guaranteed by the fact that familiar techniques had survived the test of time and were known to give certain fairly predictable results. Furthermore, if one spent a good portion of his time doing what he wanted to do, a certain practicality was assured by the fact that satisfactions were sure to follow the activity or it would not be continued. And, since goals were relatively few, simple, immediate, and attainable, the question of the practicality of a given action could quickly and easily be settled. A basic reason for the development of a concern for efficiency is undoubtedly that it is economical in terms of time or effort. But in the villages there was no great concern with time, and effort was regarded as the lot of man, who was born to toil. More efficient means of crop husbandry might have produced more abundant yields. But for what? More efficient techniques of animal husbandry might have brought about a much better quality of livestock. But why?[6]

In this general area, as in many others, there are abundant opportunities for misunderstanding and misinterpretation between Anglos and Spanish-speaking. The Anglo finds it difficult to understand why Spanish-speaking people seem to have no "ambition," why they apparently have no drive for success and are seemingly or actually content to live year after year with no observable striving for upward mobility. He is likely to interpret this in his terms and in accordance with his values as due to a lack of "gumption," or as resulting from ignorance or laziness or indifference or some other characteristic which he regards as undesirable. A frequent complaint of Anglo supervisors of Spanish-speaking employees is that they sometimes lack initiative in seeking another task when they have finished one that has been assigned them. Having finished one job, some sit and wait for someone to find another for them, a practice that makes considerable sense in terms of the attitudes and values of the village culture, but which is at almost complete variance with Anglo notions of how employees ought to behave.

   Differences in Attitudes of Acceptance and Resignation. A closely related trait of the Spanish-speaking people is their somewhat greater readiness toward acceptance and resignation than is characteristic of the Anglo. Whereas it is the belief of the latter that man has an obligation to struggle against and if possible to master the problems and difficulties that beset him, the Spanish-speaking person is more likely to accept and resign himself to whatever destiny brings him. With his eyes on the future, the Anglo tells himself and his friends that "while there is life there's hope." Greater difficulties mean greater obligations to struggle to surmount them, and the success stories that Anglos tell each other and their children are frequently of cultural heroes who were distinguished by the fact that against great odds and a high probability of failure they struggled and won success. The stories of the rise of President Lincoln from log cabin to White House and the numerous tales of young men who started with determination and a shoestring and rose to fame and fortune affirm not only a belief in democratic values but also the need to rebel against circumstances, to overcome environmental limitations, and by effort to reach the goals of one's own choosing. The environment is something to be manipulated, to be changed to suit his needs, and the Anglo reserves his deepest admiration for those who "never say die."

   The Spanish-speaking person, by contrast, is likely to meet difficulties by adjusting to them rather than by attempting to overcome them. Fate is somewhat inexorable, and there is nothing much to be gained by struggling against it. If the lot of man is hard—and it frequently is—such is the will of God, incomprehensible but just, and it is the obligation of man to accept it. Behind the Spanish-speaking person there is no tradition of heroes who conquered against great odds—unless one goes back to the time of the Spanish *conquistadores*. In the collective recollection of village life there is only the remembrance of men and women who were born, resigned themselves to suffering and hardship along with occasional joys, and died when their time came. Great and stirring deeds were not done in the villages: no one conquered disease, or changed the face of the earth, or composed memorable music, or invented a mechanical marvel, or illustrated the heights to which a man could rise if only he had vision and courage and an indomitable will. This is not to say that there were not men of vision and valor among the ancestors of the present generation of Spanish-speaking people. There were, and there are among those now alive. But the particular kinds of valor and vision required for one to feel consistenly that he not only can but should make the attempt to triumph over difficulties and obstacles, however great they may be, were not developed to any considerable degree by the kinds of experiences the Spanish-speaking villagers historically have had.

   The attitude of acceptance and resignation, to the extent that it exists, is difficult for Anglos to understand. Feeling that a person ought to rebel against circumstances, ought to master and control them, Anglos are puzzled by the behavior of persons who apparently do not share these feelings. An Anglo who falls ill feels an obligation to "do something" about his sickness, a feeling that is generally shared with an equal or greater intensity by his family and friends. Sickness is something which one must struggle against and, if possible, overcome. So the sick Anglo, with the encouragement and assistance of his relatives and friends, treats himself or seeks professional help and generally engages in or submits to a series of activities designed to restore his health. A frequently expressed fear during illness is that something that might be done is not being done; and death, when it occurs as a result of disease, is made acceptable to the survivors by the assurance that "we did everything which could be done." When the Spanish-speaking person becomes ill, he may also treat himself or seek professional assistance, but there is not so strong a feeling that he should or must do so. If the patient is uncomfortable and the onset of the disease fairly sudden, treatment may be started quickly. If the disease comes on gradually and in the early stages involves no great discomfort, the patient and his family may feel no strong obligation to do anything about it. Or, in either case, such treatment as may be given may be abandoned if it is required over too long a period of time, or is expensive, or does not produce definitely observable results.

Spanish-speaking persons suffering from chronic diseases are sometimes so indifferent to treatment that Anglo health workers become exasperated. A county health officer recently spoke of a Spanish-American father who "contributed to the murder of his daughter" by not following medical advice and sending his daughter to an institution where she might have been treated for her tuberculosis. Both father and daughter were told what would happen if the girl were not treated, but the warnings had no effect on either. The girl remained at home and died in her early twenties. The Anglo health officer and his colleagues attributed the death to virtually criminal negligence on the part of the father and spoke bitterly of his apparent callousness and lack of love for his daughter. The father and others in the family saw the death as a regrettable but natural phenomenon and were comforted by the fact that their love for the girl was such that she could spend her last days in her own home surrounded with warmth and affection, and had not been committed to the impersonal care of Anglo strangers.

The attitude of accepting rather than fighting against circumstances is sometimes given expression by withdrawal from unpleasant or potentially difficult situations. Thus, Spanish-speaking persons who need professional services may withdraw from contact with an Anglo who could give those services if they encounter evidences of hostility, or if they are being too strongly urged to make a decision or take some course of action which they are reluctant to pursue. The withdrawal may take the extreme form of refusing the Anglo admission to the home when he or she makes a professional call. It is more likely, however, to find expression in polite reticence and a passive refusal to cooperate. One aspect of the withdrawal tendency is the frequently encountered reluctance of Spanish-speaking people to make initial contacts with Anglo agencies—clinics, employment offices, and the like—where they are uncertain as to what they may expect or what may be expected of them, and where there is always the possibility of encountering some prejudiced person who is hostile, or perhaps some employee whose bureaucratic impersonality seems to imply an indifference to their problem.

Another manifestation of a general attitude of acceptance is a kind of passivity toward persons in authority, which has led Anglo employers and supervisors to comment on the "docility" of Spanish-speaking employees, who are seen to be exceedingly responsive to orders and demands made upon them by their employers. The idea of the "docile Mexican" is particularly prevalent in areas near the border and probably derives in part from the presence of large numbers of wetbacks who have no choice but to be docile since they are here illegally, and who generally are not familiar enough with Anglo ways to know how to protest. To the extent that docility as a characteristic of Spanish-speaking persons exists elsewhere in the Southwest, it is likely to be a manifestation of the general tendency to accept circumstances rather than to rebel against them, to adjust by conforming rather than by resisting.

The tendency to accept and conform, however, does not mean that the Spanish-speaking person lacks strong feelings of individuality and is content to be an undifferentiated member of a group. On the contrary, as many Spanish-speaking people themselves have noted, there is among members of the group a need for self-assertion and to be recognized for one's personal qualities, a need that finds some fulfillment in the establishing of personal relationships; in the institution of *machismo,* an exaggerated emphasis on masculinity; in outbursts of temper and, sometimes, overt aggression; and in the practice of the art of public speaking. This is not the "rugged individualism" of the Anglos, which stresses independence and the obligation of the individual by his own efforts to wrest from a hostile environment what he wants. It is rather an individualism of being rather than doing, a need that is satisfied by recognition rather than by accomplishment. This trait of "individualism" is seen in the inability of some Spanish-speaking people to orient themselves to such an abstraction as "the job" and their seeking to establish, even in situations that by Anglo standards do not warrant them, personal relationships with employers, politicians, and other persons of influence and authority. An Anglo can be "loyal" to a job and an organization and expect no more recognition than that included in his impersonal relations to those about him in the organizational hierarchy. The Spanish-speaking person is more likely to reserve his "loyalty" for some person above him in the organizational structure with whom he can establish a personal or particularized relationship. The foreman or employer who expects his Spanish-speaking workers to respond to the same kinds of impersonal incentives that result in performance from Anglos is likely to be disappointed with their response, while the "boss" who allows the formation of personal relationships and utilizes the loyalty of Spanish-speaking workers to him as a person as a means of getting performance may have reason to be much pleased with the quality and amount of work done. Likewise, Anglo professional people who permit or even encourage a personalistic quality in their relationships with Spanish-speaking patients or clients may find that they are more successful in getting their professional help accepted than those who insist on a rather rigid impersonality in their relationships.

The village environments in which the distinctive cultures of the Spanish-speaking people were produced were such that persons in them developed an orientation to people rather than to abstract ideas, and to people whom they knew rather intimately and in many roles. Impersonality could hardly exist in a village where everyone was known and shared experiences with everyone else, and it is to be expected that those who have been conditioned by the culture of such villages will feel easier in personal rather than impersonal relationships.

Differences in Attitudes Toward Dependency. Among the cherished values of the Anglo is a preference for independence and a corollary dislike and distrust of the dependent state. The ideal Anglo stands on his own two feet and, in the archaic phrase, "is beholden to no man." From the Anglo point of view, independence hardly can be overdone, while dependence, even of relatively slight degree, quickly comes to be regarded as undesirable, if not downright pathological. Anglos neither like to be dependent nor to have others dependent on them, and an implicit obligation of one who receives help is that he will at the earliest possible moment take whatever action may be necessary to make him independent again. During the depression of the 1930's, when millions of Anglos were on relief, there was much discussion of the possible damage that might be done by this wholesale dependence on the government, and there is still, among welfare workers and other Anglo professional people, considerable expression of misgiving lest their efforts somehow damage the characters of those to whom they give services by making them more dependent. Frequent expression is given to the point of view that people should be helped to help themselves and a good proportion of Anglo institutional services are deliberately designed to transfer people as rapidly as possible from a dependent to an independent state.

Underlying social casework practice is the assumption that clients are best helped, both psychologically and materially, by making it possible for them to help themselves. It is widely felt that assistance which involves no effort or participation on the part of the recipient is not only likely to be unappreciated but positively harmful, since it tends to minimize any incentive toward independence.

In the culture of the Spanish-speaking people independence is not given nearly so high a value. The unit of independence was the village community, and each village was relatively self-sufficient. Within the village, however, there was considerable interdependence, with the fortunes of individuals varying almost directly with those of the group. Between the adult individual and his family—an extended family that included three or more generations as well as uncles, aunts, cousins, nieces and nephews—was a reciprocal relationship of mutual interdependence in which each supported and was supported by the other. Intermarriages between families tied the whole community together in a network of relationships through which each individual could claim assistance from almost anyone else and was expected to give similar assistance when it was requested of him. A dependent status, when it was necessitated by misfortune or indicated by the circumstances in which an individual found himself, was not considered extraordinary. Other persons rendered whatever services or gave whatever goods were required and, in time, the individual either died or again became able to carry his share of the load. There were, of course, no agencies whose specialized function was to give material assistance of any kind—unless the *patrón* be thought of as a kind of agency—and people helped or were helped as the need arose, passing in and out of dependency relationships with each variation of their familial and individual fortunes, and with no thought that a dependent status might be wrong or dangerous or undesirable.

Dependence, thus, has one meaning for the Spanish-speaking person and quite a different meaning and significance for the Anglo. The Anglo who accepts help from another individual or an agency is supposed to do so reluctantly and to feel obligated to exert every effort to become independent at the earliest possible time. The Spanish-speaking individual who accepts professional or institutional assistance from an Anglo individual or an agency is expected to feel the same way. But to the extent that his attitudes and actions derive from the village culture, he is likely to view the giving and accepting of assistance as the normal and proper functioning of an institutional relationship in which both parties to the relationship are simply "doing what comes naturally." He needs help, so he accepts it for as long as it is available. Professional people and the agencies are expected to give help because that is their function. There is nothing in the relationship to get excited about. The Anglo, however, is likely to view the situation in moral terms and to feel that assistance should be reserved for those who deserve it or are "worthy of it"; that is, those who require assistance "through no fault of their own," who feel a bit of guilt or shame at having to accept help, and who will make an effort to change their status as rapidly as they can. The Spanish-speaking point of view is that assistance should be given to those who need it, with need being subjectively defined. Each, naturally, evaluates a given situation in terms of his own point of view. And in the difference in point of view lie the bases for many misunderstandings between members of the two groups.

Differences in Attitudes Toward Formal Organizations. One observation that is frequently made about the Spanish-speaking people of the Southwest is that the group has been unable to develop effective leadership from among its members or to organize successfully for the purpose of improving its status with respect to the rest of the population.[7] It is true that there are some large and fairly long-lived organizations of Spanish-speaking people and that there have come out of the group many individuals with considerable talent and ability for exercising leadership in their respective fields. But the organizations have been singularly ineffective in meeting the needs of the Spanish-speaking people, and most of the "leaders" have, at least until very recently, exercised their talents to a greater extent outside the group than within it.

A part of the failure to develop effective leadership from within the group has undoubtedly been due to the great differences within the Spanish-speaking population in the various parts of the Southwest, which have made interstate or regional organization almost impossible. A part of the failure must also be ascribed to the cultural trait of "individualism," mentioned above, which not only operates to hinder efforts to organize the group, but also has some relationship to a tendency of potential leaders to be hostile and to undermine each other's work. Probably more important than any of these is the fact that there is no strong tradition of either achieved leadership or organization within the culture.

Anglos, as many observers have noted, are great joiners, and their way of meeting a group problem is first to set up a committee to study and report on it and then to create an organization to deal with it. Rare is the Anglo who does not have membership in one or more formal organizations, and some belong to so many that they have difficulty remembering them all. Societies, clubs, associations, and other types of organization exist in abundance, and practically any specialized interest that an individual may have can be given expression by joining an existing organization made up of those with similar interests. If there is no such organization, it is usually easy to find enough other interested people to set up one. In these organizations there exist innumerable opportunities for the development and exercise of leadership skills, so that one who has talent for and interest in organizational and leadership activities can easily find opportunities to practice and perfect his skills. Thus, there is in the Anglo culture not only a well-developed tradition of organization but also a considerable body of collective experience in how to go about setting up an organization and making it effective, as well as an expectation that special interest groups will organize to promote and, if possible, attain their ends.

In the village culture of the Spanish-speaking people there were almost no formal organizations (possible exceptions being the church, the *penitente* order, and, in some Spanish-American villages, an irrigation ditch committee) and few or no opportunities for the development and exercise of the qualities of achieved leadership.[8] Whatever needed to be done could be accomplished largely through the informal relationships of the community itself, and there was little need to set up any additional organization to pursue any special interest or goal. Relationships between members of the community were such that the relatively few interests sanctioned by the culture could be expressed and satisfied within the existing patterns of association. The whole community constituted in a sense a single primary group in which each member had intimate access to every other member and each had an opportunity to know the others in nearly all of their several roles. The range of community activities and interests was limited to those in which every member of the community could, at some stage in his development, be expected to share. For each type of activity and each interest area there were well-understood pre-existing patterns of relationships into which individuals were fitted on the basis of ascribed characteristics. "Leadership" was probably more nominal than actual, since in any case it consisted largely of carrying out prescribed routines in a prescribed manner and included but minimal opportunity for the exercise of judgment or invention. One was a "leader" only in the sense that a person who is at the head of a procession of people, all of whom know where they are going, is a leader, and even this restricted role was reserved for persons with requisite institutional rather than personal qualities.

Persons close to the culture of the village thus have but little understanding of formal organization, little orientation toward a type of leadership based on personal, individual characteristics, and almost no tradition of responding to leadership of this type. Spanish-speaking persons are harder to organize than comparable groups of Anglos, and many organizations that have seemed to get off to a good start have failed as soon as the initial enthusiasm wore off or the outside stimulus was removed. Individuals who develop a personal drive toward leadership and who have the necessary talents and skills for organization of one kind or another frequently move over into the Anglo group where their abilities are seemingly more appreciated and a given amount of effort is likely to produce greater results. Such persons are likely to be highly acculturated in the sense that they have taken on many of the attitudes, values, and techniques of the Anglos, and their activities frequently have little direct relationship to the needs and problems of the group from which they came.

There is at the present time no effective national or regional organization of Spanish-speaking people[9] and no more than a handful of leaders who have a command of the Anglo culture and can at the same time exercise strong leadership among the less acculturated members of the Spanish-speaking group. In some local areas, and in one or two instances on a statewide level, there are the beginnings of organized movements that may develop the specialized kind of leadership and organizational skill necessary to get results in the Anglo culture. Such organizations, to the extent that they are successful, may well become a bridge over which Spanish-speaking people can move toward the acquisition of enough Anglo culture to enable them to improve their collective status. One difficulty with the concept of organization as a bridge to the acquisition of Anglo culture elements, however, is that, since organization as a means of attaining group and individual goals is not an element of the village culture, a fairly long step toward acculturation must be taken before any given individual can set foot upon the bridge.

Social Roles

SOCIAL ROLE may be viewed as the link between the individual and society, as personality in social interaction. It is the relation of the individual's perception of his own role to its perception by others that largely determines the nature of his social functioning. Status is a "structural" term indicating the individual's location in a given framework of hierarchy of positions; role is a "functional" concept, indicating how the individual is expected to behave in that status. Every status has its role connotations. Thus, the status of the father refers to its location with respect to other family statuses, the status of the teacher its location in occupational ranking. The roles of father or teacher concern the ways in which the individuals are to behave in those statuses.

An individual's social role combines, in this conception, many separate roles. At any one time he occupies age, sex, family, occupational, friendship, and many other roles. These roles may be clearly defined or they may be vague and confused. They may be congruent or conflicting. They may change smoothly through the course of life, or they may involve sharp and critical redirection.

The problem of discontinuities in roles, as discussed in Ruth Benedict's classic paper, is an acute one in our society. Continuity in role means essentially "that the child is taught nothing it must unlearn later," and is taught enough about what will be expected of him later so that the expectation will not come as a shock. Discontinuity involves both contradictions in expectations (as in attitudes toward sex expression at different age levels) and the absence of preparation of the individual for future roles. A child may be expected to behave in ways which ill prepare him for an adolescent role; and in adolescence, the failure to build into his experience adult expectations may cause difficulty in his transition to adulthood and to the assumption of occupational, marital, and parental roles. Benedict points out that there is no "natural" path to maturity from child to man. Each society sets its own patterns for the ways in which the child becomes the parent. In some simpler cultures the child is continuously conditioned to responsible social participation while at the

of the child are adapted to his capacity
trasts within our own society are great,
g the transitions of role expectation from
dulthood and to old age. The tensions
re not easily resolved, and can lead to
d expectations of oneself and of others.
temming from the interrelationship of
onjugal family, the basis of the inter-
at it is the father's occupation which
of the family. The "occupational
., therefore, be evaluated solely in the job
seen also in relation to its effect on family status,
way it fortifies or weakens the father's role, on mobility expectations of husband and wife. Reconciling the demands of occupational
and kinship roles is an endemic problem and has other manifestations.
The father or mother whose work interferes with familial obligations,
the man whose close relatives work in positions subordinate to him, are
familiar examples.

Within the occupational roles themselves, strains often appear when
there are conflicting demands. In their analysis of the social worker in
parole and probation, for example, Ohlin, Piven, and Pappenfort show
the nature and consequence of such conflicting demands. The social
worker in this setting is subject to irreconcilable pressures from his clientele, the organizational context of the agency in which he functions, and
community expectations. The concept of conflicting demands on the
individual involved in competing roles also helps explain the tendency
toward inactive majorities in large associations. Despite the official ideology of the association toward maximum participation, the multiple roles
men occupy result in a diminished capacity (in time and effort) for
investment on the part of most members in any one association. The
consequences, in what often appears to be "apathy," are examined in
Barber's discussion of "Participation and Mass Apathy in Associations."

Role strains in old age have come increasingly under scientific
scrutiny as the proportion of population over sixty-five has steadily risen
in the United States, as in most technically developed societies. As
Belknap and Friedsam indicate, old age is a complex social status, and
when the individual's life experience has not prepared him for the roles
of "later maturity," the shift may be conducive to mental illness. The
discontinuity in the transition from middle to old age may be even more
striking than from childhood to adolescence. Where the adult has felt
his social position to be primarily dependent on his dual roles of father
and wage-earner, has invested himself emotionally largely in these roles,

the loss of job due to retirement coupled with the departure of his grown children from the household during the same period, can bring in their wake a devastating sense of loneliness, ineffectuality, and bewilderment.

The future of work in this field may lie not only in the direction of more and better attention to the needs of individual elderly persons and couples, in casework, group work, and institutional settings. It may lie as well in helping our society to redefine the status and roles of the elderly so that self-esteem may remain intact and capacities can be used to their maximum. It may mean identifying ways in which society through its institutions can build into the life experience of individuals prior to old age those interests, perceptions, and capacities which would minimize the discontinuity in drastically shifting roles, and lead instead to more continuous self-fulfillment.

Problems presented by clients and patients in clinic situations often involve difficulty in clarifying existing roles or adjusting to new roles—e.g., the girl who maintains the role of the carefree adolescent even after marriage, or the immigrant patriarchal father whose paternal role is threatened by the incursion of external authorities, or the foreman who finds it hard to separate his supervisory from his friendship roles. The clinician himself often has a problem in defining his professional role in terms acceptable to the client, and in communicating his expectations of the client's role in the clinic or agency setting. The very concept of relationship through which the clinician operates to treat the client, involves a continuous process of role clarification.

Since role conflicts and strains abound in all complex societies, the perception of such conflict and strain is of major importance to the clinician. In a complex society such as ours, roles become increasingly segmented and differentiated—"functionally specific," in Parson's phrase. This means, for example, that a doctor is expected to behave in a specified way, confine himself to the medical area, is seen at special times under specified circumstances, and in general, as a doctor, would not be expected to behave as a friend or as an authority on any but medical matters. The clerk in a supermarket (in contrast to the one-man grocery store) would have particular functions to perform, would not do any others, would not be expected to behave as a neighbor or give special consideration to any customer. In other words, as the number of social relationships that are formalized increases in our society, roles in these situations become more specific and less amorphous.

By contrast, family and friendship are prime examples of groups where there are less differentiated, more "diffuse" roles. A friend may be called on for recreation, advice, or a loan. In the family, limits of what may or may not be discussed, or when, are rarely set. It is within the family, therefore, and to a lesser extent in the friendship group, that it is possible for the individual to experience his most significant emotional relationships. As relationships in the external environment become more formalized, the family becomes more important as the medium through which the emotional development of the individual takes place, and as the primary source of the individual's learning, perception, and testing of roles outside the family. For the clinician, concentration on the clarity and soundness of familial roles in the client's experience becomes crucial in evaluating the nature of difficulties experienced in other roles he occupies.

All the roles occupied at one time by a given individual in a complex society can not be specified. There are large areas of ambiguity in role definition, not only because roles change but because society's perception and expectation of given roles are not always uniform or specified, and may even be contradictory. The more obscure the perception of role, the greater the problems in living it. Whenever the question is asked "What is the proper way to behave in this situation," "What is really expected of me," there is an implicit problem of role definition. It becomes the clinician's task to be sensitive to such problems and strains on the part of the client or patient, and to help him sort out and clarify those roles with which he experiences stress so that the attendant conflicts may be resolved.

STATUS AND ROLE

Ralph Linton

. . . THE FUNCTIONING OF SOCIETIES depends upon the presence of patterns for reciprocal behavior between individuals or groups of individuals. The polar positions in such patterns of reciprocal behavior are technically known as *statuses*. The term *status*, like the term *culture*, has come to be used with a double significance. *A status*, in the abstract, is a position in a particular pattern. It is thus quite correct to speak of each individual as having many statuses, since each individual participates in the expression of a number of patterns. However, unless the term is qualified in some way, *the status* of any individual means the sum total of all the statuses which he occupies. It represents his position with relation to the total society. Thus the status of Mr. Jones as a member of his community derives from a combination of all the statuses which he holds as a citizen, as an attorney, as a Mason, as a Methodist, as Mrs. Jones' husband, and so on.

A status, as distinct from the individual who may occupy it, is simply a collection of rights and duties. Since these rights and duties can find expression only through the medium of individuals, it is extremely hard for us to maintain a distinction in our thinking between statuses and the people who hold them and exercise the rights and duties which constitute them. The relation between any individual and any status he holds is somewhat like that between the driver of an automobile and the driver's place in the machine. The driver's seat with its steering wheel, accelerator, and other controls is a constant with ever-present potentialities for action and control, while the driver may be any member of the family and may exercise these potentialities very well or very badly.

A *role* represents the dynamic aspect of a status. The individual is socially assigned to a status and occupies it with relation to other statuses. When he puts the rights and duties which constitute the status into effect, he is performing a role. Role and status are quite inseparable, and the distinction between them is of only academic interest. There are no roles without statuses or statuses without roles. Just as in the case of *status*, the term *role* is used with a double significance. Every individual has a series of roles deriving from the various patterns in which he participates and at the same time *a role*, general, which represents the sum total of these roles and determines what he does for his society and what he can expect from it.

Although all statuses and roles derive from social patterns and are integral parts of patterns, they have an independent function with relation to the individuals who occupy particular statuses and exercise their roles. To such

Reprinted from *The Study of Man* (1936), pp. 113-15, by permission of the publisher. (Copyright, 1936, by Appleton-Century-Crofts, Inc.) The article has been abridged.

individuals the combined status and role represent the minimum of attitudes and behavior which he must assume if he is to participate in the overt expression of the pattern. Status and role serve to reduce the ideal patterns for social life to individual terms. They become models for organizing the attitudes and behavior of the individual so that these will be congruous with those of the other individuals participating in the expression of the pattern. Thus if we are studying football teams in the abstract, the position of quarterback is meaningless except in relation to the other positions. From the point of view of the quarter-back himself it is a distinct and important entity. It determines where he shall take his place in the line-up and what he shall do in various plays. His assignment to this position at once limits and defines his activities and establishes a minimum of things which he must learn. Similarly, in a social pattern such as that for the employer-employee relationship the statuses of employer and employee define what each has to know and do to put the pattern into operation. The employer does not need to know the techniques involved in the employee's labor, and the employee does not need to know the techniques for marketing or accounting.

It is obvious that, as long as there is no interference from external sources, the more perfectly the members of any society are adjusted to their statuses and roles the more smoothly the society will function. In its attempts to bring about such adjustments every society finds itself caught on the horns of a dilemma. The individual's formation of habits and attitudes begins at birth, and, other things being equal, the earlier his training for a status can begin the more successful it is likely to be. At the same time, no two individuals are alike, and a status which will be congenial to one may be quite uncongenial to another. Also, there are in all social systems certain roles which require more than training for their successful performance. Perfect technique does not make a great violinist, nor a thorough book knowledge of tactics an efficient general. The utilization of the special gifts of individuals may be highly important to society, as in the case of the general, yet these gifts usually show themselves rather late, and to wait upon their manifestation for the assignment of statuses would be to forfeit the advantages to be derived from commencing training early.

Fortunately, human beings are so mutable that almost any normal individual can be trained to the adequate performance of almost any role. Most of the business of living can be conducted on a basis of habit, with little need for intelligence and none for special gifts. Societies have met the dilemma by developing two types of statuses, the *ascribed* and the *achieved*. *Ascribed* statuses are those which are assigned to individuals without reference to their innate differences or abilities. They can be predicted and trained for from the moment of birth. The *achieved* statuses are, as a minimum, those requiring special qualities, although they are not necessarily limited to these. They are not assigned to individuals from birth, but are left open to be filled through competition and individual effort. The majority of the statuses in all social systems are of the ascribed type and those which take care of the ordinary day-to-day business of living are practically always of this type.

THE PROBLEM OF THE CONCEPT OF ROLE –
A RE-SURVEY OF THE LITERATURE

Lionel J. Neiman and James W. Hughes

THE PURPOSE OF THIS PAPER is to survey the literature with specific reference to the use of the concept—"role." The method used has been to survey systematically the literature in both books and journal articles in all possible fields, attempting to cover a period of approximately fifty years, from 1900 to 1950. The years 1900 to 1920 were rather sterile as far as this concept is concerned. The paper will deal with the various definitions of role which have been used in the literature. . . .

It was not until shortly before 1900 that social psychologists began to emphasize the concept of self as the basic element in the development of the personality in a process of symbolic interaction, and to stress the importance of the individual's attitude toward himself as it is determined by the attitudes and expectations of others toward him. Possibly the earliest statement of this formulation is found in William James' chapter on "The Self"[1] in which he divided personality into four constituent elements: the material self, the social self, the spiritual self, and the pure ego. Of particular relevance to the concept of role is his description of the development of the social self:

> A man's Social Self is the recognition which he gets from his mates. . . . Properly speaking, a man has as many social selves as there are individuals who recognize him and carry an image of him in their mind. . . . But as the individuals who carry the images fall differently into classes, we may practically say that there are as many different social selves as there are distinct groups of persons about whose opinion he cares. He generally shows a different side of himself to these different groups.
>
> The particular social self of a man is his image in the eyes of his own "set" which exalts or condemns him as he conforms or not to certain requirements.[2]

These ideas were further elaborated by James Mark Baldwin, particularly in his *Mental Development* wherein he described what he calls the "dialectic of personal growth" or "the dialogue of self and others . . . the give and take between the individual and his fellows."[3] Both Cooley and Mead attribute to James and Baldwin the stimulation for their own ideas regarding the rise of the self.

John Dewey continued James' emphasis on the social self, with especial stress on the importance of language to the development of the self; criticized Wundt's conception of language as the expression of ideas; and substituted for it the conception of language as communication or symbolic interaction. While he was teaching at the University of Michigan from 1889 to 1894, Dewey's ideas had a strong influence on Cooley, whose description of the "looking glass self"[4] is very similar to Mead's idea of the social role.

Reprinted from *Social Forces* (December 1951), pp. 141-49, by permission of the authors and the publisher. (Copyright, 1951, by The Williams & Wilkins Co.) The article has been abridged.

From 1894 to 1904 Dewey was at the University of Chicago, where he was associated in the philosophy department with George Herbert Mead, and his influence is clearly shown in Mead's writings. In his description of personality development, Mead combined James' idea of the social self as the product of the mental images of a person conceived by other members of his group; Baldwin's idea of the circular response or the "dialogue of self and others"; and Dewey's emphasis on language as the basic element in the process of social interaction. He added a fourth idea of his own, "taking the role of the other," to complete the fundamental theoretical framework within which all subsequent studies of social roles have developed:

The self arises in conduct when the individual becomes a social object in experience to himself. This takes place when the individual assumes the attitude or uses the gesture which another individual would use, and responds to it himself or tends to so respond. . . . the child gradually becomes a social being in his own experience, and he acts toward himself in a manner analogous to that in which he acts toward others.[5]

This action, the social act, out of which emerges the "self," is in reality the assumption of a role for the child. The assumption of specific roles, in the Meadian sense, gives rise to the "me." The organization and integration of specific roles into a larger unity is the "generalized other."

In surveying the literature one is confronted with what seems at first to be a hopeless mass of different definitions, usages, and implications of the role concept.[6] In an attempt to systematize these definitions here, three main groups are used: (a) definitions which use role to describe the dynamic process of personality development; (b) definitions in terms of society as a whole; (c) definitions in terms of specific groups within a society. Each of these groups will be divided into sub-types. To illustrate each of these sub-types some representative examples of the use of the concept "role" have been selected.

A. DEFINITIONS IN TERMS OF THE DYNAMICS OF PERSONALITY DEVELOPMENT

1. Role as the Basic Factor in the Process of Socialization. Park and Burgess in their early introductory sociology text use such a definition of role when they talk about personality as the sum and organization of all the roles one plays in all the groups to which one belongs.[7] Also in this volume there is a section entitled, "The self as the individual's conception of his role." Self, here, is used as a synonym for personality. The use of the concept by Mead also exemplifies its definition as the basic factor in the socialization process.

Cottrell, in one of his earlier writings says:

Personality, or the most significant part of it, is the organization of the roles the person plays in group life. . . . In many, though not all personalities, there is a predominant or central role that tends to be the most characteristic of the person, while other roles, while present, are organized in subordinate relationships.

The role is the organization of habits and attitudes of the individual appropriate to a given position in a system of social relationships. For example, when we say that a given person plays a child's role, we may mean that his habitual modes of response in a situation and his attitudes towards others as well as toward himself are such that he fits into a position of dependence on, and of, the expectation of solicitous, protecting, guiding, and controlling movements from the environmental situation.

First in our use of the concept role we are prone to think of certain characteristic responses or tendencies to respond which the person makes or tends to make to persons or situations. Frequently we fail to recognize clearly enough what might be called expectations entertained by the subject as to the actions or responses which are to come from other persons. . . . There is no conception of one's role, conscious or unconscious, without a reference to what action is expected in the situation of which the role is a part.[8]

The same author, nine years later, again defines role as a basic factor in the process of socialization:

Role: an internally consistent series of conditioned responses by one member of a social situation which represents the stimulus pattern for a similarly internally consistent series of conditioned responses of the other(s) in that situation.[9]

Carr uses a similar definition:

A social role is a specific pattern of attitude and behavior which one assumes for a specific situation. Social maturation in any culture is the process of acquiring the "proper" behavior patterns—a knowledge of the social roles to be assumed in various kinds of situations. One aspect of education thus appears to be the process of developing in the young a repertoire of social roles.[10]

Bingham Dai also uses role in the same sense:

The conception an individual forms of himself usually has a social reference. It generally takes the form of some kind of relation between the self and others. In this sense, the conception of self may also be thought of as a role one intends, or is expected to play in a social situation. . . . The conceptions of the self or roles of a human individual are acquired. The individual is born with only biological needs, but acquires a self in the course of the maturation and socialization. . . . It follows from the foregoing that the nature of the self system depends largely upon the kind of personalities he is associated with and the culture after which his activities are patterned, what the significant people in the environment think of him, and the ways in which the socialization program is carried out.[11]

A further illustration of the same point is stated by Davis:

The self arises in social experience. It could not conceivably arise outside of social experience. After it has arisen it contains the social system actively within itself, and so in a way can provide its own social interaction. The person can carry on a conversation with himself (as he takes the role of the other). . . . It is astonishing how early in life the infant learns to take the role of the other. By the age of two it plays at being mother, baby, or sister. . . . Such a child has already internalized the attitudes of others. By putting itself in the role of the other it can then respond to its own words and acts in terms of the meaning they would convey to the other person. In this way the self develops and grows.[12]

Finally for a last illustration of the use of the concept role as the basic factor in the process of socialization, we quote from Cameron:

We mean by the role, a comprehensive and coherent organization in behavior of functionally related, interlocking attitudes and responses. The role is a product of social learning, which has been culturally defined by the behavior of others, and is based either upon direct personal interaction, or upon the symbolic substitutes for personal interaction in conventional language and thought. By role-taking, we shall mean the living out of such a social behavior organization, whether as play, as social institution, or as one's real-life situation.[13]

2. Role as a Cultural Pattern. The following are examples of the definitions and usages of the concept role in terms of a cultural pattern. As such, these are even less specific and well defined as are those above. For example, Sutherland and Woodward say:

Roles are—culturally determined patterns of behavior, culture sets the limits of variation of roles, but alternative roles may be available in a given culture.[14]

Ralph Linton illustrates the point as follows:

The thing which influences any given person is not culture in general—but a particular culture. The individual is never familiar with, or participates in, the whole culture. He takes its attitudes and values for granted. . . . The patterns of organization of all societies begin with the division of the entire group into certain age-sex categories and the assigning of particular activities (roles) to each. . . . The members of each society perpetuate the culture by training each succeeding generation to its behavior patterns (roles), and values.[15]

Znaniecki uses the concept similarly:

Human individuals and social groups do not exist as natural objects; they are data of evaluative and active human experiences which cannot be theoretically standardized as either objective or subjective, but can be investigated. . . . The group is not an association of concrete individuals, but a synthesis of member's roles. Member's roles and groups are cultural products, systems of values, and activities regulated in accordance with definite historical patterns.[16]

Talcott Parsons, while never saying specifically what he means by "role," uses the term as one of his central concepts, referring to normative behavior patterns in a society. In one article [included in this section], "Age and Sex in the Social Structure of the United States," he uses the concept role to refer to the behavior patterns associated with particular age and sex patterns within the social structure, describing the phenomenon of adolescence as the development of "a set of patterns and behavior phenomena" involving more complex sex roles. Women then begin to assume "the domestic role." "Organization about the function of the housewife, however, with the addition of strong affectional devotion to husband and children, is the primary focus of one of the principal patterns governing the adult feminine role—what may be called the 'Domestic Pattern.' " In this sense, then, role is the pattern of behavior normally associated with a particular category of people within the social structure.[17]

B. FUNCTIONAL DEFINITIONS IN TERMS OF SOCIETY AS A WHOLE

1. Role as a Social Norm—No Connection with Status Explicit, but Implicit. An illustration of the above sub-type definition is found in an article by E. M. Duvall in which the author uses the concept role in terms of rather indefinite social norms:

Negro mothers lean more consistently and significantly to the traditional in their expectations of their children and their conceptions of their roles as parents than do white mothers.

In its transition from the traditional institutional type of family to the person-centered unit of companionship that it is becoming, conceptions of the role of the parent and the child are shifting.[18]

Mirra Komarovsky, in "Cultural Contradictions and Sex Roles," while not defining the concept explicitly uses role as meaning culturally defined social norms which dictate reciprocal action. The author distinguishes two mutually exclusive, contradictory sex roles presented by the environment of the college woman: (1) a feminine role and (2) a modern role.[19]

Sherif uses a similar social norm definition of the concept role. Variations in culture are shown to be variations in frames of reference, common to various groups. Social frames of reference, or social norms, are such things as values, roles, customs, and stereotypes, and are regarded first as stimuli which meet the individual in his associations with others, and then become interiorized.[20] Observing alone, the individual establishes his own frame of reference, which is modified in the direction of conformity when he observes in a group.[21]

Likewise, Cameron uses role with a social norm definition of the concept. He points out that there are "three aspects of role taking in which inadequacies bridge the gap between normal and pathological behavior." These are "a.) a variety of social roles; b.) skill in shifting perspectives; and c.) socialized self reactions." The normal person would be "better" and the pathological person would be "worse" in these aspects. That is, for example, the normal individual would have a greater variety of social norm roles than would the pathological person.[22]

Ruth Benedict similarly uses a social norm definition of role with an implicit rather than explicit status association. "Contradictory roles can be played in series, in sequence, if required by society." She goes on to discuss breaks between social roles of the male child and of the adult in our society as compared with other societies and to point out that the nature of the transition of the social norm roles from the roles of children to adult roles varies with the society.[23]

In the same general pattern, Margaret Mead uses a normative definition of the concept role.[24] Her thesis is to point out, she states, that our behavior in this society has had the mark of the culture stamped upon it. She discusses in various ways different social norm roles such as, "mother's role," "father's role," and an "assertive role," and a "conspicuous role," et cetera. Role then becomes a social norm for Mead.

Stouffer's article is one of the most illustrative of this particular type for, in the article, the author uses both terms, social norm and role, and uses them interchangeably:

> The general theoretical viewpoint behind this paper involves several propositions: 1. In any social group there exists norms and a strain for conformity to these norms. 2. Ordinarily, if the norms are clear and unambiguous the individual has no choice but to conform or take the consequences in group resentment. 3. If a person has simultaneous roles in two or more groups such that simultaneous conformity to the norms of each of the groups is incompatible, he can take one of only a limited number of actions, for example: He can conform to one set of role expectations and take the consequences of non-conformity to other sets, or he can seek a compromise position by which he attempts to conform in part, though not wholly, to one or more sets of role expectations, in the hope that the sanctions applied will be minimal.[25]

2. Role as a Synonym for Behavior—Non-definitive. In the following illustrations of the use of the concept role, there are two characteristics which the authors have in common: one is using the concept as a synonym of behavior and as such adding little to the construct; and two, there is a lack of definity in the context of the concept.

Kirkpatrick and Caplow use role somewhat indiscriminately when they talk about "confusion of roles" and "courtship roles" without a clear definition. In the same article there is a further illustration of the use of the concept as a synonym for behavior: "Again we find evidence that the girl student in our sample either enjoys the role of being sought after or wishfully identifies herself with the role."[26]

Such statements as, "Personality is a role in a social situation," or role is a "pattern of behavior," or "The adolescent is an individual with a status and role in society," by Faris, Sullivan, and Reuter, respectively, are indicative of the type of usage we call non-definitive synonyms of behavior.[27]

C. FUNCTIONAL DEFINITIONS IN TERMS OF SPECIFIC GROUPS

1. Status-Role Continuity—Definitive as Activated Status. The use of the concept role in association with the concept status is one of the most concise and most frequently used in the literature. Occasionally there is some apparent confusion among some authors who use the two terms, status and role, interchangeably or synonymously.

Ralph Linton uses a status-role continuity definition as follows:

> A role represents the dynamic aspect of a status. The individual is socially assigned to a status and occupies it with relation to other statuses. When he puts the rights and duties which constitute the status into effect, he is performing a role. Role and status are quite inseparable, and the distinction between them is of only academic interest. There are no roles without statuses or statuses without roles. Every individual has a series of roles deriving from the various patterns in which

he participates, and at the same time, *a role,* general, which represents the sum total of these roles and determines what he does for his society and what he can expect from it.[28]

The same author in *The Cultural Background of Personality,* presents a similar position, but with a slight variation of emphasis:

The term, role, will be used to distinguish the sum total of the culture patterns associated with a particular status. It thus includes the attitudes, values and behavior ascribed by the society to any and all persons occupying this status. It can be even extended to include the legitimate expectations of such persons with respect to the behavior toward them of such persons in other statuses within the same system. ... The roles associated with the statuses within a single system are usually fairly well adjusted to one another and produce no conflicts as long as the individual is operating within this system.[29]

Everett Hughes, in his institutional approach to the concept role, presents a similar, though not identical view:

The conscious fulfilling of formally defined offices distinguishes social institutions from more elementary collective phenomena. . . . Status assigns individuals to various accepted social categories; each category has its own rights and duties. ... Status, in its active and conscious aspect, is an elementary form of office. An office is a standardized group of duties and privileges devolving upon a person in certain defined situations.[30]

Hughes takes cognizance of the socialized aspects of role and its relation to status as does Linton above—"A role is the dynamic aspect of a status"— but in addition Hughes adds:

Role is dynamic, but it is also something more than status. Status refers only to that part of one's role which has a standard definition in the mores or in law. A status is never peculiar to the individual; it is historic. The person, in status and in institutional office is identified with a *historic role.* The peculiar role of a prophet or a political leader may be transformed into a historic role of office or priesthood or kingship. Every office has a history, in which the informal and unique have become formal and somewhat impersonal.[31]

Kimball Young, likewise, has a status oriented definition of the concept role, when he defines it in terms of "the function or action of a person in a particular group, usually directed to some end, acceptable to other members of the group, e.g. wage-earner, parent, pastor, teacher, citizen, or soldier."[32]

E. T. Hiller, in *Social Relations and Structure* devotes a considerable portion of the book to a discussion of various aspects and types of statuses; however, he uses the concept of status and role somewhat interchangeably:

Among a person's various paired relations, there is usually one that is considered to be most distinctive, that is, one by which he or she is classified, and with reference to which his or her conduct is most widely judged. This is the *characteristic or key status.*[33]

A few pages later, however, the author asks the rather confusing question: "In what way is the *key role* assigned?" [Italics ours]

Znaniecki uses the concept in a similar manner:

Nearly every individual who participates in the activities which bring a social group into existence becomes also a part of the product itself as a group member. . . . Being a group member means a specific kind of person who performs a specific kind of role. Every concrete individual performs in the course of his life a number of social roles.

Like a theatrical role, a social role involves continual interaction between the performer and other people. The analysis of both roles shows that they are systems of values and activities practically standardized in accordance with a certain pattern—in the theatrical role, these are aesthetic; in the social role, social.

Every role involves the following components: 1) a social circle of which the performing person is the center, i.e., a circle of patients, customers, the family circle, et cetera; 2) the person's "social self" i.e., his body and mind as represented and conceived by his social circle and himself; 3) the person's status, i.e., the total "rights" which his circle and himself recognize as due to him in his role; 4) the person's function, i.e., his total "duties" which the social circle expect of him and which he tends to fulfill.[34]

In *The Social Role of the Man of Knowledge,* Znaniecki uses the concept, role, in the same framework as above when he points out that a scientist is an individual regarded by his social milieu, and who regards himself, as specializing in the cultivation of knowledge.[35] In this work role refers to specialized activities (lawyer, house-wife) or to the individuals or members of certain groups (an American, a Catholic). The synthesis of all the roles performed by an individual constitutes his social personality. Every social role presupposes a common complex of values. If the person has the qualities needed for performing the role for which he is needed, he has a definite social status. He, in turn, has a function to fulfill in connection with that status.

Merton, in his studies of the bureaucratic structure and the personality involved, while not using the term role specifically, does imply a status concept of the term. The bureaucratic structure exerts a constant pressure upon the officer to be methodical, prudent, and disciplined. The efficiency of the structure depends on infusing the participants with appropriate attitudes and sentiments. "In such an organization there is integrated a series of offices, of hierarchized statuses, in which inhere a number of obligations and privileges closely defined by the limited and specific rules."[36]

To conclude this section, we cite Gardner Murphy who offers a clear association of the concept role with status and uses the two terms in hyphenated fashion:

Role: a social task of function carried out by the individual. . . . Personality is in considerable degree a matter of role behavior; even more, however, it is a matter of role perception and self-perception in the light of the role.[37]

Murphy continues this discussion, saying that one must dress up to his "status-role," and that his car, home, and club are outlying portions of the "status-geared self."

2. Role Defined as Participation in a Specific Group. By some writers the concept role is used in the literal, dictionary sense, referring to the individual's assumption of or assignment to the performance of a "part" in a specific situation as one of the members of a group. It is in this sense that the concept is used by the Moreno group, who use the term "role-playing" or "role-practice" to refer to assuming a role in a social situation constructed for the purpose of training the person for some occupational status or for gaining therapeutic insight into his behavior.[38] This is also referred to as "reality-practice," and differs from the other definitions principally in its less generalized and less abstract nature. The frame of reference however remains similar to that of symbolic interactionism.

Coleman, for example, defines this procedure as "the playing or rehearsing of the role that the student encounters in others and must play himself in his every day life."[39] Similarly, Lawlor defines role-playing or role-practice as "a circular series of integrated patterns which may be labeled role, exhibited when the person is playing a part in a social situation."[40]

We have attempted thus far to present a basis for distinguishing the various definitions and usages of the concept role. We have noted first, definitions of role in terms of the dynamics of personality development; second, functional definitions in terms of society as a whole; and third, functional definitions in terms of specific groups. In order to achieve some degree of specificity, each major grouping in this schema was subdivided. The question may then logically be asked: What elements of similarity, if any, are found in the literature with regard to the concept role? Upon subsequent re-examination one may note that the uses of the concept role as described above have the following recurrent common elements:

1. In all the definitions and usages of the concept there is involved either an individual definition of a specific situation or an individual acceptance of a group's definition of a specific situation.

2. Role behavior, no matter how it is defined, or even when not defined, involves the assumption of a process of symbolic interaction or communication as a prerequisite, which leads then to a further generalization; namely, that man is the only role-playing animal and that this is one of the characteristics which distinguishes man from other animals.

3. Human behavior cannot be explained or described by the use of traits or other atomized concepts, but must be viewed from the framework of organized and integrated patterns of behavior.

SOCIAL DISORGANIZATION AND THE INTERRELATIONSHIP OF CULTURAL ROLES

Roland W. Warren

SOCIAL ROLE ANALYSIS affords a promising technique for additional research into the relationships and processes involved in social disorganization. The application of role analysis to social disorganization awaits the systematic conceptual study of the interrelation of role patterns in contemporary society.

At the present stage of development it is possible, at least, to offer some hypotheses, chiefly deductive, which are suggested by the growing body of literature on social role, and whose validation or invalidation through empirical research will add to our knowledge of the interrelationships involved. This paper will offer some preliminary definitions, advance some hypotheses and explain their meaning within the context of role structure and social disorganization.

Definition 1. Cultural roles are fairly clearly defined interaction patterns prescribed by the culture. The term "social role" is loosely used to denote such interaction patterns, but social role is too inclusive since it is also widely used to denote personal adjustment to role patterns as well as short-term interaction patterns worked out within a single, specific situation. For these latter meanings, the terms "personal role" and "situational role" respectively are more appropriate, so that the term "social role" can be reserved for the generic meaning, including cultural, personal, and situational roles.

Definition 2. Supplementary cultural roles are cultural roles which are not only compatible to each other within the culture, but actually reinforce each other. Examples: author-lecturer-professor, conductor-composer.

Definition 3. Compatible cultural roles are cultural roles whose confluence in one person is neither discouraged by the culture nor given a special evaluation. Examples: father-bookkeeper-commuter, sportsman-musician.

Definition 4. Incompatible cultural roles are cultural roles whose simultaneous occupancy by an individual is disapproved by the culture. Examples: preacher-playboy, physician-undertaker.

Definition 5. Cultural role clusters are combinations of cultural roles enacted by the same individual. Their importance varies, of course, with the number of people who enact the specific combination of cultural roles. A typical cultural role cluster in contemporary American life is: father, businessman, church member, citizen, service club member.

It should be pointed out that in complex cultures consensus may be lacking as to whether a certain role cluster is of supplementary, compatible, or incompatible type. The cluster teacher-bartender would be looked upon in most communities as incompatible, in a few as compatible, and conceivably in a few as supplementary.

Definition 6. Social disorganization is a condition involving lack of consensus, lack of integration of institutions, and inadequate means of social control. Where consensus is lacking, different groups work at cross-purposes with each other, and the smooth functioning of the institutional structure is hampered. The various institutions, rather than dove-tailing and complementing one another, conflict in their goals and in their functions. The problem of social control becomes difficult, since the various group expectations playing on individual members of the society are neither clear nor consistent, and to conform to one group's expectations is often to deviate from those of another group. In addition, as will be suggested below, a lack of consistency in the role structure of a society may lead to the conditioning of experienced needs which cannot be satisfied in socially approved channels. Viewed from the standpoint of the individual member of the society, this phenomenon reflects itself in individual disorganization.

Proposition 1. Social disorganization varies directly with the extent to which cultural roles place excessive demands upon biological capacities. One of the "problems" of adolescence in our culture is the inability to satisfy the sex drive within a cultural role at the adolescent level. Psychiatrists testify to the failure of "sublimation" in countless cases. Moreover, wherever the social system involves the exercise of cultural roles by persons who are not physically capable, social disorganization is present.

Proposition 2. Social disorganization varies directly with the extent to which needs are conditioned by culture which cannot be fulfilled within approved cultural roles. The conditioning of an expectation of practically unattainable standards of romantic rapture within marriage in our own culture has led to experienced needs which are often not amenable to complete satisfaction within approved marital roles.

Proposition 3. Social disorganization varies inversely with the clarity of definition of cultural roles. Lack of clarity in the range of variations permissible in a cultural role leaves to the individual the problem of devising, in interaction with other persons, his own limitations, as it were; and the chances for the acceptance of his own conception of his cultural role by others in the absence of any clear delineation of possibilities are greatly reduced. As a result, conflicting conceptions arise as to the behavior appropriate to a cultural role, and while a certain sequence of behavior may be demanded by some, that very sequence may be discouraged by others. To say that just such situations place great strain on the personalities of adolescents, marital partners, public officials, criminals, and so on, is merely to hint at the complexity of the problem. To take just one instance, much of the social disorganization involving favoritism and corruption in public office arises from the conflicting demands of a primary group to which the official belongs, on the one hand, and on the other hand those of independent citizens. What is considered a gross mismanagement of office by the wider public may be but the meeting of expectations of loyalty to a family or closely knit political group.[1]

It can be seen, then, that lack of consensus expresses itself in terms of conflicting conceptions of cultural roles by different groups. It should also be emphasized that this very lack of consensus seems to be a condition conducive to the individual freedom considered desirable in a democracy. In the absence of consensus, people are permitted, almost forced, to work out their own individual adjustments, and great deviation in personal adjustments will ensue. Choices are available where roles are not clearly defined. In addition, where consensus is lacking, the possibilities for making choices which will dissatisfy one or more groups are increased. The costs in terms of social and personal disorganization are, as it were, the other side of the mirror.

Proposition 4. Social disorganization varies directly with the proportion of role clusters which contain incompatible roles. Part of this difficulty is attenuated by the fact that not all cultural roles are activated at the same time by any one individual. Nevertheless, conditions may arise in which members of the groups corresponding to two such incompatible roles are present in the same situation, leaving upon the individual the necessity for devising a pattern of behavior which, in its goal of satisfying both groups, satisfies neither. To the extent that such situations are frequent, the society is disorganized, and this disorganization is reflected, as would be expected, in the disorganization of the individual personality.

Proposition 5. Social disorganization varies inversely with the degree of continuity in normal role sequences.[2] To take one illustration, the situations under which courtship interaction takes place, such as dances, parties, moonlit walks, movie attendance, etc., are so different from the usual situations in which marital interaction takes place (planning meals, cleaning house, talking over finances, tending to the needs of children, etc.), that satisfactory interaction within the courtship roles is neither adequate training for, nor definite assurance of, future satisfaction in the marital roles. As a result, it is frequently the case that two people who have interacted to their mutual satisfaction in the courtship roles find that they have no such basis for satisfactory interaction with the abrupt change to their marital roles.

Adequate provision within the culture for regular sequences of cultural roles through which the individual passes in his lifetime affords the possibility, at least, for early training in anticipation of future roles. The transition from role to role may be facilitated by such anticipatory training, and the breaks between them minimized. So, in England, the "public" school of Eton is designed to lay the groundwork for careers in the upper class. Youngsters are sent there whose future roles of leadership are practically ascribed on the basis of birth into the ruling class, and their training for leadership roles in later life is carefully organized. Their home environment, likewise, affords an opportunity for observation of, and participation in, the amenities of social life among those who by birth into the upper class are likely to be called upon later to participate in just such situations. Even such a triviality as the wearing of a top-hat without ostentation or signs of discomfort is ingrained into them at Eton. The transition to the student role at Oxford or Cambridge is an easy one which they have been anticipating and preparing for since their earliest days. They are reinforced by a more or less intimate group of classmates who are making the transition with them. Subsequent experience at Oxford or Cambridge prepares them further for the adult roles which they later are to assume, and in the social *savoir faire* which is so often a shibboleth for members of a ruling class. In adult life, in roles in government, industry, and the military, they interact again with classmates who have had much the same broad training experience.

Such opportunities for carefully organized and integrated careers are made possible to the extent that cultural roles are ascribed rather than achieved. And although there are always some who because of inferior native endowment cannot "grow along with" their cultural role sequence, the large proportion of those who can testifies to the adaptability of individuals so long as their careers can be planned in advance and their formative experiences keyed into the career sequence.

Proposition 6. Social disorganization varies directly with the proportion of important roles which are achieved, rather than ascribed. What gives this proposition plausibility is the possibility for a careful meshing of role to role within the sequence which constitutes the career. The throwing open of cultural roles to all comers on the basis of achievement has its advantages in terms of fulfillment of certain broad goals associated with the concept of democracy, but it takes its toll in psychic and social cost to the extent that anticipatory training for future roles is made more difficult. That a former haberdasher can become President of the United States is a symbol both of the openness of cultural role sequences, and of the wasted effort and lack of integration which characterize a culture in which many important cultural roles are of the achieved type.

"In a highly and rigidly structured society, a career consists, objectively, of a series of status and clearly defined offices. In a freer one, the individual has more latitude for creating his own position or choosing from a number of existing ones; he has also less certainty of achieving any given position," writes Hughes.[3] Here again we encounter the conditioning of needs not all of which can be satisfied within approved cultural roles for all the people who experience them. It is figuratively if not literally true that for every ten thousand who aspire to be President of the United States, or a great actress, or a captain of industry, only one can succeed. Horney has pointed out the relation of neurosis to "the stimulation of our needs and our factual frustrations in satisfying them," as well as to the contradiction existing "between the alleged freedom of the individual and all his factual limitations. These contradictions embedded in our culture are precisely the conflicts which the neurotic struggles to reconcile."[4]

Proposition 7. Conventionalizations often afford circumvention of inconsistencies in the cultural role system. "Conventionalization," wrote Sumner, "creates a set of conditions under which a thing may be tolerated which would otherwise be disapproved and tabooed."[5] Waller has used the term to refer to much the same phenomenon. "Conventionalization arises when we agree to treat a thing as true whether it is true or not."[6] In certain cultural roles, the actor is supposed to perform a function but to act as though it were being performed by another. The generally acknowledged principle of male dominance in our own culture gives rise to trying situations in which cultural roles are not appropriate to the real situation. The woman, for example, may dominate by virtue of superior intelligence or steadfastness of purpose, but is under constant pressure to keep the man thinking he is doing the leading. Many college women testify to the fact that they must keep their young man thinking that he is the one who is making all the decisions. One student reports: "I was always fearful lest I say too much in class or answer a question which the boys I dated couldn't answer." Another: "One of the nicest techniques is to spell long words incorrectly once in a while. My boy-friend seems to get a great kick out of it and writes back, 'Honey, you certainly don't know how to spell.' "[7]

"We speak of man as the wooer," Thomas wrote, "but falling in love is really mediated by the woman. By dress, behavior, coquetry, modesty, reserve, and occasional boldness she gains the attention of man and infatuates him. He does the courting, but she controls the process. *'Er glaubt zu schieben, und er wird geschoben.'* "[8]

Proposition 3 asserted that social disorganization varies inversely with the clarity of definition of cultural roles. Such clarity of definition is reduced, as Cottrell points out, by "discrepancies between what is given verbally and what is demonstrated in practice."[9] The conventionalization, however, is not at the root of the problem. At the root of the problem is the fact that the cultural role system is not completely articulated with the experienced needs and capacities of its participants. Conventionalization is a stop-gap to ease the consequent tension.

Various propositions have been given above to help pave the way toward an approach to social disorganization through cultural role analysis. They are neither finally established, nor are they merely random assertions. Their validation or invalidation will help the process of integration of these two foci of study. One can go far in the comparative study of cultures, and in an analysis of social disorganization, by pursuing such questions as: What are the cultural roles of a particular culture; what is their interrelationship; which clusters are incompatible, compatible, supplementary? How does a specific cultural role in one culture differ from that of another, both in the factors which constitute it and in its relationship to other roles in the culture? How are cultural roles related to the main theme or ethos of the culture? Which roles are ascribed, which achieved? What are the most significant role clusters? What sequences of roles for the different age groups are available? How carefully defined are the various factors in one role as compared with another? What provisions are made for continuity in the transition from role to role? What incompatible clusters in one culture are considered compatible or supplementary in another? The questions could be continued indefinitely, but enough has been given to show the significance of the approach to culture and social disorganization through role analysis.

AGE AND SEX IN THE SOCIAL STRUCTURE OF THE UNITED STATES

Talcott Parsons

IN OUR SOCIETY age grading does not to any great extent, except for the educational system, involve formal age categorization, but is interwoven with other structural elements. In relation to these, however, it constitutes an important connecting link and organizing point of reference in many respects. The most important of these for present purposes are kinship structure, formal education, occupation and community participation. In most cases the age lines are not rigidly specific, but approximate; this does not, however, necessarily lessen their structural significance.[1]

In all societies the initial status of every normal individual is that of child in a given kinship unit. In our society, however, this universal starting point is used in distinctive ways. Although in early childhood the sexes are not usually sharply differentiated, in many kinship systems a relatively sharp segregation of children begins very early. Our own society is conspicuous for the extent to which children of both sexes are in many fundamental respects treated alike. This is particularly true of both privileges and responsibilities. The primary distinctions within the group of dependent siblings are those of age. Birth order as such is notably neglected as a basis of discrimination; a child of eight and a child of five have essentially the privileges and responsibilities appropriate to their respective age levels without regard to what older, intermediate, or younger siblings there may be. The preferential treatment of an older child is not to any significant extent differentiated if and because he happens to be the first born.

There are, of course, important sex differences in dress and in approved play interest and the like, but if anything, it may be surmised that in the urban upper middle classes these are tending to diminish. Thus, for instance, play overalls are essentially similar for both sexes. What is perhaps the most important sex discrimination is more than anything else a reflection of the differentiation of adult sex roles. It seems to be a definite fact that girls are more apt to be relatively docile, to conform in general according to adult expectations, to be "good," whereas boys are more apt to be recalcitrant to discipline and defiant of adult authority and expectations. There is really no feminine equivalent of the expression "bad boy." It may be suggested that this is at least partially explained by the fact that it is possible from an early age to initiate girls directly into many important aspects of the adult feminine role. Their mothers are continually about the house and the meaning of many of the things they are doing is relatively tangible and easily understand-

Reprinted from *The American Sociological Review* (October 1942), pp. 604-16, by permission of the author and the publisher. (Copyright, 1942, by the American Sociological Society.)

able to a child. It is also possible for the daughter to participate actively and usefully in many of these activities. Especially in the urban middle classes, however, the father does not work in the home and his son is not able to observe his work or to participate in it from an early age. Furthermore many of the masculine functions are of a relatively abstract and intangible character, such that their meaning must remain almost wholly inaccessible to a child. This leaves the boy without a tangible meaningful model to emulate and without the possibility of a gradual initiation into the activities of the adult male role. An important verification of this analysis could be provided through the study in our own society of the rural situation. It is my impression that farm boys tend to be "good" in a sense in which that is not typical of their urban brothers.

The equality of privileges and responsibilities, graded only by age but not by birth order, is extended to a certain degree throughout the whole range of the life cycle. In full adult status, however, it is seriously modified by the asymmetrical relation of the sexes to the occupational structure. One of the most conspicuous expressions and symbols of the underlying equality, however, is the lack of sex differentiation in the process of formal education, so far, at least, as it is not explicitly vocational. Up through college, differentiation seems to be primarily a matter on the one hand of individual ability, on the other hand of class status, and only to a secondary degree of sex differentiation. One can certainly speak of a strongly established pattern that all children of the family have a "right" to a good education, rights which are graduated according to the class status of the family but also to individual ability. It is only in post-graduate professional education, with its direct connection with future occupational careers, that sex discrimination becomes conspicuous. It is particularly important that this equality of treatment exists in the sphere of liberal education since throughout the social structure of our society there is a strong tendency to segregate the occupational sphere from one in which certain more generally human patterns and values are dominant, particularly in informal social life and the realm of what will here be called community participation.

Although this pattern of equality of treatment is present in certain fundamental respects at all age levels, at the transition from childhood to adolescence new features appear which disturb the symmetry of sex roles, while still a second set of factors appears with marriage and the acquisition of full adult status and responsibilities.

An indication of the change is the practice of chaperonage, through which girls are given a kind of protection and supervision by adults to which boys of the same age group are not subjected. Boys, that is, are chaperoned only in their relations with girls of their own class. This modification of equality of treatment has been extended to the control of the private lives of women students in boarding schools and colleges. Of undoubted significance is the fact that it has been rapidly declining not only in actual effectiveness but as an ideal pattern. Its prominence in our recent past, however, is an important manifestation of the importance of sex role differentiation. Important light might be thrown upon its functions by systematic comparison with the related phenomena in Latin countries where this type of asymmetry has been far more accentuated than in this country in the more modern period.

It is at the point of emergence into adolescence that there first begins to develop a set of patterns and behavior phenomena which involve a highly complex combination of age grading and sex role elements. These may be referred to together as the phenomena of the "youth culture." Certain of its elements are present in pre-adolescence and others in the adult culture. But the peculiar combination in connection with this particular age level is unique and highly distinctive for American society.

Perhaps the best single point of reference for characterizing the youth culture lies in its contrast with the dominant pattern of the adult male role. By contrast with the emphasis on responsibility in this role, the orientation of the youth culture is more or less specifically irresponsible. One of its dominant features themes is "having a good time" in relation to which there is a particularly strong emphasis on social activities in company with the opposite sex. A second predominant characteristic on the male side lies in the prominence of athletics, which is an avenue of achievement and competition which stands in sharp contrast to the primary standards of adult achievement in professional and executive capacities. Negatively, there is a strong tendency to repudiate interest in adult things and to feel at least a certain recalcitrance to the pressure of adult expectations and discipline. In addition to, but including, athletic prowess the typical pattern of the male youth culture seems to lay emphasis on the value of certain qualities of attractiveness, especially in relation to the opposite sex. It is very definitely a rounded humanistic pattern rather than one of competence in the performance of specified functions. Such stereotypes as the "swell guy" are significant of this. On the feminine side there is correspondingly a strong tendency to accentuate sexual attractiveness in terms of various versions of what may be called the "glamor girl" pattern.[2] Although these patterns defining roles tend to polarize sexually—for instance, as between star athlete and socially popular girl—yet on a certain level they are complementary, both emphasizing certain features of a total personality in terms of the direct expression of certain values rather than of instrumental significance.

One further feature of this situation is the extent to which it is crystallized about the system of formal education.[3] One might say that the principal centers of prestige dissemination are the colleges, but that many of the most distinctive phenomena are to be found in high schools throughout the country. It is of course of great importance that liberal education is not primarily a matter of vocational training in the United States. The individual status on the curricular side of formal education is, however, in fundamental ways linked up with adult expectations, and doing "good work" is one of the most important sources of parental approval. Because of secondary institutionalization this approval is extended into various spheres distinctive of the youth culture. But it is notable that the youth culture has a strong tendency to develop in directions which are either on the borderline of parental approval or beyond the pale, in such matters as sex behavior, drinking, and various forms of frivolous and irresponsible behavior. The fact that adults have attitudes toward these things which are often deeply ambivalent and that on such occasions as college reunions they may outdo the younger generation, in drinking, for instance, is of great significance, but probably structurally secondary to the youth-versus-adult differential aspect. Thus the

youth culture is not only, as is true of the curricular aspect of formal education, a matter of age status as such but also shows strong signs of being a
product of tensions in the relationship of younger people and adults.

From the point of view of age grading, perhaps the most notable fact
about this situation is the existence of definite pattern distinctions from the
periods coming both before and after. At the line between childhood and
adolescence "growing up" consists precisely in ability to participate in youth
culture patterns, which are not, for either sex, the same as the adult patterns
practiced by the parental generation. In both sexes the transition to full
adulthood means loss of a certain "glamorous" element. From being the
athletic hero or the lion of college dances, the young man becomes a prosaic
business executive or lawyer. The more successful adults participate in an
important order of prestige symbols but these are of a very different order
from those of the youth culture. The contrast in the case of the feminine role
is perhaps equally sharp, with at least a strong tendency to take on a "domestic" pattern with marriage and the arrival of young children.

The symmetry in this respect must, however, not be exaggerated. It is of
fundamental significance to the sex role structure of the adult age levels that
the normal man has a "job," which is fundamental to his social status in
general. It is perhaps not too much to say that only in very exceptional cases
can an adult man be genuinely self-respecting and enjoy a respected status
in the eyes of others if he does not "earn a living" in an approved occupational role. Not only is this a matter of his own economic support but, generally speaking, his occupational status is the primary source of the income
and class status of his wife and children.

In the case of the feminine role the situation is radically different. The
majority of married women, of course, are not employed, but even of those
that are a very large proportion do not have jobs which are in basic competition for status with those of their husbands.[4] The majority of "career" women
whose occupational status is comparable with that of men in their own class,
at least in the upper middle and upper classes, are unmarried, and in the
small proportion of cases where they are married the result is a profound
alteration in family structure.

This pattern, which is central to the urban middle classes, should not be
misunderstood. In rural society, for instance, the operation of the farm and
the attendant status in the community may be said to be a matter of the joint
status of both parties to a marriage. Whereas a farm is operated by a family,
an urban job is held by an individual and does not involve other members
of the family in a comparable sense. One convenient expression of the difference lies in the question of what would happen in case of death. In the case
of a farm it would at least be not at all unusual for the widow to continue
operating the farm with the help of a son or even of hired men. In the urban
situation the widow would cease to have any connection with the organization which had employed her husband and he would be replaced by another
man without reference to family affiliations.

In this urban situation the primary status-carrying role is in a sense that
of housewife. The woman's fundamental status is that of her husband's wife,
the mother of his children, and traditionally the person responsible for a

complex of activities in connection with the management of the household, care of children, etc.

For the structuring of sex roles in the adult phase the most fundamental considerations seem to be those involved in the interrelations of the occupational system and the conjugal family. In a certain sense the most fundamental basis of the family's status is the occupational status of the husband and father. As has been pointed out, this is a status occupied by an individual by virtue of his individual qualities and achievements. But both directly and indirectly, more than any other single factor, it determines the status of the family in the social structure, directly because of the symbolic significance of the office or occupation as a symbol of prestige, indirectly because as the principal source of family income it determines the standard of living of the family. From one point of view the emergence of occupational status into this primary position can be regarded as the principal source of strain in the sex role structure of our society since it deprives the wife of her role as a partner in a common enterprise. The common enterprise is reduced to the life of the family itself and to the informal social activities in which husband and wife participate together. This leaves the wife a set of utilitarian functions in the management of the household which may be considered a kind of "pseudo-" occupation. Since the present interest is primarily in the middle classes, the relatively unstable character of the role of housewife as the principal content of the feminine role is strongly illustrated by the tendency to employ domestic servants wherever financially possible. It is true that there is an American tendency to accept tasks of drudgery with relative willingness, but it is notable that in middle class families there tends to be a dissociation of the essential personality from the performance of these tasks. Thus, advertising continually appeals to such desires as to have hands which one could never tell had washed dishes or scrubbed floors.[5] Organization about the function of housewife, however, with the addition of strong affectional devotion to husband and children, is the primary focus of one of the principal patterns governing the adult feminine role—what may be called the "domestic" pattern. It is, however, a conspicuous fact that strict adherence to this pattern has become progressively less common and has a strong tendency to a residual status—that is, to be followed most closely by those who are unsuccessful in competition for prestige in other directions.

It is, of course, possible for the adult woman to follow the masculine pattern and seek a career in fields of occupational achievement in direct competition with men of her own class. It is, however, notable that in spite of the very great progress of the emancipation of women from the traditional domestic pattern only a very small fraction have gone very far in this direction. It is also clear that its generalization would only be possible with profound alterations in the structure of the family.

Hence it seems that concomitant with the alteration in the basic masculine role in the direction of occupation there have appeared two important tendencies in the feminine role which are alternative to that of simple domesticity on the one hand, and to a full-fledged career on the other. In the older situation there tended to be a very rigid distinction between respectable married women and those who were "no better than they should be." The rigidity of this line has progressively broken down through the infiltration into the respectable sphere of elements of what may be called again the glamor pattern, with the emphasis on a specifically feminine form of attractiveness which on occasion involves directly sexual patterns of appeal. One important expression of this trend lies in the fact that many of the symbols of feminine attractiveness have been taken over directly from the practices of social types previously beyond the pale of respectable society. This would seem to be substantially true of the practice of women smoking and of at least the modern version of the use of cosmetics. The same would seem to be true of many of the modern versions of women's dress. "Emancipation" in this connection means primarily emancipation from traditional and conventional restrictions on the free expression of sexual attraction and impulses, but in a direction which tends to segregate the elements of sexual interest and attraction from the total personality and in so doing tends to emphasize the segregation of sex roles. It is particularly notable that there has been no corresponding tendency to emphasize masculine attraction in terms of dress and other such aids. One might perhaps say that in a situation which strongly inhibits competition between the sexes on the same plane the feminine glamor pattern has appeared as an offset to masculine occupational status and to its attendant symbols of prestige. It is perhaps significant that there is a common stereotype of the association of physically beautiful, expensively and elaborately dressed women with physically unattractive but rich and powerful men.

The other principal direction of emancipation from domesticity seems to lie in emphasis on what has been called the common humanistic element. This takes a wide variety of forms. One of them lies in a relatively mature appreciation and systematic cultivation of cultural interests and educated tastes, extending all the way from the intellectual sphere to matters of art, music, and house furnishings. A second consists in cultivation of serious interests and humanitarian obligations in community welfare situations and the like. It is understandable that many of these orientations are most conspicuous in fields where through some kind of tradition there is an element of particular suitability for feminine participation. Thus, a woman who takes obligations to social welfare particularly seriously will find opportunities in various forms of activity which traditionally tie up with women's relation to children, to sickness and so on. But this may be regarded as secondary to the underlying orientation which would seek an outlet in work useful to the community following the most favorable opportunities which happen to be available.

This pattern, which with reference to the character of relationship to men may be called that of the "good companion," is distinguished from the others in that it lays far less stress on the exploitation of sex role as such and more on that which is essentially common to both sexes. There are reasons, however, why cultural interests, interest in social welfare and community activities are particularly prominent in the activities of women in our urban communities. On the one side the masculine occupational role tends to absorb a very large proportion of the man's time and energy and to leave him relatively little for other interests. Furthermore, unless his position is such as to make him particularly prominent his primary orientation is to those elements of the social structure which divide the community into occupational groups rather than those which unite it in common interests and activities. The utilitarian aspect of the role of housewife, on the other hand, has declined in importance to the point where it scarcely approaches a full-time occupation for a vigorous person. Hence the resort to other interests to fill up the gap. In addition, women, being more closely tied to the local residential community, are more apt to be involved in matters of common concern to the members of that community. This peculiar role of women becomes particularly conspicuous in middle age. The younger married woman is apt to be relatively highly absorbed in the care of young children. With their growing up, however, her absorption in the household is greatly lessened, often just at the time when the husband is approaching the apex of his career and is most heavily involved in its obligations. Since to a high degree this humanistic aspect of the feminine role is only partially institutionalized it is not surprising that its patterns often bear the marks of strain and insecurity, as perhaps has been classically depicted by Helen Hokinson's cartoons of women's clubs.

The adult roles of both sexes involve important elements of strain which are involved in certain dynamic relationships, especially to the youth culture. In the case of the feminine role, marriage is the single event toward which a selective process, in which personal qualities and effort can play a decisive part, has pointed. That determines a woman's fundamental status, and after that her role patterning is not so much status determining as a matter of living up to expectations and finding satisfying interests and activities. In a society where such strong emphasis is placed upon individual achievement it is not surprising that there should be a certain romantic nostalgia for the time when the fundamental choices were still open. This element of strain is added to by the lack of clear-cut definition of the adult feminine role. Once the possibility of a career has been eliminated there still tends to be a rather unstable oscillation between emphasis in the direction of domesticity or glamor or good companionship. According to situational pressures and individual character the tendency will be to emphasize one or another of these more strongly. But it is a situation likely to produce a rather high level of insecurity. In this state the pattern of domesticity must be ranked lowest in terms of prestige but also, because of the strong emphasis in community sentiment on the virtues of fidelity and devotion to husband and children, it offers perhaps the highest level of a certain kind of security. It is no wonder that such an important symbol as Whistler's mother concentrates primarily on this pattern.

The glamor pattern has certain obvious attractions since to the woman who is excluded from the struggle for power and prestige in the occupational sphere it is the most direct path to a sense of superiority and importance. It has, however, two obvious limitations. In the first place, many of its manifestations encounter the resistance of patterns of moral conduct and engender conflicts not only with community opinion but also with the individual's own moral standards. In the second place, it is a pattern the highest manifestations of which are inevitably associated with a rather early age level—in fact, overwhelmingly with the courtship period. Hence, if strongly entered upon serious strains result from the problem of adaptation to increasing age.

The one pattern which would seem to offer the greatest possibilities for able, intelligent, and emotionally mature women is the third—the good companion pattern. This, however, suffers from a lack of fully institutionalized status and from the multiplicity of choices of channels of expression. It is only those with the strongest initiative and intelligence who achieve fully satisfactory adaptations in this direction. It is quite clear that in the adult feminine role there is quite sufficient strain and insecurity so that widespread manifestations are to be expected in the form of neurotic behavior.

The masculine role at the same time is itself by no means devoid of corresponding elements of strain. It carries with it to be sure the primary prestige of achievement, responsibility and authority. By comparison with the role of the youth culture, however, there are at least two important types of limitations. In the first place, the modern occupational system has led to increasing specialization of the role. The job absorbs an extraordinarily large proportion of the individual's energy and emotional interests in a role the content of which is often relatively narrow. This in particular restricts the area within which he can share common interests and experiences with others not in the same occupational specialty. It is perhaps of considerable significance that so many of the highest prestige statuses of our society are of the specialized character. There is in the definition of roles little to bind the individual to others in his community on a comparable status level. By contrast with this situation, it is notable that in the youth culture common human elements are far more strongly emphasized. Leadership and eminence are more in the role of total individuals and less of competent specialists. This perhaps has something to do with the significant tendency in our society for all age levels to idealize youth and for the older age groups to attempt to imitate the patterns of youth behavior.

It is perhaps as one phase of this situation that the relation of the adult man to persons of the opposite sex should be treated. The effect of the specialization of occupational role is to narrow the range in which the sharing of common human interests can play a large part. In relation to his wife the tendency of this narrowness would seem to be to encourage on her part either the domestic or the glamorous role, or community participation somewhat unrelated to the marriage relationship. This relationship between sex roles presumably introduces a certain amount of strain into the marriage relationship itself since this is of such overwhelming importance to the family and hence to a woman's status and yet so relatively difficult to maintain on a level of human companionship. Outside the marriage relationship, however, there seems to be a notable inhibition against easy social intercourse, particularly in mixed company.[6] The man's close personal intimacy with other women is checked by the danger of the situation being defined as one of rivalry with the wife, and easy friendship without sexual-emotional involvement seems to be inhibited by the specialization of interests in the occupational sphere. It is notable that brilliance of conversation of the "salon" type seems to be associated with aristocratic society and is not prominent in ours.

Along with all this goes a certain tendency for middle-aged men, as symbolized by the "bald-headed row," to be interested in the physical aspects of sex—that is, in women precisely as dissociated from those personal considerations which are important to relationships of companionship or friendship, to say nothing of marriage. In so far as it does not take this physical form, however, there seems to be a strong tendency for middle-aged men to idealize youth patterns—that is, to think of the ideal inter-sex friendship as that of their pre-marital period.[7]

In so far as the idealization of the youth culture by adults is an expression of elements of strain and insecurity in the adult roles it would be expected that the patterns thus idealized would contain an element of romantic unrealism. The patterns of youthful behavior thus idealized are not those of actual youth so much as those which older people wish their own youth might have been. This romantic element seems to coalesce with a similar element derived from certain strains in the situation of young people themselves.

The period of youth in our society is one of considerable strain and insecurity. Above all, it means turning one's back on the security both of status and of emotional attachment which is engaged in the family of orientation. It is structurally essential to transfer one's primary emotional attachment to a marriage partner who is entirely unrelated to the previous family situation. In a system of free marriage choice this applies to women as well as men. For the man there is in addition the necessity to face the hazards of occupational competition in the determination of a career. There is reason to believe that the youth culture has important positive functions in easing the transition from the security of childhood in the family of orientation to that of full adult in marriage and occupational status. But precisely because the transition is a period of strain it is to be expected that it involves elements of unrealistic romanticism. Thus significant features of youth patterns in our society would seem to derive from the coincidence of the emotional needs of adolescents with those derived from the strains of the situation of adults.

A tendency to the romantic idealization of youth patterns seems in different ways to be characteristic of modern Western society as a whole.[8] It is not possible in the present context to enter into any extended comparative analysis, but it may be illuminating to call attention to a striking difference between the patterns associated with this phenomenon in Germany and in the United States. The German "youth movement," starting before the First World War, has occasioned a great deal of comment and has in various respects been treated as the most notable instance of the revolt of youth. It is generally believed that the youth movement has an important relation to the background of National Socialism, and this fact as much as any suggests the important difference. While in Germany as everywhere there has been a generalized revolt against convention and restrictions on individual freedom as embodied in the traditional adult culture, in Germany particular emphasis has appeared on the community of male youth. "Comradeship" in a sense which strongly suggests that of soldiers in the field has from the beginning been strongly emphasized as the ideal social relationship. By contrast with this, in the American youth culture and its adult romanticization a much stronger emphasis has been placed on the cross-sex relationship. It would seem that this fact, with the structural factors which underlie it, have much to do with the failure of the youth culture to develop any considerable political significance in this country. Its predominant pattern has been that of the idealization of the isolated couple in romantic love. There have, to be sure, been certain tendencies among radical youth to a political orientation but in this case there has been a notable absence of emphasis on the solidarity of the members of one sex. The tendency has been rather to ignore the relevance of sex difference in the interest of common ideals.

The importance of youth patterns in contemporary American culture throws into particularly strong relief the status in our social structure of the most advanced age groups. By comparison with other societies the United States assumes an extreme position in the isolation of old age from participation in the most important social structures and interests. Structurally speaking, there seem to be two primary bases of this situation. In the first place, the most important single distinctive feature of our family structure is the isolation of the individual conjugal family. It is impossible to say that with us it is "natural" for any other group than husband and wife and their dependent children to maintain a common household. Hence, when the children of a couple have become independent through marriage and occupational status the parental couple is left without attachment to any continuous kinship group. It is, of course, common for other relatives to share a household with the conjugal family but this scarcely ever occurs without some important elements of strain. For independence is certainly the preferred pattern for an elderly couple, particularly from the point of view of the children.

The second basis of the situation lies in the occupational structure. In such fields as farming and maintenance of small independent enterprises there is frequently no such thing as abrupt "retirement," rather a gradual relinquishment of the main responsibilities and functions with advancing age. So far, however, as an individual's occupational status centers in a specific "job," he either holds the job or does not, and the tendency is to maintain the full level of functions up to a given point and then abruptly to retire. In view of the very great significance of occupational status and its psychological correlates, retirement leaves the older man in a peculiarly functionless situation, cut off from participation in the most important interests and activities of the society. There is a further important aspect of this situation. Not only status in the community but actual place of residence is to a very high degree a function of the specific job held. Retirement not only cuts the ties to the job itself but also greatly loosens those to the community of residence. Perhaps in no other society is there observable a phenomenon corresponding to the accumulation of retired elderly people in such areas as Florida and Southern California in the winter. It may be surmised that this structural isolation from kinship, occupational, and community ties is the fundamental basis of the recent political agitation for help to the old. It is suggested that it is far less the financial hardship[9] of the position of elderly people than their social isolation which makes old age a "problem." As in other connections we are very prone to rationalize generalized insecurity in financial and economic terms. The problem is obviously of particularly great significance in view of the changing age distribution of the population with the prospect of a far greater proportion in the older age groups than in previous generations. It may also be suggested that, through well-known psychosomatic mechanisms, the increased incidence of the disabilities of older people, such as heart disease, cancer, etc., may be at least in part attributed to this structural situation.

AGE AND SEX CATEGORIES AS SOCIOLOGICAL VARIABLES IN THE MENTAL DISORDERS OF LATER MATURITY

Ivan Belknap and Hiram J. Friedsam

RECENT DEVELOPMENTS in systematic sociological analysis of age and sex categories[1] and of the life cycle of individuals and institutional patterns[2] have a number of implications for sociological research. This paper aims to suggest a possible implication in orienting research in the mental disorders of later maturity.[3]

Most scholars in the field of abnormal psychology have assumed that the close relationship between age and sex status and the variations in specific psychoses furnishes ground for a "biological" interpretation of mental disorders.[4] This assumption no longer appears to fit research data in mental disorders. An indicated approach, as we shall try to show in the case of one class of mental disorders, is one which employs sociology and biology as co-determinants.

Senile dementia and psychosis with cerebral arteriosclerosis are the two primary mental disorders of later maturity.[5] Standard texts in abnormal psychology assume that organic (usually cerebral) deterioration "results in" these mental disorders. One text suggests that senile psychosis is the result of "damage" to the brain tissue from aging.[6]

This interpretation of mental disorders has never furnished a satisfactory account of differential incidence rates in the mental disorders of later maturity, such as the rural-urban, sex, native and foreign born, Negro-White, economic, and regional.[7]

These sociological inadequacies are the more significant in view of evidence of additional shortcomings from pathology and psychology. If cerebral deterioration by itself is a sufficient explanation for the senile psychoses, a definite correlation should exist between the deterioration and the psychotic symptoms. But research by Rothschild, Gelerstedt, Sharp and others during the past fifteen years has raised doubt as to such correlation. Rothschild writes:

> . . . When anatomic changes are scrutinized without preconceived ideas as to their significance, it becomes evident that they are but one element in the total picture. . . . Too exclusive preoccupation with . . . cerebral pathology has led to a tendency to forget that the changes are occurring in living, mentally functioning persons, who may react to a given situation, including an organic one, in various ways. The same damage which produces a psychosis in one case may not do so in another. Evidently, different persons vary greatly in their ability to withstand cerebral damage. . . . This opens up many fields of study. . . .

Such . . . study may perhaps reveal social and situational factors which may be

Reprinted from *The American Sociological Review* (June 1949), pp. 367-76, by permission of the authors and the publisher. (Copyright, 1949, by the American Sociological Society.)

susceptible to modification, and may contribute toward decreasing frequency of these disorders.[8]

In one of the few studies formulated explicitly to test the significance of "social" factors in the senile mental disorders, Williams and three co-workers attempted to determine to what degree factors of "social integration" and "financial security" were associated with senile dementia and psychosis with cerebral arteriosclerosis. The finding was that social integration had been lacking in the pre-psychotic histories of over two-thirds of the cases of senile dementia, and in about one-fourth of the cases of cerebral arteriosclerosis. Financial security was lacking in about three-fourths of the cases of senile dementia, and about one-third of the cases of cerebral arteriosclerosis. The study concluded that factors which may be translated as sociological were quite significant in the etiology of senile dementia; less so in psychosis with cerebral arteriosclerosis.[9] Sociologists will question the categories of this particular study, but the findings are suggestive.

The research of the preceding writers on the psychoses of the aged has been paralleled by similar findings in the neuroses of later life. Cameron classifies biological, cultural, and personal factors which contribute to these neuroses. The cultural factors are four-fold: Loss of Significance; Economic and Social Dependence; Retirement; and Social Restriction. The "biological" and "personal" factors in his classifications are capable of reduction, in several instances, to factors which will be recognized by sociologists and anthropologists as cultural. For example, the decline in auditory and visual powers (a biological factor) is of particular significance, according to Cameron, because it tends to isolate the individual from "participation in the activities of his social group," a process which the author calls "social dis-articulation."[10]

A large number of studies in addition to those selected[11] converge on the proposition that the mental disorders of later maturity are closely related to the character of the social relations in which the given individual is participating.[12] The most critical factor in these social relations bears an apparent resemblance to Durkheim's *anomie,* Jung's "loss of significance," in adult neuroses, and to the "isolation" of Faris and Dunham.[13]

The resemblance here suggests the possibility that the mental disorders of later maturity may be profitably analyzed in much the same frame of reference employed by Durkheim in his study of suicide, but with amplifications made possible through subsequent sociological research. We shall attempt to show that this frame of reference acquires additional research utility when it is employed in connection with systematic structural analysis of the age and sex categories through which the individual passes during his life cycle. The utility derives from the fact that this procedure enables the student to handle mental disorder rate differences as possible indices of "isolation" or *anomie* potentials in given age and sex categories.[14] A risk theory of this type may give a better account of individual susceptibility, both to organic and the so-called functional disorders than do current approaches, and it opens the way to a structural functional reinterpretation of two of the most important of the rate variations in mental disorder: those of age and sex.

Durkheim's types of suicide were thought of as occurring along a continuum of personality organization. At one extreme the *altruiste* personality was "overinstitutionalized" to such an extent that suicide occurred whenever the social system required it, the person giving up his life without any significant counter impulse toward self-preservation. At the other extreme the *anomique,* as a result of the general disintegration of the institutions of the culture itself, the personality was "under-institutionalized" to such an extent that the person had become isolated from any system of group-maintained values. The psychological manifestation of this condition of normlessness, or *anomie,* is perpetual unrest, *malaise,* an utter loss of desires, or the growth of limitless desires, so that anxiety, excessive tension, and loss of significance so loosen the hold of the individual on life that suicide occurs as a release or escape.[15]

The importance of *anomie* for sociological analysis of personality phenomena follows from the fact that Durkheim's theory of personality rests, like that of G. H. Mead,[16] on the perception that uniformities in the motivational environment for human behavior are entirely emergents in symbolic interaction.[17] For Durkheim, as for Mead, this implies complete independence of most human action from the automatic biological homeostasis of W. B. Cannon.[18] Human "desires" (wants, ends) are created in the symbolic environment, and the limits on these desires, which are necessary to define satisfaction (the analogue to Cannon's liquid equilibrium) must be created in the same environment. These limits, for Durkheim, are essentially the result of the organization of the human desires into determinate systems.

Considering these desires from his usual structural viewpoint as ends of action, Durkheim maintains that the important ends are those defined as "institutional"; those pursued not as means to any other ends, but as ends in themselves. They derive this ultimate character from the fact that they embody the superior moral authority of the group. Where these ends exist for the individual, with sufficiently-maintained force, altruistic suicide may occur, but never anomic suicide. At the other extreme, neither society nor personality can exist, and approach toward this extreme is measured by increasing rates of anomic suicide: the disorganization of self and society.[19]

As applied to the study of mental disorders in specific age categories the concept of *anomie* can be formulated in the doctrine that all human societies must provide a minimum degree of institutionalization in the age categories throughout the life cycle to insure the maintenance of social organization. The correlate of this is that, sociologically, the personality is an identity dependent for its maintenance on the institutional minima defined by the life-cycle status occupied by the individual. The two logical limiting possibilities for loss of identity of the personality system are (a) over-institutionalization to such an extent that the personality system becomes identical with its normative components (altruistic phenomena); (b) the complete disappearance of the normative minima of personality (anomic phenomena). Movements toward the second extreme by the personality system are measures of differential *anomie,* or "isolation" potentials in the age categories of the culture.

The analysis of mental disorders within the framework of age and sex categories requires a basic scheme as to the total interrelations of these categories in a given culture. The scheme which follows is intended to be abstract enough to express the universals of age-grading and the interrelation of generations, but to be amenable to employment in concrete research. The use of the scheme involves the applications of the general diagram (Figure 1, below) as the initial step in the sociological analysis of a given age status in a particular culture. The life cycles of Ego, Ego's father, and Ego's son can then be filled in by concrete data, as in Figure 2 and 3, and observations made on the concrete relationships of these statuses.[20] Next, the integration of these statuses in various stages of the life cycle may be determined, and degrees of organization, continuity, disjunction, and conflict in the life cycle of Ego inferred. These inferences can then be projected against age- and sex-specific groups of selected intervening variables, such as anomic suicide rates, mental disorders, psychosomatic phenomena, or other such expressions of degrees of integration as can be agreed upon by investigators. Once the relationships are sufficiently established by research, students may work back to inferences from the presence of the variables.[21]

The age and sex categories of particular societies are fundamentally organized in the ethos.[22] More particularly, the adult "key" age and sex status[23] is determined in the ethos, and all other statuses structured derivatively with reference to it. This determination is illustrated clearly in some of the type cases of sociology and anthropology, such as Granet's ancient Chinese noble family, Linton's Comanche, and Arensberg and Kimball's rural Irish family.[24] The key status in the Comanche culture begins with passage into the warrior status in the biological period of young maturity, while the key status in the noble Chinese family does not begin until the biological period of late maturity following the final rituals for Ego's deceased father. It is obvious how other statuses, such as "eldest son" in the Chinese culture, "youth" in the Comanche, and "boy" in the rural Irish are oriented to the key status in their respective cultures.

In the following schematic diagram, Figure 1, the term "status of orientation" will be used to refer to the key status of a given, culturally determined life cycle. The status preceding it will be designated the "status of annunciation," that following it, the "status of renunciation." The diagram is arranged to schematize the three intergeneration relations, as well as those between the three major statuses of the individual life cycle. At the right side of the statuses are shown our version of the three nuclear families of Ego which form the skeleton of all kinship structures, parallel with the age statuses of Ego. The annunciation status of Ego is parallel with Ego's family of "maturation"; the orientation status with the family of procreation; the renunciation status with the family of "gerontation." The departure from anthropological usage here is that we have changed the name, family of orientation to family of maturation, and added a third nuclear family in the family of gerontation.[25]

Figure 1 asserts only that the individual passes through a system of statuses, forming part of a moral universe defined in the ethos, that one of the statuses (orientation) is that in which he will attain the maximum integration in his life cycle with the major cultural activities as defined in the ethos; and that he must pass through a stage of preparation for (annunciation) and withdrawal from (renunciation) this major integrated status.[26] The duration, character, and subdivisions of the general life cycle statuses are determined by the particular culture.[27]

The accompanying diagrams set forth some selected concrete life cycle relations. Figure 2 is that of the middle class[28] urban, white-collar employed male in the culture of the United States;[29] Figure 3 that of the corresponding urban middle-class housewife; Figure 4 that of the eldest son in the ancient Chinese noble family.[30]

In the middle-class culture of the United States, the "key" or orientation status is that dubbed by Parsons the "male adult breadwinner." This status is structurally somewhat segregated from the family proper in that its charac-

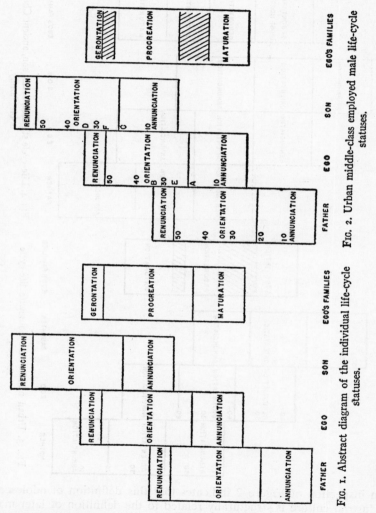

FIG. 2. Urban middle-class employed male life-cycle statuses.

FIG. 1. Abstract diagram of the individual life-cycle statuses.

teristics are determined in the occupational system. The breadwinner status is the main prestige-bearing status, and childhood, adolescence, old age, and the feminine key status of housewife and mother are derivative from this male status, carrying considerably less intrinsic prestige.[31] The exaggerated stress on the male status of orientation in the culture of the United States has created a series of observable discontinuities in the life cycles of men and women, particularly at the beginning and end of the orientation period.[32]

Students of the youth culture in the United States have long been aware[33] that processes of attrition in the family structure on one side, and the arbitrary cultural definition of industrial adulthood on the other, have created what amounts to a unique age status, generally termed adolescence, a status which appears to be not entirely a consequence of the biology of maturation.

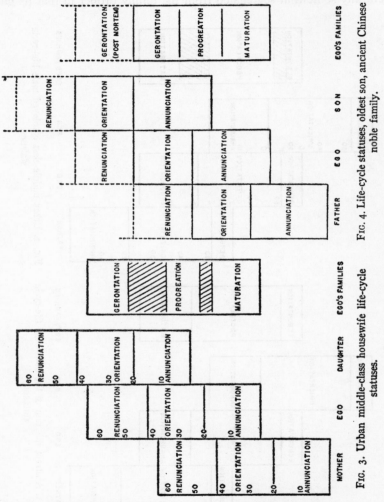

Fig. 4. Life-cycle statuses, oldest son, ancient Chinese noble family.

Fig. 3. Urban middle-class housewife life-cycle statuses.

An inspection of Figure 2 indicates that this definition of adolescence in the industrial culture is structurally related to the definition of later maturity, or old age. The male orientation status requires the functional independence of the son's job from that of the father, since succession in work in the industrial society is not provided in the family proper.[34] The associated vertical social mobility assumes that the son will choose his own mate, founding his own family of procreation independently at the beginning of his orientation period. In Figure 2, thus, Ego's life cycle is broken away from that of his father along the line AB, and the life cycle of Ego's son is broken away from Ego's life cycle along the line CD.

The break between Ego and his father at this point has a number of consequences for all the age statuses. The male Ego moves abruptly from the fairly well integrated informal peer groups of adolescence into what is essentially a new culture.[35] The novelty of this culture is accentuated by the relative narrowness and specialization of the orientation status as contrasted with the roundedness[36] of the annunciation status. At the time of passage into the orientation status, Ego's connection with his family of maturation is at its final minimum, and he has not yet founded his family of procreation. His institutional connections reach one of the minimal points in his life cycle between the ages of fifteen and twenty-five. From this point until the end of the orientation status, Ego will be connected with the specialized structure of the occupations, with the relatively narrow role of husband in the urban conjugal family, and with what secondary informal or formal organizations are available to him in the adult peer structures of the urban environment.

The immediate effect of Ego's passage into the orientation status on his father's life cycle status are not pronounced, but they have a different result for Ego's mother's status. Ego's passage, as will be indicated below, marks the end (if he is the last child) of major elements in the housewife's status of orientation, and thus the onset of the status of renunciation for Ego's mother. When Ego's father's status of renunciation is determined by retirement or superannuation from the occupations (the line EB), Ego is by this time thoroughly organized in his orientation status and his family of procreation, leaving his parents only such institutionalization as is provided by the family of gerontation. When Ego reaches this same period (the line FD) his life cycle will be at a similar period of minimal institutionalization. Even before this, the family has become the family of gerontation, a family functionally isolated from those of the children for a period which may, in the U.S. culture, last from sixteen to nineteen years after the marriage of the last child.[37] Even before this point, the maternal and paternal functions of the family of procreation have begun a steady decline. After retirement, Ego must rely heavily for institutionalization on the small universe of the gerontation family.

Comparison of the life cycle in the Chinese specimen with the contemporary cycles of Figures 2 and 3, suggests a probable lack of most of the institutional discontinuities sketched for the latter. Where status changes do occur, the continuous family structure provides the integration-maintaining rites of passage; moreover, the status of later maturity has an obviously different structure in the Chinese life cycle. With the Chinese noble eldest son, the status of orientation continues throughout all the latter part of life. He does not enter the status of renunciation until sometime after his actual death. The life cycle is probably somewhat analogous in the culture of the United States at the extremes of wealth, or in other cases in which there is family succession and control in an enterprise.[38]

If the life cycle discontinuities outlined in the middle class examples are compared with mental disorder commitment rates, there are suggestive correspondences. The determination, by sociological research, of the exact structures of the various life cycles should carry this relation beyond mere correspondence.

For the general mental disorder rates, as Landis and Page put it, "The two marked changes in incidence rates during the life span occur at the transition between adolescence and maturity, and between maturity and senility." They find that at all ages over 15, the closest approximation of the rates is between 35 and 45 years of age for the two sexes, after which the male rate rises above the female rate, but with both rates rising very rapidly after 55.[39]

Neither the theory of adolescent physiological storm and stress nor the doctrine of the female climacteric physiology gives a satisfactory account of these "marked changes." Biology does not abound in discontinuous events and sharp changes. The growth spurt, as such, is largely over before mental disorder rates climb, from ages 17 to 24; and the middle-life disorders of women begin too early, continue too long, and do not characterize enough women to explain the female rate variations.[40] No changes in the body *at the beginning* of senility can account for the rapid rise in the rates for both sexes; indeed, in view of the negative evidence as to the etiological significance of purely somatic factors cited at the beginning of this paper, the wisdom of searching for such changes seems doubtful.

If we turn to the life cycle structure as a whole in Figure 2, we find that the climb of the male mental disorder rates from ages 15 to 25 is congruent with an area of minimal institutionalization between the annunciation and orientation statuses. In the status of orientation, a number of studies have indicated other discontinuities produced by conflicts, differential male spatial mobility, Cottrell's overlapping incompatible roles, and Protestant individualistic isolation (Durkheim's *egoisme*).[41] The mental disorder, like the suicide differentials, suggests that the breadwinner prestige is a Pyrrhic triumph for the male.

Komarovsky's samples, and those of other students, show sufficient changes in the middle-class feminine life cycle between 15 and 25 years of age to explain a quota from this class in the lesser but still pronounced upsurge of the female rates.[42] Further analysis of the feminine cultural life cycle gives a fair account at other age categories.

The feminine statuses maintain, as is indicated by the lesser shading in Figure 3, a closer organization in the family universes than the masculine, even in urban areas, particularly where each generation is married.[43] There is continuity between the life-cycle statuses of mother and daughter, and this continuity may explain at least a great part of the lower female susceptibility, until extreme old age, to certain types of mental disorders.[44]

This is not to say that the female life cycle is without problematic areas. As is indicated in Figure 3, the functions of her status of orientation begin a steady attrition after the age of thirty-five. She begins to enter what is essentially her status of renunciation. The age-lateralization of her children's relationships in their statuses of annunciation in the peer groups and educational system steadily reduces both the maternal and paternal functions in the family of procreation; the difference here being that the male, at this particular time, is less dependent for integration on these functions. Census averages suggest that the unemployed housewife status, with the dwindling of the maternal functions, begins to become seriously isolated, except for secondary groupings, after thirty-five.[45]

The approximation, beginning at 35, of the general female mental disorder rates, in incidence, to those of the male, and the rise in the female involutional melancholias, furnish an intriguing possibility for research in the sociology of the mental disorders of later life. Indications from cultural anthropology are quite suggestive here, since the presence or absence of climacteric disorders seems to hinge upon whether the feminine life cycle offers sanctioned and well-institutionalized roles subsequent to the maternal function. The lack of such roles for the unemployed urban middle class housewife is obvious.[46]

Further consideration of life cycle variations is beyond the scope of this paper;[47] but the isolating factors considered above seem to offer, even in their present form, the basis of more likely hypotheses for interpretation and study of mental disorder rates in later maturity than do most current approaches.

Analysis of the life cycles of the two sexes in the culture of the United States suggests that old age, like the other age divisions, is not to be understood solely as the expression of biological processes. It is, instead, a very complex social status, defined by a particular culture, in which the roles of the individual are organized to withdraw him from the major functions of his status of orientation. When the renunciation status is analyzed in cultural terms, it is apparent that for both sexes in the culture of the United States it is associated with grave isolation potentials, given the accent of the culture on the male orientation status and the relations to this status of the female orientation status. The delineation of the varying concrete life cycles, the determination of their isolation potentials, and the subsequent correlation of these potentials with personality phenomena such as mental disorders constitute a very strongly indicated task for sociologists and anthropologists.

Research in the mental disorders of later maturity might be set up in two tentative hypotheses, one for the male, and the other for the female. Within these basic hypotheses a series of verifying investigations can be designed.[48]

The hypothesis for the male may be put, generally, as follows: When family intergenerational continuity is maintained, and when spatial and social mobility are at a minimum, and when the status of orientation is of maximum length and does not begin or terminate abruptly, the mental disorders of later maturity, organic and functional, should be at a minimum.

The hypothesis for the female, which is different because of the derivative organization of the major feminine status, is as follows: If family intergenerational continuity is maintained, and if the attrition of the feminine status of orientation is accompanied by new sanctioned statuses, feminine mental disorders, organic and functional, should be at a minimum.

Systematic research by sociologists and anthropologists along the lines suggested by these hypotheses might go far toward terminating the present dominance in the study of the mental disorders of later life of outworn ideas of unilinear organic causation. One very likely by-product of this research, in addition to its contribution to a dynamic social psychology, would be a scientific and not merely prayerful mental hygiene for the aged.

WORK CAREERS AND ASPIRATIONS
OF AUTOMOBILE WORKERS

Robert H. Guest

THE PURPOSE OF THE PRESENT STUDY[1] is to determine the extent to which modern mass production methods affect the career patterns of production workers, the degree to which aspirations are modified by long experience in this kind of mass production environment, and whether workers "question seriously the validity of the tradition of opportunity."[2]

The data are derived from personal interviews in the homes of 202 hourly production workers employed for at least twelve years in an automobile final assembly plant in an eastern metropolitan area. The sample, representing 14 per cent of the 1435 hourly production workers, was stratified according to several factors, including type of job, department, age, marital status, seniority, and others. Additional information was gathered from extended interviews with management and union officers. Personnel data were drawn from the personnel files. A certain amount of comparative data was taken from an earlier study of 180 new workers in a new automobile assembly plant.[3]

The first phase of this report is concerned with the actual career pattern of workers in the hourly production ranks. The second part of the inquiry is concerned with aspirations and more specifically with the answers to the following questions: What occupational goals do production workers set for themselves within the existing organization? Do these goals change over time? How and why do they change? What forces are at work which make men want to leave assembly line work, and what forces are operating to make them wish to remain? What kinds of total life aspirations do men have after working several years in the technological environment of an assembly line, and is there any conflict between the reality of their own experience and the tradition of vertical mobility deeply rooted in our culture?

Careers. In examining the work careers of the men in our sample of 202 assembly line operators, it was found that the great majority of men, 70 per cent, underwent a substantial rise in their economic job status, an average increase of more than 500 dollars a year, when they took a job in the assembly plant. Having made the initial jump in job status, a levelling-off process took place for those who continued over the years to work on production jobs. The leveling-off is explained by the fact that the wage differential between the lowest and highest paid jobs on the line was small. Although there were at Plant Y fifty-four different job classification titles, these classifications fell into eight pay groups.[4] Ninety-five per cent of the workers fell into four pay groups, the highest and lowest being 20 cents apart. The differen-

Reprinted from *The American Sociological Review* (April 1954), pp. 155-63, by permission of the author and the publisher. (Copyright, 1954, by the American Sociological Society.)

tial for 60 per cent of the workers was 10 cents. In other words, advancement for production workers within the hourly ranks was highly restricted.

By examining the data for each worker from the time of employment to the present—twelve to fifteen years later—it was possible to measure how much change, if any, took place during this period. To make the comparison we took each worker's first regular job and assigned today's equivalent pay rate to that job. Then we compared the difference between his first job, adjusted to present wages, and the wage rate of the job the worker held at present. The results of the comparison are shown in Table 1.

Table 1—Comparison of Wage Rates First Regular Job (Adjusted) and Present Job

Number of Workers	Per Cent of Sample	Amount of Change (in cents)
3	1.5	Increase of 26 cents or more
4	2.0	Increase of 21 to 25 cents
6	3.0	Increase of 16 to 20 cents
24	11.9	Increase of 11 to 15 cents
33	16.3	Increase of 6 to 10 cents
45	22.3	Increase of 1 to 5 cents
64	31.7	No change
12	5.9	Decrease of 1 to 5 cents
3	1.5	Decrease of 6 to 10 cents
4	2.0	Decrease of 11 to 15 cents
1	.5	Decrease of 16 cents or more
	98.6	
3	1.5	Indeterminate
202	100.1	

A slight improvement in job status is discernible—5 cents on an average, or the equivalent of one job class. The largest group (31.7 per cent) experienced no change whatsoever, and one in every ten workers held a job today which was lower in occupational status than his first job.

It must be recognized that this analysis conceals the fact that all workers *collectively* had improved themselves substantially from 1937 to the present. In 1937 a man received 65 cents an hour. In 1952 when this study was made the minimum starting wage for production workers was a dollar and eighty-two cents, or almost three times as much.[5]

Even with the increased cost of living, the over-all standard of living had clearly improved.[6] But the point here is that these gains have been collective in character. The worker, as an individual, experienced little in the way of advancement from one job to the next up the promotion ladder.

In order to understand why the wage range on hourly production jobs is narrow, and why work careers do not show much in the way of individual gains in job status, it is important to understand first the technological imperatives of assembly line jobs. It is when one examines the intrinsic nature of assembly line work that it becomes apparent why there is a negligible gradation from job to job and why there is little actual change in job status over time. A characteristic of jobs on assembly lines is the limited range of individual skill and responsibility. Each job is broken down into a relatively simple set of elements. These elements or motions are performed in a predetermined cycle of time—a cycle which is practically identical for all men working on the conveyor, regardless of the part of the product worked on or the tools used. For most workers the time cycle is of short duration, between one and two minutes, depending upon the speed of the conveyor. The work is highly repetitive.

Since differences in pay in industrial occupations are generally related to differences in skills, it is not difficult to understand why auto assembly jobs fall into a relatively narrow pay range and why, even among men with several years' experience, any upward change in job status within production departments is hardly discernible. Also to be considered is the history of union wage policy which has had the effect of compressing wages within a narrow range.

The concern of this study is with those whose work careers were limited to the hourly production ranks. It is not a study of mobility into higher supervisory ranks. Nevertheless, the extent to which other hourly production personnel could and did move into supervisory echelons is important for the later discussion of aspirations. The principal avenue of advancement for production workers was into supervisory jobs in the production departments. Almost all of the eighty-three incumbents of these jobs, comprising 3½ per cent of the total plant population, were men who started their work careers on the assembly line. The company actively promoted a promotion-from-within policy. Advancement into staff and service supervisory jobs from hourly production jobs was possible, although only seventeen of the eighty-eight supervisors in these departments began their work careers on the line. Twenty-nine of the 197 non-supervisory salary jobs were held by men who started their work careers "in production."

The exceptional production worker thus could and did move into higher supervisory jobs. From the point of view of the 1435 men the chances for advancement were limited. The demand for specialized technical knowledge virtually precluded movement into departments such as Maintenance and Engineering, Accounting, Specifications, and Personnel. Moreover, turnover in salary jobs was low when compared with turnover of hourly production workers. In the principal and direct channel of promotion up through production departments, one foreman job opened up for every 120 workers during the year the present study was made. At the time of this study, the company had instituted a program of introducing college-trained men into a few of the line supervisory jobs.

Summing up the description of work careers, it may be said that the average worker with long service in the production ranks had made a substantial economic gain in taking a job on the assembly line, and had experienced a very slight rise in individual job status over a period of twelve to fifteen years, a condition arising essentially out of the technological standardization of skills.[7] The potential for movement into supervisory jobs existed, but such movement was limited by the available openings, by low turnover of salaried positions, and by the fact that the restricted range of skills in assembly line operations had a tendency to limit movement into skilled non-production work and into certain staff positions.

Aspirations of Production Workers. It is within the framework of the above picture that workers looked at their occupational goals. The first task of the study was to find out what kind of jobs workers hoped or expected to move to within the organization. In the course of each interview workers were encouraged to describe the jobs they "would like to do most" at Plant Y and the reasons for the choice. Table 2 shows the results.

Table 2—Types of Occupation Aspired to by Production Workers

Type of Occupation Desired	Number	Per Cent	
Production work (hourly wage)		43.6	
Present job	42		20.8
Production job off the line	25		12.4
Repair	18		8.9
Utility or relief	3		1.5
Non-production work (hourly wage)		36.1	
Maintenance (craft job)	36		17.8
Quality control (inspection)	19		9.4
Materials handling	18		8.9
Supervisory	14	6.9	6.9
Clerical	7	3.5	3.5
Other		9.9	
No job at Plant Y	11		5.4
Indeterminate or does not know	9		4.5
	202	100.0	100.0

The largest group, 20.8 per cent, indicated that they preferred to stay on their present jobs. Most of these were men who held the more desirable jobs, those off the line or in repair work. The rest of the workers expressed a desire to move away from their present jobs. Interestingly enough, the overwhelming majority of this group held their aspirations down to other blue-collar jobs, and only 7 per cent expressed the desire to become supervisors. This differs considerably, as we shall see, from the supervisory aspirations of younger workers in a newer plant.

A strong desire to move into skilled jobs was evidenced by the fact that the second largest group (17.8 per cent) were men who expressed the desire to move into craft work in the Maintenance Department. The third largest group were those who wanted to get a production job off the main line.

In general it may be said that, while a desire for some kind of change was evidenced, most of these production workers were not strongly ambitious. They were setting goals which in terms of expected monetary return were modest. Even so, the availability of many of the jobs aspired to was limited. Only 6 per cent of the present skilled maintenance workers had started their careers on the assembly line. The number of off-line jobs was only a fraction of the work force, and these jobs were held by men of long seniority.

It was considered important to look back at the earlier study of Plant X where men had been on an assembly line from only six months to two years, and where the plant itself was new. We wanted to find out whether younger workers differed in their occupational outlook from men with long experience on the line.

Among the young men in the new Plant X, the desire to change one's job status was considerably greater than it was among the older workers at Plant Y. Only 8 per cent of the men at Plant X indicated they wanted to stay on their present jobs. The largest number of men, one-fifth of the group, wanted to become supervisors.

It is perhaps to be expected that young men aspire more than older men. Nevertheless, these data suggest that an important change apparently takes place the older a worker gets and the more experience he has in this kind of technological environment. It would appear that younger workers tend to approach their job future with more expectation of vertical mobility.

Workers in both plants were asked: "What do you think your chances are of getting into this kind of job?" Of the younger workers (Plant X), 60.7 per cent thought they had "poor or no chance" and the older workers (Plant Y) 81.5 per cent gave the same answer. Obviously the majority of workers in both plants were not optimistic about their chances of getting the kind of job that they had previously indicated they wanted, and the older workers were far more pessimistic, or realistic, about their chances. This fact is particularly significant when we recall that the goals which the older men at Plant Y set for themselves were considerably less ambitious than those of the younger workers at Plant X. Whatever their goals were years ago when they began work on the line, their own career experience has convinced them that they cannot expect much in the way of advancement in the traditional sense of the word. Opportunity, as will be seen shortly, is viewed more in terms of continuing to hold to a secure job, or moving on to a job which is not conveyor-paced and not as fatiguing.

The next step was to explore in greater depth the reasons men wanted to quit their jobs, and the reasons impelling them to stay. A hypothetical question was asked of every worker: "If you had a chance to take a job outside Plant Y or to stay at Plant Y, what would you do?" These responses were analyzed and scored in terms of the probability of one's leaving or staying. Slightly over half indicated they were more likely to leave than stay.

Leading the list of factors impelling men to want to leave were those which had to do with the work itself—the dislike of conveyor-paced operations, the individual work load, the restricted job cycle, and the repetitive character of the job. These were all factors intrinsic to the technological demands of this type of work. In our earlier study at Plant X, and in other phases of the Plant Y study, these factors were found to be of greatest importance in explaining job dissatisfaction. It is not surprising to find these same factors appearing among the reasons workers gave for wanting to leave their present jobs.

Lack of advancement opportunity on the present job came out next in frequency of comment among reasons impelling men to want to leave. It is recalled that workers, when focusing on aspirations for advancement to better jobs within the plant, talked very little about aspiring to higher-status jobs as such. Many wanted to get away from their present jobs, but they appeared to have resigned themselves to the fact that mobility upward was hardly possible. But here, in response to the question: "Would you leave if you had a chance?" the desire for advancement appears as a factor impelling men to want to leave the job. This suggests that an underlying desire to rise in the occupational ladder exists among these workers, but the desire comes to the surface and is articulated only when a broad freedom of choice is offered in the question, "if you had a chance."

Fear of not being able to keep up the pace of work because of age appears as another force operating to make men want to leave the job. Such fear may be found in any kind of occupation, but the condition here was especially acute because of the immediate nature of the work itself. Next in order of importance as a reason for wanting to leave is the factor of bad relationships with supervisors. Very few workers appear to have been motivated to say that the low wage on their present jobs was a reason for wanting to leave.

Workers also talked about the reasons that they would not leave even if they had a chance for another job on the outside. The most dominant theme in this phase of the remarks was the desire to maintain job security, and to these workers seniority was the symbol of security. Closely allied to the security theme were such factors as fear of being too old to get another job, fear of being laid off on another job, fear of having to start up from the bottom, and fear of not being able to make as much money. Far down the list were such positive attractions as chance for advancement, liking the work, and appreciating the working conditions. Out of a total of 435 comments from all 202 interviews, only eleven comments were of this type.

Although the above answers showed that less than half indicated they probably would stay, the fact remains that all of these men had stayed on the job for twelve to fifteen years. Their responses did not indicate therefore a true probability of leaving, but only a verbilization of a wish on the part of the worker. Another kind of question was used to probe more deeply into the reasons the men stayed. Each worker was asked: "You said you would (or would not) take a job outside of Plant Y if you had a chance. What do you suppose is the real reason why you have stayed on at Plant Y?" This question, like the previous one, was separately scored in terms of the probability of leaving or staying. The results are given in Table 3, together with the analysis of the previous question.

Table 3—Probability of Leaving or Staying on Present Job

Answer to Previous Question "Would Leave If Chance?"		Answer to Question "Why Have Stayed?"
15.8	Highly improbable would leave	59.4
29.7	More likely not to leave	24.8
45.0	More likely to leave	8.9
5.0	Highly probable would leave	1.0
4.5	Indeterminate	5.9
100.0		100.0

An overwhelming majority, 84.2 per cent, in explaining why they stayed at Plant Y, admitted directly or indirectly that they would probably continue to stay at Plant Y. The small number (9.9 per cent) indicating a likelihood of leaving were those who had clearly made up their minds to leave. Some had applied for an outside job, and two men had recently accepted other jobs at the time of the interview. A comparison of the results suggests what may be a conflict in the minds of these men on the assembly line. They want to leave, yet they want to stay. To illustrate this conflict, we have taken the comments that a worker made in response to one question and placed these comments side by side with his own comments on the other question. Typical statements made by six of the respondents appear below.

Notice the conflict in each set of remarks. When given the opportunity to answer the question about leaving Plant Y, a worker would say one thing. When asked later in the interview to express his reason for staying, he would say something quite different.

WOULD LEAVE IF CHANCE	REASON FOR STAYING
"You got a job for me? I'd leave tomorrow if you do. Why? I'll tell you: (1) No chance for advancement—they don't follow a policy of promoting from within. (2) Everything is impersonal—they don't give a damn about you as an individual, all they want is production and profits. (3) A human being can't keep up with the machine."	"Now ask me why I don't leave. I'll tell you. I'm afraid to take a gamble outside. I'm not staying because I want to. The only good thing is the pay. Besides, I've been sick in the last three years and I don't want to gamble."
"I think I would prefer to get another job somewhere else. Mass production is not too good for a fellow. Can't take too much. It works on your nervous system. It does mine; I don't know how it is on other fellows."	"Money is one. As far as seniority is concerned, I didn't care for that much. With a family you can't do much. Besides, starting rates are lower in other plants and I don't know how long I'd be working if I changed jobs. After forty years you're obsolete. Other companies wouldn't want to hire you."
"I'd take another job for this reason. Because of conditions in the plant. They make you feel when you're past so many years, when you've worked a certain amount of time, they want young blood, a guy who can keep on the grind. They figure a guy who's been working there ten years knows the angles, knows the ropes, knows too much to be of any usefulness to them."	"To tell you the truth, I'm past the age where anybody would hire me. If I go any other place, I have to start new, and any kind of a lay-off or shut-down and I would be the first laid off. In Plant Y I've got pretty good seniority. I would take a job for 30-40 cents an hour less, if I could be assured of the same seniority I've got at Plant Y."
"If somebody gave me a chance to take a job outside of Plant Y, I certainly would take it. I've no future over there. There's no room for advancement over there. It's just hard work, that's all."	"I don't know. You get on a job, you work on it for a certain time, you're used to a steady job, steady pay; you're a little reluctant to throw it over. You hesitate. After all, I've got enough seniority in Company Y so that I'll always have a job there. Money isn't the important factor; it's an agreeable job with agreeable people. After all, I worked there twelve years. I'm no better off now than when I started, only twelve years older."
"If I thought I had a half-way decent job somewhere else, I don't think I'd hesitate a minute. The automobile trade is just something that has to be done a certain way, and maybe human beings aren't cut out for that kind of work. I don't know." (What do you mean by a half-way decent job?) "One where I could see my future a lot clearer...."	"We haven't had much time to think of anything else but a steady income. I just stuck. Maybe I was afraid to take another job. Maybe that's it. Half a loaf is better than nothing."

"I'll tell you the truth. I have my eyes open now for a job on the outside, because I know that in time, when the next cutback comes, I'll be back on the line. Twelve years ago I was younger; I didn't mind it so much, but now, twelve years older, with the speed-up you just can't keep up. It's a rough job for anybody there. I don't think I'd be able to do it even if I tried. It's too much on the line."

"Mostly because I'm there so long. I wouldn't want to take a job outside when I didn't have some security. I'm here twelve years, and, although I don't like the place, at least I have a job."

He would say with considerable assurance and conviction that he would definitely leave if given the proper opportunity, then later he would admit that he probably would not leave. Job conditions, the pressures and tensions of the pace, work load and the highly repetitive operations cycles impelled him to want to get out. The fear of finding the same conditions in another factory compelled him to stay. He was afraid his age would prevent him from maintaining the pace on his present job, but he knew age was against him in finding another job. He wanted to have the opportunity to improve his social and economic status, but the uncertainty of what he might find once he broke his seniority made him think of the relatively good pay he was now getting and of the responsibilities he had toward his family. He was attracted to jobs outside which might give him the sense of independence that he appeared to want, but he understood the financial pitfalls of "opening up a little shop of my own." He wanted to learn a trade and get into skilled work, but he knew that his experience on the assembly line would help him little in such work.

In order to find out more about workers who had actually made the decision to leave and had taken the final step, a small sample of eighteen workers who had quit after twelve to fifteen years' service at Plant Y were interviewed. Considerable time was spent exploring in detail the reasons they had actually left their old jobs. The reasons given by the men in this group closely paralleled the reasons that the incumbent workers gave for wanting to leave the assembly line job. "Production pressure" (line speed, work load) topped the list, followed by lack of advancement opportunities, physical incapacity, aging, hours of work, general working conditions and others, in that order of importance. Of the eighteen men, four went into their own businesses, four went into a trade or craft, and the rest went into other kinds of jobs. Only two of the eighteen went into production work in industry.

As a final phase of the study of men who had remained at Plant Y an attempt was made to find out something more about the total life outlook of workers. Therefore, toward the end of each interview workers were encouraged to talk about their plans and aspirations for the long range future. It was found that slightly under 20 per cent were generally optimistic about the long range future. Twenty-four per cent were clearly pessimistic. The largest group, over half, made remarks which, on the verbal level at least, showed a considerable amount of mixed feeling.

Certain themes ran through the hundreds of qualitative remarks of these assembly line workers. The most prominent ones covered were aspirations for children, hopes for an independent business future, immediate desire to get out of the present line of work, no plans or aspirations for the future, and income and security of the present.

Workers spoke at length about their children's future. In general the man on the assembly line wanted his children to get a better education, and to avoid factory work. Most of these comments were in the nature of vague hopes with little indication of specific planning.

I would not let my boy work in an assembly plant, but if it was in the office that would be all right. Yes, I would like my boy to go to college and give him everything I can. (Note: the worker had said earlier in the interview about himself: "There is nothing to look forward to—nothing there at Plant Y for a man.")

No plans, no hopes, no future. Whatever happens, happens. I just hope that some day I could be established and I could give my kids a little more.

Some workers whom we interviewed were quite specific about the plans they had laid out for their children's education, as for example:

I want to send my boy to college—we started a college plan for him, and when he's ready to go the money will be there.

I'd like to see my son get an education. I've been saving and planning for it— we have an educational insurance policy for it.

I have an insurance policy on my daughter. She'll have money when she's ready to go to school. (After high school?) Yes. The boy (baby)—if he ever says he wants to work in any factory, I'll ship him out. I want him to take up a trade; plumbing would be a good one. . . . The girl ought to get a good office job.

This latter comment about encouraging a son to enter a trade was often heard among our respondents. They knew that their own confining experience in repetitive assembly line work precluded their developing craft skills. They were, therefore, anxious to see their children get an opportunity to learn a skilled trade. A few workers had at one time encouraged their sons to take a job at Plant Y. But, as one man put it:

When my kid got out of high school he didn't know what he wanted to do, so I said, "Come down to the plant and try it out." I got him an application and I took him to see ——— and he went to work. He got guts. He stuck it out for three solid months, and then he come to me and says, "Pop, I got bad news for you. You ain't going to like this, but I'm going to quit the plant. I can't take it." I says to him, "I don't blame you. If I was your age I would be out too." He is in the Navy now, and I am damn glad he quit the joint. I only wish I could do it too.

The desire to "go into a little business of my own" was another popular theme. Most of the men appeared to daydream or express a vague desire to set up their own shop, and a few indicated that they were making actual plans.

I'm going to night school, like I told you, and I would like to get connected in real estate and insurance. I've finished my insurance and passed it, but I have to take the examination for a license as an agent. I'm studying appraisals and so forth.

I want to get into that line, because a man can't live long at Plant Y. (Do you think you can connect yourself all right in insurance and real estate?) I have to. (The company president) came out once in the paper and said that the average life span of an automobile worker was five or six years.

I'm going to go into my own business, I guess. If I get enough money salted away and times look good, I'll open up for myself. I think I can make out good that way. Maybe hire a couple of men to work in my shop. I help different fellows here in (town) when they fix their cars, buddies of mine, and they all tell me I should have a shop of my own because I know the work so good. You work just as hard, but it's for yourself.

I'd like to have a little stationery store. Sell cards and stuff. But it takes a lot of money to start, and I can't give up my seniority.

I've been thinking about getting into a business of my own. I'd like to buy a gas station, but it's only a dream, I guess.

Yes, I have hopes. The only ones who don't have any hopes are dead. I've been thinking about going into business for myself, but it hasn't materialized because I can't raise the necessary capital.

Oh yeah, the wife and I always talk about selling the home and going to Florida. I have an uncle who runs a fishing fleet down there.

These comments reveal a persistent jockeying back and forth on the verbal level between wishful thinking and reality. The men yearned for the freedom which they thought "a little business of my own" would give, but they knew that to make the step would involve too much capital and not enough personal security.

To a substantial number of workers, only one thing concerning the future was important: the simple desire to get out of Plant Y. These workers, on the verbal level at least, were not concerned about broader life plans for themselves or their children. They were concerned only about the immediate present. As one said, "When you get home from that place you have no ambition. Unless it's a must and has to be done, you don't do anything. All I want is to get out of there." Or another put it simply, "I just want out of that plant."

One theme expressed as often as any other concerned the hopelessness of making any plans for the future or of having any strong aspirations whatsoever. Some of these workers were satisfied to let things drift along as at present. Others were not satisfied about the present or the prospects of the future, but they were resigned to the fact that there was little they could do to change their own personal future. As some of them said:

I think you can't plan too far ahead. You never know what's going to happen tomorrow.

I don't know. I've been there for fourteen years and I haven't accomplished a thing.

It's hard to make plans working in that place. You never know what you are going to be doing next, and with today's prices you can't get ahead at all. I just gave up hopes.

I figure I've got about ten-fifteen years more in me for the line. I take good care of myself. I don't smoke, don't drink, and I don't carouse around. I'll be on the line fifteen years in July, and I think I can last another fifteen, if I take care of myself. Then I'll get a job off the line—maybe a sweeper's job. It's not a tough job, it's easy. Wouldn't that be something, to end my years at Plant Y in a blaze of glory as a sweeper!

A small minority of workers appeared to be fully satisfied that continuing to work on the assembly line would give them the kind of future they wanted. As two of them put it:

I live close to the plant and make good pay—what else do I want? I don't want to make a pile of dough. All I want is to have my bills paid and keep this house.

I have lots of plans. I think we all have our little dream boats for something to shoot for. My immediate objective is to get my house built and moved in.

Conclusion. This study of a group of men with substantial experience on an automobile assembly line sought to determine how mass production methods affect career patterns, how the traditional culture concept of opportunity is modified by experience in this kind of technological environment, and whether workers question the tradition of opportunity.

The central fact about the work careers of those who remained as hourly production workers was lack of change in individual job status. Job rationalization had all but eliminated gradations in skills, and the intrinsic characteristics of the job of any indivdual remained substantially the same as the characteristics of the job for any other individual.

Aspirations about one's immediate job future in the plant appear to have been affected by long experience in this type of mass production work. Workers do not look for nor do they expect jobs which will give them a higher economic and social status within the existing organization. Instead, they hope for the break which will relieve them of the anonymity and impersonality of the line. They want jobs which they can handle as they grow older and which will give them more individual control over work pace. Their inability to achieve even these short-run and immediate gains was found to be a source of frustration.

In the long range picture, assembly line workers entertain hopes, on the verbal level at least, which are in keeping with the deeply rooted American tradition of opportunity. They want to quit the present job altogether and strike out on their own. Yet to leave means facing the unknown. The present imperatives of security and a reasonably steady income outweigh the attractions of the job world outside. A few workers are not troubled by this dilemma. They look to the immediate advantage they now enjoy of high wages and security. Some resolve the dilemma by building up hopes for their children's future. Others appear to resolve it simply by daydreaming about "going into an independent business of my own," knowing full well the idea is out of reach. But to the majority the dilemma is a persistent source of dissatisfaction. Our evidence in general supports Chinoy's findings, but it does not justify Chinoy's conclusion that workers are "unlikely to question seriously the validity of the tradition of opportunity."

A STUDY OF ROLE CONCEPTIONS IN BUREAUCRACY

Leonard Reissman

THE SOCIAL SCIENTIST has traversed the subject matter of bureaucracy with a variety of problems and interests, ranging from the historical descriptions of concrete instances of bureaucratic structures to theoretical frameworks designed to order the essential bureaucratic mechanisms. Its importance as an area for study increases with the realization that this form of organization[1] is becoming increasingly typical of the structures of American society as evidenced in the bureaucracies of government, education, labor, politics, and industry.

One of the major problems with which the sociologist has grappled in his approach to the subject has been that of clarifying the relation of the *informal* organization and social processes to the *formal* relationships and status positions as ordered by the bureaucratic rules. Any separation by the researcher of these two areas, which are in fact so functionally interrelated, leads to a limited or partial presentation of the real subject matter.

Phrased around the concept of "social role," the empirical study which is here presented seeks to accomplish two objectives: 1) to present data on American bureaucrats—a stratum of professionally-trained specialists in a State civil service;[2] and 2) to present the theoretical framework within which this study was conducted, as a suggested resolution of the methodologically created dichotomy of informal-formal structures in the study of bureaucratic organizations.[3]

The Theoretical Formulation. An adequate sociological presentation of bureaucracy must include the formal structure, the interpersonal relationships within it, and the effects of the surrounding social milieu. These three aspects can be interrelated in the "social role" which the bureaucratic official fulfills, as that role mirrors both the formal and informal structures, as well as the culture of which he is obviously a part. The following quotation from George H. Mead presents the social psychological mechanism of role-taking, where "role" is defined as the expected or recurrent behavior in a given situation:

... the human organism may arouse the same response ... in itself which it aroused through its gesture in the other form (other human organism) and it finds itself, therefore, in the attitude of the other in so far as this attitude which it calls out in another is called out in itself.

Such a pattern would only be present in so far as it served a function. The advantage of the individual approaching his own response from the standpoints of those also involved in the same conduct is evident enough. It would need to be present in the emphasis which it would give to appropriate responses of the individual. ...

A matter of very great importance in connection with this consideration is

Reprinted from *Social Forces* (March 1949), pp. 305-10, by permission of the author and the publisher. (Copyright, 1949, by The Williams & Wilkins Co.)

the organization of the conduct of the individual about this pattern of group activ-
ities, and in so far as these group activities are interrelated, about the pattern of
the group conduct as a whole. . . . The self, then would inevitably be organized
about the pattern of the group activities in so far as they are unitary. In various
respects this is the case, and those respects are particularly important to the individual. They are those in which the individual has specific functions, duties, rights,
and privileges in the group.[4]

Two factors are important in the use of the concept of "social role." First,
the social role must always be seen in terms of a given social situation.
Secondly, allowance must be made for a range of individual role fulfillment
based upon that person's experiences and values, if the *concept* of a social
role is to be more adequately expressive of an *acting* individual. The alternative is rejected—that of structuring the social role exclusively in terms of the
situation and ideal behavior patterns derived therefrom with little or no
concern for modifications due to individual definitions. Such an approach
would lead to formulations of behavior based solely upon logically derived
extensions of an ideal-type concept of bureaucratic organizations.[5]

The problem posed by this study was to determine what the civil servant
conceived his social role to be. In addition to "role," a corollary conceptual
tool was introduced. The content of the responses given by the bureaucrats
was viewed as constituting a synthesis of three functionally interrelated levels
of defining the situation in which the role is performed. The first consists of
the culturally prescribed behavior which conforms to the normative standards
of the society. The respect for individuality, the altruistic submergence of
individual ends for the good of the group, and the qualities of amiability in
dealing with people are indicative of such values to which the civil servant,
as a member of society, gives credence. The second level consists of the
bureaucratically defined behavior required by the formal structure of the
organization. The duties, the authority, and the responsibilities which inhere
in the office occupied by the individual civil servant carry with them highly
explicit definitions of relationships and functions. The third level is that of
the individually defined behavior which takes into account not only the
requirements already distinguished, but also adds to it the unique individual
elements. This includes the final synthesis of the individual's experience and
the conception upon which he acts.[6]

The situational background against which this particular social role was
performed was the bureaucratic form of administrative organization, which
has been given its most explicit theoretical treatment by Max Weber.[7] Briefly,
it is characterized by an emphasis upon a rational organization ordered by
rules, a high degree of disciplined behavior, an established office hierarchy,
clearly-defined areas of power for each office, and appointed specialists to
fill these offices. The civil servant of this study then, is seen as a bureaucratic
official or specialist in a midwestern State government. He has shown qualifications (by means of a technical examination) to fulfill the duties ascribed to
the given office which he holds.

Seven areas of investigation were delineated to obtain necessary content
on the role conceptions of this stratum of bureaucratic officials:

Methodology of the Study. A note on the methodology of this study will
serve not only to relate the theoretical framework presented above with

the findings which follow, but also to present more concretely the characteristics of those bureaucrats being dealt with.

Information as to salary, job assignment, education, place and extent of public contact was already available from the personnel records of a 10 per cent random sample (705 cases) of the seven thousand civil service employees of the State.[8] Three discriminating criteria, whose use was dictated by the nature of the problem, were then applied against the sample 705 cases. The first criterion, evidence of successful completion of a course of college work, was applied as the only expedient and reasonably accurate measure of possession of certain technical and professional skills. The second criterion, evidence of contact with the public, was employed because it was felt that the highest degree of role awareness would be found among those who daily were being made conscious of their bureaucratic positions by such official public contact. A final criterion selected only those civil servants whose office headquarters were in the capital city, inasmuch as the expense involved in covering all areas of the State was prohibitive.

A universe of 263 cases thus was obtained for this study, focusing on that corps of bureaucrats charged with the interpretation and daily administration of the policies handed down to them by the elected legislators in the Capitol Building. The army of highly routinized stenographic and clerical workers was excluded from the limits of the problem. The universe was stratified according to salary and place of public contact (office or community) and a sample was drawn conforming to these proportions. Intensive interviewing was accomplished for 40 cases (15 per cent), although certain statistics were obtained for an additional 60 cases from this universe.[9] Further characteristics of the bureaucrats of this study show them to average 49.8 years of age, earning $321 per month, with 17 years of continuous service.

The civil servants were interviewed on the job and their responses were recorded verbatim, except for the material gained during a free conversation period immediately following each interview. The data were analyzed by delineating categories for each question asked in the interview, and testing for the significance of the difference of the frequencies thus obtained. Replies to several questions were juxtaposed for the purposes of analysis, although they had been separated in the interview schedule to serve as cross-checks.

Findings of the Study. An informative result of this study appeared when the concept of a single individual type was broken down to order the greater flexibility which was found to exist. In the literature, the trend has been to blot out individual differences in favor of a single type which fails to capture the subtle and complex background of the individual in the bureaucratic situation. In reviewing the interview data it was found that the subjects of this study exhibited allegiances not only to their job and the government which employed them, but also to professional organizations, to particular groups who were serviced or regulated by their bureau, and to other social constellations within the community. The seven areas of investigation noted above were treated first as discrete units in each individual case to determine the direction and nature of the subject's allegiance. Abbreviated examples of the direction followed at this point will serve to clarify this procedure.

Under the first section of the interview, the reasons given for entry into civil service showed either a positive and planned decision by the subject, or a negative one such as: "It was during the depression years and this opportunity came along." From other questions in this section the extent of activity in professional societies (holding office, attendance of conventions and meetings, etc.) was determined. Finally, the subject was asked to indicate whether he would derive more satisfaction from being recognized for the work he was performing by the people in his own department or by those in a similar profession.

Responses given in the second section of the interview were surveyed to determine whether the subject insisted upon a high degree of formality in dealing with the public with whom he came into contact or whether such contact rather was characterized by a greater informality. Here, too, the extent to which the civil servant felt the public made him aware of being "a government official" was sought, and the effect which such awareness played in his relations with that public.

In the third section, the following points were focused upon: whether the source of satisfaction with the job was basically oriented toward "things" or "people";[10] from which groups were close friendships sought (other civil servants, other professions, business men, etc.); and finally was the strength of the individual's feeling of belonging with other office personnel high or low as reflected in frequent identity of interests and exchange of invitations for meeting outside of the office.

The content and self-rating of the individual's aspirations and achievements were sought in the fourth section of the interview. Did he plan to remain in civil service or was he still speaking of leaving at the first opportunity to accept employment elsewhere? Were his future aspirations tinged with concerns for promotion within the service, or with attaining greater status among members of his own profession, or did they focus more directly upon "private" aspirations of owning a home or a car? Did he feel that he ranked favorably or not when he compared himself to like professionals who were privately employed?

In the fifth section, the responses were grouped to determine whether the individual defined the "good" civil servant principally according to a standard of job proficiency or according to one of general personal qualities such as amiability, sincerity, and the like. Also surveyed here was whether a high or low degree of "rule consciousness" was present, and whether or not the conduct of civil servants in the community was predicated upon a standard which was peculiar to them as an occupational group.

The information obtained in the sixth section exhibited the strength which the requirements of the job exercised when compared with the felt demands of a professional group and of the public generally. That is, the direction in which the civil servant would tend when confronted with such a series of choices.

Finally, the limits of the individual's conception of his place in the bureaucracy were appraised as to whether he was aware of the problems of other departments in the government and what he defined as "bureaucracy."

Each individual's responses were then charted to show whether his selection of means in performing the job and the stated goals to which he felt his job was contributing were directed toward or away from the bureaucratic structure. In other words, was he appraising himself *primarily* as a civil servant or did this particular job situation rather enter into the configuration as modified and secondary to other lines of affiliation? For example, the bureaucrat who has conceived his role about a strong professional ethos considers his government employment as just a place to do the work for which he has been trained. The bureaucrat who is more deeply imbedded psychologically in the service, on the contrary, is consciously and continually aware of his position as a government official and acts accordingly. The orientation of these two extreme types toward the matter of "rules" for example, are similarly opposed and a degree of leniency in the first instance and over-strictness in the second were evident.

The substantive content for each of the four bureaucratic types which follow represents only a beginning formulation in that the necessary criteria for delineating the individual in each empirical instance have not been sufficiently sharpened in this study. They represent more accurately a potential tool in the analysis of the "bureaucratic personality"; in capturing more adequately the ranges of real variation with the formal organization. They also present a means of ordering the data within the informal organization and indicate the consequences which the behavior of each type presents. They are included as ideal-types at present for these reasons.

The first type is the *Functional Bureaucrat*—one who is orientated towards, and seeks his recognition from, a given professional group outside of, rather than within the bureaucracy. He may be portrayed as a professional who "just happens to be working for the government." His evaluations of success and accomplishment are not measured in terms of satisfactorily fulfilling a given bureaucratic policy or aim (over and above that required of him in the position), but rather in terms of the professional quality with which he does his job. Psychologically he is facing outward and away from the bureaucratic structure. He entered civil service because it offered material advantages and allowed him to do unique or specialized professional work. He is active in his professional societies and seeks appreciation and recognition on the basis of his professional specialities. Avoiding any identification with the office group, he declines any such intimacy with other civil servants because it is based only upon a common work situation. His future plans include doing research along lines of professional interests. His standards for the "good" civil servant are the standards of success in the profession, and not necessarily related to success in the bureaucracy. He feels no conflict between his professional ethics and his job because only the former standard exists for him. The bureaucracy imposes certain well-defined limitations upon him, but within these he is professionally biased.

The second type is the *Specialist Bureaucrat*. Though he resembles the first type in his professional orientations, he exhibits a greater awareness of an identification with the bureaucracy. He seeks his recognition from the department and the people with whom he works rather than from like-professionals who are privately employed. He entered civil service for "negative" reasons, i.e., he was forced in because of the depression or a business failure. Though he contacts other professional people, he remains aware of the difference between them and himself as a government employee. The ambivalent nature of his position is evident throughout—the orientation to his professional status on the one hand, and his position within the bureaucratic hierarchy on the other. This is more pointedly shown in his aspirations which evidence a desire to "get ahead" in his profession, yet realizing that this must occur through the mechanism of the bureaucratic promotion system. Overly meticulous about the rules and regulations, he attempts always to remain safely within these limits.

The third type is the *Service Bureaucrat*. Here too, as noted in the preceding type, a position of ambivalence is created. He is oriented in terms of the bureaucratic structure, but seeks recognition for the job he does from a group outside of it. He entered civil service primarily to realize certain personally-held goals which center about rendering service to a certain group.[11] The bureaucracy offers a framework through which he can best function and his task is one of utilizing that mechanism to achieve his goals.

The last type is the *Job Bureaucrat*. He is immersed entirely within the structure. Professional skills only provide the necessary entrance qualifications and determine the nature of the work to be done. He seeks recognition along departmental rather than professional lines. Satisfactions are found in the technical aspects of the work itself, and improvement of the operating efficiency of the bureau becomes an end in itself. His aspirations consist of achieving material rewards and increased status through promotions. He strongly adheres to the rules and the job constitutes his full center of attention and the end to be served.

The over-all role conceptions as they mirror the three levels of situational definitions presented in the theoretical formulations above present additional data.[12] The civil servant readily identifies himself as working for the goals of the bureaucracy at those points which explicitly embody the ideal cultural values to which a democratic form of government is traditionally dedicated. He feels, therefore, that in his position he is "working for the good of the public" and that he is constantly "aware of the best interests of the public." Such values, however, undergo modification and interpretation as the bureaucrat is faced with fulfilling the requirements of his job. Hence, he is most pleased with those people who cooperate, follow instructions, and take the advice he offers, i.e. allow *him* to determine which course of action is to the "best interests of the public." He feels, too, that "the public" treats him as "just another government official" according to popular evaluations of government administration, instead of as an individual. This situation poses a dilemma for him, in that he desires on the one hand to be treated as an individual rather than as a cog in a machine, and yet on the other hand desires to retain his superordinate position which the bureaucratic rules reserve for him in his public contacts.

The bureaucratic structure also imposes certain values which must be incorporated into these role conceptions. Hence, we find that the "good" civil servant is one "who can get along with people," who is "honest" and "loyal" to the department, and who is not so ambitious that he is constantly striving to "get ahead" even though promotions might not be immediately available. There is the recognition that higher supervisory positions carry with them more discretionary power to modify existing regulations in certain cases. Such changes will be made more readily while working in the field rather than in the office, although the civil servant feels no greater psychological tension in one place as compared to the other. It is significant to note that his conceptions of bureaucratic organization are similar to those held by the public. He believes, for example, that government administration is less efficient than that of private organizations, and that personal merit and faithful service are more readily recognized in private employment. Also, the term "bureaucracy" is for him descriptive of the operation of the Federal government and he does not believe that "we have any 'bureaucracy' in this State."

That part of the role conceptions which incorporates the values on the individual level have been partly implied in the presentation of the bureaucratic types. Personal aspirations center about raising one's standard of living rather than specifically about job promotions. However, the level of achievement is appraised most often on a standard based upon psychic as contrasted with material rewards. Accordingly, the civil servant can rate himself equally with a similar age and professional stratum in the community. However, when he uses a standard of material rewards, he ranks himself below average as a consequence. He frequently speaks of changing to private employment or going into business for himself, but such mobility is often verbalized but rarely acted upon.[13]

Finally, the civil servant does not feel that he is part of a "government class" but instead identifies himself with other class and status groups in the community. This is bolstered by seeking his close friendships from professional and business people who are not employed by the government.[14] Naturally, the civil servant feels quite certain that there is no difference in the personalities attracted to civil service as contrasted to private organizations.

Conclusions. The concept of "role" offers a valuable tool for the study of bureaucracy in at least two important ways. First, it serves to focus upon the basic content and processes in the bureaucratic situation through the individuals actually involved. A range of individual variation is thus more easily grasped from which empirically derived types can then be constructed. Secondly, it serves to synthesize information gained from other relevant areas. White's studies[15] of the public's evaluations of the prestige of government employment and Kingsley's work[16] on the historical dynamics surrounding civil service reforms in England are but two examples of valuable corollaries against which the bureaucrat's role conceptions can be placed and interpreted.

Too often the personalities are overlooked as important data in the analysis of bureaucracy, although the individuals on all administrative levels who make the mechanism function are quite obviously an integral part of such study.

PARTICIPATION AND MASS APATHY IN ASSOCIATIONS

Bernard Barber

AMONG BOTH THE CITIZENS and the social scientists of American society there has been a continuous concern about what is very often called "mass apathy."[1] A journalist, for example, refers to apathy as "our fifth column."[2] A social reformer and quasi-social scientist sees "mass apathy" all about him. "What is this apathy that infects John Smith, American citizen, to the point where in utter frustration, despair, and hopelessness he exchanges life for existence?[3] And the attitudes of the ordinary citizen, who regards "mass apathy" as a simple fact and a social problem, may be seen in the following typical letter-to-the-editor: "Most people are active for personal objects, but regarding public welfare they are passive. Rather than bestir themselves, they let such things go. Their apathy paves the way for bosses, and bossing protracts inertia."[4]

Always implicit and sometimes explicit in such judgments is the view that "mass apathy" refers to a state of affairs which is wholly bad for a democratic society. This view places an absolute emphasis on the democratic values which are involved. But such an absolute emphasis can lead to unrealistic, utterly utopian demands for "voluntary" participation by the individual citizen in the affairs of his society. The following is a typical expression of this utopian ideology: "Democracy does not exist unless each man is doing his part fully every minute, unless everyone is taking his part in building the state-to-be."[5] Now whatever the expressive and inspirational significance of the foregoing ideological statements may be, they cannot be accepted by the social scientist or the interested citizen as accurate scientific diagnosis. They are inadequate because they ignore certain facts about institutional structure in general, and certain fundamental features of American social structure in particular. The most general purpose of this essay is to demonstrate the necessity of putting the behavior to which the notion "mass apathy" refers, in the context of American social structure *as well as* of American democratic values. An enlarged understanding of this kind should contribute to the fuller realization of the democratic values themselves.

THE VOLUNTARY ASSOCIATION

The voluntary association is peculiarly characteristic of American social structure as over against other types of society.[6] In American society, kinship and occupational roles and their associated interests are, to a relatively large extent, segregated both from each other and from other interests. In the occupational and kinship spheres, members of our society achieve success and happiness by their own individual efforts and achievements. In other

Reprinted from *Studies in Leadership: Leadership and Democratic Action* (1950), Alvin W. Gouldner, ed., pp. 477-504, by permission of the editor, the author and the publisher. (Copyright, 1950, by Harper & Brothers.) The article has been abridged.

types of society, by contrast, kin, caste, and community groups determine many of these interests that are segregated in our society. It is for the organized accomplishment of these segregated interests, and for such of the interests related to occupation and kinship as cannot be achieved by the individual himself on the job or in his "isolated conjugal" family, that associations exist in great numbers in the United States.

The characteristics of the association as a sociological type derive from its functions for the American social structure. Since it pursues specific interests, it always has at least some explicit purpose. Usually, moreover, certain new purposes emerge, purposes which are important to the several members in different degree. The members are also differentially aware of the existence of these emergent purposes. In a later part of this essay we shall see how this differential importance and awareness cause certain problems for the executives of democratic associations.

Since there is a multiplicity of discrete, relatively less important interests in our society which are not determined by kin or community groups, the individual has considerable choice in the matter of which he shall pursue. It is in this sense that membership in particular associations is voluntary. We must carefully note, however, that voluntary membership is never simply psychological willingness, but rather is always patterned by a complex of social, structural, and value considerations. For example, the increasing control by trade unions of access to jobs, manifested in "closed shop" practices, has altered the sense in which any individual worker's membership in a union is "voluntary."[7] The institutional factors which define the differential significance of voluntary membership have important consequences for participation behavior in the association.

A written constitution is typical of the association. This embodies a statement of the explicit purpose of the group and of the way in which the association will be organized to pursue this purpose. The chief feature of this type of organization is a set of offices defining the delimited obligations and responsibilities of those who fill the offices. These officeholders, these "officials," are chosen by the members. Sometimes only a few members, an oligarchy, choose the officials, but usually, in the voluntary association, all the members are given a vote in the election of officials since each and every member is assumed to have an equal interest. In principle, therefore, most voluntary associations are democratic. We shall examine, below, some of the conditions that limit the full realization of this democratic principle.

Although the association is characteristic of the United States, for the structural reasons which have been specified, it is not unique to our type of society. When similar structural conditions occur in small areas of societies which are, on the whole, structurally different from our society, voluntary associations emerge in those small areas.[8] It is only the vast proliferation of associations that is unique to our society.

Participation in Associations. Close investigation of the empirical data about participation in the voluntary association in the United States reveals three basic facts: (1) There is an almost countless number of associations in this country; (2) There is a large number of people who have no memberships in any association at all; (3) There exists, in any given association, an active minority and an inactive majority among the members. Each of these facts requires some further comment and illustration.

1. The phenomenon that has been called "the proliferation of associations" in American society has been remarked upon countless times. Even after one hundred years, however, the *locus classicus* for the observation is still de Tocqueville, who was one of the first to be struck by the prevalence and significance of associations in the American Democracy. After his visit of 1831 he wrote: "In no country in the world has the principle of association been more successfully used, or applied to a greater multitude of objects than in America. Americans of all ages, all conditions, and all dispositions constantly form associations."[9]

Seventy-five years later, the most distinguished British observer of American life, Lord Bryce, was similarly impressed. "Associations," he said, "are created, extended, and worked in the United States more quickly and effectively than in any other country."[10] This from the inhabitant of a country which is not without its own multitude of voluntary associations![11] But American observers themselves were overwhelmed by what they did not fully understand: instance the following from Charles and Mary Beard's *The Rise of American Civilization*: "The tendency of Americans to unite with their fellows for varied purposes . . . now became a general mania. . . . It was a rare American who was not a member of four or five societies. . . . Any citizen who refused to affiliate with one or more associations became an object of curiosity, if not suspicion."[12] There is, almost literally, a countless number of voluntary associations in the United States. An endless variety of specific purposes does not begin to exhaust the possibilities for associations, for any two or more of these highly specific purposes may multiply themselves in several combinations. And to increase still further the possible number, there is always the fact of local and regional differentiation in a country so large as the United States. The following statistical data, therefore, are intended only to be illustrative.

Associations abound in cities and towns of all sizes. In 1924, there were almost 3000 local voluntary organizations in a group of 140 rural villages.[13] Yankee City, with a population of 17,000, had 357 associations when it was studied in the early thirties; Boulder, Colorado, a city of 12,000, has 245 associations.[14] In 1935, there were 200 associations for 7500 Negroes in Natchez; in Chicago, with 275,000 Negroes, there were 4000 associations.[15] The total number of associations in even a single major metropolitan area may be inferred from these figures.

Business and professional associations are large in number and usually are subdivided into many constituent parts. In the American Medical Association, for example, there are 2000 county, parish, and district societies. There are a great many welfare, charity, and reform associations, of which the so-called "youth-serving" organizations alone comprise 320 national organizations.[16] In 1928, the General Federation of Women's Clubs included 14,000 constituent clubs.[17] The "service clubs"—Rotary, Kiwanis, Lions, Exchange, Civitan, and Optimist—number more than 9000.[18]

2. Although in comparative perspective the United States may well be a "nation of joiners," a survey of the available data on the number of people with memberships in voluntary associations reveals the little-known fact that many have not even a single such affiliation.[19] This uniformity too holds for all types of areas in the United States, whether urban, suburban, small city, small town, or rural. The universality of this pattern indicates the pervasive

effect of American kinship and occupational structures on urban and rural areas alike.

Two studies in metropolitan areas yield the same results. Among a sample of 5500 Chicago residents, Goldhamer found that approximately 30 per cent of the men and 40 per cent of the women had no memberships at all in associations.[20] Komarovsky reports for New York City that "in the bulk of the city's population, the unaffiliated persons constitute a majority."[21] In her sample, 60 per cent of the working class and 53 per cent of the white-collar men did not belong to a single association, with the possible exception of a church. Lundberg describes a similar participation situation in the suburban sections of the New York Metropolitan area.[22] In Erie County, Ohio, a medium-sized city with a surrounding rural area, a little less than 50 per cent of the population belong to no associations at all.[23] In Yankee City, with only 17,000 population, only 41 per cent of the total population are members of even one association.[24] The large amount of nonjoining has been documented most extensively of all perhaps for the rural areas.[25]

3. "Who says organization, says oligarchy." Thus has Robert Michels stated in another form his "iron law of oligarchy."[26] Gaetano Mosca has also noted the tendency toward activity and control by a few in all organizations, governmental and nongovernmental alike.[27] Such large generalizations are really statements of the problem rather than adequate analyses, but they do indicate the extent to which the pattern of active minority and inactive majority occurs.

"Apathetic" memberships are not a new phenomenon in the United States, despite the widespread myth that voluntary participation was complete in a "golden age" of the town meeting in New England. It was writers of the nineteenth century, de Tocqueville, for example, who first "assigned to New England towns attributes they never possessed."[28] Present examples of both the direct and the representative types of town meeting are just like their prototypes in this respect.[29]

The Scope of Oligarchy. No matter what interest any particular association represents, we find the existence of an active minority in control. In the "service clubs," for example, there is a very active nucleus and a large group who are "just members." Although each club has many committees and every member is expected to be active on at least one of them, many members are wholly inactive.[30] The American Legion was founded in 1919 by a small group and is run by a self-perpetuating oligarchy who have been called "kingmakers" by those who are critical of their power to name national commanders.[31] Goldhamer summarizes the situation for fraternal organizations as follows: "Though fraternal organizations are subject to democratic control, it appears that the actual formulation of policy . . . is largely the function of a few interested individuals, with the great bulk of the membership acquiescing so long as these policies do not interfere with their private lives."[32]

The Consumer Coöperative Movement, which stresses equal and active participation by all members more than most other associations do, is no exception to the active minority pattern. J. P. Warbasse, former President of the Coöperative League of America, says: "It is true that there is much indifference; usually a minority of the membership of local societies carry on the business."[33] Even in avowedly activist organizations, there is minimal participation. ". . . in the most powerful and deeply rooted People's Organizations known in this country the degree of popular participation reached a point varying between five and seven percent!"[34]

Figures for attendance at meetings of a wide variety of associations are another index of minority participation. In Boulder, Colorado, the average attendance for all types of organizations, including the churches, is only 51.4 percent.[35] In the organizations of the small town of Mineville in the Rockies, "usual attendance" consists of only a minority of the members.[36] Studies of local societies of the Coöperative Movement in different parts of the United States bear out the same facts.[37] Minority attendance in associations persists despite the frequent attempt to choose a time and place for meetings which least conflicts with the job and family obligations of the members. It persists also despite the enactment of bylaws imposing sanctions for nonattendance. Where they exist, such rules are more honored in the breach than in the observance.[38]

Social Sources of Participation Patterns. Can we account for these three uniformities of participation in voluntary associations simply by applying the value-laden term "mass apathy"? It is perhaps already apparent that a more adequate analysis requires consideration of certain features of the American social structure in which this behavior occurs.

We have already largely anticipated the explanation of the first uniformity, that of a vast proliferation of particular associations. American social structure, by segregating a large number of specific interests from kinship and occupational ties, with which they are usually fused in other societies, creates the need for a corresponding number of voluntary associations to pursue these interests. This large number is in turn multiplied many times by the great social and geographical diversity of the United States.

But American social structure does more than segregate these other interests from family and job obligations. *It defines them as being of less importance than family and job obligations.* The relatively peripheral significance of the interests to which associations devote themselves explains in large measure the second and third uniformities: many people have no memberships at all; and, among those with memberships in any given association, the majority are inactive and participate minimally. Because of the individual's culturally prescribed preoccupation in the United States with obligations to his job and his "isolated conjugal family," there exists a socially structured pull away from membership in even those voluntary associations relevant to his interests.[39] Further, even when he is a member of an association, the individual's interest is so limited that it leads to minimal participation. This definitely limited interest can be illustrated by the attitudes of members of such voluntary associations as farmers' coöperatives and trade unions.

But the general consensus among the farmers was that "as long as they give me good quality at low prices and a bonus besides, I do not care how or who runs the organization."[40]

The ordinary member sees no particular reason for "wasting" his time at meetings. "Let the officials run the union, that's what they're getting paid for," just about expresses his attitude. . . . As long as things go well, the average union member doesn't want self-government and is annoyed and resentful when an attempt is made to force its responsibilities on him.[41]

There is, in addition, another very important structural factor which contributes to the tendency toward inactive majorities in voluntary associations. The internal structure of the voluntary association itself, that is, with its formal organization and division of functions among members, makes it possible for a minority to achieve the interests of the association with the majority participating very little or not at all. This possibility, however, brings in its train certain consequences for the executives and the members of voluntary associations alike, consequences which are serious problems for both of them. Since these problems become especially acute in associations which stress democratic values, we shall examine both the sources and the consequences of these problems in such associations.

Values of Democratic Associations. Practically all voluntary associations are democratic associations, that is to say, formal authority resides in the whole membership. Indeed, this is the typical pattern of organization throughout American society: the state itself, the major and minor political parties and groups, occupational associations—whether executive, professional, or labor—and special interest groups are democratic associations.

Note that this definition runs in terms of the nature of the internal structure of the association, not in terms of the nature of the interest it represents. Some "democratic" associations have particularistic criteria for membership, for example, interests relevant to kinship as such, religion, sex, nativity, or race—interests deriving from "ascribed" rather than "achieved" statuses. Other associations stress universalistic criteria; there is an almost "utopian" emphasis on such criteria in the Consumers' Coöperative Movement. Formulated in what are known as the Rochdale Principles, they include the ethical desirability of voluntary affiliation and membership rights open to all without regard to sex, race, occupation, nationality, social class, religious creed, or political attachment.[42] In an important sense, the associations with universalistic criteria are more democratic than those with particularistic criteria, but for our present purposes it is important only that both types have an internal structure based on the democratic authority of the membership.

By definition, the democratic association states the desirability of and makes provision for the active participation of all members, that is, for their regular and frequent attendance at meetings, their taking part in discussion, their working on committees and holding office at some time: in short, for their participation in the formulation and realization of policy. The fundamental democratic instrument is what Barnard calls "decision by vote."[43] Most democratic associations implicitly guarantee this right. The Coöperative Movement states explicitly, as a cardinal principle, "one member, one vote," and even bans the use of proxies.[44] Where the membership of a democratic association is widely scattered, the referendum may be used to sound the will of the group.[45]

As a means to the distribution of responsibility and control, the democratic association is characterized by frequent and regular election of officers, short terms of office, and the rotation of any given official position among as large a number of members as possible. This value, we shall see, has a special relevance to the problem of security of tenure for executives in the democratic association. Where the association is large enough to be divided into many branches, it is considered desirable to have relatively large local autonomy, that is, a flow of power up from the local groups to the central coördinating group. In the large association, where national conventions are held, the democratic election of delegates to the convention is valued as a means of achieving total group influence on the policy of the association.

So that effective control over the executive may be guaranteed, the democratic association requires that the elected executive furnish regular, complete, and detailed reports on its implementation of policy and on all financial transactions. Members who are critical of the executive, or otherwise dissident, have a right to express their views, to communicate such criticism to fellow members, to organize groups with the association to foster their dissent, and, if these rights are denied by the executive, to inform the general public of their protest or to form a new association. The right of free speech in the national convention and in the official publication of the association gives the critical member the opportunity to transmit his opinion to the whole membership.

These are the several procedures for fulfilling the democratic values of participation. In practice, however, democratic associations typically fall considerably short of this fulfillment. It is our purpose here to analyze certain structural necessities in democratic associations which impede the full realization of the democratic values.

PROBLEMS OF THE EXECUTIVE IN DEMOCRATIC ASSOCIATIONS

We can best achieve our purpose by considering some problems of the executive in the democratic association. These problems are commonly thought to arise simply out of "mass apathy" or out of the corruption and weakness of the particular men who are executives in democratic associations.[46] Corrupt men and indifferent members do aggravate these problems, perhaps, but they are due also to the nature of formal organization and to the functions of executives therein.[47]

There exists for every association, democratic or not, the necessity to take action in the interests of that association. An undifferentiated group of members is uncoördinated and cannot act effectively. Internal specialization of function and the coördination of differentiated functional roles are required both for efficient organizational effort and for adequate handling of changes in the external situation that affect the group purposes. Responsibility for the coördination of internal effort and for decision about external situations are among the necessary executive functions in any organized group. "Authority" is the attribute by virtue of which obedience to orders of the executive is granted and maintained. By definition, then, in every association there will be specialized functions; and authority to pursue those functions will be granted by members of the association to the occupants of executive roles.

"Taking action" is not in itself a simple matter. When an association is part of and adjusting to a relatively stable situation, it must maintain a relatively continuous and stable set of actions with respect to its purposes. When the association is expanding rapidly or when the external situation is changing, executives must make adequate diagnosis of organizational needs occasioned by the changes and must take prompt and firm action to meet these needs. Two kinds of knowledge are required for action by executives, in both stable and changing situations. These two kinds of knowledge may be called "general" and "special." "General" knowledge includes a high level of ability in the executive functions themselves and in the technical knowledge relevant to the purposes of the association. "Special" knowledge consists in acquaintance with the series of decisions that has constituted any particular association in its immediate and perhaps more distant past. Without the special knowledge of how his association has performed in the past, the executive cannot predict how it will act in the future. And on his ability to predict depends the possibility of competent executive decisions.[48]

The democratic association shares with other types of association the necessity for specialized executive functions and legitimate authority. But if executive functions in the democratic association are to be described adequately, we must keep in mind one of Barnard's dicta: "Executive processes are specialized functions in what we know as 'organizations.' If these functions are to be adequately described, the description must be in terms of the nature of the organization itself."[49] That is what we shall do here.

In the democratic association, it is the active minority that takes responsibility and becomes the executive. Barnard has also referred to the "persistent disposition to avoid responsibility" on the part of most men in the oligarchic type of organization he describes.[50] In the democratic association, members may also desire to avoid responsibility, but this is due at least in part to their preoccupation with other interests and to their willingness to have the active minority discharge the major concern for the interests of the association. In any case, the existence of an inactive majority often requires the active minority to take more power than is formally granted to it under a democratic constitution.

Full-Time Officials. Beyond a certain point, the size and interests of a democratic association compel it to have full-time officials. It is probably impossible to make any general statement for all associations about where this point may be fixed. It is determined by the peculiar needs of each group. However, when these needs require that at least one person devote so much of his time to the purposes of the association that he cannot continue in his regular occupational role, the association must appoint or elect a full-time executive. If the former part-time executive now becomes the paid, full-time official, he has changed his regular occupational role. A new career opens up for him.

In the democratic association, to conform with the value that equal participation requires rotation of officers, the formal rules provide for regular election of officials for short terms. It is, however, an empirical uniformity that at least a few of the officials serve continuously and for a long time. The long-tenure officials are the ones who have the requisite "special" knowledge of the history of the association. In some democratic associations, most of the long-tenure officials are elected; in some others, most of them are appointed; but in all democratic associations at least a few of them are elected. These few are responsible for the appointment of hired assistants, and in some cases this paid staff includes a large number of people. Where members of the association itself are not trained or available to fill the paid staff positions, outsiders are hired. These several uniformities in the term and tenure of executives may be found in many different democratic associations. For example, in the local and parent groups of the American Medical Association, the president, president-elect, and the vice-president have "almost universally short tenure." However, the secretary and treasurer are reëlected time after time.[51] In the American Legion, a National Commander is elected each year for one year and the constitution forbids reëlections. But the National Adjutant, once elected, becomes a permanent official, and in many ways the key official in the association.[52] In American trade unions, it is the pattern for practically all elected executives to have long and continuous tenure.[53] Some of the special factors that influence the tenure of trade union executives will be analyzed below.

In any democratic association, the long-tenure elected officials become a center of power that may prevent democratic practices. Where these officials occupy the highest offices, they are often attacked by dissident members either for taking power inappropriate to their office or for continuing too long in that office in violation of democratic values. Both of these criticisms are made against trade union officials. Where the long-tenure officials occupy positions below the topmost ones, with the top ones being filled with rotating personnel, they are often criticized for usurpation of power. . . .

Emergence of Career Interests. Any "career" may become a goal in itself, partially independent of the purposes of the organization in which the career is pursued. Careers in democratic associations are no exceptions to this tendency. Whereas the original interest of full-time and permanent officials were wholly like those of all other members, they soon develop additional, emergent interests in their "jobs." An elected official of a democratic association must of course be a member, and membership implies possession of the relevant interests. In many associations in the United States, these interests are based on professional and occupational skills. When a member is elected a full-time official, he may come to have a greater or more valuable skill as an executive than in his previous occupational role. Consequently, he has a great interest in maintaining his new skill and position. Moreover, occupational and professional skills that are not used are subject to a process of atrophy, the rate of which will vary with the type of skill and with the extent of change going on in the knowledge on which the skill is based. For example, the scientific knowledge on which medicine rests has been changing very rapidly, much more rapidly than the principles and substantive content of the law. The professional skill of doctors-turned-executive will, accordingly, have a greater rate of atrophy than that of lawyers in the same position.

The atrophy of a former skill establishes new interests for the executives of the democratic association. So also does the higher general social status which comes with being the executive of a large and powerful group. For both reasons, there is a strain on the executive to preserve his new interests and advance them. *He has no formal protection for his position: hence the various informal ways in which he circumvents the formal prescriptions of rotation in office and actually secures extended tenure in an office in which he now has a great stake. . . .*

Thus, where there is no formal guarantee of security of tenure in an organization and where careers in that organization emerge, various informal devices for maintaining some security will be found. In many large democratic associations, the organization is "controlled" in such a way that officials are assured of reëlection. These control devices will be discussed later.

Role Conflicts. In the democratic association, since only members can be elected officers, the officials will have the appropriate symbols of the role and interest on which membership is based. . . . It is implicit in the values of the democratic association that the officers should be "one of us." There exists a recognition, perhaps inarticulate, of the desirability that the executive be a man who through shared and common experiences, through a "style of life" even, has come to have and symbolically manifests the same values as the rest of the membership. The symbolic identification of the leader with the membership reassures the inactive majority that their interests are being safeguarded.

However, when he is the executive of a democratic association representing lower-class people, it is also necessary for the leader to have the established symbols of status and power, since in our society access to these symbols is granted to all men. When their executives have these symbols, the lower-class membership can feel that "our power" is adequate, for they know that these are the necessary instruments of achieving their interests. To this extent, therefore, it is useless for opposing interests to try to undermine the authority of leaders by exposing their possession of upper-class status and power. The members may even take a vicarious pleasure in the middle-class status, remuneration, and style of life of their leaders.

But such power and style of life may involve the executive of a working-class association in conflicts of roles. Such conflict, for example, occurs for what has been called the "progressive" type of union leader. This is the trade union executive who thinks of his work as a "calling," in which he works for "principles" and "humanity." He believes that there should be "rank and file" participation and that the officers should be of the same class origin as the members. Personal modesty, indifference to "getting ahead," dislike for "big shots" are among his ideals. When this type of executive marries, however, he accepts the middle-class "culturally normative definitions of the role of husband and father . . . [of] 'good provider' . . . [of] 'companion.' . . ." Because of his long hours on the job, he must often choose between job obligations and the expectations of his wife that he will conform to middle-class patterns. The conflict may be resolved by making the trade union office "just a job."[54]

Executives in democratic associations face still other problems. In the democratic association the membership grants authority to the executive to carry out the purposes of the group. But general statements of policy never cover all possible concrete cases. In a complex and changing situation especially, new and unforeseen cases arise continually. In these circumstances, the executives must act to adjust the purposes of the association to the external situation. In short, the executive must formulate the interests of the group to some extent, as well as realize them. Continuous, day-to-day, *ad hoc* decisions may cumulate into policy for the association. This process may be called "executive legislation," on the analogy of "judicial legislation" as analyzed by Cardozo.[55] This executive legislation may be approved *ex post facto* by the membership in convention or by referendum. But there is always the possibility that the executive will get out of touch with the wishes of the membership, as the judiciary may get out of touch with the wishes of the majority as expressed in legislation. The membership of an association often accepts a certain amount of executive legislation of which it mildly disapproves only because it considers the alternative course, abrogation, more costly or more harmful to the purposes of the association.

Where especially quick action is required, there are certain inherent difficulties in the democratic process of decision which causes strain for executives anxious to take appropriate action. There is, in short, what Barnard calls "the dilemma of the time-lag," that is, a conflict between the requirement of immediate action and the slowness of the democratic process of approval.[56] This dilemma adds to the need for executive legislation.

Still further, on technical matters especially, the members of a democratic association may not be able to judge what their interests are, and therefore the executives often have the task of formulating those interests. Moreover, insofar as there emerge new purposes in an association—purposes relating either directly to the original ones or arising from changes in the situation or in the needs of the organization—there may be a period in which these new interests are not manifest to the membership. In this period the executive may be more aware of the existence of these new purposes and of the need to take action than is the membership. The latter may complain that the executive is "wasting its time." They may not see the relevance and importance of the new problems. There may also be a difference of time-perspectives. The members may be taking the short-run view while the executive is taking the long-run view. Such differences about the nature and existence of purposes, about the relative importance of different purposes, and about time-perspectives create special problems in the democratic association, where the executive must justify its actions to the membership. Although these problems are often thought to arise simply out of the apathy of members, we can now see in what way they are inherent in the structure of the democratic association.

One final problem for the executives in the democratic association requires our attention. There are strains implicit in the executive role in all groups. For example, the decisions of the executive, although often considered simply technical decisions, are almost always moral decisions as well.[57] The executive must choose among values. Moreover, the strain on the executive is increased by the existence of uncontrollable and unpredictable elements in the situation in which he must act and by the limitations, sometimes very large, on the knowledge he can use in that situation. Such strains are great enough where authority is oligarchically structured. But they probably become greater in the democratic association, where actions must be justified to a membership ideologically confused about the nature of authority and attendant strains. It has been noted that there is, in modern Western society, "a certain 'utopianism' which tends to minimize the significance of authority, coercive power, and physical force in human affairs. . . ."[58] This is particularly characteristic of the "liberal" credo, and in the United States the democratic association has a strong "liberal" tradition. The consequent undermining of what the executive considers necessary power and authority can be destructive of effective action in particular cases.[59]

Techniques of Control. We have seen that there are special strains on the executive in the democratic association. It must formulate purposes and take "unauthorized" action, yet it must also justify these purposes and this action to the membership. It develops special interests of its own in job tenure within the association, yet this conflicts with the democratic requirement of rotation in office. We shall now consider some of the methods whereby the executive provides the necessary conditions for effective action and insures itself security of tenure. These techniques of control are often criticized as "undemocratic" and "oligarchic." In any given association they may be "undemocratic" and nothing else. But we have seen that they may also have certain positive functions owing to the internal structure of the democratic association.

It is now a sociological truism that "informal" social organization is very important. This means that the scientific observer must always look at the actual behavior of a group as well as at the written rules governing the group. This is certainly true if one wants to understand the technique of control by the executive over the membership in the democratic association. Many of the formal instruments designed especially to secure control by the membership over the excutive actually function in the opposite way. In practice they are employed by the executive to control the inactive majority.

For example, in the large democratic association, the regular convention is designated the supreme source of authority. It passes laws and determines policy for the executive. The executive is required to report on its actions since the last convention for the approval of the present convention. In practice, however, the convention is so much controlled by the executive that it is often merely a rubber-stamp approval mechanism.[60] Serious criticism of the incumbent executives is rare at conventions. In effect, for example, the permanent officials of the American Medical Association are "virtually free, in practice, of critical supervision."[61] Reports of past executive performance become empty formalities, glossed over by automatic acceptance.

There are techniques of control that operate after the convention has been held. The permanent executive may moderate its wishes or alter them in the resolutions that are presented to the convention for approval and then realize its actual purpose through subsequent "interpretation" of established policy. In most large democratic associations, the permanent executives publish an official journal which is the main medium of communication among the members. Once again, however, in practice, "the main purpose is to promote the policies of the national administration."[62]. . . Control of the established instruments of protest and communication by the executive thus reinforces the inactivity of a majority which has other important interests.

IMPLICATIONS

In brief conclusion, it is desirable to bring out some implications of our analysis for democratic values and democratic action. The essential conclusion of our analysis has been that *both* democratic values and structural factors are relevant to the problem of "mass apathy" in the voluntary association. Both interact to create a certain kind of behavior. Perhaps the chief defect of those utopian views of participation which talk about "mass apathy" is that they look at the democratic values only. In this perspective, any discrepancy from full realization of the values seems to indicate alienation from those values. A great danger of the utopian attitude is that it sometimes, in its disappointment, becomes disillusioned or cynical rejection of the values themselves. A structural view of the whole of American society, such as we have taken here, can save us from this unwarranted pessimism. It is our hope that with this more adequate understanding of the problem of "mass apathy," democratic citizens and democratic administrators will be able to make concrete plans for enlarging participation in the democratic association.

CONTINUITIES AND DISCONTINUITIES IN CULTURAL CONDITIONING

Ruth Benedict

ALL CULTURES MUST DEAL in one way or another with the cycle of growth from infancy to adulthood. Nature has posed the situation dramatically: on the one hand, the new born baby, physiologically vulnerable, unable to fend for itself, or to participate of its own initiative in the life of the group, and, on the other, the adult man or woman. Every man who rounds out his human potentialities must have been a son first and a father later and the two roles are physiologically in great contrast; he must first have been dependent upon others for his very existence and later he must provide such security for others. This discontinuity in the life cycle is a fact of nature and is inescapable. Facts of nature, however, in any discussion of human problems, are ordinarily read off, not at their bare minimal but surrounded by all the local accretions of behavior to which the student of human affairs has become accustomed in his own culture. For that reason it is illuminating to examine comparative material from other societies in order to get a wider perspective on our own special accretions. The anthropologist's role is not to question the facts of nature, but to insist upon the interposition of a middle term between "nature" and "human behavior"; his role is to analyze that term, to document local man-made doctorings of nature and to insist that these doctorings should not be read off in any one culture as nature itself. Although it is a fact of nature that the child becomes a man, the way in which this transition is effected varies from one society to another, and no one of these particular cultural bridges should be regarded as the "natural" path to maturity.

From a comparative point of view our culture goes to great extremes in emphasizing contrasts between the child and the adult. The child is sexless, the adult estimates his virility by his sexual activities; the child must be protected from the ugly facts of life, the adult must meet them without psychic catastrophe; the child must obey, the adult must command this obedience. These are all dogmas of our culture, dogmas which in spite of the facts of nature, other cultures commonly do not share. In spite of the physiological contrasts between child and adult these are cultural accretions.

It will make the point clearer if we consider one habit in our own culture in regard to which there is not this discontinuity of conditioning. With the greatest clarity of purpose and economy of training, we achieve our goal

Reprinted, by special permission of Margaret Mead, the William Alanson White Psychiatric Foundation, Inc., and Patrick Mullahy, from *A Study of Interpersonal Relations*, edited by Patrick Mullahy and published by Thomas Nelson and Sons, New York. Copyright 1949, by Hermitage Press. (Originally published in *Psychiatry*, 1938, 1:161-67.)

of conditioning everyone to eat three meals a day. The baby's training in regular food periods begins at birth and no crying of the child and no inconvenience to the mother is allowed to interfere. We gauge the child's physiological make-up and at first allow it food oftener than adults, but, because our goal is firmly set and our training consistent, before the child is two years old it has achieved the adult schedule. From the point of view of other cultures this is as startling as the fact of three-year-old babies perfectly at home in deep water is to us. Modesty is another sphere in which our child training is consistent and economical; we waste no time in clothing the baby and in contrast to many societies where the child runs naked till it is ceremonially given its skirt or its pubic sheath at adolescence, the child's training fits it precisely for adult conventions.

In neither of these aspects of behavior is there need for an individual in our culture to embark before puberty, at puberty, or at some later date upon a course of action which all his previous training has tabued. He is spared the unsureness inevitable in such a transition.

The illustration I have chosen may appear trivial, but in larger and more important aspects of behavior our methods are obviously different. Because of the great variety of child training in different families in our society, I might illustrate continuity of conditioning from individual life histories in our culture, but even these, from a comparative point of view, stop far short of consistency and I shall therefore confine myself to describing arrangements in other cultures in which training which with us is idiosyncratic, is accepted and traditional and does not therefore involve the same possibility of conflict. I shall choose childhood rather than infant and nursing situations, not because the latter do not vary strikingly in different cultures but because they are nevertheless more circumscribed by the baby's physiological needs than is its later training. Childhood situations provide an excellent field in which to illustrate the range of cultural adjustments which are possible within a universally given, but not so drastic, set of physiological facts.

The major discontinuity in the life cycle is of course that the child who is at one point a son must later be a father. These roles in our society are strongly differentiated; a good son is tractable, and does not assume adult responsibilities; a good father provides for his children and should not allow his authority to be flouted. In addition the child must be sexless so far as his family is concerned, whereas the father's sexual role is primary in the family. The individual in one role must revise his behavior from almost all points of view when he assumes the second role.

I shall select for discussion three such contrasts that occur in our culture between the individual's role as child and as father: 1. responsible—nonresponsible status role; 2. dominance—submission; 3. contrasted sexual role. It is largely upon our cultural commitments to these three contrasts that the discontinuity in the life cycle of an individual in our culture depends.

1. *Responsible—Non-Responsible Status Role.* The techniques adopted by societies which achieve continuity during the life cycle in this sphere in no way differ from those we employ in our uniform conditioning to three meals a day. They are merely applied to other areas of life. We think of the child as wanting to play and the adult as having to work, but in many societies the mother takes the baby daily in her shawl or carrying net to the

garden or to gather roots, and adult labor is seen even in infancy from the pleasant security of its position in close contact with its mother. When the child can run about it accompanies its parents still, doing tasks which are essential and yet suited to its powers, and its dichotomy between work and play is not different from that its parents recognize, namely the distinction between the busy day and the free evening. The tasks it is asked to perform are graded to its powers and its elders wait quietly by, not offering to do the task in the child's place. Everyone who is familiar with such societies has been struck by the contrast with our child training. Dr. Ruth Underhill tells me of sitting with a group of Papago elders in Arizona when the man of the house turned to his little three-year-old granddaughter and asked her to close the door. The door was heavy and hard to shut. The child tried, but it did not move. Several times the grandfather repeated, "Yes, close the door." No one jumped to the child's assistance. No one took the responsibility away from her. On the other hand there was no impatience, for after all the child was small. They sat gravely waiting till the child succeeded and her grandfather gravely thanked her. It was assumed that the task would not be asked of her unless she could perform it, and, having been asked, the responsibility was hers alone just as if she were a grown woman.

The essential point of such child training is that the child is from infancy continuously conditioned to responsible social participation, while at the same time the tasks that are expected of it are adapted to its capacity. The contrast with our society is very great. A child does not make any labor contribution to our industrial society except as it competes with an adult; its work is not measured against its own strength and skill but against high-geared industrial requirements. Even when we praise a child's achievement in the home we are outraged if such praise is interpreted as being of the same order as praise of adults. The child is praised because the parent feels well disposed, regardless of whether the task is well done by adult standards, and the child acquires no sensible standard by which to measure its achievement. The gravity of a Cheyenne Indian family ceremoniously making a feast out of the little boy's first snowbird is at the furthest remove from our behavior. At birth, the little boy was presented with a toy bow, and from the time he could run about serviceable bows suited to his stature were specially made for him by the man of the family. Animals and birds were taught him in a graded series beginning with those most easily taken, and as he brought in his first of each species his family duly made a feast of it, accepting his contribution as gravely as the buffalo his father brought. When he finally killed a buffalo, it was only the final step of his childhood conditioning, not a new adult role with which his childhood experience had been at variance.

The Canadian Ojibwa show clearly what results can be achieved. This tribe gains its livelihood by winter trapping and the small family of father, mother, and children live during the long winter alone on their great frozen hunting grounds. The boy accompanies his father and brings in his catch to his sister as his father does to his mother; the girl prepares the meat and skins for him just as his mother does for her husband. By the time the boy is twelve, he may have set his own line of traps on a hunting territory of his own and return to his parent's house only once in several months—still bringing the meat and skins to his sister. The young child is taught consistently that it has only itself to rely upon in life, and this is as true in the dealings it will have with the supernatural as in the business of getting a livelihood. This attitude he will accept as a successful adult just as he accepted it as a child.[1]

2. *Dominance—Submission.* Dominance—submission is the most striking of those categories of behavior where like does not respond to like but where one type of behavior stimulates the opposite response. It is one of the most prominent ways in which behavior is patterned in our culture. When it obtains between classes, it may be nourished by continuous experience; the difficulty in its use between children and adults lies in the fact that an individual conditioned to one set of behavior in childhood must adopt the opposite as an adult. Its opposite is a pattern of approximately identical reciprocal behavior, and societies which rely upon continuous conditioning characteristically invoke this pattern. In some primitive cultures the very terminology of address between father and son, and more commonly, between grandfather and grandson or uncle and nephew, reflects this attitude. In such kinship terminologies one reciprocal expresses each of these relationships so that son and father, for instance, exchange the same term with one another, just as we exchange the same term with a cousin. The child later will exchange it with his son. "Father—son," therefore, is a continuous relationship he enjoys throughout life. The same continuity, backed up by verbal reciprocity, occurs far oftener in the grandfather-grandson relationship or that of mother's brother-sister's son. When these are "joking" relationships, as they often are, travellers report wonderingly upon the liberties and pretensions of tiny toddlers in their dealings with these family elders. In place of our dogma of respect to elders such societies employ in these cases a reciprocity as nearly identical as may be. The teasing and practical joking the grandfather visits upon his grandchild, the grandchild returns in like coin; he would be led to believe that he failed in propriety if he did not give like for like. If the sister's son has right of access without leave to his mother's brother's possessions, the mother's brother has such rights also to the child's possessions. They share reciprocal privileges and obligations which in our society can develop only between age mates.

From the point of view of our present discussion, such kinship conventions allow the child to put in practice from infancy the same forms of behavior which it will rely upon as an adult; behavior is not polarized into a general requirement of submission for the child and dominance for the adult.

It is clear from the techniques described above by which the child is conditioned to a responsible status role that these depend chiefly upon arousing in the child the desire to share responsibility in adult life. To achieve this little stress is laid upon obedience but much stress upon approval and praise. Punishment is very commonly regarded as quite outside the realm of possibility, and the natives in many parts of the world have drawn the conclusion from our usual disciplinary methods that white parents do not love their children. If the child is not required to be submissive however, many occasions for punishment melt away; a variety of situations which call for it do not occur. Many American Indian tribes are especially explicit in rejecting the ideal of a child's submissive or obedient behavior. Prince

Maximilian von Wied who visited the Crow Indians over a hundred years ago describes a father's boasting about his young son's intractibility even when it was the father himself who was flouted; "He will be a man," his father said. He would have been baffled at the idea that his child should show behavior which would obviously make him appear a poor creature in the eyes of his fellows if he used it as an adult. Dr. George Devereaux tells me of a special case of such an attitude among the Mohave at the present time. The child's mother was white and protested to its father that he must take action when the child disobeyed and struck him. "But why?" the father said, "he is little. He cannot possibly injure me." He did not know of any dichotomy according to which an adult expects obedience and a child must accord it. If his child had been docile he would simply have judged that it would become a docile adult—an eventuality of which he would not have approved.

Child training which brings about the same result is common also in other areas of life than that of reciprocal kinship obligations between child and adult. There is a tendency in our culture to regard every situation as having in it the seeds of a dominance-submission relationship. Even where dominance-submission is patently irrelevant we read in the dichotomy, assuming that in every situation there must be one person dominating another. On the other hand some cultures, even when the situation calls for leadership, do not see it in terms of dominance-submission. To do justice to this attitude it would be necessary to describe their political and especially their economic arrangements, for such an attitude to persist must certainly be supported by economic mechanisms that are congruent with it. But it must also be supported by—or what comes to the same thing, express itself in—child training and familial situations.

3. *Contrasted Sexual Role.* Continuity of conditioning in training the child to assume responsibility and to behave no more submissively than adults is quite possible in terms of the child's physiological endowment if his participation is suited to his strength. Because of the late development of the child's reproductive organs continuity of conditioning in sex experience presents a difficult problem. So far as their belief that the child is anything but a sexless being is concerned, they are probably more nearly right than we are with an opposite dogma. But the great break is presented by the universally sterile unions before puberty and the presumably fertile ones after maturation. This physiological fact no amount of cultural manipulation can minimize or alter, and societies therefore which stress continuous conditioning most strongly sometimes do not expect children to be interested in sex experience until they have matured physically. This is striking among American Indian tribes like the Dakota; adults observe great privacy in sex acts and in no way stimulate children's sexual activity. There need be no discontinuity in the sense in which I have used the term, in such a program if the child is taught nothing it does not have to unlearn later. In such cultures adults view children's experimentation as in no way wicked or dangerous but merely as innocuous play which can have no serious consequences. In some societies such play is minimal and the children manifest little interest in it. But the same attitude may be taken by adults in societies where such play is encouraged and forms a major activity among small

children. This is true among most of the Melanesian cultures of Southeast New Guinea; adults go as far as to laugh off sexual affairs within the prohibited class if the children are not mature, saying that since they cannot marry there can be no harm done.

It is this physiological fact of the difference between children's sterile unions and adults' presumably fertile sex relations which must be kept in mind in order to understand the different mores which almost always govern sex expression in children and in adults in the same culture. A great many cultures with preadolescent sexual license require marital fidelity and a great many which value pre-marital virginity in either male or female arrange their marital life with great license. Continuity in sex experience is complicated by factors which it was unnecessary to consider in the problems previously discussed. The essential problem is not whether or not the child's sexuality is consistently exploited—for even where such exploitation is favored in the majority of cases the child must seriously modify his behavior at puberty or at marriage. Continuity in sex expression means rather that the child is taught nothing it must unlearn later. If the cultural emphasis is upon sexual pleasure the child who is continuously conditioned will be encouraged to experiment freely and pleasurably, as among the Marquesans;[2] if emphasis is upon reproduction, as among the Zuni of New Mexico, childish sex proclivities will not be exploited, for the only important use which sex is thought to serve in his culture is not yet possible to him. The important contrast with our child training is that although a Zuni child is impressed with the wickedness of premature sex experimentation he does not run the risk as in our culture of associating this wickedness with sex itself rather than with sex at his age. The adult in our culture has often failed to unlearn the wickedness or the dangerousness of sex, a lesson which was impressed upon him strongly in his most formative years.

Discontinuity in Conditioning. Even from this very summary statement of continuous conditioning the economy of such mores is evident. In spite of the obvious advantages, however, there are difficulties in its way. Many primitive societies expect as different behavior from an individual as child and as adult as we do, and such discontinuity involves a presumption of strain.

Many societies of this type, however, minimize strain by the techniques they employ, and some techniques are more successful than others in ensuring the individual's functioning without conflict. It is from this point of view that age-grade societies reveal their fundamental significance. Age-graded cultures characteristically demand different behavior of the individual at different times of his life and persons of a like age-grade are grouped into a society whose activities are all oriented toward the behavior desired at that age. Individuals "graduate" publicly and with honor from one of these groups to another. Where age society members are enjoined to loyalty and mutual support, and are drawn not only from the local group but from the whole tribe as among the Arapaho, or even from other tribes as among the Wagawaga of Southeast New Guinea, such an institution has many advantages in eliminating conflicts among local groups and fostering intra-tribal peace. This seems to be also a factor in the tribal military solidarity of the similarly organized Masai of East Africa. The point that is of chief interest for our present discussion, however, is that by this means an individual who at any time takes on a new set of duties and virtues is supported not only by a solid phalanx of age mates but by the traditional prestige of the organized "secret" society into which he has now graduated. Fortified in this way, individuals in such cultures often swing between remarkable extremes of opposite behavior without apparent psychic threat. For example, the great majority exhibit prideful and non-conflicted behavior at each stage in the life cycle even when a prime of life devoted to passionate and aggressive head hunting must be followed by a later life dedicated to ritual and to mild and peaceable civic virtues.[3]

Our chief interest here, however, is in discontinuity which primarily affects the child. In many primitive societies such discontinuity has been fostered not because of economic or political necessity, or because such discontinuity provides for a socially valuable division of labor, but because of some conceptual dogma. The most striking of these are the Australian and Papuan cultures where the ceremony of the "Making of Man" flourishes. In such societies it is believed that men and women have opposite and conflicting powers, and male children, who are of undefined status, must be initiated into the male role. In Central Australia the boy child is of the woman's side and women are tabu in the final adult stages of tribal ritual. The elaborate and protracted initiation ceremonies of the Arunta therefore snatch the boy from the mother, dramatize his gradual repudiation of her. In a final ceremony he is reborn as a man out of the men's ceremonial "baby pouch." The men's ceremonies are ritual statements of a masculine solidarity, carried out by fondling one another's *churingas,* the material symbol of each man's life, and by letting out over one another blood drawn from their veins. After this warm bond among men has been established through the ceremonies, the boy joins the men in the men's house and participates in tribal rites.[4] The enjoined discontinuity has been tribally bridged.

West of the Fly River in southern New Guinea there is a striking development of this Making of Men cult which involves a childhood period of passive homosexuality. Among the Keraki it is thought that no boy can grow to full stature without playing the role for some years.[5] Men slightly older take the active role, and the older man is a jealous partner. The life cycle of the Keraki Indians includes, therefore, in succession, passive homosexuality, active homosexuality, and heterosexuality. The Keraki believe that pregnancy will result from postpubertal passive homosexuality and see evidences of such practices in any fat man whom, even as an old man, they may kill or drive out of the tribe because of their fear. The ceremony that is of interest in connection with the present discussion takes place at the end of the period of passive homosexuality. This ceremony consists in burning out the possibility of pregnancy from the boy by pouring lye down his throat, after which he has no further protection if he gives way to the practice. There is no technique for ending active homosexuality, but this is not explicitly tabu for older men; heterosexuality and children, however, are highly valued.

I have chosen illustrations of discontinuous conditioning where it is not too much to say that the cultural institutions furnish adequate support to the individual as he progresses from role to role or interdicts the previous behavior in a summary fashion. The contrast with arrangements in our culture is very striking, and against this background of social arrangements in other cultures the adolescent period of *Sturm und Drang* with which we are so familiar becomes intelligible in terms of our discontinuous cultural institutions and dogmas rather than in terms of physiological necessity. It is even more pertinent to consider these comparative facts in relation to maladjusted persons in our culture who are said to be fixated at one or another pre-adult level. It is clear that if we were to look at our social arrangements as an outsider, we should infer directly from our family institutions and habits of child training that many individuals would not "put off childish things"; we should have to say that our adult activity demands traits that are interdicted in children, and that far from redoubling efforts to help children bridge this gap, adults in our culture put all the blame on the child when he fails to manifest spontaneously the new behavior or, overstepping the mark, manifests it with untoward belligerence. It is not surprising that in such a society many individuals fear to use behavior which has up to that time been under a ban and trust instead, though at great psychic cost, to attitudes that have been exercised with approval during their formative years. Insofar as we invoke a physiological scheme to account for these neurotic adjustments we are led to overlook the possibility of developing social institutions which would lessen the social cost we now pay; instead we elaborate a set of dogmas which prove inapplicable under other social conditions.

ROLE CONFLICT AND THE
GENESIS OF DEVIANCE

Talcott Parsons

THE CONSEQUENCES of the factors in the genesis of deviant motivation and behavior so far dealt with may be and often are compounded by the factor of role conflict. By this is meant the exposure of the actor to conflicting sets of legitimized role expectations such that complete fulfillment of both is realistically impossible. It is necessary to compromise, that is, to sacrifice some at least of both sets of expectations, or to choose one alternative and sacrifice the other. In any case the actor is exposed to negative sanctions and, so far as both sets of values are internalized, to internal conflict. There may, of course, be limited possibilities of transcending the conflict by redefining the situation, as well as of evasion as, for example, through secrecy, and segregation of occasions.

Role conflict in this sense is continuous with the elements of uncertainty and malintegration which have already been discussed. This is particularly true of the conflict of rules, and of exposure to alters who though not explicitly deviant, "stretch a point" in their reaction to ego. The beginnings of a role conflict may thus be present in the difficulty of living up both to the expectations of one alter who interprets a norm in the direction of a "perfectionistic" compulsive conformity pattern, and those of another who is also in close interaction with ego, and who stretches the same normative pattern to the verge of active rebellion, both of them expecting active reciprocation from ego.

There is a certain endemic potentiality of role conflict inherent in the fact that any actor has a plurality of roles, which involve differences of pattern, thus of relations to alters whose interests and orientations mesh with ego's in different ways. These differences have to be adjusted by an ordering or allocation of the claims of the different role-expectations to which the actor is subject. This ordering occurs by priority scales, by occasion, e.g., time and place, and by distribution among alters. There are thus always a variety of activities which have their appropriate partners, which would not be appropriate with other partners, and which have their appropriate time and place. This allocative ordering of any given actor's role-system is often delicately balanced. Any serious alteration in one part of it may encroach on others and thus necessitate a whole series of adjustments.

In the present context it is particularly important to note that a deviant motivation component relative to one set of role-expectations will have a tendency to upset this delicate balance. Thus a compulsive need to excel in an occupational role may cause the actor to encroach on times appropriately allocated to kinship roles, and make him feel that he is exposed to a conflict of expectations as between his boss and his wife. This may in turn accentuate elements of strain in his marital relationship with the possibility

Reprinted from *The Social System*, (1951), pp. 280-83, by permission of the author and the publisher. (Copyright, 1951, by The Free Press.)

that this should lead to stimulation of the deepening of the vicious circle from there on.

But the source of the conflict may not be ego-made. It may be imposed upon the actor from the malintegration of the social system itself. Not all social malintegration belongs in this category, there may for example be conflicts between groups with no overlapping membership. But, even here, in the pattern sense, there may well be role conflict because only part of the role-pattern defining participation in each group justifies the expectations of the ground vis à-vis the adversary group. This would, for example, be the case in white-negro relations in the South (and in less accentuated form throughout the United States). This may be put as a conflict of roles in that, for example, the white man has in his role as American citizen internalized participation in the universalistic values of the wider society, the "American creed," but also as a Southerner in the pattern of "white supremacy." The conflict can, however, be mitigated in that he relatively seldom has to act in roles where the significant alters hold up the conflicting expectations to him in such a way that he must directly choose. He deals universalistically in some contexts, for example vis-à-vis white colleagues in his occupational sphere, and particularistically vis-à-vis negro-white situations. This segregation is essential to minimize the strain. This situation may be regarded as a main basis of the Southern resentment against "northern interference" in the race problem. It introduces an active conflict of the expectations of significant alters whose differences cannot be ignored. This forces a decision which the segregation of contexts has tended to make it possible to evade.

The significance of role conflict as a factor in the genesis of alienative motivation should be clear from the above. Exposure to role conflict is an obvious source of strain and frustration in that it creates a situation incompatible with a harmonious integration of personality with the interaction system. There must be external frustrations, internal conflicts, or both, in the severer cases always both. Indeed what, on the interaction level if not the fully developed social role level, is exposure to conflicting expectations of some kind may be presumed to be the generic situation underlying the development of ambivalent motivational structures with their expression in neuroses, in deviant behavior or otherwise.

When, however, the element of conflict is present on the level of institutionalized role-expectations, a further element is introduced which can be of great significance. The fact that both sides of the conflicting expectations are institutionalized means that there is the basis for a claim to *legitimacy* for both patterns. As distinguished then from alienative need-dispositions which are clearly stigmatized by the moral sentiments common to ego and alter, and later, hence are the foci of feelings of guilt and shame, there is the possibility of the justification of the alienative as well as the originally conformative motivation.

On one level this should serve as a factor in the intensification of internal conflict, and therefore call for greater pressure to resort to defensive and adjustive mechanisms. An example would be the "touchiness" of the Southern white with regard to outside interference. But the obverse of intensification of conflict is that in a certain sense the defenses against overt deviance are greatly weakened if the alienative need-disposition (from the point of view of one of the given expectation patterns) is given a basis of legitimation. Both internal sanctions and those from significant alters are weakened. Then on the one hand role conflict can be seen to be very important as a source of motivations leading to social change, through some sort of undermining of the motivational bases of an established order which includes the provision of motivationally acceptable alternatives. On the other hand this possibility is potentially so dangerous to the stability of a given institutional system that it may be presumed that one of the major functions of the mechanisms of social control is to forestall the establishment of a claim to legitimacy for the expression of need-dispositions which are alienative relative to the major institutionalized patterns of the social system. Of course the establishment of such a "functional need" of the social system does not in any way explain the actual structures and processes related to it. But it does serve to focus our attention on certain points in the motivational equilibrium of the social system in such a way that our attention will be called to certain problems of the determination of processes which might otherwise have been overlooked.

MAJOR DILEMMAS OF THE SOCIAL WORKER IN PROBATION AND PAROLE

Lloyd E. Ohlin, Herman Piven, and Donnell M. Pappenfort

WHEN A FIELD OF SERVICE strives toward professionalization of its training requirements and its practice, two basic problems of general significance occur: (1) those charged with the responsibility for professional education must maintain a close integration between preparation and practice; (2) educators and practitioners alike must create conditions in the field which will make professional behavior possible.

The integration of preparation and practice must be maintained if changing needs of field workers are to be met by appropriate educational revision, consistent with professional goals:

> The function of a profession in society and the demands implicit in its practice determine the objectives of education for that profession. The responsibilities which its practitioners must assume designate the content of knowledge and skill to be attained. They determine also the character of the educational experience which students must have to become the kinds of people required both for competent service and to contribute to the ongoing development of the profession in a changing social order.[1]

This is not difficult to sustain when professionalization of the field of service has gained general acceptance. In such a case, the existing body of theory, principles, and methods will provide appropriate responses for the majority of problems encountered in the field; situations of practice will have been standardized and the roles of practitioners clearly defined. It is then relatively easy to control or modify the content of educational experience to train persons adjusted to the work realities of the field.

The situation is far more difficult when there is no general agreement on appropriate professional functions in the field. This usually occurs where the claim to control over professional education by one group is met by equally strong claims from competing groups who envision different training requirements. In such a case, different precepts and techniques of practice compete for recognition, and the work settings and orientations undergo constant change. Under these conditions the practitioners' need for theoretical, conceptual, and technical support from the centers of professional education is most acute. However, it is also at this point in the struggle for professional recognition that the schools of professional education are least well equipped to provide this support in the form of integration of the service needs of the emerging field of practice into the generic educational curriculum. This problem can be solved only through the coordinated efforts of educators, practitioners, and research workers in an impartial assessment of the prob-

Reprinted from *The National Probation and Parole Association Journal* (July 1956), pp. 211-25, by permission of the authors and the publisher. (Copyright, 1956, by the National Probation and Parole Association.) The article has been abridged.

lems and needs of the field service and an objective reconstruction of the educational curriculum to meet these needs.

The second major problem involved in the professionalization of a new field of service relates to the organizational arrangement and systems of expectations within which the emerging professional practitioner must carry on his work. The need for reorganization, as well as the amount of conflict and resistance encountered, is likely to be at a maximum when an established system of professional education and practice extends its professional mandate to lay claim to a new field of service. An effort is then made to reorganize the new field in the image of allied services where the profession is generally accepted. This movement focuses the resulting struggle of competing groups on such basic problems as definition of the objectives of the field of service, standards of recruitment, methods of job performance, redefinition of administrative and practitioner roles, and reorganization of the expectations of other agencies and the general public as to the nature of the service to be provided. Conflict develops on these points precisely because the professional cannot work effectively in a setting which does not give him adequate freedom to implement his professional skills and knowledge. In the transition period the professional is faced with special dilemmas and problems that make it extremely difficult for him to work effectively and to retain a professional identification with other members of the profession who are unaware of or relatively unconcerned about his position. The problem is further complicated by the fact that the professional knowledge and skills of the practitioner have not been adjusted to the requirements of the new work setting. Consequently, though the need for reorganization of the work setting to provide greater professional freedom is evident, there is no clear-cut understanding of the form and direction which such reorganization should take. A pertinent example of this problem is the situation of the psychiatrist and other therapists in correctional institutions. Although they have achieved general public acceptance, they feel severely hampered in their work because the custodial and administrative staff, as well as clients, have not properly defined their roles and granted them the power and freedom necessary to function professionally.

SOCIAL WORK EDUCATION FOR PROBATION AND PAROLE

Since World War II the social work profession has increasingly become a source of recruitment for probation and parole field services. This occupational expansion takes place at a time when social work education is built on a generic program applicable to all social work settings, subject only to specific on-the-job training. The special requirements of correctional work are a dramatic challenge to this program. Practitioners and social work educators interested in the correctional field have pressed for broadening the system of generic social work education to incorporate theoretical knowledge and methodological skills which would prepare practitioners to handle the problems of serving the offender client in the correctional agency setting. They are convinced that social work training provides the best available professional preparation for this work.

It [probation] is rather a *process of treatment* aimed at effecting a readjustment within the community setting, of the attitudes, habits and capabilities of the offender. If this is the goal of probation, then casework becomes the best method for achieving this goal, since the sole aim and purpose of casework is to strengthen the individual's ability to "regulate his own life" in society.[2]

This concern that social work educators and practitioners have in the professional development of the correctional field has raised many questions. Is probation and parole social work? Does social work education as presently constituted adequately prepare practitioners for the correctional field? Can the theoretical and methodological requirements for correctional work be successfully incorporated into generic social work education?

All these questions call for more detailed exploration than has thus far occurred.

One of the functions of research, under such circumstances, is to inform the educator and the field administrator of the empirical problem of implementing the professional position. It seeks to describe the conflicts and limitations which beset the practitioner and to highlight the discrepancy between what is taught in the schools and what is demanded in practice. The results of such research should provide the basis for the rational development and strengthening of educational programs and a core of knowledge and understanding for the professional reorganization of the field of work itself. This article is an attempt to outline the major dilemmas in which the social worker often finds himself as he tries to carry out his professional obligations as a social worker while fulfilling his job obligations as a probation-parole officer.

The professional in any field is more than the possessor of certain knowledge, skills, and techniques for doing his job. He is identified with a profession which constitutes for him a subculture. This subculture defines for its members the purposes, aspirations, and obligations of the profession as a whole and makes a meaningful pattern of the complex experiences of the occupational life.

Professional education as a re-educative process has to fulfill a task that is essentially equivalent to a change in culture. Since the individual's attitudes have been formed through his dependence on relationships and through his response to authority pressures within the family and other organized groups, Kurt Lewin holds that one of the outstanding needs for bringing about acceptance in re-education is the establishment of an "in-group," that is, a group in which the members experience a sense of belonging.[3]

Insofar as the practitioner is a professional man he has internalized this subculture, drawing from it the roots of his professional "identity"—his professional "self." The significance of this identification is dramatically experienced by many social workers in the correctional field. Correctional work is generally conceived by the larger profession of social work as a marginal activity[4] and it receives neither the recognition and status nor the educational and organizational support accorded to other fields of service in the profession. Consequently, correctional practitioners often feel that they are alienated from and not accepted by the general profession. This results in a confusion of professional identification which inhibits the continuity and progress of their personal careers and retards the general professionalization and development of correctional services.

The social worker, because of his practical concern with human development, has become especially aware of the fact that he is a man with a mission as well as a technical expert.[5] The social work school deliberately instills in its graduates a set of expectations about the role of the worker in relation to his client, agency, and community. It has consciously organized its curriculum to produce graduates who are oriented to the needs of traditional agency settings (best illustrated by the private family agency and the out-patient psychiatric clinic). These expectations are not always fulfilled in the correctional setting and the discrepancy between expectation and actuality is a measure of the "reality shock" experienced by the new worker. His reaction to the dilemmas in which he is placed has profound consequences for himself, his clients, the probation-parole service, and the wider field of social work.

THE PROBATION-PAROLE SETTING

The probation-parole occupation has undergone continuous change, with the entrance of the social worker representing a significant turning point in its professional development. The social work recruit comes to an agency in which many clients have not voluntarily sought casework service, are not "motivated for treatment," and are limited by lack of capacity even if they could be motivated. In addition, other occupational and interest groups and occasionally general public opinion view him with watchful suspicion, even hostility. Like other public institutions in a democratic society, his agency has organized its directives and structure partly in response to the pressures and counterpressures of public opinion. The nature of the clientele and agency organization poses for him many serious theoretical and practical problems which make his adjustment and the exercise of his professional competence far more problematic than he had been led to expect during his educational and field work training experience.

The social worker often finds the agency organized in terms of pre-social work theories of probation and parole. From the point of view of work orientations, two types of probation-parole workers have dominated the field. The "punitive officer" is the guardian of middle-class community morality; he attempts to coerce the offender into conforming by means of threats and punishment and his emphasis is on control, protecting the community *against* the offender, and systematic suspicion of those under supervision. The "protective agent," on the other hand, vacillates between protecting the offender *and* protecting the community. His tools are direct assistance, lecturing, and praise and blame. He is recognized by his ambivalent emotional involvement with the offender and others in the community as he shifts back and forth in taking sides with one against the other.

A third type, the "welfare worker," is entering correctional work with increasing frequency. His ultimate work goal is the improved welfare of the client, a condition achieved by helping him in his individual adjustment, within limits imposed by the client's capacity. He feels that the only genuine guarantee of community protection lies in the client's personal adjustment since external conformity will only be temporary and in the long run may make a successful adjustment more difficult. Emotional neutrality permeates his relationships. The diagnostic categories and treatment skills which he employs stem from an objective and theoretically based assessment of the client's situation, needs, and capacities. His primary identification is with the social work profession.

The three types of workers are often found as colleagues in the same organization, particularly during the period of emerging agency professionalization. Their differing work orientations frequently generate conflict and impose limits on the extent to which any of these work patterns can achieve full expression.

OCCUPATIONAL DILEMMAS

Three conditions structure the occupational dilemmas of the social worker:[6] (1) the nature of the clientele, (2) agency organization, and (3) community expectations.

The Client. By virtue of the control which traditional casework agencies exert over their intake policies, the profession is able to insist on the fulfillment of certain norms which are sometimes inapplicable or opposed to the requirements of probation-parole practice. The model in social casework presumes that the individual applicant selects an agency,[7] asks to become its client for service,[8] defines the service appropriately,[9] and is acceptable to the agency on the basis of his motivation and capacity for treatment.[10] With the possible exception of the last of these criteria, the probationer or parolee appears to be excluded from generic casework consideration as a client. The ramifications of this disparity between social work norms and correctional practice are manifold. The social worker in corrections feels he has not been sufficiently prepared to deal with clients who are unmotivated, who lack capacity for treatment, or who do not require his help. His expectations for providing helpful service are frustrated by clients who refuse help or fail to acknowledge the existence of problems which require help of the kind the practitioner feels professionally equipped to offer. In addition, he is confronted by a work load which does not allow him enough time to concentrate on trying to overcome these difficulties and render appropriate casework service. The basic problem is that his academic training had not given him the skills and guides to action for converting a relationship of control and authority into one of consent and treatment.

The social worker desires a warm, neutral, and nonjudgmental relationship with his client.[11] He recognizes, however, that the client regards him as a participant in the punitive and condemning system of apprehension, judgment, and correction. He knows that the offender is compelled to come to him as a condition of probation or parole and often approaches him with hostility and an interest in concealing facts and feelings. The social worker knows that his authority is real. For example, both he and the client know that the actual decision on revocation usually is the worker's, even though the formal authority is lodged elsewhere. His profession tells him that this is "an initial obstacle to be worked through," but it does not teach him what to do. This is a major though not an insuperable barrier for the recruit who has no specific training to apply.

Failing to find guidance from the social work profession in dealing with this problem, the social work practitioner sometimes turns to older workers or supervisors in the probation and parole system itself. Since many of these persons do not share a common theoretical and conceptual background of training with the social work recruit, the advice he receives often sharpens rather than resolves his dilemma. To meet his own need to overcome client hostility toward him as an authoritarian figure in order to establish conditions requisite to treatment, and at the same time to satisfy the pressures of the community (and, in some agencies, the pressures of his superiors) for client conformity, he frequently attempts to play two roles. On the one hand, he tries to offer a caseworker's sympathetic understanding and help; on the other, he is the agent of law and respectability, attempting to explain one function as separate from the other. Because he has no clear conception of how or when to integrate control and treatment functions, and lacks knowledge of the skills by which they might be made mutually supportive, his attempt to play two roles is frequently unsuccessful.

> Because humans tend to react to any one phase of an agency experience in terms of the total self and in terms of a totality of needs, it may not be a simple matter to render services clearly distinguished one from another. An agency may conveniently divide itself into two sets of services and proffer them like two different commodities. But a man has not two separate sides to his head or to his heart.[12]

This makes his dilemma clear, but it does not resolve it.

The social work recruit brings with him a model of treatment purpose and process from the classroom, casework literature, and field placement experience. He grants the possibility of incorporating the "wise use of authority,"[13] but in a work situation where the anticipated traditional process does not unfold he feels bewildered and betrayed because he has never been taught techniques appropriate to other than nonauthoritarian and nonjudgmental relationships.[14]

The social caseworker in probation and parole also experiences difficulty in classifying the problems represented in his caseload. He finds many clients with whom he would have difficulty establishing a treatment relationship even under ideal working conditions because of personality structures and lack of capacities, and because of the paucity of available knowledge and techniques. Many of the types of cases which he encounters in his agency experience have not been included in the theoretical and methodological training with case materials received during his educational preparation. Although he usually learns to classify his caseload and provide service for many who need and can use it, the probation-parole officer trained in casework first goes through the painful process of rebuff, dismay, and experimentation. He often finds it necessary to seek guidance from sources other than social work itself, sources which deal with his specific clients and problems.[15]

The difficulties which the social worker encounters with his caseload are further complicated by lack of familiarity with the criminal and delinquent subcultures from which most offenders emerge. Social casework emphasizes the importance of identifying the social environment with which the client is interacting in order to understand how he perceives and feels about his situation and how he may be helped. This requires knowledge and familiarity with the cultural and social backgrounds from which offenders come, a familiarity which the officer does not usually bring from his own background and knowledge which his formal education does not specifically give him.[16]

Agency Organization. Democratic administration has been defined as the art of compromise through which divergent and contradictory social forces modify one another and reach a final expression simultaneously reflecting the wishes of all but those of no group completely.[17] Because the probation-parole agency must adapt itself to the threat of powerful and antagonistic groups in its environment,[18] it occasionally represents an extreme case of the generalization that every organization displays a discrepancy between its stated purposes and the objective consequences of the actions of its functionaries.

The failures of probation and parole are more spectacular than those in most other professions, and newsmen have the occupational motive of "good copy" to encourage them to scrutinize correctional practice and organize critical public opinion around a dramatically destructive episode. Elected judges, legislators, and other public officials have a vested interest in being on the popular side of a crisis, and occupational groups whose interests are inherently in opposition to client-centered probation and parole supervision are able to use periods of public excitement to further their own purposes. Consequently the administrator is under pressure to anticipate possible criticism and to organize the agency and its policies in self-protection. The problem is frequently intensified for the social work administrator who feels a professional obligation to expand his program and recruit social work officers, thus requiring support from important officials and citizens not only to protect the agency but to aid in its development.

The accommodation to external threat is expressed in an emphasis on public relations revealed not only in positive educational campaigns, but also in organization of the agency and the development of policies on client supervision and the worker's role in the community.

During this transitional period, however, when the agency is striving for public acceptance of its work through increased professionalization of staff and operation, the interests of the administrator and the caseworker tend to diverge. The caseworker often perceives the public relations interest of the agency as a compromise with enforcement concepts promoted by other occupational groups in the community. He frequently feels that the agency's treatment objectives are being sacrificed for agency protection. He feels that he is under pressure to make nonprofessional decisions on his cases. This divergence of interests between the agency-centered administrator and the client-centered caseworker is illustrated below by problems arising in (1) the area of supervising the caseworker, (2) the rules for supervision of clients, and (3) informal policies about agency-community conflicts.

1. In the eyes of the social work profession, supervision by personnel skilled in imparting knowledge and techniques and in helping workers to recognize and profit by their errors without ego-destructiveness is mandatory for client welfare and workers' professional growth. The emphasis on agency protection in probation and parole, however, often results in promoting men who are successful in public relations rather than skilled in casework supervision. Also, when agencies are in a period of transition, the protection of morale and seniority leads to promotion of older employees trained in fields other than social work. Under these conditions, the social worker feels that the central focus of these supervisors is to prevent him from acting in ways

which might embarrass the agency. He feels that treatment problems not involving the possibility of public condemnation are of secondary concern, and that aiding his professional growth very seldom becomes a work function. The limitations imposed by the supervisor oriented to public relations, and the consequent variance in understanding the subtleties of casework, pose for the social worker many problems which penetrate a large number of his daily activities. He has been taught to expect supervision of a learning-helping nature; when this source of support and professional guidance is absent, he feels that he has lost one of the main links to his professional identity and competent professional performance.

2. The "rules of client supervision" are an inheritance from an earlier phase of probation-parole when control over the client was more openly advocated. For the social work administrator, however, they are functional, since they are a formal expression of community expectations concerning control of offenders which can be used as a defense against public criticism that the agency "coddles" its clients, or enforced to achieve other administrative ends with clients and workers. The "rules" sometimes are extended by informal policies and official requirements into a structure unacceptable to the social worker because he cannot interpret it as reasonable and necessary for his client. If a client must, by virtue of court order, parole decision, or informal agency requirement, abstain from drinking or observe a curfew, neither the worker nor the client can escape the realization that these are restrictions from which other adults are formally immune. The effect of this is to deny the client participation in normal activities and to reinforce his conception that he is somehow different *in kind* from other persons in the community. For the worker it reinforces the conception that the agency and the community regard his goals, methods, and clients as different *in kind* from those of other social agencies. The caseworker further feels that the "rules" may prevent individualization according to his client's needs.

3. Agency policy controlling the agent-community system of relationships also has important consequences for the casework task. The degree of emphasis on public relations varies greatly from one agency to another. An urban agency may generally achieve more autonomy than a rural one: in districts of similar population density, community pressure increases from federal to state to county levels of jurisdiction. Two extremes of agency structure exist—the relatively "autonomous" agency and the "restricted" agency.

(a) In the "autonomous" agency the social worker has far greater freedom to reject the control function and to pursue the treatment objectives of casework. For example, he makes definite recommendations for disposition, which are followed with few exceptions, and he feels free to circumvent court or parole board directives which he regards as opposed to his client's welfare. He is in a position to reject pressure from finance companies and to persuade the judge to remit court costs and restitution. He contacts clients as seldom or as often as casework needs and caseload requirements dictate and will usually arrange appointments before making home visits. He feels free to inform clients explicitly that their drinking, sex habits, hours, driving, purchases, etc., are of concern to him only when they constitute casework problems. He frequently feels the obligation to inform the client of discriminatory practices by certain employers and may even encourage him to conceal his criminal record in approaching them for employment.

It is within the "autonomous" agency that the social caseworker feels he can act most consistently with the professional directives received in his academic training. He feels he can confine his role essentially to the treatment function and permit other agencies to discharge the control function as they do with other citizens in the community. In short, he seeks to structure the performance of his work and the organization of his work relationships according to the model of social casework in traditional agency settings.

(b) In the "restricted" agency this freedom to pursue the treatment orientation and to reject the control function as a significant part of the worker's role is impossible to achieve. The social worker in the "restricted" agency encounters many points of conflict in fulfilling agency policy and maintaining a service-treatment relationship in the interests of the client—each of which is a professional norm. A uniform policy of mandatory home visits, for example, prevents individualization according to client needs. Other agency policies forbid undertaking treatment with clients whose problems may require occasional "acting out" as a prerequisite to eventual adjustment, a situation the worker has been trained to anticipate and accept as appropriate to casework. More importantly, the social worker often feels that he is forced to emphasize immediate client conformity to unrealistic standards; e.g., early curfew, abstention from drinking, from sexual relationships, etc. He frequently feels that such action keeps the client from being integrated into his own legitimate groups, prevents the client from viewing him as a treatment resource, and denies the worker the opportunity to move beyond the question of conformity in interviews. He thus has difficulty in "motivating" the unmotivated or strengthening a client's weak capacities. When he also feels compelled by agency policy to make unexpected night visits, to look in bars and poolrooms, to check on clients at work—in short, to practice "surveillance" —the problem is intensified. One social worker reported: "My God! My clients won't talk to me; they don't even want to see me. They pull the curtains when I drive up to the house."

Community Expectations. As generally portrayed in social work education, the "community" is composed of heterogeneous individuals who share certain basic values and interests. Problems of casework clients involving other people are seen as personal problems of the client, and alternative solutions are explored in the counseling relationship to aid the client's decision. The worker-client relationship is conceived as private and confidential, and the only responsibility of the worker is his client's welfare. For example, it would be unusual for a businessman to request the cooperation of a family, medical, or psychiatric social agency in persuading a client to pay a debt, and it would be regarded as clearly improper for a caseworker of such an agency to accept this responsibility.

The social worker in corrections, however, soon recognizes that the community consists of a number of interest groups with varying and conflicting demands upon him and the offender client. He finds that many officials and citizens have a negative attitude toward his client and that this is reciprocated by the client. His task is not only to alter both conceptions, but to deal with the problems raised by these conflicts of ideas and interests during the conduct of the case. He finds himself subjected to various pressures to act in ways which violate his own conception of the proper role and function of a social worker. He feels that his profession has not provided him with realistic conceptions of the "community," expectations of the pressures he will encounter, or prescriptions for appropriate action.

The probation-parole worker feels, for example, that the police pursue enforcement objectives without sufficient regard for the consequences of their actions on the offender's adjustment.[19] Such acts as indiscriminate arrest on suspicion are perceived by the worker as not only impeding the client's adjustment but re-enforcing the offender's conception of himself as a person apart from and rejected by the community. The worker experiences widespread pressure by the police and other official functionaries to define his role as that of an enforcement officer who should use control measures to restrict the client's freedom and coercion to punish him for wrongdoing. When he attempts to resist these pressures, he finds probation and parole interpreted as leniency and himself identified as a "sob sister." Recognizing that police, prosecutors, judges, and others are often guided by values and objectives different from those which he considers primary, he is uncertain as to how to proceed, especially at those points where he is required to commit what he feels are gross violations of professional norms. An illustration is often found in the use made of the worker's presentence report, where the judge not only may dispose of cases on grounds other than treatability and humanitarian equality,[20] but also may violate confidentiality by making the report public. Powerless to prevent police and others from pursuing their own interests in the client in ways which he defines as interference with the treatment and adjustment of the client, yet requiring their cooperation in his daily work, he feels untrained to deal satisfactorily with either the client or the officials.

Social workers have tended to adjust to this situation in a variety of ways. Some have expended considerable effort in seeking to educate and influence officials and citizens to understand the rehabilitative approach of the worker, the nature of the client-worker relationship, and casework methods for effecting client adjustment. Others resort to evasions, sentimental appeals, and "slanted" or safe reports. Still other workers have sought to withdraw in some measure from the norms of client service and confidentiality, accounting for apparent norm violations as limitations of the setting.

A final group of problems experienced by social workers in corrections relates to their identification with the profession. Since community officials and citizens with whom he frequently deals, as well as his own supervisor in many instances, are not social workers, the officer is usually restrained from employing the diagnostic and treatment vocabulary he has been trained to use. This limitation frequently creates anxiety in the worker, who fears the hazards of daily communication and the loss of familiarity with the technical tools of his profession. Probably more important is the difficulty experienced in maintaining a professional identification with other social workers. Not infrequently social agencies look with suspicion and distrust on the probation officer who seeks collateral information from their records. The stereotyped image maintained by social workers in traditional welfare agencies concerning the nature of casework practice in corrections often leads them to share the general community conception of the probation-parole worker as a law enforcement agent. This lack of understanding and acceptance of his position and problems by social work colleagues and educators contributes to a process of professional alienation, thus promoting further anxiety in the worker as to his professional identification.

RESPONSES OF THE SOCIAL WORKER

As a result of these barriers to professional practice in probation-parole, as conceived in traditional social casework terms, many social workers leave the field. Some give up social work entirely, disillusioned and convinced that both social work as a discipline and corrections as an area of practice are without genuine reward or meaning. Some return to more traditional case-work settings, convinced that it is not possible, at least for them, to operate professionally in probation-parole work. Others remain in corrections, unhappy with their most recent job experience, but feeling committed to this specialty because of an awareness of casework needs in the field, because of the nature of the contacts and experience they have acquired, and because of a genuine conviction that the necessary knowledge and structure can be created for professional casework in this setting. As to the social workers who remain in corrections, five general types of adjustment have been distinguished, varying principally with the length of time the officer has worked, the nature of the agency organization, and the character of community conditions.

1. One type of adjustment is found in the relatively "autonomous" agency directed by a social work oriented administrator. The worker feels that the agency is moving toward increased professionalization and that he is able to function significantly as a professional in spite of the obstacles. He identifies himself primarily as a social worker but hastens to point out major differences between the ideas and practices of the larger profession and those of the correctional field.

2. In the "restricted" agency, the worker is often harried and bewildered by demands made upon him by clients, supervisors, officials of other agencies, and the community at large for "unprofessional" behavior. He gradually accepts the "protective" definition at various important points and explicitly identifies himself as a probation-parole officer divorced from the field of social work.

3. Also found in the "restricted" agency is the worker who completely rejects what he regards as "anti-professional" demands and seeks to come to terms with these pressures by manipulation and evasion. Since the extent to which he can achieve this by himself is limited and because the effort—itself a violation of social work norms—tends to isolate him from the agency in which he works, he blames both the profession and the agency for his predicament. He derives his ultimate justification for evasion from the social work ideology of client service, however, and therefore retains a professional identity—albeit an alienated one—and he hopes to transfer to a correctional agency where the climate will be more conducive to treatment efforts.

4. Quite commonly the recent recruit to the field of corrections operates as a marginal and ambivalent worker. He experiments with various "new methods and techniques," including client coercion, in attempting to solve

his work problems. Seriously disturbed by the "reality shock" of his first contact with correctional work, he already feels disenchanted with social work. The career patterns in the field suggest that he will continue experimenting for a while and will eventually resolve his conflicts by becoming one of the other types.

5. Finally, the social worker may accept the protective measures of the "restricted" agency as more or less natural and necessary for probation-parole work, trying to give service and treatment to clients as fully as possible within the given framework. He sees himself as a special kind of social worker and explains the imposed restrictions on clients as "necessary reality," identifying the client's difficulties in accepting these restrictions as a lack of capacity to adjust "to society."

CONCLUSION

The problems of the social worker in probation and parole have been related to the generic education he receives and to the special circumstances he faces in an area of practice where his caseload differs from that of more traditional settings, where powerful community forces oppose his ideals, and in which his agency attempts to protect itself by demanding of him decisions which seem unprofessional to him. His responses to the unexpected and painful dilemmas include withdrawal to another setting, experimental-evasive-manipulative tactics, and alienation from his professional identification. These symptoms indicate a lag between social work education and the requirements of probation-parole practice.

If social work is to retain probation-parole as an area of application, it will have to participate in the solution of three problems, each demanding revision of social work preparation for the field: (1) community expectations about probation and parole must be modified to allow the professional sufficient freedom to pursue treatment interests; (2) he must be given the knowledge and skills which will enable him to do constructive work when alternatives are limited by public opinion and agency organization; (3) the practitioner must be provided with the knowledge required for work with his particular clientele. . . .

SECTION III
The Impact of Values on Practice

Values determine the choices men make, and the ends they live by. What is considered good and what is evil, what is right and wrong, success and failure, what is important and unimportant, desirable and undesirable, beautiful and ugly, are all value questions. Whether the values lie in the realm of ethics, economics, aesthetics, or religion, they exist as they are experienced in human minds and translated into human action—that they substantially determine the direction of human actions is generally agreed. In this section we are concerned not with the philosophical study of values—their objective reality, or their relation to ultimate truth—but with the recognition of their sources and variations in society, the ways in which such values are transmitted, their consequences for behavior, and their implications for practice.

Commonly held values form the basis for strong social cohesion. Opposing values have been the basis of conflict ranging from individual argument to national and religious wars. The individual who holds a consistent set of values throughout his development, values transmitted by his family which holds the same values as does the surrounding society, has his life's guide-posts clearly laid out. What he lives by and what he should live by presents no problem. Many peasant societies have provided such consistency. By contrast, the individual who receives one set of values from his family as a child, and another as an adolescent, one set of values from home and other sets from school, peer group and mass media, or simultaneously incompatible values from the same source, may easily be ridden with conflict in his decisions and in his direction in many areas of his life. Many technologically developed societies, and contemporary American society in particular, with its highly differentiated social structure, contain such value conflicts. It is part of the price to be paid, in a sense, for our economic progress and cultural diversity.

To social work, the study of values is important on a number of levels. It is a way of understanding our society and of understanding individual behavior. It also compels an examination of values underlying the profession itself. It involves awareness of changing values, of premises which the social worker and client, or the social agency and the community, or the social worker and his host agency, may hold in common or hold at variance with one another. It may fairly be said that throughout the world the tendency exists to regard one's own values as "best" or "natural" (ethnocentricity) and others as "wrong" or 'inferior." While the acceptance of difference comes easily to social workers, conflicts in values are not always readily seen, whether these values have their source in religious, class, ethnic, regional, or other groups with which the individual identifies.

In the ensuing section, the thesis is presented, in selections from Tawney's work, that a relationship exists between Puritanism and the growth of capitalism, thus delineating, if one accepts this interpretation, one of the sources of values which have helped shape America. From the "demonstration that distress is a proof of demerit" and "the doctrine of the danger of pampering poverty" came the rationale for England's Poor Law, whose premises determined public welfare legislation and public attitudes in this country well into the twentieth century. At the same time, in its accent on individual responsibility, on the importance of activity and work and status to be achieved through accomplishment in life, Puritan teaching spurred our economic development. The field of social work has clearly dissociated itself from the doctrine that to be in need is to be inferior, and in so doing has come in conflict with values long and deeply held. Its non-judgmental view in the treatment of deviant behavior is another source of conflict with prevailing norms.

Social work has, however, been imbued with other facets of the American ideology stemming from Puritan sources. Social workers, most of whom come from the middle class, may tend to hold as intrinsic and "natural" values common to the middle-class—for example, striving for greater and greater achievement, thrift, holding high educational expectations for capable children. Clients who do not maintain such values may be regarded as automatically having "problems" in their adjustment. Kingsley Davis' provocative article on "Mental Hygiene and the Class Structure" has many implications for social work in this regard. Furthermore, social workers, like other practitioners in the clinical professions, may unwittingly communicate their own standards when these may be at variance with those of the client population. Group work agencies have often seen the stress by professionals on middle-class attitudes toward sex and physical aggression, conflicting with the lower-class or ethnic attitudes held by the youth being served. This situation sometimes leads to a gradual self-selection of clientele, confined to those having reached or aspiring to middle-class position. This is not to say that social workers or social work agencies should not have values of their own to which they adhere and which they should communicate. Such determination of value premises, however, need be explicit and the consequences recognized. Otherwise, social worker and agency may find themselves in the anomalous position of conveying "total acceptance" of clientele on the surface, while in reality, however unwittingly, selecting conforming clientele and bringing pressure to bear on others to accept the agency's implicit values.

A further illustration of the impact of values on practice is provided by multi-function agencies. Professional social work services are disseminated through a variety of organizations, many of which are not under social work direction—such as prisons, courts, hospitals, and industries. In these settings, the values of the organization may not be entirely consistent with those of professional social work, yet may have the effect of penetrating social work practice and transforming its ends. For example, at times court officials exert pressure on the parole and probation officer to forego the ends of treatment solely in the interests of surveillance. In effect, the ends of social work can become submerged in organizational ends. It is less a question of conflict of values that arises under these conditions, than the whittling down or distortion of professional ends under the dominance of organizational ends, particularly when the organizational goals maximize control values.

Robin Williams approaches the concept of values as a "means of organizing conduct" and traces the principal value systems operative in American society; achievement and success, activity and work, moralistic orientation, humanitarian mores, efficiency and practicality, material comfort, equality, external conformity, science and secular rationality, nationality-patriotism, democracy, individual responsibility, racism. It will readily be seen that these value systems, modal as they may be for society as a whole, are not uniformly distributed throughout the society. They vary with social class, ethnic group, geography, religious education. Thus the emphasis on achievement and success, as Herbert Hyman points out, is far greater in the middle than the lower class. The Spanish-American does not tend to value efficiency and practicality, or science and secular rationality to the same degree as does the "old American." Racial prejudice is unevenly distributed geographically.

For the field of social work it is important to consider which values pervade the profession and are fundamental premises to which all social workers are bound, and which may vary. For the individual social worker, it becomes essential to make explicit his own values for himself, in order to recognize those of others.

ECONOMIC VIRTUES AND PRESCRIPTIONS FOR POVERTY

Richard H. Tawney

THE TRIUMPH OF ECONOMIC VIRTUES

"ONE BEAM IN A DARK PLACE," wrote one who knew the travail of the spirit, "hath exceeding much refreshment in it. Blessed be His name for shining upon so dark a heart as mine."[1] While the revelation of God to the individual soul is the center of all religion, the essence of Puritan theology was that it made it, not only the center, but the whole circumference and substance, dismissing as dross and vanity all else but this secret and solitary communion. Grace alone can save, and this grace is the direct gift of God, unmediated by any earthly institution. The elect cannot by any act of their own evoke it; but they can prepare their hearts to receive it, and cherish it when received. They will prepare them best, if they empty them of all that may disturb the intentness of their lonely vigil. Like an engineer, who, to canalize the rush of the oncoming tide, dams all channels save that through which it is to pour, like a painter who makes light visible by plunging all that is not light in gloom, the Puritan attunes his heart to the voice from Heaven by an immense effort of concentration and abnegation. To win all, he renounces all. When earthly props have been cast down, the soul stands erect in the presence of God. Infinity is attained by a process of subtraction.

To a vision thus absorbed in a single intense experience, not only religious and ecclesiastical systems, but the entire world of human relations, the whole fabric of social institutions, witnessing in all the wealth of their idealism and their greed to the infinite creativeness of man, reveal themselves in a new and wintry light. The fire of the spirit burns brightly on the hearth; but through the windows of his soul the Puritan, unless a poet or a saint, looks on a landscape touched by no breath of spring. What he sees is a forbidding and frost-bound wilderness, rolling its snow-clad leagues towards the grave—a wilderness to be subdued with aching limbs beneath solitary stars. Through it he must take his way, alone. No aid can avail him: no preacher, for only the elect can apprehend with the spirit the word of God; no Church, for to the visible Church even reprobates belong; no sacrament, for sacraments are ordained to increase the glory of God, not to minister spiritual nourishment to man; hardly God himself, for Christ died for the elect, and it may well be that the majesty of the Creator is revealed by the eternal damnation of all but a remnant of the created.[2]

His life is that of a soldier in hostile territory. He suffers in spirit the perils which the first settlers in America endured in body, the sea behind, the untamed desert in front, a cloud of inhuman enemies on either hand. Where Catholic and Anglican had caught a glimpse of the invisible, hovering

Reprinted and abridged from *Religion and the Rise of Capitalism* (1926), pp. 227-73, by permission of the publisher. (Copyright, 1926, by Harcourt, Brace & Co.)

like a consecration over the gross world of sense, and touching its muddy vesture with the unearthly gleam of a divine, yet familiar, beauty, the Puritan mourned for a lost Paradise and a creation sunk in sin. Where they had seen society as a mystical body, compact of members varying in order and degree, but dignified by participation in the common life of Christendom, he saw a bleak antithesis between the spirit which quickened and an alien, indifferent or hostile world.

The moral self-sufficiency of the Puritan nerved his will, but it corroded his sense of social solidarity. For, if each individual destiny hangs on a private transaction between himself and his Maker, what room is left for human intervention? A servant of Jehovah more than of Christ, he revered God as a Judge rather than loved him as a Father, and was moved less by compassion for his erring brethren than by impatient indignation at the blindness of vessels of wrath who "sinned their mercies." A spiritual aristocrat, who sacrificed fraternity to liberty, he drew from his idealization of personal responsibility a theory of individual rights, which, secularized and generalized, was to be among the most potent explosives that the world has known. He drew from it also a scale of ethical values, in which the traditional scheme of Christian virtues was almost exactly reversed, and which, since he was above all things practical, he carried as a dynamic into the routine of business and political life.

For, since conduct and action, though availing nothing to attain the free gift of salvation, are a proof that the gift has been accorded, what is rejected as a means is resumed as a consequence, and the Puritan flings himself into practical activities with the daemonic energy of one who, all doubts allayed, is conscious that he is a sealed and chosen vessel. Once engaged in affairs, he brings to them both the qualities and limitations of his creed in all their remorseless logic. Called by God to labor in his vineyard, he has within himself a principle at once of energy and of order, which makes him irresistible both in war and in the struggles of commerce. Convinced that character is all and circumstances nothing, he sees in the poverty of those who fall by the way, not a misfortune to be pitied and relieved, but a moral failing to be condemned, and in riches, not an object of suspicion—though like other gifts they may be abused—but the blessing which rewards the triumph of energy and will. Tempered by self-examination, self-discipline, self-control, he is the practical ascetic, whose victories are won not in the cloister, but on the battlefield, in the counting-house, and in the market.

This temper, of course with infinite varieties of quality and emphasis, found its social organ in those middle and commercial classes who were the citadel of the Puritan spirit, and whom, "ennobled by their own industry and virtue,"[3] Milton described as the standard-bearers of progress and enlightenment. We are so accustomed to think of England as *par excellence* the pioneer of economic progress, that we are apt to forget how recently that rôle has been assumed. In the Middle Ages it belonged to the Italians, in the sixteenth century to the Netherland dominions of the Spanish Empire, in the seventeenth to the United Provinces and, above all, to the Dutch.

The England of Shakespeare and Bacon was still largely medieval in its economic organization and social outlook, more interested in maintaining customary standards of consumption than in accumulating capital for future production, with an aristocracy contemptuous of the economic virtues, a peasantry farming for subsistence amid the organized confusion of the open-field village, and a small, if growing, body of jealously conservative crafts-men. In such a society Puritanism worked like the yeast which sets the whole mass fermenting. It went through its slack and loosely knit texture like a troop of Cromwell's Ironsides through the disorderly cavalry of Rupert. Where, as in Ireland, the elements were so alien that assimilation was out of the question, the result was a wound that festered for three centuries. In Eng-land the effect was that at once of an irritant and of a tonic. Puritanism had its own standards of social conduct, derived partly from the obvious interests of the commercial classes, partly from its conception of the nature of God and the destiny of man. These standards were in sharp antithesis, both to the considerable surviving elements of feudalism in English society, and to the policy of the authoritarian State, with its ideal of an ordered and graded society, whose different members were to be maintained in their traditional status by the pressure and protection of a paternal monarchy. Sapping the former by its influence and overthrowing the latter by direct attack, Puritan-ism became a potent force in preparing the way for the commercial civiliza-tion which finally triumphed at the Revolution.

The complaint that religious radicalism, which aimed at upsetting the government of the Church, went hand in hand with an economic radicalism, which resented the restraints on individual self-interest imposed in the name of religion or of social policy, was being made by the stricter school of religious opinion quite early in the reign of Elizabeth.[4] Seventeenth-century writers repeated the charge that the Puritan conscience lost its delicacy where matters of business were concerned, and some of them were sufficiently struck by the phenomenon to attempt an historical explanation of it. The example on which they usually seized—the symbol of a supposed general disposition to laxity—was the indulgence shown by Puritan divines in the particular matter of moderate interest. It was the effect, so the picturesque story ran,[5] of the Marian persecution. The refugees who fled the continent could not start busi-ness in a foreign country. If, driven by necessity, they invested their capital and lived on the proceeds, who could quarrel with so venial a lapse in so good a cause? Subsequent writers embellished the picture. The redistribution of property at the time of the Dissolution, and the expansion of trade in the middle of the century, had led, one of them argued, to a great increase in the volume of credit transactions. The opprobrium which attached to loans at interest—"a sly and forbid practice"—not only among Romanists and Angli-cans, but among honest Puritans, played into the hands of the less scrupulous members of "the faction." Disappointed in politics, they took to money-lending, and, without venturing to justify usury in theory, defended it in practice. "Without the scandal of a recantation, they contrived an expedient, by maintaining that, though usury for the name were stark naught, yet for widows, orphans and other impotents (therein principally comprising the saints under persecution) it was very tolerable, because profitable, and in a manner necessary." Naturally, Calvin's doctrine as to the legitimacy of mod-erate interest was hailed by these hypocrites with a shout of glee. "It took with the brethren like polygamy with the Turks, recommended by the example of divers zealous ministers, who themselves desired to pass for orphans of the first rank."[6] Nor was it only as the apologist of modern interest that

Puritanism was alleged to reveal the cloven hoof. Puritans themselves complained of a mercilessness in driving hard bargains, and of a harshness to the poor, which contrasted unfavorably with the practice of followers of the unreformed religion. "The Papists," wrote a Puritan in 1653, "may rise up against many of this generation. It is a sad thing that they should be more forward upon a bad principle than a Christian upon a good one."[7]

Such, in all ages, is history as seen by the political pamphleteer. The real story was less dramatic, but more significant. From the very beginning, Calvinism had comprised two elements, which Calvin himself had fused, but which contained the seeds of future discord. It had at once given a whole-hearted *imprimatur* to the life of business enterprise, which most earlier moralists had regarded with suspicion, and had laid upon it the restraining hand of an inquisitorial discipline. At Geneva, where Calvinism was the creed of a small and homogeneous city, the second aspect had predominated; in the many-sided life of England, where there were numerous conflicting interests to balance it, and where it was long politically weak, the first. Then, in the late sixteenth and early seventeenth centuries, had come the wave of commercial and financial expansion—companies, colonies, capitalism in textiles, capitalism in mining, capitalism in finance—on the crest of which the English commercial classes, in Calvin's day still held in leading-strings by conservative statesmen, had climbed to a position of dignity and affluence.

Naturally, as the Puritan movement came to its own, these two elements flew apart. The collectivist, half-communistic aspect, which had never been acclimatized in England, quietly dropped out of notice, to crop up once more, and for the last time, to the disgust and terror of merchant and landowner, in the popular agitation under the Commonwealth. The individualism congenial to the world of business became the distinctive characteristic of a Puritanism which had arrived, and which, in becoming a political force, was at once secularized and committed to a career of compromise. Its note was not the attempt to establish on earth a "Kingdom of Christ," but an ideal of personal character and conduct, to be realized by the punctual discharge both of public and private duties. Its theory had been discipline; its practical result was liberty.

Given the social and political conditions of England, the transformation was inevitable. The incompatibility of Presbyterianism with the stratified arrangement of English society had been remarked by Hooker.[8] If the City Fathers of Geneva had thrown off by the beginning of the seventeenth century the religious collectivism of Calvin's régime, it was not to be expected that the landowners and *bourgeoisie* of an aristocratic and increasingly commercial nation, however much Calvinist theology might appeal to them, would view with favor the social doctrines implied in Calvinist discipline. In the reign of the first two Stuarts, both economic interests and political theory pulled them hard in the opposite direction. "Merchants' doings," the man of business in Wilson's *Discourse upon Usury* had observed, "must not thus be overthwarted by preachers and others that cannot skill of their dealings."[9] Behind the elaborate façade of Tudor State control, which has attracted the attention of historians, an individualist movement had been steadily developing, which found expression in opposition to the traditional policy of stereotyping economic relations by checking enclosure, controlling food supplies and prices.

interfering with the money-market, and regulating the conditions of the wage contract and of apprenticeship. In the first forty years of the seventeenth century, on grounds both of expediency and of principle, the commercial and propertied classes were becoming increasingly restive under the whole system, at once ambitious and inefficient, of economic paternalism. It was in the same sections of the community that both religious and economic dissatisfaction were most acute. Puritanism, with its idealization of the spiritual energies which found expression in the activities of business and industry, drew the isolated rivulets of discontent together, and swept them forward with the dignity and momentum of a religious and a social philosophy.

For it was not merely as the exponent of certain tenets as to theology and church government, but as the champion of interests and opinions embracing every side of the life of society, that the Puritan movement came into collision with the Crown. In reality, as is the case with most heroic ideologies, the social and religious aspects of Puritanism were not disentangled; they presented themselves, both to supporters and opponents, as different facets of a single scheme. "All that crossed the views of the needy courtiers, the proud encroaching priests, the thievish projectors, the lewd nobility and gentry . . . whoever could endure a sermon, modest habit or conversation, or anything good—all these were Puritans."[10] The clash was not one of theories—a systematic and theoretical individualism did not develop till after the Restoration —but of contradictory economic interests and incompatible conceptions of social expediency.

The economic policy haltingly pursued by the Government of Charles I bore some resemblance to the system of which a more uncompromising version was developed between 1661 and 1685 by Colbert in France. It was one which favored an artificial and State-promoted capitalism—a capitalism resting on the grant of privileges and concessions to company promoters who would pay for them, and accompanied by an elaborate system of State control, which again, if partly inspired by a genuine solicitude for the public interest, was too often smeared with an odious trail of finance. It found its characteristic expression in the grant of patents, in the revival of the royal monopoly of exchange business, against which the City had fought under Elizabeth, in attempts to enforce by administrative action compliance with the elaborate and impracticable code controlling the textile trades and to put down speculation in foodstuffs, and in raids on enclosing landlords, on employers who paid in truck or evaded the rates fixed by assessment, and on justices who were negligent in the administration of the Poor Laws. Such measures were combined with occasional plunges into even more grandiose schemes for the establishment of county granaries, for taking certain industries into the hands of the Crown, and even for the virtual nationalization of the cloth manufacture."[11]

"The very genius of that nation of people," wrote Strafford to Laud of the Puritans, "leads them always to oppose, as well civilly as ecclesiastically, all that ever authority ordains for them."[12] Against this whole attempt to convert economic activity into an instrument of profit for the Government and its hangers-on—against, no less, the spasmodic attempts of the State to protect peasants against landlords, craftsmen against merchants, and consumers against middlemen—the interests which it thwarted and curbed revolted with increasing pertinacity. Questions of taxation, on which attention has usually been concentrated, were in reality merely one element in a quarrel which had its deeper cause in the collision of incompatible social philosophies. The Puritan tradesman had seen his business ruined by a monopoly granted to a needy courtier, and cursed Laud and his Popish soap. The Puritan goldsmith or financier had found his trade as a bullion-broker hampered by the reëstablishment of the ancient office of Royal Exchanger, and secured a resolution from the House of Commons, declaring that the patent vesting it in Lord Holland and the proclamation forbidding the exchanging of gold and silver by unauthorized persons were a grievance. The Puritan money-lender had been punished by the Court of High Commission, and railed at the interference of bishops in temporal affairs. The Puritan clothier, who had suffered many things at the hands of interfering busy-bodies despatched from Whitehall to teach him his business, averted discreet eyes when the Wiltshire workmen threw a more than usually obnoxious Royal Commissioner into the Avon, and, when the Civil War came, rallied to the Parliament. The Puritan country gentleman had been harried by Depopulation Commissions, and took his revenge with the meeting of the Long Parliament. The Puritan merchant had seen the Crown both squeeze money out of his company, and threaten its monopoly by encouraging interlopers to infringe its charter. The Puritan member of Parliament had invested in colonial enterprises, and had ideas as to commercial policy which were not those of the Government. Confident in their own energy and acumen, proud of their success, and regarding with profound distrust the interference both of Church and of State with matters of business and property rights, the commercial classes, in spite of their attachment to a militant mercantilism in matters of trade, were, even before the Civil War, more than half converted to the administrative nihilism which was to be the rule of social policy in the century following it. Their demand was the one which is usual in such circumstances. It was that business affairs should be left to be settled by business men, unhampered by the intrusions of an antiquated morality or by misconceived arguments of public policy.[13]

The separation of economic from ethical interests, which was the note of all this movement, was in sharp opposition to religious tradition, and it did not establish itself without a struggle. Even in the very capital of European commerce and finance, an embittered controversy was occasioned by the refusal to admit usurers to communion or to confer degrees upon them; it was only after a storm of pamphleteering, in which the theological faculty of the University of Utrecht performed prodigies of zeal and ingenuity, that the States of Holland and West Friesland closed the agitation by declaring that the Church had no concern with questions of banking.[14] In the French Calvinist Churches, the decline of discipline had caused lamentations a generation earlier.[15] In America, the theocracy of Massachusetts, merciless alike to religious liberty and to economic license, was about to be undermined by the rise of new States like Rhode Island and Pennsylvania, whose tolerant, individualist and utilitarian temper was destined to find its greatest representative in the golden common sense of Benjamin Franklin.[16] "The sin of our too great fondness for trade, to the neglecting of our more valuable interests," wrote a Scottish divine in 1709, when Glasgow was on the eve of a triumphant outburst of commercial enterprise, "I humbly think will be written upon our judgment. . . . I am sure the Lord is remarkably frowning upon our trade . . . since it was put in the room of religion."[17]

In England, the growing disposition to apply exclusively economic standards to social relations evoked from Puritan writers and divines vigorous protests against usurious interest, extortionate prices and the oppression of tenants by landlords. The faithful, it was urged, had interpreted only too literally the doctrine that the sinner was saved, not by works, but by faith. Usury, "in time of Popery an odious thing,"[18] had become a scandal. Professors, by their covetousness, caused the enemies of the reformed religion to blaspheme.[19] The exactions of the forestaller and regrater were never so monstrous or so immune from interference. The hearts of the rich were never so hard, nor the necessities of the poor so neglected. "The poor able to work are suffered to beg; the impotent, aged and sick are not sufficiently provided for, but almost starved with the allowance of 3*d.* and 4*d.* a piece a week. . . . These are the last times indeed. Men generally are all for themselves. And some would set up such, having a form of religion, without the power of it."[20]

These utterances came, however, from that part of the Puritan mind which looked backward. That which looked forward found in the rapidly growing spirit of economic enterprise something not uncongenial to its own temper, and went out to welcome it as an ally. What in Calvin had been a qualified concession to practical exigencies appeared in some of his later followers as a frank idealization of the life of the trader, as the service of God and the training-ground of the soul. Discarding the suspicion of economic motives, which had been as characteristic of the reformers as of medieval theologians, Puritanism in its later phases added a halo of ethical sanctification to the appeal of economic expediency, and offered a moral creed, in which the duties of religion and the calls of business ended their long estrangement in an unanticipated reconciliation. Its spokesmen pointed out, it is true, the peril to the soul involved in a single-minded concentration on economic interests. The enemy, however, was not riches, but the bad habits sometimes associated with them, and its warnings against an excessive preoccupation with the pursuit of gain wore more and more the air of after-thoughts, appended to teaching the main tendency and emphasis of which were little affected by these incidental qualifications. It insisted, in short, that money-making, if not free from spiritual dangers, was not a danger and nothing else, but that it could be, and ought to be, carried on for the greater glory of God.

The conception to which it appealed to bridge the gulf sprang from the very heart of Puritan theology. It was that expressed in the characteristic and oft-used phrase, "a Calling."[21] The rational order of the universe is the work of God, and its plan requires that the individual should labor for God's glory. There is a spiritual calling, and a temporal calling. It is the first duty of the Christian to know and believe in God; it is by faith that he will be saved. But faith is not a mere profession, such as that of Talkative of Prating Row, whose "religion is to make a noise." The only genuine faith is the faith which produces works. "At the day of Doom men shall be judged according to their fruits. It will not be said then, Did you believe? but, Were you doers or talkers only?"[22] The second duty of the Christian is to labor in the affairs of practical life, and this second duty is subordinate only to the first. "God," wrote a Puritan divine, "doth call every man and woman . . . to serve him in some peculiar employment in this world, both for their own and the common good. . . . The Great Governour of the world hath appointed to every man his proper post and province, and let him be never so active out of his sphere, he will be at a great loss, if he do not keep his own vineyard and mind his own business."[23]

From this reiterated insistence on secular obligations as imposed by the divine will, it follows that, not withdrawal from the world, but the conscientious discharge of the duties of business, is among the loftiest of religious and moral virtues. "The begging friars and such monks as live only to themselves and to their formal devotion, but do employ themselves in no one thing to further their own subsistence or the good of mankind...yet have the confidence to boast of this their course as a state of perfection; which in very deed, as to the worthiness of it, falls short of the poorest cobbler, for his is a calling of God, and theirs is none."[24] The idea was not a new one. Luther had advanced it as a weapon against monasticism. But for Luther, with his patriarchal outlook on economic affairs, the calling means normally that state of life in which the individual has been set by Heaven, and against which it is impiety to rebel. On the lips of Puritan divines, it is not an invitation to resignation, but the bugle-call which summons the elect to the long battle which will end only with their death. "The world is all before them." They are to hammer out their salvation, not merely *in vocatione,* but *per vocationem.* The calling is not a condition in which the individual is born, but a strenuous and exacting enterprise, to be undertaken, indeed, under the guidance of Providence, but to be chosen by each man for himself, with a deep sense of his solemn responsibilities. "God hath given to man reason for this use, that he should first consider, then choose, then put in execution; and it is a preposterous and brutish thing to fix or fall upon any weighty business, such as a calling or condition of life, without a careful pondering it in the balance of sound reason."[25]

Laborare est orare. By the Puritan moralist the ancient maxim is repeated with a new and intenser significance. The labor which he idealizes is not simply a requirement imposed by nature, or a punishment for the sin of Adam. It is itself a kind of ascetic discipline, more rigorous than that demanded of any order of mendicants—a discipline imposed by the will of God, and to be undergone, not in solitude, but in the punctual discharge of secular duties. It is not merely an economic means, to be laid aside when physical needs have been satisfied. It is a spiritual end, for in it alone can the soul find health, and it must be continued as an ethical duty long after it has ceased to be a material necessity. Work thus conceived stands at the very opposite pole from "good works," as they were understood, or misunderstood, by Protestants. They, it was thought, had been a series of single transactions, performed as compensation for particular sins, or out of anxiety to acquire merit. What is required of the Puritan is not individual meritorious acts, but a holy life—a system in which every element is grouped round a central idea, the service of God, from which all disturbing irrelevancies have been pruned, and to which all minor interests are subordinated.

His conception of that life was expressed in the words "Be wholly taken up in diligent business of your lawful callings, when you are not exercised in the more immediate service of God."[26] In order to deepen his spiritual life, the Christian must be prepared to narrow it. He "is blind in no man's cause, but best sighted in his own. He confines himself to the circle of his own affairs and thrusts not his fingers in needless fires. . . . He sees the falseness of it [the world] and therefore learns to trust himself ever, others so far as not to be damaged by their disappointment."[27] There must be no idle leisure: "those that are prodigal of their time despise their own souls."[28] Religion must be active, not merely contemplative. Contemplation is, indeed, a kind of self-indulgence. "To neglect this [i. e., bodily employment and mental labor] and say, 'I will pray and meditate,' is as if your servant should refuse your greatest work, and tye himself to some lesser, easie part. . . . God hath commanded you some way or other to labour for your daily bread."[29] The rich are no more excused from work than the poor, though they may rightly use their riches to select some occupation specially serviceable to others. Covetousness is a danger to the soul, but it is not so grave a danger as sloth. "The standing pool is prone to putrefaction: and it were better to beat down the body and to keep in subjection by a laborious calling, than through luxury to become a cast-away."[30] So far from poverty being meritorious, it is a duty to choose the more profitable occupation. "If God show you a way in which you may lawfully get more than in another way (without wrong to your soul or to any other), if you refuse this, and choose the less gainful way, you cross one of the ends of your Calling, and you refuse to be God's steward." Luxury, unrestrained pleasure, personal extravagance, can have no place in a Christian's conduct, for "every penny which is laid out . . . must be done as by God's own appointment." Even excessive devotion to friends and relations is to be avoided. "It is an irrational act, and therefore not fit for a rational creature, to love any one farther than reason will allow us. . . . It very often taketh up men's minds so as to hinder their love to God."[31] The Christian life, in short, must be systematic and organized, the work of an iron will and a cool intelligence. Those who have read Mill's account of his father must have been struck by the extent to which Utilitarianism was not merely a political doctrine, but a moral attitude. Some of the links in the Utilitarian coat of mail were forged, it may be suggested, by the Puritan divines of the seventeenth century.

The practical application of these generalities to business is set out in the numerous works composed to expound the rules of Christian conduct in the varied relations of life. If one may judge by their titles—*Navigation Spiritualized, Husbandry Spiritualized, The Religious Weaver*[32]—there must have been a considerable demand for books conducive to professional edification. A characteristic specimen is *The Tradesman's Calling*,[33] by Richard Steele. The author, after being deprived of a country living under the Act of Uniformity, spent his declining years as a minister of a congregation at Armourers Hall in London, and may be presumed to have understood the spiritual requirements of the City in his day, when the heroic age of Puritanism was almost over and enthusiasm was no longer a virtue.

In reality, however, the characteristic of *The Tradesman's Calling,* as of the age in which it was written, is not the relics of medieval doctrine which linger embalmed in its guileless pages, but the robust common sense, which carries the author lightly over traditional scruples on a tide of genial, if

Philistine, optimism. For his main thesis is a comfortable one—that there is no necessary conflict between religion and business. "Prudence and Piety were always very good friends. . . . You may gain enough of both worlds if you would mind each in its place." His object is to show how that agreeable result may be produced by dedicating business—with due reservations—to the service of God, and he has naturally little to say on the moral casuistry of economic conduct, because he is permeated by the idea that trade itself is a kind of religion. A tradesman's first duty is to get a full insight into his calling, and to use his brains to improve it. "He that hath lent you talents hath also said, 'Occupy till I come!' Your strength is a talent, your parts are talents, and so is your time. How is it that ye stand all the day idle? . . . Your trade is your proper province. . . .Your own vineyard you should keep. . . . Your fancies, your understandings, your memories . . . are all to be laid out therein." So far from their being an inevitable collision between the requirements of business and the claims of religion, they walk hand in hand. By a fortunate dispensation, the virtues enjoined on Christians—diligence, moderation, sobriety, thrift—are the very qualities most conducive to commercial success. The foundation of all is prudence; and prudence is merely another name for the "godly wisdom [which] comes in and puts due bounds" to his expenses, "and teaches the tradesman to live rather somewhat below than at all above his income." Industry comes next, and industry is at once expedient and meritorious. It will keep the tradesman from "frequent and needless frequenting of taverns," and pin him to his shop, "where you may most confidently expect the presence and blessing of God."

If virtue is advantageous, vice is ruinous. Bad company, speculation, gambling, politics, and "a preposterous zeal" in religion—it is these things which are the ruin of tradesmen. Not, indeed, that religion is to be neglected. On the contrary, it "is to be exercised in the frequent use of holy ejaculations." What is deprecated is merely the unbusinesslike habit of "neglecting a man's necessary affairs upon pretence of religious worship." But these faults, common and uncommon alike, are precisely those to be avoided by the sincere Christian, who must not, indeed, deceive or oppress his neighbor, but need not fly to the other extreme, be righteous overmuch, or refuse to "take the advantage which the Providence of God puts into his hands." By a kind of happy, preëstablished harmony, such as a later age discovered between the needs of society and the self-interest of the individual, success in business is in itself almost a sign of spiritual grace, for it is proof that a man has labored faithfully in his vocation, and that "God has blessed his trade." "Nothing will pass in any man's account except it be done in the way of his calling. . . . Next to the saving his soul, [the tradesman's] care and business is to serve God in his calling, and to drive it as far is it will go."

When duty was so profitable, might not profit-making be a duty? Thus argued the honest pupils of Mr. Gripeman, the schoolmaster of Love-gain, a market-town in the country of Coveting in the north.[34] The inference was illogical, but how attractive! When the Rev. David Jones was so indiscreet as to preach at St. Mary Woolnoth in Lombard Street a sermon against usury on the text "The Pharisees who were covetous heard all these things and they derided Christ," his career in London was brought to an abrupt conclusion.[35]

The springs of economic conduct lie in regions rarely penetrated by moralists, and to suggest a direct reaction of theory on practice would be paradoxical. But, if the circumstances which determine that certain kinds of conduct shall be profitable are economic, those which decide that they shall be the object of general approval are primarily moral and intellectual. For conventions to be adopted with wholehearted enthusiasm, to be not merely tolerated, but applauded, to become the habit of a nation and the admiration of its philosophers, the second condition must be present as well as the first.

The transition from the anabaptist to the company promoter was less abrupt than might at first sight be supposed. It had been prepared, however unintentionally, by Puritan moralists. In their emphasis on the moral duty of untiring activity, on work as an end in itself, on the evils of luxury and extravagance, on foresight and thrift, on moderation and self-discipline and rational calculation, they had created an ideal of Christian conduct, which canonized as an ethical principle the efficiency which economic theorists were preaching as a specific for social disorders. It was as captivating as it was novel. To countless generations of religious thinkers, the fundamental maxim of Christian social ethics had seemed to be expressed in the words of St. Paul to Timothy: "Having food and raiment, let us be therewith content. For the love of money is the root of all evil." Now, while as always, the world battered at the gate, a new standard was raised within the citadel by its own defenders. The garrison had discovered that the invading host of economic appetites was, not an enemy, but an ally. Not sufficiency to the needs of daily life, but limitless increase and expansion, became the goal of the Christian's efforts. Not consumption, on which the eyes of earlier sages had been turned, but production, became the pivot of his argument. Not an easy-going and open-handed charity, but a systematic and methodical accumulation, won the meed of praise that belongs to the good and faithful servant. The shrewd, calculating commercialism which tries all human relations by pecuniary standards, the acquisitiveness which cannot rest while there are competitors to be conquered or profits to be won, the love of social power and hunger for economic gain—these irrepressible appetites had evoked from time immemorial the warnings and denunciations of saints and sages. Plunged in the cleansing waters of later Puritanism, the qualities which less enlightened ages had denounced as social vices emerged as economic virtues. They emerged as moral virtues as well. For the world exists not to be enjoyed, but to be conquered. Only its conqueror deserves the name of Christian. For such a philosophy, the question "What shall it profit a man?" carries no sting. In winning the world, he wins the salvation of his own soul as well.

The idea of economic progress as an end to be consciously sought, while ever receding, had been unfamiliar to most earlier generations of Englishmen, in which the theme of moralists had been the danger of unbridled cupidity, and the main aim of public policy had been the stability of traditional relationships. It found a new sanction in the identification of labor and enterprise with the service of God. The magnificent energy which changed in a century the face of material civilization was to draw nourishment from that temper.

The contemporary progress of economic thought fortified no less the mood which glorified the economic virtues. Economic science developed in England, not, as in Germany, as the handmaid of public administration, nor, as in France, through the speculations of philosophers and men of letters, but as the interpreter of the practical interests of the City. With the exception of Petty and Locke, its most eminent practitioners were business men, and the questions which excited them were those, neither of production nor of social organization, but of commerce and finance—the balance of trade, tariffs, interest, currency and credit. The rise of Political Arithmetic after the Restoration, profoundly influenced, as it was, by the Cartesian philosophy and by the progress of natural science, stamped their spontaneous and doctrineless individualism with the seal of theoretical orthodoxy. Knowledge, wrote the author of the preface to a work by one of the most eminent exponents of the new science, "in great measure is become mechanical."[36] The exact analysis of natural conditions, the calculations of forces and strains, the reduction of the complex to the operation of simple, constant and measurable forces, was the natural bias of an age interested primarily in mathematics and physics. Its object was "to express itself in terms of number, weight or measure, to use only arguments of sense, and to consider only such causes as have visible foundations in nature; leaving those that depend upon the mutable minds, opinions, appetites and passions of particular men to the consideration of others."[37]

In such an atmosphere, the moral casuistry, which had occupied so large a place in the earlier treatment of social and economic subjects, seemed the voice of an antiquated superstition. Moreover, the main economic dogma of the mercantilist had an affinity with the main ethical dogma of the Puritan, which was the more striking because the coincidence was undesigned. To the former, production, not consumption, was the pivot of the economic system, and, by what seems to the modern reader a curious perversion, consumption is applauded only because it offers a new market for productive energies. To the latter, the cardinal virtues are precisely those which find in the strenuous toils of industry and commerce their most natural expression. The typical qualities of the successful business life, in the days before the rise of joint-stock enterprise, were intensity and earnestness of labor, concentration, system and method, the initiative which broke with routine and the foresight which postponed the present to the future.

To such a generation, a creed which transformed the acquisition of wealth from a drudgery or a temptation into a moral duty was the milk of lions. It was not that religion was expelled from practical life, but that religion itself gave it a foundation of granite. In that keen atmosphere of economic enterprise, the ethics of the Puritan bore some resemblance to those associated later with the name of Smiles. The good Christian was not wholly dissimilar from the economic man.

THE NEW MEDICINE FOR POVERTY

To applaud certain qualities is by implication to condemn the habits and institutions which appear to conflict with them. The recognition accorded by Puritan ethics to the economic virtues, in an age when such virtues were rarer than they are today, gave a timely stimulus to economic efficiency. But it naturally, if unintentionally, modified the traditional attitude towards social obligations. For the spontaneous, doctrineless individualism, which became the rule of English public life a century before the philosophy of it was propounded by Adam Smith, no single cause was responsible. But, simultaneously with the obvious movements in the world of affairs—the discrediting of the ideal of a paternal, authoritarian Government, the breakdown of central control over local administration, the dislocation caused by the Civil War, the expansion of trade and the shifting of industry from its accustomed seats— it is perhaps not fanciful to detect in the ethics of Puritanism one force contributing to the change in social policy which is noticeable after the middle of the century.

The loftiest teaching cannot escape from its own shadow. To urge that the Christian life must be lived in a zealous discharge of private duties—how necessary! Yet how readily perverted to the suggestion that there are no vital social obligations beyond and above them! To insist that the individual is responsible, that no man can save his brother, that the essence of religion is the contact of the soul with its Maker, how true and indispensable! But how easy to slip from that truth into the suggestion that society is without responsibility, that no man can help his brother, that the social order and its consequences are not even the scaffolding by which men may climb to greater heights, but something external, alien and irrelevant—something, at best, indifferent to the life of the spirit, and, at worst, the sphere of the letter which killeth and of the reliance on works which ensnares the soul into the slumber of death! In emphasizing that God's Kingdom is not of this world, Puritanism did not always escape the suggestion that this world is no part of God's Kingdom. The complacent victim of that false antithesis between the social mechanism and the life of the spirit, which was to tyrannize over English religious thought for the next two centuries, it enthroned religion in the privacy of the individual soul, not without some sighs of sober satisfaction at its abdication from society. Professor Dicey has commented on the manner in which "the appeal of the Evangelicals to personal religion corresponds with the appeal of Benthamite Liberals to individual energy."[38] The same affinity between religious and social interests found an even clearer expression in the Puritan movement of the seventeenth century. Individualism in religion led insensibly, if not quite logically, to an individualist morality, and an individualist morality to a disparagement of the significance of the social fabric as compared with personal character.

A practical example of that change of emphasis is given by the treatment accorded to the questions of Enclosure and of Pauperism. For a century and a half the progress of enclosing had been a burning issue, flaring up, from time to time, into acute agitation. During the greater part of that period, from Latimer in the thirties of the sixteenth cenury to Laud in the thirties of the seventeenth, the attitude of religious teachers had been one of condemnation. Sermon after sermon and pamphlet after pamphlet—not to mention Statutes and Royal Commissions—had been launched against depopulation. The appeal had been, not merely to public policy, but to religion. Peasant and lord, in their different degrees, are members of one Christian commonwealth, within which the law of charity must bridle the corroding appetite for economic gain. In such a mystical corporation, knit together by mutual obligations, no man may press his advantage to the full, for no man may seek to live "outside the body of the Church."

Sabotaged by the unpaid magistracy of country gentlemen, who had been the obstructive agents of local administration, the practical application of such doctrines had always been intermittent, and, when the Long Parliament struck the weapon of administrative law from the hands of the Crown, it had ceased altogether. But the politics of Westminster were not those of village and borough. The events which seemed to aristocratic Parliamentarians to close the revolution seemed to the left wing of the victorious army only to begin it. In that earliest and most turbulent of English democracies, where buff-coat taught scripture politics to his general, the talk was not merely of political, but of social, reconstruction. The program of the Levellers, who more than any other party could claim to express the aspirations of the un-privileged classes, included a demand, not only for annual or biennial Parliaments, manhood suffrage, a redistribution of seats in proportion to population, and the abolition of the veto of the House of Lords, but also that "you would have laid open all enclosures of fens and other commons, or have them enclosed only or chiefly for the benefit of the poor."[39]

Nor was it only from the visionary and the zealot that the pressure for redress proceeded. When the shattering of traditional authority seemed for a moment to make all things new, local grievances, buried beneath centuries of dull oppression, started to life, and in several Midland counties the peasants rose to pull down the hated hedges. At Leicester, where in 1649 there were rumors of a popular movement to throw down the enclosures of the neighboring forest, the City Council took the matter up. A petition was drafted, setting out the economic and social evils attending enclosure, and proposing the establishment of machinery to check it, consisting of a committee without whose assent enclosing was not to be permitted. A local minister was instructed to submit the petition to Parliament, "which hath still a watchful eye and open ear to redress the common grievances of the nation."[40]

Half a century before, such commotions would have been followed by the passing of Depopulation Acts and the issue of a Royal Commission. But, in the ten years since the meeting of the Long Parliament, the whole attitude of public policy towards the movement had begun to change. Confiscations, compositions and war taxation had effected a revolution in the distribution of property, similar, on a smaller scale, to that which had taken place at the Reformation. As land changed hands, customary relations were shaken and new interests were created. Enclosure, as Moore complained,[41] was being pushed forward by means of law suits ending in Chancery decrees. It was not to be expected that City merchants and members of the Committee for Compounding, some of whom had found land speculation a profitable business, should hear with enthusiasm a proposal to revive the old policy of arresting enclosures by State interference, at which the gentry had grumbled for more than a century.

In these circumstances, it is not surprising that reformers should have found the open ear of Parliament impenetrably closed to agrarian grievances. Nor was it only the political and economic environment which had changed. The revolution in thought was equally profound. The theoretical basis of the policy of protecting the peasant by preventing enclosure had been a conception of landownership which regarded its rights and its duties as inextricably interwoven. Property was not merely a source of income, but a public function, and its use was limited by social obligations and necessities of State. With such a doctrine the classes who had taken the lead in the struggle against the monarchy could make no truce. Its last vestiges finally disappeared when the Restoration Parliament swept away military tenures, and imposed on the nation, in the shape of an excise, the financial burden previously borne by themselves.

The theory which took its place, and which was to become in the eighteenth century almost a religion, was that expressed by Locke, when he described property as a right anterior to the existence of the State, and argued that "the supreme power cannot take from any man any part of his property without his own consent." But Locke merely poured into a philosophical mould ideas which had been hammered out in the stress of political struggles, and which were already the commonplace of landowner and merchant. The view of society held by that part of the Puritan movement which was socially and politically influential had been expressed by Ireton and Cromwell in their retort to the democrats in the army. It was that only the freeholders con- stituted the body politic, and that they could use their property as they pleased, uncontrolled by obligations to any superior, or by the need of consulting the mass of men, who were mere tenants at will, with no fixed interest or share in the land of the kingdom.[42] Naturally, this change of ideas had profound reactions on agrarian policy. Formerly a course commending itself to all public-spirited persons, the prevention of enclosure was now discredited as the program of a sect of religious and political radicals. When Major-General Whalley in 1656 introduced a measure to regulate and restrict the enclosure of commons, framed, apparently, on the lines proposed by the authorities of Leicester, there was an instant outcry from members that it would "destroy property," and the bill was refused a second reading.[43] After the Restoration the tide began to run more strongly in the same direction. Enclosure had already become the hobby of the country gentleman. Experts advocated it on economic grounds, and legislation to facilitate it was intro- duced into Parliament. Though its technique still remained to be elaborated, the attitude which was to be decisive in the eighteenth century had already been crystallized.

The change of policy was striking. The reason of it was not merely that political conditions made the landed gentry omnipotent, and that the Royalist squirearchy, who streamed back to their plundered manors in 1660, were in no mood to countenance a revival, by the Government of Charles II, of the administrative interference with the rights of property which had infuriated them in the Government of Charles I. It was that opinion as to social policy had changed, and changed not least among men of religion themselves. The pursuit of economic self-interest, which is the law of nature, is already coming to be identified by the pious with the operation of the providential plan, which is the law of God. Enclosures will increase the output of wool and grain. Each man knows best what his land is suited to produce, and the general interest will be best served by leaving him free to produce it. "It is an unde- niable maxim that every one by the light of nature and reason will do that which makes for his greatest advantage. . . . The advancement of private persons will be the advantage of the public."[44]

It is significant that such considerations were adduced, not by an economist, but by a minister. For the argument was ethical as well as economic, and, when Moore appealed to the precepts of traditional morality to bridle pecuniary interests, he provoked the retort that a judicious attention to pecuniary interests was an essential part of an enlightened morality. What the poor need for their spiritual health is—to use the favorite catchword of the age—"regulation," and regulation is possible only if they work under the eye of an employer. In the eyes of the austere moralists of the Restoration, the first, and most neglected, virtue of the poor is industry. Common rights encourage idleness by offering a precarious and demoralizing livelihood to men who ought to be at work for a master. It is not surprising, therefore, that the admonitions of religious teachers against the wickedness of joining house to house and field to field should almost entirely cease. Long the typical example of uncharitable covetousness, enclosure is now considered, not merely economically expedient, but morally beneficial. Baxter, with all his scrupulousness—partly, perhaps, because of his scrupulousness—differs from most earlier divines in giving a qualified approval to enclosure "done in moderation by a pious man," for the characteristic reason that a master can establish a moral discipline among his employees, which they would miss if they worked for themselves. What matters, in short, is not their circumstances, but their character. If they lose as peasants, they will gain as Christians. Opportunities for spiritual edification are more important than the mere material environment. If only the material environment were not itself among the forces determining men's capacity to be edified!

The temper which deplored that the open-field village was not a school of the severer virtues turned on pauperism and poor relief an even more shattering criticism. There is no province of social life in which the fashioning of a new scale of ethical values on the Puritan anvil is more clearly revealed. In the little communities of peasants and craftsmen which composed medieval England, all, when Heaven sent a bad harvest, had starved together, and the misery of the sick, the orphan and the aged had appeared as a personal calamity, not as a social problem. Apart from a few precocious theorists, who hinted at the need for a universal and secular system of provision for distress, the teaching most characteristic of medieval writers had been that the relief of the needy was a primary obligation on those who had means. St. Thomas, who in this matter is typical, quotes with approval the strong words of St. Ambrose about those who cling to the bread of the starving, insists on the idea that property is stewardship, and concludes—a conclusion not always drawn from that well-worn phrase—that to withhold alms when there is evident and urgent necessity is mortal sin.[45] Popular feeling had lent a half-mystical glamour both to poverty and to the compassion by which poverty was relieved, for poor men were God's friends. At best, the poor were thought to represent our Lord in a peculiarly intimate way—"in that sect," as Langland said, "our Saviour saved all mankind"—and it was necessary for the author of a religious manual to explain that the rich, as such, were not necessarily hateful to God.[46] At worst, men reflected that the prayers of the poor availed much, and that the sinner had been saved from hell by throwing a loaf of bread to a beggar, even though a curse went with it. The alms bestowed today would be repaid a thousandfold, when the soul took its dreadful journey amid rending briars and scorching flames.

The social character of wealth, which had been the essence of the medieval doctrine, was asserted by English divines in the sixteenth century with redoubled emphasis, precisely because the growing individualism of the age menaced the traditional conception. "The poor man," preached Latimer, "hath title to the rich man's goods; so that the rich man ought to let the poor man have part of his riches to help and to comfort him withal."[47] Nor had that sovereign indifference to the rigors of the economic calculus disappeared, when, under the influence partly of humanitarian representatives of the Renaissance like Vives, partly of religious reformers, partly of their own ambition to gather all the threads of social administration into their own hands, the statesmen of the sixteenth century set themselves to organize a secular system of poor relief. In England, after three generations in which the attempt was made to stamp out vagrancy by police measures of hideous brutality, the momentous admission was made that its cause was economic distress, not merely personal idleness, and that the whip had no terrors for the man who must either tramp or starve. The result was the celebrated Acts imposing a compulsory poor-rate and requiring the able-bodied man to be set on work. The Privy Council, alert to prevent disorder, drove lethargic justices hard, and down to the Civil War the system was administered with fair regularity. But the Elizabethan Poor Law was never designed to be what, with disastrous results, it became in the eighteenth and early nineteenth centuries, the sole measure for coping with economic distress. While it provided relief, it was but the last link in a chain of measures—the prevention of evictions, the control of food supplies and prices, the attempt to stabilize employment and to check unnecessary dismissals of workmen—intended to mitigate the forces which made relief necessary. Apart from the Poor Law, the first forty years of the seventeenth century were prolific in the private charity which founded alms-houses and hospitals, and established funds to provide employment or to aid struggling tradesmen. The appeal was still to religion, which owed to poverty a kind of reverence.

It was inevitable that, in the anarchy of the Civil War, both private charity and public relief should fall on evil days. In London, charitable endowments seem to have suffered from more than ordinary malversation, and there were complaints that the income both of Bridewell and of the Hospitals was seriously reduced.[48] In the country, the records of Quarter Sessions paint a picture of confusion, in which the machinery of presentment by constables to justice has broken down, and a long wail arises, that thieves are multiplied, the poor are neglected, and vagrants wander to and fro at their will.[49] The administrative collapse of the Elizabethan Poor Law continued after the Restoration, and twenty-three years later Sir Matthew Hale complained that the sections in it relating to the provision of employment were a dead letter.[50] Always unpopular with the local authorities, whom they involved in considerable trouble and expense, it is not surprising that, with the cessation of pressure by the Central Government, they should, except here and there, have been neglected. What is more significant, however, than the practical deficiencies in the administration of relief, was the rise of a new school of opinion, which regarded with repugnance the whole body of social theory of which both private charity and public relief had been the expression.

"The generall rule of all England," wrote a pamphleteer in 1646, "is to whip and punish the wandring beggars . . . and so many justices execute one branch of that good Statute (which is the point of justice), but as for the point of charitie, they leave [it] undone, which is to provide houses and convenient places to set the poore to work."[51] The House of Commons appears to have been conscious that the complaint had some foundation; in 1649 it ordered that the county justices should be required to see that stocks of material were provided as the law required,[52] and the question of preparing new legislation to ensure that persons in distress should be found employment was on several occasions referred to committees of the House.[53] Nothing seems, however, to have come of these proposals, nor was the Elizabethan policy of "setting the poor on work" that which was most congenial to the temper of the time. Upon the admission that distress was the result, not of personal deficiencies, but of economic causes, with its corollary that its victims had a legal right to be maintained by society, the growing individualism of the age turned the same frigid scepticism as was later directed against the Speenhamland policy by the reformers of 1834. Like the friends of Job, it saw in misfortune, not the chastisement of love, but the punishment for sin. The result was that, while the penalties on the vagrant were redoubled, religious opinion laid less emphasis on the obligation of charity than upon the duty of work, and that the admonitions which had formerly been turned upon uncharitable covetousness were now directed against improvidence and idleness. The characteristic sentiment was that of Milton's friend, Hartlib: "The law of God saith, 'he that will not work, let him not eat.' This would be a sore scourge and smart whip for idle persons if . . . none should be suffered to eat till they had wrought for it."[54]

The new attitude found expression in the rare bursts of public activity provoked by the growth of pauperism between 1640 and 1660. The idea of dealing with it on sound business principles, by means of a corporation which would combine profit with philanthropy, was being sedulously preached by a small group of reformers.[55] Parliament took it up, and in 1649 passed an Act for the relief and employment of the poor and the punishment of beggars, under which a company was to be established with power to apprehend vagrants, to offer them the choice between work and whipping, and to set to compulsory labor all other poor persons, including children without means of maintenance.[56] Eight years later the prevalence of vagrancy produced an Act of such extreme severity as almost to recall the suggestion made a generation later by Fletcher of Saltoun, that vagrants should be sent to the galleys. It provided that, since offenders could rarely be taken in the act, any vagrant who failed to satisfy the justices that he had a good reason for being on the roads should be arrested and punished as a sturdy beggar, whether actually begging or not.[57]

The protest against indiscriminate almsgiving, as the parade of a spurious religion, which sacrificed character to a formal piety, was older than the Reformation, but it had been given a new emphasis by the reformers. Luther had denounced the demands of beggars as blackmail, and the Swiss reformers had stamped out the remnants of monastic charity, as a bride ministered by Popery to dissoluteness and demoralization. "I conclude that all the large givings of the papists," preached an English divine in the reign of Elizabeth, "of which at this day many make so great brags, because they be not done in a reverent regard of the commandment of the Lord, in love, and of an inward being touched with the calamities of the needy, but for to be well reported of before men whilst they are alive, and to be prayed for after they are dead . . . are indeed no alms, but pharisaical trumpets."[58] The rise of a commercial civilization, the reaction against the authoritarian social policy of the Tudors, and the progress of Puritanism among the middle classes, all combined in the next half-century to sharpen the edge of that doctrine. Nurtured in a tradition which made the discipline of character by industry and self-denial the center of its ethical scheme, the Puritan moralist was undisturbed by any doubts as to whether even the seed of the righteous might not sometimes be constrained to beg its bread, and met the taunt that the reputation of good works was the cloak for a conscienceless egoism with the retort that the easy-going open-handedness of the sentimentalist was not less selfish in its motives and was more corrupting to its objects. "As for idle beggars," wrote Steele, "happy for them if fewer people spent their foolish pity upon their bodies, and if more shewed some wise compassion upon their souls."[59] That the greatest of evils is idleness, that the poor are the victims, not of circumstances, but of their own "idle, irregular and wicked courses," that the truest charity is not to enervate them by relief, but so to reform their characters that relief may be unnecessary—such doctrines turned severity from a sin into a duty, and froze the impulse of natural pity with the assurance that, if indulged, it would perpetuate the suffering which it sought to allay.

Few tricks of the unsophisticated intellect are more curious that the naïve psychology of the business man, who ascribes his achievements to his own unaided efforts, in bland unconsciousness of a social order without whose continuous support and vigilant protection he would be as a lamb bleating in the desert. That individualist complex owes part of its self-assurance to the suggestion of Puritan moralists, that practical success is at once the sign and the reward of ethical superiority. "No question," argued a Puritan pamphleteer, "but it [riches] should be the portion rather of the godly than of the wicked, were it good for them; for godliness hath the promises of this life as well as of the life to come."[60] The demonstration that distress is a proof of demerit, though a singular commentary on the lives of Christian saints and sages, has always been popular with the prosperous. By the lusty plutocracy of the Restoration, roaring after its meat, and not indisposed, if it could not find it elsewhere, to seek it from God, it was welcomed with a shout of applause.

A society which reverences the attainment of riches as the supreme felicity will naturally be disposed to regard the poor as damned in the next world, if only to justify itself for making their life a hell in this. Advanced by men of religion as a tonic for the soul, the doctrine of the danger of pampering poverty was hailed by the rising school of Political Arithmeticians as a sovereign cure for the ills of society. For, if the theme of the moralist was that an easy-going indulgence undermined character, the theme of the economist was that it was economically disastrous and financially ruinous. The Poor Law is the mother of idleness, "men and women growing so idle and proud that they will not work, but lie upon the parish wherein they dwell for maintenance." It discourages thrift; "if shame or fear of punishment makes him earn his dayly bread, he will do no more; his children are the charge of the parish and his old age his recess from labour or care." It keeps up wages, since "it encourages wilful and evil-disposed persons to impose what wages they please upon their labours; and herein they are so refractory to reason and the benefit of the nation that, when corn and provisions are cheap, they will not work for less wages than when they were dear."[61] To the landowner who cursed the poor-rates, and the clothier who grumbled at the high cost of labor, one school of religious thought now brought the comforting assurance that morality itself would be favored by a reduction of both.

As the history of the Poor Law in the nineteenth century was to prove, there is no touchstone, except the treatment of childhood, which reveals the true character of a social philosophy more clearly than the spirit in which it regards the misfortunes of those of its members who fall by the way. Such utterances on the subject of poverty were merely one example of a general attitude, which appeared at times to consign to collective perdition almost the whole of the wage-earning population. It was partly that, in an age which worshiped property as the foundation of the social order, the mere laborer seemed something less than a full citizen. It was partly the result of the greatly increased influence on thought and public affairs acquired at the Restoration by the commercial classes, whose temper was a ruthless materialism, determined at all costs to conquer world-markets from France and Holland, and prepared to sacrifice every other consideration to their economic ambitions. It was partly that, in spite of a century of large-scale production in textiles, the problems of capitalist industry and of a propertyless proletariat were still too novel for their essential features to be appreciated. Even those writers, like Baxter and Bunyan, who continued to insist on the wickedness of extortionate prices and unconscionable interest, rarely thought of applying their principles to the subject of wages. Their social theory had been designed for an age of petty agriculture and industry, in which personal relations had not yet been superseded by the cash nexus, and the craftsman or peasant farmer was but little removed in economic status from the half-dozen journeymen or laborers whom he employed. In a world increasingly dominated by great clothiers, iron-masters and mine-owners, they still adhered to the antiquated categories of master and servant, with the same obstinate indifference to economic realities as leads the twentieth century to talk of employers and employed, long after the individual employer has been converted into an impersonal corporation.

When philanthropists were inquiring whether it might not be desirable to reëstablish slavery, it was not to be expected that the sufferings of the destitute would wring their hearts with social compunction. The most curious feature in the whole discussion, and that which is most sharply in contrast with the long debate on pauperism carried on in the sixteenth century, was the resolute refusal to admit that society had any responsibility for the causes of distress. Tudor divines and statesmen had little mercy for idle rogues. But the former always, and the latter ultimately, regarded pauperism primarily as a social phenomenon produced by economic dislocation, and the embarrassing question put by the genial Harrison—"at whose handes shall the bloude of these men be required?"[62]—was never far from the minds even of the most cynical. Their successors after the Restoration were apparently quite unconscious that it was even conceivable that there might be any other cause of poverty than the moral failings of the poor. The practical conclusion to be drawn from so comfortable a creed was at once extremely simple and extremely agreeable. It was not to find employment under the Act of 1601, for to do that was only "to render the poor more bold." It was to surround the right to relief with obstacles such as those contained in the Act of 1662, to give it, when it could not be avoided, in a workhouse or house of correction, and, for the rest, to increase the demand for labor by reducing wages.

The grand discovery of a commercial age, that relief might be so administered as not merely to relieve, but also to deter, still remained to be made by Utilitarian philosophers. But the theory that distress was due, not to economic circumstances, but to what the Poor Law Commissioners of 1834 called "individual improvidence and vice," was firmly established, and the criticism of the Elizabethan system which was to inspire the new Poor Law had already been formulated. The essence of that system was admirably expressed a century later by a Scottish divine as "the principle that each man, simply because he exists, holds a right on other men or on society for existence."[63] Dr. Chalmers' attack upon it was the echo of a note long struck by Puritan moralists. And the views of Dr. Chalmers had impressed themselves on Nassau Senior,[64] before he set his hand to that brilliant, influential and wildly unhistorical Report, which, after provoking something like a rebellion in the north of England, was to be one of the pillars of the social policy of the nineteenth century.

It would be misleading to dwell on the limitations of Puritan ethics without emphasizing the enormous contribution of Puritanism to political freedom and social progress. The foundation of democracy is the sense of spiritual independence which nerves the individual to stand alone against the powers of this world, and in England, where squire and parson, lifting arrogant eyebrows at the insolence of the lower orders, combined to crush popular agitation, as a menace at once to society and to the Church, it is probable that democracy owes more to Nonconformity than to any other single movement. The virtues of enterprise, diligence and thrift are the indispensable foundation of any complex and vigorous civilization. It was Puritanism which, by investing them with a supernatural sanction, turned them from an unsocial eccentricity into a habit and a religion. Nor would it be difficult to find notable representatives of the Puritan spirit in whom the personal authority, which was the noblest aspect of the new ideal, was combined with a profound consciousness of social solidarity, which was the noblest aspect of that which it displaced. Firmin the philanthropist, and Bellers the Quaker, whom Owen more than a century later hailed as the father of his doctrines, were pioneers of Poor Law reform. The Society of Friends, in an age when the divorce between religion and social ethics was almost complete, met the prevalent doctrine, that it was permissible to take such gain as the market offered, by insisting on the obligation of good conscience and forbearance in economic transactions, and on the duty to make the honorable maintenance of the brother in distress a common charge.[65]

The general climate and character of a country are not altered, however, by the fact that here and there it has peaks which rise into an ampler air. The distinctive note of Puritan teaching was different. It was individual responsibility, not social obligation. Training its pupils to the mastery of others through the mastery of self, it prized as a crown of glory the qualities which arm the spiritual athlete for his solitary contest with a hostile world, and dismissed concern with the social order as the prop of weaklings and the Capua of the soul. Both the excellences and the defects of that attitude were momentous for the future. It is sometimes suggested that the astonishing outburst of industrial activity which took place after 1760 created a new type of economic character, as well as a new system of economic organization. In reality, the ideal which was later to carry all before it, in the person of the inventor and engineer and captain of industry, was well established among Englishmen before the end of the seventeenth century. Among the numerous forces which had gone to form it, some not inconsiderable part may reasonably be ascribed to the emphasis on the life of business enterprise as the appropriate field for Christian endeavor, and on the qualities needed for success in it, which was characteristic of Puritanism. These qualities, and the admiration of them, remained, when the religious reference, and the restraints which it imposed, had weakened or disappeared.

VALUE ORIENTATIONS IN
AMERICAN SOCIETY

Robin M. Williams

. . . "AMERICAN VALUES" are not values necessarily exclusive to, or even peculiar to, the United States, nor do all Americans share them. We wish to discover the extent to which any particular value or value complex is in fact present in this society.

There are, however, important grounds for expecting American culture to be characterized by a value system appreciably different from other cultures. Most obvious perhaps is the different environment—different location, physical surroundings, climate, resources, and so on. Equally impressive are the many diverse cultural strains and the subsequent crosscultural contacts within the American aggregate. Aside from these, and from any possible genetic selectivity, we have the general theorem that a society separated from others by spatial and socio-political barriers will, over a period of time, develop a relatively distinctive culture.

Americans currently face a period in which few institutions, beliefs, or values can any longer be taken for granted. All are under strain; all are challenged. Basic transformations of man and society are now underway, and many vital choices of values must be made.

It is essential for *this* analysis that we secure a clear conception of what values are and of how we may recognize and analyze their role in a system of motivated social action. We are concerned with values as observable variables in human conduct, not with an appraisal of various values as being better or worse than others, nor with the meaning and ontological status of value as a concept, however important these problems may be. For our purposes, we must seek a conception of value that can be referred to definite evidence.

We will begin by regarding value as any aspect of a situation, event, or object that is invested with a *preferential interest* as being "good," "bad," "desirable," and the like. What we can recognize as values have these qualities: (1) They have a conceptual element—they are more than pure sensations, emotions, reflexes, or so-called needs. Values are abstractions drawn from the flux of the individual's immediate experience. (2) They are affectively charged: they represent actual or potential emotional mobilization. (3) Values are not the concrete goals of action, but rather the *criteria* by which goals are chosen. (4) Values are important, not "trivial" or of slight

---

Reprinted from *American Society: A Sociological Interpretation* (1951), pp. 388-442, by permission of the author and the publisher. (Copyright, 1951, by Alfred A. Knopf, Inc.) The chapter has been abridged.

concern. (Although this statement is circular, it suggests the possibility of studying values through the study of choices.)

For present purposes we may follow Linton in treating all shared values as *cultural* values by definition. *Social* values, however, not only are shared by a number of individuals but are regarded as matters of collective welfare by an effective consensus of the group.[1] Neither of these classes of value is necessarily identical with ethical or moral values; the latter involve relatively systematic ideas of the good as apart from sheer interest, desirability, or expediency.

Values are thus "things" in which people are interested—things that they want, desire to be or become, feel as obligatory, worship, enjoy. Values are *modes of organizing conduct*—meaningful, affectively invested pattern principles that guide human action.

Empirically considered, value is not an all-or-none matter, but a continuum. At one pole, we find those intense and rigid moral values that are true matters of conscience—integral components of the superego. Values of this order are present when the individual who violates them shows a reaction of strong guilt or overwhelming shame and the group imposes strong censure upon the offender. Such moral values are the core of the individual's internalized conscience. They also define the central institutional structure of the society—although the accepted mores do not necessarily coincide with the "highest" social ethics and the ethical position of any given individual may not be identical with either the mores or the highest ethics. From the point on the value continuum at which the moral quality is emphasized, values shade off into those evoking less intense guilts and less severe social sanctions—for example, aesthetic standards, conventional properties, and simple norms of expediency or technical efficiency. Only careful research testing can establish the position of any "alleged" value along this continuum in the actual functioning of a society.

Values concern the goals or ends of action and are, as well, components in the selection of adequate means. Even in so far as choice is not deliberate or conscious, all action nevertheless is of one kind rather than another. Some balancing of alternatives must occur whenever alternatives exist. Since acts, including failures to act, typically involve a renunciation of other possible courses of behavior, every act "costs something." In this sense, values and their arrangement into hierarchies are defined by choices.

Data on choices may be derived from direct observation of spontaneous behavior, from testimony of witnesses, from self-reporting, and from various indirect evidences. Thus, for example, in a society with a highly developed money economy, much can be learned about the patterns of general values from the patterns of money expenditure, since money is a particular measure of economic "value"—that is, of value in exchange. The study of family budgets, general patterns of consumer expenditure, public expenditures, the flow of the national income, and so on, is subject to interpretation in these terms. . . .

. . . The explicit statements of value positions are, of course, not completely reliable. They may represent "mere lip service," largely divorced from realistic conduct. No student of human conduct can accept uncritically, as final evidence, people's testimony as to their own values. Yet actions may deceive as well as words, and there seems no reason for always giving one precedence over the other. Even when not explicitly stated, values can often be inferred directly from verbal materials. In argument, for instance, the statements arousing "heat," emotion, and so on, are clues to values. . . .

Verbal materials may also be analyzed by more complex methods going beyond the explicit, manifest, or apparent content. Systematic attention should be given to those implicit premises necessary for a meaningful account of (to "make sense of") explicit statements. It is commonly observed, for example, that what is *not* said is often more significant than what is said, reminding us again that the things in a culture that are most completely taken for granted typically turn out to be of fundamental importance in that culture.[2]

The material thus uncovered or reconstructed does not, of course, consist wholly of values, but includes "beliefs" and other cognitive elements. In its most simple and somewhat misleading formulation, a belief is a conviction that something is real, whereas a value is a preference. . . .

Still another source of evidence is found by observing the reward-punishment system of a group or society, noting the incidence of *social sanctions*. What behavior is rewarded and praised? What is censured, disapproved, and punished? How great are the rewards and how severe the penalties? Under what circumstances is a given act, ordinarily disapproved, held excusable? . . .

Starting with the initial location of value in a relation of a person to an object of interest, the sources of evidence mentioned above indicate just so many "operational definitions" of value: value as *overt choice or preference,* as *attention or emphasis,* as *statement* or *assertion,* as *implicit premise,* as a referent of *social sanctions*. These various evidences are "pointers" that say "this is what is meant."[3] Not all are of equal usefulness for every purpose, but all are useful. When used in combination, these several different approximations gain reliability in so far as they are mutually consistent.

Dominant and subordinate values *for a group or social system as a whole* can be roughly ordered to these criteria:

1. *Extensiveness* of the value in the total activity of the system. What proportion of a population and of its activities manifest the value?

2. *Duration* of the value. Has it been persistently important over a considerable period of time?[4]

3. *Intensity* with which the value is sought or maintained, as shown by: effort, crucial choices, verbal affirmation, and by reactions to threats to the value—for example, promptness, certainty, and severity of sanctions.

4. *Prestige of value carriers*—that is, of persons, objects, or organizations considered to be bearers of the value. Culture heroes, for example, are significant indexes of values of high generality and esteem.

It is clear that in our society the range of interests, beliefs, values, knowledges, and so on is so great that *precise and detailed* characterizations can be done only for carefully delimited segments of the society. Any attempt to delineate a national character or typical American values or a national basic personality type is extremely hazardous not only because of serious gaps in the requisite data but also because of the enormous value-diversity of the nation. This diversity we know to be so marked that a common core of values that could be said to hold for even a plurality of the population would probably be quite thin and abstract. Furthermore, values change rapidly, especially in modern times, rendering any static cross-section inventory of only temporary validity.

These considerations explain why the present chapter speaks of American value-*systems,* rather than of American values. Certain common values and symbols may be of great importance in national integration, but we cannot be certain without further evidence. On the other hand, there are sound reasons for seeking value systems rather than discrete and isolated values. We might conceivably find that there are in fact no systems deserving the name; but looking for systems will keep us looking for relationships and interconnections, consistencies and inconsistencies, and hence help us to see form, order, and equilibrium where these actually appear.

"System" here refers to some determinate arrangement of parts or entities —that is, to a set of relationships that is more than a chance ordering of parts. To speak of value systems is, then, to imply that values are not simply distributed at random, but are instead interdependent, arranged in a pattern, and subject to reciprocal or mutual variation.[5]

Even the brief illustrative material so far considered suggests that American society does not have a completely consistent and integrated value-structure.[6] We do not seem to find a neatly unified "ethos" or an irresistible "strain toward consistency." Rather, the total society is characterized by diversity and change in values. Complex division of labor, regional variations, ethnic heterogeneity, and the proliferation of specialized institutions and organizations all tend to insulate differing values from one another. Much potential conflict and strain—as well as much potential integration—is thereby avoided. Yet such insulation is itself peculiarly difficult to maintain in the American social order. For one of the most important features of that order is its delicate interdependence, especially in its economic and political structure. Because of this fundamental interdependence, individuals and groups holding different and often incompatible values not only become aware of one another but often interact directly. Millions of contact points involving problems of values are created in economic dealings, political activity, education, and other major areas of life. Simultaneously, mass communication creates gigantic magnetic fields of common and conflicting knowledges, judgments, beliefs, and values.

There are limits—although rather wide ones—to the degree of incompatibility of beliefs and values that can exist in cultures or in individuals short of the disappearance of a meaningful system. Clashes of value become crucial for social organization when they emerge in those areas of person-to-person interaction that are essential to the maintenance of the system—for example, in family life or in work relations. Persistent value-conflicts in these areas will lead, variously, to personality disorganization, to the emergence of insulating social mechanisms, or to the disruption of the system of interaction. Similarly, in mass behavior, persistent and widespread value-tension leads to political struggle, schismatic cleavages, or to the segregation of various groupings into a kind of mosaic society.

We can now outline certain major value-configurations in American culture. For convenience, we will proceed by abstracting certain dominant themes from the many important regional, class, and other intracultural variations. The simplified picture that results will, of course, be inaccurate in every concrete detail—it will be a series of ideal types, subject to numerous exceptions. Nevertheless, these abstracted patterns will serve as working models against which variations and contradictions can be more clearly seen; the value configurations thus identified will represent *tendencies* only, but they will bring out certain regularities that would not otherwise be easily seen.

"Achievement" and "Success." First, American culture is marked by a central stress upon personal achievement, especially secular occupational achievement. The "success story" and the respect accorded to the self-made man are distinctly American, if anything is. Our society has been highly competitive—a society in which ascribed status in the form of fixed, hereditary social stratification has been minimized. It has endorsed Horatio Alger and has glorified the rail splitter who becomes president: "Periodic public opinion polls are not needed to justify the selection of Abe Lincoln as the culture hero who most fully embodies the cardinal American virtues. . . . Even the inevitable schoolboy knows that Lincoln was thrifty, hard-working, eager for knowledge, ambitious, devoted to the rights of the average man, and eminently successful in climbing the ladder of opportunity from the lowermost rung of laborer to the respectable heights of merchant and lawyer. . . ."[7]

Emphasis upon achievement must be distinguished from the broader valuation of personal excellence. All societies have standards of character and proficiency, and accord rewards to those best meeting whatever standards are most highly appraised, whether of military prowess, ritual knowledge, asceticism, piety, or what not. The comparatively striking feature of American culture is its tendency to identify standards of personal excellence with competitive occupational achievement. In the pure type, the value attached to achievement does not comprehend the person as a whole, but only his accomplishments, emphasizing the objective results of his activity. Because of the preoccupation with business, the most conspicuous achievements have been those centered in business enterprise. We can say, with Laski and many others, that the "values of the business man" dominate and permeate national life. Yet achievement has never been completely identified with sheer business success; for example, such an assumption does not account for the respect and prestige accorded to the professions. Seen in the context of other major value themes,[8] business success seems to be a dominant focus, but not the dominant value-pattern, in American society.

Adequate research evidence is not as yet available to allow an accurate appraisal of the extent to which success rather than achievement has moved to the center of the values of our culture. Such evidence is greatly needed, for the question thus raised is fundamental to any real diagnosis of the current value-system. Whereas achievement refers to valued accomplishments, success lays the emphasis upon rewards. Amoral success-striving may not have gone to the lengths suggested by some observers,[9] but the important point is that once success goals are divorced from the ultimate values of society, the way is opened for a corrosion of regulative norms.[10] . . .

The dimensions of success values may perhaps be clarified by an examination of the place of wealth and its attainment in the culture. Many foreign and native observers have viewed American society as grossly acquisitive and materialistic, as naively impressed by bigness, speed, wealth, and power. Such a view is too simple, as an examination of American attitudes toward money will illustrate.

We may begin by eliminating any interpretation such as "of course money is wanted because it is the universal agency for satisfying any desires that can be met by purchasable goods."[11] For many profitable activities are socially condemned and not widely carried on; and people strive intensely for wealth long after their basic physical needs have been met or even after they have achieved nearly every conceivable means for satisfying their desires. Santayana's insight has more accurately indicated the central function of money in the American value system: "It is the symbol and measure he (the American) has at hand for success, intelligence, and power; but as to money itself he makes, loses, spends and gives it away with a very light heart."[12] In a society of relatively high social mobility, in which position in the scale of social stratification basically depends upon occupational achievement, wealth is one of the few obvious signs of one's place in the hierarchy. Achievement is difficult to index, in a highly complex society of diverse occupations, because of the great differences in abilities and effort required for success in various fields. At the same time, the central type of achievement is in business, manufacturing, commerce, finance; and since traditionalized social hierarchies, fixed estates, and established symbols of hereditary rank have had only a rudimentary development, there is a strong tendency to use money as a symbol of success. Money comes to be valued not only for itself and for the goods it will buy, but as symbolic evidence of success and, thereby, of personal worth.

"Activity" and "Work." In the United States is to be found what is almost the ideal type of a culture that stresses activity; it is no accident that the business so characteristic of the culture can also be spelled "busy-ness." Although one might quibble over Laski's flat statement that few Americans "find it easy to be happy unless they are doing something,"[13] we know that a notable series of observers have overwhelmingly agreed that America is the land of haste and bustle, of strenuous competition, of "ceaseless activity and agitation."[14] In this culture the individual tends to "face outward"—to be interested in making things happen in the external world. In ideal type, he seeks to dominate the world of nature, to subdue and exploit the physical world around him. This pattern—which forms a *leit motif* in American history—may be explained historically, of course, as developing out of religious tradition, frontier experience,[15] ceaseless change, vast opportunity, and fluid social structure. Whatever its sources, the sheer fact of this emphasis on "action" is enough for present purposes.[16]

A strong cultural emphasis upon disciplined productive activity was to be expected in America during the first two centuries in which value systems were being generalized out of experience.[17] Work was required for *group* survival along the moving frontier from the first settlements until the continent had been won. The rule "he who does not work shall not eat" expressed the deadly struggles of the early settlement period. To this compulsion was added the dawning sense of the rich rewards to be had in a land of relatively unappropriated resources. Furthermore, the population was mainly recruited from the working classes of Britain and Europe;[18] except in a few areas of the South and New England, there was no aristocratic class to give prestige to leisure and to stigmatize manual labor and trade. Finally, there was the influence of the so-called Puritan tradition—that is, of all those varieties of Protestantism in which secular occupational activity was invested with religious sanction and in which successful works became a sign of grace. This "metaphysical drive to work"[19] permeated the older agrarian culture of this country[20] and exists even today in rural areas and among certain other subgroups that have not yet fully assimilated the more recent cult of success and conspicuous consumption.

In short, the emphasis upon work as an end in itself represented a convergence of factors all operating in one direction—a mutual reinforcement of self-interest, social recognition, and ethical and religious precepts; "work" therefore became a value incorporated into the ego ideal of the representative personality types of the culture and often approached the intensity of a true matter of conscience.

Although, as later discussion will show, work as an end in itself has lost a great deal of its earlier potency, it is still important to remember that it has formed one of the core elements in the historic culture. It was, however, closely linked to an agrarian social structure in which the independent farmer and the small business man were representative social types. In such a society, work was embedded in the wider meanings attached to these statuses. As the social structure has become more and more differentiated, as manual labor has lost its connection with the control of private property, and as differentials of wealth and power have become crystallized, work as such has been devalued. The focus of positive valuation is now shifting to certain patterns of achievement and success.

"Moral Orientation." A third major value-configuration relates to a particular type of ethical quality in the total cultural orientation. Authoritative observers from De Tocqueville, through Bryce, Siegfried and others, down to such recent studies as those of Vernon L. Parrington, Margaret Mead, Gunnar Myrdal, and Harold Laski, have agreed on at least one point: Americans tend to "see the world in moral terms." They do not mean mere conformity to the detailed prescriptions of a particular moral code, but rather to a systematic moral orientation by which conduct is *judged*. It is asserted that the quasi-mythical figure, the "typical American," thinks in terms of right or wrong, good or bad, ethical or unethical. This attitude goes beyond questions of expediency or immediate utility—and beyond purely traditional or customary criteria of behavior—to test conduct against some systematic ethical principles. For example, Mead cites the query of a student who asked whether we *ought* to have a conscience.[21] And Myrdal says explicitly: "The conflict in the American concept of law and order is only one side of the 'moral overstrain' of the nation. America believes in and aspires to something much higher than its plane of actual life."[22] The presence of an element of moral overstrain in our culture seems to be established. It seems likely that this ethical tension is directly related to certain patterns of child-rearing in the society generally—however, this hypothesis remains to be proved. At least middle-class groups seem to teach children a moral code considerably more stringent than that practiced by

adults in the same group. Parents hold themselves up as exemplary models —as "much better than they really are."[23] The emerging generation then becomes disillusioned about its parents and the contrast between nominal moral principles and actual practice;[24] yet the earlier ingrained ideals cannot be given up completely. This partial blocking in normative training has a wide range of consequences, including ritualism, "lip service," vacillating or compensatory behavior, "split between theory and practice," so-called "hypocrisy," and so on. Individuals facing severe tension between their incorporated ethics and current social "realities" may resolve the conflict by developing a militant reform mentality[25] or becoming "cynical"—we often suspect that the self-styled cynic is a highly moral person who is reacting to loss of faith in the efficacy of his code. Often ideals are insulated from action or restricted to limited groups and narrowly circumscribed situations.

"Humanitarian Mores." We shall use the term "humanitarianism" to refer to another important value cluster in American society, meaning by it, emphasis upon any type of disinterested concern and helpfulness, including personal kindliness, aid and comfort, spontaneous aid in mass disasters, as well as the more impersonal patterns of organized philanthropy. Do these things represent important values in America?

It would be easy to amass contrary evidence. We could cite the expulsion and extermination of the Indians, the harsher aspects of slavery, the sweatshop pattern in industry, and a long catalog of child labor, lynching, vigilantes, and social callousness in many forms. Probably few peoples have so copiously documented and analyzed what they themselves consider to be the "bad" aspects of their history—a revealing fact in itself, for it was broadly the same culture that produced the behavior, and then pronounced it undesirable or wrong. Even so, the evidences of humanitarian values meet all our tests for a major value. Certain patterns of mutual helpfulness and generosity were already apparent in colonial America—despite the stern theology and stringently disciplined individualism—and have persisted to an important extent down to the present time. Of course, it is only in a wide comparative perspective that the importance of the humanitarian mores can clearly be seen, making probable such hypotheses as "Americans are especially likely to identify with the 'underdog' rather than the 'bully.'" This identification is indicated in a quick, impulsive sympathy for people who are in distress "by no fault of their own"; in anger at the overbearing individual, group, or nation; in pride in America as a haven for the downtrodden and oppressed.[26] The proverbial generosity of American people toward other societies facing mass disaster—for example, earthquakes, floods, fire, famine—has elements of exaggeration and myth; but it does index a real and persistent theme broadly based on religious or quasi-religious ideas of brotherhood, even though it has often been overridden by dividing interests and competing values. The enormous range of relatively disinterested humanitarian activities in America—the commonplace Community Chest, the "service club" activities, the public welfare agencies, the numerous private philanthropies, and so on[27]—stands in striking contrast to the treatment meted out to "the poor" and the "sturdy beggars" in many other parts of Western society within the past two centuries.

As always, however, this value pattern does not stand alone but is reinforced and complemented, or checked and limited, by other values. Humanitarianism is closely related to the cluster of values implicit in the conception of a progressing equalitarian democracy. In the form of what might be called pseudo-humanitarian philanthropy, on the other hand, the pattern sometimes has lent itself to the justification of economic inequalities. Throughout American history, the humanitarian theme has clashed in a variety of ways with the conception of rugged individualism.

Efficiency and Practicality. American emphasis upon *efficiency* has consistently impressed outside observers. The Germans even coined the term *Fordismus* to refer to the standardization, mass production, and "streamlined" efficiency of American industrialism personified on the Continent by the name of Ford. "Efficient" is a word of high praise in a society that has long emphasized adaptability, technological innovation, economic expansion, up-to-dateness, practicality, expediency, "getting things done." The mere listing of these words and phrases serves to bring out the multiple extensions of efficiency as a standard against which activity is judged. Such a standard is premised in the first place upon that active orientation to the world of the here and now, so characteristic of our culture. As we have emphasized, this crucially important canalization of interest at once sets this society apart from societies placing greater emphasis upon aesthetic, contemplative, ritualistic, mystical, or otherworldly concerns.

That being active is emphasized, however, tells us nothing about the kind of activity sanctioned. Even a culture centering its interest upon purposive technical mastery of its physical environment (and, to some degree, of its social problems also) might conceivably act in relatively traditionalistic ways. The Western world generally, however, has tended to unite activity and substantive rationality, focusing upon a choice of the most effective means for a given end. Since systematic wealth-getting, technological achievement, and productive organization of effort have been strongly sanctioned, pressure has been created to search for "better methods," with the result that America epitomizes high regard for efficiency in techniques. In this kind of social climate, there is high sensitivity to such epithets as "backward," "inefficient," "useless." "Technical values" are greatly appreciated; especially in skilled trades, technical, quasi-professional, and professional vocations there is systematic indoctrination in the standards of "doing a good job"—the difference between a skilled and an unskilled performance. Despite the continual pressure of pecuniary or profit-making considerations, the values of good technical performance certainly have a measure of independent influence.[28]

The elevation of sheer technique into something closely approaching a value in its own right involves the familiar tendency to turn means values into goal values through a gradual withdrawal of attention and affect from the original ends[29]—a development that is re-enforced in so far as immediate interests and short-run goals are stressed. A culture that in the first place tends toward an unhistorical and utilitarian orientation will be especially likely to encourage just those behavior patterns in which technical efficiency can become valued for its own sake.

Although efficiency can and has become in this way a true value, in certain areas of our culture it is a derivation rather than a basic theme. In economic activities and other fields that have acquired considerable autonomy apart from the ultimate-value systems of the society, the stress upon efficiency is a complex derivation from the values attached to action, to material comfort, and perhaps especially, to mastery over nature and disorder. For efficiency—like cleanliness, work, and systematic-universal ethics—is a *discipline,* and its meaning depends finally upon the broader meanings of the primary "orderliness" that underlies it.

Emphasis upon efficiency is obviously related to the high place accorded science (especially as translated into technology) and to the overweening importance attributed to practicality.[30] One of the blackest public curse-words we have is "impractical"—in the culture at large, the practical man is the good man, an embodiment of a major value. . . .

The practicality theme represents at least three quite different although closely related dimensions: (1) the nature of the immediate ends for activity; (2) the guiding criteria for arranging ends into a hierarchy of value; (3) the implicit conceptual framework—the absolute social logics—within which values are perceived. With respect to the sanctioned immediate ends of conduct, we have already seen a convergence upon the goals of certain kinds of success, as defined by secularized Puritanism. Practicality as to concrete goals of actions correspondingly has meant the canalizing of action in the service of those specific life-models most highly approved in the general culture—broadly speaking, rational, strenuous, competitive striving for personal validation through occupational success. In so far as this definition of the situation has been accepted, only those things have been considered practical that contributed to this end. Second, as a guiding principle for arranging value priorities, practicality represents a particular form of what Max Weber called *Zweckrationalität* as over against *Wertrationalität*—the rational weighting of values in a pluralistic framework rather than overwhelming concern with a single value or end. In the latter case, all other considerations except the achievement of that end become irrelevant; in prototype this is the stand of the political or religious fanatic, the insatiable hedonist, the monomaniacal economic man. American standards of practicality seem to have led mainly in the direction of a multifaceted balancing of values. Finally, practicality affects the conceptual schemes (explicit and implicit) that broadly characterize the culture. Even American philosophy displays a practical and critical cast and has been in various ways pragmatic, instrumental, relativistic.[31]

Thus, the theme of practicality points us again to activistic, rational, and secular (but "ethical") emphases of the culture; at the same time, it hints of possible tendencies toward the dissipation of the content of "ultimate" values in favor of immediate adaptability to immediate interests and satisfactions. As a highly derivative pattern, practicality does not provide in itself any sure anchorage for continuing organization and integration of individual activity. In common with the emphasis on *procedure* in American concepts of freedom and democracy, the emphasis upon practicality indicates a society that has tended to take for granted the implicit value framework within which practical action acquires meaning and rationale.

"Progress." From the society's earliest formation there has been a diffuse constellation of beliefs and attitudes that may be called the cult of progress. This broad theme has no unitary value such as would tangibly regulate

specific individual behavior, but is rather a certain "set" toward life that has permeated a wide range of behavior patterns. Various aspects of this complex are those allegedly typical American traits discussed earlier—"optimism," an emphasis upon the future rather than the past or present, "boosterism," receptivity to change, faith in the perfectibility of the common man.[32] At least in the enterprising middle classes, progress has been a prime article of faith. Our rich vocabulary of epithets ("backward," "outmoded," "old-fashioned," "stagnant," and the like) can be understood *as epithets* only against the unquestioning assumption that the new is the better—that "forward" is better than "backward."

From De Tocqueville to Laski, inquiring foreign observers have been impressed with the faith in progress and the high evaluation of the future in the United States as contrasted with Europe. Americans have felt their present to be better than their past and have felt adequate to deal with a future that will be still better.

"Throughout their history Americans have insisted that the best was yet to be. . . . The American knew that nothing was impossible in his brave new world. . . . Progress was not, to him, a mere philosophical ideal but a commonplace of experience. . . ."[33]

In the form in which it had been molded by Enlightenment, progress was conceived as the beneficent unfolding of man's capacities for reason and goodness. In the course of its later development, however, the idea picked up dominant overtones of Social Darwinism ("the survival of the fittest") at about the same time that its application was being more and more restricted to economic and technological realms. By the late nineteenth century, the concept had been largely assimilated to the values of a complex and expanding industrial order. Progress could now become a slogan to defend the course of technological innovation and economic rationalization and concentration. Progress became identified with "free private enterprise," in fact, at a time when the individual entrepreneur was already clearly certain to be supplemented by vast economic organizations the development of which was to change the traditional *laissez faire* concepts of "private property" and "economic freedom."

Material Comfort. In the 1920's during the triumph of the so-called New Era (of Permanent Prosperity), a highly critical French observer could say of Americans that they "consider it only natural that their slightest whim should be gratified."[34] Even during this period there were millions of Americans who would have considered themselves fortunate to secure basic necessities for nutrition and shelter; yet notwithstanding its exaggeration, Siegfried's comment points attention to the value placed upon a *high level of material comfort.* . . .

The fact that material comfort undoubtedly is highly approved and sought after in the culture[35] tells us very little in itself about what specific values are involved; the "American standard of living" has its undertones and overtones of meanings—from nationalistic identification, to symbol of success, competence, and power and from a token of moral excellence to something very close to a terminal "value" at the level of hedonistic gratification.

There is some criticism that passive gratification elements in American society have been receiving increased emphasis in recent decades. The most obvious although probably not the most important index of this trend is provided by commercial advertising that emphasizes comfort and effortless gratification: eat this, chew this, drink that; take a vacation; be catered to; and so on. The major focus is upon receiving, looking at, being catered to, in short, maximum pleasurable sensation with minimum effort or activity. . . .

The gratification motif appears in modern mass entertainment with all the clarity of a caricature. For motion pictures, Dorothy Jones's analysis of a hundred films appearing in 1941-42 showed a predominance of the "happy ending"—at the end of the picture, about 60 per cent of all major characters were indulged with respect to all of their wants; about 10 per cent were deprived as to all of their wants; about 14 per cent were indulged as to some wants and deprived as to others.[36]

The American experience gives some support to the hypothesis that in so far as a group or society is able to attain a high plane of material comfort, it will tend increasingly to emphasize the "hedonistic values," unless checked by internal social danger or outside threat. Apparently, at least in Western societies, the objective opportunity to secure material comforts elicits, in the long run, a desire for them. Once a high standard of living has been enjoyed, however, it is extremely difficult to reduce the level of sensation. As new wants emerge and are satisfied over a period of time, they become accepted, expected, "normal," and in this process they at the same time come to be felt as rights to which one has a moral claim. When the level of material comfort of a whole people has been rising over a considerable period of time, it will be reduced only reluctantly even under the duress of great social emergency.

Equality. The avowal of "equality," and often its practice as well, has been a persistent theme through most of American history. Even modern economic organization, which in many ways epitomizes inequality,[37] has stressed "equality of opportunity." Yet few other value complexes are more subject to strain in modern times.

The United States began its independent political existence as a congeries of societies, which in the main had broken sharply with the traditions of social deference and with the hierarchical social structures that still characterized Britain and Europe. The generalization has its exceptions. New England had been ruled by an elite of the religiously elect. Remnants of feudal land customs had persisted for a time in various areas in such forms as quit-rents and primogeniture. Indentured servitude and imprisonment for debt had represented direct transmissions of neofeudal practices. But in general all individual arrangements embodying traditional social inequalities were dissolving.[38] In retrospect, as always, this result now seems to have been inevitable. Actually it was the consequence of a highly complex constellation of factors: laxity of political control by England partly as a result of the distance from Britain and Europe; only a small number of the colonists had been aristocrats, the majority was middle and lower class and many actively opposed some features of their parent society; mass accessibility to abundant resources, which made it possible for "anyone to become a king on his own" and thus helped to dissolve old hierarchies and social forms through movement, acquisition, independence, potential equality of all sorts and manners of men; the ideological forces; the deeply individualistic strain brought in through Protestantism, as well as philosophical and political ideas that worked in the same direction. (Locke and the French rationalists, for instance, affected not only the Founding Fathers but much wider circles of eighteenth century America.)

Other factors encouraging the emergence of equality as a value may be left aside for present purposes.[39] It will suffice here to see that this society in its formative periods was one that could, and wished to, break with its hierarchical tradition and that this result was favored by fundamental objective and ideological conditions. Thus, until the late nineteenth century America was able to develop without having to face widespread conflict between the principle of equality and the principles of achievement or freedom. In this remarkable historical experience, through generation after generation the values of equality were crystallized and elaborated. People saw the disappearance of primogeniture, the abolition of indentured servitude, of imprisonment for debt, of slavery, of property qualifications for voting and public office; there was provision for the common man to acquire a stake in the land and to secure a free public education; women gained one legal right after another; and even discriminations against minorities were sharply challenged time after time.

However, as De Tocqueville saw more than a century ago, America had to face sooner or later a conflict of values that he described as a contradiction between the principle of freedom and the principle of equality. For instance, the cumulative effect of freedom to pursue individual advantage, given the opportunities and institutional framework of nineteenth century America, was to destroy equality of condition. The liberty of which De Tocqueville spoke was a freedom from feudal or mercantilistic restraints on the economic individualism so congenial to the early American situation. But this freedom could only lead under the historical circumstances to the emergence of what he called a manufacturing aristocracy, an outcome far from the perfect commonwealth of equal citizens that some idealizers of a yeoman republic desired.

If equality is a basic value in our society, it must meet our operational tests: (1) the individual must feel guilt, shame, or ego deflation when he acts in inequalitarian ways; and (2) there must be sanctions supported by the effective community for conformity or nonconformity. The extensiveness of these reactions must be weighed against parallel responses to any behavior manifesting hierarchical principles of human relations. Although no such quantitative assessment can be made from the available evidence, it is nevertheless reasonably clear that inequalities, hierarchical emphases, and various kinds of discriminations are common in American life. Taken as a whole America appears to present a highly confused situation in which conflicts and compromises are accompanied by myths, legends, and conventional fictions until the main value directions become excessively difficult to trace.

The problems can be grasped more readily if we differentiate among the several senses in which equality may be a value. It is useful to distinguish between intrinsic and extrinsic valuations. Extrinsic valuations are those judgments of value that depend upon generalized social categories and external symbols of status such as sex, age, nationality, occupation, rank, income, wealth, medals, race, authority. Intrinsic valuation has to do with the immediately personal qualities of the individual apart from any categorical social attributes, and its presence is demonstrated wherever one person feels an obligation to treat another person as—in any degree—an end in himself rather than purely as a means. To put it negatively, the person is given an intrinsic value when we feel guilt or shame if we do not act with some regard for his presumed human sensibilities, regardless of his categorical social status or group membership.

At the level of explicit doctrine, intrinsic equality is widespread in American culture, both in the form of a specifically religious conception (the equality of souls before God, the divine nature within every person, and so on), and in the more secularized formulations that attribute an irreducible quantum of value to every person: "a man's a man for all that," "after all they are human beings," or the categorical imperative to "treat others as ends rather than means." As the level of overt interpersonal relations, adherence to a sense of intrinsic human value is discernible in a wide variety of specific behaviors—perhaps most obviously in "democratic manners." America has always impressed observers from more rigid and hierarchical societies as being marked by an extraordinary informality, directness, and lack of status consciousness in person-to-person contacts.[40] This general openness of social relations can only be maintained in a culture in which intrinsic personal value is a widespread and effective assumption.[41]

In more concrete terms, equality is exhibited in the way individuals actually *relate* to others in ordinary interpersonal activities. Are individuals in American culture typically related to others by superordination and subordination, or are interpersonal relations typically horizontal? The answer to so sweeping a question can be built up only by induction from the enormous variety of social rules actually existing in our society; a definitive analysis must wait upon a great amount of further systematic research. . . . Nevertheless, in our provisional appraisal equality rather than hierarchy seems on the whole characteristic of concrete social relations—although perhaps more clearly at the level of the *goals and standards* of conduct than in the uneven compromises of going practice. On this point, something approaching a crucial "experiment of nature" is available to us in the reactions of American soldiers to military life in World War II. Military organization is the example par excellence of hierarchy; in time of war its norms are supported by all the enormous social assent that war can generate. In World War II, the vast majority of American soldiers accepted the necessity of war and the legitimacy of military authority. Yet, as hundreds of specific studies showed, these same soldiers resented almost above all else the unequal privileges of officers and enlisted men and the insistence upon detailed observance of rituals of subordination and deference. It was clear also that one of the strongest forces that kept men working and fighting as organized groups was loyalty to their comrades and equals, that "team work" (the term is significant) rather than psychological dependence upon authority figures was the crux of the American version of military morale.[42]

A second major type of equality consists of specific formal rights and obligations. In the United States the strain toward equality of legal rights for all citizens or even residents has been strong and continuing. Formally equal civil rights—from military service to voting, from public education to taxation

—represent not only freedom but also equality. In the sense of freedom these rights may be said to guarantee the individual a certain openness in his life-space; in the sense of equality, they nominally establish a minimum life-space for every one. It is in this equality of specified rights that the second major theme of American equality has developed, rather than in doctrines of equal individual potentialities, achievements, or rewards.

The third type of equality is substantive equality of social and, above all, economic rewards. Here it seems quite clear that the principles of economic freedom and individual achievement have strongly dominated principles of equality.[43] The reigning conception has been that of *equality of opportunity* rather than *equality of condition*. Concessions toward substantive equality of condition—for example, the income tax in so far as it is graduated—have not leveled differences in wealth, and the upper and middle classes of the society continually have insisted upon a moral claim to the existing differentials. It is quite striking that one of the earliest and most widespread reactions to Marxism, as popularly understood, was to select precisely the idea of "equal distribution of wealth" as the target of censure and moral outrage.

Every principle of equality is subject to its sharpest violation in the case of minority groups, especially the American Negro. Few other aspects of our society are so well documented as this one.

In widest perspective it appears that the inequalities that are felt in American culture to contravene equality values most severely are of two kinds: first, the denial of nominally universal rights of citizenship and violations of nominally universal rules of impersonal justice; second, the denial of opportunities for achievement in the formally open competitive order. It is certainly true that American culture has never found it overly difficult to tolerate great differences in certain types of individual privileges or rewards. The tautology that inequality is not resented unless considered to be undeserved takes on an important meaning, however, as soon as we are able to specify what "undeserved" actually means. By and large in the United States, it has meant *categorical* privileges—rewards not earned by effort and achievement (including moral achievement) within the basic institutional rules for fair competition. Here is the core of "the American tradition" of equality. The dominant cultural value is not an undifferentiated and undiscriminating equalitarianism, but rather a two-sided emphasis upon basic social rights and upon equality of opportunity.

It has been part of the fundamental ethos of American culture to believe that virtue should and will be rewarded—and more particularly that such economic virtues as hard work, frugality and prudence should receive a proportionate reward. The axiomatic value of this moral equation has been closely linked with the premise that everyone (at least, all in "one's own" group) has an equal right to fundamental opportunities. Without question, this whole principle is currently undergoing severe strain and extensive redefinition. . . . Values of equality in the received American culture of the modern period have centered around the dual themes of civil rights and economic opportunity.

Freedom. We need no research to tell us that verbal affirmation of the value of freedom is widespread and persistent.[44] The widespread positive reaction to the symbolic value of the word is illustrated in many ways. . . .

That something real in actual social relations lies back of the word freedom cannot be doubted. Yet the reality is not in the unconditional listing of categorical freedoms, for it can quickly be shown that actual social life and "unconditional freedom" are contradictions in terms.[45] Furthermore, what are restraints from one point of view may be rights or "privileges" from another, as when a person wants "to do his duty" (and finds it to his advantage to do so).

American conceptions of freedom mainly stem from an orientation that characterized European thought for several centuries: freedom is compatible with causality and determinism; it does not mean uncaused behavior, but rather behavior that is not subject to restraints that are in some sense external and arbitrary. In this view, although behavior is always determined—that is, influenced, caused, or conditioned—it is nevertheless possible to give a definite meaning to the statement that it may also be "free." All life in society involves the limitation of behavior not only by the physical world, including the limitations of the human body and mind, but also by reciprocal rights and obligations among persons; every social group furthermore must cope with problems of authority and power. What, then, is to be said of the American emphasis on freedom?

The historical context of freedom as a value pattern in our culture begins with the centuries-long process whereby area after area of life was removed from the web of interlocking controls of feudal Europe. With the rise of nation-states and of urban life and with the expansion of industry and trade, the settled, hierarchical society of Europe moved into an unprecedented colonizing phase. The American colonies were one result, and in them the trend toward emancipation was intensified. At one point it might be a struggle against quit-rents; at another, restiveness under mercantilistic restraints; still elsewhere, a revolt against an established religious hierarchy. Always the demand was for freedom *from* some existing restraint. That the major American freedoms were in this sense negative does not mean, of course, that they were not also positive: they were rights to *do,* by the same token that they were rights to be protected from restraint. Nevertheless, the historical process left its mark in a culturally standardized way of thought and evaluation—a tendency to think of rights rather than duties, a suspicion of established (especially personal) authority, a distrust of central government, a deep aversion to acceptance of obviously coercive restraint through visible social organization. At the time in which the primary political and economic structure of the new society was laid down, the great threat to freedom was perceived as coming from the centralized, absolutistic state, and the obvious course seemed to be to erect every possible barrier to centralized governmental control; the main import of the doctrine of checks and balances was to prevent the central state as much as possible from undertaking any positive action beyond a very few carefully defined areas of authority. Such a view of government reflected a society in which the politically effective elements of the community wanted above all to have "room" to make their own decisions, to develop their own spheres of social power, to escape from the surveillance of kings and ministers of state. This particular sort of freedom was premised on a sweeping faith: the confidence of the individual in his own competence and mastery.

. . . A major implicit cultural premise in the dominant valuation of freedom has been *the equating of "freedom" with control by diffuse cultural structure rather than by a definite social organization.* Thus, it has seemed to make a great difference whether the individual receives a certain income or has a certain type of occupation as a result of an apparently impersonal, anonymous, diffuse competitive process, as against "being forced" to accept that employment or remuneration by law or by the command of a visible social authority. A foreclosed mortgage has been culturally defined in a radically different way from governmental confiscation of the same property. To be tied to a given locality by diffuse cultural pressure and lack of economic opportunity is regarded as a quite different kind of constraint from such controls as a police order or a governmental regulation.

Upon this kind of axiomatic base, American culture has tended to identify a very great variety of forms of personal dependence as not freedom. To "work under a boss" was not so long ago regarded as a loss of freedom. The widespread reluctance to take employment as a domestic servant and the low evaluation attached to this type of occupation appear to reflect in part the same complex. One of the earliest and most persistent criticisms of American society by aristocratically minded foreign observers has concerned the absence of a docile serving-class and the impertinence of the lower orders.[46]

Viewed in these terms, the theme of freedom is far broader than any particular institutional sector of the society. It rests in the last analysis upon an even more basic conception of the individual as an integral agent, relatively autonomous and morally responsible. Above all, a sociological analysis must make explicit the difference between *freedom as a value* and the *particular historic definitions of freedom in terms of special institutional forms.* Liberty in America began as a release from certain political restraints; the economic liberty thus secured was eventually accompanied in its turn by discords and dislocations in the social structure. In our day the greatest threats to freedom, conceived in liberal democratic terms, appear in economic dislocation and class conflict. The reaction to this situation has given us a "welfare state" in which freedom is no longer so clearly tied to a social system of private property and inactive government. The necessary implications for freedom as value are by no means wholly clear; it is patent, however, that the dated and localized definition of freedom as practically synonymous with eighteenth century economic philosophies is no longer accepted by the great majority of people in our society.

The core meaning of this shift can perhaps be illustrated by a glance at the so-called *laissez faire* economics, which was so much more than either *laissez faire* or economics; it constituted, in fact, a whole system of social philosophy, an elaborate and interconnected set of social values and beliefs. The conception of man around which the doctrine centered was that of the discrete human atom, calculating his economic self-interest and acting "rationally" in the unlimited pursuit of gain. The "perfect system of natural liberty," suitable to this concept, would guarantee the sanctity of contracts, the stability of media of exchange, and the rights of private property. In such a system, so its proponents believed, "when men are free from all governmental interference, virtue finds its tangible reward in wealth and vice its penalty in economic failure."[47] In this way religious axioms were assimilated to the theory of universal social good through economic competition. Support of such a system, under a political democracy, was sought through an additional doctrine, which in this case held that the economically successful are fittest because this very success attests to their moral superiority. Freedom then becomes the economic freedom of the entrepreneur, and democracy becomes a form of government giving maximum protection of property rights. Progress becomes technological advance and economic expansion. Individualism is equated with the right of the individual to use his property as he sees fit, within very broad limits, and to complete freely with others. Society is a neo-Darwinian jungle in which only the fittest *should* survive, and the fittest are those who can win out by intelligence, industry, or ruthlessness.

This "organic" cluster of doctrines has foundered against twentieth-centuries realities. Because the cultural definition of freedom has changed and because the threats to freedom are now apprehended in different quarters it is easy to assume that the emergence of the welfare state signalizes our departure on a "road to serfdom." We suggest that the status of freedom *as value* must not be prejudged because of changing social mechanisms. There probably is no such psychological entity as freedom; rather it inheres in the *logical implications* of certain types of behavior, of interpersonal relations, and of institutional control structures. So long as American society safeguards the right of the individual to a wide range of moral autonomy in decision making, so long as the representative character structure of the culture retains a conscience that is more than simple group conformity—so long will freedom be a major value. Emphatically, institutional forms are not unimportant; but their significance must be found by specific analysis and not by uncritical prejudgment.

External conformity. Even as early as the 1830's De Tocqueville commented on the necessity of safeguards against a possible "tyranny of the majority" in America and thought that public compulsion had already penetrated into private affairs in a censorious way not usual in the France of his day. Nearly a century later Siegfried, another and more critical Frenchman, visualized America as a land of vast uniformity in speech, manners, housing, dress, recreation, and politically expressed ideas. In 1948, Laski pointed to an "amazing uniformity" of values, thought that "business *mores*" had permeated the culture, and tried to show that "the American spirit required that the limits of uniformity be drawn with a certain tautness."[48] Many Europeans in the period prior to World War II had thought American conformity-behavior to have a certain harried, compulsive quality, and have referred to standardization, "flatness," and lack of individuality in comparison with the Continent. In the period between 1920 and World War II European observers seem to have been especially (and overly) impressed with conformity themes in America. Thus, Muller-Freienfels, in a book published in 1929: "Distance, uniqueness, and originality are European values, which are foreign to the American. His values are the very reverse of these: adherence to type, agreement, similarity."[49]

These appraisals—which in fact have often been biased and exaggerated— come as something of a shock to a people that has made much of individual initiative, the rights of the individual, personal independence, "rugged individualism." Yet it should be no surprise that an intensely active, democratic society should define tolerance of individual nonconformity largely in terms of sanctioning technological and economic innovation. . . . American "individualism," taken in broadest terms, has consisted mainly of a rejection of the state and impatience with restraints upon economic activity; it has not tended to set the autonomous individual up in rebellion against his social group. In a nation of joiners, individualism tends to be a matter of "group individualism," of the particularized behavior of subcultures.

Men universally seek the approval of *some* of their fellows and therefore try to be "successful" by some shared standards of achievement or conformity. This characteristic is the outcome of universal requirements of group life and of the basic nature of the socialization process; otherwise stated, conformity and the desire for social approval are formal qualities that are part of the very definition of society. Our real interest is in knowing how rigid the conformity is and what specific content defines conformity or success in a particular group or culture. . . .

It is useful to examine American conformity emphases for the light they may throw upon other dimensions of the value system. Several general sociological hypotheses are relevant to this examination. We know that where a functioning group or society feels threatened from the outside, it tends to tighten social controls over behavior involving the group's solidarity and striking power. Wars supply the most dramatic examples, but the political "witch hunts" in periods of international tension are equally in point. We know further that a group ridden by internal insecurities and tensions will, under certain conditions that need not be specified here, tend to raise its threshold of toleration for nonconformity: "The looser the package, the tighter must be the string"—if the package is to hold together at all.[50]

Some preoccupation with external conformity is to be expected in a society in which upward social mobility is highly prized and frequently achieved. The competitive striving of an upwardly mobile group in a society organized around the economic enterprise requires stringent discipline over the expression of sexual and aggressive impulses, over patterns of consumption, over the uses of time and resources. In this aspect, conformity is derivative from equality of opportunity in conjunction with success-striving. Furthermore, an emphasis upon external conformity easily develops out of the premise of basic human equality: if all are equal, then all have an equal right to judge their fellows and to regulate their conduct accordingly to commonly accepted standards; some such cultural equation has been widely accepted in the broad middle classes of American society. The exceptions to the pattern occur in those classes and groups in which special license follows from exclusion of the group from the application of principles of equality (for example, Negroes, the very rich, certain *declassé* strata, and so on).

Interestingly enough, the very heterogeneity of American culture tends to produce a stress upon external conformity. Given the varied cultural backgrounds of the population and the desire that the various groups should continue to live together in the same society, conformity in externals becomes a sort of "social currency" making it possible to continue the society in spite of many clashes of interests and basic values. If it is gradually learned that the exhibition of cultural differences—whether they be of dress, or language, or religious faith, or political philosophy—seems to lead to friction in interpersonal relationships or even to public disturbances, a whole series of complex adjustments are set in motion. Among the possible responses to such a situation is the practice of withdrawing tension-producing items from general social circulation: for example, one finds popular maxims such as "never argue about religion or politics."[51] The individual comes to reserve controversial matters to an intimate social circle of like-minded persons; public discourse and behavior is correspondingly more highly standardized. An elaborate social currency develops; set conversation-pieces, clichés, and standardized public opinions that can be passed smoothly along the channels of social interaction almost as a counterpart to the flow of money in the exchange economy.

The economic system itself contributes to the conformity theme in two other main respects. First, the high degree of specialization of economic roles in a highly developed money economy means that much social interaction is functionally specific, impersonal, transitory, and frequently laden with clashes of immediate economic interests. These are precisely the kinds of conditions most likely to produce conventionalized or stereotyped behavior.[52] Secondly, the relations of individual economic dependence are often such as to permit stringent conformity demands: a pattern caricatured in the Hollywood "yes-man," or *The Hucksters.*

Science and secular rationality. It has become a commonplace observation that the application of science and related secular rational approaches have transformed the external conditions of American culture—along with many other major cultures of the world.[53] Applied science is highly esteemed as a tool for controlling nature. Significant here is the interest in order, control, and calculability—the passion of an engineering civilization. This interest is congruent with the externalized orientation that we have already met in several previous guises; historically it is linked also to the fundamental assumption of an ordered universe in which rational human beings can continually improve their situation and themselves.[54]

But the prime quality of "science" is not in its applications but in its basic method of approaching problems—a way of thought and a set of procedures for interpreting experience. We need only mention the long history of the "warfare of science and theology" in order to suggest the conflicts of belief and value that have accompanied the rise of science. However, it may be well to remember that the antievolution trials occurred only a few years ago, and that popular attitudes toward science still contain strong ambivalences. The caricature of the "diabolical scientist" co-exists with the stereotype of the benevolent laboratory magician. Faith in science is a faith; its continued existence is dependent upon other convictions, and these other convictions are interdependent with the real social structure. Science is a particular manifestation of the rational-theoretic theme, which Northrop among others regards as a distinguishing feature of our entire culture.[55] It is this ordering and stabilizing component that links science to the broader tendency in our culture to translate experience into systematic abstract concepts—to transform the fleeting, confused flow of immediate experience into standardized categories that permit, and in part create, prediction and control. Thus, science, socially considered, is above all a *discipline,* as Max Weber has so eloquently shown.[56] Our main interest here is accordingly to ask: a discipline for what?

Very broadly, emphasis upon science in America has reflected the values of the rationalistic-individualistic tradition. Science is disciplined, rational, functional, active; it requires systematic diligence and honesty; it is congruent with the "means" emphasis of the culture—the focus of interest upon pragmatism and efficiency and the tendency to minimize absolutes and ultimates. The applications of science profusely reward the strivings for self-externalizing mastery of the environment. We think it fair to say that science is at root fully compatible with a culture orientation that attempts to deny frustration and refuses to accept the idea of a fundamentally unreasonably and capricious world.

In recent years certain social scientists have held that science is "morally neutral." If they mean merely that science cannot allow its findings to be distorted by value presuppositions extraneous to its accepted methods and models of proof, then these statements are acceptable. But it must be quite obvious that the findings of science will often have important value implications. It must be clear that the problems chosen for study are, or may be, selected in part on the basis of nonscientific values. Finally, the existence of basic theoretic science and the free exercise of scientific method presuppose a definite social structure and system of values.[57] Honesty and clarity are not just luxury virtues in science; on the contrary, they are essential defining characteristics. The same can be said for the faith in the order of nature and the faith in human reason—these are elements of a definite credo, manifesting values that are widely assaulted in the contemporary world. Their preservation in America apparently depends upon the continued and adequate functioning of an orderly, pluralistic society.

Nationalism-Patriotism. In every society we find men participating in certain groups to which they feel they owe loyalty and with which they identify themselves—and we find other groups identified as outgroups toward which the individual feels estrangement, sense of difference, or enmity. This distinction, in small, localistic nonliterate societies, is often so sharp that others are not considered "men." Analogous situations exist in the so-called complex civilizations, perhaps most strikingly in the denial of a common humanity to the enemy in time of war. Such intergroup cleavages involve that scaling of values called ethnocentrism, that is, the diffuse value-attitude making one's own group the point of reference for judging all others. All known societies are to some extent ethnocentric; individuals everywhere give a preferential value to their own culture. Strictly speaking, ethnocentrism applies to every distinctive group from the smallest clique to the largest civilization. Today, however, the sentiments attached to the nation-state have overwhelming importance, and nationalistic feelings seem the prime example of ethnocentric values. For this reason, it is particularly important to examine the place of nationalistic or patriotic values in the social system of America. We are dealing here with a diffuse and extremely complex phenomenon, and can do no more than to suggest a few very elementary points.

First, we distinguish between two polar types of nationalistic values that are inextricably mingled in concrete situations. The first type may be described as undifferentiated or totalistic nationalism, demanding total and unquestioning allegiance to national symbols and slogans and tending to make "Americanism" a rigid orthodoxy. Criticisms of any features of American life are close to treason, and "un-American" is the epithet for any deviation from a rigid, although vaguely defined, cult of conformity. The quasi-religious character of this complex is manifest in its creedal emphasis, its concern with ritual and symbolism, its elaboration of dogma and its correlative "inquisitions." The contrasting ideal type of national-patriotic orientation tends to place less emphasis upon undifferentiated loyalty, rather conceiving of patriotism as loyalty to national institutions and symbols because and in so far as they *represent* values that are the primary objects of allegiance. . . .

Nationalism in the modern sense is, of course, a relatively recent development in Western history. In the case of American nationalism, it is clear that the early colonists for a long time thought of themselves as Englishmen (or Germans, Swiss, etc.) rather than "Americans." Even after the establishment of the new nation it was not uncommon to find that "my country" might as well mean Dinwiddie county, Virginia, or the state of Vermont, as the nation taken as a whole.[58] It took the Civil War and a whole series of subsequent developments[59] to really displace provincial patriotism in favor of national feeling.

An important component of American nationalistic values is that a generalized sense of fulfilment and confident hope has been built into the culture for over two centuries, and even the shocks of recent depressions, wars, and other deep crises have not dissipated the widespread satisfaction of a people who feel that the country "has been good to them." Indeed, in some respects World War II and its aftermath seem to have reinforced the attitude by producing a vivid sense of the misery of other areas of the world. . . .

This sense of satisfaction incorporates supposedly *universal* values. A purely tribal patriotism conceives of its culture as having a unique destiny and does not think of extending its values to the rest of mankind. But American nationalism, like the religions that have contributed so heavily to the culture, involves the idea that the American way of life is so obviously morally superior that it should be widely adopted elsewhere.[60] This secular counterpart of the missionary spirit is both an index of the strength of nationalistic feeling and a potent source of understanding and resentment in international affairs. In peace as well as in war, the United States must appear to itself to have a mission as a crusader for righteousness.[61] Other peoples have not always regarded the matter in that light.

The universalistic elements in national feeling, however, have conflicted with certain kinds of expansionism, on the one hand, and tendencies toward isolationism and national autarchy on the other. American expansionism in its earliest phases was undertaken by the pioneer, the speculator, the trader, and the missionary, and aimed at the possession of the land, chiefly through purchase, rather than at the conquest and the rule of alien peoples. It was only toward the close of the nineteenth century when the economic exploration of our own backwoods was nearing completion that chauvinism of an expansionist turn became widespread.[62]

Perhaps the most important sociological generalization that can be invoked here is that intense nationalistic conflict will always have drastic consequences upon the value systems of a democratic society. In particular, it inevitably brings in its train a large military class—and a centralization of social power. The military state must by its own terms of existence have centralized control of production; it must regulate consumption—there is actually no more infallible prescription for the destruction of *laissez faire,* the free market and the individual entrepreneur.

Democracy. Like freedom or progress, democracy in American culture is a highly complex and derivative theme. The nation that fought a great war under the slogan of making the world safe for democracy lives under a Constitution that contains no direct reference to democracy; the democracy of the Founding Fathers is not that of twentieth century industrial society; the meaning of democracy is one thing to the American Negro and another to the Ku Klux Klan. Here again the cultural meanings of a value theme and its actual role in social structure are full of complex variations, conflicts, and shadings through time and from one part of the society to another at a given time. Furthermore, the content of democracy is in considerable part subsumed under other value complexes discussed elsewhere in this chapter: for example, freedom, equality, humanitarianism; and, in any case, a reference to democracy does not denote a clear, unitary value but a multiple nexus of more specific beliefs and primary values.[63] Nevertheless, no matter how elaborately qualified, the sheer prevalence of culturally sanctioned attention to something called democracy[64] forces us to include it in our listing of major value-themes.

Along with majority rule, representative institutions, and the rejection of the monarchical and aristocratic principles under which the society began, early American democracy stressed the reservation of certain "inalienable rights" as unalterable by majority rule.[65] Basically this sort of democracy rested upon the implicit belief in natural law as opposed to personal rule, and in the moral autonomy of the individual. The actual shape of the democratic credo was a synthesis of clashing ideologies; but it was the insistence of the average citizen upon equality of political rights that actually forced the Bill of Rights into the Constitution. Major themes in the gradual crystallization of the main democratic creed thus included equality of certain formal rights and formal equality of opportunity, a faith in the rule of impersonal law, optimistic rationalism, and ethical individualism. What the Kluckhohns have called the cult of the common man[66] was a major expression of the democratic ethos that developed out of these definitions of man and society. As already suggested in the discussion of freedom, the theme of democracy was, concretely, an agreement upon *procedure* in distributing power and in settling conflicts. Liberal democracy, American model, arose in reaction to an epoch in which the great threats to security and freedom were seen in strong, autocratic central government. The new system was devised in such a way as to limit and check centralized governmental power and to establish an ordered pattern for agreeing to disagree. Such a pluralistic view of social power was clear and explicit on questions of procedure while it left the common ends of the society largely undefined.

As can be seen, the theme of democracy has converged with those of equality and freedom, and all three have been interpreted and reinterpreted along with the moralistic optimism of the doctrines of progress. . . . The cumulative review of major value-orientations seems more and more clearly to point to one central constellation that gives coherence to a wide range of others, including democracy. This nuclear or focal theme we shall call the value of individual personality. In one aspect, its relation to democracy has been given a classic statement by Carl Becker:

> Its [modern liberal democracy's] fundamental assumption is the worth and dignity and creative capacity of the individual, so that the chief aim of government is the maximum of individual self-direction, the chief means to that end the minimum of compulsion by the state. Ideally considered means and ends are conjoined in the concept of freedom: freedom of thought, so that the truth may prevail; freedom of occupation, so that careers may be open to talent; freedom of self-government, so that no one may be compelled against his will.[67]

Thus, in so far as majority rule and conditional and limited authority based upon uncoerced consensus are highly evaluated in the culture, the main American concepts of democracy are consistent with a particular set of value postulates concerning the nature and significance of the individual in society.

Individual Personality. Writing in 1897, Émile Durkheim incisively described a pattern of value in Western civilization that he called the cult of individual personality.[68] Basically this cult sets a high value on the development of individual personality and is correspondingly averse to invasion of individual integrity; to be a person is to be independent, responsible, and self-respecting, and thereby to be worthy of concern and respect in one's own right. To be a person, in this sense, is to be an autonomous and responsible agent, not merely a reflection of external pressures, and to have an internal center of gravity, a set of standards and a conviction of personal worth. Above all, the individual is not considered to be released from all sociocultural controls. As Parsons has put it: "This is not a matter simply of freeing the individual from ethical restraints imposed by society, it is a matter of the imposition of a different *kind* of restraint. Individuality is a product of a certain social state. . . ."[69] Not the unrestrained biologic human being, but the ethical, decision-making, unitary social personality is the object of this cult of the individual. What is positively valued in the tradition now under examination, in other words, is not just any kind of personality whatsoever, but rather a certain kind of individual.

The personality that is the object of high value in this particular tradition is something of intrinsic worth, not valued simply as a member of a group nor as a means to some ulterior end. This orientation to the person, it must be repeated, is the product of a definite social situation. There is no real paradox in saying that individuality can be a social product and a common social value; the development of individual personality is a *shared value* rather than a *collective end* in a group or social system. The emergence and maintenance of this state, however, is intimately related to other aspects of the society. To maintain a high evaluation of individual personality in this peculiar sense is surely a difficult and precarious feat, for there are factors inherent in society that continually threaten the value. The crucial fact in this connection is that other persons are always potential tools or threats in relation to the attainment of any one individual's separate interests; control over others is always a potentially efficient means to securing one's individual desires. There is always some measure of this centrifugal bombardment of interest that creates pressures toward "using" other people in an essentially amoral utilitarian fashion. Under certain social conditions, the integrity of the individual *qua* personality may thus largely disappear. Slaves in the ancient world were not persons in the modern meaning. The fate of the laboring population during certain phases of the Industrial Revolution further illustrates how strong interests sometimes break through protective values centering around the person. A high valuation of the individual in the present sense, is difficult to maintain under conditions of great social stress, crisis, and privation—in war, famine, natural disaster, revolution, plague, and the like. In general, whenever great urgency is felt for the accomplishment of a collective task, requiring co-ordination, speed, and great differentials of sacrifice, there is a tendency to regard individuals as tools rather than values in themselves. . . .

The reality of the value of individualism in our culture is observed not only in derivative forms such as manifest ideology, law, and formalized behavior patterns but also at the level of implicit assumptions and unconscious practices. For example, it is typical of the culture that the question as to whether there is actually such an entity as "the individual," "self," or "ego" is usually not even thought of, and, if raised, is greeted with surprise or shock. *Of course* individuals exist, of course they have separate individual needs and rights. . . . A society that draws up a Declaration of Rights for Children, that is revolted by self-immolation of the individual for the group, that perceives groups as aggregates of co-operating but separate individuals—such a society incorporates the value of the individual at the deepest levels of its unconscious presuppositions. As a matter of fact the sociologically alert student is likely to guess at once that so pervasive a theme is maintained by quite special modes of child training and basic socialization; the hypothesis would be that this value complex is embedded in the central affective-cognitive structure of the representative personalities of the culture.

Racism and Related Group-Superiority Themes. The commitment of large segments of American society to doctrines stressing the value and dignity of the individual has been real, deep, and widespread. The same can be said of the principles of equality, of humanitarian values, of political freedoms—and so on through the list of "publicly dominant" value patterns already listed. Once full weight has been given to all these "rational-humane" values in the received traditions of the society, it must be recognized at the same time that the values of the Creed have continually struggled against pervasive and powerful counter-currents of valuation. One of the chief conflicts, and in many ways the most important conflict, has centered around those diverse patterns which have as their common element *the ascription of value and privilege to individuals on the basis of race or particularistic group membership* according to birth in a particular ethnic group, social class, or related social category.

Racialistic doctrines were first given widespread currency and intellectual elaboration in the slavery controversy during the decades immediately prior to the Civil War. The value anomalies into which the pro-slavery position led,[70] in a culture so strongly stressing an individualistic religion and a democratic political system, gradually produced an explicit system of thought which relied upon assumptions of biological superiority to buttress the existing system of power and privilege.[71]

Space forbids anything like full documentation of the pervasiveness of organic, or more narrowly racist, orientations in our society. Adequate evidence is to be found in works already cited. It is enough to say that categorical discriminations are widespread in established practice, and are often crystallized into whole systems of legislation. It is not necessary here to explore the fears, vested interests, and multiple sociopsychological sources of the superiority-exclusiveness theme indexed by these legal acts. We must agree with Opler,[72] however, that these facts—only a tiny sample of other similar manifestations—reflect a view of society that in its extreme forms implicitly rejects "freedom" and individual ethical responsibility, certain conceptions of progress, and rational mastery of culture. Thus, the organic-racist view of man—in so far as its logical implications are actually worked out in human relations—stands in sharp opposition to most of the value orientations already reviewed. If a society begins with the premise that the human nature of individuals is biologically fixed and that different physical types or "races" are innately superior or inferior, then the unlimited development of this theme will make meaningless, or positively evil, the values of equality, democracy, freedom, rationality, progress (in the sense of human improvement through learning), humanitarianism, individual achievement linked with moral autonomy, and the central values of personality. The ultimate logical outgrowth of complete organicism is an exclusionistic society, rigidly organized in a static hierarchy.

It becomes apparent that a very important part of the conflict of value systems in the United States can be economically summarized in terms of tension between *values centering around the concept of the responsible individual personality versus values organized around categorical organic conceptions.*

CONCLUSION

. . . It must be always kept in mind that these themes, values, and systems of belief *do not operate as single and separate units* but *are in continually shifting and recombining configurations* marked by very complex interpenetration, conflict, and reformulation. Furthermore, our descriptive scheme that necessitated separate isolation and labeling of themes must not be allowed to leave the impression—to repeat an earlier caution—that values are disembodied elements which somehow function apart from concrete social relations and personalities. Everything described in this chapter must be capable of observation, in some sense, in the behavior of real personalities and in actual social structures, or else we have mistaken fancy for fact.

Perhaps the total picture may be clarified by a summary classification. In the first place, there are the quasi-values or *gratifications,* taken at a hedonic or physiological level, implicit in the entire analysis, and especially important in the section on "material comfort." Second, we may identify the *instrumental interests* or means-values, for example, wealth, power, work, efficiency. Although these interests may become values in themselves, it is convenient to consider them primarily as instrumental to the achievement of other values. Third, we have the *formal-universalistic values of Western tradition*: rationalism, impersonal justice and universalistic ethics, achievement, democracy, equality, freedom, certain religious values, value of individual personality. Fourth, there is a class of *particularistic, segmental, or localistic values* that are best exemplified in racist-ethnic superiority doctrines and in certain aspects of nationalism.

Running through these patterns of interests and values are certain still more general "dimensions" or "orientations" that are not typically explicit but must be identified by highly abstract inference. Because of this abstract quality, the inadequacy of the data, and the removal from observed phenomena by several stages of inference, the statement of such basic dimensions is hazardous and the following propositions must be taken as of only suggestive usefulness:

1. American culture is organized around the attempt at *active mastery* rather than *passive acceptance*. Into this dimension falls the low tolerance of frustration; the refusal to accept ascetic renunciation; the positive encouragement of desire; the stress on power; the approval of ego-assertion, and so on.

2. It tends to be interested in the *external world* of things and events, of the palpable and immediate, rather than in the inner experience of meaning and affect. Its genius is manipulative rather than contemplative.

3. Its world-view tends to be *open* rather than closed: it emphasizes change, flux, movement; its central personality types are adaptive, accessible, outgoing and assimilative.

4. In wide historical and comparative perspective, the culture places its primary faith in *rationalism* as opposed to *traditionalism;* it de-emphasizes the past, orients strongly to the future, does not accept things just because they have been done before.

5. Closely related to the above, is the dimension of *orderliness* rather than unsystematic *ad hoc* acceptance of transitory experience. (This emphasis is most marked in the urban middle classes.)

6. With conspicuous deviations, a main theme is a *universalistic* rather than a *particularistic* ethic.

7. In interpersonal relations, the weight of the value system is on the side of *"horizontal"* rather than "vertical" emphases: peer-relations, not superordinate-subordinate relations; equality rather than hierarchy.

8. Subject to increased strains and modifications, the received culture emphasizes *individual personality* rather than group identity and responsibility.

THE VALUE SYSTEMS OF DIFFERENT CLASSES:
A SOCIAL PSYCHOLOGICAL CONTRIBUTION
TO THE ANALYSIS OF STRATIFICATION

Herbert H. Hyman

INTRODUCTION. The existence of stratification in American society is well known. The corollary fact—that individuals from lower strata are not likely to climb far up the economic ladder is also known. However, what requires additional analysis are the factors that account for this lack of mobility. Many of these factors of an objective nature have been studied. Opportunity in the society is differential; higher education or specialized training, which might provide access to a high position, must be bought with money—the very commodity which the lower classes lack. Such objective factors help maintain the existing structure. But there are other factors of a more subtle psychological nature which have not been illuminated and which may also work to perpetuate the existing order. It is our assumption that an intervening variable mediating the relationship between low position and lack of upward mobility is a system of beliefs and values within the lower classes which in turn reduces the very *voluntary* actions which would ameliorate their low position.

The components of this value system, in our judgment, involve less emphasis upon the traditional high success goals, increased awareness of the lack of opportunity to achieve success, and less emphasis upon the achievement of goals which in turn would be instrumental for success. To put it simply the lower class individual doesn't want as much success, knows he couldn't get it even if he wanted to, and doesn't want what might help him get success. Of course, an individual's value system is only one among many factors on which his position in the social hierarchy depends. Some of these factors may be external and arbitrary, quite beyond the control of even a highly motivated individual. However, within the bounds of the freedom available to individuals, this value system would create a *self-imposed* barrier to an improved position.

Presumably this value system arises out of a realistic appraisal of reality and in turn softens for the individual the impact of low status. Unfortunately, we have at the moment little information on its genesis. However, we aim to document in this paper the presence of these values as a contemporary factor to be considered in discussions of the larger problems of stratification and mobility.

There are implications in such an analysis that go far beyond the specific problem of understanding the lack of upward mobility. The study of the psychological correlates of the objective class structure is in itself a problem to which social psychologists have and continue to address themselves for its relevance to the larger theoretical problem of attitude formation. And the

Reprinted from *Class, Status and Power* (1953), Reinhard Bendix and Seymour M. Lipset, eds., pp. 426-42, by permission of the author, the editors, and the publisher. (Copyright, 1953, by The Free Press.)

study of values specific to the economic realm contributes much to the social psychological analysis of adjustment and deviant behavior. Thus in Merton's influential paper, *Social Structure and Anomie,* deviant behavior is analyzed as a phenomenon concentrated in certain strata and emerging out of strains that differentially burden those lower in the social structure.[1] For example, one type of deviance is hypothesized as resulting from the frustration of the lower class individual's desire to achieve the cultural goal of economic success because the access to the means for such success is less available to him. "This syndrome of lofty aspirations and limited realistic opportunities . . . is precisely the pattern which invites deviant behavior." (p. 148.) It is clear that Merton's analysis assumes that the cultural goal of success is in actuality internalized by lower class individuals. Perhaps it also requires that the lower class individual *recognize* that the means to success are not available to him. It is certainly true *at a given point in time* that an individual frustrated in his goal because access to means is not open to him, will experience the incident as frustrating *whether or not he realizes* that the means are beyond his grasp. But it seems also true in the larger time perspective that if he continues to think that the means for a *future* success are available to him that the frustration will be milder and that deviance might not occur.[2] Conversely, if the individual regarded his chances to achieve his goal of success as negligible, when in reality they were good, there would be a psychologically produced strain toward deviance.

What is obviously required is empirical evidence on the degree to which individuals in different strata value the culturally prescribed goal of success, believe that opportunity is available to them, and hold other values which would aid or hinder them in their attempts to move towards their goal. This paper, in a preliminary way, is thus complementary to Merton's theoretical analysis.

While there is considerable literature on the beliefs and attitudes of the different economic classes, the specific realm that concerns us seems to have been generally neglected. Kornhauser's early writings come close to our problem and we shall allude to his findings in considerable detail. While Centers gives considerable attention to such values, he concentrates much more on the problem of the politico-economic ideology of individuals in different positions in the class structure. These studies provide the only quantitative evidence predicated on representative samples of large universes. Knupfer's study, while concerned with the problem and guided by the explicit hypothesis that there are "psychological restrictions which reinforce the economic," is essentially a characterology of the lower class individual describing in qualitative terms a diversity of attitudes, behaviors, and values. Similarly, Davis, Gardner and Gardner give some evidence on the way in which the class structure is experienced by individuals in different objective positions, but the reports are qualitative and literary in character. A number of quantitative studies are relevant but are limited in scope to specialized samples. Chinoy's study deals directly with our problem but is confined to a homogeneous group of 62 industrial workers in one automobile plant. Similarly, Hollingshead provides information on one aspect of the problem, the occupational goals of youth in different classes, but the study is limited to one community of about 6000 people in the Middle West. Form presents data on occupational and educational aspirations for contrasted groups of white collar and manual workers living in the relatively homogeneous planned community of Greenbelt, Maryland. Galler also presents information on the occupational goals of children in two contrasted classes for a sample limited to Chicago.[3]

A variety of other psychological concomitants of objective class position have been explored. The political ideology of the different classes is a classic realm for research by social scientists. Aesthetic values such as tastes and preferences have been mapped for the different classes by communication research specialists. Attitudes towards child rearing in the different classes have been studied by Allison Davis and Erickson.[4]

In seeking additional information in the realm of values, we shall avail ourselves of the accumulated findings of public opinion surveys, and use a procedure of secondary analysis. It is our belief that public opinion surveys have much rich information on many social science problems, such information often being an accidental by-product of the continuing inquiry into the characteristics of the public which opinion polls have been conducting for the past 15 years. While these inquiries often deal with applied problems of a transitory and insignificant character, from the great mass of data available much can be extracted by re-analysis which bears on problems of fundamental theoretical interest. We shall limit this analysis to the United States, but it should be noted that surveys parallel in content have been conducted in other countries, for example, Germany and England. Ultimately the analyses of these studies would permit us to examine the psychological variations between the classes as a function of the larger societal setting.

Most such inquiries also have the unusual advantage of being conducted on the basis of scientific sampling of the national population, and therefore permit more precise and generalized inferences than is usually the case in academic research. By contrast, Erickson's analysis of class and child rearing practices was based on 100 families in the Chicago area and the major study by Havighurst and Davis on differences in child-rearing was based on 100 white and 100 Negro families living in Chicago.[5]

Such studies while pioneering in character were limited in size by lack of resources. We are suggesting that even with minimal resources, academicians can fall heir to massive data collected at considerable expense for other purposes, and achieve greater generality in their findings.

Limitations are present, of course. The area of inquiry that interests us may have been touched only tangentially in the original survey, and possibilities for analysis may be scanty. Particularly, where the published account of the survey has to be used rather than the original data, the re-analysis is gravely limited. However, what we sacrifice in these respects is compensated for by the efficiency of the procedure and the great gain in generality. The sections to follow seek to demonstrate that secondary analyses are worthwhile, and that implicit in many surveys are data of great theoretical significance.[6]

Achievement in any realm is dependent upon two factors; the possession of both the necessary ability and the motivation to reach the goal. Ability is of course limited by *socially imposed* barriers to training and lack of channels to given types of positions. However, ability may also be retarded by lack of individual striving to obtain whatever training in turn is instrumental to economic advancement.

Consequently if we find that both motivation to advance to high positions and to obtain the training which is instrumental in achieving such positions are reduced in the lower class individual we shall have established our hypothesis. The same formula as applies to achievement, with minor modification, is relevant to Merton's theory. We need evidence here on the acceptance of success goals and on the belief in the accessibility of such goals.

The Value Placed on Formal Education. Part of the ideology of American life is that important positions are not simply inherited by virtue of the wealth of one's parents, but can be achieved. Such achievement, however, requires for many types of important positions considerable formal education. One cannot, for example, become a physician or a lawyer or an engineer without advanced education. Consequently, insofar as the lower classes placed less value on higher education, this would constitute an aspect of a larger value system which would work detrimental to their advancement. That such is really the case is evidenced in data collected by the National Opinion Research Center in a nationwide survey in 1947.[7] Within the total sample of approximately 2500 adults and 500 youths about half indicated that they regarded "some college training" as their answer to the question: "About how much schooling do you think most young men need these days to get along well in the world?" That this value is not equally shared by the lower groups is clear from the data presented in Table I below where the value is distributed by various stratification measures.

Table I—The Differential Emphasis Among Economic Classes Upon College Education as an Essential to Advancement

Interviewer's Rating Of Economic Level	Per Cent recommending College Education	N
Wealthy and prosperous	68	512
Middle class	52	1531
Lower class	39	856
Occupation		
Professional	74	301
Businessmen and proprietors	62	421
White collar workers	65	457
Skilled labor	53	392
Semi-skilled	49	416
Domestic and personal service workers	42	194
Farmers	47	417
Non-farm laborers	35	132
Highest Education Achieved		
Attended college	72	564
Attended high school	55	1411
Attended grammar school	36	926
Among renters, Monthly rental		
Above $60	70	327[a]
$40-60	64	666
$20-40	54	990
Below $20	37	403

It is clear that whatever measure of stratification is employed the lower groups emphasize college training much less.[9] Insofar as such training is one avenue to upward movement, this value would operate to maintain the present system.

These data emphasize the difference in the belief in the value of higher education. A related finding is available from a survey done by Roper in 1945 in which a more direct question was put to adults on their desire for their own children to go on to college. The exact question and the data are presented in Table II.

Table II—Preference for a College Education for the Children of the Different Classes

"After the war, if you had a son (daughter) graduating from high school would you prefer that he (she) go on to college, or would you rather have him (her) do something else, or wouldn't you care one way or the other?"

	Per Cent preferring college[10]
Prosperous	91
Upper Middle	91
Lower Middle	83
Poor	68

In terms of the perpetuation of the present system of stratification, however, these values as measured among adults only take on relevance insofar as they would be passed on to the children.[11] As a possible contribution to a more precise treatment of the consequences of this adult value we present in Table III, the same datum for groups varying in age and sex. Thus, if one were to hypothesize that American mothers are more important in the indoctrination of children than fathers, and that this value becomes crucial among those who would have children of college age, one could determine

Table III—The Emphasis Upon the Need for College Education as Related to the Sex and Age Composition of the Classes

	Per Cent recommending College Education	N
Males Over 40		
Wealthy and prosperous[12]	58	147
Middle Class	47	312
Lower Class	29	202
Difference between wealthy and poor +29%[13]		
Females Over 40		
Wealthy and prosperous	73	139
Middle Class	63	330
Lower Class	41	189
Difference between wealthy and poor +32%		
Males between 21-39 years of age		
Wealthy and prosperous	56	66
Middle Class	54	334
Lower Class	35	143
Difference between wealthy and poor +21%		
Females between 21-39 years of age		
Wealthy and prosperous	79	78
Middle Class	64	327
Lower Class	43	187
Difference between wealthy and poor +36%		

from the table above whether this reduced emphasis on college education impinges at the most crucial points in the developmental process. Incidental to this analysis, one can note whether or not the major finding of a differential value system by class continues to be demonstrated even when one controls factors of age and sex simultaneously.

It is clear that even when factors of age and sex composition are controlled that the differential emphasis upon education persists. There is a suggestion that women, presumably the more significant group in the rearing of children than men, are more likely to vary in their values as their class position changes. While women thus appear to be more conscious of their class, it can also be noted that women emphasize the value of education more than their male counterparts *for every age and class* group in the table, i.e., women in general place greater premium on formal education. Such phenomena of sex differences *per se* can also be observed in other findings yet to be presented. Parenthetically, it might be noted in the data of both Tables I and III that the middle class groups approximate closer to the value system of the prosperous, rather than being a kind of halfway group between lower and upper.

While we cannot clearly establish any major differences within the family structure of the different classes with respect to the distribution of this value, it is clear from additional data that the children of the different classes show value systems parallel to their parents.[14] In this survey, a sample of youths between the ages of 14 and 20 were studied in addition to the regular sample of the adult population. Table IV presents the distribution of this value for youths of the different classes. The data are presented separately for males and females. In addition to demonstrating the persistence of the difference when sex is controlled, this breakdown would permit us again to examine whether the differential value of the classes is most prominent in the very place in the social structure where it would have greatest significance. Insofar as male youth are the major future participants in economic life, the difference between upper and lower groups would have most social consequences if it were greater in males. It is interesting to note that the youth of both sexes and all classes are closer in their values to adult women than to adult men. This can be noted by comparing Tables III and IV and it is suggestive of the greater influence of mothers in the transmission of values.

Table IV—The Differential Emphasis Upon the Need for College Education Among Youths of the Different Classes

	Per Cent recommending College Education	N
Males between 14-20		
Wealthy and prosperous families	74	39
Middle Class	63	100
Lower Class	42	62
Difference between wealthy and lower classes +32%		
Females between 14-20		
Wealthy and prosperous families	85	45
Middle Class	71	128
Lower Class	49	73
Difference between wealthy and lower classes +36%		

Motivation to Advance in the Economic Structure. Achievement in any realm is as previously noted a function of motivation. Of course, *motivation* is only one of the factors leading toward success; the other being *ability* to succeed which would be dependent on degree of competence or training or barriers imposed on those of lowly position. Given the strongest motivation, a man might still be incapable of advancement if other factors reduced his ability to advance. A variety of data suggest that the lower class individual holds values of such a nature as to reduce his striving towards those ends which would result in his moving up the class structure.

In the same study where values with respect to higher education were ascertained, the respondents were asked a question which provided evidence on the desiderata the different classes considered in choosing an occupation. The findings show that lower class individuals emphasize those factors which would lead them to strive for careers which would be less high in the economic structure. The sample was asked, "what do you think is the most important *single* thing for a young man to consider when he is choosing his life's work?" The major considerations fell into two groups, 49% of the total sample answering in terms of the congeniality of the career pattern to the individual's personality, interests, and individual qualifications, and 32% answering in terms of direct economic considerations such as security, wages or subsidiary economic benefits, the steadiness of employment, etc. It can be clearly shown that the lower classes emphasize the latter desiderata, and the upper classes the more personal aspects of the work.[15] It is our belief that this difference in what would be sought in a career would lead the lower class individuals into occupations that would be less likely to enhance their position. Such desiderata will be achieved in a "good job" but not in such positions as managerial or professional jobs. These latter careers have greater elements of risk and are the very ones that would not mesh with the desire for stability, security and immediate economic benefits, but would mesh with the goal of congeniality to the individual's interests. Admittedly, this is only inferential, but it will be clear from related questions to be presented shortly that interpreting these respective orientations in the above terms is warranted. The data for adults of the different classes, separated by age and sex, are presented in Table V below.

It can be noted that the influence of class position on the desiderata mentioned declines with age. This might appear paradoxical, in that one would expect the younger poor still to have their illusions whereas the older individuals among the poor would have confronted reality longer and any illusions they might have would have been dissipated. Therefore, one might expect among the old a greater difference among the classes. However, what seems to be the case is that with age *all* individuals regardless of class give greater emphasis to such factors as stability and security, and therefore the differences while sizeable are somewhat reduced.

Findings of a parallel nature are found for the sample of youth. The data are presented in Table VI.[16]

We have some confirmatory data on the desiderata in choice of an occupation from surveys conducted by Roper. In 1942, a national sample of high school students were asked to express their preference for one of three types of jobs: a low income but secure job, a job with good pay but with a

50-50 risk of losing it, or a job with extremely high income and great risk. Data are presented for the different classes in Table VII below.

The poor youth cannot accept the risk involved in becoming less poor. Similar data are available for adults from surveys conducted by Roper. In

Table V—The Desiderata in Choosing an Occupation as Related to Class Position

	PER CENT MENTIONING THE FACTOR OF		Ratio of Congeniality to Economic Answers	N
	Congeniality to person	Economic Benefit		
Males between 21-39				
Wealthy or prosperous	72	17	4.2	66
Middle Class	55	20	2.7	334
Lower Class	37	32	1.2	143
Difference between upper and lower classes	+35%	—15%		
Females between 21-39				
Wealthy or prosperous	72	7	10.0	78
Middle Class	53	24	2.2	327
Lower Class	37	30	1.2	187
Difference between upper and lower classes	+35%	—23%		
Males Over 40				
Wealthy or prosperous	58	22	2.7	147
Middle Class	49	21	2.3	312
Lower Class	32	31	1.0	202
Difference between upper and lower classes	+26%	—9%		
Females Over 40				
Wealthy or prosperous	61	14	4.3	137
Middle Class	48	19	2.5	330
Lower Class	32	33	1.0	189
Difference between upper and lower classes	+29%	—19%		

Table VI—The Desiderata in Choosing an Occupation Among Youth of the Different Classes

	THE FACTOR OF PER CENT MENTIONING		Ratio of Congeniality to Economic Answers	N
	Congeniality to Person	Economic Benefit		
Males between 14-20				
Wealthy or prosperous	61	15	4.1	39
Middle Class	57	17	3.4	100
Lower Class	42	29	1.4	62
Difference between upper and lower classes	+19%	—14%		
Females between 14-20				
Wealthy or prosperous	60	14	4.3	45
Middle Class	55	19	2.9	128
Lower Class	45	27	1.7	73
Difference between upper and lower classes	+15%	—13%		

Table VII—Type of Occupation Chosen by Youth of the Different Classes[17]

Among High School Youth	Per Cent Preferring Job that Offers All-or-nothing Opulence
Poor	14
Prosperous, upper middle	29
From laboring parents	16
From executive and professional parents	31

1947, in answer to the identical question, one obtains a similar pattern by class. Thus, for example, a low income but secure job is chosen by 60% of factory workers but only by 26% of professional and executive persons. In 1949, a question presenting a similar choice situation between a secure job and a risky but promising career in one's own business yielded parallel results.[18]

Table VIII—Types of Occupations Recommended by the Different Classes

| | PER CENT RECOMMENDING | | |
	Professional Occupation	Skilled Manual Work	N
Males Between 21-39			
Wealthy and prosperous	45	5	66
Middle Class	49	13	334
Lower Class	38	22	143
Difference between wealthy and poor	+7%	—17%	
Females Between 21-39			
Wealthy and prosperous	51	3	78
Middle Class	55	7	327
Lower Class	44	17	187
Difference between wealthy and poor	+7%	—14%	
Males Over 40			
Wealthy and prosperous	49	9	147
Middle Class	43	20	312
Lower Class	27	22	202
Difference between wealthy and poor	+22%	—13%	
Females Over 40			
Wealthy and prosperous	54	3	139
Middle Class	49	13	330
Lower Class	32	15	189
Difference between wealthy and poor	+22%	—12%	

The inference that the desideratum of economic benefit rather than congeniality of work would lead the lower class individual to prefer occupations which are lower in the hierarchy can be supported by other data from a more direct question in this same NORC survey.[19] The respondents were asked: "Suppose some outstanding young man asked your advice on what would be one of the best occupations to aim toward. What *one* occupation do you think you would advise him to aim towards?" Partial data for the different classes are presented in Table VIII above, where it can be noted that the upper classes are more likely to stress professional careers whereas the lower groups emphasize skilled manual occupations.

Parallel data are presented for youths of the different classes in Table IX below.

That the occupational goals of the lower classes are limited is evidenced by other data in the area of personal income aspirations. In a number of different surveys, respondents have been asked to indicate the level of future income they would like to have, or expect to be earning. The exact question varies from survey to survey in terms of the time perspective involved and the level of reality emphasized. Correspondingly the measure obtained is expressive variously of an aspiration that is geared either to realistic expectations or to rather wild hopes and remote strivings. In general, these data show for the lower class a pattern of more limited expectations and/or striv-

Table IX—Types of Occupations Recommended by Youth of the Different Classes

| | PER CENT RECOMMENDING | | |
	Professional Occupation	Skilled Manual Work	N
Males Between 14-20			
Wealthy or prosperous	76	5	39
Middle Class	52	6	100
Lower Class	21	27	62
Difference between wealthy and poor	+55%	—22%	
Females Between 14-20			
Wealthy or prosperous	81	4	45
Middle Class	64	5	128
Lower Class	42	18	73
Difference between wealthy and poor	+39%	—14%	

ings.[20] Thus, in 1942 in Roper's national survey of youth, the question was put: "How much a week do you think you should be earning about ten years from now?" The average for the entire sample was $49.81 but the children of the prosperous and middle classes gave a figure of $58.94, whereas the children of the poor gave an average estimate of $40.26.[21]

Centers and Cantril report in 1946 on a survey conducted with a national sample of about 1200 adults. The question that was asked was: "About how much more money than that (the current income) do you think your family would need to have the things that might make your family happier or more comfortable than it is now?" As one goes up in the economic ladder, the increment of income desired decreases.

Relatively speaking the wealthier need and want less of an increase.[22] However, in terms of *absolute aspiration* level, the situation is quite different. The poor do not aspire to achieve the same dollar level as the wealthier. Thus, the absolute increase in dollars among those with a current income of less than $20 is only $16.20 on the average, whereas for those with a weekly income between $60 and $100, the absolute increase wanted is $41.60. As Centers and Cantril remark, "Individuals in the lowest income group do want a great deal more than they are now getting, but, in comparison to the sums wanted by those above them, theirs is a modest want indeed. An individual's present earnings obviously provide him with a frame of reference by means of which he sets his aspirations and judges his needs."[23]

Similar data are available from a study involving the sampling of male college students conducted by NORC in 1947.

The students were asked the weekly income they expected to be earning five years out of college. Among those students who come from families were the father is in a professional or managerial occupation, the median expectation was $119 a week whereas among those students whose fathers are in semi-skilled or skilled jobs the median figure was $103. Thus the aspirations vary with the class origins of the student. However, this particular study bears on certain interesting subtle aspects of reference group processes. The very fact that some children from lower class families entered college implies that they deviated in their behavior from the modal pattern of this class. A similar interpretation is made of this phenomenon of lower class college attendance by Havighurst and Rogers and was alluded to earlier.

Consequently, one might expect such individuals to show the lower class motivational pattern but in an attenuated form. That it is somewhat attenuated is suggested by the fact that the difference between the students of different classes is not as striking in magnitude as the differences we have just reported from other studies. In an early study by Gould there is some evidence of an even more extreme form of deviant value system among lower class college students.[24] In an experimental study of levels of aspirations among 81 male college students, two groups contrasted with respect to the size of their discrepancy score on six experimental tasks were studied. The group whose aspiration far exceeded their achievement were of predominantly *lower* class backgrounds and from minority ethnic groups. This appears to contradict our findings that lower class individuals set their goals lower than upper class groups. However, the apparent contradiction may imply the very interesting fact—that among those lower class individuals who do orient themselves to upper class patterns, i.e., enter college, their goal striving can be even more extreme.

In the NORC study of college students, one other datum suggests the attenuation of the expected pattern in the lower class college student. The students indicated those items within a list which were the three major desiderata in their choosing a job. It can be noted that this question corresponds very closely to the question previously analyzed in Table V for a national sample of adults. If we analyze these answers in terms of the differential emphasis upon factors of "economic benefit" vs. factors of "congeniality" for the different classes the differences by occupation of father are generally in the expected direction, but are of much smaller magnitude than those previously reported. They are presented in Table X.

Table X—The Desiderata in Choosing an Occupation Among College Students of Different Class Origins

	PER CENT AMONG STUDENTS WHOSE FATHERS	
Per Cent Mentioning Desideratum of:[25]	Professional or Managerial	Skilled or Semi-skilled
Adventure—Excitement	7	8
Being one's own boss	27	18
Congenial atmosphere	31	23
Intellectual challenge	55	42
Advancement	50	55
Money	26	30
Security	58	58
N=	301	106

Beliefs in Opportunity. This pattern of reduced personal aspirations and reduced appeal or valence of given occupations among the lower classes seems to derive from the perception of reality that the lower classes have. The goals of *all* individuals are governed to some extent by the appraisal of reality. Since a variety of data indicate that the poor are more aware of their lack of opportunity, presumably they would set their goals in the light of such beliefs.[26] In a national survey in 1947 by Roper, a series of questions dramatically demonstrate the difference in the beliefs of the lower classes about opportunity. The data are presented in Table XI.

Table XI—Beliefs in Economic Opportunity Among the Different Classes[27]

	AMONG EMPLOYEES WHO ARE	
	Professional or Executives	Factory Workers
Per cent believing that years ahead hold good chance for advancement over present position[28]	63	48
Per cent believing that following factor is important consideration in job advancement:[29]		
quality of work	64	43
energy and willingness	56	42
getting along well with boss	12	19
friend or relative of boss	3	8
being a politician	6	4
Per cent believing that harder work would net them personally a promotion	58	40

A parallel finding is available from 1937 when Roper asked a national sample of adults the question: "Do you think that today any young man with thrift, ability, and ambition has the opportunity to rise in the world, own his own home, and earn $5000 a year?" Among the prosperous 53% indicated categorically that such an aspiration was realistic, whereas among the poor only 31% indicated their belief in this possibility.

Evidence from a variety of psychological studies sheds further light on the way in which the person's own expectations and striving for a goal are affected by his social position. These are all based on the analysis of levels of aspiration with respect to experimental tasks.[30] Although these tasks do not have a direct relevance to behavior in the economic sphere and constitute mere analogies, the analysis of the process of setting of goals may contribute much to our problem.

In one experimental level of aspiration study, there is a graphic demonstration of the way in which the socially defined opportunity of a group affects specific aspirations, and specific responses to past success. Adams matched groups of white and Negro subjects on a series of characteristics and compared successive aspirations in an experimental task involving dart throwing. Among the white college subjects, achievement of their aspiration on the task was followed by raising of the aspiration level on the next trial, whereas for the matched Negro college group past success on the task was less likely to result in their raising their goal on the next trial.[31]

In a series of other experiments, beginning with the work of Chapman and Volkmann individuals alter their level of aspiration on experimental tasks when informed of the achievement on that task of some other social group. When this fictitious standard represents a group ostensibly superior in standing to the individual, he reduces his estimate of his own future performance.[32] Implicitly, these findings demonstrate that the individual in lowly position sets his strivings and expectancies for success in the light of the established social hierarchy of groups and a belief in differential opportunities within the hierarchy.

Two illustrative experiments show this process graphically for groups with well defined social positions. Preston and Bayton found that an experimental group of Negro college students reduced their aspiration levels when informed that white college students had achieved a certain level in the task more than the control group of Negro students informed that the same fictitious standard of achievement had been achieved by other Negroes. The mirror image of this experiment was conducted by MacIntosh who used white college students as subjects and presented them with the fictitious standard of performance of a Negro group. In the case of the white students, they orient themselves to the knowledge of Negro achievement by raising their estimates.[33]

Altered Forms of Striving for Success. Thus far the data presented show clearly that there is reduced striving for success among the lower classes, an awareness of lack of opportunity, and a lack of valuation of education, normally the major avenue to achievement of high status. However, there may well be subtle ways in which the lower class individual shows the effect of the cultural emphasis on success. Conceivably, our data might be interpreted to indicate that the person *really* wants to achieve the goal of great success, but that he has merely accommodated himself to his lesser opportunities and reduced his aspirations so as to guard against the experience of frustration and failure. Yet, the fact that the data for the sample of youth parallel so closely the findings on adults suggests that this explanation is not generally tenable. Such a dynamic readjustment of goals in relation to reality would be expected to come later. Youth seem to have internalized differentiated goals dependent on their class at an age too early to represent a kind of secondary re-setting of their sights.[34]

Similarly, one might argue that adults would have accommodated *themselves* to reality, but that the cultural emphasis upon success would be reflected by a vicarious aspiration for their children to achieve high success. Chinoy, for example, remarks on the existence of this pattern among his automobile workers. He notes that everyone of his 26 subjects with young children had greater hopes for them and believed in better opportunities for their children.[35] Merton notes the same process, and reports preliminary data from his housing studies. He notes that the lower the occupational level of the parent, the larger the proportion having aspirations for a professional career for their children.[36]

Yet, if such were *generally* the case, we would expect our youth sample to reflect such a pattern of indoctrination. They seem instead to show the pattern of aspirations of the adult members of their class.

Another possibility that presents itself is that the cultural emphasis upon success is reflected in the lower class groups in substitute forms. They cannot achieve occupational success, and so substitute other goals more readily achieved, and regard these symbolically as equivalents. Chinoy remarks on such a "shift in the context of advancement from the occupational to the consumption sphere."[37] We have no data on the problem unfortunately for large samples.

We have some data, however, on one substitute form of motivation for success in the economic sphere.

Deviant Occupational Goals. In general, it has been shown that the lower class individual has less opportunity and less motivation to advance in the hierarchy. However, there are certain occupations in America which provide wealth and benefits to which he might have singular access. These would be occupations which the more genteel classes might regard with disdain and consequently, the lower class person would have less competition. Insofar as the lower class person would have a value system which would endorse the pursuit of such occupations, this would provide a deviant and "sheltered" avenue to success. Such occupations might, for example, exist in the entertainment realm, the realm of politics, and in certain specialized jobs which appear distasteful in character.[38]

Inferential evidence in support of such a pattern is available from a series of measures of the prestige accorded by the different classes to certain selected types of occupations.

Each individual in the sample rated the prestige of a series of occupations. We shall assume that according high prestige to an occupation would so-to-speak correspond to that occupation having a strong positive valence for the individual, i.e., he would be more likely to direct his strivings toward occupations he regards as prestigious and not towards occupations he regards as non-prestigious. The hierarchy of prestige has been found in past investigations to be uniform among different occupational groups and, among groups geographically diverse, to be stable over long periods of time.[39] In the national sample studied by NORC, there was similarly, a general uniformity to the prestige accorded to different occupations by persons in widely different groups. However, despite this cultural norm, we note certain interesting differences in the prestige accorded by the different classes to occupations which we have labelled deviant. County Judge is used in this analysis as exemplifying a political career goal; singer in a night club as exemplifying an entertainment career goal, and undertaker as exemplifying a distasteful but lucrative occupation. It will be noted from Table XII below that the lower classes are more likely to accord high prestige to these careers. Conceivably the judge and singer could be regarded as positions of respectability in the judiciary and cultural world or the reactions could be predicated on the intrinsic content of the work. Therefore in the table we present results for two "control" occupations, Supreme Court Justice and musician in a symphony orchestra. Insofar as the responses of the different classes were to the intrinsic contents and the respectability of the occupation, one would expect a similar pattern to the two judicial posts and the two musical positions. However, it can be noted that the classes reverse themselves for the control occupation. In other words, a judicial post of respectability is differentially favored by the upper classes; a judicial post of a *political* nature is favored by the lower classes. Similarly, a *long haired* musical post is favored by the upper classes, and a popular musical position by the lower classes.

It can be noted that there is one inversion in the table which violates the general hypothesis. However, among the 20 possible regressions by class in the table, this is the only inversion found.

Evidence of a more direct nature supports the conclusions just presented.

Table XII—The Prestige Accorded to Deviant Occupations by the Different Classes

	Supreme Court Justice	Musician in Symphony Orchestra	County Judge	Singer in Night Club	Undertaker	N
		PER CENT GIVING THE RATING OF EXCELLENT STANDING TO:				
Males Between 21-39						
wealthy or prosperous	88	31	32	0	12	66
middle class	85	25	42	1	10	334
lower class	82	21	44	6	16	143
difference between upper and lower classes	+6%	+10%	—12%	—6%	—4%	
Females Between 21-39						
wealthy or prosperous	95	37	41	3	8	78
middle class	83	31	44	1	13	327
lower class	72	30	55	5	22	187
difference between upper and lower classes	+23%	+7%	—14%	—2%	—14%	
Males Over 40						
wealthy or prosperous	84	25	48	0	12	147
middle class	81	26	49	2	14	312
lower class	79	23	52	4	17	202
difference between upper and lower classes	+5%	+2%	—4%	—4%	—5%	
Females Over 40						
wealthy or prosperous	92	37	52	0	11	139
middle class	81	36	55	2	18	330
lower class	72	29	49	6	20	189
difference between upper and lower classes	+20%	+8%	+3%	—6%	—9%	

In 1944, the NORC asked a national sample of 2500 cases, "If you had a son just getting out of school, would you like to see him go into politics as a life work?" About two-thirds of the total sample disapproved of such a career, but the disapproval was much more characteristic of the upper classes.

Table XIII—Disapproval of a Career in Politics by the Different Classes

Economic Level	Per Cent Disapproving[40]
wealthy or prosperous	78
middle class	73
lower class	54

Reference Group Processes and the Deviant Case. While the evidence thus far presented provides consistent and strong evidence that lower class individuals *as a group* have a value system that reduces the likelihood of individual advancement, it is also clear from the data that there is a sizeable proportion of the lower group who do not incorporate this value system. Similarly, there are individuals in the upper classes who do not show the modal tendency of their group. In part, such deviant instances can be accounted for in terms of the crudity of the measurements used. In part, one must recognize that the members of these classes have much heterogeneity in such other social respects as their ethnic, religious, and other memberships and have been exposed to a variety of idiosyncratic experiences.

Table XIV—Reference Group Processes as Revealed in the Influence of the Class History of the Individual on His Values

| | AMONG RESPONDENTS WHOSE OCCUPATIONS ARE | | | |
| | PROFESSIONAL OR BUSINESS | | SKILLED OR SEMI-SKILLED | |
Per Cent Who—	Father prof. or bus.	Father skilled or semi	Father prof. or bus.	Father skilled or semi
Recommend College Education	71	60	57	50
Recommend as Best Occupation:				
Professional Work	44	29	31	25
Skilled Manual Work	10	29	23	44
Mention the Desideratum in Choosing an Occupation of:				
Congeniality	65	62	52	46
Economic Benefit	15	19	23	27
N	(377)	(140)	(298)	(397)

The value systems would be correspondingly diverse. However, one systematic factor that can be shown to account for the deviant cases which confirms at *a more subtle psychological level* the influence of class factors is that of the reference group of the individual. Some of our lower class individuals may well be identifying themselves with upper groups, and absorbing the value system of another class to which they refer themselves. Some of our upper class individuals may for a variety of reasons refer themselves psychologically to other classes. That the reference group of the individual affects his value system, was suggested by data presented earlier on lower class college students and can be shown inferentially from additional data collected in the NORC survey. Evidence was available on the occupation of the parent of each respondent. If we classify each individual in a lower class occupation in terms of whether his parental background is that of a lower or higher occupation group, we presumably have a contrast between individuals of objectively identical class, but who differ in the class with which they might identify. We shall assume that those with upper class origins would not think so much in lower class terms and would continue to reflect their more prestigious origins. If we, similarly, take individuals who are now objectively in upper class occupations and divide them in terms of parental occupation we shall presumably be classifying respondents in more psychological terms. For these four groups we shall contrast their values in each of the realms previously analyzed purely by *current* objective class membership.[41] The patterning of the findings is presented in Table XIV above. It can be noted that the values are a resultant of both the "class history" of the individual and his current position. Individuals of equal current position reflect the values of their parents' class. This can be noted by comparing Col. 1 with Col. 2 of the table and Col. 3 with Col. 4. It is also true, however, that individuals with the same class origins have different values depending on their current position. This requires the comparison of Col. 1 with Col. 3 and Col. 2 with Col. 4. Where the two sets of class factors combine in an additive way, the effect on the value system is maximal as seen in the comparison of Col. 1 with Col. 4. The residues of earlier class experiences in some manner are present suggesting that reference group processes are at work.

MENTAL HYGIENE AND THE CLASS STRUCTURE

Kingsley Davis

MENTAL HYGIENE CONSTITUTES for the sociologist a two-fold interest, first as a social movement (preparing now to celebrate its twenty-ninth anniversary), and second as an applied science (drawing upon several pure sciences of which sociology is one). Both sides of this interest fit with our present subject—the relation of mental hygiene to the vertical dimension of society—because any phenomenon which is at once a social movement and an applied human science cannot escape on two counts having some connection, however obscure it may seem, with the invidious, discriminatory aspect of social life.

We should like to define mental hygiene in terms of its chief aim, but the general goal as usually stated—improvement of mental health in the community, promotion of personal efficiency, or provision for personality expression and happiness—is ambiguous. It is difficult to determine whether mental hygiene practises are really conducive to such a goal, or whether the practises of any well-intentioned movement are not equally conducive to it. Our conception of mental hygiene, then, will embrace simply the movement and the point of view called by that name. The diffuseness of its main goal and the proliferation of subsidiary ends[1] will be viewed as symptomatic of its social role and function.

Now let us turn briefly to the vertical dimension in society. Its essence is the relative inferiority and superiority of persons in one another's eyes. It is manifest on the one hand in a *crystallized hierarchy* of positions (offices and statuses) which is supported by a correlative system of sentiments and a constraining set of legal and moral sanctions; and on the other hand in *interpersonal relations* where (in rough accord with the crystallized attitudes) every act, word and thought of the person is unremittingly subjected to the praising and condemning scrutiny of others. The vertical dimension is thus not limited to the wider or smaller circles; it is coextensive with the social.

Persons occupying similar positions in the hierarchy constitute a social class, in most cases a statistical rather than a real group. Class implies the division of persons into broad strata according to their final score in the summation of estimable tallies—the precipitate of all the countless criteria of invidious distinction. The strata may be so organized with reference to one another than movement up or down the scale is facilitated or blocked.

The first type we call a system of mobile classes, the second a system of immobile castes. Each type possesses its appropriate world philosophy common to its members, absolutistic in expression, and conceived as an order of justice. Its principles penetrate to every phase and aspect of life, taking hold of the person in the dynamic maze of communicative, especially interpersonal and primary, contacts.

Our interest lies in our own mobile class system and its accompanying world philosophy. The latter, which may conveniently be called the Protestant ethic, and which receives its severest expression in Puritanism, is: (1) *Democratic* in the sense of favoring equal opportunity to rise socially by merit rather than by birth. (2) *Worldly* in emphasizing earthly values such as the pursuit of a calling, accumulation of wealth, and achievement of status. (3) But at the same time *ascetic* in stressing physical abstinence and stern sobriety, thrift, industry, and prudence. (4) *Individualistic* in placing responsibility upon the individual himself for his economic, political, and religious destiny, and in stressing personal ambition, self-reliance, private enterprise, and entrepreneurial ability.[2] (5) *Rationalistic* and *empirical* in assuming a world order discoverable through sensory observation of nature.[3] (6) *Utilitarian* in pursuing practical ends with the best available means, and conceiving human welfare in secularized terms as attainable by human knowledge and action.

It can be demonstrated, we think, that this ethic is functionally related to an open-class society. Not only are the two historically connected, but it seems that an open-class society could scarcely work without such a philosophy.[4]

But what has this Protestant ethic, plus the underlying system of mobile classes, to do with mental hygiene? Our discussion of this point, suggestive rather than conclusive, will embrace the following propositions: first, that mental hygiene, being a social movement and a source of advice concerning personal conduct, has inevitably taken over the Protestant ethic inherent in our society, not simply as the basis for conscious preachment but also as the unconscious system of premises upon which its "scientific" analysis and its conception of mental health itself are based. Second, that this unconscious incorporation of the open-class ethic has made mental hygiene doubly susceptible to the psychologistic approach to human conduct, though the latter has represented, in part, a contradictory feature. Third, that the unconscious assumption of the dominant ethic, together with the psychologistic interpretation, has served to obscure the social determinants of mental disease, and especially the effects of invidious or emulative relationships. And finally, that mental hygiene will probably fail as a preventive movement because it cannot overcome its defects, the free analysis and manipulation of invidious social elements never being permitted in an integrated society.

The relation between mental hygiene and the open-class ethic is an unconscious one. Tacitly the textbooks for teachers and practitioners of the subject assume the existence of a mobile class structure and teach by implication the congruent moral norms. Frequently they interpret these norms as somehow given in the individual, and in the last analysis always define mental health itself in terms of them.[5]

Vertical mobility, for example, is taken for granted, and social advancement accepted as a natural goal. Democracy, in the form of equal opportunity to advance, is regarded as desirable. Lack of ambition is felt to represent a definite symptom of maladjustment, to be eliminated if possible. The normal person is considered to be one who chooses a calling and tries to distinguish himself in it, while the mentally sick person is one who needs occupational therapy.[6]

Likewise *competition* is assumed, life being regarded as a battle or a game in which victory goes to him who uses wit and strength to best advantage.[7] Since the morality of the competitive system requires that we not violate the rules of the game, and that we not envy the other fellow his accomplishments or gloat over his failures, this morality is incorporated into the mental hygiene teaching—the prevention of mental illness becoming at the same time the prevention of delinquency and the encouragement of good sportsmanship.[8] The healthy person is regarded as achieving victory against others only within the rules, by empirico-rational ingenuity and ascetic self-discipline. The maladjusted person must learn to face reality, i.e., the competitive facts.[9] He must not achieve victories in fancy only, or flee the memory of his failures. Parents must not coddle their child and thus make him unfit for the competition of adult life. Yet since to face reality means not only to grasp the fact of competition, but also to estimate correctly one's chances, and since one's chances depend upon capacity and circumstances as well as effort, a safety valve for the competitive drive is provided by the advice that one should not aspire beyond one's ability.[10]

Because competition has for its goal a worldly prize, but a prize not to be won by self-indulgence, the implied existence of competition as a sane way of life is buttressed by the tacit preachment of *worldly asceticism*. Mental hygiene does not frown upon enjoyment for itself, but it does insist that recreation shall be "wholesome." In other words, one should not choose a type of recreation that makes one unfit for the serious business of life,[11] or which violates the canons of Protestant morality. One's behavior should manifest prudence, rationality, and foresight, and material possessions should not be dissipated by whimsical extravagance.[12]

Individualism is tacitly assumed in three ways. (1) The person is held responsible for his own destiny. In case of neurosis his will is the object of treatment. In short he is the entrepreneur.[13] (2) Individual happiness is the ultimate good. Mental health is interpreted as the satisfaction of individual needs.[14] (3) Human behavior is assumed to be understandable in terms of individuals abstracted from their society. Needs, desires, and mental processes are frequently discussed as if inherent in the organism.[15]

Specialization is implicitly taken for granted in the emphasis upon the value of a particular kind of work adapted to one's talents and identified with one's own personality.

Utilitarianism is obviously assumed in the action philosophy of mental hygiene. To function, to grow, to do is regarded as the purpose of life. Tangible ends and Progress are regarded as the goals. Human welfare is seen as attainable by the application of rational science.[16]

If the thesis is true that mental hygiene unconsciously incorporates the open-class ethic, it should be further indicated by a study of the movement's personnel. Such a study, constituting a type of circumstantial evidence,[17] was made, and it shows that the persons prominently connected with the movement are of the type one would expect to uphold the Protestant principles. They are mostly upper middle class professionals, predominantly of British ancestry, identified with a Protestant church, and frequently reared and educated in New England. Many of them apparently had well-to-do parents who themselves had risen in life through effort and initiative. Some of them are self-made men of undistinguished parentage in our own or in the old country. In general they seem to have taken to heart the necessity of a calling and have worked, abstained, and striven sufficiently to succeed. It follows from their background and is exemplified in their writings, that they believe in empirical science and have taken the American humanitarian religion seriously enough to apply scientific results zealously to the mental welfare of society. They are (without cavil) idealistic, respectable, and capable, and their sentiments lean on the side of humanitarian individualism.

Aside from the personnel of the movement, there exists for our main thesis still another (and more direct) evidence—derived from examining a central and recurrent concept in the mental hygiene literature, namely, "mental health." This concept is usually defined as the "integration," the "balance," the "successful" or "happy functioning" of the personality;[18] but these words are as vague as the initial phrase. Furthermore, no adequate criteria for establishing the presence of this "integration" or "balance" are provided. The only consistent criterion, and in the last analysis the substance of every definition, is normal behavior. Consequently we shall examine what the mental hygiene literature means by "the normal."

Does "normal" refer to the statistical average of actual behavior, or to ideal behavior? It seems that mental hygienists have not seen the issue. In practice they employ the concept in both senses, though ultimately the normative sense prevails. There is in the literature much criticism of *selected* moral rules and attitudes. Sometimes the apparent basis of criticism is that the rules are unrealistic—i.e., that they are too far removed from the average actual behavior. Generally, however, the criticism springs (as it inevitably must) from value-judgments of the author. On the basis of his own conscious or unconscious values, the selected norm may be judged to be "irrational," "unenlightened," and detrimental to mental health. But whence come the author's values? Due to his position in society, and the nature of his work, they must come from the central valuational system of his culture.[19] He can and he will criticize particular norms, but he cannot impugn the basic institutions of his society, because it is in terms of these that conduct is ultimately judged to be satisfactory (i.e., adjusted) or unsatisfactory.[20]

The ethical meaning of "normal" is further borne out by the fact that when specific advice is given concerning life problems, the conduct prescribed is ordinarily such as would conform to our ideals, not to the statistical average. The mental hygienist tends to justify such advice, however, not on moral but on rational or "scientific" grounds. One can best secure mental health, best satisfy one's needs, by conforming. But since for certain selected norms he does not advise conformity, the hygienist violates his own contention. Furthermore, he never brings the question of conformity or nonconformity to a clear issue, because he does not define "individual needs" or "adjustment" apart from moral norms, and because he does not admit that the delinquent may escape detection and hence punishment.[21]

If we are to understand the logic by which mental hygiene identifies mental health with normality, and normality with an unconsciously assumed open-class ethic, we must turn our attention to a central factor in this logic, to what may be called the psychologistic conception of human nature. By the psychologistic approach is meant the explanation of human conduct in terms of traits originating within the individual, as over against traits originating within society. Any explanation is psychologistic, for example, which builds its analysis upon motives, drives, instincts, urges, prepotent reflexes, or what not, ignoring the social genesis of what is called by these names. In mental hygiene these elements are taken as given in the individual, existing prior to social forces and determining concrete actions. Since they are prior to the social, the only other alternative in accounting for them is that they are biologically given. The psychologistic interpretation is individualistic, then, in the sense that it bases its explanation upon that which is purely individual, i.e., the biologically inherited constitution (the purely nonsocial part) of the person.

It is natural that mental hygienists have adopted this conception of human nature. Protestant individualism finds here a scientific rationalization. The philosophy of private initiative, personal responsibility, and individual achievement falls easily into an interpretation of human nature in individualistic terms. Furthermore, for those who are naive in the analysis of social relations and generally unaware of the sociological premises of their own thinking, it is extremely easy to read into the individual, as given in his nature, the characteristics that are really given in his society. By thus reading social traits into original nature a degree of permanence and certainty is given them which would disappear if they were realized to be merely socially acquired. In other words, psychologism is a means whereby an unconsciously held ethic may be advantageously propagated under the guise of "science." It protects the hygienist from a disconcerting fact—the relativity of moral judgments.

Yet, if applied with logical rigor to matters of conduct, the psychologistic approach would become an incompatible element in mental hygiene doctrine. Since mental hygiene constantly judges life-situations to be wholesome or hygienic according to whether or not they satisfy individual needs, the concept of "individual needs" calls for strict definition. If defined according to a logical application of the psychologistic approach, individual needs would reduce to those that are biologically inherited—namely, the organic. Applying this point of view to conduct, mental hygiene would urge us to satisfy our physiological needs independently of social standards and ideals, and to observe such standards and ideals only in so far as they can be proven to satisfy our needs. Of course, the hygienists do not do this. Instead they inculcate the dominant morality of a mobile society. They do not, then, apply the psychologistic approach with logical rigor, but misinterpret it by including as given in the individual many things which are in reality not genetically but socially determined, such as desires and standards. These social desires and standards construed as inherent in the individual are precisely the Protestant standards that the mental hygienist implicitly follows. It is no wonder, then, that the "scientific" hygiene yields results in striking conformity to the ethical configuration, seeing that the ethical configuration is intrinsically contained in the very definition of the goal to be achieved— namely, satisfaction of individual needs.[22]

We have shown thus far, by its preachments, its personnel, and its conception of mental health and normality, that mental hygiene tacitly assumes the Protestant open-class ethic. Let us now turn to the *results,* rather than the evidences, of the implicit assumptions. We shall argue that the ethical presuppositions, plus the psychologistic approach, necessarily vitiate the scientific validity of much mental hygiene work by limiting and biasing the study of mental disorder and consequently the working conceptions behind mental hygiene practice. Specifically, the presuppositions lead to neglect of the invidious element, and in fact social elements generally, as a determining factor in mental disorder.

An aspect of social relations possessing strong presumptive evidence of responsibility in mental disorders is precisely that which embraces invidious, discriminatory differences. If we suspect already that social forces are implicated, our suspicion becomes doubly certain for this particular branch of social phenomena. Sociological analysis of personality has long stressed the individual's conception of his role in the eyes of others. It has maintained that the self develops through the acquisition and internalization of the attitudes of others. It has shown that these attitudes, laden with approval or disapproval, not only become in time the foundation of the self but also assume tremendous emotional importance for the individual.[23] Since the attitudes of others are acquired only by symbolic communication, which is social in the strictest sense and necessarily connected with the cultural heritage, it can be seen that the key to the relation between organism and culture lies precisely in the dynamics of the social role. And since the social role is largely a matter of the communicated approval or disapproval of others, involving a constant comparison of one's own position with that of others, the invidious, emulative element is inevitably present. In so far as personality and mentality are socially determined, they are also emulatively determined.

As a slight test of this theory, an analysis of 70 hospitalized cases, reported in the psychiatric literature and mostly with functional disorders, was made.[24] All but four instances showed clear evidence of status involvements. Furthermore, the evidence would seem to bear out Campbell's contention that in the functional disorders the emotional problems are of sufficient intensity and consistency as to indicate a causal relationship.[25]

It follows that in the study of mental disorder, some attention should be devoted to the invidious elements in the social past of the patients. This holds true especially for the functional derangements—those, presumably, with which mental hygiene is most concerned.[26] But in mental hygiene at least, this phase of the subject has been neglected.[27] Much attention has perforce been devoted to guilt feelings, inferiority complexes, anxiety states, and emotional conflicts. Yet though these clearly reflect the power of invidious comparison, they are hardly seen to be social at all. The vertical element is merely assumed; it remains unanalyzed while attention is turned to "instincts," "reflexes," "habits," or other bio-individual determinants.

Now if we ask why this neglect, the answer seems obvious. It is a product of the implicit assumption of an open-class philosophy of life. Little attention is paid to the emulative, discriminatory social factors because to analyze them would bring to awareness the unconscious ethical premises. Such analysis would force recognition of the vertical dimension of our society and the axiological judgments associated with it, which have been assumed as premises. Hence it would destroy the myth of scientific objectivity and the myth of the universal individual—myths necessary to the self-confident optimism of the mental hygiene movement.

The logical device by which this blindness to invidious social determinants is made to appear satisfactory to the conscious minds of the mental hygienists, is the psychologistic approach. If human personality is understandable without reference to social reality, then naturally social reality need not be analyzed. The latter can be accepted superficially as something to which the personality must adjust, something which represses or facilitates original wishes; but the more fundamental social forces are not reckoned with. If they are treated at all it is erroneously—the social elements being regarded as inherently given in the individual (i.e., as non-social).

To show that mental hygiene has neglected genuine factors, and to indicate further why it has done so, it is worth while to reflect upon some possible connections between the class structure and mental disorder.

Be the causes of mental disorder what they may, it is easy to show that the criteria are always social. Sanity lies in the observance of the normative system of the group. This allows wide latitude, of course, and we constantly make allowances for a person's rearing in the specialized culture of his particular groups. But sanity assumes acculturation in some group, and basically it is acculturation in the central mores of the widest society in which the person is an effective social unit. Furthermore, we do not judge by one lapse. We judge, rather, by systematized behavior and ideas in a direction contrary to the accepted motivational complex. Thus a criminal is not regarded as insane because he does something contrary to mores and law. Stealing is an occurrence inherent in our social organization, and we all can see the logic of motives for stealing. But a man who steals because of a motivational complex contrary to the accepted one—say, a kleptomaniac—is judged to be mentally disordered: not because he steals, but because his reasons for stealing are removed from "reality." A man who forgets is not insane. We all forget. But a man who forgets the wrong things, such as his own name, his own city, or the excretory separation of the sexes, is definitely crazy.

In a class society the motivation of one class is understood by the members of other classes, because they each, in conforming to their class standards, are really conforming to the system of standards that constitutes the society. It may be that class ideologies, considered in themselves, vary in the degree of mental health they give their adherents; but this opinion assumes something that we do not possess—namely, a standard of reality by which all ideologies may be judged. In any culture the class ideologies are merely specialized parts of the central ideology, which is not identified simply with the outlook of the dominant class, but with that of all classes.[28] It is not necessarily true, therefore, that the more divergent the class ideology from the cultural standard, the greater the incidence of mental derangement in this class. It is a particular kind of divergence that counts, a divergence in the ultimate norms which unify the entire society and knit together its specialized groups.[29] In case of such divergence other classes will focus attention upon the errant one and will seek to control its thinking and behavior through methods conforming to the sanctions of the society. But the important point is that a specialized part is not necessarily divergent in this latter sense. The ideological peculiarities of a particular class may be adequately provided for and incorporated in the central ideology.

This conclusion seems valid in a caste as well as an open-class organization, and is partially valid even where class struggle exists. So far as mental disorder is concerned, the significant question is not whether there is a caste or class system, for neither one is inherently destructive of sanity, but whether the system, whatever it is, is unified by a nucleus of common values. When the structure embraces conflicting principles of social organization based on incompatible values, psychic conflicts inevitably result. For example, ends may be presented to one group as possible and desirable, when in fact they are made impossible for that group by a conflicting mode of dominance. A clear illustration appears in the Southern part of the United States, where the avowed morality of equal opportunity to all is categorically denied in practice to Negroes.[30] The behavior of individuals caught in this situation manifests frequent attempts to escape an unbearable reality. Reality seems unbearable, however, only when another reality exists as a *conceivable* alternative; and another is conceivable only when it forms part of the social system and exists as a possibility within the cultural ideology. Mental conflict is engendered, then, not so much by the vertical structure itself as by inconsistency within the structure.

It might seem that a mobile class organization would have deleterious effects upon mental health because of the constant readjustments it requires of its circulating individuals. But the open-class system is protected against this adverse result by the fact that, as distinguished from a caste society, the limits of difference between the mores of different strata are narrow. If the differences were wide, vertical mobility, entailing a shift from one set of mores to a radically different set, would certainly have profound effects upon the person so shifting, and would tend by prohibiting the change. But actually there is a tendency in an open-class system for differences in class modes of thinking to take the form of an infinite number of small gradations, and to reduce themselves to superficial externalities; so that though vertical mobility places the strain of rapid change, responsibility, and adaptation upon the individual,[31] it compensates for this by the pulverization and externalization of differences. The class variations in mores become one of degree rather than kind. The same fundamental wants and values pervade the whole hierarchy, the only difference being that members of the various classes satisfy these wants and attain these values in different amounts. The climber who moves from the bottom to the top finds that he can still utilize practically all of his old habituations. No fundamental reorganization is required. He merely satisfies the same old wants more readily and in greater abundance. Thus does the mobile society safeguard the sanity of the mobile person.[32]

Basically its members, of whatever class, all share a common set of values—the ethic of an open-class world.

In all this, however, it should be remembered that social class is but the roughest descriptive phrase for the invidious vertical aspect of society. Actually it is not class differences alone that count, but all differences describable in terms of inferiority and superiority. A person's class position offers but the first (though necessary) index of the social determinants in his life. It may be important or unimportant in his particular case, but in either event an indispensable consideration is the sequence of his invidious experiences within limited circles of association—particularly within primary groups. Yet it is precisely these relations, as well as general class factors, that (as already pointed out) have been neglected by mental hygiene.[33]

Our speculations suggest that the vertical structure and mentality are intimately related, and that a neglect of social factors is a vital neglect for the mental hygienist. We have already said that there must be, and is, a reason for such neglect. It is obviously not our view that the mental hygienist is consciously enforcing alien class standards upon unwilling members of a lower stratum. Doubtless there is a tendency to spread the middle class Protestant ethic to classes which are not middle and hence not so mobile, but this could scarcely be interpreted as class "exploitation." We believe, rather, that the mental hygienist is really enforcing, in a secular way and under the guise of science, the standards of the entire society. This leads him beyond the goal of mental health, strictly defined, and to undertake such things as increasing the efficiency of the ordinary individual and readjusting some of our (more superficial) mores. Thus the diffuseness of the mental hygiene goal is integrally related to the hygienist's actual function. Mental hygiene can plunge into evaluation, into fields the social sciences would not touch, because it possesses an implicit ethical system which, since it is that of our society, enables it to pass value judgments, to get public support, and to enjoy an unalloyed optimism. Disguising its valuational system (by means of the psychologistic position) as rational advice based on science, it can conveniently praise and condemn under the aegis of the medico-authoritarian mantle.

Few will doubt that mental hygiene has thus far been less successful in achieving the avowed goal of prevention than has the regular public health movement. Does this represent a lag which will shortly be overcome, or does it represent a circumstance inherent in the nature of the case? The latter view seems more tenable, for the following reasons.

Scientific knowledge of mental disorder requires knowledge of social determinants. But there is a social restriction upon the impersonal analysis of personal relations, and especially upon the use of knowledge thus gained. Such knowledge must be employed only for culturally prescribed ends and persons who believe in these ends. Unfortunately, if one serves and believes these cultural ends, one cannot analyze social relations objectively.[34] If this is true of an individual, it is even truer of a movement. The latter, dependent upon public enthusiasm, must inevitably adhere to ethical preconceptions. Mental hygiene hides its adherence behind a scientific façade, but the ethical premises reveal themselves on every hand, partly through a blindness to scientifically relevant facts. It cannot combine the prestige of science with the prestige of the mores, for science and the mores unavoidably conflict at some point, and the point where they most readily conflict is precisely where "mental" (i.e., social) phenomena are concerned. We can say, in other words, that devotion to the mores entails an emotional faith in illusion. Devotion to science, on the other hand, when social illusion constitutes the subject matter of that science, entails the sceptical attitude of an investigator rather than of the believer toward the illusion. In so far as the mental hygienist retains his ethical system, he misses a complete scientific analysis of his subject and hence fails to use the best technological means to his applied-science goal. But if he forswears his ethical beliefs, he is alienated from the movement and suffers the strictures of an outraged society. Actually the mental hygienist will continue to ignore the dilemma. He will continue to be unconscious of his basic preconceptions at the same time that he keeps on professing objective knowledge. He will regard his lack of preventive success as an accident, a lag, and not as an intrinsic destiny. All because his social function is not that of a scientist but that of a practising moralist in a scientific, mobile world.

SCHOOL AND SETTLEMENT HOUSE

Albert K. Cohen

ONE OF THE SITUATIONS in which children of all social levels come together and compete for status in terms of the same set of middle-class criteria and in which working-class children are most likely to be found wanting is in the school. American educators are enamored of the idea of "democracy" as a goal of the schools. An examination of their writings reveals that "democracy" signifies "the fullest realization of the individual's potentialities," "the development of skills to an optimal level," "the development of character and abilities which can be admired by others," "preparation for effective participation in the adult vocational world."[1] Despite reservations such as "with due regard to individual differences," this conception of "democratic" education implies that a major function of the schools is to "promote," "encourage," "motivate," "stimulate," in brief, *reward* middle-class ambition and conformity to middle-class expectations. However sincerely one may desire to avoid odious comparisons and to avoid, thereby, injury to the self-esteem of those who do not conform to one's expectations, it is extremely difficult to reward, however subtly, successful conformity without at the same time, by implication, condemning and punishing the non-comformist. That same teacher who prides himself on his recognition and encouragement of deserving working-class children dramatizes, by that very show of pride, the superior merit of the "college-boy" working-class child to his less gifted or "corner-boy" working-class classmates.[2]

There are three good reasons why status in the school, insofar as it depends upon recognition by the teacher, should be measured by middle-class standards.

First, the teacher is *hired* to foster the development of middle-class personalities. The middle-class board of education, the middle-class parents whom they represent and, it is to be presumed, many of the working-class parents as well expect the teacher to define his job as the indoctrination of middle-class aspirations, character, skills and manners.[3]

Second, the teacher himself is almost certain to be a middle-class person, who personally values ambition and achievement and spontaneously recognizes and rewards these virtues in others.[4]

The third relates to the school itself as a social system with certain "structural imperatives" of its own. The teacher's textbooks in education and his own supervisors may stress "individualization" and "consideration for the needs, limitations and special problems of each student." Nonetheless, the teacher actually handles 20, 30 or 40 students at a time. Regardless of what he conceives his proper function to be, he necessarily looks with favor on the quiet, cooperative, "well-behaved" pupils who make his job easier and with disapproval and vexation on the lusty, irrepressible, boisterous youngsters who are destructive of order, routine and predictability in the classroom.

Reprinted from *Delinquent Boys: The Culture of the Gang* (1955), pp. 112-20, by permission of the author and the publisher. (Copyright, 1955, by The Free Press.)

Furthermore, the teacher himself is likely to be upwardly mobile or at least anxious about the security of his tenure in his present job. He is motivated, therefore, to conform to the criteria in terms of which *his* superiors evaluate *him*. Those superiors may themselves be "progressive" and in teacher meetings preach "democracy in the classroom" and "individualization" and indeed genuinely believe in those goals. However, the degree to which a teacher tries to achieve these goals or succeeds in doing so is not highly visible and readily determined. On the other hand, grades, performance on standardized examinations, the cleanliness and orderliness of the classroom and the frequency with which children are sent to the "front office" are among the most easily determined and "objective" bases for the evaluation of teacher performance. A good "rating," then, by his supervisors is possible only if the teacher sacrifices to some degree the very "individualization" and "tolerance" which those same supervisors may urge upon him.

Research on the kinds of behavior which teachers regard as the most "problematical" among their pupils gives results consistent with our expectations.[5] The most serious problems, from the standpoint of the teacher, are those children who are restless and unruly, who fidget and squirm, who annoy and distract, who create "discipline" problems. The "good" children are the studious, the obedient, the docile. It is precisely the working-class children who are most likely to be "problems" because of their relative lack of training in order and discipline, their lack of interest in intellectual achievement and their lack of reinforcement by the home in conformity to the requirements of the school. Both in terms of "conduct" and in terms of academic achievement, the failures in the classroom are drawn disproportionately from the lower social class levels. The child has little or no choice in selecting the group within which he shall compete for status and, in the words of Troyer, he is "evaluated against the total range of the ability distribution."

It is here that, day after day, most of the children in the lower fourth of the distribution have their sense of worth destroyed, develop feelings of insecurity, become frustrated and lose confidence in their ability to learn even that which they are capable of learning.[6]

In settlement houses and other adult-sponsored and managed recreational agencies similar conflicts may often be seen between the middle-class values of the adults in charge and the working-class values of the children for whose benefit the institutions ostensibly exist. Such organizations smile upon neat, orderly, polite, personable, mannerly children who "want to make something of themselves." The sponsors, directors and group work leaders find it a pleasure to work with such children, whose values are so like their own, and make them feel welcome and respected. They do indeed feel a special responsibility toward the boy whose family and neighborhood culture have not equipped him with those values, the "rough" boy, the "dirty" boy, the "bum" who just "hangs around" with the gang on the corner, in the pool hall or in the candy store. But the responsibility they feel toward him is to encourage him to engage in more "worthwhile" activities, to join and be a "responsible" member of some "wholesome" adult-supervised club or other group, to expurgate his language and, in general, to participate in the "constructive" program of the institution. Indeed, like the school, it functions to select potentially upwardly mobile working-class children and to help and encourage them in the upward climb. It is a common experience of such organizations that they "are very successful and do a lot of good but don't seem to get the children who need them most." The reason is that here, as in the school, it is almost impossible to reward one kind of behavior without at the same time, by implication or quite openly, punishing its absence or its opposite. The corner boy, as Whyte has shown vividly and in detail,[7] quickly senses that he is under the critical or at best condescending surveillance of people who are "foreigners" to his community and who appraise him in terms of values which he does not share. He is aware that he is being invidiously compared to others; he is uncomfortable; he finds it hard to accommodate himself to the rules of the organization. To win the favor of the people in charge he must change his habits, his values, his ambitions, his speech and his associates. Even were these things possible, the game might not be worth the candle. So, having sampled what they have to offer, he returns to the street or to his "clubhouse" in a cellar where "facilities" are meager but human relations more satisfying.

Not only in terms of standards of middle-class adults but in terms of their children's standards as well, the working-class boy of working-class culture is likely to be a "failure." Despite the existence among middle-class children of a "youth culture" which may differ in significant ways from the culture of their parents, the standards these children apply are likely to relegate to an inferior status their working-class peers. Coyle quotes from a fieldworker's report:

> Gradually the group became more critical of prospective members. A process somewhat evident from the beginning became more obvious. In general only boys who measured up to the group's unwritten, unspoken and largely unconscious standards were ever considered. These standards, characteristics of their middle-class homes, required the suppression of impulsive disorderly behavior and put a high value on controlled cooperative attitudes. Hence even these normally healthy and boisterous boys were capable of rejecting schoolmates they considered too wild and boisterous. Coincident with this was an emphasis on intellectual capacity and achievement. They preferred "smart" as contrasted with "dumb" prospects. The boys seemed to use their club unconsciously to express and reinforce the standards learned in their homes and the community.[8]

Havighurst and Taba point out that not only teachers but schoolmates, in evaluating the character of other children, tend to give the highest ratings to the children of the higher social levels, although the correlation between social class and character reputation is far from perfect.[9] Positive correlations between various indices of social class status of the home and social status in the school as measured by pupils' choices have been found by Bonney and others.[10] Hollingshead has shown how social class and the behavior and personality associated with social class membership operate to determine prestige and clique and date patterns among high school boys and girls. "This process operates in all classes, but it is especially noticeable in contacts with class V [lower-lower]. This class is so repugnant socially that adolescents in the higher classes avoid clique and dating ties with its members."[11]

Furthermore, working-class children are less likely to participate, and if they participate are less likely to achieve prominence, in extra-curricular activities, which are an important arena for the competition for status in the eyes of the students themselves. In the area of organized athletics the working-class boy is perhaps least unfitted for successful competition. Even here, however, he is likely to be at a disadvantage. Adherence to a training regimen and a schedule does not come to him as easily as to the middle-class boy and, unless he chooses to loosen his ties to his working-class friends, he is likely to find some conflict between the claims of the gang and those of his athletic career. Finally, although we must not minimize the importance of athletic achievement as a status-ladder, it is, after all, granted to relatively few, of whatever social class background, to achieve conspicuously in this area.[12]

In summary, it may confidently be said that the working-class boy, particularly if his training and values be those we have here defined as working-class, is more likely than his middle-class peers to find himself at the bottom of the status hierarchy whenever he moves in a middle-class world, whether it be of adults or of children. To the degree to which he values middle-class status, either because he values the good opinion of middle-class persons or because he has to some degree internalized middle-class standards himself, he faces a problem of adjustment and is in the market for a "solution."

SECTION IV
Social Stratification

PATTERNS OF INEQUALITY, of ranking, characterize all human groups. When we consider these patterns of inequality as they are presented in a group or in aggregates of groups, we speak of a system of social stratification. Social stratification would not otherwise be of direct interest to social workers except that behavior tends to vary predictably from one rank to another in the group. In American society, for example, patterns of sexual behavior vary widely from the lower to the middle to the upper levels of the social structure. Hence we gain better perspective on the individual if we identify the sexual mores characteristic of the position in the society which he occupies. Similarly, one finds predictable variations from one position to another in the characteristics of family organization, child-rearing practices, political attitudes, mental illness, and a host of other phenomena. In other words, the position which a person occupies in the system of social stratification tends to be an important determinant of his behavior. A full appreciation of why the individual feels and acts as he does must therefore take into account influences stemming from his position in the ranking system of his society.

The way men view the world is always influenced by their social environment. This general proposition is amply illustrated by the comparison of European and American approaches to the study of social stratification. Although no method of classifying these approaches is very satisfactory, there are several broad divisions which are helpful to keep in mind. In Europe, the development of literature on social stratification was very much conditioned by the existence of stable and traditional social divisions between men. One of the most highly visible components of this social division was, of course, a great disparity in wealth and income. Consequently, it was not at all surprising that the concept of social class came to be defined in essentially economic terms. In general, social class was any aggregate of individuals who occupied the same general position in the economic structure. To measure the position which a person occupied, largely external indices were employed, such as the individual's economic function, his wealth or income, or his relation to the means of production (e.g., owner or wage-earner, etc.). These indices were independent of the individual; they did not depend on his attitudes or values, his interests or aspirations. Quite the contrary, for the European theorist — such as those in the Marxian tradition — viewed man as being the product of his environment. Hence a man's values and interests were taken to be the effects of (largely economic) forces stemming from the particular environment which characterized his position in the social structure.

If the European theorist stressed objective, external phenomena as the determinants of social position, then the reverse was so among American theorists. Here, subjective, internal phenomena were stressed. For the American student of society, attitudes and sentiments were seen as paramount in interpreting the social system. And just as their predecessors were influenced by the social climate of the Old World, the American student was conditioned by the social climate of the New World. Here there were no traditional social divisions, but only a forest wilderness from which a society was to be hewn by the dissidents and heretics who fled from the rigid social structure of Europe. Furthermore, America was in many respects a land of opportunity, a land in which talent and merit rather than social origins were to be the determinants of one's station in life. Equality of opportunity and individual achievement came to be dominant ideological themes in the social thought of American life. And whenever the possibilities of social mobility are afforded to large numbers of men, what becomes important is not the class to which one belongs but the class to which one is oriented. Conditioned by this social climate, American theorists resisted the notion of objective, external sources of social position. They looked not so much at the class into which the individual was born as to the class with which he identified. The theoretic emphasis was not placed on the discrepancies in wealth and power which separated men, even in the new-found democracy, but rather on the extraordinary diffusion of a common, democratic, and optimistic value system which seemingly bound men of many stations together and made them one. The American theorist was impressed (and perhaps overly so) by the fact that men who occupied different economic positions appeared to display many similar attitudes and values, pursued many of the same interests, and otherwise engaged in a more or less common style of life. Hence social class came to be subjectively defined; as Giddings put it, a social class was to be defined as any aggregate of individuals who exhibited "consciousness of kind." And because there was a "consciousness of kind," a sharing of the great middle-class values throughout much of our society, the American theorist tended to become preoccupied with this vast middle sector of the society rather than with the upper and lower extremes of wealth and poverty. In fact, some scholars were so impressed by the way in which a common value system had diffused throughout the social structure as to assert that here, for all practical purposes, was a classless society.

A second division in the classification of approaches to stratification emerges if we ask whether the scholar was addressing himself to the question of how the society maintains itself, or how it changes. For reasons we shall note, an interest in social change logically followed from the objective approach, while an interest in social equilibrium logically followed from the subjective approach. As suggested above, the objective approach presupposes that aggregates of men who occupy the same general position tend to think and act alike because they respond to the same environmental conditions. As these conditions change, so, presumably, do human feelings and actions. In other words, those concerned with the economic conditions of life have also tended to focus on processes of social change.

Scholars oriented to the subjective approach, however, have tended to focus more on system-maintenance or social equilibrium. These scholars have inquired about the way in which the individual fits into the status system of the society. They have asked particularly how his attitudes and actions reinforce and buttress the existing social structure. In the *Yankee City Series*—a classic set of studies of social stratification in American communities by W. Lloyd Warner and his associates—an emphasis on equilibrium is readily detectable. Where the student of social change tends to focus on social class, the student of social equilibrium tends to focus on social status. Thus, Warner examined the status system or prestige hierarchy of the American community. Although he employed some objective indices of social position (e.g., income), he gave greater priority to essentially subjective phenomena, such as the symbolic phrases which people used invidiously to locate one another (e.g., "the river rats," "solid folk but not society," "one of the 400," etc.). These essentially subjective appraisals and evaluations provide few clues to processes of social change, however; rather, they illustrate the way in which subjective definitions contribute to the equilibrium and stability of the society.

The clinician may usefully employ knowledge about both the objective and subjective approaches to social stratification. It goes without saying that a unique social environment characterizes each social class in our society. Since human beings can only assimilate culture from other human beings, knowledge of these social class environments enables us to predict the typical characteristics and problems of individuals distributed among them. It is useful to know, for example, that individuals from the lower and middle classes tend to define their problems differently. The lower-class individual typically locates the sources of his difficulties in the external environment, while the middle-class individual is more likely to assign the difficulty to problems in his personality. General predispositions of this kind are a direct consequence of socialization in one or another of our various class cultures. Yet not all individuals in the same position invariably exhibit the same subjective predispositions. Some lower-class individuals, for example, have essentially middle-class attitudes, which may be diagnostically strategic. Lower-class individuals may internalize middle-class values for a number of reasons. For some, this may occur because they interact differentially with members of the middle class—as in schools, settlement houses, and in many occupations such as chauffeurs and domestic servants. As a consequence of selectively internalizing middle-class values, problems often arise. The individual may come to be at odds with others in his immediate environment because of value differences, and this may lead to strain and alienation. Or, to cite a further problem, the individual sometimes assimilates the middle-class emphasis on upward mobility and thus develops ambitions for himself which cannot be fulfilled because he does not have access to the required educational facilities and the like. As we shall have occasion to note in the section on deviant behavior, frustrations generated by unfulfilled aspirations are an important source of personal maladjustment.

The divergence between the European and American approaches to social stratification suggests that the individual's position in the social structure may be viewed in different ways, for any position represents a composite of analytically distinct dimensions. Max Weber, a nineteenth century sociologist, enumerated three dimensions in his classic work on social stratification, and most scholars continue to find this classification useful today. Weber designated the first of these dimensions as the person's *class,* by which he meant the individual's life chances in the market-place, his access to material goods and services, his wealth and income. In other words, for Weber, class referred to the individual's economic position. Weber called the second dimension of the individual's position *status,* which means roughly the individual's ability to exact deference and homage from others. Finally, Weber suggested that every social position is characterized by some element of *power,* by which he meant the ability of the individual to realize his own will in communal action. The way in which an individual is located with respect to these three dimensions describes what is usually meant by social position; the way a whole group of people are distributed with respect to these dimensions describes what is usually meant by social stratification.

For the most part, the positions which the bulk of the people in a society occupy represent a high correlation between these three dimensions. Thus an individual who commands a high income is also likely to be both respected and influential. As it happens, however, the correlation sometimes breaks down, and this generates strains which often lead to unusual forms of behavior. One of the familiar examples of this kind is the tendency among the nouveaux riches to engage in conspicuous consumption. Although the nouveaux riches have secured wealth and power, they are not accorded respect, especially by members of the traditional elites in the society. Hence their admission to the top echelon of the society is resisted. The nouveaux riches typically respond to "prestige barriers" by consuming their wealth conspicuously—which represents an effort to dramatize their eligibility for membership in the established elites. But members of the established elites—in an effort to preserve their advantageous position—define conspicuous consumption as common and vulgar, emphasizing instead specialized modes of language and dress, the tradition of family, and the cultivation of leisure. In other words, various aspects of the behavior of the nouveaux riches may be understood as a response to the strains generated by lack of correlation between the various dimensions of their social position.

A variety of human problems encountered in social work practice also lend themselves to this kind of analysis. Take, for example, the observation among experienced practitioners that middle-class Negroes are sometimes quite rigid in their child-rearing practices, emphasizing especially impulse renunciation and sexual morality. They are, so to say, more middle class than the middle class—a condition which frequently leads to behavioral problems among their children. Several observations may be made by way of identifying the sources of these child-rearing emphases. First, the constellation of values which facilitates upward mobility in our society undoubtedly includes deferment of gratification or impulse renunciation. Since successfully mobile individuals are more likely to have developed an ability to forego immediate satisfactions in the interests of securing future goals, it is hardly surprising that they impose this value-orientation upon their children. Yet this explanation does not go far enough, for we are still confronted by the question of why whites from the lower class become upwardly mobile without the same degree of over-identification with middle-class child-rearing mores. The answer probably lies in the fact that the three dimensions of social position to which we have referred are not, in the case of the Negro, highly correlated. Although Negroes may become mobile along economic and power dimensions, they are nevertheless denied prestige or social recognition by the white society. Despite objective differences between the behavior of the middle-class Negro and that of the lower-class Negro (e.g., standards of cleanliness, language, sexual morality, etc.), the former are still defined in terms of the prevailing stereotype of the Negro (e.g., unclean, vulgar, promiscuous). These invidious cultural definitions are buttressed by the social structure: in particular, social interaction between whites and Negroes is patterned and constrained so as to prohibit access by the otherwise mobile Negro to the white middle class. And one common reaction to this lack of prestige, to this sense of not belonging and not being accepted, is over-conformity to the style of life of the white middle-class society. Furthermore, because his newly achieved position in the social structure is so precarious, the middle-class Negro is constantly fearful of becoming downwardly mobile. Consequently, he responds to these status insecurities by repudiating the mores of the lower-class Negro and by engaging increasingly in a conspicuous conformity to the mores of that stratum of society to which he aspires but cannot belong. And from the stand-point of child-rearing emphases, the point to be observed is that over-conformity is selectively exhibited in precisely those areas of conduct for which the Negro is renounced: dress, language, cleanliness, sex, and the like. By selectively over-incorporating middle-class behavioral patterns, the middle-class Negro seeks to have his status redefined, thereby permitting him to secure a more desirable position in the prestige structure of American society. Hence discrepancies in social position help to explain particular types of behavior exhibited by individuals located in different parts of the social structure.

CLASS, STATUS, PARTY

Max Weber

Economically Determined Power and the Social Order. Law exists when there is a probability that an order will be upheld by a specific staff of men who will use physical or psychical compulsion with the intention of obtaining conformity with the order, or of inflicting sanctions for infringement of it.[1] The structure of every legal order directly influences the distribution of power, economic or otherwise, within its respective community. This is true of all legal orders and not only that of the state. In general, we understand by "power" the chance of a man or of a number of men to realize their own will in a communal action even against the resistance of others who are participating in the action.

"Economically conditioned" power is not, of course, identical with "power" as such. On the contrary, the emergence of economic power may be the consequence of power existing on other grounds. Man does not strive for power only in order to enrich himself economically. Power, including economic power, may be valued "for its own sake." Very frequently the striving for power is also conditioned by the social "honor" it entails. Not all power, however, entails social honor: The typical American Boss, as well as the typical big speculator, deliberately relinquishes social honor. Quite generally, "mere economic" power, and especially "naked" money power, is by no means a recognized basis of social honor. Nor is power the only basis of social honor. Indeed, social honor, or prestige, may even be the basis of political or economic power, and very frequently has been. Power, as well as honor, may be guaranteed by the legal order, but, at least normally, it is not their primary source. The legal order is rather an additional factor that enhances the chance to hold power or honor; but it cannot always secure them.

The way in which social honor is distributed in a community between typical groups participating in this distribution we may call the "social order." The social order and the economic order are, of course, similarly related to the "legal order." However, the social and the economic order are not identical. The economic order is for us merely the way in which economic goods and services are distributed and used. The social order is of course conditioned by the economic order to a high degree, and in its turn reacts upon it.

Now: "classes," "status groups," and "parties" are phenomena of the distribution of power within a community.

Reprinted from *Max Weber: Essays in Sociology* (1946), translated by H. H. Gerth and C. Wright Mills, pp. 180-95, by permission of the translators and the publishers. (Copyright, 1946, by Oxford University Press, Inc.)

Determination of Class-Situation by Market-Situation. In our terminology, "classes" are not communities; they merely represent possible, and frequent, bases for commercial action. We may speak of a "class" when (1) a number of people have in common a specific causal component of their life chances, in so far as (2) this component is represented exclusively by economic interests in the possession of goods and opportunities for income, and (3) is represented under the conditions of the commodity or labor markets. [These points refer to "class situation," which we may express more briefly as the typical chance for a supply of goods, external living conditions, and personal life experiences, in so far as this chance is determined by the amount and kind of power, or lack of such, to dispose of goods or skills for the sake of income in a given economic order. The term "class" refers to any group of people that is found in the same class situation.]

It is the most elemental economic fact that the way in which the disposition over material property is distributed among a plurality of people, meeting competitively in the market for the purpose of exchange, in itself creates specific life chances. According to the law of marginal utility this mode of distribution excludes the non-owners from competing for highly valued goods; it favors the owners and, in fact, gives to them a monopoly to acquire such goods. Other things being equal, this mode of distribution monopolizes the opportunities for profitable deals for all those who, provided with goods, do not necessarily have to exchange them. It increases, at least generally, their power in price wars with those who, being propertyless, have nothing to offer but their services in native form or goods in a form constituted through their own labor, and who above all are compelled to get rid of these products in order barely to subsist. This mode of distribution gives to the propertied a monopoly on the possibility of transferring property from the sphere of use as a "fortune," to the sphere of "capital goods"; that is, it gives them the entrepreneurial function and all chances to share directly or indirectly in returns on capital. All this holds true within the area in which pure market conditions prevail. "Property" and "lack of property" are, therefore, the basic categories of all class situations. It does not matter whether these two categories become effective in price wars or in competitive struggles.

Within these categories, however, class situations are further differentiated: on the one hand, according to the kind of property that is usable for returns; and, on the other hand, according to the kind of services that can be offered in the market. Ownership of domestic buildings; productive establishments; warehouses; stores; agriculturally usable land, large and small holdings— quantitative differences with possibly qualitative consequences—; ownership of mines; cattle; men (slaves); disposition over mobile instruments of production, or capital goods of all sorts, especially money or objects that can be exchanged for money easily and at any time; disposition over products of one's own labor or of others' labor differing according to their various distances from consumability; disposition over transferable monopolies of any kind—all these distinctions differentiate the class situations of the propertied just as does the "meaning" which they can and do give to the utilization of property, especially to property which has money equivalence. Accordingly, the propertied, for instance, may belong to the class of rentiers or to the class of entrepreneurs.

Those who have no property but who offer services are differentiated just as much according to their kinds of services as according to the way in which they make use of these services, in a continuous or discontinuous relation to a recipient. But always this is the generic connotation of the concept of class: that the kind of chance in the *market* is the decisive moment which presents a common condition for the individual's fate. "Class situation" is, in this sense, ultimately "market situation." The effect of naked possession *per se,* which among cattle breeders gives the non-owning slave or serf into the power of the cattle owner, is only a forerunner of real "class" formation. However, in the cattle loan and in the naked severity of the law of debts in such communities, for the first time mere "possession" as such emerges as decisive for the fate of the individual. This is very much in contrast to the agricultural communities based on labor. The creditor-debtor relation becomes the basis of "class situations" only in those cities where a "credit market," however primitive, with rates of interest increasing according to the extent of dearth and a factual monopolization of credits, is developed by a plutocracy. Therewith "class struggles" begin.

Those men whose fate is not determined by the chance of using goods or services for themselves on the market, e.g., slaves, are not, however, a "class" in the technical sense of the term. They are, rather, a "status group."

Communal Action Flowing from Class Interest. According to our terminology, the factor that creates "class" is unambiguously economic interest, and indeed, only those interests involved in the existence of the "market." Nevertheless, the concept of "class-interest" is an ambiguous one: even as an empirical concept it is ambiguous as soon as one understands by it something other than the factual direction of interests following with a certain probability from the class situation for a certain "average" of those people subjected to the class situation. The class situation and other circumstances remaining the same, the direction in which the individual worker, for instance, is likely to pursue his interests may vary widely, according to whether he is constitutionally qualified for the task at hand to a high, to an average, or to a low degree. In the same way, the direction of interests may vary according to whether or not a *communal* action of a larger or smaller portion of those commonly affected by the "class situation," or even an association among them, e.g. a "trade union," has grown out of the class situation from which the individual may or may not expect promising results. [Communal action refers to that action which is oriented to the feeling of the actors that they belong together. Societal action, on the other hand, is oriented to a rationally motivated adjustment of interests.] The rise of societal or even of communal action from a common class situation is by no means a universal phenomenon.

The class situation may be restricted in its effects to the generation of essentially *similar* reactions, that is to say, within our terminology, of "mass actions." However, it may not have even this result. Furthermore, often merely an amorphous communal action emerges. For example, the "murmuring" of the workers known in ancient oriental ethics: the moral disapproval of the work-master's conduct, which in its practical significance was probably equivalent to an increasingly typical phenomenon of precisely the latest industrial development, namely, the "slow down" (the deliberate

limiting of work effort) of laborers by virtue of tacit agreement. The degree
in which "communal action," and possibly "societal action," emerges from
the "mass actions" of the members of a class is linked to general cultural
conditions, especially to those of an intellectual sort. It is also linked to the
extent of the contrasts that have already evolved, and is especially linked to
the *transparency* of the connections between the causes and the consequences
of the "class situation." For, however different life chances may be, this
fact in itself, according to all experience, by no means gives birth to "class
action" (communal action by the members of a class). The fact of being
conditioned and the results of the class situation must be distinctly recogniz-
able. For only then the contrast of life chances can be felt not as an absolutely
given fact to be accepted, but as a resultant from either (1) the given distribution of property, or (2) the structure of the concrete economic order. It is
only then that people may react against the class structure not only through
acts of an intermittent and irrational protest, but in the form of rational
association. There have been "class situations" of the first category (1), of a
specifically naked and transparent sort, in the urban centers of Antiquity and
during the Middle Ages; especially then, when great fortunes were accumulated by factually monopolized trading in industrial products of these localities
or in foodstuffs. Furthermore, under certain circumstances, in the rural
economy of the most diverse periods, agriculture was increasingly exploited
in a profit-making manner. The most important historical example of the
second category (2) is the class situation of the modern "proletariat."

Types of "Class Struggle." Thus every class may be the carrier of any
one of the possibly innumerable forms of "class action," but this is not
necessarily so. In any case, a class does not in itself constitute a community.
To treat "class" conceptually as having the same value as "community" leads
to distortion. That men in the same class situation regularly react in mass
actions to such tangible situations as economic ones in the direction of those
interests that are most adequate to their average number is an important and
after all simple fact for the understanding of historical events. Above all, this
fact must not lead to that kind of pseudo-scientific operation with the concepts
of "class" and "class interests" so frequently found these days, and which has
found its most classic expression in the statement of a talented author, that
the individual may be in error concerning his interests but that the "class" is
"infallible" about its interests. Yet, if classes as such are not communities,
nevertheless class situations emerge only on the basis of communalization.
The communal action that brings forth class situations, however, is not
basically action between members of the identical class; it is an action between
members of different classes. Communal actions that directly determine the
class situation of the worker and the entrepreneur are: the labor market, the
commodities market, and the capitalistic enterprise. But, in its turn, the
existence of a capitalistic enterprise presupposes that a very specific communal
action exists and that it is specifically structured to protect the possession
of goods *per se,* and especially the power of individuals to dispose, in principle
freely, over the means of production. The existence of a capitalistic enterprise
is preconditioned by a specific kind of "legal order." Each kind of class
situation, and above all when it rests upon the power of property *per se,*
will become most clearly efficacious when all other determinants of reciprocal

relations are, as far as possible, eliminated in their significance. It is in this way that the utilization of the power of property in the market obtains its most sovereign importance.

Now "status groups" hinder the strict carrying through of the sheer market principle. In the present context they are of interest to us only from this one point of view. Before we briefly consider them, note that not much of a general nature can be said about the more specific kinds of antagonism between "classes" (in our meaning of the term). The great shift, which has been going on continuously in the past, and up to our times, may be summarized, although at the cost of some precision: the struggle in which class situations are effective has progressively shifted from consumption credit toward, first, competitive struggles in the commodity market and, then, toward price wars on the labor market. The "class struggles" of Antiquity—to the extent that they were genuine class struggles and not struggles between status groups—were initially carried on by indebted peasants, and perhaps also by artisans threatened by debt bondage and struggling against urban creditors. For debt bondage is the normal result of the differentiation of wealth in commercial cities, especially in seaport cities. A similar situation has existed among cattle breeders. Debt relationships as such produced class action up to the time of Cataline. Along with this, and with an increase in provision of grain for the city by transporting it from the outside, the struggle over the means of sustenance emerged. It centered in the first place around the provision of bread and the determination of the price of bread. It lasted throughout antiquity and the entire Middle Ages. The propertyless as such flocked together against those who actually and supposedly were interested in the dearth of bread. This fight spread until it involved all those commodities essential to the way of life and to handicraft production. There were only incipient discussions of wage disputes in antiquity and in the Middle Ages. But they have been slowly increasing up into modern times. In the earlier periods they were completely secondary to slave rebellions as well as to fights in the commodity market.

The propertyless of Antiquity and of the Middle Ages protested against monopolies, pre-emption, forestalling, and the withholding of goods from the market in order to raise prices. Today the central issue is the determination of the price of labor.

This transition is represented by the fight for access to the market and for the determination of the price of products. Such fights went on between merchants and workers in the putting-out system of domestic handicraft during the transition to modern times. Since it is quite a general phenomenon we must mention here that the class antagonisms that are conditioned through the market situation are usually most bitter between those who actually and directly participate as opponents in price wars. It is not the rentier, the shareholder, and the banker who suffer the ill will of the worker, but almost exclusively the manufacturer and the business executives who are the direct opponents of workers in price wars. This is so in spite of the fact that it is precisely the cash boxes of the rentier, the share-holder, and the banker into which the more or less "unearned" gains flow, rather than into the pockets of the manufacturers or of the business executives. This simple state of affairs has very frequently been decisive for the role the class situation has played in the formation of political parties. For example, it has made possible the varieties of patriarchal socialism and the frequent attempts—formerly, at least —of threatened status groups to form alliances with the proletariat against the "bourgeoisie."

Status Honor. In contrast to classes, *status groups* are normally communities. They are, however, often of an amorphous kind. In contrast to the purely economically determined "class situation" we wish to designate as "status situation" every typical component of the life fate of men that is determined by a specific, positive or negative, social estimation of *honor*. This honor may be connected with any quality shared by a plurality, and, of course, it can be knit to a class situation: class distinctions are linked in the most varied ways with status distinctions. Property as such is not always recognized as a status qualification, but in the long run it is, and with extraordinary regularity. In the subsistence economy of the organized neighborhood, very often the richest man is simply the chieftain. However, this often means only an honorific preference. For example, in the so-called pure modern "democracy," that is, one devoid of any expressly ordered status privileges for individuals, it may be that only the families coming under approximately the same tax class dance with one another. This example is reported of certain smaller Swiss cities. But status honor need not necessarily be linked with a "class situation." On the contrary, it normally stands in sharp opposition to the pretensions of sheer property.

Both propertied and propertyless people can belong to the same status group, and frequently they do with very tangible consequences. This "equality" of social esteem may, however, in the long run become quite precarious. The "equality" of status among the American "gentlemen," for instance, is expressed by the fact that outside the subordination determined by the different functions of "business," it would be considered strictly repugnant—wherever the old tradition still prevails—if even the richest "chief," while playing billiards or cards in his club in the evening, would not treat his "clerk" as in every sense fully his equal in birthright. It would be repugnant if the American "chief" would bestow upon his "clerk" the condescending "benevolence" marking a distinction of "position," which the German chief can never dissever from his attitude. This is one of the most important reasons why in America the German "clubbyness" has never been able to attain the attraction that the American clubs have.

Guarantees of Status Stratification. In content, status honor is normally expressed by the fact that above all else a specific *style of life* can be expected from all those who wish to belong to the circle. Linked with this expectation are restrictions on "social" intercourse (that is, intercourse which is not subservient to economic or any other of business's "functional" purposes). These restrictions may confine normal marriages to within the status circle and may lead to complete endogamous closure. As soon as there is not a mere individual and socially irrelevant imitation of another style of life, but an agreed-upon communal action of this closing character, the "status" development is under way.

In its characteristic form, stratification by "status groups" on the basis of conventional styles of life evolves at the present time in the United States out of the traditional democracy. For example, only the resident of a certain street ("the street") is considered as belonging to "society," is qualified for social intercourse, and is visited and invited. Above all, this differentiation evolves in such a way as to make for strict submission to the fashion that is dominant at a given time in society. This submission to fashion also exists among men in America to a degree unknown in Germany. Such submission is considered to be an indication of the fact that a given man *pretends* to qualify as a gentleman. This submission decides, at least *prima facie,* that he will be treated as such. And this recognition becomes just as important for his employment chances in "swank" establishments, and above all, for social intercourse and marriage with "esteemed" families, as the qualification for dueling among Germans in the Kaiser's day. As for the rest: certain families resident for a long time, and, of course, correspondingly wealthy, e.g. "F. F. V., i.e. First Families of Virginia," or the actual or alleged descendants of the "Indian Princess" Pocahontas, of the Pilgrim fathers, or of the Knickerbockers, the members of almost inaccessible sects and all sorts of circles setting themselves apart by means of any other characteristics and badges . . . all these elements usurp "status" honor. The development of status is essentially a question of stratification resting upon usurpation. Such usurpation is the normal origin of almost all status honor. But the road from this purely conventional situation to legal privilege, positive or negative, is easily traveled as soon as certain stratification of the social order has in fact been "lived in" and has achieved stability by virtue of a stable distribution of economic power.

"Ethnic" Segregation and "Caste." Where the consequences have been realized to their full extent, the status group evolves into a closed "caste." Status distinctions are then guaranteed not merely by conventions and laws, but also by *rituals.* This occurs in such a way that every physical contact with a member of any caste that is considered to be "lower" by the members of a "higher" caste is considered as making for a ritualistic impurity and to be a stigma which must be expiated by a religious act. Individual castes develop quite distinct cults and gods.

In general, however, the status structure reaches such extreme consequences only where there are underlying differences which are held to be "ethnic." The "caste" is, indeed, the normal form in which ethnic communities usually live side by side in a "societalized" manner. These ethnic communities believe in blood relationship and exclude exogamous marriage and social intercourse. Such a caste situation is part of the phenomenon of "pariah" peoples and is found all over the world. These people form communities, acquire specific occupational traditions of handicrafts or of other arts, and cultivate a belief in their ethnic community. They live in a "diaspora" strictly segregated from all personal intercourse, except that of an unavoidable sort, and their situation is legally precarious. Yet, by virtue of their economic indispensability, they are tolerated, indeed, frequently privileged, and they live in interspersed political communities. The Jews are the most impressive historical example.

A "status" segregation grown into a "caste" differs in its structure from a mere "ethnic" segregation: the caste structure transforms the horizontal and unconnected coexistences of ethnically segregated groups into a vertical social system of super- and subordination. Correctly formulated: a comprehensive societalization integrates the ethnically divided communities into specific political and communal action. In their consequences they differ precisely in this way: ethnic coexistences condition a mutual repulsion and disdain but allow each ethnic community to consider its own honor as the highest one; the caste structure brings about a social subordination and an acknowledgment of "more honor" in favor of the privileged caste and status groups. This is due to the fact that in the caste structure ethnic distinctions as such have become "functional" distinctions within the political societaliza- tion (warriors, priests, artisans that are politically important for war and for building, and so on). But even pariah people who are most despised are usually apt to continue cultivating in some manner that which is equally peculiar to ethnic and to status communities: the belief in their own specific "honor." This is the case with the Jews.

Only with the negatively privileged status groups does the "sense of dignity" take a specific deviation. A sense of dignity is the precipitation in individuals of social honor and of conventional demands which a positively privileged status group raises for the deportment of its members. The sense of dignity that characterizes positively privileged status groups is naturally related to their "being" which does not transcend itself, that is, it is to their "beauty and excellence." Their kingdom is "of this world." They live for the present and by exploiting their great past. The sense of dignity of the nega- tively privileged strata naturally refers to a future lying beyond the present, whether it is of this life or of another. In other words, it must be nurtured by the belief in a providential "mission" and by a belief in a specific honor before God. The "chosen people's" dignity is nurtured by a belief either that in the beyond "the last will be the first," or that in this life a Messiah will appear to bring forth into the light of the world which has cast them out the hidden honor of the pariah people. This simple state of affairs, and not the "resentment" which is so strongly emphasized in Nietzsche's much admired construction in the *Genealogy of Morals,* is the source of the religiosity cul- tivated by pariah status groups. In passing, we may note that resentment may be accurately applied only to a limited extent; for one of Nietzsche's main examples, Buddhism, it is not at all applicable.

Incidentally, the development of status groups from ethnic segregations is by no means the normal phenomenon. On the contrary, since objective "racial differences" are by no means basic to every subjective sentiment of an ethnic community, the ultimately racial foundation of status structure is rightly and absolutely a question of the concrete individual case. Very frequently a status group is instrumental in the production of a thoroughbred anthro- pological type. Certainly a status group is to a high degree effective in producing extreme types, for they select personally qualified individuals (e.g. the Knighthood selects those who are fit for warfare, physically and psychi- cally). But selection is far from being the only, or the predominant, way in which status groups are formed: Political membership or class situation has at all times been at least as frequently decisive. And today the class situation is by far the predominant factor, for of course the possibility of a style of life expected for members of a status group is usually conditioned eco- nomically.

Status Privileges. For all practical purposes, stratification by status goes

hand in hand with a monopolization of ideal and material goods or opportunities, in a manner we have come to know as typical. Besides the specific
status honor, which always rests upon distance and exclusiveness, we find all
sorts of material monopolies. Such honorific preferences may consist of the
privilege of wearing special costumes, of eating special dishes taboo to others,
of carrying arms—which is most obvious in its consequences—the right to
pursue certain non-professional dilettante artistic practices, e.g. to play certain
musical instruments. Of course, material monopolies provide the most effective motives for the exclusiveness of a status group; although, in themselves,
they are rarely sufficient, almost always they come into play to some extent.
Within a status circle there is the question of intermarriage: the interest of
the families in the monopolization of potential bridegrooms is at least of
equal importance and is parallel to the interest in the monopolization of
daughters. The daughters of the circle must be provided for. With an increased inclosure of the status group, the conventional preferential opportunities for special employment grow into a legal monopoly of special offices
for the members. Certain goods become objects for monopolization by status
groups. In the typical fashion these include "entailed estates" and frequently
also the possessions of serfs or bondsmen and, finally, special trades. This
monopolization occurs positively when the status group is exclusively entitled to own and to manage them; and negatively when, in order to maintain
its specific ways of life, the status group must *not* own and manage them.

The decisive role of a "style of life" in status "honor" means that status
groups are the specific bearers of all "conventions." In whatever way it may
be manifest, all "stylization" of life either originates in status groups or is
at least conserved by them. Even if the principles of status conventions differ
greatly, they reveal certain typical traits, especially among those strata which
are most privileged. Quite generally, among privileged status groups there is
a status disqualification that operates against the performance of common
physical labor. This disqualification is now "setting in" in America against
the old tradition of esteem for labor. Very frequently every rational economic
pursuit, and especially "entrepreneurial activity," is looked upon as a disqualification of status. Artistic and literary activity is also considered as degrading
work as soon as it is exploited for income, or at least when it is connected
with hard physical exertion. An example is the sculptor working like a mason
in his dusty smock as over against the painter in his salon-like "studio" and
those forms of musical practice that are acceptable to the status group.

Economic Condition and Effects of Status Stratification. The frequent
disqualification of the gainfully employed as such is a direct result of the principle of status stratification peculiar to the social order, and of course, of this
principle's opposition to a distribution of power which is regulated exclusively
through the market. These two factors operate along with various individual
ones, which will be touched upon below.

We have seen above that the market and its processes "knows no personal
distinctions": "functional" interests dominate it. It knows nothing of "honor."
The status order means precisely the reverse, viz.: stratification in terms of
"honor" and of styles of life peculiar to status groups as such. If mere economic acquisition and naked economic power still bearing the stigma of its
extra-status origin could bestow upon anyone who has won it the same

honor as those who are interested in status by virtue of style of life claim for themselves, the status order would be threatened at its very root. This is the more so as, given equality of status honor, property *per se* represents an addition even if it is not overtly acknowledged to be such. Yet if such economic acquisition and power gave the agent any honor at all, his wealth would result in his attaining more honor than those who successfully claim honor by virtue of style of life. Therefore all groups having interests in the status order react with special sharpness precisely against the pretensions of purely economic acquisition. In most cases they react the more vigorously the more they feel themselves threatened. Calderon's respectful treatment of the peasant, for instance, as opposed to Shakespeare's simultaneous and ostensible disdain of the *canaille* illustrates the different way in which a firmly structured status order reacts as compared with a status order that has become economically precarious. This is an example of a state of affairs that recurs everywhere. Precisely because of the rigorous reactions against the claims of property *per se,* the "parvenu" is never accepted, personally and without reservation, by the privileged status groups, no matter how completely his style of life has been adjusted to theirs. They will only accept his descendants who have been educated in the conventions of their status group and who have never besmirched its honor by their own economic labor.

As to the general *effect* of the status order, only one consequence can be stated, but it is a very important one; the hindrance of the free development of the market occurs first for those goods which status groups directly withheld from free exchange by monopolization. This monopolization may be effected either legally or conventionally. For example, in many Hellenic cities during the epoch of status groups, and also originally in Rome, the inherited estate (as is shown by the old formula for indiction against spendthrifts) was monopolized just as were the estates of knights, peasants, priests, and especially the clientele of the craft and merchant guilds. The market is restricted, and the power of naked property *per se,* which gives its stamp to "class formation," is pushed into the background. The results of this process can be most varied. Of course, they do not necessarily weaken the contrasts in the economic situation. Frequently they strengthen these contrasts, and in any case, where stratification by status permeates a community as strongly as was the case in all political communities of antiquity and of the Middle Ages, one can never speak of a genuinely free market competition as we understand it today. There are wider effects than this direct exclusion of special goods from the market. From the contrariety between the status order and the purely economic order mentioned above, it follows that in most instances the notion of honor peculiar to status absolutely abhors that which is essential to the market: higgling. Honor abhors higgling among peers and occasionally it taboos higgling for the members of a status group in general. Therefore, everywhere some status groups, and usually the most influential, consider almost any kind of overt participation in economic acquisition as absolutely stigmatizing.

With some over-simplification, one might thus say that "classes" are stratified according to their relations to the production and acquisition of goods; whereas "status groups" are stratified according to the principles of their *consumption* of goods as represented by special "styles of life."

An "occupational group" is also a status group. For normally, it successfully claims social honor only by virtue of the special style of life which may be determined by it. The differences between classes and status groups frequently overlap. It is precisely those status communities most strictly segregated in terms of honor (viz. the Indian castes) who today show, although within very rigid limits, a relatively high degree of indifference to pecuniary income. However, the Brahmins seek such income in many different ways.

As to the general economic conditions making for the predominance of stratification by "status," only very little can be said. When the bases of the acquisition and distribution of goods are relatively stable, stratification by status is favored. Every technological repercussion and economic transformation threatens stratification by status and pushes the class situation into the foreground. Epochs and countries in which the naked class situation is of predominant significance are regularly the periods of technical and economic transformations. And every slowing down of the shifting of economic stratifications leads, in due course, to the growth of status structures and makes for a resuscitation of the important role of social honor.

Parties. Whereas the genuine place of "classes" is within the economic order, the place of "status groups" is within the social order, that is, within the sphere of the distribution of "honor." From within these spheres, classes and status groups influence one another and they influence the legal order and are in turn influenced by it. But "parties" live in a house of "power."

Their action is oriented toward the acquisition of social "power," that is to say, toward influencing a communal action no matter what its content may be. In principle, parties may exist in a social "club" as well as in a "state." As over against the actions of classes and status groups, for which this is not necessarily the case, the communal actions of "parties" always mean a societalization. For party actions are always directed toward a goal which is striven for in planned manner. This goal may be a "cause" (the party may aim at realizing a program for ideal or material purposes), or the goal may be "personal" (sinecures, power, and from these, honor for the leader and the followers of the party). Usually the party action aims at all these simultaneously. Parties are, therefore, only possible within communities that are societalized, that is, which have some rational order and a staff of persons available who are ready to enforce it. For parties aim precisely at influencing this staff, and if possible, to recruit it from party followers.

In any individual case, parties may represent interests determined through "class situation" or "status situation," and they may recruit their following respectively from one or the other. But they need be neither purely "class" nor purely "status" parties. In most cases they are partly class parties and partly status parties, but sometimes they are neither. They may represent ephemeral or enduring structures. Their means of attaining power may be quite varied, ranging from naked violence of any sort to canvassing for votes with coarse or subtle means: money, social influence, the force of speech, suggestion, clumsy hoax, and so on to the rougher or more artful tactics of obstruction in parliamentary bodies.

The sociological structure of parties differs in a basic way according to the kind of communal action which they struggle to influence. Parties also differ according to whether or not the community is stratified by status or by classes.

Above all else, they vary according to the structure of domination within the community. For their leaders normally deal with the conquest of a community. They are, in the general concept which is maintained here, not only products of specially modern forms of domination. We shall also designate as parties the ancient and medieval "parties" despite the fact that their structure differs basically from the structure of modern parties. By virtue of these structural differences of domination it is impossible to say anything about the structure of parties without discussing the structural forms of social domination *per se*. Parties, which are always structures struggling for domination, are very frequently organized in a very strict "authoritarian" fashion. . . .

Concerning "classes," "status groups," and "parties," it must be said in general that they necessarily presuppose a comprehensive societalization, and especially a political framework of communal action, within which they operate. This does not mean that parties would be confined by the frontiers of any individual political community. On the contrary, at all times it has been the order of the day that the societalization (even when it aims at the use of military force in common) reaches beyond the frontiers of politics. This has been the case in the solidarity of interests among the Oligarchs and among the democrats in Hellas, among the Guelfs and among Ghibellines in the Middle Ages, and within the Calvinist party during the period of religious struggles. It has been the case up to the solidarity of the landlords (international congress of agrarian landlords), and has continued among princes (holy alliance, Karlsbad decrees), socialist workers, conservatives (the longing of Prussian conservatives for Russian intervention in 1850). But their aim is not necessarily the establishment of new international political, i.e. *territorial,* dominion. In the main they aim to influence the existing dominion.[2]

THE WARNER APPROACH TO
SOCIAL STRATIFICATION

Ruth Rosner Kornhauser

Introduction. In the past two decades investigations in the area of social stratification have increased considerably.[1] Among the most prolific contributors to this burgeoning field have been W. Lloyd Warner and his associates. Three community surveys were conducted with the purpose of showing the operation of the system of stratification throughout the entire community; in addition, there have been numerous smaller studies directed by Warner or his associates on special aspects of social stratification. The primary object of this paper is to present a summary of the major research findings and the conceptual apparatus of the Warner approach.

Inquiries into the nature of social stratification have been characterized by a diversity of theoretical orientations and research methods, and by conflicting interpretations of previously existing or currently reported data. Consequently, the efforts of students of this subject have met with varying appraisals. It is particularly in the criticisms leveled at any given approach that the main problems of investigation and analysis are made apparent. Therefore, the secondary object of this paper is to present a brief summary of the critical reactions to the Warner publications.

General Orientation. Warner was trained as a social anthropologist, and his earliest research was a study of a group of primitive tribes in Australia. In his subsequent research on modern communities Warner utilized the "anthropological approach," in which the investigator attempts to delineate the culture and social structure of an entire society. The first Warner study of the social system of a modern community was planned in collaboration with Elton Mayo. Mayo and his associates, in their researches on the relationships and behavior of factory personnel, came to the realization that psychological and social factors arising from the web of social relations in which workers participated outside the factory were important in determining their in-plant behavior. This provided the impetus for Warner's initial effort to study an American community. The research, therefore, was at first conceived as an attempt to ascertain the social organization of an entire community, in the social anthropological manner, in order thereby to place the factory in the context of the total social system.[2]

Warner analyzes the social organization of a community in terms of its constituent sub-groupings, each of which is called a social structure. The social structures in contemporary communities are the family, the clique, voluntary associations, classes, castes, the school, the church, economic institutions, the political organization, and age and sex groupings. It is

Reprinted from *Class, Status and Power* (1953), Reinhard Bendix and Seymour M. Lipset, eds., pp. 224-55, by permission of the author, the editors, and the publisher. (Copyright, 1953, by The Free Press.)

asserted that all societies "place emphasis on one structure which gives form to the total society and integrates the other structures into a social unity."[3] In some primitive societies the fundamental or integrative structure is the kinship system; in others it is the age grades and sex divisions. Membership in a kinship unit, age grades, and sex divisions, however, provide only some of the bases upon which the members of a society may be stratified. Social stratification refers to any system of ranked statuses by which all the members of a society are placed in superior and inferior positions. Besides kinship and age and sex typing, various other criteria, such as economic position, power, and so on, may provide the bases of stratification in any given society. In American society the investigators initially felt that the "fundamental structure" ultimately lay in the economic order, and in this way they were led to a consideration of class as the basic ordering mechanism in social relations. Warner and Lunt accordingly began their investigations with the view that class was largely determined by economic factors:

> Most of the several hypotheses . . . were subsumed under a general economic interpretation of human behavior in our society. It was believed that the fundamental structure of our society, that which ultimately controls and dominates the thinking and actions of our people, is economic, and that the most vital and far-reaching value systems which motivate Americans are to be ultimately traced to an economic order.[4]

At first the interview data appeared to confirm this view:

> Our first interviews tended to sustain . . . [the original] hypothesis. They were filled with references to the "big people with money" and "the little people who were poor." They assigned people high status by referring to them as bankers, large property owners, people of high salary, and professional men, or they placed people in a low status by calling them laborers, ditchdiggers, and low-wage earners. Other similar economic terms were used, all designating superior and inferior positions.[5]

However, as the interviewing progressed, it was found that while informants viewed money and occupation as very important in ranking people in superior and inferior positions, these were not the *only* factors used in ranking and did not in themselves guarantee a certain social position. These other findings, then, did not support the initial formulation:

> . . . certain groups . . . were at the bottom of the social order, yet many of the members of these groups were making an income which was considerably more than that made by people whom our informants placed far higher in the social scale.[6]

Consequently, the "simple economic hypothesis" was abandoned:

> An analysis of comparative wealth and occupational status in relation to all other factors in the total social participation of the individuals we studied demonstrated that, while occupation and wealth could and did contribute greatly to the rank-status of an individual, they were but two of many factors which decided a man's ranking in the whole community. For example, a banker was never at

the bottom of the society, and none in fact fell below the middle class, but he was not always at the top. Great wealth did not guarantee the highest social position. Something more was necessary.[7]

Warner then adopted a different view of class and eventually was led to pose his changed conception of class as an alternative to what he identified as the Marxian formulation:

> There is fundamental disagreement among theorists about how strongly social stratification is dependent upon the economic and technological base. Karl Marx and his followers insist our class system and ideology are phenomena of a capitalism base. . . . Other writers, admitting economic determinism, argue that class is a multi-factored phenomenon. The present writers belong to the second group.[8]

The definition of class Warner finally decided on was therefore designed to encompass the effects of *whatever* factors the members of a society use to rank each other in an over-all prestige hierarchy. Class, then, refers to "two or more orders of people who are believed to be, and are accordingly ranked by all members of the community, in socially superior and inferior positions."[9] The layer of equally ranked statuses which comprises a class cross-cuts the entire society; that is, in contrast to segmental hierarchies, like, for example, a church hierarchy, which ranks only *some* of the members of a society, a class hierarchy is an *inclusive* hierarchy which ranks *all* the members of a society into a vertical series of horizontal layers.[10] In such a system children are born into the same class as their parents, but mobility up or down the class hierarchy is possible. While marriage normally occurs between members of the same class, out-marriage is permissible. Finally, a "class society distributes rights and privileges, duties and obligations, unequally among its superior and inferior grades."[11]

As a result of the general orientation embodied in this conceptualization of class. there emerge in Warner's work three main emphases. (1) Warner takes an essentially subjective approach to the study of class. Though reflecting the operation of both subjective and objective factors in stratification, Warner's definition of class emphasizes the subjective factors, for it is concerned with the ratings the members of a society themselves give to each other. These ratings are "subjective" in that they are based on values, attitudes, and beliefs which determine what positions and behaviors in a society will be deemed prestigeful. When investigators use an "objective" definition or mode of determining class, all persons occupying the same position along a selected scale are placed by the investigator in the same category, regardless of the way that position is ranked by the members of the society. In the Warner scheme it is not the objective position a person occupies on an occupation or income scale, for example, that is being ranked; it is the way that position is *evaluated* by the members of the society and the way in which the person occupying that position behaves in other ways as well, that is being ranked. (2) Warner has been concerned primarily with the prestige dimension of stratification. Inquiries on the nature of class have tended to divide along two lines. Some investigators have been concerned with the ways in which persons occupying given socio-economic positions tend to exercise power in the economic and political realms in accordance with their interests. Others have investigated the ways in which the system of prestige ranks is organized. Warner's effort is mainly of the second type, for the "strata are ranked upon the basis of their prestige value in the thinking of the inhabitants of the community."[12] Thus he describes the ways in which people are accorded status in terms of the standards by which the members of a society rate different styles of life. (3) This way of defining class and the mode of procedure used to arrive at this conception of class have led Warner to claim that the classes he describes are empirically existing entities. Some sociologists have employed the notion of class as a hypothetical construct, in order to investigate the effects of a specified type of hierarchy. In the latter usage, the purpose is to ascertain the consequences of similarities and differences in socio-economic status regardless of whether or not people are aware of those consequences and regardless of whether or not people similarly situated with respect to the designated criteria exist as a concrete group in the society. Warner, on the other hand, claims that because he describes classes in terms of the way people themselves think of class, and because he assigns individuals to a class in terms of the way the members of the society themselves make assignments, the classes he describes are not constructs but actually existing entities. Thus Warner states: "We worked out empirically, by direct observation . . . the existence of six stratified social classes."[13] Warner, therefore, insists that

. . . these social levels are not categories invented by social scientists to help explain what they have to say; they are groups recognized by the people of the community as being higher or lower in the life of the city. The social scientist, when he hears that certain groups are superior or inferior, records what he hears and observes. . . . The designations of social levels are distinctions made by the people themselves in referring to each other.[14]

Method. Warner and his colleagues studied the class structure of three communities: Yankee City,[15] a New England town of about 17,000 population; Old City,[16] a Southern town of about 10,000 population; and Jonesville[17] (also called Elmtown, Prairie City, and Hometown in the several publications reporting the research), a Midwestern town of about 6,000 population.

The original intention had been to study the area around Chicago in which the Western Electric factory under investigation by Mayo and his students was located. This notion was abandoned because "these districts seemed to be disorganized; they had a social organization which was highly disfunctional, if not in partial disintegration."[18] Instead, it was decided to choose a community "with a social organization which had developed over a long period of time under the domination of a single group with a coherent tradition."[19] On the basis of this criterion the communities in New England and the South were chosen. More specifically, the town of Yankee City was chosen because it was a "well-integrated community" with a minimum of conflict relations and exhibited a social organization in which "the relations of the various members of the society [were] exactly placed and known by the individuals who made up the group."[20] It was predominantly old American but nevertheless contained a number of ethnic groups, and it contained a few industries and factories. In the choice of Jonesville various criteria of a similar sort were used to insure that Jonesville was a "typical" American community.[21] On this basis Warner asserts that the cities studied were "made to serve as a microcosmic whole, representing the total American community."[22]

In the earlier studies of Yankee City and Old City the exact method by which the investigators placed individuals in the social class hierarchy is not recorded. In the interviews it was noted that people used various terms for designating individuals who were their equals and other terms for those who were above or below them in status. In placing people in the class system, respondents referred to an individual's place of residence, the kinds of people with whom he was in intimate association, the clubs and associations he joined, and such characteristics as income, education, and occupation. Consequently, the investigators used all these kinds of data to determine an individual's social class.[23] The manner in which these factors were combined is not specified; the authors simply state that they were used:

> With the use of all structural participation [i.e., family, clique, and associational membership], and with the aid of such additional testimony as the area lived in, the type of house, kind of education, manners, and other symbols of class it was possible to determine very quickly the approximate place of any individual in the society. In the final analysis, however, individuals were placed by the evaluations of the members of Yankee City itself, e.g., by such explicit statements as "she does not belong" or "they belong to our club."[24]

In the study of Jonesville two methods for determining social class were developed. These are called the method of evaluated participation (E.P.) and the index of status characteristics (I.S.C.). The method of evaluated participation is based on the proposition that the kinds of participations an individual has in both formal and informal groups or in various areas of activity are known and evaluated by the people who know him. These activities and groups are themselves ranked. Members of the community are "explicitly or implicitly aware of the ranking and translate their evaluations of such social participation into social-class ratings that can be communicated to the investigator."[25] The method of E.P. is comprised of several subsidiary rating techniques, called rating by matched agreements, by symbolic placement, by status reputation, by comparison, by simple assignment to a class, and by institutional membership. These techniques are used to order interview data provided by a panel of informants who supply the investigator with evaluations of other individuals' participations, on the basis of which the latter are ranked. To illustrate: in the technique called rating by matched agreements, the investigator secures from the several informants on the panel a list of the named social classes recognized by each. For example, in the Jonesville study one panel member who was a professional man named the following categories during the course of the interviews: "the society class" or "the 400 class," "the fringe of society," "the upper-middle class," "the working class," and the "lulus"; another panel member who was a mill worker viewed the class hierarchy as being divided into three groups: a top group composed of powerful landowners, wealthy industrialists, and professional people, a second level of ordinary, poor people like himself, and a third group of people poorer than himself.[26] The class system of the community is then established by assembling the various designations of status levels supplied by all the panel members, and "comparing" and "aligning" them until one over-all picture of the class hierarchy emerges. Then the investigator secures the names of individual persons known to the informant, who places them in one or another of the rank orders he has mentioned. When it has been ascertained that the rank orders (i.e., the social class categories) used by the different informants are similar, the interviews are examined to see which names appear in two or more interviews. It is then possible for the investigator to count the pairs of agreements among the informants about the class positions of various people in the community. When there is a high degree of agreement among informants, the social class position of the individuals concerned has been determined. In another of the techniques, symbolic placement, the symbols used by an informant in referring to another individual (as, e.g., "he comes from the wrong side of the tracks") are noted and used by the analyst to determine social class placement. A combination of all or many of the subsidiary techniques is used to ascertain the class composition of a community.

The index of status characteristics is the sum of weighted sub-indices of occupation, source of income, house type, and dwelling area. Each of these four characteristics is rated on a seven-point scale; then each rating is assigned a weight (based on the importance of each status characteristic in social class prediction) and the four weighted ratings are totaled. Several methods are then given for converting the I.S.C. score into its social class equivalent. Two of these methods require the investigator to ascertain the E.P. ratings for some individuals in the community he is studying; the third employs a conversion scale based on E.P. data for Jonesville.[27] The I.S.C. is apparently not simply an index of "objective" characteristics, for the authors state that "it is not the house, or the job, or the income, or the neighborhood that is being measured so much as the evaluations that are in the backs of all of our heads."[28] That is, the ratings for each sub-index of the I.S.C. are determined according to the prestige value of that type of item in the community. The I.S.C. was found to correlate at .97 with class rating based on E.P. rankings for 209 old American families in Jonesville.[29] The corresponding correlation coefficients for samples of various ethnic groups were considerably lower.[30]

The System of Social Classes. As portrayed by Warner, the unequally ranked social levels called classes are distinguished from each other in two principal ways. On the one hand each social class has a distinct style of life; it is this style of life which is the object of ranking by the members of the community. Style of life includes objective factors like occupational position and income and subjective factors like values and attitudes. It is perhaps most clearly exemplified in activities which reveal the taste patterns of individuals; hence the consumption patterns, family rituals, and leisure time activities of the several classes provide good evidence of their different styles of life. A second and equally crucial mark of a class system is the way in which it limits and is an expression of social participation. Davis and the Gardners state that

. . . a "social class" is to be thought of as the largest group of people whose members have intimate access to one another. A class is composed of families and social cliques. The interrelationships between these families and cliques, in such informal activities as visiting, dances, receptions, teas, and larger informal affairs, constitute the structure of a social class. A person is a member of that social class with which most of his participations, of this intimate kind, occur.[31]

In the communities studied, either five or six social classes were distinguished. These are called the upper-upper, lower-upper, upper-middle, lower-middle, upper-lower and lower-lower classes. In Yankee City and in Old City there are reported to be six classes, for these regions are sufficiently old to have developed differentiation between "old" and "new" families within the upper class. In the smaller and more recently settled midwestern community (Jonesville), no distinction between the upper-upper and lower-upper classes is made. Hence this town exhibited only five class levels.

The upper-upper class is an "aristocracy of birth and wealth." It is made up of "old families" who can "trace their lineage through many generations participating in a way of life characteristic of the upper class" and whose wealth has been inherited through several generations.[32] The members of this class consequently display a minute interest in and knowledge of genealogies and take great pride in their distinguished ancestry. Upper-upper class people tend to be closely inter-married and hence are frequently related to each other in complicated kinship ties; even when this is not the case, they often symbolically extend the kinship system to include all or a large portion of other upper-upper class members.[33] Skilled in ritual behavior and intricate codes of etiquette, the upper-upper class members are the social arbiters of the community.

The lower-upper class is similar in many respects to the upper-upper class. They both live in large, expensive houses in exclusive residential sections[34] and have similar patterns of participation in associations and informal social life.[35] They are found to have similar occupations (as financiers, industrialists, members of the higher professions).[36] But they are crucially lacking in ancestry, for the lower-upper class members are *parvenus*. In Yankee City lower-upper class individuals had a slightly higher average income[37] than upper-upper class members and a higher median value for their homes,[38] but their new wealth was not sufficiently legitimated by a long tradition of upper class behavior to make them members of the upper-upper group.

On the average, the new families, socially inferior to the old ones, have more money, better houses, more expensive automobiles, and other material goods that are superior in dollars and cents to those of their social superiors. But if the success of the new families is due to wealth, their money is felt to be too new; if due to occupational triumph, their achievement is too recent. . . . The inherited culture of an upper class . . . is more highly regarded.[39]

The consumption pattern of these *nouveaux riches* seems to be conspicuously exaggerated when contrasted with that of the "old families."

The upper-middle class is composed of substantial businessmen and professional people. These are respected members of the community who often act as civic leaders.[40] They are "solid" folk, but not "society." While they live in comfortable houses in the better residential sections, in Yankee City their average income and the median value of their homes is less than that of the two upper classes.[41]

These three higher classes comprise what Warner calls the "level above the common man." The "level of the common man"—the "typical" and most numerous segment of the community—is composed of the lower-middle and upper-lower classes. Members of the lower-middle class are most frequently small businessmen, clerical workers, other lower level white collar workers, and a few skilled workmen.[42] Their small neat houses are located in the "side streets." "Proper and conservative," they are said to approximate the ideal of the Protestant ethic, "being careful with their money, saving, farsighted, forever anxious about what their neighbors think, and continually concerned about respectability."[43]

The upper-lower class are the "honest workmen" and the clean poor. They are mostly semiskilled workers—operatives in factories or service workers—plus a few small tradesmen.[44] Though they live in the less desirable sections of town and have lower incomes than the classes above them, they are still "respectable."[45]

Respectable is what the lower-lower class is not. This class forms the "level below the common man." It is composed of semiskilled and unskilled workers.[46] In Yankee City this class contributed a higher proportion of its members to the relief rolls than any other class.[47] Lower-lower class people live in the worst sections of town and are thought by the other classes to be immoral.

Their reputation is such that they are believed to lack the cardinal virtues in which Americans pride themselves. Although in standards of sexual behavior many differ from the classes above, others are different only because they are less ambitious and have little desire to fulfill the middle-class goal of "getting ahead." Their reputation for immorality often is no more than the projected fantasy of those above them. . . .[48]

In Yankee City and Jonesville the proportions of the total populations represented by each class are fairly similar, except that in Jonesville the lower-lower class is smaller and the upper-low and lower-middle classes correspondingly larger. The upper-upper class comprises 1.4% of the population in Yankee City, the lower-upper 1.6%, the upper-middle 10%, the lower-middle 28%, the upper-lower 33%, and the lower-lower 25%. In Jonesville the upper class represents 3% of the population, the upper-middle 11%, the lower-middle 31%, and the upper-lower 41%, and the lower-lower 14%. The distribution of the classes in the South appears to be somewhat different, due to the different rural-urban ratio and the effect of the caste structure on class differentiation.[49]

Warner asserts that despite some minor variations the class system as just described is general throughout America. The same class levels, exhibiting the same characteristics, and conforming to the same pattern of organization are said to exist throughout the country.[50]

As has already been noted, Warner also maintains that the social classes he has differentiated are not categories imposed by him and his associates but that they actually exist as real entities: "the designations of social levels are distinctions made by the people themselves in referring to each other."[51] This seems to imply that all the social classes exist in the community just as he has portrayed them and that all or most of the members of the community recognize each of the class levels. Evidence for this assertion is provided, Warner holds, by the fact that people in their interviews actually had names for the different layers. For example, some informants in the Jonesville study used such terms as "the 400," "the aristocrats," or "the people with family and money," to refer to the upper class. Or they would refer to the upper-middle class as "above average but not tops," to the lower-middle class with designations like "good common people," to the upper-lower class with appellations like "the poor but hardworking people," and to the lower-lower class with such expressions as "the poor but not respectable," the "river rats," or "the lulus."[52] All the class levels, it would seem, are named and visible to most of the members of the community.

On the other hand, somewhat contradictory assertions are made, for we are also told that not all people in the community recognize all the class distinctions made by Warner:

It must not be thought that all the people in Yankee City are aware of all the minute distinctions made in this book. The terms used to refer to such definitions as are made vary according to the class of the individual. . . . The terms Hill Streeter, Side Streeter, Homeviller, and Riverbrooker would be known to all classes. Occasionally such terms are used only in their geographical sense, but far more often they are applied as terms of status and rank.[53]

Thus it appears that in Yankee City only four class groupings are generally recognized. Yet, at other times we are told that only three broad groupings are generally distinguished by the bulk of the population. Besides the "level of the common man" (which includes the lower-middle and upper-lower classes), only the "level above the common man" (the upper-middle and upper classes), and the "level below the common man" (the lower-lower class) "are recognized by everyone in Jonesville."[54] Davis and Gardner also indicate that three broad groups are the only ones recognized by all, but it is apparent that the three they mention—the upper class, the middle class, and the lower class—are somewhat different groups from the ones recognized in Jonesville.[55] In still other passages, it appears that the number of classes demarcated by the members of a community is not constant at all, but varies according to the social class of the informant. In general, the higher classes make more class distinctions than the lower classes. In addition, for the members of all classes, "the greater the social distance from the other classes the less clearly are fine distinctions made." Moreover, the criteria for judging class membership vary from class to class, with the lower levels making designations primarily in terms of money, the middle classes in terms of money and morality, and the upper classes giving more emphasis to style of life and ancestry.[56]

Whatever the variations may be, Warner nevertheless points to the generally similar levels that are distinguished in the various communities studied and emphasizes the pervasive influence exerted by the class system on all aspects of the social structure and on the personalities and subjective orientations of persons living in a class-stratified society.

Class and Social Structure. Warner and his associates seek to show the operation of the class system within the community by locating differential behavior patterns within the several social structures of the community and treating these patterns as correlates of class status. A brief summary of some of these findings follows.

The family. In Yankee City upper class behavior, even within the home, tends to be highly ritualized. Upper class families often reside in a house which has long been in the family or is otherwise sanctified by historic tradition. Dining arrangements, and even gatherings of the immediate family in the living room are stylized. The child is trained to a code of behavior traditional for one of his position—a position which emphasizes his role as a member of a distinguished lineage. Family rituals in the lower-upper class may often be an exaggerated emulation of upper-upper behavior. Disruption in the parent-child relationship occurs frequently in this class due to the strains attending a newly gained position.[57]

Family life in the white middle classes of Old City proceeds according to definitely established rules, but it may be said to be regulated rather than ritualized. Meals must be taken at definite times, duties must be accomplished on schedule, and household effects must be respected; but etiquette observed in the home is less elaborate than in the upper classes. Like upper class families, upper-middle class families may have servants. While very few women in the three higher classes are employed outside the home, some lower-middle class mothers may be. Children are vigorously supervised and brought up to value high achievement patterns and "sound" moral codes.[58]

If the emphasis of the upper class family is on living according to a certain style, and that of the middle class family on living for high achievement (both materially and morally), then the emphasis of the lower class family may be said to be simply on living. The economic situation of members of these classes is often precarious.[59] In Old City the instability of white lower class marriages was marked, and illegal unions were common. Though discipline is often harsh, there is little supervision of children outside the home and a minimum of regulated activities within the home. Families are large and space scarce. Upper-lower class parents live in neater homes, supervise their children more, and observe more ritual in familial activities like eating than do lower-lower class parents.[60]

Cliques. Outside the family the clique is crucial in determining class status, as well as in inculcating class culture. "A man's status is judged 'by the company he keeps,' that is, by the rank of his clique."[61] People desiring upward mobility must attempt to gain access to cliques of higher status, in order thereby to absorb the culture of the superior group and to gain acceptance as a member of it. Families and cliques have a very narrow class range; families usually draw their members from one class and cliques from not more than two classes.[62]

Voluntary associations. The proportion of each class group belonging to associations decreases with class status. Thus in Yankee City 72% of the people in the upper classes belonged to associations, 64% of the upper-middle class, 49% of the lower-middle class, 39% of the upper-lower class and 22% of the lower-lower class.[63] The pattern is similar in Jonesville but appears to deviate somewhat in Old City, for Davis and Gardner report that in Old City the upper class members seldom participate actively in community organizations and limit their associational activity almost exclusively

The types of associations joined differ by social class. In Jonesville the upper classes participate most frequently in social clubs (like the Monday Club, the Country Club, and the Daughters of the American Revolution) and in charity clubs. The members of the upper-middle class are also found in many of these same clubs but take a less active part in them. The associations with which they are most closely identified are service and civic clubs, such as Rotary, the Woman's Club, and the P.T.A. Again, the lower-middle class is found in some of the high status associations of the class above it, but they are frequently in intermediate groups like Lions, Masons, and Eastern Star. Lodges and their auxiliaries draw a large portion of their members from lower-middle and upper-lower class men and women. Religious associations are also popular with the members of these two classes. Members of the lower-lower class, when they do join associations, are found primarily in the lodges and auxiliaries.[65]

The church. Churches, too, tend to draw their congregations from different class levels. For example, in Jonesville the upper and upper-middle classes are members of the Federated Church (Presbyterian and Congregational), the Methodist Church is primarily a middle class church, and the Baptist Church is the lower class church of the community.[66] Of course, the rank order of the several churches varies in different communities. The percentage of each class belonging to a church decreases with class status, from 77% in the upper class to 28% in the lower-lower class.[67] However, the higher classes cannot be said to be the most religious, for it is primarily the lower-middle and the upper-lower classes that not only join but also attend church.[68]

The school. Members of the upper class ordinarily send their children to private schools, especially at the high school level.[69] For the rest of the population the public schools may serve as an instrument of social mobility, for the schools teach the technical and academic skills necessary for advancement. They also aid mobility by providing a place where lower status children can learn the social skills needed for advancement through association with teachers and children of superior status.

In both Yankee City and Jonesville the schools were very overcrowded and in disrepair, due to the efforts of the largest property owners in each city in preventing the classes below them from securing the funds necessary to improve the schools. These funds are normally secured through increase in property taxes but such increases were successfully resisted by the affluent classes.[70] Furthermore, in Yankee City the funds that were dispersed were given in disproportionately greater amounts to the schools in the better sections of town.[71] The lower classes therefore have the most inadequate school facilities.

The proportion of children of school age that actually are enrolled in school decreases with class status. When intelligence is held constant, the proportion of high school graduates in each socio-economic level that goes on to college decreases with socio-economic status. It is therefore likely that many able children are prevented from advancement because of their families' financial status.[72] The curricula selected by students reflect their class backgrounds, with the college preparatory curricula favored by the higher classes and the commercial and general curricula favored by the lower classes.

In Yankee City the children taking non-college programs are accorded a lower status by their teachers and peers. They receive poorer instruction from the teachers and participate less in school activities than children in the college curriculum.[73] Each grade in Old City schools is divided into A, B, and C sections, presumably on the basis of ability alone; yet there was testimony that the high social position of certain students led to their being placed in the A group despite their lack of the requisite ability.[74] Teachers themselves are members of the upper-middle class in Yankee City and Old City and of the lower-middle class in Jonesville; they have often been mobile from the lower-middle and upper-lower classes, respectively.[75] The school culture is therefore dominated by middle class standards, and the dominance of middle class children in the social life of the school as well, sometimes leads to unfortunate consequences for the lower class children who do not conform to the standards of the middle class.

The factory. During the course of the Yankee City study all the factories in the major industry (shoe manufacturing) of the community were shut down by a strike. The workers won the strike and the industry became unionized for the first time. Hitherto, the Yankee City workers had been considered "docile" and had resisted unionization. Warner and Low sought to determine the conditions generating this industrial conflict and the resulting unionization.

They concluded that one of the principal factors involved was the breakdown of the skill hierarchy in the industry, and the consequent inability of workers to rise in the industrial hierarchy. When shoemaking was in the handicraft stage there was a definite hierarchy of jobs based on skill, and the worker progressed from apprentice to journeyman to master craftsman. In the modern shoe factory, however, "no longer is it possible for him to start in low-skilled jobs and progressively prepare himself for higher-skilled jobs."[76] Mechanization and minute division of labor have reduced nearly all jobs to the same relatively low skilled level. There is therefore no hierarchy of graded jobs in which to ascend. Furthermore the operatives have little chance of training themselves to enter the managerial hierarchy; managers no longer come from the ranks of the workers, but instead are college-trained men and often the sons of executives.[77]

The frustration arising from this blocked mobility has been reinforced by the increasing social distance between labor and management emerging from absentee ownership of the industry. The major factories in the community no longer are owned and operated by local people, but by regional and national enterprises. As management becomes emancipated from community control, the conflicts of interest between management and worker "become more pronounced because they lack the bonds of mutuality."[78] In short, workers as a class responded to decreasing mobility and decreasing community control over economic functions by seeking status and security in labor organization.

Warner and Low generalize these conclusions when they state that there is "strong evidence from many sources to indicate that the worker group is becoming less mobile and creating a class of its own with its own social machinery and its own hierarchy in which the ambitious rise to places of leadership and power."[79] This suggests increasing class conflict, but Warner believes that opportunities for mobility provided by the schools partially counteract these developments in industrial organization.

> Mobility in our class system for the worker and his family through advance in the skill hierarchy has never been the only route upward. There have been others, the principal one being education. The American school system has been organized largely to teach people the necessary skills to get ahead.[80]

> Today education is the principal avenue of advancement. The change is summarized in the phrase, "social mobility in the school; blocked mobility in the factory."

> From a careful scrutiny of a number of communities, life careers, and occupations, the authors believe that education has become the preeminent and most-used route to power and prestige for all classes of men in American society.[81]

However, Warner and Low believe that even this path to class mobility is becoming less certain. They therefore conclude that mobility has decreased for the working class as a whole.

> The evidence from Yankee City and other places in the United States strongly indicates that mobility through the schools is also slowing up and that the higher positions tend to be filled in each succeeding generation by the sons and daughters of families who already enjoy high positions. The evidence from a great variety of studies clearly demonstrates the truth of this last statement. While newer educational routes are being formed for the ambitious, the older ones are becoming increasingly tight, and it seems predictable that in time education may not be a certain route for those who seek success. It seems probable that our class system is becoming less open and mobility increasingly difficult for those at the bottom of the social heap.[82]

In his writings Warner has therefore emphasized the necessity for "unblocking" the educational channels of mobility, for "as long as this route remains open to the . . . lower class, their frustrations will not be sufficient to be explosive."[83]

Class, Ethnic Groups, and Caste. Ethnic groups are minorities which differ from members of the dominant culture in religious, national, or cultural origins. These groups typically become partially or wholly assimilated into the larger American society as a result of the opportunities for class mobility open to their members. As members of ethnic groups seek and achieve class mobility, they tend to detach themselves from their ethnic identifications and thereby lessen the cohesiveness and distinctive identity of these groups.

However, the extent to which ethnic groups have become assimilated and the extent to which they are permitted to assimilate varies from group to group. Among the factors influencing the degree of mobility and acculturation are the extent to which the ethnic culture is the same or different from the dominant American culture, the initial socio-economic status of the migrant group, the size of the ethnic group, and the length of time it has been in America.

In Yankee City Warner and Srole found that each immigrant group usually began in the lowest socio-economic positions, but through time their members moved upward.[84] Residential indexes (reflecting the ratings of the ecological areas in which the ethnic groups were distributed) and occupational indexes tended, with some exceptions, to vary with the length of time the group had been in the community. Thus ethnic groups like the Irish, who had been in Yankee City the longest time, tended to live in better dwelling areas and to have better jobs than the Poles or Russians, who were the most recent immigrant groups. There were several exceptions; for example, the French Canadians had a lower residential index than other groups who were newer to the community; the Jews had a higher occupational index than any other group, including the Old Americans. The distribution of ethnics throughout the several classes was also roughly related to the time each group had been in the community.[85] However, as has been indicated, time alone is not sufficient to account for the amount of mobility experienced by the members of various ethnic groups. The picture is complicated by the fact that some groups, for various reasons, resist amalgamation. For example, although the Norwegians were among the first settlers of the Midwestern region, the Norwegian-Lutheran group in Jonesville has remained isolated and developed sectarian characteristics.[86] Equally important is the fact that the dominant group is more resistant to assimilating some ethnic groups than others.[87] With respect to ethnic groups, Warner concludes that it is quite likely that "most, if not all of them, will ultimately disappear from American life."[88]

The caste situation, however, is quite different. Castes, like classes, are inclusive ranked orders which cross-cut the whole community. Unlike classes the caste system does not permit out-marriage, and mobility into another caste is impossible.[89] Hence an individual's caste position is fixed at birth and cannot be changed. In America the system of castes relegates the Negro to the inferior caste and whites to the superior caste. The caste system not only taboos intermarriage, but regulates the social relations between the castes through intricate codes of conduct which symbolize the inferior status accorded Negroes. In addition to enforcing social inferiority, the caste system systematically results in deprivation in the educational, occupational, and political realms for the Negro. No attempt can be made here to discuss the vast influence of the system of color castes. Only the relationship between caste and class will be discussed.

Within each caste, classes exist, so that it is possible for class mobility within a caste to take place. The development of social differentiation within the Negro caste has been one of the most crucial factors affecting the changing pattern of caste relations in this country. Robert Park was among the first to call attention to the changing nature of Negro-white relations. He pointed out that the castes were originally separated by a horizontal line, with all whites above all Negroes; but with the development of occupational classes within the Negro caste, the caste line has shifted to a vertical position. The white and Negro classes now occupied parallel positions and looked across the caste line at each other. Park contrasted the old and new situations as follows:

Originally race relations in the South could be rather accurately represented by a horizontal line, with all the white folk above, and all the Negro folk below.... With the development of industrial and professional classes within the Negro race, the distinction between the races tends to assume the form of a vertical line.... The situation *was* this:

All white

All colored

It is *now* this:

White	*Colored*
Professional occupation	Professional occupation
Business occupation	Business occupation
Labor	Labor

The result is to develop in every occupational class professional and industrial bi-racial organizations.... The races no longer look up and down; they look across.[90]

On the basis of his and his collaborators' investigations into caste and class relations Warner portrays current Negro-white relations as in an intermediate stage, for he concluded that the second situation depicted by Park has not yet been reached. White members of the same class as Negroes do not look *across* the caste line at their Negro counterparts; they still look down on them. However, the situation *has* changed to the extent that not *all* whites are considered to be superior to *all* Negroes. The caste rules theoretically demand that all whites be considered superior to all Negroes in every way. Formerly, when there was little differentiation within the

Warner's Diagram[92]

LEGEND: W — White. N — Negro.
U — Upper class.
M — Middle class.
L — Lower class.
AB — Present caste line.
de — Ultimate position of caste line.

Negro caste, nearly all Negroes occupied the lowest skilled jobs. Consequently, very few Negroes were superior in class position to any white people, and in this respect the caste dogmas were approximated in reality. But as class differentiation within the Negro caste has progressed, some Negroes have risen to very high positions. At present there are clearly demarcated upper, middle, and lower class groups among both Northern and Southern Negroes. As a result, there are some Negroes who are higher in class status than some whites.[91] The upper class Negro, for example, though still inferior in caste to any white person, is considered to be superior in class to the lower class white. Therefore, Warner maintains that the present caste line is neither horizontal (all whites above all Negroes) nor vertical (whites and Negroes of the some class equal but in separate, parallel hierarchies) but diagonal (higher class Negroes, though not equal to their white counterparts, superior to lower class whites). Warner illustrates this situation in the diagram on the previous page.

Nevertheless, Warner considers it probable that, if occupational, educational, and social opportunities for the Negro continue to improve, the caste situation will improve correspondingly and the caste line will move from its present diagonal position AB to the vertical position de. As indicated, there will then be identical hierarchies on each side of the vertical caste line and Negroes and whites having similar class positions will be separate but equal. Even this situation, however, is not envisaged as necessarily being final. Warner speculates about the possibility of drastic changes in the caste system that might attend the disappearance of caste differentials in power and prestige:

It is possible that the ordinary social sanctions which apply to cross-caste "social" relations might finally be weakened with the increasing differentiation in the Negro community and the disappearance of the caste differentials in power and prestige. Even the taboo on intermarriage might be relaxed. . . . Unless further sanctions were developed to maintain endogamy, the whole system of separate caste groups might disappear and new social forms develop to take its place.[93]

Differentiation within the Negro community has progressed sufficiently far for Davis and others to assert that the influence of class on behavior is greater than the influence of caste. There is found to be very great similarity between the styles of life of white and Negro middle class families and between that of white and Negro lower class families. In many ways people of the same class but different caste are more like each other than people of the same caste but different class.[94]

This by no means minimizes the vast differences between the situations of whites and Negroes. Drake and Cayton[95] in their Chicago study and Davis and Gardner[96] in their study of a Southern town show in detail the vast disadvantages visited on Negroes in all areas of economic, political, and social life, as compared with whites. One of the principal ways in which the caste system acts to disadvantage Negroes is through its influence on class differentiation within the Negro group. By restricting opportunities for Negroes, what the caste system really does is to force the vast majority of Negroes, even at present, to remain in the lower class. As a result, the Negro middle and upper classes are far smaller, proportionally, than the white middle and upper classes.[97]

One result of this *relative* lack of occupational differentiation has been the development of a somewhat more fluid class system within the Negro group. Although, as has been noted, class cultures, regardless of caste, are remarkably similar, some differences do occur. In Old City Davis and Gardner found that class sanctions could not always be so strongly imposed within the Negro community and class standards were somewhat less developed. Secondly, the occupational status required to move into the Negro upper and middle classes was lower than would be the case in white society.[98] In the North Negroes have been able to secure somewhat greater economic, educational, and political advantages, though these are still far below white opportunities.[99] However, the enlargement of opportunity has led to the development of a class system among Northern Negroes that more closely approximates its white counterpart. Nevertheless, the effects of limited opportunities are still crucial and are reflected in some of the standards developed in the Negro class structure. For example, a few wealthy and powerful individuals whose source of income is not considered "respectable" may be in the Negro upper class in Chicago;[100] this would probably not occur in the white class hierarchy. In broad outline, however, it appears that the separate class hierarchies may be very slowly approaching a condition of parallelism.

Class and Socialization. Some of Warner's colleagues have attempted to show the influence of class on the socialization of the child. Their studies describe the processes through which children learn modes of behavior and adopt orientations characteristic of their class.

In this connection the work of Allison Davis and his collaborators has focused on the child-rearing practices characteristic of middle and lower class parents. In a study done in Chicago about 100 white and 100 Negro mothers were interviewed. In each group 50 of the families were classified as middle class and 50 were lower class. The results showed that feeding practices are more highly regulated, and weaning and toilet training are instituted earlier in the middle than in the lower classes.[101] Middle class children are trained to assume certain kinds of responsibility at an earlier age than lower class children. For example, middle class children are expected to help around the house and to aid in caring for younger children earlier than are lower class children. Since it appears obvious that lower class parents have more actual need of their children's aid in these matters, Davis and Havighurst assert that the explanation of this phenomenon

probably lies in a tendency on the part of middle-class people to train their children early for achievement and responsibility, while lower-class people train their children to take responsibility only after the child is old enough to make the effort of training pay substantial returns in the work the child will do. Middle-class parents can afford to use time to train children . . . at such an early age that the children cannot repay this training effort by their actual performance, although they may repay it by adopting attitudes of self-achievement and responsibility.[102]

However, somewhat contradictory findings in the area of responsibility training are that lower-class children are expected to get jobs after school earlier and to quit school and go to work earlier than are middle class children. It was also found that middle class parents expect their children to achieve a higher occupational and educational status than do lower class parents. All these differences between middle and lower class child rearing practices are true of both Negro and white groups. Hence Davis and Havighurst conclude that "the striking thing about this study is that Negro and white middle-class families are so much alike, and that white and Negro lower-class families are so much alike."[103] A few color differences in training practices were noted (e.g., Negroes are more permissive in weaning but more strict in toilet training than whites), but these were minor in comparison with the great similarities in class behavior across caste lines.

On the basis of the data collected in the various community studies, Davis has developed generalized descriptions of the different training patterns in lower and middle class families. Davis views "adaptive anxiety" as essential for successful socialization. That is, individuals learn the behavior that is expected of them by striving to avoid the punishment that accompanies failure and to reap the rewards that accompany success in learning; this striving is maintained by socially inculcated anxiety.

It is this striving for reward, for status, this uneasiness lest the reward be not attained, which constitutes the adaptive social function of anxiety. Adolescents with a strongly developed social anxiety, therefore, usually strive for the approved social goals most eagerly and learn most successfully. In this sense the most fully socialized individuals are those with the most effective, socially directed anxiety.[104]

In each class the goals set up as desirable for the child are quite different. In the lower class physical aggression is viewed as a socially acceptable form of behavior, while in the middle class physical aggression is punished and aggressiveness through successful competition for economic and social gains is rewarded. In the lower class sexual impulses are permitted freer expression, while among the middle class adolescents "anxiety and guilt, with respect to . . . sexual intercourse, are proof of their normal socialization in their culture."[105] In the middle class the child's friends, recreation, school work, and institutional affiliations are closely supervised by the parents; in the lower class these controls are largely absent. In addition, the middle class child is urged to strive for high occupational and educational status. As a result of such class-determined training differences, Davis asserts that middle class people have a high degree of anxiety and are "culturally motivated to suffer, to renounce, to postpone gratifications in order to achieve."[106] Consequently, says Davis, it is the middle class that is the backbone of America:

Almost all of the good things in American life . . . are the achievements of middle-status persons: care of and pride in property, careful child-training with emphasis upon renunciation and sacrifice for future gains, long and arduous education, development of complex and demanding skills, working and learning one's way up in the complex processes of business, industry, government, church, and education—all of them administered . . . by the upper-middle class in the American status system.[107]

The prestige strivings of middle class people are the result of anxiety over (a) losing present status and (b) failing to reap the rewards of upward status-mobility. Lower class children have not learned to value achievement goals and therefore, Davis suggests, they must be "recruited" to a middle class way of life in order that they may reap the privileges of upward mobility and in order that the society may function more efficiently. This task can be accomplished by the school, but only if educators are aware of the reality of lower class motivation and accordingly diminish the punitive effect of a middle-class dominated school system on the lower class child.

> In order to motivate the great masses of lower-class children who crowd our schools . . . educators must first know lower-class culture. . . . If these old habits . . . of the lower-class child are to be replaced by new learning which will enable the school to recruit the child into the middle-class way of life (with an attendant increase in the social and economic efficiency of our society), the school must (1) remove the class punishments from the lower-class child within the school society and (2) concretely reward his tentative strivings for prestige in the school community.[108]

> In order, however, to make low-status children *anxious* to work hard, study hard, save their money and accept stricter sex mores, our society must convince them of the *reality* of the rewards at the end of the anxiety-laden climb.[109]

It seems, however, that this goal—of converting everyone to the anxiety-propelled status-strivings of the middle class—is not unambiguously held by Davis. Elsewhere he writes:

> Whether the middle-class or the lower-class practices are preferable is, of course, largely a matter of private opinion. But it is significant that there is now a considerable body of scientific and lay judgment operating in the middle class to make child-rearing practices more permissive. It is contended that the orthodox middle-class practices make children too anxious, and frustrate them too much. . . . On the other hand, it may be contended that civilized life requires the individual to be tamed and to learn to take constructive control of his impulses. A certain degree of anxiety is valuable, in that it puts the individual on his toes to learn the lessons and meet the demands of modern society in order to win the very considerable rewards of modern civilized social life.

> Our own view is that the better child-rearing practices can be drawn from both middle and lower-class life and made into a combination which is superior to both of the norms as they emerge in this study.[110]

In addition to the family, the peer group and the school are important influences in the socialization of the child. Davis has emphasized the predominance of middle class standards in the school. As a result of these discriminatory standards, lower class children are often at odds with their teachers, who have not succeeded in motivating them to learn.[111] Studies by Neugarten and others have shown the relationship of school children's friendship choices and character reputations to class position.[112] In this area, too, lower class children were found to be at a disadvantage. The higher the status of the child, the more often was he desired as a friend. Also, children of *all* classes rated higher status children favorably for items of character reputation more often than they did lower status children. These findings reinforced the earlier conclusions that those children who conform to middle class behavior patterns at school are rewarded by teachers and peers. In this difficult situation, many lower class children may "become increasingly hostile and aggressive" and "welcome the first opportunity to drop out of school and limit their associations to members, of their own social class."[113] Thus, the family, the school, and the peer group all reflect and reinforce the influence of class-related behavior patterns.

Controversial Issues. In the preceding sections an attempt was made to present the main contributions of the Warner school. Warner's studies have been accorded widespread acclaim and his concepts and methods have been adopted by a large number of investigators. However, like all formulations in this field, the Warner approach to stratification has met with varied evaluations. The present effort is not another appraisal, nor is it an attempt to review both the positive and negative evaluations which have been made. It is simply a brief summary of a few of the more general comments of some of Warner's critics, in order to exhibit the principal issues which have provoked controversy.

(1) The first issue to be raised concerns the utility of Warner's definition of class. It has been noted that in Warner's system a class is composed of persons of equal rank who are willing to associate intimately with one another. In order to find out on what basis class stratification takes place people are asked to tell what factors they take into account when ranking each other. In this view class is "what people say it is."[114] Warner's conception of the bases upon which class stratification takes places therefore reflects whatever factors people say they use in ranking each other. These factors, as we have seen, include such things as wealth, area lived in, style of life, occupation, ancestry, associational membership, and a host of others. Several critics have pointed to the problems which arise from the use of such a definition of class.

Following Weber, Mills distinguishes three different types of stratification and asserts that Warner's definition of class includes all three types:

"Class" as defined and used [by Warner] . . . indiscriminately absorbs at least three items, which, when considering "stratifications," it is very important to separate analytically. (1) The word swallows up the sheerly economic. . . . For convenience, this dimension will be referred to in this review as *class*. It includes the sheerly economic and nothing else. (2) Warner's "class" also points at the distribution of "prestige," "deference," "esteem," "honor": in general, *status*. This term will here be used to point at the prestige dimension, and only at it. On the whole Warner's "class" comes closest to status, thus defined. (3) Lastly, Warner's "class" may be taken to mean the distribution of *power*, i.e., who can be expected to obey whom in what situations.

From the insistence upon merely *one* vertical dimension and the consequent absorbing of these three analytically separable dimensions into the one sponge word "class" flow the chief confusions . . . [of] this study.[115]

The use of a definition of class which embodies these several elements prevents the investigator from ascertaining the effects of each separate factor on stratification:

. . . a feature of a good definition is its one-dimensionality. If you define a concept along one line, then you can study other items that vary with it. But if you define it so as to make it a sponge word, letting it absorb a number of variables, then you cannot ask questions with it concerning the relations of the analytically isolable items which it miscellaneously harbors. The central term of this study, "class," falls clearly into this case.[116]

The dispute does *not* center on what "class" actually is, or what type of stratification should be called "class." To repeat: Mills' point is rather that there are three different *bases* of stratification and the amalgamation of all three into one term prevents the investigator from ascertaining the relationships that exist among them. What, for example, is the influence of economic stratification (class, in Mills' definition) on prestige stratification (status, in Mills' definition)? The fact that Warner found economic factors were not sufficient to account for an individual's prestige position does not mean that economic stratification is of no importance. It simply means that the *prestige* hierarchy is based on other factors as well as wealth. There is, nevertheless, an *economic* hierarchy and there are important consequences of economic stratification, of which the members of a society need not necessarily be aware. In order to investigate those consequences it is necessary to separate the economic factors from all others and to distinguish between class and the awareness of class. Conversely, one might just as well wish to investigate the influence of prestige stratification on the economic hierarchy. Whatever the focus of inquiry may be, Mills is saying, it is necessary to use concepts which distinguish the several different *bases* of stratification, and which distinguish between stratification and people's *awareness* of stratification.

A further lack of distinction with direct consequences is the equating of "class" with "class-awareness." The gross facts of economic differences—in amount and in source—do not necessarily result in the awareness of those differences on the part of the participants. Yet Warner throws out *economic* class (by absorbing it indiscriminately with other dimensions) because of the fact of *status-awareness*. It is a double confusion: first, of class with status; and second, of class with status-awareness.

The first and direct result of such blurring is that the role of sheerly economic differences cannot be stated hypothetically, much less tested. This (original presupposition) is ruled out because of status-awareness on the part of some participants in the system. All that the "evidence" in terms of which the sheerly economic factor in stratification was miscellaneously absorbed indicates is that a number of persons did not pronounce *status* judgments on the basis of *mere* wealth. If the distinctions between class and status, between class and class awareness, and between status and status-awareness had been known and used, the observations from interviews would have set interesting problems and hypotheses concerning their precise relations and might have enabled their precise answering by further observation.[117]

Finally, it is implied that the basis upon which Warner adopted his many-sided definition of class is unsound. In defining class, and in investigating the importance of any variable in stratification, the social scientist cannot use people's opinions as a substitute for rigorous conceptual distinctions. The fact that people may use a variety of factors in ranking does not provide a valid reason for a composite definition of class when such a definition results in an analytical impasse. Nor do people's opinions necessarily provide valid clues to the actual importance or ramified effects of the various factors in stratification. Concepts should rather be defined with reference to their theoretical relevance and analytical utility, in order to permit the answering of significant problems.[118]

(2) A second problem now arises. Several commentators, including Mills,

have observed that Warner's conception of class, while it *includes* several dimensions of stratification, primarily *emphasizes* the prestige (or status) dimension. However, many other students of class have been concerned with problems quite different from the one implied by the emphasis on the prestige aspect of stratification. The type of class structure these writers have described is therefore different from the one described by Warner. Consequently, Warner's critics point out that his discussion of class concerns only a limited number of the problems conventionally associated with inquiries on class. Pfautz and Duncan describe the two main approaches to the study of class, and the different problems at the focus of each type of inquiry, as follows:

> On the one hand . . . many theorists . . . consider class relative to the distribution of *power* in the economic and/or political sense. On the other hand, much stratification theory and research centers on the phenomenon of *prestige,* classes being located relative to a hierarchy of esteem rather than power. . . . Thus, whereas research on power classes seems to be done on the more abstract national level, prestige class data are usually obtained from . . . local communities. Again, the power type of class is usually pictured as a mass phenomenon—an unorganized aggregate—while the prestige type is usually thought of as associational in character. . . . Power classes are generally assumed to come into existence on the basis of identity of economic and/or political "interests," and interclass relations are studied primarily in terms of conflict. Prestige classes usually are assumed to involve shared attitudes held in common—not simply like attitudes held by individuals. Further, such interclass relations are viewed as essentially accommodative in quality. Finally, whereas homogeneity of social origins is irrelevant in the case of power classes, such homogeneity is regarded as the *sin qua non* of prestige classes. While both approaches seem valuable for their respective insights, the limited relevancies of each should be recognized. A confusion enters in when the protagonists of prestige class . . . as in the case of Warner, assume that the study of prestige classes encompasses the whole field.[119]

It should be noted that the point now at issue is different from the one previously discussed. In the foregoing discussion the object of Mills' comments was to show the consequences of *combining* several analytically separate bases of stratification into one definition of class. Several critics now point to another feature of Warner's definition of class and the attempt is made to show that although *many* elements are amalgamated into the Warner definition of class, *one* dimension—namely, prestige—is *stressed*. The question now is: granted that there are two different approaches to the study of class, what are the consequences of Warner's emphasis on prestige stratification? Warner's claims are said to require qualification at several points. (a) Warner has not, as he claims, described *the* class system in America, but only the system of prestige classes. While this is a legitimate endeavour, it does not exhaust the description of class in America. (b) Therefore, Warner's formulation cannot, as he claims, be viewed as an alternative approach to the study of class, but only as a complementary approach. Each of the two perspectives focuses on different kinds of problems; both are necessary. (c) For several reasons Warner's results cannot be considered as *prima facie* disconfirmation of the Marxian view of class, or of the so-called "economic interpretation" of class in general. First, "the 'social' classes with which Warner is concerned are not necessarily the same phenomena with which Mosca, or Marx, or Veblen ... were concerned."[120] Therefore, data which indicate that non-economic factors are important in prestige stratification do not *necessarily* discount the importance of economic factors in the political sphere, in conflicts of interest, or in social change—in short, in the areas in which the Marxian approach postulates the primacy of economic factors. Secondly, some writers assert that Warner has not made clear what specific doctrines of the "economic interpretation" presumably require revision as a result of his findings. Either, it is claimed, he has defined the "economic interpretation" so narrowly as to raise issues that are not really problematical when reviewed from the perspective of any of the more sophisticated versions of the "economic interpretation" currently extant. Or else, he has at times discounted the importance of economic factors when the data do not conclusively warrant it. A case in point is his treatment of the fact that some individuals who were accorded high status had less money than some others of lower status. It will be recalled that on the basis of such evidence Warner abandoned his "original economic interpretation" of class. Concerning this decision, Merton writes:

> By stressing esteem or prestige gradients as the gist of the class structure, they [Warner and Lunt] seem to have over-reacted to their original "general economic interpretation." If they intend only to assert that *contemporary* income, wealth and occupation are insufficient to assign all members of the community to their "correct" position within the prestige-hierarchy, their evidence is adequate. But this is a perilously narrow conception of an "economic" interpretation. Unfortunately, the volume does not include case studies of families who, *over a period of generations,* have not had their claims to upper-upper status validated by "economic" criteria which must serve as means for maintaining the behavioral attributes of that status. The occurrence of lags in the imputation of status is to be expected. We may hazard the guess that, had historical dimensions been taken into account, the initial dilemma of a "general economic interpretation" *or* a cultural interpretation would have been perceived as a pseudo-problem.[121]

Third, some writers claim that Warner's own data show that more, not less, attention to the role of economic factors in stratification is warranted. The fact that Warner found occupation correlates at .91 with social class (as determined by evaluated participation) shows the importance of economic position even for prestige stratification. It is *this,* Chinoy contends, that requires further investigation:

> In all of Professor Warner's work on the status structure of American communities, economic position remains a dependent variable, or, as in the I.S.C., it is only used as an index. This fact rests upon the methodological decision made in the early stages of the Yankee City research to organize behavior and attitudes along the status axis rather than along the job or income axis. Professor Warner has never justified this decision in theoretical terms and has never supported it empirically by demonstrating that social status correlates more highly with other variables than does economic position. The .91 correlation between status and occupation found in Jonesville demands even more strongly an explanation of the nature of the relationship between the two.[122]

It should be stressed that the general point at issue in these several comments is not whether economic factors are in actuality preeminent, but rather, the dispute centers on what type of evidence should be reviewed as providing legitimate grounds for discounting the importance of economic factors in any given case.

(3) Assuming, then, that Warner has been describing a prestige hierarchy, some critics have gone on to raise a third issue: what is the relevance of the study of prestige classes for an understanding of the general pattern of stratification in America? As we have seen, Warner maintains that the social class structure he observed in the communities that were studied provides a valid picture of the class system throughout America. Objections to this contention arise on the grounds that the places studied by Warner and his collaborators have been relatively small, and findings based on them are not applicable to highly urbanized communities. The existence of the type of class structure Warner describes depends on the ability of most members of the community to make status evaluations of each other's conduct. In a small town, an individual's family background, his clique and associational participations are likely to be known and talked about. Similarly, his occupation and financial situations are highly visible and are often closely related to his other participations in the community. In this regard, Hall writes:

> One wonders how this type of analysis would apply to a less specialized community. The one dealt with [Jonesville] has many of the earmarks of a company town. One-third of all the gainfully employed work in one factory. In such a case three very special considerations are fulfilled: (1) the range of occupations is narrow; (2) occupations are objects of common understanding in the community; and (3) one's occupational designation and institutional position overlap and mutually reinforce each other. Therefore, the proportion of families who are involved in a common order is exceptionally high. But the order may be better described as an institutional order than as a class order.[123]

In a large city, on the other hand, there are such a wide range of opportunities that occupational hierarchies may be segregated. Ethnic and racial divisions, occupational and financial divisions break the metropolis up into a mosaic of separate worlds. In such a situation there is likely to be not one over-all ranked hierarchy but several disparate hierarchies, each having its own scale of esteem.

In the large city contacts are mainly secondary rather than primary; hence the type of intimate participation patterns by which prestige class placement is effected in small towns are largely absent in the great metropolis. By virtue of sheer size, the city guarantees anonymity for its inhabitants in large areas of their lives; as a result, the information necessary to place people in a prestige hierarchy is not available except to one's intimates. Reputational assessment is therefore impossible: in the large metropolises "the only class of people who know and rank one another are Warner's 'upper-uppers,' i.e., those who are known as society," but "the other 'five classes' are too numerous to permit that degree of personal acquaintance, which alone would make a system of interlocking status evaluations feasible."[124]

For all these reasons it is felt that the relevance of the study of prestige classes may be limited to small towns. In the metropolis, it is suggested, the study of power hierarchies and groups based on "interests" may prove to be a more fruitful focus of inquiry for the class analyst. Warner's choice of a "well-integrated community" having an "absence of conflict" does not permit extrapolation of his results to the metropolis, which may be loosely integrated and the locus of conflicts of interest groups.

Moreover, the same range of characteristics that produces a given class in a small community cannot be assumed to produce the same class in a large city. Lipset and Bendix state:

> The upper class of . . . small American cities is largely composed of people who are middle class when we look at class from the perspective of the metropolis. Transferred to New York, Chicago, or San Francisco, they probably would not even make the society page, and would not be members of the elite clubs of the community. . . . Every town has its exclusive country club but the members of the exclusive country clubs the country over do not belong to the same position in the social structure.[125]

Hatt makes the same point in a more general way:

> . . . the "five classes" (which the author assures us *were there* . . . , and not brought by the researcher) would not be present in New York, New Orleans, or Seattle. Or should they be, their I.S.C. (Index of Status Characteristics) would be vastly different. By the book's definition, they would thus be different classes.[126]

Therefore, it is claimed, Warner has not delimited the class structure for all of America, but only the system of prestige classes in the small towns of America. The conditions of modern urban society do not permit unqualified use of the "anthropological approach," in which the local community is viewed as a replica of the whole society. Hence Warner's claim that Jonesville (and the other towns) are laboratories for studying America

> fails to consider some of the most fundamental characteristics of a complex society. Theoretical problems which immediately rise from such an assumption of the identity of the local community with the national life are that modern industrial society is characterized by, among other things, regional specialization, local differentiation, impersonality and mobility. These are factors which cannot by definition exist on the level of the local community. To this extent, Jonesville *cannot* be taken as America.[127]

(4) A fourth controversy turns on the question of whether or not Warner has accurately portrayed the status structure, even for a small town. The validity of Warner's description is challenged on two grounds, namely, that it reveals only a limited perspective of the class system as it appears to small town residents and that it depicts a class hierarchy that is made to appear static and uniform rather than variable and complex.

(a) Some writers maintain that Warner has not described the status structure as it actually exists in a small town, but only the way in which the status structure looks when seen through the eyes of the upper-middle and upper-class residents. In his discussion of class Warner has emphasized the importance of "acting right"; though certain objective criteria are important, the crucial thing is an individual's style of life and participation pattern:

Money must be translated into socially approved behavior and possessions, and they in turn must be translated into intimate participation with, and acceptance by, members of a superior class.[128]

On the basis of these criteria Warner has located five or six classes and claims that most of the people in the community not only recognize these divisions but rank themselves and others on the basis of such criteria. This is so, Warner maintains, because the criteria he uses are the criteria used by the members of the community themselves. Some writers take exception to this claim. They point to certain clues in Warner's and his colleagues' publications to show that the view of class adopted by Warner is only accurate for the upper levels of the community. Warner himself has stated that not all members of the community make all the fine distinctions he has recorded.[129] Davis and Gardner have observed that "individuals in the two upper strata make the finest gradations in the stratification of the whole society and that class distinctions are made with decreasing precision as social position becomes lower."[130] They also show that the criteria used for ranking are different in the several classes: the upper classes think largely in term of the length of time a family has had an upper class style of life; the upper-middle class uses "moral attitudes and . . . definite conceptions of the role and importance of wealth"; the lower-middle class accords status to others "mainly because they have money"; members of the upper-lower class "like the middle classes . . . think of social stratification . . . as an absolute hierarchy of wealth"; the lower-lower class also believes status is "based entirely on . . . economic superiority."[131] Because of such variations, Chinoy contends that the class structure Warner describes "is actually a composite version of the prestige hierarchy which is built from the varied perspectives of the local residents. It is basically a construction of the researcher rather than the consensus of the community."[132] It is a construction, moreover, which some writers claim reflects most heavily the perspective of the higher classes. Why, it is asked, does Warner describe a large number of classes, when only the upper strata recognize that many? Why are six divisions more "real" than the three or four that are recognized by the lower strata? Why has Warner adopted the view that class is based on style of life and social reputation when members of the lower-middle, upper-lower and lower-lower classes (the vast majority of the population) are said to base *their* rankings *solely* on money? These critics claim that the answer is that Warner has himself adopted the view of class held by the upper and upper-middle class. They point to other indications that this may be the case. Lipset and Bendix point out that the informants selected by Warner in the Jonesville study were people who were "explicitly class-conscious"; further, of the ten informants for whom information was available, Lipset and Bendix estimate that nine of the ten are probably upper-middle class, while only one is from the working class.[133] They note that Warner says of the one working class informant "he sees class as purely a matter of income and power." Lipset and Bendix therefore conclude that Warner's studies

reveal the perspective of the social climbers just below the upper crust of small-town society. To people at this level class appears as a matter of interpersonal relations, manners, family, and so on. It is not polite to suggest that class is a reflection of one's economic position. . . .

If this is the view of the upper-middle class then the question arises whether other social groups in the community look at class in the same way. A careful reading reveals that the subjective definition of class is by no means the same for all residents. . . .[134]

. . . the one representative of the lower classes on the panel sees a class and power structure differently from the "upper-class" members . . . the group of which he is a part forms a larger proportion of the community than do the groups to which the nine other panel members belong. Why, we wonder is the upper-class view of the social structure more acceptable than the lower-class view. It would have been equally possible to approach the problem of analyzing the social structure of Jonesville from . . . [his] point of view. There is some evidence that he is, in fact, accurately describing the power structure of the town.[135]

Other data elicited from the Warner studies show that the upper-lower class is not so sharply defined as the other classes, and Pfautz and Duncan have shown that prediction errors (for predicting class level from I.S.C.) are highest for this class.[136] This further suggests that the fluidity of class lines varies from class to class. For all these reasons various commentators allege that Warner's view of a rigidly stratified class structure based on reputation is valid only for the upper reaches of the society. His classes, they claim, are not "real" entities, for not only are any investigator's results the product of his conceptual scheme and his methods,[137] but also because in this case the concepts used reflect the social reality primarily as seen from the perspective of the higher strata.

(b) As has been indicated previously, one of the reasons some critics object to the extension of the Warner results to large cities is that conditions in the metropolis lead to far more complex stratification structures than in small towns. Certain writers further contend that the Warner scheme is too simplified for a complete understanding of stratification even in small towns. Small towns also have a diversity of stratification groupings which may not necessarily be integrated into one over-all class hierarchy. The presence of disjunctive status hierarchies produces situations in which all individuals cannot be ranked according to a uniformly applied scale of stratification. Thus, for example, in commenting on the Yankee City strike, Lipset and Bendix show how status solidarity based on anti-Semitism may obliterate interclass antagonisms among non-Jews and result in status contradictions for Jews.[138] Moreover, small towns may exhibit a degree of complexity in social life and in economic functions sufficient to result in the inhabitants' inability to place exactly all the members of the community. Hence in some circumstances ambiguity in status evaluations may characterize the small town as well as the metropolis. In addition, even in small towns the fluidity of conditions in modern times, as manifested, for example, in geographical mobility and in technological change, produces constant fluctuations in social relationships. The system of stratification, therefore, is itself in a continuous state of flux. These considerations have led to the claim that Warner's image of a precisely ordered, integrated, and relatively static class hierarchy may not accurately reflect all the relevant aspects of stratification in small towns.

Recently, certain of these structures have been illustrated afresh by the findings of two investigators who attempted unsuccessfully to use Warner's scheme for describing the class structure of a small city they studied. Stone and Form found that quite a large number of people in the community could not adequately be placed in a class hierarchy due to the vagueness of their "status reputations"; that consensus on the prestige ratings of occupations existed only at the extremes but not in the middle-ranking ranges of occupations; and that movement into the town of managerial personnel from a nearby large city who resisted integration into the old "upper class" resulted in a "vertical cleavage" in the class structure.[139] They conclude that, even in a small town, the status order is characterized by typical instabilities in status, by great variation in the degree and kind of status solidarity, and hence by the presence of many different types of status grouping which cannot be viewed as arranged into one over-all social class hierarchy. Thus the authors were unable to interpret their results in terms of the conventional Warner scheme because of the complexity and the constantly changing nature of status ascription in the town they studied.

In sum, Warner's description of the class structure in small towns is said to reflect the perspective of some, not all, of the members of the society and to ignore the complex and variable aspects of class relations.

(5) Some writers maintain that Warner's work is marked by insufficient attention to historical data. As a result historical trends are said to be either ignored or at times inaccurately assessed.

(a) Mills remarks that the Yankee City study is "trendless."[140] Hence there is no indication of the manner in which the class system has changed through time. (In the preceding discussion one of the points made was that Warner does not examine variations in the class structure due to short-run fluctuations; now, the point under discussion is the importance of long-run changes in the system of stratification.) According to some commentators, the lack of historical perspective may in part account for the relative lack of emphasis, in Warner's work, on such topics as strains and conflicts in the class structure and of other attendant phenomena of social change. Goldschmidt, for example, scores Warner's neglect of social movements bearing ideologies which seek to change the present class system.[141] Merton writes:

Little is said of the dynamics of the class system. Forces which make not only for mobility of personnel within the structure but also for change in the structure itself are virtually ignored. Despite allusions to lineage and ancestral achievements, there is no systematic examination of changes in the criteria and determinants of class position in such fashion that Yankee-City-1932 is identified as a particular moment in a continuing historical process. As a result we are given a picture of a basically stable and practically unchanging system. . . .[142]

Lipset and Bendix state that the problems of social change—e.g., the analysis of the origin of political movements like Communism or Fascism—should be a central focus of class analysis. Since values, sources of power and authority, and political and religious movements change through time, "sociologists . . . [who] analyse these social phenomena, as if they were static . . . tell us in effect that they are compelled to distort the facts owing to the limitations of their research methods."[143]

(b) Other writers allege that in some cases where Warner has taken note of historical trends he has described them on the basis of insufficient or inaccurately evaluated data. For example, Warner asserts that there has been a trend toward decreasing social mobility in America, yet several writers have noted that he has nowhere presented data in support of this assertion.[144] Handlin contends that Warner's description of Yankee City as being "stable" and "predominantly old American" is in direct violation of historical fact:

> There is no need here to point to the economic changes that have caused sharp reversals in the social trends of the city at least three times in the last hundred years. But the following . . . [data] will give a more accurate picture of the "old American" population. . . . When one realizes that in 1930 about 40% of the native born had foreign parents, that the foreign birth rate was never lower than the native, and that a constant stream of Yankees was leaving the city throughout the last century, it is clear that the vast majority of the city's residents in 1930 were foreigners or the descendants of those who had immigrated in the previous nine decades.[145]

In other cases, it is claimed, Warner has accepted people's opinions about past conditions instead of seeking to ascertain what changes actually did occur. An illustration of the shortcomings of this procedure is provided in Warner's analysis of the Yankee City strike. Warner gives as one reason for the strike the change from local control to outside control of the shoe industry. He states that when local ownership was the rule relatively harmonious relationships between employers and owners prevailed. Yet May shows that this view of the past is based largely on social myths which, though they may be prevalent among the inhabitants of Yankee City, are not in accord with other available accounts of conditions in that period.

> Professors Warner and Low lay great . . . stress on local traditions regarding the benevolence, public-spiritedness, and fairness of the earlier local employers. Yankee City, they point out, continually contrasts this beautiful memory with the lack of local responsibility characteristic of the New York "outsiders" who have recently come into partial control. This contrast, they believe, accounts in large part for the increased solidarity of the employees and the lack of a strong local support for the employers. . . .
> To describe the old . . . employers, the authors make use of the composite sketch. . . . One notes, however, that in the sketches of the bygone giants . . . they make use largely of local memories. They admit, to be sure, that these memories are probably not entirely reliable. But the sketches of . . . [the present] "foreign" capitalists and their agents are drawn from recent actuality. . . . surely it is somewhat unscientific to juxtapose recent actuality and rose-colored tradition without providing ample corrective analysis. By the time of the strike, say the authors,
>> The workers and managers in the shoe industry had lost their sense of worth and mutual loyalty. No longer were they men who had a common way of life in which each did what he had to do and, in so doing, worked for himself and for the well-being of all.
> The implications in this statement concerning the affairs before the loss of local control, that is in the late nineteenth century, are based in the book on little but tradition. They certainly do not square with other impressions of life in New England industrial towns of that era.[146]

Thus, while popularly held beliefs are useful in understanding certain aspects of the strike, they cannot legitimately be used to reconstruct the past. Consequently, May shows, Warner cannot accurately assess the role of changed worker-management relations in causing present disaffection, since it is uncertain (from the data presented) what conditions actually prevailed in the past.

(6) A sixth group of criticisms is concerned with the methods employed by Warner in stratifying the communities studied. Earlier reviewers pointed out that in Warner's first group of studies no precise method for placing the members of a society in the class hierarchy was specified. Davis noted that although Warner indicated that various criteria, such as associational membership, dwelling area, and the like, were used, no information was given concerning the weighting of these several factors.[147] Furthermore, Mills observed that not *all* of the criteria listed above were *always* used.[148] Hence it is impossible to know in any given case exactly which factors were used to determine class membership. Warner also stated that actually it was the respondents themselves who rated each other. Yet it was not shown just how this was accomplished or how disagreements among informants were handled. Moreover, it is not clear whether the interviewer's judgment or the informant's judgment was the final determinant of an individual's class position.[149]

The techniques developed during the Jonesville research have also been criticized. The method of evaluated participation, since it is based on class placement through interviewing a core of informants, is said to be impossible to use in a large city.[150] The methods for the E.P. are not thought to be sufficiently precise to yield reliable results. It is alleged that instructions for choosing the panel of judges are not given (and the particular method used in Jonesville has already been criticized);[151] the method for choosing a sample of persons to be classed is not specified (and the particular sample used in Jonesville has been shown to be unrepresentative by Pfautz and Duncan);[152] criteria for summarizing the interview data are ambiguous; no procedure is specified for equating the "social levels" named by the several informants; and no satisfactory way of dealing with cases where informants disagree about the social class placement of an individual is mentioned.[153] Hence Swanson asserts that the method of evaluated participation "does not present . . . a clean, operational definition of how to use these techniques without involving the imponderables of 'artistic' judgment."[154]

With respect to the index of status characteristics, some reviewers state that it is not clear what this index measures (whether it rates objective socio-economic position or evaluations of objective factors) or what relationship it has to E.P.[155] Yet E.P. and I.S.C. are assumed to measure separate things and correlations are made between them. Hall gives several reasons why the high correlation obtained between I.S.C. and E.P. is of questionable meaning.

The authors . . . [rate] occupations in terms of skill and the prestige values accorded them in the community. One is led to suspect that this procedure for classifying occupations might of itself guarantee a high coefficient when correlating occupational status with the evaluation of participation. . . .

The same solution is offered for the delineation of residential areas. . . . Areas . . . are distinguished in terms of their social reputation. It seems here that the authors have defined their units in terms of the units with which they are to be correlated. This is particularly the case when the residential areas are defined by noting the distribution of persons whose class position has been tentatively specified. The argument is of a circular nature, and the high-order correlations (.972) may be the product of the procedures rather than of the data.[156]

Pfautz and Duncan make a similar point when they assert that the independence of the I.S.C. and the E.P. "is factitious, for we have Warner's own evidence that members of the community 'evaluate' each other, in part, on the basis of such 'status characteristics' as dwelling area" and others included in the I.S.C.[157] In addition, the unrepresentative sample used (over-represented at the higher class levels) and the fact that cases of uncertain class placement were discarded would also affect the results.[158]

(7) A seventh focus of controversy has been the value orientation alleged to characterize the Warner approach. Some writers have endeavored to criticize the values implied in Warner's work by contrasting them with an alternative set of values. Usually efforts of this type involve the assertion that Warner sanctions modes of activity which uphold the *status quo*. Thus he emphasizes mobility striving, and concomitantly he stresses the necessity of "adjusting" the individual to his station in life, in those cases where mobility is not possible. In partial support of this contention, Goldschmidt points to a remark of Warner's which occurs in *Social Class in America:* "It is the hope of the author that this book will provide a corrective instrument which will permit men and women better to evaluate their social situations and thereby better adapt themselves to social reality and fit their dreams and aspirations to what is possible."[159] By advocating the desirability of fitting the individual into the class system rather than considering the possibility of changing the system, Warner is alleged to show a "conservative" bias.[160]

Others have attempted to show that Warner's values have influenced his choice of concepts and biased some of his interpretations. Only a brief example of this type of endeavor can be given. In one such effort, it is alleged that Warner endorses the views of the higher classes and therefore views mobility "in terms of an increased desire for social prestige."[161] This is the reason, it is declared, that he views trade unions as retarding mobility. Warner states: "Where previously many laborers were interested only in their own mobility, they are working now for the advancement of the total labor group. In this process mobility is slowed down."[162] Lipset and Bendix claim that such an assertion does not recognize the importance of material gains attending unionization, which may be as important, or more so, to workers, as prestige gains are to the higher strata. They write:

It is certainly a moot point whether the aggregate of upward mobility by individual persons is equal to the aggregate gain in the standard of living of the industrial workers as a result of trade union organization. But it is surely true that these industrial workers have gained far more materially than they have in social prestige, if we make the invidious comparison between the individual and the collective type of upward mobility. In our judgment Mr. Warner's purpose is not only to study, but also to endorse the social class system of the small town, and especially its pattern of social mobility. That is to say, only if one defines upward mobility primarily in terms of a gain in social prestige, can one conclude that economic gain (without prestige gain) is synonymous with a decrease of mobility. Only if one identifies upward mobility in American society with upward mobility in a small town can one claim that mobility, when it is not solely the result of family background, is primarily dependent on an individual's ability to make himself socially acceptable by the superior classes.[163]

These, then, are the principal issues which have provoked controversy in the discussions of Warner's work.[164] As yet the issues remain unresolved. It is possible, however, that the dimensions of controversy may be narrowing. In connection with some of the points of contention listed above, it is worth-while to note several statements made by Warner in his most recent book. In *American Life,* published earlier this year, Warner writes: ". . . community studies give only part of the evidence about the vast superstructure of American life. The greatly extended economic and political hierarchies, for example, whose centers of decision are in New York and Washington, can only be partly understood by these studies."[165] He also states that "social class in America is not the same as economic class."[166] Whether these remarks will be taken to mean that Warner's views and those of his critics may be drawing closer, or whether they only augur a re-focusing of the issues in dispute, remains to be seen in future discussions of the many problems attending the study of the complex subject of social stratification.

COMMUNITY POWER STRUCTURE
AND SOCIAL WELFARE

Floyd Hunter

ONE OF THE FIRST TASKS in making a theoretical analysis of the community is that of delimiting and defining it as a structure.[1] The task of delimitation may take into account four basic elements [developed by E. T. Hiller], namely (1) personnel (members), (2) test(s) of admission and membership, (3) distinctive roles or functions of the members, and (4) norms regulating the conduct of the personnel.[2] The physical limits of the structure with which this study is concerned have been set, or at least an awareness of such limits has been indicated. We shall presently be concerned with all of the elements suggested here, and most particularly with the first three, but only in relation to a segment of the community—the power element. The fourth item, norms regulating conduct within the community of Regional City, presents problems with which the present study does not deal, except in a passing fashion. All of the norms of behavior of power personnel in Regional City are not known, but some specifications of men which may indicate norms will be outlined.

The personnel with which the current discussion is concerned represents but a minute fraction of the community in which it moves and functions. It does represent a definite group, however, and a very important one in Regional City. No pretense is made that the group to be discussed represents the totality of power leaders of the community, but it is felt that a representative case sample is presented, and that the men described come well within the range of the center of power in the community.

The leaders selected for study were secured from lists of leading civic, professional, and fraternal organizations, govermental personnel, business leaders, and "society" and "wealth" personnel suggested by various sources. These lists of more than 175 persons were rated by "judges" who selected by mutual choice the top forty persons in the total listings. These forty were the object of study and investigation in Regional City. Some data were collected about the total number. Twenty-seven members of the group were interviewed on the basis of a prepared schedule plus additional questions as the investigation proceeded. Any figures used in the study will need to be tied fairly rigidly to the twenty-seven members on whom there are comparable data.

Reprinted from *Community Power Structure: A Study of Decision Makers* (1953), pp. 60-113, by permission of the author and the publisher. (Copyright, 1953, by the University of North Carolina Press.) The chapter has been abridged.

The fourteen under-structure professionals in civic and social work who were interviewed have also provided data which may be considered comparable.

The system of power groups which is being examined may not be called a closed system. The groups are links in a total pattern, which may offer suggestive clues to total power patterns in the operating system of Regional City. There are gaps in the power arc which investigation may not be able to close. Actually the discussion here is primarily concerned with the structuring of power on a policy-making level. Only a rudimentary "power pyramid" of Regional City will be presented. One may be content to do this because I doubt seriously that power forms a single pyramid with any nicety in a community the size of Regional City. There are *pyramids* of power in this community which seem more important to the present discussion than *a* pyramid. Let me illustrate this point.

In the interviews, Regional City leaders were asked to choose ten top leaders from the basic list of forty. The choices of the twenty-seven persons answering this question showed considerable unanimity of opinion. . . .

George Delbert . . . was chosen . . . more than Charles Homer, and Homer is consequently lower down the scale than Delbert. Delbert is considered a "big man" in Regional City affairs, but he is not as big as Homer, according to most of the informants in answer to the simple question, "Who is the 'biggest' man in town?"

The question on which Delbert came to the top of the voting poll was phrased, "if a project were before the community that required *decision* by a group of leaders—leaders that nearly everyone would accept—which *ten* on the list of forty would you choose?" Delbert came out on top in this question, but not on the one related to who is the biggest man in town. Thus the pyramid scheme suggested by the voting poll of leaders, related to making projects move, must be modified in relation to the factors which weigh in Homer's favor in other areas related to power. Quite possibly some of these factors are Homer's wealth, his social position, and his business position. Homer is from an old family of wealth in Regional City. He is the wealthiest man in the community according to most reports. He is chairman of the board of the community's largest industry in volume of sales. Delbert, on the other hand, is the president of a large corporation but is a salaried man—with a very large reputed salary. There is a distinction made between salaried personnel and owners of enterprises in Regional City whether the salary be large or small. Delbert's family background is also not comparable to Homer's.

This is not to say that Delbert is not a powerful man. He is. He can command the services of more than 50,000 employees, and he has a very large voice in community matters—a larger voice perhaps than Homer's, since he uses it oftener. Delbert is willing to serve on top-flight community committees and boards. Homer is not. Homer says of himself, "I will work on no boards or committees. I work entirely through other men." His attitude on this matter is well known in the community, and consequently he was chosen fewer times than Delbert on the question under discussion. In spite of his methods of work he was chosen by almost half the men voting on the question.

The high consensus regarding the top leaders on the list of forty, plus the lack of any concerted opinion on additional individuals, would indicate that the men being interviewed represented at least a nucleus of a power grouping.

The question was also put to interviewees, "How many men would need to be involved in a major community project in Regional City 'to put it over'?" The answers to this question varied from, "You've got the men right here on this list—maybe ten of them," to "fifty or a hundred." One informant said, "Some of the men on this list would undoubtedly be in on getting the project started. After it got moving, perhaps six hundred men might be involved either directly or indirectly." This was the largest figure any informant gave. The informant elaborated on the answer by saying that a large fund-raising campaign was the thing he had in mind, and he illustrated the point by speaking of a fund drive for a hospital building program that had recently been completed in Regional City. He said that he could count the men on his hands who had "sparked" the drive, but hundreds of volunteers had been used from the civic associations and the general community to "put the drive over the top." He felt that any project for civic improvement would likely involve the same type of organization.

In the above illustration of structured action, the "men of independent decision" are a relatively small group. The "executors of policy" may run into the hundreds. This pattern of a relatively small decision-making group working through a larger under-structure is a reality, and if data were available, the total personnel involved in a major community project might possibly form a pyramid of power, but the constituency of the pyramid would change according to the project being acted upon.

In other words, the personnel of the pyramid would change depending upon what needs to be done at a particular time. Ten men might, for example, decide to bring a new industry into the community. Getting the industry physically established and operating might take the disciplined and coordinated action of a few more men or several hundred men, depending on the size of the project. Some of the same decision men in another instance might be involved in starting a program for some local governmental change, but another group of men would be involved in carrying out the decisions reached. Both projects are power orientated, but each requires different personnel in the execution. The men in the under-structure may have a multiplicity of individual roles within the totality of the community structure which can be set in motion by the men of decision.

As I became familiar with the list of forty names through the interviewing process, it became evident that certain men, even within the relatively narrow range of decision leaders with whom I was dealing, represented a top layer of personnel. Certain men were chosen more frequently than others, not only in relation to who should be chosen to decide on a project, as has already been indicated, but the same men interacted together on committees and were on the whole better known to each other than to those outside this group. Through analyzing the mutual choices made by those interviewed, it will be shown that there is an *esprit de corps* among certain top leaders, and some of them may be said to operate on a very high level of decision in the community; but this will not necessarily mean that one of the top leaders can be considered subordinate to any other in the community as a whole. On specific projects one leader may allow another to carry the ball, as a leader is said to do when he is "out front" on a project which interests him. On the next community-wide project another may carry the ball. Each may subordinate himself to another on a temporary basis, but such a structure of subordination is quite fluid, and it is voluntary.

In a scale of mutual choices among twenty of the top leaders (that is, when two leaders chose each other in the leadership poll), there is indication of a selective process in leadership choices made by the men of decision. Again, these choices were made on the basis of "who might best decide on a project." The fact that the mutual choices remain well within the upper limits of the ranking scale indicates definite selectivity.

The question was asked each person interviewed, "Indicate how many persons (in the list of forty) you have worked with on committees within the past five years?" The upper-limits group indicated that they had worked with an average of twenty-nine persons on the list. The lower-limits group indicated that they had worked with an average of only twenty-one persons on the list. The professional under-structure of civil and social workers were asked the same question and indicated that they had worked with an average of only ten persons on the list. There is a definite drop, therefore, in the rate of interaction between each of the three groups and the group of forty leaders. Each group has access to the other, but those in the upper-limits group are in contact with other leaders more frequently, in committee work, at least. The under-structure professionals, with few exceptions, interact with persons immediately above them and with other professionals close to them in the power scale.

Another index used to discover the degree of relationship existing between the leaders interviewed and the total group of forty leaders was based upon a question which asked, on a six-point scale, how well known each person on the list of forty was to the interviewee. The scale read: "How well do you know each person (on the list of forty): (1) related_____, (2) know socially_____, (3) know well_____, (4) know slightly_____, (5) heard of him_____, (6) not known_____." By again utilizing the upper-limits and lower-limits groups of leaders, and through comparison of these two groups with the professional under-structure personnel, we see a definite differentiation between the groups. In order not to present too confusing an array of figures, we shall indicate only the average number of persons known well or better in each group.

The upper-limits group knew well or better an average of thirty-four persons in the list of forty. The lower-limits group of top leaders knew an average of 28.7 leaders well or better. The professional under-structure averaged only 7.3 persons for their same degree of acquaintance with the total group of top leaders, in addition to having a higher rate of committee interaction with this same group. The professional persons who carry out the decisions of the policy-making group are definitely differentiated from the top leaders in rates of interaction and in degree of acquaintance with the top leaders.

Our rudimentary statistical conclusions on the degrees of relationship among the persons named were borne out in qualitative interviewing. Over and over, the same persons were named as influential and consequently able to "move things" in Regional City. The significance of a high degree of inter-action is suggested by Homans' hypothesis, "The more nearly equal in social rank a number of men are, the more frequently they will interact with one another."[3] Our findings bear out this hypothesis.

One other index was used to determine how closely integrated the upper-limits group was in relation to the lower-limits group. By ranking the leaders according to the number of leadership choices received from other leaders and analyzing how far up the scale or how far down the scale each went in making his choice, one finds a differentiating picture of the two groups. Members of the upper-limits group would go both up and down the scale from their own position in their choices, but not very far. They would go up an average of 5.4 places. They would go down an average of 4.9 places in their choices. These figures indicate a tendency to choose persons as leaders who are fairly close to the choosers in the scale.

The lower-limits personnel, on the other hand, tended almost entirely to choose men above them in rank. They would go up the scale an average of 13.1 places, and would go down only 0.6 places in their choices. It would seem from this evidence that the under group defers to the upper group, and that there is some solidarity in the upper echelons of policy-makers.

As shown earlier, power has been defined in terms of policy leadership, and the data given in the present chapter make a beginning at defining structural power relations. A group of men have been isolated who are among the most powerful in Regional City. It has been shown that they interact among themselves on community projects and select one another as leaders. Their relations with one another are not encompassed in a true pyramid of power, but some degree of ranking, even in the top-level policy leadership group, has been indicated. Let us now look at policy personnel patterns in another way.

In sizing up any individual one often asks, "What do you do for a living?" The reply to this question allows one rather quickly to rank another in a rough scale of social values. The men under discussion hold commercial, industrial, financial, and professional positions in Regional City that tend to classify them in the minds of any observer. In order to make a beginning at seeing the relations among the men of power in more personal terms than statistics will allow, let us examine a list of positions held by some of the leaders of the policy-determining groups in Regional City (Table 1).

It can be seen at a glance that most of the leaders hold positions as presidents of companies, chairmen of boards, or professional positions of some prestige. Generally speaking, the companies represented in the listing are of major enterprise proportions. More than half the men may be said to be businessmen, if the term is used broadly. The major economic interests of the community are overwhelmingly represented in the listing. The pattern of business dominance of civic affairs in Regional City is a fact. No other institution is as dominant in community life as the economic institution, and this phenomenon will be dealt with at greater length under an appropriate heading.

Table 1—Policy-Making Leaders in Regional City by Occupational Position

Type of Occupation	Name of Leader	Name of Organizational Affiliation	Position
Banking, Finance, Insurance	Hardy	Investment Company of Old State	President
	Mines	Producer's Investments	President
	Schmidt	First Bank	President
	Simpson	Second Bank	Vice-President
	Spade	Growers Bank	President
	Tarbell	Commercial Bank	Executive Vice-President
	Trable	Regional City Life	President
Commercial	Aiken	Livestock Company	Chairman, Board
	Black	Realty Company of Regional City	President
	Delbert	Allied Utilities	President
	Dunham	Regional Gas Heat Company	General Manager
	Graves	Refrigeration, Incorporated	President
	Parker	Mercantile Company	Executive Manager
	Parks	Paper Box Company	Chairman, Board
	Smith	Cotton Cloth Company	Manager
	C. Stokes	Oil Pipe Line Company	President
	Webster	Regional City Publishing Company	Managing Editor
	Williams	Mercantile Company	Chairman, Board
Government	Barner	City Government	Mayor
	Gordon	City Schools	Superintendent
	Rake	County Schools	Superintendent
	Worth	County Government	Treasurer
Labor	Gregory	Local Union	President
	Stone	Local Union	President
Leisure	Fairly	None	Social Leader
	Howe	None	Social Leader
	Mills	None	Social Leader
	Moore	None	Social Leader
	Stevens	None	Social Leader
Manufacture and Industry	Farris	Steel Spool Company	Chairman, Board
	Homer	Homer Chemical Company	Chairman, Board
	Spear	Homer Chemical Company	President
	E. Stokes	Stokes Gear Company	Chairman, Board
	Treat	Southern Yarn Company	President
Professional*	Farmer	Law Firm	Attorney
	Gould	Law Firm	Attorney
	Latham	Private Office	Dentist
	Moster	Law Firm	Attorney
	Street	Law Firm	Attorney
	Tidwell	Law Firm	Attorney

*Attorneys' affiliations not given. Without exception they are corporation lawyers.

One of the first interviews had in Regional City was with James Treat of the Southern Yarn Company. He gave a great deal of information concerning power relations in the community. Among other things, he supplied a clue to certain existing clique relationships and considerable information about them which was later verified. Several times in his conversation he had used the term "crowds" in describing how certain men acted in relation to each other on community projects, and he was asked to explain the term. His reply ran in this vein:

"I simply mean that there are 'crowds' in Regional City—several of them—that pretty well make the big decisions. There is the crowd I belong to (the Homer Chemical crowd); then there is the First State Bank crowd—the Regional Gas Heat crowd—the Mercantile crowd—the Growers Bank crowd —and the like."

Each man mentioned by Mr. Treat as belonging to a crowd also belongs to a major business enterprise within the community—at least the clique leader does. His position within the bureaucratic structure of his business almost automatically makes him a community leader, if he wishes to become one. The test for admission to this circle of decision-makers is almost wholly a man's position in the business community in Regional City. The larger business enterprises represent pyramids of power in their own right, as work units within the community, and the leaders within these concerns gather around them some of the top personnel within their own organization. They then augment this nucleus of leadership by a coterie of selected friends from other establishments to form knots of interest called "crowds" by Mr. Treat. The outer edges of any crowd may pick up such men as Percy Latham, the dentist, who in turn picks up others in relation to any specific activity in which the crowd may be interested. The top men in any crowd tend to act together, and they depend upon men below them to serve as intermediaries in relation to the general community.

The crowds described by Mr. Treat were also mentioned by numerous other informants. These crowds did not, however, exhaust the possibilities of clique relations within the larger group of policy leaders. Twenty-one distinct groupings were picked up within the forty persons on the list, as the study proceeded, but the crowds mentioned by Treat seemed to be the most generally recognized groupings. Several of the top leaders within the crowds would "clear with each other" informally on many matters. The older men, as mentioned earlier, tended to get their heads together on most matters, as did the younger group, but such relationships were not completely stable. Each man at the top of a "crowd pyramid" depended upon those close to him in business to carry out decisions when made. An older man, for example, could not command another older man to do something, but within his own crowd there would be a hierarchy he could put to work. In most instances decision-making tended to be channeled through the older men at some point in the process of formulation, but many things may be done on the initiative of any combination of several powerful leaders in the crowds named. None of the leaders indicated that he could work alone on any big project, nor did any feel that there was any man in the community with such power. The individual power leader is dependent on others in Regional City in contrast to mill or mining company towns where one man or one family may dominate the community actions which take place.

Society prestige and deference to wealth are not among the primary criteria for admission to the upper ranks of the decision-makers according to the study of Regional City. The persons who were included in the listing of forty top leaders purely on the basis of their wealth or society connections did not, with three or four exceptions, make the top listing of persons who might be called upon to "put across a community project." As has been mentioned before, a distinction is made between persons of wealth and social prestige who engage in work and those who do not. The persons of wealth are perhaps important in the social structure of the community as symbolic persons. They may be followed in matters of fashion and in their general manner of living. Their money may be important in financing a given project, but they are not of themselves doers. They may only be called decisive in the sense that they can withhold or give money through others to change the course of action of any given project. Gloria Stevens spends large sums of money on Regional City projects, but the expenditures are made through her lawyer, Ray Moster. She does not interact with any of the top leaders whom we interviewed, other than Moster, so far as could be ascertained. Hetty Fairly, another woman of wealth, spends her charitable monies through a foundation handled by a lawyer not on the list of leaders. The lawyers may be vigilant in serving the interests of their clients in both instances, and a part of the vigilance exercised is in keeping abreast of possible tax incursions on the "frozen wealth" of the foundations. In this there may be some connection with power, but it is rather obscure in terms of the definition of power as being the ability of persons to move goods and services toward defined goals. If there is power in the charitable foundation structures, it resides in the lawyers who operate them, rather than in the donors who are largely inactive in the affairs of the foundations.

Political eminence cannot be said to be a sole criterion for entry into the policy echelons of Regional City's life, generally speaking. The two exceptions to this statement are embodied in Mayor Barner and County Treasurer Truman Worth. Both Barner and Worth were successful businessmen before becoming involved in local politics to the point of seeking public office. Their interests may be said to be primarily business in the strict sense of the word. Both have a popular following that has kept them in office, but their close associates are businessmen. Mayor Barner had only one picture in his office—that of Charles Homer, the biggest businessman in the community. Both Barner and Worth look to businessmen constantly for advice before they make a move on any project concerning the whole community. Furthermore, they do not ordinarily "move out front" on any project themselves, but rather follow the lead of men like Delbert, Graves, or any one of the other leaders of particular crowds.

The point made at this turn of the discussion is not a new one. Businessmen are the community leaders in Regional City as they are in other cities. Wealth, social prestige, and political machinery are functional to the wielding of power by the business leaders in the community. William E. Henry puts the matter this way:

The business executive is the central figure in the economic and social life of the United States. His direction of business enterprise and his participation in informal social groupings give him a significant place in community life. In both its economic and its social aspects the role of the business executive is sociologically a highly visible one.[4]

The "visibility" suggested by Henry is a highly applicable concept in connection with an analysis of Regional City leadership. One need not labor the point. This study has already shown that business leaders take a prominent position in Regional City civic affairs.

In the general social structure of community life social scientists are prone to look upon the institutions and formal associations as powerful forces, and it is easy to be in basic agreement with this view. Most institutions and associations are subordinate, however, to the interests of the policy-makers who operate in the economic sphere of community life in Regional City. The institutions of the family, church, state, education, and the like draw sustenance from economic institutional sources and are thereby subordinate to this particular institution more than any other. The associations stand in the same relationship to the economic interests as do the institutions. We see both the institutions and the formal associations playing a vital role in the execution of determined policy, but the formulation of policy often takes place outside these formalized groupings. Within the policy-forming groups the economic interests are dominant.

The economic institution in Regional City, in drawing around itself many of the other institutions in the community, provides from within itself much of the personnel which may be considered of primary influence in power relationships. A lengthy discussion on institutions per se is not proposed. Their existence as channels through which policy may be funneled up and down to broader groups of people than those represented by the top men of power is easily recognized. Some of the institutions would represent imperfect channels for power transmission, however. For example, the family as an institution is not a channel of itself for bringing about general community agreement on such a matter as the desirability of building a new bridge across Regional River. On the other hand, the church might represent a more potent force on this question. The preacher could preach a sermon on the matter in any given church, and the members could sign petitions, attend meetings at the behest of the church bureaucracy, and go through a whole series of activities motivated by the institution in question.

It may be noted here that none of the ministers of churches in Regional City were chosen as top leaders by the persons interviewed in the study. The idea was expressed several times by interviewees that some minister *ought* to be on the listing, but under the terms of power definitions used in the study they did not make "top billing." It is understood, however, that in order to get a project well under way it would be important to bring the churches in, but they are not, as institutions, considered crucial in the decision-making process. Their influence is crucial in restating settled policies from time to time and in interpreting new policies which have been formed or are in the process of formulation. Church leaders, however, whether they be prominent laymen or professional ministers, have relatively little influence with the larger economic interests.

One cannot, in Regional City at least, look to the organized institutions as policy-determining groupings, nor can one look to the formal associations which are part of these institutions. But let us briefly be specific concerning the role of organizations. There is a multiplicity of organized groups in Regional City. The Chamber of Commerce lists more than 800 organizations from bee-keeping societies to federated industrial groups. The membership lists of some of these organizations often run into the hundreds. In this study organizations were considered as being influential in civic affairs and some ranking of the most important was deemed necessary. Consequently, all persons interviewed were asked to give their opinion on a selected list of supposedly top-ranking organizations in the community. An initial selection of thirty organizations was made by a panel of judges from lists supplied by the Chamber of Commerce and the local Community Council. The persons interviewed in the list of forty leaders narrowed their selections of organizations to seven—organizations to which the majority of these top leaders belonged. They were (in rank order of importance) the Chamber of Commerce, Community Chest, Rotary Club, Y.M.C.A., Community Council, Grand Juror's Association, and Bar Association. There was a scattering of votes for the Christian Council and for one of the larger labor organizations. The Retail Merchants Association was added to our list by two merchants. The under-structure professional personnel in civic and social work who were interviewed indicated that they recognized the influence of the same organizations chosen by the top leaders. It may be noted that they generally belonged to only the Community Chest and the Community Council in conjunction with the top leaders.

Some of the top leaders may hold board positions within the associational groupings to lend prestige to the organization, but such members are more noted for their absence than for their attendance at meetings of the respective boards. They can be called upon in an organizational crisis or emergency, and at such times they may function decisively. One leader explained his position in this way: "If I attend meetings too regularly, I am asked to be chairman of this or that committee. I don't have time for that kind of work, but you hate to refuse before a bunch of people. There are usually two or three listening posts, people who can keep me in touch with things, on these boards. I get reports from them from time to time and that way keep a hand in. I also read the minutes of important meetings. Most of the time I know about where any board I belong to stands on various matters. I attend meetings only when I'm really needed."

Occasionally a top leader will take the presidency of one of the associations, but such position is usually unsought and avoided if possible—particularly by the older leaders. The younger leaders may be pushed to take some of the top associational posts as training assignments. They take on such duties, they say, with reluctance and make feeble protests of being terribly busy and pressed for time. The less powerful understructure associational personnel may scramble (in a dignified way, of course) for the top positions in these groupings.

In crisis situations, such as during World War II, many of the older leaders were called to active duty on civic boards. This was particularly true in the large fund-raising organizations where campaign goals were doubled or tripled over previous ones and the prestige of the older leaders was needed to insure the success of particular drives. During the crisis of depression in the 1930's several of the older leaders served on the local welfare board, but as the economic situation improved, they were replaced by "second-rate" and "third-rate" community leaders.[5]

Many of the persons interviewed belonged to many more organizations than those previously indicated, but the groups listed represent those that the power leaders consider most important in carrying out or interpreting a community-wide project. Two formal organizations were mentioned which are not generally known to the community at large but which are considered quite influential by the men of power. One is called the "49 Club" and the other the "Committee of 101." The 49 Club is a highly selective group organized in Regional City at the turn of the century. It is composed of a group of men who are prominent in community life and who have in some instances inherited a place on the membership roster. The club discusses major issues before the community and the general body politic seeking agreement on general policy matters. Its meetings are not formal and are often held in the homes of members. When a member dies, his vacancy is not filled for a considerable time. The one chosen to fill the vacancy is highly honored. Several of the top men on our list belonged to this club.

The Committee of 101 is almost exclusively devoted to a discussion of political matters. It discusses candidates and issues but takes no action on any matter which comes before it, nor are any formal records kept of the meetings. These latter stipulations also apply to the 49 Club. Membership in the Committee of 101 is considered a privilege, but it does not rank as high as the 49 Club. Both have high dues, the proceeds of which are spent on entertainment of the members.

Comparable data were gathered on twenty-four Regional City leaders concerning club memberships. Figure 1 shows the interlocking nature of these memberships. Attention may be called to Club C. This club is comparable to Club B. Both are civic luncheon clubs, but Club B has a higher status in the community than Club C, as indicated by its apparent popularity among the

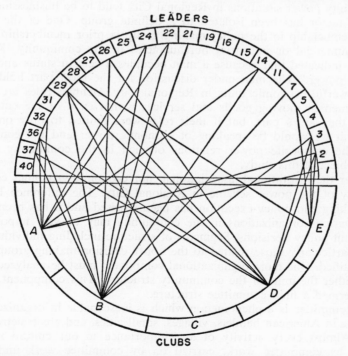

LEADERS

CLUBS

Fig. 1—Interlocking Club Memberships of 24 Regional City Leaders

top leaders. Clubs A, D, and E are social clubs of prominence. None of the under-structure professional personnel interviewed belong to any of these clubs.

None of the men interviewed considered any of the associational groupings crucial in policy determination. Their role, like that of the organized institutional groupings, is one of following rather than leading. They may provide a forum for discussing and studying community issues, needs, and policies; but, when decision is called for, another structure must come into play before action becomes the order of the day. The organizations may serve as training grounds for many of the men who later become power leaders. Most of the leaders had "graduated" from a stint in the upper positions of the more important organizations. Most associational presidents, however, remain in the under-structure of the power hierarchy. The organizations are not a sure route to sustained community prominence. Membership in the top brackets of one of the stable economic bureaucracies is the surest road to power, and this road is entered by only a few. Organizational leaders are prone to get the publicity; the upper echelon economic leaders, the power.

It was indicated at the beginning of this chapter that there would be a discussion of leadership groupings in a framework developed by E. T. Hiller, and by implication, at least, two of his criteria for analyzing community structure have been touched upon, namely, personnel and tests of admission of members. In a sense the third criterion has been bordered upon, that is, the distinctive roles of members. It has been said that the leading personnel in community power situations in Regional City tend to be businessmen. The personnel factor has been isolated to a definite group. One of the critical tests of membership in the policy-making group is prior membership in one of the commercial or industrial bureaucracies in the community. Kingsley Davis has indicated that because a man occupies a certain status and office, he enjoys power.[6] The men under discussion for the most part hold offices within powerful economic units in Regional City. Definite roles are played by these men in moving goods and services within each of the enterprises of which they are a part, but if their roles were limited to only one community unit we would be speaking of economic power and not community power. The composite power relations of men in the community are the primary object of this study.

Neither the institutional, associational, nor economic groupings comprise the totality of the power scheme in Regional City. The difference between policy-making and policy-execution has been stressed and it has been shown that the various organizations in the community may be very important in carrying out policy decisions. Segments of structure including individuals and cliques, particularly those related to the upper decision-making groups, have been identified. One more organizational component must be analyzed before tying together the units of the community structure. This component is what may be termed a fluid committee structure.

The committee is a phenomenon which is inescapable in organized community life in American hamlets, villages, small cities, and great metropolitan centers. Almost every activity of any importance in our culture must be preceded by committee work, carried on by committee work and finally posthumously evaluated by a committee. Regional City is no exception to the general rule. Day after day the hotel, club, and associational meeting rooms are packed with men going through the familiar motions of calling meetings to order and dismissing them. Committees may have short lives or they may go on for years. An example of the latter is the Committee of 101 previously discussed. Committees may be quite formally organized, utilizing parliamentary rules of order, or they may be loosely organized and informal in their procedures. They may be accompanied by food and drink or they may be devoid of such amenities. They may have serious or light purposes and consequently solemn or gay occasions as the case may be. Withal, each is accompanied by a certain degree of ritual befitting the occasion. Men used to committee work are sharp to detect poorly conducted meetings. No meeting, for example, can be said to have amounted to much if at least one motion is not put, passed, or put down—that is, in the more formally organized meetings. Men trained in conducting meetings are in demand, and such a person may display rare skills in ordering a group as it goes about its business.

Meetings are often a substitute for group action. As one Regional City professional phrased it, "There are those who believe in salvation by luncheon!" There is great faith manifest in certain quarters of our society that if people can just be got together in a meeting all problems will be solved. And there is some justification for this faith, since so many matters of community business, as well as private transactions, are brought to successful conclusions in meetings.

Meetings have the functions of clarifying objectives of a group and of fixing and delegating responsibilities for action on any matter. They may in like manner hold action in abeyance. Decisions reached in meetings may be solemnly binding, or they may not be. Decisions arrived at in one meeting may be changed in the next meeting. Responsibilities may be shifted and membership changed according to the will of the group as a series of meetings proceeds. Rarely are committee meetings bound by "constitutional" prohibitions or heavy legalistic trappings which characterize so many associational and institutional gatherings. The outstanding characteristic of the ordinary committee meeting is its fluidity and its adaptability in adjusting to changing conditions, which are so essentially a part of our modern urban culture. The importance of the committee in power relations cannot be overstressed.

While it is important to stress the fluidity of committee structure, it must also be pointed out that there is a stable base of personnel who are seen time and again in a variety of committee meetings. There are men in any community who devote large portions of their waking hours to attendance at one meeting or another. Public-relations men in industry and associational secretaries are paid to devote considerable of their time to meeting attendance. It becomes commonplace among this latter personnel group to see one another at committee meetings, and such personnel become familiar with community leaders who operate on a similar level with them. There is a tendency to judge the importance of these meetings by who is in attendance.

Most of the top personnel of the power group are rarely seen at meetings attended by the associational under-structure personnel in Regional City. The exception to this general statement may be found in those instances in which a project is broad enough so that the "whole community needs to be brought in on the matter." Such meetings as bring in the under-structure personnel are usually relatively large affairs, rather than smaller, more personal meetings which characterize policy-determination sessions. The interaction patterns of the two groups discussed here have shown a much higher rate of interaction among the top groups than between the top and lower groups. In matters of power decision the committee structure assumes keystone importance. . . .

Not all the institutions and associations in Regional City were identified as being related to the power leaders studied. For example, none of the leaders in a power relationship could be identified as representing the institution of the family or a cultural association. This does not mean that either of these groupings was unimportant for some of the top leaders, but in the specific power relations studied no identification could be made of persons within these groupings as such.

A few generalized remarks may be made concerning Figure 2, using a hypothetical example, after which it will be illustrated concretely how the structure worked in relation to a specific community project in Regional City.

If a project of major proportions were before the community for consideration—let us say a project aimed at building a new municipal auditorium—a policy committee would be formed. This may be called Project Committee A. Such a policy committee would more than likely grow out of a series of informal meetings, and it might be related to a project that has been on the discussion agenda of many associations for months or even years. But the time has arrived for action. Money must be raised through private subscription or taxation, a site selected, and contracts let. The time for a policy committee is propitious. The selection of the policy committee will fall largely to the men of power in the community. They will likely be businessmen in one or more of the larger business establishments. Mutual choices will be agreed upon for committee membership. In the early stages of policy formulation there will be a few men who make the basic decisions. As the project is trimmed, pared, and shaped into manageable proportions there will be a recognition that the committee should be enlarged. Top-ranking organizational and institutional personnel will then be selected by the original members to augment their numbers, i.e., the committee will be expanded. The civic associations and the formalized institutions will next be drawn into certain phases of planning and initiation of the project on a community-wide basis. The newspapers will finally carry stories of the proposals, the ministers will preach sermons, and the associational members will hear speeches regarding plans. This rather simply is the process, familiar to many, that goes on in getting any community project under way.

Project B might be related to changing the tax structure of the community. Much the same organizational procedure will be repeated, but different associations may be drawn into the planning and execution stages. The policy-making personnel will tend to be much the same as in Project A and this is an important point in the present discussion. There will be a hard core of policy leadership on Policy Committee B that was also present on Project Committee A. This relative stability of the top policy-making group is a pattern quite apparent in Regional City civic affairs. A similar pattern of stable committee membership exists in the under-structure of the

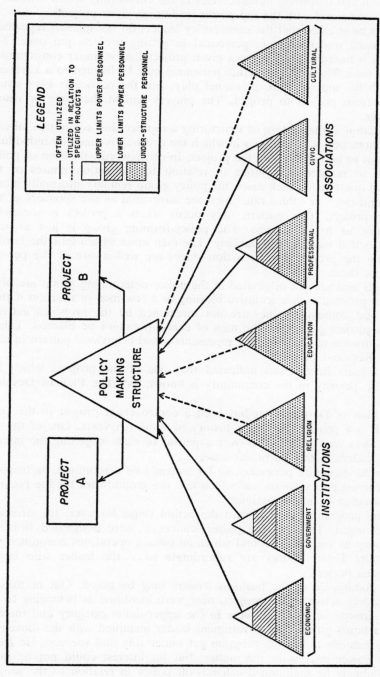

Fig. 2—Generalized Pattern of Policy Committee Formation Utilizing Institutional and Associational Structures

associational and corporate bureaucracies in the community which interact in a chain of command with the top power leaders on given projects.

It must be stressed that the same policy leaders do not interact repeatedly with the same under-structure personnel in getting projects put over. The interaction is based entirely upon a given project that is under consideration at a given time. The under-structure personnel may be likened to a keyboard over which the top structure personnel play, and the particular keys struck may vary from project to project. The players remain the same or nearly so, however.

A variation in the pattern of structuring a top-decision committee may be found in those policy committees in which the decision is made by individuals who are not to be out front on the project. In other words, the men of policy may wish to remain anonymous in relation to the action phases of the program in question. In such cases, the policy group remains informally intact, and "second-rate" or "third-rate" men are advertised as the sponsors of the particular project. This pattern may occur when a project is somewhat questionable as to its success. The policy-forming group is just as real, however, as if it were named publicly. The men upon whom falls the burden of carrying the project into its action stages are well aware of the persons who choose them.

Projects that are not originated in the policy-determining group are often allowed to proceed with a tentative blessing of a few men of decision if their interests and dominant values are not threatened by the proposed activity. If such a project goes sour, the men of decision cannot be blamed. This is another variation of structure and represents a real behavioral pattern in civic affairs in Regional City.

The leaders interviewed indicated that one of the projects which has current top priority in the community is known as "The Plan of Development."

The Plan of Development has been a controversial project in the community. It is a project that has a history of some ten years. One of the top policy leaders was quite active over a period of time in getting the interest of other leaders in this particular case. . . .

No under-structure personnel, so far as could be determined, participated in the informal policy committee which laid the groundwork for the program and determined its major outlines.

As the program moved toward the action stage, however, the structural picture changed. Three of the power leaders . . . were designated from the policy group as a nucleus around which an official operations committee was to be built. These leaders are subordinate to . . . the leader who largely initiated the project.

The dominance of the business leaders may be noted. Out of thirteen policy leaders active in the project, nine were identified as belonging to the business group, six of whom were in the upper-limits category and three in the lower-limits group. The government leader identified with the movement was very anxious to see the program get under way and succeed. He had a personal power interest in the matter, but his interest could not be made public. Publicly he maintained a hands-off policy in relation to the project, but in policy formulation he was quite active. . . .

After the policy line had been set and before the project could be activated, it was necessary to go to the state legislature for enabling legislation. In this process the legislators bargained with the policy group concerning the membership of the proposed official committee. During the horse-trading, some of the names proposed by the policy-makers were dropped in favor of local politicos agreeable to the state political leaders. The local "politicians" might be classified as semi-politicians. They have business connections which are their primary interest, but in at least four instances these businesses involve contracting or motor transport in which it is profitable to have good political relations with state officials.

One labor representative from a relatively weak union was put on the committee. He was chosen because he was identified with a joint union committee on community affairs devoted to interpreting welfare projects to the various labor groups. It does not seem desirable or necessary to describe all of the leaders of the activating committee, but mention will be made of one more individual, since his position in the scheme of project operation seems significant. This leader represents the upper-limits power leaders in the policy group. He is also a person identified with big business in the community. When the Plan of Development project was to be officially launched . . . he was asked to take the presidency of one of the more powerful civic associations for a year to "swing that group into line." He was given an impressive build-up by the newspapers for his broad civic interests and for a year he devoted a great deal of time to getting the Plan of Development under way. His leadership was well received generally, and apparently he was well supported, for the project has been put across successfully.

. . . The policy-makers generally move out of the picture at the stage of project execution. This pattern holds true generally for major community projects. The men in the under-structure of power become the doers and are activated by the policy-makers—the initiators.

The project discussed above is one related to Regional City *as a community*. Of course the affairs of the community do not stop at its borders. There are relationships between personnel in the city and persons in state and national power groups. Robert K. Merton observed in a recent study that community leaders fall into "cosmopolitan" and "local" groupings.[7] This generalized concept seems to hold true in Regional City. Some men tend to confine their activities almost entirely within the community, while others are active on state and regional matters.

Homer, Parks, Hardy, Aiken, Parker, and Rake appear to be the men in Regional City who act largely as liaison persons between the community and national policy-making groups. These men average three committees each on the national level, in comparison to 1.2 for the group as a whole. Hardy claims to belong to the most national policy-making boards and committees, with ten as his total. Homer and Aiken are definitely more interested in national than in local affairs. This fact came out strongly in interviews with them. Aiken said, "There are plenty of men who can keep an eye on things here at home. Some of these matters like inflation and national defense need to be got at in Washington, and my interest is in these things."

On the state level of operations in relation to the city, Hardy is also active along with Stone, Rake, and Parker. These men average four state committees each in comparison with an average of 1.3 for the remainder of the group. Stone confines his policy-making committee work entirely to the state. He belongs to a few local committees but is not active on them. The other persons interested in state affairs tend to divide their remaining committee time between local and national groups. The majority of the top leaders belong to an average of six policy-making boards or committees in comparison to an average of 1.3 in the state and 1.2 nationally.

The professional under-structure persons belong to fewer local committees and boards on a policy-making level than do the top leaders, but they compare favorably with the leaders on the national and state levels. They average 4.7 local committees, 1.0 state committees, and 1.3 national committees. Qualitatively their committees and boards differ from the upper power group. They most generally belong to professional association groupings which are different from the trade and other economic groupings of the top leaders.

The community politicians almost entirely operate locally on boards and committees, but the Mayor has many individual contacts with the two levels of government above him on a less formalized basis than boards and committees of policy would imply. During an interview with the Mayor he was interrupted by a phone call which he had put through to Washington regarding a project which concerned the community, and one cannot say that he is not an influential man in national and state affairs. On the phone he sounded influential. He is not the most influential man in Regional City in local-national policy matters, and when the dynamics of the power structure is elaborated upon, this will become apparent. The Mayor denies much influence in state matters. When questioned on this area he said, "I was saying to Rafferty Jones [a state politician] the other day, 'Rafferty, I'll bet that I could not be elected to the lowest job in state government!' " State and local politics are differentiated, but not entirely distinct. As in other states where a large metropolitan center is located there is much friction and conflict of interest between the two political groupings. The two are joined often at that point at which major economic interests are involved, and the leaders of economic bureaucracies have much personal influence in bridging the formal structural gaps between the levels of government on specific matters.

In one of our postulates it is stated that, "Power is structured socially, in the United States, into a dual relationship between governmental and economic authorities on national, state, and local levels." In the light of the present analysis, there is less of a "dual" relationship than had been assumed. This is particularly true in Regional City, where the dominant factor in political life is the personnel of the economic interests. It is true that there is no formal tie between the economic interests and government, but the structure of policy-determining committees and their tie-in with the other powerful institutions and organizations of the community make government subservient to the interests of these combined groups. The governmental departments and their personnel are acutely aware of the power of key individuals and combinations of citizens' groups in the policy-making realm, and they are loathe to act before consulting and "clearing" with these interests.

Brady is enlightening on this point when he says that the same interests tend to dominate politics and business, particularly in the realm of policy. "The same individuals, the same groups and cliques, [and] the same interests dominate each sphere [of property and politics]," he says.[8] One is compelled to agree with him from observations of the two groups in Regional City. There is evidence, too, that the local economic interests tie into larger groupings of like interests on the state and national levels which tend to overshadow the policy-making machinery of government at all levels. The structure is that of a dominant policy-making group using the machinery of government as a bureaucracy for the attainment of certain goals coordinate with the interests of the policy-forming group. . . .

The structural relationship between the economic policy-determining groups and the operating units of government have often been looked upon as inherently immoral. The ethical implications of the domination by one set of men in manipulating government for specific and limited purposes may be avoided, but some concern must be expressed in relation to a functional difficulty which such domination presents in our society. "Common to all the national, social, and economic crises of our day," says von Beckerath, "is the fundamental problem of rebuilding a constant workable connection between the political structure . . . and its economic structure."[9] A consistent and workable connection between the political and economic structures appears to be an extremely pertinent concept, which highlights a weakness of the power structure of Regional City as it relates to other units on the political level. There are gaps in the power arc which are closed on many issues by the narrower-interest groups. In other words, it has been pointed out that the power personnel do not represent a true pyramid of political power. The power personnel may decisively influence most policies that concern legislative groups, and they are acutely aware of their own interests in such policy matters. However, on many issues they are not interested, and there is consequently no continuing structure which may transmit to the legislative bodies the general interests of the underlying groups within the body politic. This is no new problem, but it is a structurally significant one. If the formalized structures of government are under the domination of a group of policy leaders who are isolated from direct responsibility to the mass of people in a democratic society, then, values aside, the scheme is at best dysfunctional. No patent remedy is suggested in this writing but there is a structural weakness in the policy-making machinery and power-wielding mechanism as it has been observed in a particular locality. Correction of the difficulty may come from an open recognition of actual operating elements in power relations unobscured by abstract value descriptions which do not fit reality. Simply put, power structure is looked at here, not from the point of view of what one may think we have, or what one may think we ought to have, but rather in terms of what we've got. . . .

The Mayor of Regional City says, "We have got a citizen-run town here." And one can agree with him, but policy is controlled by a relatively small group of the citizenry. In such a situation an obvious question is, "What holds the system together?" This question was asked of our informants. The question was put in this way: "It is evident that we are dealing with a small group of policy leaders in this study, but the whole community of Regional City is comprised of some half million persons. What holds the whole group together in relation to the influence exerted by so few leaders?"

Boiled down, the more significant answers ran along the following lines: "It is a sense of obligation which some men have toward others which keeps the system operating." "It is obligation plus confidence in the ability of some men to get things done, while other men cannot get things done." "Some men are interested in working on community projects, others are not." "Money holds them together." "Some people just naturally work together better than others." "You get to know certain people and when anything comes up you tend to call on the same men over and over to work on community projects." "You watch to see who is moving—when you see a man on the move, pick him up. He'll work for you!"

There is merit in all of these answers. Within the primary groups, or separate crowds clustered around specific interests, it is evident that similar interests and resulting common sentiments have a great deal to do with holding the groups together. Men who work together over a long period of time become comfortable in their working relationships with one another. Mutual sentiments of liking will grow up between them, and these sentiments in turn will lead to further interactions.[10] The ability of a top leader to retain a position of prestige depends to some extent on how well he conforms to the norms of the group he leads. The men of Regional City tend to be exponents of the "common man" in appearance and manner of speech, at least during the workday. Some of the men of top wealth and position are spoken of as "common as an old shoe." Their private lives hidden from the general mass of people may be uncommon, but their everyday behavior tends toward a confirmation of what one Regional City professional in the under-structure has called the "patched pants theory." "The biggest ones act like they have patches on their pants," he said. "The higher the rank of the person within a group, the more nearly his activities conform to the norms of the group," says Homans.[11]

Common interests, cutting across the lines of all separate crowds, tend to hold the community structure intact. James Treat said, "If you want to know what is going on, you have to be where the money is. It is capitalism, I suppose you would say. The men who make things move are interested in the larger issues—making money, keeping power." Joseph Hardy and Harvey Aiken agreed with Treat, but Aiken modified his statement by saying, "Money is only good so long as it is backed up by material goods. Inflation can ruin money, and it can ruin all the people who have money." He told of being in France recently where he inquired of some of the banking men who lived along one of the old boulevards whether their neighbors had suffered from post-war inflation. They indicated that most of their neighbors were the newly rich who had profited in the black markets resulting from World War II, and many of the new men of power were those who had been able to hold goods during the inflation rather than depend upon income from securities. The writer shares Aiken's caution about money as a sole source of power. It represents power in a stable economy when it is backed by tangible resources. With this limitation noted, it must be admitted that money still has meaning in power terms in Regional City. It is an important element.

Force is also an element of power but it is not an independent element. Von Beckerath says, "A state built upon *mere* force of a minority against the will of the majority is never possible in the long run."[12] One must look deeper than the elements of money or force to analyze adequately the power structure of Regional City. Both of these elements have their place, but both are interconnected with a complex set of habitual relationships of men which are described in terms of group relations.

Homans says, "The higher a man's social rank, the larger will be the number of persons that originate interaction for him, either directly or through subordinates." Also, "The higher a man's social rank, the larger number of persons for whom he originates interaction, either directly or through intermediaries."[13] The actions indicated are a two-way process. The men of high social rank—in this discussion, policy-makers—are acted upon and they act upon others, and because of their position they influence large numbers of people. Homans also says that high social rank presages a wide range of interactions. If Homans were to leave the matter at the latter point, I should have to disagree with him, since I found that the men of power tended to act within a limited range of contacts in Regional City, but Homans has an answer to this:

An increasing specialization of activities will bring about a decrease in the range of interaction of a person . . . and will limit the field in which he can originate action. . . . Thus an increase in the size of the group and in the specialization of activity will tend to increase the numbers of positions in the chain of interaction between the top leader and the ordinary member [in our case, citizen].[14]

The group of men dealt with here have a specialized function, namely, policy-making. It would not be physically possible for the men of decision to interact with great numbers of citizens on a face-to-face basis in Regional City. The contacts with the average citizen must be limited, but there must be channels of interaction open for decisions to flow down, and for issues to rise, at times, from the underlying population. These channels are open through the institutions and associations previously outlined in this chapter. The men of decision will not go far up or down the scale of leadership to choose others with whom to work, and these findings are in conformity with another of Homan's theories: "If a person does originate interaction for a person of higher rank, a tendency will exist for him to do so with the member of his own sub-group who is nearest him in rank."[15]

The tendency works the other way, too. Persons in the higher ranks most often work with persons close to them and rely on men immediately below them to originate interaction with persons in turn below them. As a matter of custom and practice, the person of higher rank originates interaction for those below him more often than the latter originate interaction for him.[16] This process has the following results:

Channels of interaction will become established, and the leader will not become overburdened with interaction. The relative frequency of interaction with immediate superiors and interaction with the top leader must differ from group to group according to the number of circumstances, two of which are the size of the group and the severity of the environment. . . . The more severe the environment in which the group must survive—ships and armies [for example]—the more likely it is that interaction will be strictly channeled.[17]

The channels of interaction are established in Regional City to conserve the time of the men of power. Even with the channels that are opened, there is still considerable burden of responsibility placed upon these men.

The power leaders do get around with considerable facility in the area of economic activity. When a new corporation is started, as for example a new television company, or a multi-million dollar apartment building project recently established in the city, one or more of the leaders were observed to "find time" to be identified with such developments. Certainly, the top leaders would appear to have time for policy considerations of such economic projects, if one takes into account the reports in the business section of the local press. The day-to-day working arrangements of the corporations are put into the hands of trusted under-structure administrative personnel. The pattern of power implicit in the situation matches that of civic enterprises in formation and development.

"If two institutions," says Hughes, "draw upon the same people . . . they may compete in some measure, for people have but a limited amount of time and money to expend."[18] The leaders of Regional City tend to protect themselves from too many demands by channeling policy execution through an under-structure on matters of policy. This under-structure is not a rigid bureaucracy, as has been pointed out, but is a flexible system. It has elements of stability and tends to operate by levels. The men at each level are spoken of as first, second, third and fourth rate by the power leaders, who operate primarily in conjunction with individuals of the first two ratings. The types of personnel which may be found in each rating by a sample classification are as follows:

EXAMPLES OF PERSONNEL FROM FIRST TO FOURTH RATE IN
REGIONAL CITY

FIRST RATE: Industrial, commercial, financial owners and top executives of large enterprises.

SECOND RATE: Operations officials, bank vice-presidents, public-relations men, small businessmen (owners), top-ranking public officials, corporation attorneys, contractors.

THIRD RATE: Civic organization personnel, civic agency board personnel, newspaper columnists, radio commentators, petty public officials, selected organization executives.

FOURTH RATE: Professionals such as ministers, teachers, social workers, personnel directors, and such persons as small business managers, higher paid accountants, and the like.

These ratings might be expanded. They are given simply to indicate a suggested ranking of selected personnel who operate below the policy-making leaders in Regional City. The first two ratings are personnel who are said to "set the line of policy," while the latter two groups "hold the line." The ratings are very real to the under-structure professional personnel.

The "little fellows" are continually moved to perform their proper tasks by those above them. The roles defined for the under-structure of power personnel are carefully defined in keeping with the larger interests. Their movements are carefully stimulated and watched at all times to see that their various functions are properly performed.

Stability of relationships is highly desirable in maintaining social control, and keeping men "in their places" is a vital part of the structuring of community power. Andrew Carnegie expressed the idea of every man in his place in this manner: "It is the business of the preacher to preach, of the physician to practice, of the poet to write, the business of the college professor to teach. . . ."[19] Each of these professions also has a role to play in the community activities consistent with its economic or professional role. Such roles do not ordinarily include policy-making. If one of these under-structure men should be presumptuous enough to question policy decisions, he would be immediately considered insubordinate and "punished," first by a threat to his job security, followed possibly by expulsion from his job if his insubordination continued. To quote Homans:

A social system is in a moving equilibrium and authority exists when the state of the elements that enter the system and the relations between them, including the behavior of the leader(s), is such that disobedience to the orders of the leader(s) will be followed by changes in the other elements tending to bring the system back to the state the leader(s) would have wished to reach if the disobedience had not occurred.[20]

There may be isolated dissatisfactions with policy decisions in Regional City, but mainly there is unanimity. The controversial is avoided, partly by the policy-making group's not allowing a proposal to get too far along if it meets stiff criticism at any point in decision-making. A careful watch is kept for what "will go" and for what "will not go." Luke Street says, "Most of the carping comes from people who are envious of some of the bigger crowds. When there is such envy, the crowds are talked about and criticized." Such criticism usually is not open. When criticism is open it is generally directed toward some of the under-structure men who are fronting for the larger interests. If criticism is directed toward the top leaders, the critic is liable to job dismissal in extreme cases or more subtle pressures in less flagrant cases. The omnipresent threat of power sanctions used against recalcitrant underlings is recognized by the lower echelons of power, and they generally go along with most decisions, grumbling in private with close associates, if at all. Most of these third- or fourth-rate leaders rationalize their behavior—particularly when upper decisions are in conflict with their professional or private value systems.

There is one more element in Regional City's power structure which must be discussed. It is the element of power residing in the Negro community of the city. . . . The Negro community represents a sub-structure of power as well as a sub-community. As a community grouping it calls up many issues which tend to mobilize the total power structure. As a sub-community power structure it is inextricably interwoven with the elements discussed in the present chapter, but for analytical purposes it calls for special treatment.

Two of the hypotheses of the study have been discussed in some measure in the preceding analysis. These hypotheses, restated, are as follows:

1. The exercise of power is limited and directed by the formulation and extension of social policy within a framework of socially sanctioned authority.

2. In a given power unit a smaller number of individuals will be found formulating and extending policy than those exercising power.

A corollary of the latter hypothesis was also touched upon: All policy-makers are men of power, but all men of power are not, per se, policy-makers.

The top group of the power hierarchy has been isolated and defined as comprised of policy-makers. These men are drawn largely from the business-men's class in Regional City. They form cliques or crowds, as the term is more often used in the community, which formulate policy. Committees for formulation of policy are commonplace, and on community-wide issues policy is channeled by a "fluid committee structure" down to institutional, associational groupings through a lower-level bureaucracy which executes policy.

It has been pointed out that intra-community and extra-community policy matters are handled by essentially the same group of men in this city, but there is a differentiation of functional activity within this policy group. Some men operate on different levels of policy decision, particularly in matters concerning governmental action. Some structural weaknesses in the power structure have been touched upon but at no great length. Finally, it was found that the structure is held together by common interests, mutual obligations, money, habit, delegated responsibilities, and in some cases by coercion and force.

SOCIAL CLASS AND COLOR DIFFERENCES IN CHILD-REARING

Allison Davis and Robert J. Havighurst

IN RECENT YEARS, cultural anthropologists and social psychologists have made intensive studies of the relationships between personality and socialization.[1] They have arrived at a methodological distinction which has proved helpful in the analysis of personality. In the light of their comparative data on the socialization of individual children in different societies, they have set up the operational principle that personality can best be studied in terms of two basic interacting systems of behavior.

One system of actions, feelings, and thoughts is (1) cultural. It is learned by the individual from his basic social groups: his family, his age-groups, his sex group, his social-class group, and so on. The other system of responses is (2) individual, or "idiosyncratic," or "private." It derives in part from (a) genetic factors and in part from (b) learning. These learned individual traits are responses to (a') organic, (b') affectional and (c') chance factors, and likewise to (d') the particular deviations of a child's training from the standard cultural training for his group.

The use of this hypothesis and its various derivative forms seems likely to bring some order into the chaotic field of personality-studies. As a methodological distinction, it is useful both in the exploration of the life-history, and likewise in the cross-sectional study of personality-traits in a population. As a method of securing and organizing data, it has the virtue of directing the researcher's attention to increasingly *smaller systems* of behavior in his search for the formants of personality. As an hypothesis about the dynamics of personality, this distinction between the cultural and the individual "personalities" leads to the useful effort to understand "adjustment" and "maladjustment," or "normal" and "neurotic" behavior, in terms of the degree of "fit" between a person's *individual* motivation, and the *cultural* demands made upon him to adhere to those roles and those traits approved by his particular society.

The research whose findings will be summarized below is concerned primarily with the cultural aspects of personality.[2] In a later report on a second part of our research, the development of individuality in children will be approached through intensive studies of the development of siblings. In this report, however, our purpose is to describe differences in the *cultural training* of children whose families are of different social and cultural status.

The nature of social stratification in the United States, and the cultural patterns of American social classes have been defined in extensive studies by Professor W. Lloyd Warner and his colleagues.[3] Furthermore, the powerful influence of this social-class system upon the American educational system, and upon what the child learns in school has been documented in a summary of recent studies.[4]

To students of learning, and especially to those who wish to study the processes of socialization, a detailed understanding of American social-class cultures and motivational patterns is now a *sine qua non* of both research and therapy. For the social class of the child's family determines not only the neighborhood in which he lives and the play-groups he will have, but also the basic cultural acts and goals toward which he will be trained. The social-class system maintains cultural, economic, and social barriers which prevent intimate social intermixture between the slums, the Gold Coast, and the middle class. We know that human beings can learn their culture only *from other human beings,* who already know and exhibit that culture. Therefore, by setting up barriers to social participation, the American social-class system actually prevents the vast majority of children of the working classes, or the slums, from learning any culture but that of their own groups. *Thus the pivotal meaning of social class* to students of human development is that it defines and systematizes different learning environments for children of different classes.[5]

There are three major types of cultural systems in the United States. The first is (1) *the general American system of cultural behaviors;* these include some form of the American language, certain broad similarities, such as wearing "clothing," living in "houses," using machinery etc.; the monogamous family; the prohibition of incest and murder; and certain democratic "ideals."

The other major cultural systems are (2) *the social-class cultures,* and (3) the *ethnic-group cultures.* So powerful are the social-class cultures that they tend to influence all the *general American cultural behaviors.* It is a fact that the specific form of the American language used, or of clothes, or of food, or of house, or even the social definition of a monogamous relationship varies by social class.

It has been assumed generally that the basic *areas* of training young children were very similar in all social strata, including weaning, toilet-training, property-training, etc. This seems to be true. Our purpose, however, was to determine to what extent *the methods, the timing,* and *the pace* of this early training differed in the various social classes. We attempted to make the same comparison with regard to the training demands in middle childhood.

Throughout this research, we have conceived of personality as an organization consisting of (1) learned responses, (habits, thoughts, feelings, values, goals) and (2) the genetic factors of organic irritability, growth tempo, fatigue rate, etc. *The CULTURAL aspects of personality are the responses learned in conformity with the incentives and demands of a human group (a family, a gang, a social class). The INDIVIDUAL aspects of personality include genetic factors, and in addition all other traits which distinguish between men who have been trained in the same culture, but whose responses to this training have varied according to the particular conditions under which the training took place.*

The primary questions which this research attacked were: (1) What are the training demands exerted upon the white and the Negro child in lower class and middle class in Chicago, and (2) What is the extent of the difference in the time of beginning, the length of, and the other conditions surrounding the training? The part of this study dealing with the differences between middle class and lower class white families in their child-rearing practices has been reported by Ericson.[6]

A forerunner to this study is that made by John Anderson for the White House Conference of 1930.[7] Anderson found that child-rearing practices are related to social status. The present study investigates some of the differences and relates them systematically to a theory of social structure and the socialization of the individual.

PROCEDURE

The study consisted of holding guided interviews with mothers of young children, recording their responses on a schedule, and making a statistical analysis of the data from the schedules. All the mothers were residents of Chicago, and most of them lived on the South Side of Chicago.

There were fifty mothers in each of four groups, white middle class, white lower class, Negro middle class, and Negro lower class. Data on the ages of the mothers and fathers, the number of children, and the ages of their children are given in Table I.

Table I—Data on Families in the Study

	Middle Class		Lower Class	
	White	Negro	White	Negro
Number of mothers	48	50	52	50
Median age of mother at marriage	23	21	20	18
Median age of father at marriage	25	25	25	21
Median age of mother at interview	33	29	29	29
Median age of father at interview	35	33	33	32
No. of children at time of interview	107	109	167	184
No. of families with 2 children only	34	28	12	14
No. of families with 3 or more children	11	14	34	32
Median age of children at interview	4	4	6	6

The interviewers were five women, who were trained specifically for the interviewing task in several sessions with the authors of this study. The interview was a lengthy one, lasting usually from two to three hours, and often taking place in two separate sessions.

The schedule for the interview was developed by one of the authors (A.D.) on the basis of previous work of this kind. It consisted of three main parts: The first and longest section dealt with the actual training of the child or children by the mother, and with individual differences in personality

Table II—Median Ages in Months for Various Aspects of Feeding and Toilet Training

	White				Negro			
	Middle		Lower		Middle		Lower	
	No.	Median	No.	Median	No.	Median	No.	Median
Breast feeding finished	75	3.8	114	4.9	88	8.5	159	9.4
Bottle feeding finished	95	10.7	123	12.9	74	12.5	99	12.6
Sucking finished	99	10.5	147	12.8	104	12.0	177	12.2
Bowel training begun	99	7.5	158	10.2	105	5.5	172	8.5
Bowel training complete	91	18.4	152	18.8	95	13.4	160	18.6
Bladder training begun	93	11.2	156	12.2	102	9.2	124	11.1
Bladder training complete	81	24.6	139	24.0	76	18.0	143	19.0

Table III—Proportions of Children with Certain Kinds of Feeding and Toilet-Training Experience

| | White | | | | Negro | | | |
| | Middle | | Lower | | Middle | | Lower | |
	No/Total	%	No/Total	%	No/Total	%	No/Total	%
Children breast fed only	5/106	5	28/163	17	32/107	30	80/179	45
Children bottle fed only	31/100	31	49/151	32	19/106	18	20/179	11
Children both breast and bottle fed	63/ 99	64	90/147	61	58/104	56	84/174	48
Children breast fed one month or more	76/106	72	118/163	72	90/107	83	164/179	92
Children breast fed longer than 3 months	34/106	32	66/163	41	63/107	59	145/179	81
Children sucking longer than 12 months	21/ 99	21	66/147	45	32/104	31	51/177	29
Children fed when they seemed hungry	3/106	3	53/153	35	6/108	6	87/175	50
Children having pacifiers	1/107	1	22/167	13	8/105	7	17/184	9
Children held for bottle or breast fed only	53/ 79	67	72/166	43	78/108	72	99/179	55
Children weaned sharply	20/101	20	23/154	15	7/105	7	39/182	21
Children who sucked thumb	54/105	51	30/166	18	50/104	48	54/183	30
Bowel training begun at 6 mo. or earlier	48/ 99	49	36/158	23	91/105	87	49/172	29
Bowel training complete at end of 12 mo.	25/ 91	28	31/152	21	46/ 95	49	37/160	23
Bladder training begun at 6 mo. or earlier	17/ 95	18	22/157	14	4/102	40	22/124	18
Bladder training complete at end of 18 mo.	26/ 81	32	67/139	48	51/ 76	67	73/143	51
No. of children who have masturbated	56/104	54	27/162	17	30/102	29	27/182	15

among the children in the family. The second section dealt with the mother's expectations concerning the occupation, education, and responsibilities and privileges of her children, with the child's regimen (meals, sleep, recreation) relations with father, etc. The third section dealt with socio-economic data concerning the mother and father and their families.

The families were classified into middle and lower social classes by using data from the interview which have been found to be closely correlated with social class placement as defined and described by Warner and Lunt[8] and by Davis, Gardner, and Gardner.[9]

The principal factors used in making the classification were occupation of parents and their siblings, education of parents, their siblings, and grandparents, property ownership, membership in churches and other associations, and section of the city. One of the authors (A.D.) discussed these data with the interviewer in each case, and made the classification. There was seldom any doubt as to the proper classification. For the Negro group, the criteria were parallel to those for the classification of the white families, but shifted systematically because of restrictions on opportunity for Negroes in American society. For example, where the occupation of mail carrier would have suggested lower-class status for a white man, it suggested middle-class status for a Negro.

Table IV—Mothers' Reports on Strictness of Regime

	White		Negro	
	Middle %	Lower %	Middle %	Lower %
Do children take nap in daytime?				
Yes	89	52	86	63
No	9	46	12	21
Sometimes	2	2	2	16
Total No. answering	46	50	50	48
Age at which boys go to movie alone				
5-7 years	17	35	35	70
Over 8	83	65	52	30
Doesn't approve of movies for child	0	0	13	0
Total No. answering	23	40	23	40
Age at which girls go to movie alone				
5-7	14	45	0	5
Over 8	86	55	72	95
Doesn't approve of movies for child	0	0	28	30
Total No. answering	28	42	32	37
Time boys in house at night				
5-6 o'clock	59	33	31	2
7-8 o'clock	32	33	63	57
9-10 o'clock	5	26	0	41
At will	4	8	0	0
Children not allowed on street	0	0	6	0
Total No. answering	22	39	32	44
Time girls in house at night				
5-6 o'clock	68	33	35	8
7-8 o'clock	29	39	56	63
9-10 o'clock	3	23	0	26
At will	0	5	0	0
Children not allowed on street	0	0	9	3
Total No. answering	31	39	34	38

Since all the mothers were native-born, the factor of foreign parentage was ruled out of the study to a considerable extent. Nevertheless, this factor did appear in the white lower-class sample to a limited degree, due to the fact that about a third of this group were of fairly recent foreign extraction, largely Italian, living in South Chicago. The remainder of the lower-class white group live in the Woodlawn and Hyde Park Areas, and are practically all of "old American" stock.

The middle-class sample is probably more representative of upper-middle than of lower-middle class people, with a high proportion of fathers in professions and managerial positions in business. The lower-class sample is definitely upper-lower rather than lower-lower class. The fathers were mainly steady, hard-working people at the semi-skilled and skilled levels.

The sample was not secured by a random procedure. Rather, it consisted mainly of people who had children in certain nursery schools, some private, and some war nurseries supported mainly by public funds. The South Chicago group consisted mainly of people who lived in the neighborhood in which one of the interviewers had grown up. The Woodlawn lower-class group was

Table V—Class Differences in Child Rearing

Feeding and Weaning

More lower-class children are breast-fed only.
More lower-class children breast-fed longer than 3 months (Negro only).
More lower-class children are fed at will.
Weaning takes place earlier (on the average) among middle-class children (white only).
More lower-class children suck longer than 12 months (white only).
More lower-class children have pacifiers (white only).
(c) More middle-class children are held for feeding.
(c) More lower-class children are weaned sharply (Negro only).

Toilet Training

Bowel training is begun earlier (on the average) with middle-class children.
Bladder training is begun earlier (on the average) with middle-class children.
Bowel training is completed earlier by middle-class children (Negro only).
More middle-class parents begin bowel training at 6 months or earlier.
More middle-class parents begin bladder training at 6 months or earlier (Negro only).
More middle-class parents complete bowel training at 12 months or earlier (Negro only).
More middle-class parents complete bladder training at 18 months or earlier (Negro only).
(c) More lower-class parents complete bladder training at 18 months or earlier (white only).

Father-Child Relations

Middle-class fathers spend more time with children.
Middle-class fathers spend more time in educational activities with children (teaching, reading, and
    taking for walks).
Lower-class fathers discipline children more (Negro only).

Occupational Expectations for Children

Middle class expect higher occupational status for children.

Educational Expectation (Length of Education)

More middle-class children expected to go to college.

Age of Assuming Responsibility

Middle-class expect child to help at home earlier.
Middle-class girls cross street earlier (whites only).
(c) Lower-class boys and girls cross street earlier (Negro only).
Middle-class boys and girls expected to go downtown alone earlier.
Middle-class girls expected to help with younger children earlier.
Middle-class girls expected to begin to cook earlier (white only).
Middle-class girls expected to begin to sew earlier (white only).
Middle-class girls expected to do dishes earlier (Negro only).
(c) Lower-class children expected to get job after school earlier.
(c) Lower-class children expected to quit school and go to work earlier.

Strictness of Regime

Middle-class children take naps in daytime more frequently.
Lower-class boys and girls allowed at movies alone earlier.
Middle-class boys and girls in house at night earlier.

obtained by calling at random in certain areas where housing was obviously
poor, and passing from one family to another with whom the person being
interviewed was acquainted. Any systematic bias introduced by these procedures lay probably in the direction of getting a middle-class group which
had been subjected to the kind of teaching about child-rearing which is prevalent among middle-class people who send their children to nursery schools.

Table VI—Color Differences in Child Rearing

Feeding and Weaning

More Negro children are breast fed only.
More Negro children are breast fed for three months or more.
More Negro children are fed at will (lower class only).
More Negro children have pacifiers (middle class only).
More white children are weaned sharply (middle class only).
Weaning takes place earlier (on the average) among white children (middle class only).
(c) More white children suck longer than 12 months (lower class only).

Toilet Training

Bowel training is begun earlier with Negro children.
Bladder training is begun earlier with Negro children.
Bowel training is completed earlier with Negro children (middle class only).
Bladder training is completed earlier with Negro children.
More Negro parents begin bowel training at 6 months or earlier (middle class only).
More Negro parents begin bladder training at 6 months or earlier (middle class only).
More Negro parents complete bowel training at 12 months or earlier (middle class only).
More Negro parents complete bladder training at 18 months or earlier (middle class only).

Father-Child Relations

White fathers spend more time with children (lower class only).
White fathers teach and play more with children (lower class only).
Negro fathers discipline children more (lower class only).

Educational Expectations (Length of Education)

More Negro children expected to go to college (lower class only).

Age of Assuming Responsibility

Negro boys and girls cross street earlier (lower class only).
(c) White girls cross street earlier (middle class only).
Negro boys go downtown alone earlier (lower class only).
Negro girls expected to dress selves earlier.
Negro girls expected to go to store earlier.
Negro girls expected to begin to cook earlier (lower class only).
(c) Negro children expected to quit school and go to work later.

Strictness of Regime

Negro boys allowed to go to movies alone earlier.
(c) White girls allowed to go to movies alone earlier.
White boys and girls in house at night earlier.

RESULTS

There are a large number of reliable differences between classes and between colors. The following tables report the differences between classes and colors on certain parts of the schedule. Those differences which are statistically reliable are summarized in Tables V and VI.

Feeding, Weaning and Toilet Training. Table II shows the median ages for various aspects of feeding and toilet training, while Table III shows the proportions of children in the various class and color groups who had certain kinds of feeding and toilet training experience.

Strictness of Regime. There were several questions in the interview which explored the degree of strictness of the regime set up by parents. These questions dealt with daytime naps, time children are due in the house at night, and age of going to the movies alone; all things in which the impulses of the child sometimes run counter to parental desires. Table IV shows the results on these questions.

Age of Assuming Responsibility. A number of the questions dealt with the age at which certain things are expected, such as dressing oneself, helping with younger children, learning to cook and to sew; and with the age at which certain responsibilities would be permitted, such as crossing the street alone. In general these questions dealt with the theme of *assuming responsibility.* "At what age does your child assume responsibility for one thing or another?" was asked in a variety of forms. There is not space enough to report the results of this section in detail, but the reliable differences are summarized in Tables V and VI. In general, it may be said that middle-class children are expected by their parents to assume responsibility earlier than lower-class children are expected to assume similar responsibilities by their parents.

Summary of Class Differences and Color Differences. Table V summarizes the class differences which are statistically reliable at the five per cent level, while Table VI summarizes the color differences which are statistically reliable at the same level. It will be seen that the differences tend to go together; a letter (c) indicates that the finding contradicts the general tendency of the results. For example, the general tendency is for lower-class children to be treated more permissively than middle-class children with respect to feeding and weaning. Contradictory to this tendency, however, more middle-class children are held for feeding.

Comparison of Class and Color Differences. In Table VII are summarized quantitatively the differences in the results which are statistically reliable at the five per cent level. All differences which are statistically reliable are also practically significant, for the small numbers of cases prevent us from securing reliable differences which are quantitatively small and therefore of little practical significance.

The procedure in making this table was to count all differences which were statistically reliable and independent. By independent differences we mean differences which could not be calculated from other differences already on our list. For example, if we note the difference in percentages of parents in two groups who report their children as taking naps in the daytime, we do not include the difference between these same groups who report their children as not taking naps, since this difference depends on the first one. We listed all of the reliable and independent differences—which included differences in training procedure, symptoms of maladjustment, age and sex expectations; as well as education, property ownership, associational membership, etc., of parents and their relatives. We then counted these differences with the results shown in Table VII. There were more class differences than color differences, and the class differences occurred approximately equally often in Negro and white groups.

We then put as many of the differences as possible into the categories of Table VII. Three categories of permissivity are summed up in the total Permissivity score. The category of Training for Assumption of Responsibility is not included in the Permissivity score, and it is scored in the opposite direction, a high score on Training for Assumption of Responsibility being analogous to a low score on Permissivity.

Individual Personality Traits. In addition to studying class and color differences in child-rearing we attempted to secure information on the rela-

Table VII—Summary of Class and Color Differences

Number of Statistically Reliable Differences
Between Classes and Between Colors

White	Class	Negro	Middle Class	Color	Lower Class
50	between classes	52	37	between colors	39
	Middle Class	*Permissivity (Total)*		*Whites*	
2	more permissive	2	9	more permissive	5
13	less permissive	15	8	less permissive	6
	Middle Class	*Food Training*		*Whites*	
1	more permissive	2	0	more permissive	1
5	less permissive	3	5	less permissive	3
	Middle Class	*Toilet Training*		*Whites*	
1	more permissive	0	8	more permissive	3
3	less permissive	7	0	less permissive	0
	Middle Class	*Regimen*		*Whites*	
0	more permissive	0	1	more permissive	1
5	less permissive	5	3	less permissive	3
	Middle Class	*Training for Responsibility*		*Whites*	
8	more severe	6	1	more severe	0
2	less severe	4	4	less severe	8

tions between children's experiences during training and their personality traits. This was done through questions about birth-order, physical activity, generosity, jealousy, happiness, and other characteristics.

A number of difficulties prevented us from making a great deal out of this part of the study. Chief among these difficulties was the fact that mothers' testimony on personality traits of their children is somewhat ambiguous. For example, one mother may report a child as selfish for behavior which would not be considered especially selfish by another mother. Again, mothers with several children will be able to make comparative statements, such as "this child was hard to train," or "this child was very generous," with more certainty of being right than mothers of one or two children. Another difficulty undoubtedly lay in the fact that personality traits are results of multiple causation. For example, the causes of aggressive behavior in one child may be quite different from the causes of apparently similar behavior in another child.

Despite these difficulties, we have succeeded in discovering a few statistically reliable relationships between children's early experience and their personality characteristics, as reported by these mothers.

Physical Activity Related to Personality Traits. Considering all families, *except those with only one child,* we attempted to find the relations between degree of physical activity when young and other characteristics. Physical activity was taken as an index of physical vigor, combined with a drive for exploration. Since the mothers were asked which child was most active when young, and which was most quiet when young, we could compare the "most active" and the "most quiet" for other characteristics. The children who were most active when young, compared with those who were most quiet when young, tend to be: most active now, most punished, more aggressive, and less neat.

Generosity Related to Other Personality Traits. When the children reported as "most generous" are compared with those reported as "most selfish" the following relationships occur. The "most generous" children tend to be the happiest, and to fight less. In the white but not the Negro group, the "most generous" children tend to have been more quiet as infants. There is no consistent relation between selfishness and neatness as reported by the mothers.

Birth Order and Personality. In studying the relation of birth-order to personality traits, we were forced to content ourselves with a study of the differences between first and second children in middle-class families with only two children. It would not have been wise to group all second children together because those with younger siblings would be in a different family constellation from those without younger siblings. If birth-order influences personality, it probably does so through placing children of different birth-order in different emotional relationships with other members of the family. Consequently, since a second child in a family with only two children would be in quite a different situation than a second child in a family with several children, we restricted our study to families with two children. Among both white and Negro middle-class families with only two children, the following pattern emerges.

The first child tends to be: more jealous, more selfish, and neater.

The second child tends to be: happier, more generous, and more punished.

DISCUSSION

The answer is clear to the principal question which this study was designed to answer. There are considerable social class differences in child-rearing practices, and these differences are greater than the differences between Negroes and whites of the same social class.

Personality Implications of Social Class Differences in Child-Rearing. Middle-class families are more rigorous than lower class families in their training of children for feeding and cleanliness habits. They generally begin training earlier. Furthermore, middle-class families place more emphasis on the early assumption of responsibility for the self and on individual achievement. Finally, middle-class families are less permissive than lower-class families in their regimen. They require their children to take naps at a later age, to be in the house at night earlier, and, in general, permit less free play of the impulses of their children.

Generalizing from the evidence presented in the tables, we would say that middle-class children are subjected earlier and more consistently to the influences which make a child an orderly, conscientious, responsible, and tame person. In the course of this training middle-class children probably suffer more frustration of their impulses.

In the light of these findings, the data with respect to thumb-sucking are interesting. Three times as many white middle-class children are reported to suck their thumbs as white lower-class children, and almost twice as many Negro middle-class children do likewise. Thumb-sucking is generally thought of as a response to frustration of the hunger drive, or of the drive to seek pleasure through sucking. Since middle-class children are fed less frequently and are weaned earlier, the higher incidence of thumb-sucking would be expected. The Negro middle-class children are treated much more permissively than the white middle-class children with respect to feeding and weaning, but much more rigorously with respect to toilet-training. Yet the proportion of Negro middle-class children reported as sucking their thumb is almost the same as the proportion of white middle-class children so reported. *Perhaps thumb-sucking is a response to frustration of any sort, rather than to frustration in the feeding area alone.*

The data with respect to masturbation are also of interest in this connection. Three times as many white middle-class as compared with lower-class children are reported as masturbating. Twice as many Negro middle-class children as compared with Negro lower-class children are reported as masturbating. The meaning of these findings is obscured by the possibility that some lower-class mothers may not have understood the question. Or it may be that some of them did not watch as carefully for masturbation as middle-class mothers do, or some lower-class mothers may have been more hesitant than middle-class mothers in admitting that their children followed this practice. Yet none of these explanations seems probable, and perhaps the data should be taken at their face value. Perhaps masturbation is much more common among middle-class infants than among lower-class infants. If this is true, it might be explained in terms of the hypothesis that masturbation is in part a palliative to frustration. Children who are frustrated more would masturbate more, according to the hypothesis.

It is a surprising fact that the middle-class mothers, in general, expected their children to assume responsibility earlier in the home, to help with the younger children, and to cook and sew at an earlier age. For it seems obvious that there is more actual need of the children's help in lower-class families, where the work of children to be cared for is greater and the mother has very little help with the housework. The explanation probably lies in a tendency on the part of middle-class people to train their children early for achievement and responsibility, while lower-class people train their children to take responsibility only after the child is old enough to make the effort of training pay substantial returns in the work the child will do. Middle-class parents can afford to use time to train children to dress themselves, help around the home, sew, cook, and so on, at such an early age that the children cannot repay this training effort by their actual performance, although they may repay it by adopting attitudes of self-achievement and responsibility.

In addition to training their children to take responsibility early and to adopt attitudes favorable to self-achievement, middle-class families attempt to curb those impulses of the child which would lead to poor health, waste of time, and bad moral habits, according to middle-class views. Therefore they require their children to take day-time naps longer, to come into the house at night earlier and they do not permit their children to go alone to movies at an early age. Nevertheless, they encourage their children to be venturesome in the more "constructive" activities, from the middle-class point of view, of going downtown alone to museums, department stores, dancing lessons and the like.

Whether the middle-class or the lower-class practices are preferable is, of course, largely a matter of private opinion. But it is significant that there is now a considerable body of scientific and lay judgment operating in the middle class to make child-rearing practices more permissive. It is contended that the orthodox middle-class practices make children too anxious, and frustrate them too much for the best mental health in later life. On the other hand, it may be contended that civilized life requires the individual to be tamed and to learn to take constructive control of his impulses. A certain degree of anxiety is valuable, in that it puts the individual on his toes to learn the lessons and meet the demands of modern society in order to win the very considerable rewards of modern civilized social life.

Our own view is that the better child-rearing practices can be drawn from both middle and lower-class life and made into a combination which is superior to both of the norms as they emerge in this study.

Personality Implications of Color Differences in Child-Rearing. The striking thing about this study is that Negro and white middle-class families are so much alike, and that white and Negro lower-class families are so much alike. The likenesses hold for such characteristics as number of children, ages of parents when married, as well as child-rearing practices and expectations of children.

There are, however, some very interesting color differences. The major color differences are found in the areas of feeding and cleanliness training.

Negroes are much more permissive than whites in the feeding and weaning of their children. The difference is greater in the middle class. Negro babies have a markedly different feeding and weaning experience from white babies.

The situation is reversed with respect to toilet-training. Here the Negro parents are much stricter than white parents, both in middle and lower-class circles. For example, 87 per cent of Negro middle-class mothers said they commence bowel training at 6 months or earlier, compared with 49 per cent of white middle-class mothers; and the comparable figures for bladder training are 40 and 18 per cent.

If feeding, weaning, and toilet-training have much influence on the personality, we should expect systematic differences between Negro and white people *of the same social class,* though it is not at all clear just what these differences should be, since one group is more rigorous in its training in one area while the other group is more rigorous in the other area.

There is another noticeable color difference. Negroes of both classes tend to give their girls an earlier training for responsibility in washing dishes, going to the store, and dressing themselves. This is probably traceable to the fact that Negroes of both classes have less outside help in the home than whites do and consequently the help of the girls is more urgently needed. It is noticeable, also, that middle-class Negro girls are not allowed to play across the street or to go to the movies alone as early as white middle-class girls. This may be due to the fact that most middle-class Negroes are forced to live in much less desirable neighborhoods, from their point of view, than those in which middle-class whites live.

Personality Implications of Intra-Family Differences. The questionnaire was designed to get information on personality characteristics of children as they might be related to birth order, training experience, and kinds of discipline used. Very few pronounced relationships appeared. This may have been due to several factors. Perhaps the interview method as we used it is not suited to getting information on individual personality characteristics. Again, perhaps such relations as exist are too complicated to be seen clearly in a study like this with a relatively small number of subjects. Nevertheless, there were a few interesting intra-family relationships.

For instance, the relation of "activity when young" to other characteristics is of considerable importance, since the degree of physical activity when young may be taken as an index of native vitality and of whatever inborn drive there may be for exploration or for physical activity. As we should expect, those "most active when young" were reported as most frequently punished, and as most active now. They were also reported as fighting most now, and as least neat. They were reported as happiest, except in the case of the white middle class. In general, it appears that various types of expressive, impulsive behavior tend to go together, and to characterize the happy child. An exception must be made of the white middle class, where happiness is reported by the mothers as associated with quietness rather than activity in the young child.

There are only a few characteristics clearly related to generosity and selfishness, though happiness and absence of fighting seem to be tied up with generosity. On the basis of simple Freudian principles one might expect selfishness and neatness to go together, but this hypothesis is not borne out by the data.

The data on birth order in relation to personality characteristics show some interesting trends. The first child in middle-class families of two children tends to be more jealous and more selfish than the second child. This may be taken as evidence in favor of the hypothesis of downward sibling rivalry as strongly influential in personality formation. Still, it is well to remember that mothers of young children, when there are only two in the family, may report the older as more jealous and selfish merely because the older is bigger and more able to assert himself. The second child was reported as happier and more generous, and also as more punished.

CONCLUSIONS

This study has given clear evidence of the following things:

1. There are significant differences in child-rearing practices between the middle and lower social classes in a large city. The same type of differences exist between middle and lower-class Negroes as between middle and lower-class whites.

2. Middle-class parents are more rigorous than lower-class parents in their training of children for feeding and cleanliness habits. They also expect their children to take responsibility for themselves earlier than lower-class parents do. Middle-class parents place their children under a stricter regimen, with more frustration of their impulses, than do lower-class parents.

3. In addition to these social-class differences, there are some differences between Negroes and whites in their child-rearing practices. Negroes are more permissive than whites in the feeding and weaning of their children, but they are much more rigorous than whites in toilet-training.

4. Thus there are *cultural differences* in the personality formation of middle-class compared with lower-class people, *regardless of color,* due to their early training. And for the same reason there should be further but less marked cultural differences between Negroes and whites of the same social class.

5. In addition to the cultural differences between individuals due to early training experience, there are individual personality differences between children in the same family. These are probably due to physiological differences and to differences in emotional relationships with other members of the family.

SOCIAL LEVEL AND
SEXUAL OUTLET

Alfred C. Kinsey, Wardell B. Pomeroy, and Clyde E. Martin

WITHIN ANY SINGLE social level there are, of course, considerable differences between individuals in their choice of sexual outlets, and in the frequencies with which they engage in each type of activity. The range of individual variation in any level is not particularly different from the range of variation in each other level. Within each group, each individual pattern is more or less duplicated by the patterns of individuals in every one of the other social levels. Nevertheless, the frequencies of each type of variant are so different for different social levels that the means and the medians and the general shapes of the frequency curves for the several groups are perfectly distinct. Translated into everyday thinking, this means that a large proportion of all the individuals in any group follows patterns of sexual behavior which are typical of the group, and which are followed by only a smaller number of the individuals in other groups.

If the mean or median frequencies for each type of sexual activity, at each social level, are brought together in a single chart (Figures 1, 2), it becomes possible to see what material differences there are in these patterns of behavior. Each horizontal line, followed across the chart, epitomizes the story for one social level. It is, as it were, a silhouette, a profile representing the essence of the group's attitudes on matters of sex, and the translation of those attitudes into overt sexual activity.

Even a child would comprehend that the creature represented in each of these silhouettes is distinct and unlike the creatures represented in the other silhouettes.

It is, of course, of prime concern to ask why patterns of sexual behavior differ as they do in different social levels. It is of scientific importance to understand how such patterns originate, how they are passed on to each individual, and how they become standards of behavior for such a high proportion of all the individuals in each group. It is of equal importance to understand the social significances of these patterns of sexual behavior. Few of us have been aware that there were such differences in patterns in the various subdivisions of our culture. An understanding of the facts may contribute something toward easing the tensions that arise because individuals and whole segments of the population fail to understand the sexual philosophies and the sexual behavior of groups in which they have not been raised.

We do not yet understand, to the full, the origins of these diverse sexual philosophies; but it will be possible to record what the thinking of each group is in regard to each type of activity.

Masturbation. At lower social levels, and particularly among the older generations of the lowest levels, masturbation may be looked down upon as

Reprinted with editorial adaptations from *Sexual Behavior in the Human Male* (1948), pp. 374-84, by permission of the authors and the publisher. (Copyright 1948, by W. B. Saunders Co.)

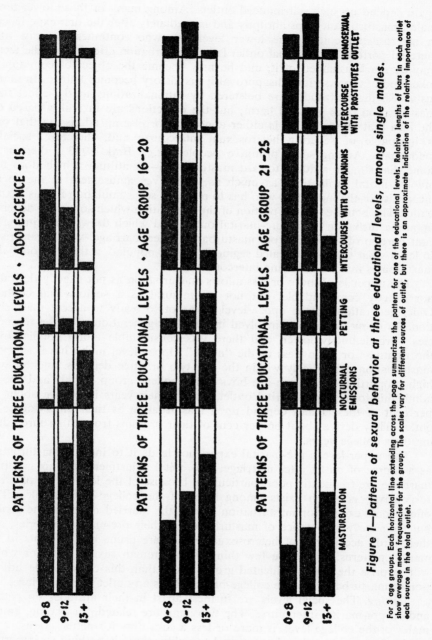

PATTERNS OF THREE EDUCATIONAL LEVELS · ADOLESCENCE - 15

PATTERNS OF THREE EDUCATIONAL LEVELS · AGE GROUP 16-20

PATTERNS OF THREE EDUCATIONAL LEVELS · AGE GROUP 21-25

MASTURBATION NOCTURNAL EMISSIONS PETTING INTERCOURSE WITH COMPANIONS INTERCOURSE WITH PROSTITUTES OUTLET HOMOSEXUAL OUTLET

0-8 9-12 13+

Figure 1—Patterns of sexual behavior at three educational levels, among single males.

For 3 age groups. Each horizontal line extending across the page summarizes the pattern for one of the educational levels. Relative lengths of bars in each outlet show average mean frequencies for the group. The scales vary for different sources of outlet, but there is an approximate indication of the relative importance of each source in the total outlet.

abnormal, a perversion, and an infantile substitute for socio-sexual contacts. Although most lower level boys masturbate during their early adolescence, many of them never have more than a few experiences or, at the most, regular masturbation for a short period of months or years, after which they rarely again depend on such self-induced outlets. Among many of those lower level males, masturbation stops abruptly and immediately after the first experiences in heterosexual coitus. The lower level boy who continues to draw any material portion of his sexual outlet from masturbation after his middle teens may be much ashamed of it, and he may become the object of community jokes and of more serious disapproval if his history becomes known. In many instances, these attitudes are bolstered by rationalizations to the effect that masturbation does physical harm; but the objections are in reality based on the idea that masturbation is either abnormal, or else an admission that one is incapable of securing heterosexual intercourse and, therefore, socially inadequate. Among some primitive peoples (*e.g.,* Bryk 1933), there is a somewhat similar attitude toward masturbation—an attitude which does not involve moral evaluations as much as it involves amusement at the social incapacity of the individual who has to resort to self stimulation for his sexual outlet. The better educated portion of the population which so largely depends upon masturbation for its pre-marital outlet, and which draws a not insignificant portion of its outlet from masturbation after marriage, will be surprised to learn what the less educated segments of the population think of one who masturbates instead of having intercourse.

The upper level more or less allows masturbation as not exactly desirable nor exactly commendable, but not as immoral as a socio-sexual contact. Older generations of the upper level were not so ready to accept masturbation. As many males were involved in the older generations, but the frequencies were definitely lower, and there was considerable moral conflict over the rightness or wrongness of the "habit." Upper level males have accepted masturbation more freely within the last two or three decades, and today a high proportion of the teen-age boys of the college group frankly and openly admit this form of pre-marital outlet. During their years in college about 70 per cent of these males depend upon masturbation as their chief source of outlet. They derive about 66 per cent of their orgasms from this source during their college years.

The upper-level's pre-marital experience leads it to include masturbation as a source of outlet after marriage. The coital adjustments of this group in marriage are frequently poor, particularly because of the low degree of erotic responsiveness which exists among many of the college-bred females. This offers some excuse for masturbation among the married males of the group; but their early acceptance of masturbation in their pre-marital histories, and their tardy acceptance of heterosexual coitus, are prime determinants in the marital patterns. There are few things in all human sexual behavior which will surprise the poorly educated groups more than this considerable utilization of masturbation by the college-bred male as an outlet after marriage.

Petting. The social levels are furthest apart in their attitudes on petting and on pre-marital intercourse. The two items are related, for petting, among males of the college level, is more or less a substitute for actual coitus.

In the upper level code of sexual morality, there is nothing so important as the preservation of the virginity of the female and, to a somewhat lesser degree, the preservation of the virginity of the male until the time of marriage. The utilization of pre-marital petting at this level is fortified by the emphasis which the marriage manuals place upon the importance of pre-coital tech-

Table 1—Sources of Sexual Outlet for Single Males, at Three Educational Levels Showing Percentages of Total Outlet Derived by Each Group from Each Source

Sources	Adol.-15	16-20	21-25	26-30	31-35	36-40
			SOURCES OF ORGASM: SINGLE MALES % OF TOTAL OUTLET			
			EDUCATIONAL LEVEL 0-8			
Masturbation	52.26	29.15	20.15	20.68	24.24	28.95
Nocturnal emissions	1.82	4.83	5.02	6.26	5.49	5.97
Petting to climax	1.06	1.66	1.23	1.96	0.68	0.05
Intercourse with companions	35.00	50.62	52.84	42.71	23.74	23.08
Intercourse with prostitutes	0.97	6.21	12.55	14.34	18.42	23.35
Homosexual outlet	8.03	6.85	8.06	14.04	27.43	18.60
Animal contacts	0.86	0.68	0.15	0.01		
Total outlet	100.00	100.00	100.00	100.00	100.00	100.00
Number of cases	712	720	361	159	61	47
Total solitary outlets	54.08	33.98	25.17	26.94	29.73	34.92
Total heterosexual outlets	37.03	58.49	66.62	59.01	42.84	46.48
Total homosexual outlet	8.03	6.85	8.06	14.04	27.43	18.60
			EDUCATIONAL LEVEL 9-12			
Masturbation	59.09	37.17	29.67	27.69	18.48	
Nocturnal emissions	4.44	6.33	8.10	7.48	8.21	
Petting to climax	1.46	2.37	2.77	1.82	1.35	
Intercourse with companions	24.93	39.49	38.02	29.75	42.81	
Intercourse with prostitutes	0.44	2.75	4.66	6.46	10.32	
Homosexual outlet	8.73	10.81	16.31	25.95	18.83	
Animal contacts	0.91	1.08	0.47	0.85		
Total outlet	100.00	100.00	100.00	100.00	100.00	100.00
Number of cases	606	607	263	117	41	
Total solitary outlets	63.53	43.50	37.77	35.17	26.69	
Total heterosexual outlets	26.83	44.61	45.45	38.03	54.48	
Total homosexual outlet	8.73	10.81	16.31	25.95	18.83	
			EDUCATIONAL LEVEL 13+			
Masturbation	79.61	66.37	53.30	45.88	44.28	
Nocturnal emissions	12.15	15.65	15.67	11.93	10.67	
Petting to climax	1.54	5.26	7.50	5.17	4.98	
Intercourse with companions	2.74	9.13	18.45	24.97	21.52	
Intercourse with prostitutes	0.11	0.80	1.27	3.16	0.65	
Homosexual outlet	3.14	2.43	3.72	8.82	17.90	
Animal contacts	0.71	0.36	0.09	0.07		
Total outlet	100.00	100.00	100.00	100.00	100.00	100.00
Number of cases	2799	2861	1898	487	87	
Total solitary outlets	91.76	82.02	68.97	57.81	54.95	
Total heterosexual outlets	4.39	15.19	27.22	33.30	27.15	
Total homosexual outlet	3.14	2.43	3.72	8.82	17.90	

niques in married relations; and the younger generation considers that its experience before marriage may contribute something to the development of satisfactory marital relations. Compared with coitus, petting has the advantage of being accessible under conditions where coitus would be impossible; it provides a simpler means of achieving both arousal and orgasm, it makes it possible to experience orgasm while avoiding the possibility of a pregnancy, and, above all, it preserves one's "virginity." Whether consciously or unconsciously, petting is chosen by the upper level because intercourse

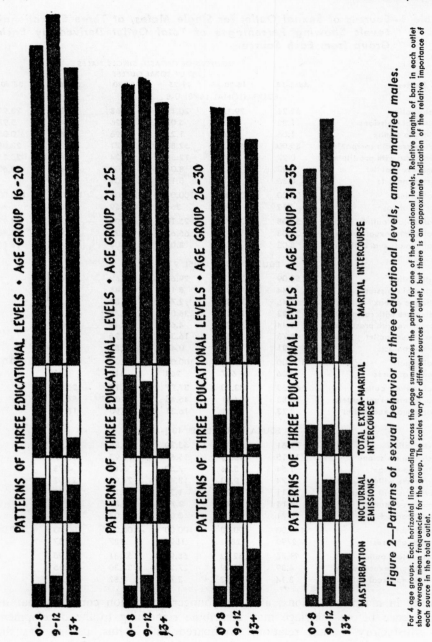

MASTURBATION   NOCTURNAL   TOTAL EXTRA-MARITAL   MARITAL INTERCOURSE
               EMISSIONS   INTERCOURSE

Figure 2—*Patterns of sexual behavior at three educational levels, among married males.*

For 4 age groups. Each horizontal line extending across the page summarizes the pattern for one of the educational levels. Relative lengths of bars in each outlet show average mean frequencies for the group. The scales vary for different sources of outlet, but there is an approximate indication of the relative importance of each source in the total outlet.

destroys virginity and is, therefore, unacceptable. It is significant to note what different values are attached, at that level, to erotic arousal and orgasm achieved through the union of genitalia, and to erotic arousal and orgasm achieved through physical contact of other portions of the body, or even through genital contact or genital manipulation which does not involve actual copulation. There are many males in the upper level who develop a fine art of achieving orgasm by petting techniques which avoid intercourse. The youth who may have experienced orgasm scores or hundreds of times in petting, and who may have utilized every type of petting technique, including mouth-genital contacts, still has the satisfaction of knowing that he is still a virgin, as his level defines virginity. There are even cases of males who effect genital union; but because they avoid orgasm while in such union they persuade themselves that they are still virgins. The illogic of the situation emphasizes the fact that the basic issue is one of conforming with a code (the avoidance of pre-marital intercourse, the preservation of one's virginity), which is of paramount importance in the mores of this social level.

The lower educational levels see no sense in this. They have nothing like this strong taboo against pre-marital intercourse and, on the contrary, accept it as natural and inevitable and a desirable thing. Lower level taboos are more often turned against an avoidance of intercourse, and against any substitution for simple and direct coitus. Petting involves a considerable list of techniques which may be acceptable to the college group, and to some degree to the high school group, but which are quite taboo at lower levels (as discussed above). It is just because petting involves these techniques, and because it substitutes for actual intercourse, that it is considered a perversion by the lower level.

In particular cases, older persons, even at upper levels, have objected to pre-marital petting; but individual objections do not have the force of long-established mores. Pre-marital intercourse is condemned by mores which go back hundreds and thousands of years. Such taboos are very different from the criticisms which lone individuals have levied against petting within the last few decades, and for the most part the younger generation has paid little attention to such criticisms.

There is nothing in the behavior of the upper level which is more responsible than petting is for the general opinion that college students are sexually wild. The lower level has many times as much pre-marital intercourse as the college male has, and it is not the intercourse of the college student which is the source of the lower level's criticism. It is the fact that petting may be engaged in for many hours without arriving at intercourse—it is the fact that intercourse itself is not more often accepted as a pre-marital outlet by the upper social level.

Pre-marital Intercourse. With the upper educational level, the question of pre-marital intercourse is largely one of morals. Some of the younger generation find it modern to insist that they do not avoid pre-marital intercourse because it is wrong, but because they consider intercourse too precious to have with anyone except the girl that they marry, or because they consider that marriages work out better when there has been no pre-marital intercourse. To this extent the younger generation is "emancipated"; but the change in the form of its rationalizations has not affected its overt behavior one whit.

A large portion of the 85 per cent of the population which never goes to college accepts pre-marital intercourse as normal and natural. Most of this group would insist that there is no question of right or wrong involved. Even some lower level clergymen, of the group that has never gone beyond grade school or high school, may react as the rest of the community of which they are a part, preaching against profanity, smoking, drinking, gambling, and extra-marital intercourse, but considering that no moral issue is involved in pre-marital intercourse. So nearly universal is pre-marital intercourse among grade school groups that in two or three lower level communities in which we

Table 2—Sources of Sexual Outlet for Married Males, at Three Educational Levels Showing Percentages of Total Outlet Derived by Each Group from Each Source

			SOURCES OF ORGASM: MARRIED MALES				
			% OF TOTAL OUTLET				
Sources	16-20	21-25	26-30	31-35	36-40	41-45	46-50
			EDUCATIONAL LEVEL 0-8				
Masturbation	2.40	2.43	2.44	1.79	1.59	1.41	1.4
Nocturnal emissions	3.08	2.79	3.41	3.03	1.85	2.25	2.6
Intercourse, marital	79.92	81.03	86.15	88.07	88.09	89.96	89.9
Interc., extra-m., comp.	10.91	11.62	6.38	5.51	7.24	4.84	4.7
Interc., extra-m., prost.	0.61	0.80	1.16	1.46	0.93	1.46	1.4
Homosexual outlet	3.08	1.33	0.46	0.14	0.30	0.08	0.0
Total outlet	100.00	100.00	100.00	100.00	100.00	100.00	100.00
Number of cases	158	324	292	186	143	100	70
Total solitary outlets	5.48	5.22	5.85	4.82	3.44	3.66	4.0
Total hetero. outlets	91.44	93.45	93.69	95.04	96.26	96.26	96.0
Total homo. outlet	3.08	1.33	0.46	0.14	0.30	0.08	0.0
			EDUCATIONAL LEVEL 9-12				
Masturbation	2.75	3.70	5.05	4.04	3.15	1.68	2.8
Nocturnal emissions	2.04	2.85	3.22	3.79	4.48	5.29	2.9
Intercourse, marital	82.19	81.56	81.67	85.18	88.19	89.18	91.0
Interc., extra-m., comp.	9.43	9.35	7.61	4.62	1.76	3.15	3.1
Interc., extra-m., prost.	1.48	1.49	1.49	0.99	1.69	0.70	0.2
Homosexual outlet	2.11	1.05	0.96	1.38	0.73		
Total outlet	100.00	100.00	100.00	100.00	100.00	100.00	100.00
Number of cases	87	164	135	82	58	34	24
Total solitary outlets	4.79	6.55	8.27	7.83	7.63	6.97	5.7
Total hetero. outlets	93.10	92.40	90.77	90.79	91.64	93.03	94.3
Total homo. outlet	2.11	1.05	0.96	1.38	0.73		
			EDUCATIONAL LEVEL 13+				
Masturbation	8.53	8.79	8.67	9.28	8.26	9.71	9.0
Nocturnal emissions	2.99	4.65	4.69	5.71	6.06	5.87	5.4
Intercourse, marital	85.41	83.94	82.76	78.34	74.41	76.39	68.5
Interc., extra-m., comp.	2.86	1.86	2.72	5.51	9.85	6.07	13.7
Interc., extra-m., prost.	0.05	0.23	0.20	0.41	0.53	0.32	0.4
Homosexual outlet	0.16	0.53	0.96	0.75	0.89	1.64	3.0
Total outlet	100.00	100.00	100.00	100.00	100.00	100.00	100.00
Number of cases	46	440	532	301	189	138	81
Total solitary outlets	11.52	13.44	13.36	14.99	14.32	15.58	14.4
Total hetero. outlets	88.32	86.03	85.68	84.26	84.79	82.78	82.6
Total homo. outlet	0.16	0.53	0.96	0.75	0.89	1.64	3.0

have worked we have been unable to find a solitary male who had not had sexual relations with girls by the time he was 16 or 17 years of age. In such a community, the occasional boy who has not had intercourse by that age is either physically incapacitated, mentally deficient, homosexual, or earmarked for moving out of his community and going to college.

Lower level males may have a certain respect for virginity, and this may lead them to insist (in 41 per cent of the cases) that they would not marry a girl who had had previous intercourse; but this may be more of a profession than a matter on which they will stand when it comes to the actual choice of a mate. Lower level males are likely to acquire weekly or more than weekly frequencies in intercourse soon after they start in early adolescence, or at least by the middle teens. They are often highly promiscuous in their choice of pre-marital partners, and there are many who have no interest in having intercourse with the same girl more than once. This strikingly parallels the promiscuity which is found among those homosexual males who are "oncers," as the vernacular term puts it. Some lower level males may have pre-marital intercourse with several hundred or even a thousand or more different girls before marriage, and here their behavior is most different from the behavior of the college-bred males.

Extra-marital Intercourse. In lower social levels there is a somewhat bitter acceptance of the idea that the male is basically promiscuous and he is going to have extra-marital intercourse, whether or not his wife or society objects. There is some continuation of the group attitude on pre-marital intercourse into the realm of extra-marital intercourse, at least in the early years of marriage. On the other hand, the upper level male who has been hetero-sexually restrained for 10 or 15 years before marriage does not freely let down and start extra-marital intercourse as soon as he has learned to have coitus with his wife. As a matter of fact, a male who has been so restrained often has difficulty in working out a sexual adjustment with his wife, and it is doubtful whether very many of the upper level males would have any facility in finding extra-marital intercourse, even if they were to set out deliberately after it. The lower level's extra-marital intercourse does cause trouble, but we do not yet understand all the factors which account for the fact that with advancing age there is a steady decline and finally a near dis-appearance of extra-marital intercourse from lower level marital histories.

The development of extra-marital intercourse in the histories of the older males of the upper level is done with a certain deliberation which in some cases may be acceded to and encouraged by the wife.

Homosexual Contacts. The considerable differences which exist in the incidences and frequencies of the homosexual in the three educational levels would seem to indicate basic differences in attitudes toward such activity; but we are not sure that we yet understand what these differences are.

The fewest objections to the homosexual are found in the very lowest of the social levels, in the best educated groups, and in top society. At the lowest social levels sex, whether it be heterosexual or homosexual, is more or less accepted as inevitable. The children here are the least restrained sexually and usually become involved in both heterosexual and homosexual activities at an early age. Since this is the group in which pre-adolescent behavior most often carries over into adult behavior, it is not surprising to find a fair number of the males at this level continuing both types of activity through the major portion of their lives. It is notable, however, that there are few individuals in this group who become exclusively homosexual. There are some who definitely condemn the homosexual, but there are many who accept it simply as one more form of sex. Rarely do they interfere with other persons who are involved, even though they themselves may not enter into such activities.

The acceptance of the homosexual in top educational and social levels is the product of a wider understanding of realities, some comprehension of the factors involved, and more concern over the mental qualities and social capacities of an individual than over anything in his sexual history.

The highest incidences of the homosexual, however, are in the group which most often verbalizes its disapproval of such activity. This is in the group that goes into high school but never beyond in its educational career. These are the males who most often condemn the homosexual, most often ridicule and express disgust for such activity, and most often punish other males for their homosexuality. And yet, this is the group which has the largest amount of overt homosexual activity. Their involvement may be due to curiosity, to the fact that one may profit financially by accepting homosexual relations, or to the fact that one may derive a sadistic satisfaction from beating up the partner after orgasm has been achieved in the homosexual activity. In a certain segment of this group the idea is more or less accepted that one may uphold the heterosexual mores while "playing the queers," provided one punishes them after orgasm is achieved in the homosexual relation. As a group these males may strenuously deny that their sexual contacts have anything to do with homosexuality; but the full and complete record indicates that many of them have stronger psychic reactions to other males than they care to admit. When they no longer find themselves being paid for such contacts, many of them begin paying other males for the privilege of sexual relations.

If there are group attitudes in regard to the homosexual, they are not as freely discussed at most social levels. It may be that this explains why community thinking is not so well crystallized on this subject as it is in regard to other forms of sexual activity.

A SLUM SEX CODE

William Foote Whyte

RESPECTABLE MIDDLE-CLASS PEOPLE have very definite standards of sex behavior. They are inclined to assume that behavior which does not conform to these standards is unorganized and subject to no set of ethics. It is my purpose to point out that, in one particular area commonly thought to be characterized by laxness of sex behavior, there is an elaborate and highly developed sex code. A study of the social and sex life of the slum will also yield certain clues as to the nature of the process of assimilation of an alien people into American society.

My information is based upon a three-and-a-half-year study of the Italian slum district of "Cornerville" in "Eastern City."[1] By discussions with a number of men in corner gangs, in which I was a participant observer, I was able to learn the sex code of the slum, as it appears to the corner boys.

The story must be told against a background of local social life. In peasant Italy, as in other peasant societies, the family group undertook to regulate the social and sexual relations of the children. Marriages were arranged by the parents of the couple, and no young man was allowed to visit a girl's home unless he had been accepted as her suitor. The influence of this system is still to be observed in Cornerville. Parents try to keep a strict watch upon their daughters. In most cases they are unable to arrange the marriage for their children, but they retain control over the home. The corner boy knows that if he once visits a girl in her home it will be assumed by her parents (and by everyone else) that he intends to marry her. Consequently, until he is completely sure of his own intentions, the corner boy remains outside of the house. He even hesitates to make a date with a girl, for if he does take her out alone it is assumed that he is her "steady."

Dances given by local clubs mark the high point of the social activities. Except for those who are "going steady," groups of men and groups of girls go separately to the dances. The man chooses his girl for each dance and, at the conclusion of the number, leaves her with her friends. There is no cutting in. When the dance is over, the men and women go home separately. Parties in a girl's home, picnics, evenings at the bowling alleys, and other social activities all tend to take this group form.

When a man centers his attention upon one girl, he arranges to meet her on the street corner. Good girls are not expected to "hang" on the corner, but the men consider it perfectly respectable for them to keep appointments on the corner. Most parents object to this practice more or less strongly and try to insist that the man shall come to the home. The insistence of the parents and the reluctance of the corner boy place the girl in a difficult position. Of course, she herself may not wish to give the relationship the permanent form which a visit to the home would involve. If they work outside of the home, most girls are able to insist upon some right to govern their social relations; but this always involves friction with the parents, its serious-

Reprinted from *The American Journal of Sociology* (July 1943), pp. 24-31, by permission of the author and the publisher. (Copyright, 1943, by the University of Chicago Press.)

ness depending upon the strength of parental control and the strenuousness, of the daughter's efforts to gain independence.

The sex life of the corner boy begins when he is very young. One of them writes:

> In Cornerville children ten years of age know most all the swear words and they have a good idea of what the word "lay" means. Swearing and describing of sex relations by older people and by the boys that hang on the corner are overheard by little children and their actions are noticed and remembered. Many of the children when they are playing in the streets, doorways and cellars actually go through the motions which pertain to the word "lay." I have seen them going through these motions, even children under ten years of age.
>
> Most all the boys that I know and all my friends carry safes [condoms]. Most boys start carrying safes when they are of high school age.
>
> Safes are purchased from necktie salesmen as cheap as a dozen for fifty cents. Some boys buy them and then make a profit by selling them to the boys at school. You can get them in some of the stores around here.

The sex play of young boys is relatively unregulated. The code of sex behavior crystallizes only as the corner boys reach maturity.

Relations between corner boys and women cannot be described in uniform terms, since there are tremendous variations in behavior, depending upon the category in which the woman is placed and the man's qualifications for access to women of various categories. The local classification of women which is explicit or implicit in corner-boy attitudes and behavior may be represented in the three categories shown in the accompanying tabulation. The most highly valued type of woman is placed at the top of each category.

Sex Experience	Physical Attractiveness	Social- and Ethnic-Group Position
1. "Good" girls	Beautiful	1. Superior groups
2. "Lays"		2. Italian nonslum
a) One-man girls	to	3. Italian slum
b) Promiscuous		
c) Prostitutes	ugly	

One evening the corner boys were discussing a beautiful girl in the neighborhood. Danny said that he would take three months in any jail in the country, even Alcatraz, for the privilege of being in bed with her for eight hours. Doc said that Danny felt this way because the girl was a virgin. Danny agreed but added: "I would take one week in any jail even if she was a lay; that's how good I think she is." The difference between three months and one week strikingly illustrates the different valuations placed upon "good girls" and "lays." Doc explained the desirability of a virgin in this way: "No one has been there before. You are showing her the way. It's a new discovery. . . . We all say we would like to lay a virgin, but we really wouldn't."

The corner-boy code strongly prohibits intercourse with a virgin. Thus the most desirable of women is also the most inaccessible. A good girl may submit to a limited amount of kisses and caresses without compromising her reputation. She must not be a "teaser" (one who attempts to excite the man as much as possible without granting him sexual access). The virginity of a "teaser" is thought to be only a technicality, and if she is raped it serves her right. Otherwise a girl's virginity must be protected.

"Good girls" are the kind that one marries. A man who takes her virginity from a "good girl," seriously affecting her marriageability, will marry her because he is responsible. The man who seeks to evade his responsibility, especially if he has made the girl pregnant, may be forced into marriage by the priest and the girl's parents. The alternative is going to jail and being held liable for the support of the child to the age of twenty-one.

While strong legal and institutional sanctions uphold virginity, corner boys do not abide by the code simply from fear of the consequences of violation. They have strong sentiments supporting the sanctity of virginity. It is felt that only the lowest type of man would have intercourse with a virgin.

If the ban on intercourse with virgins were never violated, the only nonvirgins would be girls who had had sex relations with men outside of the district. This is obviously not the case. Several stories indicate that some early-adolescent boys and girls introduce each other to sex activity. The young boy who has never had intercourse himself does not feel so strongly the protective attitude toward virgins that he will assume later. There are a few local men who break the rule, but the danger of entanglements within the district is so great that most such activity must be confined to outsiders. In any case a corner boy cannot admit having "laid" a virgin without incurring the scorn of his fellows.

The corner boys believe that a man's health requires sexual intercourse at certain intervals. "Good girls" are not available for this purpose, and even casual social relations with them are likely to lead to commitments and responsibilities that the man is not prepared to assume. The corner boy has much more freedom, and much less responsibility in dealing with "lays"; freedom increases and responsibility decreases as he establishes relations lower down in this class.

From the standpoint of prestige and social advantage, the ideal girl in the "lay" class is the one who will have sexual relations with only one man in one period, but there are great risks involved in such a relationship. As one corner boy said:

If you go with a girl too long, even if she lays, you're bound to get to like her. That's human nature. I was going out with a girl, and I was banging her every date. After about four months, I saw I was really getting fond of the girl, so I dropped her just like that.

While a man should marry only a good girl, he may become attached to the one-man girl and allow his emotions to override his judgment. Furthermore, if it is not widely known that the girl is a "lay" and she consequently enjoys a good reputation, her family will be able to exert a good deal of pressure to force a marriage. If he makes her pregnant, marriage is hardly to be avoided.

The promiscuous girl is less desirable socially, but there is also less risk in having relations with her. Only pregnancy can impose a responsibility; and, since the identity of the father is difficult to prove, such entanglements may frequently be avoided.

In practice it is hard to distinguish between these two types of "lays" because the promiscuous girl usually tries to pass herself off as a one-man "lay" and one-man girls are constantly slipping into the lower category. Nevertheless, there is a real distinction in the mind of the corner boy, and he acts differently according to his conception of the girl's sexual status. He talks freely about the promiscuous girl and is glad to share her with his friends. He keeps the higher type of "lay" to himself, says little about his relations with her, and treats her with more respect. The reputation of the one-man "lay" is not, however, permanently protected. If she breaks off with the corner boy and takes up with another man, the corner boy is likely to boast openly that he had her first.

The professional prostitute or "hustler" is the least desirable of women. I have heard some men advocate having relations with prostitutes on the ground that no social risk is involved; but generally the corner boys feel that to go to a house of prostitution would be to admit that they could not "pick up" any girls. One corner boy expressed his opinion in this way:

> I never go to a whore house. What do you get out of that? It's too easy. You just pay and go in and get it. Do you think the girl gets any fun out of that? . . . I like to take a girl out and bull her into it [persuade her]. Then when you lay her, you know she's enjoying it too. . . . And after you're through, you feel that you have accomplished something.

Another had this to say:

> You might pay a hustler a dollar and that's all there is to it, it's a business proposition. If you pick up a girl, you may spend three to five dollars on food and drinks, but I'd rather do that any time. . . . You figure, the other way, it's just a business proposition. When you go out with a girl that ain't a hustler, you figure, she must like you a little anyway or she wouldn't go out with you. A hustler will take any man she can get, but this girl is just for you tonight anyway. You take her out, have something to eat and drink, you go for a ride, you begin muggin' her up, then you get in there. . . . That's the way I like to do it. You're staking out new territory. You get the feeling you really done something when you get in there.

The corner boys make a distinction between a house of prostitution and a "line-up." In a line-up one of the men brings a prostitute to some room in the district and allows his friends to have intercourse with her, each man paying the girl for the privilege. While this is a commercial arrangement, nevertheless, it is handled by the boys themselves, and some who would not think of going to a house of prostitution are willing to participate with their friends in a line-up.

The code not only differentiates different types of women in corner-boy attitudes; it also involves strikingly different behavior with women of the different categories, as the following stories indicate.

Danny had picked up a "hustler" and taken her to his gambling joint on the understanding that she would receive a dollar a man. When she was finished, he handed her an envelope containing the bills. She had counted the bills when he pretended to be alarmed and snatched the envelope away from her, replacing it in his pocket. She protested. Danny handed her another envelope of the same size which contained only slips of paper. She was satisfied and went away without looking into the envelope. Danny felt that he had played a clever trick upon the girl.

Doc told me another story about Danny:

There are some noble things down here, Bill. . . . You take Danny's wife, as we call her. She goes to church all the time—what a good kid she is, and she's nice looking too. She goes for Danny. She wants to marry him. Now she goes for him so much that he could probably belt her if he wanted to. But he doesn't want to marry her. He hasn't a job to support a wife. So he stays away from her. . . . Then take Al Mantia. He was a hound. He was after women all the time. One time he and Danny went out with a girl—she said she was a virgin. She had one drink, and she was a little high. They were up in a room, and they had her stripped—stripped! She still said she was a virgin, but she wanted them to give her a belt. But they wouldn't do it. . . . Can you imagine that, Bill? There she was stripped, and they wouldn't do anything to her. . . . The next day she came around and thanked both of them. They can't be such bad fellows if they do that.

The Danny who spared the virgin is the same Danny who cheated the "hustler." In one case the code imposed a strong responsibility; in the other case no responsibility was involved.

The physical-attractiveness criterion needs little comment, for here the corner boys are simply evaluating women in much the same terms as those used by men everywhere in their society. The only significant local variation is found in the strong preference for blondes in sexual relationships. Most of the local Italian girls tend to have black hair and olive complexions. While a good example of this type may appear strikingly attractive to the outsider, the corner boys are more impressed by blonde hair and a fair skin.

In the social- and ethnic-group category, the most desirable woman for non-marital sex relations is the girl of old American-stock background, preferably blonde, who has a higher status than the corner boy. Once I was walking through the aristocratic section of Eastern City with a corner boy when we passed a tall and stately blonde, fashionably dressed, and very attractive. My companion breathed deeply as he said: "The old Puritan stock! . . . The real McCoy! Wouldn't I like to give her a belt."

The attraction of the native stock is not confined to the lower-class Italian. Mario Martini was born in Cornerville, but as he became successful in business he moved out to a fashionable suburb. He married an Italian girl and raised a family, sending his children to private school. He had many business relations and some social relations with upper-class Yankees. He made a practice of hiring only girls of native background for his secretarial work, and on some of his business trips he would take one of these girls along—for sexual as well as secretarial purposes. One of Martini's former secretaries, who told me this story, was a girl of rather plain features, which emphasizes the prestige of the native background even for a man who was as successful as Mario Martini.

If an old-stock American girl is not accessible, then a socially superior member of an ethnic group living outside of Cornerville is the next best thing. There is little prestige involved in having relations with a Cornerville "lay," unless she is especially attractive on a physical basis.

The three categories so far discussed give us a rating scale in terms of feminine desirability. There is one important factor which limits access to certain women, however desirable they may be in terms of these categories. We must consider the social ties between the man and the woman. The incest taboo operates in Cornerville, as elsewhere, to prohibit access to females of certain specified familial ties. While marriages may be contracted beyond these incest limits, the corner-boy code also prohibits nonmarital access to relatives who are not blood relations (for example the brother-in-law's cousin) and to relatives of friends. A corner boy described such a case to me. He was careful to explain that his friend, the girl's cousin, knew that she was a "lay" and would have been glad to have him enjoy himself. Furthermore, the girl was chasing after him so that she was practically forcing the sex relationship upon him. When he was about to have intercourse, he thought of his friend, and, as he says, "I couldn't do a thing." It is only with an outsider, with someone who is not related to him or to a friend, that the corner boy feels free to have sexual relations.

The three categories of "Sex Experience," "Physical Attractiveness," and "Social- or Ethnic-Group Position" are not, of course, the product of any individual's evaluation. They represent, implicitly, the standards of the group —the corner gang. The standards are being continually defined in action and in group discussion. The corner boys are continually talking over the girls that they know and others that they have observed in terms of all these categories. Consequently, a high degree of consensus tends to arise in placing the individual girl in her position in each category. The men then know how they are supposed to act in each case; and the observer, equipped with this conceptual scheme, is able to predict how, as a general rule, the men will attempt to act.

One feature of this classificatory scheme should be noted. The standards for marriage and for nonmarital sex relations are quite different. For non-marital sex relations the ideal girl is a one-man "lay," blonde and fair skinned, belonging to a socially superior old-stock group, and having no familial connection with the corner boy or any of his friends. For marriage, preference is for the virgin of Italian extraction and having some family connection with friends or relatives of ego. (The girl fitting this description would usually, but not always, be a dark brunette.)

Different sorts of evaluation are involved in the two cases. The corner boy thinks of casual sex relations in terms of personal prestige as well as physical satisfaction. If he were able to persuade an attractive blonde to drive down to his corner and pick him up in an expensive-looking car, he could make a great impression on his fellows. Wives are thought of in terms of long-run compatibility and utility. Corner boys express their preference for a wife of Italian extraction because "she would understand my ways," "she would know how to cook for me," and "I could trust her more than the others"; "the Italian women make faithful wives; it's their upbringing."

The corner boy's relations with the opposite sex are not determined simply by his evaluation of feminine desirability. He must possess certain qualifications in order to gain access to the most desirable women. Talk is important. The man who can talk entertainingly and "bull the girl to her ears" gains in prestige with his fellows, as well as in his social opportunities. However, talk is not enough. Social position, money, and possession of a car weigh heavily in the balance. It is a common complaint of the corner boys that the most desirable women are most difficult of access because they demand more in position, money, and a car than most corner boys can provide. I once asked a corner boy if it was necessary to have a car in order to pick up a girl for sexual purposes. He answered:

No, you can take her up to a room. . . . But no nice girl will go up to a man's room. If you take her out in the car, that's all right. If she goes up to your room with you, she's really a bum.

Under the influence of a car, a ride in the country, drinks, and heavy petting, a girl can allow a man to have sexual intercourse with her without any premeditation on her part. But if he suggests to her that they go to a room she can no longer pretend that she does not know what he is about. By consenting, she stamps herself as the kind of girl who goes to rooms with men. Even the most promiscuous like to maintain the pretense that they do it seldom and never in such a premeditated fashion. Thus the man with a car is generally able to have intercourse with a more desirable class of women than are available to the man who must rely upon rented rooms.

If the observer can classify the corner boy in terms of these criteria and classify the women within his social orbit in terms of the categories described above, then the individual's social and sexual behavior becomes still more subject to close prediction. No invariable rules can be set up, for the corner boy's code, like all other codes, is sometimes violated; but the discussion so far should clearly indicate that the relations between the sexes in the slums are subject to definite rules of behavior. The corner boys, while deviating from respectable middle-class standards, lead an organized sex life.

Our discussion has been confined to pre-marital sex and social relations. Little change is required in order to apply our conclusions to the post-marital behavior of the corner boy. The wife is expected to be completely faithful, and even the slightest flirtations are seriously regarded. The husband is expected to be a good provider and to have an affection for his wife and children. Nevertheless, the field of sexual adventure is not barred to him, and he endeavors to keep this quite separate from his married life. While the wives object, the men see nothing wrong in extra-marital sex relations, as long as they are not carried to the extremes of an open scandal or serious neglect of the family. Within these limits, the married man looks upon the feminine world just as he did before marriage.

While the slum sex code has now been described in outline form, it remains for us to consider the effect of this code and of the behavior it involves upon some of the broader social processes.

It is not easy for the Cornerville girl to maintain a good reputation if she has social relations with Cornerville men. Once I went to a dance outside of the district with two corner boys and three girls. It was late when we drove back to Cornerville. The driver stopped the car just outside of the district, and all the girls and one of the men got out to walk home. Later I asked why the girls had not been driven home. The driver answered:

Well, you know, Bill, the people of Cornerville are very suspicious people. They can make up a story about nothing at all. . . . If the girls came home alone, people would talk. If we all drove up in a car at one o'clock in the morning, they would wonder what we had been doing. . . . If the three of them walk home with Nutsy, then people will say, "Well, they have been in good company."

It is not only the older generation which gossips about the girls. The corner gang is continually defining and redefining reputations. Not even the "good girl" is safe from suspicion, and her local field of action is sharply circumscribed if she does not want to commit herself to marriage at an early age. As we have seen, the one-man "lay" cannot afford to have her "boy friend" in Cornerville because, if the relationship broke down, her reputation could be destroyed.

While social life outside of Cornerville has a great appeal to most girls, those who center their activities beyond the local boundaries seem to fit largely into two categories that represent the top and the bottom of Cornerville feminine society. There are a number of "good girls" who work outside of the district and use contacts made in this way in order to move into superior social circles. Then there are the "lays," who find greater freedom elsewhere. Most of the "good girls," being limited by their backgrounds, are unable to build up a social life outside of Cornerville. They have a romantic picture of a non-Cornerville, non-Italian of superior educational and economic status who will some day come along and marry them. While the social restrictions of Cornerville weigh particularly heavily upon the girls and influence many of them to wish for an escape through marriage outside the district, most marriages are contracted within Cornerville or between Cornerville and adjoining districts of similar social background. Nevertheless, the character of Cornerville social life operates to withdraw a significant number of local women from the orbit of the corner boys.

This situation is recognized by the corner boys. One of them commented:

There are lots of lays in Cornerville. You take Market Street from Norton Street down; nine out of ten of those girls will lay. But they won't lay for a Cornerville fellow. You know why? Because they figure if they lay for me, I'll tell my friends the girl's a lay, and they'll want to lay her, and it'll get around. . . . Can you beat it, Bill, they're all around us yet we can't get them.

My informant was disgruntled over his failure to "get" Cornerville girls, and his 90 per cent figure is not to be taken seriously. If these girls actually did go outside of the district, he was in no position to know their sexual status, and any estimate can be no more than a guess. Probably the percentage of "lays" among local girls is very small. In any case, the fact remains that Cornerville men find most local girls barred to them except for marriage. In this situation they also must look outside of Cornerville for social and sexual satisfactions. The men, with their highly organized and localized corner gangs, tend to be even more restricted than the women in their social movements, and only a minority are able to operate at all effectively outside of Cornerville. However, even that minority contributes toward changing the social structure of Cornerville and Eastern City.

The restrictions of the peasant Italian family mores, plus the close watch kept upon their behavior, tend to push some of the young Italian girls out of Cornerville. Finding local fields restricted, some of the young men follow the girls in reaching for outside social contacts. This operates to stimulate intermarriage, illegitimate births out of interethnic sex relations, and social mobility. The study of the assimilation of the Italian population would be incomplete if we did not analyze the social and sex life of the slums in these terms.

SOCIAL STRATIFICATION AND PSYCHIATRIC DISORDERS

August B. Hollingshead and Frederick C. Redlich

THE RESEARCH REPORTED HERE grew out of the work of a number of men, who, during the last half century, have demonstrated that the social environment in which individuals live is connected in some way, as yet not fully explained, to the development of mental illness.[1] Medical men have approached this problem largely from the viewpoint of epidemiology.[2] Sociologists, on the other hand, have analyzed the question in terms of ecology,[3] and of social disorganization.[4] Neither psychiatrists nor sociologists have carried on extensive research into the specific question we are concerned with, namely, interrelations between the class structure and the development of mental illness. However, a few sociologists and psychiatrists have written speculative and research papers in this area.[5]

The present research, therefore, was designed to discover whether a relationship does or does not exist between the class system of our society and mental illnesses. Five general hypotheses were formulated in our research plan to test some dimension of an assumed relationship between the two. These hypotheses were stated positively; they could just as easily have been expressed either negatively or conditionally. They were phrased as follows:

I. The *expectancy* of a psychiatric disorder is related significantly to an individual's position in the class structure of his society.

II. The *types* of psychiatric disorders are connected significantly to the class structure.

III. The type of *psychiatric treatment* administered is associated with patient's positions in the class structure.

IV. The *psycho-dynamics* of psychiatric disorders are correlative to an individual's position in the class structure.

V. *Mobility* in the class structure is neurotogenic.

Each hypothesis is linked to the others, and all are subsumed under the theoretical assumption of a functional relationship between stratification in society and the prevalence of particular types of mental disorders among given social classes or strata in a specified population. Although our research was planned around these hypotheses, we have been forced by the nature of the problem of mental illness to study *diagnosed* prevalence of psychiatric disorders, rather than *true* or *total* prevalence.

Methodological Procedure. The research is being done by a team of four psychiatrists,[6] two sociologists,[7] and a clinical psychologist.[8] The data are being assembled in the New Haven urban community, which consists of the city of New Haven and surrounding towns of East Haven, North Haven, West Haven, and Hamden. This community had a population of some 250,000 persons in 1950.[9] The New Haven community was selected because the

Reprinted from *The American Sociological Review* (April 1953), pp. 163-69, by permission of the authors and the publisher. (Copyright, 1953, by the American Sociological Society.)

community's structure has been studied intensively by sociologists over a long period. In addition, it is served by a private psychiatric hospital, three psychiatric clinics, and 27 practicing psychiatrists, as well as the state and Veterans Administration facilities.

Four basic technical operations had to be completed before the hypotheses could be tested. These were: the delineation of the class structure of the community, selection of a cross-sectional control of the community's population, the determination of who was receiving psychiatric care, and the stratification of both the control sample and the psychiatric patients.

August B. Hollingshead and Jerome K. Myers took over the task of delineating the class system. Fortunately, Maurice R. Davie and his students had studied the social structure of the New Haven community in great detail over a long time span.[10] Thus, we had a large body of data we could draw upon to aid us in blocking out the community's social structure.

The community's social structure is differentiated *vertically* along racial, ethnic, and religious lines; each of these vertical cleavages, in turn, is differentiated *horizontally* by a series of strata or classes. Around the socio-biological axis of race two social worlds have evolved: A Negro world and a white world. The white world is divided by ethnic origin and religion into Catholic, Protestant, and Jewish contingents. Within these divisions there are numerous ethnic groups. The Irish hold aloof from the Italians, and the Italians move in different circles from the Poles. The Jews maintain a religious and social life separate from the gentiles. The *horizontal* strata that transect each of these vertical divisions are based upon the social values that are attached to occupation, education, place of residence in the community, and associations.

The vertically differentiating factors of race, religion and ethnic origin, when combined with the horizontally differentiating ones of occupation, education, place of residence and so on, produce a social structure that is highly compartmentalized. The integrating factors in this complex are twofold. First, each stratum of each vertical division is similar in its cultural characteristics to the corresponding stratum in the other divisions. Second, the cultural pattern for each stratum or class was set by the "Old Yankee" core group. This core group provided the master cultural mold that has shaped the status system of each sub-group in the community. In short, the social structure of the New Haven community is a parallel class structure within the limits of race, ethnic origin and religion.

This fact enabled us to stratify the community, for our purposes, with an *Index of Social Position*.[11] This *Index* utilizes three scaled factors to determine an individual's class position within the community's stratificational system: ecological area of residence, occupation, and education. Ecological area of residence is measured by a six point scale; occupation and education are each measured by a seven point scale. To obtain a social class score on an individual we must therefore know his address, his occupation, and the number of years of school he has completed. Each of these factors is given a scale score, and the scale score is multiplied by a factor weight determined by a standard regression equation. The factor weights are as follows: Ecological area of residence, 5; occupation, 8; and education, 6. The three factor scores are summed, and the resultant score is taken as an index of this individual's position in the community's social class system.

This *Index* enabled us to delineate five main social class strata within the horizontal dimension of the social structure. These principal strata or classes may be characterized as follows:

Class I. This stratum is composed of wealthy families whose wealth is often inherited and whose heads are leaders in the community's business and professional pursuits. Its members live in those areas of the community generally regarded as "the best"; the adults are college graduates, usually from famous private institutions, and almost all gentile families are listed in the New Haven *Social Directory,* but few Jewish families are listed. In brief, these people occupy positions of high social prestige.

Class II. Adults in this stratum are almost all college graduates; the males occupy high managerial positions, many are engaged in the lesser ranking professions. These families are well-to-do, but there is no substantial inherited or acquired wealth. Its members live in the "better" residential areas; about one-half of these families belong to lesser ranking private clubs, but only 5 per cent of Class II families are listed in the New Haven *Social Directory.*

Class III. This stratum includes the vast majority of small proprietors, white-collar office and sales workers, and a considerable number of skilled manual workers. Adults are predominately high school graduates, but a considerable percentage have attended business schools and small colleges for a year or two. They live in "good" residential areas; less than 5 per cent belong to private clubs, but they are not included in the *Social Directory.* Their social life tends to be concentrated in the family, the church, and the lodge.

Class IV. This stratum consists predominately of semi-skilled factory workers. Its adult members have finished the elementary grades, but the older people have not completed high school. However, adults under thirty-five have generally graduated from high school. Its members comprise almost one-half of the community; and their residences are scattered over wide areas. Social life is centered in the family, the neighborhood, the labor union, and public places.

Class V. Occupationally, class V adults are overwhelmingly semi-skilled factory hands and unskilled laborers. Educationally most adults have not completed the elementary grades. The families are concentrated in the "tenement" and "cold-water flat" areas of New Haven. Only a small minority belong to organized community institutions. Their social life takes place in the family flat, on the street, or in neighborhood social agencies.

The second major technical operation in this research was the enumeration of psychiatric patients. A Psychiatric Census was taken to discover the number and kinds of psychiatric patients in the community. Enumeration was limited to residents of the community who were patients of a psychiatrist or a psychiatric clinic, or were in a psychiatric institution on December 1, 1950. To make reasonably certain that all patients were included in the enumeration, the research team gathered data from all public and private psychiatric institutions and clinics in Connecticut and nearby states, and all private practitioners in Connecticut and the metropolitan New York area. It received the cooperation of all clinics and institutions, and of all practitioners except a small number in New York City. It can be reasonably assumed that we have data comprising at least 98 per cent of all individuals who were receiving psychiatric care on December 1, 1950.

Forty-four pertinent items of information were gathered on each patient and placed on a schedule. The psychiatrists gathered material regarding symptomatology and diagnosis, onset of illness and duration, referral to the practitioner and the institution, and the nature and intensity of treatment. The sociologists obtained information on age, sex, occupation, education, religion, race and ethnicity, family history, marital experiences, and so on.

The third technical research operation was the selection of a control sample from the normal population of the community. The sociologists drew a 5 per cent random sample of households in the community from the 1951 New Haven *City Directory.* This directory covers the entire communal area. The names and addresses in it were compiled in October and November, 1950 —a period very close to the date of the Psychiatric Census. Therefore there was comparability of residence and date of registry between the two population groups. Each household drawn in the sample was interviewed, and data on the age, sex, occupation, education, religion, and income of family members, as well as other items necessary for our purposes were placed on a schedule. This sample is our Control Population.

Our fourth basic operation was the stratification of the psychiatric patients and of the control population with the *Index of Social Position.* As soon as these tasks were completed, the schedules from the Psychiatric Census and 5 per cent Control Sample were edited and coded, and their data were placed on Hollerith cards. The analysis of these data is in process.

Selected Findings. Before we discuss our findings relative to Hypothesis I, we want to reemphasize that our study is concerned with *diagnosed* or *treated* prevalence rather than *true* or *total* prevalence. Our Psychiatric Census included only psychiatric cases under treatment, diagnostic study, or care. It did not include individuals with psychiatric disorders who were not being treated on December 1, 1950, by a psychiatrist. There are undoubtedly many individuals in the community with psychiatric problems who escaped our net. If we had *true* prevalence figures, many findings from our present study would be more meaningful, perhaps some of our interpretations would be changed, but at present we must limit ourselves to the data we have.

Hypothesis I, as revised by the nature of the problem, stated: *The diagnosed prevalence of psychiatric disorders is related significantly to an individual's position* in the class structure. A test of this hypothesis involves a comparison of the normal population with the psychiatric population. If no significant difference between the distribution of the normal population and the psychiatric patient population by social class is found, Hypothesis I may be abandoned as unproved. However, if a significant difference is found between the two populations by class, Hypothesis I should be entertained until more conclusive data are assembled. Pertinent data for a limited test of Hypothesis I are presented in Table I. The data included show the number of individuals in the normal population and the psychiatric population, by class level. What we are concerned with in this test is how these two populations are distributed by class.

When we tested the reliability of these population distributions by the use of the chi square method, we found a *very significant* relation between social class and treated prevalence of psychiatric disorders in the New Haven community. A comparison of the percentage distribution of each population by class readily indicates the direction of the class concentration of psychiatric cases. For example, Class I contains 3.1 per cent of the community's popula-

Table I—Distribution of Normal and Psychiatric Population by Social Class

Social Class	Normal Population*		Psychiatric Population	
	Number	Per cent	Number	Per cent
I	358	3.1	19	1.0
II	926	8.1	131	6.7
III	2500	22.0	260	13.2
IV	5256	46.0	758	38.6
V	2037	17.8	723	36.8
Unknown**	345	3.0	72	3.7
Total	11,422	100.0	1,963	100.0

Chi square = 408.16, P less than .001.
*These figures are preliminary. They do not include Yale students, transients, institutionalized persons, and refusals.
**The unknown cases were not used in the calculation of chi square. They are individuals drawn in the sample, and psychiatric cases whose class level could not be determined because of paucity of data.

tion but only 1.0 per cent of the psychiatric cases. Class V, on the other hand, includes 17.8 per cent of the community's population, but contributed 36.8 per cent of the psychiatric patients. On the basis of our data Hypothesis I clearly should be accepted as tenable.

Hypothesis II postulated a significant connection between the *type* of psychiatric disorder and social class. This hypothesis involves a test of the idea that there may be a functional relationship between an individual's position in the class system and the type of psychiatric disorder that he may present. This hypothesis depends, in part, on the question of diagnosis. Our psychiatrists based their diagnoses on the classificatory system developed by the Veterans Administration.[12] For the purposes of this paper, all cases are grouped into two categories: the neuroses and the psychoses. The results of this grouping by social class are given in Table II.

Table II—Distribution of Neuroses and Psychoses by Social Class

Social Class	Neuroses		Psychoses	
	Number	Per cent	Number	Per cent
I	10	52.6	9	47.4
II	88	67.2	43	32.8
III	115	44.2	145	55.8
IV	175	23.1	583	76.9
V	61	8.4	662	91.6
Total	449		1,442	

Chi square = 296.45, P less than .001.

A study of Table II will show that the neuroses are concentrated at the higher levels and the psychoses at the lower end of the class structure. Our team advanced a number of theories to explain the sharp differences between the neuroses and psychoses by social class. One suggestion was that the low percentage of neurotics in the lower classes was a direct reaction to the cost of psychiatric treatment. But as we accumulated a series of case studies, for tests of Hypotheses IV and V, we became skeptical of this simple interpretation. Our detailed case records indicate that the social distance between psychiatrist and patient may be more potent than economic considerations in determining the character of psychiatric intervention. This question therefore requires further research.

The high concentration of psychotics in the lower strata is probably the product of a very unequal distribution of psychotics in the total population. To test this idea, Hollingshead selected schizophrenics for special study. Because of the severity of this disease it is probable that very few schizophrenics fail to receive some kind of psychiatric care. This diagnostic group comprises 44.2 per cent of all patients, and 58.7 per cent of the psychotics, in our study. Ninety-seven and six-tenths per cent of these schizophrenic patients had been hospitalized at one time or another, and 94 per cent were hospitalized at the time of our census. When we classify these patients by social class we find that there is a very significant inverse relationship between social class and schizophrenia.

Hollingshead decided to determine, on the basis of these data, what the probability of the prevalence of schizophrenia by social class might be in the general population. To do this he used a proportional index to learn whether or not there were differentials in the distribution of the general population, as represented in our control sample, and the distribution of schizophrenics by social class. If a social class exhibits the same proportion of schizophrenia as it comprises of the general population, the index for that class is 100. If schizophrenia is disproportionately prevalent in a social class the index is above 100; is schizophrenia is disproportionately low in a social class the index is below 100. The index for each social class appears in the last column of Table III.

Table III—Comparison of the Distribution of the Normal Population with Schizophrenics by Class, with Index of Probable Prevalence

Social Class	Normal Population		Schizophrenics		Index of Prevalence
	Number	Per cent	Number	Per cent	
I	358	3.2	6	.7	22
II	926	8.4	23	2.7	33
III	2,500	22.6	83	9.8	43
IV	5,256	47.4	352	41.6	88
V	2,037	18.4	383	45.2	246
Total	11,077	100.0	847	100.0	

The fact that the Index of Prevalence in class I is only one-fifth as great as it would be if schizophrenia were proportionately distributed in this class, and that it is two and one-half times as high in class V as we might expect on the basis of proportional distribution, gives further support to Hypothesis II. The fact that the Index of Prevalence is 11.2 times as great in class V as in class I is particularly impressive.

Hypothesis III stipulated that the type of psychiatric treatment a patient receives is associated with his position in the class structure. A test of this hypothesis involves a comparison of the different types of therapy being used by psychiatrists on patients in the different social classes. We encountered many forms of therapy but they may be grouped under three main types: psychotherapy, organic therapy, and custodian care. The patient population, from the viewpoint of the principal type of therapy received, was divided roughly into three categories: 32.0 per cent received some type of psychotherapy; 31.7 per cent received organic treatments of one kind or another; and 36.3 per cent received custodial care without treatment. The percentage of persons who received no treatment care was greatest in the lower classes.

The same finding applies to organic treatment. Psychotherapy, on the other hand, was concentrated in the higher classes. Within the psychotherapy category there were sharp differences between the types of psychotherapy administered to the several classes. For example, psychoanalyses was limited to classes I and II. Patients in class V who received any psychotherapy were treated by group methods in the state hospitals. The number and percentage of patients who received each type of therapy is given in Table IV. The data clearly support Hypothesis III.

Table IV—Distribution of the Principal Types of Therapy by Social Class

| | Psychotherapy | | Organic Therapy | | No Treatment | |
Social Class	Number	Per cent	Number	Per cent	Number	Per cent
I	14	73.7	2	10.5	3	15.8
II	107	81.7	15	11.4	9	6.9
III	136	52.7	74	28.7	48	18.6
IV	237	31.1	288	37.1	242	31.8
V	115	16.1	234	32.7	367	51.2

Chi square = 336.58, P less than .001.

At the moment we do not have data available for a test of Hypotheses IV and V. These will be put to a test as soon as we complete work on a series of cases now under close study. Preliminary materials give us the impression that they too will be confirmed.

Conclusions and Interpretations. This study was designed to throw new light upon the question of how mental illness is related to social environment. It approached this problem from the perspective of social class to determine if an individual's position in the social system was associated significantly with the development of psychiatric disorders. It proceeded on the theoretical assumption that if mental illnesses were distributed randomly in the population, the hypotheses designed to test the idea that psychiatric disorders are connected in some functional way to the class system would not be found to be statistically significant.

The data we have assembled demonstrate conclusively that mental illness, as measured by diagnosed prevalence, is not distributed randomly in the population of the New Haven community. On the contrary, psychiatric difficulties of so serious a nature that they reach the attention of a psychiatrist are unequally distributed among the five social classes. In addition, types of psychiatric disorders, and the ways patients are treated, are strongly associated with social class position.

The statistical tests of our hypotheses indicate that there are definite connections between particular types of social environments in which people live, as measured by the social class concept, and the emergence of particular kinds of psychiatric disorders, as measured by psychiatric diagnosis. They do not tell us what these connections are, nor how they are functionally related to a particular type of mental illness in a given individual. The next step, we believe, is to turn from the strictly statistical approach to an intensive study of the social environments associated with particular social classes, on the one hand, and of individuals in these environments who do or do not develop mental illnesses, on the other hand. Currently the research team is engaged in this next step but is not yet ready to make a formal report of its findings.

THE ORGANIZATION OF LEISURE-TIME SERVICES FOR YOUTH

August B. Hollingshead

ADOLESCENT ORGANIZATIONS

THE APPROVED CHARACTER-BUILDING organizations especially for teen-aged youngsters are sponsored by the churches, the American Legion, and the Farm Bureau. Membership in each is theoretically open to any boy or girl in the age range we studied with the exception of two lodge-sponsored groups, which are restricted to youngsters who can meet fraternal requirements.[1] Since they are restrictive in their membership, we shall not discuss them further.

Boy Scouts. After a lapse of several years, the Boy Scouts were reorganized in May, 1937, by an influential class II boy and his father. The boy and his 6 clique mates, 3 class II's, 2 class III's, and 1 class I, composed the troop's nucleus. Five of the 7 belonged to families prominent in the Federated Church, the other 2 came from leading Lutheran families. As a result, the Federated Church sponsored the troop. A young class II professional man, also in the Federated Church, was asked to become Scout Master. A rival troop was organized in the Methodist Church in the fall of that year. The latter troop selected its members from families prominent in the Methodist Church, that is, largely from classes II and III; the Scout Master was a Methodist who came from class II. Early in 1939 the Baptists organized a third troop to "take care" of their boys, and in 1940 the American Legion was induced by the adult leaders of these troops to sponsor a troop of older boys from the three junior troops. This troop was composed of boys from 15 to 17 years of age. Its Scout Master was a popular, civic-minded, young non-legionnaire from class II, but a Rotarian.

The Boy Scouts are not looked upon as a cross section of young teen-age Elmtowners either by the boys, their adult leaders, or Elmtowners in general. The president of the district Boy Scout Council summed up the official position in these words: "Scout officials represent the better type of people. They have to—they are in scout work." On the other hand, the organization is criticized severely by members of the mill workers' union and many parents in class IV as "a wealthy boys'" group.

This criticism is in large part valid, for the Boy Scouts are very selective in their membership. In 1941-1942, 41 high school boys belonged to the Boy Scouts. By class the membership was: class II, 32 per cent; class III, 44 per cent; class IV, 22 per cent; and 1 class V, 2 per cent. These figures show the proportion each class contributes rather than what each might contribute if all the boys in each class belonged to the organization. All boys in the study are theoretically eligible for membership by age, so we may assume that they are all potential members; that is, if all other factors are equal. When the number of members is compared with the number that

Reprinted from *Elmtown's Youth* (1949), pp. 389-412, by permission of the author and the publisher. (Copyright, 1949, by John Wiley and Sons, Inc.) This chapter has been abridged.

might join, the picture has very different dimensions. For instance, 13 of the 21 boys in class II (62 per cent) were Boy Scouts; however only 1 of the 116 boys in class V was a Boy Scout. Obviously, the chances for a class V boy to belong to the Boy Scouts are not the same as for a class II boy.

An index of membership was constructed to measure the difference between potential and actual membership. In this index, if each class belongs in the ratio that is theoretically possible, the index for each will be 100. If a class belongs more frequently than its proportion of the total group indicates, the index is above 100; if its membership is less than proportionate the index is below 100. The bias for or against membership in each class as revealed by the index of membership is given in the last column of the following tabulation.

Class	Number of Boys*	Number of Boy Scouts	Index of Membership
I and II	21	13	549
III	80	18	203
IV	152	9	54
V	116	1	8
Total	369	41	100

*The total number of boys in the study was used here rather than the high school group, because the Boy Scouts were supposed to be community wide, not merely for students. Actually, however, only students belonged. When a boy left school he left the Scouts.

The index of membership shows that the class II's are attracted very strongly to the Boy Scouts, the class III's to a less extent, whereas the class IV's, and particularly the class V's, are repelled. If the class II's and the class V's are compared, it is evident that the chances of a class II boy belonging are 69 to 1 as compared to the chances of a class V boy. Clearly, there is a very strong class factor at work in the Boy Scouts.

The Boy Scouts, although sponsored nominally by three churches and the American Legion, are controlled by a tightly knit clique of class II civic leaders, all members of Rotary, who take great pride in "their" movement, "their" camp, and "their" campaign for funds. In the spring of 1942, they organized a financial campaign and raised over $1,200 to support the Boy Scouts. Four of the five members of the financial committee were class II's; the chairman belonged to class I. The financial chairman told how he "put the pressure" on some people "who could see this thing at all."

When I first started raising money for campaigns, I used to ask people to help, but I soon learned that doesn't do any good; so now I call them up and I say, "I want you to give ten dollars to the Boy Scouts, and I want ten dollars from your firm."

Last year I had the tough ones to handle. John Austin and the Townsends were the worst. I called up John and said, "I want you to give ten dollars, and I want ten dollars from Mary [his wife] and ten dollars from John, Jr., and, do you hear, I want twenty-five dollars from the Hummer Corporation!"

John hemmed and hawed around, and I said, "You rich tightwad, you can afford to give a lot more than that. I'm not going to take no for an answer." He came through, but it hurt him.

Now Jim Townsend is really a tight boy. I called him up and said, "I want twenty bucks from you and twenty bucks from Tom [Jim Townsend's brother], and twenty bucks from each of your wives. And I want fifty bucks from the company." He tried to put me off. Then he said, "Let me talk it over with Tom. I'll drop the checks in the mail in two or three days." The two or three days went by, and then I called up the cashier and said, "Billingsley, write out two twenty-dollar checks to the Boy Scouts from the Townsends' personal accounts and one for fifty dollars to the Boy Scouts from the company's accounts, and take them to Tom, and tell him I said for him to sign them, and you get them in the mail today." Tom just wouldn't back out. He's not small enough for that, and the checks came through. But I'd never been able to get the money out of them without having Billingsley put the squeeze on.

Camp Fire Girls. Two "maiden ladies" organized the Camp Fire Girls shortly after the Boy Scouts were reorganized. These women (one was on the fringe of class I; the other was in class II) knew how to organize a club with the "right kind" of support. Therefore, when they decided "to do something for the girls," they privately discussed the idea with old Mrs. Woodson and Mrs. Homer McDermott. After they had gained the approval of these worthies, the idea was presented to the Friday Morning Club. The Club voted its approval, and several members became unofficial sponsors. Inevitably the Federated Church offered its parlors to the girls for their meetings; gradually the group became identified with this church, although members of the Friday Morning Club continued to finance its activities. Originally, membership was by personal invitation rather than by sex and age groups as it had been in the Boy Scouts. This policy more or less limited membership to girls from the first three classes, with a heavy emphasis upon the upper two; but in 1939 the ranks were opened to any girl 10 years old or older who desired to join. The girls already in the organization, however, exerted informal pressures to restrict the membership to class II and class III girls and within these classes to a few cliques.

Adults in the three upper classes believe that the Camp Fire Girls is "a fine organization." They are also in general agreement that the two women who worked with these girls are doing "a remarkable piece of work." The high school girls in the group are very sure of themselves and smug in their awareness that they belong to the "right" organization. However, the girls who do not belong hold other opinions. Some are indifferent, others envious, and a minority vocal in their criticism of these girls as "snobs" and "social climbers." The Camp Fire Girls, like the Boy Scouts, really represent the

Class	Number of Girls*	Number of Members	Index of Membership
II	14	8	772
III	78	15	260
IV	160	4	34
V	114	0	0
Total	366	27	100

*The total number of girls in the study by class.

girls in the upper one-fourth of the prestige structure rather than the whole, as the index of membership reveals. (No class V girl belongs or has belonged to the Camp Fire Girls.)

Girl Scouts. Although only 10 girls, 3 class III's and 7 class IV's, belong to the Girl Scouts, this organization merits considerable discussion, for it reveals the difficulty encountered by an organization which has the "wrong kind of leadership." It was organized about the same time as the Boy Scouts and the Camp Fire Girls. Its original sponsor was a civic-minded young woman in class III who believed that the community should do "something constructive" for its boys and girls. She was convinced that the ones to be reached were "those whose families could not help them understand what was going on around them." She got permission from the Methodists to use a room in the church as a meeting place for the proposed troop. She broached the idea to the Women's Club, the Sunday Schools, and the public schools, stressing the fact that this was a "wholesome organization" open to any girl between 10 and 14 years of age. After several months of hard work, she managed to organize a small troop, largely among the Methodist girls. This woman carried on practically alone for two years, then gave up, and the troop disbanded. One girl who did not want to see the organization die wrote to the national headquarters and asked what she could do to keep it going. The national office sent her a set of instructions and a form to be filled in by a prospective leader. When these materials arrived, she showed them to several of her clique mates who had been members. The group decided the first girl's mother would make a good leader; so they asked her to take over the troop. Even though she said she had "no qualifications," she became the leader.

The Girl Scouts never had the backing of the women from the two upper classes, nor that of the class III's until the fall of 1940, when a class III Girl Scout was able to interest her mother and a nun in the parochial school in the organization. The nun later interested a prominent Catholic class III mother. This woman was a close friend of a third woman who was influential in the American Legion Auxiliary. Through the latter woman's efforts the American Legion Auxiliary became involved. These women were instrumental in the organization of a Girl Scout Mothers' Club. This interest and activity produced a lively troop of 40 girls from the seventh and eighth grades of the parochial school and the Elmtown Central School.

The Girl Scout leader and the Mothers' Club in the fall of 1941 attempted to organize a Senior Troop among the high school girls. Their efforts, however, were quietly and effectively blocked by the high school principal and the Superintendent of Schools, with the tacit approval of certain members of the Board of Education. The principal was the son of a Presbyterian minister; he had been taught to hate and fear Catholics, so he had "his guard up" against the Catholics. When he learned from a high school teacher who had been asked to lead the proposed senior troop that the invitation had been extended by a leading Catholic woman, his deep-seated prejudices became active. He questioned the teacher closely as to "who is behind this anyway." The teacher told him the new troop was to meet in the Methodist Church, but it was sponsored by the nuns of the parochial school, the American Legion Auxiliary, and the Mothers' Club. After he had listened to the teacher's explanation, he gave her a number of reasons why she should not take on "such a responsibility in her first year."

The next day the principal consulted the Superintendent and asked his advice about what the teacher should do. His story to the Superintendent was different from the one he gave the teacher. He explained that his teachers were busy, but he thought that Miss X could take on the work if the Super-intendent deemed it advisable; the Superintendent did not think it advisable "under the circumstances." The principal returned to his office and notified the teachers that they should consult him before they entered into any community activities which might "interfere" with their school work. The Superintendent later told us that he believed the decision not to allow the teachers to lead the Senior Girl Scout Troop was "wise." He then went on to explain that he did not want to give "the Board" the idea that he was trying to set up a "rival organization" to the Camp Fire Girls. (Two members of the Board had daughters in the Camp Fire Girls; the Superintendent's daughter was also in this organization.)

An old personal quarrel between two members of the School Board and certain Legionnaires, one that had nothing to do with educational policy, was also a factor in this action.[2] Several years before, a former Legionnaire on the Board had been the leader in an acrimonious squabble with the clique which was in control of American Legion affairs in 1941-1942. The Superintendent, aware of this hostility, believed that by encouraging the Girl Scouts in the high school he would run into trouble with his Board because the Auxiliary of the American Legion was helping the movement along with the Catholics. The members of the School Board were aware of the moves the Girl Scout leaders were making, and two of them were in private severely critical of these efforts. One Board member said:

They are just trying to copy what we did last spring in the Boy Scouts, but you can't organize the class they have in that oufit. Last year they tried to go in with us when we raised our budget, but I said, "Nothing doing."[3]

One Board member was instrumental in blocking the efforts of the county judge to organize a Big Brother movement in Elmtown. He said he did not want to see the judge "build a political machine in that class"; yet he claimed on numerous occasions that "you can't organize that class." The boys and girls in the lower classes are the victims of these personal rivalries, jealousies, and efforts of a handful of community leaders, largely in class II, to maintain prestige. The latter are in control of the schools, churches, and adolescent organizations; thus, they are able to use the institutional machinery they control to block any movement of which they do not approve.

The girls understand the sharp differences between the prestige rating of the Girl Scouts and the Camp Fire Girls. A class III girl, who had belonged to the Girl Scouts in another town and whose family had moved to Elmtown in 1939, summarized the situation neatly when she related how the Girl Scouts rated in her old home town and how active she had been there. When the family moved to Elmtown, she joined the Girl Scouts and took up where she had left off, only to drop out in three months; "Mother did not think the kids were socially what they should be. She thought the kids looked crummy." The following year she joined the Camp Fire Girls. "They are much nicer."

4-H Club. An active 4-H Club, which was sponsored by the Farm Bureau and led by the county agent, had 30 student members, 16 boys and 14 girls.

drawn mainly from the farm population. The 4-H Club was far more popular among rural boys and girls than the Boy Scouts, Camp Fire Girls, and Girl Scouts were in town. Nevertheless, its members were drawn disproportionately from classes II and III. Since the number of rural dwellers was small in classes II and V, the class II's were combined with the class III's, and the class V's with the class IV's for purposes of measuring the potential membership against the actual in the index of membership. After these combinations were made, the index of membership for the boys in classes II and III was 202; and for those in classes IV and V, 54. The index for the girls was little different from that for the boys; for classes II and III it was 282; and for class IV, 88. (There were no class V girls in 4-H.)

The objectives of the 4-H Club are similar to those of the Boy Scouts, Girl Scouts, and Camp Fire Girls, but they are implemented with a very different program. The Boy Scouts and Girl Scouts and Camp Fire Girls hope, through directed recreation and study for about two hours at a weekly meeting and an annual two-week summer camp, to teach boys and girls to use their leisure hours constructively. The 4-H Club leadership has the same conception of its function, except that it reflects rural beliefs that leisure should involve the production of something useful. This is expressed in the statement of a class III farmer, "My father used to say when I wanted to play baseball, 'While you're resting, chop wood.' " The 4-H Club builds its program around this philosophy; thus, instead of meeting once a week to play games or to simulate living on a long-dead frontier, its members are engaged in individual projects.

The county agent, who is interested keenly in county, regional, and state livestock-growing contests, favors calf, hog, and chicken projects rather than a balanced program for both boys and girls. Although the woman who runs the Home Bureau in the county agent's office works with the girls on home-making projects, stock-feeding projects are of major interest to most of the young people. All the boys and 5 of the 7 class IV girls in the club, but none of the class III girls, are engaged in livestock-growing projects. Class II and class III girls do not approve of a girl's feeding stock; this is considered a boy's job. Consequently, they are occupied with needlework and canning projects. The class III boys, however, are avid stock feeders; this is a man's role, and they fill it ably. Year after year, Elmtown farm boys bring home their share of blue and red ribbons from the State Fair in 4-H and adult competition. In 1941, a class III boy won the state junior championship with a Hereford steer and went on to win in open competition at the International Livestock Exposition in Chicago.

INFORMAL RECREATION

In spite of the emphasis public-spirited adults place upon the Boy Scouts, Girl Scouts, Camp Fire Girls, and 4-H Club, only 28 per cent of the students belong or have belonged to them. Even among the most active members they never occupy more than a third of a youngster's free time. The informal, largely unsupervised, activity of the clique consumes from 64 to 99 per cent of the students' leisure hours. The percentage spent in the different kinds of recreation and pleasures, discussed in successive paragraphs below, varies significantly from class to class. The total amount also varies inversely with class position, as the following percentages indicate:

Class	Boys	Girls
I and II	77	64
III	86	78
IV	95	87
V	99	96

These figures tell us that, even though most of the class II's and many class III's are members of clubs, these boys and girls believe that from two-thirds to seven-eighths of their leisure time is spent in informal group activities. Practically all the free time of adolescents in class V is whiled away with other adolescents far from the eyes of adults who might constrain their activities. The activities of adolescents in these leisure hours sometimes give rise to trouble—primarily those stimulating sensations connected with the illicit violation of taboos: smoking, gambling, alcohol, driving automobiles fast, and sex.

Visiting. Visiting in the homes of one's clique mates is a popular pastime that occurs twice as frequently among the girls as among the boys; 26 per cent of the boys and 52 per cent of the girls report that they visit in a friend's house once a week or oftener. Practically all others say that they visit in their friend's home about once a month.[4] Boys in all classes are far more likely to spend their leisure time away from their own or a friend's home than the girls, for they are more or less free to wander around town and to go to other towns in search of adventure and pleasure, whereas the culture places limits on a girl's freedom away from home.

The girls' visiting patterns differ significantly from class to class. The class II girl's free hours are oriented around a series of activities which involve the clique in extracurricular affairs at the high school, church parties, or music. When she is free of this round of work and fun she is usually getting ready to go to a dance or a party where she will participate once more with the clique. When the clique, or a part of it, is not busy in these ways, its members are very likely to be visiting in a clique mate's home. The same pattern applies to the class III's, except that the percentage of girls engaged in such activities is significantly lower. The class III girls in this whirl are generally members of the same clique as the class II girls. These girls appear to be lost when they are alone. If they are not engaged in some group enterprise, they are probably talking to a boy or girl friend on the telephone. These telephone visits are usually very long, and they often end with plans for a visit to continue the discussion. Perhaps a second pal is called, and the "gang" goes to some girl's house to talk, to lay future plans, to discuss something or someone, to listen to records, and inevitably to raid the refrigerator. It is not unusual for a few boys to drop in for a while, but the boys are always from the cliques the girls date. These are gay times; indeed, a pleasant way to while away the hours.

The non-social portion of class III and most of the class IV girls visit in the homes of their friends once a week or oftener, but these visits are between best friends and only one or two clique mates. The long telephone conversations are not so prevalent; neither are the record-playing sessions, raids on the ice box, and visits from the boys. The class IV girls' families do not have so many telephones, few have record players or records, and kitchen raids and spontaneous parties are not allowed in most of these homes. Thus, the home visits tend to be on a smaller scale and to take the form of discussions between close friends.

Frequent visits between girls in class V are the exception; 17 per cent report visits to friends' homes once a week or less. This level is characterized by a high degree of anonymity and individuality both within the class and in its relations to the community. Each person tends to go his own way without paying attention to his neighbors, or often even to his family. The young people belong to few, if any, community associations; they are inclined to distrust and fear, if not to hate, society; so they both isolate themselves from the other classes and are isolated by them. Their clique and recreational contacts occur on the street, in a tavern or a hangout rather than in the home.

Motion Pictures. The motion picture show is the most popular recreation participated in by the students. Any night of the week some boys and girls may be seen going in or coming out of one of Elmtown's movie theaters. The peak attendance for the students who do not attend high school affairs is reached on Friday night, when they go to the ten-cent show at the Silver Bell.[5] The high school authorities believe that these ten-cent shows are presented in direct competition with plays, parties, dances, and athletic games sponsored by the school. This may be true, but it is doubtful whether the students who go to the movies would go to the high school parties even if this counter-attraction were not present because most of the Friday theater goers are from class IV, and the non-participants in extracurricular activities from class III. Saturday is the big show night for the many class II's and class III's and the few class IV's who participate in high school activities on Friday nights. The favorite theater is the Elmtown, particularly of those who have dates. Students who work on Saturday generally take advantage of the half-price matinees between one and five o'clock on Sunday afternoon. The current picture attracts some to a particular theater, but the guiding factor week after week is the show where one's friends go. This means that the class II's and class III's and a few upwardly mobile class IV's go to the Elmtown, whereas the majority of the class IV's and class V's go to the Bright Star or the Silver Bell.[6]

Ninety-six per cent of the boys and 91 per cent of the girls attend motion picture shows with some regularity; 68 per cent of the boys and 73 per cent of the girls go to at least one show a week. More than one-fourth (28 per cent of the boys and 27 per cent of the girls) attend two or three shows a week. Three is the normal maximum, but occasionally a boy or girls goes to four in one week. The frequency of attendance differs significantly from class to class in both sexes. Class II boys attend far more shows than might be expected on the basis of chance, whereas class IV's, particularly the boys, go to fewer shows than probability would indicate. Another way of stating the differences in the attendance patterns for the four classes is to say that the modal figure for class II's and class III's is two or three shows a week, for class IV's the mode is one show a week, and for class V's less than one a week.

The boys and girls who stay away from motion picture shows are principally Lutherans. The minister is so fanatical on this question that he made his young people pledge that they would not "contaminate their souls" in a commercial motion picture palace.

Dancing and Dances. Dancing, like the motion picture, is the center of controversy in some churches and in many homes. The Lutherans, Free Methodists, and Methodists condemn dancing on moral and doctrinal grounds. The Baptists are opposed to dancing but not so openly as the churches named above. Many parents, who object to public dances, approve of high school dances and dances held in private homes. Some parents who fear that dancing will corrupt their children's morals find their prejudices bolstered by religious beliefs. Others do not want their children to stay out late at night. Another segment, largely in class IV, is hostile to dancing since dancing and dating go together; to these people the close physical contacts of boys and girls at a dance is tantamount to the arousal of sexual desires. The persistence of these prejudices about dancing and fears of what it might lead to is marked; the young people, however, dance. Where they dance, how often, and under what circumstances are very closely associated with their family's position in the class structure.

Periodic private parties and dances are held during the year by 7 out of 8 students in class II, by 1 out of 3 in class III, but by only 1 out of 13 in class IV, and by none in class V. Home dances at which the boys and girls dance to music furnished by the radio or records are the most popular type of party in class II and the social segment of class III; however, seven private dances were given at the Country Club in the spring of 1942. A total of 27 different boys and 37 girls attended these Country Club dances. The sex disparity between the boys and the girls resulted from the tendency of girls to invite older boys they had dated in earlier years, boys who had finished high school and were going to college and were home for a week end or during vacation. (The older girls who had graduated from high school a year to two before and were either in college or in town considered the dating of a high school boy beneath their dignity.) The percentage of boys and girls from each class who attended one or more of these Country Club parties was: class II, 63; class III, 21; class IV, 7. The 4 boys and 8 girls from class IV, who were included within the narrow circle of Country Club party guests, were "smooth," and active in extracurricular high school affairs— athletics, student government, music, and dramatics. These were the same young people we mentioned earlier as being upwardly mobile persons in cliques composed of adolescent from the two higher classes; thus, they were able to participate in activities not commonly associated with their class position.

The boys and girls who attend these Country Club parties represent "the society bunch," but to some they are "the snobs." The youngsters in this little band not only attend these Country Club affairs, but also private home parties, as well as the high school dances and games. To them, life is one party and gay time after another. The pace setters within this elite group belong to the very exclusive Tenderfoot Club, which is sponsored by two mothers of class I boys and a socially ambitious mother of a class II girl. Its membership is composed of 7 boys and 7 girls who are also in the G.W.G.'s and the Cadet Club. Twelve of the 14 belong to families in four adult cliques among which there is little intercourse, but this does not preclude their children from uniting into the most exclusive association in high school. This is the "silk stocking" younger set which John Bingham says runs the high school, and in large part he is right. Although it is not a secret group, its members operate so unobstrusively that several teachers and the majority of the students do not know of its existence. It is one of "those things one does not mention" outside the charmed circle of "we few." Those who are aware of its existence and affairs are largely class II's and class III's; the few class IV's who know about it often refer to it as that "snob bunch—they have a club and think they are somebody."

The Tenderfoot Club was organized two years before as a dance group by two mothers who controlled its membership and managed its affairs. In 1941-1942, its membership by class was: class I, 3 boys; class II, 3 boys and 6 girls; class III, 1 boy and 1 girl. The real leader of the group, the mother of a class I boy, explained its membership in this way:

Those boys and girls are about William's age, and it just happened most of them are the sons and daughters of the girls I knew as a child.

William traced its membership to the neighborhood where he had lived since he was five years old (the 400 area).

We lived out on the ranch until the folks built this house in 1929. I was five when we moved here and I started running with this bunch of kids. We were together when we went to Washington School. We picked up a few new ones there. All through the first four grades we ran in a bunch. When we moved over to Central, we picked up a few more. Some moved away and some were added, but we had about the same crowd when we finished grammar school. When we got in high school, we picked up four new ones, Cliff Hendricks, Bill Warren, George Simonds, and Marge Whitney. Wilbur Sorenson [class IV] dropped out when we were freshmen. He had always been kind of on the edge though. Now he doesn't run with us at all. Then Catherine Alexander [from a class II family that moved to Elmtown when Catherine was in the seventh grade] came into the group while we were freshmen.

We started to have parties around at one another's house when we were freshmen. Then in the fall of our sophomore year Mr. and Mrs. Strayer let John [class I] have a dance at the Country Club. We had such a swell time we decided to organize into a club. The folks said it was all right, and mother agreed to sponsor us. We have lost three members in the last two years and added one. We used to have sixteen members, but we only have fourteen now. A member may invite a guest to a dance if the kids and the sponsor approve. At the annual Country Club dance, each member may invite one non-member, but that person's family must belong to the Country Club.

The Tenderfoot Club transfers the exclusive, private club idea so characteristic of the class I's and to a less extent of the class II's from the parental to the adolescent generation. There is also a hint of the "old family" tradition in its membership.

Public, Saturday night dances at Morrow's Hall on the lower end of Freedom Street are the complementary lower class form of the elaborately planned, closely supervised private dance at the Country Club. Few adolescents have the opportunity to attend the Country Club dances, but every boy with seventy-five cents, and any girl by her presence, may participate in the fun at Morrow's. But do all avail themselves of this opportunity?

Class II girls *do not go to Morrow's,* and only 4 class II boys go there regularly—to "pick up a babe." Class III boys and girls, in general, avoid Morrow's and other public dance halls, but 9 per cent, 7 boys and 6 girls, go either to Morrow's Hall or to some other public dance place in the community. The favorite non-high school dance of the class III's is the semi-private, semi-public lodge party. The class III's, however, avoid the Mill union's dances unless they are sons or daughters of skilled workers.

In the main, the public dances at Morrow's Hall and at the several dance barns scattered over the countryside are patronized by post-high school and out-of-school persons, but 33 per cent of the class IV boys and 44 per cent of the class IV girls attend them at one time or another. The comparable figures for the class V's are: 75 per cent for the boys and 61 per cent for the girls. The reputation of public dances is decidedly unsavory in the upper half of the social structure and among many conservative class IV parents. The chief criticism directed at the public dance from the "better elements" is the sale of liquor either on the premises or nearby. Even if liquor is not sold in the dance hall, it is drunk there more or less openly. Another criticism is that the dance halls are "common"; anyone may go there. Frequent fights start there, and public brawls are not a part of the action pattern of the three higher classes. A tangible effect of these attitudes is the significantly low attendance at public dances by students from classes II and III and the disproportionately high attendance from classes IV and V.

The lower class boys and girls do not have access to the Country Club, and, in large part, they cannot attend lodge dances, because few of their parents belong. They could participate in the high school dances, but they are not "comfortable" there. This self-feeling is very important in the determination of where an adolescent goes and what he does. If his friends go to a certain place and do a given thing, he feels "comfortable." If his friends are not there and the activity is outside his action pattern, he feels "uncomfortable." The boys and girls in classes IV and V who attend the dances at Morrow's Hall or Scrugg's Tavern would be uncomfortable at the Country Club, because experience has not prepared them to go to the Country Club in any capacity other than as caddy, waitress, janitor, garbage collector, or workman. Conversely, the "Country Club crowd" would be morally outraged to be invited to a dance at Scrugg's. The net effect is the segregation of the young people along class lines at the private, semi-public, and public dances. The corrected coefficient of contingency of 0.62 demonstrates that there is a very real relationship between a high school boy's or girl's class position and his or her attendance at private, semi-private, or public dances.

Bowling and Roller Skating. Bowling is a popular indoor sport in the higher classes, as roller skating is in the lower classes. These sports are related inversely to class position in both sexes, as the following tabulation indicates:

Class	Percentage of Boys Who		Percentage of Girls Who	
	Bowled	Skated	Bowled	Skated
I and II	52	9	64	14
III	23	18	30	38
IV	17	23	20	48
V	00	50	00	69

A second interesting thing that became evident in this phase of the study was the small amount of overlapping between these sports; that is, the skaters do not bowl, and the bowlers do not skate, except in classes III and IV where the overlap is 6 and 9 per cent respectively.

Bowling occupies the highest prestige in the socially correct list of winter sports, as golf does in the summer, among the elite students in classes II and III. These students look upon roller skating as "low class stuff," "a cheap sport." Skating is a much cheaper sport than bowling, a fact which appeals to youngsters who have little money, and it is not coincidence that these young people come disproportionately from classes IV and V. A boy or girl can skate from four to six o'clock in the afternoon for 10 cents and all evening for 20 cents, whereas it costs 15 cents to bowl a line in the afternoon and 25 cents in the evening. This does not appeal to very many youngsters with only 10 or 20 cents to spend in an afternoon or an evening. Such persons have more fun at the skating rink where they skate to the music of an electric gramophone with an oversized loudspeaker. There they may waltz, fox-trot, speed-skate, crack the whip, or skate with a date and neck in the corners, for hours on end, cheaply.

The high school authorities frown upon students' skating, except Tuesday afternoon and evening, when all other patrons are barred. Young people in classes II and III, particularly the girls, if they do not want to be suspected of loose morals, avoid the skating rink, for many young men go there to pick up dates; and frequent quarrels, which end in fights, are common. Most students skate on Tuesday afternoon and evening, but 14 boys (2 class III's, 10 class IV's, and 2 class V's) and 45 girls (5 class III's, 34 class IV's, and 6 class V's) skate regularly on Friday and Saturday nights. All these adolescents are rated as "grubbies" by their peers. One clique of 5 girls (4 class IV's and a class V) in this larger group skate four or five nights a week. All of them have shady reputations; they are known as "easy marks" among the boys and as "fast numbers" among the girls. The other girls ignore them in school and around the skating rink. The boys even avoid them around school, but on Friday and Saturday nights the "clippers" and "wolves" hang around them like flies around sugar on a summer's day. These girls are often the center of fights between lower class high school boys and boys in the out-of-school group. That sex is the object of attack and counter-attack is understood in the adolescent world. Three of the girls admit that they have had sex relations with their "boy friends"; another one said, "We've gone all the way lots of times." Questioned as to the meaning of this she explained circuitously, in conformance with the linguistic usages associated with the sex game, that all five girls in the clique had sex relations with the "right fella."

If a high school girl hangs around the bowling alley in the evening, she invariably has a bad reputation among her peers. After eight o'clock the alley is taken over by couples (mainly young adults who work in Elmtown's stores and offices) and middle-aged businessmen. Women from classes I and II who bowl in the afternoon in teams and cliques do not go to the alley in the evening, because the proprietor allows players and spectators to drink hard liquor after eight o'clock. He has a small corner room where customers mix whiskey, gin, or rum, which they bring with them with the "cokes" they buy there, or drink from the bottle. Those who "spike" their cokes drink openly in the spectators' gallery or on the players' benches. The association of illegal liquor, commercial pleasure, and innuendo combine to taboo the alley for most girls at night.

Team Games. Baseball, football, field hockey, and basketball are common pre-adolescent activities without a significant association with class which carries over into high school among a considerable number of the freshman and sophomore boys. Although 41 per cent of the boys report that they play the team game in season with pals once a week or oftener, the distribution is skewed definitely toward the younger boys. Almost two players out of three (64 per cent) are freshmen, and an additional 17 per cent are sophomores. Three factors produce this situation: First, unless he is highly skilled or large for his age, it is difficult for a younger boy to "make the team"; if he has free time (and most younger boys manage to find some a few times each week), he rounds up his pals or they look him up, and an informal game is started. Second, younger boys do not have equal opportunity with older boys to find part-time work. Finally, they are not so likely to be interested in girls, pool, bowling, or high school extracurricular activities.

The shift from informal team games played in the open to team games carried on inside buildings is part of the maturation process that occurs during the middle years of high school. Since the culture frowns upon the big boy who acts like a youngster, the approved role in the junior and senior years is to watch the highly skilled, carefully trained varsity team play. We believe that the subtle process of identification of self with the team enables the non-player to play the game vicariously and simultaneously to enjoy its thrills through deep ego involvement. After the game, he experiences the warm glow of glamorizing the players with those who shared the experience with him. This process was evident to us as we went to the shower rooms with the players after the games, and then on to the "coke spots" with "the gang," where the players were the center of attention.

Pool. The pool hall is strictly male territory, and the taboo against a female entering it is never broken. If a female has to communicate with a male in the pool hall, she either sends in a man with a message or goes next door to the drug store and telephones. Even tapping on the window or calling through the door is never done. Yet the pool hall is a respected establishment. The proprietor does not allow any "rough stuff," profanity, loud talk, or vulgar stories; even petty gambling between the players is carried on in a discreet way.

The pool hall is a center of gossip, news, and story telling. If a boy does not play, he is always welcome in the gallery if he is not a recognized member of class V. The owner of the pool hall discourages this class from frequenting his place for he does not want it to become, as he said, "a hangout for such bums." Part of the pool hall's popularity among the young men may have grown out of the fact that it is the most convenient place for a boy to go to get out of the weather. It is always warm inside, and any sober man is welcome there as long as he behaves; few middle-aged or older men frequent the place. This is the favorite hangout of farm boys when they are in town. During the week, if a country boy has to wait for a member of his family, he usually goes to the pool hall. On Saturday night, from 25 to 30 farm boys may be found there some time during the evening. They drift in before a date, after the show, and sometimes after a date.

Pool is the most popular male game in all classes; 63 per cent of the boys play. In addition, it is not associated with class position except in class V; no class V boy plays pool.

Eighty per cent of the pool players play once a week or oftener, about a fourth of this group play four or five times a week, and an additional third two or three times a week. The remainder play once a week; the minority, 20 per cent, play two or three times a month. Frequent play or none is encouraged by the custom which prevails that the loser pay for the game. Each player knows the relative ability of the others; if one is a poor player, it is to his advantage to improve, move to another clique, or stop playing. The unskilled boy, if he likes the game (and under the competitive conditions most do) works to improve. The only way he can do this is to play as often as his finances permit. The boys who try to win at all times are ostracized by their pals, and the "pool shark" who lies in wait for the unwary novice is soon unmasked. The boys simply refuse to play with him; so he is forced to play the game like the rest or move into the older youth group where skilled players keep him in check. Pool, like other games, is played by cliques, and there is little social interaction other than casual stray remarks between the different groups. For instance, one clique of boys from classes II and III play almost daily at the front table, and another composed of boys in classes III and IV play at the back table; but there is practically no interaction between them.

SOCIAL MOBILITY AND INTERPERSONAL RELATIONS

Peter M. Blau

SOCIAL LIFE can be conceptualized as a series of dilemmas. Choices between alternatives that confront people typically require the sacrifice of some ends in the interest of others. In the course of solving one problem, new ones are created. This is not a new idea. It is at least as old as the Socratic method of argument and the Christian doctrine of original sin. It is fundamental to Hegel's and Marx's dialectical approach. Recently, Parsons and Shils have made the concept of dilemma a central element in their theory of action,[1] and so has Bales (using the term "strain") in his interaction theory.[2] Merton's concept of disfunction has similar implications.[3]

Occupational mobility, both upward and downward, poses special dilemmas for establishing interpersonal relations and becoming integrated in the community. Attributes and orientations associated with socio-economic status do not furnish unambiguous criteria of social acceptance for mobile persons. They are marginal men, in some respects out of tune with others both in their new and original strata in the occupational hierarchy. Difficult adaptations are necessary, whether they seek to cultivate friendships among the one group or the other. The upwardly mobile must choose between abandoning hope of translating his occupational success into social acceptance by a more prestigeful group and sacrificing valued social ties and customs in an effort to gain such acceptance. The downwardly mobile must choose between risking rejections for failure to meet social obligations that are beyond his financial resources and resigning himself to losing his affiliation with a more prestigeful group. These conditions are not conducive to the development of integrative social bonds. The central hypothesis of this paper is that the dilemmas faced by mobile individuals in their interpersonal relations inhibit social integration and are responsible for many aspects of their attitudes and conduct.

Acculturation. If the occupational hierarchy is divided into two broad strata, four categories can be distinguished, two of persons who have remained in the stratum in which they originated, and two of those who have experienced occupational mobility: stationary highs, stationary lows, upwardly mobile, and downwardly mobile. Empirical data on the ways of acting and thinking of people in these four categories reveal several distinct patterns. In the first of these, the behavior of both mobile groups is intermediate between that of the two non-mobile ones, so that the frequency distributions have the following rank order: stationary highs first, upwardly and downwardly mobile sharing second place, and stationary lows last. Restriction of family size manifests this pattern and so does political behavior. On the average, upwardly and downwardly mobile have fewer children than others in working-class occupations and more children than others in middle-class occupations.[4]

Reprinted from *The American Sociological Review* (June 1956), pp. 290-95, by permission of the author and the publisher. (Copyright, 1956, by the American Sociological Society)

Similarly, the upwardly mobile are more likely to vote Republican than people who have remained workers and less likely to do so than those who have originated in the middle class.[5] Finally, the downwardly mobile are less apt to join unions than workers whose parents were workers, too.[6]

This pattern, which may be called the pattern of acculturation, can be explained in terms of the hypothesis that mobile persons are not well integrated in either social class. Without extensive and intimate social contacts, they do not have sufficient opportunity for complete acculturation to the values and style of life of the one group, nor do they continue to experience the full impact of the social constraints of the other. But both groups exert some influence over mobile individuals, since they have, or have had, social contacts with members of both, being placed by economic circumstances amidst the one, while having been socialized among the other. Hence, their behavior is expected to be intermediate between that of the two non-mobile classes. Verification of this explanation of the observed differences would require evidence that the differences tend to disappear if extent of interpersonal relations is held constant.[7] Those mobile persons who have established extensive interpersonal relations with others in their new social class should not differ in their conduct from the rest of its members. Correspondingly, those non-mobile persons who are relatively isolated should also be prone to manifest deviating tendencies, for only this would show that lack of integration is indeed a main source of deviation. It is, therefore, among the malintegrated non-mobiles that we would expect to find the social striver, the individual who adopts the style of life of a more prestigeful class to which he does not belong, and the disenchanted member of the elite, the individual who adopts the political orientation of a less powerful class than his own.

Social Insecurity. In a second pattern, the main contrast is between the mobile and the non-mobile with relatively little difference between socioeconomic strata. The rank order of frequency distributions in this case is: downwardly and upwardly mobile sharing first place, stationary lows second, and stationary highs a close third. The extreme position of the mobile dramatically indicates that occupational mobility rather occupational status is of primary significance here. Prejudice against minorities tends to assume this pattern. Specifically, mobile persons are more likely than non-mobile ones to feel that various minorities are getting too much power, and to stereotype Jews as dishonest and Negroes as lazy and ignorant.[8] (In nine out of ten comparisons, a larger proportion of the mobile is prejudiced, an average difference of 9 per cent.) Quite a different attitude reveals the same pattern, namely, that toward health. Mobile individuals, whatever the direction of their mobility, are more apt to be preoccupied with their health than non-mobile ones, whether in high or in low socio-economic positions.[9]

Feeling threatened by the power of such groups as Negroes or foreigners and holding hostile stereotypes of them may be considered expressions of insecurity, and so may preoccupation with one's health.[10] If this inference is correct, the hypothesis used to account for the first pattern can also help to explain this second one, different as the two are. For if it is true that the mobile individual is poorly integrated, it follows not only that there is relatively little communication between him and others, but also that he does not receive much social support from them. In the absence of extensive communication, he cannot fully assimiliate the style of life of the members of his new social class, with the result that his beliefs and practices are intermediate between theirs and those of the members of his class of origin. Simultaneously, lack of firm social support engenders feelings of insecurity, and this has the result that the mobile person tends to assume the extreme position, not the intermediate one, in respect to those attitudes that constitute expressions of insecurity.

Two kinds of findings support this interpretation. First, relatively direct indications of insecurity—nervousness and mental disorders—reveal the same contrast: the upwardly as well as the downwardly mobile are more troubled by nervousness than the non-mobile,[11] and they are also more prone to become mentally ill.[12] Second, according to the hypothesis, among the non-mobile, too, those with less extensive interpersonal relations should experience greater insecurity. The working class is therefore expected to exhibit more insecurity, since its members have fewer close associates and belong to fewer voluntary associations than the members of the middle class.[13] Indeed, among the non-mobile, the lows are more likely to have prejudiced images of minorities than the highs.[14] Of course, such inferential evidence only makes the hypothesis more plausible. To test it requires data on social integration, which we plan to obtain in our research at the University of Chicago.

The Appearance of Overconformity. In a third pattern, the upwardly mobile and the stationary lows are at the opposite extremes, so that the rank order of frequency distributions is: upwardly mobile first, stationary highs and downwardly mobile sharing second place, and stationary lows last. For example, discrimination against Negroes as neighbors, in contrast to having prejudiced ideas about them, is more pronounced among stationary highs than stationary lows. The downwardly mobile—persons who have moved from high to low—discriminate just as much as the stationary highs, and the upwardly mobile—those who have moved from low to high—discriminate most of all.[15] In other words, downward mobility seems to have no effect in this instance, while upward mobility has a considerable effect. This is also the case for identification with the conjugal family. Two thirds of the stationary highs are very interested in spending time with their families, compared with less than one-half (45 per cent) of the stationary lows. The downwardly mobile express such family identification in exactly the same proportion (66 per cent) as the highs, and the upwardly mobile do so in greater numbers than any other group (75 per cent).[16] Status consciousness, as indicated by a scale that measures concern with the impression made on others, reveals the same pattern.[17]

The combined influences of acculturation and insecurity seem to be responsible for this pattern. Since middle-class people are more inclined than working-class people to discriminate against minorities, to be concerned with social status, and to be identified with their conjugal family, the process of acculturation alone would place the upwardly and downwardly mobile in intermediate positions. But these three items of behavior are also affected by feelings of social insecurity, which often arise consequent to occupational mobility. Just as it engenders prejudicial beliefs about minorities, insecurity intensifies discriminatory tendencies against them. Without integrative social relations to define and support his standing in the community, the individual becomes anxiously concerned about his social status. And the less security a person derives from close relations with friends, colleagues, and neighbors, the more apt he is to turn to his conjugal family for emotional support.

For the downwardly mobile, social insecurity exerts pressures that increase discriminatory practices, status consciousness, and family identification, whereas the process of acculturation to the style of life of the lows exerts pressures in the opposite direction, since the lows discriminate less than the highs, are less status conscious, and identify less with their family. As these pressures in opposite directions neutralize one another, the behavior of the downwardly mobile remains the same as that of members of their class of origin (the highs). For the upwardly mobile, on the other hand, the pressures exerted by insecurity and acculturation to the style of life of the highs are in the same direction. Both kinds of pressure intensify discriminatory tendencies, concern with social status, and attachment to spouse and children. As a result, the upwardly mobile differ widely in these respects from members of their class of origin (the lows) and seem to overconform with the practices prevalent among their new social class (the highs). It may well be that the label of overconformity often conceals, as it would here, the influences of more complex social forces.[18]

Dimensions of Social Mobility. So far, the discussion has dealt with detrimental consequences of occupational mobility for integrative social relationships. But a dilemma implies a choice between alternatives as well as impending difficulties. Occupational mobility increases the chances that an individual's social contacts will include people who occupy a wide range of socio-economic positions. In the course of selecting from among occasional contacts persons with whom he enters into closer association, the mobile individual therefore chooses, more than the non-mobile does, between associates from different social classes. To be sure, this choice is not entirely up to him; it also depends on the attitudes of others toward him. Neither members of his former socio-economic stratum nor those of his present one are prone to accept him readily, since his style of life differs in some respects from that which prevails in either group, and this is the very reason for his lesser social integration. Nevertheless, few mobile individuals remain completely isolated, and the effective choice they make by establishing friendly relations with people in one social position rather than another has important implications.

In examining the social status of the companions of the occupationally mobile, we are, in fact, looking at the relationship between two dimensions of social mobility, movement between occupational strata—socio-economic categories—and movement between social classes—prestige groups with distinct styles of life which restrict intimate social access. Persons upwardly mobile in the occupational hierarchy who continue to associate largely with working-class people, and downwardly mobile persons who continue to associate mostly with middle-class people, have changed their economic position but not their social affiliation. Their occupational status and social status do not coincide. Economic changes are transformed into shifts in social affiliation only by those occupationally mobile individuals most of whose friends are members of their terminal social stratum, the middle class in case of the upwardly mobile, the working class in case of the downwardly mobile.[19]

Changes in style of life are expected to be most evident among the latter groups, that is, the occupationally mobile who have shifted their social affiliation. The mobile individual is not likely to be accepted by members of a social class in which he did not originate unless he has started to adapt his behavior to their style of life. Moreover, it is only after he has established social ties with some of his new peers that they and their values can exert a profound influence over his beliefs and practices.

On the other hand, the psychological impact of the experience of occupational success or failure is apt to be most pronounced and persistent for those mobile persons who maintain friendly relations primarily with members of their class of origin and thus do not change their social affiliation. If the upwardly mobile still associates largely with members of his former, lower socio-economic stratum, his occupational success is recurrently called to his attention by contrast with their less fortunate position. But if he loses contact with them and finds his companions among middle-class people, he fails to be reminded of the ascent he has experienced. The same is true for the downwardly mobile, although it has the opposite significance for him. If most of his social life is spent with members of his former, higher stratum, his inability properly to repay social obligations in this circle keeps alive his feelings of deprivation and occupational failure. But if he ceases to associate with them and befriends instead people as poor as himself, he is socially permitted to forget how much more fortunate he could have been, and his occupation is not a sign of failure in this group.

In short, regardless of the direction of occupational mobility, interpersonal relations that do not involve a change in social affiliation reinforce the invidious significance of the mobility experience itself, whereas interpersonal relations that do involve a change in social affiliation reduce its significance as a symbol of achievement. His social companions play, therefore, different roles for the occupationally mobile individual before and after he moves into a new social class, although they constitute a point of reference in terms of which he orients his outlook in both situations. As long as he remains attached to his class of origin, the economic position of his friends differs from his present one, and social interaction serves as a continual reminder of his economic success or failure. Once he cultivates friendships with his new economic peers, regular social contacts no longer furnish a contrast of occupational achievement but now provide channels of communication and influence through which he is encouraged to adopt their style of life.

The dilemmas that confront the upwardly and the downwardly mobile in their interpersonal relations are, of course, not identical. Fundamentally, the one has to choose between two kinds of social gratification, the other, between two kinds of social deprivation. Besides, there is another difference that is no less important. If an upwardly mobile person is anxious to become affiliated with a more prestigeful social class, he must make difficult adaptations in his behavior and still is unlikely to attain a fully integrated position. But if he is willing to forego the advantages of a higher social status, he can remain an integrated member of his class of origin and simultaneously enjoy the respect his occupational achievement commands among his less successful associates. Hence, one of the alternatives available to the upwardly mobile preserves social integration. In contrast, both alternatives open to the downwardly mobile inhibit social integration. If he attempts to maintain his affiliation with his class of origin, social interaction with friends whose superior economic position continually revives his sense of frustration and failure undermines his security, his relations with these friends, and thus his integrated position as one of them. And if, to escape from such experiences, he seeks the companionship of members of the working class, differences between his values and theirs make it most difficult for him to accept them unequivocally and to become completely accepted among them. Few people reject an individual simply because he has been unsuccessful in his career, but the predicament of the downwardly mobile is that the social conditions of his existence make is nevertheless likely that he will find himself without close friends.

Summary. To summarize, three implications of the hypothesis that occupational mobility creates special dilemmas for interpersonal relations have been explored. First, if the mobile person is neither well integrated among those whose similar economic position is of long standing, nor among those whose socio-economic status he once shared, his behavior can be expected to deviate from that prevalent in both groups. This expectation is borne out by the finding that many beliefs and practices of the upwardly and of the downwardly mobile are intermediate between those of the stationary highs and those of the stationary lows. Second, the lesser social integration of the mobile is expected to be manifest in stronger feelings of insecurity. Indeed, both categories of mobile persons are found to be more prone than either non-mobile group to express feelings of insecurity in various ways, such as hostility against minority groups. Third, the mobile person's choice of associates determines which of two functions, in addition to that of social support, interaction with regular companions has in his case. Social interaction with members of his class of origin serves to perpetuate the rewarding or threatening meaning of the experience of occupational success or failure, while social interaction with members of his terminal class serves to constrain him to change his style of life.

SECTION V

Deviant Behavior as a Property of Groups

IN GENERAL, the clinical professions tend to be preoccupied with individual behavior, and thus there has been a tendency to view deviant behavior largely as the consequence of intrapsychic conflicts and pressures. However, strains arise within the social environment, strains which exert pressure on various individuals to engage in nonconforming behavior. A full understanding of deviance depends on a thorough knowledge of these environmental pressures. In this section, various sociocultural approaches to the problem of deviant behavior are presented.

The sociocultural perspectives on deviant behavior rest upon a seeming paradox: that deviance is generated by the act of conformity itself. The student of the social environment does not view the deviant as unsocialized, as untouched or unreached by the society of which he is a part; on the contrary, deviance is said to arise out of the very processes by which the society attempts to elicit conformity.

The very nature of this sociocultural proposition—that deviance can arise from conformity itself—directs attention to the social environment, for what is being assumed is that strains which result in deviance stem from the process of conforming to some malintegrated state of the social environment. If we assume, for example, an instance of *extreme* conflict between two roles, three modes of adaptation to this conflict are possible. The individual may (1) devalue both roles, or (2) devalue one and accord priority to the other, or (3) attempt to fulfill the conflicting expectations of both. To the extent that the individual is *expected* to fulfill both roles, then the third adaptation constitutes the fullest act of conformity. Yet by virtue of his efforts to conform to both roles, the individual may experience extreme strain, anxiety and personality conflict. These strains may lead in turn to adaptations (1) or (2), either of which, by definition, entails a failure to meet one's role obligations. Or, to cite a further example, Durkheim observes that Protestants experience the greatest predisposition to suicide because conformity to certain theological mandates then leads to a breakdown in social solidarity and to a corresponding sense of social isolation. It is in this sense, then, that the sociocultural approach assumes that deviance flows from the processes of conformity.

These sociocultural approaches may be subsumed under a threefold classification: *variations in cultural integration, variations in social integration,* and *malintegration between cultural and social structures.* Although major theories are included, this section hardly represents an exhaustive list of the sociocultural approaches to deviance. Rather, it contains a selection of what seem to us to be the most useful theories to which social workers might turn at this time in an effort to broaden the existing conceptual basis of practice.

The cultural structure refers to the system of normative values which characterizes a group. Depending on the extent to which these social norms are integrated or conflicted, deviant behavior may ensue. It often happens, for example, that particular categories of individuals are exposed to situations characterized by conflicting social norms, as in the case of native born children of foreign born parents, and these conflicts may lead to deviant adaptations. Caught between the conflicting expectations of old world and new, second generation children experience considerable strain. Without consistent social definitions of themselves to internalize, these children often exhibit profound uncertainty about who they are. Because they lack a clear self-image, anxiety is generated— and they may seek relief either by withdrawing from social relationships or by striking out at the world through rebellious behavior. Frequently, too, these pressures lead to the formation of groups, for it is certainly no accident that individuals who lack a sense of social indentity or who otherwise experience a common problem often band together. The terror of uncertainty is allayed through the subcultures which result, for social norms arise which define the individual, which generate inner security, and which give meaning to his existence. Some observers, in fact, assert that such groups are among the most important controlling influences in the lives of these children. Furthermore, to the extent that the group channels anxious, aggressive feelings toward anti-social ends, organized juvenile delinquency may result. In short, one theory of delinquent behavior among second generation children refers to the pressures generated by conflicting social norms.

A further aspect of the problem of conflicting values arises in connection with the types of delinquency which occur in various types of neighborhoods. In an article entitled, "The Conflict of Values in Delinquency Areas," Solomon Kobrin attempts to show that variations in the types of delinquent behavior may be attributed to variations in the integration of conventional and deviant (i.e., criminal) values. Kobrin describes two types of "delinquency areas." The first is characterized by a high degree of integration between conventional and deviant values; this value integration is accompanied by various forms of structural integration, as indicated by accommodative and cooperative relationships among racketeers, politicians, police and local businessmen. According to Kobrin, this type of cultural and structural integration lends stability to the neighborhood, a stability which is reflected in the activities of delinquents. The delinquency which arises in these "integrated" areas is not characterized by unrestrained violence, maliciousness and apparent purposelessness. On the contrary, delinquent activities here constitute a socializing process by which the young prepare for ultimate assimilation into adult criminal roles. By contrast, however, the malicious, aggressive type of delinquent behavior is said to appear in a second type of "delinquency area." This area does not exhibit the cultural and structural integration referred to earlier. For various reasons, the conventional and deviant value systems are in open conflict with one another. Relations between the politician, the police, the racketeer, and local businessmen are not accommodative and cooperative. Again, for reasons which Kobrin specifies, delinquency in these neighborhoods takes on the character of untrammeled violence and aggression. In this way, conflicts in values condition the emergence of deviant behavior as well as its precise form.

Variations in the degree of integration of the social structure are also thought to constitute a source of deviant behavior. The social structure may be defined roughly as the systems of social relationships in which individuals are involved. One approach to deviance which utilizes concepts of the social structure refers to the strength or weakness of social bonds. Thus, for example, students of mental illness have suggested that the higher rates of neurotic behavior among middle-class in contrast to lower-class individuals emerge in part because of differences in the cohesiveness of social relationships in these two locations. In particular, they point to the tendency among middle-class individuals to be more preoccupied with upward mobility, which leads to greater social isolation than is presumably characteristic of individuals who are not similarly oriented toward higher status. Such isolation is thought to come about in several ways. First, the upward-oriented individual commonly attempts to make himself more acceptable to the group in which he seeks membership by taking over the norms of that group. But these behavioral prescriptions are not always wholly congruent with the norms of one's immediate membership groups. As a result, interpersonal strains may occur, strains which lead to alienation from peer groups. Second, the individual who seeks passage from one position to another in the social structure must allocate his energies and time somewhat differently than the individual who is oriented toward his own position. For one thing, he must acquire the skills and knowledge requisite to movement into a higher position, all of which means that he cannot invest as much energy in the maintenance of existing group memberships. This alone tends to increase isolation.

Finally, if the upward-oriented individual does in fact become successfully mobile, a whole set of existing relationships must be disrupted and new relationships formed. But these newly-formed relationships may not be particularly stable. As the individual successfully moves on from one position to another, the cycle in which relationships are continuously formed and disrupted may of necessity lead him to view relationships as more or less transient; the less involved the individual is with his immediate peers, the less traumatic will be the transition from one set of relationships to another. Hence a certain degree of interpersonal isolation may be imposed upon the mobile individual, an isolation which may be functional in that it eases the process of transition itself. At the same time, however, such individuals do not enjoy the group supports commonly available to the stationary individual. The burden of anxiety engendered by the competitive quest for higher status must, therefore, be carried alone, for interpersonal relationships through which these anxieties may be ventilated are not as readily available as they are to others in the society. In other words, variations in the degree of social isolation may contribute to the emergence of mental illness, by facilitating or impeding the ventilation of anxiety. Similarly, in a selection from the classic work of Emile Durkheim, the impact of variations in the solidarity of social relationships upon the suicide rate is examined. For example, Durkheim attempts to explain the greater propensity to suicide among Protestants than among either Catholics or Jews by examining the relative solidarity of social relations among individuals who participate in one or another of these religious confessions. As any who study Durkheim can hardly fail to see, his work constitutes a brilliant exposition of the way in which variations in the social environment affect the emergence of deviant behavior.

The third approach to deviance refers to those situations in which there is a marked malintegration between the cultural and social structures. One form of malintegration arises when the social structure is organized in such a way as to prevent realization by individuals of their culturally-induced aspirations. Under such conditions, deviant behavior often results. The selections by Durkheim ("Anomic Suicide"), Merton ("Social Structure and Anomie," and "Continuities in Social Structure and Anomie"), and Green ("Culture, Normality and Personality Conflict") all deal in full or in part with this theme. For example, Merton attempts to account for various forms of deviant behavior by reference to this theory. On the one hand, our normative system prescribes that each individual should hold high levels of aspiration with respect to securing success goals which are presumably accessible to all, independent of social origins; in reality, however, the social structure limits access to these goals for large parts of the population, notably the lower classes and various ethnic groups. The resultant frustrations lead many lower-class individuals to adopt illegal means in order to realize their culturally-induced ambitions. In other words, criminal activity can arise as a way of securing those goals to which access by legitimate means is otherwise denied. But criminal activity is not the only mode of adaptation which arises in response to discrepancies between one's culturally-induced aspirations and the objective possibilities of achievement. From the viewpoint of social work, one of the special merits of Merton's article is his attempt to define and describe typical adaptations to these pressures which emerge in other locations throughout the social structure. The reader's attention is particularly directed to what is thought to be a characteristic adaptation among lower middle-class individuals ("ritualism"), for this adaptation bears a distinct resemblance to several types of neurotic behavior.

The sociocultural approaches to deviance would appear to hold much promise for applications to social work practice. However, these theories require much greater elaboration and refinement, for, as Merton observes, "we still have much to learn about the processes through which social structures generate the circumstances in which infringement of social codes constitutes a 'normal' (that is to say, an expectable) response."

CULTURE, NORMALITY, AND PERSONALITY CONFLICT

Arnold W. Green

A GROWING GROUP of anthropologists has in recent years been engaged in constructing cultural configurations as psychic, rather than formal-structural, entities. That neither methodological exactitude nor validated results have been secured is hardly to be expected since the other behavioral fields from which various formulations have been borrowed possess no common frame of reference. And further, this new approach has only recently appeared: Betty J. Meggers[1] elects 1932 as the year that the psychological tide set in. And while the older anthropology required years of training to develop the requisite *technical* proficiency, the haste with which mutually unconnected, and even contradictory borrowings from other fields were thrown together in the new approach tempted many to sweeping generalizations, such as H. G. Van Loon's statement that the psyche of "primitive races" resembles very much the psyche of children.[2]

Part of the difficulty stems from an uneven application of pertinent psychological and psychiatric materials: Clyde Kluckhohn[3] claims that anthropologists are too steeped in the writings of psychoanalysts, to the exclusion of nonanalytic psychiatrists. But far more important is the fact that much of this new literature has been written with an implicit or explicit social-reform orientation. Many of the new anthropologists, reversing the role of the nineteenth-century missionary, who descended upon a primitive people to show them the true light emanating from *our* culture, insist that all mores are relative to the society in which they operate, i.e., we must not criticize peoples with cultures differing from ours in fundamental assumptions, yet we should use those differences in applying reforms to our own culture.[4]

It is against this background of inchoate theoretical formulation, controversy, and unvalidated generalization that attempts to establish criteria of "normality" have appeared in the literature. This concept has long bedevilled investigators in other fields as well. Typically, "normality" has been used on two different levels of meaning, oftentimes simultaneously, and unwittingly, by the same writer: as a statistical average of attitude or behavior; and as "an ideal fictional state never completely reached, to which only approximations are possible."[5] On one score, however, the anthropologists with a psychological bent are unanimous: that standards of normality are relevant only *within* a given cultural system. And taking the statistical horn of the dilemma, the claim is made that a norm, for the given society, can be established. The following quotation is quite typical of opinion today:

Reprinted from *The American Anthropologist* (April/June 1948), pp. 225-37, by permission of the author and the publisher. (Copyright, 1948, by the American Anthropological Society.)

If . . . we acquaint ourselves with the modal behavior of individuals in a series of totally different cultures and develop norms based on such a standard of reference, we discover that there always are individuals deviant from the norm in every society, and some of these exhibit definite pathological symptoms.[6]

This point of view has become conventionally acceptable as stating the relationship between culture and personality conflict, and persists when contrary empirical evidence is presented. Thus Margaret Mead states that neurotics may be either physiologically inadequate *or* culture deviants,[7] after demonstrating that the statistically normal Tchambuli male is neurotic. And Abram Kardiner states that the Alorese individual becomes "disorganized"[8] who has been cut off from the approved social goals, after demonstrating that this characterizes the entire range of Alorese society.

In a word, personality conflict is represented as arising from individual deviation from the standards of conduct operating within the given culture. It is the purpose of this paper to offer a different criterion, that will have no reference to cultural relativity, to the fact that standards of normality differ and are even often antithetical, from society to society.

The difficulties in using the field-results of other investigators to establish a common criterion for personality conflict are enormous. Nevertheless, while the materials used below do represent a diversity of approaches, and while the key formulation of this paper is nowhere explicitly stated in any one of them, it is hoped that a successful demonstration is made of that formulation's being implicit in all of them.

It is the thesis of this paper that the cultural causes of personality conflict can be explained in terms of the extent to which any given culture imposes roles, goals, and self-conceptions which are internally inconsistent, upon various social categories of persons—most commonly, age and sex. In most cases the inconsistency is found in a chronological context: at different stages in the life-history mutually contradictory roles to be enacted, and goals to be striven for, receive cultural sanction. Less frequently, roles and goals which are supposed to be fulfilled *at the same time* are mutually contradictory. Examples of how these two types of inconsistencies operate within different cultural contexts are cited below, along with an evaluation of their effects upon personality.

With this formulation, the problem of cultural relativism in "normality" is by-passed, and the two troublesome aspects of normality, statistical deviation on the one hand, and ideal-normative fulfillment on the other, are simply ignored. Much of the personality conflict described below is neither deviation nor failure to strive toward current ideals of behavior, appropriate for sex and age. In other words, it is hoped that here may prove to be a formulation that will reconcile Dr. Megger's rigid compartmentalization of culture, society, and man. Whether this remains within the province of anthropology the present writer is not competent to judge, but the formulation might afford a common focus of attention to investigators in tangential social science fields who desire to use anthropological materials.

The thesis under consideration can be demonstrated most strikingly in those native cultures with economic, political, and philosophical bases radically different from those of the modern west, and yet which have been subjected to considerable "acculturation." Nevertheless, in some relatively isolated cultures, conflicting demands are made on various categories of persons, and personality conflict is endemic. Introduced below are some summary-descriptions of a few representative cultures, some of which have become dominated by western influences, others relatively little. It should be pointed out that rarely do the investigators cited use the terms "role," "goal," and "self-conception." Yet a checking of any source cited will demonstrate that no untoward violence has been practiced; no new terminology has been manufactured; instead, an implicitly common focus of attention has been delineated.

The Ojibwa Indians of Southeastern Ontario.[9] While very young, the Ojibwa boy is surrounded by near and dear siblings and parents. But this psychic protection is short lived, for he soon learns that only the role of successful hunter and warrior, a highly individualized, solitary pattern among the Ojibwa, will bring the respect and adulation of others, for, unlike the neighboring Dakota Sioux, there is available no flight for the timorous deviant to the camp of the *berdache,* where the role of peaceful craftsman receives a secondary, but real, valuation. The "Ojibwa ethos" is saturated with anxiety, which has a realistic base in recurrent periods of starvation, yet similar harsh conditions among the Eskimos to the north strengthen community bonds for available supplies of food are shared.

But the Ojibwa have no possibility of gratifying a self-conception through such sacrifice, for only the individualized hunter who "exerts power over people for his private ends" is highly regarded. Yet *goal-attainment is psychologically penalized,* for he becomes more vulnerable, instead of secure. The boy is trained not to rely upon the "weak and competing humans about him," but to seek the aid of supernatural beings. Attainment of this power forces the respect of others, but they fear him, leave him alone, and other hunters, jealous of his power, direct *their* power against him.

The constant pressure to attain a goal which is self-defeating leads to "severe anxiety neuroses" on a large scale, manifesting themselves in "melancholia, violence, and obsessive cannibalism"—all subsumed under the Ojibwa term *windigo.* We are dealing here with the most logically traumatic goal-frustration experience imaginable. The position of the Ojibwa adult male is analogous to the laboratory situation described by A. H. Maslow.[10] A rat, deprived of food for twenty-four hours, will not inevitably break down, for we must distinguish between a situation in which the animal must give up something, and one in which it must give up nothing: it is the necessity of a self-defeating *choice* which is the clue to extreme goal-conflict. When the rat is both hungry and thirsty, and is made to choose between food and water, he experiences more threat than if he were forced to endure both deprivations. Similarly, the adult Ojibwa male is threatened by failure to attain his two supreme goals, safety and prestige, by the one avenue of means available to him.

The Ojibwa recognize two types of male deviants: those who fulfill the prestige and power drives in the culture beyond the statistical norm, and those who withdraw from all efforts to compete with others. Significantly, it is in the former that personality disintegration is most frequent, while the latter preserve a "coolness" in ignoring the "usual standards." In other words, *those who deviate most from the statistical and ideal norm suffer less than those who fulfill the ideal to excess.* The conclusion is inescapable that the source of male personality conflict is *in* the cultural imperatives, and not in overt behavioral deviation from them.[11]

From a mental hygiene point of view, the Ojibwa female's culturally defined roles and goals are far superior to the male's. She works in company with others. Her appropriate sex role is not rigidly defined: under duress, she can take to the warpath if a relative's blood "is crying for revenge"; she can hunt if she is orphaned, widowed, or divorced, but this is a practical matter with her, free from power drives and with no stress on controlling the supernatural. Women do not "go windigo," i.e., developed neurosis or psychosis. Except that she must do all of the house chores, her training is more haphazard, allowing for a greater range of interest expression. Those women who follow masculine pursuits are honored rather than vilified. The only deviant type of behavior not tolerated for women is non-marriage.

The Hopi of Northeastern Arizona.[12] Although Eggan is more impressed by the range of personality difficulties among the Hopi than are Thompson and Joseph, it is abundantly evident that such conflict is not nearly so endemic here as among the Ojibwa. What culturally induced stress and strain does exist stems from two sources: that which is indigenous to the Hopi culture, and that which results from training in the government boarding school.

Hopi experience cannot be cited as evidence for the widely accepted psychoanalytical theory of personality conflict as resulting from impulse deprivation in infancy and childhood. Maternal care is indulgent, weaning is late, there is no early and severe anal training, nor oral frustration nor masturbation taboos. The anxiety Eggan finds among them during childhood is said to result from the severely enforced curtailment of aggression *after* "the first few years of pampered childhood," cooperative behavior being of the essence in later childhood; and anxiety also results from impressing on the child supernatural horrors, in the form of ghosts and evil spirits.[13] And during the first initiation of the boy into the Kachina society, he learns that the Kachinas (ancestral gods) are not real gods, but human representations. So the double burden of cessation of indulgence and disenchantment, according to Eggan, causes much psychic distress.[14]

As for acculturation, Eggan notes that the white man's restrictions have fostered antagonism, dependence, have lessened self confidence, security, and pride. In the boarding school "their personal dignity was systematically offended"—clothes burned, hair cut without permission, and names summarily changed, a matter for transition rituals among the Hopi. There is an important sex differentiation, however, for, as is noted below, the boarding school *continues* female life experience, while it disrupts that of the male, fostering an independence that will be disrupted when he returns to the matriarchal system of the tribe.

Thompson and Joseph separate sex conditioning more radically. Descent is unilateral, through the female line; girls are more prized than boys, and have a more stable position and greater security through the rest of their lives. While the female remains continuously with a closely knit, powerful group of female relatives, the male, at four or five, must break away for the less stable and more hazardous world outside the household. With the male's adulthood initiation, he must *suddenly* become a man, assume adult responsibilities and eschew all quarreling, demands that are exacted more slowly on the female.

For both sexes there is much limitation and frustration of impulse expression *that is allowed free play in earliest childhood.* Yet the boy experiences more personality conflict than does the girl. The girl is consistently trained from earliest childhood for the ultimate role of clan mother. While she has less freedom outside the household than the boy, she is not concerned about it, and she is not subjected to so many contrary experiences:

The responsibilities and tasks which, for the Hopi boy, are only limiting duties and hard work without much fun, are those which he has to perform at home to help his mother—hauling water and chopping wood. . . . At the same time he observes, and feels, at home, the more or less firmly established authoritative position of his mother, and his father's peripheral significance. He also hears that his sister and not he himself will become the real head of the clan. Thus, while away from home he feels himself as an important and useful assistant to his father and the whole family, while back at his mother's house he has to become the obedient little boy again. And in fact this would not be so unpleasant, considering the warm security of food and bed and the affection given him by his mother, other relatives and friends, if the different position of the males and the females were not noticeable in the home atmosphere. This may explain why we find in boys the vague anxiety of bewilderment which the girls show less frequently.[15]

And in the boarding school, the boy must sacrifice the adult status accorded him in the initiation ceremonies, sacrifice the goal of independent action, return once more to the role of small, obedient child. Under these circumstances, and in terms of the key formula of this paper, why are personality conflicts *less* serious among the Hopi than among the Ojibwa and the Alorese (*see below*)?

The two polar points of orientation among the Hopi are the household and the ceremonial system. While the former is dominated by the women, the latter is the sole province of the men. While everyone is initiated, and learns the secrets of the masks, only the males take an active part in the Kachina rituals. From earliest childhood the boys are enabled to *project* into the future a secure and culturally highly prized role. And while contradictory demands are made of the boy in childhood, these arise out of a clash *between* situations defined within and outside the household, not as defined *within* the household. Mother and siblings remain a warm, nurturing unit. The close identification with relatives, which makes possible a deep internalization of impulse repression, is not subjected to a radical change in affectional attitudes, as occurs among the Alorese.

Finally, there is the peculiar function of the supernatural and of witchcraft in Hopi society. While Hopi children have many "unreal" fears, these are transferred into the supernatural realm, "a fact which implicitly will accentuate (on the other side) the security represented by the mother's lap, the familiar house, the laws and rules, and finally the group itself."[16] The intensive cooperation demanded by Hopi culture has led them to decry exceptional ability and to emphasize moderation in all things. The supernatural fears inculcated in them to enforce this pattern have given rise to widespread fear of, and accusations of, witchcraft.[17] These activities serve to funnel off aggressions that would receive no other sanctioned outlet, serving as a *compensation* for the repression of culturally non-acceptable goal-seeking.[18]

The Alorese of the Netherlands East Indies.[19] The Alorese infant's situation is not too difficult: walking and talking are not forced, bowel training is disregarded during the pre-walking period, and a certain amount of fondling is customary. Early childhood, on the other hand, is extremely traumatic; this is not so much the result of institutionalized conditioning as of an "accident,"[20] resulting from the mother's having to work in the fields all day. There is no system of rewards for good behavior, however, and discipline is inconsistent, the child being indulged one minute, struck the next, and, since adults feel no compunction to keep promises made to children, there is little emotional security. But because of the chaotic punishment and reward system, *little internalized identification with adult relatives takes place,* so that while social standards are imposed, they are not deeply rooted, and there is little turning of aggression upon the self.

For the young child, temper tantrums comprise the inefficient and diffused means for achieving his goals. At the same time, the child is subjected to a great deal of teasing and ridicule, deliberately provoked to aggressive response in order to provide adults with amusement. This is one of the poorest forms of training imaginable for adult life in Alor, for the interlocking affinal kinship system and the individual-initiated system of finance which ramifies out to involve the whole community require an extreme forebearance in the overt expression of aggression.

Boys especially must forego aggressiveness in order to avoid fines that the group must pay. Since parental imagos are not deeply internalized, he does escape the neurotic symptom of guilt, but the systematic teasing, and being given food of the less choice kind, does lead to the feeling of being undervalued, so that anxiety and inferiority—in a word, damaged self conceptions—are commonplace. Later, he will seek a mother-provider in a wife, a goal severely frustrated in childhood, but the mother-provider is a role that girls are ill-trained to fulfill.

Women are the basic economic producers in Alor, but they have less official status than men and "the feminine role in this society is synonymous with being exploited and worked to exhaustion."[21] Yet the women directly control the male striving for food and sex; and for the men, the acquisition of wealth directly interferes with the goal of sex-gratification because marriage, and the birth of each child, requires that he surrender more "gifts" to *her* male relatives. The general psychological picture which emerges is one of "frustration, confusions, and surrendered goals."

In certain ways, the Alor adult male's position is similar to that of the Ojibwa's: the attainment of the supreme goal in Alor society is self-defeating. In Alor, the powerful male is one who accumulates a large stock of gongs and mokos through financial manipulation. Very few succeed; the rest become satellites, and revert to the culturally denigrated role of protected child. But those who succeed are little better off, for their affinal responsibilities increase, other powerful men organize to impoverish them, they must constantly be on guard against the pilfering of children, and the women threaten them at too many actual points of power. At no period in his life may the Alor male feel secure, at no time may he have a high regard for himself.

The Fijians of Kambara.[22] The Lauans of Kambara present a total picture of but little personality conflict, owing to the fact that severe goal and role clashes are not indigenously fostered, and that the British colonial government has wisely attempted to integrate Western innovations with the going native culture.

Infant care is "good," i.e., children are highly prized, are nursed for a year and gradually weaned, and are "petted and encouraged" by female relatives. Walking and bowel-control are neither suddenly forced nor traumatic. Yet the boy's life, from age seven to his initiation at eight to thirteen, is difficult. Ignored, teased, overworked, and called by an obscene name, *"pilo,"* he "suffers from feelings of inferiority, becomes self-conscious, awkward, silent, and retiring."[23]

As was pointed out above, roles, goals, and self-conceptions operate on two levels—anticipation (projected) and realization. Unlike the Alorese youth, the Lauan boy's ego is supported by the knowledge that self-satisfying roles and goals are soon to be realized, definitely so, upon his initiation into manhood. Since personality conflict is not a matter of a single traumatic episode, or series of episodes, but a life-history trend,[24] the arresting of that trend will diminish the effects of earlier experiences:

A youth's life changes radically after his initiation. He is accepted immediately as an adult male in the community and as such has all the privileges of a full grown man. He now begins to prepare food for the earth oven, sail on trading expeditions, learn a craft if he is a member of a hereditary carpenter clan, and participate in ceremonies and adult games. Women and girls defer to him and he begins to have secret love affairs with those who are not tabu to him. From a self-conscious inverted *pilo* he rapidly grows into a loud swaggering and aggressive youth, arrogant and condescending to women, and with great interest in the figure he cuts in the village.[25]

Great Britain has imposed an *indirect* rule; the old elaborate rank structure has not been radically modified, and native chiefs have been given colonial political posts. It is a British policy to retain land title in the clans, so there is no unemployment, and a man who wanders may always return and work his ancestral holdings. Although the elimination of warfare and the inauguration of a paternalistic policy have "weakened" the Lauans, and the traditional ceremonial exchanges are being buffeted by new economic policies, the "fundamental cultural drives persist," for the natives have retained economic independence, the basic social system of ranked clans has been made the basis of the new political order, and contact with the old sacred places has been maintained. Interestingly enough, Christianity has been blended with native beliefs, and the native chiefs have been used as missionaries! The general picture presented is one that is not too unfavorable to personality development: the indigenous culture does not force impossible individual alternatives, as is the case in Alor and Ojibwa; and western influence has not driven a wedge between the generations.

Java and Omaha. Far different "acculturation processes" are presented by B. Schrieke and Margaret Mead. In Java,[26] the "old society" had the primary aim of leaving things as previous generations had found them; it was a world without competition, individualism, or desire for improvement. Today, under the impact of western *economic* domination, the individual, not genealogy, assumes importance—money, not land; and the sale of land, formerly forbidden, is now common. To succeed, the modern native *must* break away from the unity of traditional society. And, unlike the Fijian experience, old and new have not been brought into harmony. Feelings of distress, exploitation, and impotence are common, and a "social inferiority complex" results which is "actuated from latency and charged with energy by every feeling of belittlement of the ego in our own eyes."[27]

The "Antler,"[28] American Indian tribe is depicted as a morass of inertia, loss of pride, conflict of generations, intra-group and personality conflict. Within a short period, a culture oriented about the male activities of war and hunting, about free land and free giving, ancestral rank, maternal descent, polygamy, and native religion, was by fiat abolished by the American government. Supposed to become farmers, the males ceased all productive activity; becoming in fact ward-landowners, through inheritance and sale of land, they were wealthy one year, poverty-stricken parasites on their relatives the next.

The women, not the men, are now the core of the battered Antler culture. Their culturally traditional roles and goals were not smashed with one blow. From generation to generation, they were able to continue their traditional gardening, house tending, and child raising. Both sexes have one paramount compensation—blame of the white man for all their own defections. The men thus explain away their vegetative existence, the women console themselves for the well-nigh universal deviation from the cultural ideal of female chastity.

In spite of all the qualifications noted in the first part of this paper, enough material has been presented to warrant a few tentative conclusions. In the first place, the role, goal, and self-conception formulation appears to be a useful tool of analysis that can be applied regardless of the range of cultural diversity. Any two cultures can be compared in terms of (1) the extent to which culturally defined roles, goals, and self-conceptions, appropriate for social categories such as age and sex, are inherently inconsistent at any given moment in time; and (2) the extent to which these cultural definitions regarded at different points in time, for the same social categories, are inconsistent. It is important to emphasize that early life conditioning is not the *source* of personality conflict; but the conflict *between* earlier and later self-incorporated cultural elements is predictive of personality conflict at this level of abstraction. Even Abram Kardiner, who stresses the importance of early family conditioning perhaps more than any other investigator, admits that earlier personal-conflict trends must be reinforced by later experience in this connection.[29]

Second, roles and goals must be distinguished as *projection* and *realization*. The projection is the personal seeking of assurance that a desirable future state will ensue. Where this is true, more *present* frustration, role and goal conflict, invidious distinctions, are personally assimilable. This was noted in Hopi and Fiji. This is a form of compensation for one's present condition. Different cultures develop varying kinds and degrees of compensations for conflicting roles and goals *presently* played as well, and in such cases offset much personality conflict that would logically be expected to ensue.

Third, deviation, in and of itself, is not linked in any one-to-one relationship with personality conflict. It has been demonstrated that the statistically-

and ideal-normal male in Ojibwa and Alor is ridden with conflict. Interestingly enough, the claim was made that the statistically- and ideal-deviant male was better "adjusted" among the Ojibwa. This is not to say that the temperamental or overt deviant does not develop personality conflicts, but merely that the assumption of deviation where conflict is found, and vice versa, is likely to confuse the issue.

Fourth, the degree of identification fostered with the persons directly mediating the culture during the period of maximum socialization of the child is important. The tentative hypothesis is offered that the lesser identification engendered, the more inconsistency and the more failure to attain desired roles and goals can be assimilated, precisely because failure elicits less guilt. The Alorese, considering the stresses they "normally" experience, would unquestionably be the most conflict-ridden society on record unless spared a high degree of identification with the mother.[30] James Clark Moloney[31] has shown the Okinawan child being firmly emancipated from his mother's influence at the age of four, in order to develop independent adult roles and goals early in life, able to withstand shelling, dirt, hunger, and infectious diseases without becoming neurotic. He further observes that this is not true of *other* Orientals who have accepted Christian "identification," which

. . . tends to erase ego boundaries, and many individuals seem to become unable to distinguish between themselves and the "little son" being "mutilated" by surgery.[32]

It is significant, Moloney writes, that the all-powerful God is also called father, demanding submission.

Finally, the data presented have implications for much of the popular explanation for personality conflict in modern society. For example, the allegation is frequently encountered that the swift pace, the dirt, noise, hustle-and-bustle of modern urban living *causes* "neurosis." In many more studies than those few cited it has been abundantly shown that extreme personality conflict is endemic in societies with a simple technology, and spared all these urban stimuli. This is not to deny that nervous tension increases under modern urban conditions, but merely that the physical fact of residence in megalopolis is not a sufficient explanation of personality conflict. It may be that the formulation stated here can be applied in terms of the range of choices afforded in the modern city. Primitive cultures restrict the range of roles and goals available to any individual; the modern metropolis indefinitely extends and diversifies them. The possibility of conflict *within* the modern culture is thus magnified. And in conjunction with this, we know that the majority of our urban residents were either born in rural areas, or are the children of parents with a rural background. The possibility that in the city there are greater clashes developed between *earlier* and *later* roles, goals, and self conceptions than in rural areas remains to be explored.

EGOISTIC SUICIDE

Emile Durkheim

LET US SEE HOW the different religious confessions affect suicide.

If one casts a glance at the map of European suicide, it is at once clear that in purely Catholic countries like Spain, Portugal, Italy, suicide is very little developed, while it is at its maximum in Protestant countries, in Prussia, Saxony, Denmark. The following averages compiled by Morselli confirm this first conclusion:

	Average of Suicides per Million Inhabitants
Protestant states	190
Mixed states (Protestant and Catholic)	96
Catholic states	58

Nevertheless, this first comparison is still too summary. In spite of undeniable similarities, the social environments of the inhabitants of these different countries are not identical. The civilizations of Spain and Portugal are far below that of Germany and this inferiority may conceivably be the reason for the lesser development of suicide which we have just mentioned. If one wishes to avoid this source of error and determine more definitely the influence of Catholicism and Protestantism on the suicidal tendency, the two religions must be compared in the heart of a single society.

Of all the great states of Germany, Bavaria has by far the fewest suicides. There have been barely 90 per million inhabitants yearly since 1874, while Prussia has 133 (1871-75), the duchy of Baden 156, Wurttemberg 162,

Bavarian Provinces (1867-75)*

Provinces w. Catholic Minority (less than 50%)	Suicides per Million Inhabitants	Provinces w. Catholic Majority (50 to 90%)	Suicides per Million Inhabitants	Provinces w. More Than 90% Catholic	Suicides per Million Inhabitants
Rhenish Palatinate	167	Lower Franconia	157	Upper Palatinate	64
Central Franconia	207	Swabia	118	Upper Bavaria	114
Upper Franconia	204			Lower Bavaria	19
Average	192	Average	135	Average	75

*The population below 15 years has been omitted.

Saxony 300. Now, Bavaria also has most Catholics, 713.2 to 1,000 inhabitants. On the other hand, if one compares the different provinces of Bavaria, suicides are found to be in direct proportion to the number of Protestants and in inverse proportion to that of Catholics (See Table above). Not only

Reprinted, in abridged form, from *Suicide: A Study in Sociology* (1951), translated by John A. Spaulding and George Simpson, pp. 152-212, by permission of the publisher. (Copyright, 1951, by The Free Press.) This book was originally published in Paris in 1897.

the proportions of averages to one another confirm the law but all the numbers of the first column are higher than those of the second and those of the second higher than those of the third without exception.

The aptitude of Jews for suicide is always less than that of Protestants; in a very general way it is also, though to a lesser degree, lower than that of Catholics. Occasionally, however, the latter relation is reversed; such cases occur especially in recent times. Up to the middle of the century, Jews killed themselves less frequently than Catholics in all countries but Bavaria; only towards 1870 do they begin to lose their ancient immunity. They still very rarely greatly exceed the rate for Catholics. Besides, it must be remembered that Jews live more exclusively than other confessional groups in cities and are in intellectual occupations. On this account they are more inclined to suicide than the members of other confessions, for reasons other than their religion. If therefore the rate for Judaism is so low, in spite of this aggravating circumstance, it may be assumed that other things being equal, their religion has the fewest suicides of all.

These facts established, what is their explanation?

If we consider that the Jews are everywhere in a very small minority and that in most societies where the foregoing observations were made, Catholics are in the minority, we are tempted to find in these facts the cause explaining the relative rarity of voluntary deaths in these two confessions.[1] Obviously, the less numerous confessions, facing the hostility of the surrounding populations, in order to maintain themselves are obliged to exercise severe control over themselves and subject themselves to an especially rigorous discipline. To justify the always precarious tolerance granted them, they have to practice greater morality. Besides these considerations, certain facts seem really to imply that this special factor has some influence. In Prussia, the minority status of Catholics is very pronounced, since they are only a third of the whole population. They kill themselves only one third as often as the Protestants. The difference decreases in Bavaria where two thirds of the inhabitants are Catholics; the voluntary deaths of the latter are here only in the proportion of 100 to 275 of those Protestants or else of 100 to 238, according to the period. Finally, in the almost entirely Catholic Empire of Austria, only 155 Protestant to 100 Catholic suicides are found. It would seem then that where Protestantism becomes a minority its tendency to suicide decreases.

But first, suicide is too little an object of public condemnation for the slight measure of blame attaching to it to have such influence, even on minorities obliged by their situation to pay special heed to public opinion. As it is an act without offense to others, it involves no great reproach to the groups more inclined to it than others, and is not apt to increase greatly their relative ostracism as would certainly be the case with a greater frequency of crime and misdemeanor. Besides, when religious intolerance is very pronounced, it often produces an opposite effect. Instead of exciting the dissenters to respect opinion more, it accustoms them to disregard it. When one feels himself an object of inescapable hostility, one abandons the idea of conciliating it and is the more resolute in his most unpopular observances. This has frequently happened to the Jews and thus their exceptional immunity probably has another cause.

Anyway, this explanation would not account for the respective situation of Protestants and Catholics. For though the protective influence of Catholicism is less in Austria and Bavaria, where it is in the majority, it is still considerable. Catholicism does not therefore owe this solely to its minority status. More generally, whatever the proportional share of these two confessions in the total population, wherever their comparison has been possible from the point of view of suicide, Protestants are found to kill themselves much oftener than Catholics. There are even countries like the Upper Palatinate and Upper Bavaria, where the population is almost wholly Catholic (92 and 96 per cent) and where there are nevertheless 300 and 423 Protestant suicides to 100 Catholic suicides. The proportion even rises to 528 per cent in Lower Bavaria where the reformed religion has not quite one follower to 100 inhabitants. Therefore, even if the prudence incumbent on minorities were a partial cause of the great difference between the two religions, the greatest share is certainly due to other causes.

We shall find these other causes in the nature of these two religious systems. Yet they both prohibit suicide with equal emphasis; not only do they penalize it morally with great severity, but both teach that a new life begins beyond the tomb where men are punished for their evil actions, and Protestantism just as well as Catholicism numbers suicide among them. Finally, in both cults these prohibitions are of divine origin; they are represented not as the logical conclusion of correct reason, but God Himself is their authority. Therefore, if Protestantism is less unfavorable to the development of suicide, it is not because of a different attitude from that of Catholicism. Thus, if both religions have the same precepts with respect to this particular matter, their dissimilar influence on suicide must proceed from one of the more general characteristics differentiating them.

The only essential difference between Catholicism and Protestantism is that the second permits free inquiry to a far greater degree than the first. Of course, Catholicism by the very fact that it is an idealistic religion concedes a far greater place to thought and reflection than Greco-Latin polytheism or Hebrew monotheism. It is not restricted to mechanical ceremonies but seeks the control of the conscience. So it appeals to conscience, and even when demanding blind submission of reason, does so by employing the language of reason. None the less, the Catholic accepts his faith ready made, without scrutiny. He may not even submit it to historical examination since the original texts that serve as its basis are proscribed. A whole hierarchical system of authority is devised, with marvelous ingenuity, to render tradition invariable. All *variation* is abhorrent to Catholic thought. The Protestant is far more the author of his faith. The Bible is put in his hands and no interpretation is imposed upon him. The very structure of the reformed cult stresses this state of religious individualism. Nowhere but in England is the Protestant clergy a hierarchy; like the worshippers, the priest has no other source but himself and his conscience. He is a more instructed guide than the run of worshippers but with no special authority for fixing dogma. But what best proves that this freedom of inquiry proclaimed by the founders of the Reformation has not remained a Platonic affirmation is the increasing multiplicity of all sorts of sects so strikingly in contrast with the indivisible unity of the Catholic Church.

We thus reach our first conclusion, that the proclivity of Protestantism for suicide must relate to the spirit of free inquiry that animates this religion. Let us understand this relationship correctly. Free inquiry itself is only the effect of another cause. When it appears, when men, after having long received their ready made faith from tradition, claim the right to shape it for themselves, this is not because of the intrinsic desirability of free inquiry, for the latter involves as much sorrow as happiness. But it is because men henceforth need this liberty. This very need can have only one cause: the overthrow of traditional beliefs. If they still asserted themselves with equal energy, it would never occur to men to criticize them. If they still had the same authority, men would not demand the right to verify the source of this authority. Reflection develops only if its development becomes imperative, that is, if certain ideas and instinctive sentiments which have hitherto adequately guided conduct are found to have lost their efficacy. Then reflection intervenes to fill the gap that has appeared, but which it has not created. Just as reflection disappears to the extent that thought and action take the form of automatic habits, it awakes only when accepted habits become disorganized. It asserts its rights against public opinion only when the latter loses strength, that is, when it is no longer prevalent to the same extent. If these assertions occur not merely occasionally and as passing crises, but become chronic; if individual consciences keep reaffirming their autonomy, it is because they are constantly subject to conflicting impulses, because a new opinion has not been formed to replace the one no longer existing. If a new system of beliefs were constituted which seemed as indisputable to everyone as the old, no one would think of discussing it any longer. Its discussion would no longer even be permitted; for ideas shared by an entire society draw from this consensus an authority that makes them sacrosanct and raises them above dispute. For them to have become more tolerant, they must first already have become the object of less general and complete assent and been weakened by preliminary controversy.

Thus, if it is correct to say that free inquiry once proclaimed, multiplies schisms, it must be added that it presupposes them and derives from them, for it is claimed and instituted as a principle only in order to permit latent or half-declared schisms to develop more freely. So if Protestantism concedes a greater freedom to individual thought than Catholicism, it is because it has fewer common beliefs and practices. Now, a religious society cannot exist without a collective *credo* and the more extensive the *credo* the more unified and strong is the society. For it does not unite men by an exchange and reciprocity of services, a temporal bond of union which permits and even presupposes differences, but which a religious society cannot form. It socializes men only by attaching them completely to an identical body of doctrine and socializes them in proportion as this body of doctrine is extensive and firm. The more numerous the manners of action and thought of a religious character are, which are accordingly removed from free inquiry, the more the idea of God presents itself in all details of existence, and makes individual wills converge to one identical goal. Inversely, the greater concessions a confessional group makes to individual judgment, the less it dominates lives, the less its cohesion and vitality. We thus reach the conclusion that the superiority of Protestantism with respect to suicide results from its being a less strongly integrated church than the Catholic Church.

This also explains the situation of Judaism. Indeed, the reproach to which Jews have for so long been exposed by Christianity has created feelings of unusual solidarity among them. Their need of resisting a general hostility, the very impossibility of free communication with the rest of the population, has forced them to strict union among themselves. Consequently, each community became a small, compact and coherent society with a strong feeling of self-consciousness and unity. Everyone thought and lived alike; individual divergences were made almost impossible by the community of existence and the close and constant surveillance of all over each. The Jewish church has thus been more strongly united than any other, from its dependence on itself because of being the object of intolerance. By analogy with what has just been observed apropos of Protestantism, the same cause must therefore be assumed for the slight tendency of the Jews to suicide in spite of all sorts of circumstances which might on the contrary incline them to it. Doubtless they owe this immunity in a sense to the hostility surrounding them. But if this is its influence, it is not because it imposes a higher morality but because it obliges them to live in greater union. They are immune to this degree because their religious society is of such solidarity. Besides, the ostracism to which they are subject is only one of the causes producing this result; the very nature of Jewish beliefs must contribute largely to it. Judaism, in fact, like all early religions, consists basically of a body of practices minutely governing all the details of life and leaving little free room to individual judgment.

In conclusion, we see why, generally speaking, religion has a prophylactic effect upon suicide. It is not, as has sometimes been said, because it condemns it more unhesitatingly than secular morality, nor because the idea of God gives its precepts exceptional authority which subdues the will, nor because the prospect of a future life and the terrible punishments there awaiting the guilty give its proscriptions a greater sanction than that of human laws. The Protestant believes in God and the immortality of the soul no less than the Catholic. More than this, the religion with least inclination to suicide, Judaism, is the very one not formally proscribing it and also the one in which the idea of immortality plays the least role. Indeed, the Bible contains no law forbidding man to kill himself and, on the other hand, its beliefs in a future life are most vague. Doubtless, in both matters, rabbinical teaching has gradually supplied the omissions of the sacred book; but they have not its authority. The beneficent influence of religion is therefore not due to the special nature of religious conceptions. If religion protects man against the desire for self-destruction, it is not that it preaches the respect for his own person to him with arguments *sui generis;* but because it is a society. What constitutes this society is the existence of a certain number of beliefs and practices common to all the faithful, traditional and thus obligatory. The more numerous and strong these collective states of mind are, the stronger the integration of the religious community, and also the greater its preservative value. The details of dogmas and rites are secondary. The essential thing is that they be capable of supporting a sufficiently intense collective life. And because the Protestant church has less consistency than the others it has less moderating effect upon suicide.*

---

*Editor's note: In like manner, Durkheim analyzes the effects on suicide rates of variations in social cohesion in domestic and in political life. These two sections have been omitted.

We have thus successively set up the three following propositions:

Suicide varies inversely with the degree of integration of religious society.
Suicide varies inversely with the degree of integration of domestic society.
Suicide varies inversely with the degree of integration of political society.

This grouping shows that whereas these different societies have a moderating influence upon suicide, this is due not to special characteristics of each but to a characteristic common to all. Religion does not owe its efficacy to the special nature of religious sentiments, since domestic and political societies both produce the same effects when strongly integrated. This, moreover, we have already proved when studying directly the manner of action of different religions upon suicide. Inversely, it is not the specific nature of the domestic or political tie which can explain the immunity they confer, since religious society has the same advantage. The cause can only be found in a single quality possessed by all these social groups, though perhaps to varying degrees. The only quality satisfying this condition is that they are all strongly integrated social groups. So we reach the general conclusion: suicide varies inversely with the degree of integration of the social groups of which the individual forms a part.

But society cannot disintegrate without the individual simultaneously detaching himself from social life, without his own goals becoming preponderant over those of the community, in a word without his personality tending to surmount the collective personality. The more weakened the groups to which he belongs, the less he depends on them, the more he consequently depends only on himself and recognizes no other rules of conduct than what are founded on his private interests. If we agree to call this state egoism, in which the individual ego asserts itself to excess in the face of the social ego and at its expense, we may call egoistic the special type of suicide springing from excessive individualism.

But how can suicide have such an origin?

First of all, it can be said that, as collective force is one of the obstacles best calculated to restrain suicide, its weakening involves a development of suicide. When society is strongly integrated, it holds individuals under its control, considers them at its service and thus forbids them to dispose wilfully of themselves. Accordingly it opposes their evading their duties to it through death. But how could society impose its supremacy upon them when they refuse to accept this subordination as legitimate? It no longer then possesses the requisite authority to retain them in their duty if they wish to desert; and conscious of its own weakness, it even recognizes their right to do freely what it can no longer prevent. So far as they are the admitted masters of their destinies, it is their privilege to end their lives. They, on their part, have no reason to endure life's sufferings patiently. For they cling to life more resolutely when belonging to a group they love, so as not to betray interests they put before their own. The bond that unites them with the common cause attaches them to life and the lofty goal they envisage prevents their feeling personal troubles so deeply. There is, in short, in a cohesive and animated society a constant interchange of ideas and feelings from all to each and each to all, something like a mutual support, which instead of throwing the individual on his own resources, leads him to share in the collective energy and supports his own when exhausted.

But these reasons are purely secondary. Excessive individualism not only results in favoring the action of suicidogenic causes, but it is itself such a cause. It not only frees man's inclination to do away with himself from a protective obstacle, but creates this inclination out of whole cloth and thus gives birth to a special suicide which bears its mark. This must be clearly understood for this is what constitutes the special character of the type of suicide just distinguished and justifies the name we have given it. What is there then in individualism that explains this result?

It has been sometimes said that because of his psychological constitution, man cannot live without attachment to some object which transcends and survives him, and that the reason for this necessity is a need we must have not to perish entirely. Life is said to be intolerable unless some reason for existing is involved, some purpose justifying life's trials. The individual alone is not a sufficient end for his activity. He is too little. He is not only hemmed in spatially; he is also strictly limited temporally. When, therefore, we have no other object than ourselves we cannot avoid the thought that our efforts will finally end in nothingness, since we ourselves disappear. But annihilation terrifies us. Under these conditions one would lose courage to live, that is, to act and struggle, since nothing will remain of our exertions. The state of egoism, in other words, is supposed to be contradictory to human nature and, consequently, too uncertain to have chances of permanence.

In this absolute formulation the proposition is vulnerable. If the thought of the end of our personality were really so hateful, we could consent to live only by blinding ourselves voluntarily as to life's value. For if we may in a measure avoid the prospect of annihilation we cannot extirpate it; it is inevitable, whatever we do. We may push back the frontier for some generations, force our name to endure for some years or centuries longer than our body; a moment too soon for most men, always comes when it will be nothing. For the groups we join in order to prolong our existence by their means are themselves mortal; they too must dissolve, carrying with them all our deposit of ourselves. Those are few whose memories are closely enough bound to the very history of humanity to be assured of living until its death. So, if we really thus thirsted after immortality, no such brief perspectives could ever appease us. Besides, what of us is it that lives? A word, a sound, an imperceptible trace, most often anonymous,[2] therefore nothing comparable to the violence of our efforts or able to justify them to us. In actuality, though a child is naturally an egoist who feels not the slightest craving to survive himself, and the old man is very often a child in this and so many other respects, neither ceases to cling to life as much or more than the adult; indeed we have seen that suicide is very rare for the first fifteen years and tends to decrease at the other extreme of life. Such too is the case with animals, whose psychological constitution differs from that of men only in degree. It is therefore untrue that life is only possible by its possessing its rationale outside of itself.

Indeed, a whole range of functions concern only the individual; these are the ones indispensable for physical life. Since they are made for this purpose only, they are perfected by its attainment. In everything concerning them, therefore, man can act reasonably without thought of transcendental purposes.

These functions serve by merely serving him. In so far as he has no other needs, he is therefore self-sufficient and can live happily with no other objective than living. This is not the case, however, with the civilized adult. He has many ideas, feelings and practices unrelated to organic needs. The roles of art, morality, religion, political faith, science itself are not to repair organic exhaustion nor to provide sound functioning of the organs. All this supraphysical life is built and expanded not because of the demands of the cosmic environment but because of the demands of the social environment. The influence of society is what has aroused in us the sentiments of sympathy and solidarity drawing us toward others; it is society which, fashioning us in its image, fills us with religious, political and moral beliefs that control our actions. To play our social role we have striven to extend our intelligence and it is still society that has supplied us with tools for this development by transmitting to us its trust fund of knowledge.

Through the very fact that these superior forms of human activity have a collective origin, they have a collective purpose. As they derive from society they have reference to it; rather they are society itself incarnated and individualized in each one of us. But for them to have a raison d'etre in our eyes, the purpose they envisage must be one not indifferent to us. We can cling to these forms of human activity only to the degree that we cling to society itself. Contrariwise, in the same measure as we feel detached from society we become detached from that life whose source and aim is society. For what purpose do these rules of morality, these precepts of law binding us to all sorts of sacrifices, these restrictive dogmas exist, if there is no being outside us whom they serve and in whom we participate? What is the purpose of science itself? If its only use is to increase our chances for survival, it does not deserve the trouble it entails. Instinct acquits itself better of this role; animals prove this. Why substitute for it a more hesitant and uncertain reflection? What is the end of suffering, above all? If the value of things can only be estimated by their relation to this positive evil for the individual, it is without reward and incomprehensible. This problem does not exist for the believer firm in his faith or the man strongly bound by ties of domestic or political society. Instinctively and unreflectively they ascribe all that they are and do, the one to his Church or his God, the living symbol of the Church, the other to his family, the third to his country or party. Even in their sufferings they see only a means of glorifying the group to which they belong and thus do homage to it. So, the Christian ultimately desires and seeks suffering to testify more fully to his contempt for the flesh and more fully resemble his divine model. But the more the believer doubts, that is, the less he feels himself a real participant in the religious faith to which he belongs, and from which he is freeing himself; the more the family and community become foreign to the individual, so much the more does he become a mystery to himself, unable to escape the exasperating and agonizing question: to what purpose?

THE CONFLICT OF VALUES
IN DELINQUENCY AREAS

Solomon Kobrin

THE CIRCUMSTANCE that less than one-quarter of the boys in the urban areas of high rates of delinquents are brought into the juvenile court charged as delinquents appears to invalidate the hypothesis that in the disorganized city areas delinquency is primarily a product of cultural rather than of personality or psychological processes.[1] Some of the official statistics of delinquency seem to suggest that most children conform to the legal norms of the wider society even in those urban areas where the culture of the local community is relatively favorable to the transmission of delinquent conduct patterns.[2] These statistics therefore leave the inference that even in this situation variables other than culture are of possibly greater importance in delinquency causation than the customary sociological explanations would concede.

While the literature of juvenile delinquency is replete with discussions of the inadequacy of delinquency statistics in general as a basis for measuring the extent of officially proscribed behavior in the larger administrative areas,[3] the present paper will attempt to provide a demonstration of the inadequacies of these statistics with respect to the extent of delinquent behavior in the urban slum areas. This is deemed necessary only because the high proportion of official non-delinquency in these areas is sometimes construed as vital evidence bearing on the nature of the problem of delinquency. In addition, an attempt will be made to formulate a hypothesis with reference to delinquency in the high rate urban areas consistent with the statistical evidence of its extent in such areas, and to subject this hypothesis to preliminary examination in terms of slum delinquency and its enveloping social structure.

As is well known, enumerations of delinquents based on different measures of delinquency produce different impressions of its extent. With increasing degrees of inclusiveness these measures range from commitments to training schools and other custodial institutions, through official and unofficial juvenile court cases, to police complaint cases. On the grounds of either accuracy or completeness no conclusive arguments may be adduced for regarding any of these enumerations as preferable, since each may serve to measure accurately a defined level of deviational behavior, or official action, or both.[4]

Thus, the range of possible enumerations of delinquents in the high rate areas may be illustrated by the data from one representative jurisdiction. During the seven-year period 1927-1933 the rate of commitment per 100 boys of juvenile court age residing in Chicago in the ten square mile areas with highest rates was 6.1.[5] In the highest rate square mile area this rate was 9.2. During the same period the rate of official court delinquents in the ten square mile areas of highest rates was 14.6, with a rate of 18.9 in the top square mile area.

In contrast to both commitments and juvenile court appearances, police complaint cases, as may be anticipated, include in the delinquent classification

Reprinted from *The American Sociological Review* (October 1951), pp. 653-61, by permission of the author and the publisher. (Copyright, 1951, by the American Sociological Society.)

a considerably larger proportion of boys residing in urban delinquency areas. Thus, the Chicago data show that the average rate of delinquents based on police complaints for the ten square mile areas of highest rates for the year 1926 was 20.6. In this police series the top area had a rate of 26.6.[6] However, these rates are not computed on the basis of the seven-year period of age eligibility, and therefore do not parallel rates of commitments or court appearances. To restore comparability between the rates of police complaints here presented and rates of commitments and court appearances it is necessary to multiply by seven the annual rate given. Since the data for the police series do not eliminate duplications of individuals, the multiplication required would result in a rate which exceeds the total age eligible boy population of these areas. Unfortunately, a count of unduplicated individuals who became police cases in the ten highest rate areas of Chicago is not available for 1926.

However, such a count is available for an area of moderate rates for the standard seven-year period of juvenile court eligibility. A count of the unduplicated juveniles dealt with by the police during the 1927-1933 period disclosed that the police complaint rate for this area was 28.8, as compared to an average annual rate of police cases of 9.2 for the area. This indicates that the proportion of unduplicated individuals who become police cases during their seven-year period of eligibility is approximately three times larger than the rate of police cases for a single given year. Since the rate of police cases for the ten highest rate areas in Chicago in the single year 1926 was 20.6, the suggested relative magnitudes of single and seven-year rates indicate that the rate of police cases for the top ten square mile areas in Chicago during the seven-year period centering on 1926 was 65.9.[7] This is the proportion of individuals who, as they moved from their first to their seventh year of age eligibility, engaged in misbehavior serious enough to warrant recorded police attention. And this is the rate which is more nearly comparable, in terms of the basis of computation, to the rates of commitment and court appearance of 6.1 and 14.6 respectively, cited above. Thus, it is evident that when the most inclusive measure based on official records is used, not one-fifth but almost two-thirds of the boys in delinquency areas may be regarded as official delinquents.

The validity of such official cases for the measurement of delinquency rests not only on its inclusiveness of all official delinquents, but on its capacity to mark out as well a homogeneous segment of the juvenile population which is consistently delinquent in terms of behavior content. It is of course with reference to the latter function that the official statistics of delinquency are more severely limited. After making the distinctions between the types of measures discussed, and concluding that police complaints probably represent the most inclusive measure, we are still confronted with the question whether the group thus identified is a distinctively delinquent group in contrast to the balance of the juvenile population. In other words, does even this inclusive measure include all juveniles who engage in delinquent activity? The answer, of course, is that it does not, since it is well known that many delinquent juveniles who are never apprehended are known to social agencies, neighbors, friends, and associates.

Even if a defensible division of boys between delinquent and non-delinquent could be made, the prognostic value of the concept "delinquent," in its official sense, would still be uncertain. This is indicated by the findings of a recent follow-up of the careers of 83 public school boys who in 1929 resided in one of Chicago's delinquency areas. The individuals in this group were ascertained to be without records of appearances before the juvenile court prior to 1929. In 1949 an examination of their records of law violations during their adult careers revealed that 51 per cent of this group had been arrested for offenses other than infraction of the traffic laws. While a sample of 69 boys with juvenile court records drawn from the same neighborhood during the same year exhibited an adult arrest rate of 75 per cent, illustrative of the tendency of juvenile courts to deal primarily with the more serious and persistent offenders, the fact remains that over half the boys in the group of putative non-delinquents became adult offenders.[8]

It is altogether unlikely that these individuals stoutly resisted influences in the direction of delinquency during their youth only to succumb as adults. It is more reasonable to assume that as children they, too, engaged in delinquent activity, but perhaps less persistently or with greater success in avoiding detection and treatment in the court. If the terms "delinquent" and "non-delinquent" had dependable descriptive value the large proportion of boys who were non-delinquent officially would not have appeared as adult offenders.

Taken together, the data presented above indicate that enumerations of delinquents in urban areas of high rates of delinquents exhibit a wide range. It is clear that (a) assertions of the preponderance of non-delinquency in these areas are based on relatively uninclusive official records, and (b) the more inclusive official records indicate the proportion of delinquents to be approximately two-thirds of the age eligibles. Moreover, even so inclusive a category as police complaint cases cannot be regarded as including the total number of offenders, since the police neither know of all offenses committed nor apprehend all offenders.

These observations suggest that delinquency is widely diffused in the urban high rate areas and therefore represents normative behavior which, like all normative behavior, generates a systematic scheme of values and institutional forms for its expression. The statistics of delinquency also indicate that a significantly large number of boys in these areas are free of the kind of involvement in delinquent practices which ordinarily results in the acquisition of a police record or in the development of adult criminality. With respect to the careers of these individuals it seems necessary to assume the ultimate dominance of the norms of conventional society. Thus, a duality of conduct norms in the high rate areas rather than the hegemony of either conventional or criminal value systems may be regarded as the fundamental sociological fact in the culture of these communities.[9] This conclusion is suggested largely by the statistics of delinquency. Its validity may be subjected to further examination by using it in an attempt to explain selected aspects of the problem of delinquency in the high rate urban areas.

(a) *The Variability of Behavior Status in the Delinquency Area.* The facts indicate that in areas of high rates of delinquents there are not only many boys who engage in delinquent activity without becoming official delinquents, but that a substantial number of boys who do possess police and court records become conventional and law-abiding adults. Moreover, there is evidence that of those who are without juvenile records, many become adult offenders. These apparent reversals of career lines are incomprehensible except on the assumption that the individual participates simultaneously in both criminal and conventional value systems. Observation of the social experiences of young persons in the delinquency areas supports this assumption and indicates that the simultaneous participation occurs in two ways.[10]

First, groupings of boys based on play interests frequently include at any given moment of time three types of individuals with reference to delinquent conduct: those who at the time are occasionally delinquent; those who at the time are actively and persistently delinquent; and those who at the time refrain completely from delinquent activity. In terms of propinquity and opportunity for association, delinquents have many contacts with non-delinquents and vice versa. The play of influence with respect to the development of values and goals is simultaneously exerted in both directions, even though delinquents may be expected to have more frequent and more intimate contacts with other delinquents than with non-delinquents.

Second, taken from the standpoint of the development pattern of the individual, marked variability is encountered, particularly in the younger age groups, with respect to the degree of delinquent activity in which the individual is involved from time to time. Thus, the same person, either within the same group or in a succession of groups, may interchangeably occupy the role of persistent delinquent, occasional delinquent, or non-delinquent. He is thus provided an opportunity to experience in a direct and personal manner the full meaning of the alternative value systems implicit in each mode of conduct.

Simultaneous participation in the conventional and criminal value systems in either of the ways indicated is not inconsistent with the fact that over a long period of time persons in delinquency areas who come to occupy either the conventional or the delinquent role will develop more intimate associations and relationships with persons of the same role traits. As a result, progressive alienation from either the criminal or the conventional value scheme ensues, and the person may come in time to live more completely in terms of one rather than in terms of the other value scheme.

These observations emphasize the inadequacy, for purposes of either description or analysis, of designating boys in delinquency areas as delinquent or non-delinquent. In a real sense they are neither and they are both. The world of meanings in which they must find their way is an amalgam compounded in widely varying proportions of two implicitly inharmonious codes of conduct. As an amalgam of this character the world of the delinquency area represents an experience for the growing child which is qualitatively different from either the conventional world of the middle class child or the world of the child reared in an outcast society. It is, in fact, a world in which, because of its two scale value orientation, boys move readily between the delinquent and the non-delinquent classifications. Thus, when applied to the boy who resides in an urban area of high rate of delinquents, the term "non-delinquent" becomes ambiguous. This designation has stable meaning primarily in the social world of those who are conventional and law-abiding.

(b) *Varieties of Delinquency Areas.* The culture of delinquency areas and specific group patterns of delinquency in these areas may be regarded as in large part determined by the character of the interaction between the conventional and the criminal value systems. This fact suggests the possibility of a typology of delinquency areas based on variations in the relationship between these two systems.

Delinquency areas exhibit important differences in the degree to which integration between the conventional and criminal value systems is achieved.[11] Areas range from those in which the integration is well advanced to those in which it is minimal. The two polar types on this continuum may be briefly described.

In areas where the two systems are highly integrated adult violative activity tends to be systematic and organized. This tendency is revealed in the development in these areas of groups of adults engaged in the promotion and management of consistently profitable illegal enterprises. Leaders in these enterprises frequently maintain membership in such conventional institutions of their local communities as churches, fraternal and mutual benefit societies, and political parties. While participation in the political party organizations is usually required by the character of their occupational activity, participation in churches and the other social organizations of the community represents a spontaneous quest for status in the social structure within which they have become acculturated. Within this framework the influence of each of the two value systems is reciprocal, the leaders of illegal enterprise participating in the primary orientation of the conventional elements in the population, and the latter, through their participation in a local power structure sustained in large part by illicit activity, participating perforce in the alternate, criminal value system.

The stable position of illicit enterprise in the adult society of the community is reflected in the character of delinquent conduct on the part of children. While delinquency in all high rate areas is intrinsically disorderly in that it is unrelated to official programs for the education of the young, in the type of community under discussion boys may more or less realistically recognize the potentialities for personal progress in the local society through success in delinquency. In a general way, therefore, delinquent activity in these areas constitutes a training ground for the acquisition of skill in the use of violence, concealment of offense, evasion of detection and arrest, and the purchase of immunity from punishment. Those who come to excel in these respects are frequently noted and valued by adult leaders in the rackets who are confronted, as are the leaders of all income-producing enterprises, with problems of the recruitment of competent personnel.

As a consequence of this situation delinquency tends to occur within a partial frame-work of social controls, insofar as delinquent activity in these areas represents a tolerated means for the acquisition of an approved role and status. Thus, while delinquent activity here possesses the usual characteristics of violence and destructiveness, there tend to develop effective limits of permissible activity in this direction. Delinquency is, in other words, encompassed and contained within a local social structure, and is marginally but palpably related to that structure.

The contrasting polar type of delinquency area is characterized principally by the absence of systematic and organized adult activity in violation of law, despite the fact that many adults in these areas commit violations. The presence of violators as adult models in the community legitimizes activity in opposition to law from the point of view of delinquent juveniles. In this situation conventional and criminal systems of values are not merely not integrated, but are in extreme and open opposition to one another. As a consequence, the delinquency in areas of this type tends to be unrestrained by controls originating *at any point* in the adult social structure.

Areas of this type are frequently produced by drastic changes in the class, ethnic, or racial characteristics of its population. Such transitions, as is well known, tend to devitalize the older institutions of the area, and to introduce a period during which institutional and other controls are at a minimum. During these interim periods the bearers of the conventional culture and its value system are without the customary institutional machinery, and therefore in effect partially demobilized with reference to the diffusion of their value system. In these conditions the alternative criminal value system is able to gain both ground and vigor, and to persist on the local scene without effective opposition.

Because adult crime in this type of area is itself unorganized, its value system remains implicit and hence incapable of generating norms which function effectively on a groupwise basis. As a result, juvenile violators readily escape not merely the controls of the conventional persons in the community, but those of adult violators as well. It should be noted that the emergence of group norms on the part of persistent and systematic violators in the contemporary urban milieu is usually accompanied by regularized and dependable accommodations with such representatives of the wider society as police and politicians. It is at this point that the implicit value system of criminality becomes explicit, moves toward integration with conventionality, and undergoes an enhancement of its capacity to exert control over the behavior of violators.

In areas where such integration is absent the delinquencies of juveniles tend to acquire a wild, untrammelled character. Delinquents in this kind of situation more frequently exhibit the personality traits of the social type sometimes referred to as the hoodlum. Both individually and in groups violent physical combat is engaged in for its own sake, almost as a form of recreation. Here groups of delinquents may be seen as excluded, isolated conflict groups dedicated to an unending battle against all forms of constraint. The escape from controls originating in any social structure, other than that provided by unstable groupings of the delinquents themselves, is here complete.

All delinquency areas fall somewhere between the polar types described. Moreover, changes in the character of a given delinquency area may be explained in terms of changes in the degree of integration existing from time to time between the criminal and the conventional value systems. It is, in fact, the specific form of the interaction between these opposing value systems which helps to explain the character of juvenile group activity in specific delinquency areas, as well as changes in these activities in either a criminal or a conventional direction.

Thus, duality of value orientation in the high rate urban areas may be regarded as a fundamental property of a wide variety of specific community situations. While delinquency areas may move toward or away from the integration of these opposing systems of values, the basic character of the social life of these communities appears to be determined in large part by the explicit presence of this duality.

(c) *Personality of the Delinquent and Conflicting Value Systems.* Juvenile groupings based on common interest in the pursuit of delinquent activity develop a body of shared attitudes which may be regarded as making up a distinctive culture. In a thoughtful analysis of the origin of this culture, Albert K. Cohen[12] has suggested that it arises in a framework of lower socio-economic class status in which many persons are unable, in terms either of achievement or the disciplining of behavior necessary for achievement, to acquire the symbols of success current in the conventional, respectable, and dominant middle class culture of the wider society.[13] As a result, young persons are exposed to the invidious judgments of those who, within the range of social contacts of the lower-class child, represent and exemplify the norms of middle-class culture. Such persons, moreover, symbolize, by virtue both of their roles and their class position, the power and prestige of the wider society in which the lower-class areas is set.[14] One of several adjustive responses available to young males in this situation is to reject the imputation of inferiority and degradation by emphasizing those activities and personal traits which distinguish them from striving, upward mobile persons. The common response inaugurates new norms of conduct out of which develop the distinctive criteria of status in the delinquent group. Thus, a coherent social milieu is created in which status is distributed according to success in attacking the symbols of middle-class respectability. Since property represents a central symbol of merit and virtue in the culture of this class, stealing and destructiveness become a principal though not the only form taken by the attack.

This analysis constitutes a framework within which personality process and culture process may be in part related for purposes of understanding the delinquent as a person. This analysis also throws light on a further aspect of the conflict of value systems which has been seen as an essential characteristic of delinquency areas.

The aggressively hostile response of the young male in the delinquency area to his devaluation by representatives of the conventional culture arises entirely from the fact that the criteria of status in the conventional culture have validity for him. This is indicated not in the hostile response as such, but in certain sentiments and emotions which accompany the hostility. These associated sentiments are reflected in the acts of defiance and contempt which frequently accompany ordinary depredations of property. Nowhere is this more apparent than in the not uncommon burglaries of schools in delinquency areas in which the delinquent escapade is sometimes crowned, as it were, by defecating upon the school principal's desk. This supreme gesture of defiance and contempt can be understood as an effort on the part of the delinquents to counteract their own impulses to accept and accede to the superior status of such representatives of the conventional order as school principals. In a sense, such an act is a dramatically exaggerated denial of a system of values which the delinquent has at least partially introjected, but which for the sake of preserving a tolerable self-image he must reject. In this interplay of attitudinal elements the vigor of the rejection of the value system is the measure of its hold upon the person. In other words, the mood of rebellion which characterizes these young males is created not alone by the negative judgments of the surrogates of middle-class culture, but by the negative self-judgment as well.

Such overtones of rebellion, on the other hand, do not characterize members of subculture groups who are totally excluded from participation in the dominant culture of the wider society. For example, those groups which live by systematic depredations upon property, like the criminal castes of India or the professional thieves of our own society, are relatively impervious to the negative judgments of conventional persons, and do not ordinarily resort to the kind of behavior described.[15] Their devaluation and rejection by conventional society is not transmuted into self-rejection, since their criteria of worthiness diverge sharply from those encountered in conventional society. In contrast, the young male who occupies the role of delinquent in the delinquency area resorts to purposive destructiveness and exaggerates the differences between himself and conventional persons precisely because he cannot exclude from his system of values the conventional criteria of personal worth. His delinquency may hence be seen as a defensive adaptation in which he creates an opposing system of values, since by virtue of his lower-class culture background he remains relatively unequipped to move toward the goals explicit in the middle-class culture of the wider society.

The general conclusions suggested by these observations are (a) that a delinquent subculture originates in a setting of cross-group hostility; (b) that this subculture is a groupwise elaboration of individual adaptations serving ego-defense needs; and (c) that the conflict of cultures generated in this situation is reflected on its social psychological side in the introjection by the delinquent of a dual value orientation as exhibited principally in the delinquent's aggressive destructiveness.[16]

SUMMARY

Analysis of the problem of the causation of delinquency in urban areas of high rates of delinquents is frequently confused by allusions to statistical data which suggest that, while the proportion of delinquents in these areas is high, this class nonetheless represents a distinct minority of the age eligible population. Examination of delinquency statistics indicates that no conclusive judgments regarding this matter may be made on the basis of these statistics.

On the other hand, the statistics do support the proposition that urban areas of high rates of delinquents are characterized by a duality of conduct norms rather than by the dominance of either a conventional or a criminal culture.

This hypothesis appears to be useful in explaining the variability of behavior status on the part of boys in delinquency areas; in constructing a typology of delinquency areas based on degrees of integration of opposing value schemes; and in accounting for certain psychological mechanisms involved in the origin and persistence of the subculture of the delinquent boys' gang.

ANOMIC SUICIDE

Emile Durkheim

SOCIETY is not only something attracting the sentiments and activities of individuals with unequal force. It is also a power controlling them. There is a relation between the way this regulative action is performed and the social suicide-rate.

It is a well-known fact that economic crises have an aggravating effect on the suicidal tendency.

In Vienna, in 1873 a financial crisis occurred which reached its height in 1874; the number of suicides immediately rose. From 141 in 1872, they rose to 153 in 1873 and 216 in 1874. . . . The same crisis occurring at the same time in Frankfurt-on-Main produced the same effects there. In the years before 1874, 22 suicides were committed annually on the average; in 1874 there were 32, or 45 per cent more.

But to what do these crises owe their influence? Is it because they increase poverty by causing public wealth to fluctuate? Is life more readily renounced as it becomes more difficult? The explanation is seductively simple; and it agrees with the popular idea of suicide. But it is contradicted by facts.

Actually, if voluntary deaths increased because life was becoming more difficult, they should diminish perceptibly as comfort increases. Now, although when the price of the most necessary foods rises excessively, suicides generally do the same, they are not found to fall below the average in the opposite case. In Prussia, in 1850 wheat was quoted at the lowest point it reached during the entire period of 1848-81; it was at 6.91 marks per 50 kilograms; yet at this very time suicides rose from 1,527 where they were in 1849 to 1,736, or an increase of 13 per cent, and continued to increase during the years 1851, 1852 and 1853 although the cheap market held. In 1858-59 a new fall took place; yet suicides rose from 2,038 in 1857 to 2,126 in 1858, and to 2,146 in 1859. From 1863 to 1866 prices which had reached 11.04 marks in 1861 fell progressively to 7.95 marks in 1864 and remained very reasonable for the whole period; suicides during the same time increased 17 per cent (2,112 in 1862, 2,485 in 1866). . . .

So far is the increase in poverty from causing the increase in suicide that even fortunate crises, the effect of which is abruptly to enhance a country's prosperity, affect suicide like economic disasters.

The conquest of Rome by Victor-Emmanuel in 1870, by definitely forming the basis of Italian unity, was the starting point for the country of a process of growth which is making it one of the great powers of Europe. Trade and industry received a sharp stimulus from it and surprisingly rapid changes took place. Whereas in 1876, 4,459 steam boilers with a total of 54,000 horse-power were enough for industrial needs, the number of machines in 1887 was 9,983 and their horse-power of 167,000 was threefold more. Of course the amount of production rose proportionately during the

Reprinted, in abridged form, from *Suicide: A Study in Sociology* (1951), translated by John A. Spaulding and George Simpson, pp. 241-58, by permission of the publisher. (Copyright, 1951, by The Free Press.) This book was originally published in Paris in 1897.

same time. Trade followed the same rising course; not only did the merchant marine, communications and transportation develop, but the number of persons and things transported doubled. As this generally heightened activity caused an increase in salaries (an increase of 35 per cent is estimated to have taken place from 1873 to 1889), the material comfort of workers rose, especially since the price of bread was falling at the same time. Finally, according to calculations by Bodio, private wealth rose from 45 and a half billions on the average during the period 1875-80 to 51 billions during the years 1880-85 and 54 billions and a half in 1885-90.

Now, an unusual increase in the number of suicides is observed parallel with this collective renaissance. From 1866 to 1870 they were roughly stable; from 1871 to 1877 they increased 36 per cent.

1864-70	29 suicides per million	1874	37 suicides per million
1871	31 suicides per million	1875	34 suicides per million
1872	33 suicides per million	1876	36.5 suicides per million
1873	36 suicides per million	1877	40.6 suicides per million

And since then the movement has continued. The total figure, 1,139 in 1877, was 1,463 in 1889, a new increase of 28 per cent.

What proves still more conclusively that economic distress does not have the aggravating influence often attributed to it, is that it tends rather to produce the opposite effect. There is very little suicide in Ireland, where the peasantry leads so wretched a life. Poverty stricken Calabria has almost no suicides; Spain has a tenth as many as France. Poverty may even be considered a protection. In the various French departments the more people there are who have independent means, the more numerous are suicides.

Departments Where, per 100,000 Inhabitants, Suicides Were Committed (1878-1887)		Average Number of Persons of Independent Means per 1,000 Inhabitants in Each Group of Departments (1886)
Suicides	Number of Departments	
From 48 to 43	5	127
From 38 to 31	6	73
From 30 to 24	6	69
From 23 to 18	15	59
From 17 to 13	18	49
From 12 to 8	26	49
From 7 to 3	10	42

. . . If therefore industrial or financial crises increase suicides, this is not because they cause poverty, since crises of prosperity have the same result; it is because they are crises, that is, disturbances of the collective order. Every disturbance of equilibrium, even though it achieves greater comfort and a heightening of general vitality, is an impulse to voluntary death. Whenever serious readjustments take place in the social order, whether or not due to a sudden growth or to an unexpected catastrophe, men are more inclined to self-destruction. How is this possible? How can something considered generally to improve existence serve to detach men from it?

For the answer, some preliminary considerations are required.

No living being can be happy or even exist unless his needs are sufficiently proportioned to his means. In other words, if his needs require more than can be granted, or even merely something of a different sort, they will be under continual friction and can only function painfully. Movements incapable of production without pain tend not to be reproduced. Unsatisfied tendencies atrophy, and as the impulse to live is merely the result of all the rest, it is bound to weaken as the others relax.

In the animal, at least in a normal condition, this equilibrium is established with automatic spontaneity because the animal depends on purely material conditions. All the organism needs is that the supplies of substance and energy constantly employed in the vital process should be periodically renewed by equivalent quantities; that replacement be equivalent to use. When the void created by existence in its own resources is filled, the animal, satisfied, asks nothing further. Its power of reflection is not sufficiently developed to imagine other ends than those implicit in its physical nature. On the other hand, as the work demanded of each organ itself depends on the general state of vital energy and the needs of organic equilibrium, use is regulated in turn by replacement and the balance is automatic. The limits of one are those of the other; both are fundamental to the constitution of the existence in question, which cannot exceed them.

This is not the case with man, because most of his needs are not dependent on his body or not to the same degree. Strictly speaking, we may consider that the quantity of material supplies necessary to the physical maintenance of a human life is subject to computation, though this be less exact than in the preceding case and a wider margin left for the free combinations of the will; for beyond the indispensable minimum which satisfies nature when instinctive, a more awakened reflection suggests better conditions, seemingly desirable ends craving fulfillment. Such appetites, however, admittedly sooner or later reach a limit which they cannot pass. But how determine the quantity of well-being, comfort or luxury legitimately to be craved by a human being? Nothing appears in man's organic nor in his psychological constitution which sets a limit to such tendencies. The functioning of individual life does not require them to cease at one point rather than at another; the proof being that they have constantly increased since the beginnings of history, receiving more and more complete satisfaction, yet with no weakening of average health. Above all, how establish their proper variation with different conditions of life, occupations, relative importance of services, etc.? In no society are they equally satisfied in the different stages of the social hierarchy. Yet human nature is substantially the same among all men, in its essential qualities. It is not human nature which can assign the variable limits necessary to our needs. They are thus unlimited so far as they depend on the individual alone. Irrespective of any external regulatory force, our capacity for feeling is in itself an insatiable and bottomless abyss.

But if nothing external can restrain this capacity, it can only be a source of torment to itself. Unlimited desires are insatiable by definition and insatiability is rightly considered a sign of morbidity. Being unlimited, they constantly and infinitely surpass the means at their command; they cannot be quenched. Inextinguishable thirst is constantly renewed torture. It has been claimed, indeed, that human activity naturally aspires beyond assignable limits and sets itself unattainable goals. But how can such an undetermined state be any more reconciled with the conditions of mental life than with the demands of physical life? All man's pleasure in acting, moving and exerting himself implies the sense that his efforts are not in vain and that by walking he has advanced. However, one does not advance when one walks toward no goal, or—which is the same thing—when his goal is infinity. Since the distance between us and it is always the same, whatever road we take, we might as well have made the motions without progress from the spot. Even our glances behind and our feeling of pride at the distance covered can cause only deceptive satisfaction, since the remaining distance is not proportionately reduced. To pursue a goal which is by definition unattainable is to condemn oneself to a state of perpetual unhappiness. Of course, man may hope contrary to all reason, and hope has its pleasures even when unreasonable. It may sustain him for a time; but it cannot survive the repeated disappointments of experience indefinitely. What more can the future offer him than the past, since he can never reach a tenable condition nor even approach the glimpsed ideal? Thus, the more one has, the more one wants, since satisfactions received only stimulate instead of filling needs. Shall action as such be considered agreeable? First, only on condition of blindness to its uselessness. Secondly, for this pleasure to be felt and to temper and half veil the accompanying painful unrest, such unending motion must at least always be easy and unhampered. If it is interfered with only restlessness is left, with the lack of ease which it, itself, entails. But it would be a miracle if no insurmountable obstacle were never encountered. Our thread of life on these conditions is pretty thin, breakable at any instant.

To achieve any other result, the passions first must be limited. Only then can they be harmonized with the faculties and satisfied. But since the individual has no way of limiting them, this must be done by some force exterior to him. A regulative force must play the same role for moral needs which the organism plays for physical needs. This means that the force can only be moral. The awakening of conscience interrupted the state of equilibrium of the animal's dormant existence; only conscience, therefore, can furnish the means to re-establish it. Physical restraint would be ineffective; hearts cannot be touched by physio-chemical forces. So far as the appetites are not automatically restrained by physiological mechanisms, they can be halted only by a limit that they recognize as just. Men would never consent to restrict their desires if they felt justified in passing the assigned limit. But, for reasons given above, they cannot assign themselves this law of justice. So they must receive it from an authority which they respect, to which they yield spontaneously. Either directly and as a whole, or through the agency of one of its organs, society alone can play this moderating role; for it is the only moral power superior to the individual, the authority of which he accepts. It alone has the power necessary to stipulate law and to set the point beyond which the passions must not go. Finally, it alone can estimate the reward to be prospectively offered to every class of human functionary, in the name of the common interest.

As a matter of fact, at every moment of history there is a dim perception, in the moral consciousness of societies, of the respective value of different social services, the relative reward due to each, and the consequent degree of comfort appropriate on the average to workers in each occupation. The different functions are graded in public opinion and a certain coefficient of well-

being assigned to each, according to its place in the hierarchy. According to
accepted ideas, for example, a certain way of living is considered the upper
limit to which a workman may aspire in his efforts to improve his existence,
and there is another limit below which he is not willingly permitted to fall
unless he has seriously demeaned himself. Both differ for city and country
workers, for the domestic servant and the day-laborer, for the business clerk
and the official, etc. Likewise the man of wealth is reproved if he lives the
life of a poor man, but also if he seeks the refinement of luxury overmuch.
Economists may protest in vain; public feeling will always be scandalized if
an individual spends too much wealth for wholly superfluous use, and it even
seems that this severity relaxes only in times of moral disturbance. A genuine
regimen exists, therefore, although not always legally formulated, which fixes
with relative precision the maximum degree of ease of living to which each
social class may legitimately aspire. However, there is nothing immutable
about such a scale. It changes with the increase or decrease of collective
revenue and the changes occurring in the moral ideas of society. Thus what
appears luxury to one period no longer does so to another; and the well-being
which for long periods was granted to a class only by exception and supererogation,
finally appears strictly necessary and equitable.

Under this pressure, each in his sphere vaguely realizes the extreme limit
set to his ambitions and aspires to nothing beyond. At least if he respects
regulations and is docile to collective authority, that is, has a wholesome
moral constitution, he feels that it is not well to ask more. Thus, an end and
goal are set to the passions. Truly, there is nothing rigid nor absolute about
such determination. The economic ideal assigned each class of citizens is
itself confined to certain limits, within which the desires have free range. But
it is not infinite. This relative limitation and the moderation it involves, make
men contented with their lot while stimulating them moderately to improve it;
and this average contentment causes the feeling of calm, active happiness, the
pleasure in existing and living which characterizes health for societies as well
as for individuals. Each person is then at least, generally speaking, in harmony with his condition, and desires only what he may legitimately hope for
as the normal reward of his activity. Besides, this does not condemn man to
a sort of immobility. He may seek to give beauty to his life; but his attempts
in this direction may fail without causing him to despair. For, loving what he
has and not fixing his desire solely on what he lacks, his wishes and hopes
may fail of what he has happened to aspire to, without his being wholly
destitute. He has the essentials. The equilibrium of his happiness is secure because it is defined, and a few mishaps cannot disconcert him.

But it would be of little use for everyone to recognize the justice of the
hierarchy of functions established by public opinion, if he did not also consider the distribution of these functions just. The workman is not in harmony
with his social position if he is not convinced that he has his desserts. If he
feels justified in occupying another, what he has would not satisfy him. So
it is not enough for the average level of needs for each social condition to be
regulated by public opinion, but another, more precise rule, must fix the way
in which these conditions are open to individuals. There is no society in which
such regulation does not exist. It varies with times and places. Once it re-

garded birth as the almost exclusive principle of social classification; today it recognizes no other inherent inequality than hereditary fortune and merit. But in all these various forms its object is unchanged. It is also only possible, everywhere, as a restriction upon individuals imposed by superior authority, that is, by collective authority. For it can be established only by requiring of one or another group of men, usually of all, sacrifices and concessions in the name of the public interest.

Some, to be sure, have thought that this moral pressure would become unnecessary if men's economic circumstances were only no longer determined by heredity. If inheritance were abolished, the argument runs, if everyone began life with equal resources and if the competitive struggle were fought out on a basis of perfect equality, no one could think its results unjust. Each would instinctively feel that things are as they should be.

Truly, the nearer this ideal equality were approached, the less social restraint will be necessary. But it is only a matter of degree. One sort of heredity will always exist, that of natural talent. Intelligence, taste, scientific, artistic, literary or industrial ability, courage and manual dexterity are gifts received by each of us at birth, as the heir to wealth receives his capital or as the nobleman formerly received his title and function. A moral discipline will therefore still be required to make those less favored by nature accept the lesser advantages which they owe to the chance of birth. Shall it be demanded that all have an equal share and that no advantage be given those more useful and deserving? But then there would have to be a discipline far stronger to make these accept a treatment merely equal to that of the mediocre and incapable.

But like the one first mentioned, this discipline can be useful only if considered just by the peoples subject to it. When it is maintained only by custom and force, peace and harmony are illusory; the spirit of unrest and discontent are latent; appetites superficially restrained are ready to revolt. This happened in Rome and Greece when the faiths underlying the old organization of the patricians and plebeians were shaken, and in our modern societies when aristocratic prejudices began to lose their old ascendancy. But this state of upheaval is exceptional; it occurs only when society is passing through some abnormal crisis. In normal conditions the collective order is regarded as just by the great majority of persons. Therefore, when we say that an authority is necessary to impose this order on individuals, we certainly do not mean that violence is the only means of establishing it. Since this regulation is meant to restrain individual passions, it must come from a power which dominates individuals; but this power must also be obeyed through respect, not fear.

It is not true, then, that human activity can be released from all restraint. Nothing in the world can enjoy such a privilege. All existence being a part of the universe is relative to the remainder; its nature and method of manifestation accordingly depend not only on itself but on other beings, who consequently restrain and regulate it. Here there are only differences of degree and form between the mineral realm and the thinking person. Man's characteristic privilege is that the bond he accepts is not physical but moral; that is, social. He is governed not by a material environment brutally imposed on him, but by a conscience superior to his own, the superiority of which he feels. Because the greater, better part of his existence transcends the body, he escapes the body's yoke, but is subject to that of society.

But when society is disturbed by some painful crisis or by beneficent but abrupt transitions, it is momentarily incapable of exercising this influence; thence come the sudden rises in the curve of suicides which we have pointed out above.

In the case of economic disasters, indeed, something like a declassification occurs which suddenly casts certain individuals into a lower state than their previous one. Then they must reduce their requirements, restrain their needs, learn greater self-control. All the advantages of social influence are lost so far as they are concerned; their moral education has to be recommenced. But society cannot adjust them instantaneously to this new life and teach them to practice the increased self-repression to which they are unaccustomed. So they are not adjusted to the condition forced on them, and its very prospect is intolerable; hence the suffering which detaches them from a reduced existence even before they have made trial of it.

It is the same if the source of the crisis is an abrupt growth of power and wealth. Then, truly, as the conditions of life are changed, the standard according to which needs were regulated can no longer remain the same; for it varies with social resources, since it largely determines the share of each class of producers. The scale is upset; but a new scale cannot be immediately improvised. Time is required for the public conscience to reclassify men and things. So long as the social forces thus freed have not regained equilibrium, their respective values are unknown and so all regulation is lacking for a time. The limits are unknown between the possible and the impossible, what is just and what is unjust, legitimate claims and hopes and those which are immoderate. Consequently, there is no restraint upon aspirations. If the disturbance is profound, it affects even the principles controlling the distribution of men among various occupations. Since the relations between various parts of society are necessarily modified, the ideas expressing these relations must change. Some particular class especially favored by the crisis is no longer resigned to its former lot, and, on the other hand, the example of its greater good fortune arouses all sorts of jealousy below and about it. Appetites, not being controlled by a public opinion become disoriented, no longer recognize the limits proper to them. Besides, they are at the same time seized by a sort of natural erethism simply by the greater intensity of public life. With increased prosperity desires increase. At the very moment when traditional rules have lost their authority, the richer prize offered these appetites stimulates them and makes them more exigent and impatient of control. The state of de-regulation or anomy is thus further heightened by passions being less disciplined, precisely when they need more disciplining.

But then their very demands make fulfillment impossible. Overweening ambition always exceeds the results obtained, great as they may be, since there is no warning to pause here. Nothing gives satisfaction and all this agitation is uninterruptedly maintained without appeasement. Above all, since this race for an unattainable goal can give no other pleasure but that of the race itself, if it is one, once it is interrupted the participants are left empty-handed. At the same time the struggle grows more violent and painful, both from being less controlled and because competition is greater. All classes contend among themselves because no established classification any longer exists. Effort grows, just when it becomes less productive. How could the desire to live not be weakened under such conditions?

This explanation is confirmed by the remarkable immunity of poor countries. Poverty protects against suicide because it is a restraint in itself. No matter how one acts, desires have to depend upon resources to some extent; actual possessions are partly the criterion of those aspired to. So the less one has the less he is tempted to extend the range of his needs indefinitely. Lack of power, compelling moderation, accustoms men to it, while nothing excites envy if no one has superfluity. Wealth, on the other hand, by the power it bestows, deceives us into believing that we depend on ourselves only. Reducing the resistance we encounter from objects, it suggests the possibility of unlimited success against them. The less limited one feels, the more intolerable all limitation appears. Not without reason, therefore, have so many religions dwelt on the advantages and moral value of poverty. It is actually the best school for teaching self-restraint. Forcing us to constant self-discipline, it prepares us to accept collective discipline with equanimity, while wealth, exalting the individual, may always arouse the spirit of rebellion which is the very source of immorality. This, of course, is no reason why humanity should not improve its material condition. But though the moral danger involved in every growth of prosperity is not irremediable, it should not be forgotten.

If anomy never appeared except, as in the above instances, in intermittent spurts and acute crisis, it might cause the social suicide-rate to vary from time to time, but it would not be a regular, constant factor. In one sphere of social life, however—the sphere of trade and industry—it is actually in a chronic state.

For a whole century, economic progress has mainly consisted in freeing industrial relations from all regulation. Until very recently, it was the function of a whole system of moral forces to exert this discipline. First, the influence of religion was felt alike by workers and masters, the poor and the rich. It consoled the former and taught them contentment with their lot by informing them of the providential nature of the social order, that the share of each class was assigned by God himself, and by holding out the hope for just compensation in a world to come in return for the inequalities of this world. It governed the latter, recalling that worldly interests are not man's entire lot, that they must be subordinate to other and higher interests, and that they should therefore not be pursued without rule or measure. Temporal power, in turn, restrained the scope of economic functions by its supremacy over them and by the relatively subordinate role it assigned them. Finally, within the business world proper, the occupational groups by regulating salaries, the price of products and production itself, indirectly fixed the average level of income on which needs are partially based by the very force of circumstances. However, we do not mean to propose this organization as a model. Clearly it would be inadequate to existing societies without great changes. What we stress is its existence, the fact of its useful influence, and that nothing today has come to take its place.

Actually, religion has lost most of its power. And government, instead of regulating economic life, has become its tool and servant. The most opposite schools, orthodox economists and extreme socialists, unite to reduce government to the role of a more or less passive intermediary among the various social functions. The former wish to make it simply the guardian of individual contracts; the latter leave it the task of doing the collective bookkeeping, that is, of recording the demands of consumers, transmitting them to producers, inventorying the total revenue and distributing it according to a fixed formula. But both refuse it any power to subordinate other social organs to itself and to make them converge toward one dominant aim. On both sides nations are declared to have the single or chief purpose of achieving industrial prosperity; such is the implication of the dogma of economic materialism, the basis of both apparently opposed systems. And as these theories merely express the state of opinion, industry, instead of being still regarded as a means to an end transcending itself, has become the supreme end of individuals and societies alike. Thereupon the appetites thus excited have become freed of any limiting authority. By sanctifying them, so to speak, this apotheosis of well-being has placed them above all human law. Their restraint seems like a sort of sacrilege. For this reason, even the purely utilitarian regulation of them exercised by the industrial world itself through the medium of occupational groups has been unable to persist. Ultimately, this liberation of desires has been made worse by the very development of industry and the almost infinite extension of the market. So long as the producer could gain his profits only in his immediate neighborhood, the restricted amount of possible gain could not much overexcite ambition. Now that he may assume to have almost the entire world as his customer, how could passions accept their former confinement in the face of such limitless prospects?

Such is the source of the excitement predominating in this part of society, and which has thence extended to the other parts. There, the state of crisis and anomy is constant and, so to speak, normal. From top to bottom of the ladder, greed is aroused without knowing where to find ultimate foothold. Nothing can calm it, since its goal is far beyond all it can attain. Reality seems valueless by comparison with the dreams of fevered imaginations; reality is therefore abandoned, but so too is possibility abandoned when it in turn becomes reality. A thirst arises for novelties, unfamiliar pleasures, nameless sensations, all of which lose their savor once known. Henceforth one has no strength to endure the least reverse. The whole fever subsides and the sterility of all the tumult is apparent, and it is seen that all these new sensations in their infinite quantity cannot form a solid foundation of happiness to support one during days of trial. The wise man, knowing how to enjoy achieved results without having constantly to replace them with others, finds in them an attachment to life in the hour of difficulty. But the man who has always pinned all his hopes on the future and lived with his eyes fixed upon it, has nothing in the past as a comfort against the present's afflictions, for the past was nothing to him but a series of hastily experienced stages. What blinded him to himself was his expectation always to find further on the happiness he had so far missed. Now he is stopped in his tracks; from now on nothing remains behind or ahead of him to fix his gaze upon. Weariness alone, moreover, is enough to bring disillusionment, for he cannot in the end escape the futility of an endless pursuit.

We may even wonder if this moral state is not principally what makes economic catastrophes of our day so fertile in suicides. In societies where a man is subjected to a healthy discipline, he submits more readily to the blows of chance. The necessary effort for sustaining a little more discomfort costs him relatively little, since he is used to discomfort and constraint. But when every constraint is hateful in itself, how can closer constraint not seem intolerable? There is no tendency to resignation in the feverish impatience of men's lives. When there is no other aim but to outstrip constantly the point arrived at, how painful to be thrown back! Now this very lack of organization characterizing our economic condition throws the door wide to every sort of adventure. Since imagination is hungry for novelty, and ungoverned, it gropes at random. Setbacks necessarily increase with risks and thus crises multiply, just when they are becoming more destructive.

Yet these dispositions are so inbred that society has grown to accept them and is accustomed to think them normal. It is everlastingly repeated that it is man's nature to be eternally dissatisfied, constantly to advance, without relief or rest, toward an indefinite goal. The longing for infinity is daily represented as a mark of moral distinction, whereas it can only appear within unregulated consciences which elevate to a rule the lack of rule from which they suffer. The doctrine of the most ruthless and swift progress has become an article of faith. But other theories appear parallel with those praising the advantages of instability, which, generalizing the situation that gives them birth, declare life evil, claim that it is richer in grief than in pleasure and that it attracts men only by false claims. Since this disorder is greatest in the economic world, it has most victims there.

Industrial and commercial functions are really among the occupations which furnish the greatest number of suicides (see Table 1). Almost on a level with the liberal professions, they sometimes surpass them; they are especially more afflicted than agriculture, where the old regulative forces still make their appearance felt most and where the fever of business has least penetrated. Here is best recalled what was once the general constitution of the economic order. And the divergence would be yet greater if, among the suicides of industry, employers were distinguished from workmen, for the former are probably most stricken by the state of anomy. The enormous rate of those with independent means (720 per million) sufficiently shows that the possessors of most comfort suffer most. Everything that enforces subordination attenuates the effects of this state. At least the horizon of the

Table I—Suicides per Million Persons of Different Occupations

	Trade	Transportation	Industry	Agriculture	Liberal* Professions
France (1878-87)†	440	....	340	240	300
Switzerland (1876)	664	1,514	577	304	558
Italy (1866-76)	277	152.6	80.4	26.7	618‡
Prussia (1883-90)	754	....	456	315	832
Bavaria (1884-91)	465	....	369	153	454
Belgium (1886-90)	421	....	160	160	100
Wurttemberg (1873-78)	273	....	190	206	....
Saxony (1878)		341.59§		71.17	....

*When statistics distinguish several different sorts of liberal occupations, we show as a specimen the one in which the suicide-rate is highest.
†From 1826 to 1880 economic functions seem less affected (see *Compte-rendu* of 1880); but were occupational statistics very accurate?
‡This figure is reached only by men of letters.
§Figure represents Trade, Transportation and Industry combined for Saxony.

lower classes is limited by those above them, and for this same reason their desires are more modest. Those who have only empty space above them are almost inevitably lost in it, if no force restrains them.

Anomy, therefore, is a regular and specific factor in suicide in our modern societies; one of the springs from which the annual contingent feeds. So we have here a new type to distinguish from the others. It differs from them in its dependence, not on the way in which individuals are attached to society, but on how it regulates them. Egoistic suicide results from man's no longer finding a basis for existence in life; altruistic suicide, because this basis for existence appears to man situated beyond life itself. The third sort of suicide, the existence of which has just been shown, results from man's activity's lacking regulation and his consequent sufferings. By virtue of its origin we shall assign this last variety the name of *anomic suicide.*

Certainly, this and egotistic suicide have kindred ties. Both spring from society's insufficient presence in individuals. But the sphere of its absence is not the same in both cases. In egoistic suicide it is deficient in truly collective activity, thus depriving the latter of object and meaning. In anomic suicide, society's influence is lacking in the basically individual passions, thus leaving them without a check-rein. In spite of their relationship, therefore, the two types are independent of each other. We may offer society everything social in us, and still be unable to control our desires; one may live in an anomic state without being egoistic, and vice versa. These two sorts of suicide therefore do not draw their chief recruits from the same social environments; one has its principal field among intellectual careers, the world of thought—the other, the industrial or commercial world.

SOCIAL STRUCTURE AND ANOMIE

Robert K. Merton

UNTIL RECENTLY, and all the more so before then, one could speak of a marked tendency in psychological and sociological theory to attribute the faulty operation of social structures to failures of social control over man's imperious biological drives. The imagery of the relations between man and society implied by this doctrine is as clear as it is questionable. In the beginning, there are man's biological impulses which seek full expression. And then, there is the social order, essentially an apparatus for the management of impulses, for the social processing of tensions, for the "renunciation of instinctual gratifications," in the words of Freud. Nonconformity with the demands of a social structure is thus assumed to be anchored in original nature.[1] It is the biologically rooted impulses which from time to time break through social control. And by implication, conformity is the result of an utilitarian calculus or of unreasoned conditioning.

With the more recent advancement of social science, this set of conceptions has undergone basic modification. For one thing, it no longer appears so obvious that man is set against society in an unceasing war between biological impulse and social restraint. The image of man as an untamed bundle of impulses begins to look more like a caricature than a portrait. For another, sociological perspectives have increasingly entered into the analysis of behavior deviating from prescribed patterns of conduct. For whatever the role of biological impulses, there still remains the further question of why it is that the frequency of deviant behavior varies within different social structures and how it happens that the deviations have different shapes and patterns in different social structures. Today, as then, we have still much to learn about the processes through which social structures generate the circumstances in which infringement of social codes constitutes a "normal" (that is to say, an expectable) response.[2] This chapter is an essay seeking clarification of the problem.

The framework set out in this essay is designed to provide one systematic approach to the analysis of social and cultural sources of deviant behavior. Our primary aim is to discover how some *social structures exert a definite pressure upon certain persons in the society to engage in non-conforming rather than conforming conduct.* If we can locate groups peculiarly subject to such pressures, we should expect to find fairly high rates of deviant behavior in these groups, not because the human beings comprising them are compounded of distinctive biological tendencies but because they are responding normally to the social situation in which they find themselves. Our perspective is sociological. We look at variations in the *rates* of deviant behavior, not at its incidence.[3] Should our quest be at all successful, some

Reprinted from *Social Theory and Social Structure*, revised and enlarged edition (1957), pp. 131-60. (Copyright, 1957, by The Free Press.) The article was published originally in Ruth Nanda Ashen, ed., *The Family: Its Function and Destiny* (1949), pp. 226-57. (Copyright, 1949, by Harper & Brothers.) It appears here by permission of the author and the editor and publisher of that volume.

forms of deviant behavior will be found to be as psychologically normal as conformist behavior, and the equation of deviation and psychological abnormality will be put in question.

PATTERNS OF CULTURAL GOALS AND INSTITUTIONAL NORMS

Among the several elements of social and cultural structures, two are of immediate importance. These are analytically separable although they merge in concrete situations. The first consists of culturally defined goals, purposes and interests, held out as legitimate objectives for all or for diversely located members of the society. The goals are more or less integrated—the degree is a question of empirical fact—and roughly ordered in some hierarchy of value. Involving various degrees of sentiment and significance, the prevailing goals comprise a frame of aspirational reference. They are the things "worth striving for." They are a basic, though not the exclusive, component of what Linton has called "designs for group living." And though some, not all, of these cultural goals are directly related to the biological drives of man, they are not determined by them.

A second element of the cultural structure defines, regulates and controls the acceptable modes of reaching out for these goals. Every social group invariably couples its cultural objectives with regulations, rooted in the mores or institutions, of allowable procedures for moving toward these objectives. These regulatory norms are not necessarily identical with technical or efficiency norms. Many procedures which from the standpoint of particular individuals would be most efficient in securing desired values—the exercise of force, fraud, power—are ruled out of the institutional area of permitted conduct. At times, the disallowed procedures include some which would be efficient for the group itself—*e.g.,* historic taboos on vivisection, on medical experimentation, on the sociological analysis of "sacred" norms—since the criterion of acceptability is not technical efficiency but value-laden sentiments (supported by most members of the group or by those able to promote these sentiments through the composite use of power and propaganda). In all instances, the choice of expedients for striving toward cultural goals is limited by institutionalized norms.

Sociologists often speak of these controls as being "in the mores" or as operating through social institutions. Such elliptical statements are true enough, but they obscure the fact that culturally standardized practices are not all of a piece. They are subject to a wide gamut of control. They may represent definitely prescribed or preferential or permissive or proscribed patterns of behavior. In assessing the operation of social controls, these variations—roughly indicated by the terms *prescription, preference, permission* and *proscription*—must of course be taken into account.

To say, moreover, that cultural goals and institutionalized norms operate jointly to shape prevailing practices is not to say that they bear a constant relation to one another. The cultural emphasis placed upon certain goals varies independently of the degree of emphasis upon institutionalized means. There may develop a very heavy, at times a virtually exclusive, stress upon the value of particular goals, involving comparatively little concern with the institutionally prescribed means of striving toward these goals. The limiting case of this type is reached when the range of alternative procedures is governed only by technical rather than by institutional norms. Any and all procedures which promise attainment of the all-important goal would be permitted in this hypothetical polar case. This constitutes one type of malintegrated culture. A second polar type is found in groups where activities originally conceived as instrumental are transmuted into self-contained practices, lacking further objectives. The original purposes are forgotten and close adherence to institutionally prescribed conduct becomes a matter of ritual.[4] Sheer conformity becomes a central value. For a time, social stability is ensured—at the expense of flexibility. Since the range of alternative behaviors permitted by the culture is severely limited, there is little basis for adapting to new conditions. There develops a tradition-bound, 'sacred' society marked by neophobia. Between these extreme types are societies which maintain a rough balance between emphases upon cultural goals and institutionalized practices, and these constitute the integrated and relatively stable, though changing, societies.

An effective equilibrium between these two phases of the social structure is maintained so long as satisfactions accrue to individuals conforming to both cultural constraints, *viz.,* satisfactions from the achievement of goals and satisfactions emerging directly from the institutionally canalized modes of striving to attain them. It is reckoned in terms of the product and in terms of the process, in terms of the outcome and in terms of the activities. Thus continuing satisfactions must derive from sheer participation in a competitive order as well as from eclipsing one's competitors if the order itself is to be sustained. If concern shifts exclusively to the outcome of competition, then those who perenially suffer defeat may, understandably enough, work for a change in the rules of the game. The sacrifices occasionally—not, as Freud assumed, invariably—entailed by conformity to institutional norms must be compensated by socialized rewards. The distribution of statuses through competition must be so organized that positive incentives for adherence to status obligations are provided *for every position* within the distributive order. Otherwise, as will soon become plain, aberrant behavior ensues. It is, indeed, my central hypothesis that aberrant behavior may be regarded sociologically as a symptom of dissociation between culturally prescribed aspirations and socially structured avenues for realizing these aspirations.

Of the types of societies which result from independent variation of cultural goals and institutionalized means, we shall be primarily concerned with the first—a society in which there is an exceptionally strong emphasis upon specific goals without a corresponding emphasis upon institutional procedures. If it is not to be misunderstood, this statement must be elaborated. No society lacks norms governing conduct. But societies do differ in the degree to which the folkways, mores and institutional controls are effectively integrated with the goals which stand high in the hierarchy of cultural values. The culture may be such as to lead individuals to center their emotional convictions upon the complex of culturally acclaimed ends, with far less emotional support for prescribed methods of reaching out for these ends. With such differential emphases upon goals and institutional procedures, the latter may be so vitiated by the stress on goals as to have the behavior of many individuals limited only by considerations of technical expediency. In this context, the sole significant question becomes: Which of the available procedures is most efficient in netting the culturally approved value?[5] The technically most effective procedure, whether culturally legitimate or not, becomes typically preferred to institutionally prescribed conduct. As this process of attenuation continues, the society becomes unstable and there develops what Durkheim called "anomie" (or normlessness).[6]

The working of this process eventuating in anomie can be easily glimpsed in a series of familiar and instructive, though perhaps trivial, episodes. Thus, in competitive athletics, when the aim of victory is shorn of its institutional trappings and success becomes construed as "winning the game" rather than "winning under the rules of the game," a premium is implicitly set upon the use of illegitimate but technically efficient means. The star of the opposing football team is surreptitiously slugged; the wrestler incapacitates his opponent through ingenious but illicit techniques; university alumni covertly subsidize "students" whose talents are confined to the athletic field. The emphasis on the goal has so attenuated the satisfactions deriving from sheer participation in the competitive activity that only a successful outcome provides gratification. Through the same process, tension generated by the desire to win in a poker game is relieved by successfully dealing one's self four aces or, when the cult of success has truly flowered, by sagaciously shuffling the cards in a game of solitaire. The faint twinge of uneasiness in the last instance and the surreptitious nature of public delicts indicate clearly that the institutional rules of the game are *known* to those who evade them. But cultural (or idiosyncratic) exaggeration of the success-goal leads men to withdraw emotional support from the rules.[7]

This process is of course not restricted to the realm of competitive sport, which has simply provided us with microcosmic images of the social macrocosm. The process whereby exaltation of the end generates a literal *demoralization, i.e.,* a de-institutionalization, of the means occurs in many[8] groups where the two components of the social structure are not highly integrated.

Contemporary American culture appears to approximate the polar type in which great emphasis upon certain success-goals occurs without equivalent emphasis upon institutional means. It would of course be fanciful to assert that accumulated wealth stands alone as a symbol of success just as it would be fanciful to deny that Americans assign it a place high in their scale of values. In some large measure, money has been consecrated as a value in itself, over and above its expenditure for articles of consumption or its use for the enhancement of power. "Money" is peculiarly well adapted to become a symbol of prestige. As Simmel emphasized, money is highly abstract and impersonal. However acquired, fraudulently or institutionally, it can be used to purchase the same goods and services. The anonymity of an urban society, in conjunction with these peculiarities of money, permits wealth, the sources of which may be unknown to the community in which the plutocrat lives or, if known, to become purified in the course of time, to serve as a symbol of high status. Moreover, in the American Dream there is no final stopping point. The measure of "monetary success" is conveniently indefinite and relative. At each income level, as H. F. Clark found, Americans want just about twenty-five per cent more (but of course this "just a bit more" continues to operate once it is obtained). In this flux of shifting standards, there is no stable resting point, or rather, it is the point which manages always to be "just ahead." An observer of a community in which annual salaries in six figures are not uncommon, reports the anguished words of one victim of the American Dream: "In this town, I'm snubbed socially because I only get a thousand a week. That hurts."[9]

To say that the goal of monetary success is entrenched in American culture is only to say that Americans are bombarded on every side by precepts which affirm the right or, often, the duty of retaining the goal even in the face of repeated frustration. Prestigeful representatives of the society reinforce the cultural emphasis. The family, the school and the workplace—the major agencies shaping the personality structure and goal formation of Americans—join to provide the intensive disciplining required if an individual is to retain intact a goal that remains elusively beyond reach, if he is to be motivated by the promise of a gratification which is not redeemed. As we shall presently see, parents serve as a transmission belt for the values and goals of the groups of which they are a part—above all, of their social class or of the class with which they identify themselves. And the schools are of course the official agency for the passing on of the prevailing values, with a large proportion of the textbooks used in city schools implying or stating explicitly "that education leads to intelligence and consequently to job and money success."[10] Central to this process of disciplining people to maintain their unfulfilled aspirations are the cultural prototypes of success, the living documents testifying that the American Dream can be realized if one but has the requisite abilities. Consider in this connection the following excerpts from the business journal, *Nation's Business,* drawn from a large amount of comparable materials found in mass communications setting forth the values of business class culture.

The Document (Nation's Business, Vol. 27, No. 8, p. 7)	*Its Sociological Implications*
'You have to be born to those jobs, buddy, or else have a good pull.'	Here is a heretical opinion, possibly born of continued frustration, which rejects the worth of retaining an apparently unrealizable goal and, moreover, questions the legitimacy of a social structure which provides differential access to this goal.
That's an old sedative to ambition.	The counter-attack, explicitly asserting the cultural value of retaining one's aspirations intact, of not losing "ambition."
Before listening to its seduction, ask these men:	A clear statement of the function to be served by the ensuing list of "successes." These men are living testimony that the social structure is such as to permit these aspirations to be achieved, *if one is worthy.* And correlatively, failure to reach these goals testifies only to one's own personal shortcomings. Aggression provoked by failure should therefore be directed inward and not outward, against oneself and not against a social structure which provides free and equal access to opportunity.

Elmer R. Jones, president of Wells-Fargo and Co., who began life as a poor boy and left school at the fifth grade to take his first job.

Frank C. Ball, the Mason fruit jar king of America, who rode from Buffalo to Muncie, Indiana, in a boxcar along with his brother George's horse, to start a little business in Muncie that became the biggest of its kind.

J. L. Bevan, president of the Illinois Central Railroad, who at twelve was a messenger boy in the freight office at New Orleans.

Success prototype I: *All* may properly have the *same* lofty ambitions, for however lowly the starting-point, true talent can reach the very heights. Aspirations must be retained intact.

Success prototype II: Whatever the present results of one's strivings, the future is large with promise; for the common man may yet become a king. Gratifications may seem forever deferred, but they will finally be realized as one's enterprise becomes "the biggest of its kind."

Success prototype III: If the secular trends of our economy seem to give little scope to small business, then one may rise within the giant bureaucracies of private enterprise. If one can no longer be a king in a realm of his own creation, he may at least become a president in one of the economic democracies. No matter what one's present station, messenger boy or clerk, one's gaze should be fixed at the top.

From divers sources there flows a continuing pressure to retain high ambition. The exhortational literature is immense, and one can choose only at the risk of seeming invidious. Consider only these: The Reverend Russell H. Conwell, with his *Acres of Diamonds* address heard and read by hundreds of thousands and his subsequent book, *The New Day, or Fresh Opportunities: A Book for Young Men;* Elbert Hubbard, who delivered the famous *Message to Garcia* at Chautauqua forums throughout the land; Orison Swett Marden, who, in a stream of books, first set forth *The Secret of Achievement,* praised by college presidents, then explained the process of *Pushing to the Front,* eulogized by President McKinley and finally, these democratic testimonials notwithstanding, mapped the road to make *Every Man a King.* The symbolism of a commoner rising to the estate of economic royalty is woven deep in the texture of the American culture pattern, finding what is perhaps its ultimate expression in the words of one who knew whereof he spoke, Andrew Carnegie: "Be a king in your dreams. Say to yourself, 'My place is at the top.' "[11]

Coupled with this positive emphasis upon the obligation to maintain lofty goals is a correlative emphasis upon the penalizing of those who draw in their ambitions. Americans are admonished "not to be a quitter" for in the dictionary of American culture, as in the lexicon of youth, "there is no such word as 'fail.' " The cultural manifesto is clear: one must not quit, must not cease striving, must not lessen his goals, for "not failure, but low aim, is crime."

Thus the culture enjoins the acceptance of three cultural axioms: First, all should strive for the same lofty goals since these are open to all; second, present seeming failure is but a way-station to ultimate success; and third, genuine failure consists only in the lessening or withdrawal of ambition.

In rough psychological paraphrase, these axioms represent, first, a symbolic secondary reinforcement of incentive; second, curbing the threatened extinction of a response through an associated stimulus; third, increasing the motive-strength to evoke continued responses despite the continued absence of reward.

In sociological paraphrase, these axioms represent, first, the deflection of criticism of the social structure onto one's self among those so situated in the society that they do not have full and equal access to opportunity; second, the preservation of a structure of social power by having individuals in the lower social strata identify themselves, not with their compeers, but with those at the top (whom they will ultimately join); and third, providing pressures for conformity with the cultural dictates of unslackened ambition by the threat of less than full membership in the society for those who fail to conform.

It is in these terms and through these processes that contemporary American culture continues to be characterized by a heavy emphasis on wealth as a basic symbol of success, without a corresponding emphasis upon the legitimate avenues on which to march toward this goal. How do individuals living in this cultural context respond? And how do our observations bear upon the doctrine that deviant behavior typically derives from biological impulses breaking through the restraints imposed by culture? What, in short, are the consequences for the behavior of people variously situated in a social structure of a culture in which the emphasis on dominant success-goals has become increasingly separated from an equivalent emphasis on institutionalized procedures for seeking these goals?

TYPES OF INDIVIDUAL ADAPTATION

Turning from these culture patterns, we now examine types of adaptation by individuals within the culture-bearing society. Though our focus is still the cultural and social genesis of varying rates and types of deviant behavior, our perspective shifts from the plane of patterns of cultural values to the plane of types of adaptation to these values among those occupying different positions in the social structure.

We here consider five types of adaptation, as these are schematically set out in the following table, where (+) signifies "acceptance," (−) signifies "rejection," and (±) signifies "rejection of prevailing values and substitution of new values."

A Typology of Modes of Individual Adaptation[12]

Modes of Adaptation	Culture Goals	Institutionalized Means
I. Conformity	+	+
II. Innovation	+	−
III. Ritualism	−	+
IV. Retreatism	−	−
V. Rebellion[13]	±	±

Examination of how the social structure operates to exert pressure upon individuals for one or another of these alternative modes of behavior must be prefaced by the observation that people may shift from one alternative to another as they engage in different spheres of social activities. These categories refer to role behavior in specific types of situations, not to personality. They are types of more or less enduring response, not types of personality organization. To consider these types of adaptation in several spheres of conduct would introduce a complexity unmanageable within the confines of this chapter. For this reason, we shall be primarily concerned with economic activity in the broad sense of "the production, exchange, distribution and consumption of goods and services" in our competitive society, where wealth has taken on a highly symbolic cast.

I. Conformity. To the extent that a society is stable, adaptation type I—conformity to both cultural goals and institutionalized means—is the most common and widely diffused. Were this not so, the stability and continuity of the society could not be maintained. The mesh of expectancies constituting every social order is sustained by the modal behavior of its members representing conformity to the established, though perhaps secularly changing, culture patterns. It is, in fact, only because behavior is typically oriented toward the basic values of the society that we may speak of a human aggregate as comprising a society. Unless there is a deposit of values shared by interacting individuals, there exist social relations, if the disorderly interactions may be so called, but no society. It is thus that, at mid-century, one may refer to a Society of Nations primarily as a figure of speech or as an imagined objective, but not as a sociological reality.

Since our primary interest centers on the sources of *deviant* behavior, and since we have briefly examined the mechanisms making for conformity as the modal response in American society, little more need be said regarding this type of adaptation, at this point.

II. Innovation. Great cultural emphasis upon the success-goal invites this mode of adaptation through the use of institutionally proscribed but often effective means of attaining at least the simulacrum of success—wealth and power. This response occurs when the individual has assimilated the cultural emphasis upon the goal without equally internalizing the institutional norms governing ways and means for its attainment.

From the standpoint of psychology, great emotional investment in an objective may be expected to produce a readiness to take risks, and this attitude may be adopted by people in all social strata. From the standpoint of sociology, the question arises, which features of our social structure predispose toward this type of adaptation, thus producing greater frequencies of deviant behavior in one social stratum than in another?

On the top economic levels, the pressure toward innovation not infrequently erases the distinction between business-like strivings this side of the mores and sharp practices beyond the mores. As Veblen observed, "It is not easy in any given case—indeed it is at times impossible until the courts have spoken—to say whether it is an instance of praiseworthy salesmanship or a penitentiary offense." The history of the great American fortunes is threaded with strains toward institutionally dubious innovation as is attested by many tributes to the Robber Barons. The reluctant admiration often expressed privately, and not seldom publicly, of these "shrewd, smart and successful" men is a product of a cultural structure in which the sacrosanct goal virtually consecrates the means. This is no new phenomenon. Without assuming that Charles Dickens was a wholly accurate observer of the American scene and with full knowledge that he was anything but impartial, we cite his perceptive remarks on the American

love of "smart" dealing: which gilds over many a swindle and gross breach of trust; many a defalcation, public and private; and enables many a knave to hold his head up with the best, who well deserves a halter. . . . The merits of a broken speculation, or a bankruptcy, or of a successful scoundrel, are not gauged by its or his observance of the golden rule, "Do as you would be done by," but are considered with reference to their smartness. . . . The following dialogue I have held a hundred times: "Is it not a very disgraceful circumstance that such a man as So-and-so should be acquiring a large property by the most infamous and odious means, and notwithstanding all the crimes of which he has been guilty, should be tolerated and abetted by your Citizens? He is a public nuisance, is he not?" "Yes, sir." "A convicted liar?" "Yes, sir." "He has been kicked and cuffed, and caned?" "Yes, sir." "And he is utterly dishonorable, debased, and profligate?" "Yes, sir." "In the name of wonder, then, what is his merit?" "Well, sir, he is a smart man."

In this caricature of conflicting cultural values, Dickens was of course only one of many wits who mercilessly probed the consequences of the heavy emphasis on financial success. Native wits continued where alien wits left off. Artemus Ward satirized the commonplaces of American life until they seemed strangely incongruous. The "crackerbox philosophers," Bill Arp and Petroleum Volcano [later Vesuvius] Nasby, put wit in the service of iconoclasm, breaking the images of public figures with unconcealed pleasure. Josh Billings and his alter ego, Uncle Esek, made plain what many could not freely acknowledge, when he observed that satisfaction is relative since "most of the happiness in this world konsists in possessing what others kant git." All were engaged in exhibiting the social functions of tendentious wit, as this was later to be analyzed by Freud, in his monograph on *Wit and Its Relation to the Unconscious,* using it as "a weapon of attack upon what is great, dignified and mighty, [upon] that which is shielded by internal hindrances or external circumstance against direct disparagement. . . ." But perhaps most in point here was the deployment of wit by Ambrose Bierce in a form which made it evident that *wit* had not cut away from its etymological origins and still meant the power by which one knows, learns, or thinks. In his characteristically ironical and deep-seeing essay on "crime and its correctives," Bierce begins with the observation that "Sociologists have long been debating the theory that the impulse to commit crime is a disease, and the ayes appear to have it—the disease." After this prelude, he describes the ways in which the successful rogue achieves social legitimacy, and proceeds to anatomize the discrepancies between cultural values and social relations.

The good American is, as a rule, pretty hard on roguery, but he atones for his austerity by an amiable toleration of rogues. His only requirement is that he must personally know the rogues. We all "denounce" thieves loudly enough if we have not the honor of their acquaintance. If we have, why, that is different—unless they have the actual odor of the slum or the prison about them. We may know them guilty, but we meet them, shake hands with them, drink with them and, if they happen to be wealthy, or otherwise great, invite them to our houses, and deem it an honor to frequent theirs. We do not "approve their methods"—let that be understood; and thereby they are sufficiently punished. The notion that a knave cares a pin what is thought of his ways by one who is civil and friendly to himself appears to have been invented by a humorist. On the vaudeville stage of Mars it would probably have made his fortune.

[And again:] If social recognition were denied to rogues they would be fewer by many. Some would only the more diligently cover their tracks along the devious paths of unrighteousness, but others would do so much violence to their consciences as to renounce the disadvantages of rascality for those of an honest life. An unworthy person dreads nothing so much as the withholding of an honest hand, the slow, inevitable stroke of an ignoring eye.

We have rich rogues because we have "respectable" persons who are not ashamed to take them by the hand, to be seen with them, to say that they know them. In such it is treachery to censure them; to cry out when robbed by them is to turn state's evidence.

One may smile upon a rascal (most of us do many times a day) if one does not know him to be a rascal, and has not said he is; but knowing him to be, or having said he is, to smile upon him is to be a hypocrite—just a plain hypocrite or a sycophantic hypocrite, according to the station in life of the rascal smiled upon. There are more plain hypocrites than sycophantic ones, for there are more rascals of no consequence than rich and distinguished ones, though they get fewer smiles each. The American people will be plundered as long as the American character is what it is; as long as it is tolerant of successful knaves; as long as American ingenuity draws an imaginery distinction between a man's public character and his private—his commercial and his personal. In brief, the American people will be plundered as long as they deserve to be plundered. No human law can stop, none ought to stop it, for that would abrogate a higher and more salutary law: "As ye sow, ye shall reap."[14]

Living in the age in which the American robber barons flourished, Bierce could not easily fail to observe what became later known as "white-collar crime." Nevertheless, he was aware that not all of these large and dramatic departures from institutional norms in the top economic strata are known, and possibly fewer deviations among the lesser middle classes come to light. Sutherland has repeatedly documented the prevalence of "white-collar criminality" among business men. He notes, further, that many of these crimes were not prosecuted because they were not detected or, if detected, because of "the status of the business man, the trend away from punishment, and the relatively unorganized resentment of the public against white-collar criminals."[15] A study of some 1,700 prevalently middle-class individuals found that "off the record crimes" were common among wholly "respectable" members of society. Ninety-nine per cent of those questioned confessed to having committed one or more of 49 offenses under the penal law of the State of New York, each of these offenses being sufficiently serious to draw a maximum sentence of not less than one year. The mean number of offenses in adult years—this excludes all offenses committed before the age of sixteen— was 18 for men and 11 for women. Fully 64% of the men and 29% of the women acknowledged their guilt on one or more counts of felony which, under the laws of New York is ground for depriving them of all rights of citizenship. One keynote of these findings is expressed by a minister, referring to false statements he made about a commodity he sold, "I tried truth first, but it's not always successful." On the basis of these results, the authors modestly conclude that "the number of acts legally constituting crimes are far in excess of those officially reported. Unlawful behavior, far from being an abnormal social or psychological manifestation, is in truth a very common phenomenon."[16]

But whatever the differential rates of deviant behavior in the several social strata, and we know from many sources that the official crime statistics uniformly showing higher rates in the lower strata are far from complete or reliable, it appears from our analysis that the greatest pressures toward deviation are exerted upon the lower strata. Cases in point permit us to detect the sociological mechanisms involved in producing these pressures. Several researchers have shown that specialized areas of vice and crime constitute a "normal" response to a situation where the cultural emphasis upon pecuniary success has been absorbed, but where there is little access to conventional and legitimate means for becoming successful. The occupational opportunities of people in these areas are largely confined to manual labor and the lesser white-collar jobs. Given the American stigmatization of manual labor *which has been found to hold rather uniformly in all social classes*,[17] and the absence of realistic opportunities for advancement beyond this level, the result is a marked tendency toward deviant behavior. The status of unskilled labor and the consequent low income cannot readily compete *in terms of established standards of worth* with the promises of power and high income from organized vice, rackets and crime.[18]

For our purposes, these situations exhibit two salient features. First, incentives for success are provided by the established values of the culture *and* second, the avenues available for moving toward this goal are largely limited by the class structure to those of deviant behavior. It is the *combination* of the cultural emphasis and the social structure which produces intense pressure for deviation. Recourse to legitimate channels for "getting in the money" is limited by a class structure which is not fully open at each level to men of good capacity.[19] Despite our persisting open-class-ideology,[20] advance toward the success-goal is relatively rare and notably difficult for those armed with little formal education and few economic resources. The dominant pressure leads toward the gradual attenuation of legitimate, but by and large ineffectual, strivings and the increasing use of illegitimate, but more or less effective, expedients.

Of those located in the lower reaches of the social structure, the culture makes incompatible demands. On the one hand, they are asked to orient their conduct toward the prospect of large wealth—"Every man a king," said Marden and Carnegie and Long—and on the other, they are largely denied effective opportunities to do so institutionally. The consequence of this structural inconsistency is a high rate of deviant behavior. The equilibrium between culturally designated ends and means becomes highly unstable with progressive emphasis on attaining the prestige-laden ends by any means whatsoever. Within this context, Al Capone represents the triumph of amoral intelligence over morally prescribed "failure," when the channels of vertical mobility are closed or narrowed in a *society which places a high premium on economic affluence and social ascent for* all *its members.*[21]

This last qualification is of central importance. It implies that other aspects of the social structure, besides the extreme emphasis on pecuniary success, must be considered if we are to understand the social sources of deviant behavior. A high frequency of deviant behavior is not generated merely by lack of opportunity or by this exaggerated pecuniary emphasis. A comparatively rigidified class structure, a caste order, may limit opportunities far beyond the point which obtains in American society today. It is only when a system of cultural values extols, virtually above all else, certain *common* success-goals *for the population at large* while the social structure rigorously restricts or completely closes access to approved modes of reaching these goals *for a considerable part of the same population,* that deviant behavior ensues on a large scale. Otherwise said, our egalitarian ideology denies by implication the existence of non-competing individuals and groups in the pursuit of pecuniary success. Instead, the same body of success-symbols is held to apply for all. Goals are held to transcend class lines, not to be bounded by them, yet the actual social organization is such that there exist class differentials in accessibility of the goals. In this setting, a cardinal American virtue, "ambition," promotes a cardinal American vice, "deviant behavior."

This theoretical analysis may help explain the varying correlations between crime and poverty.[22] "Poverty" is not an isolated variable which operates in precisely the same fashion wherever found; it is only one in a complex of identifiably interdependent social and cultural variables. Poverty as such and consequent limitation of opportunity are not enough to produce a conspicuously high rate of criminal behavior. Even the notorious "poverty in the midst of plenty" will not necessarily lead to this result. But when poverty and associated disadvantages in competing for the culture values approved for *all* members of the society are linked with a cultural emphasis on pecuniary success as a dominant goal, high rates of criminal behavior are the normal outcome. Thus, crude (and not necessarily reliable) crime statistics suggest that poverty is less highly correlated with crime in southeastern Europe than in the United States. The economic life-chances of the poor in these European areas would seem to be even less promising than in this country, so that neither poverty nor its association with limited opportunity is sufficient to account for the varying correlations. However, when we consider the full configuration—poverty, limited opportunity and the assignment of cultural goals—there appears some basis for explaining the higher correlation between poverty and crime in our society than in others where rigidified class structure is coupled with *differential class symbols of success.*

The victims of this contradiction between the cultural emphasis on pecuniary ambition and the social bars to full opportunity are not always aware of the structural sources of their thwarted aspirations. To be sure, they are often aware of a discrepancy between individual worth and social rewards. But they do not necessarily see how this comes about. Those who do find its source in the social structure may become alienated from that structure and become ready candidates for Adaptation V (rebellion). But others, and this appears to include the great majority, may attribute their difficulties to more mystical and less sociological sources. For as the distinguished classicist and sociologist-in-spite-of-himself, Gilbert Murray, has remarked in this general connection, "The best seed-ground for superstition is a society in which the fortunes of men seem to bear practically no relation to their merits and efforts. A stable and well-governed society does tend, speaking roughly, to ensure that the Virtuous and Industrious Apprentice shall succeed in life, while the Wicked and Idle Apprentice fails. And in such a society people tend to lay stress on the reasonable or visible chains of causation. But in [a society suffering from anomie] . . ., the ordinary virtues of diligence, honesty, and kindliness seem to be of little avail."[23] And in such a society people tend to put stress on mysticism: the workings of Fortune, Chance, Luck.

In point of fact, both the eminently "successful" and the eminently "unsuccessful" in our society not infrequently attribute the outcome to "luck." Thus, the prosperous man of business, Julius Rosenwald, declared that 95% of the great fortunes were "due to luck."[24] And a leading business journal, in an editorial explaining the social benefits of great individual wealth, finds it necessary to supplement wisdom with luck as the factors accounting for great fortunes: "When one man through wise investments—aided, we'll grant, by good luck in many cases—accumulates a few millions, he doesn't thereby take something from the rest of us."[25] In much the same fashion, the worker often explains economic status in terms of chance. "The worker sees all about him experienced and skilled men with no work to do. If he is in work, he feels lucky. If he is out of work, he is the victim of hard luck. *He can see little relation between worth and consequences.*"[26]

But these references to the workings of chance and luck serve distinctive functions according to whether they are made by those who have reached or those who have not reached the culturally emphasized goals. For the successful, it is in psychological terms, a disarming expression of modesty. It is far removed from any semblance of conceit to say, in effect, that one was lucky rather than altogether deserving of one's good fortune. In sociological terms, the doctrine of luck as expounded by the successful serves the dual function of explaining the frequent discrepancy between merit and reward while keeping immune from criticism a social structure which allows this discrepancy to become frequent. For if success is primarily a matter of luck, if it is just in the blind nature of things, if it bloweth where it listeth and thou canst not tell whence it cometh or whither it goeth, then surely it is beyond control and will occur in the same measure *whatever the social structure.*

For the unsuccessful and particularly for those among the unsuccessful who find little reward for their merit and their effort, the doctrine of luck serves the psychological function of enabling them to preserve their self-esteem in the face of failure. It may also entail the dysfunction of curbing motivation for sustained endeavor.[27] Sociologically, as implied by Bakke,[28] the doctrine may reflect a failure to comprehend the workings of the social and economic system, and may be dysfunctional inasmuch as it eliminates the rationale of working for structural changes making for greater equities in opportunity and reward.

This orientation toward chance and risk-taking, accentuated by the strain of frustrated aspirations, may help explain the marked interest in gambling—an institutionally proscribed or at best permitted rather than preferred or prescribed mode of activity—within certain social strata.[29]

Among those who do not apply the doctrine of luck to the gulf between merit, effort and reward there may develop an individuated and cynical attitude toward the social structure, best exemplified in the cultural cliché that "it's not what you know, but who you know, that counts."

In societies such as our own, then, the great cultural emphasis on pecuniary success for all and a social structure which unduly limits practical recourse to approved means for many set up a tension toward innovative practices which depart from institutional norms. But this form of adaptation presupposes that individuals have been imperfectly socialized so that they abandon institutional means while retaining the success-aspiration. Among those who have fully internalized the institutional values, however, a comparable situation is more likely to lead to an alternative response in which the goal is abandoned but conformity to the mores persists. This type of response calls for further examination.

III. Ritualism. The ritualistic type of adaptation can be readily identified. It involves the abandoning or scaling down of the lofty cultural goals of great pecuniary success and rapid social mobility to the point where one's aspirations can be satisfied. But though one rejects the cultural obligation to attempt "to get ahead in the world," though one draws in one's horizons, one continues to abide almost compulsively by institutional norms.

It is something of a terminological quibble to ask whether this represents genuinely deviant behavior. Since the adaptation is, in effect, an internal decision and since the overt behavior is institutionally permitted, though not culturally preferred, it is not generally considered to represent a social problem. Intimates of individuals making this adaptation may pass judgment in terms of prevailing cultural emphases and may "feel sorry for them," they may, in the individual case, feel that "old Jonesy is certainly in a rut." Whether this is described as deviant behavior or no, it clearly represents a departure from the cultural model in which men are obliged to strive actively, preferably through institutionalized procedures, to move onward and upward in the social hierarchy.

We should expect this type of adaptation to be fairly frequent in a society which makes one's social status largely dependent upon one's achievements. For, as has so often been observed,[30] this ceaseless competitive struggle produces acute status anxiety. One device for allaying these anxieties is to lower one's level of aspiration—permanently. Fear produces inaction, or more accurately, routinized action.[31]

The syndrome of the social ritualist is both familiar and instructive. His implicit life-philosophy finds expression in a series of cultural clichés: "I'm not sticking *my* neck out," "I'm playing safe," "I'm satisfied with what I've got," "Don't aim high and you won't be disappointed." The theme threaded through these attitudes is that high ambitions invite frustration and danger whereas lower aspirations produce satisfaction and security. It is a response to a situation which appears threatening and excites distrust. It is the attitude implicit among workers who carefully regulate their output to a constant quota in an industrial organization where they have occasion to fear that they will "be noticed" by managerial personnel and "something will happen" if their output rises and falls.[32] It is the perspective of the frightened employee, the zealously conformist bureaucrat in the teller's cage of the private banking enterprise or in the front office of the public works enterprise.[33] It is, in short, the mode of adaptation of individually seeking a *private* escape from the dangers and frustrations which seem to them inherent in the competition for major cultural goals by abandoning these goals and clinging all the more closely to the safe routines and the institutional norms.

If we should expect *lower-class* Americans to exhibit Adaptation II—
"innovation"—to the frustrations enjoined by the prevailing emphasis on large
cultural goals and the fact of small social opportunities, we should expect
lower-middle class Americans to be heavily represented among those making
Adaptation III, "ritualism." For it is in the lower middle class that parents
typically exert continuous pressure upon children to abide by the moral
mandates of society, and where the social climb upward is less likely to meet
with success than among the upper middle class. The strong disciplining for
conformity with mores reduces the likelihood of Adaptation II and promotes
the likelihood of Adaptation III. The severe training leads many to carry a
heavy burden of anxiety. The socialization patterns of the lower middle class
thus promote the very character structure most predisposed toward ritualism,[34] and it is in this stratum, accordingly, that the adaptive pattern III
should most often occur.[35]

But we should note again, as at the outset of this chapter, that we are here
examining *modes of adaptation* to contradictions in the cultural and social
structure: we are not focusing on character or personality types. Individuals
caught up in these contradictions can and do move from one type of adaptation to another. Thus it may be conjectured that some ritualists, conforming
meticulously to the institutional rules, are so steeped in the regulations that
they become bureaucratic virtuosos, that they over-conform precisely because
they are subject to guilt engendered by previous nonconformity with the rules
(*i.e.*, Adaptation II). And the occasional passage from ritualistic adaptation
to dramatic kinds of illicit adaptation is well-documented in clinical case-
histories and often set forth in insightful fiction. Defiant outbreaks not infrequently follow upon prolonged periods of over-compliance.[36] But though
the psychodynamic mechanisms of this type of adaptation have been fairly
well identified and linked with patterns of discipline and socialization in the
family, much sociological research is still required to explain why these patterns are presumably more frequent in certain social strata and groups than
in others. Our own discussion has merely set out one analytical framework
for sociological research focused on this problem.

IV. Retreatism. Just as Adaptation I (conformity) remains the most frequent, Adaptation IV (the rejection of cultural goals and institutional means)
is probably the least common. People who adapt (or maladapt) in this fashion
are, strictly speaking, *in* the society but not *of* it. Sociologically, these constitute the true aliens. Not sharing the common frame of values, they can be
included as members of the *society* (in distinction from the *population*) only
in fictional sense.

In this category fall some of the adaptive activities of psychotics, autists,
pariahs, outcasts, vagrants, vagabonds, tramps, chronic drunkards and drug
addicts.[37] They have relinquished culturally prescribed goals and their behavior does not accord with institutional norms. This is not to say that in
some cases the source of their mode of adaptation is not the very social
structure which they have in effect repudiated nor that their very existence
within an area does not constitute a problem for members of the society.

From the standpoint of its sources in the social structure, this mode of
adaptation is most likely to occur when *both* the cultural goals and the institutional practices have been thoroughly assimilated by the individual and

imbued with affect and high value, but accessible institutional avenues are not productive of success. There results a twofold conflict: the interiorized moral obligation for adopting institutional means conflicts with pressures to resort to illicit means (which may attain the goal) and the individual is shut off from means which are both legitimate and effective. The competitive order is maintained but the frustrated and handicapped individual who cannot cope with this order drops out. Defeatism, quietism and resignation are manifested in escape mechanisms which ultimately lead him to "escape" from the requirements of the society. It is thus an expedient which arises from continued failure to near the goal by legitimate measures and from an inability to use the illegitimate route because of internalized prohibitions, *this process occurring while the supreme value of the success-goal has not yet been renounced*. The conflict is resolved by abandoning *both* precipitating elements, the goals and the means. The escape is complete, the conflict is eliminated and the individual is asocialized.

In public and ceremonial life, this type of deviant behavior is most heartily condemned by conventional representatives of the society. In contrast to the conformist, who keeps the wheels of society running, this deviant is a non-productive liability; in contrast to the innovator who is at least "smart" and actively striving, he sees no value in the success-goal which the culture prizes so highly; in contrast to the ritualist who conforms at least to the mores, he pays scant attention to the institutional practices.

Nor does the society lightly accept these repudiations of its values. To do so would be to put these values into question. Those who have abandoned the quest for success are relentlessly pursued to their haunts by a society insistent upon having all its members orient themselves to success-striving. Thus, in the heart of Chicago's Hobohemia are the book stalls filled with wares designed to revitalize dead aspirations.

The Gold Coast Book Store is in the basement of an old residence, built back from the street, and now sandwiched between two business blocks. The space in front is filled with stalls, and striking placards and posters.

These posters advertise such books as will arrest the attention of the down-and-out. One reads: ". . . Men in thousands pass this spot daily, but the majority of them are not financially successful. They are never more than two jumps ahead of the rent men. Instead of that, they should be more bold and daring," "Getting Ahead of the Game," before old age withers them and casts them on the junk heap of human wrecks. If you want to escape this evil fate—the fate of the vast majority of men—come in and get a copy of *The Law of Financial Success*. It will put some new ideas in your head, and put you on the highroad to success. 35 cents.

There are always men loitering before its stalls. But they seldom buy. Success comes high, even at thirty-five cents, to the hobo.[38]

But if this deviant is condemned in real life, he may become a source of gratification in fantasy-life. Thus Kardiner has advanced the speculation that such figures in contemporary folklore and popular culture bolster "morale and self-esteem by the spectacle of man rejecting current ideals and expressing contempt for them." The prototype in the films is of course Charlie Chaplin's bum.

He is Mr. Nobody and is very much aware of his own insignificance. He is always the butt of a crazy and bewildering world in which he has no place and from which he constantly runs away into a contented do-nothingness. *He is free from conflict because he has abandoned the quest for security and prestige, and is resigned to the lack of any claim to virtue or distinction.* [A precise characterological portrait of Adaptation IV.] He always becomes involved in the world by accident. There he encounters evil and aggression against the weak and helpless which he has no power to combat. Yet always, in spite of himself, he becomes the champion of the wronged and oppressed, not by virtue of his great organizing ability but by virtue of homely and insolent trickiness by which he seeks out the weakness of the wrongdoer. He always remains humble, poor, and lonely, but is contemptuous of the incomprehensible world and its values. He therefore represents the character of our time who is *perplexed by the dilemma either of being crushed in the struggle to achieve the socially approved goals of success and power* (he achieves it only once—in *The Gold Rush*) or of *succumbing to a hopeless resignation and flight from them.* Charlie's bum is a great comfort in that he gloats in his ability to outwit the pernicious forces aligned against him if he chooses to do so and affords every man the satisfaction of feeling that the ultimate flight from social goals to loneliness is an act of *choice* and not a symptom of his defeat. Mickey Mouse is a continuation of the Chaplin saga.[39]

This fourth mode of adaptation, then, is that of the socially disinherited who if they have none of the rewards held out by society also have few of the frustrations attendant upon continuing to seek these rewards. It is, moreover, a privatized rather than a collective mode of adaptation. Although people exhibiting this deviant behavior may gravitate toward centers where they come into contact with other deviants and although they may come to share in the subculture of these deviant groups, their adaptations are largely private and isolated rather than unified under the aegis of a new cultural code. The type of collective adaptation remains to be considered.

V. Rebellion. This adaptation leads men outside the environing social structure to envisage and seek to bring into being a new, that is to say, a greatly modified social structure. It presupposes alienation from reigning goals and standards. These come to be regarded as purely arbitrary. And the arbitrary is precisely that which can neither exact allegiance nor possess legitimacy, for it might as well be otherwise. In our society, organized movements for rebellion apparently aim to introduce a social structure in which the cultural standards of success would be sharply modified and provision would be made for a closer correspondence between merit, effort and reward.

But before examining "rebellion" as a mode of adaptation, we must distinguish it from a superficially similar but essentially different type, *ressentiment.* Introduced in a special technical sense, by Nietzsche, the concept of *ressentiment* was taken up and developed sociologically by Max Scheler.[40] This complex sentiment has three interlocking elements. First, diffuse feelings of hate, envy and hostility; second, a sense of being powerless to express these feelings actively against the person or social stratum evoking them; and third, a continual re-experiencing of this impotent hostility.[41] The essential point distinguishing *ressentiment* from rebellion is that the former does not involve a genuine change in values. *Ressentiment* involves a sour-grapes pattern which asserts merely that desired but unattainable objectives do not actually embody the prized values—after all, the fox in the fable does not say that he abandons all taste for sweet grapes; he says only that these particular grapes are not sweet. Rebellion, on the other hand, involves a genuine transvaluation, where the direct or vicarious experience of frustration leads to full denunciation of previously prized values—the rebellious fox simply renounces the prevailing taste for sweet grapes. In *ressentiment,* one condemns what one secretly craves; in rebellion, one condemns the craving itself. But though the two are distinct, organized rebellion may draw upon a vast reservoir of the resentful and discontented as institutional dislocations become acute.

When the institutional system is regarded as the barrier to the satisfaction of legitimized goals, the stage is set for rebellion as an adaptive response. To pass into organized political action, allegiance must not only be withdrawn from the prevailing social structure but must be transferred to new groups possessed of a new myth.[42] The dual function of the myth is to locate the source of large-scale frustrations in the social structure and to portray an alternative structure which would not, presumably, give rise to frustration of the deserving. It is a charter for action. In this context, the functions of the counter-myth of the conservatives—briefly sketched in an earlier section of this chapter—become further clarified: whatever the source of mass frustration, it is not to be found in the basic structure of the society. The conservative myth may thus assert that these frustrations are in the nature of things and would occur in *any* social system: "Periodic mass unemployment and business depressions can't be legislated out of existence; it's just like a person who feels good one day and bad the next."[43] Or, if not the doctrine of inevitability, then the doctrine of gradual and slight adjustment: "A few changes here and there, and we'll have things running as ship-shape as they can possibly be." Or, the doctrine which deflects hostility from the social structure onto the individual who is a "failure" since "every man really gets what's coming to him in this country."

The myths of rebellion and of conservatism both work toward a "monopoly of the imagination" seeking to define the situation in such terms as to move the frustrate toward or away from Adaptation V. It is above all the renegade who, though himself successful, renounces the prevailing values that becomes the target of greatest hostility among those in rebellion. For he not only puts the values in question, as does the out-group, but he signifies that the unity of the group is broken.[44] Yet, as has so often been noted, it is typically members of a rising class rather than the most depressed strata who organize the resentful and the rebellious into a revolutionary group.

THE STRAIN TOWARD ANOMIE

The social structure we have examined produces a strain toward anomie and deviant behavior. The pressure of such a social order is upon outdoing one's competitors. So long as the sentiments supporting this competitive system are distributed throughout the entire range of activities and are not confined to the final result of "success," the choice of means will remain largely within the ambit of institutional control. When, however, the cultural emphasis shifts from the satisfactions deriving from competition itself to almost exclusive concern with the outcome, the resultant stress makes for the breakdown of the regulatory structure. With this attenuation of institutional controls, there occurs an approximation to the situation erroneously held by the utilitarian philosophers to be typical of society, a situation in which calculations of personal advantage and fear of punishment are the only regulating agencies.

This strain toward anomie does not operate evenly throughout the society. Some effort has been made in the present analysis to suggest the strata most vulnerable to the pressures for deviant behavior and to set forth some of the mechanisms operating to produce those pressures. For purposes of simplifying the problem, monetary success was taken as the major cultural goal, although there are, of course, alternative goals in the repository of common values. The realms of intellectual and artistic achievement, for example, provide alternative career patterns which may not entail large pecuniary rewards. To the extent that the cultural structure attaches prestige to these alternatives and the social structure permits access to them, the system is somewhat stabilized. Potential deviants may still conform in terms of these auxiliary sets of values.

But the central tendencies toward anomie remain, and it is to these that the analytical scheme here set forth calls particular attention.

The Role of the Family. A final word should be said drawing together the implications scattered throughout the foregoing discussion concerning the role played by the family in these patterns of deviant behavior.

It is the family, of course, which is a major transmission belt for the diffusion of cultural standards to the oncoming generation. But what has until lately been overlooked is that the family largely transmits that portion of the culture accessible to the social stratum and groups in which the parents find themselves. It is, therefore, a mechanism for disciplining the child in terms of the cultural goals and mores characteristic of this narrow range of groups. Nor is the socialization confined to direct training and disciplining. The process is, at least in part, inadvertent. Quite apart from direct admonitions, rewards and punishments, the child is exposed to social prototypes in the witnessed daily behavior and casual conversations of parents. Not infrequently, *children detect and incorporate cultural uniformities even when these remain implicit and have not been reduced to rules.*

Language patterns provide the most impressive evidence, readily observable in clinical fashion, that children, in the process of socialization, detect uniformities which have not been explicitly formulated for them by elders or contemporaries and which are not formulated by the children themselves. Persistent errors of language among children are most instructive. Thus, the child will spontaneously use such words as "mouses" or "moneys," *even though he has never heard such terms or been taught "the rule for forming plurals."* Or he will create such words as "falled," "runned," "singed," "hitted," though he has not been taught, at the age of three, "rules" of conjugation. Or, he will refer to a choice morsel as "gooder" than another less favored, or perhaps through a logical extension, he may describe it as "goodest" of all. Obviously, he has detected the implicit paradigms for the expression of plurality, for the conjugation of verbs, and the inflection of adjectives. The very nature of his error and misapplication of the paradigm testifies to this.[45]

It may be tentatively inferred, therefore, that he is also busily engaged in *detecting and acting upon the implicit paradigms of cultural evaluation, and categorization of people and things, and the formation of estimable goals* as well as assimilating the explicit cultural orientation set forth in an endless stream of commands, explanations and exhortations by parents. It would appear that in addition to the important researches of the depth psychologies on the socialization process, there is need for supplementary types of direct observation of culture diffusion with the family. It may well be that the child retains the implicit paradigm of cultural values detected in the day-by-day behavior of his parents even when this conflicts with their explicit advice and exhortations.

The projection of parental ambitions onto the child is also centrally relevant to the subject in hand. As is well known, many parents confronted with personal "failure" or limited "success" may mute their original goal-emphasis and may defer further efforts to reach the goal, attempting to reach it vicariously through their children. "The influence may come through the mother or the father. Often it is the case of a parent who hopes that the child will attain heights that he or she failed to attain."[46] In a recent research on the social organization of public housing developments, we have found among both Negroes and Whites on lower occupational levels, a substantial proportion having aspirations for a professional career for their children.[47] Should this finding be confirmed by further research it will have large bearing upon the problem in hand. For if compensatory projection of parental ambition onto children is widespread, then it is precisely those parents least able to provide free access to opportunity for their children—the "failures" and "frustrates"—who exert great pressure upon their children for high achievement. And this syndrome of lofty aspirations and limited realistic opportunities, as we have seen, is precisely the pattern which invites deviant behavior. This clearly points to the need for investigation focused upon occupational goal-formation in the several social strata if the inadvertent role of family disciplining in deviant behavior is to be understood from the perspectives of our analytical scheme.

CONCLUDING REMARKS

It should be apparent that the foregoing discussion is not pitched on a moralistic plane. Whatever the sentiments of the reader concerning the moral desirability of coördinating the goals-and-means phases of the social structure, it is clear that imperfect coördination of the two leads to anomie. In so far as one of the most general functions of social structure is to provide a basis for predictability and regularity of social behavior, it becomes increasingly limited in effectiveness as these elements of the social structure become dissociated. At the extreme, predictability is minimized and what may be properly called anomie or cultural chaos supervenes.

This essay on the structural sources of deviant behavior remains but a prelude. It has not included a detailed treatment of the structural elements which predispose toward one rather than another of the alternative responses open to individuals living in an ill-balanced social structure; it has largely neglected but not denied the relevance of the social-psychological processes determining the specific incidence of these responses; it has only briefly considered the social functions fulfilled by deviant behavior; it has not put the explanatory power of the analytical scheme to full empirical test by determining group variations in deviant and conformist behavior; it has only touched upon rebellious behavior which seeks to refashion the social framework.

It is suggested that these and related problems may be advantageously analyzed by use of this scheme.

CONTINUITIES IN THE THEORY
OF SOCIAL STRUCTURE AND ANOMIE

Robert K. Merton

RECENT YEARS have seen the appearance of a sizable sociological literature which bears upon one or another aspect of anomie. This provides an enlarged basis for clarifying and extending the formulations set out in the preceding paper. Interest in the concept of anomie has indeed grown rapidly enough for it to become (almost inevitably) vulgarized as it diffuses to wider and wider social circles. As one example of vulgarization, consider the case of the news-weekly which seizes upon a sober and careful inquiry by Gerhart Niemeyer into the social consequences of anomie and promptly imbues the account with 'reader appeal' by beginning in these folksy and shrill terms: " 'Boy, that's what I call acute anomie," whistled Bleecker Totten, one of 225 students at Oglethorpe University."[1] Less sibilant but more instructive are the theoretical, substantive, and procedural studies of anomie now to be examined.

THE EXTENDED CONCEPT OF ANOMIE

As initially developed by Durkheim, the concept of anomie referred to a condition of relative normlessness in a society or group. Durkheim made it clear that this concept referred to a property of the social and cultural structure, not to a property of individuals confronting that structure. Nevertheless, as the utility of the concept for understanding diverse forms of deviant behavior became evident, it was extended to refer to a condition of individuals rather than of their environment.

This psychological conception of anomie has been simultaneously formulated by R. M. MacIver and by David Riesman. Since their formulations are substantially alike, what is said of one may be said of both.

"Anomy"—MacIver is resurrecting the sixteenth-century and long obsolete spelling of the word—"signifies the *state of mind* of one who has been pulled up by his moral roots, who has no longer any standards but only disconnected urges, who has no longer any sense of continuity, of folk, of obligation. The anomic man has become spiritually sterile, responsive only to himself, responsible to no one. He derides the values of other men. His only faith is the philosophy of denial. He lives on the thin line of sensation between no future and no past." And again: "Anomy is a *state of mind* in which the individual's sense of social cohesion—the mainspring of his morale—is broken or fatally weakened."[2]

As has been noted, "MacIver's approach is thus psychological (i.e., anomie is for him a state of *mind,* not a state of society—though the state of mind may reflect social tensions), and his psychological types [of anomie] correspond to the elements (anxiety-isolation-purposeless) which form the

Reprinted from *Social Theory and Social Structure,* revised and enlarged edition (1957), pp. 161-94, by permission of the author and the publisher. (Copyright, 1957, by The Free Press.)

subjective aspect of Durkheim's concept."[3] That the psychological concept of anomie has a definite referent, that it refers to identifiable "states of mind" of particular individuals, is beyond question, as the crowded casebooks of psychiatrists attest. But the psychological concept is nevertheless a counterpart of the sociological concept of anomie, and not a substitute for it.

The sociological concept of anomie, as developed in the preceding pages, [Social Structure and Anomie] presupposes that the salient environment of individuals can be usefully thought of as involving the cultural structure, on the one hand, and the social structure, on the other. It assumes that, however intimately connected these in fact are, they must be kept separate for purposes of analysis before they are brought together again. In this connection, cultural structure may be defined as that organized set of normative values governing behavior which is common to members of a designated society or group. And by social structure is meant that organized set of social relationships in which members of the society or group are variously implicated. Anomie is then conceived as a breakdown in the cultural structure, occurring particularly when there is an acute disjunction between the cultural norms and goals and the socially structured capacities of members of the group to act in accord with them. In this conception, cultural values may help to produce behavior which is at odds with the mandates of the values themselves.

On this view, the social structure strains the cultural values, making action in accord with them readily possible for those occupying certain statuses within the society and difficult or impossible for others. The social structure acts as a barrier or as an open door to the acting out of cultural mandates. When the cultural and the social structure are malintegrated, the first calling for behavior and attitudes which the second precludes, there is a strain toward the breakdown of the norms, toward normlessness. It does not follow, of course, that this is the sole process making for the social condition of anomie; further theory and research are directed toward searching out other patterned sources of a high degree of anomie.

An effort has been made to catch up the psychological and sociological concepts in a distinction between "simple" and "acute" anomie.[4] Simple anomie refers to the state of confusion in a group or society which is subject to conflict between value-systems, resulting in some degree of uneasiness and a sense of separation from the group; acute anomie, to the deterioration and, at the extreme, the disintegration of value-systems, which results in marked anxieties. This has the merit of terminologically ear-marking the often stated but sometimes neglected fact that, like other conditions of society, anomie varies in degree and perhaps in kind.

Having identified some of the processes conducing to anomie, the preceding chapter sets out a typology of adaptive responses to this condition and the structural pressures making for a greater or less frequency of each of these responses among the several strata of the class structure. The underlying premise here is that class strata are not only differentially subject to anomie but are differentially subject to one or another type of response to it. Talcott Parsons has taken up this typology and has derived it, in motivational terms, from his conceptual scheme of social interaction.[5] This analysis proceeds from the assumption that neither tendencies toward deviant behavior nor tendencies toward reequilibration of a system of social interaction can develop at random; instead, they work out in one or more of a limited number of identifiable directions. This is to say, that deviant behavior is itself patterned.

In the words of Parsons and Bales, "Deviance was shown to involve four basic directions, according to whether the need to express alienation from the normative pattern—including the repudiation of attachment to alter as an object—or to maintain compulsive conformity with the normative pattern and attachment to alter, and according to whether the mode of action was actively or passively inclined. This yielded four directional types, those of aggressiveness and withdrawal on the alienative side, and of compulsive performance and compulsive acceptance, on the side of compulsive conformity. It was furthermore shown that this paradigm, independently derived, is essentially the same as that previously put forward by Merton for the analysis of social structure and anomie."[6]

This first extension of the typology of response, it will be noted, continues to take account of *both* the cultural structure—"the normative pattern"—and the social structure—patterned attachments to other people or alienation from them. It goes on, however, to characterize the types of response in terms of their being either active or passive, meaning by this that the deviant behavior can involve either actively " 'taking the situation in hand,' doing more in attempting to control it than the [institutionalized] expectations" call for, or passively "falling short of asserting the degree of active control" required by these expectations. The types of deviant behavior can be further subdivided by distinguishing between cases in which the strains are primarily in the social relations with others or in the cultural norms with which conformity is expected.[7] Such concrete manifestations of reaction to anomic strains as delinquency, crime, and suicide, as well as such conceptually intermediate types of responses as innovation, ritualism, retreatism and rebellion thus become classifiable as resultants of certain abstract properties of interaction systems identified by Parsons. Having been developed so recently, this more complex classification of types of deviant behavior has yet to be extensively utilized in empirical investigations.

INDICATORS OF ANOMIE

Like many of us who have tried to follow in his large footsteps and consequently wobble a bit in these excessively spacious areas, Durkheim did not afford explicit and methodical guidance to the various signs of anomie, to the observables of normlessness and deteriorated social relationships. Yet it is plain that indicators must be developed if the concept of anomie is to be utilized in empirical research.

A step in this direction has been taken by Leo Srole in developing a preliminary "scale of anomie."[8] In part, the scale incorporates items referring to the individual's perception of his social environment; in part, to his perception of his own place within that environment. More specifically, the five items comprising this preliminary scale refer to (1) the perception that community-leaders are indifferent to one's needs; (2) the perception that little can be accomplished in the society which is seen as basically unpredictable and lacking order; (3) the perception that life-goals are receding rather than being realized; (4) a sense of futility; and (5) the conviction that one cannot count on personal associates for social and psychological support.[9] As Srole indicates in some detail, this effort to develop a scale of anomie has various limitations and some inadequacies, but it does furnish a beginning toward a standardized measure of anomie, as perceived and experienced by individuals in a group or community.

This scale can be taken to measure anomie as *subjectively* experienced; manifestly needed is a further measure of anomie, as an *objective* condition of group life. A symptomatic advance toward this latter type of measure has been made by Bernard Lander.[10] Through factor analysis of eight properties of census tracts in an American city, he has identified two clusters of variables, one of which he designates as "an *anomic* factor." By this he means that this cluster of variables—having the values of a high delinquency rate, a large percentage of non-white residents in the area and a small percentage of dwellings occupied by the owner—seems, on inspection, to characterize areas of relative normlessness and social instability. As Lander is the first to recognize, the anomic factor is at best only roughly measured by this particular cluster of variables. Its decisive limitation derives from a circumstance which regularly confronts sociologists seeking to devise measures of theoretical concepts by drawing upon the array of social data which *happen* to be recorded in the statistical series established by agencies of the society—namely, the circumstance that these data of social bookkeeping which happen to be on hand are not necessarily the data which best measure the concept. That is why I have described Lander's ingenious effort as a "symptomatic" rather than a decisive advance. For just as the mere availability of official statistics constrained Durkheim to employ such rough, indirect and highly provisional measures of anomie as occupational status, marital status and family disintegration (divorce), so the fortuity that census tract records in Baltimore include data on delinquency, racial composition and house-ownership led Lander to use these as a rough, indirect and highly provisional measure of anomie. Pragmatic considerations of this sort are of course no suitable alternative to theoretically derived indicators of the concept. Turnover in residence may be an indirect measure of the rate of breakdown in established social relationships, but it is evident that the measure would be substantially improved if provision were made to obtain data directly on rates of disrupted social relationships. And so with the other objective components of anomie, conceived as both normative and relational breakdown. This is no mere counsel of unattainable perfection. It merely states, what is abundantly evident, that just as scales of the subjective aspects of anomie must be further improved, so must scales of its objective aspects. The utilization of available social-bookkeeping data is only a pragmatically enforced and interim substitute.

Growing out of the conception of both subjective and objective components of anomie is the further evident requirements that research on the sources and consequences of anomie deal *simultaneously* with the interaction of the two types of components. Concretely and illustratively, this means that the behavior of "anomic" and "eunomic" *individuals* within groups having a designated degree of objective anomie could be systematically compared, just as the behavior of individuals of the same type could be examined in groups with varying degrees of anomie. This kind of research plainly constitutes the next step forward in the study of anomie.[11]

Recent theoretical and procedural contributions have thus somewhat clarified the concept of anomie and have begun to fashion the tools needed for its systematic study. Other substantive contributions have lately appeared which have direct bearing on one or another part of the structural and functional analysis of anomie set forth in the preceding paper.

THE SUCCESS-THEME IN AMERICAN CULTURE

It will be remembered that we have considered the emphasis on monetary success as *one* dominant theme in American culture, and have traced the strains which it differentially imposes upon those variously located in the social structure. This was not to say, of course—as was repeatedly indicated—that the disjunction between cultural goals and institutionally legitimate means derives only from *this* extreme goal-emphasis. The theory holds that *any* extreme emphasis upon achievement—whether this be scientific productivity, accumulation of personal wealth or, by a small stretch of the imagination, the conquests of a Don Juan—will attenuate conformity to the institutional norms governing behavior designed to achieve the particular form of "success," especially among those who are socially disadvantaged in the competitive race. It is the conflict between cultural goals and the availability of using institutional means—whatever the character of the goals—which produces a strain toward anomie.[12]

The goal of monetary success was selected for illustrative analysis on the assumption that it, in particular, has been firmly entrenched in American culture. An array of studies in history and historical sociology has recently lent further support to that widely-held assumption. In his detailed monograph on the American gospel of economic success through self-help—the achievement motif—Irvin Gordon Wyllie has shown that, although "success" has of course been diversely defined in American culture (and variously among the several social strata), no other definition "enjoys such universal favor in America as that which equates success with making money."[13]

This heavy accent on financial success is of course not peculiar to Americans. Max Weber's analytical and long-standing observation is still much in point: "The impulse to acquisition, pursuit of gain, of money, of the greatest possible amount of money, has in itself nothing to do with capitalism [and, in the present instance, with the specifically American culture]. This impulse exists and has existed among waiters, physicians, coachmen, artists, prostitutes, dishonest officials, soldiers, nobles, crusaders, gamblers and beggars. One may say that it has been common to all sorts and conditions of men at all times and in all countries of the earth, wherever the objective possibility of it is or has been given."[14]

But what makes American culture relatively distinctive in this regard and what was taken as central to the analysis of this case in the foregoing chapter is that this is "a society which places a high premium on economic affluence and social ascent for *all* its members." As a success-primer of the late nineteenth century admirably pictured this cultural belief: "The road to fortune, like the public turnpike, is open alike to the children of the beggar, and the descendant of kings. There are tolls to be paid by all, yet all have rights, and it only remains for us to avail ourselves of these."[15] The distinctive nature of this cultural doctrine is twofold: first, striving for success is not a matter of individuals *happening* to have acquisitive impulses, rooted in human nature, but is a socially-defined expectation, and second, this patterned expectation is regarded as appropriate for everyone, irrespective of his initial lot or station in life. Not, of course, that identical standards of achievement are concretely exacted of everyone in the society; the nature and extent of this movement up the economic ladder can become differently defined among the several social strata. But the prevailing cultural orientations assign great emphasis to this form of success and hold it appropriate that all should strive for it. (As we shall soon see, this is far removed from the empirical proposition that the same proportions of people in all social classes in fact accept this cultural emphasis and assimilate it into their personal value-structure.) It is only that in pulpit and in press, in fiction and in motion pictures, in the course of formal education and of informal socialization, in the various public and private communications which come to the attention of Americans, there is a comparatively marked emphasis on the moral obligation as well as the factual possibility of striving for monetary success, and of achieving it.

As Wyllie shows, inspirational lectures in lyceums, mercantile library associations and business colleges and a large library of success-manuals insistently propagated this theme. This is further documented by what amounts to a series of content-analyses of widely-read novels, of endlessly reprinted primers used in grammar schools throughout the land, and of the values reaffirmed in the obituaries of some of America's most famous men of business. Kenneth S. Lynn traces the pervasive theme of rags-to-riches in the novels of Theodore Dreiser, Jack London, David Graham Phillips, Frank Norris and Robert Herrick. The enduring presence of the same theme in the seemingly inexhaustible series of McGuffey readers is demonstrated by Richard D. Mosier.[16] And in *The Reputation of the American Businessman*,[17] Sigmund Diamond analyzes a large array of obituaries, those depositories of moral sentiment, published after the death of Stephen Girard, John Jacob Astor, Cornelius Vanderbuilt, J. P. Morgan, John D. Rockefeller, and Henry Ford and detects the theme that as long as a man "has the requisite qualities, success will be his at any time in any place, under any circumstances."

This cultural theme not only holds that monetary success is possible for all, irrespective of station, and that striving for success is incumbent on all, but, on occasion, that the seeming disadvantages of poverty are actually advantages for, in the words of Henry Ward Beecher, it is " 'the hard but kind bosom of Poverty, who says to them, 'Work!' and, working, makes them men.' "[18]

This leads naturally to the subsidiary theme that success or failure are results wholly of personal qualities; that he who fails has only himself to blame, for the corollary to the concept of the self-made man is the self-unmade man. To the extent that this cultural definition is assimilated by those who have not made their mark, failure represents a double defeat: the manifest defeat of remaining far behind in the race for success and the implicit defeat of not having the capacities and moral stamina needed for success. Whatever the objective truth or falsity of the doctrine in any particular instance, and it is important that this cannot be readily discovered, the prevailing definition exacts a psychic toll of those who do not measure up. It is in this cultural setting that, in a significant proportion of cases, the threat of defeat motivates men to the use of those tactics, beyond the law or the mores, which promise "success."

The moral mandate to achieve success thus exerts pressure to succeed, by fair means if possible and by foul means if necessary. The moral norms of course continue to reiterate the rules of the game and to call for "fair play," even while behavior departs from the norm. On occasion, however, even success-manuals urge men "to 'go in and win' by making use of all available means of scrambling ahead of competitors," as in the understandably anonymous tract of 1878, *How to Become Rich*. And, "in the period between 1880 and 1914, Populists, single-taxers, muckrakers, and Socialists looked behind the moral façade of business to examine the practice. What they found scarcely squared with the wealth-through-virtue theme. Their findings were not entirely new, for skeptics had long suspected that something other than virtue might be involved in the making of money. What was new was the documentation—concrete evidence that the greatest barons were robber barons, men who made their way by corrupting legislatures, appropriating resources, organizing monopolies, and crushing competitors."[19]

These recent studies thus confirm what has often been noticed before: that an extreme cultural emphasis on the goal of success attenuates conformity to institutionally prescribed methods of moving toward this goal. "Ambition" comes to approximate the meaning of its etymological origins: "to run around" and not only in the form practiced by the little politicians of ancient Rome who solicited votes from one and all in their "precincts" and used all manner of devices to ensure a plenty of appropriate votes. It is in this way that the culturally established goal moves toward sanctifying all those means which enable one to attain it. This is what was meant in the foregoing essay by the process of "demoralization," in which norms are robbed of their power to regulate behavior, and the "normlessness" component of anomie ensues.

This process making for anomie need not, however, continue unimpeded. Under conditions still to be identified, countervailing tendencies may develop. To some degree, to judge from the historical record, this may have occurred in American society. The cultural emphasis on success-open-to-all has become qualified, partly, it may be, in response to cumulative recognition of the actual structure of opportunity and partly in response to the occasionally observed demoralizing consequences of the unqualified theme. This is to say that, although the original theme persists, it is occasionally hedged in by qualifications advising some to lower their aspirations. That popular missionary of the gospel of success, Orison Swett Marden, advises his readers: " 'The fact is that most of us can never hope to be rich.' " A handbook of success, published at the turn of the century, offers a philosophy of consolation which re-defines success: "It is just as much to be a common soldier in the ranks as to be a general that leads. We cannot all be generals. If you are a good soldier in a select crowd, and have a good reputation, that is success in itself." Even such a journal as the *American Banker* finds it possible to assert that "only a few of us that share the common lot are destined to accumulate great wealth, or achieve conspicuous stations. The number of such stations and the chances for such accumulations never did correspond, and never will, to the number of energetic, ambitious and capable men which is hopeful of achieving them. This unpalatable truth the literature of success abhors."[20]

But though these doctrines, accommodating to the visible facts of the case, find periodic expression and provide a rationale for slow and limited ascent in the economic hierarchy, Wyllie and other recent students of the subject indicate that they are still only secondary emphases in the culture of the time. To a considerable extent, the success-theme still dominates in the public communications of American culture.

But if the communications addressed to generations of Americans continue to reiterate the gospel of success, it does not follow that Americans in all groups, regions and class strata have uniformly assimilated this set of values. There is no swift and unbroken passage from the values expressed in the popular culture to the values by which men actually live. It would be equally mistaken, however, to assume that the two are wholly unrelated simply because they are not identical. It is a matter for inquiry, not a matter of supposition, to find out how widely the values under examination have been assimilated. That is why, in "Social Structure and Anomie," it was said that "among the problems calling for further research [is] the following: the extent to which Americans in different social strata have in fact assimilated the *same* culturally induced goals and values. . . ." This problem can be further clarified by examining research which has been focused on it.

DIFFERENTIALS IN ASSIMILATION OF SUCCESS-VALUES

In a recent paper, Herbert H. Hyman has addressed himself to the problem of collating and re-analyzing data available in public opinion surveys which bear directly or tangentially on the distribution of success-values among economic and social strata.[21] As he first puts the general issue, "It is clear that Merton's analysis assumes that the cultural goal is in actuality internalized by lower class individuals." In view of the data which are subsequently presented, it becomes essential to state this assumption more clearly by qualifying it: the analysis assumes that *some* individuals in the lower economic and social strata actually adopt the success-goal. For, after all, the analysis holds not that *all* or *most* members of the lower strata are subject to pressure toward nonconformist behavior of the various kinds set out in the typology of adaptation, but only that *more* of them are subject to this pressure than of those in the higher strata. On the hypothesis under review, deviant behavior is still the subsidiary pattern and conformity the modal pattern. It is therefore sufficient that a *sizable minority* of the lower strata assimilate this goal for them to be differentially subject to this pressure as a result of their relatively smaller opportunities to achieve monetary success.

Hyman further prefaces his paper by observing that "what is obviously required is empirical evidence on *the degree to which individuals in different strata* value the culturally prescribed goal of success, believe that opportunity is available to them, and hold other values which would aid or hinder them in their attempts to move towards their goal. This paper, in a preliminary way, is thus complementary to Merton's theoretical analysis."[22] Here again, if the data in hand are to be appropriately connected with the hypothesis, the statement must be qualified. It is true that the analysis calls for empirical evidence on "the degree to which individuals in different strata" set store by the success-goal; patently, the success-value will provide little by way of motivation unless they are significantly committed to it. As it happens, the survey data available to Hyman do not discriminate between the *degrees* of commitment to the goal but indicate only the relative *frequency* with which individuals in the samples drawn from the several social strata express some unknown degree of acceptance of the success-goal and of related values. From the outset, then, it appears that subsequent inquiry might be usefully directed toward studying the intensity as well as the extent to which these values are held in diverse groups, social strata, and communities.

We should take note, then, that the hypothesis of the foregoing chapter requires that an appreciable minority, not all or most, of those in the lower social strata will have assimilated the cultural mandate for monetary success, and that it presupposes affectively significant assimilation of this value rather than merely verbal acquiescence with it. These two qualifications provide a context for locating the theoretical implications of the empirical evidence brought together in Hyman's germane and compact paper.

By and large, the array of evidence, which is not reviewed here in full detail since it is readily accessible, uniformly shows *differentials* in the *proportions* of both adults and youth in the lower, middle and upper social strata who are positively oriented toward occupational success and toward established means for aiding the achievement of such success. For example: one national survey of opinion in the late nineteen-thirties found class differentials in the belief in occupational opportunity as registered by responses to the question: "Do you think that today any young man with thrift, ability and ambition has the opportunity to rise in the world, own his own home, and earn $5000 a year?" Among "the prosperous," 53% affirmed the belief that this was so, compared with what Hyman describes as "only" 31% among "the poor."[23] Another national survey found 63% of professional and executive employees expressing their belief that the years ahead held a good chance for advancing beyond their present position, in comparison with 48% of factory workers; furthermore, 58% of the first aggregate of more highly placed employees maintained that harder work would net them a promotion, while 40% of the second aggregate of manual workers held this optimistic view.

To these data, cited by Hyman, can be added others, drawn from a sociological study of white and Negro residents in a low-rent housing development.[24] These 500 residents, at different levels within the lower reaches of the occupational hierarchy, set out their appraisals of opportunity for advancement, in their occupation at large, and in their own workplace in particular.[25] Three significant patterns of appraisal emerge. First, there is a pattern of mounting optimism about the chances for "getting ahead" in the occupation at large at each successively higher level in this modest hierarchy of jobs. It is as though the sheer existence of others in occupational strata lower than one's own supports the conviction that ascent up the ladder is possible, for one *is,* after all, in a relatively higher stratum. Among Negroes in white-collar or skilled jobs, 63% believe that the chances for advancement in their occupation are good or fair, compared with 44% of those in semi-skilled jobs and 31% in unskilled or domestic service jobs. Though not as pronounced, the same pattern obtains among whites.

Second, much the same pattern, though with a significantly narrower range of variation, occurs in the estimates of chances prevailing in *their own* place of employment. The higher the job-level, the larger the proportion believing that chances for advancement in their place of work are good or fair. Among the Negroes, the percentages recording their optimism are respectively 43, 32 and 27; among the whites, 58, 47 and 44.

The third pattern in the appraisal of opportunity, however, definitely distinguishes the outlook of Negro and white workers as aggregates. White workers tend to see little difference between prospects in the occupation at large and in their own workplace: what they take to hold true in general they assume to hold true in their immediate surroundings. Among the Negro workers, particularly among those in the somewhat higher-status jobs, all this changes. However they estimate the opportunities in their occupation in general, they tend to be decidedly more pessimistic in appraising the opportunities where they themselves work. What these statistics of occupational expectation appear to show is the frequent conviction among Negro workers on each occupational level that they are barred from equitable access to advancement.

To this evidence on class and racial differentials in the belief in occupational opportunities can be added evidence, cited by Hyman, on class differentials in the value placed upon formal education as a means for enlarging the prospect of occupational success. For example: substantially larger proportions of the higher than of the lower social strata express the belief that "some college training" is required "to get along well in the world"; again, 91% of the "prosperous" individuals interviewed in one national survey, compared with 68% of the "poor" individuals expressed a preference that their children go on to college rather than take a job immediately after having been graduated from high school; further, 74% of a sample of teen-age boys from "wealthy and prosperous" families compared with 42% of those from "the lower class" preferred college education to a job as the sequel to graduation from high school; and finally, in this selection from the numerous data summarized by Hyman, 14% of high school youths from "poor" families stated a preference for a job that provided high income but great risk as compared with 31% of those from families of business executives or professional people.[26]

The available though still scanty evidence, then, consistently exhibits *differentials in the proportions* of the several social strata (and perhaps, of Negroes and whites) affirming the culturally patterned belief in opportunities for occupational success, aspiring to high-paying though risk-laden jobs and placing value upon higher education as a means for occupational advancement. But what Hyman fails to note, in his otherwise instructive and useful collation of the evidence, is that from the standpoint of the hypothesis advanced in the preceding paper, *it is not the relative proportions of the several social classes adopting the cultural goal of success that matter, but their absolute numbers.* To say that a larger *percentage* of the upper social and economic strata hold fast to the cultural goal of success is not to say that larger *numbers* of them than of lower-class people do so. Indeed, since the number of people in the topmost stratum identified in these studies is substantially smaller than the number in the lowest stratum, it is sometimes the case that *more* lower-class than upper-class people abide by this goal.

By centering almost exclusively[27] on the *comparative proportions* in the several social strata having one or another value-orientation—a matter which of course holds interest in its own right—Hyman fails to consider the facts most directly germane to the hypothesis under review. For, as has been repeatedly said, the hypothesis does not require that larger proportions or even larger numbers in the lower social strata be oriented toward the success-goal, but only that a *substantial number* be so oriented. For it is the *disjunction* between culturally induced high aspirations and socially structured obstacles to realization of these aspirations which is held to exert distinct pressure for deviant behavior. By a "substantial number," then, is meant a number sufficiently large to result in a more frequent *disjunction* between goals and opportunity among the lower-class strata than among the more advantaged upper-class strata. It may even be, though adequate empirical data on this are still wanting, that this disjunction is more frequent in the lower strata than in the middle strata, since the evidently larger number of middle-class Americans adopting the success-goal may include a sufficiently smaller proportion who are seriously impeded in their efforts to reach out toward this goal.

In any event, the fundamental analytical requirement is to distinguish systematically between the findings on relative proportions and on absolute numbers[28] in the several social classes accepting the cultural goal and to recognize that it is the frequency of disjunction between the goal and socially structured access to it which is of theoretical moment. Further research will have to solve the difficult problem of obtaining systematic data on *both* goals and on patterned access to opportunity and of analyzing these *jointly* to see whether the combination of lofty aspirations and small opportunity occurs with substantially different frequency in various social strata, groups, and communities and whether, in turn, these differentials are related to differing rates of deviant behavior. Schematically, this would call for data on *socially patterned differentials in*

1. *exposure* to the cultural goal and norms regulating behavior oriented toward that goal;
2. *acceptance* of the goal and norms as moral mandates and internalized values;
3. *relative accessibility to the goal:* life-chances in the opportunity-structure;
4. *the extent of discrepancy* between the accepted goal and its accessibility;
5. *the degree of anomie;* and
6. *the rates of deviant behavior* of the various kinds set out in the typology of modes of adaptation.

It is plainly no easy matter to assemble adequate data on all these distinct though related items. Until now, sociologists have had to work with avowedly rough and imperfect measures of almost all these variables—using the extent of formal education, for example, as an indicator of access to opportunity. But it is increasingly the case in sociology that once theoretically strategic variables have been identified, improved measures of them have been devised. There is a growing interplay between theory, which states the case for the significance of certain variables; methodology, which works out the logic of empirical inquiry involving these variables; and technique, which develops the tools and procedures for measuring the variables. As we have seen, definite beginnings have lately been made in developing measures of both the subjective and the objective components of anomie. It may not be too much to assume that these measures will continue to be improved, and that suitable measures of the other variables will be developed—in particular, improved measures of the still loosely-utilized but important concept of what Weber called "life-chances" in the opportunity-structure.

In this way, it will become possible to discover the social topography of anomie. It will become possible to locate the structural places in American society, for example, where the disjunction between the cultural values enjoining people to aim for certain goals and the patterned possibilities of living up to these values is at a maximum. Such inquiry would counter any unthinking tendency to assume that American society is uniformly riddled with anomie. It would search out, on the contrary, the statuses in the structure of American society which entail the greatest difficulty for people to live up to the normative requirements, for this is what is meant by saying that the disjunction between accepted norms and opportunities for socially rewarded conformity to these norms "exerts pressure" for deviant behavior and produces anomie.

Just as it is in point to identify the sources of differing degrees of anomie in different sectors of society, so it is in point to examine the varying adaptations to anomie and the forces making for one rather than another type of adaptation. A number of recent studies bear on this general problem.

ANOMIE AND FORMS OF DEVIANT BEHAVIOR

Innovation. The first form of deviant behavior identified in the typology set out in the preceding chapter was described as innovation. This, it may be remembered, refers to the rejection of institutional practices but the retention of cultural goals. This would seem to characterize a substantial part of the deviant behavior which has been accorded the greatest share of research attention—namely that which is loosely caught up in the blanket-concepts of "crime" and "delinquency." Since the law provides formal criteria of this form of deviance, it is relatively visible and readily becomes a focus for study. In contrast, other forms of behavior which are sociologically though not legally departures from accepted norms—what we have called "retreatism," for example—are less visible and receive little attention.

Several studies have lately indicated that the received concepts of "crime" and "delinquency" may serve to obscure rather than to clarify our understanding of the numerous variety of deviant behavior to which they refer. Aubert, for example, observes that "the legal definition of crime . . . probably [represents] little in common between all the phenomena covered by the concept. And the same seems to be true of white-collar crime. This type can also differ very much in its nature, and may need quite different causal explanations."[29]

In the course of assigning a term such as crime or delinquency to a class of behavior, there develops a tendency to attend primarily to the similarities —consequential or not—between the items of behavior encompassed in that class. Sociologically quite distinct forms of behavior by youngsters, for example, come to be designated by the generic term, "juvenile delinquency." This often carries with it the assumption that the wide diversity of behavior or the individuals engaging in one or another form of this behavior are of theoretically like kind. Yet, it is questionable that the behavior of the youngster who has purloined some baseball equipment is significantly similar to that of the youngster who periodically assaults members of an out-group.

Furthermore, the decision to encompass a wide array of behavior in the one rubric of crime or delinquency tends to lead to the assumption that a single theory will account for the entire range of behavior placed in this category. This is not too remote, in logical structure, from the assumption of a Benjamin Rush or a John Brown that there must be *a* theory of disease, rather than distinct theories of disease—of tuberculosis and arthritis, of Mèniere's syndrome and syphilis. Just as classifying enormously varied conditions and processes under the one heading of disease led some zealous medical systematists to believe that it was their task to evolve a single overarching theory of disease, so, it seems, the established idiom, both vernacular and scientific, of referring to "juvenile delinquency" as though it were a single entity, leads some to believe that there must be *a* basic theory of "its" causation. Perhaps this is enough to suggest what is meant by referring to crime or juvenile delinquency as a blanket-concept which may get in the way of theoretical formulations of the problem.

Once it is recognized that the behavior ordinarily described as criminal or delinquent is, from the sociological standpoint, quite varied and disparate, it becomes evident that theory under review does not purport to account for all such forms of deviant behavior. In his theoretically sensitive book, Albert K. Cohen suggests that this theory is "highly plausible as an explanation for adult professional crime and for the property delinquency of some older and semi-professional juvenile thieves. Unfortunately," he goes on to say, "it fails to account for the non-utilitarian quality of the subculture. . . . Were the participant in the delinquent subculture merely employing illicit means to the end of acquiring economic goods, he would show more respect for the goods he has thus acquired. Furthermore, the destructiveness, the versatility, the zest and the wholesale negativism which characterizes the delinquent subculture are beyond the purview of this theory."[30]

The first and major point made by Cohen commands assent and deserves reiteration. The foregoing theory of anomie is designed to account for some, not all, forms of deviant behavior customarily described as criminal or delinquent. The second point is important if it turns out to be true and, in any case, has the merit of focusing future inquiry on its implications. This is the point that the theory of social structure and anomie does not account for the "non-utilitarian" character of much of the behavior occurring in the delinquency-groups. But in exploring this matter further, it should be remembered, for purposes of theoretical clarity, that this theory does *not* maintain that the resulting deviant behavior is rationally calculated and utilitarian. Instead, it centers on the *acute* pressures created by the discrepancy between culturally induced goals and socially structured opportunities. The responses to these pressures with the consequent strains upon individuals subject to them may involve a considerable degree of frustration and of non-rational or of irrational behavior.[31] "Destructiveness" has often been psychologically identified as one form of response to continued frustration. So, too, it would appear that "wholesale negativism" can be construed, without enlarging the theory to incorporate new *ad hoc* variables, as a sustained repudiation of the authorities which exemplify the contradiction between legitimized cultural aspirations and socially restricted opportunities.

It seems to be the case, however, that the "versatility" and the "zest" with which some boys are observed to pursue their group-supported deviations are not directly accounted for by the theory of social structure and anomie. For the sources of these properties of the deviant behavior, one must presumably look to the social interaction among these likeminded deviants who mutually reinforce their deviant attitudes and behavior which, in the theory, result from the more or less common situation in which they find themselves. It is to this phase of the total process of gang-supported deviant behavior that Cohen primarily applies his instructive analysis. But, as he indicates later in his book, before proceeding to analyze the types of "solutions" to the difficulties which the "delinquent boys" encounter in their immediate social milieu, one must account for the varying frequencies with which these difficulties turn up. In this part of his analysis, Cohen does, in fact, examine the social and cultural sources of these pressures in much the same terms as those we have been considering. His thoroughly sociological analysis considerably advances our understanding of certain forms of deviant behavior commonly found in delinquency-groups and does so by extending the type of structural and functional theory now under review.

In examining the delinquency subculture, Cohen is of course in a direct line of continuity with the earlier studies by Shaw, McKay, and, particularly, Thrasher.[32] However, he goes on to observe that these studies were principally concerned with the problem of how the delinquency subculture is *transmitted* to youngsters, and that the correlative problem, to which he addresses himself, concerns the *origin* of these cultural patterns. In much the same way, it is possible to distinguish between a theory which deals only with the responses of individuals to culturally-induced stresses, like that advanced by Karen Horney, for example, and a theory which deals also with *the effects of the aggregated and sometimes socially organized responses upon the normative structure itself.*

The social process linking anomie and deviant behavior. To put this problem in its appropriate theoretical context requires us to see the emergence and growth of anomie as a resultant of ongoing social process and not simply as a condition which happens to obtain.[33] Within this context, the process can be provisionally pictured in the following way. Owing to their objectively disadvantaged position in the group as well as to distinctive personality configurations,[34] some individuals are subjected more than others to the strains arising from the discrepancy between cultural goals and effective access to their realization. They are consequently more vulnerable to deviant behavior. In some proportion of cases, again dependent upon the control-structure of the group, these departures from institutional norms are socially rewarded by "successful" achievement of goals. But these deviant ways of achieving the goals occur within social systems. The deviant behavior consequently affects not only the individuals who first engage in it but, in some measure, it also affects other individuals with whom they are inter-related in the system.

A mounting frequency of deviant but "successful" behavior tends to lessen and, as an extreme potentiality, to eliminate the legitimacy of the institutional norms for others in the system. The process thus enlarges the extent of anomie within the system so that others, who did not respond in the form of deviant behavior to the relatively slight anomie which first obtained, come to do so as anomie spreads and is intensified. This, in turn, creates a more acutely anomic situation for still other and initially less vulnerable individuals in the social system. In this way, anomie and mounting rates of deviant behavior can be conceived as interacting in a process of social and cultural dynamics, with cumulatively disruptive consequences for the normative structure, unless counteracting mechanisms of control are called into play. In each specific case under examination, then, it is essential, as we have said before, to identify the control mechanisms which "minimize the strains resulting from seeming [or actual] contradictions between cultural goals and socially restricted access" to them.

Further Assumptions of the Theory. A preceding section of this chapter examines evidence bearing upon forms of response to anomie encompassed in the affectively and ethically neutral concept of "innovation": the use of institutionally proscribed means for attaining a culturally valued goal. Before turning to evidence on other major types of response—ritualism, retreatism, and rebellion—we must emphasize again that the general theory of social structure and anomie is *not* confined to the specific goal of monetary success and of social restrictions upon access to it. The theory has been found applicable, for example, to a case of interdisciplinary research in science, and to cases of mass communications behavior,[35] to a case of deviations from religious orthodoxy,[36] and to a case of conformity with and deviation from social norms in a military prison[37]—cases which, at least, on the face of them, would otherwise seem to have little in common and that little, assuredly not the dominant goal of monetary success. As was said in the initial exposition of the theory, "monetary success was taken as the major cultural goal" only "for purposes of simplifying the problem . . . although there are, of course, alternative goals in the repository of common values." In terms of the general conception, *any* cultural goals which receive extreme and only negligibly qualified emphasis in the culture of a group will serve to attenuate the emphasis on institutionalized practices and make for anomie.

In the same way, it is necessary to reiterate that the typology of deviant behavior is far from being confined to the behavior which is ordinarily described as criminal or delinquent. From the standpoint of sociology, other forms of departure from regulatory norms may have little or nothing to do with violation of the established law of the land. Merely to identify some types of deviation is itself a difficult problem of sociological theory which is being progressively clarified. For example, a distinct theoretical advance was effected by Parsons's conception that *illness* is, in one of its principal aspects, "to be defined as a form of deviant behavior, and that the elements of motivation to deviance which are expressed in the sick role are continuous with those expressed in a variety of other channels, including types of compulsive conformity which are not socially defined as deviant."[38]

As another example, the behavior describable as "over-conformity" or "over-compliance" with institutional norms has been sociologically analyzed as deviant even though it too may at first glance appear to represent overt conformity.[39] As the *typology* of responses to anomie is intended to make clear, these are distinct kinds of behavior which, in contrast to their manifest appearance of conformity to institutionalized expectations, can be shown upon further sociological analysis to represent departures from these expectations.

Finally, by way of preamble to this review of other types of deviant behavior, it should be noted once again that, from the standpoint of sociology, not all such deviation from the dominant norms of the group is necessarily dysfunctional to the basic values and adaptation of the group. Correlatively, strict and unquestioned adherence to all prevailing norms would be functional only in a group that never was: a group which is completely static and unchanging in a social and cultural environment which is static and unchanging. Some (unknown) degree of deviation from current norms is probably functional for the basic goals of all groups. A certain degree of "innovation," for example, may result in the formation of new institutionalized patterns of behavior which are more adaptive than the old in making for realization of primary goals.

It would be a shortsighted view and a concealed ethical judgment, moreover, to assume that even the deviant behavior which is dysfunctional to the current values of the group is also ethically deficient. For, as we have had frequent occasion to note in this book, the concept of social dysfunction is not a latter-day terminological substitute for "immorality" or "unethical practice." A particular pattern of behavior which departs from the dominant norms of the group may be dysfunctional in lessening the stability of the group or in reducing its prospect of achieving the goals it values. But, judged by one or another set of ethical standards, it may be the norms of the group which are at fault, not the innovator who rejects them. This has been put with characteristic insight and eloquence by one of the truly great men of our time:

> In the primitive tribe every class has its appointed *Moira* or portion, its *Ergon* or function, and things go right if each class and each individual fulfills his *Moira* and performs his *Ergon,* and does not transgress or trespass on those of others. In modern language each has his social service to perform and his consequent rights. It is the old *Themis* [law or justice personified, the things which "are done"]; but a *Themis* vastly extended by the imagination and made more positive. A *Themis* in which you may be called upon not merely to die for your country—the oldest tribal laws involved that—but to die for the truth, or, as he explains in a wonderful passage in the second book, to defy the whole conventional law of your society for the sake of the true law which it has forsaken or forgotten. No one who has read it can easily forget the account of the righteous man in the evil or mistaken society, how he is to be scourged and blinded and at last impaled or crucified by the society that misunderstands him, because he is righteous and seems the reverse, and how after all it is better for him so to suffer than to follow the multitude in doing wrong.[40]

All this would require no repetition were it not for the occasional and, it seems, increasingly frequent, assumption that deviant behavior is necessarily equivalent to social dysfunction, and social dysfunction, in turn, to violation of an ethical code. In the history of every society, presumably, some of its culture heroes have been regarded as heroic precisely because they have had the courage and the vision to depart from norms then obtaining in the group.

As we all know, the rebel, revolutionary, nonconformist, individualist, heretic or renegade of an earlier time is often the culture hero of today.

It should also be said again, since it is so easily forgotten, that to center this theory upon the cultural and structural sources of deviant behavior is *not* to imply that such behavior is the characteristic, let alone the exclusive, response to the pressures we have been examining. This is an analysis of varying *rates and types* of deviant behavior, not an empirical generalization to the effect that *all* those subject to these pressures respond by deviation. The theory only holds that those located in places in the social structure which are particularly exposed to such stresses are more likely than others to exhibit deviant behavior. Yet, as a result of countervailing social mechanisms, most even of these stressful positions do not *typically* induce deviation; conformity tends to remain the modal response. Among the countervailing mechanisms, as has been suggested in the preceding chapter, is access to "alternative goals in the repository of common values. . . . To the extent that the cultural structure attaches prestige to these alternatives and the social structure permits access to them, the system is somewhat stabilized. Potential deviants may still conform in terms of these auxiliary sets of values." Inquiry has been begun into the workings of such alternatives as curbs upon deviant behavior.[40a]

In quick summary, then, it should be evident that (1) the theory under review deals with culturally emphasized goals of diverse kinds and not only with the goal of monetary success which was examined for the purpose of illustration; (2) that it distinguishes forms of deviant behavior which may be far removed from those which represent violations of the law; (3) that the deviant behavior is not *necessarily* dysfunctional to the effective operation and development of the group; (4) that the concepts of social deviation and social dysfunction do not harbor concealed ethical premises; and (5) that alternative cultural goals provide a basis for stabilizing the social and cultural systems.

Ritualism. As located in the typology, ritualism refers to a pattern of response in which culturally defined aspirations are abandoned while "one continues to abide almost compulsively by institutional norms." As was said when this concept was introduced, "it is something of a terminological quibble to ask whether this represents 'genuinely deviant behavior.' Since the adaptation is, in effect, an internal decision and since the overt behavior is institutionally permitted, though not culturally preferred, it is not generally considered to represent a 'social problem.' Intimates of individuals making this adaptation may pass judgment in terms of prevailing cultural emphases and may 'feel sorry for them'; they may, in the individual case, feel that 'old Jonesy is certainly in a rut.' Whether this is described as deviant behavior or no, it clearly represents a departure from the cultural model in which men are obliged to strive actively, preferably through institutionalized procedures, to move onward and upward in the social hierarchy."

In this way, it was suggested, the acute status-anxiety in a society which emphasizes the achievement-motif may induce the deviant behavior of "over-conformity" and "over-compliance." For example, such over-compliance may be found among "bureaucratic virtuosos," some of whom may "over-conform precisely because they are subject to guilt engendered by previous nonconformity with the rules."[41] There is still little by way of systematic evidence on this particular hypothesis, apart from a psychoanalytic study of twenty "bureaucrats" which did find that they tended to be "compulsive neurotics."[42] Even this scanty evidence, however, does not bear directly on the present theory which has to do, not with types of *personality,* important as this is for other purposes, but with types of *role-performance* in response to socially structured situations.

Of more direct relevance is the study of the behavior of bureaucrats by Peter M. Blau.[43] He suggests that observed cases of overconformity are "not due to the fact that ritualistic adherence to existing operating procedure had become an inescapable habit" and that "ritualism results not so much from overidentification with rules and strong habituation to established practices as from lack of security in important social relationships in the organization." It is, in short, when the structure of the situation does not allay the status-anxiety and anxiety over the capacity to measure up to institutionalized expectations that individuals in these organizations respond with over-compliance.

The situations patterned by the social structure which invite the retreatist response of overconformity to normative expectations have been experimentally and, of course, only homologously reproduced among sheep and goats. (The reader will surely resist the temptation of concluding that no more symbolically appropriate animals could possibly have been selected for the purpose.) The situation inviting retreatism, it will be recalled, involves either the repeated frustration of strongly-held goals or the continued experience of finding that reward is not proportioned to conformity. The psychobiologist, Howard S. Liddell, has in effect reproduced both these conditions in his series of experiments.[44] As one among many examples,

A goat . . . is brought to the laboratory every day and subjected to a simple test: every two minutes a telegraph sounder clicks once a second for ten seconds followed by a shock to the foreleg. After twenty signal-shock combinations the goat returns to the pasture. It soon acquires a satisfactory level of motor skill and seemingly adapts well to this assembly-line procedure. Within six or seven weeks, however, the observer notes that a change in the animal's deportment has insidiously developed. It comes willingly to the laboratory but, upon entering, it exhibits a certain mannered deliberation and its conditioned responses are exceedingly precise. It seems to be trying 'to do just the right thing.' Some years ago our group began calling such animals 'perfectionists.' . . . We discovered that in Pavlov's laboratory the expression 'formal behavior' was used to characterize such conduct in the dog.

This does seem to bear more than a passing resemblance to what we have described as "the syndrome of the social ritualist" who "responds to a situation which appears threatening and excites distrust" by "clinging all the more closely to the safe routines and the institutional norms."[45] And indeed, Liddell goes on to report that "what we may infer to be similar behavior in man under threatening circumstances is to be found in Mira's portrayal of the six stages of human fear [the first of which is described as follows]:

Prudence and Self Restraint: Observed from without, the subject appears modest, prudent, and unpretending. By means of voluntary self-restraint he limits his aims and ambitions, and renounces all those pleasures which entail risk or exposure. The individual in this stage is already under the inhibitory influence of fear. He reacts with a prophylactic avoidance of the approaching situation. *Intro-*

spectively, the subject is not yet conscious of being afraid. On the contrary, he is rather self-satisfied and proud because he considers himself endowed with greater foresight than other human beings.[46]

This characterological portrait of the compulsive conformist who thanks God that he is not as other men limits the essential elements of a kind of retreatist response to threatening situations. It is the office of sociological theory to identify the structural and cultural processes which produce high rates of such conditions of threat in certain sectors of the society and negligible rates in others, and it is that type of problem to which the theory of social structure and anomie addresses itself. In this way, there develops a consolidation of "psychological" and "sociological" interpretations of observed patterns of behavior, such as that exemplified by retreatism.

Further apposite data and ideas, focused on personality rather than on role-performance in designated types of situations, are found in the studies centered on "intolerance of ambiguity."[47] What these studies lack by way of systematic incorporation of variables and dynamics of social structure is largely compensated by their detailed characterization of the components which presumably enter into retreatist responses to patterned situations and not only into the structure of the rigid personality. As set forth in a recent rapid inventory, the components of intolerance of ambiguity include: "undue preference for symmetry, familiarity, definiteness, and regularity; tendency toward black-white solutions, over-simplified dichotomizing, unqualified either-or solutions, premature closure, perseveration and stereotypy; a tendency toward excessively 'good' form (that is, excessive *Prägnanz* of *Gestalt* organization), achieved either by diffuse globality or by over-emphasis on concrete detail; compartmentalization, stimulus-boundness; avoidance of uncertainty as accomplished by the narrowing of meanings, by inaccessibility to experience, by mechanical repetition of sets, or by a segmentary randomness and an absolutizing of those aspects of reality which have been preserved."[48]

The substantive significance of each of these components cannot be apparent from this compact listing; the details are set forth in numerous publications. But what is evident, even from the list, is that the concept of intolerance of ambiguity refers to "an excess" of designated kinds of perception, attitudes and behavior (as indicated by such terms as "undue preference," "over-simplified," "unqualified," "over-emphasis," and the like). The norms in terms of which these are judged to be "excessive," however, need not be confined to the statistical norms observed in an aggregate of personalities under observation or to norms of "functional appropriateness" established by considering individuals *seriatim* in abstraction from their social environments. The norms can also be derived from the standardized normative expectations which obtain in various groups so that behavior which, by the first set of standards, may be regarded as "psychological over-rigidity" can, on occasion, be regarded by the second set of standards, as adaptive social conformity. This is only to say that although there is probably a linkage between the concept of overly-rigid personalities and the concept of socially induced ritualistic behavior, the two are far from being identical.

Retreatism. The retreatist pattern consists of the substantial abandoning both of the once-esteemed cultural goals and of institutionalized practices directed toward those goals. Approximations to this pattern have recently been identified among what has been described as "problem families"—roughly, those families who do not measure up to the normative expectations prevailing in their social environment.[49] Further evidence of this mode of response is found among workers who develop a state of psychic passivity in response to some discernible extent of anomie.[50]

Generally, however, retreatism seems to occur in response to acute anomie, involving an abrupt break in the familiar and accepted normative framework and in established social relations, particularly when it appears to individuals subjected to it that the condition will continue indefinitely. As Durkheim noted with characteristic insight,[51] such disruptions may be found in the "anomie of prosperity," when Fortune smiles and many experience radical upward shifts from their accustomed status, and not only in the "anomie of depression," when Fortune frowns and apparently exits for good. Much the same anomic condition often obtains in those patterned situations which "exempt" individuals from a wide array of role-obligations, as, for example, in the case of "retirement" from the job being imposed upon people without their consent and in the case of widowhood.[52]

In a study of the widowed and those retired from their job, Zena S. Blau examines in detail the circumstances making for retreatism, as one of several patterns of response.[53] As she points out, both the widowed and the "retirants" have lost a major role and, in some measure, experience a sense of isolation. She finds that retreatism tends to occur more often among isolated widows and widowers, and goes on to account for its even greater frequency among widowed women than widowed men. Retreatism is manifested in nostalgia for the past and apathy in the present. Retreatists are even more reluctant to enter into new social relations with others than are those described as "alienated," with the result that they tend to continue in their apathetic condition.

Possibly because retreatism represents a form of deviant behavior which is not publicly registered in social bookkeeping statistics, as is decidedly the case for such deviant behavior as crime and delinquency, and because it has not the same dramatic and highly visible effect upon the functioning of groups as violations of law, it has tended to be neglected as a subject for study by sociologists, if not by psychiatrists. Yet the syndrome of retreatism has been identified for centuries and under the label of accidie (or variously, acedy, acedia, and accidia) was regarded by the Roman Catholic Church as one of the deadly sins. As the sloth and torpor in which the "wells of the spirit run dry," accidie has interested theologians from the Middle Ages onward. It has engaged the attention of men and women of letters from at least the time of Langland and Chaucer, down through Burton, to Aldous Huxley and Rebecca West. Psychiatrists without number have dealt with it in the form of apathy, melancholy, or anhedonia.[54] But sociologists have accorded the syndrome singularly little attention. Yet it would seem that this form of deviant behavior has its social antecedents as well as its manifest social consequences, and we may look for more sociological inquiry into it of the kind represented by Zena Blau's recent study.

It remains to be seen whether the kinds of political and organizational apathy now being investigated by social scientists can be theoretically related to the social forces which, on this theory, make for retreatist behavior.[55] This possibility has been stated in the following terms:

> . . . rejection of norms and goals includes the phenomenon of cultural apathy with respect to standards of conduct. Qualitatively different aspects of the latter condition are variously connoted by terms such as indifference, cynicism, moral fatigue, disenchantment, withdrawal of affect, opportunism. One prominent type of apathy is the loss of involvement in a previously sought cultural goal, such as occurs when continued striving results in persistent and seemingly unavoidable frustration. The loss of central life-goals leaves the individual in a social vacuum, without focal direction or meaning. But another crucial kind of apathy seems to emerge from conditions of great normative complexity and/or rapid change, when individuals are pulled this way and that by numerous conflicting norms and goals, until the person is literally dis-oriented and de-moralized, unable to secure a firm commitment to a set of norms that he can feel as self-consistent. Under certain conditions, not yet understood, the result is a kind of 'resignation from responsibility': a discounting of principled conduct, a lack of concern for the maintenance of a moral community. It seems that this lostness is *one* of the basic conditions out of which some types of political totalitarianism emerge. The individual renounces moral autonomy, and is subjected to an external discipline.[56]

Rebellion. It should be plain by now that the theory under review sees the conflict between culturally defined goals and institutional norms as one *source* of anomie; it does not *equate* value-conflict and anomie.[57] Quite the contrary: conflicts between the norms held by distinct subgroups in a society of course often result in an increased adherence to the norms prevailing in each subgroup. It is the conflict between culturally accepted values and the socially structured difficulties in living up to these values which exerts pressure toward deviant behavior and disruption of the normative system. This outcome of anomie, however, may be only a prelude to the development of new norms, and it is this response which we have described as 'rebellion' in the typology of adaptation.

When rebellion is confined to relatively small and relatively powerless elements in a community, it provides a potential for the formation of subgroups, alienated from the rest of the community but unified within themselves. This pattern is exemplified by alienated adolescents teaming up in gangs or becoming part of a youth movement with a distinctive subculture of its own.[58] This response to anomie tends, however, to be unstable unless the new groups and norms are sufficiently insulated from the rest of the society which rejects them.

When rebellion becomes endemic in a substantial part of the society, it provides a potential for revolution, which reshapes both the normative and the social structure. It is in this connection that a recent study of the changing role of the bourgeoisie in eighteenth century France significantly extends the present theory of anomie. This extension is compactly stated as follows:[59]

> It has been suggested that . . . too great a discrepancy between the expectation of mobility and actual fulfillment results in a state of *anomie*, that is, a partial social disintegration reflecting the weakening of moral norms. The same demoralization will very likely also arise when there is *de facto* mobility without the accompanying moral approval, and it was with discrepancies of both these kinds that the 18th century French bourgeoisie was faced to an increasing extent as the century progressed.

Quite apart from the particular historical case in point, this directs theoretical attention to the general conception that anomie may result from two kinds of discrepancy between objective rates of social mobility and cultural definition of the moral right (and obligation) to move up in a hierarchical social system. Throughout, we have been considering only the one type of discrepancy in which culturally valued ascent is objectively restricted, and it may turn out that this is historically the more frequent type of instance. But the correlative discrepancy, as Dr. Barber observes, also introduces severe strains upon the system. In general terms, this can be identified as the familiar pattern, increasingly familiar to Americans, in which both caste and open-class norms obtain in a society, with a resulting widespread ambivalence toward the *de facto* class *and* caste mobility of those assigned by many to a lower caste. The phase of demoralization which results from a structural situation of this kind is exemplified not only in the relations between the races in various parts of the United States but in a large number of societies once colonized by the West. These familiar facts would seem to be of a piece, in terms of sociological theory, with the facts regarding the bourgeoisie of the *ancien régime* which Dr. Barber has put in this theoretical setting.[60]

CHANGING SOCIAL STRUCTURE AND DEVIANT BEHAVIOR

In terms of the theory under review, it is plain that differential pressures for deviant behavior will continue to be exerted upon certain groups and strata only as long as the structure of opportunity and the cultural goals remain substantially unchanged. Correlatively, as significant changes in the structure or goals occur, we should expect corresponding changes in the sectors of the population most severely exposed to these pressures.

We have had frequent occasion to note that criminal "rackets" and sometimes associated political machines persist by virtue of the social functions they perform for various parts of the underlying population who constitute their acknowledged and unacknowledged clientele.[61] It should be expected, therefore, that as legitimate structural alternatives for performing these functions develop, this would result in substantial changes in the social distribution of deviant behavior. It is precisely this thesis which is developed by Daniel Bell in an analytically perceptive paper.[62]

Bell observes that "the mobsters, by and large, had immigrant roots, and crime, as the pattern showed, was a route of social ascent and place in American life." And as sociological students of the subject have often observed, each new immigrant group found itself occupying the lowermost social stratum lately quitted by an immigrant group which had come before. For example, by the time the Italians had experienced a generation or two of American life, they found the "more obvious big city paths from rags to riches pre-empted" by the Jews and Irish. And as Bell goes on to say,

Excluded from the political ladder—in the early '30's there were almost no Italians on the city payroll in top jobs, nor in books of the period can one find discussion of Italian political leaders—[and] finding few open routes to wealth, some turned to illicit ways. In the children's court statistics of the 1930's, the largest group of delinquents were the Italian. . . .

It was the one-time racketeer, seeking respectability, says Bell, who "provided one of the major supports for the drive to win a political voice for Italians in the power structure of the urban political machines." And a decisive change in the sources of funds for the urban political machines provided the context facilitating this alliance of the racketeer and the political organization. For the substantial funds which formerly came from big business were now being diverted from municipal to national political organizations. One of the substitute sources for financing these machines was ready to hand in "the new, and often illegally earned, Italian wealth. This is well illustrated by the career of Costello and his emergence as a political power in New York. Here the ruling motive has been the search for an entrée—for oneself and one's ethnic group—into the ruling circles of the big city." In due course, Italians came to achieve a substantial degree of political influence for the first time.

In abbreviated summary, these are the terms in which Bell traces a "distinct ethnic sequence in the modes of obtaining illicit wealth." Although the evidence is still far from adequate, there is some basis for concluding, as Bell does, that "men of Italian origin appeared in most of the leading roles in the high drama of gambling and mobs, just as twenty years ago the children of East European Jews were the most prominent figures in organized crime, and before that individuals of Irish descent were similarly prominent."

But with changes in the structure of opportunity, "a growing number of Italians with professional training and legitimate business success . . . both prompts and permits the Italian group to wield increasing political influence; and increasingly it is the professionals and businessmen who provide models for Italian youth today, models that hardly existed twenty years ago."

Finally, and ironically, in view of the close connection of Roosevelt with the large urban political machines, it is a basic structural change in the form of providing services, through the rationalized procedures of what some call "the welfare state," that largely spelled the decline of the political machine. It would be figurative but essentially true to say that it was the system of "social security" and the growth of more-or-less bureaucratically administered scholarships which, more than direct assaults of reformers, have so greatly reduced the power of the political machine. As Bell concludes,

with the rationalization and absorption of some illicit activities into the structure of the economy, the passing of an older generation that had established a hegemony over crime, the rise of minority groups to social position, and the breakup of the urban boss system, the pattern of crime we have discussed is passing as well. Crime, of course, remains as long as passion and the desire for gain remain. But big, organized city crime, as we have known it for the past seventy-five years, was based on more than these universal motives. It was based on characteristics of the American economy, American ethnic groups, and American politics. The changes in all these areas means that it too, in the form we have known it, is at an end. (154)

We need seek no more fitting close, in terms of an essentially structural and functional analysis, to this review of continuities in the analysis of the relation of social structure to anomie.

SECTION VI
Bureaucratic Structure

THE STUDY of bureaucratic organization has immense importance for the field of social welfare. In this context the term "bureaucratic" has a technical rather than a popular meaning. The popular use of the term conjures up a host of invidious connotations which are imputed to this form of organization—red tape, inefficiency, and wholesale waste. Here, however, we depart from popular usage, and employ the term to refer to a very specialized form of human organization which in itself is neither good nor bad, but which differs in various salient respects from other modes of grouping, such as the family or peer group.

The opening selection by Max Weber has been included to provide the reader who is not familiar with this material with a basis for thinking about the way in which this type of organization is differentiated from other systems of social arrangements in which men engage. Weber observes, for example, that "the spirit in which the ideal official conducts his office" is one of "formalistic impersonality, *Sine ira et studio,* without hatred or passion, and hence without affection or enthusiasm." If, in the mass bureaucratic organization, each functionary permitted his personal feelings to govern his actions, the organization would shortly be plunged into chaos. Hence, the requirement for emotional detachment and emotional neutrality arises simply as a means of preserving equilibrium, making it possible for the organization to get its work done. In the peer group, by contrast, feelings and interests are the subject of immediate consideration. Thus the peer group and bureaucratic organization differ in the extent to which expression of personal feelings is encouraged or constrained. Similarly, Weber enumerates a variety of characteristics which differentiate the bureaucratic organization from other modes of human grouping.

Without doubt, the growth of bureaucratic organization is among the more important trends of the modern era. Since the large-scale emergence of corporate structures following the Civil War, for example, our economic system has become increasingly bureaucratized. Many other institutional spheres of the society—governmental, recreational, religious,

(560)

educational, political, labor—have been developing in the same direction. And on the basis of available evidence, there is every reason to believe that this development will continue. As we once spoke of the "industrial revolution," therefore, we may now speak of the "bureaucratic revolution."

The field of social welfare—including such professions as education, social work, and medicine—has not been exempted from this organizational transformation which has so profoundly affected social life in other segments of our society. The practice of social work, for example, is mediated almost exclusively through "agencies"—which is to say, through bureaucracies. Whether one speaks of correction, child welfare, family services, health, recreation, or community planning, what is immediately called to mind are the bureaucratic organizations unique to that field of practice. In corrections, one thinks of court clinics, parole and probation systems, and various residential institutions for juvenile and adult offenders. Similarly, we have child guidance clinics, social group work agencies, day centers for the young and old, community chests and councils, departments of social welfare, social casework agencies, and the like. It is evident, of course, that many of our agencies do not fully fit the model described by Weber. This is particularly true of the smaller, private agencies in contrast to the larger, public agencies. The former are characterized by much less clarity of role definition, somewhat more blurred distinctions between superordinates and subordinates, and a greater diffusion of power among staff. Yet we should not let these departures from the ideal-typical bureaucratic model obscure the fact that we are essentially an agency-centered or, rather, a "bureaucracy-centered" field.

Bureaucratization has many implications for the field of social welfare. For the present purposes, two major areas of relevance may be identified. First, knowledge of bureaucratic organization provides a host of clues which facilitate the process of study, diagnosis, and treatment. Secondly, familiarity with the consequences of alternative modes of organization enables the skillful administrator to improve the effectiveness of his staff as well as the quality of its services.

The clinician who understands bureaucratic organization has a source of valuable insights for diagnosis as well as for treatment. The individual who is employed in an organization, at whatever level, is subject to satisfactions and to strains that depend in part on the conditions which obtain in his occupational setting. In addition to considerations of pay and physical comfort, there are many other essentially organizational factors which generate satisfaction or strain: the extent of control of the individual over his job, the clarity with which he can see his contribution to the total product, the fairness with which he is evaluated, the opportunities for advancement, the norms governing interpersonal relations with peers, supervisors and subordinates, and the like. The clinician can trace out the relationship between these organizational factors and the needs and capacities which the individual brings to his job. Thus, an individual who seeks satisfactions from essentially creative activities will tend to be frustrated in a setting which is characterized by rigid supervisory controls; on the other hand, where work is not so much an end in itself, such controls will appear less oppressive. For some individuals, routinized work—as is characteristic of many bureaucracies —is an important source of security; demands for competitive and aggressive behavior, or for innovation, would tend to be experienced as threatening and overwhelming. Because the individual does not wholly control his choice of work setting, or may not make an appropriate choice when the opportunity affords itself, his needs and capacities are not always matched with the requirements of his occupation. Sensitive help requires sorting out the relationships between the individual's capacities and organizational requirements in order to clarify the sources of strain.

From the viewpoint of the administrator, knowledge of bureaucratic organization is essential. Given such knowledge, he may alter or modify internal organizational arrangements so as to improve the performance of his staff. In the same way, the quality of services to people is to a large extent affected by internal characteristics of the organization. With respect to the matter of staff performance, the fact that we spend so much of our professional lives within these structures has consequences for the kind of people we become—for our values, our behavior, and our thought-ways. This is hardly a startling assertion, for individuals are always influenced by the groups in which they move and have their being. Some of the articles in this section represent an attempt to identify various consequences for individuals who are located within bureaucratic organizations. In an article entitled "Bureaucratic Structure and Personality," for example, Merton identifies various organizational pressures which lead to what is sometimes referred to invidiously as the "bureaucratic personality"—a mode of adaptation which is characterized by over-concern with rules, by rigid, ritualistic adherence to bureaucratic procedures. The important point made in Merton's article is that certain identifiable features of the organization *itself* give rise to such behavior. Hence one reason for thinking about bureaucratic structure is to acquaint ourselves with the way in which we are influenced by the organizational contexts in which we work. Having identified structural sources of malfunctioning, we may then seek alternative and hopefully more satisfactory organizational arrangements.

Because differences in organizational arrangements have a crucial impact upon the people being served, we may also use our knowledge of bureaucratic structure to improve services. For example, the way in which the agency is organized will affect the relationship between worker and client; this relationship—whether located in a penal institution or a social group work agency—is in no sense fully described by the characteristics of the worker and client alone. One must also describe those ways in which the organization intervenes and modifies their interaction. Peter Blau's article—"Cooperation and Competition in a Bureaucracy"— illustrates how the interaction between the worker and client is directly affected by the existence of cooperative or competitive relationships among the workers themselves; when staff relations are highly competitive, the quality of service to clients deteriorates. One of the special merits of this article for our purposes is the way in which Blau traces out and identifies the different types of organizational arrangements which give rise to competition or cooperation. Similarly, the articles by Gouldner and Schwartz contain materials which suggest ways in which various modes of organization further or impede achievement of agency goals.

Unfortunately, few references to the developing knowledge of bureaucratic organization appear in our administrative literature. Yet the art of administration in the modern era must rest on a science of bureaucratic structure, for this type of human organization is spreading rapidly to every part of the vast field of social welfare. This section is intended to provide the reader with a glimpse of the extraordinary complexity of bureaucratic organization as well as to stimulate further study of this important subject.

THE ESSENTIALS OF BUREAUCRATIC ORGANIZATION: AN IDEAL-TYPE CONSTRUCTION

Max Weber

THE EFFECTIVENESS OF LEGAL AUTHORITY rests on the acceptance of the validity of the following mutually inter-dependent ideas.

1. That any given legal norm may be established by agreement or by imposition, on grounds of expediency or rational values or both, with a claim to obedience at least on the part of the members of the corporate group. This is, however, usually extended to include all persons within the sphere of authority or of power in question—which in the case of territorial bodies is the territorial area—who stand in certain social relationships or carry out forms of social action which in the order governing the corporate group have been declared to be relevant.

2. That every body of law consists essentially in a consistent system of abstract rules which have normally been intentionally established. Furthermore, administration of law is held to consist in the application of these rules to particular cases; the administrative process is the rational pursuit of the interests which are specified in the order governing the corporate group within the limits laid down by legal precepts and following principles which are capable of generalized formulation and are approved in the order governing the group, or at least not disapproved in it.

3. That thus the typical person in authority occupies an "office." In the action associated with his status, including the commands he issues to others, he is subject to an impersonal order to which his actions are oriented. This is true not only for persons exercising legal authority who are in the usual sense "officials," but, for instance, for the elected president of a state.

4. That the person who obeys authority does so, as it is usually stated, only in his capacity as a "member" of the corporate group and what he obeys is only "the law." He may in this connexion be the member of an association, of a territorial commune, of a church, or a citizen of a state.

5. In conformity with point 3, it is held that the members of the corporate group, in so far as they obey a person in authority, do not owe this obedience to him as an individual, but to the impersonal order. Hence, it follows that there is an obligation to obedience only within the sphere of the rationally delimited authority which, in terms of the order, has been conferred upon him.

Reprinted from *The Theory of Social and Economic Organization* (1947), translated by A. M. Henderson and Talcott Parsons, pp. 329-40, by permission of the translators and the publisher. (Copyright, 1947, by Oxford University Press.)

The following may thus be said to be the fundamental categories of rational legal authority:

(1) A continuous organization of official functions bound by rules.

(2) A specified sphere of competence. This involves (a) a sphere of obligations to perform functions which has been marked off as part of a systematic division of labour. (b) The provisions of the incumbent with the necessary authority to carry out these functions. (c) That the necessary means of compulsion are clearly defined and their use is subject to definite conditions. A unit exercising authority which is organized in this way will be called an "administrative organ."

There are administrative organs in this sense in large-scale private organizations, in parties and armies, as well as in the state and the church. An elected president, a cabinet of ministers, or a body of elected representatives also in this sense constitute administrative organs. This is not, however, the place to discuss these concepts. Not every administrative organ is provided with compulsory powers. But this distinction is not important for present purposes.

(3) The organization of offices follows the principle of hierarchy; that is, each lower office is under the control and supervision of a higher one. There is a right of appeal and of statement of grievances from the lower to the higher. Hierarchies differ in respect to whether and in what cases complaints can lead to a ruling from an authority at various points higher in the scale, and as to whether changes are imposed from higher up or the responsibility for such changes is left to the lower office, the conduct of which was the subject of complaint.

(4) The rules which regulate the conduct of an office may be technical rules or norms.[1] In both cases, if their application is to be fully rational, specialized training is necessary. It is thus normally true that only a person who has demonstrated an adequate technical training is qualified to be a member of the administrative staff of such an organized group, and hence only such persons are eligible for appointment to official positions. The administrative staff of a rational corporate group thus typically consists of "officials," whether the organization be devoted to political, religious, economic—in particular, capitalistic—or other ends.

(5) In the rational type it is a matter of principle that the members of the administrative staff should be completely separated from ownership of the means of production or administration. Officials, employees, and workers attached to the administrative staff do not themselves own the nonhuman means of production and administration. These are rather provided for their use in kind or in money, and the official is obligated to render an accounting of their use. There exists, furthermore, in principle complete separation of the property belonging to the organization, which is controlled within the sphere of office, and the personal property of the official, which is available for his own private uses. There is a corresponding separation of the place in which official functions are carried out, the "office" in the sense of premises, from living quarters.

(6) In the rational type case, there is also a complete absence of appropriation of his official position by the incumbent. Where "rights" to an office exist, as in the case of judges, and recently of an increasing proportion

of officials and even of workers, they do not normally serve the purpose of appropriation by the official, but of securing the purely objective and independent character of the conduct of the office so that it is oriented only to the relevant norms.

(7) Administrative acts, decisions, and rules are formulated and recorded in writing, even in cases where oral discussion is the rule or is even mandatory. This applies at least to preliminary discussions and proposals, to final decisions, and to all sorts of orders and rules. The combination of written documents and a continuous organization of official functions constitutes the "office"[2] which is the central focus of all types of modern corporate action.

(8) Legal authority can be exercised in a wide variety of different forms which will be distinguished and discussed later. The following analysis will be deliberately confined for the most part to the aspect of imperative coordination in the structure of the administrative staff. It will consist in an analysis in terms of ideal types of officialdom or "bureaucracy."

In the above outline no mention has been made of the kind of supreme head appropriate to a system of legal authority. This is a consequence of certain considerations which can only be made entirely understandable at a later stage in the analysis. There are very important types of rational imperative coordination which, with respect to the ultimate source of authority, belong to other categories. This is true of the hereditary charismatic type, as illustrated by hereditary monarchy and of the pure charismatic type of a president chosen by plebiscite. Other cases involve rational elements at important points, but are made up of a combination of bureaucratic and charismatic components, as is true of the cabinet form of government. Still others are subject to the authority of the chief of other corporate groups, whether their character be charismatic or bureaucratic; thus the formal head of a government department under a parliamentary regime may be a minister who occupies his position because of his authority in a party. The type of rational, legal administrative staff is capable of application in all kinds of situations and contexts. It is the most important mechanism for the administration of everyday profane affairs. For in that sphere, the exercise of authority and, more broadly, imperative coordination, consists precisely in administration.

The purest type of exercise of legal authority is that which employs a bureaucratic administrative staff. Only the supreme chief of the organization occupies his position of authority by virtue of appropriation, of election, or of having been designated for the succession. But even *his* authority consists in a sphere of legal "competence." The whole administrative staff under the supreme authority then consists, in the purest type, of individual officials who are appointed and function according to the following criteria:[3]

(1) They are personally free and subject to authority only with respect to their impersonal official obligations.

(2) They are organized in a clearly defined hierarchy of offices.

(3) Each office has a clearly defined sphere of competence in the legal sense.

(4) The office is filled by a free contractual relationship. Thus, in principle, there is free selection.

(5) Candidates are selected on the basis of technical qualifications. In the most rational case, this is tested by examination or guaranteed by diplomas certifying technical training, or both. They are *appointed,* not elected.

(6) They are remunerated by fixed salaries in money, for the most part with a right to pensions. Only under certain circumstances does the employing authority, especially in private organizations, have a right to terminate the appointment, but the official is always free to resign. The salary scale is primarily graded according to rank in the hierarchy; but in addition to this criterion, the responsibility of the position and the requirements of the incumbent's social status may be taken into account.

(7) The office is treated as the sole, or at least the primary, occupation of the incumbent.

(8) It constitutes a career. There is a system of "promotion" according to seniority or to achievement, or both. Promotion is dependent on the judgment of superiors.

(9) The official works entirely separated from ownership of the means of administration and without appropriation of his position.

(10) He is subject to strict and systematic discipline and control in the conduct of the office.

This type of organization is in principle applicable with equal facility to a wide variety of different fields. It may be applied in profit-making business or in charitable organizations, or in any number of other types of private enterprises serving ideal or material ends. It is equally applicable to political and to religious organizations. With varying degrees of approximation to a pure type, its historical existence can be demonstrated in all these fields.

1. For example, this type of bureaucracy is found in private clinics, as well as in endowed hospitals or the hospitals maintained by religious orders. Bureaucratic organization has played a major role in the Catholic Church. It is well illustrated by the administrative role of the priesthood in the modern church, which has expropriated almost all of the old church benefices, which were in former days to a large extent subject to private appropriation. It is also illustrated by the conception of the universal Episcopate, which is thought of as formally constituting a universal legal competence in religious matters. Similarly, the doctrine of Papal infallibility is thought of as in fact involving a universal competence, but only one which functions "ex cathedra" in the sphere of the office, thus implying the typical distinction between the sphere of office and that of the private affairs of the incumbent. The same phenomena are found in the large-scale capitalistic enterprise; and the larger it is, the greater their role. And this is not less true of political parties, which will be discussed separately. Finally, the modern army is essentially a bureaucratic organization administered by that peculiar type of military functionary, the "officer."

2. Bureaucratic authority is carried out in its purest form where it is most clearly dominated by the principle of appointment. There is no such thing as a hierarchy of elected officials in the same sense as there is a hierarchical organization of appointed officials. In the first place, election makes it impossible to attain a stringency of discipline even approaching that

in the appointed type. For it is open to a subordinate official to compete for elective honours on the same terms as his superiors, and his prospects are not dependent on the superior's judgment.

3. Appointment by free contract, which makes free selection possible, is essential to modern bureaucracy. Where there is a hierarchical organization with impersonal spheres of competence, but occupied by unfree officials—like slaves or dependents, who, however, function in a formally bureaucratic manner—the term "patrimonial bureaucracy" will be used.

4. The role of technical qualifications in bureaucratic organizations is continually increasing. Even an official in a party or a trade-union organization is in need of specialized knowledge, though it is usually of an empirical character, developed by experience, rather than by formal training. In the modern state, the only "offices" for which no technical qualifications are required are those of ministers and presidents. This only goes to prove that they are "officials" only in a formal sense, and not substantively, as is true of the managing director or president of a large business corporation. There is no question but that the "position" of the capitalistic entrepreneur is as definitely appropriated as is that of a monarch. Thus at the top of a bureaucratic organization, there is necessarily an element which is at least not purely bureaucratic. The category of bureaucracy is one applying only to the exercise of control by means of a particular kind of administrative staff.

5. The bureaucratic official normally receives a fixed salary. By contrast, sources of income which are privately appropriated will be called "benefices." Bureaucratic salaries are also normally paid in money. Though this is not essential to the concept of bureaucracy, it is the arrangement which best fits the pure type. Payments in kind are apt to have the character of benefices, and the receipt of a benefice normally implies the appropriation of opportunities for earnings and of positions. There are, however, gradual transitions in this field with many intermediate types. Appropriation by virtue of leasing or sale of offices or the pledge of income from office are phenomena foreign to the pure type of bureaucracy.

6. "Offices" which do not constitute the incumbent's principal occupation, in particular "honorary" offices, belong in other categories. . . . The typical "bureaucratic" official occupies the office as his principal occupation.

7. With respect to the separation of the official from ownership of the means of administration, the situation is essentially the same in the field of public administration and in private bureaucratic organizations, such as the large-scale capitalistic enterprise.

8. . . . At the present time [collegial bodies] are rapidly decreasing in importance in favour of types of organization which are in fact, and for the most part formally as well, subject to the authority of a single head. For instance, the collegial "government" in Prussia have long since given way to the monocratic "district president." The decisive factor in this development has been the need for rapid, clear decisions, free of the necessity of compromise between different opinions and also free of shifting majorities.

9. The modern army officer is a type of appointed official who is clearly marked off by certain class distinctions. . . . In this respect such officers differ radically from elected military leaders, from charismatic condottieri, from the type of officers who recruit and lead mercenary armies as a capitalistic

enterprise, and, finally, from the incumbents of commissions which have been purchased. There may be gradual transitions between these types. The patrimonial "retainer," who is separated from the means of carrying out his function, and the proprietor of a mercenary army for capitalistic purposes have, along with the private capitalistic entrepreneur, been pioneers in the organization of the modern type of bureaucracy. . . .

The Monocratic Type of Bureaucratic Administration. Experience tends universally to show that the purely bureaucratic type of administrative organization—that is, the monocratic variety of bureaucracy—is, from a purely technical point of view, capable of attaining the highest degree of efficiency and is in this sense formally the most rational known means of carrying out imperative control over human beings. It is superior to any other form in precision, in stability, in the stringency of its discipline, and in its reliability. It thus makes possible a particularly high degree of calculability of results for the heads of the organization and for those acting in relation to it. It is finally superior both in intensive efficiency and in the scope of its operations, and is formally capable of application to all kinds of administrative tasks.

The development of the modern form of the organization of corporate groups in all fields is nothing less than identical with the development and continual spread of bureaucratic administration. This is true of church and state, of armies, political parties, economic enterprises, organizations to promote all kinds of causes, private associations, clubs, and many others. Its development is, to take the most striking case, the most crucial phenomenon of the modern Western state. However many forms there may be which do not appear to fit this pattern, such as collegial representative bodies, parliamentary committees, soviets, honorary officers, lay judges, and what not, and however much people may complain about the "evils of bureaucracy," it would be sheer illusion to think for a moment that continuous administrative work can be carried out in any field except by means of officials working in offices. The whole pattern of everyday life is cut to fit this framework. For bureaucratic administration is, other things being equal, always, from a formal, technical point of view, the most rational type. For the needs of mass administration to-day, it is completely indispensable. The choice is only that between bureaucracy and dilettantism in the field of administration.

The primary source of the superiority of bureaucratic administration lies in the role of technical knowledge which, through the development of modern technology and business methods in the production of goods, has become completely indispensable. In this respect, it makes no difference whether the economic system is organized on a capitalistic or a socialistic basis. Indeed, if in the latter case a comparable level of technical efficiency were to be achieved, it would mean a tremendous increase in the importance of specialized bureaucracy.

When those subject to bureaucratic control seek to escape the influence of the existing bureaucratic apparatus, this is normally possible only by creating an organization of their own which is equally subject to the process of bureaucratization. Similarly the existing bureaucratic apparatus is driven to continue functioning by the most powerful interests which are material and objective, but also ideal in character. Without it, a society like our own—

with a separation of officials, employees, and workers from ownership of the means of administration, dependent on discipline and on technical training—could no longer function. The only exception would be those groups, such as the peasantry, who are still in possession of their own means of subsistence. Even in case of revolution by force or of occupation by an enemy, the bureaucratic machinery will normally continue to function just as it has for the previous legal government.

The question is always who controls the existing bureaucratic machinery. And such control is possible only in a very limited degree to persons who are not technical specialists. Generally speaking, the trained permanent official is more likely to get his way in the long run than his nominal superior, the Cabinet minister, who is not a specialist.

Though by no means alone, the capitalistic system has undeniably played a major role in the development of bureaucracy. Indeed, without it capitalistic production could not continue and any rational type of socialism would have simply to take it over and increase its importance. Its development, largely under capitalistic auspices, has created an urgent need for stable, strict, intensive, and calculable administration. It is this need which gives bureaucracy a crucial role in our society as the central element in any kind of large-scale administration. Only by reversion in every field—political, religious, economic, etc.—to small-scale organization would it be possible to any considerable extent to escape its influence. On the one hand, capitalism in its modern stages of development strongly tends to foster the development of bureaucracy, though both capitalism and bureaucracy have arisen from many different historical sources. Conversely, capitalism is the most rational economic basis for bureaucratic administration and enables it to develop in the most rational form, especially because, from a fiscal point of view, it supplies the necessary money resources.

Along with these fiscal conditions of efficient bureaucratic administration, there are certain extremely important conditions in the fields of communication and transportation. The precision of its functioning requires the services of the railway, the telegraph, and the telephone, and becomes increasingly dependent on them. A socialistic form of organization would not alter this fact. It would be a question whether in a socialistic system it would be possible to provide conditions for carrying out as stringent bureaucratic organization as has been possible in a capitalistic order. For socialism would, in fact, require a still higher degree of formal bureaucratization than capitalism. If this should prove not to be possible, it would demonstrate the existence of another of those fundamental elements of irrationality in social systems—a conflict between formal and substantive rationality of the sort which sociology so often encounters.

Bureaucratic administration means fundamentally the exercise of control on the basis of knowledge. This is the feature of it which makes it specifically rational. This consists on the one hand in technical knowledge which, by itself, is sufficient to ensure it a position of extraordinary power. But in addition to this, bureaucratic organizations, or the holders of power who make use of them, have the tendency to increase their power still further by the knowledge growing out of experience in the service. For they acquire through the conduct of office a special knowledge of facts and have available a store of documentary material peculiar to themselves. While not peculiar to bureaucratic organizations, the concept of "official secrets" is certainly typical of them. It stands in relation to technical knowledge in somewhat the same position as commercial secrets do to technological training. It is a product of the striving for power.

Bureaucracy is superior in knowledge, including both technical knowledge and knowledge of the concrete fact within its own sphere of interest, which is usually confined to the interests of a private business—a capitalistic enterprise. The capitalistic entrepreneur is, in our society, the only type who has been able to maintain at least relative immunity from subjection to the control of rational bureaucratic knowledge. All the rest of the population have tended to be organized in large-scale corporate groups which are inevitably subject to bureaucratic control. This is as inevitable as the dominance of precision machinery in the mass production of goods.

The following are the principal more general social consequences of bureaucratic control:

(1) The tendency to "levelling" in the interest of the broadest possible basis of recruitment in terms of technical competence.

(2) The tendency to plutocracy growing out of the interest in the greatest possible length of technical training. To-day this often lasts up to the age of thirty.

(3) The dominance of a spirit of formalistic impersonality, *"Sine ira et studio,"* without hatred or passion, and hence without affection or enthusiasm. The dominant norms are concepts of straightforward duty without regard to personal considerations. Everyone is subject to formal equality of treatment; that is, everyone in the same empirical situation. This is the spirit in which the ideal official conducts his office.

SOCIAL INTEGRATION, BUREAUCRATIZATION, AND THE PROFESSIONS

Walter I. Wardwell

IT IS GENERALLY AGREED that the central problem of modern society is the integration of differentiated activities into some kind of meaningful and coordinated whole. Among these differentiated activities are occupations, or occupational roles. It is the emergence of occupational roles which more than anything else distinguishes modern society from the folk type; and the integration of modern society is tied directly to its occupational and economic systems.

An occupational role is a pattern of activity organized primarily around the functional, or instrumental, contribution a person makes to society.[1] It is focussed on what a person *does* rather than *who* he is in terms of some relational tie such as kinship.[2] Using the concepts of differentiation and integration as a basis of classification we can distinguish three general types of occupational roles: (1) those which involve high degrees of specialization and proficiency within a relatively narrow range of knowledge or skill; (2) those which involve responsibility for integrating or coordinating the differentiated activities of others; and (3) a residual group of occupations which involve neither a high degree of knowledge or skill nor responsibility for coordinating the activities of others. Following Parsons we shall designate these as "professional" roles, "executive" roles, and "labor" roles, respectively.

As defined, these roles are "ideal" or "pure" types. Actual occupations usually combine elements of more than one type. Nevertheless there are some nearly pure types even of labor roles, such as the ditch-digger who is guided by lines drawn on the ground to show him where to dig and who has someone to tell him when to stop digging. The term "hand," whether applied to workers on farms, on ships, or in factories, connotes that it is not intellect but mainly physical strength that is hired. Numerous professional occupations approximate the pure type of professional role, particularly specialists in such fields as medicine, law, and science. The presidents of business corporations may be former engineers, financiers, lawyers, or salesmen; hence they do not hold their position by virtue of any one of these specialized competencies but because of their executive ability. As administrators their job is to coordinate the "parts" of their organization so that it will endure as a going concern, which in the case of business enterprises means among other things making a profit.

The chief executive of a hospital or university, who is usually also a physician or an academician, as the case may be, exemplifies an occupational

Reprinted from *Social Forces* (May 1955), pp. 356-59, by permission of the author and the publisher. (Copyright, 1955, by the Williams & Wilkins Co.)

role which combines the two elements of specialized competence and executive responsibility, although increasingly the tendency has been to place men whose experience has been principally in the executive role in these positions. Midway between the pure types of professional role and labor role is that of the skilled craftsman or artisan, who has a highly specialized skill without the high degree of abstract knowledge and generalized competence of the "learned" professions. On the dimension of executive responsibility there is a wide range of positions from the "straw" (or working) boss to the top executive of an organization, as well as numerous combinations of administrative responsibility with specialized technical knowledge.

The executive role is never found apart from a "formal" or "bureaucratic" organization which needs administrative direction. By "bureaucratic organization" we mean a pyramidal structure of authority relations consciously established to accomplish a specific purpose by rationally efficient means.[3] Bureaucratic organizations of this type are as peculiar to our type of society as are occupational roles themselves. Included in an industrial bureaucracy complementary to executive roles are the various labor roles of mass-production workers. They are mostly the semi-skilled "operatives" or "operators" of our industrial machine. In the case of non-industrial bureaucracies (i.e., governmental, military, educational, religious,[4] etc.) the mass of participants (i.e., citizens, soldiers, students, parishioners, etc.) do not fill occupational roles strictly speaking, but the roles they fill are complementary to the executive or professional roles in their respective bureaucratic structures and are homologous to the labor roles of an industrial bureaucracy. We may refer to all these occupational roles as "bureaucratized" in contrast to those independent of the kind of authority relations that bureaucracy implies.

A bureaucratic organization is both a *differentiated* and an *integrated* unit. Durkheim would say that its solidarity is primarily of the "organic"[5] type, by which he means that its various parts fit together in an interdependent and complementary fashion. Parsons' term "instrumental authority"[6] characterizes the relationship of the executive to the bureaucratic organization which he administers. The executive's authority involves four elements which we may sum up as follows: (1) *responsibility* for the (2) *decision-making* necessary to (3) *coordinate* an organization (4) *as a going concern*. These ideas are not new but it seems useful to bring them together in one sentence. Stated in another way: if a bureaucratic organization of the type we are discussing is to survive, its parts must somehow fit into or contribute to the over-all goal or purpose of the organization; this requires that some person, or group, have the acknowledged right and ability to make the decisions necessary to coordinate the whole into an organic unity.

The instrumental authority of the executive makes it possible for him to perform this function for the organization even though his actual *power* over participants in the organization is only conditional—that is, as long as they participate in the organization they are subject to his authority, but they are free (in a democratic society, at least) to withdraw from the organization if they wish. Empirical evidence for the attributes of the executive role that we have emphasized is found in the *transferability* of executive talents from one bureaucracy to another that has been so prevalent in the United States during World War II and its aftermath, when executives have freely moved among industrial, military, governmental, and educational bureaucracies. The ability to integrate the "parts" of these bureaucracies into "going concerns" is transferable because the function performed for each of the bureaucracies is the same.

Bureaucratic organizations also increasingly include professional roles within them. The need for specialized abilities, particularly at the staff level, is apparent even in production organizations of industry. Engineers, lawyers, accountants, and experts in economics, psychology, labor relations, public relations, etc., must be "integrated" into the organization and their contributions must be "coordinated" with those of the production departments which they assist the executive in coordinating.

Nevertheless professional roles in general resist bureaucratization. The specialized technical knowledge which makes a professional man an *authority* in a limited field differs in kind from the delegated *authority* of a bureaucracy, especially that of the "line" as distinct from staff. A professional man such as a doctor or lawyer does not need delegated authority and the weight and sanction of an authoritarian organization to support his professional decisions. The only social relationships which professional men need with their professional colleagues are those that protect them from the indiscretions of other professional men, particularly in such matters as the maintenance of standards of competence and ethics and the profession's reputation with the public. The appropriate basis of social organization for a profession is therefore the "group of equals" pattern[7] of the professional association rather than the bureaucratic type of organization.

And we in fact find that the representative mode of association, at least in the "free" professions, is the partnership, i.e., an egalitarian form of organization. Even where professions function in bureaucratic-type organizations there are indications that the group of equals pattern exists. In a hospital the physicians on any one service tend to be related to each other as equals, toward whom the "chief" of the service is a *primus inter pares* rather than a superior. The faculty of a college or university is a "body of scholars" in spite of differences in academic rank (which correspond more to stages in a career than to levels of authority). Such democratic processes as rotating or elected department chairmanships and all-faculty voting on important issues signalize the basic equality of status of the faculty. And at Commencement, the most important ritual occasion of the college year, the faculty, except for a few administrative officers, usually take precedence in order not of academic rank but of length of tenure, which is the least status-differentiating principle (other than lot) for ordering equals.

In the skilled trades the organizational principle is comparable to that of the professions, no doubt for the same reasons. It is relevant to note that the professions and the crafts both descended from the guilds of the late medieval period. Modern craftsmen such as plumbers and electricians are licensed much as members of the independent professions are and in their negotiations with "clients" are free from pressures other than those affecting the welfare of the craft as a whole. However, the organizational trend in these trades seems to be toward permanent or semi-permanent arrangements with one contractor of services and hence toward eventual absorption into a bureaucratic structure.

In the professions, too, there are bureaucratic pressures, as well as counter-pressures.[8] For example, there is need for coordination of specialized activities within the confines of a single profession. This need could be met by the *primus inter pares* principle of the elected president of a professional society, the senior partner, the chairman of a department, the professor administrant,[9] etc. But particularly when the work of a profession becomes large-scale and/or complex there are additional pressures toward bureaucratization, and this is especially true in a society that is largely bureaucratized in other areas and when these bureaucracies incorporate professional roles into their structure. In medicine, law, and teaching the work environment has become increasingly that of large-scale, impersonal organization rather than that of the intimate personal relationship of free professional and client. Physicians more and more use hospitals and clinics, with their large array of specialized services and technicians, as their base of operations. Frequently the patient has not one doctor but many doctors, and when this is the case the independence of the individual physician is severely limited.

It should be noted, however, that this tendency toward bureaucratization and resulting loss of independence of the physician has nothing to do with the question of socialized medicine but is inherent in the structure of modern medical practice. Complete bureaucratization of a profession such as medicine would produce real problems, as can be illustrated by the story of the American Army dental officer in charge of a clinic who would not permit the dentists subordinate to him to fill or extract teeth until he had personally checked the teeth and approved the recommended course of action. Although the subordinate dentists were naturally infuriated at this insult to their professional competence they were powerless to do anything but comply with orders. This story also indicates the nature of the resistance that can be expected to full bureaucratization of a profession.

In the legal profession the term "law factory" suggests the kind of organization that large law firms have become.[10] They include senior and junior partners and numerous salaried "associates," younger lawyers serving their apprenticeship at low wages. Some law firms have even found it necessary to employ full-time lawyer administrators to handle internal management of the firm. Thus far, however, the legal profession has shown the least tendency toward bureaucratization of all the professions, although the reasons for this resistance are somewhat difficult to determine. The tradition of independence in the legal profession is so strong that it still is comprised mainly of "solo" practitioners despite the many advantages of organizing into partnerships which make possible a greater degree of specialization and competence in particular fields of law. Perhaps the fact that the administration of law in our courts involves a series of legal contests has obviated the need for the kind of over-all coordination which a hospital or university requires. That is, emphasis has been on *conflicts* of interest rather than on ways of obtaining *cooperation*. The closest thing to an administrator in law is the presiding judge of a circuit court or the chief justice of certain state supreme courts, but these officers, even though governmental, are certainly not chief executives of bureaucratic organizations.

In colleges and universities, despite the manifestations of a "group of equals" pattern that have been mentioned, there are stronger pressures toward bureaucratization than in law and medicine. An important factor working in this direction has been the very large number of students to be educated which has made centralized coordination more necessary. Then too the "independent professional" pattern of medicine and law has never characterized teaching in the United States. Teachers in an educational institution cannot refuse to accept a student any more than a student can refuse to study under a particular teacher. One has only to look at our public school system to see how bureaucratized education can become.[11]

We have now come full circle. It is principally the professions, crafts, and small entrepreneurs that have resisted bureaucratization in our urban society. Yet even they are subject to its influence for the reasons we have noted: the "free" professions, crafts, and enterprises seem to be undergoing modification in favor of emerging bureaucratic-type structures such as hospitals and universities, in the case of professions, and industrial bureaucracies in the case of "free" enterprise. However, the relation between executive and professional roles in these organizations has received little attention either theoretically or practically, probably because of greater interest in labor roles and in relations between organized labor and management.[12] Yet it is clear that not only the greatest amount of technological specialization but also the most tenacious resistance to bureaucratic control exists in the professions.

Nor has the problem of coordinating the activities of different bureaucracies been solved. It is one thing to devise techniques of coordination for a single bureaucracy and another to establish procedures for the harmonious interrelationship of many potentially conflicting bureaucratic structures. Here the analysis requires a more definite consideration of power relations than it is the purpose of this paper to undertake. However, we should not forget that it may be the specialized roles of the professions themselves that can provide the techniques, the principles, and the beliefs that can make possible a successful solution to this problem. Humanistic patterns derived from religion, philosophy, and science are integrative patterns for society, if not in fact at least in fancy. If the various bureaucratic structures do not actually constitute an integrated whole, the student of religion, philosophy, or science fashions an ideal to shoot for, a model to think about, or a conceptual scheme for analyzing societal integration. Is it a paradox that executive roles, although their function is coordination and integration, achieve it only in limited areas (due to the fact that bureaucratic organizations are limited in purpose and tend to have only "instrumental" authority) while professional roles such as those of law, religion, and science, which as social roles are focused on technical competence in relatively narrow fields of specialization, seem to offer the likeliest bases for societal integration?

BUREAUCRATIC STRUCTURE AND PERSONALITY

Robert K. Merton

A FORMAL, RATIONALLY ORGANIZED social structure involves clearly defined patterns of activity in which, ideally, every series of actions is functionally related to the purposes of the organization.[1] In such an organization there is integrated a series of offices, of hierarchized statuses, in which inhere a number of obligations and privileges closely defined by limited and specific rules. Each of these offices contains an area of imputed competence and responsibility. Authority, the power of control which derives from an acknowledged status, inheres in the office and not in the particular person who performs the official role. Official action ordinarily occurs within the framework of pre-existing rules of the organization. The system of prescribed relations between the various offices involves a considerable degree of formality and clearly defined social distance between the occupants of these positions. Formality is manifested by means of a more or less complicated social ritual which symbolizes and supports the pecking order of the various offices. Such formality, which is integrated with the distribution of authority within the system, serves to minimize friction by largely restricting (official) contact to modes which are previously defined by the rules of the organization. Ready calculability of others' behavior and a stable set of mutual expectations is thus built up. Moreover, formality facilitates the interaction of the occupants of offices despite their (possibly hostile) private attitudes toward one another. In this way, the subordinate is protected from the arbitrary action of his superior, since the actions of both are constrained by a mutually recognized set of rules. Specific procedural devices foster objectivity and restrain the "quick passage of impulse into action."[2]

The Structure of Bureaucracy. The ideal type of such formal organization is bureaucracy and, in many respects, the classical analysis of bureaucracy is that by Max Weber.[3] As Weber indicates, bureaucracy involves a clear-cut division of integrated activities which are regarded as duties inherent in the office. A system of differentiated controls and sanctions is stated in the regulations. The assignment of roles occurs on the basis of technical qualifications which are ascertained through formalized, impersonal procedures (e.g., examinations). Within the structure of hierarchically arranged authority, the activities of "trained and salaried experts" are governed by general, abstract, and clearly defined rules which preclude the necessity for the issuance of specific instructions for each specific case. The generality of the rules requires the constant use of *categorization,* whereby individual problems and cases are classified on the basis of designated criteria and are treated accordingly. The pure type of bureaucratic official is appointed, either by a superior or through the exercise of impersonal competition; he is not elected. A measure of flexibility in the bureaucracy is attained by electing higher functionaries who presumably express the will of the electorate (e.g., a body of citizens or a board of directors). The election of higher officials is designed to affect the purposes of the organization, but the technical procedures for attaining these ends are carried out by continuing bureaucratic personnel.[4]

Most bureaucratic offices involve the expectation of life-long tenure, in the absence of disturbing factors which may decrease the size of the organization. Bureaucracy maximizes vocational security.[5] The function of security of tenure, pensions, incremental salaries and regularized procedures for promotion is to ensure the devoted performance of official duties, without regard for extraneous pressures.[6] The chief merit of bureaucracy is its technical efficiency, with a premium placed on precision, speed, expert control, continuity, discretion, and optimal returns on input. The structure is one which approaches the complete elimination of personalized relationships and nonrational considerations (hostility, anxiety, affectual involvements, etc).

With increasing bureaucratization, it becomes plain to all who would see that man is to a very important degree controlled by his social relations to the instruments of production. This can no longer seem only a tenet of Marxism, but a stubborn fact to be acknowledged by all, quite apart from their ideological persuasion. Bureaucratization makes readily visible what was previously dim and obscure. More and more people discover that to work, they must be employed. For to work, one must have tools and equipment. And the tools and equipment are increasingly available only in bureaucracies, private or public. Consequently, one must be employed by the bureaucracies in order to have access to tools in order to work in order to live. It is in this sense that bureaucratization entails separation of individuals from the instruments of production, as in modern capitalistic enterprise or in state communistic enterprise (of the midcentury variety), just as in the post-feudal army, bureaucratization entailed complete separation from the instruments of destruction. Typically, the worker no longer owns his tools nor the soldier, his weapons. And in this special sense, more and more people become workers, either blue collar or white collar or stiff shirt. So develops, for example, the new type of scientific worker, as the scientist is "separated" from his technical equipment—after all, the physicist does not ordinarily own his cyclotron. To work at his research, he must be employed by a bureaucracy with laboratory resources.

Bureaucracy is administration which almost completely avoids public discussion of its techniques, although there may occur public discussion of its policies.[7] This secrecy is confined neither to public nor to private bureaucracies. It is held to be necessary to keep valuable information from private economic competitors or from foreign and potentially hostile political groups. And though it is not often so called, espionage among competitors is perhaps as common, if not as intricately organized, in systems of private economic enterprise as in systems of national states. Cost figures, lists of clients, new technical processes, plans for production—all these are typically regarded as essential secrets of private economic bureaucracies which might be revealed if the bases of all decisions and policies had to be publicly defended.

The Dysfunctions of Bureaucracy. In these bold outlines, the positive attainments and functions of bureaucratic organization are emphasized and the internal stresses and strains of such structures are almost wholly neglected. The community at large, however, evidently emphasizes the imperfections of bureaucracy, as is suggested by the fact that the "horrid hybrid," bureaucrat, has become an epithet, a *Schimpfwort*.

The transition to a study of the negative aspects of bureaucracy is afforded by the application of Veblen's concept of "trained incapacity," Dewey's notion of "occupational psychosis" or Warnotte's view of "professional deformation." Trained incapacity refers to that state of affairs in which one's abilities function as inadequacies or blind spots. Actions based upon training and skills which have been successfully applied in the past may result in inappropriate responses *under changed conditions*. An inadequate flexibility in the application of skills, will, in a changing milieu, result in more or less serious maladjustments.[8] Thus, to adopt a barnyard illustration used in this connection by Burke, chickens may be readily conditioned to interpret the sound of a bell as a signal for food. The same bell may now be used to summon the trained chickens to their doom as they are assembled to suffer decapitation. In general, one adopts measures in keeping with one's past training and, under new conditions which are not recognized as *significantly* different, the very soundness of this training may lead to the adoption of the wrong procedures. Again, in Burke's almost echolalic phrase, "people may be unfitted by being fit in an unfit fitness"; their training may become an incapacity.

Dewey's concept of occupational psychosis rests upon much the same observations. As a result of their day to day routines, people develop special preferences, antipathies, discriminations and emphasis.[9] (The term psychosis is used by Dewey to denote a "pronounced character of the mind.") These psychoses develop through demands put upon the individual by the particular organization of his occupational role.

The concepts of both Veblen and Dewey refer to a fundamental ambivalence. Any action can be considered in terms of what it attains or what it fails to attain. "A way of seeing is also a way of not seeing—a focus upon object *A* involves a neglect of object *B*."[10] In his discussion, Weber is almost exclusively concerned with what the bureaucratic structure attains: precision, reliability, efficiency. This same structure may be examined from another perspective provided by the ambivalence. What are the limitations of the organizations designed to attain these goals?

For reasons which we have already noted, the bureaucratic structure exerts a constant pressure upon the official to be "methodical, prudent, disciplined." If the bureaucracy is to operate successfully, it must attain a high degree of reliability of behavior, an unusual degree of conformity with prescribed patterns of action. Hence, the fundamental importance of discipline which may be as highly developed in a religious or economic bureaucracy as in the army. Discipline can be effective only if the ideal patterns are buttressed by strong sentiments which entail devotion to one's duties, a keen sense of the limitation of one's authority and competence, and methodical performance of routine activities. The efficacy of social structure depends ultimately upon infusing group participants with appropriate attitudes and sentiments. As we shall see, there are definite arrangements in the bureaucracy for inculcating and reinforcing these sentiments.

At the moment, it suffices to observe that in order to ensure discipline (the necessary reliability of response), these sentiments are often more intense than is technically necessary. There is a margin of safety, so to speak, in the pressure exerted by these sentiments upon the bureaucrat to conform to his patterned obligations, in much the same sense that added allowances (precautionary overestimations) are made by the engineer in designing the supports for a bridge. But this very emphasis leads to a transference of the sentiments from the *aims* of the organization onto the particular details of behavior required by the rules. Adherence to the rules, originally conceived as a means, becomes transformed into an end-in-itself; there occurs the familiar process of *displacement of goals* whereby "an instrumental value becomes a terminal value."[11] Discipline, readily interpreted as conformance with regulations, whatever the situation, is seen not as a measure designed for specific purposes but becomes an immediate value in the life-organization of the bureaucrat. This emphasis, resulting from the displacement of the original goals, develops into rigidities and an inability to adjust readily. Formalism, even ritualism, ensues with an unchallenged insistence upon punctilious adherence to formalized procedures.[12] This may be exaggerated to the point where primary concern with conformity to the rules interferes with the achievement of the purposes of the organization, in which case we have the familiar phenomenon of the technicism or red tape of the official. An extreme product of this process of displacement of goals is the bureaucratic virtuoso, who never forgets a single rule binding his action and hence is unable to assist many of his clients.[13] A case in point, where strict recognition of the limits of authority and literal adherence to rules produced this result, is the pathetic plight of Bernt Balchen, Admiral Byrd's pilot in the flight over the South Pole.

According to a ruling of the department of labor Bernt Balchen . . . cannot receive his citizenship papers. Balchen, a native of Norway, declared his intention in 1927. It is held that he has failed to meet the condition of five years' continuous residence in the United States. The Byrd antarctic voyage took him out of the country, although he was on a ship carrying the American flag, was an invaluable member of the American expedition, and in a region to which there is an American claim because of the exploration and occupation of it by Americans, this region being Little America.

The bureau of naturalization explains that it cannot proceed on the assumption that Little America is American soil. That would be *trespass on international questions* where it has no sanction. So far as the bureau is concerned, Balchen was out of the country and *technically* has not complied with the law of naturalization.[14]

Structural Sources of Overconformity. Such inadequacies in orientation which involve trained incapacity clearly derive from structural sources. The process may be briefly recapitulated. (1) An effective bureaucracy demands reliability of response and strict devotion to regulations. (2) Such devotion to the rules leads to their transformation into absolutes; they are no longer conceived as relative to a set of purposes. (3) This interferes with ready adaptation under special conditions not clearly envisaged by those who drew up the general rules. (4) Thus, the very elements which conduce toward efficiency in general produce inefficiency in specific instances. Full realization of the inadequacy is seldom attained by members of the group who have not divorced themselves from the meanings which the rules have for them. These rules in time become symbolic in cast, rather than strictly utilitarian.

Thus far, we have treated the ingrained sentiments making for rigorous discipline simply as data, as given. However, definite features of the bureaucratic structure may be seen to conduce to these sentiments. The bureaucrat's official life is planned for him in terms of a graded career, through the organizational devices of promotion by seniority, pensions, incremental salaries, *etc.*, all of which are designed to provide incentives for disciplined action and conformity to the official regulations.[15] The official is tacitly expected to and largely does adapt his thoughts, feelings, and actions to the prospect of this career. But *these very devices* which increase the probability of conformance also lead to an over-concern with strict adherence to regulations which induces timidity, conservatism, and technicism. Displacement of sentiments from goals onto means is fostered by the tremendous symbolic significance of the means (rules).

Another feature of the bureaucratic structure tends to produce much the same result. Functionaries have the sense of a common destiny for all those who work together. They share the same interests, especially since there is relatively little competition in so far as promotion is in terms of seniority. In-group aggression is thus minimized and this arrangement is therefore conceived to be positively functional for the bureaucracy. However, the *esprit de corps* and informal social organization which typically develops in such situations often leads the personnel to defend their entrenched interests rather than to assist their clientele and elected higher officials. As President Lowell reports, if the bureaucrats believe that their status is not adequately recognized by an incoming elected official, detailed information will be withheld from him, leading him to errors for which he is held responsible. Or, if he seeks to dominate fully, and thus violates the sentiment of self-integrity of the bureaucrats, he may have documents brought to him in such numbers that he cannot manage to sign them all, let alone read them.[16] This illustrates the defensive informal organization which tends to arise whenever there is an apparent threat to the integrity of the group.[17]

It would be much too facile and partly erroneous to attribute such resistance by bureaucrats simply to vested interests. Vested interests oppose any new order which either eliminates or at least makes uncertain their differential advantage deriving from the current arrangements. This is undoubtedly involved in part in bureaucratic resistance to change but another process is perhaps more significant. As we have seen, bureaucratic officials affectively identify themselves with their way of life. They have a pride of craft which leads them to resist change in established routines; at least, those changes which are felt to be imposed by others. This nonlogical pride of craft is a familiar pattern found even, to judge from Sutherland's *Professional Thief*, among pickpockets who, despite the risk, delight in mastering the prestige-bearing feat of "beating a left breech" (picking the left front trousers pocket).

In a stimulating paper, Hughes has applied the concepts of "secular" and "sacred" to various types of division of labor; "the sacredness" of caste and *Stände* prerogatives contrasts sharply with the increasing secularism of occupational differentiation in our society.[18] However, as our discussion suggests, there may ensue, in particular vocations and in particular types of organization, the *process of sanctification* (viewed as the counterpart of the process of secularization). This is to say that through sentiment-formation, emotional dependence upon bureaucratic symbols and status, and affective involvement in spheres of competence and authority, there develop prerogatives involving attitudes of moral legitimacy which are established as values in their own right, and are no longer viewed as merely technical means for expediting administration. One may note a tendency for certain bureaucratic norms, originally introduced for technical reasons, to become rigidified and sacred, although, as Durkheim would say, they are *laïque en apparence*.[19] Durkheim has touched on this general process in his description of the attitudes and values which persist in the organic solidarity of a highly differentiated society.

Primary vs. Secondary Relations. Another feature of the bureaucratic structure, the stress on depersonalization of relationships, also plays its part in the bureaucrat's trained incapacity. The personality pattern of the bureaucratic is nucleated about this norm of impersonality. Both this and the categorizing tendency, which develops from the dominant role of general, abstract rules, tend to produce conflict in the bureaucrat's contacts with the public or clientele. Since functionaries minimize personal relations and resort to categorization, the peculiarities of individual cases are often ignored. But the client who, quite understandably, is convinced of the special features of *his* own problem often objects to such categorical treatment. Stereotyped behavior is not adapted to the exigencies of individual problems. The impersonal treatment of affairs which are at times of great personal significance to the client gives rise to the charge of "arrogance" and "haughtiness" of the bureaucrat. Thus, at the Greenwich Employment Exchange, the unemployed worker who is securing his insurance payment resents what he deems to be "the impersonality and, at times, the apparent abruptness and even harshness of his treatment by the clerks. . . . Some men complain of the superior attitude which the clerks have."[20]

Still another source of conflict with the public derives from the bureaucratic structure. The bureaucrat, in part irrespective of his position within the hierarchy, acts as a representative of the power and prestige of the entire structure. In his official role he is vested with definite authority. This often leads to an actually or apparently domineering attitude, which may only be exaggerated by a discrepancy between his position within the hierarchy and his position with reference to the public.[21] Protest and recourse to other officials on the part of the client are often ineffective or largely precluded by the previously mentioned *esprit de corps* which joins the officials into a more or less solidary ingroup. This source of conflict *may* be minimized in private enterprise since the client can register an effective protest by transferring his trade to another organization within the competitive system. But with the monopolistic nature of the public organization, no such alternative is possible. Moreover, in this case, tension is increased because of a discrepancy between ideology and fact: the governmental personnel are held to be "servants of the people," but in fact they are often superordinate, and release of tension can seldom be afforded by turning to other agencies for the necessary service.[22] This tension is in part attributable to the confusion of the status of bureaucrat and client; the client may consider himself socially superior to the official who is at the moment dominant.[23]

Thus, with respect to the relations between officials and clientele, one structural source of conflict is the pressure for formal and impersonal treatment when individual, personalized consideration is desired by the client. The conflict may be viewed, then, as deriving from the introduction of inappropriate attitudes and relationships. Conflict with*in* the bureaucratic structure arises from the converse situation, namely, when personalized relationships are substituted for the structurally required impersonal relationships. This type of conflict may be characterized as follows.

The bureaucracy, as we have seen, is organized as a secondary, formal group. The normal responses involved in this organized network of social expectations are supported by affective attitudes of members of the group. Since the group is oriented toward secondary norms of impersonality, any failure to conform to these norms will arouse antagonism from those who have identified themselves with the legitimacy of these rules. Hence, the substitution of personal for impersonal treatment within the structure is met with widespread disapproval and is characterized by such epithets as graft, favoritism, nepotism, apple-polishing, etc. These epithets are clearly manifestations of injured sentiments.[24] The function of such virtually automatic resentment can be clearly seen in terms of the requirements of bureaucratic structure.

Bureaucracy is a secondary group structure designed to carry on certain activities which cannot be satisfactorily performed on the basis of primary group criteria.[25] Hence behavior which runs counter to these formalized norms becomes the object of emotionalized disapproval. This constitutes a functionally significant defense set up against tendencies which jeopardize the performance of socially necessary activities. To be sure, these reactions are not rationally determined practices explicitly designed for the fulfillment of this function. Rather, viewed in terms of the individual's interpretation of the situation, such resentment is simply an immediate response opposing the "dishonesty" of those who violate the rules of the game. However, this subjective frame of reference notwithstanding, these reactions serve the latent function of maintaining the essential structural elements of bureaucracy by reaffirming the necessity for formalized, secondary relations and by helping to prevent the disintegration of the bureaucratic structure which would occur should these be supplanted by personalized relations. This type of conflict may be generically described as the intrusion of primary group attitudes when secondary group attitudes are institutionally demanded, just as the bureaucrat-client conflict often derives from interaction on impersonal terms when personal treatment is individually demanded.[26]

Problems for Research. The trend towards increasing bureaucratization in Western Society, which Weber had long since foreseen, is not the sole reason for sociologists to turn their attention to this field. Empirical studies of the interaction of bureaucracy and personality should especially increase our understanding of social structure. A large number of specific questions invite out attention. To what extent are particular personality types selected and modified by the various bureaucracies (private enterprise, public service, the quasi-legal political machine, religious orders)? Inasmuch as ascendancy and submission are held to be traits of personality, despite their variability in different stimulus-situations, do bureaucracies select personalities of particularly submissive or ascendant tendencies? And since various studies have shown that these traits can be modified, does participation in bureaucratic office tend to increase ascendant tendencies? Do various systems of recruitment (e.g., patronage, open competition involving specialized knowledge or general mental capacity, practical experience) select different personality types?[27] Does promotion through seniority lessen competitive anxieties and enhance administrative efficiency? A detailed examination of mechanisms for imbuing the bureaucratic codes with affect would be instructive both sociologically and psychologically. Does the general anonymity of civil service decisions tend to restrict the area of prestige-symbols to a narrowly defined inner circle? Is there a tendency for differential association to be especially marked among bureaucrats?

The range of theoretically significant and practically important questions would seem to be limited only by the accessibility of the concrete data. Studies of religious, educational, military, economic, and political bureaucracies dealing with the interdependence of social organization and personality formation should constitute an avenue for fruitful research. On that avenue, the functional analysis of concrete structures may yet build a Solomon's House for sociologists.

CO-OPERATION AND COMPETITION
IN A BUREAUCRACY

Peter M. Blau

THIS PAPER discusses performance and variations in competitiveness among twelve interviewers in two small sections of a public employment agency.[1] The duties of the interviewers in both sections were essentially alike. They received requests for workers over the phone. The order forms on which job openings were described were filed in a common pool in each section. Most of the official's time was spent interviewing applicants for jobs. After ascertaining the client's qualifications, the interviewer searched the sectional files for suitable vacancies. If an acceptable job was found, he referred the client to it and later phoned the employer to determine whether the client had been hired.

"The statistics which show how many interviews and how many placements each person in the section did are passed around to all interviewers. Of course, you look at them and see how you compare with others. This creates a competitive spirit," said one of the interviewers, voicing the sentiments of most of his fellows. In a period of job shortages, competition took the form of trying to utilize job openings before anybody else did. Interviewers were so anxious to make placements that they even resorted to illicit methods. Said one:

When you take an order, instead of putting it in the box, you leave it on your desk. There was so much hiding of orders under the blotter that we used to ask, "Do you have anything under your rug?" when we looked for an order. You might leave an order you took on the desk, or you might leave it on the desk after you made no referral. . . . Or, you might take an order only partially; you write the firm's name, and a few things; the others you remember. And you leave it on the pad [of order blanks]. You keep on doing this, and all these orders are not in the box.

You can do some wrong filling out. For instance, for a rather low-salary job, you fill out "experience required." Nobody can make a placement on that except you, because you, alone, know that experience isn't required. Or, if there are several openings [on one order], you put the order into "referrals" [file category for *filled* job openings] after you make one placement. You're supposed to put it into "referrals" but stand it up, so that the others can see it. If you don't, you have a better chance of making the next placement than somebody else. And time and again you see four, five openings on one order filled by the same person. [In one case on file eight out of nine openings on one order had been filled by the same interviewer.]

The major opportunity for competitive monopolization of job openings occurred when they were received from employers. Since illicit practices were concealed from the observer, the extent of competitition could not be determined through questioning or direct observation[2] but was betrayed by the record of official transactions. The extent to which an interviewer filled the vacancies he had received over the phone with his own clients in excess of

Reprinted from *The American Journal of Sociology* (May 1954), pp. 530-35, by permission of the author and the publisher. (Copyright, 1954, by the University of Chicago Press.)

chance expectations furnishes an index of competitiveness. (Col. 4 in Table 1 shows this index; cols. 1-3 present the data on which it is based.)

Table 1—Competitiveness and Productivity in Section A and in Section B

	Openings Received* (1)	Referrals Made by Recipient (2)	Ratio of Referrals to Openings (3)	Competi- tiveness† (4)	Productiv- ity‡ (5)	Number of Placements (6)
Section A:						
Adams	34	19	0.56	3.9	0.70	100
Ahman	62	27	.44	3.1	.49	70
Ajax	40	28	.70	4.9	.97	139
Akers	71	32	.45	3.2	.71	101
Ambros	69	18	.26	1.8	.45	65
Atzenberg	106	43	.41	2.9	.61	87
Auble	10	3	.30	2.1	.39	56§
Section B:						
Babcock	16	7	.44	2.2	.53	46
Beers	58	19	.33	1.6	.71	62
Bing	51	15	.29	1.5	.75	65
Borden	17	7	.41	2.1	.55	48§
Bush	43	19	0.42	2.1	0.97	84
Section A	392	170	0.43	3.0	0.59	590
Section B	185	67	0.36	1.8	0.67	289

*The great differences between interviewers in this column show that some were much more successful than others in inducing employers, or telephone operators, to channel requests for workers to them personally. This form of rivalry does not involve competitive interaction.

†Competitiveness index (col. 4): The proportion of job openings received to which the recipient made a referral (col. 3) times the number of members of the section. (This represents the observed divided by the expected frequency of referrals made by the recipient of a job opening.) Base period: First half of April, 1949.

‡Productivity index (col. 5): The number of placements made (col. 6) divided by the number of job openings available, that is, the number of openings in the section per interviewer. Base period: April, 1949.

§The number of placements was adjusted for the two interviewers absent for more than five days during April. Since the sectional numbers of placements were not revised, the values in col. 6 add up to more than the two totals shown.

Structural Conditions and Competitiveness. The members of Section A were more competitive than those of Section B. The last two columns in Table 1 also show that the interviewer's competitiveness was related to his productivity in Section A (Pearsonian $r = +.92$), but this was not the case in Section B ($r = -.20$). In other words, hoarding of jobs was an effective way to improve an interviewer's placement record only in one of these two groups.

The members of Section B were more cooperative: they discouraged competitive practices by making them ineffective. When they learned about interesting vacancies, they often told one another, but an interviewer who manifested competitive tendencies was excluded from the network of reciprocal information and lost the respect of his co-workers. Any advantage of hoarding jobs was, at least, neutralized by such lack of cooperation, as is indicated by the absence of a relation between competitiveness and productivity in this group. Since competitive practices made an interviewer unpopular and failed to raise his productivity, they were infrequent.

These officials themselves attributed the greater competitiveness in Section A to the ambitiousness of several members: "There is usually one individual who starts it, who becomes a pace-setter. Once it has started, it is too late." The others, so interviewers claimed, have to follow suit. However, the most competitive member of Section A in recounting her reactions when production records were first introduced made it clear that this explanation of competition on the basis of personality characteristics is inadequate:

When they introduced statistics, I realized how fast I worked. I even wanted to drop lower. I didn't mind working fast as long as it didn't show, but when it showed up like that on the record, I wanted to work less. But you know what happened? Some of the others started to compete with each other and produced more than I did. Then I thought to myself, "Since I can do it, it's silly to let them get ahead of me." I'm only human. So I worked as fast as before.

When statistical records made the superior performance of this interviewer public knowledge, she decided to work less, possibly in response to pressures the others had brought to bear upon her. While complaining about her unfair standards, however, the other members of the section also improved their own performance. Consequently, this interviewer, just like the others, felt constrained by colleagues to compete for an outstanding record. One or two members of Section B, on the other hand, were also accused of competitive tendencies, but their colleagues successfully discouraged their expression in monopolistic practices. It is in this sense that the competitive practices of one group and the co-operative practices of the other were social factors, calling for explanation in sociological rather than psychological terms, as Durkheim has long since emphasized.[3]

Differential conditions affected the development of these two groups. First, the supervisor in Section A relied heavily on performance records in evaluating interviewers: "And here, in the production figures, is the answer to the question: How good are you? Here you see exactly how good the work you did was." Interviewers often mentioned the pressure thus exerted: "[Especially] around rating time, you get this competition. You don't care whether the best person gets the job, but you try to make the placement yourself." In contrast, the new supervisor in Section B surprised his subordinates by rating them more leniently than they had expected, and not primarily on the basis of production records. Consequently, as one interviewer reported, "we became less anxious about statistics; another experience like that, and we might forget all about placement credit."

Second, a common professional orientation existed only in Section B. While the members of Section A had been assigned, and had received their training, at different times, the majority of those in Section B received their training together after World War II, at a time when intensive counseling had been stressed, since many returning veterans needed occupational advice. One official said of this period:

When I first came here, in May, 1946, we had a very nice bunch. It was like an all-day consultation; we discussed placements with each other all day long. At that time, the veterans came back, and there was a lot of emphasis on counseling. Nobody asked you how many placements you made, then. The emphasis was on quality, and we consulted with each other all day.

In this situation, the group developed a common professional code, which discouraged speedy placement as constituting defective employment service. In effect, this orientation transformed competitive practices from illegitimate means for desirable ends into illegitimate means for worthless ends. If such practices did occur, they were vigorously opposed on moral grounds as violating the interest of clients. Nevertheless, as will be shown presently, competition could not have been effectively curbed if the supervisor's evaluation practice had engendered acute anxiety over productivity. However, the existence of this code would have made it difficult for the supervisor to judge performance mainly by productivity, since doing so would have stamped him as ignorant of the essentials of good employment service.

No opportunity for the development of a *common* professional code had existed in Section A. Since competitiveness prevailed in this group, the individual whose personal professional standards made him reluctant to compete either became the deviant whose productivity suffered or modified his standards and entered the race with the others.

Third, most members of Section A had been appointed to temporary civil service positions during World War II. They were on probation pending permanent appointments when production records were originally introduced and even afterward remained subject to layoffs due to reductions in staff. Their insecurity led them to strive to impress superiors with outstanding performance. In contrast, all but one of the members of Section B were veterans, whose employment could not be terminated except for cause. As one envious colleague put it, "They felt that nothing could happen to them, because they were veterans, and had super-seniority."

Differences in these three conditions—security of employment, opportunity for the development of a common professional orientation, and the evaluation practice of the supervisor—gave rise to two dissimilar social structures. Productivity was highly valued in Section A and became associated with the individual's standing in the group, while striving for sheer productivity was disparaged in Section B. Thus, whereas the most productive and most competitive member of Section A was considered the best interviewer by her co-workers and was most popular with them,[4] the most productive member of Section B was least respected and least popular. As a result of these structural differences, co-operative norms prevailed only in Section B.

The interviewers in *both* sections disliked working in a competitive atmosphere. A member of Section A said: "If I see that an interviewer keeps orders on her desk, I take them and put them in the box. . . . Of course, you don't make friends that way." Since the majority in this section, including its most popular members, were highly competitive, to antagonize them was to threaten one's own standing in the group. This deterred interviewers from discouraging competitive practices. Antagonizing a deviant, however, does not endanger one's status. Consequently, since a striver was unpopular in Section B, its members could use sanctions freely to combat competitive practices and enforce co-operative norms.

Social Cohesion and Productivity. Table 1 shows that the group most concerned with productivity was less productive than the other group. Fifty-nine per cent of the job openings received in Section A were filled, in contrast to 67 per cent in Section B. (The 8 per cent difference is significant on the .01 level.) Another implicit paradox is that competitiveness and productivity were directly related for individuals in Section A but inversely related for the two groups.[5]

Anxious concern with productivity induced interviewers in Section A to concentrate blindly upon it at the expense of other considerations. In their eagerness to make many placements they often ignored their relationships with others as well as official rules. Competitiveness in this group weakened social cohesion, while co-operativeness in Section B strengthened it. This difference is further shown by the fact that usually none of the members of Section A spent their rest periods together, whereas all but one of those of Section B, a newcomer when this study was being made, did. Social cohesion enhanced operating efficiency by facilitating co-operation and by reducing status anxiety.

Although the members of both groups had occasion to assist one another, greater effort was required to elicit such co-operation in Section A. The social interaction that occurred in the office during the twenty-four busiest hours of one week was recorded and classified as official and private contacts, that is, those directly concerned with a specific job or client, and all others. The frequency of an interviewer's official contacts with colleagues was related to his productivity in Section A (rank correlation $= +.98$) but not in Section B (rank correlation $= +.08$). This suggests that only interviewers who kept, as one puts it, "hopping around all the time" to retrieve job orders that others kept on their desks were able to make many placements in the competitive section. In the cohesive group, on the other hand, the co-operation needed for making placements occurred as a matter of course, and not only in response to special requests. This effort was not required for high productivity.

To maximize his placements, the interviewer in Section A hoarded jobs and simultaneously tried to prevent others from doing so, thereby antagonizing his co-workers, whose co-operation he needed if he was to do well. The members of this section therefore attempted to conciliate colleagues whom their competitive practices had alienated. Often, shortly after having interfered with her operations, an interviewer paid another a compliment about her work or her apparel. The most competitive interviewer was in the habit of taking time out to joke with her co-workers and was proud of making more placements than anybody else, "nevertheless." Actually, this compensating friendliness, which made her popular despite her competitiveness, helped her to be productive.

In Section A, interviewers had to make special efforts at conciliation in order to make placements, but this was not necessary in Section B. At least, this impression is corroborated by the finding that frequency of private contacts with others was also related to productivity in Section A (rank correlation $= +.84$) but not in Section B (rank correlation $= +.13$). The members of the cohesive group, whose operating practices did not put colleagues at a disadvantage, did not have to devote time and energy to solicit and encourage co-operation, since it was not extended reluctantly. Their spontaneous co-operation improved operating efficiency.

Social cohesion also lessened the status anxiety generated by the evaluation system. Such anxiety is most acute in the individual who does not feel integrated in his work group and therefore seeks to derive social recognition from excelling at his task and from approval of superiors. Friendly relations with co-workers made the standing of the individual in the cohesive group independent of his productivity, particularly since fast work was disparaged as a sign of superficial service. The consequent reduction of anxiety in the antiproductivity-oriented group actually raised its productivity.

Fluctuations in productivity illustrate the dysfunction of status anxiety. Section B had not always operated more efficiently than Section A. Its productivity had been lower during the two months preceding the last rating but had abruptly increased then, while that of Section A had declined, as Table 2 shows.

The two groups found themselves in different situations before and after

Table 2—Productivity Before and After Rating

	Section A	Section B
December, 1948	0.64 (619)*	0.56 (317)
January, 1949	.70 (941)	.56 (472)
February, 1949 (rating)	.56 (1,342)	.60 (477)
March, 1949	.59 (1,335)	.71 (448)
April, 1949	0.59 (1,001)	0.67 (433)

*Numbers in parentheses are the numbers of job openings available on which the productivity index—the proportion of these openings that were filled—is based.

they were rated. The members of Section A were familiar with the rating standards of their supervisor, for she had rated them in previous years. Their anxiety led them to work especially hard immediately before the annual rating. The members of Section B, on the other hand, had never before been rated by their new supervisor. They were also concerned about their record but could not calm their anxiety by concentrating upon certain tasks, because they did not know what the supervisor would stress; the explanation he gave to his subordinates was too vague and adhered too strictly to official procedures to help them to foresee his actual practices. This unfocused anxiety was particularly detrimental to efficient performance. Later, when the interviewers found out that they were not rated primarily on the basis of statistical records, their anxiety largely subsided and their productivity increased. In contrast, the experience of the members of Section A, whose rating was strongly influenced by their status anxiety, but, when the rating was over, anxiety was no longer channeled into exceptionally hard work, with the result that their productivity declined below that of Section B.

Social cohesion is no guaranty against anxiety in a bureaucracy. Civil service status is too important to officials for them to remain immune to the threat of losing it. But when no such threat is felt, social cohesion reduces anxiety by divesting productivity of its significance as a symbol of status in the work group. Diminished anxiety as well as smoother co-operation then enable those in the cohesive group to perform their tasks more efficiently than the others.

In the absence of social cohesion, competitive striving for an outstanding performance record became a substitute means for relieving status anxiety in Section A. This psychological function of competition is illustrated by the following incident: The interviewers in this section became very irritable, and one of them even became physically ill, when a temporary supervisor, who tried to prevent competitive practices, interfered with their method of allaying anxiety. Status anxiety reduced operating efficiency. Even in the cohesive group, productivity was low when the unknown rating standards of a new supervisor produced acute and diffuse anxiety. Otherwise, however, the cohesive group was more productive, because social cohesion relieved status anxiety by making the individual's standing in the group independent of his productivity. The very competitive striving that undermined the group's cohesiveness also served to lessen the individual's status anxiety in a noncohesive situation. The hypothesis that the cohesiveness of the group and the competitiveness of the individual in the less cohesive group both reduce status anxiety explains the paradox that the *less competitive group* as well as the *more competitive individual* in the competitive group each was particularly productive.

SOCIAL RESEARCH IN THE MENTAL HOSPITAL

Morris S. Schwartz

IN THE PAST FEW YEARS the mental hospital has increasingly come to be used by social scientists as a research site. This growth in interest and research activity might be attributed to the special advantages the mental hospital affords for the study of social interaction, as well as to the kinds of problems that can be investigated therein. In this paper I will indicate some of these advantages and discuss some problems that have been and that might be investigated in the mental hospital.

The segregation of the mentally ill in a separate institution, the limitations placed upon patients, and the institutional controls and organization devised to regulate and carry out hospital functions all combine to create certain research opportunities for the investigator. The first of these is ready accessibility of "captive" research subjects. Many patients, especially those who reside on a locked ward, live their lives in a limited physical space where they are readily accessible to observation. This means that the number and kinds of activities in which these subjects can engage is severely circumscribed and that the investigator can include in his examination a large part of their social interactions. In effect, many parts of the mental hospital, for example a ward, can be delimited as a small-scale social system in which the current interactions of the patient participants are only minimally modified by activity occurring outside the system. Thus, there is a considerable restriction on the number of variables entering into their social interaction.

In addition, the covert aspects of these subjects' transactions—their feelings and sentiments—are more readily observable and more easily inferred. This is so because the mental hospital tolerates and accepts the direct expression of patients' feelings and attitudes. This means that patients will reveal their feelings in unconventional ways and the investigator will not have to contend with the cultural disguises and defenses people ordinarily maintain to prevent observation of their inner emotional life. This opportunity for observing the feeling-life of the subjects is also increased because of the nature of the patient's mental illness. Many patients have their feelings and attitudes easily evoked and cannot control their expression. They have to express their feelings openly because they have scarcely any defensive armor behind which to hide them. This greater accessibility to the inner feeling-life does not mean that the meanings and motivations related to their covert and overt behavior are more easily understood; they merely lend themselves to observation by an investigator in a way that would not be available if the subjects were being studied in more conventional areas of our society.

There is one final advantage in studying patients in the mental hospital— an investigation of deviant and "desocialized" persons and the kind of interactions they carry on may throw light on our conventional structures and processes.

In addition to studying patients, the investigator might also study the interrelations among personnel and the nature of the social organization created and maintained by the staff. This organization has a direct and important therapeutic impact upon the patient. If a patient gets well in this context, the observer can try to specify those aspects of the social structure and those social processes which contributed to this. If a patient remains ill, the investigator can try to discover those aspects of the social system which contributed to the maintenance of his mental illness. In this way patients can be used as an index of the therapeutic effects of the social structure.

Social Structure and Mental Health. Many of the social-research projects in the mental hospital have been interested in evaluating the relation of the social structure to the therapeutic course of patients. These studies have ranged from the delineation of cultural or institutional patterns to the identification of minute and detailed social contexts. For example Devereux[1] was concerned with identifying general structural factors in the mental hospital that facilitated the patient's recovery. He found these to be the simplicity of hospital life, the concreteness of the social structure, its high degree of consistency and uniformity, and the relatively slow rate of change. Bateman and Dunham[2] found, on the other hand, that the functioning of the attendant culture and the difference in value systems of patients and staff had untherapeutic effects on patients. The dynamics of this culture was such that it tried to preserve its inner form and structure, and its aim was to bring about complete control of patients without regard to patient welfare. Other studies[3] have pointed to the hierarchical structuring of staff relations and the social distance between various levels of personnel, as well as between patients and staff, as factors that might deter patient improvement. Caudill and his coworkers, especially, emphasized the two separate and distinct cultural milieus maintained by patients and staff in the mental hospital they studied. This sharp dichotomy between the patient world and the staff world resulted in a lack of awareness on the part of the staff of the highly organized culture of the patients and the nature of its functioning. Because of this they found that the patient's therapeutic needs were being inadequately met. Barrabee[4] studied the effect of a mental-hospital structure on the fulfillment of its functions. He delineated the kinds of problems the social organization of the hospital had to cope with and the strains engendered in the process of integrating structure and function. He found the conflict between the therapeutic needs of the patient and the needs of the social system to be an important strain in the hospital structure, especially in the area of "control" of patients.

Stanton and I[5] have studied a small mental hospital as an integrated social system in which the various subparts function together more or less adequately to fulfill the various purposes of the hospital. We have operated on the assumption that different forms of social organization and different interactional processes will have varying effects on patient behavior and improvement. We have identified detailed and specific ways in which interactional processes and concrete aspects of the social structure affect patients.

On the institutional level we devoted our attention to the differentiation of roles, the communication and decision-making process, and the influence of stereotypes on the operations of personnel. Where the roles of various categories of personnel were not clearly defined, or were overlapping, it became difficult for them to function effectively in the social system. Role-confusion among staff reflected itself in confusion among patients. There is a need to determine the most appropriate and effective ways of differentiating, defining, and organizing roles in the mental hospital; what alterations in conventional roles need to be brought about; how the prestige attached to various roles can best be distributed; what value systems are associated with various roles and how role-conflict develops; and how various roles can complement and be integrated with each other in order to provide the most effective therapeutic context.

We gathered data on the system and processes of communication of staff members and also between patients and staff. We found that the formal organization of the system of communication and the informal means for transmitting and receiving information play an important role in the patient's therapeutic progress. Defects in communicative organization, breakdowns, blocks, distortions, omissions in the transmission of information, the passing on of inadequate or inaccurate data—all may contribute to misunderstandings between and among hospital participants. These misunderstandings tend to perpetuate the patient's mental illness. In one of our investigations[6] we found that an interference in communication between two staff members who were in direct contact with the patient, and who were also in covert disagreement over the patient's management, was regularly accompanied by pathological excitement on the patient's part. When the interferences and barriers to communication were removed and the staff members discussed their disagreement, the patient's excitement disappeared. Caudill[7] found that the patient group was lacking in adequate channels of communication to the staff and as a consequence developed their own social structure which was insulated as much as possible from friction with the hospital routine. Much more investigative work needs to be done in studying communicative networks in the mental hospital. We need to know the ways in which communicative channels are either deficient or effective in the transmission of information, with what effects on the functioning of personnel, with what influence on the patient's therapeutic course. These data need to be gathered in sufficient detail so that the consequences of the communicative system for patient welfare can be accurately evaluated.

The structure and process of decision-making, that is, the system and methods of distributing authority and responsibility and the exercise of power in the mental hospital, has an important effect on patients. Where we were able to delineate defective organization of decision-making we also found difficulties in performance of function on the part of personnel. Where there was, in addition, an inadequate method of locating these deficiencies in the power arrangements, problems created by an ineffective arrangement for the making of decisions tended to perpetuate themselves. Research needs to be done to acquire detailed information on the participation in the decision-making process of various categories of personnel and the ways in which their participation influences their approaches to and attitudes toward patients. When we have been able to trace with sufficient precision the consequences of different types of power organizations for patient welfare, we can then start to think in terms of what kind of power relations, with what types of participation in the decision-making process, will facilitate patients' mental health. There may be general types of authority arrangements that are universally therapeutic, or there may be specific types of authority structures that are beneficial for only certain kinds of patients.

In one study[8] we pointed out the kinds of stereotypes that are used by personnel to justify or rationalize a course of action. The precise ways in which these stereotypes develop, their specific effects on patients, and the ways in which they can be recognized and altered in the direction of more realistic appraisal of a social situation await further intensive investigation.

In trying to identify specific and delimited social contexts that tend to elicit or maintain the patient's mental illness, we found it fruitful to view the patient's mental illness as a way of participating in the social process—a process within which and with which he lives, and to which he contributes in making it what it is. This is in contrast to a view that conceives of the patient's mental illness as an entity he has within himself. In our view the illness is not an individual phenomenon independent of the patient's milieu but a phenomenon of a total situation which is part of and takes into account the current social situation. Thus, the patient's mental illness may be stable because it is part of a stable social equilibrium, and a significant alteration in this equilibrium might also occasion a change in the patient's mode of participation (his illness). With this frame of reference the social scientist can try to identify specific social contexts that maintain the patient's mental illness (his "ill" ways of participating) and those that facilitate his mental health (his "more mature" ways of participating). For example, we investigated the influence of certain social situations and constellations of staff attitudes on the continuation of patients' incontinent behavior.[9] We found that attitudes such as antipathy, disgust, and devaluation of and discouragement about the patient tended to reinforce the patient's habitual mode of incontinent participation. Similarly, situations of conflict or those in which the patient was isolated, abandoned, or devalued precipitated the overwhelming majority of directly observed incidents of patients' incontinence. These attitudes and social situations constituted part of a stable equilibrium in which incontinence was a regularly recurring aspect. On the other hand, when a different type of social context was structured, the same patients who were incontinent in the old contexts rarely participated with incontinence in the new context. The delineation of the social phase of a segment of the patient's behavior, that is, its function and meaning in the social equilibrium, may continue to be a rewarding area of social research.

With a similar orientation we studied the fulfillment of patients' needs on a mental-hospital ward. Staff reactions to the more withdrawn patients included exasperation and anxiety in contacting them, difficulty in communicating with them, and not taking the patients' requests seriously. These reactions tended to work in the direction of maintaining the patient's withdrawal, to which the staff members responded in kind—by withdrawal. In this way an equilibrium of mutual withdrawal was established. This kind of equilibrium was not established with patients whose modes of participation more closely approximated conventional behavior. Thus, a differential in need fulfillment was maintained in which the needs of the more withdrawn patients were less frequently fulfilled.

Interpersonal processes that are considered to be fundamental for patient improvement can be observed closely in the mental hospital. For example, respect for the patient is considered to be such a basic condition. Answers to questions such as the following can be pursued: What are the conditions under which respect and disrespect develop? What are the components of each of these attitudes and how are they identifiable? What are the various manifestations of these attitudes in the mental hospital? What are the ways in which and the means whereby a staff member changes from an attitude of disrespect to one of respect, and vice versa? In order to answer some of these questions the relations between a staff member and a patient might be followed over a time—especially those relations in which the staff member began with a noticeable disrespectful or respectful attitude. The changes and the bases for these changes in the staff members' attitudes on the respect-disrespect continuum could then be carefully noted.

An investigator who is interested in empathic phenomena can find them in profusion on a mental-hospital ward. Personnel are frequently reporting their own nonverbal empathic responses to patients and patients' nonverbal responses to them, as well as making predictions about patients' behavior that are subsequently found to be accurate. Methods need to be worked out for systematically recording and analyzing these empathic phenomena as they occur within this "natural" setting, and for evaluating the relevance of these phenomena for facilitating the patient's mental health.

There are many possibilities for research on the institution of interventions in those social configurations that are found to be illness-maintaining. How these interventions originate, how they are designed and planned for, their effects and their evaluation and revision are all important aspects that need to be studied. For example, Tudor[10] demonstrated how one might intervene into the process of mutual withdrawal. She found that the withdrawal had to be brought into the nurse's awareness, and that the meaning of the nature of the nurse's mode of withdrawn participation, its psychological basis, and the nature of the equilibrium she established with the patient also had to be clearly seen and understood. After such awareness had developed through discussion with a consultant outside the situation, the nurse could reverse her withdrawal. The interruption of the nurse's withdrawal then contributed to interrupting the patient's withdrawal. G. T. Will and I also were able to intervene into the process of mutual withdrawal by interrupting a nurse's low morale.[11] We found that a nurse's low morale was constituted by a pattern of interpersonal processes, such as feelings of failure, anger and resentment, guilt and blame, and constriction of perspective. Further, this pattern of low morale was found to contribute to an integration of mutual withdrawal, in which the patient's withdrawal is in part a function of the nurse's withdrawal and the nurse's withdrawal is a function of her low morale. An interruption of the nurse's low morale was accomplished by the nurse's discussing and analyzing with a consultant outside the situation the ways in which her low morale was initiated, developed, and maintained, and the nature of its contribution to an integration of mutual withdrawal. The raising of the nurse's morale was followed by a cessation of the integration of mutual withdrawal.

At the institutional level Jones and his co-workers[12] have initiated widespread institutional change, especially in the alteration of the communicative network, in an attempt to study the effects on patient improvement. Hyde, Greenblatt and York and co-workers, in studies supported by Russell Sage Foundation and as yet unpublished, have done experimental work in various mental hospitals in an attempt to determine the most effective institutional ways of improving ward patient care.

The intervention procedure can be a significant tool in the study of social change. When a particular configuration has been identified as illness-maintaining and an intervention instituted to alter this configuration, the social scientist can study the antecedents and consequences of this intervention with a view toward establishing connections between events. Such questions as the following might be explored: How does a particular social context emerge from another social context that preceded it in time? What are the significant transition points in this sequence of events? What is the relation, and how is it established, of any event sequence or configuration of event sequences to the improvement of the patient? These questions are difficult to answer because of the following methodological problems implicit in them which as yet have not been adequately solved and which could be explored in the mental hospital: (a) the delineation of the boundaries of any event or event sequence; (b) the assessment of the relevance of any event or sequence of events to another event or sequence of events; (c) following the complex relation between one configuration and other configurations; (d) isolating and evaluating accurately the significant transition points that have presumably modified a previous context and are shaping an emergent context; (e) developing precision in tracing connections between events and establishing these interconnections in an unbroken flow.

The study of intervention along the lines indicated could most effectively be conducted by the method of participant observation. This method, too, needs careful appraisal and evaluation to insure the collection of valid data. Some important aspects of this process that require further intensive investigation are: (a) the reciprocal influence of the observer and observed, (b) the covert transactions entering into the process, (c) the definition of the observer's role in its formal and informal aspects, (d) the advantages and disadvantages of active and passive participant observation, and (e) the role of anxiety and bias in distorting the data gathered by this method.[13]

I have tried to indicate above the value of using a sociological frame of reference in studying the mental hospital. With this perspective the mental hospital can be viewed as an on-going social system in which institutional structures and processes, as well as substructures and subprocesses, are patterned in definable ways. These patterns must be seen in both their formal and informal aspects. Viewed over time, the structure as a whole and specific processes that are part of it produce varying therapeutic effects. The task of an investigator might be to identify and delineate the larger institutional patterns, as well as the more specific social contexts, to see the various processes in their interrelations, and to evaluate and test the relation of these varied social contexts to improvement in the patient's mental health. In developing and testing hypotheses on the relation between mental-hospital structure and mental health it would be important to make comparative studies of large and small mental hospitals. Significant differences in size of hospital, staff-patient ratios, and complexity of organization may reveal different therapeutic or untherapeutic contexts in these different types of institutions; at the same time some common factors may be found that are generally therapeutic, regardless of the size of the hospital.

Studying the relation between the social structure and mental health in the mental hospital, with the patient as the focus, has the advantages of the extreme case: Any alterations that occur in the patient's mental health may be more readily observable and stand out more sharply, especially when the patient makes dramatic changes. However, the study of the relation between social structure and mental health has important implications beyond the mental hospital. It seems reasonable to assume that many of the institutional structures, social contexts, and interpersonal processes that facilitate the recovery of a mentally ill patient will also contribute to the development of mental health in the child while he is being socialized. Specific hypotheses need to be formulated on the basis of findings in the mental hospital and then further tested for their applicability to the process of socialization.

The Study of Group Life. There are some problems that have been of continuing sociological interest that can be studied in the mental hospital and that need not be considered in terms of their therapeutic implications. The staff carries on a highly organized form of group life in the mental hospital. Alongside of this, there are some types of patients who live together but are lacking organization among themselves and remain on the level of an aggregate. In between these two extremes there are, of course, various degrees of cohesiveness in patient groupings.[14] These gradations in the cohesiveness, complex organization, and persistence of various groups in the mental hospital afford the social scientist the opportunity for close comparison. Seeing these groups side by side, as well as in interaction with each other, may enable us to develop knowledge about the bases and factors that account for the differences in group functioning and for the differences in group organization of mentally ill persons.

Patients who maintain only a very tenuous form of group life may provide a critical area for study of the evaluation, persistence, and dissolution of groups in a "natural" setting. In these groups the fluctuations in anxiety of the participants seem to play an important role. Studies need to be formulated to examine the effects of anxiety in such groups. What is the point beyond which anxiety makes group life impossible? Where the group persists in tenuous form, what are the various forms and orientations it takes with increasing or decreasing anxiety? Asking these questions about the relation between anxiety and group life brings us into the problem of the relation between the individual and the group. In these tenuous groups we might be able to trace the effects produced by anxiety in the individual members, who in turn direct or fashion the nature of the group activity under the pressure of their anxiety. Conversely, data can be gathered on the ways in which the group helps allay or minimize the individual's anxiety so that the group cohesiveness is maintained.

Collective Behavior. The susceptibility of patients to anxiety contributes to a type of collective phenomenon we have called collective disturbance, which is readily available for investigation in the mental hospital.[15] We found[16] that collective disturbances of patients on a ward that were intense and persistent over a time were a function of general institutional disturbances. We were able to trace the development of institutional disturbance through the various hierarchical levels until it reached the patients. The failure in effective functioning of many staff members formed a pattern of reciprocity in which the disturbance of one contributed to that of another so as to increase and spread the effects of the disturbance. The collective disturbance among patients spread in the context of generalized tension in the institution as a whole. From our study we arrived at the conclusion that the communication of tension between and among patients had to be looked at in its complex interrelatedness to the rest of the institution.

The study of such collective phenomena in the mental hospital may provide more detailed and valid generalizations about the development of generalized tensions and the precise ways in which they are communicated. In addition, through the study of collective disturbance, processes of organization, disorganization, and reorganization and their interrelations can be examined.

Because much of the social research in mental hospitals is of recent origin, a great deal of the work in the field is in progress and as yet unpublished. Caudill and Stainbrook, Dunham and Weinberg, Gillin, Le Bar and co-workers, and others have all done broad studies of the social organization and culture of a mental hospital. Von Mering is now conducting a survey of developments in ward-patient care in various hospitals throughout the country; and Mishler is studying staff motivations and commitment to organizational goals in a mental hospital. The interest in studying the mental hospital and the increase of research activity within its confines seems to hold much promise for developing our understanding of the relation between mental health and social structure as well as contributing to our knowledge of human behavior in general.

RED TAPE AS A SOCIAL PROBLEM

Alvin W. Gouldner

"These clients came to plead with us. Instead of storming the office and knocking everything to smithereens, they came to plead."—FRANZ KAFKA

IT IS NOW SOMETHING more than a century since the term "red tape" was introduced into the English language in its figurative sense. Sidney Smith (1771-1845), an Englishman who could not make up his mind whether he wished to be remembered as a clergyman or as a wit, did much to popularize the satirical connotations of the term.

In 1838, Lord Lytton averred that "the men of dazzling genius began to sneer at the red-tape minister as a mere official manager of details." The redoubtable Carlyle once described someone as "little other than a red-tape talking machine." Probably the first person to give red tape its sociological baptism was Herbert Spencer (about 1873). It was not, however, until 1889 and 1890 that the term began to appear in American newspapers and periodicals.

Present day interest in red tape on the part of sociologists largely derives from studies in bureaucratic structure. Alexander Leighton[1] and Robert Merton have analyzed it as a dysfunctional behavioral pattern which impairs the persistence or continuity of an organization.[2]

Here, and in similar approaches to the subject, red tape is interpreted as being the actual behavior engaged in by the bureaucrat, or of its consequences, interpreted in terms of the ends of the *organization*.[3]

There is, however, one set of observations which this approach to red tape was not designed to encompass. Namely, that red tape is a popular and widespread complaint which is explicitly articulated. There is, then, a second, not an alternative but an additional, context in terms of which red tape may be analyzed—i.e., as a "social problem" taken cognizance of by large numbers of laymen.

The implications of this further analysis may be clarified if two questions are asked:

(1) Why is it, for example, that not all means which have become transformed into ends are thought of as red tape, e.g., the American Constitution?

(2) Why is it, also, that the very same procedures or practices which one group may characterize as red tape may be viewed by another group as deserving no invidious label? The latter may, in fact, attach an approving (possibly, "green-tape") label to the procedure. For example, some landlords but few tenants characterize rent control procedures as red tape[4]

Commonplace as those observations are, they, nevertheless, suggest that red tape involves phenomena of two orders: (1) the perceiving individual

---

Reprinted from *Reader in Bureaucracy* (1952), Robert K. Merton, Ailsa P. Gray, Barbara Hockey, Hanan C. Selvin, eds., pp. 410-18, by permission of the author, the editors and the publisher. (Copyright, 1952, by The Free Press.)

who, with a given frame of reference, comes into some relationship with (2) objective, perhaps bureaucratic, practices or behavior patterns.

Thus red tape as a social problem cannot be explained unless the frame of reference employed by the individual who uses this label is understood, as well as the objective attributes of the situations with which he comes into contact. Both elements are interrelated and changes in either alter the scope and formulation of the problem.

This analysis of red tape as a social problem does not seek to attach a new meaning to a familiar term. Rather, it seeks to identify the frame of reference of people who are hostile to red tape and for whom it therefore comprises a problem, as well as to describe the structural context and the social functions of red tape.

The data upon which this tentative account is partly based are of two kinds: first, secret ballot, group interviews, qualitatively analyzed; second, interviews with a small sample of 124 respondents stratified in terms of status and ethnic group.[5]

Red Tape as the Unnecessary. As might be expected, the meanings ascribed by our interviewees to the term "red tape," as indicated both by their general definitions and concrete illustrations, are most often stated in the language of efficiency. For example, "going through a lot of unnecessary beating around the bush." Another: "Red tape is something which disagrees with the theory that the shortest distance between two points is a straight line." And again: "It means a lot of unnecessary rigmarole and delay in filling out forms."

The language of efficiency is not a valueless and detached judgment on the part of people in our society. "Efficiency"—the choice of those alternatives that maximize the realization of objectives, or minimize expenditures in their pursuit—is widely regarded as a good in and of itself. It is in this sense that a belief in efficiency is one critical element in the frame of reference for the perception and judgment of red tape.

Since efficiency is a widely acknowledged value in a society priding itself upon its "technique" and "know-how," it is apparently employed to mask negative judgment based on less universally accredited values or less easily articulated sentiments. It is not merely that there are other non-rational elements in the red-tape frame of reference, but that these may be implicit in seemingly rational judgments expressed in terms of efficiency.[6] This will be evident from the discussion following.

The Separation of Public and Private Spheres. In describing the meaning red tape has for them, interviewees tend to emphasize presumably "unnecessary" or dispensable features. These, however, are condemned not solely because they violate the canons of efficiency, but because they transgress less easily expressed values. One of the most important of these is the sacredness of privacy, or a belief that the individual should be privileged to withhold certain information about himself from anyone. In this context, the unnecessary is that which violates privacy.

The clichés and common places of complaints regarding red tape repeatedly strike this same keynote: too many people have a chance to observe something of a nature which the respondent deems private; he feels that he is being forced to divulge matters construed as intimate. For some, red tape means: "filling out forms," "going through many hands," "too many details asked," "being investigated," or "too many interviews needed."

One respondent remarks: "When I wanted to withdraw $300 from my bank account, they wouldn't let me take it out unless I first saw a vice-president. They could see that I had the money in my account from my bank book. He wanted to know what I wanted the money for, and I had to explain I was moving and buying new furniture. Why was it his business?" This theme is compactly summarized by another: "Many questions that are asked are of a personal nature and should not be the ordinary business of a stranger."

Not only is the individual's privacy invaded by the information demanded of him, but he is himself investigated, and thus placed on the defensive. One respondent, describing an experience with what he called red tape, reports:

"A commercial vehicle struck my automobile. To settle the matter, I had to give a report to my insurance company. They had to send out a man to inspect my damage to see if the estimate I had given them was correct. . . ." Another says that a "mild example" of red tape "would be in the attempt to borrow money from a finance company. All your references have to be *checked,* your source of income *checked,* your honesty, reliability, etc." A respondent describing efforts of a married couple to adopt a child says: "They must undergo *investigation* for moral and financial reasons. After they finally get a child, they must be *investigated* again before they can legally adopt the child. . . ." Finally, a respondent complains that "You are asked questions which have to be *verified* by so and so and so and so."

In these instances regarded as red tape, the individual's ego is challenged on two counts: (1) A claim which he believes legitimate is not taken "at face value." He must either supply proof or allow it to be investigated. He is, as one remarked, "treated as a criminal"—he may feel his worth is questioned, his status impugned. (2) Not only are his claims and assertions challenged, but other details of his "private life" are investigated. The individual enters the situation on "official," "technical," or "public" business, and feels that he ends up by being investigated as a person.

It seems clear that this conception of red tape would turn up only if the individual accepted the current value which insists upon the division of social activity into the spheres of the public and the private.[7] In such cases, the individual responds to the violation of the value by feeling, as some expressed it, that "he is getting involved;" that he is experiencing the fusion of spheres which should be kept separated.

The Belief in Equality. The foregoing comments of interviewees may have suggested that the situation is defined as red tape when pursuit of an end is obstructed and especially so when the ends themselves are defined in a particular way—namely, as rights. One respondent mentions that veterans encounter red tape when "trying to get the V. A. to approve dental work to a veteran who is *entitled to it.* . . ." Another tells of his difficulty in obtaining an army promotion when he was "due for" it. A third speaks of his difficulty in collecting back flying pay, even though "I had papers with me verifying my *entitlement* to the flying pay. . . ."

It is not necessarily the absolute, but rather the relative complexity of demands made by an organization upon its clientele which leads these to be regarded as red tape. Ordinary routines are so regarded if there is the suspicion that special privilege exempts others from these routines. A commercial aviator thus considers the customs procedures encountered in international flights as red tape, going on to declare that if you belong to the "right organizations" you pass through customs much more quickly. A respondent speaking of banks says that they "act as if they are doing you a favor to take your money. When you first open your account, they keep you waiting until they are ready. . . . They really don't want a small account. They're interested in the big accounts."

The democratic creed with its accent on equality of rights may thus provide a value component of the red tape frame of reference,[8] one which would presumably not be common in a nondemocratic society.

Powerlessness. Sensitivity to disparities of power seems to be another element in the red tape frame of reference. A veteran refers to his army experiences to illustrate his conception of red tape: "If a soldier wishes to go on leave, first of all the G. I. must present the claim to his platoon sergeant. Then it is referred to the top sergeant who, in turn, goes over the request and gives either his approval or disapproval. He then presents this to the C. O. who will either approve or disapprove your request."

Another: "In factories, when persons have grievances, they are usually sent to many different persons before 'hitting' the particular one who will handle the case, rather than being sent directly to the person who will give you the satisfaction."

A student discussing an encounter with what he calls red tape says:

"To secure permission to use school records for the purpose of doing an attendance survey, I was first directed to an employee at the Board of Education, then to another employee, then to the deputy superintendent, the superintendent, the first employee asked, the superintendent again, then to the attendance director and, finally, permission to use the records was obtained."

These and similar statements suggest that the individual who decries red tape feels that he is unable to "get to" the people who have the power, or get to them readily enough. You first have to go before the powerless people —they seem to be saying—who though they may be able to deny your request, are often unable to approve it finally. They can say, "no," but not "yes." Power centers are felt to be out of reach and the individual experiences himself and those with whom he can have some face to face contact as powerless.[9] This feeling of powerlessness may in some cases be a character trait rather than an artifact of a social situation.

Suspicion and the Inability to Defer Gratifications. Two further character traits of clients apparently encourage them to perceive red tape where others do not. These are suspiciousness and an apparent inability to defer gratifications. The prevalence of suspicion manifests itself in the motives that respondents ascribe to those who present them with the red tape obstacles. "Apparently the only thing to be gained in making this application complicated, which resulted in many applications rejected," said one informant, "was the increase and duration of political jobs." Red tape, says another, "seems to be used in order to have only the very anxious ones receive whatever they're after and discourage those who are not too eager." These remarks, among others, seem to imply that there exists deliberate intent to frustrate the client. For some, the world of red tape is not merely "unnecessary," "complicated," or "meaningless"; it becomes meaningful as willful maliciousness when viewed in the context of suspicion.[10]

Those who are particularly sensitive to "waiting," when they emphasize the time it takes to comply with their requests or to get a decision on them, may include some whose capacity to defer gratification has become weakened. It would seem that suspicion and an inability to defer gratifications are closely interlocked. For, to the extent that the world is felt to be peopled with those who would do us harm and who cannot be trusted, safety lies only in the *immediate* satisfaction. The satisfaction that has to be deferred is imperiled by all manner of hostile forces that may prevent its realization.

Inadequate "Substantial Rationality." One further characteristic of the red-tape-sensitive frame of reference deserves special mention: its apparent inhibition of an "intelligent insight into the interrelations of events in a given situation," what Karl Mannheim called[11] "substantial rationality." Persons complaining of red tape often say, in effect, that the things they experience are meaningless and make no sense to them. They describe red tape as "complicated," "unnecessarily complex," a "mix-up" or "befuddlement."

We need not presuppose that the demands placed upon a client, or the procedures with which he is forced to comply, are actually necessary or unnecessary. The only question of interest here is whether anything can be learned about the client and his frame of reference from his repeated references to red tape as "confused" or "mixed-up." Our data do not permit us to say whether, in some objective sense, the situation is really "befuddled." We can be reasonably certain, however, that it does "confuse" the client, and that it provides him with experiences which are meaningless in his frame of reference.

As Lundberg has indicated,[12] the degree to which a situation appears complicated or simple is not only determined by the situation itself. It is also influenced by the frame of reference through which it is viewed. Thus individuals coming upon a situation which they label "red tape" and finding it confusing are likely to have a frame of reference that cannot make sense of their experience.

What are some reasons for this eclipse of substantial rationality and for the inadequacy of the red-tape-sensitive frame of reference? Some clues may be provided by examining the kinds of organizations alleged to have the least red tape. Most respondents mention nonprofit, private associations, as having least red tape. These include churches, Y's, the American Legion, the Salvation Army, fraternities, and trade unions. In part, these groups are distinguished by their relatively personalized and informal relationships. The tendency to choose "least red tape" groups on the basis of this criterion is epitomized by one person who nominated, "the home."

A second criterion apparently used by respondents involves the effectiveness of the possible cash transactions. Thus one respondent, who declared that second-hand car dealers have little red tape, went on to say, "Here, money talks!"

The organizations listed as having least red tape in general appear to have well-developed, personalized, and informal relations or effective cash relationships. Among privately owned businesses believed to have little red tape, *small* businesses were prominent. These, providing "service with a smile," also effectively fuse informal and pecuniary ties.

Apparently, many individuals in our society expect organizations to operate on one or both of these bases. But a distinctive feature of contemporary bureaucracies is their use of relationships which are neither personalized nor pecuniary, neither informal nor contractual. Instead, they are attuned to abstract and impersonal rules. These considerations suggest that those who pronounce red tape to be a "mix-up" and "befuddlement" are utilizing a frame of reference which relies upon somewhat outmoded techniques for realizing goals. A frame of reference which depends upon market and informal arrangements as instrumentalities will be less and less effective as bureaucratic organization invades ever-widening spheres of the society.

Red Tape as "Resentment." Other social sources of the red-tape-sensitive frame of reference are indicated in Max Scheler's concept of "resentment." According to Scheler, "resentment" is a compound of envy and suppressed aggression, a compound which sometimes bursts into the open and is directed against some diffusely defined group or object. Scheler maintains that, "The wider the gulf existing between the juridical condition of divergent social groups established by the political system or tradition, on the one side, and their actual power on the other, the more powerful will be the charge of psychological explosiveness implicit in the situation."[13]

In certain major respects the red tape frame of reference and Scheler's description of resentment converge. Both involve a belief in quality which is violated by a sense of powerlessness. Like the "man of resentment," the individual hostile to red tape also feels that there are things to which he is entitled but never receives. Essentially, however, what distinguishes the man of resentment is not his frustration, but his feeling of powerlessness. He has little hope of rectifying the situation. It would appear, therefore, that a full analysis of the social roots of the red-tape-sensitive frame of reference must link up with the phenomenon of alienation.

Alienation of the Conservative. If this is so, it is likely that we are confronted with the alienation of a distinct ideological group, roughly characterizable as "conservatives." For it is the conservatives, rather than the "radicals," who seem most concerned with red tape as a social problem.[14] To designate this group simply as "conservative," without specifying its other attributes, especially its status properties, is clearly inadequate. Further analysis of our data is required, however, before the other characteristics of this group can be stated with confidence.

For the present, a tentative formulation might hold that red tape, as a culturally familiar epithet, has largely developed under conservative sponsorship.[15] This may explain why those indignant at red tape frequently direct their aggression against clerks at the bottom of a structure, while higher echelons escape unscathed. Their hostility is, moreover, aimed at *means*— e.g., forms and questionnaires—rather than at group *ends*. Criticisms embodied in the term "red tape" enable the individual to express aggression against powerful and prestige-laden organization, while still permitting him to be "counted in." As such, "red tape" is a social critique readily acceptable to conservatives.

The significance of the red tape stereotype seems, however, to be even deeper. Social institutions during the last century or so have undergone profound changes partly describable as bureaucratization. The red tape stereotype gives compact but blurred expression to the resentment against the alienation, the impersonalization, and the dull routines that afflict bureaucracy. This suggests that the growth of concern with "red tape" may indicate new types of social problems.

BUREAUCRATIC ORGANIZATION
AND THE VOLUNTEER

Bernard Barber

. . . DESPITE THEIR DEMOCRATIC WILLINGNESS to volunteer for community welfare activities, American citizens are pulled away from greater voluntary participation by their job and family obligations, which are also essential components of a democratic society. We have now to examine another paradox, namely, that the nature and needs of the organizations in which social work is carried on make it difficult to use volunteers except under limited and special conditions, and this even when social work executives are genuinely convinced of the value of voluntary participation.

Social work and public welfare agencies are not all alike, of course, but most of them are characterized by a type of organization which sociologists have recently come to call "formal organization." This type of organization is not peculiar to social work; indeed, it is characteristic of practically all of American industry as well as of the bureaus of the Government and the Armed Forces. In social work, the largest of such bureaucratically structured organizations may be found in the larger Community Fund Drives and in the American Red Cross, where tens of thousands of professionals and volunteers are coordinated in an efficient and smoothly functioning group. Such organizations are efficient instruments for the achievement of social purposes, indeed, they have been called social machines. Their efficiency depends, however, upon a certain set of conditions.

Formal organizations are composed of carefully defined positions, called "offices," arranged in a clear pattern of hierarchical authority. The incumbent of each office must be trained and regularly available to perform his technical functions according to the schedule fixed for the whole organization. His absence may do more than deprive the organization of one worker; it may disrupt the entire organization, or a large part of it, because a connecting link in the routine of performance is missing. Each office-holder, moreover, is responsible for something else than technical functions. His position in the hierarchy of offices requires of him both effective supervision of his subordinates and loyal obedience to his superiors. In this respect too, the absence or irregularity of a single worker may disrupt a large part of the organization or considerably diminish its effectiveness. We may think of these conditions as emergent imperatives of the existence of formal organizations. Such imperatives, indeed, operate for *all* formal organizations, whether they are staffed by paid employees entirely or in part by volunteers. As a result, social work organizations find themselves with many of the same problems of recruitment, training, incentives, and recognition that industrial and military organizations have.

Volunteers have certain shortcomings from the point of view of formal

This is a previously unpublished article based on Bernard Barber, " 'Mass Apathy' and Voluntary Social Participation in the United States" (unpublished Ph.D. Dissertation, Harvard University, 1948).

organizations and the professional social work executives who run them. Executives of such organizations require trained, reliable, disciplined, and responsible subordinates. On the whole, volunteers are less suitable in these respects than paid employees. At least so far as large groups of workers are concerned, money income is the most effective incentive for securing the regular efforts of workers in American society. This is not because Americans are mercenary, but simply because, as we have indicated above, a paid job is terribly important as the primary determinant of the social status and livelihood of each individual and his family. When a worker is paid, his job takes precedence over other obligations. But when a middle-class woman takes a volunteer position, that job at best is always competing with her other obligations. It cannot, in the nature of the case, be as important to her as a job is to a paid worker. Hence it is inevitable that the other obligations of the volunteer will often win out and cause disrupting absences and irregularities in organizations using volunteers. Chester I. Barnard, formerly President of the New Jersey Bell Telephone Company and now President of the Rockefeller Foundation, has commented on this inferiority of volunteers in formal organizations:

> After much experience, I am convinced that the most ineffective services in a continuing effort are in one sense those of volunteers, or of semi-volunteers; for example, half-pay workers. What appears to be inexpensive is in fact very expensive, because non-material incentives—such as prestige, toleration of too great personal interest in the work with its accompanying fads and "pet" projects, the yielding to exaggerated conceptions of individual importance—are causes of internal friction and many other undesirable consequences.[1]

For such reasons, and even though they are themselves sometimes unaware of them, executives of social work agencies are reluctant to use volunteers. This reluctance can be seen in the following excerpt from a manual of instructions on the use of volunteers intended for the professional executives in the Boys Club movement:

> Long experience has led men in the Boys Club field to believe that a Boys Club functions most effectively with a full-time, professionally trained leadership, and that there is no wholly adequate substitute for such personnel. . . . The Boys Club, however, like every other sort of agency which is not directly tied in with our war effort, is being stripped today of its full-time manpower. . . . They are not to be found even though funds are available for them. Thus we are *forced* to look to volunteers and part-time leaders . . .[2]

Such statements indicate no lack of democratic belief in the value of volunteers but only the problems of executives in formal organizations trying to get certain jobs done.

The volunteer's job in a formal organization is, in important respects, like any paid job, requiring definitely scheduled contributions of work and the ready performance of tasks assigned by superiors regardless of the personal preferences of the individual volunteer. Yet it is apparently difficult to be guaranteed such performance by volunteers, witness the following injunctions to them contained in a pamphlet issued by the Volunteer Bureau of Greater Hartford:

Be dependable, come when you say you will and be on time.

Be loyal, take constructive criticism to an agency supervisor rather than the outside world.

Respect the policies, standards, rules and personnel practices of the agency. Be willing to accept supervision.

Some executives may find these problems of dealing with volunteers insoluble or think them more trouble than volunteer work is worth. Moved by voluntarist values, however, most executives are striving to cope with them. There is developing in social work a group of specialists who have considerable experience and knowledge of these problems and who know how to minimize them. The Office of Price Administration, for example, had great success in using such volunteer specialists and therefore appointed one for each of its regional offices.[3] These specialists, and other social work executives, have been slowly formulating a rationalized technology for using volunteers.[4]

Here are some principles and procedures of this technology for the recruitment, placement, training, and rewarding of volunteers:

Professionals are now learning that "not everyone who volunteers can be accepted. . . ."[5] Over-enthusiastic recruitment often results in excessive mortality rates for volunteers, with consequent disruptions of the established routines and schedules of the organization. To prevent disappointment, the volunteer must be told that he may not like the work or that he may not be suited to a particular agency. Volunteers apparently prefer to attach themselves directly to a particular social work agency rather than pass through an employment clearing-house like a central volunteer service bureau. Therefore, their needs and the needs of any given agency which they happen to choose may not coincide or may even be in conflict.

Social work organizations have discovered the need for very careful job placement.[6] At best, this is difficult, since job needs are often for special skills at particular times and volunteers usually have limited skills and limited time. In the best practice, it is now recommended that one person in each agency should be responsible for initial contact with the volunteer. The first contact should be cordial and hospitable, since the volunteer, unlike the paid employee, still has to be "sold" to some extent. The first contact should determine just which carefully defined job in the organization the volunteer can fill. Next, the volunteer "should be given knowledge about the agency, its staff and their duties, its rules and regulations, policies, standards, facilities and any training courses conducted by the agency."[7]

Both pre-service and in-service training are desirable, with considerable training on the job under careful supervision being preferred. Some social workers recommend that wherever possible groups that are already organized, such as church groups and lay clubs, be used in volunteer projects in order to reduce the need for professional supervision. Since the volunteer is free to leave at any time, even if he is a trained and presumably satisfied member of the organization, professionals are advised to have periodic contact with the volunteer to make sure that he is getting the job satisfaction he desires. It is considered important that volunteers feel their work is worth doing. Note, however, that such procedures for personnel recruitment, training, and supervision are quite different and more time-consuming than those customarily used in American industry.

Finally, in acknowledgment of the special motivation of the volunteer, it is necessary to reward her with some public recognition, with some standardized symbol of her type and length of service. The Advisory Committee on Volunteer Service of Community Chests and Councils has recently published a "Plan of Recognition with Awards for Community Volunteer Service" that is typical of such systems of recognition. Under this plan, recognition consists of certificates and metal emblems to be awarded the volunteer upon the completion of stated numbers of hours of volunteer work. It is recommended that these rewards be distributed at "appropriate community recognition ceremonies" with the "participation of public officials, leading citizens and impressive speakers."

In all these ways, the professional social work executive who uses volunteers must consider the special problems of volunteer motivation as well as the needs of his organization in a somewhat different way from that required of the successful executive of an organization using only paid workers. It would be unfair not to see that these problems impose an additional burden on the executive who uses volunteers.

There is still another important problem. Because of the different relations which volunteers and professionals have to the formal organizations in which they collaborate, problems of adjustment between their *different* needs and attitudes arise, problems which some executives may wish to avoid by excluding volunteers. For the professional, his place in the organization is essentially a "job," with established routines, patterned hierarchical relationships, problems of security and a career, and definite, limited goals. In short, he is likely to have vested interests of emotion and values in the organization itself and in its effective functioning. The volunteer, however, because she is motivated by enthusiasm for the final goals of the organization, may be impatient with the needs of the organization itself and of its full-time, regular professional employees. There is some evidence that professional social workers need to be reassured in their relations with volunteers. A volunteer guide addressed to professionals says: "Volunteer jobs complement and augment the work of a professional staff; they do not displace paid workers."[8] Also, it is frequently recommended in professional social work literature that "schools of social work give special attention to training social workers for more cooperative work with volunteers."[9] In some agencies, *esprit de corps* is promoted by social gatherings of the whole staff, professional and volunteer.

These and other problems of using volunteers, then, are inevitable because efficient social work is carried on in formal organizations and because that kind of organization has certain conditions for its efficiency. These problems are not, we see, insoluble, but neither can they be overlooked by those social workers whose democratic values and needs for personnel lead them to use volunteers.

Notes

I – FAMILY STRUCTURE AND ETHNIC PATTERNS

THE KINSHIP SYSTEM OF THE CONTEMPORARY UNITED STATES

Talcott Parsons

1. Probably the most significant contribution to this field thus far has been made by Kingsley Davis in a series of articles starting with his "Structural Analysis of Kinship," *American Anthropologist*, April, 1937, in collaboration with W. Lloyd Warner, and going on to "Jealousy and Sexual Property," *Social Forces*, March, 1936; "The Sociology of Prostitution," *American Sociological Review*, October, 1937; "The Child and the Social Structure," *Journal of Educational Sociology*, December, 1940; "The Sociology of Parent-Youth Conflict," reprinted in this volume.

I am greatly indebted to Dr. Davis's work, starting with the significance of his first article for the systematic relating of the biological and the social levels of kinship structure. Much of the present analysis is implicit in his later articles, which have proved to be very suggestive in working out the somewhat more explicit formulations of the present study.

2. It is proposed in a later article to enter into certain of these comparative problems of kinship structure in an attempt to arrive at a higher level of dynamic generalization about kinship than has yet come to be current in the sociological or even the anthropological literature.

3. The diagramming conventions adopted in this paper are somewhat different from those commonly used by anthropologists. They are imposed by the peculiar structural features of our system, especially: a) Its "openness," i.e. absence of preferential mating. Hence the two spouses of any given conjugal family are not structurally related by family of orientation and it is not possible to portray "the" marriage system in terms of a limited number of lines of descent. Each marriage links ego's kinship system to a complete system. b) The consequent indefinite "dispersion" of the lines of descent.

The best that can be done in two dimensions is to take *ego* as a point of reference and show *his* significant kin. It is strictly impossible to diagram the system as a whole—that would require a space of n-dimensions. Similarly, "vertical" and "horizontal" or "lateral" "axes" have only a very limited meaning." Lines of descent" and "generations" are significant. But there is a geometrically progressive increase in the number of lines of descent with each generation away from ego and the distinctions cannot be made in terms of a linear continuum. I am indebted to Miss Ai-li Sung of Radcliffe College for assistance in drafting the diagram.

4. The most important exception is its usage in upper class circles to denote what Warner calls a "lineage," i.e., a group possessing continuity over several generations, usually following the "name line," e.g., the "Adams family." See W. L. Warner and Lunt, *Social Life of a Modern Community* (New Haven: Yale University Press, 1941). The significance of this exception will be commented upon below.

5. See Ralph Linton, *The Study of Man*, (New York: Appleton-Century-Crofts), Chap. VIII, for the very useful distinction between "conjugal" and "consanguine" kinship types.

6. Excluding, of course, those who do not marry. But failure to marry has no positive structural consequences in relation to kinship —only negative.

7. It is of course possible for two pairs—or even more—of siblings to intermarry. This case is, however, without structural significance.

8. In any finite population, lines of descent are bound to cross somewhere, and in our society the marriage of fairly close relatives is not infrequent. But there is no consistent pattern in this intermarriage, and it is hence without structural consequences.

Most of the essentials of an open conjugal system can be maintained, while a high level of generation continuity in at least one line is also maintained, by a systematic discrimination between lines of descent—especially through primogeniture. The extent to which this has and has not occurred is the most important range of variation within the basic pattern and will have to be discussed in some detail below.

9. It should perhaps be explicitly stated that though sometimes called a "descriptive" system by some of the older anthropologists, our terminology is by no means literally descriptive of exact biological relationships. Above all it fails to distinguish relatives whose relation to *ego* is traced through different lines of descent. But it also fails to distinguish by birth order, or to distinguish siblings' spouses from spouses' siblings—both are brothers- or sisters-in-law. Finally, as just noted, it stops making distinctions very soon, treating all collaterals as "cousins."

10. Though perhaps the commonest pattern, primogeniture has by no means been universal. Cf. Arensberg and Kimball, *Family and Society in Ireland*, and G. C. Homans, *English Villagers of the 13th Century*.

11. Indeed a wealthy man who completely neglected philanthropies in his will would be criticized.

12. Cf. Warner and Lunt, *op. cit.* and A. Davis and Burleigh and Mary Gardner, *Deep*

South (Chicago: University of Chicago Press, 1941).

13. Cf. Davis and Gardner, *op. cit.*, Ch. VI; E. Franklin Frazier, "The Negro Family in the United States," reprinted in this volume and Lynd, *Middletown in Transition* (New York: Harcourt Brace, 1937). Mrs. Florence Kluckhohn of Wellesley College has called my attention to a fourth deviant type which she calls the "suburban matriarchy." In certain suburban areas, especially with upper-middle class population, the husband and father is out of the home a very large proportion of the time. He tends to leave by far the greater part of responsibility for children to his wife and also either not to participate in the affairs of the local community at all or only at the insistence of his wife. This would apply to informal social relationships where both entertaining and acceptances of invitations are primarily arranged by the wife or on her initiative.

14. This is conspicuously true, for example, in a unilateral clan system, of the members of the sex group on which the continuity of the clan rests. The situation of the other, the "out-marrying," sex is, on the other hand, quite different.

15. See Simmel's well-known essay on the significance of number in social relationships, *Soziologie*, Ch. II. This is an illuminating case of the "Triadic" group. It is not, however institutionally that of *tertius gaudens* since that implies one playing off the other two against each other, though informally it may sometimes approach that. Institutionally, however, what is most important is the requirement of impartiality between the two families of orientation. Essentially the same considerations apply as between an older couple and two or more of their married children's families of procreation—impartiality irrespective of sex or birth order is expected.

16. This tendency for multiple-membered social systems to repress spontaneous manifestations of sentiment should not be taken too absolutely. In such phenomena as cliques, there is room for the following of personal inclinations within the framework of institutionalized statuses. It is, however, probable that it is more restrictive in groups where, as in kinship, the institutionalized relationships are particularistic and functionally diffuse than in universalistic and functionally specific systems such as modern occupational organizations. In the latter case personal affective relationships can, within considerable limits, be institutionally ignored as belonging to the sphere of "private affairs."

17. See Abraham Kardiner, *The Individual and His Society*.

18. Cf. the various writings of Margaret Mead, especially her *Coming of Age in Samoa* and *Sex and Temperament*.

19. Cf. N. J. Demerath, "Schizophrenia and the Sociology of Adolescence." Dissertation, Harvard University, 1942, (unpub.).

20. Cf. Talcott Parsons, "An Analytical Approach to the Theory of Social Stratification," *American Journal of Sociology*, May, 1940, and "Age and Sex in the Social Structure of the United States," *American Sociological Review*, October, 1942.

21. For the meaning of these technical terms, see Talcott Parsons, "The Professions and Social Structure," *Social Forces*, May, 1939.

22. An example of disturbing indeterminacy of family status without occupational competition between husband and wife in the case where inherited wealth and family connections of a wife involve the couple in a standard of living and social relations to which the husband's occupational status and income would not give access. Such a situation is usually uncomfortable for the husband, but also very likely for the wife.

23. There is no intention to imply that the adult masculine role in American society is devoid of comparably severe strains. They are not, however, *prima facie* so intimately connected with the structure of kinship as are those of the feminine role.

24. These pressures are, of course, likely to be by far most acute in the case of widows and widowers, especially the former. They are also considerably the more numerous and often there is no other at all tolerable solution than to live in the family of a married child. Being, joined and cared for by an unmarried child, especially a daughter, is another way out for the aged which often involves acute tragedies for the younger person.

THE CONTEMPORARY AMERICAN FAMILY AS AN ANTHROPOLOGIST SEES IT

Margaret Mead

1. Anthropological contributions to the study of the American family have taken the form of (1) detailed studies of American culture made by anthropologists trained as ethnologists, (2) detailed studies of American culture on the basis of some of the premises and methods which had been developed in ethnological research, (3) diagnostic studies of regularities in American culture against the background of research in several other cultures, and (4) use of anthropological concepts in the theoretical analysis of American problems. Among these various contributions the following studies may be mentioned: G. Bateson, "Morale and National Character," in *Civilian Morale, Second Yearbook of the Society for the Psychological Study of Social Issues*, ed. Goodwin Watson (New York: Houghton Mifflin Co., 1942), pp. 71-91; Allison Davis and Burleigh and Mary Gardner, *Deep South* (Chicago: University of Chicago Press, 1942); Allison Davis and John Dollard, *Children of Bondage* (Washington, D. C.: American Council on Education, 1940); John Dollard, *Caste and Class in a Southern Town* (New Haven: Yale University Press, 1937);

E. H. Erikson, "Ego Development and His-torical Change," in *The Psycho-analytic Study of the Child*, ed Anna Freud, Heinz Hartmann, and Ernst Kris (New York: International University Press, 1947), Vol. II; Geoffrey Gorer, *The American People* (New York: W. W. Norton & Co., 1948); Robert S. and Helen M. Lynd, *Middletown* (New York: Harcourt, Brace & Co., 1929); *Middletown in Transition* (New York: Harcourt, Brace & Co., 1937); Margaret Mead, *And Keep Your Powder Dry* (New York: William Morrow & Co., 1942); "On the Institutionalized Role of Women and Character Formation," *Zeitschrift für Sozialforschung*, V, No. 1 (1936), 69-75; "Contracts and Comparisons from Primitive Society," *Annals of the American Academy of Political and Social Science*, CLX (March, 1932), 23-28; "Broken Homes," *Nation*, CXXVIII (February, 1929), 253-55; "What Is Happening to the American Family," *Journal of Social Case Work*, November, 1947, pp. 323-30; "Conflict of Cultures in America," *Proceedings of the 54th Annual Convention of the Middle States Association of Colleges and Secondary Schools and Affiliated Associations*, November, 1940; Talcott Parsons, "Certain Primary Sources and Patterns of Aggression in the Social Structure of the Western World," *Psychiatry*, Vol. X, No. 2 (May, 1947); "Age and Sex in the Social Structure of the United States," *American Sociological Review*, VII (October, 1942), 604-16; "The Kinship System of the Contemporary United States," *American Anthropologist*, XLV, No. 1 (January-March, 1943), 22-38; Hortense Powdermaker, *After Freedom* (New York: Viking Press, 1939); W. Lloyd Warner and Paul Lunt, *The Social Life of a Modern Community* ("Yankee Town Series," Vol. I [New Haven: Yale University Press, 1941]); *The Status System of a Modern Community* "Yankee City Series," Vol. II [New Haven: Yale University Press, 1942]); W. Lloyd Warner and Leo Strole, *The Social Systems of American Ethnic Groups* ("Yankee City Series," Vol. III [New Haven: Yale University Press, 1945]); James West, *Plainsville, U. S. A.* (New York: Columbia University Press, 1945).

THE MIDDLE-CLASS MALE CHILD AND NEUROSIS

Arnold W. Green

1. Arnold W. Green, "Sociological Analysis of Horney and Fromm," *American Journal of Sociology* (1946) 51:533-540.

2. *Neurotic Personality of Our Time* (W. W. Norton & Co., N. Y., 1937, xii and 299 pp.) page 80: The "basic evil is invariably a lack of genuine warmth and affection." Since "love" represents a not too radical departure from "libido" and "Oedipus," it is not surprising that the initial revolt against Freudian theory should find Freudian-trained analysts huddling

close to the fence of familiar pastures. See, for example, Adolph Stern. "Psychoanalytic Therapy in the Borderline Neuroses," *The Psychoanalytic Quarterly* (1945) 14:190-198. Stern finds "affect-hunger," especially in the relationship of mother and child, the root of borderline neuroses. The revolt probably stems more from a distaste of the moral nihilism implicit in Sigmund Freud's theoretical structure, rather than primarily from a rejection of the theory itself.

3. *New Ways in Psychoanalysis* (W. W. Norton & Co., N. Y., 1939, 313 pp.), pp. 75-76. Fromm's position remains more theoretically consistent. In *Escape from Freedom* (Farrar & Rinehart, Inc., N. Y., 1941, ix and 305 pp.) institutional authority as developed in a historical framework is designated as the cause of both neurosis and "normal escapes" in modern western culture; as for the *individual* etiology of neurosis and "pathological normalcy," Fromm points to the experience of irrational authority in the family of orientation: see "Individual and Social Origins of Neurosis," *Amer. Sociol. Rev.* (1944) 9:380-384.

4. This seems to conform to Robert M. MacIver's dictum: ". . . any effective causal enquiry should be addressed to a specific difference between comparable situations." Page 85 of *Social Causation* (Ginn & Co., 1942, x and 414 pp.). The question might be raised that "comparable situations" are not being dealt with here, but both Fromm and Horney use "the family" and "the modern family" as generic terms, without differentiation according to class, ethnic group, etc.

5. Arnold W. Green, "The 'Cult of Personality' and Sexual Relations," *Psychiatry* (1941) 4:343-348.

6. "In all the relations between parents and children the familial organization leaves no place for merely personal affection. Certainly this affection exists, but it cannot express itself in socially sanctioned acts. The behavior of the parents toward the children and the contrary must be determined exclusively by their situations as family members, not by individual merits or preferences." (W. I. Thomas and Florian Znaniecki, *The Polish Peasant in Europe and America*, Knopf, N. Y., 1927, Vol. I, p. 94.) In other words, parental authority, while usually unleavened with "love," is based not so much on personal caprice (Fromm's "irrational authority") but mutual respect for common rules of behavior and labor functions within the household unit.

Respect, not love, is the tie that binds in the peasant family. And within a rigid set of rules, parental authority is almost absolute: ". . . a rebellious child finds nowhere any help, not even in the younger generation, for every member of the family will side with the child's parents if he considers them right, and everyone will feel the familial will behind him and will play the part of a representative of the group" (*ibid.*, pp. 91-92). If the male child's will is considered, it is not because of respect for his individual personality, but because of the increasing power and control the child will assume; he will finally assume the father's place as head of the household.

7. The author is no psychiatrist, and the reader may wonder at the foolhardiness of making such a statement. Yet in the overt behavior of an entire generation in the village, whom the author has intimately known as children, adolescents, and young adults, there was no expression of anxiety, guilt-feelings, rigidity of response, repressed hostility, and so on, the various symptoms described by Horney as characteristic of the basic neurotic character structure. It is impossible to check directly on the reasons for rejection at the local induction center, yet a Polish informant has assured me there is no known case of army rejection because of psychoneurosis within the local Polish community.

Of course, the argument might be raised that only a psychiatrist could discover the unconscious personality conflicts which were present. There is no adequate answer to this charge, just as there is no adequate answer to the orthodox Freudian's charge that only a Freudian can criticize classical psychoanalysis because only a Freudian can understand it. Admittedly, this is no water-tight rebuttal; about all that can be said here is that the total description of the socialization process taking place in the local Polish community at least leaves open the door to the possibility that many who experienced it did not become neurotic. And it is pertinent to remember that analysts have knowledge of only upper middle-class and upper-class behavior.

According to Horney the neurotic develops one of three trends, or some combination of them: masochistic (making the self small and insignificant), narcissistic (appearing unduly significant to one's self and insatiably craving admiration from others) and perfectionistic (need for other's recognition of the self's infallibility, particularly moral infallibility). These trends are all accessible to direct observation within a field of personal interaction, without psychoanalytic techniques. The only personality-trend in these Polish youngsters which resembles any of Horney's formulations is the narcissistic; it is not so much "neurotic," however, as sheer crass egocentrism. According to middle-class standards the socialization process has simply been left uncompleted, with but an elementary self, and social-awareness resulting. And it is *because* these youngsters remain egocentric, with little identification of self with others, that they are spared such neurotic symptoms as anxiety and guilt-feelings. This does not mean they are never unhappy and miserable; far from it, but these feeling-states have nothing in common with the neurotic trends and symptoms described by psychoanalysts, which are all dependent upon intensive identification.

8. Demonstrations of affection are not al-together lacking, but they have little in common with the definitions of parent-child love found in the middle-class women's magazines. A fairly common positive attitude is a fleeting, rather grimly humorous appreciation of the other's alleged shortcomings On occasions where an expression of sentiment would seem to be appropriate, such as a funeral within the family, parents and children are clumsy, awkward, embarrassed with one another. Too many avenues of approach have been sealed off in the past. Relations with parents tend to improve as the children become economically independent; while extremely rare, it does happen occasionally that a father and his grown son may be observed drinking beer together at one of the tables in the Polish Club. It must be remembered that while the local Polish community is an industrial slum, it is also a rural community, and there is sufficient cohesiveness within it to enforce at least the outward appearance of intrafamily solidarity; this is not experienced to any great degree, however, until the children reach young adulthood, and only if they take up residence within the community.

No claim is being made that the early training of all Polish youth in this community is exactly alike, nor that the attitudes of parents and children toward one another are exactly duplicated from family to family. It is here that the "subjective element" in insight (where the observer himself constructs patterns of behavior, at least in part, or merely interprets field-conjuncture?) and in the participant-observer technique becomes potentially dangerous: a single description of a behavior-type or development is applied to various individual personalities, families, situations. And so, in the local Polish community, there is the boy who cripples his father in a fist-fight, runs away from home never to return; another lad, married and raising a family of his own, wistfully wishes he "had gotten to know the old folks better." One girl leaves home at sixteen to become a prostitute; another delays marriage to care for an ailing mother. Thus reality, compressed into a single formulation, becomes distorted.

This is not the place for justification of abstraction. I am convinced, however, that if another observer could spend many years in the village, and find some means of participating in the life of a large number of families representing all groups, as did the author, he would agree that the training of any second-generation Polish child would deviate but slightly from the above general description, while the training of any lower middle-class Protestant child would deviate from that de-description to a marked degree.

9. The problem here is defining "middle-class" in such a way as to maximize psychological relevance. Robert S. Lynd has defined middle class as that class which is off the economic floor (objective) and conceives of itself as going places (subjective). For

present purposes this can be revised as follows: the middle class is that class whose members have welded their attitudes and value into a life-long striving toward an improvement of personal socioeconomic position within the class-structure. By this definition the lower class then becomes made up of those who acquiesce to inferior status and the upper class those with an assured superior status. The only "objective criterion" which can be admitted in conjunction with the foregoing definition of middle class is that a given person not be permanently blocked in his striving by reason of race, color, ethnic-group, which are essentially caste elements.

10. Not only has "middle-class" been loosely defined, but also the claim is not being made that all middle-class children are equally affected by the ideal-type conditioning described, which is a deliberate exaggeration of the factor-conjunction which maximizes personality-absorption. In individual cases there will be different combinations of the factors enumerated, as well as deviations from individual factors.

11. Fromm's formulation of the "pseudo self" must not be confused with "personality absorption." Fromm views the self as having a dynamism of its own, apart from its social context: the pseudo self arises when the self accepts the ideas, values, and goals of others as its own. The present author accepts no such demarcation of self and social: the self is derived within the given social context; personality absorption occurs when that context is narrowed for the child to include little more than one or two adults.

12. Peculiarly enough, parents are viewed either as constant factors or as the villains in the piece in most discussions of "individual factors" in neurosis. But it is rather important to find out what there is to being a modern middle-class parent that fertilizes the soil of the child's neurosis however the individual seed may be planted. It will not suffice to dismiss the matter with "the parents' own neuroses," as does Horney.

13. See Arnold W. Green, "Duplicity," *Psychiatry* (1943) 6:411-424.

14. This obligation, as an individual experience, is fast passing. See Robert M. Dinkel, "Attitudes of Children Toward Supporting Aged Parents," *Amer Sociol. Rev.* (1944) 9:370-379. The government bureaus are planning old-age assistance benefits on the assumption that an increasing proportion of the aged will fail to secure support from their children. See W. S. Woytinsky, *Labor in the United States* (Social Science Research Council, Washington, 1938, xxii and 33 pp.).

15. Basing their estimates on a family income of $2,500, Dublin and Lotka figure that the parents spend between $9,180 and $10,485 in rearing a child through the age of 18. (Quoted in Kinsley Davis, "Reproductive Institutions and the Pressure for Population,"

Sociological Rev. (1937) 29:1-18—a British publication).

16. The child must not be spanked, parents should be "patient" with him, his ego-growth must not be curbed, etc. The assumption of much of the child-care literature seems to be that the parents have a combined culinary, nursing, and psychiatric function, and nothing more. But note that in a mobile, industrial, specialized job-world, with its emphasis upon contractual relations, cooks, nurses, and psychiatrists are paid for what they do.

17. It would be impossible to ascertain directly the extent of this ambivalence. Asking a man whether or not he approves of the Bretton Woods Proposal differs from asking him whether he loves his little daughter—to be indicated on a ten-point scale. It differs, first, because Bretton Woods is relatively extraneous to the core of the self and is publicly defined as something upon which one may express a wide divergence of opinion, and, second, because a man's attitude toward his daughter is made up of a series of personal experiences, some delightful, others not, all complicated by a cultural compulsive to repress consciousness of ambivalence toward one's own children. Recall George Babbitt: of course he *loved* his wife, Myra, and sometimes he almost liked her!

18. See Willard Waller, *The Family* (Cordon, N. Y., 1938, 621 pp.).

19. The extent of the actual emancipation of women has been commonly exaggerated. Within all classes in our culture, as in all other cultures, women are trained to regard themselves as inferior to men in some degree. It is usually desired that the first child shall be a boy, by wife as well as husband.

20. Clara Thompson, "The Role of Women in This Culture," *Psychiatry* (1941) 4:1-8, p. 6.

21. See Ernest W. Burgess and Leonard S. Cottrell, Jr., *Predicting Success or Failure in Marriage* (Prentice-Hall, Inc., N. Y., 1939, xxiii and 472 pp.), esp. page 413. In their sample they found a slight negative correlation between number of children and self-rating of marital adjustment. Lewis M. Terman, *et al.*, *Psychological Factors in Marital Happiness* (McGraw-Hill, N. Y., 1938, xiv and 474 pp.) apparently remain unaware that their characterization of "Happily married women," derived from statistical manipulations, is a classic statement of the middle-class Victorian housewife-and-mother role. If "happiness" for married women must be something founded in a fading tradition the future looks black. Fortunately, Terman and associates have probably not established isolable unit-factors; instead, sifted elements out of a total middle-class cultural setting which is rapidly changing, *i.e.*, their "factors" may not be applicable in the immediate future.

22. The addition of one more child, which is the outside limit in most middle-class homes, probably does nothing to diminish the

possibility of the first child's developing a neurosis *if* there is an appreciable gap in their ages, because of the likehood of sibling rivalry. See David M. Levy, *Maternal Overprotection* (Columbia University Press, N. Y., 1943, ix and 417 pp.). Levy's valuable monograph has not been used in the present discussion because Levy conceives of the overprotective mother as a person who has voluntarily renounced the world and all its works to devote her entire life to the sacred cause of her own child: the "middle-class mother" is here conceived as a type which has not resolved a conflict between "duty" and individualism. The latter is much more common.

23. Children are being more and more regarded by young middle-class couples as a symbol of *romantic* consummation. "And soon we'll be three," the popular song goes; the child is, then, considered more in terms of being a product of wedded egos than of having an integral place of his own in a family unit. Also, as parents no longer secure economic good and security from children, the affectional element is stepped up to give the parents a reason for having children. In fact, William F. Ogburn has made affection his only hope for preserving our present family form.

24. Margarethe Ribble, in "Disorganizing Factors in Infant Personality," *American Journal of Psychiatry* (1941) 98:459-463, says: "There is a necessity for a long and uninterrupted period of consistent and skillful 'psychological mothering' by one individual. This must continue at least until speech is well-developed and the child has acquired a feeling of self-security and voluntary control of his body equilibrium. . . . It seems that the tone of the gastro-intestinal tract in this early period depends in some special way on reflex stimulation from the periphery. Thus the touch of the mother has a definite, biological implication in the regulation of the breathing and nutritive functions of the child" (page 463). Two things should be noted here: while a certain amount of handling during infancy by one person may be necessary, that person need not be the biological mother; and it would be difficult to measure the extent of the need.

There are several excellent empirical studies of the socialization process now available and in all of them a great deal is made of the child's need for love and affection. But in every single instance studied the child had either been early conditioned to regard love as the most important thing in the world, or had had the opportunity of observing other youngsters receiving something which he did not have. This is not to deny that some affirmation of personal ties to others in primary-group relationships, if not a biological need, is at least universal, but it is doubtful that it need be the type of parent-child love discussed in such studies. Primitive children, brought up in large dwelling-units among many kinsmen, in a sense spread thin their affection over a wide area, and this affection is relatively less in total intensity as well. Polish children, in the village above described, receive short shrift from their mothers when they begin to walk, and even during infancy there is little dandling and cooing; in fact, after weaning the child is most frequently literally handed over to the eldest daughter who gives the child the strictest minimum of attention. Among the siblings there is little demonstrativeness: there is, however, the fierce loyalty of an in-group on the defensive; this loyalty comprises the principal matrix for the imposition of the actual moral code by which they live. Describing "genuine love" *in and of itself* as a necessity for preventing neurosis is sociologically naïve.

25. I am immeasurably indebted to Dr. Franklin J. Shaw, for long stimulating conversations about his work at the University of New Hampshire Psychological Clinic. He states that male students seeking psychotherapy invariably recall ridicule and ego-attacks by the father during the period of first testing male roles.

As for the "authority" formulation, is it not possible that it may be subsumed under "love withdrawal"? From the child's point of view, even corporal punishment becomes unbearable primarily because it represents the father's withdrawal of love and support. During adolescence, authority as such does become a problem for the child, but the "normal" child suffers from it then as much, and oftentimes more, than does the neurotic.

26. All middle-class children certainly do not become neurotic. But to the extent that their experience approaches the polar type described, they will tend to. This picture is often exaggerated by the parents' own unacknowledged hostile impulses toward the child, stemming from the individualistic values and strivings described.

27. Erich Fromm, "Individual and Social Origins of Neurosis," *American Sociological Review* (1944) 9:380-384; page 381.

28. *Ibid., loc. cit.*

29. The play-group has immeasurable sociological significance for it is secondary in importance only to the family of orientation in the socialization process. Unfortunately, the only good empirical studies of the play-group available are of institutionalized children or slum children whose gang behavior is regarded as a social problem.

30. See Ruth Benedict, "Continuities and Discontinuities in Cultural Conditioning," *Psychiatry* (1938) 1:161-167. On page 161 appears this statement:

"From a comparative point of view our culture goes to great extremes in emphasizing contrasts between the child and the adult. The child is sexless, the adult estimates his virility by his sexual activities; the child must be protected from the ugly facts of life, the adult must meet them without psychic catastrophe; the child must obey, the adult must command this obedience."

THE SOCIOLOGY OF
PARENT-YOUTH CONFLICT

Kingsley Davis

1. In the absence of statistical evidence, exaggeration of the conflict is easily possible, and two able students have warned against it. E. B. Reuter, "The Sociology of Adolescence," and Jessie R. Runner, "Social Distance in Adolescent Relationships," both in *The American Journal of Sociology*, November, 1937, 43:415-16, 437. Yet sufficient nonquantitative evidence lies at hand in the form of personal experience, the outpour of literature in adolescent problems, and the historical and anthropological accounts of contrasting societies to justify the conclusion that in comparison with other cultures our exhibits an exceptional amount of such conflict. If this paper seems to stress conflict, it is simply because we are concerned with this problem rather than with parent-youth harmony.

2. Cf. Nathan Miller, *The Child in Primitive Society* (New York: 1928); Miriam Van Waters, "The Adolescent Girl Among Primitive Peoples," *Journal of Religious Psychology*, 1913, 6:375-421 (1913) and 7:75-120 (1914); Margaret Mead, *Coming of Age in Samoa* and "Adolescence in Primitive and Modern Society," *The New Generation* (ed. by V. F. Calverton and S. Schmalhausen); A. M. Bacon, *Japanese Girls and Women*.

3. Partially done by Mead and Van Waters in the works cited above.

4. Soviet Russia and Nazi Germany are examples. See Sigmund Neumann, "The Conflict of Generations in Contemporary Europe from Versailles to Munich," *Vital Speeches of the Day*, August 1, 1939. Parents in these countries are to be obeyed only so long as they profess the "correct" (i.e., youthful, revolutionary) ideas.

5. See Footnote 11 for necessary qualifications.

6. When discussing a youthful ideal, however, the older person is quick to take a dialectical advantage by pointing out not only that this ideal affronts the aspirations of the multitude but that it also fails to correspond to human behavior either now or (by the lessons of history) probably in the future.

7. See amusing but accurate article, "Fathers are Liars," *Scribner's*, March, 1934.

8. Evidence from mental growth data which point to a leveling off of the growth curve at about age 16. For charts and brief explanations, together with references, see F. K. Shuttelworth, The Adolescent Period, Monographs of the Society for Research in Child Development, III, Serial No. 16 (Washington, D. C., 1938), Figs. 16, 230, 232, 276, 285, 308.

Maturity of judgment is of course another matter. We are speaking only of logical capacity. Judgment is based on experience as well as capacity; hence, adolescents are apt to lack it.

9. An illustration of youthful reformation was afforded by the Laval University students who decided to "do something about" prostitution in the city of Quebec. They broke into eight houses in succession one night, "whacked naked inmates upon the buttocks, upset beds and otherwise proved their collegiate virtue. . . ." They ended by "shoving the few remaining girls out of doors into the cold autumn night." *Time*, October 19, 1936.

10. This holds only for expressed cynicism, but so close is the relation of thought to action that the possibility of an entirely convert cynic seems remote.

11. This tentative analysis holds only insofar as the logic of personality development in a complex culture is the sole factor. Because of other forces, concrete situations may be quite different. When, for example, a person is specifically trained in certain rigid, other worldly, or impractical ideals, he may grow increasingly fanatical with the years rather than realistic, while his offspring, because of association with less fanatical persons, may be more pragmatic than he. The variation in group norms within a society produces persons who, whatever their orientation inside the group, remain more idealistic than the average outsider, while their children may, with outside contacts, become more pragmatic. Even within a group, however, a person's situation may be such as to drive him beyond the everyday realities of that group, while his children remain undisturbed. Such situations largely explain the personal crises that may alter one's orientation. The anlysis, overly brief and mainly illustrative, therefore represents a certain degree of abstraction. The reader should realize, moreover, that the terms "realistic" and "idealistic" are chosen merely for convenience in trying to convey the idea, not for any evaluative judgments which they may happen to connote. The terms are not used in any technical epistemological sense, but simply in the way made plain by the context. Above all, it is not implied that ideals are "unreal" to observer and actor are complex indeed. See Talcott Parsons, *The Structure of Social Action*, 396, and V. Pareto, *The Mind and Society*, III: 1300-1304.

12. House slaves, for example, are generally treated much better than field slaves. Authority over the former is of a personal type, while that over the latter (often in the form of a foreman-gang organization) is of a more impersonal or economic type.

13. Sometimes compensated for by an interest in the grandchildren, which permits them partially to recover the role of the vigorous parent.

14. The essential point is not that there are other authorities—in every society there are extrafamilial influences in socialization—but that, because of specialization and individualistic enterprise, they are *competing* authorities. Because they make a living by their work and are specialists in socialization, some authorities have a competitive advantage over par-

ents who are amateurs or at best merely general practitioners.

15. Margaret Mead, "Social Organization of Manua, 84" Honolulu, Bernice P. Bishop Museum Bulletin 76, 1930. Large heterogeneous households early accustom the child to expect emotional rewards from many different persons. D. M. Spencer, "The Composition of the Family as a Factor in the Behavior of Children in Fijian Society," *Sociometry* (1939) 2:47-55.

16. The principle of substitution is widespread in familism, as shown by the wide distribution of adoption, leviate, sororate, and classificatory kinship nomenclature.

17. M. Mead, *Coming of Age in Samoa*, 200*ff*.

18. Cf. L. K. Frank, "The Management of Tensions," *American Journal of Sociology*, March 1928, 33:706-22; M. Mead, *op. cit.*, 216-17, 222-23.

19. "Even among the essentially 'unrepressed' Trobrianders the parent is never the confidant in matters of sex." Bronislaw Malinowski, *Sex and Reproduction in Savage Society*, 36*n*, London. Cf. the interesting article "Intrusive Parents," *The Commentator*, September, 1938, which opposes frank sex discussion between parents and children.

20. For further evidence of this incompatibility, see the writer's "Reproductive Institutions and the Pressure for Population," *British Sociological Review*, July, 1937, 29:289-306.

CLASS DIFFERENCES IN FAMILY STABILITY

August B. Hollingshead

1. W. Lloyd Warner and P. S. Lunt, *The Social Life of a Modern Community* (New Haven: Yale University Press, 1941), pp. 60-61, 92-104; James West, *Plainville, U.S.A.* (New York: Columbia University Press, 1945), pp. 57-69, 115-41; Allison Davis, Burleigh B. Gardner, and Mary R. Gardiner, *Deep South* (Chicago: University of Chicago Press, 1941), pp. 59-136; August B. Hollingshead, *Elmtown's Youth* (New York: John Wiley and Sons, 1949), pp. 66-126, 335-88, 414-36; August B. Hollingshead, "Class and Kinship in a Middle Western Community," *American Sociological Review*, Vol. 14 (Aug. 1949), pp. 469-75.

2. For a discussion of this concept see Paul C. Glick, "The Family Cycle," *American Sociological Review*, Vol. 12 (April, 1947), pp. 164-74.

3. The effects of a nuclear family's mobility, both upward and downward, on its relations to the kin group will be explored in a forthcoming paper by the author, published elsewhere.

4. All names are pseudonyms; they are used because some of the quotations have meaning only in terms of them.

5. Hollingshead, *Elmtown's Youth*, *op. cit.* note 1 *supra*, p. 99.

6. Paul Oren, "Becoming a Milltown American," unpublished doctoral dissertation, Yale University, 1950.

7. Hollingshead, *Elmtown's Youth*, *op. cit.* note 1 *supra*, p. 106.

8. *Op. cit.* note 6 *supra*.

9. See Floyd Dotson, "The Associations of Urban Workers," unpublished doctoral dissertation, Yale University, 1950, for an excellent analysis of urban working-class culture.

10. Davis, Gardner and Gardner, *Deep South*, *op. cit.* note 1 *supra*, pp. 118-36; Hollingshead, *Elmtown's Youth*, *op. cit.* note 1 *supra*, pp. 116-20.

THE NEGRO FAMILY IN THE UNITED STATES

E. Franklin Frazier

1. Bureau of the Census, *Current Population Reports* ("Population Characteristics," Series P-20 No. 10), p. 12.

2. Sixteenth Census of the United States: 1940 Population and Housing, Families, "General Characteristics," p. 31.

3. *Ibid.*

HYPOTHESES CONCERNING THE EASTERN EUROPEAN JEWISH FAMILY

Ruth Landes and Mark Zborowski

1. "The values and patterns discussed here are the ones characteristic of the *shtetl*—the Jewish community in the small town or village of Eastern Europe, i.e., in Ukraine, Poland (Galicia and Russian Poland), Lithuania, Romania (Bessarabia and Bukovina), Hungary, and Carpatho-Russia." Mark Zborowski, "The Place of Book-Learning in Traditional Jewish Culture," *Harvard Educational Review* (1949), 19:97-109; see p. 88.

2. Informants included 74 women and 64 men, ranging in age from the 20's to the 90's, of different social classes and degrees of education.

3. To be reported in the forthcoming book describing shtetl culture, prepared by Research in Contemporary Cultures.

4. In addition to the references listed elsewhere in this paper, cf. also the following: Sholem Asch, *Mary* (New York: G. P. Putnam's Sons, 1949); Hanan J. Ayalti (ed.), *Yiddish Proverbs* (New York: Schocken Books, 1949); Joseph Block, *My Reminiscences*, R. Lowit, ed., (Vienna: Ch. Bloch, 1923); Sol Bloom, *The Autobiography of Sol Bloom* (New York: G. P. Putnam's Sons, 1948); P. D. Bookstaber, *Judaism and the American Mind in Theory and Practice* (New York: Bloch Publishing Co., 1941); S. R. Brav, *Jewish Family Solidarity: Myth or Fact?* (Vicksburg, Norgales Press, 1940); Earl Bennett Cross, *The Hebrew Family. A Study in Historical Sociology* (Chicago: University of Chicago Press, 1927); Rudolph

Dreikurs, "The Jewish Family: A Psychiatrist Looks at Jewish Family Life," *New Currents* (1944), 2:28-31; L. Epstein, *Jewish Marriage Contract* (New York: Jewish Theological Seminary of America, 1927); Louis M. Epstein, *Marriage Laws in the Bible and the Talmud* (Cambridge: Harvard University Press, 1942); Louis M. Epstein, *Sex Laws and Customs in Judaism* (New York: Bloch Publishing Co., 1948); S. E. Goldstein, *Meaning of Marriage and Foundation of the Family: A Jewish Interpretation* (New York: Bloch Publishing Co., 1942); Sidney B. Hoenig, *Jewish Family Life: The Duty of the Woman* (New York: Committee of the Rabbi D. Miller Foundation, 1942); Irving Howe, "The Lost Intellectual," *Commentary*, II (1946); 361-67; Irving Howe, "Daniel Fuchs: Escape from Williamsburg," *Commenary*, VI (1948), 29-34; Simon Kaplan, *Once a Rebel* (New York: Farrar & Rinehart, 1941); A. Myerson, "Neuroses and Alcoholism among Jews," *Medical Leaves*, III (1941), 104-107; Harold Orlansky, "Jewish Personality Traits: A Review of Studies on an Elusive Problem," *Commentary*, II (1946), 377-83; Bernard Sachs, *Multitude of Dreams* (Johannesburg: Kayor Publishing House, 1949); Jo Sinclair, *Wasteland* (New York: Harper, 1946); Ruth Tennenbaum, "Jewish Parents in a Child Guidance Clinic: A Study of Culture and Personality," *Smith College Studies in Social Work*, X (1939), 50-76; J. J. Trunk, *Poilen* (Poland), Book IV (Yiddish) (New York: Unzer Tsalt, 1949).

Also, cf. the following films: "Eternal Song," Poland, ca. 1938; "Green Fields," United States, 1938; "Long Is the Road," Palestine, 1948; "Mirele Efros," United States, 1939 (based on the original stage play); "Road to Israel," Palestine, 1948; "Vilna Legend," United States, 1939 (originally filmed in Poland, 1929); "Yiddl Mit Dem Fiddl," Poland, 1938; "Purim Spieler," "Tevya," 1939; "The Songs of Moyshe Oysher."

5. Described in "The Covenant" manuscript by Mark Zborowski, in the files of Research in Contemporary Cultures.

6. Within it we find reminders of Freud's familial formulations, but embedded among relationships and values that were unrealized by him.

7. For references dealing with "prescribed" behavior, the following sources are used, if not specified otherwise: A. Cohen, *Everyman's Talmud* (New York: E. P. Dutton & Co., 1949); Salomon Gansfried, *Code of Jewish Law* (Kitzur Schulchan Aruch), Hyman E. Goldin, tr. (New York: Hebrew Publishing Co., 1927).

8. Marriage is seen as a legal outlet for man's sexual desire, which is given to man in order to procreate (Schulchan Aruch, CL, 9.) This desire if not satisfied, handicaps a man's prescribed study of sacred law. Therefore, man must find a legal sexual partner as soon as possible and early marriages between the ages of eighteen and twenty are highly recommended. (Schulchan Aruch, CXLV, 1.)

Procreation, however, is not the only reason for marriage. The Code insists upon the obligation to marry even when the man or woman is unable to procreate. The Law states that it is not good for a man to be alone. (Schulchan Aruch CXLV, 3; cf. Talmud, p. 162.)

Striking physical and age differences should be avoided in marriage, and the partners should have the same social background. (Schulchan Aruch CXLV, 6, 8; Talmud, pp. 163-164.) The most highly recommended partner for a girl is a learned man; and for a boy, the daughter of a learned father. Romantic love is ignored by the Code. (Bernard Horwich, *My First Eighty Years* [Chicago: Argus Books, 1939], pp. 5, 159; Lucy Robins Lang, *Tomorrow Is Beautiful* [New York: Macmillan, 1948], p. 1.) Relationships between husband and wife are phrased exclusively in terms of mutual duties and obligations. (Schulchan Aruch, CXLV, 10; Talmud, p. 165.)

9. Schulchan Aruch CXLV, 4; Talmud, p. 168.

10. Schulchan Aruch, CXLV, 1.

11. Ignatz Maybaum, *The Jewish Home* (London: James Clarke & Co., 1945), pp. 45, 27.

12. Mishna Aboth Pirke Aboth (*Sayings of the Fathers*, 4th ed. [New York: Block Publishing Co., 1929]).

13. The Kashruth observances are dietary prohibitions and regulations, without which the functioning of a Jewish traditional household is inconceivable. They were elaborated over centuries by generations of Jewish sages, on the basis of an original set of dietary regulations stated in the Pentateuch. The observances of Kashruth are prime criteria in the orthodox definition of a household as "Jewish." Although the traditional theory of Kashruth is studied by the men, its application belongs mainly to the women, who are responsible for the handling of food. Any doubts which may arise in connection with the application of Kashruth laws are to be referred for decision to the religious authority in the community, the Rabbi.

14. Mikvah is the ritual bath which every Jewish wife must take after the menstrual period. During this period all physical contact between husband and wife is prohibited, and by extension avoided between all members of opposite sex. Deformed children are regarded as divine punishment for violation of the taboo. Detailed rules govern the relationship between husband and wife during the impure period; the responsibility for the observances rests with the married women. An unmarried girl is not subject to these prohibitions.

15. Schulchan Aruch CXLIII, 20.

16. A story tells of a female Chassidic leader who disconcerted the community with her male scholarly behavior until the elders were able to lead her into marriage and thus

into a familiar female role. Cf. also Mary Antin, *The Promised Land* (New York: Houghton Mifflin, 1941).

17. Schulchan Aruch, CXLIII, 1.

18. For separate sex play-groups, cf. Antin, *op. cit.*, p. 105 and Shemariah Levin, *Childhood in Exile* (New York: Harcourt Brace, 1929), p. 63.

19. This technical reference from the vocabulary of cultural anthropology refers to a society's traditional ways of preventing incest or related improprieties.

20. Cf. Ruth Landes, "The Abnormal Among the Ojibwa Indians," *Journal of Abnormal and Social Psychology*, XXXIII (1938), 14-33, esp. p. 24; and Gregory Bateson, *Naven* (London: Cambridge University Press, 1936), esp. p. 32.

21. *Oxford English Dictionary*.

22. Bateson, *op. cit.*

23. Horwich, *op. cit.*, p. 5.

24. Nathan Ausubel, *A Treasury of Jewish Folklore* (New York, Crown Publications, 1948), p. 638.

25. Furthermore, the Talmudic commentary accepts the obviousness of respect for the mother, and expresses the need to insist upon equal reverence for the father.

26. Ignztz Bernstein, *Yiddishe Sprichwerter* (Yiddish) (Warsaw. 1912), p. 97, Cf. Bava Bathra 100, 1; in the Talmud.

27. Horwich, *op. cit.*, p. 9.

28. Levin, *op. cit.*, p. 6.

29. Levin, *op. cit.*, pp. 3-7.

30. Cf. the Talmud where pouring olive oil on olives is a dream symbol of incest with the mother; this is interpreted by us as symbolizing in part a "return to the source." Berachoth, 56.

31. Avoidance appears in alternating forms of silence and of nagging and quarrels.

32. Schulchan Aruch CLII, 10. The ancient Teachers emphasize the sexual desirability of woman as well as her dangerous character. She is considered sexually aggressive and therefore is to be strictly avoided. She is considered unreliable and generally possesses undesirable traits of character. Talmud, p. 160.

33. Berachoth 56.

34. Levin, *op. cit.*, pp. 6-7.

35. Bernstein, *op. cit.*, p. 11. Proverb 4, p. 96 expresses the same idea: "One's son is given, but one's son-in-law is chosen."

36. Chassidism was a socioreligious movement which arose in Poland in the eighteenth century and spread over all of Eastern Europe. It was characterized by the intense belief of the followers in the personality of the leader, called the *tsaddik*. The followers centered about "courts" composed of the leader, his family, and servants. The leadership became hereditary.

37. Food as a social control is the monopoly of women, as learning is the monopoly of men.

38. The intellectual interest of the husband and his "childish" helplessness in domestic affairs often lead the wife to decry his practical abilities; thus she calls him "my breadwinner" with an ironical intonation. But she always admires his intellectual abilities and boasts of them to outsiders.

39. Bernstein, *op. cit.*, p. 96.

40. Levin, *op. cit.*, p. 14.

41. Daniel Charney, *Barg Arof* (Yiddish) (Warsaw: Uphill, 1935), p. 65.

42. Morris R. Cohen, *A Dreamer's Journey* (Boston: Beacon Press, 1949) pp. 15-62, ff.

43. An informant aptly states that "From the moment the boy is taken from the maternal environment into school, he is considered an adult in study, synagogue, and community; but he is always a child in the area of physical needs. His mother, his sister, and his wife consider him a child even when he is old, though he was considered a man intellectually by the age of three."

44. Footnote 24, p. 638.

45. Chaim Tchernowitz, "Grandfather Mendele as I Remember Him," *Commentary* VI (1948), 436-43, see p. 442.

46. Cf. film "Mamele" (Poland, 1938); Lang, *op. cit.*, p. 16; Antin, *op. cit.*, p. 144.

47. Schulchan Aruch CLIII, 1.

48. The daughter may utilize her father's indulgence to advance herself beyond the limitations of her status, as when she secures permission to share her brother's studies.

49. "When father returned home after work, he would embrace me tenderly for my day's work and after dinner, when the dishes were washed and the house put in order, he would braid my hair." Lang, *op. cit.*, p. 7.

50. "We live in a generation which has rebelled against the father. . . . We possess a whole literature full of complaints of sons against the father. Psychology and literature united in order to voice the oppressed son's complaints." Maybaum, *op. cit.*, p. 27.

51. "God, Flesh and the Devil," New York City, 1949. In this drama, a pious, childless couple rears the orphaned daughters of the wife's sister. When the elder ward reaches marriageable age, her foster father proposes marriage to her, saying that he will divorce his wife, whom the girl addresses as "second mother"; legally he may divorce his wife because she is still barren after twenty years. The foster daughter accepts the proposal and her "second mother" resigns herself to the situation.

52. On the other hand, informants indicate that mother enjoys showing her son how to cook as he assists her in the kitchen. She wants his company and is flattered by his interest.

53. Intellectual training is presented to her as of secondary importance, and is often completely neglected. Folk sayings belittle women's mental capacities.

54. Romantic love was considered "un-Jewish" by the better families, though songs and stories show it interested young people. Parents chose marital partners for their children of opposite sex, often aided by a profes-

sional matchmaker, and without consulting the children's preferences.

55. Bernstein, *op. cit.*, p. 96.

56. After the period of the kest, if the husband continues to devote himself to study, his wife is expected to take over all the burden of providing subsistence for the family. A wife who supports her learned husband who is devoted to the correct functioning of the household, who sacrifices herself for the well-being of her husband and children, is highly praised in the community, and is expected to be rewarded after death by sharing her husband's life in heaven. The ideal arrangement is achieved when two people of more or less similar backgrounds live together, fulfilling their culturally expected roles—the man devoting most of his time to intellectual pursuits and conjugal duties, the woman devoting her life to husband, children, and household, and providing the material support of the family.

Where the husband is not a learned man but is engaged in some business, his work is nevertheless considered "mental" and his relationship to his wife is similar to that of a learned man. But an ignoramus who is dependent upon his wife is despised by the community, and is considered a parasite.

57. When pleased with his wife, the husband may tell her that she is "almost as good as mother," according to some informants.

58. Cf. Antin, re disappointment in son-in-law. *Op. cit.*, p. 65.

59. A man may be jealous of his sister's husband partly because of the stranger's sudden claim upon his sister and upon his mother, but also because of the formality and stereotyped tensions in his relation with his father. According to a saying "Great men have lesser sons." But a man's traditional attitude is that his son-in-law whom he chose in the arranged marriage is smarter or more desirable than his son. The Lubavitcher Rabbi in his Memoirs (Joseph I. Schneersohn, *Luba-vitcher Rabbi's Memoirs* [Brooklyn: Otzer Hachassidim, 1949], p. 79), quotes a smith in the Russian town of Dobramysi thusly: "I must say that I am more than satisfied with my daughters. . . . They are married to fine, well-learned men and are nicely settled in a house I had built for them. My sons-in-law spend their time in study, but as for my son, Samuel Nahum, I have to admit he is a great disappointment to me. I had hoped he too would be a scholar, but unfortunately he has no talent whatsoever for studying." This is a conventional statement of the situation, and suggests how forlorn the unmarried man can feel in the father-son relationship. Relief may come when he marries, leaving the parental home, and in his turn shining forth as the beloved son, perhaps supported by his father-in-law on kest. But even after marriage, resentment of the father can persist a life long, having its roots in the didactic demands laid down in early childhood.

60. This attitude connotes expectations of aid, analogous to ceremonies in other cul-

tures where greetings are expressed with offerings of tobacco, food, drink, baths.

61. "We inherited from Momma and Poppa two sets of tantehs and uncles, who produced in turn an abundance of cousins, who got hitched to other people's cousins and uncles and tantehs,—and they all came to our house. And, as usually happens, Momma's side of the family was favored—the Chosen People." Sammy Levenson, *Meet the Folks* (New York: Citadel Press, 1948), p. 24.

62. That is, the Jewish man must marry his brother's widow if she is childless.

63. The plots of Yiddish language films—for example, "I Want to Be a Mother," "Bar Mitsvah," "Mamele"—includes these themes.

64. They follow the form: A man (woman) sees himself (herself) in his (her) son-in-law (daughter-in-law).

65. In New York City the National Desertion Bureau, a Jewish Community Agency established in 1914, devotes itself exclusively to this problem. Miriam Shomer Zunser, in *Yesterday* (New York: Stackpole Sons, 1939), pp. 64-74; 160-179ff., suggests other factors in desertion among Eastern European Jewish men, such as sheer displeasure with the ugliness or age of the bride. One informant said sheyne men deserted less often than proste, for they were more sensitive to public opinion.

66. For example, in Sabbath and holiday ritual, and in child rearing.

67. Individual women occasionally rebelled by repudiating the unattractive spouse arranged for them, but only after the marriage ceremony. There were also some suicides by married women who felt trapped. Men acted similarly much more often. Cf. Zunser, *op. cit.*, pp. 64-74; pp. 160-179ff. Folk songs and stories reflect conflicts over arranged marriages.

68. It seems to us, for example, that these elements played an important role in the history of eighteenth century mystical Chassidism which developed out of traditional rational Judaism, and in the secularized Socialist labor movement of the nineteenth and twentieth centuries which scorned the religious tradition and advocated assimilation with the non-Jewish world.

69. "He is a guest in his own house," is a popular turn of phrase.

THE ITALIAN FAMILY IN THE UNITED STATES

Paul J. Campisi

1. During the decade of 1900-1910, of the 2,045,877 Italians who came to America, the majority were from southern Italy.

2. The observations in this paper are based on the literature in the field, on my own specific research in America on the acculturation of Italians, and finally, on personal impressions and conclusions as a participant observer. A visit to southern Italy and Sicily three years ago gave me an opportunity to

come in contact with the Old World peasant-type family. While this type of family has changed considerably from the time of the mass migration to America, enough structural and functional family lags exist to make the reconstruction of it in this paper reasonably valid.

3. See Robert Redfield, "The Folk Society," *American Journal of Sociology*, L11 (1947), 293-308.

4. For an excellent analysis of the importance of a strong family and community culture see Margaret Park Redfield, "The American Family: Consensus and Freedom," *American Journal of Sociology*, LII (1946), 175-83.

5. See Carlo Sforza, *The Real Italians* (New York: Columbia University Press, 1942), for an interesting account of Italian-Americans who change their names.

CULTURE PATTERNS OF PUERTO RICO

Julian H. Steward

1. The present essay is a résumé of the study entitled *The People of Puerto Rico* (Urbana: University of Illinois, 1956), written not only by the present author, but by those who did the field research in Puerto Rico: Robert A. Manners, Sidney Mintz, Elena Padilla, Raymond L. Scheele, and Eric Wolf. My co-workers should share full credit and responsibility for the analyses herein offered.

CULTURAL COMPONENTS IN RESPONSES TO PAIN

Mark Zborowski

1. James D. Hardy, Harold G. Wolff and Helen Goodell, *Pain Sensations and Reactions* (Baltimore: Williams and Wilkins, 1952), p. 23.

2. *Ibid.*, p. 204.

3. *Ibid.*, p. 262.

4. Italian respondents are mainly of South Italian origin; the Jewish respondents, with one exception, are all of East European origin. Whenever the Jews are mentioned they are spoken in terms of the culture they represent and not in terms of their religion.

ENGLISH-SPEAKING AND SPANISH-SPEAKING PEOPLE OF THE SOUTHWEST

Lyle Sanders

1. "A culture is more than a collection of customs; it is a system of customs, each more or less meaningfully related to the others. Culture has structure as well as content. Recognition of this fact would enable us to understand the tenacity of certain customs:

they are hard to move because they are geared to other customs . . ." Paul, Benjamin D., "Respect for Cultural Differences," *Community Development Bulletin*, vol. 4, June, 1953, p. 44.

2. The orientation to time of Spanish-Americans is specifically discussed in *Cultural Patterns and Technical Change*, edited by Margaret Mead, United Nations Educational, Scientific, and Cultural Organization, 1953, Paris, pp. 179-180. See also Florence Kluckhohn's discussion of what she has called the *manana* configuration in *Los Atarquenos*, Ph.D. dissertation, Radcliffe College, 1941.

3. Campa, Arthur L., "Manana is Today," *New Mexico Quarterly*, vol. 9, 1939, pp. 3-11.

4. These and other Anglo characteristics have been discussed by many competent observers. Among the better accounts are: "Major Value-Orientations in America" in Williams, Robin M., Jr., *American Society: A Sociological Interpretation*, Alfred A. Knopf, New York, 1951; Kluckhohn, Clyde, and Florence R. Kluckhohn, "American Culture: Generalized Orientations and Class Patterns," *Conflicts of Power in Modern Culture*, edited by Lyman Bryson and others, Seventh Symposium of the Conference on Science, Philosophy, and Religion, New York, 1948; Gorer, Geoffrey, *The American People: A Study in National Character*, Cresset Press, London, 1948; Coleman, Lee, "What is American: A Study of Alleged American Traits," *Social Forces*, vol. 19, May, 1941, pp. 492-499; Laski, Harold, *The American Democracy*, Viking Press, New York, 1948.

5. Cultural differences in attitudes toward work and success are illustrated in the story, frequently heard in the Southwest and related by Bennett Cerf in the "Trade Winds" column of the *Saturday Review*, about an eastern businessman. While strolling the railway station platform at Albuquerque, he observed a number of Pueblo Indian men sitting in the sun and was moved to indignation by what he considered an appalling waste of manpower. He approached one of the Indians and, with some asperity, asked, "Why aren't you working?"

"Why should I work?" replied the Indian.

"To earn money," said the businessman.

"Why should I want to earn money?" asked the Indian.

"If you work and earn money and save it, some day you will have enough so that you can retire and won't have to work any more."

"I'm not working now," said the Indian.

6. The low value on practicality and efficiency in the culture of the Spanish-speaking is clearly illustrated in *Human Problems and Technological Change: A Casebook*, edited by Edward H. Spicer, Russell Sage Foundation, New York, 1952, pp. 35-40. Case 2, "Corn and Custom" describes the failure of an attempt to introduce an unfamiliar strain of high-producing corn into the agriculture of a New Mexican village. Even though the yields

were much greater than with old strains, the use of the new hybrid was soon abandoned because the appearance and flavor were thought to be inferior to those of the corn traditionally grown in the village.

7. Leadership among Spanish-Americans and the amount of membership and participation in various types of formal organizations are discussed at length by Julian Samora, in *Minority Leadership in a Bi-Cultural Community*, Ph.D. dissertation, Washington University, October, 1953.

8. The reciprocal of leadership is, of course, followership. It should be emphasized that, just as the village culture of the Spanish-speaking people offered few opportunities for the development of leadership, there were equally few chances for anyone to learn how to be a follower.

9. Possible exceptions to this rather sweeping generalization are the American Council for Spanish-Speaking People, under the very able leadership of Dr. George I. Sanchez; the American G.I. Forum, which has been rapidly expanding and is providing opportunities for the development and testing of talents of young leaders; and the Community Service Organization, which has been doing effective organizational work in and around Los Angeles.

II – SOCIAL ROLES

THE PROBLEM OF THE CONCEPT OF ROLE—A RE-SURVEY OF THE LITERATURE

Lionel J. Neiman and James W. Hughes

1. William James, *Psychology* (New York: Henry Holt, 1892), pp. 179-81.

2. *Ibid.*

3. James M. Baldwin, *Mental Development in the Child and in the Race* (New York: Macmillan, 1898).

4. Charles H. Cooley, *Human Nature and the Social Order* (New York: Scribners, 1902), p. 183 *et seq.*

5. George Herbert Mead, *Mind, Self and Society* (Chicago: University of Chicago Press, 1934), p. 138 *et seq.*

6. For a recent addition to the furtherance of confusion see Walter Coutu, "Role-Playing vs. Role-Taking," *American Sociological Review*, 16 (April 1951), pp. 180-187. The "versus" is an interesting approach, but clarifies nothing, except perhaps another dichotomy.

7. Robert E. Park and E. W. Burgess, *An Introduction to the Science of Sociology* (Chicago: University of Chicago Press, 1921), pp. 114-17.

8. Leonard S. Cottrell, "Roles and Marital Adjustment," *Publications of the American Sociological Society*, 27 (May 1933), pp. 107-12.

9. Leonard S. Cottrell, "The Adjustment of the Individual to His Age and Sex Roles," *American Sociological Review*, 7 (October 1942), pp. 617-20.

10. Lowell J. Carr, *Situational Analysis* (New York: Harpers, 1948), pp. 32-33.

11. Bingham Dai, "Some Problems of Personality Development Among Negro Children," in *Personality in Nature, Society and Culture*, ed. by Kluckhohn and Murray (New York: Knopf, 1948), p. 439.

12. Kingsley Davis, *Human Society* (New York: Macmillan, 1949), p. 210. See also chap. IV.

13. Norman Cameron, *The Psychology of Behavior Disorder* (New York: Houghton Mifflin, 1947), p. 90. Also for a similar approach see such books as Richard T. La Piere, *Sociology* (New York: McGraw-Hill, 1946), and Logan Wilson and William L. Kolb, *Sociological Analysis* (New York: Harcourt Brace, 1949).

14. Robert L. Sutherland and Julian L. Woodward, *Introductory Sociology* (New York: Lippincott, 1940), pp. 250-53.

15. Ralph Linton, "Culture, Society and the Individual," *Journal of Abnormal and Social Psychology*, 33 (October 1938), pp. 425-36. Also see Linton's *The Study of Man* (New York: Appleton-Century, 1936), especially chap. 8, "Status and Role."

16. Florian Znaniecki, "Social Groups as Products of Participating Individuals," *American Journal of Sociology*, 44 (May, 1939), pp. 799-812.

17. Talcott Parsons, "Age and Sex in the Social Structure of the United States," *American Journal of Sociology*, 42 (July, 1936), pp. 81-94.

18. E. M. Duvall, "Conceptions of Parenthood," *American Journal of Sociology*, 52 (November, 1946), pp. 193-203.

19. Mirra Komarovsky, "Cultural Contradictions and Sex Roles," *American Journal of Sociology*, 52 (November 1946), pp. 184-89.

20. Muzafer Sherif, *The Psychology of Social Norms* (New York: Harpers, 1936); see particularly chaps. III, IV, and V. The notion of "interiorization" of which Sherif speaks here is a neat shorthand explanation—or an attempt at such. Concepts such as "internalization" and "interiorization" themselves need to be explained, but they are frequently found as explanations of how one acquires roles.

21. Most of the work quoted by Sherif in this volume are studies of perception as affected by social norms of perceiving. For the same orientation see also, Muzafer Sherif, *An Outline of Social Psychology* (New York: Harpers, 1948) and Muzafer Sherif and

Hadley Cantril, *The Psychology of Ego-Involvements* (New York: John Wiley, 1949).

22. Norman Cameron, "Role Concepts in Behavior Pathology," *American Journal of Sociology*, 55 (March 1950), pp. 464-67.

23. Ruth Benedict, "Continuities and Discontinuities in Cultural Conditioning," *Psychiatry*, 1 (May 1938), pp. 161-67. See also Ruth Benedict, *Patterns of Culture* (Boston: Houghton Mifflin, 1932), and Ruth Benedict, *The Chrysanthemum and the Sword* (Boston: Houghton Mifflin, 1946), for a similar exposition of role.

24. Margaret Mead, *And Keep Your Powder Dry* (New York: Morrow, 1942).

25. Samuel A. Stouffer, "An Analysis of Conflicting Social Norms," *American Sociological Review*, 14 (December 1949), pp. 707-17.

26. Clifford Kirkpatrick and Theodore Caplow, "Courtship in a Group of Minnesota Students," *American Journal of Sociology*, 51 (September 1945), pp. 114-125.

27. Ellsworth Faris, "The Social Psychology of George Mead," *American Journal of Social Psychology*, 43 (November 1937), pp. 391-403; Harry Stack Sullivan, "A Note on Formulating the Relationship of the Individual and the Group," *American Journal of Sociology*, 44 (May 1939), pp. 932-37; Edward B. Reuter, "Sociological Research in Adolescence," *American Journal of Sociology*, 42 (July 1936), pp. 81-94.

28. Ralph Linton, *The Study of Man* (New York: Appleton-Century, 1936), p. 114.

29. Ralph Linton, *The Cultural Background of Personality* (New York: Appleton-Century, 1945), p. 18, *et seq.*

30. Everett C. Hughes, "Institutional Office and the Person," *American Journal of Sociology*, 43 (November 1937), pp. 404-13.

31. *Ibid.* See also Everett C. Hughes, "Dilemmas and Contradictions of Status," *American Journal of Sociology*, 50 (March 1945), pp. 353-59.

32. Kimball Young, *Social Psychology* (New York: Crofts, 1946), p. 564. See also chap. VII.

33. E. T. Hiller, *Social Relations and Structures* (New York: Harpers, 1947), p. 339, *et seq.*

34. Florian Znaniecki, "Social Groups as Products of Participating Individuals," *American Journal of Sociology*, 44 (May 1939), pp. 799-812.

35. Florian Znaniecki, *The Social Role of the Man of Knowledge* (New York: Columbia University, 1940), pp. 13-14.

36. Robert K. Merton, "Bureaucratic Structure and Personality," *Social Forces*, 18 (May 1940), pp. 560-68.

37. Gardner Murphy, *Personality: A Biosocial Approach to Origins and Structure* (New York: Harpers, 1947), p. 516, *et seq.*

38. See for example, Joseph L. Moreno, "Psychodramatic Treatment of Marriage Problems," *Sociometry*, 3 (May 1940), pp. 1-23; and also by the same author, *Who Shall Survive* (Washington, D. C.: Beacon Hill. 1934). Also see, Julian B. Rotter and Delso D. Wickens, "The Consistency and Generality of Ratings of 'Social Aggressiveness' Made from Observations of Role Playing Situations," *American Psychology*, 2 (1947), pp. 333-35. Also, T. Lippitt, "The Psychodrama in Leadership Training," *Sociometry*, 6 (August 1943), pp. 286-92.

39. William Coleman, "Role Playing as an Instructional Aid," *Journal of Educational Psychology*, 39 (November 1948), pp. 429-35.

40. Gordon Lawlor, "Role Therapy," *Sociatry*, 1 (1947), pp. 51-55.

SOCIAL DISORGANIZATION AND THE INTERRELATIONSHIP OF CULTURAL ROLES

Roland W. Warren

1. Cf. L. L. Bernard, "The Conflict between Primary Group Attitudes and Derivative Group Ideals in Modern Society," *American Journal of Sociology*, March, 1936.

2. Cultural role sequences are different cultural roles which significantly sized groups of people are expected to occupy consecutively in the course of their lives. From the standpoint of the individual who occupies them, they constitute a career. Some attention to the question of continuity or discontinuity in cultural role sequences has been given by Ralph Linton in *The Study of Man*, Ruth Benedict in "Continuities and Discontinuities in Cultural Conditioning," *Psychiatry*, May, 1938, Mirra Komarovsky in "Cultural Contradictions and Sex Roles," *American Journal of Sociology*, November, 1946, and Leonard S. Cottrell, Jr. in "The Adjustment of the Individual to his Age and Sex Roles," *American Sociological Review*, October, 1942 and in "Roles and Marital Adjustment," *Publication of the American Sociological Society*, Volume XXVII, No. 2, May, 1933.

3. Everett C. Hughes, "Institutional Office and the Person," *American Journal of Sociology*, November, 1937, p. 409.

4. Karen Horney, *The Neurotic Personality of Our Time* (New York: W. W. Norton & Company, 1937), pp. 288-289.

5. William Graham Sumner, *Folkways* (Boston: Ginn and Company, 1906), p. 68.

6. Willard Waller, *The Family: A Dynamic Interpretation* (New York: The Dryden Press, 1938), p. 387.

7. Mirra Komarovsky, "Cultural Contradictions and Sex Roles," *American Journal of Sociology*, November, 1946, p. 187.

8. W. I. Thomas, "The Adventitious Character of Woman," *American Journal of Sociology*, July, 1906, p. 39.

9. Leonard S. Cottrell, Jr., "The Adjustment of the Individual to his Age and Sex Roles," *American Sociological Review*, October, 1942, p. 618.

AGE AND SEX IN THE
SOCIAL STRUCTURE OF THE
UNITED STATES

Talcott Parsons

1. The problem of organization of this material for systematic presentation is, in view of this fact, particularly difficult. It would be possible to discuss the subject in terms of the above four principal structures with which age and sex are most closely interwoven, but there are serious disadvantages involved in this procedure. Age and sex categories constitute one of the main links of structural continuity in terms of which structures which are differentiated in other respects are articulated with each other; and in isolating the treatment of these categories there is danger that this extremely important aspect of the problem will be lost sight of. The least objectionable method, at least within the limits of space of such a paper, seems to be to follow the sequence of the life cycle.

2. Perhaps the most dramatic manifestation of this tendency lies in the prominence of the patterns of "dating," for instance among college women. As shown by an unpublished participant-observer study made at one of the Eastern women's colleges, perhaps the most important single basis of informal prestige rating among the residents of a dormitory lies in their relative dating success—though this is by no means the only basis. One of the most striking features of the pattern is the high publicity given to the "achievements" of the individual in a sphere where traditionally in the culture a rather high level of privacy is sanctioned—it is interesting that once an engagement has occurred a far greater amount of privacy is granted. The standards of rating cannot be said to be well integrated, though there is an underlying consistency in that being in demand by what the group regards as desirable men is perhaps the main standard.

It is true that the "dating" complex need not be exclusively bound up with the "glamor girl" stereotype of ideal feminine personality—the "good companion" type may also have a place. Precisely, however, where the competitive aspect of dating is most prominent the glamor pattern seems heavily to predominate, as does, on the masculine side, a somewhat comparable glamorous type. On each side at the same time there is room for considerable differences as to just where the emphasis is placed—for example as between "voluptuous" sexuality and more decorous "charm."

3. A central aspect of this focus of crystallization lies in the element of tension, sometimes of direct conflict, between the youth culture patterns of college and school life, and the "serious" interests in and obligations toward curricular work. It is of course the latter which defines some at least of the most important foci of adult expectations of doing "good" work and justifying the privileges granted. It is not possible here to attempt to analyze the interesting ambivalent attitudes of youth toward curricular work and achievement.

4. The above statement, even more than most in the present paper, needs to be qualified in relation to the problem of class. It is above all to the upper middle class that it applies. Here probably the great majority of "working wives" are engaged in some form of secretarial work which would, on an independent basis, generally be classed as a lower middle class occupation. The situation at lower levels of the class structure is quite different since the prestige of the jobs of husband and wife is then much more likely to be nearly equivalent. It is quite possible that this fact is closely related to the relative instability of marriage which Davis and Gardner (*Deep South*) find, at least for the community they studied, to be typical of lower class groups. The relation is one which deserves careful study.

5. This type of advertising appeal undoubtedly contains an element of "snob appeal" in the sense of an invitation to the individual by her appearance and ways to identify herself with a higher social class than that of her actual status. But it is almost certainly not wholly explained by this element. A glamorously feminine appearance which is specifically dissociated from physical work is undoubtedly a genuine part of an authentic personality ideal of the middle class, and not only evidence of a desire to belong to the upper class.

6. In the informal social life of academic circles with which the writer is familiar there seems to be a strong tendency in mixed gatherings—as after dinner—for the sexes to segregate. In such groups the men are apt to talk either shop subjects or politics whereas the women are apt to talk about domestic affairs, schools, their children, etc., or personalities. It is perhaps on personalities that mixed conversation is apt to flow most freely.

7. This, to be sure, often contains an element of romanticization. It is more nearly what he wishes these relations had been than what they actually were.

8. *Cf.* E. Y. Hartshorne, "German Youth and the Nazi Dream of Victory," *America in a World at War*, Pamphlet, No. 12, New York, 1941.

9. That the financial difficulties of older people in a very large proportion of cases are real is not to be doubted. This, however, is at least to a very large extent a consequence rather than a determinant of the structural situation. Except where it is fully taken care of by pension schemes, the income of older people is apt to be seriously reduced, but, even more important, the younger conjugal family does not feel an obligation to contribute to the support of aged parents. Where as a matter of course both generations shared a common household, this problem did not exist.

AGE AND SEX CATEGORIES AS SOCIOLOGICAL VARIABLES IN THE MENTAL DISORDERS OF LATER MATURITY

Ivan Belknap and Hiram J. Friedsam

1. T. Parsons, "Age and Sex in the Social Structure of the United States," *American Sociological Review*, VII (Dec. 1942), 604-620; R. Linton, "Age and Sex Categories," *American Sociological Review*, VII (Dec. 1942), 589-603; L. S. Cottrell, Jr., "The Adjustment of the Individual to His Age and Sex Roles," *Readings in Social Psychology* (Ed. T. Newcomb, and E. L. Hartley), New York: Henry Holt, 1947. Actually, as Ralph Linton remarks, the analysis of age categories is implicit in many culture studies. E. T. Hiller (*Social Relations and Structures*, New York: Harpers, Chs. 22-25) has made a thorough sociological application.

2. P. C. Glick, "The Family Life Cycle," *American Sociological Review*, XII (April, 1947), 164-74; A. Beegle, and C. P. Loomis, "Life Cycles of Farm, Rural Non-Farm, and Urban Families in the United States as Derived from Census Materials," *Notes, Rural Sociology*, XIII (March, 1948), 70-74, R. E. L. Faris, "Interaction of Generations and Family Stability," *American Sociological Review*, XII (April, 1947), 159-164.

3. Research in other age categories is of course implied in the theory, but it has been omitted from the present paper.

4. "Biological" in the sense that these disorders are an expression of organic events associated with genetic sexual, maturation, or senescence patterns. See J. D. Page, *Abnormal Psychology*, New York: McGraw-Hill Book Co., 1947, p. 216; C. Landis, and M. Bolles, *Textbooks of Abnormal Psychology*, New York: The Macmillan Co., 1946, p. 156. N. Munn, *Psychology*, Boston: Houghton Mifflin Co., 1946, p. 481.

5. Recent literature deals also with the neuroses of later maturity.

6. Munn, *Psychology, loc. cit.*

7. H. W. Dunham, "Social Psychiatry," *American Sociological Review*, XIII (April, 1948), 183-197, has reviewed these inadequacies, for mental disorders in general, quite comprehensively.

8. D. Rothschild, "Senile Psychoses and Cerebral Arteriosclerosis," in O. J. Kaplan (Ed.), *Mental Disorders in Later Life*, Stanford University: Stanford University Press, 1945.

9. H. W. Williams, *et al.*, "Studies in Senile and Arteriosclerotic Psychoses," *American Journal of Psychiatry*, 99 (1942), 712-715.

10. N. Cameron, "Neuroses of Later Maturity," in Kaplan, *Mental Disorders in Later Life, op. cit.*

11. See citations in Rothschild, Note 8, *supra*. This type of convergence begins to appear in psychosomatic research. See E. Weiss, and S. O. English, *Psychosomatic Medicine*, Philadelphia: Saunders, 1943.

12. This does not exclude the biological factor, as we have pointed out above, but treats it as only one co-determinant.

13. E. Durkheim, *Le suicide: etude de sociologie*, Paris: Felix Alcan, 1897. C. Jung, *Modern Man in Search of a Soul*, New York: Harcourt Brace, 1933. R. E. L. Faris, and H. W. Dunham, *Mental Disorders in Urban Areas*, Chicago: University of Chicago Press, 1939. See particularly Faris' concept of "cultural malnutrition" ("Interactions of Generations and Family Stability," *op cit.*, p. 164).

14. The possibility of applying quantitative checks through these rates is one of the merits of this approach.

15. E. Durkheim, *Le Suicide, op. cit.*, pp. 272-285. This formulation is not entirely satisfactory. Ultimately, *suicide altruiste* may also be an anomic phenomenon, since the group actually extrudes the particular individual, providing no further "place" for him. *Egoisme*, another of Durkheim's types of suicide, is also perhaps significant only as a cause of *anomie*. These theoretical problems are important, but they do not affect the use of Durkheim in this paper.

16. G. H. Mead, *Mind, Self, and Society*, Chicago: University of Chicago Press, 1934, Part III, 18, 19, 29; Part IV, 30-34.

17. This does not deny the idiosyncratic elements in concrete human motivation, but it does insist that these elements cannot be the object of a science, since they are always, by definition, unique.

18. W. B. Cannon, "Stresses and Strains of Homeostasis," *American Journal of Medical Science*, 189, pp. 1-14. Durkheim considers this point at great length in analyzing the conditions of want satisfaction posed by the fact that man's wants are defined exterior to his biology (*Le Suicide, op. cit.*, pp. 272-280). Cf. Mead's similar treatment, Note 16, *Supra*.

19. Durkheim, *loc. cit.* W. L. Warner in *A Black Civizilation* (New York: Harper & Bros., 1936, pp. 240-3) gives an excellent analysis of the drastic results for the individual personality when, as in the case of the victim of black magic, disarticulation of institutionalization is deliberately carried out by the tribe.

The basic theory on which the position taken here rests is that set forth by T. Parsons, *The Structure of Social Action*, New York: McGraw-Hill Book Co., 1937, particularly in the commentary on Emile Durkheim, Chs. II, IV-XI. Cf. F. Znaniecki, *The Method of Sociology*, New York: Farrar & Rinehart, 1934, pp. 90-130; 3-26. Cf. P. A. Sorokin, *Sociocultural Causality, Space, Time*, Durham: Duke University Press, 1943, Chs. I, V.

20. The distinction between concrete and analytical levels is that suggested by Parsons, *The Structure of Social Action, op. cit.*, pp. 48-49, and F. Znaniecki, *The Method of Sociology, op. cit.*, pp. 90-130.

21. The mental disorders may actually be more direct measures of *anomie* than suicide. Variations in the psychosomatic rates, particularly those involving hypochondriasis, are another likely measurement. J. L. Halliday, a British physician, has recently attempted to show that variations in psychosomatic disorders of this type among Scottish coal miners are paralleled unmistakably by *anomie* (his term is "social sickness") resulting from the destruction of their community and work groupings (*Psychosocial Medicine*, New York: W. W. Norton, 1948).

22. "Ethos" in this usage is that of W. G. Sumner (*Folkways*, Boston: Ginn and Co., 1940, p. 36), in the Greek meaning in which he used it: as "the sum of characteristic usages, ideas, standards, and codes by which a group was individualized in character from other groups." Cf. R. Benedict, *Patterns of Culture*, Boston: Houghton Mifflin, 1934.

23. This term is that of E. T. Hiller, *Social Relations and Structures*, op. cit., Ch. 22. Our treatment of these statuses has been influenced by, and is in part based on Hiller's treatment, that of T. Parsons' "Age and Sex in the Social Structure of the United States," *op. cit.*, Ralph Linton's "Age and Sex Categories," *op. cit.*, and Kingsley Davis' "Sociology of Parent-Youth Conflict," *American Sociological Review*, V, (August, 1940), 523-535.

24. Marcel Granet, *Chinese Civilization*, New York: A. Knopf, 1930, Chs. II, III, IV, Bk. 3; A. Kardiner, and Associates, *The Psychological Frontiers of Society*, New York: Columbia University Press, 1945, Chs. II, IV; C. Arensberg, and S. Kimball, *Family and Community in Ireland*, Cambridge: Harvard University Press, 1940.

25. If we draw the correct conclusions from the article by W. L. Warner and Kingsley Davis ("Structural Analysis of Kinship," *American Anthropologist* 39, April-June, 1937), the term "maturation" expresses better than "orientation" (the term now used by Warner) the idea of selection, by the kinship system, of given features of man's biology for organization. The period of biological maturation is employed by the culture for socialization as, in turn, sexual maturity is employed for procreation. The biological correlates of our family of gerontation are the general consequences of the fact that human beings live long past their peak physical and reproductive capacities, thus overlapping the life cycles of generations. Where length of life is not great, and integrated kinship reciprocities are maintained by a well-organized family system, the family of gerontation is hardly discernible. In the industrial culture this family is becoming more evident with every decade, and is an important element in the sociological analysis of later maturity.

26. Cf. E. D. Chapple, and C. S. Coon, *Principles of Anthropology*, New York: Holt, 1942, pp. 486-488.

27. Figure 1 is based largely on the suggestion of Kingsley Davis ("The Sociology of Parent-Youth Conflict," *op. cit.*, p. 525) except that we are considering three rather than two generations.

28. The class concept is used with the qualifications recently suggested by A. B. Hollingshead, "Community Research," *American Sociological Review*, XIII, (April, 1948), 141-144, and L. Mendieta y Nunez, "The Social Classes," *American Sociological Review*, XI, (April, 1946), 166-176.

29. The chronological divisions in the life cycles of Figures 2 and 3 are drawn from the recent estimates of family life cycles of Glick, Beegle, and Loomis (*supra*, Note 2).

30. The divisions of Figure 4 are inferred roughly from the material on the ancient Chinese noble family in Marcel Granet's *Chinese Civilization*, *op. cit.*, esp. Bk. 3.

31. Parsons, "Age and Sex in the Social Structure of the United States," *op. cit.*, pp. 605-606.

32. The effects ramify into all classes and all other age statuses, but the present treatment is occupied mainly with the middle classes and the statuses of later maturity.

33. Since the analysis of Reuter, the study of the romantic pattern by Merrill and Elliott, and Waller's functional interpretation of the rating and dating complex. See E. B. Reuter, "The Sociology of Adolescence," *American Journal of Sociology*, 43, (1937), 414-427; F. Merrill, and M. Elliott, *Social Disorganization* (Rev. Ed.), New York: Harper & Bros., 1941, Ch. XXIII; Willard Waller, "The Rating and Dating Complex," *American Sociological Review*, II, (Oct., 1937), 727-734, Cf. Parsons, "Age and Sex in the Social Structure of the United States," *op. cit.*

34. Parsons and others have indicated the necessary relationship of this independence to the requirements of the industrial occupations and to the norms of achievement which are a necessary part of the incentive structure of these occupations. See, e.g., T. Parsons, *Essays in Sociological Theory*, Glencoe: Free Press, 1949, pp. 142-144.

35. P. H. Landis, *Adolescence and Youth*, New York: McGraw-Hill Book Co., 1947, Chs. 4, 15-17. T. Parsons, "Age and Sex in the Social Structure of the United States," *op. cit.*

36. Parsons, *ibid.*, pp. 605-608.

37. Glick, "The Family Life Cycle," *op. cit.*, Beegle and Loomis, "Life Cycles of Farm, Rural Non-Farm and Urban Families in the United States," *op. cit.* Cf. Parsons, "The Kinship System of the Contemporary United States," *American Anthropologist*, XLV (Jan.-March, 1943), 22-38.

38. Yankee City upper-uppers until the past generation were examples. (See W. L. Warner, and Paul Lunt, *The Social Life of a Modern Community*, New Haven: Yale University Press, 1941). Other students have confirmed this observation.

39. Landis and Page, *Modern Society and Mental Disease, op. cit.* pp. 30-32.

40. Many psychiatrists have dwelt on this point. See O. S. English and G. H. J. Pearson, *Emotional Problems of Living*, New York: W. W. Norton, 1945, Ch. XV.

41. L. S. Cottrell, Jr., and R. Gallagher, *Developments in Social Psychology*, Sociometry Monograph No. 1, New York: Beacon House, 1941, pp. 12-58. Isidor Thorner, "Sociological Aspects of Affectional Frustration," *Psychiatry*, VI (May, 1943), 157-173. Cf. R. E. L. Faris, "Interaction of Generations and Family Stability," *op. cit.*

42. M. Komarovsky, "Cultural Contradictions and Sex Roles," *American Journal of Sociology*, 42 (Nov., 1946), 184-189.

43. The life cycle of the unmarried woman in the urban United States culture requires special analysis. She is heir to disjunctions blending some of the problematic character of both the major sanctioned sex roles.

44. Even here it is probably only her greater average length of life that makes her susceptibility equivalent.

45. Cf. Parsons, "Age and Sex in the Social Structure of the United States," *op. cit.*, p. 609.

46. Ralph Linton, "Age and Sex Categories," *op. cit.*

47. It is almost certain that in the case of many ethnic minorities, the migratory, skilled and unskilled, the slum-dweller, and the rural-urban migrant, the life-cycle discontinuities will be much greater even than those of the middle-class groups. Cf. A. B. Hollingshead's findings as to family integration in his lowest economic class, "Selected Characteristics of Classes in a Middle Western Community," *American Sociological Review*, XII (Aug., 1947), 385-395. See also Allison Davis, "The Motivations of the Underprivileged Worker," in *Industry and Society* (Ed. by W. F. Whyte), Chicago: University of Chicago Press, 1945.

48. These investigations will find a wealth of data in the present literature which may be capable of new interpretations.

WORK CAREERS AND ASPIRATIONS OF AUTOMOBILE WORKERS

Robert H. Guest

1. The data upon which this report is based were taken from a large body of research material gathered in connection with a project for studying the general effects of mass production methods on human behavior, under the direction of Charles R. Walker, Director of Research in Technology and Human Relations of Yale University.

2. See Ely Chinoy, "The Tradition of Opportunity and the Aspirations of Automobile Workers," *American Journal of Sociology*, 57 (March, 1952), pp. 453-459. Chinoy's findings closely parallel those of the present study in most respects. The present writer differs in some measure with Chinoy's conclusions.

3. See Charles R. Walker and Robert H. Guest, *The Man on the Assembly Line*, Cambridge: Harvard University Press, 1952.

4. This assembly plant will be called Y to distinguish it from Plant X, which was a new plant described in *The Man on the Assembly Line*.

5. This figure includes the cost-of-living bonus.

6. The actual wage increase approximated 300 per cent, while the consumers' price index figure was 187.9. See "Consumers' Price Index and Retail Food Prices," Department of Labor, Bureau of Labor Statistics, March 1952, for the month of February, 1952.

7. Robert C. Stone's evidence supports this comment in "Factory Organization and Vertical Mobility," *American Sociological Review*, 18 (February, 1953), pp. 28-35. He concludes: "Investigation of production methods . . . reveals that those factories with modern production methods tend to have low mobility rates, and those with mixed production methods have high mobility rates."

A STUDY OF ROLE CONCEPTIONS IN BUREAUCRACY

Leonard Reissman

1. H. H. Gerth and C. W. Mills, "A Marx for the Managers," *Ethics*, 52:200-215 (January 1942).

2. This might be considered as the middle stratum, between the policy-makers at the top the highly routinized clerical workers at the bottom.

3. *Cf.* Philip Selznick, "An Approach to a Theory of Bureaucracy," *American Sociological Review*, 8: 4754 (February 1943), as an example of emphasis upon the informal structures. Also, Robert K. Merton, "Bureaucratic Structure and Personality," *Social Forces*, 18: 560-568 (May 1940), as an example of emphasis upon the formal structure and the personality characteristics to be deduced from it.

4. George H. Mead, *Philosophy of the Act*, edited by Charles W. Morris and others (Chicago: University of Chicago Press, 1938), pp. 448-9. (Italics mine).

5. The reasoning followed in this instance derives the personality characteristics most suited for a given ideal form of bureaucratic organization. Cf. Merton, *op. cit.*

6. It would be unreal to omit the individual category in our framework. Even though it is methodologically necessary to concentrate upon a single role among the many which individuals fulfill, there is obviously a psychological unity (the total individual) throughout this segmentalized behavior.

7. *From Max Weber: Essays in Sociology*, transl. & edited by H. H. Gerth and C. W. Mills (New York: Oxford University Press, 1946), chap. VIII. *The Theory of Social and Economic Organization*, transl. by A. M. Henderson and T. Parsons (New York: Oxford

University Press, 1947), pp. 329-341.

8. Prof. Useem had drawn this sample after excluding those who were assigned either to: 1) state hospitals, penal institutions, and colleges; or 2) an agency which had less than 10 persons assigned to it.

9. Tests of significance between those cases interviewed and the additional 60 cases were computed for differences in age, place of birth, year of entry into civil service, and salary. These tests further assured the representativeness of the sample interviewed.

10. *Cf.* Alexander H. Leighton, *The Governing of Men* (Princeton: Princeton University Press, 1943).

11. He need not himself be a member of that group as, for example, in the case of the civil servant who renders service to handicapped children.

12. These conclusions are based upon a statistically significant frequency of responses in each generalization.

13. This generalization is limited by the fact that the sample interviewed obviously includes only those civil servants who have chosen to remain in the service.

14. All responses to this point indicated that those who are employed in the State university are not considered as "other civil servants" although a strict definition would most certainly include them.

15. Leonard D. White, *Prestige Value of Public Employment* (Chicago: University of Chicago Press, 1929); *Further Contributions to the Prestige Value of Public Employment* (Chicago: University of Chicago Press, 1932).

16. J. Donald Kingsley, *Representative Bureaucracy* (Yellow Springs: Antioch Press, 1944).

PARTICIPATION AND MASS APATHY IN ASSOCIATIONS

Bernard Barber

1. The problem of "mass apathy" has lately been receiving more attention from academic social scientists, perhaps because of Professor Robert Lynd's remarks on apathy in his *Knowledge for What?* (Princeton, 1939). Professor Robert Merton of Columbia University will make the problem of "mass apathy" an important theme in his forthcoming study of a planned housing community.

2. John M. Dumas, "Apathy—Our Fifth Column," *National Municipal Review*, xxxvi (1947), 494-496, 502.

3. Saul D. Alinsky, *Reville for Radicals* (Chicago, 1946), p. 66.

4. John Daniels, "To Vitalize Democracy," *The Harvard Alumni Bulletin*, June 26, 1948.

5. Mary P. Follett, *The New State* (New York, 1918), p. 335.

6. Much of what is said here about the United States applies equally to Great Britain and, in somewhat lesser degree, to the other countries of western Europe.

7. American Civil Liberties Unions, *Democracy in Trade Unions* (New York, November, 1943).

8. See, for example, Louis D. Hartson, "A Study of Voluntary Associations, Educational and Social, in Europe during the Period from 1100 to 1700," *Pedagogical Seminary*, xvii (1911), pp. 10-31.

For the "paucity" of associations in non-literate societies, as he calls it, see R. M. MacIver, "Interests," *Encyclopedia of the Social Sciences* (New York, 1934). Also, on the lack of associations in the "folk society," see Robert Redfield, "The Folk Society," *American Journal of Sociology*, LII (1947), pp. 293-308.

9. *Democracy in America* (1862), I, 216, as cited in Herbert Goldhamer and Noel P. Gist, "Social Clubs and Fraternities," *Development of Collective Enterprise*, Seba Eldridge, ed. (Lawrence, Kansas, 1943).

10. *The American Commonwealth* (1911), II, 281, cited in Goldhamer and Gist, *op. cit.*

11. See Crane Brinton, *The United States and Britain* (Cambridge, Mass., 1945), p. 72, for a comment on the proliferation of associations in Great Britain.

12. (New York, 1930), pp. 730-731.

13. Edmund deS. Brunner and J. H. Kolb, *Rural Social Trends* (New York, 1933), pp. 102, 244, 372.

14. W. Lloyd Warner and Paul S. Lunt, *The Social Life of a Modern Community*, Vol. I, Yankee City Series (New Haven, 1941); F. A. Bushee, "Social Organizations in a Small City," *American Journal of Sociology*, LI (1945), 217-226.

15. Gunnar Myrdal, *An American Dilemma*, 2 vols. (New York, 1944), pp. 952-955.

16. Merritt Chambers, *Youth Serving Organizations* (Washington, D. C.: American Youth Commission of the National Council on Education, 1941).

17. Gladys Meyerand, "Women's Organizations," *Encyclopedia of the Social Sciences* (New York, 1935).

18. C. F. Marden, *Rotary and Its Brothers* (Princeton, 1935).

19. In England, the same is true. One study of two large urban areas in 1945 found that 59 per cent of the whole sample belonged to no organization at all. Forty-one per cent of the men and 79 per cent of the women had no memberships at all in associations. See "Clubs, Societies, and Democracy," *Planning, a Broadsheet* issued by *Political and Economic Planning*, No. 263, March 21, 1947.

20. Herbert Goldhamer, *Some Factors Affecting Participation in Voluntary Associations* (Unpublished Ph.D. Dissertation, University of Chicago, 1943), p. 19.

21. Mirra Komarovsky, "The Voluntary Associations of Urban Dwellers," *American Sociological Review*, 11 (1946), 686-698.

22. G. A. Lundberg, M. Komarovsky, and M. A. McInerny, *Leisure, A Suburban Study* (New York, 1934), p. 128, pp. 135ff.

23. P. F. Lazarsfeld, B. Berelson, and H. Gaudet, *The People's Choice: How the Voter*

Makes Up His Mind in a Presidential Campaign (New York, 1944), p. 145.

24. Warner and Lunt, *op. cit.*, p. 323, p. 339. See also Bushee, *op. cit.*

25. W. A. Anderson, *Farm Women in the Home Bureau* (Ithaca, N. Y.: Cornell University Agricultural Experiment Station, mimeo., 1941); W. A. Anderson, *Farm Families in the Grange* (Ithaca, N. Y.: Cornell University Agricultural Experiment Station, mimeo., 1943); W. A. Anderson and Dwight Sanderson, *Membership Relations in Cooperative Organizations* (Ithaca, N. Y.: Cornell University Agricultural Experiment Station, mimeo., 1943); W. A. Anderson and D. B. Fales, *Farm Youth in the 4-H Club* (Ithaca, N. Y.: Cornell University Agricultural Experiment Station, mimeo., 1944); and W. A. Anderson, "The Family and Individual Social Participation," *American Sociological Review*, 8 (1943), 420-425.

26. Robert Michels, *Political Parties, A Sociological Study of the Oligarchical Tendencies of Modern Democracy*, trans. by Eden and Cedar Paul (New York, 1915), pp. 377, 401.

27. Gaetano Mosca, *The Ruling Class*, trans. by Arthur Livingston (New York, 1939).

28. John F. Sly, *Town Government in Massachusetts* (Unpublished Ph.D. Dissertation, Harvard University, 1925), pp. 166-167.

29. L. L. Barber, *Modifications of Town Government in New England* (Unpublished Ph.D. Dissertation, Harvard University, 1941), Ch. X; and Lane W. Lancaster, *Government in Rural America* (New York, 1937), pp. 44ff.

30. Marden, *op. cit.*

31. William Gellerman, *The American Legion as Educator* (New York, 1938); Marcus Duffield, *King Legion* (New York, 1931), Ch. I.

32. Goldhamer and Gist, *op. cit.*, p. 175.

33. James Peter Warbasse, *Cooperative Democracy* (New York, 1923), I, 21.

34. Alinsky, *op. cit.*, p. 198.

35. Bushee, *op. cit.*

36. Albert Blumenthal, *Small Town Stuff* (Chicago, 1932), Table XIII, p. 265.

37. L. C. Kercher, V. W. Kebker, and W. C. Leland, Jr. *Consumers' Cooperatives in the North Central States* (Minneapolis, 1941), p. 44; and H. Haines Turner, *Case Studies of Consumers' Cooperatives* (New York, 1941), p. 267.

38. Marden, *op. cit.*, p. 68.

39. Lack of space prevents our presenting here the detailed sketch of the American social structure which would provide a complete basis for this statement. For an indication of both the method and substance of such a sketch, see Talcott Parsons, *Essays in Social Theory* (Glencoe, Illinois, 1948).

40. W. A. Anderson and D. Sanderson, *op. cit.*, p. 18.

41. Will Herberg, *Bureaucracy and Democracy in Labor Unions*. Reprinted for Great Island Conference, New York City, 1947, from the *Antioch Review*, Fall, 1943, p. 18.

42. Kercher *et al.*, *op. cit.*, pp. 5ff.

43. C. I. Barnard, *Dilemmas of Leadership in the Democratic Process* (Princeton: Published under the University Extension Fund, 1939).

44. Kercher *et al.*, *op cit.*, pp. 5ff.

45. Oliver Garceau, *The Political Life of the American Medical Association* (Cambridge, Mass., 1941), p. 19, discusses the use of the referendum in the A.M.A.

46. Cf. Michels, *op. cit.*, p. 205, "The desire to dominate, for good or evil, is universal."

47. Some of the problems analyzed here arise in even the smallest democratic association, but they are present in their full number and clearest form in the large democratic association. The present discussion is, in effect, limited to the latter type.

48. This highly condensed statement of the nature of executive functions is introductory to the following discussion, in which it will be amplified. This statement derives chiefly from the following sources: Max Weber, *From Max Weber: Essays in Sociology*, trans. and ed. by H. H. Gerth and C. Wright Mills (New York, 1946); and Chester I. Barnard, *The Functions of the Executive* (Cambridge, Mass., 1938).

See also, for futher abstract and concrete studies of the functions of the executive: H. C. Metcalf and L. Urwick, *Dynamic Administration: The Collected Papers of Mary Parker Follett* (New York, 1942); Grace Coyle, *Social Process in Organized Groups* (New York, 1930), Ch. V; and Marshall E. Dimock, *The Executive in Action* (New York, 1945).

49. Barnard, *op. cit.*

50. *Ibid.*, p. vii.

51. Garceau, *op. cit.*, p. 48.

52. Richard Seelye Jones, *A History of the American Legion* (Indianapolis, 1946), Ch. XXVI. Although the foreword claims this is not an "official" history, it would seem to be so.

53. American Civil Liberties Union, 1943, p. 52. See also, C. Wright Mills, *The New Men of Power* (New York, 1948).

54. Alvin W. Gouldner, "Attitudes of 'Progressive' Trade Union Leaders," *American Journal of Sociology*, LII (1947), 389-392.

55. Benjamin N. Cardozo, *The Nature of the Judicial Process* (New Haven, 1921).

56. Barnard, *op. cit.*, pp. 8, 13.

57. *Ibid.*, p. 281.

58. See Introduction, pp. 56ff., to Max Weber, *The Theory of Social and Economic Organization*, trans. by A. R. Henderson and Talcott Parsons, ed. and with an introduction by Talcott Parsons (New York, 1947).

59. C. Wright Mills, "Grass Roots Union with Ideas," *Commentary* 5 (1948), 240-247, describes a "grass roots" union the members of which "disrespect authority even when they have elected it."

60. American Civil Liberties Union, 1943; V. O. Key, Jr., *Politics, Parties, and Pressure*

Groups (New York, 1947), pp. 70ff.; Garceau, *op. cit.*

61. Garceau, *op. cit.*, p. 84.

62. American Civil Liberties Union, 1943, pp. 53-55.

CONTINUITIES AND DISCONTINUITIES IN CULTURAL CONDITIONING

Ruth Benedict

1. Landes, Ruth, *The Ojibwa Woman*, Part 1, Youth—Columbia University Contributions to Anthropology, Volume XXXI.

2. Ralph Linton, class notes on the Marquesans.

3. Henry Elkin, manuscript on the Arapaho.

4. Spencer, B., and Gillen, F. J., *The Arunta;* N. Y., Macmillan, 1927 (2 vols.). Roheim, Geza, Psycho-Analysis of Primitive Cultural Types. *Internat. J. Psychoanal.* (1932) 13:1-224—in particular, Chapter III, on the Aranda, The Children of the Desert.

5. Williams, Francis E., *Papuans of the Trans-Fly;* Oxford, 1936.

MAJOR DILEMMAS OF THE SOCIAL WORKER IN PROBATION AND PAROLE

Lloyd E. Ohlin, Herman Piven, and Donnell M. Pappenfort

1. Charlotte Towle, "The General Objectives of Professional Education," *Social Service Review*, December, 1951, p. 427.

2. Ben Meeker, "Probation Is Casework," *Federal Probation*, June, 1948, p. 52. Cf. Arthur E. Fink, *The Field of Social Work*, New York, Henry Holt, 1942, pp. 213-261; Frank T. Flynn, "Probation and Individualized Justice," *Federal Probation*, June, 1950, pp. 70-76; Elliot Studt, "Casework in the Correctional Field," *Federal Probation*, September, 1954, pp. 19-26; *Training Personnel for Work with Juvenile Delinquents*, U. S. Department of Health, Education, and Welfare, Children's Bureau Publication No. 348, Washington, D. C. 1954.

3. Charlotte Towle, "The Contribution of Education for Social Casework to Practice," Cora Kasius, ed., *Principles and Techniques in Social Casework*, New York, Family Service Association of America, 1950, p. 262.

4. Cf. U. S. Bureau of Labor Statistics, *Social Worker in 1950*, New York, American Association of Social Workers, 1952, p. 23.

5. "Competencies expected of social workers were grouped into three categories: (1) Perceptual and Conceptual Knowledge; (2) Skills, Methods, Processes, and Procedures; (3) Personal Professional Qualities. Attitudes permeated all three. The first two of these categories have been referred to graphically as 'must know' and 'must do' items. Perhaps the third should be designated as the 'must

be and must feel' category." Ernest V. Hollis and Alice L. Taylor, *Social Work Education in the United States*, New York, American Association of Social Workers, 1952, p. 27.

6. A complete study of probation-parole requires analysis of problems encountered by the "punitive officer" and the "protective agent" as well as the "welfare worker" as represented by persons recruited from the field of social work. In this article only the problems and dilemmas of social workers will be considered. It should be noted, however, that each of the other types of workers faces equally serious and consequential problems in their work adjustment.

7. Helen L. Witmer, *Social Work—An Analysis of a Social Institution*, New York, Rinehart, 1942, pp. 179-180.

8. Swithun Bowers, "The Nature and Definition of Social Casework," *Principles and Techniques in Social Casework, op. cit.*, p. 108.

9. *Ibid.*, p. 11.

10. Delwin K. Anderson and Frank Kiesler, "Helping Toward Help: The Intake Interview," *Social Casework*, February, 1954, p. 72.

11. Cf. Charlotte Towle, "Social Case Work in Modern Society," *Social Service Review*, June, 1946, pp. 168-169, for the casework model of this relationship and the treatment process.

12. Charlotte Towle, *Common Human Needs*, Chicago, University of Chicago Press, 1945, p. 61.

13. Elliot Studt, "An Outline for Study of Social Authority Factors in Casework," *Social Casework*, June, 1954, pp. 231-238.

14. In the article by Charlotte Towle, "Social Case Work in Modern Society," *op. cit.*, it is noted that some clients "become confused, anxious and frustrated" in the neutral casework relationship and that it is then advisable "to be supportive—i.e., . . . to use authority, meet dependency, impose demands, and convey moral judgments in a sustaining way so that the individual may become more self-determining or, at least, less self-destructive in his behavior." The social worker points out, however, that the school has not shown him when or how to do this.

15. In one study, all but one of the social work officers in the probation and parole agency gave as his first reading choice either the NPPA JOURNAL or *Federal Probation*, in preference to social work journals. This is an indication of the partial alienation from the social work profession which practitioners trained in social work frequently experience under the pressure of solving their immediate work problems.

16 Cf. Otto Pollak, "Cultural Dynamics in Casework," *Social Casework*, July, 1953, pp. 279-284; Melitta Schmideberg and Jack Sokol, "The Function of Contact in Psychotherapy with Offenders," *Social Casework*, November, 1953, p. 386; and Elliot Studt, "Casework in the Correctional Field," *op. cit.*, p. 25.

17. Reinhard Bendix, "Bureaucracy: The Problem and Its Setting," *American Sociological Review*, October, 1947, pp. 493-507.

18. Cf. Philip Selznick, "An Approach to a Theory of Bureaucracy," *American Sociological Review*, February, 1943, pp. 47-54.

19. Other major interest groups frequently mentioned with varying degrees of similar criticism by workers are lawyers, judges, finance companies, bonding companies, used-car companies, and institutional personnel. Cf. U. S. Department of Justice, *Attorney General's Survey of Release Procedures*, Vol. IV, *Parole*, Washington, D. C., 1939, pp. 220-221.

20. *Ibid.*, Vol. II, *Probation*, pp. 470-471.

III – VALUES

ECONOMIC VIRTUES AND PRESCRIPTIONS FOR POVERTY

Richard H. Tawney

1. Carlyle, *Cromwell's Letters and Speeches*, Letter ii.

2. See on these points Max Weber, *Die protestantische Ethik und der Geist des Kapitalismus*, first published in the *Archiv für Sozialwissenschaft und Sozialpolitik Statistik*, vols. xx, xxi, and since reprinted in vol. i of his *Gesammelte Aufsätze zur Religionssoziologie*, 1920, p. 94, whose main conclusions I paraphrase.

3. Milton, *A Defence of the People of England* (1692 ed), p. xvii.

4. See, *e.g.*, Thos. Wilson, *A Discourse upon Usury*, Preface, 1925 ed., p. 178: "There bee two sortes of men that are alwayes to bee looked upon very narroly, the one is the dissembling gospeller, and the other is the wilfull and indurate papiste. The first under colour of religion overthroweth all religion, and bearing good men in hande that he loveth playnesse, useth covertelie all deceypte that maye bee, and for pryvate gayne undoeth the common welfare of man. And touching thys sinne of usurie, none doe more openly offende in thys behalfe than do these counterfeite professours of thys pure religion."

5. Fenton, *A Treatise of Usurie*, 1612, pp. 60-1.

6. *Brief Survey of the Growth of Usury in England*, 1673.

7. S. Richardson, *The Cause of the Poor Pleaded*, 1653, Thomason Tracts, E. 703 (9), p. 14. For other references, see note 72 below. For extortionate prices, see Thomason Tracts, E. 399 (6), *The Worth of a Penny, or a Caution to keep Money*, 1647. I am indebted for this and subsequent references to the Thomason Tracts to Miss P. James.

8. Hooker, Preface to *The Laws of Ecclesiastical Polity*, Everyman ed., 1907, vol i, p. 128.

9. Wilson, *op. cit.*, p. 250.

10. *Memoirs of the Life of Colonel Hutchinson, written by his Widow Lucy*, Everyman ed., 1908, pp. 64-5.

11. See the references given in note 13.

12. *The Earl of Strafforde's Letters and Despatches*, by William Knowler, D.D., 1739 vol. ii, p. 138.

13. No attempt has been made in the text to do more than refer to the points on which the economic interests and outlook of the commercial and propertied classes brought them into collison with the monarchy, and only the most obvious sources of information are mentioned here. For patents and monopolies, including the hated soap monopoly, see G. Unwin, *The Gilds and Companies of London*, 1908, chap. xvii, and W. Hyde Price, *The English Patents of Monopoly*, 1906, chap. xi, and *passim*. For the control of exchange business, *Cambium Regis, or the Office of his Majesties Exchange Royall, declaring and justifying his Majesties Right and the Convenience thereof*, 1628, and Ruding, *Annals of the Coinage*, 1819, vol. iv, pp. 201-10. For the punishment of speculation by the Star Chamber, and for projects of public granaries, Camden Society, N.S., vol xxxix, 1886, *Reports of Cases in the Courts of Star Chamber and High Commission*, ed. S. R. Gardiner, pp. 43 *seqq.*, 82 *seqq.*, and N.S.B. Gras, *The Evolution of the English Corn Market*, 1915, pp. 246-50. For the control of the textile industry and the reaction against it, H. Heaton, *The Yorkshire Woollen and Worsted Industries*, 1920, chaps. iv, vii; Kate E. Barford, *The West of England Cloth Industry: A seventeenth-century Experiment in State Control*, in the *Wiltshire Archaelogical and Natural History Magazine*, Dec., 1924, pp. 531-42; R. R. Reid, *The King's Council in the North*, 1921, pt. iv, chap. ii; *Victoria County History, Suffolk*, vol. ii, pp. 263-8. For the intervention of the Privy Council to raise the wages of textile workers and to protect craftsmen, Tawney, *The Assessment of Wages in England by the Justices of the Peace*, in the *Vierteljahrschrift für Sozial- und Wirthschaftzgeschichte*, Bd. xi, 1913, pp. 307-37, 533-64; Leonard, *The Early History of English Poor Relief*, pp. 160-3; *Victoria County History, Suffolk*, vol. ii, pp. 268-9; and Unwin, *Industrial Organization in the Sixteenth and Seventeenth Centuries*, 1904, pp. 142-7. For the Depopulation Commissions, Tawney, *The Agrarian Problem in the Sixteenth Century*, pp. 376, 391. For the squeezing of money from the East India Company and the infringement of its Charter, Shafa'at Ahmad Khan, *The East India Trade in the XVIIth Century*, 1923, pp. 69-73. For the colonial interests of Puritan members, A. P. Newton, *The Colonising Activities of the English Puritans*, 1914, and C. E. Wade, *John Pym*, 1912.

14. E. Laspeyres, *Geschichte der Volkswirthschaftlichen Anschauungen der Nieder-*

länder und ihrer Literatur zur Zeit der Repub-lik, 1863, pp. 256-70. An idea of the points at issue can be gathered from the exhaustive (and unreadable) work of Salmasius, *De Modo Usurarum*, 1639.

15. John Quick, *Synodicon in Gallia Re-formata*, 1692, vol. i, p. 99.

16. For the change of sentiment in America, see Troeltsch, *Protestantism and Progress*, pp. 117-27; for Franklin, *Memoirs of the Life and Writings of Benjamin Franklin*, and Som-bart, *The Quintessence of Capitalism*, 1915, pp. 116-21.

17. Rev. Robert Woodrow (quoted by Som-bart, *op. cit.*, p. 149).

18. John Cooke, *Unum Necessarium or the Poore Man's Case* (1648), which contains a plea for the regulation of prices and the es-tablishment of *Monts de Piété*.

19. For the scandal caused to the Protestant religion by its alleged condonation of covet-ousness, see T. Watson, *A Plea for Alms*, 1658 (Thomason Tracts, E. 2125), pp. 21, 33-4: "The Church of Rome layes upon us this aspersion that we are against good workes . . . I am sorry that any who go for honest men should be brought into the indightment; I mean that any professors should be im-peached as guilty of this sinne of covetous-nesse and unmercifulnesse . . . I tell you these devout misers are the reproach of Christianity . . . I may say of penurious votaries, they have the wings of profession by which they seem to fly to heaven, but the feet of beasts, walking on the earth and even licking the dust . . . Oh, take heed, that, seeing your religion will not destroy your covetousnesse, at last your covetousnesse does not destroy your re-ligion." See also Sir Balthazar Gerbier, *A New Year's Result in favour of the Poore*, 1651 (Thomason Tracts, E. 651 [14], p. 4: "If the Papists did rely as much on faith as the reformed professors of the Gospel (ac-cording to our English tenets) doe, or that the reformed professors did so much practice charity as the Papists doe?"

20. S. Richardson, *op. cit.* (see note 7 above), pp. 7-8, 10.

21. The first person to emphasize the way in which the idea of a "calling" was used as an argument for the economic virtues was Weber, to whose conclusions I am largely in-debted for the following paragraphs.

22. Bunyan, *The Pilgrim's Progress*.

23. Richard Steele, *The Tradesman's Call-ing, being a Discourse concerning the Nature, Necessity, Choice, etc., of a Calling in general*, 1684, pp. 1, 4.

24. *Ibid.*, pp. 21-2.

25. *Ibid.*, p. 35.

26. Baxter, *Christian Directory*, 1678 ed., vol. i, p. 336*b*.

27. Thomas Adams (quoted Weber, *op. cit.*, p. 96 n.)

28. Matthew Henry, *The Worth of the Soul* (quoted *ibid.*, p. 168 n.)

29. Baxter, *op. cit.*, vol. i, p. 111*a*.

30. Steele, *op. cit.*, p. 20.

31. Baxter, *op. cit.*, vol. i, pp. 378*b*, 108*b*; vol. iv, p. 253*a*.

32. *Navigation Spiritualized: or a New Compass for Seamen, consisting of xxxii Points:*

of { *Pleasant Observations*
     Profitable Applications and
     Serious Reflections.

All concluded with so many spiritual poems. Whereunto is now added,

i. *A sober conversation of the sin of drunkenness.*

ii. *The Harlot's face in the scripture-glass, etc.*

Being an essay towards their much desired Reformation from the horrible and detestable sins of Drunkenness, Swearing, Uncleanness, Forgetfulness of Mercies, Violation of Prom-ises, and Atheistical Contempt of Death. 1682. The author of this cheerful work was a Devonshire minister, John Flavell, who also wrote, *Husbandry Spiritualized, or the Heavenly Use of Earthly Things*, 1669. In him, as in Steele, the Chadband touch is unmistakable. *The Religious Weaver*, apparently by one Fawcett, I have not been able to trace.

33. Steele, *op. cit.* (see note 23 above).

34. Bunyan, *The Pilgrim's Progress*.

35. David Jones, *A Farewell Sermon at St. Mary Woolnoth's*, 1692.

36. Sir Dudley North, *Discourses upon Trade*, 1691, Preface.

37. Petty, *Political Arithmetic*, Preface.

38. Dicey, *Law and Public Opinion in Eng-land*, 1905, pp. 400-1.

39. *The Humble Petition of Thousands of well-affected Persons inhabiting the City of London, Westminster, the Borough of South-wark, Hamlets, and Places adjacent* (Bodleian Pamphlets, The Levellers' Petitions, c. 15, 3 Linc.). See also G. P. Gooch, *English Demo-cratic Ideas in the Seventeenth Century*, 1898.

40. *Records of the Borough of Leicester*, 1603-88, ed. Helen Stocks, 1923, pp. 370, 414, 428-30.

41. John Moore, *The Crying Sin of England of not caring for the Poor; wherein Inclosure, viz. such as doth unpeople Townes, and un-corn Fields, is arraigned, convicted and con-demned*, 1653, p. 13. See also E. C. K. Gon-ner, *Common Land and Enclosure*, 1912, pp. 53-5.

42. Camden Society, *The Clarke Papers*, vol. i, pp. 299 seqq., lxvii seqq.

43. *The Diary of Thomas Burton*, ed. J. T. Rutt, 1828, vol. i, pp. 175-6. A letter from Whalley, referring to agitations against en-closure in Warwickshire, Nottinghamshire, Lincolnshire and Leicestershire, will be found in Thurloe, *State Papers*, vol. iv, p. 686.

44. Joseph Lee, *A Vindication of a Regu-lated Enclosure*, 1656, p. 9.

45. Aquinas, *Summa Theol.*, 2a 2ae, Q. xxxii, art. v.

46. *Dives et Pauper*, 1493, Prol., chap. vii; cf. Pecock, *The Repressor of over-much Blaming of the Clergy*, pt. iii, chap. iv, pp. 296-7. For an excellent account of the medie-

val attitude towards the poor, see B. L. Manning, *The People's Faith in the Time of Wyclif,* 1919, chap. x.

47. Latimer, *The fifth Sermon on the Lord's Prayer* (in *Sermons,* Everyman ed., p. 336). Cf. Tyndale, *The Parable of the Wicked Mammon* (in *Doctrinal Treatises of William Tyndale,* Parker Society, 1848, p. 97): "If thy brother or neighbour therefore need, and thou have to help him, and yet showest not mercy, but withdrawest they hands from him, then robbest thou him of his own, and art a thief."

48. *A True Report of the Great Cost and Charges of the foure Hospitals in the City of London,* 1644 (quoted, *ibid.,* p. 66).

49. See, *e.g., Hist. MSS. Comm., Reports on MSS. in various Collections,* vol. i, 1901, pp. 109-24; Leonard, *Early History of English Poor Relief,* pp. 268-9.

50. Sir Matthew Hale, *A Discourse touching Provision for the Poor,* 1683.

51. *Stanley's Remedy, or the Way how to reform wandering Beggars, Thieves, Highway Robbers and Pick-pockets,* 1646 (Thomason Tracts, E. 317 [6]), p. 4.

52. *Commons' Journals,* March 19, 1648/9, vol. vi, p. 167.

53. *Ibid.,* vol. vi, pp. 201, 374, 416, 481; vol. vii, p. 167.

54. Samuel Hartlib, *London's Charity Inlarged,* 1650, p. i.

55. Hartlib, *op. cit.*

56. Firth and Rait, *Acts and Ordinances of the Interregnum,* 1911, vol. ii, pp. 104-10. An ordinance creating a corporation had been passed Dec. 17, 1647 (*ibid.,* vol. i, pp. 1042-5).

57. *Ibid.,* vol. ii, pp. 1098-9.

58. Stockwood, at Paul's Cross, 1578 (quoted by Haweis, *Sketches of the Reformation,* p. 277).

59. Richard Steele, The Tradesman's Calling, being a Discourse concerning the Nature, Necessity, Choice, etc. of a Calling in general, 1684, p. 22.

60. R. Younge, *The Poores' Advocate,* 1654 (Thomason Tracts, E. 1452 [3]), p. 6.

61. For these and other passages from Restoration economists to the same effect, see a striking article by Dr. T. E. Gregory on *The Economics of Employment in England* (1660-1713) in *Economica,* no. i, Jan., 1921, pp. 37 seqq., and E. S. Furniss, *The Position of the Labourer in a System of Nationalism,* 1920, chaps. v, vi.

62. Harrison, *The Description of Britaine,* 1587 ed., bk. ii, chap. x, *Of Provision made for the Poor.*

63. H. Hunter, *Problems of Poverty: Selections from the . . . Writings of Thomas Chalmers, D. D.* 1912, p. 202.

64. For the influence of Chalmer's idea on Senior, and, through him, on the new Poor Law of 1834, see T. Mackay, *History of the English Poor Law,* vol. iii, 1899, pp. 32-4. Chalmers held that *any* Poor Law was in itself objectionable. Senior, who described

Chalmers' evidence before the Committee on the State of the Poor in Ireland as "the most instructive, perhaps, that ever was given before a Committee of the House of Commons," appears to have begun by agreeing with him, but later to have adopted the principle of deterrence, backed by the test workhouse, as a second best. The Commissioners of 1832-4 were right in thinking the existing methods of relief administration extremely bad; they were wrong in supposing distress to be due mainly to lax administration, instead of realizing, as was the fact, that lax administration had arisen as an attempt to meet the increase of distress. Their discussion of the causes of pauperism is, therefore, extremely superficial, and requires to be supplemented by the evidence contained in the various contemporary reports (such, *e.g.,* as those on the hand-loom weavers) dealing with the industrial aspects of the problem.

65. W. C. Braithwaite, *The Second Period of Quakerism,* 1919, pp. 560-2. Defoe comments on the strict business standards of the Quakers in *Letter xvii (Of Honesty in Dealing)* in *The Complete English Tradesman.* Mr. Ashton (*Iron and Steel in the Industrial Revolution,* p. 219) remarks, "The eighteenth century Friend no less than the medieval Catholic held firmly to some doctrine of Just Price," and quotes examples from the conduct of Quaker iron-masters.

VALUE ORIENTATIONS IN AMERICAN SOCIETY

Robin M. Williams

1. These distinctions can be maintained without confusion only by recognizing other possible usages of the terms "social" and "cultural" as applied to values. *Social* values have been considered variously as: (1) conducive or essential to the welfare of a collectivity taken as a whole; (2) constituting models or goals of personal behavior in social interaction; or (3) common to the members of a given social aggregate. The term "cultural value" is sometimes reserved for the value inherent in culture objects (systems of thought and belief, art, artifacts, and so on) as distinct from actual social relations. In the present analysis, values attached to timeless objects of culture are of interest only in so far as they play a role in social interaction.

2. In one respect, the residue-derivation technique of Vilfredo Pareto helps identify such implicit configurations. Much of the work of psychiatrists and clinical psychologists, and much of psychological testing (for example, the use of projective techniques) is directed to the discovery of meaning, beliefs, and values that are not readily made explicit by the person himself.

3. It should be noted at this point that "group value" is an ambiguous term that may refer either to (a) a *shared* value, as when "getting ahead" (as individuals) represents a value complex held in common throughout a

group, or (b) a value *for* the group taken collectively (as military security may be so regarded). A "group goal" we may define as a future state of affairs intended to be reached by group (collective) action. ("Intended" means either explicitly stated, or inferred, by an observer.) Thus, a group goal is *not* necessarily identical, or even congruent, with the values, motives, or goals of individual members considered distributively.

4. Or has it been thought important through time by the population in question? Not antiquity as objective fact, but antiquity as belief may be the more significant factor. This observation was suggested to the writer by R. Lauriston Sharp.

5. James H. Tufts: *America's Social Morality* (New York: 1933), p. 24: "In studying the character of a group or of a people it is in point to look not only at this and that detail of conduct-business, politics, crime, philanthropy, vice—but also at the main end or ends, if there be such, which the group more or less consciously pursues."

6. "A simple society with a culture all its own and with no disturbing contacts with the outside enjoys a success in conditioning its members no modern society can expect."—Ralph Linton: *The Study of Man* (New York: 1936), p. 110.

The theme of value diversity and change has been taken as the central thesis of a recent book with the revealing title *Problems of American Society: Values in Conflict* by John F. Cuber and Robert Harper (New York: 1948).

7. Robert K. Merton: "The Self-Fulfilling Prophecy," *The Antioch Review* (Summer, 1948), p. 199.

8. The so-called success philosophy attains its full cultural meaning only along with a particular kind of moral individualism. See Cuber and Harper: *Problems of American Society*, p. 356: "The basic premise of this philosophy is that individuals, not classes, are the real competing units. A man is said to reap his reward by 'his own' efforts, skills, and perseverance."

9. Geoffrey Gorer: *The American People: A Study in National Character* (New York: 1948), pp. 169 and 172.

10. Some of the more important personality strains engendered by high levels of aspiration in a competitive order have been compactly analyzed by Karen Horney in several works; see, for example, *The Neurotic Personality of Our Time* (New York: 1937).

11. The American sociologist Charles Horton Cooley pointed out as long ago as the turn of the century that "wealth as an object of ambition and a measure of success owes its ascendency to its social implications, and the pursuit of it is by no means a proof of materialism or sensuality. . . . The fact that a man desires it, throws little or no light upon the real object of his ambition."—*Sociological Theory and Social Research* (New York: 1930), pp. 222; the quotation is from the

esssay "Personal Competition," which first appeared as an article in 1899.

12. *Character and Opinion in the United States* (New York: 1920), p. 185, Cf. Gorer: *The American People*, p. 177: "It can be said that, as a general rule, the acquisition of money is very important to Americans, but its retention relatively unimportant."

13. Laski: *The American Democracy*, p. 15.

14. See the summary in Lee Coleman, "What Is American?" pp. 492-9; also, Henry Steele Commager: *America in Perspective* (New York: 1947), p. xii.

15. Cf. Constance Rourke's characterization of the man of the frontier: "Strength was his obsession—size, scale, power: he seemed obliged to shout their symbols as if after all he were not wholly secure in their possession." *American Humor: A Study of the National Character* (New York: 1931), p. 36.

16. For interpretations of this theme in literature see: Vernon L. Parrington: *Main Currents in American Thought* (New York: 1930); Henry A. Myers: *Are Men Equal?* (New York: 1945); Henry B. Parkes: *The American Experience* (New York: 1947).

17. Cf. E. T. Hiller: *Social Relations and Structures* (New York: 1947), p. 313.

18. Max Savelle: *Seeds of Liberty* (New York: 1948), p. 219. "From the beginning, America was made up of what they call in England the middle and laboring classes, and it has always remained so. This is, in fact, one of the important points about it."—James Truslow Adams: *The American: The Making of a New Man* (New York: 1943), p. 49.

19. The phrase used by Goetz Briefs: *The Proletariat* (New York: 1937).

20. For a clear description see James M. Williams: *Our Rural Heritage* (New York: 1925).

21. Margaret Mead: *And Keep Your Powder Dry* (New York: 1942), chap. 6.

22. Myrdal et al.: *An American Dilemma*, Vol. I, p. 21. This phrase, however, is question-begging formulation, as we shall see in more detail later. "Overstrain" is itself a value-laden concept. However, it does suggest a strong tension between nominally dominant ethical principles and the pragmatic codes and exigencies of actual social life.

23. Mead: *And Keep Your Powder Dry*, chap. 6.

24. Cf. chap. 4 above.

25. Thus Harold D. Lasswell has suggested that anxiety from severe conscience assumed to be typical of much of middle-class America often leads to the attempt to enforce moralistic legislation upon others: "Emotional fixation upon the unqualified reaffirmation of 'principles' is one result of the anxieties generated by the threatened conscience." *World Politics and Personal Insecurity* (New York: 1935), p. 226.

26. As in many other instances, the orientation has not been constant, and there are indications that the welcoming symbolism of the Statue of Liberty has lost much of its

Chr

Mr. Gilkirin

RETURN TO

OFFICE OF REGISTRAR

BY SEPT. 10

appeal in the mature economy of a world power in a time of international tension and crisis. Once again we must remind ourselves that values are subject to fluctuations and trends. Cf. Tufts: *America's Social Morality*, p. 35: "To speak of any single interest or end, as though the mind of the people were one and were settled upon the same objective throughout a period, is to assume too much unity and stability."

27. The phenomenon of the "volunteer worker" is further evidence. There are reputed to be some thirty million persons in the United States who give unpaid help to various religious, social, political, civic, and service organizations. *Survey Graphic* (March, 1949), p. 137.

28. On the psychological side, closely related to Gordon W. Allport's "autonomy of motives."

29. Robert K. Merton: "The Unanticipated Consequences of Purposive Social Action," *American Sociological Review*, vol. I, no. 6 (December, 1936), pp. 891-904.

30. Laski: *The American Democracy*, p. 12.

31. Charles A. Beard and Mary R. Beard: *The American Spirit* (New York: 1942), pp. 661-70.

32. Coleman reports this general complex among the traits upon which writers on America have usually agreed.

33. Henry Steele Commager (ed.): *America in Perspective* (New York: Random House, Inc., 1947), pp. xi and xiv.

34. André Siegfried: *America Comes of Age* (New York: 1927).

35. Cf. Laski: "No church which urged the desirability of asceticism had any hope of influence or much hope of survival." *The American Democracy*, p. 13.

36. Dorothy B. Jones: "Quantitative Analysis of Motion Picture Content," *Public Opinion Quarterly*, Vol. VI, no. 3 (Fall, 1942), pp. 411-28.

37. Note how far the ideology of Soviet Russia is from indicating the actual hierarchy of industrial organization there.

38. "Feudalism never got a real footing in America. . . . The most striking feature of the land system of the colonists generally was the departure from the English system of primogeniture." W. Paschal Larkin: *Property in the Eighteenth Century* (London: 1930), pp. 140-1.

39. For example, the influence of geographic mobility, mutual dependence under frontier conditions, the lack of a complex division of labor and highly developed urban life, etc.

40. The references are numerous. See the works by Commager and by Parkes, already cited. Also Kurt Lewin: "Some Social-Psychological Differences Between the United States and Germany," *Character and Personality*, Vol. IV (1936), pp. 265-93.

41. Cf. H. D. Lasswell: *World Politics and Personal Insecurity* (New York: 1935), p. 229: "The democratization of manners resulted in those 'man to man' forms of social intercourse which are so potent in reducing hostility against anybody who gets rich and stays a 'good fellow.' This relative universalization of deference claims has tended to nullify the consequences of a steep pyramid of wealth distribution."

42. See the findings presented in Samuel A. Stouffer *et al.*: *The American Soldier*, Vols. I and II (Princeton, N. J.: 1949), especially chaps. 6, 8, 9, and 10 of Vol. I, and chaps. 3, 6, and 7 of Vol. II.

43. Lewin: "Some Social-Psychological Differences Between the United States and Germany," p. 16: "In spite of the democratic idea of equality of men, proclaimed in the American Constitution as one of its basic principles, there are probably no other people as interested in *individual accomplishments* . . . as the Americans."

44. Savelle's conclusion from his study of the eighteenth century is: "Thus the great common denominator of American social thinking was the ideal of social freedom—freedom to rise, that is—individualism, and social fluidity. If the Americans still believed in aristocracy, it was now, in theory at least, predominantly . . . based upon the ideal of an aristocracy of merit, of individual worth." *Seeds of Liberty* (New York: Alfred A. Knopf, Inc., 1948), p. 280.

45. Cf. Linton: *The Study of Man*, chaps. 8 and 16.

46. Beard and Beard: *The American Spirit*, p. 488.

47. Myers: *Are Men Equal?*, p. 140. The passage cited is a paraphrase of the doctrines of Sumner, the Yale sociologist and economist, whose theories are a quintessence of social Darwinism.

48. *The American Democracy*, pp. 49-51.

49. Richard Muller-Freienfels: *Mysteries of the Soul*, trans. by Bernard Miall (London: 1929). This view has been common among those who feel that if industry turns out standardized goods for a mass market it follows that the whole culture is "standardized."

50. An alleged insecurity factor in American conformity has been often suggested. A representative statement is: "Today America shows perhaps more conformity in externals than any other country. . . . Americans had to establish a social tradition of their own to hold them together." H. M. Spitzer: "Presenting America in American Propaganda," *Public Opinion Quarterly*, Vol. IX (Summer, 1947), p. 219.

51. Obviously if people felt strongly enough about these difference-provoking symbols, this would not happen. The American situation implies that agreement on procedure has dominated over disagreement on other values.

52. Cf. James W. Woodward: "The Role of Fictions in Cultural Life," in *Transactions of the New York Academy of Sciences* (1944).

53. Compare the statement of a prominent physicist: "Our culture has the outstanding property of striving to convert all experience

into rational scientific knowledge."—Henry Margenau: "Western Culture and Scientific Method," in Lyman Bryson, Louis Finkelstein, and Robert M. MacIver (eds.): *Conflicts of Power in Modern Culture,* Seventh Symposium of the Conference on Science, Philosophy and Religion (New York: 1948), p. 16.

54. Clyde Kluckhohn and Florence R. Kluckhohn: "American Culture: Generalized Orientations and Class Patterns," in ibid., p. 111: "Our glorification of 'science' and our faith in what can be accomplished through 'education,' are two striking aspects of our generalized conviction that secular, humanistic effort will improve the world in a series of changes, all or mainly for the better."

55. F. S. C. Northrop: *The Meeting of East and West* (New York: 1946).

56. Especially in his *"Wissenschaft als Beruf,"* in H. H. Gerth and C. Wright Mills (trans. and eds.): *From Max Weber: Essays in Sociology* (New York: 1946).

57. There are societies where biological theories must conform to political doctrines.

58. Merle Curti: *The Roots of American Loyalty* (New York: 1946), chap. I. Even in World War II, an appreciative chord was struck by the Secretary of the Navy when he told a Texas gathering that he had been assured that Texas would not make a separate peace.

59. For example, modern methods of communication and transportation which break down the barriers between local communities. It may be added that the modern cult of nationalism has emerged concurrently with the dramatic weakening of family and other *gemeinschafliche* structures, and there are apparently definite functional connections between these two developments.

60. Concerning the very tangible influence of a moralistic orientation, with its attendant "sense of mission," upon America's role in world affairs, see chap. 14 of Henry B. Parkes: *The American Experience.*

61. This is abundantly documented in many studies. See for example Curti: *The Roots of American Loyalty,* pp. 48 ff.

62. James Truslow Adams: *The American,* pp. 304 ff. and 346 ff.; Miriam Beard: *A Short History of the Business Man,* chaps. 24 and 25; Curti: *The Roots of American Loyalty,* p. 6.

63. Cf. Carl Becker's comment that democracy is a word "which has no 'referent'— there is no precise or palpable thing or object which we all think of when the word is pronounced." *Modern Democracy* (New Haven, Conn.: 1941), p. 4.

64. It is sufficient to note that Coleman ("What is American?", p. 498) found that democracy is one of the few "national traits" mentioned by observers in all major historical periods.

65. James Truslow Adams: *The American,* p. 258.

66. Clyde Kluckhohn and Florence R.

Kluckhohn: "American Culture: Generalized Orientations and Class Patterns," in Bryson, Finkelstein, and MacIver (eds.): *Conflicts of Power in Modern Culture,* pp. 106-28.

67. Carl Becker: *Modern Democracy* (New Haven, Conn.: Yale University Press, 1941), p. 27.

68. *Le suicide* (Paris: 1897; new ed.: 1930), Book III, chap. I.

69. Parsons: *The Structure of Social Action,* pp. 333-4.

70. Wilbert E. Moore and Robin M. Williams, Jr., "Stratification in the Ante-Bellum South," *American Sociological Review,* Vol. VII, no. 3 (June: 1942), pp. 343-51.

71. "The race dogma is nearly the only way out for a people so moralistically equalitarian, if it is not prepared to live up to its faith." Myrdal, *et al., An American Dilemma,* Vol. I, p. 89.

72. Morris E. Opler: "Cultural and Organic Conceptions in Contemporary World History," *American Anthropologist,* Vol. XLVI, no. 4 (October-December, 1944), pp. 448-9.

THE VALUE SYSTEMS OF DIFFERENT CLASSES: A SOCIAL PSYCHOLOGICAL CONTRIBUTION TO THE ANALYSIS OF STRATIFICATION

Herbert H. Hyman

1. R. K. Merton, Social Structure and Anomie, reprinted as Chapter IV, *Social Theory and Social Structure,* Glencoe, The Free Press, 1949.

2. Farber has demonstrated that the experience of suffering as a consequence of some objective frustration is dependent on the time perspective of the individual. See M. L. Farber, Suffering and Time Perspective of the Prisoner, *Univ. Iowa Stud. Child Welf.,* 1944, 20, 155-227.

3. See, Arthur W. Kornhauser, Analysis of "Class Structure" of Contemporary American Society—psychological bases of class divisions, in, *Industrial Conflict,* G. W. Hartmann and T. Newcomb (ed.), New York: Dryden Press, 1939; A. Davis, B. B. Gardner and M. Gardner, *Deep South, A Social Anthropological Study of Caste and Class,* Chicago, U. of Chicago Press, 1941; Centers, R., *The Psychology of Social Classes,* Princeton, Princeton Univ. Press, 1949, see especially Chap. IX for a treatment of other values; also see his paper Motivational Aspects of Occupational Stratification, *J. Soc. Psychol.,* 28, 1948, pp. 196-197; Knupfer, G., Portrait of the Underdog, *Publ. Opin. Quart.,* 11, 1947, 103-114; E. Chinoy, The Tradition of Opportunity and the Aspirations of Automobile Workers, *Amer. J. Sociol.,* LVII, 1952, 453-459; A. B. Hollingshead, *Elmtown's Youth,* New York: Wiley, 1949; Wm. H. Form, Toward an Occupational Social Psychology, *J. Soc. Psy-*

chol., 1946, 24, 85-99; E. H. Galler, Influence of Social Class on Children's Choices of Occupations, *Elem. School J.*, LI, 1951, 439-445.

4. For summaries of literature on attitudes as related to objective class position the reader is referred to H. Hyman, The Psychology of Status, *Arch. Psychol.*, No. 269, 1942, especially Chapter VI; for summaries of aesthetic values as related to class factors the reader is referred to J. T. Klapper, *The Effects of Mass Media*, Columbia University, Bureau of Applied Social Research, 1950 (mimeo); for studies in the child-rearing realm see, Erickson, M. C., Social Status and Child-rearing Practices, in T. Newcomb, and E. L. Hartley, *Readings in Social Psychology*, New York: Holt, 1947; Allison Davis, *Social-class Influences Upon Learning*, Cambridge, Harvard Univ. Press, 1951.

5. *Ibid.*

6. The basic source for such analyses is now available in H. Cantril and M. Strunk, *Public Opinion*, 1935-1946, Princeton Press.

7. For a summary report of this survey, the reader is referred to *"Opinion News,"* Sept. 1, 1947, National Opinion Research Center, University of Chicago. The survey was conducted in conjunction with Ohio State University; Profs. Hatt and North representing that institution and Don Cahalan of the Center acting as Study Director.

8. The numbers do not add to the total sample because farm respondents and certain other groups are excluded from the rental question.

9. On the basis of a variety of studies, Havighurst and Rodgers confirm these findings. They remark "the motivational reasons for not going to college may be summarized as follows: Practically all of the superior youths who do not continue their education beyond high school are children of people who have had less than a high school education. These families participate in a culture which has little personal contact with higher education. They value a job and an earning career highly for their young people. . . . While these people have come to look favorably on a high school education for their children, they do not regard colleges really within the reach of their aspirations or their financial means." Havighurst and Rodgers do, however, point to the interesting phenomenon of the deviant case, and note that a substantial *minority* of the working class do view higher education for their children in favorable terms. They attribute this to exposure to "upper middle class culture." See, *Who Should Go to College*, Columbia University Press, 1952. p. 162.

10. Taken from Cantril, *op. cit.*, p. 186. The number of cases in the different classes is unfortunately not given. The measure of stratification is presumably an interviewer's rating of standard of living. A parallel question asked by the Fortune Poll in 1949 yielded essentially similar differences by class. See *Publ. Opin. Quart.*, 13, 1949, pp. 714-715. Confirmatory data are also available in Centers, Motivational Aspects, *op. cit.*, p. 202.

11. Merton similarly calls attention to the role of parents as central to his analysis: *op. cit.*, p. 148.

12. A variety of measures of objective class could be used in this and subsequent tables. The interviewer's rating of economic level will be used wherever possible since it is the most efficient for our purposes. However, the correlations among all these different indices are high so that the particular index chosen makes little difference. Thus the relation between interviewer's rating and monthy rental as expressed by a contingency coefficient is .74 and between the rating and education is .55.

13. Plus sign will be used to denote the fact that the difference is in the direction of greater endorsement of the value by the upper class.

14. In a national survey of high school youth conducted in 1942 by Elmo Roper, all students were asked "what do you expect to do when you finish high school?" "Continuing with education is the first choice of every occupational group, including the children of laboring and farming families." However, Roper reports that this choice "is . . . outranked by the idea of going to work among the poor and the Negroes." Thus, not only is there a difference in the value attached to education among the different classes, there is also a difference in the expectation or aspiration for higher education among the different classes. See *Fortune*, XXVI, No. 6, 1942, p. 9.

15. Similar findings are reported by Centers. When his samples were shown a card and asked which kind of job they would choose, if they had the choice, the middle class emphasized "self-expression" and the working class emphasized "security" as the basis for choice. *Op. cit.*, pp. 151-158.

16. In a comparison of children between the ages of 10-14 from a "lower class school" with children from an "upper middle class school" in Chicago, Galler obtained parallel findings. The reasons the lower class children gave for their choice of an occupation emphasized extrinsic rewards whereas the upper class children emphasized interest of the job, *op. cit.*

17. The youth data are from *Fortune, op. cit.* Unfortunately the number of cases in the different groups is not given. In 1948, the Fortune Poll repeated an almost identical question of a sample of youths aged 18-25. The stratification measure available in the published report was formal-education which correlates highly with other measures. The all-or-nothing opulent job was chosen by 33% of the college educated but only by 11% of those with grade school education. See *Publ. Opin. Quart.* 13, 1949, p. 168.

18. *Fortune*, 1947, p. 10; *Publ. Opin. Quart.* 14, 1950, p. 182.

19. In a study by Lipset and Bendix based on a probability sample of 1000 cases representing the city of Oakland, exclusive of **high-**

est and lowest socio-economic segments, somewhat contradictory data are reported. They note that a considerable majority of manual workers have had aspirations to own their own businesses, and that a sizeable minority have actually attempted such a career. Moreover, differences between various grades of manual workers are negligible. These data certainly do not conform to our picture of reduced aspirations among the lower groups, and increased emphasis upon desiderata such as security. However, apart from the restriction of the findings to the city of Oakland, it should also be noted, as the authors point out, that they are based on a somewhat truncated economic distribution. S. M. Lipset and R. Bendix, "Social Mobility and Occupational Career Patterns, II, Social Mobility," *Amer. J. Sociol.*, LVII, 1952, pp. 494-504. By contrast Centers found sizeable differences between various grades of workers with respect to the hope or expectation of owning one's own business. See "Motivational Aspects," *op. cit.*, pp. 199-201.

20. Hollingshead presents similar findings for Elmtown. Each youth "was asked to name the occupation he would like to follow when he reached maturity." As one goes down in the class structure, the per cent choosing a profession or business declines from 77% to 7% and indecision or lower occupational choices increases. *Op. cit.*, p. 286. Galler presents similar findings for her youth group in Chicago, *op. cit.*

21. *Fortune*, 1942, *op. cit.*

22. Merton remarks on a study conducted by H. F. Clark which appears to contradict the Centers-Cantril finding. He states that Clark indicates a constant increment of 25% for each income level. However, it is not clear on what kind of sample or research procedure these dates are based. *Op. cit.*

23. R. Centers and H. Cantril, "Income Satisfaction and Income Aspiration," *J. Abnorm. Soc. Psychol.*, 41, 1946, pp. 64-69.

24. See R. Gould, "Some Sociological Determinants of Goal Strivings," *J. Soc. Psychol.*, 1941, 13, pp. 461-473.

25. The per cents add to much more than 100% since each respondent was asked to name the *three* most important desiderata.

26. Chinoy makes the same general point on the basis of his study of automobile workers. "The aspirations of the automobile workers . . . represent a constant balancing of hope and desire against the objective circumstances in which they find themselves. . . . By and large they confine their aims to those limited alternatives which seem possible for men with their skills and resources." *Op. cit.*, p. 454. The statistical data in support of this conclusion are that: only 8 out of his 62 subjects felt they had a promising future outside of the factory; only five felt they had any real hope of becoming foremen within the factory; only 3 of the semi-skilled group felt it might be possible to move up to skilled levels. The remaining 46 subjects could see little in the

way of opportunity and hence reduced their goals. However, Kornhauser in his original analysis of class differences in attitudes and values disagrees with our interpretation. He remarks that people at the lower income levels "cling devotedly to the American belief in individual opportunity." He predicates this interpretation on a number of questions asked in his survey of attitudes in Chicago in which differences were small between income groups, and in which the majority of the lowest group endorsed the view that they and their children can get ahead. Yet, in certain other questions he asked in the realm of satisfaction with the opportunities for their children and satisfaction with their own life chances, differences between income groups were large and in the direction of our hypothesis. Admittedly, the wide variety of data that exists, some of it contradictory, permits of some qualification of the conclusions we have drawn. See A. W. Kornhauser, *op. cit.*, pp. 241-242.

27. *Fortune*, 1947. Unfortunately the size of the different groups is not reported. For the exact questions asked, the reader is referred to the original table.

28. The identical question asked seven years before shows approximately the same pattern of findings for the different classes. See Cantril, *op. cit.*, p. 830. Parallel findings are reported by Centers. See "Motivational Aspects," *op. cit.*, pp. 196-197.

29. Chinoy confirms this general picture in his study of automobile workers. His subjects stressed as criteria for achieving promotion such considerations as "pull," "connections," and various personal techniques for gaining favor. *Op. cit.*, p. 455. In 1948 the Fortune Poll queried a sample of youth aged 18-25 with a similar question and obtained parallel results by class. See *Publ. Opin. Quart.*, 13, 1949, p. 174. Also Centers reports similar findings from a national sample of adults. See *J. Soc. Psychol.*, 27, 1948, pp. 168-169.

30. For a discussion of the level of aspiration experiment, and a summary of the literature, the reader is referred to K. Lewin, T. Dembo, L. Festinger and P. Sears, "Level of Aspiration," Chap. X, in J. McV. Hunt, *Personality and the Behavior Disorders*, New York, Ronald Press, 1944.

31. D. K. Adams, "Age, Race, and Responsiveness of Levels of Aspiration to Success and Failure," *Psychol. Bull.*, 1939, 36, p. 573 (abstract).

32. K. Lewin, et al., *op. cit.*, pp. 341-342.

33. Preston and Bayton, J., "Differential Effect of a Social Variable upon Three Levels of Aspiration," *J. Exp. Psychol.*, 1941, 29, pp. 351-369. A MacIntosh, "Differential Effect of the Status of the Competing Group upon the Levels of Aspiration," *Amer. J. Psychol.*, 1942, 55, pp. 546-554. Minor differences in the findings in these two experiments on minimum and maximum aspirations do not concern us in this context.

34. Yet it is conceivable that even in the case of youth the limited occupational goals of the lower class represents a readjustment to reality occurring at a very early age. Hollingshead notes among his lower class youth *who are already employed* that the frequency of choice of professional or business careers is less than such choices among youth of the *same classes who are still in school.* He concluded that they have adjusted their hopes, in most cases, to the reality of the work world. *Op. cit.,* pp. 382-383.

35. Chinoy, *op. cit.,* p. 459.

36. Merton, *op. cit.,* p. 148.

37. Chinoy, *op. cit.*

38. Certain kinds of professional athletics might also fall into this grouping. For evidence on the way the occupation of boxer provides such an avenue to high status to ethnic minorities and lower socio-economic individuals, see S. K. Weinberg and H. Arond, "The Occupational Culture of the Boxer," *Amer. J. Sociol.,* LVII, 1952, pp. 460-469.

39. See G. S. Counts, "Social Status of Occupations," *School Review,* XXXIII, 1925, pp. 16-27; M. E. Deeg and D. G. Paterson, "Changes in Social Status of Occupations," *Occupations,* XXV, 1947, pp. 205-208; J. Tuckman, "Social Status of Occupations in Canada," *Canad. J. Psychol.,* 1, No. 2, 1947, pp. 71-75; "Jobs and Occupations, Soldiers' Evaluation," *Opinion News* (NORC), June 15, 1948.

40. Unfortunately, the number of cases in each of the economic groups was not available in the published report.

41. Lipset and Bendix on the basis of noting the large amount of "temporary" mobility or shifting of jobs within the careers of workers, make the basic point that such changes contribute much to reference group selection and to beliefs about mobility. Thus, they remark: "Those in the middle and upper brackets of the occupational hierarchy may continue to insist that ready opportunities for social and economic advancement exist, because from 40 to 80% of their numbers have at one time or another worked in the manual occupations. While this is not the place to explore the subjective aspects of mobility, we want to emphasize the importance of considering the impact of casual job experiences on the subjective appraisals of opportunities and on the presence or absence of subjective class identifications." By extension, the same theory can be generalized from mobility within the life history of the individual to mobility between generations. *Op. cit.,* p. 495.

MENTAL HYGIENE AND THE CLASS STRUCTURE

Kingsley Davis

1. "The ultimate in mental hygiene means mental poise, calm judgment, and an understanding of leadership and fellowship—in other words, cooperation, with an attitude that tempers justice with mercy and humility."—Dr. M. J. Rosenau, "Mental Hygiene and Public Health," *Mental Hygiene,* xix (Jan. 1935): 9. Bromberg attributes to a prominent spokesman of the movement the following statement: "Mental hygiene . . . presents many wider aspects. Industrial unrest to a large degree means bad mental hygiene, and is to be corrected by good mental hygiene. The various antisocial attitudes that lead to crime are problems for the mental hygienist. Dependency, insofar as it is social parasitism not due to mental or physical defect, belongs to mental hygiene. But mental hygiene has a message also for those who consider themselves quite normal, for, by its aims, the man who is fifty per cent efficient can make himself seventy per cent efficient. . . ."—W. Bromberg, *The Mind of Man,* New York, 1937, p. 217. So many similar statements can be found in mental hygiene texts, articles, and credos, that these quotations are typical.

Mental hygiene thus possesses a characteristic that is essential to any social movement—namely, that its proponents regard it as a panacea. Since mental health is obviously connected with the social environment, to promote such health is to treat not only particular minds but also the customs and institutions in which the minds function. To cure so much is to cure all.

A sane way to discuss mental hygiene is to assume that the purpose of mental hygiene is the prevention of positive mental disorder, and that it is therefore a branch of the public health movement, which intends not so much to make everybody bouncingly robust as to prevent the onset and spread of definite diseases. But since mental hygienists dub this limited goal as old fashioned, our realistic treatment cannot make the assumption.

2. The individualistic and worldly-ascetic qualities were delineated by Max Weber. See his *General Economic History,* trans. by F. H. Knight, Part IV; and *The Protestant Ethic and the Spirit of Capitalism,* trans. by Talcott Parsons, London, 1930.

3. R. K. Merton, "Puritanism, Pietism, and Science," *Sociological Review,* xxviii (Jan. 1936): 1-30. Max Weber, *op. cit.,* also points out the rationalistic character of Protestantism, as does W. Sombart in his *Quintessence of Capitalism,* trans. by M. Epstein, London, 1915, in his article on "Capitalism" in *Ency. Soc. Sciences,* 1930, and in his *Jews and Modern Capitalism,* London, 1913. Sombart, in the article cited, sums up the capitalist spirit in the concepts: acquisition, competition, and rationality. Following this lead we could regard capitalism as the competition for social status in terms of the acquisition of goods by rational manipulative processes.

4. The Protestant ethic was perhaps most characteristic of early capitalism, and it has doubtless fallen into some desuetude with subsequent social changes, but it still tends to

form the unconscious premises of our thinking about conduct, even when in practice we do not follow its precepts. Veblen was particularly impressed with the archaic character of our present 18th century moral philosophy. (See his *Vested Interests and the Common Man*, N. Y., 1920). The Protestant ethic is still the living message of our departed moral authorities—Jefferson, Franklin, Lincoln, and Emerson—and is woven into poetry, song, and precept.

5. Our generalizations are based upon a systematic study of selected literature in the field, chosen from a list sent out by the National Committee for Mental Hygiene, Inc. In addition, a few other standard works were read with a view to sampling. All told, thirteen volumes were gone through, with the aid of a fixed questionnaire designed to discover certain things about each book. The books systematically perused are as follows: V. V. Anderson, *Psychiatry in Education*, N. Y., 1932; W. J. Burnham, *The Wholesome Personality*, N. Y., 1932; E. R. Groves and P. Blanchard, *Introduction to Mental Hygiene*, N. Y., 1930; Howard and Patry, *Mental Health*, N. Y., 1935; D. W. La Rue, *Mental Hygiene*, N. Y., 1927; J. J. B. Morgan, *Keeping a Sound Mind*, N. Y., 1934; W. V. Richmond, *Personality: Its Study and Hygiene*, N. Y., 1937; L. F. Shaffer, *The Psychology of Adjustment*, Boston, 1936; G. S. Stevenson and G. Smith, *Child Guidance Clinics*, N. Y., 1934; D. A. Thom, *Everyday Problems of the Everyday Child*, N. Y., 1928 J. E. W. Wallin, *Personality Maladjustments and Mental Hygiene*, N. Y., 1935; F. L. Wells, *Mental Adjustments*, N. Y., 1917; C. B. Zachry, *Personality Adjustments of School Children*, N. Y., 1929. Other literature, especially recent contributions in psychiatry dealing with the relation of mental disorder to social phenomena, was of course read.

6. Burnham, p. 522: "The democratic ideal in its higher form is based, not on an abstract myth of human equality, made concrete in an equal share of human necessities and social privileges, but based rather on the psychological fact of profound individual differences." "The ideal democratic group today is one where each member of the group has the opportunity to become superior in something according to his special ability."

Howard and Patry consider mobility on the whole a desirable condition, since it offers a goal for effort. But they criticize the mad scramble for money and "material" things. In other words, they condemn some of the particular goals of vertical movement, but they do not condemn (or indeed consciously treat) mobility itself.

La Rue says that we must learn to adapt ourselves to any surroundings. "But that is no reason why we should rest satisfied with all these things, or make no effort to improve our condition."—p. 280. Ambition is assumed all through the book. Self-confidence, a necessary entrepreneurial virtue, is extolled and Emerson

is quoted as saying that "Self-trust is the secret of success."

Wells assumes that the aim of life is to get ahead, and that ambition is a prerequisite to a well-functioning mind. P. 11: "The free imagination of wished-for things results well for the mind through painting in more glowing colors the excellence of what is wished for, and firing the ambition to strive for it the more intensely." The success vs. failure motif is apparent.

7. Morgan, p. 166: "Your birth means that you have been selected as a player in the greatest game ever devised. . . ."

Wells, p. 7: "Yet the worth of existence depends on success in a game infinitely more complicated than that of chess, in which no mistake is ever overlooked and no move ever taken back, and where knowledge from one's own experience often comes too late for use."

8. Morgan, p. 38: "The fight of the mature adult is thus transformed from the childish attempt to resist all conditions which produce physical discomfort to the battle against any infraction against his self-imposed standards of behavior."

9. Shaffer states, p. 152, that one symptom of bad adjustment found in the inferiority complex is "a poor reaction to competition."

A literal translation of the phrase "personal efficiency," found so frequently in the literature, would be "competitive ability."

10. One of the five goals of "progressive" education, as listed by Zachry, p. 271, is: "The cultivation of ambitions which can be attained."

Morgan, p. 151: "Ambition must not be excessive." P. 22: "Facing life squarely is the first principle of mental health."

11. Groves and Blanchard, p. 302: "The devotion of some leisure time to recreational pursuits is of positive value outside of the enjoyment which it affords, for it enables the individual to return reinvigorated to the more serious routine of study or work."

Another of the five goals of "progressive" education which Zachry lists is "healthful recreation."

12. Wells, p. 276: "In life, the lubricating function of money to the social machinery is well known. It plays an equally essential part in the smooth operation of one's mental trends."

Shaffer, p. 539: The individual should "employ the scientific method for the solution of his personal problems." P. 382: It is assumed that rationality and insight are possible and desirable.

13. Shaffer, p. 539: "The chief requirements for hygienic work are freedom and success. Each person must be free to select the kind of task that is most suitable and most satisfying to him. He must have freedom to plan it and to carry it to completion in his own way."

Another of Zachry's five goals of "progressive" education is "personal indepedence—intellectual and emotional."

14. La Rue, pp. 11-12: "Happiness is, in general, the sign of mental health."

Stevenson and Smith, p. 1: "The child guidance clinic is an attempt to marshal the resources of the community in behalf of children who are in distress because of unsatisfied inner needs. . . ."

15. Shaffer assumes that individuals possess four types of motives which then come into conflict with the environment.—p. 86.

Zachry says that that child's "instinctive tendencies often conflict with one another. . . ." —p. 45.

16. Shaffer, p. 539: The individual should "employ the scientific method for the solution of his personal problems." P. 382: Assumes that rationality and insight are possible and desirable.

Another of Zachry's five goals is "purposeful and rational activity."

Morgan, p. 1: Life is ever-changing and demands continuous readjustment. It is "a game with a continual challenge which you must meet if you are to keep alive. Stagnation and death come when you cease to rise to the challenge."

17. The survey includes data on the lives of 51 persons, leaders of the mental hygiene movement. With no funds for detailed historical or questionnaire research, we could not secure as many facts as we wished. Our conclusions are therefore tentative, but on the information we do have, taken from available bibliographical sources in obituaries, *Who's Who*, etc., they seem quite justified.

18. Howard and Patry, p. 24: "We have seen that the prime condition of mental health is the integration of the psychophysical and psychosocial organism through the development of stable major circuits of energy or good patterns of behavior." La Rue, p. 13: "Happiness is, in general, the sign of mental health. But it should be lasting happiness; for of course one can be happy for the moment, like the maniac or the drunkard, without having a mind that is really healthy." Richmond: The healthy personality is one which "functions more or less perfectly in its cultural milieu."—p. 248. Shaffer, p. 138: "For a person to satisfy all his motives with regard for their functioning as an interrelated system, is good adjustment. To achieve this requires unified and integrated behavior." Thom, p. 135: "The well-adjusted personality, which characterizes a happy and efficient man or woman, is a harmonious blending of these varied emotions and character traits, resulting in self-control and habits of conformity." Wallin, p. 32: "That individual may be considered to be mentally sound and efficient who is able to react to his physical and social environment in an effective, consistent, and integrated manner. That is, an individual's mental soundness can be judged by the appropriateness and rationality of his behavior patterns on the psychological and social levels."

19. In the following passage quoted from Howard and Patry, pp. 146-148, we find an illustration of typical reasoning along this line:

"The moralists and theologians who were not able to give sex a rational explanation sought to stamp sex interest out of life. This only tended to dam up its force. [Condemnation of an old moral attitude on ground of its effects.] When psychoanalysis began to disclose it as a factor in mental conflicts, the so-called realists . . . began to play fast and loose with sex themes, with the result . . . a flood of sex liberalism. [Condemnation of current attitude.] . . . There is at present the need of a middle ground between the old attitude of avoidance and the present indiscriminate flaunting of sex themes. [Advocacy of a particular attitude.] Wholesome-minded people are not averse to frank consideration of sex under proper conditions and right motives, but they do not enjoy having it dragged into prominence on every possible pretext and occasion. Dignity and decency are the marks of successful sex adjustment. [Bolstering the proposed attitude with words and phrases of praise and redundant identification of it with health and the right people.] In our approach to the problems and in procedures for the enlightenment of the young these qualities should be our guide and goal." [Assertion that everybody *should* accept the author's goal.] "In our attempts at sex education we have not yet learned to appeal to the highest motive-family formation. . . . Morality for its own sake no longer makes an appeal to young people. All moral codes should be tested by the degree to which they contribute vital values and call out deeper potentialities." [Justifying the proposed attitude on the basis of its connection with a fundamental institution and hence the central system of values in the culture.]

20. Here we see an illustration of the conflict between the humanitarian mores (by which certain established practices are criticized) and the organizational mores (the more basic and unconsciously accepted standards). See W. Waller, "Social Problems and the Mores," *Amer. Soc. Rev.,* i (Dec. 1936): 922-933.

21. It is often difficult to get behind the emotionality and loquacity of mental hygiene literature to see the essential logic. This paragraph is meant to describe the general features of its main position after all the verbiage has been laboriously sifted.

22. Mental hygiene turns out to be not so much a science for the prevention of mental disorder, as a science for the prevention of moral delinquency. Thus an author may state that every individual has a need for some kind of useful work, then draw the conclusion that every individual *must* have useful work to be mentally adjusted, and finally declare that any social customs which do not permit this are irrational and unworthy. The conscious premise, that every individual has the alleged need, is a psychologistic fallacy. The other propositions, avowedly based on the initial premise, are in fact the product of

countless unverbalized values which together represent an accepted ethical system.

We are thus able to account for the extraordinary diffuseness of mental hygiene goals. Mental health being defined in terms of conformity to a basic ethic, the pursuit of mental hygiene must be carried on along many fronts. Also, since the fiction of science is maintained, the ethical character of the movement can never be consciously and deliberately stated—hence the goals must be nebulous and obscurantist in character.

23. The works of Cooley, Mead, Faris, and Dewey are here referred to.

24. This study, though merely a straw in the wind, satisfied us that significant research could be carried on in this direction.

25. C. M. Campbell, *Destiny and Disease in Mental Disorders*, N. Y., 1935.

26. In so far as mental disorder results from definite disease processes, its prevention lies within the province of the ordinary public health program, the field of physical hygiene. Only when it is seen as somehow resulting from non-physical forces (Campbell's "personal" as opposed to impersonal factors) does it fall within the province of *mental* hygiene.

27. Mental hygiene literature sadly neglects to analyze social processes, whether invidious or otherwise. Much is of course written about the importance of "environmental factors," but these so important "factors" are scarcely ever treated so as to discover their specific mode and intensity of operation.

The same criticism applies, though in lesser degree, to psychiatry and abnormal psychology. In them too, even when a school is dealing avowedly with superiority and inferiority, there is a tendency to regard these as individual traits and not explore their social origins. This is true, for example, of Adler's so-called individual school of psychology. The limitation of his point of view has caused him to miss essential features of the very phenomenon he insists is important. Again we may mention the works of Dr. Macfie Campbell, who very skilfully points out the causal importance of what he calls personal factors, but disclaims any attempt to analyze these factors systematically. What he calls "personal" could equally be called socio-genic, and studied sociologically.

Mental hygiene's neglect of social process springs partly from the fact that mental hygienists are for the most part trained psychologically to look for bio-genetic determinants, rather than sociologically to look for social determinants. But it also arises from the sociologists' own failure to clarify the role of social interaction in the etiology of mental derangement. At any rate mental hygiene seems to be limping along on one foot, because if there *are* social determinants, these are not being discovered and utilized in prevention.

Detailed proof and knowledge of determining social processes will not come until case histories are invented and utilized which give the *significant social past* of the patient. Such histories wait upon two achievements: first, the development of a conceptual scheme which, as a first approximation, indicates what facts in the social past are significant, hence guides the research from the start; and second, the perfection and standardization, and the possible invention of new techniques of social investigation. The first achievement has perhaps been realized in sociological theory, but its application in the gathering of social data about specific patients lags far behind.

While much of our sociological work has not been sufficiently detailed to apply to the etiology of mental disorder, it does point in directions where further investigation may prove fruitful. This is true, for example, of the ecological and comparative approach to the distribution of functional disorders. In other words, though we cannot give an exact description of the operation of social determinants in particular psychoses, we have strong evidence, if not proof, *that* such determinants are there. The *how* need not escape us always. In the last analysis it seems that sociologists could be expected to produce the required knowledge, because they, of all those interested in the problem, are the only ones devoting themselves purely to social relations as such.

Of the two great systems of causation with reference to personality—one the biological (cellular interaction) and the other sociological (communicative interaction)—neither can be ignored by any science of mental disorder. Thus far, however, it seems that far more energy, thought, and money has gone into the investigation of the first. Problems are even stated in such a way as to preclude investigation of the second, and concepts are used which are stop-gaps rather than invitations to a knowledge of it. And yet there exist countless evidences that sociological factors play a significant part in both normal and abnormal behavior.

28. A class structure presupposes a hierarchy of values. Who possesses the highest values, or possesses these in the greatest degree, is of the highest class. It does not follow, as some would have us believe, that the system of values was instituted for the benefit of the upper class. Rather the system of values sets the framework and determines the goals of competition for position.

29. This observation seems to be justified by the ecological studies of schizophrenia that have been made. Areas in which conduct violates the norms of the very society of which conduct the persons are a part, are areas of high incidence. *Cf.* R. E. L. Faris, "Cultural Isolation and the Schizophrenic Personality," *Amer. Jour. of Soc.*, xl (Sept. 1934): 155-164. Also, H. W. Dunham, "The Ecology of the Functional Psychoses in Chicago," *Amer. Soc. Review*, ii (Aug. 1937): 467-479.

30. See W. L. Warner, "American Caste and Class," *Amer. Jour. of Soc.*, xlii (Sept. 1936): 234-237. J. Dollard, *Caste and Class*

in *Southerntown*, New Haven, 1937, especially pp. 72, 89, 182. Also K. Davis, "The American Caste System," unpublished manuscript in possession of the author.

31. Compare P. Sorokin, *Social Mobility*, New York, 1927, Ch. 21. Sorokin concludes that since in a mobile system the individual must adapt himself to changing milieus, mobility increases the incidence of mental disease. He admits increasing superficiality and externalization, however, but he interprets them in terms of the individuals concerned and does not realize that they are even more characteristic of the cultural differences between classes and therefore constitute a compensation for the mental strain. It is only in the initial stages of becoming a mobile system that a class order may engender insanity. But this is a period of social change, and the increased incidence is due to our principle of conflicting values and not to the sheer fact of mobility itself.

32. The open-class society is also protected by the fact that the class sieves are never entirely open and hence most people move only a few rungs up or down. For this additional reason the changes required of any individual are usually not overwhelming. It should be remembered too that the open-class ethic places a positive value upon upward movement, and that even in the case of failure it always holds out hopes of recovery and progression. A person's mobility thus fulfills the values.

33. Psychiatry is waking up to the necessity of studying interpersonal relations. See H. S. Sullivan, "A Note on the Implications of Psychiatry, the Study of Interpersonal Relations, for Investigations in the Social Sciences," *Amer. Jour. of Soc.*, xlii (May 1937): 848-861. Also, Karen Horney, *The Neurotic Personality of Our Time*, New York, 1937; and the works of Macfie Campbell.

34. Psychiatry, as shown by Campbell, Horney, Sullivan, and others, has gradually come to realize the importance of social and cultural factors in the determination of mental derangement. Generally, however, there has been an overestimation of the power this places in the hands of the practitioner. As reported by a sociologist who has spent some time as an observer in a mental hospital, some doctors and psychiatrists assume that with further knowledge of social factors, these can be immediately changed so as to reduce the incidence of mental disorder. But for very profound reasons we cannot plan or alter our culture out of whole cloth. However, there is another type of optimism which is slightly more justified. This involves concentrating upon special or limited social environments as the field of social manipulation. Each of these has been studied in connection with the possible genesis of mental disease, and certain reforms advocated. But often, as in the case of the individual when he was first studied apart from his culture, the possibility of changing these particular social milieus is

easily over-estimated. They are parts of our general culture, and resistances to changing them arise which were not at first apparent. Of course one particular individual's relation to one of his special social environments (say the court) can be helpfully altered, but this is casework and does not alter the situation so far as the general population is concerned. (For a detailed consideration of the problem of manipulating limited social milieus, see K. Davis, "The Application of Science to Personal Relations, A Critique of the Family Clinic Idea," *Amer. Sociological Review*, i (April 1936): 236-251.) Some features of society, moreover, are scarcely limited to any particular milieu. One of these is the class structure which, as a phase of the entire social organization, cuts across all special parts of that organization. When speaking of such factors it is difficult to advocate their immediate removal or change without becoming involved in ethical controversies and unseen consequences far transcending the immediate problem in hand.

SCHOOL AND SETTLEMENT HOUSE

Albert K. Cohen

1. See, for example, the following statements by educators: Elizabeth M. Fuller, Helen Christianson, Neith Headley *et al.*, "Practices and Resources in Early Childhood Education," in *The Forty-Sixth Yearbook of the National Society for the Study of Education*, Part II (Chicago: University of Chicago Press, 1947), pp. 103-105 and Samuel Smith, George R. Cressman and Robert K. Speer, *Education and Society: An Introduction to Education for a Democracy* (New York: The Dryden Press, 1942), pp. 154-155.

2. On the mental hygiene implications of failure in conforming to teacher expectations, see Fritz Redl and William W. Wattenberg, *Mental Hygiene in Teaching* (New York: D. Appleton-Century Company, 1940), pp. 245-247; and an excellent short article by Roger G. Barker, "Success and Failure in the Classroom," in Wayne Dennis (ed.), *Readings in Child Psychology* (New York: Prentice-Hall, Inc., 1951). pp. 577-582, reprinted from an article in *Progressive Education*, XIX (1942), 221-224.

3. W. Lloyd Warner, Robert J. Havighurst and Martin B. Loeb, *Who Shall Be Educated?* (New York: Harper and Brothers, 1944), is an excellent discussion of the way in which school policy is shaped by middle-class values. The functions of teachers, they say, are two: "They train or seek to train children in middle-class manners and skills. And they select those children from the middle and lower classes who appear to be the best candidates for promotion in the social hierarchy." (p. 107). A public-school superintendent, critical of current guidance philosophy, states: "Boards of Education and Parent-Teacher

Associations are invariably Calvinists. . . . They believe that a Director of Guidance in the high school will be able to elevate every student, that is, to lead him into some pleasant and dignified occupation, to guide him so that his will not be a life of toil or manual work or degrading forms of labor. A school with a real guidance program should raise all pupils to a high social and economic position." Ernest W. Butterfield, "Our White-Collar Guidance Psychology," *The Clearing House,* XIII (May, 1939), 516.

4. Percival M. Symonds, "Personality Adjustment of Women Teachers," *American Journal of Orthopsychiatry,* XI (January, 1941), 15, comments, on the basis of a study of 50 biographies of women teachers:

It is because the need for achievement is so strong among teachers that competition is used as a motivating force so widely in schools. The teacher with strong drive for achievement is likely to overstimulate the bright, and show unjust discrimination against the dull and failing.

5. The best study is E. Koster Wickman, *Children's Behavior and Teachers' Attitudes* (New York: The Commonwealth Fund, 1928). The findings of later studies are consistent with Wickman's. See Harold H. Anderson, "The Construction of a Mental Hygiene Scale for Teachers," *American Journal of Orthopsychiatry,* X (April, 1940), 253-263, and Grace B. Cox and Harold H. Anderson, "A Study of Teachers' Responses to Problem Situations As Reported by Teachers and Students," *American Journal of Orthopsychiatry,* XIV (July, 1944), 528-544.

6. Maurice E. Troyer, "Squaring Evaluation Processes with Democratic Values," *American Council of Education Studies,* Series I, No. 34 (January, 1949), p. 42.

7. See William F. Whyte, *Street Corner Society* (Chicago: University of Chicago Press, 1943), especially pp. 98-104. See also E. L. Johnstone, "What Do Boys Think of Us—and Why?", *Proceedings of the American Prison Association, 1944* (New York: The American Prison Association, 1944), pp. 143-144.

8. Grace L. Coyle, *Group Work with American Youth. A Guide to the Practice of*

Leadership (New York: Harper and Brothers, 1948), p. 49.

9. Robert J. Havighurst and Hilda Taba, *Adolescent Character and Personality* (New York: John Wiley and Sons, 1949), pp. 52-55.

10. Merl E. Bonney, "A Study of Social Status on the Second Grade Level," *Journal of Genetic Psychology.* LX (June, 1952), 271-305. See also Henry P. Smith, "A Study in the Selective Character of American Secondary Education: Participation in School Activities as Conditioned by Socio-Economic Status and Other Factors," *Journal of Educational Psychology,* XXXVI (April, 1945), 229-246 and August B. Hollingshead, *Elmtown's Youth* (New York: John Wiley and Sons, 1949), pp. 192-203.

11. August B. Hollingshead, *op. cit.,* p. 241.

12. There is tangible research evidence that, at least in the school area, low status is accompanied by maladjustment. Joel B. Montague, "Social Status and Adjustment in School," *Clearing House,* XXVII (September, 1952), 19-24, investigates the relationship between the adjustment of students and the students' own estimates of the status of their parents in the community. The lowest status group, in contrast to the middle and upper status groups, strikingly more often, in response to an attitude questionnaire, indicate that school is not interesting, the studies are too hard, they don't like their courses, they are not popular, they are left out of things, it is hard to make friends, they are unable to express themselves well, they can't seem to concentrate, there is not enough time to study. Onas Scandrette, "School—through the Eyes of the Underchosen," in the same issue of *Clearing House,* 35-37, compares the attitudes of children who are frequently chosen and those who are underchosen by their classmates to be members of a classroom project committee. The underchosen are much more likely to feel that teachers have little personal interest in their students, teachers are unfair, teachers are unkind, teachers are unfriendly, other students are unkind, association with the opposite sex is not enjoyable, school work is too hard.

IV — SOCIAL STRATIFICATION

CLASS, STATUS, PARTY

Max Weber

1. *Wirtschaft und Gesellschaft,* part III, chap. 4, pp. 631-40. The first sentence in paragraph one and the several definitions in this chapter which are in brackets do not appear in the original text. They have been taken from other contexts of *Wirtschaft und Gesellschaft.*

2. The posthumously published text breaks off here. We omit an incomplete sketch of types of "warrior estates."

THE WARNER APPROACH TO SOCIAL STRATIFICATION

Ruth Rosner Kornhauser

1. The author is indebted to Herbert Hyman and Daniel Bell for their valuable suggestions.

2. W. Lloyd Warner and Paul S. Lunt, *The Social Life of a Modern Community* (New Haven: Yale University Press, 1941), vol. I, Yankee City Series, chap. i.

3. *Ibid.,* p. 35.

4. *Ibid.,* p. 81.

5. *Ibid.*

6. *Ibid.*

7. *Ibid.*, p. 82.

8. W. Lloyd Warner, Marchia Meeker, and Kenneth Eels, *Social Class in America* (Chicago: Science Research Associates, 1949), p. 129.

9. Warner and Lunt, *op. cit.*, p. 82.

10. W. Lloyd Warner, *American Life* (Chicago: University of Chicago Press, 1953), p. 52.

11. Warner and Lunt, *op. cit.*, p. 82.

12. Allison Davis, "Socialization and Adolescent Personality," in Theodore M. Newcomb and Eugene L. Hartley (eds.), *Readings in Social Psychology* (New York: Henry Holt & Co., 1947), p. 142.

13. Warner and Lunt, *op. cit.*, p. 74.

14. W. Lloyd Warner and Associates, *Democracy in Jonesville* (New York: Harper & Bros., 1949), pp. xiii-xiv.

15. Four volumes in the Yankee City Series have been published to date: W. Lloyd Warner and Paul S. Lunt, *The Social Life of a Modern Community* (New Haven: Yale University Press, 1941); W. Lloyd Warner and Paul S. Lunt, *The Status System of a Modern Community* (1942); W. Lloyd Warner and Leo Srole, *The Social System of American Ethnic Groups* (1945); and W. Lloyd Warner and J. O. Low, *The Social System of the Modern Factory* (1947).

16. Allison Davis, Burleigh B. Gardner, and Mary R. Gardner, *Deep South* (Chicago: University of Chicago Press, 1941).

17. The substantive report on the Jonesville community as a whole is contained in W. Lloyd Warner and Associates, *Democracy in Jonesville.* The methodological results are reported in W. Lloyd Warner, Marchia Meeker, and Kenneth Eels, *Social Class in America.* Robert J. Havighurst and Hilda Taba's *Adolescent Character and Personality* (New York: John Wiley & Sons, 1948) is based on data collected in Jonesville (called Prairie City in this volume). August B. Hollingshead's study, *Elmtown's Youth* (New York: John Wiley & Sons, 1949), was also conducted in Jonesville. One of the communities discussed in W. Lloyd Warner, Robert J. Havighurst and Martin Loeb, *Who Shall Be Educated?* (New York: Harper & Bros., 1944) presumably is Jonesville, although it is called Hometown in this book.

18. Warner and Lunt, *The Social Life of a Modern Community*, pp. 4-5.

19. *Ibid.*, p. 5.

20. *Ibid.*, p. 38.

21. Warner and Associates, *op. cit.*, pp. xiv-xv; Warner, *op. cit.*, pp. 32-34.

22. Warner, *op. cit.*, p. 32.

23. Warner and Lunt, *The Social Life of a Modern Community,* chap. v.

24. *Ibid.*, p. 90.

25. Warner, Meeker, and Eels, *op. cit.*, p. 35.

26. *Ibid.*, pp. 48-52, p. 61, and pp. 62-63.

27. *Ibid.*, chap. viii.

28. *Ibid.*, p. 40.

29. *Ibid.*, pp. 167-168.

30. *Ibid.*, p. 196.

31. Davis, Gardner, and Gardner, *op. cit.*, p. 59.

32. Warner, Meeker, and Eels, *op. cit.*, p. 11.

33. Warner and Lunt, *The Social Life of a Modern Community*, pp. 100-102; Davis, Gardner, and Gardner, *op. cit.*, pp. 84-88.

34. Warner and Lunt, *The Social Life of a Modern Community*, pp. 234-235 and pp. 244-245.

35. Davis, Gardner, and Gardner, *op. cit.*, p. 64.

36. Warner and Lunt, *The Social Life of a Modern Community*, p. 261; Warner, Meeker, and Eels, *op. cit.*, pp. 11-12.

37. Warner and Lunt, *The Social Life of a Modern Community*, p. 290.

38. *Ibid.*, p. 424.

39. Warner, *op. cit.*, pp. 55-56.

40. Warner, Meeker, and Eels, *op. cit.*, p. 13.

41. Warner and Lunt, *The Social Life of a Modern Community*, pp. 244-246, pp. 283-284, and p. 290.

42. Warner, Meeker, and Eels, *op. cit.*, p. 13.

43. Warner, *op. cit.*, p. 57.

44. *Ibid.*

45. Warner and Lunt, *The Social Life of a Modern Community*, p. 445 and p. 290; Warner, Meeker, and Eels, *op. cit.*, p. 15.

46. Warner and Lunt, *The Social Life of a Modern Community*, pp. 447-448; Warner, Havighurst, and Loeb, *op. cit.*, p. 26.

47. Warner and Lunt, *The Social Life of a Modern Community*, p. 279.

48. Warner, *op. cit.*, pp. 57-58.

49. *Ibid.*, pp. 58-59.

50. *Ibid.*, p. 32 and p. 60; Warner, Meeker and Eels, *op. cit.*, p. 6 and p. 24; Warner and Associates, *op. cit.*, pp. xiv-xv.

51. Warner and Associates, *op. cit.*, p. xiv.

52. Warner, *op. cit.*, pp. 62-63.

53. Warner and Lunt, *The Social Life of a Modern Community*, p. 91.

54. Warner and Associates, *op. cit.*, p. 23.

55. Davis, Gardner, and Gardner, *op. cit.*, p. 61.

56. *Ibid.*, pp. 71-72.

57. Warner, *op. cit.*, pp. 97-98.

58. Davis, Gardner, and Gardner, *op. cit.*, chap. v.

59. Warner and Lunt, *The Social Life of a Modern Community*, pp. 277-279 and p. 291.

60. Davis, Gardner, and Gardner, *op. cit.*, chap. vi.

61. Allison Davis and John Dollard, *Children of Bondage* (Washington, D. C.: American Council on Education, 1940), p. 261.

62. Warner and Lunt, *The Social Life of a Modern Community*, p. 124.

63. Warner, *op. cit.*, p. 193.

64. Davis, Gardner, and Gardner, *op. cit.*, pp. 74-75.

65. Warner and Associates, *op. cit.*, pp. 131-144.

66. *Ibid.*, pp. 156-161.

67. *Ibid.*, p. 154.

68. Warner, *op. cit.*, p. 194.

69. Warner, Havighurst, and Loeb, *op. cit.*, pp. 60-61.

70. *Ibid.*, pp. 65-66; Warner and Associates, *op. cit.*, pp. 196-198 and pp. 202-204.

71. Warner, Havighurst, and Loeb, *op. cit.*, p. 75.

72. *Ibid.*, pp. 51-53.

73. *Ibid.*, pp. 61-63; Warner and Associates, *op. cit.*, pp. 206-208.

74. Warner, Havighurst, and Loeb, *op. cit.*, p. 74.

75. *Ibid.*, p. 101.

76. Warner and Low, *op. cit.*, p. 76.

77. *Ibid.*, chap. v. See also Warner, Havighurst, and Loeb, *op. cit.*, pp. 152-153.

78. Warner and Low, *op. cit.*, p. 109.

79. *Ibid.*, p. 183.

80. *Ibid.*

81. *Ibid.*, p. 185.

82. *Ibid.*

83. *Ibid.*, p. 183. See also Warner, Havighurst, and Loeb, *op. cit.*, p. 157.

84. Warner and Srole, *op. cit.*, p. 2.

85. Warner, *op. cit.*, pp. 160-163.

86. Warner and Associates, *op. cit.*, chap. xi.

87. Warner and Srole, *op. cit.*, chap x.

88. Warner, *op. cit.*, p. 171.

89. *Ibid.*, pp. 67 ff.

90. Robert E. Park, "The Bases of Race Prejudice," *Race and Culture* (Glencoe: The Free Press, 1950), p. 243.

91. W. Lloyd Warner, "American Caste and Class," *American Journal of Sociology*, XLVII (1936), p. 235.

92. *Ibid.*

93. W. Lloyd Warner, Introduction to Davis, Gardner, and Gardner, *op. cit.*, pp. 11-12.

94. Davis and Dollard, *op. cit.*, p. 256; Allison Davis and Robert J. Havighurst, "Social Class and Color Differences in Child-Rearing," in Clyde Kluckhohn and Henry A. Murray (eds.), *Personality in Nature, Society, and Culture* (New York: Alfred A. Knopf, 1948), p. 263.

95. St. Clair Drake and Horace R. Cayton, *Black Metropolis* (New York: Harcourt, Brace & Co., 1945).

96. Davis, Gardner, and Gardner, *op. cit.*

97. *Ibid.*, p. 240; Drake and Cayton, *op. cit.*, p. 522.

98. Davis, Gardner, and Gardner, *op. cit.*, pp. 239-242.

99. Drake and Cayton, *op. cit.*, pp. 779-781.

100. *Ibid.*, pp. 524-525.

101. Davis and Havighurst, *op. cit.*, p. 258.

102. *Ibid.*, p. 262.

103. *Ibid.*, p. 263.

104. Davis, "Socialization and Adolescent Personality," *op. cit.*, p. 146. A portion of this selection is italicized in the original text.

105. *Ibid.*, p. 148. This quotation is italicized in the original text.

106. *Ibid.*, p. 149.

107. *Ibid.*

108. Allison Davis, "American Status Systems and the Socialization of the Child," in Clyde Kluckhohn and Henry A. Murray (eds.), *Personality in Nature, Society and Culture* (New York: Alfred A. Knopf, 1948), p. 468.

109. Davis, "Socialization and Adolescent Personality," *op. cit.*, p. 150.

110. Davis and Havighurst, *op. cit.*, pp. 262-263.

111. Allison Davis, *Social-Class Influences upon Learning* (Cambridge: Harvard University Press, 1952).

112. See Warner and Associates, *op. cit.*, chap. v; and Havighurst and Taba, *op. cit.*, chap. v.

113. Warner and Associates, *op. cit.*, p. 85.

114. Seymour M. Lipset and Reinhard Bendix, "Social Status and Social Structure: A Re-examination of Data and Interpretations: I," *The British Journal of Sociology*, II (1951), p. 153.

115. C. Wright Mills, review of W. Lloyd Warner and Paul S. Lunt, *The Social Life of a Modern Community, American Sociological Review*, VII (1942), pp. 264-265.

116. *Ibid.*, pp. 265-266.

117. *Ibid.*, p. 265.

118. *Ibid.*, pp. 264-266; Lipset and Bendix, *op. cit.*, pp. 154 ff.

119. Harold W. Pfautz and Otis Dudley Duncan, "A Critical Evaluation of Warner's Work in Stratification," *American Sociological Review*, XV (1950), pp. 210-211.

120. *Ibid.*, p. 210. See also Lipset and Bendix, *op. cit.*, pp. 151-152; and Seymour M. Lipset and Reinhard Bendix, "Social Status and Social Structure: A Re-examination of Data and Interpretations: II," *The British Journal of Sociology*, II (1951), 241-244.

121. Robert K. Merton, review of W. Lloyd Warner and Paul S. Lunt, *The Social Life of a Modern Community, Survey Graphic*, XXXI (1942), p. 438.

122. Ely Chinoy, "Research in Class Structure," *Canadian Journal of Economics and Political Science*, XVI (1950), pp. 259-260.

123. Oswald Hall, review of W. Lloyd Warner, Marchia Meeker, and Kenneth Eels, *Social Class in America, American Journal of Sociology*, LVI (1951), p. 368.

124. Lipset and Bendix, "Social Status and Social Structure: I," *op. cit.*, p. 168.

125. Lipset and Bendix, "Social Status and Social Structure: II," *op. cit.*, p. 232.

126. Paul K. Hatt, review of W. Lloyd Warner and Associates, *Democracy in Jonesville, American Sociological Review*, XIV (1949), p. 811.

127. Paul K. Hatt, "Stratification in the Mass Society," *American Sociological Review*, XV (1950), p. 218.

128. Warner, Meeker, and Eels, *op. cit.*, p. 21.

129. Warner and Lunt, *The Social Life of a Modern Community*, p. 91. See Lipset and

Bendix, "Social Status and Social Structure: I," *op. cit.*, pp. 153 ff.

130. Davis, Gardner, and Gardner, *op. cit.*, p. 72.

131. *Ibid.*, pp. 60-72.

132. Chinoy, *op. cit.*, p. 259.

133. Lipset and Bendix, "Social Status and Social Structure: I," *op. cit.*, p. 160.

134. *Ibid.*, p. 162.

135. *Ibid.*, p. 164.

136. Pfautz and Duncan, *op. cit.*, p. 209.

137. Lipset and Bendix, "Social Status and Social Structure: I," *op. cit.*, p. 164. See also Merton, *op. cit.*, p. 438.

138. Lipset and Bendix, "Social Status and Social Structure: II," *op. cit.*, pp. 230-233, p. 243 and p. 250.

139. Gregory P. Stone and William H. Form, "Instabilities in Status: The Problem of Hierarchy in the Community Study of Status Arrangements," *American Sociological Review*, XVIII (1953), pp. 154-156.

140. Mills, *op. cit.*, p. 268.

141. Walter R. Goldschmidt, "America's Social Classes: Is Equality a Myth?" *Commentary*, X (1950), pp. 179-181.

142. Merton, *op. cit.*, p. 438.

143. Lipset and Bendix, "Social Status and Social Structure: II," *op. cit.*, p. 247.

144. *Ibid.*, p. 237 and p. 239; Hatt, review of *Democracy in Jonesville*, *op. cit.*, p. 811.

145. Oscar Handlin, review of W. Lloyd Warner and Paul S. Lunt, *The Social Life of a Modern Community*, New England Quarterly, XV (1942), pp. 555-556.

146. Henry F. May, review of W. Lloyd Warner and J. O. Low, *The Social System of the Modern Factory*, New England Quarterly, XXI (1948), pp. 276-277. For a discussion of similar points, see Lipset and Bendix, "Social Status and Social Structure: II," *op. cit.*, pp. 234-237, p. 239, and pp. 245 ff.; and a review by Oscar Handlin in *Journal of Economic History*, VII (1947), p. 277, as cited by Lipset and Bendix, *ibid.*, p. 239, n. 2.

147. Kingsley Davis, review of W. Lloyd Warner and Paul S. Lunt, *The Status System of a Modern Community*, American Journal of Sociology, XLVIII (1943), p. 512.

148. Mills, *op. cit.*, p. 267.

149. *Ibid.*; Davis, *op. cit.*, pp. 512-513; Merton, *op. cit.*, p. 438.

150. Pfautz and Duncan, *op. cit.*, p. 210.

151. Lipset and Bendix, "Social Status and Social Structure: I," *op. cit.*, pp. 160 ff. See also Richard Centers, "Four Studies in Psychology and Social Status," *Psychological Bulletin*, XLVII (1950), pp. 265-266.

152. Pfautz and Duncan, *op. cit.*, p. 208.

153. *Ibid.*, p. 207. See also Chinoy, *op. cit.*, pp. 258-259; and Hall, *op. cit.*, p. 368.

154. G. E. Swanson, review of W. Lloyd Warner, Marchia Meeker, and Kenneth Eels, *Social Class in America*, American Sociological Review, XIV (1949), p. 823.

155. Hall, *op. cit.*, p. 367; Pfautz and Duncan, *op. cit.*, p. 207.

156. Hall, *op. cit.*, pp. 367-368.

157. Pfautz and Duncan, *op. cit.*, p. 207.

158. *Ibid.*, p. 208; Hall, *op. cit.*, p. 368.

159. Warner, Meeker, and Eels, *Social Class in America*, as quoted in Goldschmidt, *op. cit.*, p. 181.

160. Chinoy, *op. cit.*, p. 262.

161. Lipset and Bendix, "Social Status and Social Structure: II," *op. cit.*, p. 237.

162. *Life*, 12 September 1949, p. 119, as quoted in Lipset and Bendix, *ibid.*

163. Lipset and Bendix, *ibid.*

164. As indicated, this is not an exhaustive summary of all the issues that have been raised. For a critique of Warner's use of the term "caste" in describing contemporary Negro-white relations in America, see Oliver C. Cox, "Race and Caste: A Distinction," *American Journal of Sociology*, L. (1945), pp. 360-368. For a list of recent critical comments (except book reviews) on Warner's approach, see Harold W. Pfautz, "The Current Literature on Social Stratification: Critique and Bibliography," *American Journal of Sociology*, LVII (1953), p. 405.

165. Warner, *American Life*, p. 34.

166. *Ibid.*, p. 53.

COMMUNITY POWER STRUCTURE AND SOCIAL WELFARE

Floyd Hunter

1. E. T. Hiller, "The Community as a Social Group," *American Sociological Review*, VI (April 1941), 191-92.

2. *Ibid.*, p. 189.

3. George C. Homans, *The Human Group* (New York: Harcourt, Brace and Company, 1950), p. 184.

4. The Business Executive: The Psycho-Dynamics of a Social Role," *American Journal of Sociology*, LIV (January 1949), 286.

5. This classification is explained later in the chapter.

6. "A Conceptual Analysis of Stratification," *American Sociological Review*, VII (June 1942), 316.

7. Paul Lazarsfeld and Frank N. Stanton (eds.), *Communications Research* (New York: Harper and Brothers, 1949), p. 192.

8. R. A. Brady, *Business as a System of Power* (New York: Columbia University Press, 1938), p. 314.

9. Herbert von Beckerath, "Economics and Politics," *Social Forces*, XIV (October 1935), 42.

10. Homans, *op. cit.*, p. 112.

11. *Ibid.*, p. 141.

12. "Economics and Politics," *loc. cit.*, p. 52.

13. *Op. cit.*, p. 145.

14. *Ibid.* p. 406.

15. *Ibid.*, p. 184.

16. *Ibid.*, p. 145.

17. *Ibid.*, p. 184.

18. Everett C. Hughes, "Ecological Aspects of Institutions," *American Sociological Review*, I (April 1936), 186.

19. *The Empire of Business* (New York: Doubleday, Page and Company, 1902), p. 189.

20. *Op. cit.*, p. 422.

SOCIAL CLASS AND COLOR DIFFERENCES IN CHILD-REARING

Allison Davis and Robert J. Havighurst

Editors' Note: In 1951-52, Robert R. Sears and his colleagues made a study of social class and child-rearing practices in New England, a study comparable to an extent with that reported in this article. The Sears research is presented by Robert J. Havighurst and Allison Davis in an article entitled "A Comparison of the Chicago and Harvard Studies of Social Class Differences in Child-Rearing" (*American Sociological Review*, August, 1955.) Several differences were found between the findings of the two studies. Havighurst and Davis state that "changes in child-rearing ideology between 1945 and 1952 may be in some measure responsible for the differences." They also suggest that "inadequacies of sampling in both studies" may be a factor.

1. See Margaret Mead, *Sex and Temperament In Three Primitive Societies*, in *From The South Seas*. New York: William Morrow and Co., 1939. Allison Davis and John Dollard, *Children of Bondage*, Washington, D.C.: American Council on Education, 1940, W. Lloyd Warner, Buford Junker, and Walter A. Adams, *Color and Human Nature*, Washington, D.C.: American Council on Education, 1941. Cora du Bois, *The People of Alor*. Minneapolis: The University of Minnesota Press, 1944. Abram Kardiner, *The Psychological Frontiers of Society*. New York: Columbia University Press, 1945.

2. Some of the implications of this research for the understanding of child development will be found in *Father of the Man*, by Allison Davis and Robert J. Havighurst. Boston: Houghton-Mifflin Company, 1947.

3. *The Yankee City Series*. New Haven, Conn.; Yale University Press. *Deep South*. Allison Davis, Burleigh B. Gardner, and Mary R. Gardner: The University of Chicago Press, 1941.

4. *Who Shall Be Educated?* W. Lloyd Warner, Robert J. Havighurst, and Martin B. Loeb. New York: Harper and Bros., 1944.

5. Allison Davis, "Socialization and The Adolescent Personality," Chapter XI in the *Forty-Third Yearbook of the National Society For the Study of Education*, Part I, 1944, pp. 198-216.

6. Martha C. Ericson, "Child-Rearing and Social Status," *American Journal of Sociology*, 53, 190-192 (Nov. 1946).

7. John E. Anderson, *The Young Child in the Home*. White House Conference on Child Health and Protection. New York: Appleton-Century, 1936.

8. W. Lloyd Warner and Paul S. Lunt, *The Social Life of a Modern Community*. New Haven: Yale University Press, 1941.

9. Allison Davis, Burleigh B. Gardner, and Mary R. Gardner. *Deep South*. Chicago: University of Chicago Press, 1941.

A SLUM SEX CODE

William Foote Whyte

1. A detailed report of this research will be found in *Street Corner Society*, published by the University of Chicago Press, Chicago, 1943.

SOCIAL STRATIFICATION AND PSYCHIATRIC DISORDERS

August B. Hollingshead and Frederick C. Redlich

1. For example, see A. J. Rosanoff, *Report of a Survey of Mental Disorders in Nassau County, New York*, New York: National Committee for Mental Hygiene, 1916; Ludwig Stern, *Kulturkreis und Form der Geistigen Erkrankung*, (Sammlung Zwanglosen Abshandlungen aus dem Gebiete der Nervenund-Geiteskrankheiten), X, No. 2, Halle a. S:C. Marhold, 1913, pp. 1-62; J. F. Sutherland, "Geographical Distribution of Lunacy in Scotland," *British Association for Advancement of Science*, Glasgow, Sept. 1901; William A. White, "Geographical Distribution of Insanity in the United States," *Journal of Nervous and Mental Disease*, XXX (1903), pp. 257-279.

2. For example, see: Trygve Braatoy, "Is it Probable that the Sociological Situation is a Factor in Schizophrenia?" *Psychiatricia et Neurologica*, XII (1937), pp. 109-138; Donald L. Gerard and Joseph Siegel, "The Family Background of Schizophrenia," *The Psychiatric Quarterly*, 24 (January, 1950), pp. 47-73; Robert W. Hyde and Lowell V. Kingsley, "Studies in Medical Sociology, I: The Relation of Mental Disorders to the Community Socio-economic Level," *The New England Journal of Medicine*, 231, No. 16 (October 19, 1944), pp. 543-548; Robert W. Hyde and Lowell V. Kingsley, "Studies in Medical Sociology, II: The Relation of Mental Disorders to Population Density," *The New England Journal of Medicine*, 231, No. 17 (October 26, 1944), pp. 571-577; Robert M. Hyde and Roderick M. Chisholm, "Studies in Medical Sociology, III: The Relation of Mental Disorders to Race and Nationality," *The New England Journal of Medicine*, 231, No. 18 (November 2, 1944), pp. 612-618; William Malamud and Irene Malamud, "A Socio-Psychiatric Investigation of Schizophrenia Occurring in the Armed Forces," *Psychosomatic Medicine*, 5 (October, 1943) pp. 364-375; B. Malzberg, *Social and Biological Aspects of Mental Disease*, Utica, N. Y.: State Hospital Press, 1940; William F. Roth and Frank H. Luton, "The Mental Health Program in Tennessee: Statistical Report of a Psychiatric Survey in a Rural County," *American Journal*

of Psychiatry, 99 (March 1943), pp. 662-675; J. Ruesch and Others, Chronic Disease and Psychological Invalidism, New York: American Society for Research in Psychosomatic Problems, 1946; J. Ruesch and others, Duodenal Ulcer: A Socio-psychological Study of Naval Enlisted Personnel and Civilians, Berkeley and Los Angeles: University of California Press, 1948; Jurgen Ruesch, Annemarie Jacobson, and Martin B. Loeb, "Acculturation and Illness," Psychological Monographs: General and Applied, Vol. 62, No. 5, Whole No. 292, 1948 (American Psychological Association, 1515 Massachusetts Ave., N.W., Washington 5, D. C.); C. Tietze, Paul Lemkau and M. Cooper, "A Survey of Statistical Studies on the Prevalence and Incidence of Mental Disorders in Sample Populations," Public Health Reports, 1909-27, 58 (December 31, 1943); C. Tietze, P. Lemkau and Marcia Cooper, "Schizophrenia, Manic Depressive Psychosis and Social-Economic Status," American Journal of Sociology, XLVII (September, 1941), pp. 167-175.

3. Robert E. L. Faris, and H. Warren Dunham, Mental Disorders in Urban Areas, Chicago: University of Chicago Press, 1939; H. Warren Dunham, "Current Status of Ecological Research in Mental Disorder," Social Forces, 25 (March, 1947), pp. 321-326; R. H. Felix and R. V. Bowers, "Mental Hygiene and Socio-Environmental Factors," The Milbank Memorial Fund Quarterly, XXVI (April 1948), pp. 125-147; H. W. Green, Persons Admitted to the Cleveland State Hospital, 1928-1937, Cleveland Health Council, 1939.

4. R. E. L. Faris, "Cultural Isolation and the Schizophrenic Personality," American Journal of Sociology XXXIX (September, 1934), pp. 155-169; R. E. L. Faris, "Reflections of Social Disorganization in the Behavior of a Schizophrenic Patient," American Journal of Sociology, L (September, 1944), pp. 134-141.

5. For example, see: Robert E. Clark, "Psychoses, Income, and Occupational Prestige," American Journal of Sociology, 44 (March, 1949), pp. 433-440; Robert E. Clark, "The Relationship of Schizophrenia to Occupational Income and Occupational Prestige," American Sociological Review, 13 (June, 1948), pp. 325-330; Kingsley Davis, "Mental Hygiene and the Class Structure," Psychiatry, I (February, 1938), pp. 55-56; Talcott Parsons, "Psychoanalysis and the Social Structure," The Psychoanalytical Quarterly, XIX, No. 3 (1950), pp. 371-384; John Dollard and Neal Miller, Personality and Psychotherapy, New York: McGraw-Hill, 1950; Jurgen Ruesch, "Social Technique, Social Status, and Social Change in Illness," Clyde Kluckhohn and Henry A. Murray (editors), in Personality in Nature, Society, and Culture, New York: Alfred A. Knopf, 1949, pp. 117-130; W. L. Warner, "The Society, the Individual and his Mental Disorders," American Journal of Psychiatry, 94, No. 2 (September, 1937), pp. 275-284.

6. F. C. Redlich, B. H. Roberts, L. Z. Freedman, and Leslie Schaffer.

7. August B. Hollingshead and J. K. Myers.

8. Harvey A. Robinson.

9. The population of each component was as follows: New Haven, 164,443; East Haven, 12,212; North Haven, 9,444; West Haven, 32,010; Hamden, 29,715; and Woodbridge, 2,822.

10. Maurice R. Davie, "The Pattern of Urban Growth," G. P. Murdock (editor), in Studies in the Science of Society, New Haven: 1937, pp. 133-162; Ruby J. R. Kennedy, "Single or Triple Melting-Pot: Intermarriage Trends in New Haven, 1870-1940," American Journal of Sociology, 39 (January, 1944), pp. 331-339; John W. McConnell, The Influence of Occupation Upon Social Stratification, Unpublished Ph.D. thesis, Sterling Memorial Library, Yale University, 1937; Jerome K. Myers, "Assimilation to the Ecological and Social Systems of a Community," American Sociological Review, 15 (June, 1950), pp. 367-372; Mhyra Minnis, "The Relationship of Women's Organizations to the Social Structure of a City," Unpublished Ph.D. Thesis, Sterling Memorial Library, Yale University, 1951.

11. A detailed statement of the procedures used to develop and validate this Index described in a monograph on this research titled Psychiatry and Social Class by August B. Hollingshead and Fredrick C. Redlich.

12. Psychiatric Disorders and Reactions, Washington: Veterans Administration, Technical Bulletin 10A-78, October, 1947.

THE ORGANIZATION OF LEISURE-TIME SERVICES FOR YOUTH

August B. Hollingshead

1. The Order of Eastern Star sponsors a chapter of Job's Daughters for high-school-aged girls. By class its membership is: class II, 4; class III, 8; class IV, 3. The Woodmen of the World foster a small group of boys in an athletic club that has its headquarters in the lodge hall. Only 4 high school boys are in it.

2. Five of the 7 members of the School Board had been Legionnaires, and the President of the Board was formerly Commander of the local post, but none of them was active in the American Legion leadership at this time.

3. From the time the Girl Scouts were organized until the Mother's Club was formed, the girls and the leader raised all their own funds by soliciting their families and by conducting cookie sales. In 1941, the American Legion Auxiliary donated $10, and the Woman's Relief Corps in the Catholic Church gave $3.

4. The percentage of boys visiting their friends' homes by class is: class II, 38; class III, 27; class IV, 20; class V, 25. These figures are not statistically significant.

5. The best and most popular theater, the

Elmtown, located in the center of the business district, shows first-run pictures, news, and shorts. The Silver Bell, two blocks away, features westerns, second-run films, and double features on Friday nights. The Bright Star specializes in second-rate shows and sensation sex films. Local values place the theaters in a hierarchy with the Elmtown at the top, followed at some distance by the Silver Bell, and the Bright Star a very low third.

6. Class I, class II, and class III adults normally go to the Elmtown, occasionally to the Silver Bell, but seldom if ever to the Bright Star. Many class IV's but few class V's attend the Elmtown. The majority of the Silver Bell's patrons work in the mines and the mills, but a generous sprinkling of farmers is attracted by the westerns. The difference in admission may exert an influence, as the Elmtown charges 40 cents, and the Silver Bell 25, but we suspect custom is more important. The Bright Star is located near the railroad tracks on the poor end of Freedom Street, and the admission is 20 cents. Its patrons are almost exclusively drawn from classes IV and V, the scale being tipped toward class V's rather than class IV's.

SOCIAL MOBILITY AND INTERPERSONAL RELATIONS

Peter M. Blau

1. Talcott Parsons and Edward A. Shils (editors), *Toward a General Theory of Action*, Cambridge: Harvard University Press, 1951, pp. 53-109. See also Talcott Parsons, *The Social System*, Glencoe, Ill.: Free Press, 1951.

2. Robert F. Bales, *Interaction Process Analysis*, Cambridge: Addison-Wesley Press, 1949, pp. 81-84, 153-157. See also his article in Talcott Parsons, Robert F. Bales and Edward A. Shils (editors), *Working Papers in the Theory of Action*, Glencoe, Ill.: Free Press, 1953, pp. 111-161.

3. Robert K. Merton, *Social Theory and Social Structure*, Glencoe, Ill.: Free Press, 1949, pp. 49-55. See also Peter M. Blau, *The Dynamics of Bureaucracy*, Chicago: University of Chicago Press, 1955.

4. See Jerzy Berent, "Fertility and Social Mobility," *Population Studies*, 5 (March, 1952), pp. 240-260.

5. See Bernard R. Berelson, Paul F. Lazars-feld and William N. McPhee, *Voting*, Chicago: University of Chicago Press, 1954, pp. 90-91; and Patricia S. West, "Social Mobility among College Graduates," in Reinhard Bendix and Seymour M. Lipset (editors), *Class Status and Power*, Glencoe, Ill.: Free Press, 1953, p. 478.

6. See Seymour M. Lipset and Joan Gordon, "Mobility and Trade Union Membership," in Bendix and Lipset, *op. cit.*, p. 492.

7. For the methodological principle involved, see Patricia L. Kendall and Paul F. Lazarsfeld, "Problems of Survey Analysis," in Robert K. Merton and Paul F. Lazarsfeld (editors), *Continuities in Social Research*, Glencoe, Ill.: Free Press, 1950, pp. 113-196.

8. See Joseph Greenblum and Leonard I. Pearlin, "Vertical Mobility and Prejudice," in Bendix and Lipset, *op. cit., pp.* 480-488.

9. See Eugene Litwak, "Conflicting Values and Decision Making," Ph.D., dissertation, Columbia University, 1956.

10. Indeed, Greenblum and Pearlin interpret their findings in this manner; *op. cit.*, pp. 486, 491.

11. Litwak, *op. cit.*

12. See A. B. Hollingshead, R. Ellis, and E. Kirby, "Social Mobility and Mental Illness," *American Sociological Review*, 19 (October, 1954), pp. 577-584.

13. Evidence from various sources on class differences in informal as well as formal social participation is summarized in Genevieve Knupfer "Portrait of the Underdog," *Public Opinion Quarterly*, 11 (Spring, 1947), pp. 103-114.

14. Greenblum and Pearlin, *op. cit.*

15. *Ibid.*

16. Litwak, *op. cit.* (Women are more identified with their families than men, but the same pattern of distribution is found among both sexes.)

17. *Ibid.*

18. For quite a different example of apparent overconformity which analysis reveals to be the result of more complex socio-psychological processes, see Robert K. Merton and Alice Kitt, "Contributions to the Theory of Reference Group Behavior," in Merton and Lazarsfeld, *op. cit.*, pp. 70-77. See also Blau, *op. cit.*, pp. 184-189.

19. See W. Lloyd Warner and Paul S. Lunt, *The Social Life of a Modern Community*, New Haven: Yale University Press, 1941, esp. pp. 81-84, 222-224, and 350-355.

V – DEVIANT BEHAVIOR AS A PROPERTY OF GROUPS

CULTURE, NORMALITY, AND PERSONALITY CONFLICT

Arnold W. Green

1. B. J. Meggers, "Recent Trends in American Ethnology," *American Anthropologist*, XLVIII (1946), p. 183. Dr. Meggers takes a gloomy view of the new trend, claiming that the three variables, culture, society, and man, taken together, are unmanageable. Anthropology can retain its status as a special field of investigation only be remaining within its own province, culture.

2. F. H. G. Van Loon, "Amok and Lattah,

Journal of Abnormal and Social Psychology, XXI (1927), p. 437.

3. C. Kluckhohn, "The Influence of Psychiatry on Anthropology in America During the Past One Hundred Years," in J. K. Hall (ed.) *One Hundred Years of Psychiatry* (New York, Columbia University Press, 1944). p. 589.

4. Cf. E. Williams, "Anthropology for the Common Man," *American Anthropologist,* XLIX (1947), pp. 84-90.

5. F. J. Hacker, "The Concept of Normality and Its Significance," *American Journal of Orthopsychiatry,* XV (1945), p. 48.

6. A. I. Hallowell, "Psychic Stresses and Culture Patterns," *American Journal of Psychiatry,* XII (1936), p. 1293.

7. M. Mead, *Sex and Temperament in Three Primitive Societies* (New York, Morrow and Co., 1935), p. 291.

8. A. Kardiner, *The Psychological Frontiers of Society* (New York, Columbia University Press, 1945), p. 453.

9. Sources: R. Landes, "The Abnormal Among the Ojibwa Indians," *Journal of Abnormal and Social Psychology,* XXXIII (1938), pp. 14-33; and R. Landes, *The Ojibwa Woman* (New York, Columbia University Press, 1938).

10. A. H. Maslow, "Conflict, Frustration, and the Theory of Threat," in S. S. Tompkins (ed.) *Contemporary Psychopathology,* (Cambridge, Harvard University Press, 1943), pp. 588-94.

11. In comparison with the examples of other cultures given below, the peculiarity here is the absence of the time-element. The source of personality-conflict for the Ojibwa male is not one of inconsistent roles and goals inculcated at different periods in the life history, but the impossibility of attaining, in the one role of hunter and warrior, for which his entire boyhood was training and his manhood fulfillment, the two goals of safety and prestige.

12. Sources: D. Eggan, "The General Problem of Hopi Adjustment," *American Anthropologist,* XLV (1943), pp. 357-373; and L. Thompson and A. Joseph, *The Hopi Way* (Chicago, University of Chicago Press, 1944).

13. Abram Kardiner's contention, that religious systems are "replicas of the experience of the child with parental disciplines . . ." is not borne out in the Hopi. *See* Kardiner, "The Concept of Basic Personality Structure as an Operational Tool in the Social Sciences," in Ralph Linton (ed.) *The Science of Man in the World Crisis* (New York, Columbia University Press, 1945), p. 112.

14. E. A. Kennard, *Hopi Kachinas* (New York, J. J. Augustin, 1938), p. 2, states that the Hopi remain "comfortably vague" regarding the supernatural aspects of Kachinas, exhibiting interest only in the concrete details of the rituals. This may be sufficient to reopen the question as to the extent of "disenchantment" experienced by the Hopi child.

15. Thompson and Joseph, *op. cit.,* p. 114.

16. *Ibid.,* p. 105.

17. M. Titiev, "Notes on Hopi Witchcraft," *Papers of the Michigan Academy of Science, Arts, and Letters,* XXVIII (1942), p. 557.

18. *See* E. Beaglehole, "A Note on Cultural Compensation," *Journal of Abnormal and Social Psychology,* XXXIII (1938), p. 121. He states that each society tends to "emphasize one segment of the potential raw stuff of human behavior," and represses others. But compensations must be forthcoming, either in occasional ceremonial allowance of the forbidden behavior, or "for the satisfaction of emotional-impulsive drives that receive no overt expression in the generalized culture pattern." There would be a danger, however, in assuming that the same amount and range of compensations could be found in all societies.

19. Sources: C. Dubois, *The People of Alor* (Minneapolis, University of Minnesota, 1944); and Kardiner, *The Psychological Frontiers of Society.*

20. Kardiner, *The Psychological Frontiers of Society,* p. 170.

21. Du Bois, *op. cit.,* p. 115.

22. L. Thompson, *Fijian Frontier* (American Council Institute of Pacific Relations, 1940).

23. *Ibid.,* p. 44.

24. A. W. Green, "Sociological Analysis of Horney and Fromm," *American Journal of Sociology,* LI (1946), p. 533.

25. Thompson, *op. cit.,* p. 46.

26. B. Schrieke, "Native Society in the Transformation Period" in B. Schrieke (ed.) *The effect of Western Influence on Native Civilizations in the Malay Archipelago* (Batavia, Java, G. Kolff and Co., 1929).

27. *Ibid.,* p. 243.

28. Mead, *op. cit.*

29. Du Bois, *op. cit.,* p. 13.

30. *See* A. Green, "The Middle Class Male Child and Neurosis," *American Sociological Review,* XI (1946), pp. 31-31, for a discussion of socialization in a modern Polish industrial community, where it was found that a combination of "bad parental care" and failure to identify with parental images was uncorrelated with personality conflict.

31. J. C. Moloney, "Psychiatric Observations on Okinawa Shima," *Psychiatry,* VIII (1945), pp. 391-99.

32. J. C. Moloney, "On Oriental Stoicism," *American Journal of Psychiatry,* CIII (1946), p. 63.

EGOISTIC SUICIDE

Emile Durkheim

1. Legoyt, *Le Suicide Ancien et Moderne* (Paris: 1881), p. 205; Oettingen, *Moralstatistik,* p. 654.

2. We say nothing of the ideal protraction of life involved in the belief in immortality of the soul, for (1) this cannot explain why the family or attachment to political society

preserves us from suicide; and (2) it is not even this belief which forms religion's prophylatic influence, as we have shown above.

THE CONFLICT OF VALUES IN DELINQUENCY AREAS

Solomon Kobrin

1. The ecological studies of Shaw and McKay in Chicago show that the proportion of juvenile court age boys on whom delinquency petitions were filed in the highest rate square mile areas were: for the 1917-1923 series, 19.4 per cent; for the 1927-1933 series, 18.9 per cent; and for the 1934-1940 series, 21.8 per cent. C. R. Shaw and Henry D. McKay, *Juvenile Delinquency and Urban Areas*, Chicago: University of Chicago Press, 1942, pp. 53 and 59. The figure for the 1934-1940 series is based on unpublished material by the same authors.

2. Tappan observes that these statistics indicate that "most people living in such associations and under such social and psychological influences as those of the deteriorated slum do not violate the law." Paul W. Tappan, *Juvenile Delinquency*, New York: McGraw-Hill Book Co., 1949, p. 142. The ambivalence of many students in this field regarding the validity of delinquency statistics as a basis for judgments about the extent of proscribed behavior among children is revealed in the same author's assertion which appears earlier in the same work that "statistical data on the volume of delinquency give no valid picture of its actual extent." *Ibid.*, p. 37.

3. Among recent evaluations of this problem are: Negley K. Tetters and John O. Reinemann, *The Challenge of Delinquency*, New York: Prentice-Hall, Inc., 1950, pp. 12-19; and Paul W. Tappan, *op. cit.*, pp. 31-52. Relevant discussion is also provided in Sophia M. Robison, "Wanted—An Index of Crime and Delinquency," *Proceedings*, American Prison Association, 1945, pp. 203-212; Edward E. Schwartz, "Statistics of Juvenile Delinquency in the United States," *The Annals*, 261 (1949), 9-20; I. Richard Perlman, "The Meaning of Juvenile Delinquency Statistics," *Federal Probation*, September, 1949, 63-67; F. J. Murphy, M. M. Shirley, and H. L. Witmer, "The Incidence of Hidden Delinquency," *American Journal of Orthopsychiatry*, 16 (1946), 685-666; and W. S. Robinson, "Ecological Correlations and the Behavior of Individuals," *American Sociological Review*, 15 (June 1950), 351-357.

4. Insofar as any of these measures may be assumed to bear a constant ratio to the total volume of proscribed behavior they may be used as indexes of delinquency. These indexes, in turn, may be validly used only to gain a picture of the relative volume of delinquency in subdivisions of the same juvenile court jurisdiction during a period of time when administrative practices remain unchanged.

5. Clifford R. Shaw and Henry D. McKay, *op. cit.*, p. 70.

6. From police data available in the Sociology Department, Illinois Institute for Juvenile Research.

7. *Ibid.*

8. Unpublished materials available in the Sociology Department, Illinois Institute for Juvenile Research.

9. This view is related both to Sutherland's concept of "differential association" and to Sellin's emphasis on the primacy of culture conflict, in one form or another, in the etiology of crime. E. H. Sutherland, *Principles of Criminology*, New York: J. B. Lippincott Co., 1939; and T. Sellin, *Culture Conflict and Crime*, New York: Social Science Research Council, 1938. The present discussion may be regarded, in fact, as an effort to identify and describe with a modicum of detail some of the coordinate of culture conflict in the urban delinquency area, and to mark out one type of problem involved in "associating differentially."

10. Concern with the social and psychological processes resulting in delinquent careers has led to a relative neglect of those aspects of the life of the "submerged" urban areas which center on the conventional and traditional institutions of the wider community. However, the presence of an emphatic strain of conventionality in these areas is indicated in W. F. Whyte, *Street Corner Society*, Chicago: University of Chicago Press, 1943. Ample reflection of the impact of such institutions and agencies as schools, police, social settlements, and churches may be found in C. R. Shaw and H. D. McKay, "Social Factors in Juvenile Delinquency," *Report on the Causes of Crime*, Vol. II, National Commission on Law Observance and Enforcement, Washington, D. C., 1931; and C. R. Shaw et al., *Brothers in Crime*, Chicago; University of Chicago Press, 1938. There exists, in addition, a large if popular biographical literature detailing the rise of children of poor immigrant families to positions of prominence, power, and wealth within conventional hierarchies.

11. Competing value systems tend to accommodate to one another by mutual incorporation of elements common to or compatible with each. The criminal culture shares with the conventional culture the goal of a large and assured money income, and like the conventional culture utilizes the flexible processes of politics to achieve this goal. The use of the political process by organized crime entails the development of relationships with functionaries of the established power structure which transcend the symbiotic precisely because both the goal and in general form the methods of achieving the goal are truly shared by representatives of both cultures. The term "integration" as used in this connection denotes a situation in which such relationships are firmly established. When these relationships are haphazard, occasional, or unde-

pendable it appears logical to conceptualize such a situation as representing only partial integration.

12. Thesis statement submitted to Department of Human Relations, Harvard University, 1949.

13. The relation of social structure to the delinquency of the high rate urban areas is lucidly analyzed in Robert K. Merton, "Social Structure and Anomie," in *Social Theory and Social Structure*, Glencoe: The Free Press, 1949, pp. 134-140.

14. The significance of the social class identification of teachers for their attitudes toward lower-class children is in part indicated in W. Lloyd Warner, *Democracy in Jonesville*, New York: Harper & Brothers, 1949, pp. 208-210.

15. M. Kennedy, *Criminal Tribes of the Bombay Presidency*, Bombay, 1908; E. H. Sutherland, *The Professional Thief*, Chicago: University of Chicago Press, 1937.

16. Discussions of this problem in the psychoanalytic literature, illuminating and suggestive as they are, do not deal explicitly with those variables related to delinquency which originate in inter-group relations. Thus Aichhorn covers the customary range of etiologies when he observes that the child may become delinquent when his psychic apparatus is defective, when he develops defects in the superego or conscience functions of personality as a result of distorting or shocking experiences in his family relationships, or when, as in the instance of the gang boy or child of delinquent parents, he acquires an ego-ideal which is socially unacceptable. August Aichhorn, *Wayward Youth*, New York: The Viking Press, 1935, pp. 222-225. The problem of etiology is further complicated when we consider the effect upon normal personality of constraints to identify with models defined by the subculture as hostile and inimical.

SOCIAL STRUCTURE AND ANOMIE

Robert K. Merton

1. See, for example, S. Freud, *Civilization and Its Discontents* (*passim*, and esp. at 63): Ernest Jones, *Social Aspects of Psychoanalysis* (London, 1924) 28. If the Freudian notion is a variety of the "original sin" doctrine, then the interpretation advanced in this paper is a doctrine of "socially derived sin."

2. "Normal" in the sense of the psychologically expectable, if not culturally approved, response to determinate social conditions. This statement does not, of course, deny the role of biological and personality differences in fixing the *incidence* of deviant behavior. It is simply that *this* is not the problem considered here. It is in this same sense, I take it, that James S. Plant speaks of the "normal reaction of normal people to abnormal conditions." See his *Personality and the Cultural Pattern* (New York, 1937), 248.

3. The position taken here has been percep-tively described by Edward Sapir. ". . . problems of social science differ from problems of individual behavior in degree of specificity, not in kind. Every statement about behavior which throws the emphasis, explicitly or implicitly, on the actual, integral experiences of defined personalities or types of personalities is a datum of psychology or psychiatry rather than of social science. Every statement about behavior which aims, not to be accurate about the behavior of an actual individual or individuals or about the expected behavior of a physically and psychologically defined type of individual, but which abstracts from such behavior in order to bring out in clear relief certain expectancies with regard to those aspects of individual behavior which various people share, as an interpersonal or 'social' pattern, is a datum, however crudely expressed, of social science." I have here chosen the second perspective; although I shall have occasion to speak of attitudes, values and function, it will be from the standpoint of how the social structure promotes or inhibits their appearance in specified types of situations. See Sapir, "Why cultural anthropology needs the psychiatrist," *Psychiatry*, 1938, 1, 7-12.

4. This ritualism may be associated with a mythology which rationalizes these practices so that they appear to retain their status as means, but the dominant pressure is toward strict ritualistic conformity, irrespective of the mythology. Ritualism is thus most complete when such rationalizations are not even called forth.

5. In this connection, one sees the relevance of Elton Mayo's paraphrase of the title of Tawney's well-known book. "Actually the problem is *not that of the sickness of an acquisitive society; it is that of the acquisitiveness of a sick society.*" *Human Problems of an Industrial Civilization*, 153. Mayo deals with the process through which wealth comes to be the basic symbol of social achievement and sees this as arising from a state of anomie. My major concern here is with the social consequences of a heavy emphasis upon monetary success as a goal in a society which has not adapted its structure to the implications of this emphasis. A complete analysis would require the simultaneous examination of both processes.

6. Durkheim's resurrection of the term "anomie" which, so far as I know, first appears in approximately the same sense in the late sixteenth century, might well become the object of an investigation by a student interested in the historical filiation of ideas. Like the term "climate of opinion" brought into academic and political popularity by A. N. Whitehead three centuries after it was coined by Joseph Glanvill, the word "anomie" (or anomy or anomia) has lately come into frequent use, once it was re-introduced by Durkheim. Why the resonance in contemporary society? For a magnificent model of the type of research required by questions of this order,

see Leo Spitzer, *"Milieu* and *Ambiance:* an essay in historical semantics," *Philosophy and Phenomenological Research,* 1942, 3, 1-42, 169-218.

7. It appears unlikely that cultural norms, once interiorized, are wholly eliminated. Whatever residuum persists will induce personality tensions and conflict, with some measure of ambivalence. A manifest rejection of the once-incorporated institutional norms will be coupled with some latent retention of their emotional correlates. Guilt feelings, a sense of sin, pangs of conscience are diverse terms referring to this unrelieved tension. Symbolic adherence to the nominally repudiated values or rationalizations for the rejection of these values constitute a more subtle expression of these tensions.

8. "Many," not all, unintegrated groups, for the reason mentioned earlier. In groups where the primary emphasis shifts to institutional means, the outcome is normally a type of ritualism rather than anomie.

9. Leo C. Rosten, *Hollywood* (New York, 1940), 40.

10. Malcolm S. MacLean, *Scholars, Workers and Gentlemen* (Harvard University Press, 1938), 29.

11. *Cf.* A. W. Griswold, *The American Cult of Success* (Yale University doctoral dissertation, 1933); R. O. Carlson, *"Personality Schools": A Sociological Analysis,* (Columbia University Master's Essay, 1948).

12. There is no lack of typologies of alternative modes of response to frustrating conditions. Freud, in his *Civilization and Its Discontents* (p. 30 ff.) supplies one; derivative typologies, often differing in basic details, will be found in Karen Horney, *Neurotic Personality of Our Time* (New York, 1937); in S. Rosenzweig, "The experimental measurement of types of reaction to frustration," in H. A. Murray *et al., Explorations in Personality* (New York, 1938), 585-99; and in the work of John Dollard, Harold Lasswell, Abram Kardiner, Erich Fromm. But particularly in the strictly Freudian typology, the perspective is that of types of individual responses, quite apart from the place of the individual within the social structure. Despite her consistent concern with "culture," for example, Horney does not explore differences in the impact of this culture upon farmer, worker and businessman, upon lower-, middle-, and upper-class individuals, upon members of various ethnic and racial groups, *etc.* As a result, the role of "inconsistencies in culture" is *not* located in its differential impact upon diversely situated groups. Culture becomes a kind of blanket covering all members of the society equally, apart from their idiosyncratic differences of life-history. It is a primary assumption of our typology that these responses occur with different frequency within various sub-groups in our society precisely because members of these groups or strata are differentially subject to cultural stimulation and social restraints. This

sociological orientation will be found in the writings of Dollard and, less systematically, in the work of Fromm, Kardiner and Lasswell. On the general point, see note 3 of this chapter.

13. This fifth alternative is on a plane clearly different from that of the others. It represents a transitional response seeking to *institutionalize* new goals and new procedures to be shared by other members of the society. It thus refers to efforts to *change* the existing cultural and social structure rather than to accommodate efforts *within* this structure.

14. The observations by Dickens are from his *American Notes* (in the edition, for example, published in Boston: Books, Inc., 1940), 218. A sociological analysis which would be the formal, albeit inevitably lesser, counterpart of Freud's psychological analysis of the functions of tendentious wit and of tendentious wits is long overdue. The doctoral dissertation by Jeannette Tandy, though not sociological in character, affords one point of departure: *Crackerbox Philosophers: American Humor and Satire* (New York: Columbia University Press, 1925). In Chapter V of *Intellectual America* (New York: Macmillan, 1941), appropriately entitled "The Intelligentsia," Oscar Cargill has some compact observations on the role of the nineteenth century masters of American wit, but this naturally has only a small place in this large book on the "march of American ideas." The essay by Bierce from which I have quoted at such length will be found in *The Collected Works of Ambrose Bierce* (New York and Washington: The Neale Publishing Company, 1912), volume XI, 187-198. For what it is worth, I must differ with the harsh and far from justified judgment of Cargill on Bierce. It seems to be less a judgment than the expression of a prejudice which, in Bierce's own understanding of "prejudice," is only "a vagrant opinion without visible means of support."

15. E. H. Sutherland, "White collar criminality," *op. cit.;* "Crime and business," *Annals, American Academy of Political and Social Science,* 1941, 217, 112-118; "Is 'white collar crime' crime?", *American Sociological Review,* 1945, 10, 132-139; Marshall B. Clinard, *The Black Market: A Study of White Collar Crime* (New York: Rinehart & Co., 1952); Donald R. Cressey, *Other People's Money: A Study in the Social Psychology of Embezzlement* (Glencoe: The Free Press, 1953).

16. James S. Wallerstein and Clement J. Wyle, "Our law-abiding law-breakers," *Probation,* April, 1947.

17. National Opinion Research Center, *National Opinion on Occupations,* April, 1947. This research on the ranking and evaluation of ninety occupations by a nationwide sample presents a series of important empirical data. Of great significance is their finding that, despite a slight tendency for people to rank their own and related occupations higher than do other groups, there is a substantial agreement in ranking of occupations among all

occupational strata. More researches of this kind are needed to map the cultural topography of contemporary societies. (See the comparative study of prestige accorded major occupations in six industrialized countries: Alex Inkeles and Peter H. Rossi, "National comparisons of occupational prestige," *American Journal of Sociology*, 1956, 61, 329-339.)

18. See Joseph D. Lohman, "The participant observer in community studies," *American Sociological Review*, 1937, 2, 890-98 and William F. Whyte, *Street Corner Society* (Chicago, 1943). Note Whyte's conclusions: "It is difficult for the Cornerville man to get onto the ladder [of success], even on the bottom rung. . . . He is an Italian, and the Italians are looked upon by upperclass people as among the least desirable of the immigrant peoples . . . the society holds out attractive rewards in terms of money and material possessions to the 'successful' man. For most Cornerville people these rewards are available only through advancement in the world of rackets and politics." (273-74.)

19. Numerous studies have found that the educational pyramid operates to keep a large proportion of unquestionably able but economically disadvantaged youth from obtaining higher formal education. This fact about our class structure has been noted with dismay, for example, by Vannevar Bush in his governmental report, *Science: The Endless Frontier*. Also, see W. L. Warner, R. J. Havighurst and M. B. Loeb, *Who Shall Be Educated?* (New York, 1944).

20. The shifting historical role of this ideology is a profitable subject for exploration.

21. The role of the Negro in this connection raises almost as many theoretical as practical questions. It has been reported that large segments of the Negro population have assimilated the dominant caste's values of pecuniary success and social advancement, but have "realistically adjusted" themselves to the "fact" that social ascent is presently confined almost entirely to movement within the caste. See Dollard, *Caste and Class in a Southern Town*, 66 ff.; Donald Young, *American Minority Peoples*, 581; Robert A. Warner, *New Haven Negroes* (New Haven, 1940), 234. See also the subsequent discussion in this chapter.

22. This analytical scheme may serve to resolve some of the apparent inconsistencies in the relation between crime and economic status mentioned by P. A. Sorokin. For example, he notes that "not everywhere nor always do the poor show a greater proportion of crime . . . many poorer countries have had less crime than the richer countries. . . . The economic improvement in the second half of the nineteenth century, and the beginning of the twentieth, has not been followed by a decrease of crime." See his *Contemporary Sociological Theories*, (New York, 1928),

560-61. The crucial point is, however, that low economic status plays a different dynamic role in different social and cultural structures, as is set out in the text. One should not, therefore, expect a linear correlation between crime and poverty.

23. Gilbert Murray, *Five Stages of Greek Religion* (New York, 1925), 164-5. Professor Murray's chapter on "The Failure of Nerve," from which I have taken this excerpt, must surely be ranked among the most civilized and perceptive sociological analyses in our time.

24. See the quotation from an interview cited in Gustavus Meyers, *History of the Great American Fortunes* (New York, 1937), 706.

25. *Nation's Business*, Vol. 27, No. 9, pp. 8-9.

26. E. W. Bakke, *The Unemployed Man* (New York, 1934), p. 14 (I have supplied the emphasis.) Bakke hints at the structural sources making for a belief in luck among workers. "There is a measure of hopelessness in the situation when a man knows that *most of his good or ill fortune is out of his own control and depends on luck.*" (Emphasis supplied) In so far as he is forced to accommodate himself to occasionally unpredictable decisions of management, the worker is subject to job insecurities and anxieties: another "seed-ground" for belief in destiny, fate, chance. It would be instructive to learn if such beliefs become lessened where workers' organizations reduce the probability that their occupational fate will be out of their own hands.

27. At its extreme, it may invite resignation and routinized activity (Adaptation III) or a fatalistic passivism (Adaptation IV), of which more presently.

28. Bakke, *op. cit.*, 14, where he suggests that "the worker knows less about the processes which cause him to succeed or have no chance to succeed than business or professional people. There are more points, therefore, at which events appear to have their incidence in good or ill luck."

29. *Cf.* R. A. Warner, *New Haven Negroes* and Harold F. Gosnell, *Negro Politicians* (Chicago, 1935), 123-5, both of whom comment in this general connection on the great interest in "playing the numbers" among lessadvantaged Negroes.

30. See, for example, H. S. Sullivan, "Modern conceptions of psychiatry," *Psychiatry*, 1940, 3, 111-12; Margaret Mead, *And Keep Your Powder Dry* (New York, 1942), Chapter VII; Merton, Fiske and Curtis, *Mass Persuasion*, 59-60.

31. P. Janet, "The fear of action," *Journal of Abnormal Psychology*, 1921, 16, 150-60, and the extraordinary discussion by F. L. Wells, "Social maladjustments: adaptive regression," *op. cit.*, which bears closely on the type of adaptation examined here.

32. F. J. Roethlisberger and W. J. Dick-

son, *Management and the Worker*, Chapter 18 and 531 ff.; and on the more general theme, the typically perspicacious remarks of Gilbert Murray, *op. cit.*, 138-39.

33. See the three following chapters [in *Social Theory and Social Structure*.]

34. See, for example, Allison Davis and John Dollard, *Children of Bondage* (Washington, 1940), Chapter 12 ("Child Training and Class"), which, though it deals with the lower- and lower-middle class patterns of socialization among Negroes in the Far South, appears applicable, with slight modification, to the white population as well. On this, see further M. C. Erickson, "Child-rearing and social status," *American Journal of Sociology*, 1946, 53, 190-92; Allison Davis and R. J. Havighurst, "Social class and color differences in child-rearing," *American Sociological Review*, 1946, 11, 698-710: ". . . *the pivotal meaning of social class* to students of human development is that it defines and systematizes different learning environments for children of different classes." "Generalizing from the evidence presented in the tables, we would say that middle-class children [the authors do not distinguish between lower-middle and upper-middle strata] are subjected earlier and more consistently to the influences which make a child an orderly, conscientious, responsible, and tame person. In the course of this training middle-class children probably suffer more frustration of their impulses."

35. This hypothesis still awaits empirical test. Beginnings in this direction have been made with the "level of aspiration" experiments which explore the determinants of goal-formation and modification in specific, experimentally devised activities. There is, however, a major obstacle, not yet surmounted, in drawing inferences from the laboratory situation, with its relatively slight ego-involvement with the casual task—pencil-and-paper mazes, ring-throwing, arithmetical problems, *etc.*— which will be applicable to the strong emotional investment with success-goals in the routines of everyday life. Nor have these experiments, with their *ad hoc* group formations, been able to reproduce the acute social pressures obtaining in daily life. (What laboratory experiment reproduces for example, the querulous nagging of a modern Xantippe: "The trouble with you is, you've got no ambition; a real man would go out and do things"?) Among studies with a definite though limited relevance, see especially R. Gould, "Some sociological determinants of goal strivings," *Journal of Social Psychology*, 1941, 13, 461-73; L. Festinger, "Wish, expectation and group standards as factors influencing level of aspiration," *Journal of Abnormal and Social Psychology*, 1942, 37, 184-200. For a resume of researches, see Kurt Lewin *et al.*, "Level of Aspiration," in J. McV. Hunt, ed., *Personality and the Behavior Disorders* (New York, 1944), I, Chap. 10.

The conception of "success" as a ratio between aspiration and achievement pursued systematically in the level-of-aspiration experiments has, of course, a long history. Gilbert Murray (*op. cit.*, 138-9) notes the prevalence of this conception among the thinkers of fourth century Greece. And in *Sartor Resartus*, Carlyle observes that "happiness" (gratification) can be represented by a fraction in which the numerator represents achievement and the denominator, aspiration. Much the same notion is examined by William James (*The Principles of Psychology* [New York, 1902], I, 310). See also F. L. Wells, *op. cit.*, 879, and P. A. Sorokin, *Social and Cultural Dynamics* (New York, 1937), III, 161-164. The critical question is whether this familiar insight can be subjected to rigorous experimentation in which the contrived laboratory situation adequately reproduces the salient aspects of the real-life situation or whether disciplined observation of routines of behavior in everyday life will prove the more productive method of inquiry.

36. In her novel, *The Bitter Box* (New York, 1946), Eleanor Clark has portrayed this process with great sensitivity. The discussion by Erich Fromm, *Escape from Freedom* (New York, 1941), 185-206, may be cited, without implying acceptance of his concept of "spontaneity" and "man's inherent tendency toward self-development." For an example of a sound sociological formulation: "As long as we assume . . . that the anal character, as it is typical of the European lower middle class, is caused by certain early experiences in connection with defecation, we have hardly any data that lead us to understand why a specific class should have an anal social character and resulting from the experiences with the outside world, we have a key for understanding why the whole mode of life of the lower middle class, its narrowness, isolation, and hostility, made for the development of this kind of character structure." (293-4) For an example of a formulation stemming from a kind of latter-day benevolent anarchism here judged as dubious: ". . . there are also certain psychological qualities inherent in man that need to be satisfied. . . . The most important seems to be the tendency to grow, to develop and realize potentialities which man has developed in the course of history—as, for instance, the faculty of creative and critical thinking. . . . It also seems that this general tendency to grow—which is the psychological equivalent of the identical biological tendency—results in such specific tendencies as the desire for freedom and the hatred against oppression, since freedom is the fundamental condition for any growth." (287-88)

37. Obviously, this is an elliptical statement. These individuals may retain some orientation to the values of their own groupings within the larger society or, occasionally, to the values of the conventional society itself. They may, in other words, shift to other modes of adaptation. But Adaptation IV can

be easily detected. Nels Anderson's account of the behavior and attitudes of the bum, for example, can readily be recast in terms of our analytical scheme. See *The Hobo* (Chicago, 1923), 93-98, *et passim*.

38. H. W. Zorbaugh, *The Gold Coast and the Slum* (Chicago, 1929), 108.

39. Abram Kardiner, *The Psychological Frontiers of Society* (New York, 1945), 369-70. (Emphases supplied.)

40. Max Scheler, *L'homme du ressentiment* (Paris, n. d.). This essay first appeared in 1912; revised and completed, it was included in Scheler's *Abhandlungen und Aufsätze*, appearing thereafter in his *Vom Umsturz der Werte* (1919). The last text was used for the French translation. It has had considerable influence in varied intellectual circles. For an excellent and well-balanced discussion of Scheler's essay, indicating some of its limitations and biasses, the respects in which it prefigured Nazi conceptions, its anti-democratic orientation and, withal, its occasionally brilliant insights, see V. J. McGill, "Scheler's theory of sympathy and love," *Philosophy and Phenomenological Research*, 1942, 2, 273-91. For another critical account which properly criticizes Scheler's view that social structure plays only a secondary role in *ressentiment*, see Svend Ranulf, *Moral Indignation and Middle-Class Psychology: A Sociological Study* (Copenhagen, 1938), 199-204.

41. Scheler, *op cit.*, 55-56. No English word fully reproduces the complex of elements implied by the word *ressentiment;* its nearest approximation in German would appear to be *Groll.*

42. George S. Pettee, *The Process of Revolution* (New York, 1938), 8-24; see particularly his account of "monopoly of the imagination.

43. R. S. and H. M. Lynd, *Middletown in Transition* (New York, 1937), 408, for a series of cultural clichés exemplifying the conservative myth.

44. See the acute observations by Georg Simmel, *Soziologie* (Leipzig, 1908).

45. W. Stern, *Psychology of Early Childhood* (New York, 1924), 166, notes the *fact* of such errors (*e.g.,* "drinked" for "drank"), but does not draw the inferences regarding the detection of implicit paradigms.

46. H. A. Murray *et al., Explorations in Personality,* 307.

47. From a study of the social organization of planned communities by R. K. Merton, Patricia S. West and M. Jahoda, *Patterns of Social Life.*

CONTINUITIES IN THE THEORY OF SOCIAL STRUCTURE AND ANOMIE

Robert K. Merton

1. *Pathfinder*, May 17, 1950, 55.
2. R. M. MacIver, *The Ramparts We Guard*

(New York: The Macmillian Company, 1950), 84, 85, and the whole of Chapter Ten; italics supplied. Compare the independently conceived but equivalent description of 'the anomics' by David Riesman, in collaboration with Reuel Denney and Nathan Glazer, *The Lonely Crowd* (New Haven: Yale University Press, 1950), 287 ff.

3. R. H. Brookes, "The anatomy of anomie," *Political Science*, 1951, 3, 44-51; 1952, 4, 38-49—a review-article examining recent conceptual extensions of anomie. H. L. Ansbacher undertakes to relate anomie to the Adlerian notion of "lack of social interest" in a note appearing in *Individual Psychology News Letter: Organ of the International Association of Individual Psychology,* London, June-July 1956.

4. Sebastian De Grazia, *The Political Community* (University of Chicago Press, 1948), 72-74, *passim; cf.* Brookes, *op. cit.,* 46.

5. Parsons, *The Social System,* 256-267, 321-325; Talcott Parsons, Robert F. Bales and Edward A. Shils, *Working Papers in the Theory of Action* (Glencoe: The Free Press, 1953), 67-78.

6. Parsons et al., *Working Papers,* 68.

7. *Ibid.,* 74.

8. In a paper read before the American Sociological Society, 1951, entitled "Social dysfunction, personality, and social distance attitudes"; and again, in an extended but still unpublished version, entitled "Social integration and certain corollaries."

9. The specific wording of these items is reported in Alan H. Roberts and Milton Rokeach, "Anomie, authoritarianism, and prejudice: a replication," *American Journal of Sociology*, 1956, 61, 355-358, at note 14. In a published comment on this paper. Srole questions that his study has in fact been replicated; *Ibid.,* 1956, 62, 63-67.

10. *Towards an Understanding of Juvenile Delinquency* (New York: Columbia University Press, 1954), esp. Chapters V-VI. See also the instructive review-article based on this book by Ernest Greenwood, "New directions in delinquency research," *The Social Service Review,* 1956, 30, 147-157.

11. For the general logic of this kind of analysis, see the section on "statistical indices of social structure," 260-262 of this volume, and Paul F. Lazarsfeld and Morris Rosenberg, *The Language of Social Research* (Glencoe: The Free Press, 1955).

12. W. J. H. Sprott has expressed this with enviable clarity in the Josiah Mason lectures delivered at the University of Birmingham. *Science and Social Action* (London: Watts & Co., 1954), 113.

13. Irvin Gordon Wyllie, *The Self-Made Man in America* (New Brunswick: Rutgers University Press, 1954), 3-4 and throughout the book.

14. Max Weber, *The Protestant Ethic and the Spirit of Capitalism* (New York: Charles Scribner's Sons, 1930), 17.

15. A. C. McCurdy, *Win Who Will* (Philadelphia, 1872), 19, as cited by Wyllie, *op. cit.*, 22.

16. Kenneth S. Lynn, *The Dream of Success* (Boston: Little Brown, 1955); Richard D. Mosier, *Making the American Mind* (New York: King's Crown Press, 1947). See also Marshall W. Fishwick, *American Heroes: Myth and Reality* (Washington, D. C.: Public Affairs Press, 1954).

17. Cambridge: Harvard University Press, 1955.

18. Quoted by Wyllie, 22-23.

19. Wyllie, *op. cit.*, 84-85, 146.

20. For these and comparable observations, see Wyllie, 144 ff.

21. Herbert H. Hyman, "The value systems of different classes," in Bendix and Lipset, editors, *Class, Status and Power*, 426-442. Apposite evidence on the aspirations and achievements of religious and racial minorities is also presented by Gerhart Saenger and Norma S. Gordon, "The influence of discrimination on minority group members in its relation to attempts to combat discrimination," *Journal of Social Psychology*, 1950, 31, 95-120, esp. 113 ff.

22. *Ibid.*, 427-8 [italics inserted]. Empirical inquiries into the comparative frequency of the success-motif in different social groups have been begun. For one such study, see R. W. Mack, R. J. Murphy and S. Yellin, "The Protestant ethic, level of aspiration, and social mobility: an empirical test," *American Sociological Review*, 1956, 21, 295-300. This study intimates, although it was not directed to demonstrate, that the American ethos of success may be pervasive enough to override differences in cultural emphasis found among Protestants and Catholics in the United States. Another study finds that "the Horatio Alger myth is a middle class myth which percolates down to some, but not all, members of the common man class." Joseph A. Kahl, "Educational and occupational aspirations of 'common man' boys," *Harvard Educational Review*, 1953, 23, 186-203.

23. *Ibid.*, 437. Belief in the realistic prospects of opportunity for occupational advancement seems to be fairly widespread among workers, at least as recently as the late forties. For example, Roper reports that among a sample of workers, 70 per cent said that their chances of getting ahead were better than those their fathers had had and 62 per cent said that the chances for their sons would be even better than their own. This *relative* appraisal of occupational opportunity involving comparisons between consecutive generations may be more pertinent, in terms of an image of opportunity, than *absolute* appraisals for one's own generation. See Elmo Roper, "A self portrait of the American people—1947," *Fortune*, 1947, 35, 5-16.

24. R. K. Merton, P. S. West and M.

Jahoda, *Patterns of Social Life*, Chapter 3, unpublished.

25. The questions eliciting the appraisals were these: "What are the chances for a person in your occupation to get ahead if he really sets his mind to it?" "How about the place where you work now—what are the chances for getting ahead there?"

26. Hyman, *op. cit.*, 430-434.

27. At one point toward the close of his paper, Hyman clearly notes the distinction between comparative proportions and absolute proportions (and absolute numbers). But he does so in connection with a special problem of reference-group theory and does not draw the implications basic to the hypothesis in hand. His observation is as follows: "While the evidence thus far presented provides consistent and strong evidence that lower class individuals *as a group* has a value system that reduces the likelihood of individual advancement, it is also clear from the data that there is a sizable proportion of the lower group who do not incorporate this value system. [With regard to some items Hyman has reported, this 'sizable proportion' represents a substantial majority.] Similarly, there are individuals in the upper classes who do not show the modal tendency of their group." *Ibid.*, 441.

28. It should be noted, at least in passing, that the requirement for making this distinction has wide bearing on the analysis of social life. Important as it is in its own right, the *relative* proportions of those in various social strata and groups exhibiting particular attitudes, talents, wealth or any behavior-pattern should not be allowed to obscure, as they often do in sociological studies, the equally important fact of the *absolute numbers* manifesting these items in different strata and groups. From the standpoint of effects upon the society, it is often the absolute numbers and not the relative proportions that matter. For other instances of this same general consideration, see Chapter X of this book [*Social Theory and Social Structure*] at n. 16.

29. Vilhelm Aubert, "White-collar crime and social structure," *American Journal of Sociology*, 1952, 58, 263-271, at 270; *cf.* also, R. K. Merton, "The social-cultural environment and anomie," in Helen L. Witmer and Ruth Kotinsky, editors, *New Perspectives for Research on Juvenile Delinquency* (Washington, D. C.: U. S. Department of Health, Education, and Welfare, Children's Bureau, 1956), 24-50, including discussion by members of the conference; Daniel Glaser, "Criminality theories and behavioral images," *American Journal of Sociology*, 1956, 61, 433-443, at 434.

30. Albert K. Cohen, *Delinquent Boys* (Glencoe: The Free Press, 1955), 36. Since some of the principal theoretical issues are being examined in connection with Cohen's book, the following discussions which bear

upon the paradigm of social structure and anomie as a basis for analyzing criminal and delinquent behavior are only cited. Milton L. Barron, "Juvenile delinquency and American values," *American Sociological Review*, 1951, 16, 208-214; Solomon Kobrin, "The conflict of values in delinquency areas," *American Sociological Review*, 1951, 16, 653-662; Ralph H. Turner, "Value conflict in social disorganization," *Sociology and Social Research*, 1954, 38, 301-308; W. J. H. Sprott, *The Social Background of Delinquency* (University of Nottingham, 1954), as reviewed by John C. Spencer, *The Howard Journal*, 1955, 9, 163-165; Hermann Mannheim, "Juvenile delinquency," *British Journal of Sociology*, 1956, 7, 147-152; Aubert, *op. cit.;* Glaser, *op. cit.*

31. In his comment on precisely this point, Hermann Mannheim indicates that the theory "may be quite capable of explaining much more than merely the utilitarian form of expressing frustrated aspirations." *Op. cit.*, 149.

32. Among the many well-known publications by this group of sociologists, see Clifford R. Shaw and Henry D. McKay, *Juvenile Delinquency and Urban Areas* (University of Chicago Press, 1942); Frederic M. Thrasher, *The Gang* (University of Chicago Press, 1936), 2nd edition.

33. See Merton, "The social and cultural environment and *anomie*," *op. cit.*

34. It is consistent with the theory under review to recognize that distinctive family constellations can promote vulnerability to anomic pressures. For example, Franz Alexander writes of his patients drawn "from second-generation Americans, members of immigrant families, and . . . a racial minority group" that the father's role goes far toward imbuing the son with a driving concern with success. As he puts it, "one common outcome is that the son, usurping father's place in mother's affections as well as in any material respects, develops tremendous ambition. He wants to justify all the hopes and sacrifices of the mother and thus appease his guilty conscience toward the father. There is only one way to accomplish this end. He must become successful, whatever the cost. In the hierarchy of values, success becomes supreme, overshadowing everything else, and failure becomes equivalent to sin. . . . Consequently all other vices, such as insincerity in human relationships, unfairness in competition, disloyalty, disregard for everyone else, appear comparatively as nothing; and there emerges the formidable phenomenon of the ruthless careerist, obsessed by the single idea of self-promotion, a caricature of the self-made man, a threat to Western civilization, the principles of which he reduces to an absurdity." Franz Alexander, "Educative influence of personality factors in the environment," re-printed in Clyde Kluckhohn, Henry A. Murray and David M. Schneider, editors, *Personality in Nature, Society, and Culture* (New York: A. A. Knopf, 1953, 2d ed.), 421-435, at 431-433.

This essentially psychological analysis of the formation of unqualified and therefore normatively disruptive success-goals must, however, be connected with a sociological analysis, if it is to do justice to the facts of the case. For even though these strivings for success may develop anew and more or less independently in *each* of the families being described, the deviant behavior occurs in a social system which variously links up these diversely initiated patterns of behavior. In this way, whatever the initial situation for each individual, the deviant behavior of individuals *outside the family* tends to become mutually supporting and disruptive of established norms. Anomie becomes a social phenomenon, well beyond the confines of an aggregate of separate and distinct families. For a related analysis, see Ralph Pieris, "Ideological momentum and social equilibrium," *American Journal of Sociology*, 1952, 57, 339-346.

35. Warren G. Bennis, "Some barriers to teamwork in social research," *Social Problems*, 1956, 3, 223-235; Matilda White Riley and Samuel H. Flowerman, "Group relations as a variable in communications research," *American Sociological Review*, 1951, 16, 174-180; Leonard I. Pearlin, *The Social and Psychological Setting of Communications Behavior* (Columbia University, unpublished doctoral dissertation in sociology, 1957). Pearlin finds strong tendencies toward using television as "escape" among those who are both highly motivated to achieve social mobility and placed in an occupation which does not readily allow this motive to be satisfied. One of the principal conclusions of this empirical study is that "television is well established as one instrument by which people can withdraw from conflicts and stresses which have their etiology in the social system."

36. Celia Stopnicka Rosenthal, "Deviation and social change in the Jewish community of a small Polish town," *American Journal of Sociology*, 1954, 60, 177-181.

37. Richard Cloward, *The Culture of a Military Prison: A Case Study of Anomie* (Glencoe: The Free Press, to be published); and Cloward's partial summary of this study in Witmer and Kotinsky, *op. cit.*, 80-91.

38. Parsons, *The Social System*, 476-477, and the whole of Chapter X.

39. See the further discussion of this in the following section devoted to the retreatist pattern of response to anomie.

40. Gilbert Murray, *Greek Studies* (Oxford: Clarendon Press, 1946), 75. The allusion is to the second book of Plato's *Republic;* it is a nice question of judgment whether the original formulation by Plato does justice to the paraphrase by Gilbert Murray.

40a. See the forthcoming paper by Ruth B. Granick, "Biographies of popular Negro 'heroes.'" Following the procedures established by Leo Lowenthal in his study of popular biographies, Granick has analyzed the social composition of "Negro heroes" in two popular magazines designed primarily for Negro readers, within the context supplied by the theory of deviant behavior here under review. She finds different routes to success in the world of entertainment for Negroes and whites, although the apparently valued statuses seem much the same for these two subgroups. What is more in point is her provisional finding that access to alternative goals of success provides ample room for conformist, rather than deviant, behavior. The well-known study by Lowenthal is his "Biographies in popular magazines," in P. F. Lazarsfeld and F. N. Stanton (editors), *Radio Research, 1942-1943* (New York: Duell, Sloan and Pearce, 1944).

It has been pointed out also that patterns of consumption behavior—for example, the trickling-down of styles and fashion in the stratification system—serve the latent function of making the system gratifying even for those who do not rise appreciably within it. See)Bernard Barber and Lyle S. Lobel, " 'Fashion' in women's clothes and the American social system," *Social Forces*, 1952, 31, 124-131 and a correlative paper by Lloyd A. Fallers, "A note on the 'trickle effect,' " *Public Opinion Quarterly*, 1954, 18, 314-321.

For pertinent observations on differential symbols of accomplishment which serve to mitigate a sense of personal failure, see Margaret M. Wood, *Paths of Loneliness* (New York: Columbia University Press, 1953), 212 ff.

41. Page 152 [of *Social Theory and Social Structure*]. See also the discussion of "structural sources of overconformity" in Chapter VI and of the "renegade" and "convert" in Chapter VIII and IX of this book; and the observation by Parsons and Bales that "the first important insight in this connection [of relating their independently developed theories] was that 'over conformity' should be defined as deviance." Parsons *et al.*, *Working Papers*, 75.

42. Otto Sperling, "Psychoanalytic aspects of bureaucracy," *Psychoanalytic Quarterly*, 1950, 19, 88-100.

43. P. M. Blau, *The Dynamics of Bureaucracy*, Chapter XII, esp. 184-193.

44. Conveniently summarized in Howard S. Liddell, "Adaptation on the threshold of intelligence," *Adaptation*, edited by John Romano, (Ithaca: Cornell University Press, 1949), 55-75.

45. Chapter IV of this book [*Social Theory and Social Structure*], at 150-151.

46. Emilio Mira y López, *Psychiatry in War* (New York: Academy of Medicine, 1943), as quoted by Liddell, *op. cit.*, 70.

47. Else Frenkel-Brunswik, "Intolerance of ambiguity as an emotional and perceptual personality variable," *Journal of Personality*, 1949, 18, 108-143; also T. W. Adorno et al.,

The Authoritarian Personality (New York: Harper & Brothers, 1950); Richard Christie and Marie Jahoda, editors, *Studies in the Scope and Method of 'The Authoritarian Personality'* (Glencoe: The Free Press, 1954).

48. Else Frenkel-Brunswik, in Christie and Jahoda, *op. cit.*, 247.

49. W. Baldamus and Noel Timms, "The problem family: a sociological approach," *British Journal of Sociology*, 1955, 6, 318-327. The authors conclude by saying that "although individual traits of personality structure appeared to have a more powerful effect . . . than was expected, the evidence of deviant beliefs and orientations as a separate determinant is still sufficient to warrant a more elaborate inquiry into the nature and the importance of this factor. Thus it appeared that, with certain qualifications, the more extreme cases of disorganization and inefficiency in problem families approach a situation of retreatism . . .: conformity to established values is virtually relinquished especially in respect of standards of behaviour." From all indications, retreatism seems to be marked among those in the lower-lower social stratum, as this has been described by W. Lloyd Warner and Paul S. Lunt, *The Social Life of a Modern Community* (New Haven: Yale University Press, 1941).

50. Ely Chinoy, *Automobile Workers and the American Dream* (New York: Doubleday & Company, 1955); and see on this point, the review of the book by Paul Meadows, *American Sociological Review*, 1955, 20, 624.

As we noted in first presenting the types of adaptation, these refer "to role behavior . . . not to personality." It does not follow, of course, that the adaptations remain fixed throughout the life-cycle of individuals; on the contrary, there is room for systematic inquiry into patterns of *role-sequence* which develop under determinate conditions. Conformist striving, for example, may be followed by a ritualist adaptation and this, in turn, by retreatism; other types of role-sequence can also be identified. For an interesting study which begins to deal with sequences of role-adaptation, see Leonard Reissman, "Levels of aspiration and social class," *American Sociological Review*, 1953, 18, 233-242.

51. As with most insights into the behavior of men, this one had of course been "anticipated." In *The Way of All Flesh*, for example, Samuel Butler remarks: "Adversity, if a man is set down to it by degrees, is more supportable with equanimity by most people than any great prosperity arrived at in a single lifetime." (Chapter V) The difference is, of course, that Durkheim went on to incorporate his insight into an orderly set of theoretical ideas which he followed out in their implications; this was not Butler's *métier* and he went on, instead, to numerous other unconnected insights into man and his society.

52. Here again, the man of letters perceives

what the social scientist goes on to examine, in its details and implications. Charles Lamb's classic essay on *The Super annuated Man* describes the syndrome of disorientation experienced by those who are removed from the role-obligation of being tethered to a desk, with all the possibly dull but thoroughly comfortable routines which gave order to daily existence. And he goes on to "caution persons grown old in active business, not lightly, nor without weighing their own resources, to forego their customary employment *all at once,* for there may be danger in it." The italics are supplied to direct attention to what Durkheim and Butler and Lamb take as the nub of the matter: the suddenness of change of status and role.

53. Zena Smith Blau, *Old Age: A Study of Change in Status,* Unpublished doctoral dissertation in sociology, Columbia University, 1956.

54. For a few among the many accounts of accidie: Langland's *Piers Plowman* and Chaucer's "Parson's Tale"; Burton's *Anatomy of Melancholy;* the essay by Aldous Huxley in *On The Margin;* Rebecca West, *The Thinking Reed. Further,* F. L. Wells, "Social maladjustments: adaptive regression," in Carl A. Murchison, ed., *Handbook of Social Psychology,* 869 ff. and the cited paper by A. Meyerson, "Anhedonia," *American Journal of Psychiatry,* 1922, 2, 97-103.

55. *Cf.* Bernard Barber, *'Mass Apathy' and Voluntary Social Participation in the United States,* unpublished doctoral dissertation in sociology, Harvard University, 1949; B. Zawadski and Paul F. Lazarsfeld, "The psychological consequences of unemployment," *Journal of Social Psychology,* 1935, 6.

56. Robin M. Williams, Jr. *American Society* (New York: A. A. Knopf, 1951), 534-535.

57. As first formulated, the theory is evidently more than usually obscure on this point. At least, this conclusion would seem indicated by the fact that two perceptive discussions have suggested that a conflict between norms has been equated with normlessness (the cultural aspect of anomie). Ralph H. Turner, "Value conflict in social disorganization," *Sociology and Social Research,* 1954, 38, 301-308; Christian Bay, *The Freedom of Expression,* unpublished ms., Chapter III.

An historical sociologist has identified the outlines of a process of disenchantment with both cultural goals and institutional means in the later 1930's in the United States, as this was registered, for example, in journals of opinion upon the death of John D. Rockefeller. He observes: "Clearly the dissenters did not see eye to eye regarding the measures to be taken to reform society, but from the point of view of the defenders of Rockefeller and of business enterprise that disagreement was perhaps of less importance than was the evidence of distrust in the regime of enterprise and of alienation—particularly in the

lower ranks of the social order—from the goals and standards which provided its ideological security. For these critics, such goals and standards no longer possessed legitimacy, no longer could serve to exact allegiance; and with allegiance broken, how then could business enterprisers confidently expect the routine of actions and responses that characterized industrial discipline to be maintained? But more than dissent and dissatisfaction lurked in the diatribes of the critics. If the activities of an entrepreneur like Rockefeller were functions of a social organization which was itself the cause of discontent—of poverty and unemployment—then no longer, its critics maintained, did that social organization deserve to be supported and no longer would 'young men' fall into rank behind its cultural standards. With sufficient change—and it was at this point that the critics themselves differed —a new and better social organization could be achieved. This was—or could become—more than merely discussion; it was a charter for action. And because the action contemplated restricting the scope and freedom of action of enterprise, its journalistic defenders had to meet the challenge. Loyalties in jeopardy needed reaffirmation, and every new evidence that they were in jeopardy—from sit-down strikes in Flint to New Deal legislation in Washington—added urgency to the task." Sigmund Diamond, *The Reputation of the American Businessman,* 116-117.

58. See the highly instructive study by Howard Becker, *German Youth: Bond or Free* (London: Routledge & Kegan Paul, 1946); S. N. Eisenstadt, *From Generation to Generation: Age Groups and Social Structure* (Glencoe: The Free Press, 1956), esp. Chapter VI.

59. Elinor G. Barber, *The Bourgeoisie in 18th Century France* (Princeton: Princeton University Press, 1955), 56.

60. Since it is the theoretical contribution, rather than the specific empirical findings, which are of immediate interest, I do not summarize the substantive materials set forth by Dr. Barber. These are summed up in her tentative conclusion that "it was the rigidification of the class system that precipitated the alienation of this [middle] segment of the bourgeoisie from the existing class structure to which it had, up to the Revolution, given its predominant allegiance. When he was denied the right to improve his social position, the bourgeois found the strain of conflicting moralities intolerable, so that he rejected altogether the disapproval of social mobility." *Ibid.,* 144.

61. See the observation by William F. Whyte quoted in Chapter I of this book [*Social Theory and Social Structure*] (78) and see the further discussion of crime as a means of social mobility in Chapter IV.

62. Daniel Bell, "Crime as an American way of life," *The Antioch Review,* Summer 1953, 131-154.

VI – BUREAUCRATIC STRUCTURE

THE ESSENTIALS OF BUREAUCRATIC ORGANIZATION: AND IDEAL-TYPE CONSTRUCTION

Max Weber

1. Weber does not explain this distinction. By a "technical rule" he probably means a prescribed course of action which is dictated primarily on grounds touching efficiency of the performance of the immediate functions, while by "norms" he probably means rules which limit conduct on grounds other than those of efficiency. Of course, in one sense all rules are norms in that they are prescriptions for conduct, conformity with which is problematical.—Ed. [Parsons.]

2. *Bureau.* It has seemed necessary to use the English word "office" in three different meanings, which are distinguished in Weber's discussion by at least two terms. The first is *Amt,* which means "office" in the sense of the institutionally defined status of a person. The second is the "work premises" as in the expression "he spent the afternoon in his office." For this Weber uses *Bureau* as also for the third meaning which he has just defined, the "organized work process of a group." In this last sense an office is a particular type of "organization," or *Betrieb* in Weber's sense. This use is established in English in such expressions as "the District Attorney's Office has such and such functions." Which of the three meanings is involved in a given case will generally be clear from the context.—Ed. [Parsons.]

3. This characterization applies to the "monocratic" as opposed to the "collegial" type, which will be discussed below.

SOCIAL INTEGRATION, BUREAUCRATIZATION, AND THE PROFESSIONS

Walter I. Wardwell

1. Cf. Talcott Parsons, *The Social System* (Glencoe, Illinois: The Free Press, 1951), p. 474 et passim. Many of the ideas in this paper derive ultimately from Parsons' lectures and writings although it is difficult to specify precisely where and in what form they first appeared. The writer's debt to Parsons is hereby acknowledged. Expression of appreciation is also due to James H. Barnett for critical reading of the manuscript and several helpful suggestions.

2. Since all roles involve "relational ties" and "functional contributions" of one sort or other, this distinction rests on the relative emphasis of each in the definition of the role. A housewife does a lot of work but hers is not an occupational role, while the cook, nursemaid, and housekeeper functions are clearly recognized as occupational roles.

3. The kind of bureaucratic organization referred to here is thus based on "rational-legal" authority and not on "tradition." Cf.

Max Weber, *The Theory of Social and Economic Organization* (tr. by A. M. Henderson and Talcott Parsons; New York: Oxford University Press, 1947), pp. 329-58. Religious and governmental bureaucracies tend to contain important elements of traditional authority and to that extent differ from the pure type of bureaucratic organization that we have defined.

4. In the case of the episcopal type of church.

5. Emile Durkheim, *Division of Labor in Society* (tr. by George Simpson; Glencoe, Illinois: The Free Press, 1947), chap. III. Of course a bureaucratic organization also has a certain degree of "mechanical" solidarity and "esprit de corps."

6. "Toward a Common Language for the Area of Social Science," *Essays in Sociological Theory, Pure and Applied* (Glencoe, Illinois: The Free Press, 1949), p. 49. Cf. also Chester I. Barnard, *The Functions of the Executive* (Cambridge, Mass.: Harvard University Press, 1945).

7. A term suggested by Parsons in his lectures.

8. See especially in this connection C. W. Mills, *White Collar* (New York: Oxford University Press, 1951), chap. 6, "Old Professions and New Skills."

9. This is Logan Wilson's circumlocution for "dean" in *The Academic Man* (New York: Oxford University Press, 1942).

10. Roscoe Pound says: "There is danger to professional ideals and to the spirit of practice of a profession as a public service in the legal department of a great public utility or industrial enterprise or legal staff of an administrative agency or even the great law office in a metropolitan city where there is temptation to operate as a business organization in which the advocates are simply employees." *The Lawyer from Antiquity to Modern Times* (St. Paul, Minnesota: West Publishing Co., 1953), p. 183.

11. During World War II the writer had an experience which illustrates the basic incompatibility between bureaucracy and the "group of equals" pattern in the academic profession. While assigned to the ROTC department of an engineering school he was "advised" by his military superior how to cast his vote in theoretically democratic faculty voting.

12. Cf. however Peter Drucker, "Management and the Professional Employee," *Harvard Business Review,* 30, No. 3 (1952).

BUREAUCRATIC STRUCTURE AND PERSONALITY

Robert K. Merton

1. For a development of the concept of "rational organization," see Karl Mannheim, *Mensch und Gesellschaft im Zeitalter des Umbaus* (Leiden: A. W. Sijthoff, 1935), esp. 28 ff.

2. H. D. Lasswell, *Politics* (New York: McGraw-Hill, 1936), 120-21.

3. Max Weber, *Wirtschaft und Gesellschaft* (Tübingen: J. C. B. Mohr, 1922), Pt. III, chap. 6; 650-678. For a brief summary of Weber's discussion, see Talcott Parsons, *The Structure of Social Action*, esp. 506 ff. For a description, which is not a caricature, of the bureaucrat as a personality type, see C. Rabany, "Les types sociaux: le fonctionnaire," *Revue générale d'administration*, 1907, 88, 5-28.

4. Karl Mannheim, *Ideology and Utopia* (New York: Harcourt, Brace, 1936), 18n., 105 ff. See also Ramsay Muir, *Peers and Bureaucrats* (London: Constable, 1910), 12-13.

5. E. G. Cahen-Salvador suggests that the personnel of bureaucracies is largely constituted by those who value security above all else. See his "La situation matérielle et morale des fonctionnaires," *Revue politique et parlementaire* (1926), 319.

6. H. J. Laski, "Bureaucracy," *Encyclopedia of the Social Sciences*. This article is written primarily from the standpoint of the political scientist rather than that of the sociologist.

7. Weber, *op. cit.*, 671.

8. For a stimulating discussion and application of these concepts, see Kenneth Burke, *Permanence and Change* (New York: New Republic, 1935), pp. 50 ff.; Daniel Warnotte, "Bureaucratie et Fonctionnarisme," *Revue de l'Institut de Sociologie*, 1937, 17, 245.

9. *Ibid.*, 58-59.

10. *Ibid.*, 70.

11. This process has often been observed in various connections. Wundt's *heterogony of ends* is a case in point; Max Weber's *Paradoxie der Folgen* is another. See also Mac-Iver's observations on the transformation of civilization into culture and Lasswell's remark that "the human animal distinguishes himself by his infinite capacity for making ends of his means." See Merton, "The unanticipated consequences of purposive social action," *American Sociological Review*, 1936, 1, 894-904. In terms of the psychological mechanisms involved, this process has been analyzed most fully by Gordon W. Allport, in his discussion of what he calls "the functional autonomy of motives." Allport emends the earlier formulations of Woodworth, Tolman, and William Stern, and arrives at a statement of the process from the standpoint of individual motivation. He does not consider those phases of the social structure which conduce toward the "transformation of motives." The formulation adopted in this paper is thus complementary to Allport's analysis; the one stressing the psychological mechanisms involved, the other considering the constraints of the social structure. The convergence of psychology and sociology toward this central concept suggests that it may well constitute one of the conceptual bridges between the two disciplines. See Gordon W. Allport, *Personality* (New York: Henry Holt & Co., 1937), chap. 7.

12. See E. C. Hughes, "Institutional office and the person," *American Journal of Sociology*, 1937, 43, 404-413; E. T. Hiller, "Social structure in relation to the person," *Social Forces*, 1937, 16, 34-4.

13. Mannheim, *Ideology and Utopia*, 106.

14. Quoted from the *Chicago Tribune* (June 24, 1931, p. 10) by Thurman Arnold, *The Symbols of Government* (New Haven: Yale University Press, 1935), 201-2. (My italics.)

15. Mannheim, *Mensch und Gesellschaft*, 32-33. Mannheim stresses the importance of the "Lebensplan" and the "Amtskarriere." See the comments by Hughes, *op. cit.*, 413.

16. A. L. Lowell, *The Government of England* (New York, 1908), I, 189 ff.

17. For an instructive description of the development of such a defensive organization in a group of workers, see F. J. Roethlisberger and W. J. Dickson, *Management and the Worker* (Boston: Harvard School of Business Administration, 1934).

18. E. C. Hughes, "Personality types and the division of labor," *American Journal of Sociology*, 1928, 33, 754-768. Much the same distinction is drawn by Leopold von Wiese and Howard Becker, *Systematic Sociology* (New York: John Wiley & Sons, 1932), 222-25 *et passim*.

19. Hughes recognizes one phase of this process of sanctification when he writes that professional training "carries with it as a by-product assimilation of the candidate to a set of professional attitudes and controls, *a professional conscience and solidarity. The profession claims and aims to become a moral unit.*" Hughes, *op. cit.*, 762, (italics inserted). In this same connection, Sumner's concept of *pathos*, as the halo of sentiment which protects a social value from criticism, is particularly relevant, inasmuch as it affords a clue to the mechanism involved in the process of sanctification. See his *Folkways*, 180-181.

20. " 'They treat you like a lump of dirt they do. I see a navvy reach across the counter and shake one of them by the collar the other day. The rest of us felt like cheering. Of course he lost his benefit over it. . . . But the clerk deserved it for his sassy way.' " (E. W. Bakke, *The Unemployed Man*, 79-80). Note that the domineering attitude was *imputed* by the unemployed client who is in a state of tension due to his loss of status and self-esteem in society where the ideology is still current that an "able man" can always find a job. That the imputation of arrogance stems largely from the client's state of mind is seen from Bakke's own observation that "the clerks were rushed, and had no time for pleasantries, but there was little sign of harshness or a superiority feeling in their treatment of the men." In so far as there is an objective basis for the imputation of arrogant behavior to bureaucrats, it may possibly be explained by the following juxtaposed statements. "Auch der moderne, sei es öffentliche, sei es private, Beamte erstrebt immer und geniesst meist den Beherrschten gegenüber eine spezifisch gehobene, 'ständische' soziale Schätzung." (Weber, *op. cit.*, 652.) "In persons in whom the craving for prestige is uppermost, hostility

usually takes the form of a desire to humiliate others." K. Horney, *The Neurotic Personality of Our Time*, 178-79.

21. In this connection, note the relevance of of Koffka's comments on certain features of the pecking-order of birds. "If one compares the behavior of the bird at the top of the pecking list, the despot, with that of one very far down, the second or third from the last, then one finds the latter much more cruel to the few others over whom he lords it than the former in his treatment of all members. As soon as one removes from the group all members above the penultimate, his behavior becomes milder and may even become very friendly. . . . It is not difficult to find analogies to this in human societies, and therefore one side of such behavior must be primarily the effects of the social groupings, and not of individual characteristics." K. Koffka, *Principles of Gestalt Psychology* (New York: Harcourt, Brace, 1935), 668-9.

22. At this point the political machine often becomes functionally significant. As Steffens and others have shown, highly personalized relations and the abrogation of formal rules (red tape) by the machine often satisfy the needs of individual "clients" more fully than the formalized mechanism of governmental bureaucracy.

23. As one of the unemployed men remarked about the clerks at the Greenwich Employment Exchange: " 'And the bloody blokes wouldn't have their jobs if it wasn't for us men out of a job either. That's what gets me about their holding their noses up.' " Bakke, *op. cit.*, 80. See also H. D. Lasswell and G. Almond, "Aggressive behavior by clients towards public relief administrators," *American Political Science Review*, 1934, 28, 643-55.

24. The diagnostic significance of such linguistic indices as epithets has scarcely been explored by the sociologist. Sumner properly observes that epithets produce "summary criticisms" and definitions of social situations. Dollard also notes that "epithets frequently define the central issues in a society," and Sapir has rightly emphasized the importance of context of situations in appraising the significance of epithets. Of equal relevance is Linton's observation that "in case histories the way in which the community felt about a particular episode is, if anything, more important to our study than the actual behavior. . . ." A sociological study of "vocabularies of encomium and opprobrium" should lead to valuable findings.

25. *Cf.* Ellsworth Faris, *The Nature of Human Nature* (New York: McGraw-Hill, 1937), 41 ff.

26. Community disapproval of many forms of behavior may be analyzed in terms of one or the other of these patterns of substitution of culturally inappropriate types of relationship. Thus, prostitution constitutes a type-case where coitus, a form of intimacy which is institutionally defined as symbolic of the most "sacred" primary group relationship, is placed within a contractual context, symbolized by the exchange of that most impersonal of all symbols, money. See Kingsley Davis, "The sociology of prostitution," *American Sociological Review*, 1937, 2, 744-55.

27. Among recent studies of recruitment to bureaucracy are: Reinhard Bendix, *Higher Civil Servants in American Society* (Boulder: University of Colorado Press, 1949); Dwaine Marwick, *Career Perspectives in a Bureaucratic Setting* (Ann Arbor: University of Michigan Press, 1954); R. K. Kelsall, *Higher Civil Servants in Britain* (London: Routledge and Kegan Paul, 1955); W. L. Warner and J. C. Abegglen, *Occupational Mobility in American Business and Industry* (Minneapolis: University of Minnesota Press, 1955).

CO-OPERATION AND COMPETITION IN A BUREAUCRACY

Peter M. Blau

1. There were seven interviewers in Section A and five in Section B. Seven of the twelve were women.

2. This is clearly indicated by the comment of one of a group of special interviewers, who were expected to use the job openings of the regular interviewers but usually had great difficulty in doing so: "Oh, they hide everything from us. We got more orders when you [the observer] sat in the middle of that section than ever before. We laughed about it. Interviewers would hand us orders asking whether we could use them—when you were looking. That had never happened before."

3. Émile Durkheim, *The Rules of Sociological Method* (Chicago: University of Chicago Press, 1938), pp. 110 and *passim*.

4. She was most often mentioned by members of her own section in answer to the questions, respectively, "Who are the best interviewers?" and "Who are your friends in the office?"

5. For another example of such disparity between individual and corresponding group data see the discussion of promotion opportunities and attitudes toward promotion in Samuel A. Stouffer *et al.*, *The American Soldier* (Princeton: Princeton University Press, 1949), I, 250-54. Kendall and Lazarsfeld discuss the methodological significance of such findings in Robert K. Merton and Paul F. Lazarsfeld (eds.), *Continuities in Social Research* (Glencoe, Ill.: Free Press, 1950), pp. 193-95.

SOCIAL RESEARCH IN THE MENTAL HOSPITAL

Morris S. Schwartz

1. Devereux, G., "The Social Structure of the Hospital as a Factor in Total Therapy," *American Journal of Orthopsychiatry*, XIX (1949), 492-500.

2. Bateman, J. F., and Dunham, H. W., "The State Mental Hospital as a Specialized

Community Experience," *American Journal of Psychiatry*, CV (1948), 445-448.

3. Rowland, H., "Friendship Patterns in the State Mental Hospital," *Psychiatry*, II (1939), 363-373. Caudill, W., Redlich, F. C., Gilmore, H. R., and Brody, E. B., "Social Structure and Interaction Processes on a Psychiatric Ward," *American Journal of Orthopsychiatry*, XXII (1952), 314-334.

4. Barrabee, P. S., "The Study of a Mental Hospital: The Effect of its Social Structure on its Functions," Unpub. Ph.D. dissertation, Cambridge: Harvard University, 1951.

5. Stanton, A. H., and Schwartz, M. S., *The Mental Hospital*. New York: Basic Books, 1954.

6. Stanton, A. H., and Schwartz, M. S., "The Management of a Type of Institutional Participation in Mental Illness," *Psychiatry*, XII (1949), 13-26.

7. Caudill, *et al., op. cit.*

8. Stanton, A. H., and Schwartz, M. S., "Medical Opinion and the Social Context in the Mental Hospital," *Psychiatry*, XII (1949), 243-49.

9. Schwartz, M. S., and Stanton, A. H., "A Social Psychological Study of Incontinence," *Psychiatry*, XIII (1950), 399-416.

10. Tudor, G. E., "A Sociopsychiatric Nursing Approach to Intervention in a Problem of Mutual Withdrawal on a Mental Hospital Ward," *Psychiatry*, XV (1952), 193-217.

11. Schwartz, M. S., and Will, G. T., "Low Morale and Mutual Withdrawal on a Mental Hospital Ward," *Psychiatry*, XVI (1953), 337-53.

12. Baker, A. A., Jones, M., Marry, J., and Pomryn, B. A., "A Community Method of Psychotherapy," *British Journal of Medical Psychology*, XXVI, parts 3 and 4 (1953), 222-224. Jones, M., *The Therapeutic Community*. New York: Basic Books, 1953.

13. Schwartz, M. S. and C. G., "Participant Observation as a Method of Social Research" (to be published in the *American Journal of Sociology*).

14. Schwartz, M. S., "Social Interaction on a Disturbed Ward of a Mental Hospital," Unpub. Ph.D. dissertation, Chicago: University of Chicago, 1951. Slotkin, J. S., "The Nature and Effects of Social Interaction in Schizophrenia," *Journal of Abnormal and Social Psychology*, XXXVII (1942), 345-68. Rowland, H., *op. cit.*

15. Rowland, H., "Interaction Processes in the State Mental Hospital," *Psychiatry*, I (1938), 323-27.

16. Stanton, A. H., and Schwartz, M. S., *The Mental Hospital*. New York: Basic Books, 1954.

RED TAPE AS A SOCIAL PROBLEM

Alvin W. Gouldner

1. *The Governing of Men* (Princeton University Press, 1945), p. 309.

2. "Bureaucratic Structure and Personality" reprinted in this volume.

3. We have, elsewhere, suggested the possibility of analyzing this phenomenon in theoretical contexts other than the means-end schema. Alvin W. Gouldner, "Discussion of 'Industrial Sociology: Status and Prospects.'" *American Sociological Review*, XIII (August, 1948), p. 399.

4. "When at the threshold of World War II motormaker William Knudsen assumed a post of great importance in the defense effort of the nation, he said of Washington red tape, 'In Detroit we call it system.'" John A. Vieg, "Bureaucracy—Fact and Fiction," in Fritz Morstein Marx (ed.), *Elements of Public Administration* (New York: Prentice-Hall, Inc., 1946), p. 54.

5. Preliminary statistical analyses of these are reported in footnotes. Only suggestive at best, these are intended to indicate that further study is warranted.

6. Proportion of Respondents Using Differing Values in Defining and Illustrating Red Tape:

Value	Per Cent of Respondents*
Efficiency	74
Equality	17
The separation of private and public spheres	10
	(N = 124)

*Some, of course, use more than one value: 61 per cent of the respondents use "efficiency" alone; 17 per cent of those using "efficiency" use it in conjunction with either or both of the other values.

7. Respondents were asked: "On the whole, do you feel that: (a) Most of the red tape you came across is really necessary, (b) Some of the red tape you came across is necessary but some is not, (c) Practically none of the red tape you came across is necessary?" Respondents choosing either (a) or (b) were classified as "tolerant" toward red tape; those choosing (c), as "hostile." Among a battery of questions designed to explore their values, they were asked to indicate their agreement or disagreement with the following statement, (which was used as an index of their belief in the value of maintaining a separation of private and public spheres) "A man's business and private life should be kept strictly separated." Cross-tabulation of answers to the first and second questions gave the following table ("no answers" and "don't knows" eliminated).

Attitude Toward Red Tape	Attitude Toward Separation of Private and Public Spheres	
	Agree	Disagree
Tolerant	62	19
Hostile	24	2
Total	86	21	107

The probability of the corrected chi square for this table is between 0.10 and 0.20.

8. Responses to the following statement were used as an index for the respondent's attitude toward equality: "All people are born equal and should be treated that way."

Attitude Toward Red Tape	Attitude Toward Equality		
	Agree	Disagree	
Tolerant	61	19	
Hostile	26	3	
Total	87	22	109

Probability for the corrected chi square is about 0.02.

9. Agreement with the following statement (here selected from several others of like kind) was used as an index of the respondent's feeling of powerlessness: "An awful lot of people are getting stepped on these days."

Attitude Toward Red Tape	Sense of Powerlessness		
	+	—	
Tolerant	53	20	
Hostile	27	2	
Total	80	22	102

Probability for the corrected chi square is between 0.05 and 0.02.

10. Responses to the following statement were used as an index to the respondent's feeling of suspicion: "Lots of people seem to be friendly and sincere but many of them only pretend to be that way."

Attitude Toward Red Tape	Suspiciousness		
	+	—	
Tolerant	11	65	
Hostile	10	19	
Total	21	84	105

Probability for the corrected chi square is about 0.05.

11. *Man and Society in an Age of Reconstruction* (Harcourt, Brace and Company, 1941), p. 53.

12. George A. Lundberg, *Foundations of Sociology* (Macmillan Company, 1938), p. 138.

13. As quoted in Gerard de Gré, *Society and Ideology* (Columbia University Bookstore, 1943), p. 11.

14. The question here is: in what kind of a political orientation is red tape ascribed the *most importance*. To ascertain this we asked: "How important a problem would you say red tape is?" Respondents could check one of the following answers: (a) of great importance, (b) of some importance, (c) not very important, (d) not sure. Responses to the following statement were used as a crude index of "radicalism-conservatism": "The country would be better off if the trade

unions had more power." Omitting those without a definite opinion, the following table was obtained:

Importance Ascribed to Red Tape	Political Orientation	
	"Radical"	"Conservative"
High (a, b)	19	43
Low (c)	15	8
Total	34	51

Probability for the corrected chi square is better than 0.01.

15. It is an interesting fact of intellectual history that those passages of Karl Marx's writings in which he castigates alienation, impersonalization, and dull, routine work find little echo among the present Marxian epigoni.

BUREAUCRATIC ORGANIZATION AND THE VOLUNTEER

Bernard Barber

1. Barnard, C. I., *The Functions of the Executive,* Cambridge: Harvard University Press, 1938, p. 221n.

2. Boys' Clubs of America, pamphlet: "Training Volunteers and Part-time Workers for Boysclubs," New York, 1942, my italics.

3. Putnam, Imogene H., *Volunteers in OPA,* Washington, D. C.: Government Printing Office, 1947, p. 104. The Public Welfare Department, Westchester County, New York, now employs a full-time, paid Director of Volunteers. See *Volunteer Viewpoints,* no. 2, published by Community Chests and Councils.

4. See "Statement of Principles," published in 1945 by the Advisory Committee on Volunteer Service of Community Chests and Councils.

5. Boys' Clubs of America, 1942, p. 5.

6. Whitney, (Mrs.) Charles S., "The Volunteer and the Social Agency," *Highlights,* V (1944), 20-22.

7. Volunteer Bureau of Greater Hartford, 1948.

8. See fn. 7.

9. National Conference on Prevention and Control of Juvenile Delinquency, p. 12. See also, Sullivan, Dorothea F., "The Professional School Curriculum and Citizen Participation," *The Compass,* xxvii (1946), pp. 21-22.